CW00924969

# THE OXFORD DICTIONARY OF
# ORIGINAL SHAKESPEAREAN PRONUNCIATION

THE OXFORD DICTIONARY

# OF ORIGINAL SHAKESPEAREAN PRONUNCIATION

DAVID CRYSTAL

To Rachel
with looove... from
Jan & Penny

OXFORD
UNIVERSITY PRESS

Great Clarendon Street, Oxford, OX2 6DP,
United Kingdom

Oxford University Press is a department of the University of Oxford.
It furthers the University's objective of excellence in research, scholarship,
and education by publishing worldwide. Oxford is a registered trade mark of
Oxford University Press in the UK and in certain other countries



Impression: 1



Published in the United States of America by Oxford University Press
198 Madison Avenue, New York, NY 10016, United States of America

British Library Cataloguing in Publication Data
Data available

Library of Congress Control Number: 2015949663

ISBN 978–0–19–966842–7

Printed in Great Britain by
Clays Ltd, St Ives plc

# CONTENTS



www.oup.co.uk/companion/crystal_shakespeare

# PREFACE

This dictionary has been over ten years in the making. I downloaded an electronic edition of the First Folio in December 2004, once it became apparent that the initiative of Shakespeare's Globe to present plays in original pronunciation (OP) was going to result in many more such projects, and began work on a resource that I hoped would one day help anyone interested in mounting a production. It took much longer than I thought, mainly because I wanted the work to include all the data on rhymes and spelling variations that provide a great deal of the evidence for phonological reconstruction, so that those interested could evaluate my decisions for themselves.

Incorporating frequency information about the use of spellings in the First Folio was one of the reasons the project took so long, as I had to go through each count, initiated using the Find function in Word, to check on such things as word-class, compound words, and lexical status (e.g. proper vs common nouns), and also to eliminate irrelevant strings (such as speech character-identifiers). One day a fully tagged grammatical and semantic corpus of the lexical items in the canon will allow such searches to be done in seconds, and provide a level of checking that no manual approach could achieve, but that day is not yet.

I must admit that there were many days—especially (as all lexicographers know) in the middle of 'long' letters, such as C, P, and S—when I thought to abandon the project and await the time when more sophisticated software would do this aspect of the job for me. But the demand for OP materials remained pressing, and I persuaded myself that the usefulness of the dictionary would far outweigh any inaccuracies I may have inadvertently introduced. I hope that is so. Certainly, these weaknesses are far fewer than they might have been, thanks to Professor Paul Meier, who provided helpful suggestions on a draft of my Introduction, Audrey Norman for help in file-collating, and above all to Hilary Crystal, who spent I don't know how many hours inputting, collating, and checking entries during the final stages of the project.

My thanks must also go to John Davey, formerly of OUP, who commissioned the project, to Kim Allen for her copy-editing (no mean feat, with a book like this) and Michael Janes for his proofreading, to Gary Leicester, who looked after the audio-recording, and to Julia Steer who took over from John Davey, advised on the final organization of the dictionary, and saw the work through press. Nor must I forget the indirect but hugely important contribution of the many actors and directors with whom I have collaborated over the past decade, and in particular those in Ben Crystal's Passion in Practice Shakespeare Ensemble, for demonstrating the effect of OP in theatrical practice, and providing me with the confirmation I needed that my account of OP was not just an academic exercise but something that actually worked on stage.

David Crystal
*Holyhead, January 2016*

# ABBREVIATIONS

| | |
|---|---|
| *abbr* | abbreviated |
| *adj* | adjective |
| *adv* | adverb |
| *aux* | auxiliary verb |
| *det* | determiner |
| *emend* | emendation |
| *Eng* | English |
| *Epil* | Epilogue |
| f(f) | following line(s) |
| *F* | First Folio |
| *Fr* | French |
| *interj* | interjection |
| *Ital* | Italian |
| *Lat* | Latin |
| *m* | metrical choice |
| *malap* | malapropism |
| *n* | noun |
| *prep* | preposition |
| *pro* | pronoun |
| *Prol* | Prologue |
| *pron* | pronunciation |
| Q | Quarto |
| *rh* | rhyming with |
| *s.d.* | stage direction |
| *sp* | spelling |
| *Sp* | Spanish |
| *str* | stressed |
| *unstr* | unstressed |
| *usu* | usually |
| *v* | verb |
| = | OP pron same as today |
| 1.2.3 | Act 1, Scene 2, Line 3 |

## The Shakespearean Canon

* Texts not in the First Folio

| | |
|---|---|
| AC | Antony and Cleopatra |
| AW | All's Well That Ends Well |
| AY | As You Like It |
| CE | The Comedy of Errors |
| Cor | Coriolanus |
| Cym | Cymbeline |
| Ham | Hamlet |
| 1H4 | Henry IV Part 1 |
| 2H4 | Henry IV Part 2 |
| H5 | Henry V |
| 1H6 | Henry VI Part 1 |
| 2H6 | Henry VI Part 2 |
| 3H6 | Henry VI Part 3 |
| H8 | Henry VIII |
| JC | Julius Caesar |
| KJ | King John |
| KL | King Lear |
| LC* | A Lover's Complaint |
| LLL | Love's Labour's Lost |
| Luc* | The Rape of Lucrece |
| MA | Much Ado About Nothing |
| Mac | Macbeth |
| MM | Measure for Measure |
| MND | A Midsummer Night's Dream |
| MV | The Merchant of Venice |
| MW | The Merry Wives of Windsor |
| Oth | Othello |
| Per* | Pericles |
| PP* | The Passionate Pilgrim |
| PT* | The Phoenix and the Turtle |
| R2 | Richard II |
| R3 | Richard III |
| RJ | Romeo and Juliet |
| S* | Sonnets |

| | |
|---|---|
| Tem | The Tempest |
| Tim | Timon of Athens |
| Tit | Titus Andronicus |
| TC | Troilus and Cressida |
| TG | The Two Gentlemen of Verona |
| TN | Twelfth Night |
| TNK* | The Two Noble Kinsmen |
| TS | The Taming of the Shrew |
| VA* | Venus and Adonis |
| WT | The Winter's Tale |

# PART I
# INTRODUCTION

## An artistic-scientific endeavour

This dictionary has a single aim: to help those who wish to present Shakespeare using Early Modern English pronunciation—or OP ('original pronunciation'). Although this term has a much broader application, describing any period of phonological reconstruction in the history of a language, it has come to be popularly used when approaching Shakespeare in this way. It echoes another 'OP'—'original practices' (as used, for example, by Shakespeare's Globe in London), referring to the efforts that have been made to discover as much as possible about the ways in which plays of the period were originally performed.

OP is an exercise in applied linguistics—to be precise, in applied historical phonology. Phonology is the study of the sound system of a language—or, as here, of the state of a language in a particular period of time. Pronunciation always changes, as shown by the archive of recorded sound over the past century. The phonology of Early Modern English was thus different in several important respects from that of Modern English, and this dictionary gives an account of what those differences were. They are not so great as to make OP unintelligible to a modern ear: most of the consonants and almost half of the vowels haven't changed noticeably over the past 400 years, and the stress pattern on most words has stayed the same. So people listening to an OP production for the first time quickly 'tune in' to the system. But the consonants, vowels, and stresses that *have* changed are enough to produce a way of speaking that is distinctive, fresh, and intriguing, opening up new directions for linguistic, literary, and theatrical enquiry.

OP aims to meet a need that comes from outside linguistics, and in a theatre context is thus as much an artistic as a scientific endeavour. Although a great deal can be firmly established about the nature of the Early Modern English sound system, thanks to a century of research by philologists and historical phonologists, there are still several words where the evidence for a particular pronunciation is lacking or can be interpreted in more than one way—usually because alternative pronunciations were current, just as they are today. In such cases, all one can do is (as lawyers say) 'take a view'. Because of the limitations of the evidence, historical phonologists would never claim that their reconstructions were authentic, therefore; but they would say that they are plausible, and (in a situation such as a theatrical setting) usable and effective. They would also point out that several versions of OP are possible, based on different interpretations of the evidence, and my recommendations in this dictionary should be seen in that light. In this respect, a practitioner's choices as to which version of OP to use in a production involves a similar kind of decision-making to what takes place when deciding about other domains of theatrical practice, such as setting, lighting, music, movement, and costume.

In any applied linguistic venture, effectiveness is judged by the criteria laid down by practitioners. Just as the efficacy of a linguistically inspired speech therapy intervention is judged by the way a patient's language ability improves, so in the theatrical world the value of any linguistically motivated perspective is judged by the usual pragmatic criteria of artistic success. 'The play's the thing', after all, and everyone involved—director, actors, audience, and reviewers—needs to feel, after an OP production, that their theatrical experience has been enhanced by the approach. The way the OP 'movement' has grown, and the demand for support materials, suggests that this has often been the case—sufficiently often, at least, to motivate the present dictionary.

In one respect, OP isn't new at all to Shakespeare practitioners, and is already part of mainstream production. Everyone takes pains to take into account the cues provided by the metrical line, even though there are differences of opinion about just how much attention to pay to scansion in relation to other factors. And the metre shows clearly that many polysyllabic words had a different stress pattern from what they have today. So, for example, the following lines would be said with the stress brought forward:

> Instruct my daughter how she shall persever (*AW* 3.7.37)
> The dust on antique time would be unswept (*Cor* 2.3.118)

Anyone doing so, of course, is immediately doing (a bit of) OP.

Judging by the reactions to productions since Shakespeare's Globe's pioneering *Romeo and Juliet* in 2004 (described later in this introduction), it is possible to judge the theatrical potential of OP in three main ways.

- For actors, it must feel like a natural sound system—as Hamlet says, speech should come 'trippingly on the tongue'. They should find it learnable with no greater difficulty than they would experience in acquiring any other accent. And, once learned, they should feel that OP is a valuable part of their accent repertoire, offering new choices in their exploration of a character, so that they want to use it as much as they can. Directors, likewise, should find the experience fresh and illuminating, in the same way that all original practices offer an opportunity of getting 'closer to Shakespeare'.
- For dramaturges, and also for literary critics, OP should provide solutions to some of the difficulties encountered when speaking a text, and suggest fresh possibilities of character interpretation and interaction. Among the benefits here are the way it enables couplets to rhyme that fail to do so in Modern English, and the bringing to light of wordplay that is obscured by present-day pronunciation (see further below in the section 'The nature of the evidence').
- For audiences, OP offers a new auditory aesthetic, a contrast with British received pronunciation (RP) or the local modern regional accent in which they will have experienced Shakespeare hitherto. Those who speak with an accent other than RP (which in the UK comprises most of the population) say that OP reaches out to them in a way that RP does not, primarily because they recognize in it echoes of the way they themselves speak. 'We speak like that where we come from' has been the predictable audience response, regardless of where the listeners originate.[1] To a historical phonologist, this reaction—though naive—is understandable, for many of the distinctive features of present-day accents around the world can be traced back to the Early Modern sound system. OP thus offers a new kind of 'ownership' of Shakespeare—a point that has been made even more strongly by those from parts of the English-speaking world outside the UK where RP has never been the prestige accent.

This last point raises an important issue. The notion of 'Modern English pronunciation' is actually an abstraction, realized by hundreds of different accents around the world, and the same kind of variation existed in earlier states of the language. People often loosely refer to OP as 'an accent', but this is as misleading as it would be to refer to Modern English pronunciation as 'an accent'. It would be even more misleading to describe OP as 'Shakespeare's accent', as is sometimes done. We know nothing about how Shakespeare himself spoke, though we can conjecture that his accent would have been a mixture of Warwickshire and London. It cannot be stated too often that OP is a phonology—a sound system—which would have been realized in a variety of accents, all of which were different in certain respects from the variety we find in present-day English.

Shakespeare himself tells us that there was variation at the time. In *Romeo and Juliet* Mercutio contemptuously describes Tybalt as one of the 'new tuners of accent', Orlando is surprised when he hears the refined accent of disguised Rosalind in *As You Like It*; disguised Edgar adopts a West Country accent in *King Lear*. The actors on the Globe stage in 1600 would have displayed their regional origins in their speech, doubtless modified by their London living. Robert Armin was born in Norfolk, John Heminges in Worcestershire, Henry Condell probably in East Anglia, Lawrence Fletcher seems to have come down from Scotland. They would have sounded different, but they would all have reflected the phonology of the period. For example, such words as *invention, musician,* and *suspicion* would all have been said without the *-shun* ending that we use today, but with an ending more like 'see-on' (see further, p. xxxi). A pronunciation of *invention* by someone from Scotland and someone from Norfolk would have sounded different, but both speakers would have said the word in the second line in *Henry V* with four syllables. And similarly, two such speakers reading a sonnet aloud would each have respected the identity of the vowels in such rhyming word-pairs as *love* and *prove,* though one reading would have sounded recognizably Scottish and the other recognizably East Anglian.

The same sort of variation is to be expected when we encounter OP today. We hear it with some features of the accent of the present-day speaker superimposed. In the Globe production of *Romeo and Juliet* in 2004, for example, there was a Scots-tinged Juliet, a Cockney-tinged Nurse, an RP-tinged Romeo, and a Northern Irish-tinged Peter. In the Kansas University production of *A Midsummer Night's Dream* in 2010 and the University of Nevada production of *Hamlet* in 2011 the OP was heard filtered through a range of American accents. Regional differences in intonation accounted for some of the effects, but vowels were affected too, and this is possible because a vowel occupies a space in the mouth, not a point, and this is shown by a circle on the cardinal vowel diagrams (p. xli). Slight variations of vowel quality can thus be accommodated within that space, and these can signal regional or personal differences (the basis of individual voice recognition). Putting this in traditional linguistic terms: there can be several phonetic realizations of a vowel phoneme while preserving the status of that vowel within the sound system as a whole.

This dictionary codifies only the sound system of Early Modern English, and any articulation of it will be idiosyncratic to a degree. If you listen to the associated audio files you will hear my own rendition of OP, which will differ in tiny phonetic respects from anyone else's rendition, though not enough to cause the different phonemes to become confused. In performance, these tiny differences are an important element in preserving individual actor identities. And a critical element of OP training is to reign in an actor's accent so that the underlying phonological system is respected, and phonemic confusions are avoided, while at the same time not reducing all voices to an identical blandness.

The general effect of OP needs to be compared with any Modern English accent, not just RP, of course. We sometimes find present-day productions entirely in a regional accent, such as those mounted by the Northern Broadsides theatre company in a Yorkshire accent or a production of *Macbeth* entirely in Scottish, or which adopt a particular accent for a group of characters (such as playing the mechanicals with a Birmingham accent, as in Greg Doran's 2006 production of *A Midsummer Night's Dream*). The problem here is that these accents bring modern 'baggage' with them. Because we have grown up with these accents as part of our social milieu, we have developed associations and attitudes relating to them. They may be positive or negative, occupational or aesthetic, personal or public. A Yorkshire accent will remind us of someone we know, or some character on television, or some situation we have experienced, and it will prove very difficult to eliminate these associations from the characters we see on stage. But OP has no such baggage. Nobody today has heard it before, and the mixture of echoes which accompany it do not cohere into something recognizable. On the contrary, it is the unfamiliarity of the phonology which attracts the attention.

## The scope of this dictionary

OP presentations have now been made of period texts other than by Shakespeare—such as John Donne, composers John Dowland and William Byrd, and the writers who contributed to the front matter of the First Folio—and one day the entire corpus of Elizabethan English will be available for us to test hypotheses about the Early Modern English sound system. For this dictionary I have restricted the subject-matter to Shakespeare, and focused it on a single electronic edition of a First Folio. The reasons are partly pragmatic—this book contains the plays which are currently attracting greatest public interest—and partly practical, for providing a comprehensive description of all the relevant evidence in the Folio alone evidently produces a dictionary of significant size. It was also a corpus of sufficient extent to demonstrate the character of OP in fine detail. The conclusions are of course applicable to other texts of the time, including the remainder of the Shakespearean canon, even though in due course they may need to be modified in the light of wider-ranging studies.

What is this evidence? Historical phonologists use several types of data to reconstruct the sound system from a period before the advent of audio-recording, and these are discussed later in this introduction. For the Elizabethan period, chief among them are spellings and rhymes, which—judiciously interpreted, and supplemented by the observations of contemporary writers on language—provide most of the information we need in order to reconstruct OP. However, as OP studies are still in their infancy, and as any analyst frequently has to 'take a view', it is important to provide interested readers with enough of the data to allow them to evaluate the interpretations that have been made. I have thus included within the dictionary, along with the phonetic transcription of individual words, the following data.

- The entries list all the spelling variations of the words in speeches and stage directions of the First Folio, along with frequency data, but excluding any organizational content (words appearing in the front matter, play titles, lists of dramatis personae, and speaker-names, whether in full or abbreviated). Although quite extensive in its own right, this corpus can only be illustrative, and has to be seen in a wider orthographic context. For the present work, all entries were checked against the historically organized lists of spelling variations at the beginning of each entry in the online *Oxford English Dictionary* (www.oed.com), and the associated etymologies, which often contain notes on pronunciation. For example, *pollution* appears with two spellings in the Folio: *pollution* and *polusion*. While this suggests a pronunciation of the final syllable as 'see-on', the deduction is strongly reinforced by the *OED* listing of other spellings from Middle English into the fifteenth and sixteenth centuries:

> ME **pollicioun**, ME **pollucioun**, ME **pollucoun**, ME **pollusyone**, ME **polucion**, ME **polucioun**, ME–15 **pollucion**, ME–15 **polucyon**, 15–16 **pollusion**, 15– **pollution**, 16 **polusion**, 16 **polution**

No OP judgement was made without taking into account the information provided by the OED entries.

- Entries also list all the rhymes in the Shakespeare canon, using as source texts the edition of the *Collected Works* by Bate and Rasmussen and the Shakespeare's Words database (see bibliography p. xlix). This includes the poems, which provide the majority of the rhyming evidence. Judgements about whether a pair of lines rhyme are of course partly subjective. Rhyming is a conscious, creative, phonaesthetic process. Just because two lines happen to end with the same sounds doesn't necessarily mean they count as a rhyme. Because I am using rhymes as evidence for OP, I have therefore adopted a fairly strict policy of excluding any line-pairs where there is an element of doubt, such as at *Julius Caesar 1.1.32–3* where, in the middle of a scene that is entirely in prose and blank verse, we encounter adjacent lines ending in *home* and *Rome*.[2]

Cercignani (1981) repeatedly takes Kökeritz (1953) to task in these respects. Kökeritz threw his net very wide in his search for rhyming evidence, and even though he marked uncertain cases with an asterisk as 'possible or dubious' (1953: 400), there are many examples taken from blank verse where there is no real justification for including a pair of words in his index of rhymes, such as this sequence in *AC 3.13.33*: 'Do draw the inward quality after them / To suffer all alike. That he should dream'. Cercignani makes the point about such cases that 'an obvious prerequisite to the discussion of any rhyme from a phonological point of view is that two or more words are so manifestly intended to rhyme together as to justify their claim to the name of rhyme', and he concludes: 'the use of unreliable instances in support of alleged phonological developments is gravely misleading' (1981: 9–10).

For the same reason, I do not include many examples of wordplay as evidence for OP. There are a number of clear-cut cases, well-recognized by editors, and these will be found in the entries; but deciding whether a word is a pun is often a highly subjective matter. Some people have tried to read puns (especially risque ones) into virtually every word Shakespeare wrote! Although OP can be illuminating in suggesting puns that are missed in modern English pronunciation, as illustrated below, it is wise to adopt a more cautious approach than some authors (such as Kökeritz) have done in using them as evidence of phonetic identity between words.

## Entry structure

An entry in this dictionary thus consists of up to six elements, the first three of which are obligatory.

### *The headword*

The headword, along with any inflections, is shown in boldface, with an indication of word-class (part of speech). While this is conventional dictionary practice, in the case of OP the grammatical status of a word sometimes shows interesting correlations with spelling and pronunciation. For example, the adjective from *curse* is always spelled *cursed*, and pronounced as two syllables, whereas the past tense of the verb is always spelled *curs't* (or similar), and pronounced as a monosyllable.[3]

Inflected forms are abbreviated, unless wholly irregular, with an abbreviation linked to a preceding full form by a tilde:

**bear / ~est / ~s / ~eth / ~ing / bare / bore / ~st / borne** *v*
*in full*
bear / bearest / bears / beareth / bearing / bare / bore / borest / borne

If a word has an inflection that involves a spelling alternation, the point of departure in the preceding item is marked by a raised dot:

**beastl·y / ~iest** *adj*
*in full* beastly / beastliest

Any points of headword clarification are shown in square brackets:

**bark** [*animal*]
**bark** [*tree*]

If a word, or an inflected form, is only known from a non-Folio text, that text is specified next to the item (for abbreviations, see p. vii):

**impannelled** *S*
**betake /** *PP* **~s / betook** *v*

These should be read as follows: '*impannelled* occurs only in the *Sonnets*'; 'the form *betakes* occurs only in *Passionate Pilgrim*'. The exact locations are given in the rhyme line (see subsection on rhyme below).

Foreign words, chiefly from Latin or French, are also shown by an abbreviation after the headword:

**ainsi** *Fr adv*

It is important to appreciate that the list of variants reflects only the forms that occur in the First Folio. If a noun, for example, is shown without a plural form, this is simply because it is not used in this way in the Folio, and its omission says nothing about its use elsewhere in Elizabethan English. The dictionary is not an account of Early Modern English vocabulary, but only of the vocabulary of the First Folio (supplemented, as mentioned above, by words from the rest of the canon that illustrate rhymes).

A certain amount of standardization is required in the case of headwords, where variant spellings in the First Folio need to be brought together. A typical case is words beginning with *over-*, where we find *ouer, o'er, ore,* and *o're,* with sometimes all variants appearing and sometimes only an abbreviated form. In such cases, the headword is given first in full, with the spelling line showing the forms that actually appear in the text:

**overhasty**, *abbr* **o'er** *adj*
**sp** o're-hasty[1]

A by-product of grouping word-forms in this way is that it allows us to arrive at an informed conclusion about the 'number of words' in Shakespeare. The totals mentioned in the literature have varied greatly, mainly because people have not been systematic in distinguishing semantic units (lexemes, or lexical items) and words (strings of letters separated by spaces). In the *bear* example above there are clearly nine words, but they are all grammatical variants of a single semantic entity—the lexeme *bear*. We do not think of *bears* and *bearest*, for example, as 'different words', but as 'different forms of the same word'. It is this notion of 'different words' that gives us a true insight into the range of Shakespeare's vocabulary, and that is what is captured through the headwords (strictly, head lexemes) in this dictionary.

Vocabulary counting is full of difficulties, as I have pointed out elsewhere (Crystal, 2008). The dictionary contains 20,672 headwords, excluding cross-references, but these include 1,809 proper names, 495 foreign words, and 29 nonsense words (mainly the pseudo-linguistic interrogation of Parolles in *AW*), as well as 84 items from non-Folio works that are included solely because of their rhymes. If we exclude these, we are left with 18,255 English lexemes. The total is informative, but of course not definitive. It ignores a few typesetting errors where it is impossible to assign an item to any headword. And there are several instances where it is ambiguous whether a sequence of two words (such as *self* + *mettle*) should be seen as a compound word (i.e. a single lexeme) or not. I have taken a view, and not everyone may agree. Nor have I made any attempt to extract multi-word verbs (*go to, set on, lay by, pay back*, etc.) from the Folio—a difficult linguistic task in itself—as they have no bearing on OP. If these are taken as separate lexemes, the above total will be an understatement (I suspect by about a hundred) of the number of lexemes the Folio contains. Notwithstanding these riders, the figure of 18,255 is suggestive, in that—once the remaining texts in the canon are analysed in the same way—the figure of 'around 20,000' commonly cited in the literature for the size of Shakespeare's English vocabulary will not be far from the truth.

## *The pronunciations*

Pronunciation is shown using an International Phonetic Alphabet (IPA) transcription (described in detail on p. xl), but only where this is different from RP. As the main aim of this dictionary is to alert users to the points of contrast between Early Modern and Modern pronunciations, words where there is no difference are simply marked with an identity symbol (=). Most short vowels, for example, are the same, so in entries such as *bat, bashfulness*, and *baron*, the only transcription we need is shown as here:

**baron / ~s** *n*
=

The single = here applies to all the listed forms. In cases where there is a string of inflections, I repeat the = as required to show the way the pronunciations relate to the headwords, as here:

**bend / ~s / ~ing / ~ed / bent** *v*
= / = / ˈbendɪn, -ɪŋ / =

This reads: '*bend* and *bent* are the same today, as are *bended* and *bent*'. A total of 4,239 items in the entries use this symbol—around a fifth of all word-forms.

There are a few exceptions to the identity principle. The pronunciation is shown of all archaic words (such as *alarum*) and Classical names (such as *Aeson*), even if there has been no change since 1600, to help readers who may be unfamiliar with those areas of the lexicon. Also transcribed are cases where there is a risk of uncertainty because of pronunciation variation in Modern English, as in words like *fast*, which can be heard today with either a short (as in *cat*) or a long ('ah') vowel. OP uses the short vowel, so this word is transcribed as /fast/ in the dictionary, notwithstanding the fact that this pronunciation would be used by many RP speakers today. Similarly, where an RP pronunciation differs from General American, I give the OP transcription as an aid to US actors (as with *due*, *traduce*—/dju:/, not /du:/).

The identity convention would need to be extended if readers chose a basis of comparison other than RP, as several words where the OP is different from RP would show identity when compared with other accents. A case in point is the treatment of *r* after a vowel in such words as *bar* and *hair*. RP does not pronounce the *r* in this position; but because it is sounded in OP (see below) this dictionary transcribes such words using an appropriate symbol, [ɹ]. For English-speakers who do routinely pronounce *r* after a vowel, such as most speakers of American English, the presence of this symbol in the transcription thus has to be seen as a point of identity, not contrast, with OP.

Alternative pronunciations of the headword are separated by a comma, with the abbreviated forms linked to the preceding full form by a hyphen, and the place of substitution identified by a shared letter:

**abating** ə'betɪn, -ɪŋ, *in full* ə'betɪn, ə'betɪŋ [shared letter *ɪ*]
**respect** rɪ'speks, -kts, *in full* rɪ'speks, rɪ'spekts [shared letters *k* . . . *s*]

In cases like the following, the shared letters show reduced forms:

**perjury** 'pɐ:ɹdʒəˌrəɪ, -dʒər-, -dʒr-, *in full* 'pɐ:ɹdʒəˌrəɪ, 'pɐ:ɹdʒərəɪ, 'pɐ:ɹdʒrəɪ

As with headwords, the pronunciation of inflected forms is abbreviated:

**bath / ~s**
baθ / -s

In a sequence of abbreviated inflections, the point of departure is shown by a raised dot:

**ris·e / ~es / ~eth / ~ing**
rəɪz / 'rəɪz·ɪz / -əθ / -ɪn, -ɪŋ
*in full*, 'rəɪz·ɪz / 'rəɪzəθ / 'rəɪzɪn, -ɪŋ

Idiosyncratic pronunciations, such as by Welsh characters, are shown with a line reference:

**bashful** *adj*
=, *Fluellen H5 4.8.70* 'paʃfʊl

This example reads: 'the usual pronunciation of *bashful* is the same as today, but in this instance from Fluellen we find the following pronunciation'. The line references are to the editions used for the *Shakespeare's Words* website (www.shakespeareswords.com).

In many instances, a word has an unusual pronunciation (compared to Modern English), or alternative pronunciations, depending on its location within a metrical line. In such cases I draw attention to the metrical factor by preceding the transcription with *m*. I do not choose between alternatives: *m* simply indicates that the reader must take metre into account before arriving at an OP decision. And in examples such as *beautiful* below, the transcription leaves open the question of how strongly the secondary stress should be articulated.

> **thereon** *adv*
> *m* ðɛːɹˈɒn, ˈðɛːɹɒn
>
> **spiced** *adj*
> *m* ˈspəɪsɪd
>
> **beautiful** *adj*
> *m* ˈbjuːtɪˌfʊl

It is important to appreciate that transcriptions reflect the pronunciation of words only as they are used in the First Folio, and should not be taken to exclude the possibility of other pronunciations in other contexts.

### *The spellings*

Each entry has a section, introduced by **sp**, that shows the spelling(s) of the headword and its inflections as they appear in the First Folio, retaining the use of *i* for *j* and *u* for *v*, but ignoring the erratic use of an initial capital letter in common nouns. Capitalization is shown only for proper nouns. In addition, the electronic text makes use of two transcription conventions that are retained in this dictionary.

- If a word is broken at a line ending, this is shown with a hyphen.
- If a word has a diacritic indicating an omitted letter, this is shown in square brackets:

Both of these conventions are illustrated here:

> **sp** assistance[10], assista[n]ce[1], assi-stance[1]

Although these features are of little linguistic significance, I include them to enable any reader who wishes to do so to replicate my online searches in the edition of the text I used. Someone searching for all instances of *assistance* needs to know that in one instance this is found as *assista[n]ce* and in another as *assist-ance*. Similarly, the spelling line shows any isolated textual idiosyncrasies, such as an oddly spaced apostrophe or hyphen.

The superscript numerals show the number of occurrences of each form in the First Folio. The frequency with which a particular spelling is used can alert the phonologist to the relative importance of variant pronunciations; and a sense of relative frequency is important for actors who are learning OP, as it alerts them to those words which demand extra attention, simply because they are going to be often encountered. Apart from this, the frequency totals have, I believe, an intrinsic interest that goes well beyond the OP initiative, and suggest possible applications in other domains of Shakespearean language study where information about frequency of occurrence can be illuminating. The word-counts should however be seen only as a first approximation. We know from Elizabethan typesetting practice that no two Folios are identical in every respect, so a statistical count of a different copy from the one I used is going to show many small differences. In addition, word-counting is more difficult than might at first appear, as for two forms to count as the 'same' word they need to share grammatical identity, and quite often it is an analytical decision whether, for example, a word is being used as an adjective or an adverb, or whether a participle (ending in *-ing* or *-ed*) is being used adjectivally or as a verb. Semantic reasoning might lead analysts to make different decisions, and this will affect any word-count.[4]

Two other kinds of information are included in the spelling section:

- Readers using a modern edition of the plays will encounter emendations of words in the First Folio that editors have considered to be errors. As OP guidance is needed here too, emended forms are included in the dictionary, with the relevant line reference from the *Shakespeare's Words* website, as here:

  **Sackerson** *n*
  'sakəɹsən
  **sp** *MW 1.1.275 emend of* Saskerson[1]

- Occasionally, a useful piece of information regarding the pronunciation of a word comes from the way it is spelled in a different textual source, as in this example from the Second Quarto of Hamlet, where a pronunciation of *beetles* with a short vowel is clearly suggested by the following double consonant:

  **beetle / ~s** *v*
  'bi:tlz, 'be-
  **sp** beetles[1], *Q2 Ham 1.4.71* bettles

One further convention will be seen in the spellings section. The Folio typesetters often joined independent words by a hyphen: for example, *dried pear* is set as *dride-peare*. As these are not genuine compound words, it is important to locate each element in its appropriate alphabetical place, so that it can be seen alongside other instances, without losing its typographical distinctiveness. In this dictionary the secondary element is placed in square brackets. So, with this example, at *dried* you will see *dride-*[*peare*] and at *pear* the complementary [*dride*]*-peare*.

## *The rhymes*

Many entries have a section, introduced by **rh**, which lists any rhymes for the headword or its inflections found in the Shakespeare canon. Each rhyme is shown with its play or poem line reference, as given in the *Shakespeare's Words* database, as in this listing of rhymes for *abide* (for text abbreviations, see p. vii):

**rh** chide *Luc 486*; deified *LC 83*; hide *TC 5.6.30*; pride *R2 5.6.22*; putrified *Luc 1749*; slide *S 45.2*; tide *3H6 4.3.59*, *Luc 647*; wide *S 27.5*

In a number of cases, editorial decisions have introduced differences between the Folio text and *Shakespeare's Words*, so that the rhymes differ. These are marked by [F] or a related comment, as here:

**shield**
**rh** field *LLL 5.2.549* [*F end line*]

In this example, *shield* is at the end of a line in the Folio, but has been placed midline in the edition used in *Shakespeare's Words*.

Where a word has alternative rhymes in Modern English, these are distinguished numerically. The noun *regard*, for example, in OP rhymes with three types of word that would not be rhymes of each other in RP:

**rh** *1* hard *LC 213*; **rh** 2 heard *Luc 305*, *R2 2.1.28*; **rh** *3* ward *Luc 305*

A great deal of the reasoning used in reconstructing OP involves resolving such differences, in the light of the corpus of rhymes as a whole.

If a headword contains inflections that have rhymes, these are separated by forward slashes corresponding to the divisions in the headword line, as here:

**accident / ~s** *n*
'aksɪˌdent / -s
**sp** accident[21] / accedents[1], accidents[11]
**rh** lament *Ham 3.2.209*; discontent *S 124.5* / intents *S 115.5*

*Other elements*

A few entries have a section, introduced by *pun*, in which is listed any clear instance of wordplay that has relevance for OP. It is not a major feature of the dictionary, for the reason given above (p. xiii), but there are occasions when a pun can play a role in the reasoning which leads us to a decision about pronunciation. For example, part of the evidence that *ace* was pronounced /as/ is in the way it is punned with *ass*, as shown in this entry:

**ace** *n*
as
**sp** ace[3]
**pun** *Cym 2.3.2*, *MND 5.1.299* ass
> ames-ace, deus-ace

This example also illustrates one other feature of the entries in this book: the use of a cross-reference to other headwords that illustrate the same pronunciation. The aim here is to enable people to build up a more general sense of how a particular pronunciation is used. An actor who has looked up *ace*, to find out how it is pronounced in OP, is now aware of the other words in which this form is used. In an example like *bear* (meaning 'carry'), the cross-references can be numerous:

> over-, under-bear; bull-, under-bearing; high-, just-, self-, shard-, stiff-borne

For reasons of space economy, cross-references using a shared final element are clustered and abbreviated using hyphens, as in this example.

*The whole entry*

When an entry contains inflections, each form is separated by a forward slash, with abbreviated forms linked to the headword by typography, as described above. The pronunciation and spelling lines then reflect the structure of the headword line, using parallel slashes.

**bar / ~rest / ~s / ~red** *v*
bɑːɹ / -st / -z / -d
**sp** barre[17] / barr'st[1], bar'st[1] / barres[3], bars[1] / bar'd[2], bard[2], barr'd[4]
**rh** war *S 46.3* / stars *S 25.3* / reward *AW 2.1.148*
> em-, un-bar; barred, strong-barred

## The nature of the evidence

The reconstruction of OP is based on four kinds of evidence, collated by Dobson (1968), Kökeritz (1953), Barber (1976), Cercignani (1981), and others: spellings, rhymes, puns, and observations by contemporary writers. A similar approach is described in the reconstruction of Latin by Allen (1978: Foreword). Here is a brief example of each.

- In *RJ* 1.4.66, when Mercutio describes Queen Mab as having a whip with 'a lash of film', the Folio and Quarto spellings of *philome* indicate a bisyllabic pronunciation, 'fillum' (as in modern Irish English).
- In *MND* 3.2.118, Puck's couplet indicates a pronunciation of *one* that no longer exists in English: 'Then will two at once woo one / That must needs be sport alone'.
- In *LLL* 5.2.574, there is a pun in the line 'Your lion, that holds his pole-axe sitting on a close-stool, will be given to Ajax' which can only work if we recognize (see further below) that *Ajax* could also be pronounced 'a jakes' (*jakes* = 'privy').
- In Ben Jonson's *English Grammar* (1616), the letter *o* is described as follows: 'In the short time more flat, and akin to u; as . . . brother, love, prove', indicating that, for him at least, *prove* was pronounced like *love*, not the other way round.[5]

A reconstruction exercise is by no means straightforward because the textual evidence is often difficult to interpret. A distinctive spelling may genuinely indicate how a word was pronounced, or it may be a typesetter's error. Words at the ends of lines may point to a genuine rhyme (as in a sonnet) or may have a fortuitous connection (as in the examples above, p. xiii, from adjacent lines of blank verse). The possibility of eye-rhymes also needs to be considered (see further below). And what counts as a pun may be a modern interpretation rather than something Shakespeare intended.

Similarly, the evidence of the orthoepists is also often difficult to interpret because they privilege different pronunciations. This isn't surprising when we consider that they were writing throughout the whole of Shakespeare's lifetime and beyond—a period of great pronunciation change in the history of English. The changes were being brought about largely by the increased mobility of people in England (the great movement south to London from East Anglia and the Midlands had been a feature of the social scene for some decades) and the huge increase in the number of immigrants, making London a highly multilingual (and thus multidialectal) city. In population it had grown from around 120,000 in the mid-1500s to around 250,000 in 1600, and would increase further to around 400,000 by 1650. Dialect and accent diversity was an inevitable consequence, and norms were shifting as time passed. As a consequence, the orthoepists who wrote in the 1560s and 1570s often describe words differently from those who wrote in the 1620s and 1630s. In addition, there are differences which are probably due to their regional backgrounds, or to the likelihood that they were thinking of different sections of the population when they made their descriptions. The same sort of thing still happens today when we consider such pronunciation pairs as *schedule* beginning with 'sh-' or 'sk-', *garage* ending with '-ahzh' or '-idge', or *research* with the stress on the first or the second syllable. But my impression is that there was a great deal more variation in and around 1600 compared with today, and this is reflected in the many alternatives listed in this dictionary (about half the entries show some sort of variation). Moreover, attitudes towards pronunciation have to be taken into account.

Someone who feels that the Queen's English is the only acceptable style of speech today would paint a very different phonological picture from someone who thinks otherwise. Similar attitudes were present in Shakespeare's day, as Holofernes clearly illustrates.

Despite the difficulties, there are a sufficient number of clear cases of spellings, rhymes, puns, and comments to warrant a reconstruction of the English sound system of Shakespeare's day. The evidence of spellings and rhymes is particularly compelling, as they are so frequent. A systematic review of the comments made by contemporary writers is beyond the scope of this introduction (for which see Dobson), but a selection of their observations is included below.

## *Spellings*

Because spelling was not standardized in Shakespeare's day—an accepted notion of 'correct' spelling did not emerge until the eighteenth century—the choices made by the various writers and typesetters often provide pointers as to how a word was pronounced. With no agreed spelling for a word, the way it was said was likely to influence the way it was spelled. It is thus possible to work backwards from the spelling towards the pronunciation.

It is well known that a great deal of typographical randomness and error appears in the First Folio. Different spellings of a word may occur even in a single line, as in *AW* 5.3.314: 'Ile loue her dearely, euer, euer dearly'. But a typographical error is unlikely when we find the same distinctive spelling appearing in a variety of texts, a number of different spellings of a word pointing in the same direction, or a number of different words all using the same spelling. For example, in the First Folio we find *murder* and its derivative forms spelled as *murder* 84 times and as *murther* 175 times, clearly suggesting that a fricative pronunciation was routinely available. Spellings of *apparition* as *aparision* and *petitioner* as *peticioner*—as well as the *pollution* examples on p. xiii—indicate that the *-ti-* ending was pronounced /sɪ/. The spelling of *Hortentio* 10 times but *Hortensio* 30 times shows the same pronunciation in proper names. The point is confirmed by contemporary writers. Richard Mulcaster, for example, writes (p. 122 of his *Elementarie*):

> T, kepeth one force still sauing where a vowell followeth after, i, as in action, discretion, consumption, where as, t, soundeth like the full s, or strong c...

In such cases, a deduction about OP can be made with confidence. Other examples of spelling evidence are given in the description of individual sounds (p. xlii).

## *Rhymes*

A deduction based on rhyme becomes convincing when we see a word being paired with different words in a range of clear cases. *War*, for example, rhymes with *jar* in *VA* 98, with *scar* and *afar* in *Luc* 831, and with *bar* in *S* 46; *wars* rhymes with *stars* in *MND* 3.2.408. There are no instances of *war* rhyming with words like *more* and *shore*, as they would today. This clearly warrants a pronunciation as /wɑːɹ/—though exactly what phonetic value to give to the /ɑː/ vowel remains an open question (see further below in the section 'Long vowels').

A reconstruction becomes even more plausible when evidence from two sources coincides. *Again*, for example, is almost always pronounced with a long vowel /əˈgɛːn/ to rhyme with *twain, mane, plain, slain*, and so on (these examples from *Luc* 121, 209, 273, 408, 474). However, in *S* 79.8 we find *again* rhyming with *pen*, indicating that two pronunciations of this word existed, as they do today. The rhyming evidence for a short-vowel pronunciation is here further supported by the spelling, *agen*.

Where alternative pronunciations exist, it is important to take all the evidence into account when deciding on which variant to propose in cases where either would be possible. In the case of *again*, the evidence is clear. The usual spelling in the First Folio is *againe* (716 instances) or *again* (12 instances), which suggests that /ə'gɛːn/ should be the primary recommendation in a pronouncing dictionary. But the First Folio also gives us 26 instances of *agen*. Thanks to *S* 79, these cannot be viewed as merely a typographical aberration. They motivate us to use that pronunciation in those cases where the *agen* spelling occurs, and allow us to think of the short-vowel version as an option in other cases. The situation facing the actor or director is then exactly the same as it would be in a production of any modern play in which the word appears. They have to choose, and for this they will look to other criteria than the linguistic. The role of the historical linguist is to demonstrate the options, not to make dramaturgical or literary critical decisions.

A reconstruction becomes compelling when it resolves a phonological anomaly resulting from the changes between Early Modern and Modern English. For example, rhymes are an important index of play structure, being a frequent marker of scene closure: 55 per cent of all verse scenes in the canon (376 out of 684, using the *Oxford Shakespeare* scene divisions) end in a rhyming couplet or have one close by. And when a rhyme fails—something that happens in 12 per cent of cases (44 times)—the effect is really noticeable, as in this example from *RJ* 2.2:

> ROMEO: O, let us hence! I stand on sudden haste.
> FRIAR: Wisely and slow. They stumble that run fast.

The jarring effect is even more noticeable when it is the final two lines in a play, as at the end of *Macbeth*, where generations of actors have tried and failed to make something of *one* rhyming with *Scone*—a rhyme that only works in OP—or in this example from *King Lear*:

> We that are young
> Shall never see so much, nor live so long.

In the *Sonnets*, which have a transparent rhyme scheme, no less than 96 of the 154 have line-pairs which fail to rhyme in Modern English —142 instances in all (13 per cent of all lines). In two cases (*S* 72 and *S* 154), four of the seven line-pairs fail to rhyme. Here are the last ten lines of *S* 154:

> The fairest votary took up that fire,
> Which many legions of true hearts had warmed,
> And so the general of hot desire
> Was sleeping by a virgin hand disarmed.
> This brand she quenched in a cool well by,
> Which from love's fire took heat perpetual,
> Growing a bath and healthful remedy
> For men diseased; but I, my mistress' thrall,
> Came there for cure, and this by that I prove:
> Love's fire heats water, water cools not love.

In sum: only a third of the sonnets rhyme perfectly in modern English; and in eighteen instances, it is the final couplet which fails to work, leaving a particularly unsatisfactory impression in the ear. In cases of this kind, the need to apply an OP perspective is strong indeed.

It should be plain that this perspective often demands the recognition of alternative forms. For example, in *MND* we find that *gone* rhymes with *alone, anon, moan, none, on, Oberon*, and *upon*. We can divide these into three types. The rhymes with *on* and *upon*, which have always had short vowels in the history of English, along with *Oberon*, indicate the pronunciation that we still have today. The rhymes with *alone* and *moan* clearly indicate a long vowel. The rhymes with *anon* and *none* provide ambiguous evidence, as those words also had variant forms. This means that in any dictionary of Shakespearean pronunciation, both /gɒn/ and /goːn/ need to be represented. It also means that a choice is available when we encounter this word in a non-rhyming context. When Lucrece says (1051) 'O that is gone for which I sought to live', there is no way of knowing whether Elizabethans would have read this as /gɒn/ or /goːn/, or whether they would even have noticed the difference. We have a similar situation today with the vowel in *says*, which can be pronounced either short as /sez/ or long as /seɪz/. People switch from one to the other without a second thought, depending on such factors as euphony, emphasis, and speed of speaking. If a historical linguist 400 years hence had to reconstruct early twenty-first century English phonology, either version of *says* would be plausible. And it is the same today when we look back 400 years. To read Lucrece's line with a long vowel in *gone* may not be authentic (i.e. what Shakespeare intended), but it is at least plausible. And the same point applies if we read it with a short vowel.

### INEXACT RHYMES

Might some of the failed line-pairs be explained by alternative views of rhyme in which other factors than the auditory become influential? Two such notions could be relevant. In an 'eye-rhyme' (or 'printer's rhyme', as it is sometimes called), the endings are homographic but there is nothing phonologically in common: *cough* and *though*. In a 'half-rhyme' (also sometimes called 'slant rhyme'), the two syllables do share some phonological properties (distinctive features): consonants, in such cases as *dish* and *cash*; vowels, in such cases as *saver* and *later*.[6]

Once OP is taken into account, there are very few half-rhymes in the Shakespeare canon. My rhymes database contains 2842 rhyme pairings in the poems and 3927 rhyme pairings in the plays, giving 6769 rhyme pairings in all. Comparing the rhyming syllables of these pairings, only 269 of these are inexact according to the transcriptions in this dictionary (0.04%), so they are the candidates for 'half-rhymes'. Of these, 168 (62%) differ by only one distinctive feature, including many instances where the phonetic distinction is so slight that the rhymes might well have been perceived to be identical (e.g. /s/ vs /z/ in cases like *amiss/is* and *precise/flies*, where the final /z/ would have had some degree of devoicing). The remaining pairs include 71 instances separated by two distinctive features (eg *fa<u>v</u>our/la<u>b</u>our*—labio-dental vs bilabial, fricative vs plosive), 29 by three (e.g. *opportunity/infa<u>m</u>y*—voiceless, alveolar, plosive vs voiced, bilabial, nasal), and one by four (*r<u>e</u>adiness/f<u>o</u>rwardness*—mid-high, front, unrounded, short vs mid-low, back, rounded, long). It will be an interesting further investigation to explore how far these approximations suggest a more flexible view of rhyme by writers in Early Modern English—or, whether they would have been judged as simply 'bad rhymes'.[7]

Eye-rhymes, similarly, are few, once OP is taken into account, and I do not find this surprising. Certainly, as poetry became less an oral performance and more a private reading experience—a development which accompanied the availability of printed books and the rise of literacy in the sixteenth century—we might expect visual rhymes to be increasingly used as a poetic device. But from a linguistic point of view, this was unlikely to happen until a standardized spelling system had developed. When spelling is inconsistent, regionally diverse, and idiosyncratic, as it was in Middle English (with as many as 52 spellings recorded for *might*, for example, in the *OED*), a predictable graphaesthetic effect is impossible. And although the process of spelling standardization was well underway in the sixteenth century, it was still a long way from achieving the stability that would be seen a century later. As John Hart put it in his influential *Orthographie* (1569, folio 2), English spelling shows 'such confusion and disorder, as it may be accounted rather a kind of ciphring'. And Richard Mulcaster, in his *Elementarie* (1582), affirms that it is 'a very necessarie labor to set the writing certaine, that the reading may be sure'. Word-endings, in particular, were variably spelled, notably the presence or absence of a final *e* (*again* vs *againe*), the alternation between apostrophe and *e* (*arm'd* vs *armed*), the use of *ie* or *y* (*busie* vs *busy*), and variation between double and single consonants (*royall* vs *royal*). This is not a climate in which we would expect eye-rhymes to thrive.

'That the reading may be sure.' Poets, far more alert to the impact of their linguistic choices than the average language user, would hardly be likely to introduce a graphic effect when there was no guarantee that their readers would recognize it. And certainly not to the extent found in the sonnets. Given the importance attached to rhyme in this new genre, would anyone write a sonnet in which four of the seven line-pairs are eye-rhymes, as happens in sonnets 72 and 154? Or where there are three line-pairs anomalous (17, 61, 105, 116, 136)? A further 29 have two line-pairs affected. Even allowing for the occasional eye-rhyme or half-rhyme, I agree with Kökeritz (1953: 33), who says: 'No magic formula exists by means of which we can single out the eye rhymes in Shakespeare.'

If eye-rhymes were a regular device at the time, we would expect to see contemporary writers discussing them. But there is no mention of them in Samuel Daniel's *A Defence of Ryme* (1603), for example. On the contrary, there is a wholly auditory perspective in his definition of rhyme: 'number and harmonie of words, consisting of an agreeing sound in the last silables of seuerall verses, giuing both to the Eare an Eccho of a delightfull report & to the Memorie a deepe impression of what is deliuered therein.' It is the ear, not the eye, that is the theme of sixteenth-century writers. George Puttenham in *The Arte of English Poesie* (1569) heads his Chapter 2.5 as follows: 'How the good maker will not wrench his word to helpe his rime, either by falsifying his accent, or by untrue orthographie.' The auditory effect is paramount:

> Now there can not be in a maker a fowler fault, then to falsifie his accent to serue his cadence, or by vntrue orthographie to wrench his words to helpe his rime, for it is a signe that such a maker is not copious in his owne language, or (as they are wont to say) not halfe his crafts maister: as for example, if one should rime to this word *Restore* he may not match him with *Doore* or *Poore* for neither of both are of like terminant, either by good orthography or in naturall sound, therfore such rime is strained, so is it to this word *Ram* to say *came* or to *Beane Den* for the sound not nor be written alike, & many other like cadences which were superfluous to recite, and are vsuall with rude rimers who obserue not precisely the rules of *prosidie*.

He goes on to say: 'our maker must not be too licentious in his concords, but see that they go euen, iust and melodious in the eare'. And he concludes: 'a licentious maker is in truth but a bungler and not a Poet'.

Support for an auditory view also comes from some unlikely places. Benedick is a typical bungler. He is one of several lovers (such as Don Armado and Berowne) who make it clear that rhymes are prerequisite for romantic success, but he acknowledges that he himself is no good at them. 'I can find out no rhyme to "lady" but "baby"…I was not born under a rhyming planet' (MA 5.2.35). This is a half-rhyme, and his use of the example shows that he must have been aware of such phenomena as a poetic strategy; but the example also shows that he does not think of it as a very good strategy. If Benedick dismisses it in his love poem, it asks rather a lot to think of Shakespeare as welcoming it in his. I conclude that we may trust the majority of line-pairings we find in Shakespeare as guides to genuine auditory effect, while allowing the occasional visually motivated instance.[8]

### *Puns*

When it comes to puns, we are on different ground, as semantic considerations arise, and it is important, as stated above, to use only the clearest cases as evidence for OP, some of which may need to be expounded in detail for the wordplay to be understood. An example is the pronunciation of *Jaques*. The fact that this name was homophonous with *jakes* (meaning 'privy') was a standard joke at the time. Sir John Harington's remarkable proposal for a new design of privy was published in 1596 under the title *A new discovrse of a stale svbject, called the metamorphosis of Aiax* (Donno, 1962), and he actually begins his book with this anecdote (letters *s, w, i/j* and *u/v* are modernized here):

> There was a very tall & serviceable gentleman, somtime Lieutenant of the ordinance, called M. *Jaques Wingfield*; who coming one day, either of businesse, or of kindnesse, to visit a great Ladie in the Court; the Ladie bad her Gentlewoman aske, which of the *Wingfields* it was; he told her *Jaques Wingfield*: the modest gentlewoman, that was not so well seene in the French, to know that *Jaques*, was but *James* in English, was so bashfoole, that to mend the matter (as she thought) she brought her Ladie word, not without blushing, that it was *M. Privie Wingfield*; at which, I suppose the Lady then, I am sure the Gentleman after, as long as he lived, was wont to make great sport.

Harington later includes a verse in which *jakes* rhymes with *makes* (Donno, 1962: 158), leaving us in no doubt as to its pronunciation, /ʤɛːks/, modern /ʤeɪks/. Shakespeare certainly knew the word, for he uses it in *KL* 2.2.64 when Kent harangues Oswald: 'I will tread this unbolted villain into mortar and daub the wall of a jakes with him.'

We can be confident, then, about recommending this as one of the pronunciations of *Jaques* in OP. It is supported by the metre in several places, such as the dialogue between the First Lord and the Duke in *AY* 2.1.41, 54, where we find:

> Much marked of the melancholy Jaques...
> And never stays to greet him: 'Ay,' quoth Jaques...

And it is this pronunciation we need to bear in mind in order to interpret Touchstone's otherwise puzzling term of address at *AY* 3.3.67, when he euphemistically refers to Jaques as 'Master What-ye-call't'—perhaps, as with the gentlewoman in Harington's anecdote, a mite embarrassed to say the word in front of Audrey. But in the First Lord's speech we also find (*AY* 2.1.26) a disyllabic pronunciation, which must have been /ˈʤɛːkwiːz/, modern /ˈʤeɪkwiːz/:

> The melancholy Jaques grieves at that

This, along with similar usages in *AW*, remind us that we need to be careful. It will not be possible to see the 'privy' sense in all uses of the name.

We also need to note a second dimension to the *jakes* wordplay, for *Ajax* is also a pun. Harington's book is about the redesign (*metamorphosis*) of a jakes, and it is evident that this was a common pronunciation of *Ajax*. Indeed, those who criticized his invention took the pun a stage further, referring to him by such names as 'M[aister] A Jax'. It was a convenient insult—and one which was not lost on Shakespeare. In *TC* 2.1.63, Thersites rails at Ajax with the words 'But yet you look not well upon him; for whomsoever you take him to be, he is Ajax'. The insult is totally lost if one is unaware of the OP. And the pun is recapitulated at *TC* 2.3.95: 'Then will Ajax lack matter, if he have lost his argument.'

## Using original pronunciation

There are, then, two aspects to OP: the discovery procedure and the application. Once a plausible system has been established, with all its variants, it can be used to indicate the phonological options available for line readings, some of which can suggest a novel (to modern ears) interpretation of a familiar text. Whether the alternative interpretation is warranted is a separate matter. But in the first instance, we need to be aware that a possible ambiguity (in the sense of William Empson (1930), in his *Seven Types of Ambiguity*) is present. As he put it, on the opening page of his book: ambiguity is 'any verbal nuance, however slight, which gives room for alternative reactions to the same piece of language'. That is what OP does: it makes room.

### *Wordplay*

In *RJ*, for example, once we know that the two modern diphthongs /aɪ/ (as in *by*) and /ɔɪ/ (as in *boy*) were both realized as /əɪ/ in OP, then we are presented with the possibility that there is a genealogical nuance (*lines*) which can be added to the physical sense of *loins* in the Prologue: 'From forth the fatal loins of these two foes'. And once we know that a possible pronunciation of *woman* was /wo:mən/, 'woe-man', along with the more usual /wʊmən/, then several references can be interestingly re-thought (such as 'Frailty, thy name is woman', *Ham* 1.2.146). The evidence for this last option is to be found both in rhymes, as in *TG* 3.1.103,

> That man that hath a tongue, I say is no man
> If with his tongue he cannot win a woman.

but also explicitly in such lines as 'the Woeman, shee, did worke man woe' (from one of the Conscience poems by Richard Barnfield, 1598), and there are several other recorded instances of the pun in the sixteenth century (see *OED*, *woman*, sense P4a). The example makes the point that, to motivate OP in Shakespeare, we must not restrict ourselves to the canon, but use whatever data we can find from the period.

Sometimes an OP reading can remove a dramatic difficulty. An often-reported instance is in *AY* 2.7.23, where we find Jaques reporting to Duke Senior what he overheard Touchstone say.

> 'Thus we may see', quoth he, 'how the world wags:
> 'Tis but an hour ago since it was nine,
> And after one hour more 'twill be eleven,
> And so from hour to hour we ripe, and ripe,
> And then from hour to hour we rot, and rot,
> And thereby hangs a tale.'

This makes Jaques laugh for an hour—but there is nothing in the text, when read in a modern pronunciation, to motivate such a reaction. We need to know about the homophony between *hour* and *whore*, both pronounced /o:ɹ/ in OP, if we are to provide an explanation.

Similar examples of wordplay can be posited in the poems. The same homophony between *hour* and *whore* offers a fresh reading for *S 63*:

> Against my love shall be as I am now
> With Time's injurious hand crushed and o'er-worn, [whore-worn?]
> When hours have drained his blood and filled his brow [whores?]

With lines and wrinkles, when his youthful morn
Hath travelled on to age's steepy night...

Might we also read such a pun into *S* 124, talking about his love?

It fears not policy, that heretic,
Which works on leases of short-numbered hours, [whores?]
But all alone stands hugely politic,
That it nor grows with heat, nor drowns with showers.

In *S* 95.5, the words *vice* and *voice* would have sounded the same, both pronounced with /əɪ/:

That tongue that tells the story of thy days
(Making lascivious comments on thy sport)
Cannot dispraise, but in a kind of praise,
Naming thy name, blesses an ill report.
Oh what a mansion have those vices got [voices]
Which for their habitation chose out thee,

In *S* 53 there are repeated instances of *one* /o:n/. Apart from the fresh resonance in line 3, there is a new pun in line 4: *one/own* now neatly opposes *lend*. And the assonance continues into *Adonis* in line 5.

What is your substance, whereof are you made,
That millions of strange shadows on you tend?
Since every one hath, every one, one shade,
And you, but one, can every shadow lend.
Describe Adonis,

These are interesting questions which, in editions of the sonnets that ignore an OP perspective, are not mentioned as possibilities.

## *Phonaesthetic effects*

Also semantically relevant, though less directly, are those cases where the OP alters the relationships of alliteration or assonance among the words in a text, conveying a significantly different auditory impression from what would be heard in Modern English. The *Sonnets* provide many examples:

No matter then although my foot did stand
Upon the farthest earth removed from thee... (*S* 44)

In Modern English, *farthest* and *earth* have different vowels; in OP, *earth* echoes the vowel of *farthest* (/ɐ:ɹθ/.

This told, I joy, but then no longer glad... (*S* 45)

Today *I* and *joy* have different diphthongs; in OP, *joy* had the same diphthong as in *I* /əɪ/.

In the following extract from *S* 55, Modern English gives four different vowel values to the underlined syllables in *wasteful, war, overturn* / *work,* and *Mars*. In OP, the vowels of *Mars* and *war* coincide, and the front and central qualities of *waste* and *turn* / *work* become more open, resulting in a sequence of /a/-like vowels that adds an insistent urgency to the first and third lines.

> When wasteful war shall statues overturn,
> And broils root out the work of masonry,
> Nor Mars his sword nor war's quick fire shall burn
> The living record of your memory.

This is where OP offers least certainty, for assonance relies on phonetic as much as on phonological decisions. It is one thing to know that *war* was pronounced /wɑːɹ/. It is quite another to know exactly which quality of /ɑː/ to adopt. From a phonetic point of view, this vowel, with the tongue in the open back position, takes up quite a bit of articulatory space. In one direction (further forward) it could take on a hint of the quality of the vowel in *cat* (as spoken by a British northerner); in another, it could approach the vowel in *the*; in a third, it could approach the vowel heard in *cot*. There is plenty of room for disagreement over optimal readings here; but equally, the OP offers plenty of room for fresh readings of what is a very familiar text.

## *Sociolinguistic factors*

These are points relating to texts seen as poetry. When the texts are seen as drama, OP raises a further set of considerations, sociolinguistic and stylistic in character. One of the most important things to appreciate about OP is that the range of accents it generated lacked a single prestige variety such as we encounter in present-day RP. RP was an accent that developed at the end of the eighteenth century—a class accent contrived to allow the upper-classes to distinguish themselves from the way people from other classes talked. If Cockneys omitted /h/ when it was there in the spelling and inserted it when it was not (as in *I 'urt my harm*), then those who wanted to distance themselves as far as possible from Cockney speech would follow the opposite procedure, and scrupulously follow the spelling. If people from the provinces around Britain pronounced an /r/ after vowels, then those wishing to appear non-provincial would not. And slowly the phonetic character of RP evolved as the prestige, regionally neutral, educated, elite way of talking in England.

No such accent existed in Shakespeare's day. As Empson puts it at one point: 'Elizabethan pronunciation was very little troubled by snobbery' (1930: 26). People with strong regional accents could achieve the highest positions in the land (such as Raleigh and Drake with their Devonshire speech). When James came to the throne in 1603, Scottish accents became the dominant voice of the court. The only way you could show, through the way you talked, that you were a member of the educated elite was to use special vocabulary or grammar. Accent alone would not do it. Educated people would probably display their literacy by having their pronunciation reflect the way words were spelled—a practice that must have been very common, for Shakespeare plainly expected people to recognize the character of Holofernes in *Love's Labour's Lost*, with his exaggerated respect for spelling. Holofernes is horrified at the 'rackers of orthography' who omit the /b/ in such words as *doubt* and *debt* and who leave out the /l/ in *calf* and *half*. But what Holofernes' accent was is an open question.

We cannot rid ourselves entirely of the influence of Modern English phonetics and phonology, of course. The point applies equally to all aspects of 'original practices' productions—which is why Shakespeare's Globe tends to distance itself from the notion that they are being 'authentic'. Nothing can totally recreate the Jacobethan experience. The sounds, smells, and tactility of the Globe are hugely different from how it would have been. No jumbo jets rumbling overhead then. No smell of urine today. And it is the same with pronunciation, as can be seen with the use of /h/. Ever since the Middle Ages, English accents have used or dropped initial /h/. In Shakespeare's time, it would have come and gone without notice, in much the same way as people today sometimes vary their pronunciations of *again, says*, and *often*—or indeed /h/ itself in unstressed positions (as in *I saw him in the park*). So it would be perfectly possible for an educated person to pronounce a word beginning with *h* in a stressed syllable either with or without the sound. The evidence is partly in the spellings, such as *Ercles* for *Hercules, Ircanian* for *Hyrcanian*, and *dungell* for *dunghill*, as well as elisions like *t'have* and *th'harmony* and OED spellings of such words as *halcyon, halt, homage*, and *habiliments* without an *h*. But it is also in the contemporary writers, who comment on individual words. Palsgrave, for example, writing in 1530, says about *habitacion*: 'in whiche *h* is written and nat sounded with us', and various Folio citations show *h*-words preceded by *an* or *mine* suggesting *h*-lessness, as in *an habitation, an hoast, an hayre*, and *an hypocrite*. On the other hand, the spellings show a great deal of variation. The Folio gives us instances of both *a hundred* and *an hundred, an habitation*, and *a habit*, and both *my* and *mine* preceding *host, haire*, and *hostesse*. Clearly, both alternatives need to be recognized in an OP dictionary.

However, in making decisions about the forms to use in a production, we cannot rid ourselves completely of our modern associations. It may have been perfectly possible for actors to address each other as *'Amlet* and *'Oratio* in 1600, but this would introduce a distraction to modern listeners, who would not expect to hear a dropped *h* in such upper-class people. On the other hand, they would not be disturbed by *h*-dropping if lower-class characters do it, as that conforms to modern stereotypes. So here we have a set of new options for characters. In *MND*, for example, an OP perspective could keep /h/ for Theseus and Hippolyta and the lovers, and omit it for the mechanicals. But what do we do with the fairies? Do Oberon and Titania drop their *hs*, as down-to-earth beings might do, or do they keep them, as might befit a well-brought-up Fairy King and Queen? And what about Puck, whose naughtiness might have a linguistic reflex in *h*-dropping? If he is an *h*-dropper, then he has an extra option, when mimicking the voices of Lysander and Demetrius in the forest, by adding upper-class *hs* as required. Or, to take an example from towards the end of the play, a subtle theatrical effect can be achieved though the use of /h/ when the mechanicals are putting on their play, and attempting to adopt a high oratorical vein. They know there should be *hs* somewhere, but are not entirely sure where. Snout, as Wall, for example, might say this—unnecessarily pronouncing them on the grammatical words, and over-emphasizing them on the content words:

> And such a wall as I would have you think
> That had in it a crannied 'ole or chink...

These are tiny points, but they are not trivial ones, and are the kinds of issue that take up a great deal of time in the rehearsal room, as they can offer fresh ideas about character and interaction.

Many such options can be found. In *Twelfth Night*, we can well imagine Orsino and Olivia pronouncing their *hs*, given their educated background, and the Captain and Antonio not doing so. But does Sir Toby? Sir Andrew? Malvolio? And what should happen with the poetry? Were sonnets read aloud in a more declamatory 'high' style or colloquially? From the comments made by the contemporary writers on poetry, both styles would seem to have been used. Puttenham, for example, affirms a high style in his definition of poetry (p. 18):

> Poesie is a pleasant maner of vtterance varying from the ordinarie of purpose to refresh the mynde by the eares delight.

and notions such as 'delicacy' and 'cleanness' strongly suggest a care for articulation that would motivate the sounding of /h/:

> speech by meeter is a kind of vtterance, more cleanly couched and more delicate to the eare then prose is, because it is more currant and slipper vpon the tongue, and withal tunable and melodious, as a kind of Musicke, and therfore may be tearmed a musicall speech or vtterance, which cannot but please the hearer very well.

On the other hand, a more colloquial style is suggested by demotic and informal settings (pp. 8, 10):

> And the great Princes, and Popes, and Sultans would one salute and greet an other sometime in friendship and sport, sometime in earnest and enmitie by ryming verses, & nothing seemed clerkly done, but must be done in ryme:
>
> So did euery scholer & secular clerke or versifier, when he wrote any short poeme or matter of good lesson put in in ryme, whereby it came to passe that all your old Prouerbes and common sayinges, which they would haue plausible to the reader and easie to remember and beare away, were of that sorte as these.

And it is difficult to imagine a high style for the opening of *S 40*, with its markedly colloquial syntax (*yea* is /jɛ:/, 'yeah'):

> Take all my loves, my love, yea, take them all;
> What hast thou then more than thou hadst before?

Would someone who has just said 'mi luv' and 'yeah' pronounce *hast* and *hadst* with full-blown *h*s? Holofernes (*LLL* 5.1.19) would have insisted on the spelling being fully pronounced, of course. But would your average lover?

## *Character choices*

The large number of alternative pronunciations recorded in this dictionary offers actors many options to suit their interpretation of a character. In addition to the possible implications of *h*-dropping, there is the colloquial vs formal choice of *g*-dropping in the verbal *-ing* suffix (e.g. *possessing* vs *possessin'*, indicated by such spellings as *poprin* for *poppering*), or of *t*-dropping in the *-est* suffix (as shown by such spellings as *interrupts* for *interruptest*, and rhymes such as *fleet'st* and *sweete*). The colloquial elision of a syllable is very frequent (e.g. *prosp'rous, gen'rall, confedrate*) and the existence of alternative forms suggests a potential stylistic contrast, as in *buttery* along with *buttry*, *vtterance* along with *vtt'rance* and *vttrance*.

Several of these stylistic options are doubtless a consequence of a speech rate that followed Hamlet's recommendation to the players that they should speak 'trippingly upon the tongue' and not 'mouth' the lines as if they were being spoken by town criers (*Ham* 3.2.1). The increase in speed which comes from implementing this directive is immediately noticeable, with full attention paid to the elisions indicated in the orthography (*i'th*, *woo't*, etc). An OP rendition of a speech like 'It is my lady. O, it is my love! O that she knew she were!' (*RJ* 2.2.10) lacks the fuller articulation of the unstressed syllables usually heard in a Modern English production.

> MODERN: /ɪt ɪz maɪ leɪdɪ. əʊ, ɪt ɪz maɪ lʌv. əʊ ðæt ʃi: nju: ʃi: wə:/
> OP: /ɪt ɪz mɪ lɛ:dəɪ. o:, ɪt ɪz mɪ lɤv. o: ðət ʃɪ nju: ʃɪ wɑ:ɹ/

The cumulative difference in speed was seen in the Globe production of *Romeo and Juliet*, in which the same company performed the play both in OP and in Modern English: the OP version was ten minutes shorter than its modern counterpart—and it took the company a little by surprise, especially when it proved necessary to integrate the language with other activities, such as in the fight scene, or in the banquet scene (where the speaking and the dancing was carefully choreographed in Modern English, but in OP the speaking finished well before the dancing did). The Master of Movement at the Globe also observed that the actors were holding themselves differently and moving about the stage differently in the OP production compared with their performance in the Modern English one. Actors routinely report such effects, finding that OP affects their whole body, and is not simply 'an accent'.

Conveying effects of speech rate in connected speech is not the remit of a dictionary, which deals in single lexical items, but the consequences of a rapid articulation do often need to be taken into account, especially in relation to the elision of elements in consonant clusters, as with *promps* (= prompts), *temt* (= tempt), and *gransier* (= grandsire). The *-est* verb inflection is especially affected, as most instances are reduced to *-'st*—or even to *-s*, if appearing in a difficult-to-articulate consonant cluster, or followed by a similar sound, as in the examples above. In this dictionary, there are many entries where variations in formality are shown by elided pronunciations. The point also sometimes motivates a pun, as with *presence* and *presents* in *AY* 1.2.113–15.

The fact that pronunciations were changing over time during Shakespeare's lifetime offers a further option for characterization. For example, in the 1580s words like *musician* and *invention* seem to have been pronounced /mju'zɪsɪən/ and /in'vensɪən/. Forty years later we see pronunciations such as /mju'ziʃɪən/ and /ɪn'venʃɪən/, and soon after we find the modern pronunciations /-ʃən/, and /-ʃn/. So in 1600 older people would very likely have said the former, and younger people the latter. And this allows us a theatrical option, which was exploited in the *Romeo and Juliet* production. The old Montagues and Capulets said the words with /sɪən/ and the young ones with /ʃɪən/. In this dictionary, words ending in *-tion*, *-cion* (etc.) are shown with a conservative pronunciation, /-sɪən/. The choice of monosyllabic /-sɪən/ versus disyllabic /-sɪˌɒn/ depends on the metre.

Sometimes the spelling of an individual item can suggest a character choice, as in these examples from the OP production of *Henry V* mounted at Shakespeare's Globe in 2015. At *H5* 5.2.258 the French princess Katherine's maid says

> Dat it is not be de fashon pour le Ladies of Fraunce;

this is the only case in the Folio where *fashion* is spelled without its *i*. This would seem to suggest a French pronunciation rather than the usual OP 'fash-ee-on'. The point is missed in modern editions, which spell the word as *fashion*.

A little later there is a nuance that comes from the way *France* is spelled. The name of the country turns up many times in the canon, and is always spelled *France*, pronounced /frans/, apart from ten instances where it is *Fraunce*, /frɔːns/. Seven of these cases belong to people who are clearly French or who are reading French aloud: Pucelle in *1H6*, the Frenchman in *Cym*, Katherine and Lady (as in the above example), and Exeter in *H5*. But the remaining three come from Henry himself—twice when he is trying to speak French with Katherine (where an attempt at a French pronunciation is unremarkable), and the following interesting case:

> It is not a fashion for the Maids in Fraunce to kisse before they are marryed, would she say?

Henry is repeating what Katherine's maid has just said, and—although now speaking English—seems to be copying her pronunciation of *Fraunce*. In the Globe co-production, the actor playing Henry made much of this option, with humorous effect.

## The history of OP studies

Contemporary interest in reconstructing Shakespearean pronunciation should be seen as a revival rather than an innovation, as previous projects can be traced back to the mid-nineteenth century.[9] Before that, there was of course regular exploration into the prosody of his verse, and within the perspective of nineteenth-century philology attention was routinely drawn to individual puns, rhymes, and metrical idiosyncrasies. A typical example is Craik (1857). But nobody tried to construct a system of early pronunciation in real detail until an essay by the American literary critic and lawyer Richard Grant White, whose many works on Shakespeare included two editions of the plays. He was also a music critic, and it was perhaps this joint interest which led him to pay special attention to OP. In an appendix, 'Memorandum on English Pronunciation in the Elizabethan Era', he analyses rhymes, puns, and spellings as evidence of early pronunciation, and is the first to anticipate the reaction of readers (White, 1865). After giving a transcription of a *Hamlet* speech with respellings (rather than phonetic transcription, which was not available in his day), he comments:

> Some readers may shrink from the conclusions to which the foregoing memorandums lead, because of the strangeness, and, as they will think, the uncouthness, of the pronunciation which they will involve. They will imagine *Hamlet* exclaiming:—
>
> 'A *baste* that wants *discoorse* of *rayson*
> Would *haive moorn'd* longer!'...
>
> and, overcome by the astonishing effect of the passages thus spoken, they will refuse to believe that they were ever thus pronounced out of Ireland.

As mentioned above, people always hear echoes of other accents in OP, and Irish is one of the commonest impressions, though only a few of the features of OP have a direct correspondence with modern Irish accents. However, reactions of this kind have been heard every time OP has since been presented, right down to the present day. And White's riposte has often been made too:

> But let them suppose that such was the pronunciation of Shakespeare's day, and they must see that our orthoepy would have sounded as strange and laughable to our forefathers, as theirs does to us.

White's interest is paralleled by a number of other publications that appeared in the early 1860s. George P. Marsh, for example, delivered a series of lectures at Columbia College in New York in 1858–9. Lecture 22 was called 'Orthoepical change in English'. It was a general discussion, from Old English onwards, but it contained several references to Shakespeare, and some discussion of general principles, such as the use of metrics and rhyme as evidence. He warns against the uncritical use of rhymes, and he identifies the biggest difficulty facing his contemporaries: 'All the old English writers on orthography and pronunciation fail alike, in the want of clear descriptive analysis of sounds' (1861: 475). Thirty years later, the publication of the International Phonetic Alphabet would help to solve that problem.

The topic of OP was evidently being widely discussed at the time. In 1864, the work of Craik, Marsh, and White was analysed in a long review article by Charles S. Pierce and J. B. Noyes in the *North American Review*. And in Britain, a similar interest was emerging in the embryonic phonetics community. The major work was by Alexander Ellis (1869–74), *On Early English Pronunciation*, in which Chaucer and Shakespeare receive special attention. This was a massive study, over a thousand pages in its four parts. Ellis had in 1867 given a paper to the Philological Society on

'Pronunciation in the Sixteenth Century'. He was excited to be able to explore the subject using the new system of palaeotype symbols devised by Melville Bell in *Visible Speech*, replacing earlier metaphorical expressions for sound description ('thick, thin, fat, full, flat, hard, rough', etc.). In Part 3 of his book (1871: 26–7) we find the first statement of the method that has been used ever since. To begin with, we need an awareness of the principles underlying sound change:

> In tracing the alteration of vowel sounds from the XVIth through the XVIIth to the XVIIIth century a certain definite line of change came to light, which was more or less confirmed by a comparison of the changes, as far as they can be traced, in other languages.

Second, we must acknowledge the importance of auditory rhyme, in a period when few people knew how to spell:

> the rhymes to be appreciated at all must have been rhymes to the ear, and not the modern monstrosity of rhymes to the eye.

Ignoring the value-judgement, Ellis's emphasis is correct. Eye-rhymes presuppose a standardized spelling system, which did not exist in Shakespeare's day (p. xxiii); and it is always the auditory requirement of rhyming that dominates when this topic is dealt with in the books on poetics that were around at the time, such as George Puttenham's *The Arte of English Poesie*.

Third, we need to know the views of contemporary authors, of whom Ellis lists and paraphrases several. This is where we get the first collation of evidence of such pronunciations as a short vowel in *prove* and *remove* (ibid: 100–1), a detailed discussion of the phonetic quality of postvocalic *r* (ibid: 200–1), and other period effects. His account is unprecedented in its detail, and not to be surpassed until Dobson almost a century later. Ellis also comments on the effect of OP on an audience, and—despite his scholarly caution expressed on almost every page—reaches a very firm conclusion (ibid: 224):

> There can be no reasonable doubt, after the preceding discussions, of its very closely representing the pronunciation actually in use by the actors who performed Shakspere's plays in his lifetime.

Ellis's transcription was a major step forward, but his palaeotypy was limited to 'the ordinary printing types', as the title page put it, he completely ignores the evidence provided by spelling, and the representations are not always easy to interpret. A reader schooled in modern phonetics has to rethink several parameters in order to get a sense of the postulated sounds.

It is in section 8 of his book (ibid: 917ff.) that Ellis goes into the matter in real detail, evaluating the authority of the various orthoepists, and stating the internal evidence: 'puns, metre, and rhyme'. He sees straight away that the pun 'is not really of so much use as might have been expected', but he nonetheless identifies a large number of punning word pairs that do provide good evidence of pronunciation (such as *goats/Goths, dollar/dolour, Rome/room, civil/Seville*). He gives a long list of metrical variants, reproduces the orthoepist Alexander Gil's Latin account as evidence, and quotes many of the examples contained in Abbott's *Grammar*, which was being published at the time. For instance, he lists copious instances justifying the use of an extra syllable in such words as *patience* and *substantial*. He also abstracts the main findings of White (ibid: 966ff.), and makes a detailed comparison of his approach and the conclusions of Peirce and Noyes, before concluding (ibid: 917): 'we do not much differ'—an interesting remark, given that the two studies were referring their phonetic values to different regional base accents, American and British.

In relation to rhymes, Ellis cautions about trusting rhymes too much, but nonetheless makes some illuminating observations. He notes that Shakespeare is not as liberal [i.e. respecting phonetic accuracy] as Spenser, and that the most liberal rhymes are to be found in the songs, where 'he seems to have been quite contented at times with a rude approximation' (ibid: 953). But despite Ellis's caution, he concludes that, 'viewed as a whole, the system of rhymes is confirmatory of the conclusions drawn from a consideration of external authorities'. He ends with a series of specimens in palaeotype from several plays.

Like White, Ellis takes pains to anticipate the view of readers (ibid: 982–4):

> The pronunciation founded on these conclusions, and realized in the following examples, may at first hearing appear rude and provincial. But I have tried the effect of reading some of these passages to many persons, including well-known elocutionists, and the general result has been an expression of satisfaction, shewing that the poetry was not burlesqued or in any way impaired by this change, but, on the contrary, seemed to gain in power and impressiveness.

The reference to elocutionists is the Victorian temperament showing through, as is his fear of actually using any of this approach on the stage:

> it is, of course, not to be thought of that Shakspere's plays should now be publicly read or performed in this pronunciation.... As essentially our household poet, Shakspere will, and must, in each age of the English language, be read and spoken in the current pronunciation of the time, and any marked departure from it (except occasional and familiar "resolutions", sounding the final *-ed*, and shifting the position of the accent, which are accepted archaisms consecrated by usage), would withdraw the attention of a mixed audience or of the habitual reader from the thought to the word, would cross old associations, would jar upon cherished memories, and would be therefore generally unacceptable.

This was a time when RP ruled the English stage, as it did the British Empire.

The interest in OP continued over subsequent decades, especially in Germany, where the study of the history of English was an important theme in German comparative philology (e.g. Sweet, 1874; Franz, 1905). Shakespeare and Chaucer attracted especial attention. The French phonetician Paul Passy, the founder of the International Phonetics Association, reports (1905) on a vacation visit to Britain where he sat in on lectures by Henry Sweet, and he comments on Sweet's readings from Chaucer and Shakespeare in OP. The following year, the professor of English philology at Marburg, Wilhelm Viëtor, produced two books on the subject, using the new International Phonetic Alphabet (1906a, 1906b). He comments that, although there has been a great deal of German work on English historical phonetics, 'the pronunciation of Shakspere has only incidentally been treated since 1871' (1906a: 3). He has read Ellis, but finds his transcription to be 'rather archaic' (ibid: 2). His aim is 'to show that there is a far greater majority of perfect rimes in Shakespeare's poems and plays than might appear from modern usage, and also from the conclusions of Ellis' (ibid: 5). The book is predominantly about the evidence provided by the rhymes, with two-thirds of it (pp. 116–266) devoted to a comprehensive rhyme-index. Variant pronunciations receive special mention. However, in the Reader that accompanied his theoretical book, he adopts a simplified transcription which does not distinguish between strong and weak vowels. He also notes few variants—mainly uncertainties over length, by putting the length mark in parentheses, as in *hæ(:)st* for *haste*. But this was the fullest attempt at the time to present texts in OP, and his work influenced several others over the next few decades (e.g. Ayres, 1916; Blandford, 1927)—though it would later be strongly attacked by Kökeritz (1953: 48-9) for its 'archaic and artificial' style of utterance—including Daniel Jones, who first encountered phonetics while studying German at Marburg.

Jones was beginning his own explorations in OP at this time. In 1909 he made a public presentation at University College London (UCL) of 'Scenes from Shakespeare in the original pronunciation', playing Prospero and Andrew Aguecheek (*Tem* 1.2, *TN* 1.3). It was reviewed by Noël-Armfield, who later became Jones's assistant, in *Le Maître phonétique* (1910):

> Saturday, 3 July, 1909, marks an epoch in the history of Elizabethan representations of Shakespeare. On that date people living in the twentieth century heard some of Shakespeare's work in the pronunciation which may be safely accepted as that used by the poet himself and his fellow actors.

Jones, says Noël-Armfield, 'was, of course, responsible for the phonetic transcription, as well as for the actual pronunciation of the performers, and it is a testimony to the care and thoroughness with which he rehearsed his little company that we noticed very few deviations from the printed transcriptions.' The event also received a favourable mention in an *Observer* review the next day (4 July 1909), which reported some of the sound effects. The *Observer* reviewer follows listeners before and after who attempt to relate the OP to accents they already know:

> The effect of the old pronunciation on the ear was very pleasing. It strongly resembles the broad, rich dialect of the West of England, with a strong admixture of the Lancashire speech.

No mention of Irish, this time.

Jones was unimpressed with the attempts of newspaper reporters to write OP down. In a letter to the *Manchester Guardian* (30 June 1909), he castigated the writer of an article announcing the forthcoming event at UCL for its use of a system of respelling which, gives only 'the very roughest idea of what the actual pronunciation was'. He insists: 'a scientific system of phonetic transcription is essential'. And the following year he published a supplement (1910a) to *Le Maître phonétique* containing the transcription, and followed it up with some notes on his method (1910b), based on those he wrote for the programme, in which he acknowledges the prior work of Ellis, Sweet, and Viëtor. The event was such a success that he repeated it in Wimbledon (where he lived) in December 1909, with music, himself singing some madrigals. He also would give occasional recitals at social occasions, such as dinners and weddings, usually 'without book'. As part of the plans for a proposed Institute of Phonetics (which never materialized), Jones suggested (in a letter, 21 November 1919) that he could put on a shortened version of *TN* in OP, to be staged by pupils from his brother Arnold's prep school, but this never went ahead.[10]

Jones's interest in OP evidently influenced his junior colleagues. Harold Palmer joined him in 1915 and stayed there for five years, eventually being given charge of what Jones called the 'Spoken English department'. Palmer then went to Japan, where he stayed for many years, becoming a major influence on the early development of English language teaching. But he was often in England, and at the official dinner of the Second International Congress of Phonetic Sciences, held in London in 1935, he is on record as being part of the entertainment: Jones recited some Chaucer, and Palmer presented (in song) 'The Modern Phonetician'—a fluency exercise reworking Gilbert & Sullivan's 'Modern Major-General'. Although we have no example of Palmer himself using OP, he evidently was well aware of it, judging by the opening lines of the third stanza:

> I've read the works of Daniel Jones, of Ripman and of Viëtor
> (Who tells us how the Germans speak in every German theatre)...

It was Palmer's collaborator, F(rancis) G(eorge) Blandford, who was more involved with OP. Blandford had been an undergraduate at Corpus Christi College in Cambridge, later becoming a lecturer and then director of studies in the Secondary Department of the Cambridge University Training College for Schoolmasters (later, the Department of Education). As early as 1927, he had published a booklet transcribing *TN* 1.5 into OP for the Festival Theatre Company in

Cambridge, and this was used on a number of occasions. A production by Terence Gray at the Cambridge Festival Theatre in 1933 included this scene in OP (everything else was in modern English). The experiment did not impress the *Manchester Guardian* correspondent (18 May 1933), who described the OP as an experiment that was 'interesting if not entirely justified'—'an impossible mixture of Scottish, Irish, Welsh, and a Lancashire dialect.' No mention of the West Country, this time.

Although not a Jonesian, in his approach to phonetic theory, Blandford would certainly have encountered Jones on the academic circuit, as well as through the BBC. Jones had began an association with the BBC in 1926, when he became one of the founder members of the Advisory Committee on Spoken English. A decade later (15 April 1936), the BBC put out a 1-hour programme called 'London Calling—1600'. The *Manchester Guardian* radio critic loved it:

> The result was a speech that sounded as if it were made up of some of the more pleasant English country accents and something almost foreign, while the whole effect was much more soft and musical than spoken Shakespeare is to-day.

The programme was repeated on 25 February 1937. Clearly, OP was attracting a great deal of interest—and the interest now extended across the Atlantic. There was a publicity piece in the *New York Times* (21 February 1937) which refers to a Cambridge professor (i.e. Blandford) schooling the cast in 'the correct Elizabethan pronunciation, which to us today seems very strange—something like a mixture of Yorkshire dialect and Irish brogue'. And the BBC kept up its involvement. At the end of 1937 (6 December) there was a fresh broadcast of the *TN* scene in both modern pronunciation and OP for its Experimental Drama Hour, with Blandford as the consultant. Jones almost certainly was involved behind the scenes in maintaining the BBC's interest, as he was still himself actively promoting OP. The same year he made an OP recording for Linguaphone (1937a, 1937b), along with an accompanying pamphlet.[11] The speakers are Daniel Jones and a phonetician colleague Eileen Evans.

During the 1940s, the BBC developed its interest in Shakespeare production. A famous series of broadcasts in 1943–6 on individual Shakespeare characters, written by Herbert Farjeon, was produced by Mary Hope Allen, and culminated in a full production of *The Tempest* in 1953 (with John Gielgud). None of these was in OP, but the memory of the 1936–7 broadcasts evidently remained, for in 1949 Jones was asked to train a group of actors to present a programme of OP Shakespearean extracts. The result was broadcast on the Third Programme on 28 December 1949 as 'The Elizabethan Tongue: passages from the plays of Shakespeare in their original pronunciation', introduced by Jones himself. He also wrote a 1,000-word piece for *Radio Times* the same week called 'The tongue that Shakespeare spake ...' (Jones, 1949). He is in no doubt that 'we now have a pretty accurate picture of the way in which English pronunciation has developed from Anglo-Saxon times to the present day'. There must have been some worries in the BBC about possible listener reaction. The *Radio Times* announcement ends with the advice: 'Listeners may find the text useful in occasional passages.'

In the third edition of *The Pronunciation of English* (1950: 198) Jones builds on his confidence to present his own transcription of the 'Friends, Romans and countrymen' speech from *Julius Caesar* (whereas in the first edition (1909: 103), he had simply referred his readers to Viëtor). Evidently he now found Viëtor's version too conservative and stylized. However, the trend to see OP as nearer to present-day English did not satisfy Kökeritz, who strongly criticized both Viëtor and Jones (1953: 49–50) for not going far enough. Jones, as a consequence, revised his transcription, influenced also by the fresh ideas about OP coming from a new member of Jones's department,

A. C. Gimson, and also from Randolph Quirk, who would later become Professor of English at UCL. Jones's fourth edition (1956) shows several further changes, especially in the use of weak forms. However, Kökeritz's view that 'Shakespeare's pronunciation strongly resembled modern English' (ibid: 6) was in turn strongly and convincingly attacked by Cercignani (1981), whose detailed study is the latest and fullest attempt to review all the evidence of rhymes, puns, spellings, and metrics in the Shakespeare corpus. The outcome is that the Jones transcription is actually now seen to be more reliable than it was a few decades ago.

Gimson had joined the UCL Phonetics Department after World War 2, and took up the OP baton when Jones retired in 1949, later becoming its head. Gimson's interest in the history of English phonology is exemplified in the extracts from Old English to Modern English in his *Introduction to the Pronunciation of English* (1962), in which the 'dagger' speech from *Macbeth* is transcribed in OP. This book also illustrates the changes Gimson had made in the system of phonetic transcription introduced by Jones. The choice of *Macbeth* was a consequence of Gimson having advised in the OP production at the Mermaid Theatre a decade before, along with Bertram L. Joseph. Gimson was responsible for the transcription, along with his colleagues J. D. O'Connor and Gordon Arnold; Joseph (a specialist in Elizabethan stage performance) advised on gesture and movement. The unique feature of this event was that the phoneticians provided the company with a recording of the play in OP, and most of this is available in the UCL Phonetics Collection at the British Library.[12]

The OP aspect of the production received mixed reviews. A *Guardian* journalist, writing before the production, and evidently having heard the UCL recording (or perhaps one of the rehearsals), was quite positive (Our London Correspondent, 1952a):

> 'Macbeth' is being done in contemporary accents, and the phonetics department of London University has recorded the play, as a mode, for the actors, in Elizabethan speech which is smooth, less exaggerated than has sometimes been heard, and with pleasant Midland, West of England, and Irish undertones. Australians may be surprised to hear the words 'too true' coming out with the familiar sound of 'tue trew'.

The review of the year in the 1953 *Shakespeare Quarterly* (Current Theater Notes, 1953) found it an 'interesting experiment'. On the other hand, the correspondent who attended the opening night was less enthusiastic (Our London Correspondent, 1952b):

> The other interest is that here, as in a recent 'Julius Caesar' at Cambridge, an attempt is made to recapture the supposed broad vowels of the Elizabethans, whereby 'war' becomes "wahrr" and so on. This may give purists pleasure and it suits Mr Miles perfectly, for he can run the gamut of his dialect diction. But the danger is that it not only slows the pace but makes the speaking of verse perhaps even more difficult for the lesser fry.

This indicates under-rehearsal in the OP, which inevitably leads to inconsistency, as well as suggesting different levels of acting ability in the use of the accent—problems that have always beset productions. It also suggests a lack of confidence in the OP—understandable in a production which had such a short run. It was performed twice nightly for only six days, with a large gap in the middle, which is never the best of conditions for developing a fluent OP. Perfect OP production (i.e. an error-free realization of the phonetic transcription) takes a great deal of rehearsal time. It is not like the learning of a modern regional accent, where the actors have contemporary intuitions and everyday models to refer to. It requires a special kind of dialect coaching, which is not always available. The present-day OP movement has encountered the same problems (Crystal, 2005).

John Trim, who had joined the UCL Phonetics Department in 1949, confirms the impression that the OP was shaky:[13]

> Bernard Miles himself was very enthusiastic and followed the reconstruction quite accurately, but I gained the impression (confirmed by the performance I attended) that others did not wish to spend time on detailed phonetic accuracy as opposed to giving a general impression, and that his wife, who played Lady Macbeth, was rather impatient of the undertaking.

Miles would have taken further inspiration for his production from a 75-minute BBC radio play, 'The Conscience of the King', transmitted on the Third Programme in May 1952, in which a group of actors are heard rehearsing a performance of King Lear, and discussing the role of the Fool, to be interrupted by the ghost of Shakespeare, who takes part in the discussion speaking in OP. The role of Shakespeare was played by Ian Catford, who in the late 1940s was carrying on a combined career as a phonetics lecturer and actor, and who later went on to set up the School of Applied Linguistics in Edinburgh (Catford, 1998: 20). He was greatly influenced by Henry Sweet and trained partly by Daniel Jones, and in the 1940s taught actors at RADA, finding them to have very little awareness of phonetics. He was in frequent demand at the BBC whenever they wanted an actor who was able to produce regional speech at will, and this was one of his many radio broadcasts. Catford's OP interests extended well beyond the late sixteenth century—he read extracts from Langland and Chaucer, for example—but it seems to have been the Shakespearean OP that had the greatest impact on listeners.

The negative reactions of the 1950s were hardly surprising, given the general style of speech production which dominated the British theatre scene. This was a time when RP was the dominant voice of British theatre, given resonant articulation by such famous voices as Olivier and Gielgud. It was also the voice of the BBC, and Shakespeare broadcasts there were uniformly in RP. In the USA, actors struggled to acquire an RP accent for their Shakespeare performances. Putting on the plays in a regional accent was unimaginable; so a production which was perceived to be a mixture of accents was never likely to be well received.

Things might have been different if the academic community had been publicly more positive. Despite the confident conclusions of Ellis and Jones, referred to above, the general impression given by the OP philologists, phoneticians, and linguists was less stimulating. They were all careful to stress the tentative nature of many of their findings, and to draw attention to the speech variation that existed at the time. They repeatedly pointed out that the evidence of rhymes and especially puns is limited, and that agreement is often lacking among the orthoepists, who wrote in different periods, were from different parts of the country, were of different ages, held different attitudes about correctness, and presented transcriptions which are not always easy to interpret phonetically. There were also scholarly clashes between leading proponents. This was hardly the way to rebut the criticisms voiced by reviewers, or to answer the question present in the minds of everyone who attends an OP production: 'How do we know?' A negative climate thus built up about OP, which is probably why, after the 1950s, no further productions took place for fifty years.

The scholarly caution expressed by the OP researchers has led some observers to conclude that the OP exercise is pointless. Some have dismissed the whole approach out of hand, and critical attitudes can still be encountered today (Gurr, 2001; JC 2012). The philologists and phoneticians have, it must be admitted, been poor at boasting. They have focused on the difficulties (as good scholars should), and underemphasized the areas where the evidence is compelling. Casual readers, who look at the general observations but do not go through the thousands of listed examples, inevitably end up with a limited impression. But there is also a great deal of agreement, as any comparison of different transcriptions shows.

What critics have ignored is the fundamental distinction between phonetics and phonology. This perspective was missing in the early studies, as the theoretical distinction was not introduced into linguistics until the 1920s, and it is not strongly present in the work of Kökeritz and Dobson either. Their background in traditional philology motivated them to use spellings in traditional orthography along with occasional phonetic symbols, and it is often unclear, when reading their transcriptions, whether they are thinking in terms of phonemes or phones. But this distinction is crucial to the modern study of OP. It allows for the fact that there were variant forms in Elizabethan English, that the actors came from different accent backgrounds, and that recitation would have involved different styles. At the same time, it recognizes that the Early Modern English sound system was different, offering pronunciations which are worth exploring to see the effects they convey in dramatic or poetic production.

Despite the recognized difficulties of reconstruction, the exercise is well worth attempting. It is a commonplace in literary criticism and dramaturgy to acknowledge the centrality of the relationship between pronunciation and interpretation. William Empson, to take one well-known instance, emphasized the phonic dimension of text. 'The sound must be an echo to the sense', he states in the opening chapter of *Seven Types of Ambiguity* (1930: 10), and, in relation to Shakespeare, he asserts that no other poet has been more able to 'exploit their sensitivity to the sounds of language' (1930: 88). In which case, we need to try to get as close as possible to the sound system that Shakespeare himself would have heard and used, and not rely for our conclusions solely on the auditory effects introduced by a modern phonology.

## The modern OP movement

The present-day motivation to explore OP did not originate from within linguistics, but from the world of the theatre. In 2004, Shakespeare's Globe in London launched a bold experiment as part of a commitment to introduce 'original practices' into its reconstructed theatre. Along with the exploration of original music, instruments, costume, and movement, it decided to mount an OP production of *Romeo and Juliet*. This was the first staged reconstruction of Elizabethan period speech for fifty years. In 1952, John Barton had produced *Julius Caesar* in OP for the Marlowe Society in Cambridge, England. A few months later, as mentioned above, Joan Swinstead produced *Macbeth* in OP for the new Mermaid Theatre, starring Bernard Miles. In 1954 Helge Kökeritz advised on a production of *The Merry Wives of Windsor* at the Yale School of Drama. Nobody had attempted to recreate the accent on the London stage.

The reconstructed Globe opened its doors in 1997. That it took so long to mount an OP production was due to a suspicion that the accent would not be intelligible; and for a theatre which was open only six months of the year, and where the lack of a public subsidy demanded full houses to ensure survival, management was reluctant to support any venture which might put off an audience. Once the realization dawned that the differences were not as great as feared, and that OP was no more difficult for an audience to understand than any modern regional accent, director Tim Carroll was able to get a proposal accepted to mount a production. It was a 'toe-in-the-water' acceptance. The Globe was still uncertain about how an OP event would go down, so they devoted only one weekend in the middle of the season to OP performances; the rest of the run was in Modern English. The poor actors, of course, had to learn the play twice, as a result. I tell the full story in *Pronouncing Shakespeare* (2005).

The experiment was sufficiently successful, in terms of audience reaction, to motivate the Globe to mount a second production the following year, of *Troilus and Cressida*—this time with the whole run being presented in OP. American visitors to these events enthusiastically took the idea home with them, and over the next few years extracts of plays in OP were presented in New York City, Philadelphia, and at the Blackfriars theatre in Staunton, Virginia culminating in two major OP productions: *A Midsummer Night's Dream* at Kansas University in 2010 (Meier, 2010), and *Hamlet* at the University of Nevada (Reno) in 2011. Other US productions included *Cymbeline* (Portland Center Stage, Oregon, 2012), *Julius Caesar* (University of Texas, Houston, 2013), *Twelfth Night* (Classical Actors Ensemble, Minneapolis, 2014), and *The Merchant of Venice* (Shakespeare Factory, Baltimore, 2015). The UK saw productions of *As You Like It* (Bangor University, 2013), *Macbeth* (Shakespeare's Globe, 2014), and *Henry V* (Shakespeare's Globe, 2015), as well as a toured production of *Pericles* in Stockholm (2015). A full OP version of the Sonnets was also made in 2008 for performance sonneteer Will Sutton.

At the same time, interest was being shown in the expressive individuality of OP by other groups interested in the early modern period, notably those involved in early vocal music, both secular and religious. The prospect of using OP also appealed to people working at heritage sites reconstructing life in the early seventeenth century, such as those at Stratford-upon-Avon (UK) and Plimouth Plantation (USA). Other authors from the period began to be explored from an OP point of view, such as John Donne, whose 1722 Easter Sermon outside St Paul's was recreated online in 2012, with the text being read in OP (Wall, 2013). The 400th anniversary of the King James Bible led to a number of readings of biblical extracts in OP throughout 2011. The earlier sixteenth century is represented by Tyndale (British Library, 2013). And at an academic level, OP was included in a project on the comparative phonology of English accents based at the University of Edinburgh.

Meanwhile, the British Library decided to add an audio dimension to its 2010–11 exhibition on the history of the English language, *Evolving English*. This included an OP reading of extracts from Old and Middle English, such as *Beowulf* and *The Canterbury Tales*, as well as some from Early Modern English, such as the Paston letters and Shakespeare. The Shakespeare element in this exhibition attracted special interest, so the Library followed it up by publishing a CD of extracts from the plays and poems, read by a company of actors, two of whom had been part of the Globe productions in 2004–5 (British Library, 2012). A website devoted to the subject was set up as a clearing-house for information and discussion (Crystal 2011b), and several articles have been written by those involved in OP developments (see the bibliography, p. xlix).

## Transcription

All the words in this dictionary are shown in a broad phonetic transcription. This is a full transcription, in which every sound is represented by an appropriate phonetic symbol. In this respect, the transcription differs from the one used in Crystal (2005) and in the various play-transcriptions I have made hitherto with the needs of actors in mind. These have been partial transcriptions, in which the phonetic symbols identify only the sounds that *differ* from those found in the modern accent used by the speaker. The aim there was to produce a transcription which would ease the learning task for actors unfamiliar with the accent, many of whom had little or no experience of reading phonetic symbols. These transcriptions have also varied somewhat to take account of the home accent of the company. For example, British actors used to RP need to have the OP postvocalic *r* drawn to their attention, whereas this is not necessary with a company whose home accent is General American. These pragmatic and pedagogical considerations are not relevant in a dictionary which is to be used by people with all kinds of accents.

The vowel symbols used in the transcription represent qualities shown on the accompanying cardinal vowel diagram in Figure 1.1. Major differences with RP (as described by Gimson 1962 and later editions) are noted.

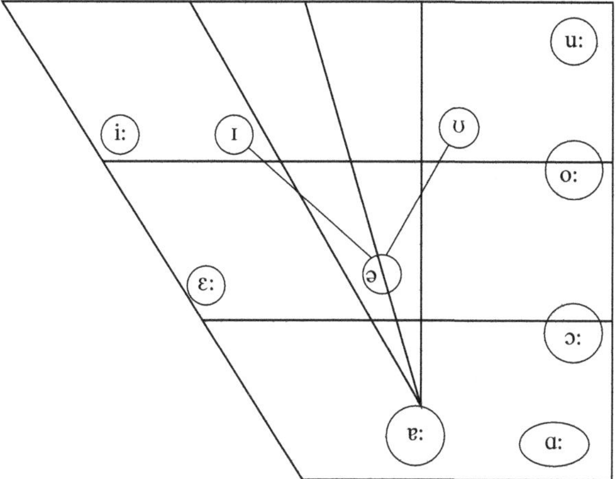


Long Vowels and Diphthongs

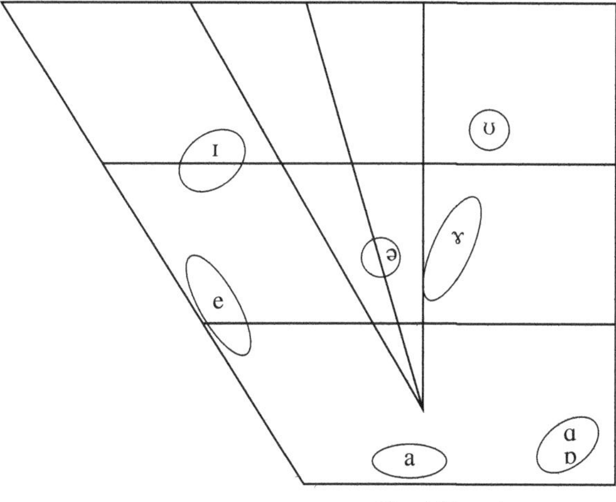


Short Vowels

**Figure 1.1** Cardinal vowels

## *Short vowels*

Most of the short vowels show little phonetic difference (p. xv), so that it is possible for whole sentences in OP to sound the same as today, such as 'Is shee gone to the king?' Rhymes and spellings do however suggest that several vowels were more open than their present-day counterparts.

### /ɪ/ AS IN *SIT, WILL, PRINCE*

This vowel must have been more open, in the direction of [e], otherwise it is difficult to explain the many spelling alternations between *i* and *e*: *hither* / *hether, seldom* / *sildom, diuision* / *deuision, deuil* / *diuel, Priscian* appearing as *Prescian,* and the many variant forms of words beginning with *im-* / *em-* and *in-* / *en-* (*imploy* / *employ, intend* / *entend*). Among the rhymes, we see *sentinel* rhyming with both *kill* and *well, shift* rhyming with both *shrift* and *theft, error* rhyming with *mirror* and *terror.* This goes against locating it high on the CV diagram, close to the present-day quality of /iː/, as suggested for example by Kökeritz (1953: 340). Jonson is one who draws attention to the open quality of *i,* observing in his *English Grammar* (ch.3) that '*e* and *i* have such a nearness in our tongue, as oftentimes they interchange places'. I transcribe syllabic past tense endings as /ɪd/, as in modern English dictionaries, unless there is a rhyme motivating an /ed/, as in *remembered* / *dead.*

It is this overlap that could throw light on some problematic cases, such as the crux at *Mac* 5.3.55, where *cyme* seems to be an error for *cynne* (= *senna*). *Cy-* was generally pronounced /sɪ/, as shown by such items as *Cynthia* and *cypress,* and *Cyprus* spelled *Ciprus. Cyme* /sɪm/ would thus have sounded more like [sem], which would have reinforced the confusion. Similarly, the Folio spelling *Ginyes case* at *MW* 4.1.57 readily suggests the reading *Jenny's case.* And when we encounter words that have alternative present-day pronunciations, such as *divest* as either /dɪvest/ or /dəɪvest/, the Folio spellings of *deuest* along with *diuest* point to the short vowel version in OP.

Hundreds of words in which a final unstressed *-y* rhymes with a stressed syllable (as in *archery* / *dye, enemy* / *fly, majesty* / *eye, remedy* / *espy*) point to a diphthongized variant, /əɪ/ in this position, though not strongly articulated. John Hart, in his *Orthographie* (1569–70), is one who transcribes the syllable in a way that suggests a diphthong: *boldlei, sertenlei, partlei,* etc. The RP version with /ɪ/, or even /i/, fails to respect the rhymes.

### /e/ AS IN *MET, TELL, HEN*

The main value for this vowel seems to have been the same as today, half-way between mid-close and mid-open, but with some speakers using a more open variant, in the direction of cardinal [ɛ]. This is suggested by those spellings where an expected *e* is replaced by *a,* as in *rellish* / *rallish, rendeuous* / *randeuous,* and *terras* / *tarrace,* as well as rhymes such as *neck* and *back.* That there was some confusion in the other direction, from *a* towards *e,* is shown by *thatcht* / *thetchd, thrash* / *thresh,* and *ambassador* / *embassador.* A closer variant, in the direction of [ɪ], pulled in that direction by a preceding palatal consonant /j/, is indicated by *yet* rhyming with *sit* and *wit.*

### /a/ AS IN *CAP, FAT, LAMB,* AND ALSO *FAST, BATH, FATHER, LAUGH, HASTE, ANY*

In view of the more open character of the above two short front vowels, it seems likely that /a/ would also have had a more open and central quality compared with the sound in present-day conservative RP (which is closer to cardinal [ɛ] than [a]), and thus much more like a northern British version of this vowel. This is supported by the occasional spelling of /a/ with a back vowel, such as *todpole* for *tadpole, strond* for *strand, loffe* for *laugh,* as well as the alternative pronunciations suggested by such spelling variants as *stanch* / *staunch*, *paltry* / *paultry*, *lance* / *launce*. Words such as *haste* and *taste* have this vowel, as shown by the rhymes with *fast*, *blast*, etc. This is an important contrast with the long /ɑː/ in such words as *bath* and *past*, which is a prominent feature of RP.

### /ɤ/ AS IN *CUP*, *STUFF*, *DRUM*

The quality is further back and closer than the equivalent vowel in RP, /ʌ/. Opinions vary as to how far back it would have been, with values proposed between [ə] and unrounded cardinal 7 [ɤ]. In my view, the latter is more likely, hence the choice of this symbol in the transcription. A *u* spelling is the norm for this vowel, and there are several instances where there is overlap with *o*, suggesting the back quality, as in *sodaine* / *sudden*, *sommer* / *summer*, *Sonday* / *Sunday*, *dombe* / *dumbe*, *tombles* / *tumble*. The emendation at *Ham* 3.3.18 of *somnet* to *summit* also reflects this quality. Contemporary writers reinforce this view, as in the quotation from Jonson (p. xx), where the *o* of *love* and *prove* is said to be 'akin to u', which in turn he describes as 'thick and flat' in such words as *us*.

As both *o* and *u* were routinely used for rounded vowels, the question arises as to whether the vowel in these words was rounded, as in many parts of northern England today. The evidence is unclear: in the same section, Jonson describes *o* as being pronounced 'with a round mouth', but immediately adds that this 'is a letter of much change, and uncertainty with us'. The spelling of *slumber* as *slomber* by Macmorris (*H5* 3.2.111) suggests a rounding that would be absent from the non-Scots form. And there are rhymes with unrounded front vowels that are also suggestive, such as *shudder* / *adder*, *Sunday* / *array*, *us* / *guess*, *punish* / *languish*. My view is that both unrounded and rounded variants were in use at the time (as they are today), but opting for the unrounded form as the default in this dictionary allows actors the choice of using the rounded variant if they want to differentiate a character. Certainly, if they were to replace all [ɤ] by [ʊ], it would result in an OP of a noticeably different auditory character (much closer to, say Yorkshire or Irish English in effect), as this vowel is very common, being used in some frequently occurring words (*must*, *us*, *under*, the *un-* and *sub-* prefixes, etc.). On the other hand, they do not have to adopt such a noticeable lip-rounding as we hear in present-day regional accents, and I would not correct a slight degree of rounding, when working with a company.

### /ʊ/ AS IN *PUT*, *LOOK*, *FOOT*, AND ALSO IN *FOOL*, *TOOTH*

This rounded vowel seems to have had the same value as in conservative RP today (though it is now losing its rounding among young people). The only uncertainty is the extent to which it was used as an alternative in words with long [uː]. Rhymes such as *tooth* and *doth*, *brood* and *blood*, *food* and *flood*, and puns such as *fool* and *full* show that it was an option in some cases, but whether it should be applied to *moon*, *afternoon*, and others is an open question. Rhymes can be suggestive, such as *boot* / *foot*, but the direction of the rhyme is often unclear. The dictionary thus shows long and short vowels in these words, with the latter more likely in regional speech, as today.

### /ɒ/ AS IN *HOT*, *FOND*, *BOG*, AND ALSO IN *TONGUE*, *YOUNG*

This back vowel may have been more open than its already fairly open position in RP, its *a*-like character being suggested by a spelling such as *aspray* for *osprey* and rhymes like *cough* / *laugh*, *bob* / *crab*. However, it could retain a degree of lip-rounding, which would differentiate it from the totally unrounded open vowel quality typical of much American speech in words like *hot*. It should also stay short, and not attract the lengthening often heard in some regional accents, such as the West Country of England. The use of this vowel in such words as *tongue* is shown by rhymes (*song, wrong,* etc.) and occasional puns (see entry at *tongue*). It is an important metrical alternative in such words as *satisfaction*: ˌsatɪsˈfaksɪən, -sɪˌɒn.

### /ɑ/ IN *WHAT, WATCH, FESTIVAL, SPECIAL*

As with the long /ɑ:/ vowel below, a short open back /ɑ/ follows a preceding /w/ or /ʍ/, rather than the mid-open quality heard today, shown by such rhymes as *want / enchant, warp / harp, waste / past, water / matter*. The same velar influence is seen when this is followed by a 'dark' /l/, as in short-vowel versions of *false, halt, Mall*. In Modern English, the quality in *burial* etc. is schwa-like, whereas in OP it is [ɑ]-like, as suggested by such rhymes as *hospital / befall, burial / all, equivocal / gall*. Alternate spellings with *o* also point to a back vowel quality, as with *capitall / capitoll*, and the rhyme of *folly* and *dally*. In an unstressed syllable, the difference between /ɑ/ and /ə/ would be very small, but for consistency I transcribe all instances of *a* before *l* as /ɑ/, as in *rascally, rehearsal*, etc.

### /ə/ AS IN *A, THE, MOTHER, ATTEMPT*

As in Modern English, /ə/ is used as the default vowel-marker in unstressed syllables. In my transcription it is never used in a stressed syllable. This works well enough when the contrast is between primary stress and unstressed, but when secondary stress is involved, and especially when required by the metre, it is a choice whether to show the vowel as /ə/ or as its nearest stressed vowel equivalent. In a line such as 'He's quoted for a most perfidious slaue', *perfidious* appears as /pəɹˈfɪdɪəs/; but in 'Men feare the French would proue perfidious', the metre requires a secondary stress on the final syllable: /pəɹˈfɪdɪˌɤs/. In this dictionary, such cases are shown with the stressed vowel, even though this would be said more weakly than when in a situation of primary stress, as also in *astronomer* /əˈstrɒnəˌmɐ:ɹ/ and *satisfaction* above.

## *Long vowels*

### /i:/ AS IN *SEE, HE, SCENE, HERE,* AND ALSO *SEA, LEAVE, DREAM*

These two types of word, phonologically distinct in Middle English, are not distinguished in this dictionary. It is not clear just how far a merger would have taken place by the end of the sixteenth century, or which words would have been affected. But there is a consensus that the gradual rising in this part of the vowel-space still had some way to go before reaching the present-day value of /i:/, which is shown in Gimson (1962) and derivative works as close to cardinal 1. In OP it seems likely to have been nearer to cardinal 2—and thus similar to the Modern French vowel in *bébé*. Transcriptionally, it could therefore be symbolized as /e:/—and this was the practice adopted in Crystal (2005). However, actors found this confusing, with the letter *e* also being used for the more open short vowel (see above); there was a persistent tendency to over-open the long vowel, so that *sleep*, for example, would be pronounced as /slɛ:p/, thus neutralizing the contrast between such pairs as *meek* and *make*. In the present dictionary I have accordingly kept the /i:/ symbol, so that in OP training it is necessary to remind practitioners of its more open character compared to RP.

### /ɛ:/ AS IN *DAY, PLACE, MAKE* AND ALSO IN *FAIR, HARE, THERE*

The same rising trend at the front of the mouth, from Middle to Modern English, is seen in this vowel, which had yet to achieve the diphthongal status it has in RP. There may have been a phonetic distinction between the two types of word, because of the influence of the following *r*, but in this dictionary I transcribe both with [ɛ:]. This value is also used in several words that would later become /i:/, such as *reason* and *season*, and as a variant, along with /i:/, in such words as *here*, which shows rhymes with both *deer* and *there*. Puns provide useful reinforcement here, as wordplay between *reason* and *raisin*, for example, would not have worked without some degree of homophony.

### /ɐ:/ BEFORE /ɹ/ IN SUCH WORDS AS *BIRD, MERCY, SIR*

The open quality of this vowel is heard today in many regional accents, on both sides of the Atlantic, reflected in dialect-writing in such spellings as the exclamatory 'marcy me…!' The spelling evidence in the Folio is seen in the use of an *a* in such words as *merchant / marchant, sterling / starling, German / Iarman*, and rhymes such as *serve / carve, stir / war*. Phonetically, there is little difference between this quality and that of /ɑ:/ below, but I have kept the transcriptions distinct, to draw attention to the different phonological relationships with their present-day equivalents.

### /ɑ:/ AS IN *WALL, WAR, ALL, FALL*

As with the short /ɑ/ vowel above, a long open back /ɑ:/ follows a preceding /w/, rather than the mid-open quality heard today, as is evident by such rhymes as *war / bar, ward / guard, warm / harm.* The influence of a following /l/ is especially striking in *all*, because this word usually has considerable semantic prominence in a speech. It must have been a noticeable feature of OP as Jonson, among others, pays special attention to it, contrasting it with the normal use of *a* ('pronounced less than the French à'): 'when it comes before l, in the end of a syllabe, it obtaineth the full French sound, and is uttered with the mouth and tongue wide opened, the tongue bent back from the teeth'. He gives *all, small, salt, calm* among his examples.

### /ɔ:/ AS IN *FAWN, CORD, TALK, HAUNT*

This vowel seems to have been much more open than in RP, where today it falls midway between half-close and half-open. This closer value in RP seems to be a relatively recent development, as Daniel Jones, for example, shows words like *lord* with a very open tongue position in the early twentieth century. Spelling alternations between *au* or *aw* and *a* also suggest a more open quality: *Auffidius / Affidius, auspitious / aspitious /, scauld / scald.* Note also such rhymes as *vaunt / want, brawl / all.*

### /o:/ AS IN *GO, SOUL, MOAN*, AND ALSO *ONE, POWER, POOR*

The important point to note about this vowel is the lack of the diphthongal quality characteristic of RP, where it has a range of values running from [oʊ] to [əʊ] to [ɛʊ]. The pure vowel is widely used in present-day accents, such as those of the Celtic areas, and its frequency in English (in very common words such as *go, know, so*) makes it a noticeable feature of OP. Rhymes show its use as a variant in words that later would have more open vowels, such as *one / throne, none / bone.* Several words and prefixes spelled with *or* or *our*, shown in this dictionary with /ɔ:/, such as *four, more, fore-, for-* could also be sounded with a closer variant.

### /u:/ AS IN *DO, SHOE, SPOON, NEW, CURE*

This value seems identical with the one we have today in conservative RP accents (younger people tend to lose some of the lip-rounding), though—as noted above—several words that today have /u:/ could be shortened, such as *fool*. Spellings such as *cooz* and *coosin* ('cousin') show that *oo* could represent a short vowel as well as a long one.

## *Diphthongs*

### /əɪ/ AS IN *MY*, *SIGH*, *FRIGHT*, *MILE*, AND ALSO IN *JOY*, *BOY*, *ENJOY*

The identity between the two diphthongs that are distinct in RP is an important source of puns in OP, such as *voice* / *vice*, *lines* / *loins*, *boil* / *bile*, and supported by such spellings as *biles*, *byle*, *byles* for *boils* (*n*) and the rhyme *groin* / *swine*. A few unexpected words take the same value, notably *juice*, rhyming with *voice*, which has *OED* spellings *ioyce* and *joice*. The central and higher quality of the opening element of the diphthong is critical here, and is one of the main auditory features of OP, in view of its use in several frequently appearing words, such as *my*, *thy*, *by*, *like*, *time*.

### /əʊ/ AS IN *NOW*, *BROWN*, *HOUSE*, *ALLOW*

The same raising and centralizing heard in /əɪ/ also affects the corresponding back diphthong, heard in RP as /ɑʊ/. Before voiceless consonants (*out*, *house*), it is well known in North America, where phoneticians have called it 'Canadian raising'. Although not such a common sound as /əɪ/, it does occur in some frequently occurring words, such as *now*, *down*, *out*, *how*.

## *Consonants*

Most of the consonants have the same phonetic value in OP as they do in RP, with the following differences.

### /ɹ/ AFTER VOWELS

The exact phonetic quality of this sound is unclear. The descriptions of the sound by contemporary writers leave it open just how r is articulated, such as how far back the tongue curls. When used in front of a vowel, it would seem to have been the same sound as in RP, a post-alveolar frictionless continuant, though there must have been a trilled variant (as today in some accents of Scotland and Wales), for Jonson describes *r* as a sound that 'hurreth [vibrates] ... with a trembling about the teeth'. But he then draws a contrast between *r* before and after vowels: 'It is sounded firm in the beginning of the words, and more *liquid* in the middle and ends; as in *rarer*, *riper*.' I interpret this to mean a continuant r, as in the West Country of England and much of America, but there is no way of knowing whether the focus of the articulation is post-alveolar or retroflex, so a great deal of variation will be heard in present-day OP productions.

### /ʍ/ AS IN *WHERE*, CONTRASTING WITH /w/ AS IN *WEAR*

RP makes no distinction between, say, *Wales* and *whales*, though the contrast is often heard in regional accents. The aspiration was noted by contemporary writers. Jonson, for example, describes words that have 'the aspiration afore', illustrating with *what*, *which*, *wheel*, and *whether*. Some transcriptions reflect his way of putting it, transcribing the sound as /hw/ (as I did in Crystal (2005)). It is not however a sequence of two sounds, but a 'voiceless w', hence the choice of /ʍ/ for this dictionary.

Apart from these, the only points to note are cases where familiar sounds appear in unfamiliar places, and these are listed in the dictionary. For example, spellings show that several words with /θ/ today were pronounced with /t/, such as *fift* and *sixt* for *fifth* and *sixth*, as well as *orthography* as *ortagriphie*. This is one of the features that makes people identify OP with Irish English. Some people would doubtless, Holofernes-like, have followed the spelling in scholarly words such as *apothecary* and *lethargy*, but variant spellings in names as well as loanwords show the use of /t/—*Katerine* / *Katherine*, *Proteus* / *Protheus*, *swart* / *swarth*, as well as such rhymes as *nothing* / *a-doting*. We also sometimes see *th* used in words where /t/ is the only pronunciation, such as *Sathan* for *Satan*, *gamoth* for *gamut*, *Athica* for *Attica*, and the interesting *authorithy* for *authority*. There was a similar voiced sound variation, as seen in *farthell* / *fardles* and *fardingales* / *farthingales*.

Other important consonantal features of OP have been mentioned earlier in this Introduction, such as the replacement of /ʃ/ by /sɪ/ in such words as *suspicious*, *pensioner*, *musician*, and the option of replacing /ŋ/ by /n/ in the *-ing* verb inflection, as well as when used adjectivally, shown by such spellings as *poprin* for *poppering* and *blush-in* for *blushing*. That the latter was a stylistic option is indicated by rhymes where it is retained, such as *niggarding* / *spring* and *prefiguring* / *sing*. Another noticeable auditory effect comes from the replacement of /tʃ/ by /t/ in such words as *nature*, *lecture*, *tempestuous*, as shown by such spelling as *lector* / *lecture*, *venter* / *venture*, *tempestious* (*OED*) for *tempestuous* (Folio), and rhymes such as *departure* / *shorter*.

Some OP practitioners, influenced by earlier sixteenth-century usage in which word-initial silent letters in such words as *know*, *gnaw*, and *write* were still being pronounced, have chosen to keep these in the OP of Shakespeare's time. Opinion among the contemporary writers is mixed. I therefore acknowledge this possibility in the dictionary entries, but am influenced more by the spellings (e.g. as *wring* / *ring*, (*OED*) *knack* / *neck*), rhymes (e.g. *knight* / *night*), and puns (e.g. *nave* / *knave*) which suggest that these consonants had fallen silent.

This is a dictionary of the pronunciation of individual words, and no account is given of assimilations and elisions between words (apart from in a few cases of grammatical-word sequences such as *i'th*). However, in view of their frequency, I do show elisions of consonants in the *-est* verb ending. For example, *settest* is transcribed as both /setst/ and /sets/—the former being the more likely option when the ending is followed by a vowel (such as *sets oath to oath*) and the latter when it is followed by a consonant (such as *set'st me free*).

## *Word stress*

It is essential to show stress in polysyllabic words, as the metre shows that this often varies between OP and RP. Primary (ˈ) and (if needed) secondary (ˌ) stress is marked before the relevant syllable. The assignment of stress is not always clear, especially in a compound word, where often either element could be primary, or both elements could have equal stress. Where possible, I have been guided by the position of the words in metrical lines.

## *Latin*

The pronunciation of Latin in the early sixteenth century was a matter of great controversy, with Erasmus, among others, attempting to reform the traditional English pronunciation of the language to make it conform more to classical models. The earlier history of Latin in Europe had been characterized by great diversity, with the classical model adapted to the phonological norms of the languages of different countries. In an appendix, Allen observes that Latin in England had 'from earliest times been affected by native speech-habits'—most notably in the application of the stress pattern of English, which altered the length of vowels. Long vowels in Latin were also influenced by the way English long vowels were changing (the Great Vowel Shift), several becoming diphthongs. The overall effect attracted an acerbic comment from Joseph Scaliger—writing at the beginning of the seventeenth century—that an English visitor speaking Latin was so difficult to understand that he might as well have been speaking Turkish.

Allen concluded that one could treat Latin in the Early Modern period as almost entirely 'equivalent to a reading in terms of English spelling conventions', so the transcription of the Latin words in this dictionary uses the same symbols as in English OP.

### *French*

The transcription of French words in the dictionary uses a different set of vowel symbols, reflecting conventional practice in such French dictionaries as (followed here) *Harrap's Concise French and English Dictionary* (1978).

/i/ *il, vie, si*
/iː/ *dire*
/e/ *assez, ces, donner*
/ɛ/ *belle, affaire, ciel*
/ɛː/ *terre, cher*
/a/ *bras, la, madame*
/aː/ *brave, car, langage*
/ɑː/ *bataille, grâce*
/ɔ/ *comme, bonne, robe*
/ɔː/ *encore, fort, mort*
/o/ *au, chaud, mot*
/oː/ *autre, gros, pauvre*
/u/ *doute, tout, couper*
/uː/ *amour, jour, cour*
/y/ *tu, perdu, coutume*
/ø/ *peu, deux, feu*
/œ/ *heureux, monsieur, veux*
/œː/ *leur, heure, honneur*
/ə/ *ce, le, cheval*
/ɛ̃/ *bien, rien, point*
/ɑ̃/ *pense, quand, anges*
/ɑ̃ː/ *apprendre, France, ensemble*
/ɔ̃/ *garçon, bon, allons*
/ɔ̃ː/ *contre, donc, monde*
/œ̃/ *un*
/ũ/ *sont*

Compared to English, there seems to have been less change between the Early Modern and Modern states of the language, judging by the classic description of historical French phonology in Pope (1934). The most notable differences in the French entries in this dictionary are the articulation of final /ə/ in such words as *autre* /ˈoːtrə/ and *pauvre* /ˈpoːvrə/, the use of a front mid value for such words as *moi* /mwɛ/ and *pourquoi* /puːɹˈkwɛ/, a close nasal back vowel in some words (e.g. *sont* /sũ/), and the use of a phonetic quality of /r/ that seems to have been closer to the one used in English OP, rather than the uvular value familiar from Modern French, hence the use of the same symbol /ɹ/. Unlike English, French is a syllable-timed language, with stress-marks of the kind used in English unnecessary; but as a pedagogical aid I have added /ˈ/ in polysyllabic words to indicate the usual point of greatest emphasis.

## REFERENCES


Allen, W. Sidney. 1978. *Vox Latina: the Pronunciation of Classical Latin*, 2nd edn. Cambridge: Cambridge University Press.

Ayres, H. M. 1916. *The Question of Shakspere's Pronunciation*. New York: Columbia University.

Barber, C. 1976. *Early Modern English*. London: Deutsch.

Bate, J. and Rasmussen, E. 2007. *William Shakespeare: Complete Works*. Basingstoke: Macmillan.

Blandford, F. G. 1927. *Shakespeare's Pronunciation: A Transcription of Twelfth Night Act I, Scene V*. Cambridge: Heffer.

British Library. 2012. *Shakespeare's Original Pronunciation*. Audio CD. London: British Library.

British Library. 2013. *Tyndale's Bible: Saint Matthew's Gospel*. Audio CD. London: British Library.

Catford, J. C. 1998. Sixty years in linguistics. In E. F. K. Koerner (ed.), *First Person Singular III: Autobiographies by North American Scholars in the Language Sciences*. Amsterdam: Benjamins.

Cercignani, F. 1981. *Shakespeare's Works and Elizabethan Pronunciation*. Oxford: Clarendon Press.

Collins, B. and Mees, I. M. 1998. *The Real Professor Higgins: The Life and Career of Daniel Jones*. Berlin & New York: Mouton de Gruyter.

Craik, George L. 1857. *The English of Shakespeare Illustrated in a Philological Commentary on his Julius Caesar*. London: Chapman & Hall.

Crystal, D. 2005. *Pronouncing Shakespeare*. Cambridge: Cambridge University Press. http://www.pronouncingshakespeare.com

Crystal, D. 2008. *Think on my Words: Exploring Shakespeare's Language*. Cambridge: Cambridge University Press.

Crystal, D. 2011a. Sounding out Shakespeare: sonnet rhymes in original pronunciation. In: V. Vasic (ed.), *Jezik u Upotrebi: Primenjena Lingvistikja u Cast Ranku Bugarskom [Language in Use: Applied Linguistics in Honour of Ranko Bugarski]* (Novi Sad and Belgrade: Philosophy faculties), 295–306. Available at: http://www.davidcrystal.com/DC_articles/Shakespeare72.pdf

Crystal, D. 2011b. http://originalpronunciation.com

Crystal, D. 2013. Early interest in Shakespearean original pronunciation. *Language and History* 56 (1): 5–17.

Crystal, D. and Crystal, B. 2002. *Shakespeare's Words*. London: Penguin.

Current Theater Notes. 1953. *Shakespeare Quarterly* 4 (1): 61–75.

Dobson, E. J. 1968. *English Pronunciation 1500–1700*. Oxford: Clarendon Press.

Donno, E. S. 1962. *Sir John Harington's A New Discourse on a Stale Subject, Called the Metamorphosis of Ajax: A Critical Annotated Edition*. London: Routledge & Kegan Paul.

Ellis, A. J. 1869–74. *On Early English Pronunciation, With Especial Reference to Shakespeare and Chaucer. Part 3 [1871]: Illustrations of the Pronunciation of the XIVth and XVIth Centuries*. London: Philological Society.

Empson, W. 1930. *Seven Types of Ambiguity*. London: Chatto & Windus.

Franz, W. 1905. *Orthographie, Lautgebung und Wortbildung in den Werken Shakespeares*. Heidelberg.

Gimson, A. C. 1962. *An Introduction to the Pronunciation of English*. London: Arnold.

Gurr, A. 2001. Other Accents: Some Problems in Identifying Elizabethan pronunciation, *Early Modern Literary Studies* 7 (1): 1–4.

JC. 2012. As she is spake. *Times Literary Supplement*, 6 April.

Jones, D. 1910a. Scenes from Shakespeare in the Original Pronunciation. Supplement to *Le Maître phonétique* 24 (2): 1–7.

Jones, D. 1910b. The pronunciation of early English, *Le Maître phonétique* 24 (2): 119–23.

Jones, D. 1937a. *Pronunciation of Early XVII Century English*. London: Linguaphone.

Jones, D. 1937b. Some notes on the Pronunciation of English at the Time of Shakespeare. In *English Pronunciation Through the Centuries*, London: Linguaphone Institute, 38–41.

Jones, D. 1949. The Tongue that Shakespeare Spake . . . *Radio Times*, 16 December: 15.

Jones, D. 1950. *The Pronunciation of English, 3rd edn*. Cambridge: Cambridge University Press; 1st edn 1909; 4th edn 1956.

Kökeritz, H. 1953. *Shakespeare's Pronunciation*. New Haven, CT: Yale University Press.

Marsh, G. P. 1861. *Lectures on the English Language*, 1st series [given in 1858–9]. Lecture 22: Orthoepical Change in English. New York: Scribner, 468–98.

Meier, P. 2010. http://paulmeier.com/shakespeare.html

Noël-Armfield, G. 2010. Scenes from Shakespeare in the Original Pronunciation, *Le Maître phonétique* 24 (2): 117–19.

Our London Correspondent. 1952a. *Guardian*, 25 July 1952, p. 6.

Our London Correspondent. 1952b. *Guardian*, 13 September 1952, p. 6.

Passy, P. 1905. Cours de vacances, *Le Maître phonétique* 20 (2): 109.

Peirce, C. S. and Noyes, J. B. 1864. Shakespearian Pronunciation, *North American Review* 98: 342–69.

Pope, M. K. 1934. *From Latin to Modern French with especial consideration of Anglo-Norman*. Manchester: Manchester University Press.

Sweet, H. 1874. *A History of English Sounds from the Earliest Period*. English Dialect Society 4. London: Trübner.

Viëtor, W. 1906a. *A Shakespeare Phonology, with a Rime-index to the Poems as a Pronouncing Vocabulary*. Marburg: Elwert; London: Nutt.

Viëtor, W. 1906b. *Shakespeare's Pronunciation: A Shakespeare Reader in the Old Spelling and with a Phonetic Transcription*. Marburg: Elwert; London: Nutt; New York: Lemcke & Buechner.

Wall, J. 2013. *Virtual Paul's Cross Project, London 1622*. http://vpcp.chass.ncsu.edu

White, R. G. 1865. Memorandum on English Pronunciation in the Elizabethan Era. Appendix to Vol. 12 of *The Works of William Shakespeare*. Boston: Little Brown.

## NOTES

1 For example: people who live in an area where they use /ɹ/ after a vowel (such as the West of England, or many parts of the USA) will tune in to that feature of OP. Those who notice the long pure vowels in words like *say* /sɛː/ will very likely be from a part of the world (such as Lancashire) where this vowel is common. The Irish recognize the double stress in such words as *ruminate*. Many Scots people have a pronunciation of *prove* that rhymes with *love*. Australians notice the high vowel in *yet*—sounding more like /yɪt/. Londoners notice the /ə/ ending of words like *window* and *shadow*.

2 Some other examples: *prove* and *love* at *TN* 3.3.10–11, *you* and *true* at *WT* 2.3.35–7, *discontent* and *argument* at *KJ* 4.2.53–4.

3 Other examples: *prenominate* adjective and verb, *presage* noun and verb, *proclaim* adjective and verb, *proposed* adjective and verb, *raven* noun and verb.

4 In a few cases of high-frequency grammatical words with different functions, where pronunciation would not be affected, I have not given separate counts. For example, *more*, which can occur as adjective, adverb, or noun, is shown with a single total for all instances. To show that no separate count has been made, the word-classes are separated by commas, not slashes: *adj, adv, n*.

5 This does not exclude the possibility of the word having a long vowel in a regional dialect—as mentioned by John Hart (a Devonshire man) in 1570, and also by Richard Mulcaster in *The Elementarie* (1582?: 116).

6 The notion of 'half' is inadequate, from a phonemic point of view. Most so-called half-rhymes in Shakespeare are in fact differentiated by a single distinctive feature—for example, the final consonants of *Valentine* and *betime* share nasality, voicing, and manner of articulation, differing only in place of articulation; the vowels in *go* and *do* are both rounded and back, differing only in height (close vs mid-close). It would be more accurate to call such cases 'two-thirds rhymes' or 'three-quarter rhymes'!

7 The full list of items involved in the distinctive feature analysis will be found on the companion website at www.oup.co.uk/companion/crystal_shakespeare.

8 See further, Crystal (2011a). A good example of a rhyming crux, where one would not wish to force an auditory identity, is *S 81.10, 12*:

> Which eyes not yet created shall o'er-read...
> When all the breathers of this world are dead.

9 This section is an adaptation of Crystal (2013).

10 For the details of Jones's early career, see, Collins and Mees (1998: 58–62, 266, 368–70, 444–8), where examples can also be found of the programme and transcriptions.

11 The list says it is in two parts, but only Part 1 is relevant, as the other side is a modern English conversation at the tobacconist's.

12 My own transcriptions have been influenced by Gimson, who taught me OP when I studied under him at UCL.

13 Personal communication, July 2012.

# PART II
# THE DICTIONARY

**a / an** *det*
=
**sp** a[13956], a-[manie][1], a-[scorne][1], an[1654], an-[fooles][1], [and]-a [*song*][1]
> at, awhile, have, he, in, of, on

**A** [letter] *n*
'ɛ:
**sp** [M.O.]A.[I.][4]

**à** *Fr prep*
a
**sp** a[9], a[sture]

**Aaron / ~'s** *n*
'arən / -z
**sp** Aaron[29], Aron[6] / Aarons[1]

**abaiss·er / ~iez** *Fr v*
abɛsi'ez
**sp** abbaisse[1]

**abandon / ~ed** *v*
= / *m* ə'bandənd, -də,nɪd
**sp** abandon[4] / abandon'd[5], abandoned[2]

**abandoned** *adj*
ə'bandənd
**sp** abandon'd[1]

**abase** *v*
ə'bɛ:s
**sp** abase[2]

**abashed** *adj*
=
**sp** abash'd[1]

**abate / ~s / ~d** *v*
ə'bɛ:t / -s / -ɪd /
**sp** abate[12], a-bate[1] / abates[1] / abated[2]
> bate

**abated** *adj*
ə'bɛ:tɪd
**sp** abated[1]

**abatement** *n*
ə'bɛ:tmənt
**sp** abatement[3]

**a-bat-fowling** *n*
ə'bat,fəʊlɪn, -ɪŋ
**sp** a bat-fowling[1]
> fowl

**abbess** *n*
=
**sp** abbesse[8]

**abbey / ~s** *n*
'abəɪ / -z
**sp** abbey[14] / abbies[1]

**abbot / ~s** *n*
=
**sp** abbot[7] / abbots[1]

**abbreviate / ~d** *v*
ə'bri:vɪ,ɛ:tɪd
**sp** abreuiated[1]

**ABC** *n*
,ɛ:bi:'si:
**sp** A.B.C.[1]
> Absey

**abed** *adv*
=
**sp** a-bed[1], a bed[7], a bedde[1]
> bed, slug-a-bed

**Abel / ~'s** *n*
'ɛ:bəl / -z
**sp** Abel[1] / Abels[1]

**Abergavenny** *n*
,abəɹ'ganəɪ
**sp** Aburgany[2], Aburgauenny[1]

**abet / ~ting** *v*
= / ə'betɪn, -ɪŋ
**sp** abett[1] / abetting[1]

**abhomination**
> abomination

**abhor / ~s / ~ring / ~red / ~redst** *v*
ə'bɔ:ɹ / -z / -ɪn, -ɪŋ / -d / -st
**sp** abhor[1], abhorre[16] / abhorres[2], abhors[1] / abhorring[2] / abhord[1], abhor'd[1], abhorr'd / abhorrd'st[1]
**rh** more *S 150.11*; abhor thee adore thee *PP 12.9*
**pun** *Oth 4.2.161* whore

**abhorred** *adj*
*m* ə'bɔ:ɹd, ə'bɒɹɪd
**sp** abhord[2], abhor'd[1], abhorr'd[2], abhorred[9]
> all-abhorred

**Abhorson** *n*
ə'bɔ:ɹsən
**sp** Abhorson[5]

**abide / ~s** *v*
ə'bəɪd / -z
**sp** abide[33] / abides[8]
**rh** chide *Luc 486*; deified *LC 83*; hide *TC 5.6.30*; pride *R2 5.6.22*; putrified *Luc 1749*; slide *S 45.2*; tide *3H6 4.3.59*, *Luc 647*; wide *S 27.5*

**abilit·y / ~ies** *n*
*m* ə'bɪlɪtəɪ, -lt- / -z
**sp** abilitie[4], abilitie's [ability is][1], ability[5] / abilities[5]

**a-billing** *VA* *v*
ə'bɪlɪn, -ɪŋ
**sp** a billing[1]
**rh** unwilling *VA 366*
> bill

**a-birding** *v*
ə'bɐːɹdɪn, -ɪŋ
**sp** a birding[4]
> bird

**abject** *adj*
'abʤekt
**sp** abiect[10]

**abject / ~s** *n*
*m* əb'ʤekt / -s
**sp** abiect[1] / abiects[1]

**abjectly** *adv*
'abʤekləɪ, -ktl-
**sp** abiectly[1]

**abjure / ~d** *v*
əb'ʤuːɹ / -d
**sp** abiure[4] / abiur'd[2]

**able / ~r** *adj*
'ɛːbəl / 'ɛːbləɹ
**sp** able[59] / abler[1]

**a-bleeding** *v*
ə'bliːdɪn, -ɪŋ
**sp** a bleeding[2]
**rh** proceeding *RJ 3.1.189*
> bleed

**aboard** *adv / prep*
ə'bɔːɹd
**sp** a-board[1], aboarde[1], aboord[20], a-boord[2] / aboord[3], a-boord[1]

**abode** *n*
ə'boːd
**sp** aboad[1], aboade[1], abode[5], a-bode[2]

**abod·e / ~ed / ~ing** *v*
ə'boːdɪd / -ɪn, -ɪŋ
**sp** aboaded[1] / aboding[1]

**abodement / ~s** *n*
ə'boːdmənts
**sp** aboadments[1]

**abominable** *adj*
ə'bɒmɪˌnabəl, *Holofernes LLL 5.1.24* ab'hɒ-
**sp** abhominable[14], abhomi-nable[1], *Holofernes describing Armado* abho-minable[1]

**abominably** *adv*
ə'bɒmɪˌnabləɪ, ab'hɒ-
**sp** ab-hominably[1]

**abomination / ~s** *n*
əˌbɒmɪ'nɛːsɪənz, abˌhɒ-
**sp** abhominations[1]
**rh** exclamation, imagination *Luc 704*; inclination, subornation *Luc 921* / invocations, lamentations *Luc 1832*

**abortive** *adj*
ə'bɔːɹtɪv
**sp** abortiue[4]

**abortive / ~z** *n*
ə'bɔːɹtɪvz
**sp** abbortiues[1]

**abound / ~est** *v*
ə'bəʊnd / -nst, -ndst
**sp** abound[6], a-bound[1] / abound'st[1]
> bound

**abounding** *adj*
ə'bəʊndɪn, -ɪŋ
**sp** abounding[1]

**about, *abbr* bout** *adv / prep*
*m* ə'bəʊt, *abbr* bəʊt
**sp** about[95], about[376] / a-bout[5], *abbr* 'bout [4]
**rh** out *Luc* 412, *MA 5.3.26, MW 5.5.55, 101, RJ 1.2.34, 3.5.40, S 113.2, TNK Prol.26*; about her without her *TS 4.4.103*
> here-, there-, where-about

**about to** [*in aux* be about to]
ə'bəʊt tə, -tʊ
**sp** about to[11], a-bout to[1], *emend of Ham 2.1.50* about say[1]

**above, *abbr* bove** *adv / prep*
*m* ə'bɤv, *abbr* bɤv
**sp** aboue[34] / aboue[87], *abbr* 'boue[4]
**rh** love *AW 2.3.81, AY 3.2.3, 1H6 1.2.114, MA 5.2.27, Per 2.3.22, S 110.6, TC 3.2.155, TN 5.1.135*

**Abraham / ~'s** *n*
*m* 'ɛːbrəˌham, 'ɛːbrəm / 'ɛːbrəmz
**sp** Abraham[4], Abram[2] / Abrahams[1]

**abram** *adj*
'ɛːbrəm
**sp** abram[1]

**abreast** *adv*
=
**sp** a-brest[2]
> breast

**a-breeding** *v*
ə'briːdɪn, -ɪŋ
**sp** a breeding[2]
**rh** proceeding *LLL 1.1.97*
> breed

**a-brewing** *v*
ə'bruːɪn, -ɪŋ
**sp** a bruing[1]
> brew

**abridge / ~d** *v*
=
**sp** abridge[2] / abridg'd[2]

**abridgement / ~s** *n*
=
**sp** abridgement[2], abridgment[1] / abridgements[1]

**abroach** *adv*
ə'broːʧ
**sp** abroach[3]

**abroad** *adv*
=
**sp** abroad[60], a-broad[1]
> broad

**abrogate** *v*
'abrəˌgɛ:t
**sp** abrogate[1]

**abrook** *v*
=
**sp** abrooke[1]

**abrupt** *adj*
ə'brɤpt
**sp** abrupt[1]

**abruption** *n*
ə'brɤpsɪən
**sp** abruption[1]

**abruptly** *adv*
ə'brɤpləɪ, -ptl-
**sp** abruptly[1]

**absence** *n*
=
**sp** absence[47], ab-sence[1], abse[n]ce[1]

**absent** *adj*
= ['absənt]
**sp** absent[28]

**absent** *v*
= [əb'sent]
**sp** absent[2]

**Absey** *adj*
'absi:
**sp** Absey[1]
> ABC

**Absirtis** *n*
ab'sɐ:ɹtɪs
**sp** Absirtis[1]

**absolute** *adj*
*m* 'absəˌlu:t, -slu:t
**sp** absolute[29]
**rh** pollute *Luc 853*

**absolutely** *adv*
ˌabsə'lu:tləɪ
**sp** absolutely[2]

**absolution** *Luc* *n*
ˌabsə'lu:sɪən
**sp** absolution[1]
**rh** dissolution, resolution *Luc 354*

**absolve / ~d** *v*
=
**sp** absolu'd[3]
> sin-absolver

**abstain / ~s** *v*
əb'stɛ:nz
**sp** abstaynes[1]

**abstaining** *Luc, TNK* *n*
əb'stɛ:nɪn, -ɪŋ
**sp** abstaining[2]
**rh** gaining, obtaining *Luc 130*

**abstemious** *adj*
əb'stɛ:nɪəs, -mɪ-
**sp** abstenious[1]

**abstinence** *n*
=
**sp** abstinence[4]

**abstract / ~s** *n*
=
**sp** abstract[5] / abstracts[2]

**absurd** *adj*
*m* əb'sɐ:ɹd, 'absəɹd
**sp** absurd[4]

**abundance** *n*
ə'bɤndəns, -'bəʊn-
**sp** aboundance[1], abundance[7], abun-dance[1]

**abundant** *adj*
ə'bɤndənt, -'bəʊn-
**sp** abundant[3]

**abundantly** *adv*
*m* ə'bɤndəntˌləɪ, -'bəʊn-
**sp** abundantly[1]

**abuse / ~s** *n*
=
**sp** abuse[22] / abuses[6], a-buses[1]
**rh** excuse *n Luc 1315, 1655, VA 792*; use *n RJ 2.3.16, S 134.12, VA 166* / excuses *n Luc 269, 1075, RJ 3.1.193*; sluices *Luc 1075*
> self-abuse

**abus·e / ~es / ~ing / ~ed** *v*
= / = / ə'bju:zɪn, -ɪŋ / *m* ə'bju:zd, -zɪd, *Grumio TS 1.2.7* rɪ'bju:zd
**sp** abuse[21] / abuses[2], a-buses[1] / abusing[1] / abusd[1], abus'd[35], a-bus'd[1], abusde[1], abused[4], *Grumio* rebus'd[1]
**rh** use *v S 4.5*; **abuse it lose it** *1H6 4.5.41*; use it *Luc 864* / perused *Luc 1529*; refused *MND 2.2.140*; used *KL 1.3.21* [*Q*], *LLL 2.1.213, S 82.14*

**abused** *adj*
*m* ə'bju:zɪd
**sp** abused[2]

**abuser** *n*
ə'bju:zəɹ
**sp** abuser[1]

**abusing** *adj / n*
ə'bju:zɪn, -ɪŋ
**sp** abusing[1] / abusing[1]

**abutting** *adj*
ə'bɤtɪn, -ɪŋ
**sp** abutting[1]

**aby** *v*
ə'bəɪ
**sp** abide[2]

**abysm** *n*
=
**sp** abisme[2]

**Academe / ~s** *n*
'akədi:m, -dɛm / -z
**sp** Achademe[1] / Achademes[1], Achademes[1]

**a-capering** *v*
ə'kɛ:prɪn, -ɪŋ
**sp** a capring[1]
> caper

**accent / ~s** *n*
=
**sp** accent[15], ac-cent[1] / accents[5]

**accept** *n*
=
**sp** accept[1]

**accept / ~s / ~ed** *v*
=
**sp** accept[29] / accepts[2] / accepted[3]

**acceptance** *n*
=
**sp** acceptance[5], ac-ceptance[1]

**access** *n*
*m* ək'ses, 'akses
**sp** accesse[22]
**rh** less *RJ 2.Chorus.9*

**accessible** *adj*
=
**sp** accessible[1]

**accessory** *n*
*m* 'aksə,sɤrəɪ, -əsr-
**sp** accessary[2]

**accidence** *n*
=
**sp** accidence[1]

**accident / ~s** *n*
'aksɪ,dent / -s
**sp** accident[21] / accedents[1], accidents[11]
**rh** lament *Ham 3.2.209*; discontent *S 124.5* / intents *S 115.5*

**accidental** *adj*
'aksɪ,dental
**sp** accidentall[3]

**accidentally** *adv*
*m* ,aksi'dentə,ləɪ, -tləɪ
**sp** accidentally[3]

**accite / ~s / d** *v*
ək'səɪt / -s / -ɪd
**sp** accite[1] / accites[1] / accited[1]

**acclamation / ~s** *n*
,aklə'mɛ:sɪənz
**sp** acclamations[1]

**accommodate / ~d** *v*
ə'kɒmə,dɛ:t / -ɪd
**sp** accommodate[1] / accommodated[5], accommoda-ted[1], accomodated[1]
> unaccommodated

**accommodation / ~s** *n*
ə,kɒmə'dɛ:sɪən / -z
**sp** accomodation[1] / accommodations[1]

**accommodo** *Lat v*
a'kɒmə,do:
**sp** accommodo[1]

**accompan·y / ~ying / ~ied** *v*
*m* ə'kɒmp·ə,nəɪ-, -pn-, -'kɤm- / -nəɪɪn, -ɪŋ / -ə,nəɪd, -pn-
**sp** accompanie[2], accompany[6] / accompanying[1] / accompanied[7], accompanyed[2]
> unaccompanied

**accomplice / ~s** *n*
ə'kɒmplɪsɪz, -'kɤm-
**sp** accomplices[1]

**accomplish / ~ing / ~ed** *v*
ə'kɒmplɪʃ, -'kɤm- / -ɪn, -ɪŋ / *m* -t, -ʃɪd
**sp** accomplish[3] / accomplishing[1] / accomplish'd[3], accomplished[2], accomplisht[1]
> well-accomplished

**accomplished** *adj*
ə'kɒmplɪʃt, -'kɤm-
**sp** accomplish'd[3]

**accomplishment** *n*
ə'kɒmplɪʃ,ment, -'kɤm-
**sp** accomplishment[1]

**accompt / ~s** *n*
ə'kɒmt, -mpt / -s
**sp** accompt[12] / accompts[1]
> account

**accomptant** *n*
ə'kɒmtənt, -mpt-
**sp** accomptant[1]

**accord / ~s** *n*
ə'kɔ:ɹd / -z
**sp** accord[7] / accords[1]
**rh** lord *TS 3.1.71* / lords *CE 2.1.25*

**accord / ~s / ~eth / ~ed** *v*
ə'kɔ:ɹd / -z / -əθ / -ɪd
**sp** accord[2] / accords[2] / accordeth[1] / *LC* accorded[1]
**rh** lord *AY 5.4.130* / reworded *LC 3*

**accordant** *adj*
ə'kɔ:ɹdənt
**sp** accordant[1]

**according** *adj / adv*
ə'kɔ:ɹdɪn, -ɪŋ
**sp** according[1] / according[1]

**according as / ~to** *prep*
ə'kɔ:ɹdɪn, -ɪŋ ,az / -,tʊ, ,tu:
**sp** according as[4] / according to[39]

**accordingly** *adv*
ə'kɔ:ɹdɪn,ləɪ, -ɪŋ-
**sp** accordinglie[1], accordingly[9]

**accost** *n*
=
**sp** *misunderstood name TN 1.3.49* accost[2]

**accost / ~ed** *v*
=
**sp** accost[4] / accosted[1]

**account** *n*
ə'kəʊnt
**sp** account[14], ac-count[1]
**rh** surmount *S 62.6*
> accompt

**account / ~s / ~ed / ~edest** *v*
ə'kəʊnt / -s / -ɪd / -ɪdst

sp account[17], ac-count[1] / accounts[1] / accounted[7] / accountedst[1]
> accompt

**accountant** *n*
ə'kəʊntənt
sp accountant[1]

**accoutered** *adj*
ə'ku:təɹd, -'ku:st-
sp accoutered[1], accoutred[1]

**acoutrement / ~s** *n*
ə'ku:trə,ment, -'ku:st- / -s
sp accoutrement[1], accustrement[1] / accoutrements[1], ac-coustrements[1]

**accrue** *v*
=
sp accrue[1]

**accumulate / ~d** *v*
ə'kju:mə,lɛ:t / -ɪd
sp accumulate[1] / accumulated[1]
rh hate *S 117.10*

**accumulation** *n*
ə,kju:mə'lɛ:sɪən
sp accumulation[1]

**accursed** *adj*
*m* ə'kɐ:ɹsɪd, ə'kɐ:ɹst
sp accurs'd[3], accursed[16], accurst[12], accur'st[2]
rh first *Ham 3.2.189, VA 1120*; worst *2H4 1.3.107, TG 5.4.71*

**accursed** *n*
ə'kɐ:ɹst
sp accurst[1]

**accusation / ~s** *n*
*m* ,akjə'zɛ:sɪən, -ɪ,ɒn / -z
sp accusation[13] / accusations[5], accus-ations[1]

**accusative** *adj*
=
sp accusatiue-[case][1]

**accusativ·us / ~o** *Lat n*
a,kju:zə'ti:vo:
sp accusatiuo[1], ac-cusatiuo[1]

**accuse** *n*
=
sp accuse[1]

**accus·e / ~es / ~eth / ~ing / ~ed** *v*
= / = / = / ə'kju:z·ɪn, -ɪŋ / *m* -ɪd, -d
sp accuse[33], ac-cuse[1] / accuses[2] / accuseth[1] / accusing[2] / accus'd[18], accusde[2], accused[3], accust[1]
rh accuse thee misuse thee *S 152.5* / excused *MA 4.1.213*

**accused** *n*
*m* ə'kju:zɪd
sp accused[1]

**accuser / ~'s / ~s** *n*
ə'kju:zəɹ / -z
sp accuser[2] / accusers[1] / accusers[5], ac-cusers[1]

**accustomed** *adj*
ə'kɤstəmd
sp accustomed[1], accustom'd[5]
> customed, unaccustomed

**ace** *n*
as
sp ace[3]
pun *Cym 2.3.2, MND 5.1.299* ass
> ames-, deus-ace

**ache / ~s** *n*
ɛ:ʧ / *m* 'ɛ:ʧɪz
sp ache[4] / aches[3]
pun *AC 4.7.8* H

**ache / ~s** *v*
ɛ:k / -s
sp ake[7] / akes[4]
rh brake *VA 875*; sake *CE 3.1.58*
> heart-, tooth-ache; aching, unaching

**Acheron** *n*
*m* 'akərɒn, -,rɒn
sp Acaron[1], Acheron[2]
rh anon *MND 3.2.357*; gone *Mac 3.5.15*

**achieve / ~s / ~d** *v*
ə'ʧi:v, ə'ʧɪv / -z / -d
sp atcheeue[4], atcheiue[2], atchieue[6] / atcheeues[2] / atchieu'd[7], atchieued[2], atchie-ued[1], atchiu'd[1]
rh live *S 67.3* / rh *1* lived *H5 Epil.7*; rh *2* grieved *R2 4.1.216*
> half-, strange-achieved; deed-achieving

**achievement / ~s** *n*
ə'ʧi:vmənt, - ʧɪv- / -s
sp atchieuement[3] / atchieuements[2], atchieuments[1]

**achiever** *n*
ə'ʧi:vəɹ, -ʧɪv-
sp atchieuer[1]

**Achilles / ~s'** *n*
ə'kɪli:z
sp Achilles[81], A-chilles[2] / Achilles[6]

**aching** *adj*
'ɛ:kɪn, -ɪŋ
sp aking[3]
> ache *v*

**Achitophel** *n*
ə'kɪtəfəl
sp Achitophel[1]

**acknow** *v*
ək'no:
> acknown, know

**acknowledge / ~d** *v*
=
sp acknowledge[19] / acknowledg'd[2], acknowledged[1]

**acknowledgement** *n*
=
sp acknowledgement[1]

**acknown** *adj*
ək'no:n
sp acknowne[1]
> acknow

**a-cold** *adj*
ə'ko:ld
sp a cold[5]
> cold

**a-coming** *v*
ə'kɤmɪn, -ɪŋ
**sp** a comming[1]
> coming

**aconitum** *n*
akə'nəɪtəm
**sp** aconitum[1]

**acordo** *nonsense word*
ə'kɔ:ɹdo:
**sp** acordo[1]

**acorn** *n*
'ɛ:kɔ:ɹn
**sp** acorne[4]
> full-acorned

**acquaint / ~s / ~ed** *v*
ə'kwɛ:nt / -s / -ɪd
**sp** acquaint[22] / acquaints[1] / acquainted[31], ac-quainted[2]
**rh** attainted *S 88.5*; painted *S 20.3*; tainted *CE 3.2.15*
> un-, well-acquainted

**acquaintance** *n*
ə'kwɛ:ntəns
**sp** acquaintance[29], ac-quaintance[1], acquain-tance[1], acquainta[n]ce[1]

**acquire / ~d** *v*
ə'kwəɪɹ / -d
**sp** acquire[4] / acquir'd[2]

**acquisition** *n*
ˌakwɪ'zɪsɪən
**sp** acquisition[1]

**acquit / ~ted** *v*
=
**sp** acquit[8] / acquitted[3]

**acquittance / ~s** *n*
=
**sp** acquittance[3] / acquittances[1]

**acre / ~s** *n*
'ɛ:kəɹ, 'ak- / -z
**sp** acre[3] / acres[3], akers[1]

**across** *adv / prep*
=
**sp** a-crosse[5] / a-crosse[1]
**rh** loss *Luc 1662*

**act / ~s** *n*
=
**sp** act[74], acte[24] / actes[1], acts[19]
**rh** fact *AW 3.7.46, Luc 350*

**act / ~s / ~ing / ~ed** *v*
= / = / 'aktɪn, -ɪŋ / =
**sp** act[12], acte[6] / acts[3] / acting[3] / acted[7]
> unacted, unactive

**Actaeon / ~'s** *n*
ək'tɛ:ən / -z
**sp** Acteon[2] / Acteons[1]

**acting** *n*
'aktɪn, -ɪŋ
**sp** acting[5]

**action / ~s** *n*
'aksɪən / -z
**sp** action[111], [kindred]-action[1], *Hostess 2H4 2.1.28* exion[1] / actions[23], ac-tions[1]
> kindred-action

**action-taking** *adj*
'aksɪən-ˌtɛ:kɪn, -ɪŋ
**sp** action-taking[1]
> take

**Actium** *n*
'aksɪəm, -ən
**sp** Action[1]

**active** *adv*
=
**sp** actiue[6]

**actively** *adv*
*m* 'aktɪvˌləɪ
**sp** actiuely[1]
> unactive

**active-valiant** *adj*
=
**sp** actiue, valiant[1]
> valiant

**activity** *n*
*m* ək'tɪvɪˌtəɪ, -vt-
**sp** actiuitie[1], actiuity[2]

**actor / ~'s / ~s** *n*
'aktəɹ / -z
**sp** actor[11] / actors[1] / actors[10]

**actual** *adj*
'aktjʊɑl, 'akʧɑl
**sp** actuall[2]

**a-cursing** *v*
ə-'kɐ:ɹsɪn, -ɪŋ
**sp** a cursing[1]
> curse

**acute** *adj*
=
**sp** acute[2]

**acutely** *adv*
ə'kju:tləɪ
**sp** acutely[1]

**ad** *Lat prep*
=
**sp** ad[6]
> adsum

**adage** *n*
'adɑ:ʒ, 'adɪʤ
**sp** adage[1], addage[1]

**Adallas** *n*
ə'dɤləs
**sp** Adullas[1]

**Adam / ~'s** *n*
=
**sp** Adam[25] / Adams[3]

**adamant** *n*
=
**sp** adamant[3]

**a-days** *adv*
ə'dɛ:z
**sp** a-dayes[1]
> day

**add / ~s / ~ing / ~ed** *v*
= / = / 'adɪn, -ɪŋ / =

sp adde[41] / addes[4], adds[1] / adding[7] / added[16]

**adder / ~'s / ~s / ~s'** *n*
'adəɹ / -z
sp adder[11] / adders[2] / adders[2] / adders[1]
rh shudder *VA 878*

**addict / ~ed** *v*
=
sp addict[1] / addicted[2]

**addiction** *n*
ə'dɪksɪən
sp addiction[1]

**addition / ~s** *n*
ə'dɪsɪən / -z
sp addition[24], additi-on[1] / additions[3]
> sur-addition

**addle** *adj*
=
sp addle[3]

**address / ~s / ~ing / ~ed** *v*
= / = / ə'dresɪn, -ɪŋ / =
sp addresse[11] / addresses[1] / addressing[1] / addressed[1], addrest[8]
rh guest *H5 3.3.58*; rest *LLL 5.2.92*

**adhere / ~s** *v*
ə'dɛːɹ, ə'diːɹ / -z
sp adhere[2] / adheres[3]

**adieu / ~s** *n*
ə'ʤuː, -djuː, *Caius MW 4.5.82, 5.3.5* adjø / ə'ʤuːz, -djuːz
sp adew[9], adieu[63], adiew[8], adue[19] / adieus[1], adieu's[1]
rh imbrue *MND 5.1.339*; Jew *LLL 3.1.132*; new *KL 1.1.186, Mac 2.4.37, R2 5.3.143*; rue *KJ 3.1.326*; true *AY 5.4.118, MA 3.1.109, R2 5.3.143, RJ 2.2.136*; you *AC 5.2.189, 1H6 4.4.45, LLL 1.1.110, 2.1.199, 5.2.226, 234, 241, MND 1.1.224, RJ 3.5.59, S 57.8, TNK 1.4.12, VA 537*
pun *LLL 5.2.623* Jude

**adjacent** *adj*
ə'ʤɛːsənt
sp adiacent[2]

**adjoin / ~ed** *v*
ə'ʤəɪnd
sp adioyn'd[1]
> join

**adjoining to** *prep*
ə'ʤəɪnɪn 'tuː, -ɪŋ-, -'tʊ
sp adioyning to[1]

**adjourn / ~ed** *v*
ə'ʤɐːɹn / -d, -'ʤɔː-
sp adiourne[1] / adiourn'd[1]
rh *1* turned *Cym 5.4.78*; rh *2* performed *Cym 5.4.78*

**adjudge / ~d** *v*
*m* ə'ʤɤʤd, -ʤɪd
sp adiudg'd[4], adiudged[1]

**adjunct** *n*
=
sp adiunct[2]

**administer** *v*
əd'mɪnɪstəɹ
sp administer[1]

**administration** *n*
əd,mɪnɪ'strɛːsɪən
sp administration[1]

**admirable** *adj*
*m* 'admɪ,rabəl, -ɪrəb-
sp admirable[15]
> admire

**admiral** *n*
*m* 'admɪ,rɑl, -ɪrəl
sp admirall[6]

**admiration** *n*
,admɪ'rɛːsɪən
sp admiration[12], ad-miration[1]

**admir·e / ~ing / ~ed** *v*
əd'məɪɹ / -rɪn, -rɪŋ / *m* -d, -rɪd, 'adməɪɹd
sp admire[6] / admiring[3] / admir'd[3], admired[2]
rh desire *S 123.5*; fire *LLL 4.2.114, PP 5.10* / desired, tired *Luc 418*
> all-admiring

**admired** *adj*
*m* əd'məɪɹd, -rɪd
sp admir'd[5], admired[4]

**admirer** *n*
əd'məɪrəɹ
sp admirer[1]

**admiring** *adj*
əd'məɪɹɪn, -ɪŋ
sp admiring[2]

**admiringly** *adv*
əd'məɪrɪnləɪ, -ɪŋ-
sp admiringly[2]

**admission** *n*
əd'mɪsɪən
sp admission[1]
> self-admission

**admit / ~s / ~ting / ~ted** *v*
= / = / əd'mɪtɪn, -ɪŋ / =
sp admit[23] / admits[7] / admitting[1] / admitted[13]

**admittance** *n*
=
sp admittance[8], admit-tance[2]

**admonish / ~ ing** *v*
= / əd'mɒnɪʃɪn, -ɪŋ
sp admonish[1] / admonishing[1]

**admonishment / ~s** *n*
=
sp admonishment[1] / admonishments[1]

**admonition** *n*
,adm∂'nɪsɪən
sp admonition[2]

**ado** *n*
=
sp ado[2], a-do[1], adoe[10], a-doe[2], adoo[3]
rh too *Tit 2.1.98*

**a-doing** *v*
ə'duːɪn, -ɪŋ
sp a doing[1]
> do

**Adonis** *n*
ə'do:nɪs
**sp** Adonis[2]

**a-doors**
> door

**adopt / ~s / ~ed** *v*
=
**sp** adopt[3] / adopts[1] / adopted[4]

**adopted** *adj*
=
**sp** adopted[2]

**adoptedly** *adv*
ə'dɒptɪdləɪ
**sp** adoptedly[1]

**adoption** *n*
ə'dɒpsɪən
**sp** adoption[4]

**adoptious** *adj*
*m* ə'dɒpsɪəs
**sp** adoptious[1]

**adoration / ~s** *n*
ˌadə'rɛ:sɪən / -z
**sp** adoration[1], odoration[1] / adorations[1]

**ador·e / ~est / ~es / ~eth / ~ing / ~ed** *v*
ə'dɔ:ɹ / -st / -z / -əθ / -rɪn, -rɪŋ / -d
**sp** adore[13] / adorest[1] / adores[2] / adoreth[1] / adoring[1] / ador'd[3]
**rh** gore *TN 2.5.103*; store *Luc 1835*; adore thee abhor thee, hie thee *PP 12.9*

**adorer** *n*
ə'dɔ:rəɹ
**sp** adorer[1]

**adorn / ~s / ~ed** *v*
ə'dɔ:ɹn / -z / *m* -d, -nɪd
**sp** adorne[3] / adornes[1] / adorned[2]

**adorning / ~s** *n*
ə'dɔ:ɹnɪnz, -ɪŋz
**sp** adornings[1]

**adornment** *n*
ə'dɔ:ɹnmənt
**sp** adornement[2]

**a-doting** *S* *n*
ə'do:tɪn, -ɪŋ
**sp** a dotinge[1]
**rh** nothing *S 20.10*
> dote

**a-down / ~-a** *adv*
ə'dəʊn / -ə
**sp** a-downe[1] / a-downe-a[1], adowne'a[1]
> down

**Adramadio** *n*
ˌadrə'mɑ:dɪo:, -'mad-
**sp** Adramadio[2]

**a-dreams**
> John-a-dreams

**Adrian** *n*
'ɛ:drɪən
**sp** Adrian[5]

**Adriana** *n*
ˌadrɪ'ɑ:nə, -'an-
**sp** Adriana[9]

**Adriano** *n*
ˌadrɪ'ɑ:no:, -'an-
**sp** Adriano[1], *emend of LLL 1.1.266* Adriana[2]

**Adriatic** *adj*
ɛ:drɪ'atɪk
**sp** Adriaticke[1]

**adsum** *Lat v*
'adsʊm
**sp** ad sum[1]

**a-ducking** *v*
ə'dɤkɪn, -ɪŋ
**sp** a ducking[1]
> duck

**adulation** *n*
adjə'lɛ:sɪən, adʒə-
**sp** adulation[1]

**Adullas**
> Adallas

**adulterate** *adj*
*m* ə'dɤltrət, -tər-
**sp** adulterate[3]

**adulterate / ~s** *v*
ə'dɤltrəts, -tər-
**sp** adulterates[1]

**adulterer / ~s** *n*
ə'dɤltrəɹz, -tər-
**sp** adulterers[1]

**adulteress** *n*
*m* ə'dɤltrəs, -təˌres
**sp** adulteresse[1], adultresse[4]

**adulterous** *adj*
ə'dɤltrəs, -tər-
**sp** adulterous[2]

**adulter·y / ~ies** *n*
*m* ə'dɤltrəɪ, -təˌrəɪ / -təˌrəɪz
**sp** adultery[6], adulte-ry[1] / adulteries[1]
**rh** flies *Cym 5.4.33*

**advance / ~d** *v*
əd'vans / *m* əd'vanst, -sɪd
**sp** aduance[27] / aduanc'd[10], aduanced[3], aduaunc'd[1]
**rh** chance, circumstance *Luc 1705*; dance *LLL 5.2.123, TNK 3.5.133*; France *H5 2.2.192, 5.2.346, 5. Chorus.44*; ignorance *S 78.13*

**advanced** *adj*
*m* əd'vanst, 'advanst
**sp** aduanc'd[1], aduanced[1], aduan'st[2]

**advancement** *n*
əd'vansmənt
**sp** aduancement[9], aduance-ment[1]

**advantage / ~s** *n*
əd'vantɪdʒ / -ɪz
**sp** aduantage[62], ad-uantage[1], [th ']aduantage[1] / aduantages[8], ad-uantages[1], aduanta-ges[1]
> disadvantage

**advantag·e / ~ing / ~ed** *v*
əd'vantɪdʒ / -ɪn, -ɪŋ / -d

**sp** aduantage[4] / aduantaging[1] / aduantaged[1]

**advantageable** *adj*
*m* əd'vantɪˌʤabəl
**sp** aduantageable[1]

**advantageous** *adj*
ˌadvən'tɛːʤɪəs
**sp** aduantageous[1], aduantagious[1]

**adventure / ~s** *n*
ə'ventəɹ, əd'v- / -z
**sp** aduenture[11], aduen-ture[1] / aduentures[3]
> mis-, per-adventure

**adventur·e / ~ing / ~d** *v*
ə'ventəɹ, əd'v- / -rɪn, -rɪŋ, -ventr- / -d
**sp** aduenture[11] / aduenturing[1] / aduentur'd[1]

**adventurous** *adj*
ə'ventrəs, əd'v-
**sp** aduentrous[1], aduenturous[2]

**adventurously** *adv*
*m* ə'ventrəsˌləɪ, əd'v-
**sp** adventurously[1]

**adversar·y / ~ies** *n*
*m* 'advəɹsˌrəɪ, -ˌsarəɪ, -sr-, *Fluellen H5 3.2.59 ff* 'að- / -z
**sp** aduersarie[3], aduersary[4], *Fluellen* athuersarie[2], athuer-sarie[1] / aduersaries[15]

**adverse** *adj*
*m* 'advəɹs, əd'vɐːɹs
**sp** aduerse[10]

**adversely** *adv*
*m* 'advəɹsˌləɪ
**sp** aduersly[1]

**adversit·y / ~y's / ~ies** *n*
*m* əd'vɐːɹsɪˌtəɪ, -ɪt- / -ɪˌtəɪz
**sp** aduersitie[4], aduer-sitie[1], aduersity[1] / aduersities[1] / aduersities[1]
**rh** cry *CE 2.1.34*

**advertis·e / ~ing / ~ed** *v*
*m* əd'vɐːɹtəɪz / -ɪn, -ɪŋ / -d
**sp** aduertise[2] / aduertysing[1] / aduertis'd[2], aduertised[3], aduertiz'd[1]

**advertisement** *n*
*m* əd'vɐːɹtəɪzˌment
**sp** aduertisement[3], ad-uertisement[1]

**advice** *n*
əd'vəɪs
**sp** aduice[31], aduise[11]
**rh** entice, nice *Luc 1409*; price *KL 2.1.120*

**advise / ~s / ~d** *v*
əd'vəɪz, ə'v- / -ɪz / *m* -d, -ɪd
**sp** aduice[3], aduise[35], ad-uise[1] / aduises[2] / aduis'd[26], aduisde[1], aduised[3], adui-sed[1], auis'd[2]
**rh** *1* companies *TS 1.1.238*; **rh** *2* flies *Per 4.3.51* / disguised *LLL 5.2.300, 434*

**advised** *adj*
*m* əd'vəɪzɪd, -zd, ə'v-
**sp** aduis'd[1], aduised[4]

**advisedly** *adv*
*m* əd'vəɪzɪdˌləɪ, ə'v-
**sp** aduisedlie[1], aduisedly[1]
**rh** by *Luc 1816*; eye, fly *Luc 180*; reply *1H4 5.1.114*

**advising / ~s** *n*
əd'vəɪzɪnz, -ɪŋz, ə'v-
**sp** aduisings[1]
> fore-, un-, well-advised

**advocate** *n*
*m* 'advəˌkɛːt, -vəkət
**sp** aduocate[7], aduocate's [advocate is][1]
**rh** hate *S 35.10*

**advocation** *n*
ˌadvə'kɛːsɪən
**sp** aduocation[1]

**a-dying** *v*
ə'dəɪɪn, -ɪŋ
**sp** a dying[1]
> die

**Aeacides** *n*
iː'asɪdiːz
**sp** Aeacides[1]

**Aeac·us / ~ida** *n*
iː'asɪdə
**sp** Aeacida[1]

**Aedile / ~s** *n*
'iːdəɪl / -z
**sp** Aedile[3], Edile[3] / Aediles[5], Ediles[2]

**Aegles** *n*
'iːgliːz
**sp** Eagles[1]

**Aemilia**
> Emilia

**Aemillius**
> Emillius

**Aeneas** *n*
ə'nɛːəs
**sp** Aeneas[40]

**Aeolus** *n*
'iːələs
**sp** Aeolus[1]

**aer** *Lat n*
ɛːɹ
**sp** aer[2]

**aerial** *n*
'ɛːrɪəl
**sp** eriall[1]

**aerie, aery**
> eyrie

**Aesculapius** *n*
ˌeskə'lɛːpɪəs
**sp** Esculapius[1]

**Aeson** *n*
'iːsən
**sp** Eson[1]

**Aesop** *n*
'iːsəp
**sp** Aesop[1]

**Aethiop**
> Ethiop

**Aetna**
> Etna

**afar** *adv*
ə'fɑ:ɹ
**sp** a far[1], afarre[9], a farre[5], a-farre[2], a farre-[off][2]
**rh** *1* scar *Luc 830*; **rh** *2* war *Luc 830*
> far

**afeared** *adj*
ə'fi:ɹd, -'fɛ:-
**sp** afeard[11], a-feard[3], afear'd[6], a-fear'd[1], affeard[4], affear'd[6]
**rh** reared *1H6 4.7.93*
> fear

**a-feasting** *v*
ə'festɪn, -ɪŋ
**sp** a feasting[1]
> feast

**affability** *n*
*m* ˌafə'bɪlɪˌtəɪ, -ɪt-
**sp** affabilitie[2], affability[1]

**affable** *adj*
*m* 'afəˌbɤl, 'afbəl
**sp** affable[5]

**affair / ~s** *n*
ə'fɛ:ɹ / -z
**sp** affaire[9], affayre[3] / affaires[46], [selfe]-affaires[1], affairs[1], affayres[17]
> love-affair, self-affairs

**affaire / ~s** *Fr n*
a'fɛ:ɹ
**sp** affaires[1]

**affect / ~s** *n*
ə'feks, -kts
**sp** affects[3]

**affect / ~s / ~eth / ~ing / ~ed** *v*
*m* ə'fekt, 'afekt / ə'fek·s, -ts / -əθ / -ɪn, -ɪŋ / -ɪd
**sp** affect[23] / affects[8] / affecteth[1] / affecting[1] / affected[17]

**affectation / ~s** *n*
ˌafek'tɛ:sɪən / -z
**sp** affectation[1] / affectations[1]

**affected** *adj*
=
**sp** affected[3]
**rh** infected *LLL 2.1.218*; rejected *VA 157*
> self-affected

**affectedly** *LC adv*
*m* ə'fektɪdˌləɪ
**sp** affectedly[1]
**rh** secrecy *LC 48*

**affecting** *adj*
ə'fektɪn, -ɪŋ
**sp** affecting[1]
> drawling-affecting

**affection / ~s** *n*
*m* ə'feksɪən, -sɪˌɒn / -z
**sp** affection[72], af-fection[1], affe-ction[1] / affections[36], affecti-ons[1]
**rh** ostentation *LLL 5.2.407*; passion *TS 3.1.74*

**affectionate** *adj*
*m* ə'feksɪəˌnɛ:t
**sp** affectio-nate[1]

**affectionately** *adv*
*m* ə'feksɪəˌnɛ:tləɪ
**sp** affectionately[1]

**affectioned** *adj*
ə'feksɪənd
**sp** affection'd[1]

**affiance / ~d** *v*
ə'fəɪəns / -t
**sp** affiance[3] / affianced[1], af-fianced[1]

**affine / ~d** *v*
ə'fəɪnd
**sp** affin'd[3]

**affinity** *n*
ə'fɪnɪtəɪ
**sp** affinitie[1]

**affirm** *v*
ə'fɐ:ɹm
**sp** affirme[4]

**affirmation** *n*
'afəɹˌmɛ:sɪən
**sp** affirmation[1]

**affirmative / ~s** *n*
ə'fɐ:ɹmətɪvz
**sp** affirmatiues[1]

**afflict / ~s / ~ed** *v*
=
**sp** afflict[13] / afflicts[1] / afflicted[3]

**afflicted** *adj*
=
**sp** afflicted[4]

**affliction / ~s** *n*
ə'flɪksɪən / *m* -z, -sɪˌɒnz
**sp** affliction[18], affli-ction[1], afflicti-on[1] / afflictions[5]

**afford / ~s / ~eth** *v*
ə'fɔ:ɹd / -z / -əθ
**sp** affoord[14], afford[6] / affoords[4], affords[7], af-fords[1] / affordeth[1]
**rh** *1* lord *LLL 4.1.39, Luc 1305, R2 1.1.177, RJ 4.1.125*; **rh** *2* word *S 79.11* / words *CE 3.1.24, Luc 1106, S 85.7, 105.12*

**affray** *n*
ə'frɛ:
**sp** affray[1]
**rh** day *RJ 3.5.33*

**affright / ~s / ~ed** *v*
ə'frəɪt / -s / -ɪd
**sp** affright[9] / affrights[5] / affrighted[5]
**rh** flight, night *Luc 971*; night *MND 5.1.140*
> fright

**affrighted** *adj*
ə'frəɪtɪd
**sp** affrighted[1]
> self-affrighted

**affront** *n*
ə'frʏnt
**sp** affront[1]

**affront / ~ed** *v*
ə'frʏnt / -ɪd
**sp** affront[3] / affronted[1]

**aff·y / ~ied** *v*
ə'fəɪ / -d
**sp** affie[1], affye[1] / affied[1]
**rh** integrity *Tit 1.1.50*

**afield** *adv*
ə'fi:ld
**sp** a-field[1], a field[3]
> field

**afire** *adj*
ə'fəɪɹ
**sp** afire[1], a fire[3]
> fire

**afloat** *adj*
ə'flo:t
**sp** a-float[1]
**rh** boat *S 80.9*
> float

**afoot** *adv*
=
**sp** afoot[4], a foot[3], a-foot[9], afoote[2], a foote[6]
> foot

**afore** *adv*
ə'fɔ:ɹ
**sp** afore[11], a-fore[1]
> before

**aforehand** *adv*
*m* ə'fɔ:ɹˌand, -ˌhand
**sp** aforehand[1]
> forehand, hand

**aforesaid** *adj*
*m* ə'fɔ:ɹsed
**sp** aforesaid[2], afore-said[1]
> foresaid, say

**afraid** *adj*
ə'frɛ:d
**sp** affraid[20], affraide[2], afraid[17], a-fraid[2], afraide[2]
**rh** dismayed *VA 898*; maid, said *LC 179*; played *PP 17.20*

**afresh** *adv*
=
**sp** afresh[3], a-fresh[1]
> fresh

**Afric** *adj*
'afrɪk
**sp** Affricke[1]

**Afric / ~a** *n*
'afrɪk / =
**sp** Affricke[3] / Affrica[1]

**African** *n*
=
**sp** African[1]

**afront** *adv*
ə'frʏnt
**sp** a-front[1]
> front

**after** *adj / adv / conj / prep*
'aftəɹ, 'ɑ:təɹ
**sp** after[1] / after[82], af-ter[3] / after[28], af-ter[1] / after[262], af-ter[3]
**rh** caught her, daughter, halter, slaughter *KL 1.4.318*; daughter *TS 1.1.236*, WT *4.1.28*
> thereafter

**after-debt / ~s** *n*
'aftəɹ-ˌdets, 'ɑ:təɹ-
**sp** after-debts[1]
> debt

**after-dinner / ~'s** *adj*
'aftəɹ-ˌdɪnəɹz, 'ɑ:təɹ-
**sp** after-dinners[1], after dinners[1]
> dinner

**after-enquiry / inquiry** *n*
'aftəɹ-ɪŋˌkwəɪrəɪ, 'ɑ:təɹ-
**sp** after-enquiry[1]
> enquiry / inquiry

**after-eye** *v*
'aftəɹ-ˌəɪ, 'ɑ:təɹ-
**sp** after-eye[1]
> eye

**after-fleet** *n*
'aftəɹ-ˌfli:t, 'ɑ:təɹ-
**sp** after fleete[1]
> fleet

**after-hours** *n*
'aftəɹ-ˌo:ɹz, 'ɑ:təɹ-
**sp** after-houres[1]
> hours

**after-loss** *S* *n*
'aftəɹ-ˌlɒs, 'ɑ:təɹ-
**sp** after losse[1]
**rh** cross *S 90.4*
> loss

**after-love** *n*
'aftəɹ-ˌlʏv, 'ɑ:təɹ-
**sp** after-loue[1], after loue[1]
> love

**after-meeting** *n*
'aftəɹ-ˌmi:tɪn, -ɪŋ, 'ɑ:təɹ-
**sp** after-meeting[1]
> meeting

**afternoon** *n*
ˌaftəɹ'nu:n, ˌɑ:təɹ-, -'nʊn
**sp** afternoone[22], after-noone[5]
**rh** done *AW 5.3.66*; son *1H6 4.5.53*
> noon

**after-supper** *n*
'aftəɹ-ˌsʏpəɹ, 'ɑ:təɹ-
**sp** after supper[1]

**after-times** *n*
'aftəɹ-ˌtəɪmz, 'ɑ:təɹ-
**sp** after-times[1]
> time

**afterward / ~s** *adv*
*m* 'aftəɹˌwɐ:ɹd, -ɹwəɹd, 'ɑ:təɹ- / -z
**sp** afterward[7], after-ward[1] / afterwards[14], af-terwards[1]

**again** *adv*
ə'gɛ:n, ə'gen
**sp** again[12], againe[705], a-gaine[11], agen[24], a-gen[2], *KJ 4.2.1 emend of* again
**rh** *1* amain, vein *LLL 5.2.540*; brain *VA 908, 1042*; complain *RJ 2. Chorus.5*; disdain *VA 499*; disdain, pain *Luc 688*; distain, pain *Luc 788*; entertain *Luc 1359*; gain *Per 5. Chorus.12*; mane *VA 273*; pain *Cym 4.2.289, MND 1.1.251, VA 1036*; plain *LLL 5.2.453, VA 408*; rain *Mac 1.1.1, VA 960, 966*; slain *1H6 4.5.19, RJ 3.1.121, S 22.14, VA 474, 1020, 1113*; stain *Luc 1707, S 109.6*; sustain *TN 4.2.123*; twain *LLL 5.2.458, MV 3.2.324, R2 5.3.132, TNK 3.5.144, VA 121, 209*; vain *2H6 4.1.78, CE 3.2.25, Luc 1666, MM 4.1.5, R2 2.2.142, 3.2.213, Tem 4.1.98, VA 769*; **rh** *2* Amen *R3 5.5.40*; Imogen *Cym 3.5.106, 5.3.82*; men *R2 3.2.78, Tim 4.2.40*; pen *S 79.8*; then *LLL 5.2.821, RJ 2.3.44*; when *R2 1.1.163*

**against,** *abbr* **gainst** *adv / conj / prep*
ə'gɛ:nst, ə'genst, *abbr* 'gɛ:nst, 'genst
**sp** against[2] / against[1], *abbr* gainst[1], / against[551], a-gainst[10], *abbr* gainst[8], 'gainst [81]

**Agamemnon / ~'s** *n*
agə'memnən / -z
**sp** Agamemnon[33], Aga-memnon[1], Agamem-non[1] / Agamemnons[6]

**agate** *n*
'agət
**sp** agat[1], agot[3]

**agate-stone** *n*
'agət-ˌsto:n
**sp** agat-stone[1]
> stone

**agaze / ~d** *v*
ə'gɛ:zd
**sp** agaz'd[1]
> gaze

**age / ~'s / ~s** *n*
ɛ:ʤ / 'ɛ:ʤɪz
**sp** age[175] / ages[3] / ages[12]
**rh** *1* assuage *LC 70*; equipage *S 32.10*; gage *Luc 1350, R2 1.1.160*; gage, rage *Luc 142*; outrage *Luc 603*; page *MW 1.3.78, S 108.10*; rage *1H6 4.6.12, 35, LC 14, S 17.9, 64.2*; sage, stage *Luc 275*; **rh** *2* pilgrimage *AY 3.2.128, Luc 962, R2 1.3.229, S 7.6*; presage *S 107.8*

**aged** *adj*
*m* 'ɛ:ʤɪd, ɛ:ʤd
**sp** aged[23], ag'd[3]

**aged** *n*
*m* 'ɛ:ʤɪd
**sp** aged[1]

**Agenor** *n*
ə'ʤɛ:nəɹ
**sp** Agenor[1]

**agent / ~s** *n*
'ɛ:ʤənt / -s
**sp** agent[10] / agents[3]

**aggravate** *v*
*m* ˌagrə'vɛ:t
**sp** aggrauate[2], ag-grauate[1], aggra-uate[1]

**Agincourt** *n*
'aʤɪnˌkɔ:ɹt
**sp** Agincourt[4]

**agitation** *n*
ˌaʤɪ'tɛ:sɪən
**sp** agitation[2]

**aglet-baby** *n*
'aglɪt-ˌbɛ:bəɪ
**sp** aglet babie[1]

**agnize** *v*
əg'nəɪz
**sp** agnize[1]

**ago** *adv*
ə'go:
**sp** ago[14], agoe[13]
**rh** Hortensio *TS 3.1.69*

**a-going** *v*
ə'go:ɪn, -ɪŋ
**sp** a going[1]
> go

**agone** *adv*
ə'gɒn
**sp** agone[3]

**agony** *n*
'agənəɪ
**sp** agonie[2], agony[4]
**rh** thee *R3 4.4.164*

**agree,** *abbr* **gree / ~s / ~ing / ~d,** *abbr* **greed** *v*
ə'gri:, *abbr* gri: / -z / -ɪn, -ɪŋ / -d, *abbr* gri:d
**sp** agree[20], *abbr* gree[1] / agrees[5] / agreeing[4] / agreed[17], *abbr* greed[3], 'greed[2]
**rh** be, me *LLL 2.1.211*; me *PP 8.1*; see *H8 Prol.10* / sees *Luc 1095, VA 288* / seeing *Ham 3.2.264, S 114.11* / bleed *R2 1.1.156*
> disagree, unagreeable

**agreement** *n*
ə'gri:mənt
**sp** agreement[4]

**aggrieved** *adj*
*Fluellen H5 4.7.158* ə'gri:ft
**sp** agreefd[1]

**Agrippa** *n*
ə'grɪpə
**sp** Agrippa[24]

**aground** *adv*
ə'grəʊnd
**sp** a ground[1]

**a-growing** *v*
ə'gro:ɪn, -ɪŋ
**sp** a growing[1]
> grow

**ague** *adj*
'ɛ:gju:
**sp** ague[1]

**ague / ~'s / ~s** *n*
'ɛ:gju: / -z
**sp** ague[8] / agues[2] / agues[3]

**Aguecheek** *n*
'ɛ:gju:ˌʧi:k
**sp** Ague-cheeke[3]
> cheek

**agued** *adj*
'ɛ:gju:d
**sp** agued[1]

**agueface** *n*
'ɛ:gju:ˌfɛ:s
**sp** agueface[1]
> face

**ague-proof** *adj*
'ɛ:gju:-ˌprɤf, -ˌpru:f
**sp** agu-proofe[1]
> proof

**ah / aha** *interj*
=
**sp** ah[146] / ah ha[7]; ah, ha[2]

**a-hanging** *v*
ə-'aŋɪn, -ɪŋ, -'ha-
**sp** a hanging[1]
> hang

**a-height** *adv*
ə-'əɪt, -'hə-
**sp** a height[1]
> height

**a-high** *adv*
ə-'əɪ, -'hə-
**sp** a high[1]
> high

**a-hold** *adv*
ə-'o:ld, -'ho:-
**sp** a hold[2]
> hold

**a-hooting** *v*
ə-'u:tɪn, -ɪŋ, -'hu:-
**sp** a hooting[1]
**rh** shooting *LLL 4.2.60*
> hoot

**a-horseback** *adv*
ə-'ɔ:ɹsbak, -'hɔ:-
**sp** a-horseback[3], a horsebacke[1], a horse-backe[2]
> horseback

**a-hungry / an-** *adj*
ə-'ɤŋgrəɪ, -'hɤ- / ən-
**sp** a-hungry[1] / an hungry[1]
> hungry

**ai** *Fr*
> avoir

**aid / ~s** *n*
ɛ:d / -z
**sp** aid[3], aide[7], ayd[8], ayde[27] / aydes[1]
**rh** *1* appaid *Luc 912*; betrayed *1H6 1.1.143*; bewrayed *Luc 1696*; conveyed *VA 1190*; decayed *S 79.1*; dismayed *R3 5.3.174*; maid *AW 5.3.326*; **rh** *2* said *Luc 912, 1696, 1784*
> inaidible

**aid / ~ing / ~ed** *v*
ɛ:d / 'ɛ:d·ɪn, -ɪŋ / -ɪd
**sp** aid[1], aide[1], ayde[8] / ayding[1] / ayded[1]

**aidance** *n*
'ɛ:dəns
**sp** aydance[1]

**aidant** *adj*
'ɛ:dənt
**sp** aydant[1]

**aiding** *adj*
'ɛ:dɪn, -ɪŋ
**sp** ayding[1]

**aidless** *adj*
'ɛ:dləs
**sp** aydelesse[1]

**ail / ~est** *v*
ɛ:l / -st
**sp** ayle[1] / ayl'st[1]

**aim / ~s** *n*
ɛ:m / -z
**sp** aime[4], ayme[19] / aimes[1]
**rh** claim *CE 3.2.63*; exclaim, maim *LC 310*; proclaim *AW 2.1.156*

**aim / ~est / ~s / ~ing / ~ed** *v*
ɛ:m / -st / -z / 'ɛ:m·ɪn, -ɪŋ / *m* -ɪd, ɪ:md
**sp** aime[2], ayme[12] / aymest[1], aym'st[1] / aymes[3] / ayming[3], ayming[3] / aim'd[1], aimed[1], aym'd[5]

**ainsi** *Fr adv*
ɛ̃'si
**sp** ainsi[2]

**aio** *Lat v*
'əɪo:
**sp** aio[1]

**air / ~s** *n*
ɛ:ɹ / -z
**sp** aire[17], ayer[2], ayre[159], ayre's [air is][1] / aires[1], ayres[4]
**rh** despair *MV 3.2.108*; fair *LLL 4.3.102, Luc 778, Mac 1.1.10, MND 1.1.183, PP 16.4, S 21.12, 70.4, TNK 1.1.16, VA 1085*; repair *LLL 5.2.293*

**air** *Fr n*
ɛɹ
**sp** air[1]

**air / ~ed** *v*
ɛ:ɹd
**sp** ayr'd[1], ayred[1]

**air-braving** *adj*
'ɛ:ɹˌbrɛ:vɪn, -ɪŋ
**sp** ayre-brauing[1]
> brave

**air-drawn** *adj*
'ɛ:ɹ-ˌdrɔ:n
**sp** ayre-drawne- [dagger][1]
> draw

**airless** *adj*
'ɛ:ɹləs
**sp** ayre-lesse[1]

**airy** *adj*
'ɛ:ɹəɪ
**sp** aiery[1], airie[1], ayrie[3], ayrie-[charme][1] / ayry[1]

**Ajax** *n*
*m* 'ɛ:ʤəks, ə'ʤɛ:ks
**sp** Aiax[67]
**pun** a jakes *LLL 5.2.574*, *TC 2.1.63ff*

**a-killing** *v*
ə'kɪlɪn, -ɪŋ
**sp** a killing[1]
> kill

**akin** *TNK* *adj*
ə'kɪn
**sp** a kin[1]
**rh** gi'en *TNK Prol.1*

**alablaster** *n*
'aləblastəɹ
**sp** alablaster[3]

**alack,** *abbr* **lack** *interj*
=, *abbr* lak
**sp** alack[14], alacke[59], *abbr* lacke[1], 'lacke[1]
**rh** back *S 65.9*; black *MND 5.1.169*; wrack *Per 4.Chorus.11*

**alacrity** *n*
ə'lakrɪtəɪ
**sp** alacratie[1], alacritie[1], alacrity[2]

**a-land** *Per* *adv*
ə'land
**sp** aland[1], a-land[1]
**rh** understand *Per 3.2.67*
> land

**Alarbus** *n*
ə'lɑ:ɹbəs
**sp** Alarbus[3]

**alarm / ~s** *n*
ə'lɑ:ɹm / -z
**sp** alarme[2] / alarmes[1]
**rh** arms *R2 1.1.205*
> night-alarm

**alarum,** *abbr* **larum** *adj*
ə'lɑ:rəm, *abbr* 'lɑ:rəm
**sp** alarum[1], *abbr* larum[1]

**alarum,** *abbr* **larum / ~s** *n*
*m* ə'lɑ:rəm, -ɑ:ɹm, *abbr* 'lɑ:rəm / -z
**sp** alarum[86], *abbr* larum[3] / alarums[20], allarums[1], *abbr* larums[2]

**alarum / ~ed** *v*
ə'lɑ:rəmd
**sp** alarum'd[1]

**alarum-bell,** *abbr* **larum-~** *n*
ə'lɑ:rəm-ˌbel, *abbr* 'lɑ:-
**sp** alarum bell[2], *abbr* larum-bell[1]

**alarumed** *adj*
ə'lɑ:rəmd
**sp** alarum'd[1]

**alas** *interj*
=
**sp** alas[227], alasse[2]

**Alban / ~s** *n*
'ɑ:lbən / -z
**sp** Albon[1], Albone[1] / Albans[1], Albones[7], Albons[8]

**Albany / ~'s** *n*
*m* 'ɑ:lbənəɪ, -bnəɪ / 'ɑ:lbnəɪz
**sp** Albanie[1], Albany[10] / Albanies[1]

**albeit** *conj*
*m* ɑl'bi:t, ˌɑlbi:'ɪt
**sp** albeit[15]

**Albion / ~'s** *n*
*m* =, 'ɑlbɪˌɒn / -z
**sp** Albion[3] / Albions[3]
**rh** confusion *KL 3.2.85*

**alchemist** *n*
'ɑlchəmɪst, 'ɒl-
**sp** alchymist[1], alcumist[1]

**alchemy** *n*
'ɑlchəməɪ, 'ɒl-
**sp** alchymie[1]
**rh** *1* eye *S 33.4*; **rh** *2* flattery *S 114.4*

**Alcibiades** *n*
*m* ˌɑlsɪ'bəɪdi:z, -'bəɪə-
**sp** Alcibiades[19]

**Alcides** *n*
ɑl'səɪdi:z
**sp** Alcides[7]

**alderliefest** *adj*
'ɑldəɹˌlɪfɪst, 'ɒl-
**sp** alder liefest[1]
> lief

**alder·man / ~man's / ~men** *n*
'ɑldəɹˌman, 'ɒl- / -z / *m* -ˌman, -mən
**sp** alderman[1] / aldermans[1] / aldermen[3]

**ale / ~s** *n*
ɛ:l / -z
**sp** ale[13] / ales[2]
**rh** tale *MND 2.1.50*
> bottle-ale

**Alecto / ~'s** *n*
ə'lekto:z
**sp** Alecto's[1]

**alehouse / ~s** *n*
'ɛ:l·əʊs, -'həʊs / -əʊzɪz, 'həʊ-
**sp** alehouse[1], ale-house[8] / alehouses[1]
> house

**Alençon / ~'s** *n*
*m* ə'lensən, 'alnsən / -z
**sp** Alanson[26], Alan-son[1] / Alansoes[1], Alansons[1]

**Aleppo** *n*
ə'lepo:
**sp** Aleppo[2]

**ale-washed** *adj*
'ɛ:lˌwɑʃt
**sp** ale-washt[1]
> wash

**ale·wife / ~wives** *n*
'ɛ:lˌwəɪf / -ˌwəɪvz
**sp** alewife[1] / ale-wiues[1]
> wife

**Alexander / ~'s / ~s** *n*
ɑlɪk'sandəɹ, *Curate LLL 5.2.561ff* ɑlɪ'sandəɹ / -z
**sp** Alexander[20], A-lexander[1], Alisander[6] / Alexanders[1] / Alexanders[1]
**rh** commander *LLL 5.2.561, 564, 566*

**Alexandria** *n*
ɑlɪk'sandrɪə
**sp** Alexandria[5]

**Alexandrian** *adj*
ɑlɪk'sandrɪən
**sp** Alexandrian[2]

**Alexas** *n*
ə'leksəs
**sp** Alexas[14], Alexias[1]

**alias** *adv*
'alɪəs
**sp** alias[4]

**Alice** *n*
*Eng* 'alɪs, *TS Induction 2.109* als / *Fr* a'lis
**sp** Alice[2], Alce[1] / Alice[2]

**alien** *n*
'ɛ:lɪən
**sp** alien[2]

**Aliena** *n*
ɛ:lɪ'enə
**sp** Aliena[7]

**alight ~ed** *v*
ə'ləɪt / -ɪd
**sp** a-light[1] / alighted[2], a-lighted[1]
**rh** plight *KL 3.4.117*
> light

**ali·us / ~is** *Lat n*
'ali:i:s
**sp** alijs[1], [cum]alijs[1]

**alike** *adj / adv*
ə'ləɪk
**sp** alike[22] / alike[17]

**Alisander**
> Alexander

**alive** *adj / adv*
ə'ləɪv
**sp** aliue[78], a-liue[1] / aliue[9]
**rh** hive, survive *Luc 1768*; strive *Per 2.Chorus.20, S 112.7*; survive *VA 174*; thrive *AW 4.3.329, VA 1009*

**all** *adj, det, n*
ɑ:l, [*later*] ɔ:l
**sp** al[23], all[3453], [with]all[4], *emend of Tim 3.4.112* Ullorxa[1], all's [all is][35], all's [ all his][1], al's [all is][1]
**rh** *1* befall *2H6 5.3.32, Tit 5.1.58*; brawl *RJ 3.1.142*; call *AW 2.1.181, MND 5.1.426, Per 5.1.242, S 40.1, 109.14, 117.1*; fall *AY 5.4.175, CE 1.1.2, H5 3.5.67, 2H6 1.2.107, KL 3.3.22, LC 42, R2 4.1.316, TNK 3.5.108, VA 720*; gall *TC 2.2.146*; hall *2H4 5.3.34*; small *Per 3.4.17, TG 1.2.30*; tall *2H4 5.3.32*; wall *MND 5.1.198, Tim 4.1.37*; **rh** *2* burial *MND 3.2.382*
**pun** *JC 1.1.21* awl

**alla** *Ital prep*
'ala
**sp** alla[2]

**all-abhorred** *adj*
'ɑ:l-əˌbɒɹɪd
**sp** all-abhorred[1]
> abhor

**all-admiring** *adj*
'ɑ:l-ədˌməɪrɪn, -ɪŋ
**sp** all-admiring[1]
> admiring

**allay / ~s / ~ing / ~ed** *v*
ə'lɛ: / -z / -ɪn, -ɪŋ / -d
**sp** alay[4], allay[9] / allayes[1] / allaying[1] / allay'd[1]
**rh** said *S 56.3*

**allaying** *adj*
ə'lɛ:ɪn, -ɪŋ
**sp** alay-ing

**allayment / ~s** *n*
ə'lɛ:mənt / -s
**sp** alaiment[1] / allayments[1]

**all-binding** *adj*
ˌɑ:l-'bəɪndɪn, -ɪŋ
**sp** *emend of MM 2.4.94* all-building-[law][1]
> bind

**all-building** *adj*
ˌɑ:l-'bɪldɪn, -ɪŋ
**sp** all-building-[law][1]
> build

**all-changing** *adj*
ˌɑ:l-'ʧɛ:nʤɪn, -ɪŋ
**sp** all-changing-[word][1]
> changing

**all-cheering** *adj*
ˌɑ:l-'ʧi:rɪn, -ɪŋ
**sp** all-cheering[1]
> cheer

**all-disgraced** *adj*
*m* ˌɑ:l-dɪs'grɛ:sɪd
**sp** all-disgraced[1]
> disgraced

**all-dreaded** *adj*
ˌɑ:l-'dredɪd
**sp** all-dreaded[1]
> dreaded

**allegation / ~s** *n*
ɑlɛ'gɛ:sɪən / -z
**sp** allegation[1] / allegations[1]

**allege / *abbr* ledges / ~d** *v*
= / *abbr* 'leʤɪz / *m* ə'leʤɪd
**sp** alledge[1] / *abbr* leges[1] / alleadged[1]

**alleged** *adj*
*m* ə'leʤɪd
**sp** alleadged[1]

**allegiance** *n*
*m* ə'lɛ:ʤɪəns, -ɪˌans
**sp** allegeance[22], allegiance[3], al-legiance[1]
**rh** *1H6 5.5.43* France

**allegiant** *adj*
ə'lɛ:ʤɪənt
**sp** allegiant[1]

**aller** *Fr v*

***allons***
a'lɔ̃
**sp** alone[2], alons[1]

***va***
va
**sp** *Pistol H5 4.1.35* vous[1]

***vais***
vɛ
**sp** voi[1]

**alley** *n*
'aləɪ
**sp** alley[2]

**all-hail** *interj*
ˌɑ:l-'ɛ:l, -'hɛ:l
**sp** all-haile[2]
> hail

**all-hail / ~ed** *v*
ˌɑ:l-'ɛ:ld, -'hɛ:-
**sp** all-hail'd[1]

**All-Hallond Eve** *n*
'ɑ:l-'ɑlənd i:v, -'hɑ-
**sp** Allhallond-Eue[1]
> eve

**All-Hallowmass** *n*
'ɑ:l-'ɑləmas, -'hɑ-
**sp** Alhallowmas[1]
> Hallowmass

**All-Hallown** *adj*
'ɑ:l-'ɑlən, -'hɑ-
**sp** Alhollown[1]

**all-hating** *n*
ˌɑ:l-'ɛ:tɪn, -ɪŋ, -'hɛ:-
**sp** all-hating[1]
> hate

**all-honoured** *adj*
ˌɑ:l-'ɒnəɹd
**sp** all-honor'd[1]
> honoured

**alliance** *n*
ə'ləɪəns
**sp** alliance[13], allyance[3]

**allicholy, allycholly** [*malap* melancholy] *n*
'aliˌkɒləɪ
**sp** allicholy[1], allycholly[1]

**alligant** [*malap* elegant *or* eloquent] *adj*
*m* 'aliˌgant
**sp** alligant[1]

**alligator** *n*
ɑli'gɑ:təɹ, -tə
**sp** *F* allegater[1] [*Q* aligarta]

**all-licensed** *adj*
ˌɑ:l-'ləɪsənst
**sp** all-lycenc'd[1]
> licence

**all-noble** *adj*
ˌɑ:l-'no:bəl
**sp** all-noble[1]
> noble

**all-obeying** *adj*
'ɑ:l-ə'bɛ:ɪn, -ɪŋ
**sp** all-obeying[1]
> obey

**allons**
> aller

**allot / ~s / *Luc* ~ted** *v*
=
**sp** allot[1] / a lots[1] / allotted[1]
**rh** rotted, unspotted *Luc 824*

**allotery** *n*
ə'lɒtrəɪ, -tər-
**sp** allottery[1]
> lottery

**allow / ~s / ~ing / ~ed** *v*
ə'ləʊ, ə'lo: / -z / -ɪn, -ɪŋ / -d
**sp** allow[23], alow[1] / allowes[3] / allowing[2] / allowd[1], allow'd[9], allowed[7], alowd[2]
**rh** bow *v*, vow *Luc 1845*; brow *S 19.11, 112.4*; now *R2 5.2.40, RJ 2.3.82, WT 4.1.29*; thou *R2 1.1.123* / house *Tim 3.3.41* / growing *WT 4.1.15* / shroud *LLL 5.2.478*

**allowance** *n*
*m* ə'ləʊəns, ə'ləʊns, ə'lo:-
**sp** allowance[10]

**allowed** *adj*
ə'ləʊd, ə'lo:-
**sp** allow'd[2], allowed[1]

**allowing** *adj*
ə'ləʊɪn, -ɪŋ, ə'lo:-
**sp** allowing[1]

**all-praised** *adj*
*m* ˌɑ:l-'prɛ:zɪd
**sp** all-praysed[1]
> praise

**all-seeing** *adj*
ˌɑ:l-'si:ɪn, -ɪŋ
**sp** all-seeing[2]
> see

**all-seer** *n*
ˌɑ:l-'si:ɹ
**sp** all-seer[1]
> see

**all-shaking** *adj*
ˌɑ:l-'ʃɛ:kɪn, -ɪŋ
**sp** all-shaking[1]
> shake

**all-smarting** *adj*
ˌɑ:l-'smɑ:ɹtɪn, -ɪŋ
**sp** all-smarting[1]
> smart

**All Souls' Day** *n*
'ɑ:l 'so:lz ˌdɛ:
**sp** Al-soules day[1], All-soules day[2]
> day

**all-telling** *adj*
ˌɑ:l-'telɪn, -ɪŋ
**sp** all-telling[1]
> tell

**all-thing** *adj*
'ɑ:l-ˌθɪŋ
**sp** all-thing[1]
> thing

**all-unable** *adj*
ˌɑ:l-ən'ɛ:bəl
**sp** all-vnable[1]
> unable

**allur·e / ~ed** *v*
ə'lu:ɹ / -d
**sp** allure[2] / allur'd[1]

**allurement** *n*
ə'lu:ɹmənt
**sp** allurement[1]

**alluring** *adj*
ə'lu:rɪn, -ɪŋ
**sp** alluring[1]

**allusion** *n*
ə'lu:zɪən
**sp** allusion[2]

**all-watched** *adj*
*m* ˌɑ:l-'wɑʧɪd
**sp** all-watched[1]
> watch

**all-worthy** *adj*
ˌɑ:l-'wɑ:ɹðəɪ
**sp** all-worthy[2]
> worthy

**all·y / ~ies** *n*
ə'ləɪ / -z
**sp** alie[1] / allies[7], allyes[1]

**all·y / ~ied** *v*
ə'ləɪd
**sp** alide[1], allied[3], ally'd[2]

**allycholly**
> allicholy

**Almain** *n*
'almɛ:n
**sp** Al-maine[1]

**almanac / ~s** *n*
'ɑ:lmənak, 'ɑl-, [*later*] 'ɔ:l- / -s
**sp** almanack[2], almanacke[1] / almanackes[1]

**almighty** *n*
ɑ:l'məɪtəɪ, [*later*] 'ɔ:l-
**sp** almightie[3], almighty[4]
**rh** fight, yea *LLL 5.2.649* [*recitation*]

**almond** *n*
'ɑ:lmənd, [*later*] 'ɔ:l-
**sp** almond[1]

**almost** *adv*
'ɑ:lmo:st, [*later*] 'ɔ:l-
**sp** almost[154], al-most[1]

**alms** *adj / n*
=
**sp** almes[1] / almes[12]

**alms-basket** *n*
=
**sp** almes-basket[1]
> basket

**alms-deed** *n*
=
**sp** almes-deed[1]
> deed

**alms-drink** *n*
=
**sp** almes drinke[1]

**alms-house / ~s** *n*
'ɑ:mz-ˌəʊzɪz, -ˌhəʊ-
**sp** almes-houses[1]
> house

**almsman, ~'s** *n*
=
**sp** almes-mans[1]
> man

**aloft** *adv*
=
**sp** aloft[22]

**alone** *adv*
ə'lo:n
**sp** alone[222], a-lone[1]
**rh** *1* bone *TC 1.3.390*; groan *Ham 3.3.22, S 131.8, 133.3, VA 786*; moan *PP 20.8*; own *TG 2.4.165*; prone *S 141.8*; stone *VA 213*; **rh** *2* none *AW 2.3.127, 1H6 4.7.9, MM 2.1.40, PP 17.35, TN 3.1.157*; one *MND 3.2.119, R3 1.1.100, RJ 2.6.36, Luc 1480, PP 9.14, S 36.4, 39.8, 42.14, 105.13, TS 1.2.244*; **rh** *3* anon *S 75.7*; gone *KJ 3.1.64, S 4.9, 31.12, 45.7, 66.14, VA 382, TG 3.1.99, TNK 1.1.2*

**along** *adv / prep*
=
**sp** along[107] / along[4]
**rh** *1* wrong *RJ 1.1.195*; **rh** *2* sung *VA 1093*

**Alonso** *n*
ə'lɒnzo:
**sp** Alonso[6]

**aloof** *adv*
=, ə'lɤf
**sp** aloofe[17]
**rh** behoof, proof *LC 166*

**aloud** *adv*
ə'ləʊd
**sp** aloud[12], alowd[12]
**rh** proud *VA 262, 886*

**alow** *interj*
ə'lo:
**sp** alow[2]
> hallow

**alphabet** *n*
=
**sp** alphabet[1]

**alphabetical** *adj*
ˌalfə'betɪkɑl
**sp** alphabeticall[1]

**Alphonso** *n*
al'fɒnso:
**sp** Alphonso[1]

**Alps** *n*
=
**sp** Alpes[4]

**already** *adv*
ɑ:l'redəɪ, [*later*] ɔ:l-
**sp** alreadie[35], already[107], al-ready[2]

**also** *adv*
'ɑlso:, [*later*] 'ɒl-
**sp** also[34]

**altar / ~s** *n*
'ɑltəɹ, [*later*] 'ɒl- / -z
**sp** altar[10] / altars[3]

**alter / ~s / ~ed** *v*
'ɑltəɹ, [*later*] 'ɒl- / -z / -d
**sp** alter[15] / alters[1] / alter'd[15], al-ter'd[1], altred[1]

**alteration** *n*
ˌɑltə'rɛ:sɪən, [*later*] ˌɒl-
**sp** alteration[8]

**altered** *adj*
'ɑltəɹd, [*later*] 'ɒl-
**sp** alter'd[1]

**altering** *adj*
'ɑltrɪn, -ɪŋ, [*later*] 'ɒl-
**sp** altring[1]

**Althea / ~'s** *n*
al'tɛ:ə / -z
**sp** Althaea[1], Althea[1] / Altheas[1]

**although** *conj*
ɑ:l'ðo:, [*later*] ɔ:l-
**sp** although[72]
> though

**altitude** *n*
'altɪˌtju:d
**sp** altitude[3]

**altogether / ~s** *adv*
*m* ɑ:ltə'geðəɹ, -'gɛ:ɹ, [*later*] ɔ:l- / -z
**sp** altogether[31], al-together[1], alto-gether[1] / *Evans MW 1.2.7* altogeathers [altogether is][1]

**Alton** *n*
'ɑ:ltən, [*later*] 'ɔ:l-
**sp** Alton[1]

**alway / ~s** *adv*
'ɑ:lwɛ:, [*later*] 'ɔ:l- / -z
**sp** alway[2] / alwaies[23], al-waies[1], alwayes[37], al-wayes[2]
**rh** dam

**am** *v*
=
**sp** am[2125], 'am[1]
**rh** dam *MND 5.1.219*
> be

***I am*** *abbr*
əɪm
**sp** I'm[8], I'me[7]

**Amaimon** *n*
ə'mamən
**sp** Amaimon[1], Amamon[1]

**amain** *adv*
ə'mɛ:n
**sp** amain[1], amaine[10], a-maine[1], a maine[1]
**rh** again, vein *LLL 5.2.542*; entertain *Tem 4.1.74*; slain *TC 5.8.13*

**a-making** *v*
ə'mɛ:kɪn, -ɪŋ
**sp** a making[2]
> make

**amaze / ~s** *n*
ə'mɛ:zɪz
**sp** amazes[1]
**rh** gazes *LLL 2.1.232*

**amaze / ~s / ~th / ~d,** *abbr* **mazed** *v*
ə'mɛ:z / -ɪz / -əθ / -d, mɛ:zd
**sp** amaze[9] / amazes[1] / amazeth[1] / amasde[1], amaz'd[4] / maz'd[1]
**rh** gazes VA 634 / gazeth *S 20.8*

**amazed,** *abbr* **mazed** *adj*
*m* ə'mɛ:zd, -zɪd, *abbr* 'mɛ:zɪd, mɛ:zd
**sp** amaz'd[28], amazed[5], *abbr* maz'd[1], mazed[1]
**rh** blazed, gazed *Luc 1356*; gazed *VA 925*

**amazedly** *adv*
*m* ə'mɛ:zɪdˌləɪ, -dl-
**sp** amazedly[4]
**rh** why *Mac 4.1.125*

**amazedness** *n*
*m* ə'mɛ:zɪdˌnes, -dnəs
**sp** amazednesse[2]

**amazement** *n*
ə'mɛ:zmənt
**sp** amazement[12]

**amazing** *adj*
ə'mɛ:zɪn, -ɪŋ
**sp** amazing[1]

**Amazon / ~s** *n*
*m* 'aməˌzɒn, -əzən / -z
**sp** Amazon[4] / Amazons[2]
**rh** *1* on *3H6 4.1.106*; **rh** *2* done *3H6 4.1.106*

**Amazonian** *adj*
amə'zo:nɪən
**sp** Amazonian[2]

**ambassador / ~s** *n*
*m* am'basəˌdɔ:ɹ, -sdəɹ / -z
**sp** ambassador[13], am-bassador[1], embassador[5], embassadour[1], em-bassadour[1] / ambassadors[11], ambassadours[1], embassadors[5]

**amber** *adj / n*
'ambəɹ
**sp** amber[2] / amber[3]
**rh** chamber *WT 4.4.224*

**amber-coloured** *adj*
'ambəɹ-ˌkɤləɹd
**sp** amber coloured[1]
> colour

**ambiguit·y / ~ies** *n*
ambɪ'gju:ɪtəɪz
**sp** ambiguities[2]

**ambiguous** *adj*
am'bɪgjəs
**sp** ambiguous[1]

**ambition / ~'s / ~s** *n*
am'bɪsɪən / -z
**sp** ambition[43], am-bition[1] / ambitions[2] / ambitions[2]

**ambitious** *adj*
am'bɪsɪəs
**sp** ambitious[36]

**ambitiously** *adv*
am'bɪsɪəsləɪ
**sp** ambitiously[2]

**amble / ~s / ~d** *v*
=
**sp** amble[1] / ambles[4] / ambled[1]

**ambling** *adj / n*
'amblɪn, -ɪŋ
**sp** ambling[2] / ambling[1]

**ambo** *Lat n*
'ambo:
**sp** ambo[2]

**ambuscado / ~s** *n*
ambəs'kɑ:do:z
**sp** ambuscados[1]

**ambush** *n*
=
**sp** ambush[6], am-bush[1]

**ameer / ~s** *n*
ə'mi:ɹz
**sp** *MW 2.1.202 emend of* an-heires[1]

**amen** *interj /* *n*
ɑ:'men
**sp** amen[80] / amen[1]
**rh** again *R3 5.5.41*; Englishmen *H5 5.2.360*; pen *S 85.6*

**amend / ~s / ~ed** *v*
ə'mend / -z / -dɪd
**sp** amend[17] / amends[2], a-mends[1] / amended[4]
**rh** blend *LC 214 /* depends *S 101.1*; friends, lends *Luc 961*; friends *MND 5.1.428 /* ended, pretended *Luc 578*; offended *AW 3.4.7*
> amends *n*

**amending** *n*
ə'mendɪn, -ɪŋ
**sp** amending
**rh** depending, ending *Luc 1614*

**a-mending** *v*
ə'mendɪn, -ɪŋ
**sp** a mending[1]
> mend

**amendment** *n*
ə'mendmənt
**sp** amendment[4]

**amends** *n*
ə'mendz
**sp** amends[20]
> amend *v*

**amerce** *v*
ə'mɐ:ɹs
**sp** amerce[1]

**America** *n*
=
**sp** America[1]

**ames-ace** *n*
'ɛ:mz-ˌas
**sp** ames-ace[1]
> ace

**amiable** *adj*
*m* 'ɛ:mɪˌabəl, -mɪəb-
**sp** amiable[7]

**amid / ~st, *abbr* midst** *prep*
=
**sp** amid[1] / amid'st[1], *abbr* 'midst[1]

**Amiens** *n*
'amɪenz [*2 sylls*]
**sp** Amiens[1], Amyens[3]

**amiss** *adj / adv / n*
ə'mɪs
**sp** amisse[19] / amis[2], amisse[13] / amisse[1]
**rh** this *PP 17.2* / **rh** *1* is *MV 2.9.65, S 59.3*; **rh** *2* bliss, iwis, kiss, this *MV 2.9.65, CE 2.2.193* / **rh** *1* this *Ham 5.2.396, S 35.7*; **rh** *2* is *Ham 4.5.18, S 151.3*

**amit·y / ~ies** *n*
*m* 'amɪˌtəɪ, 'amtəɪ / 'amɪˌtəɪz
**sp** amitie[13], amity[10] / amities[1]
**rh** *MND 4.1.86* be, me, solemnly, triumphantly, prosperity, jollity

**among, *abbr* mong** *adv / prep*
ə'mɤŋ, ə'mɒŋ, *abbr* mɤŋ, mɒŋ
**sp** among[2] / among[82], a-mong[2], amongs [among us][1], *abbr* 'mong[4]
**rh** *adv* sung *KL 1.4.174*; belong, strong *LC 256*

**amongst, *abbr* mongst** *prep*
ə'mɤŋst, -mɒ-, [*also, followed by a consonant*] ə'mɤŋs, -mɒ-, *abbr* mɤ-, mɒ-
**sp** amongest[1], amongst[20], a-mongst[1], among'st[14], *abbr* 'mongst [16], 'mong'st [3], mong'st[2]

**amorous** *adj*
*m* 'amrəs, 'aməˌrɤs
**sp** amorous[22]

**amort** *adj*
ə'mɔ:ɹt
**sp** amort[1], a-mort[1]

**amount / ~s** *v*
ə'məʊnt / -s
**sp** amount[7] / amounts[3]

**amour** *Fr n*
a'mu:ɹ
**sp** amour[1]

**Amphimacus** *n*
*m* am'fɪməˌkɤs
**sp** Amphimacus[1]

**ample / ~er / ~est** *adj*
= / 'ampləɹ / =
**sp** ample[15] / ampler[1] / amplest[2]

**amplif·y** LC **/ ~ied** *v*
*m* 'amplɪˌfəɪ / -d
**sp** amplifie[1] / amplified[1]
**rh** quality *LC 209*

**amply** *adv*
'ampləɪ
**sp** amply[3]

**Ampthill** *n*
'amtɪl
**sp** Ampthill[1]

**Amurath** *n*
*m* 'aməˌraθ, -ˌrat
**sp** Amurah[2]

**Amyntas** *n*
ə'mɪntəs
**sp** Amintas[1]

**an, an'**
> a, and

**anatomize / ~d** *v*
*m* ə'natəˌməɪz, -əm-, *Armado LLL 4.1.70* -'nɒt- / -d
**sp** anathomize[2], anatomize[1], *Armado* annothanize[1] / anathomiz'd[2]
**rh** disguised *Luc 1450*

**anatomy** *n*
*m* ə'natəˌməɪ
**sp** anatomie[2], anatomy[3]

**ancestor / ~s** *n*
*m* 'ansəsˌtɒɹ, -stəɹ-, 'ɔ:n- / -z
**sp** ancestor[4], auncestor[1] / ancestors[18], auncestors[2]

**ancestry** *n*
*m* 'ansəsˌtrəɪ, 'ɔ:n-
**sp** ancestrie[2], ancestry[1], auncestry[1]

**Anchises / ~'** *n*
an'kəɪse:z
**sp** Anchyses[2] / Anchises[1]

**anchor / ~s** *n*
'aŋkəɹ / -z
**sp** anchor[5], anchor's [anchor is][1] / anchors[2]

**anchor / ~s / ~ed** *v*
'aŋkəɹ / -z / -d
**sp** anchor[1] / anchors[3] / anchor'd[1]
> holding-anchor

**anchorage** *n*
'aŋkəˌɹɪʤ
**sp** anchorage[1]

**anchoring** *adj*
'aŋkrɪn, -ɪŋ, -kər-
**sp** anchoring[2]

**anchov·y / ~ies** *n*
'anʧəvəɪz
**sp** anchoues[1]

**ancient / ~est** *adj*
'ɛ:nsɪənt [*2 sylls*], 'ɔ:n-, [*later*] -nʃɪənt, / -ənst
**sp** ancient[55], *Fluellen* aunchiant[1], aunchient[1], aun-chient[1], *in Othello* auncient[5] / ancient'st[1]

**ancient** *n*
*m* 'ɛ:nsɪənt [*2 sylls*], -ɪˌent, 'ɔ:n-, [*later*] -nʃɪənt / -s
**sp** ancient[11], ancients[1], *Fluellen* aunchient[5], *in Othello* auncient[2], auncient[1], auntient[1]

**ancientry** *n*
'ɛ:nsɪəntrəɪ, -nʃən-, 'ɔ:n-
**sp** aunchentry[1], auncientry[1]

**Ancus** *n*
'aŋkəs
**sp** Ancus[1]

**and** *conj*
=, *unstr* ənd, ən, n
**sp** and[24362], and-[a][1] [*song*], &[562]
> to and fro

***and his** abbr*
*unstr* ənz
**sp** and's[3]

***and it** abbr*
*unstr* ant, ənt
**sp** and't[32], ant[1], an't[10]

**andiron / ~s** *n*
'andəɹnz
**sp** andirons[1]

**Andren** *n*
'andrən
**sp** Andren[1]

**Andrew** *n*
=
**sp** Andrew[24], An-drew[2]

**Andromache** *n*
*m* an'drɒməki:, -mki:
**sp** Andromache[5]

**Andronici** *n*
*m* an'drɒnɪˌkəɪ
**sp** Andronici[3]

**Andronicus** *n*
*m* an'drɒnɪˌkɤs, -ɪkəs, -ɒŋk-, *Tit 1.1.23* ˌandrə'nəɪkəs
**sp** Andronicus[53]

**anew** *adv*
=
**sp** anew[3], a-new[1], a new[1]
**rh** hue *S 82.7, Tit 1.1.265*; true *S 119.11*
> new

**ange / ~s** *Fr n*
ɑ̃:ʒ
**sp** anges[1]

**angel** *adj*
'ɛ:nʤəl
**sp** angel[1], angell[1]

**angel / ~'s / ~s / ~s'** *n*
'ɛ:nʤəl / -z
**sp** angel[4], an-gel[1], angell[37] / angells[1] / angells[1], angels[33] / angels[2]
> she-angel

**Angelica** *n*
=
**sp** Angelica[1]

**angelical** *adj*
ən'ʤɛlɪˌkɑl
**sp** angelicall[1]

**angel-like** *adj*
'ɛ:nʤəl-ˌləɪk
**sp** angel-like[1], angell-like[1]
> like

**Angelo / ~'s** *n*
*m* 'anʤəˌlo:, -ʤlo: / -ʤəˌlo:z
**sp** Angelo[85], Angelo's [Angelo is][2] / Angelo's[1]
**rh** grow *MM 3.2.257*

**anger / ~-s** *n*
'aŋgəɹ / -z
**sp** anger[43], angers [anger is][1], anger's [anger is][1] / angers[1]

**anger / ~s / ~ing / ~ed** *v*
'aŋgəɹ / -z / 'aŋgrɪn, -ɪŋ / 'aŋgəɹd

**sp** anger[10] / angers[3] / ang'ring[1] / anger'd[3], angred[4]

**angered** *adj*
'aŋgəɹd
**sp** anger'd[1]

**angerly** *adv*
*m* 'aŋgəɹˌləɪ
**sp** angerly[3]

**Angiers** *n*
*m* 'anʤɪəɹz, an'ʤiːɹz
**sp** Angiers[15], Angires[1]

**anglais** *Fr n*
ɑ̃'glwɛ
**sp** Anglois[5]

**angle** *n*
=
**sp** angle[4]

**angl·e / ~ing / ~ed** *v*
= / 'aŋglɪn, -ɪŋ / =
**sp** angle[4] / angling[1] / angl'd[1]
> angling *n*

**angler** *n*
'aŋgləɹ
**sp** ang-ler[1]

**Angleterre** *Fr n*
ɑ̃glə'tɛːɹ
**sp** Angleterre[4]

**Angli·a / ~ae** *Lat n*
'aŋglɪɛː
**sp** Angliae[1]

**angling** *n*
'aŋglɪn, -ɪŋ
**sp** angling[1], ang-ling[1]
> angle

**Anglish**
> English

**angry** *adj*
'aŋgrəɪ, *m Tim 3.5.58* 'aŋgəˌrəɪ
**sp** angrie[9], angry[83]
**rh** impiety *Tim 3.5.58*
> ever-angry

**anguish** *n*
=
**sp** anguish[6]
**rh** languish *RJ 1.2.46*

**Angus** *n*
=
**sp** Angus[7]

**an-hungry**
> a-hungry

**a-nights** *adv*
ə'nəɪts
**sp** a-nights[2], a nights[2]
> night

**animal / ~s** *n*
*m* 'anɪməl, -ˌmɑl / -z
**sp** animall[1], a-nimall[1], annimall[1] / animalls[1], animals[3], annimals[1]

**anim·us / ~is** *Lat n*
'anɪmiːs
**sp** animis[1]

**Anjou** *n*
*m* an'ʤuː, 'anʤuː, *Fr* ɑ̃'ʒuː
**sp** Aniou[11], Aniow[1], Aniowe[1]

**ankle** *n*
=
**sp** anckle[1]

**Anna** *n*
=
**sp** Anna[1]

**annals** *n*
'anɑlz
**sp** annales[1]

**Anne / ~'s** *n*
=
**sp** An[4], Anne[68] / Ans[4]

**annex / ~ed** *v*
=
**sp** annext[1]

**annexment** *n*
=
**sp** annexment[1]

**Annius** *n*
'anɪəs
**sp** Annius[1]

**annoy** *n*
ə'nəɪ
**sp** annoy[3]
**rh** destroy, Troy *Luc 1370*; joy *3H6 5.7.45, Luc 1109, R3 5.3.157, S 8.4, VA 497, 599*

**annoy / ~ing / ~ed** *v*
ə'nəɪ / -ɪn, -ɪŋ / -d
**sp** annoy[4] / annoying[1] / annoy'd[1]

**annoyance,** *abbr* **noyance** *n*
ə'nəɪəns, *abbr* 'nəɪəns
**sp** annoyance[5], *abbr* noyance[1]

**annual** *adj*
*m* 'anjɑl, -jʊɑl
**sp** annuall[4]

**anoint / ~ed,** *abbr* **nointed** *v*
ə'nəɪnt / -ɪd, *abbr* 'nəɪntɪd
**sp** annoint[2], annointed[3], anoynted[2], *abbr* nointed[1], 'noynted[1]

**anointed** *adj / n*
ə'nəɪntɪd
**sp** annointed[6], 'anointed [1], anoynted[6] / annointed[2]

**anon** *adv*
ə'nɒn, ə'noːn
**sp** anon[120], a-non[2], anone[4]
**rh** *1* Acheron *MND 3.2.356*; anon *H5 4.1.27*; gone *MND 2.1.17, RJ 1.5.143*; anon, sir gone, sir *TN 4.2.122*; **rh** *2* alone *S 75.5*

**another / ~'s** *adj*
ə'nɤðəɹ / -z
**sp** another[338], a-nother[1], an-other[1], ano-ther[9], an other[4] / anothers[21], ano-thers[1]
**rh** brother *CE 5.1.426, Tim 3.5.89*; brother, smother *Luc 632*; mother *S 3.2, 8.9*; other *Mac 1.3.13*
> other

**Anselm** *n*
=
**sp** An-selme[1]

**answer / ~s** *n*
'ansəɹ, 'ɔ:n- / -z
**sp** answer[109], an-swer[3], answere[36], an-swere[2] / answeres[6], answers[5]
> discretion-answer

**answer / ~est / ~s / ~ing / ~ed** *v*
'ansəɹ, 'ɔ:n-, *Le Beau AY 1.2.96* 'ɔ:nsəɹ / -st / -z / *m* 'ansrɪn, -ɪŋ, -səˌrɪn, -ɪŋ, 'ɔ:n- / *m* 'ansəɹd, -əˌred, 'ɔ:n-
**sp** answer[157], answere[67], an-swere[1], *Le Beau* aun-swer[1] / answerest[1], answer'st[2], / answeres[3], an-swere's[1], answers[6], answer's[2] / answering[7] / answerd[1], answer'd[36], an-swer'd[1], answered[16], an-swered[1]
**rh** answered *MND 3.2.18* head
> re-answer; quick-, un-answered

**answerable** *adj*
*m* 'ansəɹˌabəl, -srə-, 'ɔ:n-
**sp** answerable[3]

**answering** *n*
*m* 'ansrɪn, -ɪŋ, -səˌr-, 'ɔ:n-
**sp** answering[1]

**ant** *n*
=
**sp** ant[2]

**an't**
> and

**antar**
> antre

**Antenor** *n*
ən'tenəɹ
**sp** Antenor[3], Anthenor[11], An-thenor[1]

**Antenorides** *n*
ˌantə'nɒrɪˌdi:z
**sp** Antenoridus[1]

**anthem / ~s** *n*
'antəm / -z
**sp** antheme[1] / anthemes[1]

**Anthonio, Anthonius, Anthony**
> Antonio, Antonius, Antony

**anthropophagi** *n*
ˌantrə'pɒfəʤəɪ
**sp** antropophague[1]

**anthropophaginian** *n*
ˌantrəpɒfə'ʤɪnɪən
**sp** anthropophaginian[1]

**Antiat / ~s** *n*
*m* 'ansɪˌɛ:ts
**sp** Antiates[1], Antiats[2], Antients[1]

**antic** *adj*
> antique

**anticipat·e / ~est / ~es / ~ing** *v*
an'tɪsɪˌpɛ:t / -st / -s / -ɪn, -ɪŋ
**sp** anticipate[1] / anticipat'st[1] / anticipates[1] / anticipating[1]
**rh** state *S 118.9*

**anticipation** *n*
anˌtɪsɪ'pɛ:sɪən
**sp** anticipation[1]

**antick / ~ed** *v*
an'tɪkt
**sp** antickt[1]

**antidote / ~s** *n*
*m* 'antɪˌdo:t / -s
**sp** antidote[1] / antidotes[1]

**Antigonus** *n*
*m* an'tɪgəˌnɤs, -ənəs
**sp** Antigonus[9]

**Antiopa** *n*
*m* an'təɪəˌpa
**sp** Antiopa[1]

**antipathy** *n*
*m* an'tɪpəˌθəɪ, -ˌtəɪ
**sp** antipathy[1]

**Antipholus** *n*
*m* an'tɪfəˌlɤs, -ələs
**sp** Antipholus[24]
**rh** ruinous *CE 3.2.2*

**antipodes** *n*
*m* an'tɪpəˌdi:z, -əd-
**sp** antipodes[3], antypodes[1]
**rh** displease *MND 3.2.55*

**antiquary** *adj*
*m* 'antɪˌkwarəɪ
**sp** antiquary[1]

**antique, antic** *adj*
'antɪk
**sp** anticke[5], antike[1], antique[8]

**antique, antic / ~s** *n*
'antɪk
**sp** anticke[5], antique[2] / antickes[1], antiques[1]

**antiquely** *adv*
'antɪkləɪ
**sp** antiquely[1]

**antiquity** *n*
an'tɪkwɪˌtəɪ, -ɪt-
**sp** antiquitie[1], antiquity[3], anti-quity[1]
**rh** iniquity *S 62.10*

**Antium** *n*
'ansɪəm
**sp** Antium[5]

**Antoniad** *n*
*m* an'to:nɪˌad
**sp** [Th]antoniad[1]

**Antonio, Anthonio / ~'s** *n*
*m* an'to:nɪˌo:, -nɪo:
**sp** Anthonio[68], An-thonio[1], Anthonio[1], Antonio[11] / Anthonios[2], Anthonio's[4], Anthonyo's[1], Antonio's[2], *TS 1.2.188 emend of* Butonios[1]

**Antonius** *n*
*m* an'to:nɪˌɤs, -nɪəs
**sp** Anthonius[3]

**Antony / ~'s** *n*
*m* 'antəˌnəɪ, 'antnəɪ, an'to:nəɪ / -z
**sp** Anthonie[5], Anthony[163], An-thony[2], Antony[78], *abbr in s.d.*Ant[1] / Anthonies[4], Anthonie's[1], Antonies[1]

**antre / ~s** *n*
'antəɹz
**sp** antars[1]

**anvil** *n*
=
**sp** anuile[2]

**any** *det, pro*
'anəɪ, 'anɪ
**sp** any[648], any's [any is][1], anie[22], a-nie[1], a-ny[2], anyes [any is][1]
**rh** many *KL 3.2.28, S 10.1, VA 708*

**anybody** *pro*
'anɪbɒdəɪ, *Evans MW 3.3.198* 'anɪpɒdəɪ
**sp** any body[4], *Evans* any pody[1]
> body

**anyone** *pro*
*m* 'anɪ,o:n, -,wɒn, -ɪo:n, -ɪwən
**sp** any one[10]
> one

**anything** *pro*
*m* 'anɪ,θɪn, -ɪŋ, -ɪθ-
**sp** anie thing[6], anything[1], any thing[107]
> thing

**anywhere** *adv*
*m* 'anɪ,ʍɛ:ɹ, -ɪʍ-
**sp** any where[7]
**rh** swear *RJ 2.Chorus.12*
> where

**ap**
> Rhys ap Thomas

**apace** *adv*
ə'pɛ:s
**sp** apace[25]
**rh** embrace *VA 813*; face, grace *LC 284*

**apaid**
> appaid

**apart** *adv*
ə'paɹt
**sp** apart[19], a-part[5]
**rh** heart *AY 4.3.45*
> part

**apathaton**
> epitheton

**ape / ~s** *n*
ɛ:p / -s
**sp** ape[19] / apes[11]
**rh** shape *CE 2.2.208*
> dog-ape, Jack-an-apes

**ape-bearer** *n*
'ɛ:p-,bɛ:ɹəɹ
**sp** ape-bearer[1]
> bearer

**Apemantus** *n*
apɪ'mantəs
**sp** Apemantus[18], A-pemantus[1], Ape-mantus[1], Apeman-tus[1], Apermantus, *abbr in s.d.* Apeman[1]

**Apennines** *n*
'apə,nəɪnz
**sp** Appenines[1]

**apiece** *adv*
=
**sp** apeece[1], a peece[2]
> piece

**apish** *adj*
'ɛ:pɪʃ, 'apɪʃ
**sp** apish[5]
**rh** *KL 1.4.166* foppish

**Apollo / ~'s** *n*
ə'pɒlo: / -z
**sp** Apollo[18], Appollo[1] / Apolloes[1], Apollo's[5], Appollo's[1]

**Apoll·o / ~inem** *Lat n*
apə'ləɪnem
**sp** *emend of Tit 4.3.54* Appollonem[1]

**Apollodorus** *n*
ə,pɒlə'dɔ:rəs
**sp** Appolodorus[1]

**apology** *n*
a'pɒlə,ʤəɪ, -əʤ-
**sp** apologie[5]
**rh** minority *LLL 5.2.589*

**apoplexy** *n*
*m* ə'pɒplɪksəɪ
**sp** apoplexie[3], apoplexy[1]

**apostle / ~s** *n*
=
**sp** apostle[1] / apostles[1]

**apostrophus** *n*
ə'pɒstrəfəs
**sp** apostraphas[1]

**apothecary,** *abbr* **pothecary** *n*
*m* ə'pɒtə,krəɪ, -tkrəɪ, *abbr* 'pɒtə,krəɪ
**sp** apothecarie[1], apothecary[1], appothecarie[4], appothecary[1], *abbr* pothecarie[1]

**appaid** *Luc* *adj*
ə'pɛ:d
**sp** apaide[1]
**rh** *1* aid *Luc 914*; **rh** *2* said *Luc 914*

**appal / ~s** *v*
ə'pɑ:l, -'pɔ:l / -z
**sp** appall[1], apale[1] / appalls[1], appauls[1]
**rh** called *PT 37*

**appalled** *adj*
ə'pɑ:ld, -'pɔ:ld
**sp** appal'd[1], appauled[1]

**apparel,** *abbr* **parel** *n*
=, *abbr* 'parəl
**sp** apparel[1], apparell[13], apparrel[2], apparrell[18], ap-parrell[1], *abbr* parrell[1]

**apparel / ~led** *v*
=
**sp** apparell[2], apparrell[2] / apparel'd[4], apparell'd[1]
> new-, well-apparelled

**apparent** *adj*
=
**sp** apparant[25]
> heir-apparent

**apparently** *adv*
*m* ə'parənt,ləɪ
**sp** apparantly[1]

**apparition / ~s** *n*
,apə'rɪsɪən / -z
**sp** apparation[3], apparision[1], apparition[4] / apparitions[1]

**appeach / ~ed** *v*
ə'piːʧ / -t
**sp** appeach[2] / appeach'd[1]

**appeal** *n*
ə'piːl
**sp** appeale[8]

**appeal / ~s / ~d** *v*
ə'piːl / -z / -d
**sp** appeale[9] / appeales[1] / appeal'd[1]
**rh** commonweal *2H6 2.1.185*; repeal *Luc 638*

**appear / ~s / ~eth / ~ing / ~ed** *v*
ə'piːɹ, -'pɛːɹ / -z / -əθ / -ɪn, -ɪŋ / -d
**sp** appear[4], appeare[116], ap-peare[1], appeere[2] / appeares[44], ap-peares[1], appears[1], appeeres[1] / appeareth[2] / appearing[2], ap-pearing[1] / appeard[1], appear'd[18], appeared[4], appeer'd[3]
**rh** *1* dear *LC 93, 3.1.79*; dear, here *MND 3.1.80*; dear, near *MND 2.2.38*; ear *LLL 4.3.43, MND 1.1.185*; fear *Luc 116, 1434*; hear *TNK Prol.28*; here *Cor 2.3.115, KL 1.1.180, Mac 5.5.47, MND 3.2.99, 5.1.416, MV 2.9.73, R2 5.6.9*; here, there *KL 1.4.143* [*Q*]; pioneer *Luc 1382*; tear [cry] *S 31.7*; year *S 53.11*; **rh** *2* bear *CE 3.1.15, S 80.8, TC 1.2.295*; every where *S 102.2*; there *Luc 116*; wear *LC 93*; **rh** *3* were *Luc 633*; **rh** *4* murderer *Per 4.Chorus.51* / **rh** *1* fears *LC 299, Luc 458*; tears [cry] *LC 299, LLL 4.3.154, 5.2.117, MND 3.2.125, VA 1175*; **rh** *2* wears *Per Epil.9*

**appearance** *n*
ə'piːrəns, -'pɛː-
**sp** apparance[3], appearance[9]

**appearing** *adj*
ə'piːrɪn, -ɪŋ, -pɛː-
**sp** appearing[4]
> new-appearing

**appease / ~d** *v*
=
**sp** appease[4] / appeas'd[5]
**rh** Pericles *Per 3.Chorus.29* [*emend of* oppress]; pleased *TG 5.4.81*
> unappeased

**appeler / appelle / appel·ons / ~ez / ~é / ~ée / ~és** *Fr v*
a'pɛl / ap'lɔ̃, -pə-/ a'plez, -pə- / a'ple
**sp** appelle[1] / appellons[1] / appelle[1], ap-pelle[2], appelez[1] / appelle[1] / appelle[1] / appelle[1]

**appellant / ~s** *n*
ə'pelənt, -'piː- / -s
**sp** appealant[2], appellant[2] / appealants[2]

**appendix** *n*
=
**sp** appendix[1]

**apperil** *n*
ə'perɪl
**sp** apperill[1]

**appertain / ~s / ~ing** *v*
,apəɹ'tɛːn / -z / -ɪn, -ɪŋ
**sp** appertaine[2] / appertaines[1] / appertaining[1]

**appertaining** *adj*
,apəɹ'tɛːnɪn, -ɪŋ
**sp** appertaining[2]

**appertainment / ~s** *n*
,apəɹ'tɛːnmənts
**sp** appertainments[1]

**appertinent** *adj*
ə'pɐːɹtɪnənt
**sp** appertinent[2]
> pertinent

**appertinent / ~s** *n*
*m* ə'pɐːɹtɪ,nents
**sp** appertinents[1]

**appetite / ~s** *n*
*m* 'apɪ,təɪt, -ɪt-, 'aptəɪt / -s
**sp** appetite[32], appe-tite[1] / appetites[4]
**rh** delight, white *Luc 9*; might *S 56.2*; right *Luc 546*

**applaud / ~ing / ~ed** *v*
= / ə'plɔːdɪn, -ɪŋ / =
**sp** applaud[9], applau'd[2] / applaud-ing[1] / applauded[1]

**applauding** *adj*
ə'plɔːdɪn, -ɪŋ
**sp** applauding[1]

**applause / ~s** *n*
=
**sp** applause[12], 'applause[1] / applauses[1]

**apple / ~s** *n*
=
**sp** apple[9] / apples[3]

**apple-john / ~s** *n*
=
**sp** apple iohn[1], apple-iohn[1], apple-iohns[2]
> John

**appliance / ~s** *n*
*m* ə'pləɪəns, -ləɪns / -ləɪən,sɪz
**sp** appliance[3] / appliances[2]

**application / ~s** *n*
,aplɪ'kɛːsɪənz
**sp** applications[1]

**appl·y / ~ies / ~ied** *v*
ə'pləɪ / -z / *m* -ɪd, ə'pləɪd
**sp** applie[2], apply[12] / applyes[1] / appli'd[1], applyed[2]
**rh** *1* eye *MND 3.2.450*; lie *MM 3.2.265;* **rh** *2* remedy *MND 3.2.450*; simplicity *LLL 5.2.77* / divide, side *LC 68*; purified *Luc 531*
> mis-, self-applied

**appoint,** *abbr* **point / ~s / ~ed** *v*
ə'pəɪnt, *abbr* pəɪnt / -s / 'pəɪntɪd

sp appoint[12], *abbr* point[3] / appoints[1] / apointed[1], appointed[26], appoin-ted[1]
> pointed, well-appointed

**appointment / ~s** *n*
ə'pəɪntmənt / -s
sp appointment[9], appoint-ment[1] / appointments[2]

**apprehend / ~est / ~s / ~ed** *v*
ˌaprɪ'en·d, -'he- / -st, -dst / -z, -dz / -dɪd
sp apprehend[16], appre-hend[1] / apprehend'st[1] / apprehends[3] / apprehended[9]
> comprehended

**apprehension / ~s** *n*
*m* ˌaprɪ'ensɪən, -'he-, -sɪˌɒn / -z
sp apprehension[14] / apprehensions[3]

**apprehensive** *adj*
ˌaprɪ'ensɪv, -'he-
sp apprehensiue[3]

**apprendre / apprenne / appris** *Fr v*
a'prɑ̃:drə / a'prɛn / a'pri
sp apprendre[1] / append[1] / apprins[1]

**approach / ~es** *n*
ə'pro:ʧ / -ɪz
sp approach[25], approch[3], ap-proch[1] / approaches[3]

**approach / ~es / ~eth / ~ing / ~ed** *v*
ə'pro:ʧ / -ɪz / -əθ / -ɪn, -ɪŋ / -t
sp approach[39], approch[3] / approaches[7], approches[3], appro-ches[1] / approacheth[3], approcheth[1] / approaching[2] / approach'd[3], approacht[1]

**approacher / ~s** *n*
ə'pro:ʧəɹz
sp approachers[1]

**approaching** *adj / n*
ə'pro:ʧɪn, -ɪŋ
sp approaching[1], approching[1] / approaching[1]

**approbation** *n*
ˌaprə'bɛ:sɪən
sp approbation[13]

**approof** *n*
ə'prɤf, -ru:f
sp approofe[4]
> proof

**appropriation** *n*
əˌprɒprɪ'ɛ:sɪən
sp appropria-tion[1]

**approve / ~s / ~d** *v*
ə'prɤv, -ru:v / -z / *m* -d , -ɪd, -ru:-
sp approue[21], aproue[1] / approues[5] / approu'd[6], approued[3]
rh love *KL 1.1.184, MND 2.2.74, S 70.5, 147.7, Tit 2.1.35*; approve her love her *S 42.8* / beloved *TG 5.4.43*
> prove

**approved** *adj*
*m* 'aprɤvd, ə'prɤvd, -rɤvɪd, -ru:-
sp approoued[2], approu'd[2], approued[5]

**approver / ~s** *n*
ə'prɤvəɹz, -ru:-
sp approuers[1]

**appurtenance / ~s** *n*
*m* ə'pɐ:ɹtəˌnans / -ɪz
sp appurtenance[1] / appurtenances[1]

**a-praying** *v*
ə'prɛ:ɪn, -ɪŋ
sp *Ham* 3.3.73 *F* praying[1]
> pray

**apricock / ~s** *n*
'ɛ:prɪˌkɒks
sp apricocks[2]

**April** *adj*
'ɛ:prɪl
sp Aprill[2]

**April / ~'s** *n*
'ɛ:prɪl / -z
sp April[2], Aprill[7], Aprill's [April is][1] / Aprils[1]

**apron / ~s** *n*
'ɛ:prən, *2H6 2.3.74 dialect form* 'ɛ:pəɹn / -z
sp apron[1], *2H6* aporne[1] / aprons[5]

**apron-man / ~men** *n*
'ɛ:prən-ˌmen
sp apron men[1]
> man

**apt / ~er / ~est** *adj*
= / 'aptəɹ / =
sp apt[41] / apter[2] / aptest[1]
> unapt

**aptly** *adv*
'aptləɪ
sp aptly[4]

**aptness** *n*
=
sp aptnesse[2]
> unaptness

**aqua-vitae** *n*
'akwə-ˌvi:tɛ:
sp aqua-vitae[4], aqua-vitae-[bottle][1], aqua vite[1], aquavite[1]

**Aquilon** *n*
'akwɪˌlɒn
sp Aquilon[1]

**Aquitaine** *n*
ˌakwɪ'tɛ:n, -'tɛn
sp Aquitaine[7], Aquitane[1]
rh vain *LLL 1.1.135*

**Arabia** *n*
ə'rɛ:bɪə
sp Arabia[5]

**Arabian** *adj*
ə'rɛ:bɪən
sp Arabian[2], Arabian-[Bird][1]

**Aragon**
> Arragon

**araise** *v*
ə'rɛːz
**sp** arayse[1]

**arbitrat·e / ~ing** *v*
*m* 'ɑːɹbɪˌtrɛːt / -ɪn, -ɪŋ
**sp** arbitrate[5] / arbitrating[1]
**rh** hate *R2 1.1.200*; relate *Mac 5.4.20*

**arbitrator / *Luc* ~s** *n*
'ɑːɹbɪˌtrɛːtəɹ / -z
**sp** arbitrator[2] / arbitrators[1]
**rh** debaters, mediators *Luc 1017*

**arbitrement** *n*
ɑːɹ'bɪtrəˌment, -təɹ-, -əmənt
**sp** arbiterment[1], arbitrement[3], arbitre-ment[1]

**arbour / ~s** *n*
'ɑːɹbəɹ / -z
**sp** arbor[2] / arbors[1]

**Arc** *n*
ɑːɹk
**sp** *emend of 1H6 2.2.20* Acre[1], *1H6 5.4.49* Aire[1]

**arch** *adj / n*
ɑːɹʧ
**sp** arch[3] / arch[5]

**arch / ~ed** *v*
*m* ɑːɹʧt, 'ɑːɹʧɪd
**sp** arch'd[1]

**archbishop / ~'s / ~s** *n*
ɑːɹʧ'bɪʃəp / -s
**sp** archbishop[12], arch-bishop[9], archbyshop[2], arch-byshop[4] / arch-bishops[1] / archbishops[1]
> bishop

**archbishopric** *n*
ɑːɹʧ'bɪʃəpˌrɪk
**sp** archbishopricke[1]

**archdeacon** *n*
*m* ˌɑːɹʧdɪ'akən
**sp** arch-deacon[1]

**arched** *adj*
*m* ɑːɹʧt, 'ɑːɹʧɪd
**sp** arched[1], arched-[beauty][1]

**Archelaus** *n*
ˌɑːɹkɪ'lɛːəs
**sp** Archilaus[1]

**arch-enemy** *n*
*m* ˌɑːɹʧ-'enəˌməɪ
**sp** arch-enemy[1]
> enemy

**archer / ~s** *n*
'ɑːɹʧəɹ / -z
**sp** archer[1], ar-cher[1] / archers[3]

**archery** *n*
*m* 'ɑːɹʧəˌɹəɪ
**sp** archerie[1], archery[1]
**rh** *MND 3.2.103* by, dye, espy, eye, gloriously, remedy, sky

**arch-heretic** *n*
*m* ˌɑːɹʧ-'erɪˌtɪk, -'he-
**sp** arch-heretique[2]
> heretic

**Archibald** *n*
ˌɑːɹʧɪ'bɑːld
**sp** Archibald[1]

**Archidamus** *n*
ˌɑːɹkɪ'daməs
**sp** Archidamus[1]

**architect** *n*
'ɑːɹkɪˌtekt
**sp** architect[1]

**arch-mock** *n*
ˌɑːɹʧ-'mɒk
**sp** arch-mock[1]
> mock

**arch-one** *n*
'ɑːɹʧ-ˌoːn, 'ɑːɹʧən
**sp** arch-one[1]
> one

**arch-villain** *n*
ˌɑːɹʧ-'vɪlən
**sp** arch-villaine[1]
> villain

**arc·us / ~u** *Lat n*
'ɑːɹkuː
**sp** *emend of Tit 4.2.21* ar-cus[1]

**Arde** *n*
ɑːɹd
**sp** Arde[1]

**Arden** *n*
'ɑːɹdən
**sp** Arden[4]

**ardent** *adj*
'ɑːɹdənt
**sp** ar-dent[1]

**ardour** *n*
'ɑːɹdəɹ, -duːɹ
**sp** ardour[1], ardure[1]

**are** *v*
*str* ɑːɹ, ɛːɹ, *unstr* əɹ, *abbr* ɹ
**sp** are[3283]
**rh** *1* care, snare *Luc 929*; care *3H6 2.5.124, Mac 4.1.90, R2 2.3.169, S 48.5, 112.11, 147.11*; compare *S 35.8, TS 5.2.174, VA 10*; dare *Mac 3.5.2*; prepare *LLL 5.2.82, S 13.1*; rare *S 52.7*; unaware *VA 825*; **rh** *2* car *S 7.11*; scar *MND 5.1.402*; star *LLL 1.1.91*; **rh** *3* war *TC Prol.30*
> art

***they are abbr***
ðɛːɹ, *unstr* ðɛɹ
**sp** th'are[2], they'r[1], they're[6]

***we are abbr***
wɛːɹ
**sp** w'are[1]

***you/ye are abbr***
*unstr* jəɹ, *str* jɑːɹ
**sp** y'are[48], you'r[6], you're[15]

**a-repairing** *v*
ə-rɪ'pɛːrɪn, -ɪŋ
**sp** a repairing[1]
> repair

**argal** *adv*
ɐːɹ'gɑːl, -'gɔːl
**sp** argall[3]
> ergo

**Argier** *n*
ɑɹ'ʤi:ɹ
**sp** Argier[2]

**argo**
> ergo

**argos·y / ~ies** *n*
'ɑ:ɹgə,səɪ, -əs- / -z
**sp** argosie[4], argo-sie[1] / argosies[3]

**argu·e / ~es / ~ing / ~ed** *v*
'ɑ:ɹgju: / -z / -ɪn, -ɪŋ / -d
**sp** argue[5] / argues[10], ar-gues[1] / arguing[2] / argu'd[2], argued[1]

**arguing** *n*
*m* 'ɑ:ɹgu:ɪn, -ɪŋ
**sp** arguing[1]

**argument / ~s** *n*
*m* 'ɑ:ɹgə,ment, -gment / -s
**sp** argument[57], argu-ment[2] / arguments[10]
**rh** hardiment *TC 4.5.29*; invent *S 79.5*; punishment *LLL 4.3.59, PP 3.2*; spent *S 76.10, 100.8, 105.9, Tim 3.5.23*

**Argus** *n*
'ɑ:ɹgəs
**sp** Argos[1], Argus[2]

**Ariachne / ~'s** *n*
,arɪ'akni:z
**sp** Ariachnes[1]

**Ariadne** *n*
,arɪ'adni:
**sp** Ariadne[2]

**Ariel** *n*
*m* 'ɛ:rɪəl, 'ɛ:rɪ,el
**sp** Ariel[13], Ariell[22]

**Aries** *n*
'ɛ:ri:z
**sp** Aries[1]

**aright** *adv*
ə'rəɪt
**sp** aright[5], a right[1]
**rh** night *MND 2.1.42*; sight *S 148.4*

**Arion** *n*
ə'rəɪən
**sp** Orion[1]

**a-ripening** *v*
ə'rəɪpnɪn, -ɪŋ, -pən-
**sp** a ripening[1]
> ripen

**arise / ~s / ~eth / arose** *v*
ə'rəɪz / -ɪz / -əθ / ə'ro:z
**sp** arise[36] / arises[1] / ariseth[2] / arose[3]
**rh** *1* butterflies, eyes, thighs *MND 3.1.166*; despise, enterprise *Luc 186*; disguise, eyes *Luc 1818*; eyes *Cym 2.3.24, 4.2.403, 5.1.318, S 55.13*; lies *Cym 2.3.20*; **rh** *2* bees, courtesies, dewberries, mulberries *MND 3.1.166* / despising *S 29.11*

**Aristotle / ~'s** *n*
'arɪstɒtl / -z
**sp** Aristotle[1] / Aristotles[1]

**arithmetic** *n*
ə'rɪtmə,tɪk, -ət-
**sp** arethmaticke[1], arithmatique[1], arithmetick[1], arithmeticke[1], arithmetique[1]

**arithmetician** *n*
ə,rɪtmə'tɪsɪən
**sp** arithmatician[1]

**Ark** *n*
ɑ:ɹk
**sp** Arke[1]

**arm / ~'s / ~s** *n*
ɑ:ɹm, *Fr H5 3.4.26* ɑ:ɹmə / -z
**sp** arme[98], *Fr* arma[1] / armes[4] / armes[236], arms[4]
**rh** charm, harm *Luc 170* / charms *PP 11.6*; harms *1H6 4.7.29, 45, Luc 27, 197, 1693*
> coat-of-, officer-at-, pursuivant-at-, sergeant-at-arms

**arm / ~s / ~ing / ~ed** *v*
ɑ:ɹm / -z / 'ɑ:ɹmɪn, -ɪŋ / *m* 'ɑ:ɹmɪd, ɑ:ɹmd
**sp** arm[1], arme[43] / armes[1] / arming[4] / arm'd[8], armed[7], ar-med[1]
**rh** harmed *VA 625*; uncharmed *RJ 1.1.210*
> unarm

**arma**
> arm *n*

**armado / ~es** *n*
ɐ:ɹ'mɑ:do: / -z
**sp** armado[1] / ar-madoes[1]

**Armado / ~'s [name]** *n*
ɑ:ɹ'mɑ:ðo:, -ɑ:do:, *abbr LLL 1.1.185* ɑ:ɹm
**sp** Armado[8], Armatho[3], Armathor[1], *abbr* Arme[2] / Armadoes[1], Armathoes[1]

**Armagnac** *n*
'ɑ:ɹmɪ,nak
**sp** Arminack[1], Arminacke[2]

**armed** *adj*
*m* ɑ:ɹmd, 'ɑ:ɹmɪd
**sp** arm'd[32], armed[20]
> short-, un-, well-armed

**Armenia** *n*
'ɑ:ɹmi:nɪə
**sp** Armenia[2]

**arm-gaunt** *adj*
'ɑ:ɹm-,gɔ:nt
**sp** arme-gaunt[1]

**armiger / ~o** *adj*
'ɑ:ɹmɪʤro:
**sp** armigero[2]

**arming** *n*
'ɑ:ɹmɪn, -ɪŋ
**sp** arming[1]

**armipotent** *adj*
ɑ:ɹ'mɪptənt, -pət-
**sp** armipotent[2], army-potent[1]

**armour / ~s** *n*
'ɑ:ɹməɹ / -z
**sp** armor[11], ar-mor[1] armour[30], / armors[2], armours[2]

**armourer / ~'s / ~s** *n*
*m* 'ɑːɹmə,rɐːɹ, -mrəɹ / -rəɹz / -mə,rɐːɹz
**sp** armorer[5], armourer[1] / armorers[1] / armorers[1], armourers[1]

**armoury** *n*
*m* 'ɑːɹmə,rəɪ, -ər-
**sp** armorie[2], armory[1]

**arm·y / ~ies** *n*
'ɑːɹməɪ / -z
**sp** armie[19], armie's [army is][1], army[70], ar-my[1] / armies[13]

**aroint** *v*
ə'rəɪnt
**sp** aroynt[3], *Q KL 3.4.129* arint[1]

**a-rolling** *v*
ə'roːlɪn, -ɪŋ
**sp** a rowling[1]
> roll

**arose**
> arise

**arouse** *v*
ə'rəʊz
**sp** arouse[1]
> arrose

**a-row** *adv*
ə'roː
**sp** a-row[1]
> row

**aroynt**
> aroint

**Arragon** *n*
*m* 'arə,gɒn, -əgən
**sp** Arragon[3], Arra-gon[1]

**arraign / ~ing / ~ed** *v*
ə'rɛːn / -ɪn, -ɪŋ / -d
**sp** araign[1], araigne[1], arraigne[2] / arraigning[1] / arraigned[1]
> darraign

**arraignment** *n*
ə'rɛːnmənt
**sp** arraignment[1]

**arrant** *adj*
'arənt
**sp** ar-rand[1], arrant[14], ar-rant[1]

**arras** *n*
'arəs
**sp** arras[10], ar-ras[1]

**array** *n*
ə'rɛː
**sp** aray[1], a-ray[1], array[9]
**rh** day *VA 483*; stay *1H6 1.3.55*; Sunday *TS 2.1.316*

**array / ~ed** *v*
ə'rɛː / -d
**sp** array'd[1], arrayed[1]
**rh** gay *S 146.2*

**arrearage / ~s** *n*
ə'rɛːrɪdʒɪz
**sp** arrerages[1]

**arrest / ~s** *n*
=
**sp** arrest[5] / arrests[1]
**rh** interest *S 74.1*

**arrest / ~s / ~ed** *v*
=
**sp** arrest[22] / arrests[1] / arested[2], arrested[9], arre-sted[1]

**arrival** *n*
ə'rəɪvɑl
**sp** arriuall[5]

**arrivancy** *n*
*m* ə'rəɪvən,səɪ
**sp** arriuancie[1]

**arrive / ~s / ~ing / ~d** *v*
ə'rəɪv / -z / -ɪn, -ɪŋ / *m* -d, -ɪd
**sp** arriue[5] / arriues[2] / arriuing[1] / a-riu'd[1], arriu'd[19], arriued[5]
**rh** strived *Luc 50, Per 5.Chorus.14*; wived *Oth 2.1.58*

**arrogance** *n*
*m* 'arə,gans
**sp** arrogance[1]
**rh** France *AW 2.1.195*

**arrogancy** *n*
*m* 'arə,gansəɪ
**sp** arrogancie[1]

**arrogant** *adj*
*m* 'arə,gant, -əgənt, 'ɑːɹgənt
**sp** arrogant[4]

**arrow / ~s** *n*
'arə, 'aroː / -z
**sp** arrow[7], ar-row[1] / arrowes[11], arrows[2]
**rh** sparrows *Tem 4.1.99*

**art / ~s** *n*
ɑːɹt / -s
**sp** art[64] / artes[1], arts[11]
**rh** *1* depart *S 6.9*; heart *H8 3.1.12, LC 174, Luc 1394, Mac 4.1.100, MND 1.1.192, 2.2.110, S 24.4, 24.13, 125.11, 139.4, TS 4.2.9*; heart, part *LC 145*; part *AW 2.1.133, Mac 3.5.9;* **rh** *2* convert *S 14.10*

**art** *v*
*str* ɑːɹt, *unstr* əɹt, *abbr* ɹt
**sp** art[813], ar't[1], ourt[1], 'rt [19]
**rh** *1* heart *LLL 5.2.280, Luc 593, R2 5.3.135, S 22.8, 41.4, 48.10, 131.1*; smart *Cym 5.4.40;* **rh** *2* convert *Luc 593*
> are

**Artemidorus** *n*
ɐːɹ,temɪ'dɔːrəs
**sp** Artemidorus[2], Artimedorus[1]

**artere** *n*
'ɑːɹtəɹ
**sp** artire[1]
> artery

**arter·y / ~ies** *n*
*m* 'ɑːɹtə,rəɪz
**sp** arteries[1]

**Arthur / ~'s** *n*
'ɑːɹtəɹ / -z
**sp** Arthur[34] / Arthurs[13]

**article / ~s** *n*
*m* 'ɑːɹtɪkəl, -,kɤl / -z
**sp** article[16], ar-ticle[1] / articles[19]

**articulate / ~d** *v*
ɑːɹ'tɪkjəˌlɛːt / -ɪd
**sp** articulate[1] / articulated[1]

**artificer** *n*
*m* ɑːɹ'tɪfɪˌsɐːɹ
**sp** artificer[1]

**artificial** *adj*
ˌɑːɹtɪ'fɪsɪɑl
**sp** artificiall[6]

**artillery** *n*
*m* ɑːɹ'tɪləˌrəɪ, -lr-
**sp** artillerie[5]

**artist / ~s** *n*
'ɑːɹtɪst / -s
**sp** artist[1] / artists[1]

**artless** *adj*
'ɑːɹtləs
**sp** artlesse[1]

**Artois** *n*
*m* ɑːɹ'twɛ, 'ɑːɹtwɛ, *Eng* -təɪz
**sp** Artoys[1]

**arts-man** *n*
'ɑːɹtsˌman
**sp** arts-man[1]

**artus** *Lat n*
'ɑːɹtʊs
**sp** artus[1]

**Arviragus** *n*
ˌɑːɹvɪ'ragəs
**sp** Aruiragus[10], Arui-ragus[1]

**as** *conj*
*str* az, *unstr* əz, *Fluellen H5 5.1.4* as
**sp** as[5499], as't [as it][4], as[much][1], *Fluellen* asse[1]
> when as

**as / ~es** *n*
'asɪz
**sp** *Ham 5.2.43* assis[1]
**pun** ass

**as** *Fr*
> avoir

**Asaph** *n*
'asəf
**sp** Asaph[1]

**Ascanius** *n*
ə'skɛːnɪəs
**sp** Ascanius[1]

**ascend / ~s / ~ed** *v*
=
**sp** ascend[11] / ascends[4] / ascended[2]

**ascension** *n*
ə'sensɪən
**sp** ascension[1]

**Ascension Day** *n phrase*
ə'sensɪən ˌdɛː
**sp** Ascension day[3], Ascention day[1]

**ascent** *n*
=
**sp** assent[1]

**ascribe / ~s** *v*
ə'skrəɪb / -z
**sp** ascribe[3] / ascribes[1]

**ash / ~es** *n*
=
**sp** ash[1] / ashes[18]

**a-shaking** *Luc* *v*
ə'ʃɛːkɪn, -ɪŋ
**sp** a shaking[1]
**rh** taking, waking *Luc 452*
> shake

**ashamed** *adj*
*m* ə'ʃɛːmd, -mɪd
**sp** asham'd[31], ashamed[3]

**Asher-house** *n*
'aʃəɹ-ˌəʊs, -ˌhəʊs
**sp** Asher-house[1]

**Ashford** *n*
'aʃfəɹd
**sp** Ashford[2]

**ashore** *adv*
ə'ʃɔːɹ
**sp** a'shoare[1], ashore[6], a-shore[1], a'shore[1], a shore[2]

**a-shouting** *v*
ə'ʃəʊtɪn, -ɪŋ
**sp** a shouting[1]
> shout

**Ash Wednesday** *n phrase*
ˌaʃ 'wensdɛː
**sp** ashwensday[1]
> Wednesday

**ashy** *adj*
'aʃəɪ
**sp** ashy[1]
> ash

**Asia** *n*
*m* 'ɛːzɪə, -ɪˌa
**sp** Asia[4]

**aside** *adv*
ə'səɪd
**sp** aside[7]
**rh** bide *S 139.6*; denied *RJ 1.1.156*; espied, wide *Luc 362*; pride *S 76.3*

**asinico** *n*
asɪ'niːkoː
**sp** asinico[1]

**ask / ~est / ~s / ~eth / ~ing / ~ed** *v*
ask / -st / -s / 'ask·əθ / -ɪn, -ɪŋ / askt
**sp** ask[11], aske[151] / askst[1], ask'st[1] / askes[1], asks[1] / asketh[2] / asking[7] / ask'd[17], askt[12], ask't[1]
**rh** mask [*F, at* LLL 2.1.113–29], *5.2.243*; masque *RJ 1.4.49*

**askance** *adv*
ə'skɒns
**sp** a sconce[1]

**asker** *n*
'askəɹ
**sp** asker[1]

**asking** *n*
'askɪn, -ɪŋ
**sp** asking[5]

**aslant** *adv*
ə'slant
**sp** aslant[1]

**asleep** *adv*
ə'sli:p
**sp** asleep[2], asleepe[46], a-sleepe[2], a sleepe[5]
**rh** keep *S 154.1*, steep *S 153.1*
> sleep

**a-sleeping** *v*
ə'sli:pɪn, -ɪŋ
**sp** asleeping[1]
**rh** weeping *Tim 1.2.66*
> sleep

**Asmath** *n*
'azmat
**sp** Asmath[1]

**aspect / ~s** *n*
ə'spekt / -s
**sp** aspect[24], as-pect[1] / aspects[4]
**rh** decked *LLL 4.3.258*; effect *AY 4.3.54*; respect *S 26.10*

**aspen** *adj*
=
**sp** aspen[1], as-pen[1]

**aspersion** *n*
ə'spɐ:ɹsɪən
**sp** aspersion[1]

**aspic / ~'s / ~s'** *n*
'aspɪk / -s
**sp** aspicke[2] / aspickes[1] / aspickes[1]

**aspicious** [*malap* suspicious] *adj*
ə'spɪsɪəs
**sp** aspitious[1]

**aspiration** *n*
ˌaspɪ'rɛ:sɪən
**sp** aspiration[1]

**aspire / ~d** *v*
ə'spəɪɹ / -d
**sp** aspire[4] / aspir'd[2]
**rh** desire, fire *Luc 5*; fire *VA 150*; higher *MW 5.5.97, Per 1.4.5*

**aspiring** *adj*
ə'spəɪrɪn, -ɪŋ
**sp** aspiring[5], aspyring[1]

**asquint** *adv*
ə'skwɪnt
**sp** a squint[1]
> squint

**ass / ~'s / ~es** *n*
=
**sp** asse[90] / asses[2] / asses[9]
**rh** *1* grass *CE 2.2.209*; pass *AW 4.3.326, AY 2.5.48, CE 3.1.18, MND 3.2.34, 4.1.76*; **rh** *2* place *CE 3.1.47*

**assail / ~s / ~eth / ~ed** *v*
ə'sɛ:l / -z / -əθ / *m* -d, -ɪd
**sp** assaile[3], assayle[2] / assailes[2] / assayleth[1] / assayl'd[2], assayled[2]
**rh** nails *Luc 1562* / prevailed *S 41.6*
> unassailed

**assailable** *adj*
*m* ə'sɛ:ləˌbɤl
**sp** assaileable[1]
> unassailable

**assailant / ~s** *n*
ə'sɛ:lənt / -s
**sp** assaylant[1] / assailants[1]

**assailing** *adj*
ə'sɛ:lɪn, -ɪŋ
**sp** assailing[1], assayling[1]

**assassination** *n*
ə'sasɪˌnɛ:sɪən
**sp** assassination[1]

**assault / ~s** *n*
ə'sɔ:t, -lt / -s
**sp** assalt[1], assault[12] / assaults[1]

**assault / ~s / ~ed** *v*
ə'sɔ:t, -lt / -s / -ɪd
**sp** assault[3] / assaults[2] / assaulted[2]
**rh** faults *Tem Epil.17*

**assay / ~s** *n*
ə'sɛ: / -z
**sp** assay[6] / assaies[1], assayes[1]
**rh** delays, says *Luc 1720*

**assay / ~s / ~ing / ~ed** *v*
ə'sɛ: / -z / -ɪn, -ɪŋ / -d
**sp** assay[8] / assaies[1] / assaying[1] / assaid[2], assay'd[1]
**rh** stay, way *LC 156*

**assemblance** *n*
=
**sp** assemblance[1]

**assemble / ~d** *v*
=
**sp** assemble[6] / assembled[9]
**rh** resemble *S 114.8*

**assembled** *adj*
=
**sp** assembled[1]

**assembl·y / ~ies** *n*
*m* ə'sembləɪ, -bəˌləɪ / ə'sembləɪz
**sp** assembly[13], as sembly[1] / assemblies[2]

**assent** *n*
=
**sp** assent[2]

**assez** *Fr adv*
a'sez
**sp** asses[1]

**ass-head** *n*
'as-ˌed, -ˌhed
**sp** asse head[1], asse-head[2]

**assign /~s** *n*
ə'səɪnz
**sp** assignes[2]

**assign / ~ed** *v*
ə'səɪn / ə'səɪnd
**sp** assigne[3] / assign'd[3]
**rh** find, mind *LC 138*

**assigned** *adj*
ə'səɪnd
**sp** assign'd[1]

**assinico**
> asinico

**assist / ~ing / ~ed** *v*
= / ə'sɪstɪn, -ɪŋ / =
**sp** assist[20] / assisting[1] / assisted[3]

**assistance / ~s** *n*
ə'sɪstəns / *m* -ˌsɪz
**sp** assistance[10], assista[n]ce[1], assi-stance[1] / assistances[1]

**assistant / ~s** *n*
=
**sp** assistant[3], assi-stant[1] / assistants[3]

**associate / ~s** *n*
ə'so:sɪəts
**sp** associates[1]

**associate / ~d** *v*
*m* ə'so:sɪɛ:t, -ˌɛ:t / -ˌɛ:tɪd
**sp** associate[2] / associated[1]

**assuage / *VA* ~d** *v*
ə'swɛ:ʤ / -d
**sp** asswage[1] / asswag'd[1]
**rh** age *LC 69*; pilgrimage *Luc 790*; rage *VA 334* / enraged *VA 318*

**assubjugate** *v*
*m* ə'sɤbʤəˌgɛ:t
**sp** assubiugate[1]

**assume / ~s / ~d** *v*
ə'sju:m / -z / -d
**sp** assume[12] / assumes[3] / assum'd[1]
**rh** plumes *TC 1.3.385*
> self-assumption

**assurance** *n*
ə'ʃu:rəns, ə'sju:-
**sp** assurance[26], assu-rance[2]
**pun** *Mac 4.1.82* sure / *KJ 2.1.471* unsured

**assure / ~s / ~ed** *v*
ə'ʃu:ɹ, ə'sju:ɹ / -z / *m* -d, -ɪd, 'aʃu:ɹd, 'asju:ɹd
**sp** assure[49] / assures[1] / assur'd[37], assured[4], assu-red[1]
**rh** distemperature *RJ 2.3.35*; assure thee cure thee *VA 371* / recured *S 45.11*; endured *S 107.7*

**assured** *adj*
*m* ə'ʃu:ɹd, ə'sju:-, 'aʃu:ɹd, 'asju:-
**sp** assur'd[3], assured[4]
**rh** cured *S 118.10*

**assuredly** *adv*
*m* ə'ʃu:ɹɪdˌləɪ, -'sju:-
**sp** assuredly[4]

**Assyrian** *adj*
=
**sp** Assyrian[2]

**astonish / ~ed** *v*
= / ə'stɒnɪʃt, *S* -ɪˌʃed
**sp** astonish[4], astonish'd[1], astonisht[2], *S* astonished[1]
**rh** dead *S 86.8*

**Astraea / ~'s** *n*
'astri:ə / -z
**sp** Astrea[1] / Astrea's[1]

**astray** *adv*
ə'strɛ:
**sp** astray[2]
**rh** way *MND 3.2.358*

**astringer** *n*
ə'strɪnʤəɹ
**sp** astringer[1]

**astronomer / ~s** *n*
*m* ə'strɒnəˌmɐ:ɹ / -əməɹz
**sp** astronomer[1] / astronomers[1]

**astronomy** *n*
*m* ə'strɒnəˌməɪ
**sp** astronomy
**rh** quality *S 14.2*

**asture** [à cette heure] *Fr phrase*
a'styɹ
**sp** asture[1]

**asunder** *adv*
ə'sɤndəɹ
**sp** asunder[10], a-sunder[2], assunder[3]
**rh** thunder *VA 266*; wonder *1H6 4.7.47, PT 29*
> sunder

**at** *prep*
=
**sp** at[2406], at'[2], at's [at his][3], at's [at us][1], at[other][1]
**rh** fat *LLL 5.2.266*; gat *Per 2.2.7*

**Atalanta / ~'s** *n*
'atəˌlantəz
**sp** Attalanta's[2]

**a-talking** *v*
ə'tɔ:kɪn, -ɪŋ
**sp** a talking[1]
> talk

**ate**
> eat

**Ate / ~s** *n*
'ɛ:ti: / -z
**sp** Ace[1], Ate[2], Atees[2]

**Athenian** *adj*
*m* ə'ti:nɪən, -ɪˌan
**sp** Athenian[15]

**Athenian / ~'s ~s** *n*
*m* ə'ti:nɪən, -ɪˌan / -z
**sp** Athenian[6] / Athenians[3] / Athenians[4]
**rh** man *MND 3.2.41*

**Athens** *n*
'atənz
**sp** Athens[55]

**Atholl** *n*
'atəl
**sp** Atholl[1]

**athwart** *adv / prep*
ə'twɑ:ɹt, ə'θ-
**sp** athwart[2] / athwart[5]
**rh** *prep* heart *LLL 4.3.133*

**atilt** *adv*
=
**sp** a-tilt[2]
> tilt

**a-tiptoe** *adv*
ə'tɪpto:
**sp** a tip-toe[1]
> tiptoe

**Atlas** *n*
=
**sp** Atlas[2]
> demi-atlas

**atom·y / ~ies** *n*
*m* 'atəˌməɪz
**sp** atomies[2], atomyes[1]

**atone** *v*
ə'to:n
**sp** attone[7]

**atonement / ~s** *n*
ə'to:nmənt / -s
**sp** attonement[2] / attone-ments[1]

**Atropos** *n*
*m* 'atrəˌpɒs
**sp** Atropos[1]

**attach / ~ed** *v*
= / *m* ə'tatʃt, -tʃɪd
**sp** attach[10] / attach'd[5], attached[2]

**attachment** *n*
=
**sp** attachment[1]

**attain** *n*
ə'tɛ:n
**sp** attaine[1]

**attain / ~s / ~ed** *v*
ə'tɛ:n / -z / -d
**sp** attaine[9] / attaines[1] / attaind[1], attain'd[3], attayn'd[1]

**attainder** *n*
ə'tɛ:ndəɹ
**sp** attainder[2], attaindor[1]

**attaint** *n*
ə'tɛ:nt
**sp** attaint[2]
**rh** faint *VA 741*; paint *Luc 1072*; saint *CE 3.2.16*

**attaint / ~ed** *v*
ə'tɛ:nt / -ɪd
**sp** attaint[2] / attainted[3]
**rh** saint *PP 18.46* / acquainted *S 88.7*
> unattainted

**attainture** *n*
ə'tɛ:ntəɹ
**sp** attainture[1], attendure[1]

**attempt / ~s** *n*
ə'temt, -mpt / -s
**sp** attempt[11] / attempts[6]

**attempt / ~s / ~ing / ~ed** *v*
ə'temt, -mpt / -s / -ɪn, -ɪŋ / -ɪd
**sp** attempt[23] / attempts[1] / attempting[2] / attempted[2]
> unattempted

**attemptable** *adj*
ə'temtɪbəl, -mpt-
**sp** attemptible[1]

**attend,** *abbr* **tend / ~est / ~s / ~ eth / ~ing / ~ed** *v*
= / ə'tenst, -ndst / = / = / ə'tendɪn, -ɪŋ / =
**sp** attend[112], *abbr* 'tend[1] / attend'st[1] / attends[19] / attendeth[1] / attending[7] / attended[21]
**rh** end *R3 4.4.196, VA 1136*; mend *RJ Prol.13*; **attend me** defend me, lend me *Luc 1682* / lendeth *Luc 1674* / ending *Per Epil.17* / commended *LC 78*; offended *VA 809*
> unattended

**attendance** *n*
=
**sp** attendance[7]

**attendant** *adj*
=
**sp** attendant[4]

**attendant / ~s** *n*
=
**sp** attendant[5] / atendants[1], attendants[57], atten-dants[1]

**attending** *adj*
ə'tendɪn, -ɪŋ
**sp** attending[4]

**attent** *n*
=
**sp** attent[1]
**rh** spent *Per 3.Chorus.11*

**attention** *n*
ə'tensɪən
**sp** attention[5]

**attentive** *adj*
=
**sp** attentiue[5]

**attentiveness** *n*
=
**sp** attentiuenesse[1]

**attest / ~ed** *v*
=
**sp** attest[3] / attested[1]

**Attica** *n*
'atɪkə
**sp** Athica[1]

**attire / ~s** *n*
ə'təɪɹ / -z
**sp** attire[3], attyre[6] / attires[2], attyres[1]

**attire / ~d** *v*
ə'təɪɹ / *m* -d, -ɪd
**sp** attire[1], attyre[2] / attir'd[1], attired[3], attyr'd[1], attyred[1]

**attorney / ~s** *n*
ə'tu:ɹnəɪ / -z
**sp** attorney[1], attourney[1], atturney[4], attur-ney[1] / attorneyes[1], atturneyes[1], atturnies[1]

**attorney / ~ed** *v*
ə'tu:ɹnəɪd
**sp** attornyed[1], atturnied[1]

**attorneyship** *n*
*m* ə'tu:ɹnəɪ,ʃɪp
**sp** atturney-ship[1]

**attract / ~s** *v*
=
**sp** attract[1] / attracts[2]

**attraction** *n*
ə'traksɪən
**sp** attraction[2]

**attractive** *adj*
=
**sp** attractiue[2]

**attribute / ~s** *n*
*m* 'atrɪ,bju:t / -s, 'atrɪbjəts
**sp** attribute[3] / attributes[2]

**attribute / ~d** *v*
'atrɪ,bju:tɪd
**sp** attributed[1]

**attribution** *n*
,atrɪ'bju:sɪən
**sp** attribution[1]

**a-turning** *PP* *v*
ə'tɐ:ɹnɪn, -ɪŋ
**sp** a turning[1]
**rh** framing *PP 7.16*
> turn

**a-twain** *LC* *adv*
ə'twɛ:n
**sp** a twaine[1]
**rh** rain *LC 6*
> twain

**au** *Fr prep + det*
o
**sp** au[2]

**Aubrey** *n*
'ɔ:brəɪ
**sp** Aubrey[1]

**aucune** *Fr adj*
o'kyn
**sp** au-cune[1]

**audacious** *adj*
ɔ:'dɛ:sɪəs
**sp** audacious[7]

**audaciously** *adv*
*m* ɔ:'dɛ:sɪəs,ləɪ
**sp** audaciously[1]
**rh** livery, modesty *Luc 1223*; see *LLL 5.2.104*

**audacity** *n*
*m* ɔ:'dasɪ,təɪ
**sp** audacitie[2]
**rh** leisurely, saucily *Luc 1346*

**audible** *adj*
=
**sp** audible[2]
> inaudible

**audience** *n*
=
**sp** audience[30], au-dience[1]

**aud·io / ~is** *Lat v*
'əʊdɪs
**sp** audis[1]

**audit** *n*
=
**sp** audit[4], awdit[1]

**auditor / ~s** *n*
*m* 'ɔ:dɪ,tɔ:ɹ / -z
**sp** auditor[2] / auditors[1]

**auditory** *adj*
*m* 'ɔ:dɪ,trəɪ, -,tɒr-
**sp** auditory[1]

**Audrey** *n*
'ɔ:drəɪ
**sp** Audrey[9], Audrie[1], Audry[3], Awdrie[5]
**rh** bawdry *AY 3.3.86*

**Aufidius / ~s' / ~es** *n*
ɔ:'fɪdɪəs, a'f- / -ɪz
**sp** Affidious[1], Affidius[1], Auffidious[6], Auffidius[33], Auf-fidius[1] / Auffidius[1] / Auffidiuses[1]
**pun** *Cor 2.1.126* so fiddious'd

**aught** *pro*
=
**sp** aught[8]

**augment / ~ing / ~ed** *v*
= / ɔ:g'mentɪn, -ɪŋ / =
**sp** augment[4] / augmenting[2] / augmented[2]

**augmentation** *n*
,ɔ:gmən'tɛ:sɪən
**sp** augmentation[1]

**augmented** *adj*
=
**sp** augmented[1]

**augur** *adj*
'ɔ:gəɹ
**sp** augure[1]

**augur / ~'s / ~s** *n*
'ɔ:gəɹz
**sp** augors[1] / augures[1]

**augurer / ~s** *n*
*m* 'ɔ:grəɹ, -gə,rɐ:ɹ / -z
**sp** agurer[1], augurer[1] / augurers[2]

**augur-hole** *n*
'ɔ:gəɹ-,o:l, -,ho:-
**sp** augure hole[1]

**auguring** *adj*
*m* 'ɔ:grɪn, -ɪŋ, -gər-
**sp** auguring[1]

**augur·y / ~ies** *n*
*m* 'ɔ:grəɪ, -gə,rəɪ / -gə,rəɪz
**sp** augury[2] / auguries[1]

**August** *n*
=
**sp** August[2]

**Augustus** *n*
ɔ:'gɤstəs
**sp** Augustus[5]

**Aumerle** *n*
ɔ:'mɐ:ɹl
**sp** Aumerle[26]

**aunt / ~s** *n*
'ɔ:nt / -s
**sp** aunt[25] / aunts[1]
**rh** chants *WT 4.3.11*

**aunt-mother** *n*
'ɔ:nt-'mɤðəɹ
**sp** aunt mother[1]
> mother

**auricular** *adj*
ɔ:'rɪkjələɹ
**sp** auri-cular[1]

**Aurora / ~'s** *n*
ə'rɔ:rəz
**sp** Auroras[2]

**auspicious** *adj*
ɔ:'spɪsɪəs, *malap MA 3.5.43* a'-
**sp** aspitious[1], auspicious[5], auspitious[1]
> in-, un-auspicious

**aussi** *Fr adv*
o'si
**sp** ausi[1], ousie[1]

**austere** *adj*
*m* ɒ'sti:ɹ, 'ɒs-
**sp** austere[3], au-stere[1]

**austerely** *adv*
ɒ'sti:ɹləɪ
**sp** austeerely[1], austerely[1]

**austereness** *n*
ɒ'sti:ɹnəs
**sp** austeerenesse[1]

**austerity** *n*
*m* ɒ'sterɪˌtəɪ
**sp** austeritie[1], austerity[2]

**Austria / ~'s** *n*
'ɒstrɪə / -z
**sp** Austria[6] / Austrias[1], Austria's[1]

**aut** *Lat conj*
ɔ:t
**sp** aut[1]

**authentic** *adj*
ɔ:'tentɪk
**sp** authenticke[3], authentique[1]

**author / ~'s / ~s** *n*
'ɔ:təɹ / -z
**sp** author[13], authour[1] / authors[2] / authors[3], authours[1]

**authorit·y / ~ies** *n*
*m* ɔ:'tɒrɪˌtəɪ, -ɪt-, -'tɒrtəɪ / -z
**sp** authorithy[1], authoritie[29], authoritie[1], authority[23] / authorities[4]
**rh** celerity *MM 4.2.108*; simplicity *S 66.9*; thee *1H6 5.1.59*

**authorize / ~d** *v*
*m* ɔ:'tɒrəɪzd
**sp** authoriz'd[1]
> unauthorized

**Autolycus** *n*
ɔ:'tɒlɪkəs
**sp** Autolicus[7]

**autre** *Fr adj*
'o:trə
**sp** autre[foys][1]

**autumn / ~'s** *n*
=
**sp** autumne[4] / autumne's[1]

**Auvergne** *n*
o:'vɐ:ɹn
**sp** Ouergne[1]

**avail / ~s** *n*
ə'vɛ:l / -z
**sp** auaile[1] / auailes[1]

**avail / ~s** *v*
ə'vɛ:l / -z
**sp** auaile[1], a-uaile[1], auayle[1] / auailes[1]

**avarice** *n*
=
**sp** auarice[2]

**avaricious** *adj*
ˌavə'rɪsɪəs
**sp** auaricious[1]

**avaunt** *interj*
ə'vɔ:nt
**sp** auant[9], auaunt[6]

**'ave**
> have

**Ave / ~s** *n*
'ɑ:vɛ:z
**sp** Aues[1]

**Ave-Mary / ~s** *n*
ˌɑ:vɛ:-'mɑ:ri:z
**sp** Aue-Maries[2]

**avenge / ~d** *v*
*m* ə'venʤd, -ʤɪd
**sp** auenge[1] / aueng'd[4], auenged[1]

**aver / ~ring** *v*
ə'vɐ:rɪn, -ɪŋ
**sp** auerring[1]

**avert** *v*
ə'vɐ:ɹt
**sp** auert[1]

**avez** *Fr*
> avoir

**avise**
> advise

**avoid / ~s / ~ing / ~ed, *abbr* voided** *v*
ə'vəɪd / -z / -ɪn, -ɪŋ / -ɪd, *m 1H4 5.5.13* ə'vəɪd, *abbr* 'vəɪdɪd
**sp** auoid[18], a-uoid[1], auoide[6], auoyd[10], auoyde[1], avoid[1] / auoydes[1] / auoiding[1] / auoided[2], auoyded[6], *abbr* voided[1]
**rh** destroyed *H5 3.3.42, R2 1.3.241*
> unavoided

**avoir** *Fr v*

*ai*
ɛ
**sp** a[1], ay[1], [i']ay[1]

*as*
a
**sp** as[1]

*avez*
a'vez
**sp** aue[1], aues[1], [m]aves[1], *emend of H5 4.4.51* l[ayt a][1]

*ayez*
a'jez
**sp** aye[1]

**avoirdupois** *n*
ˌavəɹdə'pəɪz
**sp** haber-de-pois[1]

**avouch** *n*
ə'vəʊʧ, -'vu:ʧ
**sp** auouch[1]

**avouch / ~s / ~ed** *v*
ə'vəʊʧ, -'vu:ʧ / -ɪz / *m* -ɪd
**sp** auouch[8] / auouch't[1], auouch-it[1] / auouches[2] / auouched[1]
**rh** avouch it budget *WT 4.3.22*

**avouchment** *n*
ə'vəʊʧmənt, -'vu:ʧ-
**sp** auouchment[1]

**avow** *v*
ə'vəʊ
**sp** auou[1], avow[1]

**await / ~s** *v*
ə'wɛ:t / -s
**sp** await[2] / awaits[1]

**awak·e / ~es / ~eth / ~ing / ~ed** *v*
ə'wɛ:k / -s / -əθ / -ɪn, -ɪŋ / -t
**sp** awake[76] / awakes[4], *abbr in s.d.* awa[1] / awaketh[1] / awaking[1] / awak'd[14], awaked[1], awak't[1]
**rh** make *MND 3.2.117*; sake *MND 2.2.108, 3.2.69, R3 5.3.150, S 61.10*; take *Tem 2.1.310* / maketh, slaketh *Luc 1675*

**awaken / ~s / ~ed** *v*
ə'wɛ:kən / -z / -d
**sp** awaken[1] / awakens[1] / awakened[1]

**awaking** *n*
ə'wɛ:kɪn, -ɪŋ
**sp** awaking[1]

**award / ~s** *v*
ə'wɑ:ɹd / -z
**sp** award[1] / awards[2]

**away** *adv*
ə'wɛ:
**sp** awaie[9], away[819], a-way[6], a way[1]
**rh** bay *PP 11.14*; betray *S 96.11*; bewray *KL 3.6.108* [*Q*]; clay *Ham 5.1.210, Luc 608, R2 1.1.178*; day *AW 3.2.129, 1H4 4.1.131, H5 4.2.60, 4.3.131, JC 5.5.80, KJ 1.1.166, LLL 4.1.107, Luc 1281, MA 4.1.249, MM 4.1.1, MND 3.2.51, MV 3.2.310, PP 18.30, R2 3.2.217, RJ 3.5.26, S 73.7, 75.14, 145.12, TG 1.3.87, TNK 1.5.1*; day, gay *PP 15.14*; day, stay *Luc 1010*; decay *Luc 1169, PP 14.2, S 11.8, 64.12, 80.13*; delay *1H4 3.2.179, 1H6 4.3.45*; dismay *Ham 4.1.44*; fray, say *MND 3.2.343*; gay *S 68.6*; hay, play *LLL 5.1.150* [*F line end*]; lay *Luc 259, 1056*; lay, say *Luc 1796*; may *Tit 1.1.289*; may, stay *LLL 2.1.112*; nay *TNK 3.5.72*; obey *R2 3.2.209*; play *AW 4.4.25, Ham 3.2.283, S 98.13, TC Prol.28*; pray *TS 1.2.225*; prey *MND 2.2.155*; say *AY 3.3.93, CE 4.2.27, Luc 1711, R2 1.3.244, 5.5.96, RJ 2.4.193, 5.3.67, TG 3.1.101, VA 255, 807*; slay *VA 763*; stay *CE 3.2.193, 5.1.336, 1H6 4.5.31, 4.6.41, 2H6 5.2.72, KJ 2.1.415, 4.3.7, KL 2.4.80, LLL 4.3.210, 5.2.625, MND 2.1.144, MV 2.6.58, 3.2.323, R2 4.1.197, 5.5.96, R3 1.4.285, RJ 1.1.159, 3.1.135, 5.3.160, S 74.2, 92.1, 143.2, TN 5.1.140, TS 5.1.137*; stray *TG 1.1.75*; today *2H6 2.1.157, LLL 4.3.269, MV 3.4.83*; unsay *MND 1.1.180*
> cast-, run-away

**awe** *n*
=
**sp** awe[15]
**rh** flaw Ham *5.1.211*; law *Per Prol.36, R3 5.3.311*; saw *Luc 245*

**awe / ~d** *v*
=
**sp** awe[2], awe-[him][1] / aw'd[1]
> overawe

**a-weary** *adj*
ə'wi:rəɪ, ə'we-
**sp** awearie[1], a wearie[2], a-weary[2], a weary[2]
> weary

**a-weeping** *n*
ə'wi:pɪn, -ɪŋ
**sp** a weeping[1]
> weep

**aweless** *adj*
=
**sp** awelesse[1], awlesse[1]

**awful** *adj*
=
**sp** awefull[3], awfull[4]

**awhile** *adv*
ə'ʍəɪl
**sp** awhile[27], a-while[26], [littell]-a-while[1], a while[59]
**rh** beguile *Ham 3.2.235*; reconcile *Per 4.4.21*; smile *Per 1.4.107, TNK Epil.3*
> while

**awkward** *adj*
'ɔ:kwəɹd
**sp** aukward[2], awk-ward[1]

**awl** *n*
ɔ:l
**sp** aule[1]
**pun** *JC 1.1.21* awl, all, withal

**a-wooing** *v*
ə'wu:ɪn, -ɪŋ
**sp** a woing[1], a wooing[1]
> woo

**awork** *adv*
ə'wɔ:ɹk
**sp** aworke[1], a-worke[3]
> work

**awry** *adj*
ə'rəɪ
**sp** awrie[1], awry[4]
**rh** majesty *R2 2.2.19*

**axe / ~'s** *n*
=
**sp** axe[19] / axes[1]

**axle-tree** *n*
'aksəl-ˌtri:
**sp** axletree[1], axle-tree[1]

**ay [yes]** *adv*
əɪ
**sp** ay[2], I[699]
**rh** die *R2 3.3.175*; eye *LLL 2.1.123*; I *RJ 1.3.58*
**pun** *RJ 3.2.45ff* eye, I [pronoun, letter]

**aye [alas]** *interj*
ɛ:
**sp** ay[6], ay[-me][1], aye[18]

**aye [always]** *adv*
ɛ:
**sp** aie[1], aye[15]
**rh** obey *Tim 5.1.50*

**ayez** *Fr*
> avoir

**azure** *adj*
'azəɹ
**sp** azure[1]

**azured** *adj*
'azəɹd
**sp** azur'd[2]

**B** [letter] *n*
=
**sp** B[1]

**B** [music] *n*
=
**sp** beeme [=B mi][1]

**baa** [sheep sound] *interj*
=
**sp** ba[2], baa[1]

**babble** *n / v*
=
**sp** babble[1] / babble[1]
> bibble-babble

**babbling** *adj*
'bablın, -ıŋ
**sp** babling[6]

**babe / ~s** *n*
bɛ:b, bab / -z
**sp** babe[34], [new-borne]-babe[1] / babes[22]
**rh** drab, slab *Mac 4.1.30*
> cradle-babe

**baboon / ~'s / ~s** *n*
*m* bə'bu:n, 'bab- / -z
**sp** baboon[1], baboone[2] / baboones[1] / baboones[1]

**baby** *adj*
'bɛ:bəı
**sp** baby[1], baby-[brow, daughter, eyes][3]
> aglet-baby

**bab·y / ~y's / ~ies** *n*
'bɛ:bəı / -z
**sp** babie[3], baby[10] / babies[1] / babies[2], babyes[1]

**Babylon** *n*
=, *Evans MW 3.1.23* 'pabılɒn
**sp** Babylon[2] / *Evans* Pa-bilon[1]

**baccare** *mock Lat* *v*
*Gremio TS 2.1.73* ba'kɑ:rɛ:
**sp** bacare[1]

**Bacchanals** *n*
ˌbakə'nɑ:lz
**sp** Bachanals[1], Backenals[1]

**Bacchus** *n*
'bakəs
**sp** Bacchus[1], Bachus[1]

**bachelor / ~s** *n*
'baʧləɹ, -ʧəl- / -z
**sp** bachelor[1], batcheler[4], batcheller[3], batchellor[4], batchellour[3], batchelor[2], batchelour[1] / batchelers[1], batchellers[1], batchellors[1]

**bachelorship** *n*
'baʧləɹˌʃıp
**sp** bach'ler-ship[1]

**back** *adj*
=
**sp** back[1], backe[2]
> crook-, horse-, keeper-back; unbacked

**back** *adv*
=
**sp** back[35], [pluck]-back[1], backe[199]
**rh** alack *S 65.11*; black *Luc 1583*; slack *PP 18.24*; wrack *Luc 843, 965, S 126.6, VA 557*

**back / ~s** *n*
=
**sp** back[11], backe[71] / backes[14], backs[7]
**rh** *1* crack *KJ 2.1.145*; lack *AC 4.14.58, VA 300*; wrack *Mac 5.5.52*; **rh** *2* neck *VA 594*

**back / ~ing / ~ed** *v*
= / 'bakın, -ıŋ / =
**sp** back[2], backe[3] / backing[2] / back'd[4], back't[1], backt[2]

**back-bite** *v*
*m* ˌbak-'bəıt
**sp** backe-bite[1]

**backing** *n*
'bakın, -ıŋ
**sp** backing[2], bac-king[1]

**backside** *n*
'baksəıd
**sp** backe-side[1]
> side

**backsword** *adj*
'bakˌsɔ:ɹd
**sp** back-sword-[man][1]

**back-trick** *n*
=
**sp** backe-tricke[1]

**backward** *adj / adv / n*
'bakwəɹd
**sp** backward[2] / backeward[2], backward[13], back-ward[1] / [dark]-backward[1]

**backwardly** *adv*
'bakwəɹdləı
**sp** backwardly[1]

**backwards** *adv*
'bakwəɹdz
**sp** backwards[1]

**back-wounding** *adj*
*m* ˌbak-'wəʊndɪn, -ɪŋ
**sp** back-wounding[1]
> wounding

**bacon / ~s** *n*
'bɛ:kən / -z
**sp** bacon[1] / ba-cons[1]

**bacon-fed** *adj*
'bɛ:kən-ˌfed
**sp** bacon-fed[1]
> feed

**bad** *adj / adv / n*
=, *Evans MW 3.3.207* pad / =
**sp** bad[93], badde[1], *Evans* pad[1] / bad[1] / bad[19]
**rh** *adj* had *S 67.14*; mad *CE 5.1.67, S 140.11* / **rh** *n* glad *Per 2.Chorus.37*; mad *Luc 995*
> worse

**bade**
> bid

**badge / ~s** *n*
=
**sp** badg[1], badge[12] / badges[3]

**badge / ~d** *v*
=
**sp** badg'd[1]
> office-badge

**badly** *adv*
'badləɪ
**sp** badly[1]

**badness** *n*
=
**sp** badnesse[3]

**baffle / ~d** *v*
=
**sp** baffle[2] / baffel'd[3]

**bag / ~s** *n*
=
**sp** bag[5], bagge[3] / bagges[1], baggs[1], bags[6]
**rh** rags *KL 2.4.48*
> cloak-, honey-, money-, sand-bag

**baggage** *n*
=
**sp** baggage[7]

**Bagot** *n*
'bagət
**sp** Bagot[11]

**bagpipe** *n*
'bagpəɪp
**sp** bagpipe[1], bag-pipe[3]

**bagpiper** *n*
'bagpəɪpəɹ
**sp** bag-piper[1]
> pipe

**bail** *n / v*
bɛ:l
**sp** baile[9], bale[1], bayle[1] / baile[3], bayle[1]
**rh** jail *S 133.10*

**bailiff** *n*
'bɛ:lɪf
**sp** bayliffe[1]
> bum-baily

**baille** *Fr v*
baj
*sp MW 1.4.86 emend of* ballow[1]

**bairn / ~s** *n*
bɐɹn / -z
**sp** barne[2] / barnes[1]
**pun** *MA 3.4.43* barn

**bais·er / ~ant / ~ées** *Fr v*
bɛ'zɑ̃ / bɛ'ze
**sp** baisant[1] / baisee[1], buisse[1]

**bait / ~s** *n*
bɛ:t / -s
**sp** bait[2], baite[5], bayt[1] / baites[1], baits[1]
**rh** *1* straight *S 129.7*; **rh** *2* conceit *PP 4.11*
> bear-baiting

**bait / ~s / ~ing / ~ed** *v*
bɛ:t / -s / 'bɛ:t·ɪn, -ɪŋ / -ɪd
**sp** bait[2], baite[7] / bayts[1] / baiting[1] / baited[5], bayted[1]
**rh** state *CE 2.1.94*
**pun** *WT 2.3.92* beat

**baited** *adj*
'bɛ:tɪd
**sp** baited[1]

**baiting-place** *n*
'bɛ:tɪn-ˌplɛ:s, -ɪŋ-
**sp** bayting place[2]
> place

**Bajazeth / ~'s** *n*
ˌbajə'zets
**sp** Baiazeths[1]

**bake / ~s / ~d** *v*
bɛ:k / -s / *m* -t, 'bɛ:kɪd
**sp** bake[2] / bakes[1] / bak'd[5], baked[1], bakte[1]
**rh** snake *Mac 4.1.13*
> unbaked

**baked-meats** *n*
*m* 'bɛ:kt-ˌmi:ts, ˌbɛ:kt-'mi:ts
**sp** bakt-meats[1], bakte meates[1]

**baker / ~'s / ~s'** *n*
'bɛ:kəɹs
**sp** bakers / bakers

**baking** *n*
'bɛ:kɪn, -ɪŋ
**sp** baking

**balance** *n / v*
=
**sp** ballance[9] / ballance[1]
> well-balanced

**bald** *adj*
bɑ:ld
**sp** bald[17]

**bald-pate** *n*
'bɑ:ld-ˌpɛ:t
**sp** bald-pate[1]

**bald-pated** *adj*
'ba:ld-ˌpɛ:tɪd
**sp** bald-pated[1]

**baldric** *n*
'bɔ:drɪk
**sp** baldricke[1]

**baleful** *adj*
'bɛ:lfʊl
**sp** balefull[7]

**balk / ~ed** *v*
bɔ:k / -t
**sp** balke[1] / balk'd[1], baulkt[1]
**rh** hawk *Luc 696*

**ball / ~s** *n*
bɑ:l / -z
**sp** ball[5] / balles[4], balls[3], [Paris]-balls[1], bals[3]
> eye-, foot-, snow-ball

**ballad / ~s** *n*
'baləd, -ət / -s
**sp** ballad[10], ballet[4] / bal-lads[1], ballads[4]

**ballad / ~s** *v*
'baləds, -əts
**sp** ballads[1]

**ballad-maker / ~s** *n*
'baləd-ˌmɛ:kəɹz, -lət-
**sp** ballad-makers[2], ballet-makers[1]
> make

**ballad-monger / ~s** *n*
'baləd-ˌmɤŋgəɹz, -lət-
**sp** ballad-mongers[1]

**ballast** *n*
=
**sp** ballast[1]

**ballasting** *n*
*m* 'baləsˌtɪn, -ɪŋ
**sp** ballasting[1]

**ballow** *n*
'balə, -o:
**sp** ballow[1]
> baille

**balm / ~s** *n*
bɔ:m / -z
**sp** balme[14] / balmes[1]
**rh** palm *VA 27*
> embalm

**balm** *v*
bɔ:m
**sp** balme[1]

**balmy** *adj*
'bɔ:məɪ
**sp** balmy[1]

**balsamum** *n*
*m* 'bɑlsəˌmɤm, 'bɒl-
**sp** balsamum[1]

**balsom** *n*
'bɑlsəm, 'bɒl-
**sp** balsome[1]

**Balthazar** *n*
*m* 'bɑltəˌzɐ:ɹ, -əzəɹ, 'bɒl-
**sp** Balthasar[7], Balthaser[2], Balthazar[3], Balthazer[1]

**ban / ~s** *n*
=
**sp** ban[1] / bannes[1], bans[1]

**ban** *v*
=
**sp** ban[2], banne[1]

**'ban**
> Caliban

**Banbury** *n*
'banbrəɪ, -bər-
**sp** Banbery[1]

**band / ~s** *n*
=
**sp** band[24] / bands[14]
**rh** hand *Luc 255, MA 3.1.114, MND 3.2.110, VA 225, 363* / hands *AY 5.4.126, Ham 3.2.169, Tem Epil.9*

**band / ~ing** *v*
'bandɪn, -ɪŋ
**sp** banding[1]
> unbanded

**bandetto** *adj*
ban'deto:
**sp** bandetto[1]

**bandett·o / ~i** *n*
ban'deti:
**sp** bandetti[1]

**bandog / ~s** *n*
'bandɒgz
**sp** bandogs[1]

**band·y / ~ied** *v*
'bandəɪ / -d
**sp** bandie[2], bandy[5] / bandied[1]

**bandying** *n*
*m* 'bandəɪɪn, -ɪŋ
**sp** bandying[2]

**bane** *n*
bɛ:n
**sp** baine[1], bane[5]
**rh** Dunsinane *Mac 5.3.59*; lane *Cym 5.3.58*
> ratsbane

**bane / ~d** *v*
bɛ:nd
**sp** bain'd[1]

**bang** *n*
=
**sp** bang[1]

**bang / ~ed** *v*
=
**sp** bangd[1], bang'd[1]

**banish / ~ed** *v*
= / *m* 'banɪʃt, -ɪˌʃɪd
**sp** banish[36] / banish'd[46], banished[31], banisht[12]

**banished** *adj*
*m* 'banɪʃt, -ɪˌʃɪd
**sp** banish'd[21], banished[3], banisht[10]

**banisher / ~s** *n*
*m* 'banɪˌʃɐ:ɹz
**sp** banishers[1]

**banishment** *n*
*m* 'banɪʃˌment, -nɪʃmənt, -nʃ-
**sp** banishment[37]
**rh** consent *Luc 1855*; content *AY 1.3.136*; lent *R2 1.3.147*; spent *R2 1.3.212, RJ 3.2.131*

**Banister** *n*
*m* 'banɪˌstɐːɹ
**sp** Banister[1]

**bank / ~s** *n*
=
**sp** banke[13] / bankes[9], banks[3]
**rh** rank *VA 72* / ranks *Luc 1442*
> sea-bank

**bank / ~ed** *v*
=
**sp** bank'd[1]

**bankrupt** *adj*
'baŋkruːt, -rəʊt
**sp** bankrupt[4]

**bankrupt / ~s** *n*
'baŋkruːt, -rəʊt / -s
**sp** banckrout[1], bankerout[1], bankrout[3], bankrupt[1], banqu'rout[1] / bankrupts[1]

**bankrupt** *v*
*m* 'baŋkəˌruːt, -ˌrəʊt
**sp** bankerout[1]

**bann**
> banns

**banner / ~s** *n*
'banəɹ / -z
**sp** banner[3] / banners[7]

**banneret / ~s** *n*
'banəɹɪts
**sp** ban-nerets[1]

**banning** *adj*
'banɪn, -ɪŋ
**sp** banning[1]

**banns** *n*
bɛːnz
**sp** banes[4]

**banquet / ~s** *n*
'baŋkɪt / -s
**sp** banket[11], banquet[14] / banquets[2]

**banquet / ~ted** *v*
'baŋkɪt / -ɪd
**sp** banquet[5] / banquetted[1]

**banquetting** *n*
*m* 'baŋkɪˌtɪn, -ɪŋ
**sp** banquetting[2]

**Banquo / ~'s** *n*
'baŋkwoː / -z
**sp** Banquo[33], Banquoh[1], Banquo's [Banquo is][2] / Banquo's[3]

**baptism** *n*
'baptɪzəm
**sp** baptisme[3]

**Baptista / ~'s** *n*
bap'tiːsta / -z
**sp** Baptista[33] / Baptistas[6]

**baptize / ~d** *v*
'baptəɪzd
**sp** baptiz'd[1]

**bar / ~s** *n*
bɑːɹ / -z
**sp** bar[4], barre[8] / barres[5], bars[2]

**bar / ~rest / ~s / ~red** *v*
bɑːɹ / -st / -z / -d
**sp** barre[17] / barr'st[1], bar'st[1] / barres[3], bars[1] / bar'd[2], bard[2], barr'd[4]
**rh** war *S 46.3* / stars *S 25.3* / reward *AW 2.1.148*
> em-, un-bar; barred, strong-barred

**Bar** [name] *n*
bɑːɹ
**sp** Bar[1]

**barbarian** *adj*
bɑːɹ'barɪən
**sp** barbarian[1]

**barbarian / ~s** *n*
bɑːɹ'barɪən / -z
**sp** barbarian[1] / barbarians[1]

**barbarism** *n*
*m* 'bɑːɹbəˌrɪzm [*3 sylls*]
**sp** barbarisme[4]

**barbarous** *adj / n*
*m* 'bɑːɹbrəs, -bəˌrʏs
**sp** barbarous[18] / barbarous[1]

**Barbary** *adj / n*
*m* 'bɑːɹbrəɪ, -bəˌrəɪ
**sp** Barbarie[1], Barbary[4] / Barbarie[2], Barbary[4]

**Barbary-a** [*song*] *n*
'bɑːɹbəˌrəɪ-ə
**sp** three, a[1]
**rh** three-a *TNK 3.5.61*

**Barbason** *n*
'bɑːɹbəsən
**sp** Barbason[2]

**barbed** *adj*
*m* 'bɑːɹbɪd
**sp** barbed[2]

**barber / ~'s / ~s** *n*
'bɑːɹbəɹ / -z
**sp** barber[1] / barbers[6] / barbars[1]

**barber / ~ed** *v*
'bɑːɹbəɹd
**sp** barber'd[1]

**barber-monger** *n*
'bɑːɹbəɹ-ˌmʏŋgəɹ
**sp** barber-monger[1]

**bard / ~s** *n*
bɑːɹdz
**sp** bards[1]

**Bardolph / ~'s** *n*
'bɑːɹdɒlf / -s
**sp** Bardol[1], Bardolf[2], Bardolfe[41], Bar-dolfe[1], Bardolffe[1], Bardolph[33], Bar-dolph[1] / Bardolphs[3]

**bare** *adj*
bɛːɹ
**sp** bare[39], bare-[head][1]
**rh** care *PP 12.4*
> threadbare

**bare / ~d** *v*
bɛːɹ / -d
**sp** bear[1] / bar'd[1], bar'de[1]

**Bare** [name]
> Barnes

**bare-bone** *n*
'bɛːɹ-ˌboːn
**sp** bare-bone[1]

**bare-faced** *adj / adv*
'bɛːɹ-ˌfɛːst
**sp** bare-fac'd[1], bare fac'd[1] / bare-fac'd[1]

**barefoot** *adj / adv*
'bɛːɹˌfʊt
**sp** bare-fote[2] / barefoot[1], bare-foot[3], bare-foote[1]

**bare-gnawn** *adj*
'bɛːɹ-ˌnɔːn, -gn-
**sp** bare-gnawne[1]
> gnaw

**bare-headed** *adj*
ˌbɛːɹ-'edɪd, -'he-
**sp** bare-headed[5], bare headed[1], *in s.d.* bare head[1]
> head

**barely** *adv*
'bɛːɹləɪ
**sp** barely[4]

**bareness** *n*
'bɛːɹnəs
**sp** barenesse[2]

**bare-picked** *adj*
'bɛːɹ-ˌpɪkt
**sp** bare-pickt[1]
> pick

**bare-ribbed** *adj*
'bɛːɹ-ˌrɪbd
**sp** bare-rib'd[1]
> rib

**barful** *adj*
'bɑːɹfʊl
**sp** barrefull[1]

**bargain / ~s** *n*
'bɑːɹgɪn / -z
**sp** bargaine[17], bar-gaine[1] / bargaines[3]

**bargain / ~ed** *v*
'bɑːɹgɪn / -d
**sp** bargaine[1] / bargain'd[2]

**barge** *n*
bɑːɹʤ
**sp** barge[5]

**Bargulus** *n*
*m* 'bɑːɹgəˌlɤs
**sp** Bargulus[1]

**baring** *n*
'bɛːrɪn, -ɪŋ
**sp** baring[1]

**bark** [animal] **/ ~est / ~s /** *VA* **~eth** *v*
bɑːɹk / -st / -s / 'bɑːɹkəθ
**sp** barke[10] / barkst[1] / barkes[1] / barketh[1]
**rh** hark *Tem 1.2.383*; park *VA 240* / marketh *VA 459*

**bark** [tree] **/ ~s** *n*
bɑːɹk / -s
**sp** barke[7] / barkes[4]

**bark** [tree] **/ ~ed** *v*
bɑːɹk / -t
**sp** barke[1] / barkt[1]

**barking** *n*
'bɑːɹkɪn, -ɪŋ
**sp** barking[2]

**barky** *adj*
'bɑːɹkəɪ
**sp** barky[1]

**barlet**
> martlet

**barley** *n*
'bɑːɹləɪ
**sp** barley[1]

**barley broth** *n*
'bɑːɹləɪ ˌbrɒθ
**sp** barly broth[1]
> broth

**barm** *n*
bɑːɹm
**sp** barme[1]
**rh** harm *MND 2.1.38*

**barn / ~s** *n*
bɑːɹn / -z
**sp** barne[2] / barnes[3]
**pun** *MA 3.4.43* bairns
> bairn

**barnacle / ~s** *n*
*m* 'bɑːɹnkəlz, -nək-
**sp** barnacles[1]

**Barnardine / ~'s** *n*
'bɑːɹnəɹˌdəɪn / -z
**sp** Barnardine[17], Bernar-dine[1] / Barnardines[1]

**Barnardo** *n*
bəɹ'nɑːɹdoː
**sp** Barnardo[7]

**Barnes** *n*
bɑːɹnz
**sp** [*Q*] *emend of F 2H4 3.2.19* Bare

**Barnet** *n*
'bɑːɹnət
**sp** Barnet[2]

**baron / ~s** *n*
=
**sp** baron[1] / barons[6]

**barony** *n*
*m* 'barənəɪ, 'bɑːɹnəɪ
**sp** barony[1]

**barque** *n*
bɑːɹk
**sp** backe[1], barke[27]
**rh** hark *Per 5.Chorus.22*; mark *S 116.7*

**Barrabas** *n*
*m* 'barə,bas
**sp** Barrabas[1]

**barred** *adj*
bɑ:ɹd
**sp** barr'd[1]

**barred-up** *adj*
'bɑ:ɹd-,ɤp
**sp** barr'd vp[1]

**barrel / ~s** *n*
=
**sp** barrelles[1]
> beer-barrel

**barren** *adj / n*
=, *m S 12.5* ba'ren
**sp** barraine[3], barren[31] / barren[1]

**barrenness** *n*
'barənəs
**sp** barrennesse[1]

**barren-spirited** *adj*
'barən,sprəɪtɪd, -,spɪɹt-
**sp** barren spirited[1]
> spirited

**barricado / ~es** *n*
barɪ'kɑ:do: / -z
**sp** barracado[1], barricado[1] / bari-cadoes[1]

**barrow** *n*
'barə, -ro:
**sp** barrow[1]

**Barson** *n*
'bɑ:ɹsən
**sp** Barson[1]

**barter / ~ed** *v*
'bɑ:ɹtəɹd
**sp** barter'd

**Bartholomew** *n*
*m* 'bɑ:ɹtl,mju:
**sp** Bartholmew[2]

**Bartholomew-tide** *n*
'bɑ:ɹtlmju:-,təɪd
**sp** Bartholo-mew-tyde[1]
> tide

**Basan** *n*
'basən
**sp** Basan[1]

**base / ~r / ~est** *adj*
bas, bɛ:s / 'bas·əɹ, 'bɛ:- / -əst
**sp** bace[2], base[138], base-[mettle] [1] / baser[11] / basest[9]
**rh** disgrace *1H6 4.6.21*; face *Luc 202*; grace *Cym 4.2.26, R2 3.3.180, Tim 3.5.94*
**pun** *TS 3.1.45* bass

**base** *n / v*
bas, bɛ:s
**sp** bace[1], base[12] / base[1]

**base-born** *adj*
'bas-,bɔ:ɹn, 'bɛ:s-
**sp** base-borne[3]
> bear

**based**
> strong-based

**baseless** *adj*
'basləs, 'bɛ:s-
**sp** baselesse[1]

**basely** *adv*
'basləɪ, 'bɛ:s-
**sp** basely[9]

**baseness** *n*
'basnəs, 'bɛ:s-
**sp** basenes[2], basenesse[16]

**bashful** *adj*
=, *Fluellen H5 4.8.70* 'paʃfʊl
**sp** bashfull[6], *Fluellen* pashfull[1]
> unbashful

**bashfulness** *n*
=
**sp** bashfulnesse[1]

**basilisco-like** *adj*
basɪ'lɪsko:-,ləɪk
**sp** basilisco-like[1]

**basilisk / ~s** *n*
'basɪlɪsk / -s
**sp** basiliske[3], basilisque[1] / basiliskes[4]

**Basimecu** [name] *n*
'basmɪ,ku:
**sp** Basimecu[1]

**basin / ~s** *n*
'bɛ:sən / -z
**sp** bason[5] / basons[1]

**Basingstoke** *n*
'bɛ:zɪn,sto:k, -ɪŋ-
**sp** Basingstoke[1]

**basis** *n*
'basɪs
**sp** basis[6]

**bask / ~ed** *v*
baskt
**sp** bask'd[1]

**basket / ~s** *n*
'baskɪt / -s
**sp** basket[22], bas-ket[1] / baskets[1]
> alms-, buck-basket

**basket-hilt** *adj*
'baskɪt-,ɪlt, -,hɪlt
**sp** basket-hilt[1]
> hilt

**bass** *adj*
bas
**sp** base[1]

**bass / ~es** *n*
bas / 'basɪz
**sp** base[2] / bases[1]
**pun** *TS 3.1.45* base

**Bassanio / ~'s** *n*
bə'sɑ:nɪo: [*3 sylls*] / -z
**sp** Bassanio[39], Bassanio's [Bassanio is][1], Bassiano[1] / Bassanios[2], Bassanio's[2], Bassianos[1], Bassiano's[1]
**rh** so *MV 2.8.39*

**Basset** *n*
=
**sp** Basset[1], Bassit[1]

**Bassianus / ~'s** *n*
ˌbasɪˈɑːnəs, -ˈan-
**sp** Bassianus[21], Bassianuss[1] / Bassianus[3]

**bass-viol** *n*
ˌbas-ˈvəɪəl
**sp** base-viole[1]

**basta** *Ital interj*
ˈbasta
**sp** basta[1]

**bastard** *adj*
ˈbastəɹd
**sp** bastard[20]

**bastard / ~'s / ~s** *n*
ˈbastəɹd / -z
**sp** bastard[68], bastard-[vertues, braynes][2], ba-stard[1], basterd[1] / bastards[2] / bastards[15]

**bastardizing** *n*
ˈbastəɹdəɪzɪn, -ɪŋ
**sp** bastardizing[1]

**bastardly** *adv*
ˈbastəɹdləɪ
**sp** bastardly[1]

**bastardy** *n*
*m* ˈbastəɹˌdəɪ
**sp** bastardie[7], bastardy[1]
**rh** *1* eye *Luc 522*; **rh** *2* obloquy *Luc 522*; tree *Tit 5.1.48*

**baste / ~s / ~d** *v*
basts / ˈbastɪd
**sp** bastes[1] / basted[1]

**bastinado** *n*
ˌbastɪˈnɑːdoː
**sp** bastinado[3]

**basting** *n*
ˈbastɪn, -ɪŋ
**sp** basting[2]

**bat / ~'s / ~s** *n*
=
**sp** bat[3] / batts[1] / bats[2], batts[1]
**rh** sat *LC 64*

**bataille / ~s** *Fr n*
baˈtɑːj
**sp** battailes[1]
> battle

**batch** *n*
=
**sp** batch[1]

**bate** *n*
bɛːt
**sp** bate[1]
> breed-bate

**bate / ~s / ~ing / ~d** *v*
bɛːt / -s / ˈbɛːtɪn, -ɪŋ / ˈbɛːtɪd
**sp** bate[13] / bates[1] / bayting[1] / bated[6]
**rh** translated *MND 1.1.190*
> abate, unbated

**bated** *adj*
ˈbɛːtɪd
**sp** bated[2]

**Bates** *n*
bɛːts
**sp** Bates[2]

**bat-fowling**
> a-bat-fowling

**bath / ~s** *n*
baθ / -s
**sp** bath[3] / bathes[1]

**bath** *v*
baθ
**sp** bath[1]

**bath·e / ~ing / ~d** *v*
bɛːð / ˈbɛːðɪn, -ɪŋ / bɛːðd
**sp** bathe[5] / bathing[1] / bath'd[5]

**batler** *n*
ˈbatləɹ
**sp** batler[1]

**battalia** *n*
bəˈtaljə
**sp** battalia[1]

**battalion / ~s** *n*
=
**sp** battalians[1]

**batten** *v*
=
**sp** batten[2]

**batter / ~s / ~ing / ~ed** *v*
ˈbatəɹ / -z / -ɪn, -ɪŋ, ˈbatrɪn, -ɪŋ / -d
**sp** batter[2] / batters[3] / batte-ring[1] / batt'red[1], batter'd[1]
> unbattered

**battered** *adj*
ˈbatəɹd
**sp** batter'd[1]

**battering** *adj*
*m* ˈbatrɪn, -ɪŋ, -tər-
**sp** battering[1]

**battery** *n*
ˈbatrəɪ, -tər-
**sp** batterie[1], battery[6], batt'rie[1], battry[1], batt'ry[2]
**rh** flattery *VA 426*

**battle / ~'s / ~s** *n*
=, *Fluellen H5 4.7.93*
ˈpatl / -z
**sp** battaile[52], [scarse-cold]-battaile[1], bat-taile[2], battaile's [battle is][1], battel[1], battell[42], bat-tell[1], *Fluellen* pattle[1] / battailes[1] / battailes[17], battels[1]
> high-battled

**battle** *v*
=
**sp** battaile[1]

**battleaxe** *n*
=
**sp** battleaxe[1]

**battlements** *n*
=
**sp** battelments[1], battlements[7]

**batty** *adj*
'batəɪ
**sp** battie-[wings][1]

**bauble / ~s** *n*
'bɔ:bəl, 'bɑ:- / -z
**sp** bable[2], bauble[6] / baubles[1]

**baubling** *adj*
'bɔ:blɪn, -ɪŋ, 'bɑ:-
**sp** bawbling[1]

**baulk**
> balk

**bavin** *adj*
'bavɪn
**sp** bauin[1]

**bawcock** *n*
'bɔ:kɒk
**sp** bawcock[4]

**bawd / ~s** *n*
=
**sp** baud[13], bawd[25], bawde[1] / baudes[1], bauds[2], bawdes[2], bawds[1]
**rh** laud *Luc 623*; laud, thawed *Luc 886*

**bawdry** *n*
'bɔ:drəɪ
**sp** baudrey[1], baudry[1], bawdrie[1]
**rh** Audrey *AY 3.3.87*

**bawdy** *adj*
'bɔ:dəɪ
**sp** baudy[3], bawdy[5]

**bawdy-house / ~s** *n*
'bɔ:dəɪˌəʊs, -ˌhəʊs / -əʊzɪz
**sp** bawdy-house[4] / bawdie-houses[1]
> house

**bawling** *adj*
'bɔ:lɪn, -ɪŋ
**sp** bawling[1]

**bay** *adj*
bɛ:
**sp** bay[3]

**bay / ~s** *n*
bɛ: / -z
**sp** baie[1], bay[17] / bayes[2]
**rh** away *PP 11.13*; way *VA 877*

**bay / ~s / ~ing / ~d** *v*
bɛ: / -z / 'bɛ:ɪn, -ɪŋ / bɛ:d
**sp** bay[3] / baes[2] / baying[1] / bay'd[1], bayed[2]

**bay-tree / ~s** *n*
'bɛ:-ˌtri:z
**sp** bay-trees[1]
> tree

**bay window** *n*
ˌbɛ:-'wɪndəz, -do:z
**sp** bay windoes[1]

**Baynard / ~'s** *n*
'bɛ:nəɹdz
**sp** Baynards[2]

**Bayonne** *n*
bɛ'jɒn
**sp** Bayon[1]

**be / beest / being / been** *v*
*str* bi:, *unstr* bɪ
**sp** be[6427], bee[303], bee['t] [be it][6], be [gon][2], be[gone][1], be's [be his][3], be [sworne][1], be't [be it][8], ['twill]be[1], [wil]be[2]
**rh** *1* agree, me *LLL 2.1.209*; decree *LLL 4.3.213, S 93.11*; dignity, he *Cym 5.4.55*; fee *VA 607*; free *MM 3.2.36, Oth 1.2.99, Tem Epil.19*; free, see *LC 103*; G *R3 1.1.40, 57*; he *KJ 2.1.508, LLL 4.2.28, R2 2.1.154, TC 1.3.289, 5.9.5, TN 3.4.15*; knee *R2 5.3.97*; me *1H6 4.5.22, 2H4 4.5.221, 2H6 3.1.382, CE 2.2.211, Cym 4.2.28, H5 5.2.366, LC 223, Luc 1049, 1203, MND 4.1.85, Per 1.2.110, PP 1.14, R2 1.3.144, 2.1.91, RJ 2.3.86, S 35.13, 91.11, 132.3, 133.4, 138.14, Tem 4.1.104, TG 3.1.149, Tim 3.5.90, TN 4.1.64, TNK 3.5.9, WT 4.1.20, 4.4.304*; me, thee *Luc 1194*; see *AC 1.3.65, AY 2.4.84, Cor 5.3.129, H5 4.Chorus.53, Ham 5.1.295, LC 185, LLL 2.1.225, Luc 752, 1085, Mac 1.4.53, MM 1.3.54, MND 2.1.10, 3.2.115, 4.1.70, 5.1.272, MV 2.9.101, MW 5.5.67, RJ 1.2.31, S 56.9, 137.4, TC 1.2.285, TN 1.2.63, VA 937*; see, three *PP 15.2*; she *LLL 4.3.94, MND 1.1.226, Per 4.Chorus.20, PT62, TG 4.2.42*; thee *CE 3.2.65, Cym 3.5.159, 2H6 4.10.29, Luc 1211, R2 2.1.136, 4.1.200, 5.3.33, S 1.13, 3.13, 4.14, 44.8, 78.12, 101.12, 123.13, 126.11, 136.10, 140.12, 141.12, 142.12, 151.11, VA 155*; three *MND 5.1.398*; tree *AY 3.2.121, Ham 3.2.201, Mac 4.1.93, MW 5.5.78, PP 10.6, PT 3*; we *MND 5.1.394, Tim 3.5.46, TN 2.2.32*; ye *JC 4.3.129*; cannot be buried be *PT 62*; be it free it, see it *Luc 1209*; **rh** *2* amity, jollity, prosperity, solemnly, triumphantly *MND 4.1.85*; beggary *KJ 2.1.595*; company *LLL 5.2.225*; confederacy *MND 3.2.191*; cruelty *TN 1.5.276*; dignity *Cym 4.2.3, 5.4.55*; flattery *Tim 1.2.253*; humanity *Tim 3.6.104*; idolatry *S 105.3*; indignity *LLL 5.2.288*; infamy *Luc 1637*; infirmity *Luc 148*; integrity *LLL 5.2.355*; lady *LLL 2.1.194, 4.1.133*; mannerly *MV 2.9.101*; nativity *MND 5.1.404*; necessity *Per 2. Chorus.5*; sovereignty *LLL 4.1.37, Luc 38*; suddenly *AY 2.4.96*; **rh** *3* eye *VA 1066*
> am, are, art, is, was, were

***beest***
*str* bi:st; *unstr* bɪst
**sp** beest[12], bee'st[12], be'st[3]

***being***
*m* 'bi:ɪn, -ɪŋ; bi:n, bi:ŋ
**sp** beeing[8], bee-ing[2], being[592], be-ing[7]
**rh** seeing *S 121.2*
> being *n*

***been***
*str* bi:n, bɪn; *unstr* bɪn, bn
**sp** been[58], beene[359], bin[205], byn[1]
**rh** *1* seen *R2 5.6.28, S 97.1*; sheen Ham *3.2.167*; spleen *PP 6.8*; **rh** *2* sin *Luc 210*

***be with ye/you***
'bɪjə
**sp** b'uy[1], bu'y[1], buy'[1], buy'ye[1]

**beach** *n*
=
**sp** beach[5]

**beached** *adj*
*m* 'bi:ʧɪd
**sp** beached[2]

**beachy** *adj*
'bi:ʧəɪ
**sp** beachie[1]

**beacon** *n*
=
**sp** beacon[4]

**bead / ~s** *n*
=
**sp** bead[1] / beades[5], beads[4], beds[1]

**Bead** [name] *n*
=
**sp** Bede[1]

**beadle / ~s** *n*
=
**sp** beadle[8] / beadles[3]

**beads·man / ~men** *n*
'bi:dsmən
**sp** beades-man[1] / beads-men[1]

**beagle / ~s** *n*
=
**sp** beagle[1] / beagles[1]

**beak / ~s** *n*
=
**sp** beake[3] / beakes[1]

**beam / ~s** *n*
=
**sp** beame[11] / beames[25]
**rh** gleams [*emend*] *MND 5.1.264*; streams *MND 3.2.392*
> moon-, sun-beam

**beamed**
> daughter-beamed, sunbeamed

**bean / ~s** *n*
=
**sp** beanes[1]

**bean-fed** *adj*
=
**sp** bean-fed[1]
> feed

**bear / ~'s / ~s** *n*
bɛ:ɹ / -z
**sp** beare[38] / beares[1] / beares[13], bears[1]
**rh** *1* hair *MND 2.2.36*; **rh** *2* fear *MND 2.2.100*
> bug-, she-bear

**bear / ~est / ~s / ~eth / ~ing / bare / bore / ~st / borne** *v*
bɛ:ɹ, *Fluellen H5 4.8.35* pɛ:ɹ / -st / -z / 'bɛ:r·əθ / -ɪn, -ɪŋ / bɑ:ɹ / bɔ:ɹ / bɔ:ɹst / bɔ:ɹn
**sp** bare[2], bear[3], beare[473], bear't [bear it][2], *Fluellen* peare[1] / bearest[3], bearst[2], bear'st[6] / beares[91] / beareth[1] / bearing[46], bea-ring[1] / bare[8] / bore[27] / boar'st[1] / born[1], borne[75], [well] borne[1]
**rh** *1* appear *CE 3.1.16, S 80.6, TC 1.2.294*; clear *Tim 3.5.40*; dear, here *Luc 1292*; deer *AY 4.2.12*; ear, hear *Luc 1327*; ear *Luc 1419, S 8.8*; fear *Luc 612, Mac 3.5.30, 5.3.9, MND 5.1.22*; here *Luc 1474, R2 5.5.117*; here, tear [cry] *LC 53*; severe *MM 3.2.249*; tear [cry] *Luc 1132*; year *1H6 1.3.90*; **bear her** clear her, hear her *Luc 1321*; **bear thee** hear thee *Luc 670*; **rh** *2* hair *Luc 1132*; swear *Luc 1419, S 131.11*; tear [rip] *Luc 1474*; there *LLL 5.2.100, Tem 1.2.380*; wear *AY 4.2.12, S 77.3, VA 165*; **bear thee** tear thee [rip] *Luc 670*; **rh** *3* were *S 13.8*; **bear it** were it *Luc 1158* / **rh** *1* clears, tears [cry] *Luc 1712*; fears *LC 272*; hears *Oth 1.3.210*; tears [cry] *LC 19*; **rh** *2* characters *LC 19, Per 4.4.29* / **rh** *1* hearing *VA 430*; **rh** *2* swearing *S 152.4* / **bore it** wore it *AY 4.2.15* / scorn *Cym 5.2.6, 1H6 4.7.17*
> over-, under-bear; bull-, under-bearing; high-, just-, self-, shard-, stiff-borne

**bear-baiting / ~s** *n*
'bɛ:ɹ-ˌbɛ:tɪn, -ɪŋ / -z
**sp** beare-baiting[1], beare-bayting[1] / beare-baitings[1]
> bait

**beard** *n*
bɛ:ɹd, bɐ:ɹd, *Evans MW 4.2.182f* pɛ:ɹd, pɐ:ɹd / -z
**sp** beard[81], beard's [beard is][1], berd[1], *Evans* peard[2] / beards[13]
**rh** heard *LLL 2.1.189*; herd *S 12.8*
> grey-, lack-beard; scarce-, white-bearded

**beard / ~ed** *adj*
'bɛ:ɹdɪd, 'bɐ:ɹ-
**sp** bearded[3]

**beard / ~ed** *v*
bɛ:ɹd, bɐ:ɹd / 'bɛ:ɹdɪd, 'bɐ:ɹ-
**sp** beard[4] / bearded[1]

**beardless** *adj*
'bɛ:ɹdləs, 'bɐ:ɹd-
**sp** beardlesse[2]

**bearer / ~s** *n*
'bɛ:rəɹ / -z
**sp** bearer[6] / bearers[1]
> ape-, cup-, purse-, thunder-, torch-bearer

**bearherd, bearward** *n*
'bɛ:ɹˌɐ:ɹd, -ˌhɐ:ɹd
**sp** beard[1], beare-heard[2], berard[1], berrord[1]
> bear *n*

**bearing** *n*
'bɛ:rɪn, -ɪŋ
**sp** bearing[10], bea-ring[2]

**bearing-cloth** *n*
'bɛ:rɪn-ˌklɒθ, -ɪŋ-
**sp** bearing-cloath[1], bearing cloth[1]
> cloth

**bear-like** *adj*
'bɛ:ɹləɪk
**sp** beare-like[1]

**bearward**
> bearherd

**bear-whelp / ~s** *n*
'bɛ:ɹ-ˌʍelp / -s
**sp** beare-whelpe[1] / bear-whelpes[1]
> bear *n*

**beast / ~s** *n*
best, bi:st / -s
**sp** beast[69] / beastes[1], beasts[33]
**rh** blest *VA 326*; jest *LLL 2.1.208, VA 999*; rest *CE 5.1.84*
**pun** *MND 5.1.224* best; *Tim 4.3.327* abased
> horn-beast

**beast-like** *adj*
'best-ləɪk, 'bi:-
**sp** beast-like[1]

**beastliness** *n*
'bestlɪnəs, 'bi:-
**sp** beastlinesse[1]

**beastl·y / ~iest** *adj*
'bestləɪ, 'bi:- / -əst
**sp** beastly[15] [*Q TC 5.10.5* bestly] / beastliest[1]

**beastly** *adv*
'bestləɪ, 'bi:-
**sp** beastly[5]

**beat / ~s / ~ing / ~en** *v*
bi:t, bɛ:t, *Evans MW 1.1.66, Fluellen H5 5.1.39* pi:t, pɛ:t / -s / 'bi:tɪn, -ɪŋ, 'bɛ:t- / 'bi:tən, 'betən, *MW Evans 4.4.20* 'pi:tən, 'petən
**sp** beat[49], beate[77], *Evans* peat[1], *Fluellen* peate[1] / beates[12], beats[13] / beating[6] / beaten[38], *Evans* peaten[1]
**pun** *WT 2.3.92* bait
> dry-, over-beat

**beaten** *adj*
'bi:tən, 'betən
**sp** beaten[8]
> dry-, new-, weather-beaten

**beating** *adj / n*
'bi:tɪn, -ɪŋ, 'bɛ:t-
**sp** beating[1] / beating[9]
> bold-beating

**Beatrice** *n*
*m* 'bi:əˌtrɪs, -ət-, 'bi:t-, 'bet-
**sp** Beatrice[52], Bea-trice[1]

**Beau** [name]
> Le Beau

**Beaufort / ~'s** *n*
'bo:fəɹd / -z
**sp** Beauford[10], Beau-ford[1] / Beaufords[1]

**Beaumont** *n*
*m* bo:'mɒnt, *Fr* bo:'mɔ̃
**sp** Beaumond[1], Beaumont[2], Beumont[1]

**beauteous** *adj*
'bju:tɪəs [*2 sylls*]
**sp** beauteous[19], beautious[10]

**beautified** *adj*
*m* 'bju:tɪˌfəɪd
**sp** beautifed[1], beautified[1]

**beautiful** *adj*
*m* 'bju:tɪˌfʊl
**sp** beautiful[2], beautifull[12]

**beautif·y / ~ied** *v*
*m* 'bju:tɪˌfəɪ / -d
**sp** beautifie[3] / beautifide[1]
**rh** modesty, mortality *Luc 404*

**beaut·y / ~y's / ~ ies** *n*
'bju:təɪ / -z
**sp** beautie[64], beau-tie[1], beauties [beauty is][1], beauty[82], [arched]-beauty[1], beuty[1] / beauties[11] / beauties[10]
**rh** duty *Luc 496, VA 167* / duties *Luc 13*

**beaut·y / ~ied** *v*
'bju:təɪd
**sp** beautied[1]

**beauty-waining** *adj*
'bju:təɪ-ˌwɛ:nɪn, -ɪŋ
**sp** beautie-waining[1]
> waining

**beaver / ~s** *n*
'bi:vəɹ / -z
**sp** beauer[4], beuer[2] / beauers[1]

**became**
> become

**because,** *abbr* **cause** *conj*
=
**sp** because[178], be-cause[5], *abbr* cause[2]

**bechance / ~d** *v*
bɪ'ʧɔ:ns, -'ʧans / *m* -t, -ɪd
**sp** bechance[1] / bechanced[1], bechaunc'd[1]
> chance

**beck / ~s** *n*
=
**sp** beck[1], becke[3] / beckes[1]
**rh** check *S 58.5*

**beck / ~s / ~ed** *v*
=
**sp** becks[1] / beck'd[1]

**beckon / ~s / ~ing / ~ed** *v*
= / 'beknɪn, -ɪŋ / =
**sp** beckens[2], beckons[1] / beckning[1] / becken'd[1]
**rh** reckoning *TNK 3.5.128*

**becom·e / ~est / ~es / ~ing / ~ed / became** *v*
bɪ'kɤm / -st / -z / -ɪn, -ɪŋ / -d / bɪ'kɛ:m
**sp** becom[2], become[134], be-come[4], becom't [become it][1] / becom'st[2] / becomes[58], becoms[3] / becomming[3] / becom'd[2] / became[24]
**rh** becomes you instruct you *TS 4.2.121*
> come, misbecome

**becomed** *adj*
*m* bɪ'kɤmɪd
**sp** becomed[1]

**becoming** *adj*
bɪ'kɤmɪn, -ɪŋ
**sp** becomming[2]
> unbecoming

**becoming / ~s** *n*
bɪ'kɤmɪnz, -ɪŋ-
**sp** becommings[1]

**bed / ~s** *n*
=, *Evans MW 3.1.18* pedz

**sp** bed[242], [maiden]-bed[1], [prest]-bed[1], bedde[2] / beds[23], *Evans* peds[1]
**rh** bred *Luc 938*; dead *Cym 4.2.357, Ham 3.2.195*; dread *Luc 169*; enamelled *CE 2.1.108*; fed *TC 5.8.20, VA 397*; head *Luc 776, MND 2.2.45, 4.1.1, RJ 2.3.30, S 27.1*; head, imagined *Luc 1619*; head, misled *Luc 366*; head, shed *Luc 684*; head, sped *MV 2.9.70*; honoured *AY 5.4.139*; led *Luc 301*; maidenhead *Per 3.Chorus.9, RJ 3.2.136*; managed *CE 3.2.17*; married *RJ 1.5.135*; questioned *Luc 120*; red *VA 108*; sped *TS 5.2.183*; undishonoured *CE 2.2.154*; unwed *CE 2.1.27*; visited *MND 3.2.429*; wed *AW 2.3.90, Ham 4.5.67, Per 2.5.95, PP 18.47*; widowed *RJ 3.2.134* / heads *Per 2.3.98, TN 5.1.398*
> a-, bridal-, bride-, child-, day-, death-, field-, lily-, love-, maiden-, marriage-, standing-, truckle-bed

**bed / ~ded** *v*
=
**sp** bed / bedded[2]

**bedabble / ~ed** *v*
bɪ'dabəld
**sp** bedabbled[1]

**bedash / ~ed** *v*
bɪ'daʃt
**sp** bedash'd[1]
> dash

**bedaub / ~ed** *v*
=
**sp** bedawb'd[1]
> daub

**bedazzle / ~d** *v*
=
**sp** bedazled[1]
> dazzle

**bed-chamber** *n*
'bed-ˌʧambəɹ
**sp** bed-chamber[6]
> chamber

**bedclothes** *n*
'bed-ˌklo:z, -o:ðz
**sp** bed-cloathes[1]
> clothes

**bedded** *adj*
=
**sp** bedded[1]

**bedeck** *v*
=
**sp** bedecke[1]

**bedecking** *adj*
bɪ'dekɪn, -ɪŋ
**sp** bedecking[1]

**bedew** *v*
bɪ'dju:
**sp** bedew[1]

**bedfellow / ~s** *n*
'bedfelə, -lo: / -z
**sp** bedfellow[9], bed-fellow[3] / bed-fellowes[1], bedfel-lowes[1]
**rh** playfellow *Per Prol.33*
> fellow

**Bedford / ~'s** *n*
'bedfəɹd / -z
**sp** Bedford[22] / Bedfords[1]

**bed-hanging / ~s** *n*
'bed-ˌaŋɪnz, -ɪŋz, -ˌhaŋ-
**sp** bed-hangings[1]
> hang

**bedim / ~med** *v*
bɪ'dɪmd
**sp** bedymn'd[1]

**Bedlam** *adj / n*
=
**sp** Bedlam[2], bedlam[1], Bedlem[1] / Bedlam[2], Bedlem[1]

**bed-mate** *n*
'bed-ˌmɛ:t
**sp** bed-mate[1]
> mate

**bed-presser** *n*
'bed-ˌpresəɹ
**sp** bed-presser[1]

**bedrench** *v*
bɪ'drenʧ
**sp** bedrench[1]
> drench

**bed-rid** *adj*
=
**sp** bedrid[1], bed-rid[2]

**bed-right** *n*
'bed-ˌrəɪt
**sp** bed-right[1]
> right

**bedroom** *n*
'bed-ˌru:m, -rʊm
**sp** bed-roome[1]
> room

**bed-swerver** *n*
'bed-ˌswɐ:ɹvəɹ
**sp** bed-swaruer[1]

**bedtime** *n*
*m* ˌbed-'təɪm, 'bed-ˌtəɪm
**sp** bed-time[1], bed time[2]
> time

**bedward** *adv*
'bedwəɹd
**sp** bedward[1]

**bed-work** *n*
'bed-ˌwɔ:ɹk
**sp** bed-worke[1]
> work

**bee / ~s** *n*
=
**sp** bee[4] / bees[11]
**rh** me *Luc 836* / **rh** *1* courtesies, dewberries, mulberries *MND 3.1.163*; **rh** *2* arise, butterflies, eyes, thighs *MND 3.1.163*
> honey-, humble-bee

**beef / ~s** *n*
=
**sp** beefe[12] / beefes[1], beeues[2]

**beef-witted** *adj*
=
**sp** beefe-witted[1]

**beehive / ~s** *n*
*m* ˌbi:-'əɪvz, -'həɪ-
**sp** bee-hiues[1]
> hive

**been**
> be

**beer** *n*
biːɹ, bɛːɹ
**sp** beere[4]
**rh** were *Oth 2.1.157*

**beer-barrel** *n*
ˈbiːɹ-ˌbarəl, ˈbɛːɹ-
**sp** beere-barrell[1]
> barrel

**beetle / ~s** *n*
ˈbiːtl, ˈbe- / -z
**sp** beetle[3], [sharded, three-man]-beetle[2] / beetles[3]

**beetle / ~s** *v*
ˈbiːtlz, ˈbe-
**sp** beetles[1], *Q2 Ham 1.4.71* bettles

**beetle-brows** *n*
ˈbiːtl-ˌbrəʊz, ˈbe-
**sp** beetle-browes[1]
> brow

**beetle-headed** *adj*
ˈbiːtl-ˌedɪd, ˈbe-, -ˌhed-
**sp** beetle-headed[1]
> head

**beeves**
> beef

**befall / ~s / befell / befallen** *v*
bɪˈfɑːl / -z / = / [2 *sylls*] bɪˈfɑːln
**sp** befall[28] / befals[1] / befell[3] / befalne[8]
**rh** *1* all *2H6 5.3.33, Tit 5.1.57*; wall *MND 5.1.153*; **rh** *2* hospital *LLL 5.2.859*
> fall

**befit / ~s / ~ting / ~ed** *v*
= / bɪˈfɪtɪn, -ɪŋ / =
**sp** befits[8] / befitting[1] / befitted[1]
**rh** commits *S 41.3*
> unbefitting

**before,** *abbr* **fore** *adv / conj / prep*
bɪˈfɔːɹ, *abbr* fɔːɹ
**sp** before[183], be-fore[2] / before[161], *abbr* ’fore[2] / before[360], be-fore[2], before’ [before ’em][1], before’s [before us][1], befor’t [before it][2], *abbr* fore[9], ’fore[15], ’fore-[noone][1]
**rh** door *H5 1.2.308, Luc 1302, MND 5.1.379, R2 5.3.77*; door, sore *CE 3.1.63*; more *CE 1.1.96, PP 20.47, R2 2.1.11, S 40.2. 85.12, TN 1.1.8*; o’er *S 30.12*; roar *LLL 4.1.91*; score *AW 4.3.221*; shore *S 60.3*; store *Luc 693*; swore *LLL 5.2.110, Luc 1847*
> afore, tofore

**before-breach** *n*
bɪˈfɔːɹ-ˌbriːʧ
**sp** before breach[1]

**beforehand** *adv*
bɪˈfɔːɹand, -ha-
**sp** before hand[1]
> hand

**befortune** *v*
bɪˈfɔːɹtən
**sp** befortune[1]

**befriend / ~ed** *v*
=
**sp** befriend[3], be-friend[1] / befrended[1], befriended[1]
**rh** ended *TC 5.9.9*
> friend

**beg / ~gest / ~s / ~ging / ~ged** *v*
= / -st / -z / ˈbegɪn, -ɪŋ / =
**sp** beg[40], begge[56] / beg’st[1] / begges[4], begs[2] / begging[2] / beg’d[6], begg’d[19]
> fool-begged

**began**
> begin

**beget,** *abbr* **get / begets / begetting,** *abbr* **getting / begat / begot,** *abbr* **got / begotten,** *abbr* **gotten** *v*
= / = / bɪˈgetɪn, -ɪŋ, *abbr* ˈgetɪn, -ɪŋ / =
**sp** beget[20], be-get[1], *abbr* get[14] / begets[4] / begetting[2], *abbr* getting[4] / begot[26], *abbr* got[21] / gat[1] / begotten[5], *abbr* gotten[1]
**rh** frets *VA 768* / at *Per 2.2.6* / not *KJ 1.1.274*; shot *KJ 1.1.175*
> mis-, true-, un-begotten

**begetting,** *abbr* **getting** *n*
bɪˈgetɪn, -ɪŋ, *abbr* ˈget-
**sp** begetting[1], *abbr* getting[4]

**beggar / ~’s / ~s / ~s’** *n*
ˈbegəɹ / -z
**sp** beggar[12], beg-gar[1], begger[45], beg-ger[2] / beggars[2], beggers[6] / beggars[3], beggers[19] / beggers[2]
> she-beggar

**beggar / ~s / ~ed** *v*
ˈbegəɹ / -z / -d
**sp** begger[1] / beggars[1] / beggard[1], beggerd[1], begger’d[2]

**beggared** *adj*
ˈbegəɹd
**sp** begger’d[1]

**beggar-fear** *n*
ˈbegəɹ-ˌfiːɹ, -ˌfɛːɹ
**sp** beggar-feare[1]
> fear

**beggarly** *adj*
ˈbegəɹləɪ
**sp** beggarly[1], beggerly[9]

**beggar-maid** *n*
ˈbegəɹ-ˌmɛːd
**sp** beggar maid[1]
> maid

**beggar-man** *n*
ˈbegəɹ-ˌman
**sp** beggar-man[1]
> man

**beggar-woman** *n*
ˈbegəɹ-ˌwʊmən
**sp** beggar-woman[1]
> woman

**beggary** *n*
*m* 'begɹəɪ, -gə,ɹəɪ
**sp** beggerie[5], beggery[7]
**rh** be *KJ 2.1.596*

**begging** *adj / n*
'begɪn, -ɪŋ
**sp** begging[2] / begging[2]

**begin,** *abbr* **gin / ~s,** *abbr* **gins / ~ning / began,** *abbr* **gan / ~nest / begun** *v*
=, *abbr* gɪn / =, *abbr* gɪnz / bɪ'gɪnɪn, -ɪŋ / =, *abbr* gan / bɪ'ganst / bɪ'gɤn
**sp** begin[107], beginne[4], *abbr* 'ginne[1] / beginnes[4], begins[49], *abbr* gins[3], 'gins [1] / beginning[3] / began[32], beganne[1], began't [began it][1], begon[1], *abbr* gan[4] / beganst[1] / begun[25]
**rh** chin *Luc 470, VA 60*; in *LLL 3.1.107* [*F line ending*]; kin *TC 4.5.93*; shin *LLL 3.1.69, 103*; sin *Luc 342, Per Prol.29, R2 1.1.186, S 114.14*; therein *TG 1.1.10*; win *H5 1.2.168*; within *Cym 5.1.32* / man *VA 7, 367*; ran, than [then] *Luc 1439* / done *Ham 4.3.70, R2 1.2.60, TN 5.1.402, TS 1.1.249, VA 845*; done, sun *LC 12, Luc 26*; gun *VA 462*; run *Ham 3.2.220*; son *KJ 1.1.158, R2 1.1.158*; sun *LC 262* [*or emend* nun], *Luc 374, RJ 1.2.92*

**beginner / ~s** *n*
bɪ'gɪnəɹz
**sp** beginners[2]

**beginning / ~s** *n*
bɪ'gɪnɪn, -ɪŋ / -z
**sp** begining[1], beginning[12], begin-ning[1] / beginnings[2]

**begnaw / ~n** *v*
=, bɪ'gnɔː / -n
**sp** begnaw[1] / begnawne[1]
> gnaw

**begot, begotten**
> beget

**begotten** *adj*
=
**sp** begotten[1]

**begrime / ~d** *v*
bɪ'grəɪmd
**sp** begrim'd[1]

**beguild** Luc *v*
bɪ'gəɪld
**sp** beguild[1]
**rh** defiled, mild *Luc 1544*

**beguil·e / ~s / ~ing / ~ed** *v*
bɪ'gəɪl / -z / -ɪn, -ɪŋ / *m* -ɪd, -d
**sp** beguile[19], be-guile[4] / beguiles[5] / beguiling[1], begui-ling[1] / beguild[4], be-guild[1], beguil'd[11], be-guil'd[1], beguilde[1], beguiled[1]
**rh** awhile *Ham 3.2.236*; smile *MND 2.1.45, Oth 1.3.208*; while *LLL 1.1.77, VA 1144* / defiling, smiling *LC 170* / child *MND 1.1.239, S 59.2*; child, wild *Luc 957*; exiled *RJ 3.2.132*; smiled *PP 20.28*

**begun**
> begin

**behalf / ~s** *n*
bɪ'ɔːf, -'hɔːf, -'ɑːf, -'hɑːf / -s
**sp** behalfe[46] / behalfes[1]

**behave / ~d / ~dest** *v*
bɪ'ɛːvd, -'hɛː- / -st
**sp** behau'd[1], behaued[1] / behaued'st[1]
> haviour, well-behaved

**behaviour / ~s** *n*
bɪ'ɛːvɪəɹ, -'hɛːv- [*3 sylls*] / -z
**sp** behauior[2], behauiour[23], behaui-our[2] / behauiours[8]
> haviour, well-behaved

**behead / ~ed** *v*
bɪ'ed, -'hed / -ɪd
**sp** behead[1] / beheaded[6]
> head

**beheld**
> behold

**behest / ~s** *n*
bɪ'est, -'he- / -s
**sp** behest[1] / behests[1]
**rh** blest *Cym 5.4.122* / breasts, nests *Luc 852*

**behind** *adv / prep*
bɪ'əɪnd, -'həɪnd
**sp** behind[15], behinde[31] / behind[16], behinde[38]
**rh** *adv 1* hind *CE 3.1.76*; kind Ham *3.2.185, 3.4.180, S 143.10*; kind, mind *Luc 1425*; mind *KL 3.6.103* [*Q*], *Luc 734, 1413, Oth 2.1.154, Per 4.4.13, S 9.6, 50.14, Tim 1.2.160* / **rh** *adv 2* wind *CE 3.1.76*; **behind thee** with thee *AY 3.3.91*

**behind-door-work** *n*
bɪ'əɪnd-'doːɹ-,wɔːɹk, -'həɪ-
**sp** be-hinde-doore worke[1]
> work

**behindhand** *adv*
bɪ'əɪnd-,and, -'həɪ-, -ha-
**sp** behind-hand[1]
> hand

**behold / ~est / ~s / ~ing / beheld** *v*
bɪ'oːld, -'hoː- / -st / -z / -ɪn, -ɪŋ / bɪ'eld, -'he-
**sp** behold[147], be-hold[1], beholde[2], behold's [behold us][1] / beholdest[1], beholdst[1], behold'st[2] / beholds[2] / beholding[5] / beheld[27], be-held[1]
**rh** bold *S 131.5*; bold, cold, enfold, gold, inscrolled, old, sold, told *MV 2.7.68*; cold *S 73.1*; cold, unfold *Luc 1143*; controlled *Luc 447*; gold *2H6 4.7.93, Luc 857, VA 857*; old *LC 71, Luc 1758, S 22.3*; rolled, told *Luc 1395*; told *Luc 1326*; unfold *MND 1.1.209*; unfold, untold *Luc 751* / dwelled, stelled *Luc 1447*; excelled *VA 1129*

**beholder / ~s** *n*
bɪ'oːldəɹ, -'hoː- / -z
**sp** beholder[1] / beholders[4], behol-ders[1]

**beholding** *adj / n*
bɪ'oːldɪn, -ɪŋ, -'hoː-
**sp** beholding[19], be-holding[1] / beholding[3]

**behoof** *n*
bɪ'ʊf, -'hʊf, -'uːf, -'huːf
**sp** behoofe[1]
**rh** aloof, proof *LC 165*

**behove** *n*
bɪ'ɤv, -'hɤv, -'u:v, -'hu:v
**sp** behoue[1]
**rh** love *Ham 5.1.63*

**behove / ~s** *v*
bɪ'ɤv, -'hɤv, -'u:v, -'hu:v / -z
**sp** behooue[1], behoue[1] / behooues[3], behoues[1]

**behoveful** *adj*
bɪ'ɤvfəl, -'hɤv-, -'u:v-, -'hu:v-
**sp** behoouefull[1]

**behowl / ~s** *v*
bɪ'əʊlz, -'həʊ-
**sp** *emend of MND 5.1.362* beholds

**being** *n*
'bi:ɪn, -ɪŋ
**sp** being[16]

**being** *v*
> be

**Bel / ~'s** *n*
=
**sp** Bels[1]

**Belario / ~'s** *n*
*m* bɪ'larɪo: [*3 sylls*], -rɪ'o: / bɪ'larɪo:z
**sp** Belario[1], Bellario[7] / Bellarioes[1]

**Belarius** *n*
bɪ'larɪəs [*3 sylls*]
**sp** Belarius[11], Bellarius[2]

**belch** *v*
=
**sp** belch[4]

**Belch** [name] *n*
=
**sp** Belch[2]

**belching** *adj*
'beltʃɪn, -ɪŋ
**sp** belching[1]

**beldame** *adj*
'beldəm
**sp** beldame[1]

**beldame / ~s** *n*
'beldəm / -z
**sp** beldam[1] / beldames[1], beldams[1]

**belee / ~d** *v*
bɪ'li:d
**sp** be-leed[1]

**Belgia** *n*
'belʤə, -ʤɪə
**sp** Belgia[2]

**belie / ~est / ~d** *v*
bɪ'ləɪ / -st / -d
**sp** bely[3], belye[5], be-lye-[her][1] / beliest[1] / belied[3], belyed[2]
**rh** spied *Luc 1533*; wide *S 140.13*

**belief** *n*
bɪ'li:f
**sp** beleefe[12]

**believ·e / ~est / ~es / ~ing / ~ed** *v*
= / bɪ'li:v·st / = / -ɪn, -ɪŋ / =
**sp** beleeue[225], 'beleeue [1], belieue[1], be-leeue't [believe it][4], beleeu't [believe it][5] / beleeuest[1], beleeu'st[1] / beleeues[4] / beleeuing[4], be-leeuing[1] / beleeued[3], belee-ued[1], beleeu'd[12]
**rh** *1* give *H8 Prol.8*; **rh** *2* sleeve *CE 3.2.21, TC 5.3.95*
> misbelieving, unbelieved

**believing** *adj*
bɪ'li:vɪn, -ɪŋ
**sp** beleeuing[1]

**belike** *adv*
bɪ'ləɪk
**sp** belike[40], be-like[3]
> like

**bell / ~s** *n*
=
**sp** bell[32], [Windsor]-bell[1] / belles[2], bells[5], bels[7]
**rh** dwell *S 71.2*; knell *MV 3.2.71, Tem 1.2.405*; knell, tell *Luc 1493*; well *VA 702* [passing bell] / tells *Luc 511*
> alarum-, hare-bell

**belle** *Fr adj*
bɛl
**sp** belle[1]

**bellied** *adj*
'beləɪd
**sp** belly'd[1]
> big-, gor-bellied

**bellied** *v*
> belly *v*

**bellman** *n*
=
**sp** bell-man[1]

**Bellona / ~'s** *n*
bɪ'lo:nəz
**sp** Bellona's[1]

**bellow / ~ing / ~ed** *v*
'belə, -lo: / *m* 'belwɪn, -ɪŋ, -ləw-, -lo:- / 'beləd, -lo:d
**sp** bellow[1] / bellowing[1], bellow'd[1] / bellowed[1]

**bellowing** *n*
*m* 'belwɪn, -ɪŋ, -ləw-, -lo:-
**sp** bellowing[1]

**bellows** *n*
'beləz, -lo:z
**sp** bellowes[1]

**bellows-mender** *n*
'beləz-ˌmendəɹ, -lo:z-
**sp** bellowes-mender[3]
> mend

**bell-weather** *n*
'bel-ˌweðəɹ
**sp** bell-weather[1], bel-weather[1]
> weather

**bell·y / ~y's / ~ies** *n*
'beləɪ / -z
**sp** bel-lie[1], bellies [belly is][1], belly[35] / bellies[2] / bellies[1], bellyes[1]
> great-, thin-belly

**bell·y / ~ied** *v*
'belǝɪ / -d
**sp** belly[1] / bellied[1]

**Belman** *n*
=
**sp** Belman[1]

**Belmont** *n*
=
**sp** Belmont[7]

**belock / ~ed** *v*
bɪ'lɒkt
**sp** belockt[1]

**belong / ~s, *abbr* longs / *abbr* longeth / ~ing, *abbr* longing / ~ed** *v*
= / = / = / bɪ'lɒŋɪn, -ɪŋ, *abbr* 'lɒŋ- / =
**sp** belong[14] / belongs[16], *abbr* longs[4] / *abbr* longeth[2] / belonging[3], *abbr* longing[2] / belong'd[2]
**rh** *1* among *LC 254*; tongue *LLL 5.2.381*; young *AW 1.3.125*; **rh** *2* strong *LC 254, S 58.11*; strong, wrong *Luc 1265*; wrong *S 88.13* / **rh** *1* tongues *LLL 4.3.238*; **rh** *2* wrongs *S 92.7*

**belonging** *adj*
bɪ'lɒŋɪn, -ɪŋ
**sp** belonging[1]

**belonging / ~s** *n*
bɪ'lɒŋɪn, -ɪŋ / -z
**sp** belonging[1] / belongings[1]

**beloved** *adj*
*m* bɪ'lɤvd, -vɪd
**sp** belou'd[23], beloued[15]
**rh** approved *TG 5.4.44*; removed *S 25.13*
> dear-beloved

**beloved** *n*
*m* bɪ'lɤvd, -vɪd
**sp** belou'd[3], [well]-belou'd[1], beloued[3]

**beloving** *n*
bɪ'lɤvɪn, -ɪŋ
**sp** belouing[1]

**below** *adv / n / prep*
bɪ'lo:
**sp** below[19], be-low[1] / below[1] / below[18]
**rh** *adv* blow *Per 2.Chorus.30*; go *Ham 3.3.97, VA 923*

**belt** *n*
=
**sp** belt[2]

**Belzebub** *n*
'belzɪbǝb
**sp** Belzebub[3]

**bemet** *v*
bɪ'met
**sp** be-met[1]
> meet

**bemete** *v*
bɪ'mi:t
**sp** be-mete[1]
> mete

**bemoan / ~ed** *v*
bɪ'mo:nd
**sp** bemoan'd[1]

**bemock** *v*
bɪ'mɒk
**sp** bemocke[1]

**bemocked-at** *adj*
bɪ'mɒkt-ˌat
**sp** bemockt-at-[stabs][1]

**bemoil / ~ed** *v*
bɪ'mǝɪld
**sp** bemoil'd[1]

**ben** *Ital*
> bene

**bench / ~es** *n*
=
**sp** bench[8] / benches[2]

**bench / ~ed** *v*
=
**sp** bench'd[1]
> disbench

**bencher** *n*
'benʧǝɹ
**sp** bencher[1]

**bench-hole / ~s** *n*
'benʧ-ˌo:lz, -ˌho:-
**sp** bench-holes[1]

**bend / ~s / ~ing / ~ed / bent** *v*
= / = / 'bendɪn, -ɪŋ / =
**sp** bend[44] / bends[2] / bending[7] / bended[3] / bent[20]
**rh** commandment *PP 20.43*; discontent *S 143.6*; occident *R2 3.3.65*; repent *PP 18.25*
> unbend

**bended** *adj*
=
**sp** bended[4]

**bending** *adj / n*
'bendɪn, -ɪŋ
**sp** bending[7] / bending[3]

**bene** *Ital / Lat adv*
'bene
**sp** been[1], bene[2], bien[1] / *emend of LLL 5.1.28* boon[1]

**beneath** *adj / adv / prep*
=
**sp** beneath[1] / beneath[3] / beneath[11]

**benedic·o / ~ite** *Lat v*
*m* ˌbene'dɪsɪˌti:
**sp** benedecite[1], benedicite[1]
**rh** me *RJ 2.3.27*

**Benedick / ~'s** *n*
=
**sp** Benedick[5], Benedicke[54], Bene-dicke[2] / Benedicks[3]

**Benedict** *n*
=
**sp** Benedict[1]

**benediction** *n*
ˌbenɪ'dɪksɪǝn
**sp** benediction[4], be-nediction[1]

**benedictus** *Lat adj*
ˌbeneˈdɪktʊs
**sp** benedictus[4]

**benefactor / ~s** *n*
ˌbenɪˈfaktəɹz
**sp** benefactors[4]

**benefice** *n*
=
**sp** benefice[1]

**beneficial** *adj*
ˌbenɪˈfɪsɪɑl [*4 sylls*]
**sp** beneficiall[2], bene-ficiall[1]

**benefit / ~s** *n*
*m* ˈbenɪˌfɪt, ˈbenfit / -s
**sp** benefit[34], be-nefit[1] / benefits[5], bene-fits[1], benefitts[1]

**benefit** *v*
*m* ˈbenɪˌfɪt, ˈbenfit
**sp** benefit[2]

**benet / ~ted** *v*
bɪˈnetɪd
**sp** benetted[1]

**benevolence / ~s** *n*
=
**sp** beneuolence[1] / beneuolences[1]

**benison** *n*
*m* ˈbenɪˌzɒn
**sp** benizon[2], benyson[1]
**rh** conversation *Per 2.Chorus.10*, gone *KL 1.1.265*

**Bennet** *n*
=
**sp** Bennet[2]

**bent** *adj*
=
**sp** bent[4]
**rh** merriment *MND 3.2.145*
> unbent

**bent / ~s** *n*
=
**sp** bent[12] / bents[1]

**Bentii** *n*
ˈbentɪiː [*3 sylls*]
**sp** Bentij[1]

**Bentivolii** *n*
ˈbentɪˌvoːlɪiː [*4 sylls*]
**sp** Bentiuolij[1]

**benumbed** *adj*
*m* bɪˈnɤmɪd
**sp** benummed[1]

**Benvolio** *n*
*m* benˈvoːlɪoː [*3 sylls*], -ɪˌoː
**sp** Benuolio[14]

**bepaint** *v*
bɪˈpɛːnt
**sp** bepaint[1]

**bequeath / ~ing / ~ed** *v*
bɪˈkwe·θ, -ð; bɪˈkwiː·θ, -ð / -θɪn, -θɪŋ; -ðɪn, -ðɪŋ / *m* -θt, -θɪd; -ðd, -ðɪd
**sp** bequeath[9] / bequeathing[2] / bequeath'd[2], bequeathed[4]
**rh** breath, death *Luc 1181, MND 3.2.166* / breathed, unsheathed *Luc 1727*

**berattle / ~ed** *v*
bɪˈratld
**sp** be-ratled[1]

**bereave / ~s / ~d / bereft** *v*
bɪˈrɛːv / -z / *m* bɪˈrɛːvɪd / =
**sp** bereaue[3] / bereaues[1] / bereaued[1] / bereft[16]
**rh** leaves *VA 797* / left, theft *Luc 835*; left *CE 2.1.40, S 5.11, Tim 5.4.70*; **bereft me** left me *VA 439*

**bereaved** *adj*
*m* bɪˈrɛːvɪd
**sp** bereaued[1]

**Bergamo** *n*
ˈbɐːɹgəmoː
**sp** Bergamo[1]

**bergomask** *n*
ˈbɐːɹgəmask
**sp** bergomask[1], burgomaske[1]

**berhyme / ~d** *v*
bɪˈrəɪm / -d
**sp** berime[1] / berim'd[1]

**Berkeley** *n*
ˈbɑːɹkləɪ
**sp** Barkely[5], Barkley[3], Berkley[1], Barkloughly[1]

**berlady, berlaken**
> by Our Lady

**Bermoothes** *n*
bəɹˈmuːðəz, -uːdəz
**sp** Bermoothes[1]

**Berowne / ~'s** *n*
bəˈruːn / -z
**sp** Beroune[2], Berown[1], Berowne[29] / Berowns[1]
**rh** moon *LLL 4.3.230*

**berr·y / ~ies** *n*
ˈberəɪ / -z
**sp** berry[4] / berries[5], berryes[1]
**rh** cherry *Per 5.Chorus.6* / cherries *VA 1104*

**Bertram / ~'s** *n*
ˈbɐːɹtrəm / -z
**sp** Bertram[12], Bertrame[1] / Bertrams[1]

**Berwick** *n*
ˈberɪk
**sp** Barwicke[2], Barwicke[1]

**bescreen / ~ed** *v*
bɪˈskriːnd
**sp** bescreen'd[1]
> screen

**beseech / ~ing / ~ed** *v*
=, *Fluellen H5 5.1.21* pɪˈsiːʧ / bɪˈsiːʧɪn, -ɪŋ / =
**sp** beseech[221], 'beseech [8], beseech'[1], be-seech[1], *Fluellen* peseech[1] / beseeching[3] / beseech'd[1]
**rh** *1* speech *CE 4.2.16*; teach *TC 1.2.293*; **beseech thee** teach thee *VA 404*; **beseech you** teach you *Per 4.4.7*; **rh** *2* liege *R2 5.3.91* / empleached, enriched *LC 207*

**beseek** *v*
bɪ'si:k
**sp** beseeke[1]

**beseem / ~s / ~eth / ~ing** *v*
bɪ'si:m / -z / -əθ / -ɪn, -ɪŋ
**sp** beseeme[5] / beseemes[4] / beseemeth[1] / beseeming[2]

**beseeming** *adj / n*
bɪ'si:mɪn, -ɪŋ
**sp** beseeming[1] / beseeming[1]
> ill-, well-beseeming

**beset** *v*
=
**sp** beset[6]
**rh** cabinet *Luc 444*

**beshrew,** ***abbr*** **shrew** *v*
bɪ'ʃro:, *abbr* ʃro:
**sp** beshrew[29], beshrow[2], *abbr* shrew[1], 'shrew[1]
> shrew

**beside** *adv / prep*
bɪ'səɪd
**sp** beside[19], be-side[1] / beside[10]
**rh** *adv* bide, pride *LC 32*; denied *R2 5.3.103*; pride *S 103.4*; provide *Mac 3.5.19*; self-applied *LC 77*; supplied *H5 1.1.18*; tide *VA 981*
> side

**besides** *adv / prep*
bɪ'səɪdz
**sp** besides[69], be-sides[1] / besides[38]

**besiege / ~d** *v*
= / =, *Macmorris H5 3.2.105*
bɪ'si:ʧt
**sp** besiege[7] / besiedg'd[1], besieg'd[3], besieged[1], *Macmorris* beseech'd[1]
> siege

**beslubber** *v*
bɪ'slɤbəɹ
**sp** beslubber[1]
> slubber

**besmear / ~ed** *v*
bɪ'smi:ɹ / -d
**sp** besmeare[2] / besmear'd[3]
> smear

**besmirch / ~ed** *v*
bɪ'smɐ:ɹʧ / -t
**sp** besmerch[1], besmyrcht[1]

**besom** *n*
'bi:zəm
**sp** beesome[1]

**besort** *v*
bɪ'sɔ:ɹt
**sp** besort[2]

**besotted** *adj*
bɪ'sɒtɪd
**sp** be-sotted[1]

**bespeak / ~spake / ~spoke** *v*
bɪ'spi:k, -spɛ:k, -spek / -'spɛ:k / -'spo:k
**sp** bespeake[6] / bispake[2] / bespoke[5]
> speak

**bespice** *v*
bɪ'spəɪs
**sp** be-spice[1]

**Bess** *n*
=
**sp** Besse[1]

**best** *adj / adv / n*
=
**sp** best[213] / best[103] / best[94]
**rh** *adj* feast *RJ 1.2.98*; nest *2H6 2.1.184*; rest *Per 2.Chorus.25*; *adv* nest *Luc 1613*; rest *S 115.10*; *n* breast *3H6 2.5.10, MND 2.2.151, S 110.13*; expressed *S 106.5*; indigest *S 114.7*; rest *Per 2.3.115, PP 1.6, S 91.8, TG 1.2.21*; suppressed *S 138.6*; unrest *RJ 1.5.119*; west *TC 2.3.261*
> good

**Best / ~'s [name]** *n*
=
**sp** Bests[1]

**best-conditioned** *adj*
ˌbes-kən'dɪsɪənd, ˌbest-
**sp** best condition'd[1]

**bested** *adj*
=
**sp** bestead[1]

**best-esteemed** *adj*
=
**sp** best esteemd[1]
> esteemed

**best-governed** *adj*
ˌbes-'gɤvəɹnd, ˌbest-
**sp** best gouern'd[1]
> govern

**bestial** *adj*
'bi:stɪɑl, 'bestɪɑl [2 *sylls*]
**sp** beastiall[1], bestiall[1]

**bestilled**
> distilled

**bestir / ~red** *v*
bɪ'stɐ:ɹ / -d
**sp** bestirre[2] / bestir'd[1], bestirr'd[1]
> stir

**best-moving** *adj*
ˌbes-'mɤvɪn, -ɪŋ, ˌbest-, -mu:v-
**sp** best mouing[1]
> move

**bestow / ~est / ~s / ~ing / ~ed** *v*
bɪ'sto: / -st / -z / -ɪn, -ɪŋ / -d
**sp** bestow[45], bestowe[1], bestow't [bestow it][1] / bestow'st[1] / bestowes[5] / bestowing[3] / bestow'd[13], be-stow'd[1], bestowed[13], be-stowed[2]
**rh** know *AW 2.1.200, LLL 5.2.125*; bestow it show it *S 26.8*; bestow them owe them *LC 139* / *rh* grow'st *S 11.3* / glowed, owed *LC 326*; o'erflowed *Per 4.4.41*

**bestowing** *n*
bɪ'sto:ɪn, -ɪŋ
**sp** bestowing[2]

**bestraught** *adj*
bɪ'strɔ:t
**sp** bestraught[1]

**best-regarded** *adj*
ˌbes-rɪˈgɑːɹdɪd, ˌbest-
**sp** best regarded[1]
> regard

**bestrew / ~ed** *v*
bɪˈstroː / -d
**sp** bestrew[1], bestrow[1] / bestrew'd[1]
> strew

**bestride / ~s / bestrid** *v*
bɪˈstrəɪd / -z / bɪˈstrɪd
**sp** bestride[8], bestryde[1] / bestrides[1] / bestrid[6]
> stride

**best-tempered** *adj*
ˌbes-ˈtempəɹd, ˌbest-
**sp** best temper'd[1]
> temper

**bet / ~ted** *v*
=
**sp** betted[1]

**betake / *PP* ~s / betook** *v*
bɪˈtɛːk / -s / bɪˈtʊk
**sp** betake[6] / betakes[1] / betooke[1]
**rh** wake *Luc 125* [Q] / makes *PP 8.12*

**beteem** *v*
bɪˈtiːm
**sp** beteeme[1], beteene[1]

**bethink / bethought** *v*
bɪˈθɪŋk / bɪˈθɔːt
**sp** bethink[2], bethinke[19] / bethought[4]

**bethump / ~ed** *v*
bɪˈθɤmt, -mpt
**sp** bethumpt[1]
> thump

**betide / ~th / betid** *v*
bɪˈtəɪd / -əθ / bɪˈtɪd
**sp** betide[11] / betideth[2] / betid[1]
**rh** provide *3H6 4.6.88*

**betime** *adv*
bɪˈtəɪm
**sp** betime[4]
**rh** Valentine *Ham 4.5.49*

**betimes** *adv*
bɪˈtəɪmz
**sp** betimes[21], be-times[3]

**betoken / *VA* ~ed** *v*
bɪˈtoːkən / -d
**sp** betoken[1] / betokend[1]
**rh** opened *VA 453*

**betook**
> betake

**betossed** *adj*
bɪˈtɒsɪd
**sp** betossed[1]
> toss

**betray / ~s / ~ing / ~ed / ~edest** *v*
bɪˈtrɛː / -z / - ɪn, -ɪŋ / *m* -d, -ɪd / -dst
**sp** betraie[1], betray[32], betray's [betray us][1] / betrayes[1] / betraying[1], betraid[8], betraide[1], betraied[1], betrayd[1], betray'd[7], betrayed[6] / betrayed'st[1]
**rh** away *S 96.9*; may *S 151.5* / days *Luc 160* / aid *1H6 1.1.144*
> fore-betrayed

**betrayed** *adj*
*m* bɪˈtrɛɪd
**sp** betrayed[1]

**betrim / ~s** *v*
bɪˈtrɪm / -z
**sp** betrims[1]
**rh** brims *Tem 4.1.65*

**betroth / ~s / ~ed** *v*
bɪˈtroːðz / -ðd
**sp** betrothes[1] / betroathd[1], betroath'd[1], betroth'd[5]
> true-betrothed

**betrothed** *adj / n*
*m* bɪˈtroːðɪd, -ðd
**sp** betrothed[1] / betroathed[1], betroth'd[1]

**better** *adj / adv / n*
ˈbetəɹ / *French lady H5 5.2.261* ˈbetrə, *Fluellen H5 5.1.7, Evans MW 1.1.39ff* ˈpetəɹ
**sp** better[286], bet-ter[6], *French lady* bettre[1], *Fluellen, Evans* petter[4] / better[147], bet-ter[1] / better[65]

**better / ~s** *n*
ˈbetəɹ / -z
**sp** beter[1], better[57] / betters[11]

**better / ~s / ~ing / ~ed** *v*
ˈbetəɹ / -z / ˈbetrɪn, -ɪŋ / ˈbetəɹd
**sp** better[4] / betters[1] / bett'ring[1] / better'd[1], bettered[1], bettred[2]
**rh** debtor *AY 2.3.75, Luc 1154, Per 2.1.143*; fetter *TN 3.1.153*; letter *LLL 4.1.96, Luc 1323, TG 2.1.132*; greater *S 119.10*

**better-fashioned** *adj*
ˈbetəɹ-ˈfaʃɪənd
**sp** better fashion'd[1]

**bettering** *n*
ˈbetrɪn, -ɪŋ, -tər-
**sp** bettering[1]

**better-tempered** *adj*
ˈbetəɹ-ˈtempəɹd
**sp** better temper'd[2]

**betting** *n*
ˈbetɪn, -ɪŋ
**sp** betting[1]

**between** *adv / n*
=
**sp** betweene[8] / betweene[1]
> broker-, goer-between

**between, *abbr* tween** *prep*
=
**sp** between[25], betweene[179], be-tweene[13], between's [between us][2], betweene's [between us][2], *abbr* tween[1], 'tweene[12]
**rh** between them seen them *VA 355*

**betwixt, *abbr* twixt** *prep*
=
**sp** betwixt[52], be-twixt[2], *abbr* twixt[16], 'twixt[54]

**bevel** *S adj*
=
**sp** beuel[1]
**rh** level *S 121.11*

**beveridge** *n*
*m* 'bevəˌrɪʤ
**sp** beueridge[1]

**Bevis** *n*
'bi:vɪs
**sp** Beuis[2]

**bevy** *n*
'bevəɪ
**sp** beuy[1]

**bewail / ~s** *v*
bɪ'wɛ:l / -z
**sp** bewaile[2] / bewayles[1]
> unbewailed

**bewailing** *adj*
bɪ'wɛ:lɪn, -ɪŋ
**sp** bewailing[1]

**beware** *v*
bɪ'wɛ:ɹ
**sp** beware[29]
**rh** care *Tem 2.1.309*
> ware *interj*

**beweep / bewept** *v*
bɪ'wi:p / bɪ'wept
**sp** beweepe[3] / bewept[3]

**bewet** *v*
bɪ'wet
**sp** bewet[1]

**bewhore / ~d** *v*
bɪ'o:ɹd
**sp** bewhor'd[1]
> whore

**bewitch,** *abbr* **witch / ~ed** *v*
= / *m* bɪ'wɪʧ·t, -ɪd
**sp** bewitch[1], be-witch[1], *abbr* 'witch[1] / bewicht[1], bewitch'd[3], bewitched[1], bewitcht[2]
> witch

**bewitchment** *n*
=
**sp** bewitchment[1]

**bewray / ~ed** *v*
bɪ'rɛ: / -d
**sp** bewray[6] / bewray'd[1]
**rh** away *KL 3.6.109* [*Q*] / **rh** *1* aid *Luc 1698*; **rh** *2* said *Luc 1698, PP 18.54*

**beyond** *adv / prep*
=
**sp** beyond[4] / beyond[54], be-yond[1]

**Bezonian / ~s** *n*
bɪ'zo:nɪən / -z
**sp** Bezonian[1] / Bezonions[1]

**Bianca / ~s** *n*
bɪ'aŋka / -z
**sp** Bianca[55], Bianeu[1] / Biancas[2], Bianca's[4]

**bias** *n*
'bəɪəs
**sp** bias[6], byas[6]

**bibble-babble** *n*
=, *Fluellen H5 4.1.70* 'pɪbəl-'pabəl
**sp** bibble babble[1], *Fluellen* pibble ba-ble[1]
> babble

**Bible** *n*
*Caius MW 2.3.7* 'pəɪbəl
**sp** *Caius* Pible[1]

**bickering / ~s** *n*
'bɪkrɪnz, -ɪŋz, -kər-
**sp** bickerings[1]

**bid / ~st / ~s / ~ding / bade / baddest / bidden** *v*
=, *Evans MW 5.4.3* pɪd / -st / -z / 'bɪdɪn, -ɪŋ / bad / -st / =
**sp** bid[329], bidde[3], *Evans MW 5.4.3* pid[1] / bidst[4], bid'st[1] / biddes[1], bids[56], byds[1] / bidding[21] / bad[43], bade[1] / badst[1], bad'st[1] / bidden[1]
> out-, un-bid; unbidden

**bidding / ~s** *n*
'bɪdɪn, -ɪŋ / -z
**sp** bidding[4] / biddings[1]

**biddy** *n*
'bɪdəɪ
**sp** biddy[1]

**bid·e / ~es / ~ing** *v*
bəɪd / -z / 'bəɪdɪn, -ɪŋ
**sp** bide[13] / bides[4] / biding[1]
**rh** aside *S 139.8*; beside, pride *LC 33*; side *MND 3.2.186* / dividing, hiding *Luc 550*

**biding** *n*
'bəɪdɪn, -ɪŋ
**sp** biding[1]

**bien** *Fr adv*
bjɛ̃
**sp** bien[3]

**bier** *n*
bi:ɹ
**sp** beer[1], beere[4]
**rh** here *R2 5.6.52, RJ 3.2.60, TNK 3.6.308*; tear [cry] *Ham 4.5.166*

**big / ~er** *adj*
=, *Fluellen H5 4.7.13* pɪg / 'bɪgəɹ
**sp** big[21], bigge[26] / bigger[14], big-ger[1]

**bigamy** *n*
*m* 'bɪgəˌməɪ
**sp** bigamie[1]

**big-bellied** *adj*
*m* ˌbɪg'beləɪd
**sp** big bellied[1]
> belly

**big-boned** *adj*
'bɪg-ˌbo:nd
**sp** big-bon'd-[men][1]
> bone

**biggen** *n*
'bɪgən
**sp** biggen[1]

**bigness** *n*
=
**sp** bignesse[1]

**bigot** *n*
=
**sp** bigot[6]

**big-swollen** *adj*
'bɪg-ˌswo:ln
**sp** big-swolne[2]
> swell

**bilberry** *n*
*m* 'bɪlbrəɪ, -bər-
**sp** bill-berry[1]
**rh** sluttery *MW 5.5.45*

**bilbo / ~es** *n*
'bɪlbo: / -z
**sp** bilbo[1], bilboe[1] / bilboes[1]

**bilbo**
> elbow

**bill / ~s** *n*
=
**sp** bil[1], bill[15], byll[1] / billes[7], bils[6], bills[2]
**rh** quill *MND 3.1.119* / gills *VA 1102*

**bill / ~ing** *v*
= / 'bɪlɪn, -ɪŋ
**sp** bill[1] / billing[1]
> a-billing

**billet / ~s** *n*
'bɪləts
**sp** billets[1]

**billet / ~ed** *v*
'bɪlɪtɪd
**sp** billetted[1], billited[1]

**billiards** *n*
'bɪlɪəɹdz
**sp** billiards[1]

**billing**
> a-billing

**billow / ~s** *n*
'bɪlə, -lo: / -z
**sp** billow[2] / billowes[5]

**bind / ~s / ~eth / bound** *v*
bəɪnd / -z / 'bəɪndəθ / bəʊnd
**sp** bind[3], binde[38] / bindes[2], binds[2] / bindeth[1] / bound[165]
**rh** kind *S 134.8*; Rosalind *AY 3.2.103*
> all-binding, bound, unbind

**Biondello** *n*
ˌbi:ən'delo:
**sp** Biondello[26]

**birch** *n*
bɐ:ɹʧ
**sp** birch[1]

**bird / ~s** *n*
bɐ:ɹd / -z
**sp** bird[38], [Arabian]-bird[1] / birds[33]
**rh** herds *VA 455*

**birdbolt / ~s** *n*
'bɐ:ɹdˌbo:lt / -s
**sp** birdbolt[1] / bird-bolts[1]

**birding-piece / ~s** *n*
'bɐ:ɹdɪn-ˌpi:sɪz, -ɪŋ-
**sp** birding-peeces[1]
> a-birding, piece

**birdlime** *n*
'bɐ:ɹdˌləɪm
**sp** birdlyme[1]

**Birnam** *n*
'bɐ:ɹnən, -nəm
**sp** Birnan[1], Birnane[2], Byrnane[4], Byrnam[1], Byrnan[2]

**birth / ~s** *n*
bɐ:ɹθ / -s
**sp** birth[72], byrth[7], *emend of Ham 1.1.160* birch[1] / births[5]
**rh** earth *1H4 3.1.13, MW 5.5.83, Per 1.2.114, 4.4.38*; mirth *LLL 5.2.518*

**birthday** *n*
'bɐ:ɹθdɛ:
**sp** birth-day[2]

**birthdom** *n*
'bɐ:ɹθdəm
**sp** birthdome[1]

**birthplace** *n*
'bɐ:ɹθplɛ:s
**sp** birth-place[1]
> place

**birthright / ~s** *n*
'bɐ:ɹθrəɪt / -s
**sp** birth-right[4] / birth-rights[1]
> right

**birth-strangled** *adj*
*m* ˌbɐ:ɹθ-'straŋgld
**sp** birth-strangled[1]
> strangle

**bis** *Lat adv*
bɪs
**sp** bis[2]

**biscuit** *n*
=
**sp** bisket[2]

**bishop / ~s** *n*
=
**sp** bishop[25], byshop[2] / bishops[15], byshops[1]
> archbishop

**bisson** *adj*
'bi:səm, 'bɪsən
**sp** beesome[1], bisson[1]

**bit / ~s** *n*
=
**sp** bit[1], bitt[1], bitte[1] / bits[6]
**rh** wits *LLL 1.1.26*

**bit** *v*
> bite

**bitch / ~es** *n*
=
**sp** bitch[1] / bitches[1]

**bitch-wolf / ~'s** *n*
=
**sp** bitch-wolfes-[sonne][1]
> wolf

**bit·e / ~s / bit / bitten** *v*
bəɪt / -s / =
**sp** bite[37], bight[1], byte[1] / bites[9] / bit[4] / bitten[1]

**rh** light *R2 1.3.292* [*Q*]; white *KL 3.6.66*
> back-bite, unbitted

**biting** *adj / n*
'bəɪtɪn, -ɪŋ
**sp** biting[5], bi-ting[1], byting[2] / by-ting[1], byting[1]
> sheep-biting

**bitten** *adj*
=
**sp** bitten[1]
> fly-, weather-bitten

**bitter / ~est** *adj*
'bɪtəɹ / 'bɪtrəst, -tər-
**sp** bitter[71], bitter-[sweeting][1] / bitterest[2]

**bitterest** *n*
'bɪtrəst
**sp** bittrest[1]

**bitterly** *adv*
'bɪtəɹləɪ
**sp** bitterly[9]

**bitterness** *n*
'bɪtəɹˌnes, -ɹnəs
**sp** bitternes[1], bit-ternesse[1], bitternesse[7]

**blab / ~s / ~bed** *v*
=
**sp** blab[2] / blabs[1] / blab'd[2]

**blabbing** *adj*
'blabɪn, -ɪŋ
**sp** blabbing[1]

**black / ~er / ~est** *adj*
=, *Fluellen H5 4.7.92* plak / 'blak·əɹ / -əst, -st
**sp** black[25], black-[browes][1], blacke[113], *Fluellen* placke[1] / blacker[3], black-er[1] / blackest[2], black'st[1]
**rh** alack *MND 5.1.167*; back *Luc 1585*; crack *LLL 4.3.264*; lack *LLL 4.3.251, Oth 1.3.287, S 127.9, 132.13*
> coal-, hell-black

**black / ~s** *n*
=
**sp** blacks[1]

**blackamoor** *n*
'blakəmɔ:ɹ
**sp** black-a-moore[1], blacke a moore[1]

**blackberr·y / ~ies** *n*
'blakbrəɪ, -bər- / -z
**sp** black-berry[1] / black-berries[1], black-berryes[1]

**black-browed** *adj*
'blakˌbrəʊd, -ˌbro:d
**sp** blackebrow'd[1], blacke browd[1]

**black-cornered** *adj*
ˌblak-'kɒɹnəɹd
**sp** blacke-corner'd[1]

**black-faced** *adj*
'blakˌfɛ:st
**sp** black-fac'd[1]
> face

**Blackfriars** *n*
*m* ˌblak' frəɪɹz
**sp** Black-Fryers[1]

**Blackheath** *n*
ˌblak'ɛ:θ, -'hɛ:θ, -'i:θ, -'hi:θ
**sp** Black-Heath[1]
> heath

**Blackmere** *n*
'blakˌmɛ:ɹ
**sp** Blackmere[1]

**blackness** *n*
=
**sp** blacknesse[2], blacknessse[1]

**Black Prince** *n*
=
**sp** Black-Prince[2], Black Prince[1], black Prince[1]

**bladder / ~s** *n*
'bladəɹ / -z
**sp** bladder[1] / bladders[2]

**blade / ~s** *n*
blɛ:d / -z
**sp** blade[10] / blades[3]
**rh** shade *Luc 505, MND 5.1.145*

**bladed** *adj*
'blɛ:dɪd
**sp** bladed[2]

**blain / ~s** *n*
blɛ:nz
**sp** blaines[1]

**blame / ~s** *n*
blɛ:m / -z
**sp** blame[18] / blames[2]
**rh** defame, shame *Luc 767*; name *CE 3.1.45, VA 796*; name, shame *Luc 620*; shame *1H6 4.5.47, Luc 224, 1259, 1343, R3 5.1.29, S 129.3*
> wilful-blame

**blame / ~d** *v*
blɛ:m / -d
**sp** blame[61] / blam'd[3], blamed[2]
**rh** dame *PP 18.3*; name *VA 992*; same *LLL 1.2.98*; shame *Ham 4.5.62*

**blameful** *adj*
'blɛ:mfʊl
**sp** blamefull[3]

**blameless** *adj*
'blɛ:mləs
**sp** blamelesse[2]

**Blanche** *n*
blɔ:nʃ
**sp** Blanch[10], Blaunch[3]

**blanched** *adj*
blɔ:nʃt
**sp** blanch'd[1]

**blank** *adj*
=
**sp** blanke[3], blancke-[space][1]
> point-blank

**blank / ~s** *n*
=
**sp** blanke[6] / blankes[3]

**blank / ~s** *v*
=
**sp** blanke[1] / blankes[1]

**blank-charter / ~s** *n*
ˌblaŋk-ˈʧɑːɹtəɹz
**sp** blanke-charters[1]

**blanket** *n*
=
**sp** blanket[5], blan-ket[1]

**blaspheme / ~ing** *v*
= / blasˈfiːmɪn, -ɪŋ
**sp** blaspheme[3] / blaspheming[1]

**blaspheming** *adj*
blasˈfiːmɪn, -ɪŋ
**sp** blaspheming[1]

**blasphemous** *adj*
=
**sp** blasphe-mous[1]

**blasphemy** *n*
*m* ˈblasfəˌməɪ
**sp** blasphemie[1], blasphemy[2]

**blast / ~s** *n*
blast / -s
**sp** blast[5] / blastes[1], blasts[5]
**rh** *1* fast *Luc 1335*; last *Per Epil.5*;
**rh** *2* haste *Luc 1335*

**blast / ~s / ~ing / ~ed** *v*
blast / -s / ˈblast·ɪn, -ɪŋ / -ɪd
**sp** blast[5] / blasts[1] / blasting[2] / blasted[5]
> star-blasting

**blasted** *adj*
ˈblastɪd
**sp** blasted[3]
> half-blasted

**blasting** *adj*
ˈblastɪn, -ɪŋ
**sp** blasting[1]

**blastment / ~s** *n*
ˈblastmənts
**sp** blastments[1]

**blaz·e / ~s** *n*
blɛːz / ˈblɛːzɪz
**sp** blaze[4] / blazes[1]

**blaz·e / ~ing / ~d** *v*
blɛːz / ˈblɛːzɪn, -ɪŋ / blɛːzd
**sp** blaze[4] / blazing[1] / blaz'd[2]
**rh** amazed, gazed *Luc 1353*
> emblaze

**blazing** *adj*
ˈblɛːzɪn, -ɪŋ
**sp** blazing[1]

**blazon** *n*
ˈblɛːzən
**sp** blason[1], blazon[3]

**blazon / ~est / ~ing** *v*
ˈblɛːzən / -st / -ɪn, -ɪŋ, ˈblɛːznɪn, -ɪŋ
**sp** blason[1] / blazon'st[1] / blazoning[1]

**blazoning** *adj*
ˈblɛːznɪn, -ɪŋ, -zən-
**sp** blazoning[1]

**bleach / ~ing** *n*
ˈbliːʧɪn, -ɪŋ
**sp** bleaching[1]

**bleach / ~ing** *v*
= / ˈbliːʧɪn, -ɪŋ
**sp** bleach[1] / bleaching[1]

**bleak** *adj*
=
**sp** bleake[4]

**blear / ~ed** *v*
bliːɹd
**sp** bleer'd[1]

**bleared** *adj*
*m* ˈbliːrɪd
**sp** bleared[2]

**bleat** *n*
=
**sp** bleat[1]
**rh** feat *MA 5.4.51*

**bleat / ~s / ~ed** *v*
=
**sp** bleat[2], bleate[1] / bleates[1] / bleated[1]

**bleed / ~est / ~s / ~eth / ~ing / bled** *v*
= / bliːdst / = / = / ˈbliːdɪn, -ɪŋ / =
**sp** bleed[22], bleede[10] / blee-dest[1], bleed'st[3] / bleedes[3], bleeds[4] / bleedeth[1] / bleeding[13] / bled[3]
**rh** agreed *R2 1.1.157*; decreed *Per 1.1.59*; deed *Luc 1732*, *Tit 5.3.64*; deed, exceed *Luc 228*; indeed *VA 669*; succeed *H5 Epil.12*; weed *VA 1056* / deeds, proceeds *Luc 1824*; proceeds *Luc 1551*; sheeds *Luc 1551* / needing *PP 17.15*
> a-bleeding

**bleeding** *adj / n*
ˈbliːdɪn, -ɪŋ
**sp** bleeding[13] / bleeding[1]
> mother-bleeding

**blemish / ~es** *n*
=
**sp** blemish[5] / blemishes[3]
**rh** replenish *Luc 1358*

**blemish / ~ed** *v*
=
**sp** blemish[3] / blemish'd[2]

**blemished** *adj*
=
**sp** blemish'd[1], blemisht[1]

**blench** *v*
=
**sp** blench[5]

**blend / ~ed / blent** *v*
=
**sp** blend[1] / blended[1] / blent[2]
**rh** amend, tend *LC 215*

**blended** *adj*
=
**sp** blended[1]

**bless / ~es / ~eth / ~ing / ~ed** *v*
=, *Fluellen H5 3.6.85ff*, *Evans MW 1.1.67ff* ples / = / = / ˈblesɪn, -ɪŋ / blest
**sp** bless[1], blesse[96], 'blesse[3], [heauen]-blesse[1], *Fluellen* plesse[4],

*Evans* 'plesse[3], [Got]-plesse[1] / blesses[1] / blesseth[1] / blessing[1] / bless'd[7], blessed[3], blest[39]
**rh** *1* cesse *AW 5.3.71*; confess *VA 1119*; **rh** *2* peace *MND 5.1.407* / beast *VA 328*; behest *Cym 5.4.121*; crest *MW 5.5.64*; rest *AW 2.1.208, MND 5.1.409*; blessed them rest them *TG 3.1.146*
> unblessed

**blessed** *adj*
*m* 'blesɪd, blest, *Evans MW 1.1.245* 'plesɪd
**sp** bles'd[1], bless'd[3], blessed[66], blest[15] *Evans* plessed-[will][1]

**blessedly** *adv*
'blesɪdləɪ
**sp** blessedly[2]

**blessedness** *n*
*m* 'blesɪd,nes
**sp** blessednesse[3]

**blessing / ~s** *n*
'blesɪn, -ɪŋ, *Evans MW 1.1.70* 'plesɪn, -ɪŋ / -z
**sp** blessing[45], 'blessing[2], *Evans* plessing[1] / blessings[16], bles-sings[1]
**rh** increasing *Tem 4.1.106*

**blew**
> blow

**blind** *adj*
bləɪnd
**sp** blind[17], blind[man][1], blind-[boyes, harpers, mans, ones][4], blinde[48]
**rh** Inde *LLL 4.3.222*; find, mind *Luc 758*; find *S 148.13*; kind *KL 2.4.47*; *MND 1.1.235, S 113.3, 149.14*; unkind *Tit 5.3.48*
> gravel-, hoodman-, pur-, sand-blind

**blind** *n*
bləɪnd
**sp** blinde[1]

**blind / ~s / ~ed** *v*
bləɪnd / -z / bləɪndɪd
**sp** blinde[2] / blindes[1] / blinded[3]

**blinded** *adj*
bləɪndɪd
**sp** blinded[1]

**blindfold** *adj*
'bləɪnfo:ld, -ndf-
**sp** blindfold[1]
> fold

**blinding** *adj*
'bləɪndɪn, -ɪŋ
**sp** blinding[2]

**blindly** *adv*
'bləɪnləɪ, -ndl-
**sp** blindely[1]

**blindness** *n*
'bləɪnəs, -ndn-
**sp** blindnesse[4]
**rh** kindness *CE 3.2.8, S 152.11, TG 4.2.46*

**blindworm / ~s** *n*
'bləɪndwɔ:ɹmz
**sp** blinde-wormes[1], blinde wormes[1]

**blink** *v*
=
**sp** blinke[1]

**blinking** *adj*
'blɪŋkɪn, -ɪŋ
**sp** blinking[2]

**bliss** *n*
=
**sp** blisse[22]
**rh** *1* amiss, iwis, kiss, this *MV 2.9.67*; kiss *Luc 389, MND 3.2.144*; this *MND 5.1.177, MV 3.2.136, Tit 3.1.149*; **rh** *2* is *Luc 389, MV 2.9.67*

**blister / ~s** *n*
'blɪstəɹ / -z
**sp** blister[3] / blisters[2]

**blister / ~ed** *v*
'blɪstəɹ / -d
**sp** blister[3] / blisterd[1], blister'd[1]

**blistered** *adj*
'blɪstəɹd
**sp** blistred[1]

**blithe** *adj*
bləɪð
**sp** blithe[2], blythe[1]

**Blithild** *n*
'blɪtɪld
**sp** Blithild[1]

**block / ~s** *n*
=
**sp** block[4], blocke[11] / blockes[4], blocks[1]

**blockhead** *n*
'blɒked, -hed
**sp** blocke-head[1]
> head

**blockish** *adj*
=
**sp** blockish[1]

**blood / ~'s / ~s** *n*
blɤd, *Fluellen H5 4.7.105* plɤd / -z
**sp** blood[525], blood-[royall][1], [maiden]-blood[1], bloud[87], [new-shed, stranger]-bloud[2], bloude[1], ['s]blud [God's blood][1], *Fluellen* plood[1] / bloods[2] / bloods[12], blouds[2]
**rh** *1* good *AW 2.3.96, 1H6 2.5.128, LC 162, LLL 2.1.121, Luc 655, 1029, Mac 3.4.135, 4.1.37, MND 5.1.275, R2 2.1.131, 5.5.113, S 109.10, 121.6, Tim 3.5.54, 4.2.38, Tit 5.1.49, VA 1182*; maidenhood *1H6 4.6.16*; stood *1H6 4.5.16, Luc 1738, VA 1122, 1169*; understood *LC 198*; wood *1H6 4.7.36, VA 742*; **rh** *2* brood *S 19.4*; mood *LC 198, MND 3.2.75*; **rh** *3* flood, mud *LC 47*; flood, *Luc 655, 1738, TC 1.3.301* / woods *Tim 4.3.535*
> half-blooded, hot-bloodied; heart-, life-, maiden-blood

**blood-bespotted** *adj*
'blɤd-bɪ,spɒtɪd
**sp** blood-bespotted[1]

**blood-boltered** *adj*
'blɤd-ˌbo:ltəɹd
**sp** blood-bolter'd[1]

**blood-consuming** *adj*
'blɤd-kənˌsju:mɪn, -ɪŋ
**sp** blood-consuming[1]
> consume

**blood-drinking** *adj*
*m* ˌblɤd-'drɪŋkɪn, -ɪŋ
**sp** blood-drinking[3]
> drink

**bloodhound** *n*
'blɤdəʊnd, -həʊnd
**sp** blood-hound[1]
> hound

**bloodied** *adj*
'blɤdəɪd
**sp** bloodied[1]

**bloodily** *adv*
*m* 'blɤdɪˌləɪ
**sp** bloodily[4]

**bloodless** *adj*
'blɤdləs
**sp** bloodlesse[5]

**blood-sacrifice** *n*
ˌblɤd-'sakrɪˌfəɪs
**sp** blood-sacrifice[1]

**bloodshed** *n*
'blɤdˌʃed
**sp** blood-shed[2]
> shed

**bloodshedding** *n*
'blɤdˌʃedɪn, -ɪŋ
**sp** bloodshedding[1]

**blood-slain** *adj*
'blɤdˌslɛ:n
**sp** bloud-slaine[1]
> slain

**blood-stained** *adj*
*m* ˌblɤd-'stɛ:nɪd
**sp** blood-stained[2]
> stain

**blood-sucker / ~s** *n*
'blɤd-ˌsɤkəɹ / -z
**sp** blood-sucker[1] / blood-suckers[1]

**blood-sucking** *adj*
*m* ˌblɤd-'sɤkɪn, -ɪŋ
**sp** blood-sucking[1]

**blood-thirsty** *adj*
*m* ˌblɤd-'θɐ:ɹstəɪ
**sp** blood-thirstie[1]

**blood·y / ~ier / ~iest** *adj*
'blɤdəɪ, *Fluellen H5 5.1.40* 'plɤdəɪ / -əɹ / -əst
**sp** bloodie[17], bloody[170], bloudie[5], bloudy[26], *Fluellen* ploodie[1] / bloodier[1] / bloodiest[1]

**blood·y / ~ied** *v*
'blɤdəɪd
**sp** blou-died[1]
> unbloodied

**bloody-faced** *adj*
'blɤdəɪ-ˌfɛ:st
**sp** bloody fac'd[1]
> face

**bloody-hunting** *adj*
'blɤdəɪ-'ɤntɪn, -ɪŋ, -'hɤnt-
**sp** bloody-hunting[1]
> hunt

**bloody-minded** *adj*
'blɤdəɪ-'məɪndɪd
**sp** bloody-minded[2]
> mind

**bloom** *n*
=
**sp** bloome[2]

**bloom / ~ed** *v*
=
**sp** bloom'd[1]

**blossom / ~s** *n*
=
**sp** blossom[1], blossome[10] / blossomes[5]

**blossoming** *adj*
'blɒsmɪn, -ɪŋ, -səm-
**sp** blossoming[2]

**blot / ~s** *n*
=
**sp** blot[13] / blots [4], blottes[1]
**rh** forgot, lot *Luc 537*; got *S 95.11*; not *S 92.13*; plot *R2 4.1.324*

**blot / ~s / ~ting / ~ted** *v*
= / = / 'blɒtɪn, -ɪŋ / =
**sp** blot[6] / blots[2] / blotting[1] / blotted[3]
**rh** not *LLL 4.3.239, Luc 192* / spotted *Oth 5.1.35*

**blow / ~s** *n*
blo: / -z
**sp** blow[23] / blowes[44], blows[3]
**rh** no, trow *CE 3.1.56*; woe *Luc 1823* / knows *AC 3.11.74, LLL 5.2.291, Luc 832*

**blow / ~est / ~s / ~ing / ~ed / blew / blown** *v*
blo:, *Fluellen H5 3.2.62* plo: / -st / -z, *Fluellen H5 4.8.14* plo:z / 'blo:ɪn, -ɪŋ / blo:d / = / blo:n
**sp** blow[57], blowe[2], *Fluellen* plowe[1] / blowest[1] / blowes[22], blows[1], *Fluellen* plowes[1] / blowing[8] / blowed[1] / blew[3] / blown[2], blowne[26]
**rh** below *Per 2.Chorus.29*; know *Mac 1.3.15, TC 4.5.275*; snow *LLL 5.2.910*; so, woe *Luc 1663*; so *LLL 4.3.107, PP 16.9* / grows *MND 2.1.249* / growing *TNK 1.1.11* / own *VA 778*
> overblow

**blowed** *adj*
blo:d
**sp** blow'd[1]
> unblowed

**blower-up / ~s ~** *n*
'blo:ɹz-'ɤp
**sp** blowers up[1]

**blowing** *n*
'blo:ɪn, -ɪŋ
**sp** blowing[1]
> fly-blowing

**blown** *adj*
blo:n
**sp** blowne[6]
**rh** shown *LLL 5.2.297*
> fly-, half-, high-blown

**blowze** *n*
bləʊz
**sp** blowse[1]

**Blois** *n*
*Fr* blwɛ, *Eng* bləɪz
**sp** Bloys[1]

**blubber / ~ing** *v*
'blɤbrɪn, -ɪŋ
**sp** blubbring[2]

**blue / ~est** *adj*
=, *Fluellen H5 3.6.101* plu: / 'blu:əst
**sp** blew[23], *Fluellen* plue[1] / blewest[1]
**rh** ensue *CE 2.2.201*; hue *LLL 5.2.883*; knew *Luc 407*

**blue-bottled** *adj*
=
**sp** blew-bottel'd[1]

**blue-cap / ~s** *n*
=
**sp** blew-cappes[1]
> cap

**blue-eyed** *adj*
'blu:-ˌəɪd
**sp** blew ey'd[1]
> eye

**blueish** *adj*
=
**sp** blewish[1]

**Blumer** *n*
'blu:məɹ
**sp** Blumer[1]

**blunt / ~est** *adj*
blɤnt / 'blɤntəst
**sp** blunt[26] / bluntest[1]

**Blunt / ~s** [name] *n*
blɤnt / -s
**sp** Blunt[20] / Blunts[1]

**blunt / ~s / ~ed** *v*
blɤnt / -s / 'blɤntɪd
**sp** blunt[4] / blunts[1] / blunted[1]

**blunted** *adj*
'blɤntɪd
**sp** blunted[1]

**bluntly** *adv*
'blɤntləɪ
**sp** bluntly[3]

**bluntness** *n*
'blɤntnəs
**sp** bluntnesse[1]

**blunt-witted** *adj*
ˌblɤnt-'wɪtɪd
**sp** blunt-witted[1]

**blur / ~s / ~red** *v*
blɐ:ɹ / -z / -d
**sp** blurre[1] / blurres[1] / blurr'd[1]

**blush / ~es** *n*
blɤʃ / 'blɤʃɪz
**sp** blush[8] / blushes[6]

**blush / ~est / ~es / ~ing / ~ed** *v*
blɤʃ / 'blɤʃ·əst / -ɪz / -ɪn, -ɪŋ / blɤʃt
**sp** blush[39] / blushest[1] / blushes[4] / blushing[4] / blush'd[3], blusht[3]
**rh** bush *LLL 4.3.136*

**blushing** *adj / n*
'blɤʃɪn, -ɪŋ
**sp** blushing[9], blush-in[1] / blushing[4]

**bluster / ~s** *n*
'blɤstəɹ / -z
**sp** bluster[1] / blusters[1]

**blustering** *adj*
'blɤstrɪn, -ɪŋ
**sp** blustring[1], blust'ring[1]

**boar / ~s** *n*
bɔ:ɹ / -z
**sp** boare[5], bore[11] / boares[1], [wilde]-boares[1]
**rh** gore *VA 614, 662*; more *VA 711, 900*; sore *PP 9.10*; wore *VA 1105*

**board / ~s** *n*
bɔ:ɹd / -z
**sp** boord[10] / boords[1]
**rh** word *CE 3.2.18*
> overboard

**board / ~ing / ~ed** *v*
bɔ:ɹd / 'bɔ:ɹd·ɪn, -ɪŋ / -ɪd
**sp** board[1], boord[6] / boording[1] / boarded[1], boorded[6]
**rh** word *LLL 2.1.204*

**boarish** *adj*
=
**sp** boarish[1]

**boar-pig** *n*
'bɔ:ɹ-ˌpɪg
**sp** bore-pigge[1]
> pig

**boar-spear** *n*
'bɔ:ɹ-ˌspi:ɹ
**sp** bore-speare[2]
> spear

**boast / ~s** *n*
bo:st, bɒst / -s
**sp** boast[9] / boasts[1]
**rh** lost *Luc 1193*

**boast / ~s / ~ing / ~ed** *v*
bo:st, bɒst / -s / 'bo:st·ɪn, -ɪŋ, 'bɒst- / -ɪd
**sp** boast[18] / boasts[1] / boasting[1] / boasted[1]
**rh** *1* cost *S 91.12*; frost *LLL 1.1.102*; lost *1H6 4.5.24, VA 1077*; **rh** *2* ghost *S 86.11*; most *S 25.2*

**boastful** *adj*
'bo:stfʊl, 'bɒst-
**sp** boastfull[1]

**boasting** *adj / n*
'bo:stɪn, -ɪŋ, 'bɒst-
**sp** boasting[1] / boasting[3]

**boat / ~s** *n*
bo:t / -s
**sp** boat[2], boate[6] / boates[3], boats[3], botes[1]
**rh** *1* afloat *S 80.11*; **rh** *2* wot *1H6 4.6.33*

**boatswain** *n*
'bo:sən, 'bo:tsən
**sp** boate-swaine[1], boatswaine[1], boat-swaine[1], boteswaine[3], bote-swaine[1], boson[1]

**bob** *n*
bɒb
**sp** bob[1]
**rh** crab *MND 2.1.49*

**bob / ~bed** *v*
bɒb / -d
**sp** bob[2] / bobb'd[2], bob'd[1]

**boblibindo** *nonsense word*
ˌbɒblɪ'bɪndo:
**sp** boblibindo[1]

**bobtail** *n*
'bɒbtɛ:l
**sp** bobtaile[1]

**Bocchus** *n*
'bɒkəs
**sp** Bochus[1]

**bod·e / ~es / ~ing / ~ed** *v*
bo:d / -z / 'bo:d·ɪn, -ɪŋ / -ɪd
**sp** boad[1], boade[1], bode[5] / boades[1], boads[2], bodes[3] / boading[1] / boaded[2]

**bodement / ~s** *n*
'bo:dmənts
**sp** boadments[1], bodements[1]

**bodge / ~d** *v*
=
**sp** bodg'd[1]

**bodied**
> loose-, tender-, worse-bodied

**bodiless** *adj*
=
**sp** bodilesse[1]

**bodily** *adj*
'bɒdɪləɪ
**sp** bodily[4]

**boding** *adj*
'bo:dɪn, -ɪŋ
**sp** boading[2]
> false-, ill-boding

**bodkin / ~s** *n*
=
**sp** bodkin[2] / bodkins[1]

**body / ~'s / bodies** *n*
'bɒdəɪ, *Fluellen H5 4.7.105* 'pɒdəɪ / -z
**sp** baudie *Q RJ 2.5.42*, bodie[33], bodies [body is][1], bodie's [body is][3], body[201], bo-dy[1], *Fluellen* pody[1] / bodies[13], bodyes[1] / bodies[31], bo-dies[1], bodyes[9]
> any-, no-, some-body

**bod·y / ~ies** *v*
'bɒdəɪz
**sp** bodies[1]
> em-, un-bodied

**body-curer** *n*
'bɒdəɪ-ˌkju:rəɹ
**sp** body-curer[1]
> curer

**bodykins** *n*
'bɒdɪkɪnz, -dk-
**sp** bodykins[1], body-kins[1]

**bog / ~s** *n*
=
**sp** bog[1], bogge[1] / bogges[1], boggs[1], bogs[1]

**boggle** *v*
=
**sp** boggle[1]

**boggler** *n*
'bɒgləɹ
**sp** boggeler[1]

**Bohemia / ~'s** *n*
bo:'i:mɪə, -'hi:- / -z
**sp** Bohemia[23], Bohe-mia[1], Bohemia's [Bohemia is][1] / Bohemia's[1]

**Bohemian** *n*
bo:'i:mɪən, -'hi:-
**sp** Bohemian[1], Bohemian-[Tartar][1]

**Bohun** *n*
*m* bu:n
**sp** Bohun[1]

**boil / ~s** *n*
bəɪl / -z
**sp** byle[1] / biles[1], byles[2]
**pun** *TN 2.5.3* bile

**boil / ~ed** *v*
bəɪl / bəɪld
**sp** boile[1], boyle[5] / boyld[1], boyl'd[1]
**rh** spoil *VA 555*

**boiled** *adj*
bəɪld
**sp** boyl'd[1]

**boiled-brains** *n*
'bəɪld-'brɛ:nz
**sp** boylde-braines[1]

**boiling** *adj / n*
'bəɪlɪn, -ɪŋ
**sp** boiling[1], boyling[1] / boyling[1]

**Bois** *n*
*Fr* bwɛ, *Eng* bəɪz
**sp** Boys[2]

**boisterous** *adj*
*m* 'bəɪstrəs
**sp** boistrous[2], boysterous[4], boystrous[4], boyst'rous[3]

**boisterously** *adv*
*m* 'bəɪstrəsˌləɪ
**sp** boysterously[1]

**boisterous-rough** *adj*
'bəɪstrəs-'rɤf
**sp** boistrous rough[1]

**boîtier** *Fr n*
bwɛt'je
**sp** [vn]boyteere[1]

**bold / ~er / ~est** *adj*
bo:ld, *Evans MW 5.4.3* po:ld / 'bo:ld·əɹ / *m* -əst, bo:ldst
**sp** bold[128], bolde[1], *Evans* pold[1] / bolder[4] / boldest[2], bold'st[1]
**rh** behold *S 131.7*; behold, cold, gold, infold, inscrolled, old, sold, told *MV 2.7.70*; cold *VA 401*; cold, hold *Luc 1559*; hold *S 122.11*; sold *R3 5.3.305*; told *Luc 1282, TNK Epil.11* / shoulder *LLL 5.2.108*
> over-, sudden-bold

**bold-beating** *adj*
'bo:ld-'bi:tɪn, -ɪŋ
**sp** bold-beating-[oathes][1]
> beating

**bolden / ~ed** *v*
'bo:ldənd
**sp** bolden'd[1], boldned[1]

**bolder** *n*
'bo:ldəɹ
**sp** bolder[2]

**boldfaced** *adj*
'bo:ld,fɛ:st
**sp** bold-fac't[1]
> face

**boldly** *adv*
'bo:ldləɪ
**sp** boldly[16]

**boldness** *n*
'bo:ldnəs
**sp** boldnes[2], boldnesse[12], bold-nesse[1]

**Bolingbroke / ~'s** *n*
'bʊlɪnbrʊk, -ɪŋ- / -s
**sp** Bollingbrooke[1], Bullinbroke[1], Bullinbrook[1], Bullinbrooke[1], Bullingbroke[1], Bullingbrooke[66], Bulling-brooke[1] / Bullingbrookes[4]
**rh** look *R2 3.4.99*

**bolster** *n / v*
'bo:lstəɹ
**sp** boulster[1] / boulster[1]

**bolt / ~s** *n*
bo:lt / -s
**sp** bolt[10], boult[1] / boltes[1], bolts[3]
> thunderbolt

**bolt / ~s / ~ed** *v*
bo:lts / 'bo:ltɪd
**sp** bolts[1] / bolted[1]

**bolted** *adj*
'bo:ltɪd
**sp** boulted[2]
> unbolted

**bolter / ~s** *n*
'bo:ltəɹz
**sp** boulters[1]

**bolting** *n*
'bo:ltɪn, -ɪŋ
**sp** bolting[1], boulting[1]

**bolting-hutch** *n*
'bo:ltɪn-,ɤʧ, -ɪŋ-, -,hɤʧ
**sp** boulting-hutch[1]

**bombard / ~s** *n*
'bɒmbəɹd, 'bɤm- / -z
**sp** bombard[1], bumbard[1] / bombards[1]

**bombast** *n*
'bɒmbast, 'bɤm-
**sp** bombast[1], bumbast[2]

**bon / ~ne** *Fr adj*
bɔ̃ / bɔn
**sp** bon[3] / bon[2]

**bona** *Lat*
> bonus

**Bona** [name] *n*
'bo:nə
**sp** Bona[14]

**bona-roba / ~s** *n*
,bɒnə-'ro:bə / -z
**sp** bona-roba[1] / bona-roba's[1]

**bond / ~s** *n*
=
**sp** bond[71] / bondes[1], bonds[21]
**rh** fond *Luc 136, Tim 1.2.64*

**bondage** *n*
=
**sp** bondage[20]

**bondmaid** *n*
'bɒndmɛ:d
**sp** bondmaide[1]

**bond·man / ~'s / ~men** *n*
=
**sp** bondman[7], bond-man[2] / bond-mans[1] / bondmen[2], bond-men[2]

**bondslave / ~s** *n*
*m* 'bɒndslɛ:v / bɒnd'slɛ:vz
**sp** bondslaue[2] / bond-slaues[1]
> slave

**bone** *Lat adv (in error) Holofernes correction of Nathaniel LLL 5.1.28* 'bo:nɛ
**sp** bome[1], boon[1], *emend of LLL 5.1.27* bene

**bone / ~s** *n*
bo:n / -z
**sp** bone[12] / bones[74]
**rh** *1* alone *TC 1.3.391*; **rh** *2* one *LLL 5.2.332*; gone *VA 56*; one *LC 45, VA 294*; **rh** *3* down *TC 5.8.12*; **rh** *4* none *Tim 4.3.531* / groans *TC 5.10.51*; stones *KJ 4.3.10, Tim 3.6.117*
> big-, burly-, raw-boned

**bone-ache** *n*
'bo:n-,ɛʧ
**sp** bone-ach[1]

**boneless** *adj*
'bo:nləs
**sp** bonelesse

**bonfire** *adj*
'bɒnfəɪɹ
bone-fire-[light][1]

**bonfire / ~s** *n*
'bɒnfəɪɹ / -z
**sp** bonfire[1] / bonfires[4], bon-fires[1]
> fire

**bonjour** *Fr interj*
bɔ̃'ʒuːɹ
**sp** bon iour[2], boon-iour[1]
> jour

**bonnet** *n*
=
**sp** bonnet[5], bonet[1]

**bonnet / ~ted** *v*
=
**sp** bon-netted[1]
> unbonneted

**bonny** *adj*
'bɒnəɪ
**sp** bonnie[3], bonny[3], bony[1]
**rh** nonny *MA 2.3.65*

**bonos** [*mock Lat TN 4.2.12*] *adj*
'bɒnɒs
**sp** bonos[1]

**bonus / ~a** *Lat adj*
'bɒna
**sp** bona[1]
**melius** *Per comparative adj*
'melɪʊs
**sp** melius[1]
**rh** glorious *Per Prol.10*

**Bonville** *n*
'bɒnvɪl
**sp** Bonuill[1]

**book / ~s** *n*
=
**sp** book[2], booke[80] / bookes[32], books[3]
**rh** look *LLL 1.1.74, 4.2.24, 4.3.248, Luc 615, S 59.7, 77.14*; o'erlook *MND 2.2.128, S 82.4*; took *RJ 1.5.110* / hooks, looks *Luc 102*; looks *AY 3.2.5, LLL 1.1.87, Luc 811, 1253, RJ 2.2.156*
> copy-, horn-, love-, muster-, note-, prayer-, table-book; unbookish

**book / ~ed** *v*
=
**sp** booke[1] / book'd[1]

**bookish** *adj*
=
**sp** bookish[3]

**book·man / ~men** *n*
=
**sp** bookemen[1], book-men[1]

**book-mate / ~s** *n*
'bʊk-ˌmɛːts
**sp** booke-mates[1]
> mate

**book-oath** *n*
'bʊk-ˌoːθ
**sp** book-oath[1]
> oath

**boon** *n*
=
**sp** boon[1], boone[10]

**boor / ~s** *n*
buːɹ / -z
**sp** boore[1] / boores[1]

**boorish** *adj*
'buːrɪʃ
**sp** boorish[1]

**boot / ~s** *n*
=, bʊt / -s
**sp** boot[13], boote[14] / bootes[7], boots[10], [fishermens]-boots[1]
**rh** foot *1H6 4.6.52, R2 1.1.164, TS 5.2.175*
> overboots

**boot / ~s** *v*
=, bʊt / -s
**sp** boot[2], boote[2] / bootes[3], boots[3]

**booted** *adj*
'buːtɪd, bʊt-
**sp** booted[1]

**boot-hose** *n*
'buːt-ˌoːz, -hoːz, 'bʊt-
**sp** boot-hose[1]
> hose

**bootless** *adj*
'buːtləs, 'bʊt-
**sp** booteles[1], bootelesse[3], bootles[1], bootlesse[14]

**boot·y / ~ies** *n*
'buːtəɪ / -z
**sp** booty[3], boo-ty[1] / booties[1]

**bo-peep** *n*
ˌboː-'piːp
**sp** bo-peepe[1]
**rh** weep *KL 1.4.173*
> peep

**Borachio** *n*
bɒ'raʧɪoː
**sp** Borachio[7], Bo-rachio[1]

**Bordeaux** *adj / n*
*m* 'bɔːɹdoː
**sp** Burdeux-[stuffe][1] / Burdeaux[7], Burdeux[1]

**border / ~s** *n*
'bɔːɹdəɹ / -z
**sp** border[1] / borders[1]

**borderer / ~s** *n*
*m* 'bɔːɹdəˌrɐːɹz
**sp** borderers[1]

**bore / ~s** *n*
bɔːɹ / -z
**sp** bore[1], boare[1] / bores[1]
> bear

**bor·e / ~es / ~ing / ~ed** *v*
bɔːɹ / -z / 'bɔːɹɪn, -ɪŋ / bɔːɹd
**sp** bore[1] / bores[2] / boaring[1] / bord[1]
**rh** restore *LC 300*

**bore** [*past tense*]
> bear *v*

**Boreas** *n*
'bɒrɪəs
**sp** Boreas[1]

**bore-sprit** *n*
'bɔːɹ-ˌsprɪt
**sp** bore-spritt[1]

**born** *adj*
bɔːɹn, *Fluellen H5 4.7.11ff* pɔːɹn

**sp** born[5], borne[153], borne-[deuill][1], *Fluellen* porne[3]
**rh** forsworn *LLL 1.1.149, 4.3.216, S 66.2*; horn *AY 4.2.15*; outworn *S 68.3*; outworn, torn *Luc 1759*; scorn *AW 2.3.133, Cym 4.4.54, 5.4.126, 1H6 4.7.40, Luc 1190, Mac 4.1.79, 5.6.23, MND 2.2.129, 3.2.124*; sworn *LLL 5.2.284*; thorn *AW 1.3.126*
> base-, eldest-, first-, fool-, forest-, hag-, hedge-, high-, low-, mean-, new-, newly-, self-, still-, true-, twin-, un-, well-, youngest-born

**borne**
> bear *v*

**borough / ~s** *n*
'bɤrə / -z
**sp** borough[1], burrough[1] / boroughs[1]

**borrow / ~s / ~ed / ~edest** *v*
'bɒrə, -ro: / -z / -d / -dst
**sp** borrow[24], bor-row[1] / borrowes[3], borrows[1] / borrow'd[2], borro-wed[1], borrowed[5] / borrowd'st[1]
**rh** good-morrow *VA 861*; morrow, sorrow *Luc 1083*; sorrow *Luc 1498, Oth 1.3.213, VA 961*; tomorrow *PP 14.29*

**borrowed** *adj*
'bɒrəd, -ro:d
**sp** borrowed[12], borrow-ed[1]
> easy-borrowed

**borrower** *n*
*m* 'bɒrəwəɹ, -rw-
**sp** borrower[2]

**borrowing** *adj / n*
*m* 'bɒrəwɪn, -ɪŋ, -rw-
**sp** borrowing[1] / borrowing[3]

**bosko / boskos** *nonsense words*
'bɒsko: / 'bɒskɒs
**sp** bosko[1] / boskos[1]

**bosky** *adj*
'bɒskəɪ
**sp** boskie[1]

**bosom** *adj / v*
=
**sp** bosome[2] / bosome[1]
> unbosom

**bosom / ~s** *n*
=
**sp** bosom[5], bosome[112], [glutton]-bosome[1], bosome-[multiplied][1] / bosomes[27]

**boss / ~ed** *v*
=
**sp** bost[1]

**Bosworth** *n*
'bɒzwəɹθ, -ɹt
**sp** Bosworth[1]

**botch / ~es** *n*
=
**sp** botches[1]

**botch / ~ed** *v*
=
**sp** botch[2] / botcht[1], botch'd[1]

**botcher / ~ers** *n*
'bɒʧəɹ / -z
**sp** botcher[1] / botchers[2]

**botchy** *adj*
'bɒʧəɪ
**sp** botchy[1]

**both** *adj*
bo:θ, *Jamy H5 3.2.99* ba:θ
**sp** both[596], *Jamy* bath[1]
**rh** growth *S 99.10*; oath *Per 1.2.121*; oath, troth *Luc 572*; troth *MND 2.2.47*

**both-sides** *adj*
'bo:θ-ˌsəɪdz
**sp** both-sides[1]
> side

**bots** *n*
bɒts
**sp** bots[1], bottes[1]

**bottle / ~s** *n*
=
**sp** bottle[20], [aqua-vitae]-bottle[1] / bottles[2]
> twiggen-bottle

**bottle-ale** *adj*
'bɒtl-ˌɛ:l
**sp** bottle-ale[2]
> ale

**bottled** *adj*
=
**sp** bottel'd[2]

**bottom / ~s** *n*
=
**sp** bottom[1], bottome[31], bot-tome[1] / bottomes[2]

**Bottom / ~'s [name]** *n*
=
**sp** Bottom[1], Bottome[12] / Bottomes[2]

**bottom** *v*
=
**sp** bottome[2]
> sandy-bottomed

**bottomless** *adj*
=
**sp** bottomlesse[2]

**Bouciqualt** *n*
'bu:sɪˌkwɑl, *Fr* busi'ko:
**sp** Bouchiquald[1], Bouciquall[1]

**bough / ~s** *n*
bəʊ / bəʊz
**sp** bough[3], bow[1] / boughes[6], bowes[2], bows[1]
**rh** now *S 102.11, Tem 5.1.94, VA 37* / vows *AY 3.2.131*

**bought**
> buy

**bounce** *n*
bəʊns
**sp** bounce[1], bownce[1]

**bouncing** *adj*
'bəʊnsɪn, -ɪŋ
**sp** bouncing[1]

**bound** *adj*
bəʊnd
**sp** bound[2]
> brow-, earth-, gold-, un-bound

**bound / ~s** *n*
bəʊnd / bəʊndz
**sp** bound[10] / bounds[18]
**rh** sound *RJ 3.2.125* / hounds *MND 3.2.65*

**bound / ~eth / ~ing / ~ed / ~en** *v*
bəʊndz / 'bəʊnd·əθ / -ɪn, -ɪŋ / -ɪd / -ən
**sp** bounds[2] / boundeth[1] / bounding[1] / bounded[2] / bounden[2]
**rh** confound *Per 5.2.13* [*Chorus*]; ground *VA 226*; round *Luc 1501*; bound-a sound-a *TNK 3.5.65* [*song*] / wounds *VA 265*
> a-, re-bound

**bounded** *adj*
'bəʊndɪd
**sp** bounded[1]

**bounding** *adj*
'bəʊndɪn, -ɪŋ
**sp** bounding[1]

**boundless** *adj*
'bəʊndləs
**sp** bound-lesse[1], boundlesse[5]

**bounteous** *adj*
'bəʊntɪəs [2 *sylls*]
**sp** bounteous[16]

**bounteously** *adv*
*m* 'bəʊntɪəs,ləɪ [3 *sylls*]
**sp** bounteously[1]

**bountiful** *adj*
*m* 'bəʊntɪ,fʊl, -ɪf-
**sp** bountifull[6], boun-tifull[1]

**bountifully** *adv*
'bəʊntɪ,fʊləɪ, -ɪfləɪ
**sp** bountifully[1]

**bount·y / ~ies** *n*
'bəʊntəɪ / -z
**sp** bountie[11], bounty[26] / bounties[5]
> self-bounty

**bourbier** *Fr n*
buɹ'bje
**sp** bourbier[1]

**Bourbon** *n*
*m* 'bu:ɹbən
**sp** Bourbon[2], Burbon[5]

**Bourgogne** *n*
*m* 'bu:ɹgɔɪn
**sp** Bourgougne[1], Burgogne[1]

**bourn** *n*
bɔɹn
**sp** borne[3], bourne[3]

**bout / ~s** *n*
bəʊt / -s
**sp** bout[1], bowt[3] / bowts[1]

**bow / ~s** [weapon] *n*
bo: / -z
**sp** bow[15], bowe[3] / bowes[3]
**rh** doe *Luc 580, TC 3.1.113*; go *MND 3.2.101*; know *LLL 4.1.110, Tem 4.1.86*; woe *Per 5.1.247*
> stone-bow

**bow** [head] **/ ~s / ~ing / ~ed** *v*
bəʊ / -z / 'bəʊɪn, -ɪŋ / bəʊd
**sp** bow[22], bowe[4] / bowes[8] / bowing[2] / bow'd[12], bowed[2]
**rh** allow, vow *Luc 1846*; now *KL 3.6.107* [*Q*], *S 90.3, 120.3, VA 99, 1061* / growing *Tem 4.1.113* / proud *Luc 1372*; vowed *LLL 4.2.108, PP 5.4*
> unbowed

**bow-boy / ~'s** *n*
'bo:-,bəɪz
**sp** bowe-boyes[1]

**bow-case** *n*
'bo:-,kɛ:s
**sp** bow-case[1]
> case

**bowels** *n*
*m* 'bəʊəlz, bəʊlz
**sp** bowelles[1], bowels[21]

**bower / ~s** *n*
bo:ɹ / -z
**sp** bower[5], bowre[1] / bowres[1]
**rh** flower *MND 3.1.192*; hour *MND 3.2.7*; power *S 127.7* / flowers *TN 1.1.42*

**bower** *v*
bo:ɹ
**sp** bower[1]

**bow-hand** *n*
'bo:-,and, -,hand
**sp** bow hand[1]

**bowl / ~s** *n*
bəʊl, bo:l / -z
**sp** bole[1], bowl[1], bowle[8] / bowles[5]
**rh** *1* foal *MND 2.1.47*; **rh** *2* owl *LLL 5.2.914*

**bowl / ~ed** *v*
bəʊl, bo:l / -d
**sp** boule[2] / bowl'd[1]
**rh** foul, owl *LLL 4.1.139*

**bowler** *n*
'bəʊləɹ, 'bo:l-
**sp** bowler[1]

**bowling** *n*
'bəʊlɪn, -ɪŋ, 'bo:l-
**sp** bowling[1]

**bow-string / ~s** *n*
'bo:-,strɪŋ / -z
**sp** bow-string[1] / bow-strings[1]
> string

**bow-wow** *interj*
'bəʊ-'wəʊ
**sp** bowgh wawgh[1], bowgh-wawgh[1]
**rh** dow *Tem 1.2.382*

**box / ~es** *n*
=
**sp** box[12], boxe[6] / boxes[1]

**box-tree** *n*
=
**sp** box tree[1]
> tree

**boy / ~'s / ~s / ~s'** *n*
bəɪ / -z, *Fluellen H5 4.7.1* pəɪz
**sp** boy[365] / boyes[4], [blind]-boyes[1] / boies[1], boyes[77], [hem]-boyes[1], *Fluellen* poyes[1] / boyes[1]
**rh** coy *VA 95*; destroy *1H6 4.6.24, VA 344*; employ *MND 3.2.375*; joy *MND 2.1.26, R2 5.3.95, VA 403*; toy *TN 5.1.386, TS 2.1.396, VA 32*; Troy *TC 5.3.35* / joys *Cym 5.5.107*; noise *CE 3.1.62*; toys *Cym 4.2.194, LLL 4.3.167*
> school-, sea-, ship-, tom-boy

**boy** *v*
bəɪ
**sp** boy[1]

**Boyet** *n*
bə'jet
**sp** Boyet[15], *also sp* Boiet[2] *in speech prefixes*
**rh** debt *LLL 5.2.334*

**boyish** *adj*
'bəɪɪʃ
**sp** boyish[2]

**boy-queller** *n*
'bəɪ-ˌkweləɹ
**sp** boy-queller[1]
> quell

**Boys**
> Bois

**Brabant** *n*
*m* 'brabənt, -ɔ:nt
**sp** Brabant[5]

**Brabantio** *n*
bra'bansɪo:
**sp** Brabantio[10]

**brabble** *n*
=
**sp** brabble[2]

**brabbler** *n*
'brabləɹ
**sp** brabler[2]

**Braby**
> Bracy

**brace** *n*
brɛ:s
**sp** brace[16]

**brace / ~d** *v*
brɛ:st
**sp** brac'd[1]
> unbraced

**bracelet / ~s** *n*
'brɛ:slɪt / -s
**sp** bracelet[3] / bracelets[2]

**brach** *n*
braʧ
**sp** brach[4], brache[1]

**Bracy** *n*
'brɛ:səɪ
*sp emend of 1H4 2.4.327* Braby[1]

**brag / ~s** *n*
=
**sp** bragge[4] / bragges[2]

**brag / ~s / ~ging / ~ged** *v*
= / = / 'bragɪn, -ɪŋ / =
**sp** brag[6], bragge[2] / brags[5] / bragging[1] / bragg'd[1]

**braggard / ~s** *n*
'bragəɹd / -z
**sp** braggard[1] / braggards[1]
> braggart

**braggardism** *n*
'bragəɹdɪzəm
**sp** bragadisme[1]

**braggart / ~s** *n*
'bragəɹt / -s
**sp** bragart[2], braggart[11] / braggarts[1], braggerts[1]
> braggard

**bragged** *adj*
=
**sp** bragg'd[1]

**bragging** *adj / n*
'bragɪn, -ɪŋ, *Fluellen H5 5.1.5* 'pragɪn, -ɪŋ
**sp** bragging[5], *Fluellen* pragging[1] / bragging[2]

**bragless** *adj*
=
**sp** braglesse[1]

**braid** *adj*
brɛ:d
**sp** braide[1]
**rh** maid *AW 4.2.73*
> unbraided

**brain / ~s / ~s'** *n*
brɛ:n, *Evans MW 1.1.40, 4.1.33* prɛ:n / brɛ:nz, *Evans MW 3.1.110, Fluellen H5 4.7.27, 35* prɛ:nz / brɛ:nz
**sp** brain[3], braine[66], brayne[2], *Evans* praine[2] / braines[1] / braines[41], [boylde]-braines[1], brains[2], [bastard]-braynes, *Evans, Fluellen* praines[3]
**rh** again *VA 910, 1040*; contain *S 77.11*; reign *RJ 2.3.33*; remain *S 122.1*; Spain *LLL 1.1.163*; twain *Ham 3.2.237*
> lack-, mad-, tickle-brain

**brain / ~ed** *v*
brɛ:n / -d
**sp** braine[3] / brain'd[2]
> dull-, fat-, hare-brained

**Brainford** *n*
'brɛ:nfəɹd
**sp** Braineford[1], Brainford[3]

**brainish** *adj*
'brɛ:nɪʃ
**sp** brainish[1]

**brainless** *adj*
'brɛ:nləs
**sp** brainlesse[1]

**brain-pan** *n*
'brɛ:n-ˌpan
**sp** brain-pan[1]

**brainsick** *adj*
'brɛ:n-ˌsɪk
**sp** braine-sick[1], braine-sicke[2], brainsicke[1], brain-sicke[1]
> sick

**brainsickly** *adv*
'brɛ:n-ˌsɪkləɪ
**sp** braine-sickly[1]

**brake / ~s** *n*
brɛ:k / -s
**sp** brake[6] / brakes[2]
**rh** ache *VA 876*; take *MND 3.2.15*

**Brakenbury** *n*
*m* 'brakənbrəɪ
**sp** Brakenbury[4]

**bramble / ~s** *n*
=
**sp** brambles[1]

**bran** *n*
=
**sp** bran[6], branne[1]

**branch / ~es** *n*
branʃ, brɔ:- / 'branʃɪz, 'brɔ:-
**sp** branch[12], [top]-branch[1] / branches[15], [virgin]-branches[1]

**branch** *v*
branʃ, brɔ:-
**sp** braunch[1]

**branched** *adj*
branʃt, brɔ:-
**sp** branch'd[1]

**branchless** *adj*
'branʃləs, 'brɔ:-
**sp** branchlesse[1]

**brand / ~s** *n*
=
**sp** brand[4] / brands[6]
**rh** hand *S 111.5, 154.2*
> firebrand

**brand / ~s / ~ed** *v*
=
**sp** brand[1] / brands[1] / branded[3]

**brandish / ~ed** *v*
=
**sp** brandish[3] / brandish'd[1], brandisht[1]

**brandished** *adj*
=
**sp** brandisht[2]

**Brandon** *n*
=
**sp** Branden[1], Brandon[4]

**Brandusium** *n*
bran'du:zɪʊm
**sp** Brandusium[1]

**bras** *Fr n*
bra
**sp** bras[2]

**brass** *adj / n*
bras
**sp** brasse[2] / brasse[12]

**brassy** *adj*
'brasəɪ
**sp** brassie[1]

**brat / ~s** *n*
=
**sp** brat[8] / brats[4]

**brave / ~er / ~est** *adj*
brɛ:v, *Fluellen H5 3.6.62ff* prɛ:v / 'brɛ:v·əɪ / -əst
**sp** braue[142], *Fluellen* praue[4] / brauer[9] / brauest[3]

**brave / ~s** *n*
brɛ:v / -z
**sp** braue[2] / braues[3]

**brav·e / ~s / ~ing / ~ed** *v*
brɛ:v / -z / 'brɛ:vɪn, -ɪŋ / brɛ:vd
**sp** braue[13] / braues[1] / brauing[3] / brau'd[6], braued[2]
> outbrave

**brave** *Fr adj*
bra:v
**sp** braue[1]

**bravely** *adv*
'brɛ:vləɪ
**sp** brauely[35]

**bravery** *n*
*m* 'brɛ:vrəɪ, -vər-
**sp** brauerie[1], brauery[4], brau'ry[1]
**rh** knavery *TS 4.3.57*

**bravest** *n*
'brɛ:vəst
**sp** brauest[1]

**braving** *adj*
'brɛ:vɪn, -ɪŋ
**sp** brauing[1]
> air-braving

**brawl / ~s** *n*
brɔ:l, brɑ:l / -z, *Fluellen H5 4.8.65* prɔ:lz
**sp** brall[2], braule[2], brawle[3] / bralles[1], braules[2], brawles[1], *Fluellen* prawles[1]
**rh** all *RJ 3.1.143*
> night-brawler

**brawl / ~s / ~ing / ~ed** *v*
brɔ:l, brɑ:l / -z / 'brɔ:lɪn, -ɪŋ, 'brɑ:- / brɔ:ld, brɑ:ld
**sp** braul[1], brawle[7] / brawles[1] / brauling[2] / braul'd[1]

**brawling** *adj / n*
'brɔ:lɪn, -ɪŋ, 'brɑ:-
**sp** brawling[3] / brawling[2]

**brawn** *adj*
=
**sp** brawn[1]

**brawn / ~s** *n*
=
**sp** brawne[4] / brawnes[1]

**bray** *n*
brɛ:
**sp** bray[1]

**bray / ~ed** *v*
brɛ: / -d
**sp** bray[1] / braid[1]

**braying** *n*
'brɛ:ɪn, -ɪŋ
**sp** braying[1]

**braze / ~d** *v*
brɛ:zd
**sp** braz'd[2]

**brazen** *adj*
'brɛ:zən
**sp** brasen[1], brazen[9], brazon[1], brazon-[face][1]

**brazen-faced** *adj*
'brɛ:zən-ˌfɛ:st
**sp** brazen-fac'd[1]
> face

**brazier** *n*
'brɛ:zɪəɹ
**sp** bras-ier[1]

**breach / ~es** *n*
bri:ʧ / 'bri:ʧɪz
**sp** breach[31], breech[1] / breaches[1]
> before-, faith-, promise-breach

**bread** *n*
=, *Fluellen H5 5.1.8* pred
**sp** bread[20], [browne]-bread[1], *Fluellen* pread[1]
**rh** dead *Per 1.4.95*
> gingerbread

**bread-chopper** *n*
'bred-ˌʧɒpəɹ
**sp** bread-chopper[1]

**breadth** *n*
=
**sp** breadth[1], bredth[7]
> hairbreadth

**break / ~est / ~s / ~ing / brake / broke / ~n** *v*
brɛ:k / -st / -s / 'brɛ:kɪn, -ɪŋ / brɛ:k / bro:k / 'bro:kən
**sp** brake[1], break[11], breake[239], break't [break it][1] / break'st[1] / breakes[25], breaks[2] / breaking[13] / brake[2] / broke[83], brok's [broke his][1] / broken[25]
**rh** speak *Ham 3.2.197, LLL 1.1.131, Luc 1270, 1716, Mac 4.3.210, S 34.5, TC 3.3.215, VA 222* / speaks *Luc 566* / speaking *TC 4.4.16* / spoke *MND 1.1.175* / open *S 61.3, VA 47*
> heart-, out-break; broke, unbroke

**breaker** *n*
'brɛ:kəɹ
**sp** breaker[2]
> horseback-, promise-breaker

**breakfast** *n / v*
=
**sp** breakefast[3], breakfast[7], break-fast[4] / breakefast[1]

**breaking** *adj / n*
'brɛ:kɪn, -ɪŋ
**sp** breaking[4] / breaking[7]
> oath-, rib-breaking

**breakneck** *n*
'brɛ:kˌnek
**sp** breake-neck[1]
> neck

**break-promise** *n*
'brɛ:k-ˌprɒmɪs
**sp** breake-promise[1]

**break-vow** *n*
'brɛ:k-ˌvəʊ
**sp** breake-vow[1]
> vow

**breast / ~s** *n*
= / -s
**sp** breast[27], brest[60] / breastes[1], breasts[4], brests[5]
**rh** *1* best *3H6 2.5.11, MND 2.2.152, S 110.14*; chest *R2 1.1.181, S 48.11*; congest *LC 259*; crest *VA 396*; detest, guest *Luc 1563*; distressed *Luc 463, VA 812*; expressed *S 23.10;* guest *S 153.10*; jest *LLL 4.3.171, R2 1.3.96, 5.3.101*; nest *PT 57*; pressed *RJ 1.1.186*; protest *VA 582*; rest *3H6 2.6.30, Ham 3.2.188, LLL 5.2.811, Luc 759, 1842, MND 5.1.146, PT 57, RJ 2.2.124, 2.2.186, VA 648, 782, 855, 1183*; unrest *Luc 1723* / **rh** *2* east *LLL 4.3.223*; feast *Per 3.Chorus.3* / behests, nests *Luc 851*; guests, rests *Luc 1122*
> a-, red-breast

**breast / ~ing / ~ed** *v*
'brestɪn, -ɪŋ / =
**sp** bresting[1] / brested[1]

**breast-deep** *adj*
=
**sp** brest deepe[1]
> deep

**breastplate** *n*
'brestˌplɛ:t
**sp** brest-plate[1]
> plate

**breath / ~s** *n*
=
**sp** breath[190], breathe[2], breth[5] / breathes[3], breaths[4]
**rh** *1* death *2H4 4.2.123, 1H6 4.3.41, 4.6.4, 4.7.24, KJ 4.2.246, LLL 4.3.106, Luc 400, 1180, 1777, Mac 5.6.9, MND 3.2.168, PP 16.8, R2 1.3.66, 173, 232, 3.2.185, 5.3.71, R3 5.3.173, S 99.11, TC 4.1.74, 5.8.3, TN 2.4.52, VA 414, 510, 929, 934, 1172*; death, vanisheth *Luc 1040*; Macbeth *Mac 4.1.98*; **rh** *2* bequeath *Luc 1180, MND 3.2.168*
> self-breath

**breath·e / ~est / ~es / ~ing / ~ed** *v*
= / bri:ðst / = / 'bri:ð·ɪn, -ɪŋ / *m* -ɪd, bri:ðd
**sp** breath[48], breathe[13] / breath'st[1], / breathes[7], breaths[2], breath's[1] / breathing[6] / breath'd[21], breathed[1]
**rh** bequeathed, unsheathed *Luc 1726*

**breathed** *adj*
*m* bri:ðd, 'bri:ðɪd
**sp** breathed[2]
> out-, un-breathed

**breather** *n*
'bri:ðəɹ
**sp** breather[3]

**breathing** *adj / n*
'bri:ðɪn, -ɪŋ
**sp** breathing[9] / breathing[8], brea-thing[1]

**breathless** *adj*
=
**sp** breathles[2], breathlesse[10]

**Brecknock** *n*
=
**sp** Brecnock[1]

**bred**
> breed

**breech** *n*
=
**sp** breech[1]

**breech / ~ed** *v*
=
**sp** breech'd[1]
> unbreeched

**breeches** *n*
'bri:ʧɪz, *Evans MW 4.1.73* 'pri:ʧɪz
**sp** breeches[7], *Evans* preeches[1]

**breeching** *adj*
'bri:ʧɪn, -ɪŋ
**sp** breeching[1]

**breed** *n*
=
**sp** breed[8], breede[1]

**breed / ~s / ~ing / bred** *v*
= / = / 'bri:dɪn, -ɪŋ / =
**sp** breed[29], breede[8] / breedes[6], breeds[16] / breeding[1] / bred[35]
**rh** deed, speed *Luc 499*; feed *Per 1.1.66, 134, VA 171* / deeds *S 111.4*; deeds, feeds *Luc 907*; seeds *AW 1.3.140* / bed *Luc 937*; buried [*3 sylls*] *Per 5.1.164*; dead *Luc 490, 1188, S 108.13, 112.13, VA 214*; dishon-oured *Luc 1188*; fed *Tit 5.3.61*; head *Per 1.1.108*; head, nourished *MV 3.2.63*; honoured, unconquered *Luc 411*; red *LLL 1.2.96*
> a-breeding; heaven-, home-, inland-, mad-, near-, true-, well-bred

**breed-bate** *n*
'bri:d-ˌbɛ:t
**sp** breede-bate[1]
> bate

**breeder / ~s** *n*
'bri:dəɹ / -z
**sp** breeder[5] / breeders[2]
> soldier-breeder

**breeding** *adj / n*
'bri:dɪn, -ɪŋ
**sp** breeding[1] / breeding[22], breed-ing[1]
> ill-, still-breeding

**breeze** *n*
=
**sp** breeze[1], brieze[1]

**brethren / ~'s** *n*
*m* 'breðəˌren, 'breðrən / -z
**sp** bretheren[6], brethren[15] / bretherens[1]

**brevis** *Lat adj*
'brevɪs
**sp** breuis[1]

**brevity** *n*
*m* 'brevtəɪ, -vɪt-
**sp** breuitie[3], breuity[1]

**brew / ~s / ~ing / ~ed** *v*
= / = / 'bru:ɪn, -ɪŋ / =
**sp** brew[4] / brewes[1] / brewing[1] / breu'd[1], brew'd[2]
> a-brewing

**brewage** *n*
=
**sp** brewage[1]

**brewer / ~'s / ~s** *n*
'bru:əɹz
**sp** brewers[1] / brewers[2]

**brew-house** *n*
'bru:-ˌəʊs, -ˌhəʊs
**sp** brew-house[1]
> house

**briar / ~s** *n*
'brəɪəɹ / -z
**sp** briar[1], brier[2], bryer[3] / briars[6], briers[3]
**rh** fire *MND 2.1.3, 3.1.101, 5.1.384*; tire *MND 3.1.87* / desires *MND 3.2.443*

**Briareus** *n*
brɪ'arɪəs
**sp** Briareus[1]

**bribe / ~s** *n*
brəɪb / -z
**sp** bribe[3] / bribes[3]

**bribe / ~d** *v*
brəɪb / -d
**sp** bribe[2] / brib'd[2]

**bribed** *adj*
brəɪbd
**sp** brib'd-[bucke][1]

**briber** *n*
'brəɪbəɹ
**sp** briber[1]

**brick** *adj*
=
**sp** brick-[wall][1], bricke[1]

**brick / ~s** *n*
=
**sp** bricke[1] / brickes[1]

**bricklayer** *n*
'brɪkˌlɛ:əɹ
**sp** bricklayer[2]

**bridal** *adj / n*
'brəɪdl
**sp** bridall[4] / bridall[1]

**bridal-bed** *n*
'brəɪdl-ˌbed
**sp** bridall bed[3]
> bed

**bride / ~s** *n*
brəɪd / -z

**sp** bride[34] / brides[2]
**rh** pride *RJ 1.2.11*

**bride-bed** *n*
'brəɪd-ˌbed
**sp** bride-bed[2]
> bed

**bridegroom / ~'s / ~s** *n*
'brəɪdˌgru:m, -grʊm / -z
**sp** bridegroom[2], bridegroome[8], bride-groome[3] / bridegroomes[2], bride-groomes[1] / bride-groomes[1]
> groom

**bridge / ~s** *n*
=, *Fluellen H5 3.6.12ff* prɪʤ / =
**sp** bridge[10], *Fluellen* pridge[6] / bridges[2]
> drawbridge, London Bridge

**Bridgenorth** *n*
'brɪʤˌnɒɹθ
**sp** Bridgenorth[2]

**Bridget** *n*
=
**sp** Bridget[1], Briget[2]

**bridle** *n*
'brəɪdl
**sp** bridle[2]
> unbridled

**bridle / ~d** *v*
'brəɪdl / -d
**sp** bridle[3] / bridled[2]

**brief / ~er / ~est** *adj*
= / bri:fəɹ / =
**sp** breefe[26], brief[1], briefe[36] / briefer[1] / breefest[1]
**rh** grief *Luc 1309, R2 5.1.93*

**brief** *n*
=, *Evans MW 1.1.134* pri:f, *Jamy H5 3.2.114* bref
**sp** breefe[10], briefe[13], *Evans* priefe[1], *Jamy* breff[1]

**briefly** *adv*
'bri:fləɪ
**sp** breefely[8], briefelie[1], briefely[7], briefly[3]

**briefness** *n*
=
**sp** briefenesse[2]

**bright / ~est** *adj*
brəɪt / 'brəɪtəst
**sp** bright[59] / brightest[4]
**rh** light *LLL 4.3.28, 265, S 43.5, VA 862*; light, sight *Luc 376*; might *S 65.14*; night *RJ 1.5.44, 2.2.21, S 28.9, 147.13, TNK 3.5.124*; sight *MND 5.1.265*; write *S 21.11*

**brighten** *v*
'brəɪtən
**sp** brighten[1]

**brightly** *adv*
'brəɪtləɪ
**sp** brightly[2]

**brightness** *n*
'brəɪtnəs
**sp** brightnesse[2]

**bright-shining** *adj*
'brəɪt-ˌʃəɪnɪn, -ɪŋ
**sp** bright-shining[1]
> shine

**brim** *adj*
=
**sp** brim[1]
> full

**brim / ~s** *n*
=
**sp** brim[1], brimme[2] / brims[1]
**rh** him *PP 6.10* / betrims *Tem 4.1.64*

**brimful** *adj*
=
**sp** brim full[2], brim-full[2]

**brimstone** *n*
'brɪmsto:n
**sp** brimestone[1], brimstone[2]
> stone

**brinded** *adj*
'brɪndɪd
**sp** brinded[1]

**brine** *n*
brəɪn
**sp** brine[6], bryne[1]
**rh** eyne *LC 17*; mine, pine *Luc 796*; Rosaline *RJ 2.3.65*

**brine-pit / ~s** *n*
'brəɪn-ˌpɪts
**sp** brine-pits[1]

**bring / ~est / ~s / ~eth / ~ing / brought** *v*
= / brɪŋst / =, *Fluellen H5 5.1.8, Evans MW 1.1.41* prɪŋz / 'brɪŋgəθ / 'brɪŋgɪn, -ɪŋ / =
**sp** bring[433] / bring'st[4] / brings[49], *Fluellen H5 5.1.8, Evans MW 1.1.41* prings[2] / bringeth[2], brin-geth[1] / bringing[13] / broght[1], brought[186]
**rh** dwelling, excelling, sing, thing *TG 4.2.52*; forfeiting *H8 Prol.20*; king *Per 2.Chorus.2*; ring *AW 2.1.161*; sing *Per Prol.14, S 39.3, TNK 1.1.23*; spring *VA 658*; sting *Luc 491*; thing *TNK Prol.21* / kings *S 29.13*; things *AW 1.1.218, MND 2.2.144, RJ 5.3.305* / thought *H5 1.2.311, Luc 1578, Per 4.4.17, S 32.11, 44.3*; wrought *R2 5.6.33*; brought her daughter *AY 5.4.109*

**bringer** *n*
'brɪŋgəɹ
**sp** bringer[3]

**bringing** *n*
'brɪŋgɪn, -ɪŋ
**sp** bringing[1]

**bringing-forth / ~s-~** *n*
ˌbrɪŋgɪnz-'fɒɹθ, -ɪŋz-
**sp** bringings forth[1]

**bringing-up** *n*
ˌbrɪŋgɪn-'ɤp, -ɪŋ-
**sp** bringing vp[3]

**brinish** *adj*
'brəɪnɪʃ
**sp** brinish[2]

**brink** *n*
=
**sp** brinke[2]

**brisk** *adj*
=
**sp** brisk[1], briske[3]

**brisky** *adj*
'brɪskəɪ
**sp** brisky[1]

**bristle** *n*
=, 'brɪzəl
**sp** brissle[1]

**bristle** *v*
=, 'brɪzəl
**sp** brissle[1], bristle[2]

**bristled** *adj*
=, 'brɪzəld
**sp** bristled[1], brizled[1]

**Bristol** *n*
=, 'brɪsto:
**sp** Bristoll[1], Bristow[4]

**Britain / ~'s** *n*
=
**sp** Britaigne[1], Britain[1], Britaine[44], [not-fearing]-Britaine[1], Britaine's [Britain is][1], Brittaine[4] / Britaines[1]

**British** *adj*
=
**sp** Brittish[4]

**Briton / ~s / ~s'** *n*
=
**sp** Britaines[12], Brittaines[1] / Britaines[1]

**Brittany** *n*
*m* 'brɪtəˌnəɪ
**sp** Britanie[1], Britanny[1], Brittanie[2]
**rh** enmity *3H6 4.6.97*; speedily *3H6 4.6.101*

**brittle** *adj*
=
**sp** brittle[4]
**rh** fickle *PP 7.3*

**broach / ~ed** *v*
bro:ʧ / *m* bro:ʧt, 'bro:ʧɪd
**sp** broach[4] / broach'd[5], broached[2], broacht[2]

**broached** *adj*
*m* 'bro:ʧɪd
**sp** broached[1]

**broad / ~er** *adj*
= / 'brɔ:dəɹ
**sp** broad[13] / broader[1], broder[1]
> abroad

**broad-fronted** *adj*
'brɔ:d-ˌfrɤntɪd
**sp** broad-fronted[1]

**broadsides** *n*
*m* 'brɔ:dˌsəɪdz
**sp** broad-sides[1]
> side

**broad-spreading** *adj*
'brɔ:d-ˌspredɪn, -ɪŋ
**sp** broad-spreading[1]

**brock** *n*
=
**sp** brocke[1]

**brogue / ~s** *n*
bro:gz
**sp** brogues[1]

**broil / ~s** *n*
brəɪl / -z
**sp** broile[1], broyle[4] / broiles[2], broils[1], broyles[9]

**broil / ~s / ~ing / ~ed** *v*
brəɪlz / 'brəɪlɪn, -ɪŋ / brəɪld
**sp** broyles[1] / broiling[1] / broyl'd[1]

**Brokas** *n*
'brɒkəs
**sp** Broccas[1]

**broke** [*past tense*]
> break

**broke / ~s** *v*
bro:ks
**sp** brokes[1]

**broken** *adj*
'bro:kən
**sp** broken[33]

**Brokenbury** *n*
'brɒkənbrəɪ
**sp** Brokenbury[1]

**brokenly** *adv*
'bro:kənləɪ
**sp** brokenly[1]

**broker / ~s** *n*
'bro:kəɹ / -z
**sp** broker[7] / broakers[1], brokers[1]
> love-broker

**broker-between / brokers-~** *n*
'bro:kəɹz-bɪˌtwi:n
**sp** brokers betweene[1]
> between

**broking** *adj*
'bro:kɪn, -ɪŋ
**sp** broaking[1]

**brooch / ~es** *n*
bro:ʧ / 'bro:ʧɪz
**sp** brooch[6], browch[1] / brooches[1]

**brooch / ~ed** *v*
bro:ʧt
**sp** brooch'd[1]

**brood** *n*
=, brɤd
**sp** brood[6], broode[1]
**rh** blood *S 19.2*

**brood / ~ing** *v*
bru:dɪn, -ɪŋ, 'brɤd-
**sp** brooding[1]

**brooded** *adj*
=, 'brɤdɪd
**sp** brooded[1]

**brook / ~s** *n*
=
**sp** brooke[12] / brookes[2], brooks[2]
**rh** forsook *VA 162*; look *PP 4.1, 6.5*; took *VA 1099* / looks *Tem 4.1.128*
> Cole-, ice-brook

**brook / ~s / ~ed** *v*
=
**sp** brooke[2ɐ] / brookes[1], brooks[1] / brook'd[3]

**Brooke** [*MW* Q1]
> Broome

**broom** *n*
=, brʊm
**sp** broome[1]

**Broome / ~s** [name] *n*
=, brʊm
**sp** Broome[41] / Broomes[1]

**broom-grove / ~s** *n*
*m* 'bru:m-ˌgrɤvz, 'brʊm-
**sp** broome groues[1]
**rh** loves *Tem 4.1.66*
> grove

**broomstaff** *n*
'bru:mstaf, 'brʊm-
**sp** broome staffe[1]

**broth / ~s** *n*
=
**sp** broth[1] / brothes[1]
> barley-, hell-, snow-broth

**brothel / ~s** *n*
=
**sp** brothell[3] / brothels[1]

**brothel-house** *n*
'brɒθl-ˌəʊs, -ˌhəʊs
**sp** brothel-house[1]
> house

**brother / ~'s / ~s / ~s'** *n*
'brɤðəɹ / -z
**sp** brother[529], [twyn]-brother[1], bro-ther[6] / brothers[81] / brothers[73], bro-thers[1] / brothers[2]
**rh** another, smother *Luc* 635; another CE *5.1.425, Tim 3.5.88*; mother *Ham 3.4.30*; other *AW 1.3.161, MM 4.2.59, PP 8.2*; smother *AY 1.2.277*

**brother-cardinal / ~s** *n*
*m* 'brɤðəɹ-'kɑ:ɹdɪˌnɑlz
**sp** brother-cardinals[1]
> cardinal

**brotherhood / ~s** *n*
'brɤðəɹˌʊd, -ˌhʊd / -z
**sp** brotherhood[5], brother-hood[1] / brother-hoods[1]

**brother-in-law** *n*
'brɤðəɹ-ɪn-ˌlɔ:
**sp** brother-in-law[2], brother in law[2]
> law

**brother-justice** *n*
'brɤðəɹ-ˌʤɤstɪs
**sp** brother-iustice[1]
> justice

**brother-like** *adj*
'brɤðəɹ-ˌləɪk
**sp** brother-like[1]

**brotherly** *adj*
*m* 'brɤðəɹˌləɪ
**sp** brotherly[3]

**brought**
> bring

**brow / ~s** *n*
brəʊ, bro: / -z
**sp** brow[61], [baby]-brow[1], [gold-bound]-brow[1] / browes[39], [black]-browes[1], brows[2]
**rh** *1* allow *S 19.9, 112.2*; how *Luc 749*; how, vow *Luc 807*; now *H8 Prol.2, KJ 2.1.505, LLL 4.1.17, 118, 4.3.225, 263, S 2.1, 33.10, 63.3, 68.4, 106.6*; **rh** *2* glow *VA 339*; grow *VA 139*; mow [grass] *S 60.10*
> black-browed, eyebrow

**brow-bound** *adj*
'brəʊ-ˌbəʊnd
**sp** brow-bound[1]
> bound

**brown / ~er** *adj*
brəʊn / -ər
**sp** brown[2], browne[18], browne-[bread][1] / browner[3]

**Brownist** *n*
'brəʊnɪst
**sp** Brownist[1]

**brows·e / ~ing / ~ed** *v*
brəʊz / 'brəʊzɪn, -ɪŋ / brəʊzd
**sp** brouz[1] / brou-zing[1] / brows'd[1]

**bruis·e / ~es** *n*
=
**sp** bruise[2] / bruizes[1]
> unbruised

**bruise / ~d** *v*
= / bru:zd
**sp** bruise[6] / bruis'd[2], bruiz'd[2]

**bruised** *adj*
*m* bru:zd, 'bru:zɪd
**sp** bruised[4], bruized[1]

**bruising** *adj*
'bru:zɪn, -ɪŋ
**sp** bruising[1], brusing[2], bruzing-[stones][1]

**bruit** *n*
bru:t
**sp** bruit[1], bruite[2]

**bruit / ~ed** *v*
bru:t / 'bru:tɪd
**sp** bruite[1] / bruited[3]

**brunt** *n*
brɤnt
**sp** brunt[1]

**brush / ~es** *n*
brɤʃ / 'brɤʃɪz
**sp** brush[2] / brushes[1]

**brush / ~es / ~ed** *v*
'brɤʃɪz / brɤʃt
**sp** brushes[1] / brush'd[2]

**brute** *adj*
bru:t
**sp** bruite[1]
**pun** *Ham 3.2.114* Brutus

**Brute** *Lat n*
'bru:ˌtɛ
**sp** Brute[1]
> Brutus

**brutish** *adj*
=
**sp** brutish[6]

**Brutus / ~s'** *n*
=
**sp** Brutus[170], *abbr in text as* Bru[1], Brut[1] / Brutus[11]
**pun** *Ham 3.2.113* brute

**bubble** *adj / v*
'bɤbəl
**sp** bubble[1] / bubble[6]
**rh** trouble *Mac 4.1.11, 19; Mac 4.1.21, 36*

**bubble / ~s** *n*
'bɤbəl / -z
**sp** bubble[2] / bubbles[3]

**bubbling** *adj*
'bɤblɪn, -ɪŋ
**sp** bubling[1]

**bubukle / ~s** *n*
'bju:bəkəlz
**sp** bubukles[1]

**buck** [animal] *n*
bɤk / -s
**sp** bucke[3], [brib'd]-bucke[1]

**buck** [laundry] **/ ~s** *n*
bɤk / -s
**sp** buck[2], bucke[5] / buckes[1]

**buck-basket / ~s** *n*
'bɤk-ˌbaskɪt / -s
**sp** buck-basket[4], bucke-basket[1] / buck-baskets[1]
> basket

**bucket / ~s** *n*
'bɤkɪt / -s
**sp** bucket[3] / buckets[2]

**bucking** *n*
'bɤkɪn, -ɪŋ
**sp** bucking[1]

**Buckingham / ~'s** *n*
'bɤkɪŋəm, -ɪnəm / -z
**sp** Buckingham[104], Buc-kingham[1], Buck-ingham[1], Bucking-ham[1], Buck[ingham][1] / Buckinghams[4]
**rh** mistrusting them *R3 4.4.525*

**buckle / ~s** *n*
'bɤkəlz
**sp** buckles[2]

**buckle / ~s / ~d** *v*
'bɤkəl / -z / -d
**sp** buckle[7] / buckles[2] / buckled[5], buck-led[1]
> unbuckle

**buckler / ~s** *n*
'bɤkləɹ / -z
**sp** buckler[5] / bucklers[4]

**Bucklersbury** *n*
'bɤkləɹsˌberəɪ
**sp** bucklers-berry[1]

**buckram** *adj / n*
'bɤkrəm
**sp** buckram[1], buckrom[3] / buckram[1], buckrom[3]

**buck-washing** *n*
'bɤk-ˌwɑʃɪn, -ɪŋ
**sp** buck-washing[1]
> washing

**bud / ~s** *n*
bɤd / -z
**sp** bud[11], budde[2] / buddes[2], budds[1], buds[8]
**rh** *1* understood *LLL 5.2.295*; **rh** *2* mud *Luc 848, S 35.4* / studs *PP 19.13*

**bud / ~ded** *v*
bɤd / 'bɤdɪd
**sp** bud[1] / budded[1]
**rh** good *PP 13.3*

**budding** *adj*
'bɤdɪn, -ɪŋ
**sp** budding[2]

**budge** *v*
bu:ʤ
**sp** budge[6], boudge[2], bouge[4]

**budger** *n*
'bu:ʤəɹ
**sp** budger[1]

**budget** *n*
'bu:ʤɪt
**sp** budget[3], bowget[1]
**rh** avouch it *WT 4.3.20*

**buff** *adj*
bɤf
**sp** buffe[3], buffe-[ierkin][1]
**rh** rough *CE 4.2.36*

**buffet / ~s** *n*
'bɤfɪt / -s
**sp** buffet[1] / buffets[3]

**buffet / ~s** *v*
'bɤfɪt / -s
**sp** buffet[3] / buffets[1], buffettes[1]

**buffetting** *n*
'bɤfɪtɪn, -ɪŋ
**sp** buffetting[1]

**bug / ~s** *n*
bɤg / -z
**sp** bugge[2] / bugges[1], bugs[2]

**bugbear** *n*
'bɤgˌbɛ:ɹ
**sp** bug-beare[1]
> bear

**bugle** *n*
=
**sp** bugle[2]

**bugle-bracelet** *n*
'bju:gəl-ˌbrɛ:slɪt
**sp** bugle-bracelet[1]

**build / ~s / ~eth / ~ing / ~ed / built** *v*
= / = / = / 'bɪldɪn, -ɪŋ / =
**sp** build[18], builde[4] / buildes[1], builds[5] / buildeth[3] / building[1] / builded[1] / built[14]
**rh** field *KL 3.2.92* / shielded, yielded *LC 152*
> all-building, new-built, unbuild

**building / ~s** *n*
'bɪldɪn, -ɪŋ / -z
**sp** building[6] / buildings[5]

**built**
> build

**bulk / ~s** *n*
bɤlk / -s
**sp** builke[1], bulke[13] / bulkes[2]
> overbulk

**bull** *adj*
=
**sp** bul[1]

**bull / ~'s / ~s** *n*
=
**sp** bull[14], [towne]-bull[1] / bulles[1], bulls[1] / bulls[1], buls[3]

**bull-bearing** *adj*
ˌbʊl-'bɛ:rɪn, -ɪŋ
**sp** bull-bearing[1]
> bearing

**Bullcalf** [name] *n*
'bʊlˌkɔ:f
**sp** bul-calfe[1], bulcalfe[2], bull-calfe[5]
> calf

**bull-calf** *n*
'bʊl-ˌkɔ:f
**sp** bull-calfe[1]

**Bullen / ~'s / ~s** *n*
=
**sp** Bullen[6] / Bullens[1] / Bullens[2]

**bullet / ~s** *n*
=
**sp** bullet[2] / bullets[8], bulletts[1]

**bullock / ~s** *n*
=
**sp** bullockes[1], bullocks[1]

**bull's-pizzle** *n*
'bʊlz-'pɪsəl
**sp** bulles-pissell[1]

**bully** *adj / n*
'bʊləɪ
**sp** bully[6], bully-[doctor][1], bully-[knight][1], bully-[monster][1], bully-[rooke][3], bully-[stale][1] / bully[7]

**bulwark / ~s** *n*
'bʊlwɑ:ɹk / -s
**sp** bulwarke[4] / bulwarkes[3]

**bum / ~s** *n*
bɤm / -z
**sp** bum[2] / bummes[1]
**rh** sums *Tim 1.2.236*

**Bum** [name] *n*
bɤm
**sp** Bum[1]

**bum-baily** *n*
'bɤm-ˌbɛ:ləɪ
**sp** bum-baylie[1]
> bailiff

**bumbard**
> bombard

**bumbast**
> bombast

**bump** *n*
bɤmp
**sp** bumpe[1]

**bunch / ~es** *n*
bɤnʃ / 'bɤnʃɪz
**sp** bunch[2] / bunches[2]

**bunch-backed** *adj*
'bɤnʃ-ˌbakt
**sp** bunch-back'd[1], bunch-backt[1]

**bundle** *n*
'bɤndl
**sp** bundle[1]

**bung** *n*
bɤŋ
**sp** bung[1]

**bunghole** *n*
'bɤŋˌo:l, -ˌho:l
**sp** bunghole[1]

**bungle** *v*
'bɤŋgəl
**sp** bungle[1]

**bunting** *n*
'bɤntɪŋ
**sp** bunting[1]

**buoy** *n*
bəɪ
**sp** buoy[1]

**buoy / ~ed** *v*
bəɪd
**sp** buoy'd[1]

**burbolt** *n*
'bɐ:ɹbo:lt
**sp** burbolt[1]

**burden / ~s** *n*
'bɐ:ɹ·ðən, -dən / -z
**sp** burden[5], burthen[37], bur-then[2] / burthens[6], bur-thens[1]
**rh** heaven *H8 3.2.384*

**burden / ~s / ~ed** *v*
'bɐ:ɹ·ðən, -dən / -z / -d
**sp** burthen[4] / burthens[1] / burdened[1], burdned[1]
> unburthen

**burdened** *adj*
'bɐ:ɹ·ðənd, -dənd
**sp** burthen'd[2]

**burdening** *adj*
*m* 'bɐ:ɹ·ðnɪn, -ɪŋ, -ðən-, -dən-
**sp** burthening[1]

**burdenous** *adj*
*m* 'bɐ:ɹ·ðəˌnɤs, -də-
**sp** burthenous[1]

**burgher / ~s** *n*
'bɐ:ɹgəɹ / -z
**sp** burger[1] / burgers[2]

**burglary** *n*
'bɐ:ɹgləˌrəɪ
**sp** burglarie[1]

**Burgogne**
> Bourgogne

**burgomaster / ~s** *n*
'bɐːɹɡəˌmastəɹz
**sp** bourgomasters[1]

**burgonet** *n*
'bɐːɹɡəˌnet
**sp** burganet[1], burgonet[3]

**Burgundy** *n*
*m* 'bɐːɹɡənˌdəɪ, -ˌdiː, -nd-, -əˌnəɪ
**sp** Burgonie[15], Burgundie[15], Burgundy[17], Bur-gundy[1]
**rh** me *KL 1.1.258*; thee *1H6 4.6.14*

**burial** *adj / n*
'berɪɑl [*2 sylls*] / *m* 'berɪɑl, -ɪˌɑːl
**sp** buriall[1] / buriall[21], buryall[1]
**rh** *n* all *MND 3.2.383*; fall *Per 1.4.49, 2.4.12*

**buried** *adj*
*m* 'berəɪd, 'berɪˌed
**sp** buried[6]

**buried** *n*
'berəɪd
**sp** buried[1]

**burier** *n*
'berɪəɹ [*2 sylls*]
**sp** burier[1]

**burly-boned** *adj*
'bɐːɹləɪ-ˌboːnd
**sp** burly bon'd[1]
> bone

**burn / ~s / ~eth / ~ing / ~ed / ~t** *v*
bɐːɹn / -z / 'bɐːɹn·əθ / -ɪn, -ɪŋ / *m* -ɪd, bɐːɹnd / bɐːɹnt
**sp** burn[1], burne[74] / burnes[26], burns[1] / burneth[2] / burning[10] / burn'd[10], burned[2] / burnt[21]
**rh** overturn *S 55.7*; turn *MND 3.1.104, Per Epil.14, VA 94* / turning *RJ 1.2.45, VA 142* / turned *AY 4.3.42, S 104.7*
> heart-burn, unburnt

**burned** *adj*
bɐːɹnd
**sp** burn'd[3]

**burnet** *n*
'bɐːɹnɪt
**sp** burnet[1]

**burning** *adj / n*
'bɐːɹnɪn, -ɪŋ
**sp** burning[30] / burning[2]

**burning-glass** *n*
'bɐːɹnɪn-ˌɡlas, -ɪŋ-
**sp** burning-glasse[1]
> glass

**burnished** *adj*
'bɐːɹnɪʃt
**sp** burnisht[2]

**burr / ~s** *n*
bɐːɹ / -z
**sp** bur[1], burre[1] / burres[2], burs[2]

**burrow / ~s** *n*
'bɤrəz, -roːz
**sp** burroughes[1]

**burst / ~s** *n*
bɐːɹst / -s
**sp** burst[4] / bursts[1]

**burst** *v*
bɐːɹst
**sp** burst[23]

**bursting** *n*
'bɐɹstɪn, -ɪŋ
**sp** bursting[1]

**burthen / ~ous**
> burden / ~ous

**Burton** *n*
'bɐːɹtən
**sp** burton[1]

**Burtonheath** *n*
ˌbɐːɹtən-'ɛːθ, -'hɛːθ, -iːθ, -hiːθ
**sp** burton-heath[1]
> heath

**bur·y / ~ied** *v*
'berəɪ / *m* 'berəɪd, 'berɪˌed
**sp** burie[8], bury[31] / bu-ried[1], buried[38], buryed[6]
**rh** bred *RJ 4.5.64, Per 5.1.163*; dead *Per 2.1.77, S 31.4, TG 4.2.111*; spread *S 25.7*; buried be [*2 sylls*] cannot be, she *PT 64*
> unburied

**burying** *adj / Per n*
*m* 'berɪɪn, -ɪŋ [*2 sylls*] / 'berəɪ ˌɪn, -ɪŋ
**sp** burying[1] / burying[1]
**rh** *n* king *Per 3.2.70*

**burying-place** *n*
'berɪɪn-ˌplɛːs, -ɪŋ
**sp** burying place[1]

**bush / ~es** *n*
=, bɤʃ / =, 'bɤʃɪz
**sp** bush[35] / bushes[4]
**rh** blush *LLL 4.3.135* / rushes *VA 629*

**bushel / ~s** *n*
=
**sp** bushels[1]

**Bushy** *n*
'bʊʃəɪ
**sp** Bushie[7], Bushy[6]

**busily** *adv*
*m* 'bɪzɪˌləɪ
**sp** busily[2]

**business** *n*
*m* 'bɪznəs, 'bɤs-, *MND 1.1.124* 'bɪzəɪˌnɪs / -ɪz
**sp** busines[25], businesse[201], bu-sinesse[6] / businesses[6]
**pun** *Cor 3.2.75* bussing

**buskined** *adj*
'bɤskɪnd
**sp** buskin'd[1]

**busky** *adj*
'bɤskəɪ
**sp** busky[1]

**buss / ~es** *n*
'bɤsɪz
**sp** busses[1]

**buss / ~ing** *v*
bɤs / 'bɤsɪn, -ɪŋ
**sp** busse[2], bussing[1]

**bussing** *adj*
'bɤsɪn, -ɪŋ
**sp** bussing[1]

**bustle** *v*
'bɤsəl
**sp** bussle[1], bustle[3]

**bustling** *adj*
'bɤslɪn, -ɪŋ
**sp** bussling[1]

**busy** *adj*
'bɪzəɪ
**sp** busie[24]

**bus·y / ~ied** *v*
'bɪzəɪ / -d
**sp** busie[2] / busied[4]

**but** *conj*
bɤt, *unstr* bət
**sp** but[5981]

**butcher / ~'s / ~s** *n*
'bʊʧəɹ / -z
**sp** butcher[18] / butchers[4] / butchers[7]

**butcher / ~ed** *v*
'bʊʧəɹ / -d
**sp** butcher[1] / butcher'd[4], butchered[2]
**rh** slaughtered *R3 4.4.393*

**butchered** *adj*
'bʊʧəɹd
**sp** butcher'd[1]

**butcherly** *adv*
*m* 'bʊʧəɹˌləɪ
**sp** butcherly[1]

**butcher·y / ~ies** *n*
*m* 'bʊʧəˌrəɪ, -ʧrəɪ / -əˌrəɪz
**sp** butcherie[1], butchery[2] / butcheries[2]

**butler** *n*
'bɤtləɹ
**sp** butler[2]

**Butler** [name] *n*
'bɤtləɹ
**sp** Butler[2]

**butt** *n*
bɤt
**sp** butt[4]
> malmsey-butt

**butt / ~s** *v*
bɤts
**sp** butts[1]

**butt-end** *n*
'bɤt-ˌend
**sp** butt-end[1]
> end

**butter** *n*
'bɤtəɹ, *Evans MW 5.5.139ff* 'pɤtəɹ
**sp** butter[8], *Evans* putter[3]

**butter / ~ed** *v*
'bɤtəɹd
**sp** butter'd[1], buttered[1]

**butterfl·y / ~ies** *n*
'bɤtəɹˌfləɪ / -z
**sp** butterfly[2], but-terfly[1] / butterflies[2], butter-flies[2]
**rh** *1* arise, eyes, thighs *MND 3.1.167*;
**rh** *2* bees, courtesies, dewberries, mulberries *MND 3.1.167*
> fly

**buttering** *n*
'bɤtrɪn, -ɪŋ
**sp** butt'ring[1]

**butter-wo·man / ~man's / ~men's** *n*
'bɤtəɹ-ˌwʊmənz, -wo:m- / -wɪmɪnz
**sp** butter-womans[1] / butter-womens[1]
> woman

**buttery** *n*
*m* 'bɤtəˌrəɪ, 'bɤtrəɪ
**sp** butterie[1], buttry[1]

**buttock / ~s** *n*
'bɤtək / -s
**sp** buttocke[2], but-tocke[2] / buttockes[2]

**button / ~s** *n*
'bɤtən / -z
**sp** button[5] / buttons[2]

**button / ~ed** *v*
'bɤtənd
**sp** button'd[1]
> unbutton

**buttonhole** *n*
'bɤtənˌo:l, -ˌho:l
**sp** button hole[1]

**buttress** *n*
'bɤtrɪs
**sp** buttrice[1]

**Butts** [name] *n*
bɤts
**sp** Buts[5], Butts[1]

**butt-shaft** *n*
'bɤt-ˌʃaft
**sp** butshaft[1], but-shaft[1]
> shaft

**buxom** *adj*
'bɤksəm
**sp** buxome[1]

**buy / ~s / ~ing / bought** *v*
bəɪ / -z / 'bəɪɪn, -ɪŋ / =
**sp** buie[2], buy[101], *Mac 4.2.42* by[1] / buyes[9] / buying[1] / bought[51]
**rh** eye *LLL 2.1.229* / thought *Luc 1067*

**buyer** *n*
'bəɪəɹ
**sp** buyer[2]

**buzz** *interj / n*
bɤz
**sp** buzze[3] / buz[2]

**buzz / ~ed** *v*
bɤz / -d
**sp** buz[3], buzze[2] / buz'd[1]

**buzzard / ~s** *n*
'bɤzəɹd / -z
**sp** buzard[2], buzzard[1] / buzards[1]

**buzzer / ~s** *n*
'bɤzəɹz
**sp** buzzers[1]

**buzzing** *adj / n*
'bɤzɪn, -ɪŋ
**sp** buzing[1], buzzing[2] / buzzing[1]

**by** *adv, prep*
bəɪ, *unstr* bɪ, bə
**sp** by[3468], by-[gar][6], by'r[1], by't[8], [fast]-by[1], [goe]-by[1], [hard]-by[1], [run]-by[1], [stand]-by[1], *Caius* bee[1], be-[gar][1]
**rh** *1* cry *PP 20.14*; die *H8 3.1.11*; dye, espy, eye, sky *MND 3.2.108*; espy *VA 259*; eye *CE 3.2.56, LLL 1.1.83, MV 2.5.40, PP 6.9, RJ 1.2.93, VA 282;* I *R3 5.3.183*; lie *1H4 5.4.108, S 73.12*; nigh *LC 59*; sky *VA 347*; **by her** try her *PP 11.1*; **by him** spy him *Luc 882* / **rh** *2* advisedly *Luc 1814*; archery, gloriously, remedy *MND 3.2.108*; lunacy *Tit 5.2.69*; remedy *S 154.9*; unmannerly *1H4 1.3.41*; warily *LLL 5.2.94*
> thereby

***by the** abbr*
bɪθ, bəɪθ, -ɪð
**sp** bi'th'[1], byth'[3], by'th[5], by'th'[26]

**by and by** *adv*
'bəɪ-ən-'bəɪ
**sp** by and by[43]; by, and by[1]

**by-dependence / ~s** *n*
'bəɪ-dɪˌpendənsɪz
**sp** by-dependances[1]
> dependence

**by-drinking / ~s** *n*
'bəɪ-ˌdrŋkɪnz, -ɪŋz
**sp** by-drinkings[1]
> drink

**bygone** *adj*
'bəɪgɒn
**sp** by-gone[1], by-gone-[day][1]
> go

**by Our Lady / ~ Lakin** *interj*
bəɹ'lɛ:dəɪ, *Evans MW 1.1.26* pəɹ'lɛ:dəɪ / bəɹ'lɛ:kən
**sp** berlady[2], ber Lady[1], birladie[2], birlady[1], byrlady[6], by'r lady[1], *Evans* per-lady / berlaken[1], by'r lakin[1]
> lady

**by-path / ~s** *n*
*m* ˌbəɪ-'paθs
**sp** by-pathes[1]
> path

**by-room** *n*
'bəɪ-ˌru:m, -ˌrʊm
**sp** by-roome[1]
> room

**by-word / ~s** *n*
'bəɪˌwɔ:ɹdz
**sp** by-words[1]
> word

**Byzantium** *n*
bɪ'zansɪˌʊm
**sp** Bizantium[1]

**C [letter]** *n*
=
**sp** C's[2]

**C [note]** *n*
=
**sp** Cfavt [C fa ut][1]

**ça** *Fr adv*
sa
**sp** *emend of H5 3.7.12* ch'[1]

**cabbage** *n*
=
**sp** cabidge[1]

**cabin / ~s** *n*
=
**sp** cabin[3], cabine[4], cabyn[1] / cabines[1]

**cabin / ~ed** *v*
=
**sp** cabbin[1] / cabin'd[1]

**cabinet** *n*
*m* 'kabɪˌnet
**sp** cabinet[2]
**rh** beset *Luc 442*

**cable / ~s** *n*
'kɛ:bəl / -z
**sp** cable[4] / cables[1]

**cackl·e / ~ing** *v*
'kaklɪn, -ɪŋ
**sp** cackling[2]

**Cacodemon** *n*
ˌkakə'di:mən
**sp** Cacodemon[1]

**caddis / ~es** *n*
=
**sp** caddysses[1]

**caddis-garter** *n*
'kadɪs-ˌgɑ:ɹtəɹ
**sp** caddice garter[1]
> garter

**cade** *n*
kɛ:d
**sp** cade[1]
**pun** *2H6 4.2.32* Cade

**Cade / ~s [name]** *n*
kɛ:d / -z
**sp** Cade[32] / Cades[1]

**cadence** *n*
'kɛ:dəns
**sp** cadence[1]

**cadent** *adj*
'kɛ:dənt
**sp** cadent[1]

**Cadmus** *n*
'kadməs
**sp** Cadmus[1]

**caduceus** *n*
ka'dju:sɪəs
**sp** caduceus[1]

**Cadwal**
> Cadwallader

**Cadwallader** *abbr*
**Cadwal** *n*
kad'wɑlədəɹ, *abbr* 'kadwɑl
**sp** Cadwallader[1], *abbr* Cadwal[1], Cadwall[6]

**cael·us / ~um** *Lat n*
'si:lʊm
**sp** *emend of LLL 4.2.5* celo[1]

**Caesar / ~'s / ~s** *n*
'si:zəɹ / -z
**sp** Caesar[372], Cae-sar[1], Caesars [Caesar is][1], Caesar's [Caesar is][1], Cesar[1] / Caesars[71], Cesars[1] / Caesars[2]

**Caesarian** *adj*
sɪ'zarɪən
**sp** Caesarian[1]

**Caesarion** *n*
sɪ'zarɪən
**sp** Caesarion[1]

**cage** *n*
kɛ:ʤ
**sp** cage[7]

**caged** *adj*
kɛ:ʤd
**sp** caged[1]
> incaged

**Cain / ~'s** *n*
kɛ:n / -z
**sp** Cain[1], Caine[3] / Caines[1], Cains[1]

**cain-coloured** *adj*
'kɛ:n-ˌkɤləɹd
**sp** caine colourd[1]
> colour

**Caithness** *n*
'kaθnes
**sp** Cathnes[2]

**caitiff / ~s** *n*
'kɛ:tɪf / -s
**sp** caitiffe[7], caytiffe[5] / caitifs[1]

**Caius** *n*
'kəɪəs
**sp** Caius[65]

**cake / ~s** *n*
kɛ:k / -s
**sp** cake[4] / cakes[5]

**caked** *adj*
kɛ:kd
**sp** cak'd[1]

**Calaber** *n*
'kalə,bɛɹ
**sp** Calaber[1]

**Calais** *n*
'kalɪs
**sp** Calice[2], Calis[1], Callice[7], Callis[2]

**calamit·y / ~ies** *n*
*m* kə'lamɪ,təɪ, -mtəɪ / -ɪ,təɪz
**sp** calamitie[5], calamity[5] / calamities[1]
**rh** majesty *1H6 1.2.81*

**Calchas / ~'** *n*
'kalkəs
**sp** Calcas[2], Calchas[1], Chalcas[4] / Calcas[1], Calcha's[1], Chalcas[1]

**calculate** *v*
'kalkjə,lɛ:t
**sp** calculate[2]

**calendar / ~s** *n*
'kaləndəɹ / -z
**sp** calender[3], kalender[4] / kalenders[1]

**calf / calves** *n*
kɔ:f, *Holofernes LLL 5.1.22* kɑlf / kɔ:vz
**sp** calfe[15], [cole-blacke]-calfe[1], *Holofernes* calf[1], *describing Armado* caufe[1] / calues[2]
**rh** half *LLL 5.2.247, 248*
> Bull-, moon-calf

**calf-like** *adj*
'kɔ:f-,ləɪk
**sp** calfe-like[1]

**calf's-guts / calves'-~** *n*
'kɔ:fs-,gɤts, kɔ:vz-
**sp** calues-guts[1]
> guts

**calf's-head** *n*
'kɔ:fs-,ed, -,hed, 'kɔ:vz-
**sp** calues head[1]

**calf's-skin / ~s** *n*
'kɔ:f-,skɪn, 'kɔ:v- / -z
**sp** calues-skin[5], calues skin[2] / calue-skinnes[1]
> skin

**Caliban / ~s, *abbr* ban / *chant* Cacaliban** *n*
'kalɪ,ban, *abbr* ban / -z / *m chant Tem 2.2.180* 'kakalɪ'ban
**sp** Caliban[15], Calliban[1], *abbr* ban'[2], *abbr in s.d.* Cal.[1] / Calibans[1] / Cacalyban[1]
**rh** man Tem *2.2.180*

**Calipolis** *n*
kə'lɪpə,lɪs
**sp** Calipolis[1]

**caliver** *n*
kə'li:vəɹ
**sp** caliuer[1], calyuer[2]

**call / ~est / ~s / ~ing / ~ed / ~edest** *v*
kɑ:l / -st / -z / 'kɑ:lɪn, -ɪŋ / kɑ:ld / -st
**sp** cal[3], call[546], cal't [call it][1], call't [call it][2] / call'st[5], calst[2], cal'st[4] / calles[18], calls[24], call's[6], cals[36] / calling[15], cal-ling[1] / cald[8], cal'd[28], call'd[144], called[15], cal-led[1] / calldst[1], call'dst[2]
**rh** all *AW 2.1.182, MND 5.1.425, Per 5.1.244, S 40.3, 109.13, 117.3*; fall *S 151.13*; prodigal *PP 20.38*; withal *VA 849* / falls *MND 3.2.26, S 124.8* / appalled *PT 40*
> miscall, recall

**callet** *n*
'kalət
**sp** callat[1], callet[2], callot[1]

**calm** *adj*
kɔ:m
**sp** calme[17]

**calm / ~s** *n*
kɔ:m / -z
**sp** calme[6] / calmes[1]

**calm / ~est / ~s / ~ed** *v*
kɔ:m / 'kɔ:məst / kɔ:m·z / -d
**sp** calme[10] / calmest[1] / calmes[1] / calm'd[3]

**calmie** *unclear Fr*
*Pistol H5 4.4.4* 'kalmi:
**sp** calmie[1]

**calmly** *adv*
'kɔ:mləɪ
**sp** calmely[3]

**calmness** *n*
'kɔ:mnəs
**sp** calmenesse[1]

**Calphurnia / ~'s** *n*
kal'pɐ:ɹnɪə / -z
**sp** Calphurnia[8] / Calphurnia's[2]

**calumniate** *v*
kə'lɤmnɪ,ɛ:t
**sp** calumniate[1]

**calumniating** *adj*
kə'lɤmnɪ,ɛ:tɪn, -ɪŋ
**sp** calumniating[1]

**calumnious** *adj*
kə'lɤmnɪəs
**sp** calumnious[2], calum-nious[1]

**calumny** *n*
*m* 'kaləm,nəɪ, -mn-
**sp** calumnie[4], calumny[1]
**rh** mortality *MM 3.2.176*

**calve / ~d** *v*
kɔ:vd
**sp** calued[1]

**calves**
> calf

**Calydon** *n*
'kalɪdən
**sp** Calidon[1]

**Cambio** *n*
*m* 'kambɪo:, -ɪˌo:
**sp** Cambio[8]

**Cambria** *n*
=
**sp** Cambria[2]

**cambric / ~s** *n*
=
**sp** cambrick[1] / cambrickes[1]

**Cambridge** *n*
'kɛ:mbrɪʤ
**sp** Cambridge[12]

**Cambyses / ~'** *n*
kəm'bəɪsi:z
**sp** Cambyses[1]

**came**
> come

**camel / ~s** *n*
=
**sp** camell[5] / cammels[1]

**Camelot** *n*
=
**sp** Camelot[1]

**Camidius**
> Canidius

**Camillo / ~'s** *n*
kə'mɪlo: / -z
**sp** Camillo[45], Ca-millo[1] / Camillo's[2]

**camomile** *n*
'kaməməɪl
**sp** camomile[1]

**camp** *n / v*
=
**sp** camp[4], campe[21] / campe[1]
> encamp

**Campeius** *n*
kam'pɛ:əs
**sp** Campeius[4], *emend of s.d. H8 3.1.23* Campian[1]

**camping** *n*
'kampɪn, -ɪŋ
**sp** camping[1]

**can** *n*
=
**sp** canne[1]
> Half-Can

**can / ~st / ~not / ~'t** *v*
=, *unstr* kn / kanst / =
**sp** can[1145], ca[n][1] / canst[144], can'st[20] / cannot[741], ca[n]not[1], can-not[6], canot[1] / cant[1], can't[1]
**rh** *1* Englishman *R2 1.3.308*; man *AC 4.8.21, 1H6 4.3.43, LLL 4.1.129, MND 2.2.132, Per 2.Chorus.12, R2 5.3.87, S 141.9*; **rh** *2* swan *PT 14*
> could

**canar·y / ~ies** *n*
kə'nɛ:rəɪ / -z
**sp** canari[1], canarie[3], ca-narie[2] / canaries[2]

**cancel / ~s / ~ling / ~led** *v*
= / = / 'kansəlɪn, -ɪŋ / =
**sp** cancell[5] / cancells[1] / cancelling[1] / cancell'd[1]

**cancer** *n*
'kansəɹ
**sp** cancer[1]

**candidatus** *Lat n*
ˌkandɪ'dɑ:tʊs
**sp** candidatus[1]

**candied** *adj*
'kandəɪd
**sp** candied[1]
> candy

**candle / ~s** *n*
=
**sp** candle[17], candell[1] / candles[6]

**candle-case / ~s** *n*
'kandl-ˌkɛ:sɪz
**sp** candle-cases[1]

**candle-holder** *n*
'kandl-ˌo:ldəɹ, -ˌho:-
**sp** candle-holder[1]

**candle-mine** *n*
'kandl-ˌməɪn
**sp** candle-myne[1]

**candlestick / ~s** *n*
=
**sp** candlestick[1] / candlesticks[1]

**candle-waster / ~s** *n*
'kandl-ˌwastəɹz
**sp** candle-wasters[1]

**candy** *adj*
'kandəɪ
**sp** *emend of 1H4 1.3.247* caudie[1]

**Candy** [name] *n*
'kandəɪ
**sp** Candy

**cand·y / ~ied** *v*
'kandəɪd
**sp** candied[2]

**Canidius** *n*
kə'nɪdɪəs, -'mɪd-
**sp** Camidias[1], Camidius[6], Camindius[1]

**canker** *adj*
'kaŋkəɹ
**sp** canker[3]

**canker / ~s** *n*
'kaŋkəɹ / -z
**sp** canker[11] / cankers[3]

**canker / ~s / ~ed** *v*
'kaŋkəɹ·z / -d
**sp** cankers[1] / cankred[1]

**canker-bit** *adj*
'kaŋkəɹ-ˌbɪt
**sp** canker-bit[1]

**cankered** *adj*
'kaŋkəɹd
**sp** canker'd[1], cankred[4]

**canker-sorrow** *n*
'kaŋkəɹ-ˌsɒrə, -roː
**sp** canker-sorrow[1]
> sorrow

**cannakin** *n*
=
**sp** cannakin[2]

**cannibal / ~s** *n*
'kanɪˌbɑlz
**sp** caniballes[1], caniballs[2], canibals[1]

**cannibally** *adv*
'kanɪˌbɑləɪ
**sp** cannibally[1]

**cannon / ~s** *n*
=
**sp** cannon[11], canon[3] / cannons[4], canons[3]
> demi-cannon

**cannon-bullet / ~s** *n*
=
**sp** cannon bullets[1]

**cannoneer** *n*
'kanəˌniːɹ
**sp** cannoneer[1], cannoneere[1]

**cannon-fire** *n*
'kanən-ˌfəɪɹ
**sp** cannon fire[1]
> fire

**cannon-shot** *n*
=
**sp** cannon-shot[1]
> shot

**cannot**
> can

**canon / ~s** *n*
=
**sp** cannon[3], canon[2] / cannons[1]

**canonize / ~d** *v*
*m* kə'nɒnəɪz / *m* -d, -ˌzɪd
**sp** canonize[1] / canoniz'd[2], canonized[2]

**canonized** *adj*
*m* kə'nɒnəɪzd
**sp** canonized[1]

**canop·y / ~ies** *n*
*m* 'kanəˌpəɪ, -əp- / -əˌpəɪz
**sp** canopie[2], canopy[6] / canopies[2]
**rh** eternity *S 125.1*

**canop·y / ~ied** *v*
*m* 'kanəˌpəɪd
**sp** canopied[1], canopy'd[1]
> overcanopied

**Canterbury / ~'s** *n*
*m* 'kantəɹˌbriː, -ˌbɤrəɪ / -ɹbriːz
**sp** Canterburie[1], Canterbury[17] / Canterburies[1]

**cantherizing** *n*
'kantəˌrəɪzɪn, -ɪŋ
**sp** *emend of Tim 5.1.131* capac-itie[1]

**cantle** *n*
=
**sp** cantle[2]

**canton / ~s** *n*
=
**sp** cantons[1]

**canus** *Lat n*
*adaptation of canis LLL 5.2.585* 'kanʊs
**sp** canus[1]
**rh** manus *LLL 5.2.585* [*Lat*]

**canvas** *adj / v*
=
**sp** canuas[1] / canuas[2]

**canzonet** *n*
ˌkanzə'net
**sp** cangenet[1]

**cap / ~s** *n*
=
**sp** cap[36], cappe[9] / cappes[1], caps[16]
**rh** hap *LLL 2.1.195*
> blue-, corner-, half-, mad-, night-, sea-, statute-cap

**cap** *v*
=
**sp** cap[1]
> cloud-capped, off-cap

**capable** *adj*
*m* 'kɛːpəˌbɤl, -pbəl
**sp** capable[8], capeable[8]
> in-, un-capable

**capacit·y / ~ies** *n*
*m* kə'pasɪˌtəɪ, -sɪtəɪ / -sɪtəɪz
**sp** capacitie[5], capacity[6] / capaci-ties[1]
**rh** *1* eye *LLL 5.2.376*; **rh** *2* simplicity *MND 5.1.105*

**cap-and-knee** *adj*
= , 'kap-ən-'kniː
**sp** cap and knee-[slaues][1]

**cap-a-pe** *adv*
ˌkap-ə-'pɛː
**sp** cap-a-pe[1], cap a pe[1]

**caparison / ~ed** *v*
*m* kə'parɪˌsɒn, -ɪsən / -ɪsənd
**sp** caparison[3] / caparison'd[1], capari-son'd[1]

**cape** *n*
kɛːp
**sp** cape[6]
**rh** tape *WT 4.4.314*
> uncape

**Capel / ~'s** *n*
=
**sp** Capels[2]

**caper / ~s** *n*
'kɛːpəɹ / -z
**sp** caper[1] / capers[1]
> a-capering

**caper / ~s / ~ing / ~ed** *v*
'kɛːpəɹ / -z / 'kɛːprɪn, -ɪŋ / 'kɛːpəɹd
**sp** caper[1], ca-per[1], capre[1] / capers[2] / capring[1] / caper'd[1]

**Caper** [name] *n*
'kɛ:pəɹ
**sp** Caper[1]

**Capet / ~'s** *n*
=
**sp** Capet[2] / Capets[1]

**Caphis** *n*
'kafɪs
**sp** Caphis[4]

**Capilet** *n*
'kapɪlet
**sp** Capilet[3]

**capitaine** *Fr n*
kapɪ'tɛn
**sp** capitaine[1]

**capital** *adj*
*m* 'kapɪˌtɑl, -ɪt-, 'kaptɑl
**sp** capitall[13]
**pun** *Ham 3.2.114* capitol

**capite** *Lat*
> caput

**capitol** *n*
*m* 'kapiˌtɒl, -ɪt-, 'kaptɒl
**sp** capitall[1], capitol[2], capitoll[36]
**pun** *Ham 3.2.113* capital

**capitulate** *v*
kə'pɪtjəˌlɛ:t
**sp** capitulate[2]

**capocchia** *n*
kə'po:ʧɪə
**sp** *emend of TC 4.2.31* chipochia[1]

**capon / ~'s / ~s** *n*
'kɛ:pən / -z
**sp** capon[8] / capons-[leg][1] / capons[3]

**Cappadocia** *n*
ˌkapə'do:sɪə
**sp** Cappadocia[1]

**capriccio** *n*
kə'prɪʧɪo:
**sp** caprichio[1]

**capricious** *adj*
kə'prɪsɪəs
**sp** capricious[1]

**captain / ~'s / ~s** *n*
= / 'kaptɪnz, *Jamy H5 3.2.99* 'kaptenz
**sp** captain[2], captaine[131], cap-taine[1] / captaines[4], captains[2], captaine's[1] / captaines[23], *Jamy* captens[1]

**captainship** *n*
=
**sp** captainship[1], captain-ship[1]

**captious** *adj*
'kapsɪəs
**sp** captious[1]

**captivate / ~s / ~d** *v*
'kaptɪˌvɛ:t / -s / -ɪd
**sp** captiuate[2] / captiuates[1] / captiuated[1]

**captive** *adj*
=
**sp** captiue[5]

**captive / ~s** *n*
=
**sp** captiue[8] / captiues[9]

**captive / ~d** *v*
=
**sp** captiu'd[1]

**captivity** *n*
*m* kap'tɪvɪˌtəɪ, -ɪt-, -vt-
**sp** captiuitie[6]
**rh** thee *1H6 4.7.3*

**captus / ~um** *Lat n*
'kaptʊm
**sp** captam[1]

**Capuchius** *n*
kə'pu:ʧɪəs
**sp** Capuchius[2]

**Capulet / ~'s / ~s** *n*
*m* 'kapjəˌlet, -ələt, -pl- / -s
**sp** Capulet[22] / Capulets[2] / Capulets[5]
**rh** debt *RJ 1.5.117*; set *RJ 2.3.54*

**cap·ut / ~ite** *Lat n*
'kapɪˌtɛ
**sp** capite[1]

**car / ~s** *n*
kɑ:ɹ / -z
**sp** car[2], carre[8] / cars[1]
**rh** are *S 7.9*; far, mar *MND 1.2.31*

**car** *Fr conj*
ka:ɹ
**sp** car[1]

**Car** [name] *n*
kɑ:ɹ
**sp** Car[3]

**carat** *n*
=, 'karəkt
**sp** charect[1], charract[1]

**carbonado** *n / v*
ˌkɑ:ɹbə'nado:
**sp** carbinado[1], carbonado[1] / carbonado[1]

**carbonadoed** *adj*
ˌkɑ:ɹbə'nado:d
**sp** carbinado'd[1], carbonado'd[1]

**carbuncle / ~s** *n*
*m* 'kɑ:ɹbəŋˌkɤl, -ŋkəl / -z
**sp** carbuncle[3] / carbuncles[2]

**carbuncle / ~d** *v*
*m* 'kɑ:ɹbəŋˌkɤld
**sp** carbunkled[1]

**carcanet** *n*
'kɑ:ɹkəˌnet
**sp** carkanet[1]
**rh** set *S 52.8*

**carcass / ~es** *n*
'kɑ:ɹkəs / -ɪz
**sp** carkasse[5] / carcasses[1], carkasses[2]

**card / ~s** *n*
kɑ:ɹd / -z
**sp** card[4], carde[1] / cards[2]
> Surecard

**card / ~ed** *v*
'kɑ:ɹdɪd
**sp** carded[1]

**cardecue** *n*
'kɑ:ɹdɪkju:
**sp** cardceue[1], cardecue[1]

**carder / ~s** *n*
'kɑ:ɹdəɹ / -z
**sp** carders[1]

**cardinal** *adj*
'kɑ:ɹdnɑl, -dɪn-
**sp** cardinall[2]

**cardinal / ~'s / ~s** *n*
*m* 'kɑ:ɹdɪ,nɑl, -ɪn-, -dn- / -z
**sp** cardinal[3], cardinall[89], cardinall's [cardinal is][2], cardnall[3], card'nall[2] / cardinalls[7], cardinals[7] / cardinalls[2], cardinals[5]
**pun** *H8 3.1.1.104* carnal
> brother-, count-, king-cardinal

**cardinally** *adv*
*m* 'kɑ:ɹdɪ,nɑləɪ
**sp** cardinally[1]

**cardmaker** *n*
'kɑ:ɹd,mɛ:kəɹ
**sp** cardmaker[1]
> make

**carduus** *Lat n*
'kɑ:ɹdju:əs
**sp** carduus[1]

**care / ~s** *n*
kɛ:ɹ / -z
**sp** care[134] / cares[22]
**rh** *1* bare *PP 12.2*; beware *Tem 2.1.308*; compare *Luc 1100*; fare *1H6 4.6.26*; hare *VA 681*; mare *VA 383*; prepare *LLL 5.2.508*; rare *S 56.13*; share *PP 14.3*; snare *Luc 926* / fares *Luc 720*; fares, stares *Luc 1593*; **rh** *2* are *3H6 2.5.123, Luc 926, Mac 4.1.89, R2 2.3.170, S 48.7, 112.9, 147.9* / **rh** 3 tears [cry] *3H6 3.3.14*

**care / ~est / ~s / ~ed** *v*
kɛ:ɹ / -st / -z / -d
**sp** care[77] / car'st[1] / cares[14] / car'd[4]

**care-crazed** *adj*
'kɛ:ɹ-,krɛ:zd
**sp** care-cras'd[1]

**career / ~s** *n*
kə'ri:ɹ / -z
**sp** careere[2], cariere[1], carreere[1], car-reere[1], carriere[1] / car-eires[1], carreeres[1]
**rh** spear *R2 1.2.49*

**careful** *adj*
'kɛ:ɹfʊl
**sp** carefull[20]
> overcareful

**carefully** *adv*
*m* 'kɛ:ɹfʊ,ləɪ
**sp** carefully[8]

**careless** *adj*
'kɛ:ɹləs
**sp** carelesse[12], care-lesse[1]

**carelessly** *adv*
*m* 'kɛ:ɹləs,ləɪ
**sp** carelesly[3], carelessely[2]

**carelessness** *n*
*m* 'kɛ:ɹləs,nes
**sp** carelesnesse[1]

**care·o / ~t** *Lat v*
'karet
**sp** caret[2]
**pun** *MW 4.1.59* carrot

**care-tuned** *adj*
'kɛ:ɹ-,tju:nd
**sp** care-tun'd[1]
> tune

**cargo** *nonsense word*
'kɑ:ɹgo:
**sp** cargo[7]

**carl** *n*
kɑ:ɹl
**sp** carle[1]

**Carlisle** *n*
*m* kɑ:ɹ'ləɪl, 'kɑ:ɹləɪl
**sp** Carlile[7]

**carlot** *n*
'kɑ:ɹlət
**sp** carlot[1]

**carman** *n*
'kɑ:ɹmən
**sp** carman[1]

**carnal** *adj*
'kɑ:ɹnɑl
**sp** carnall[3]

**carnally** *adv*
'kaɹnɑləɪ
**sp** carnallie[1]

**Carnarvonshire** *n*
kəɹ'nɑ:ɹvən,ʃəɪɹ
**sp** Carnaruanshire[1]

**carnation** *adj*
kɑ:ɹ'nɛ:sɪən
**sp** carnation[1]

**carnation / ~s** *n*
kɑ:ɹ'nɛ:sɪən / -z
**sp** carnation[1] / carnations[1]

**carol** *n*
=
**sp** caroll[1], carroll[1]

**carouse / ~s** *n*
kə'rəʊzɪz
**sp** carowses[2]

**carous·e / ~es / ~ing / ~ed** *v*
kə'rəʊz / -ɪz / -ɪn, -ɪŋ / -d
**sp** carowse[2] / carowses[1] / carowsing[2] / carows'd[2], carrows'd[1]

**carp** *n*
kɑ:ɹp
**sp** carpe[1]

**carp / ~ed** *v*
kɑ:ɹp / -t
**sp** carpe[1] / carp'd[1]

**carpenter** *n*
'kɑ:ɹpɪntəɹ
**sp** carpenter[7]

**carper** *n*
'kɑ:ɹpəɹ
**sp** carper[1]

**carpet / ~s** *n*
'kɑ:ɹpɪt / -s
**sp** carpet[2] / carpets[1]

**carpet-monger / ~s** *n*
'kɑ:ɹpɪt-ˌmɤŋgəɹz
**sp** car-pet-mongers[1]

**carping** *adj / n*
'kɑ:ɹpɪn, -ɪŋ
**sp** carping[3] / carping[1]

**carrack / ~s** *n*
'karəkt / -s
**sp** carract[1] /carrects[1]

**carraway / ~s** *n*
'karəwɛ:z
**sp** carrawayes[1]

**carriage / ~s** *n*
=
**sp** carriage[21] / carriages[7]

**carrier / s** *n*
'karɪəɹ / -z
**sp** cariere[1], carrier[5] / carriers[2]

**carrion / ~s** *n*
=
**sp** carion[1], carrion[12] / carrions[2]

**carr·y / ~ies / ~ying / ~ied** *v*
'karəɪ / -z / -ɪn, -ɪŋ / *m* -d, -ˌɪd, -ˌed
**sp** carie[1], carrie[15], carry[66], carry't[4], carry-[her][1] / carries[20], car-ries[1], carryes[2] / carrying[7], car-rying[1] / caried[1], ca-ried[1], carried[22], car-ried[1], carryed[4]
> miscarry

**carry-tale** *n*
'karəɪ-ˌtɛ:l
**sp** carry-tale[1]
> tale

**cart / ~s** *n*
kɑ:ɹt / -s
**sp** cart[5] / carts[1]

**carter / ~s** *n*
'kɑ:ɹtəɹ / -z
**sp** carters[3]

**Carthage** *n*
'kɑ:ɹtɪʤ
**sp** Carthage[7]

**carv·e / ~es / ~ing / ~ed** *v*
kɑ:ɹv / -z / 'kɑ:ɹvɪn, -ɪŋ / kɑ:ɹvd
**sp** carue[9] / carues[1] / caruing[2] / caru'd[4], carued[2]
**rh** serve *LLL 4.1.58*

**carved** *adj*
kɑ:ɹvd
**sp** carued[1]

**carved-bone** *adj*
'kɑ:ɹvd-ˌbo:n
**sp** caru'd-bone[1]

**carver / ~s** *n*
'kɑ:ɹvəɹ / -z
**sp** caruer[1] / caruers[1]

**casa** *Ital n*
'ka:sa
**sp** casa[1]

**Casca / ~'s** *n*
'kaskə / -z
**sp** Caska[30] / Caska's[1]

**case / ~s** *n*
kɛ:s / 'kɛ:sɪz
**sp** case[95], [accusatiue]-case[1] / cases[10]
**rh** disgrace *R2 1.1.134*; face *CE 4.2.5, LLL 5.2.387*; face, place *Luc 313, KJ 1.1.147*; grace *TS 4.2.45*; grace, pace *Luc 711*; grace, place *LC 116*; place *1H6 2.1.72, RJ 1.1.101, S 108.9* / faces *LLL 5.2.273*
> bow-, lute-, watch-case

**case / ~d** *v*
kɛ:s / kɛ:st
**sp** case[5] / cas'd[2]
> dis-, un-case

**cased** *adj*
kɛ:st
**sp** cased[1]

**casement / ~s** *n*
'kɛ:smənt / -s
**sp** case-ment[1], casement[8] / casements[3]

**cash** *n*
=
**sp** cash[1]

**cashier / ~ed** *v*
kə'ʃi:ɹ / -d
**sp** casheere[1] / casheerd[1], casheer'd[2]

**cashiered** *adj*
kə'ʃi:ɹd
**sp** casheer'd[1]

**casing** *adj*
'kɛ:sɪn, -ɪŋ
**sp** casing[1]

**cask / ~s** *n*
kask / -s
**sp** caske[1] / caskes[1]

**casket / ~s** *n*
'kaskɪt / -s
**sp** casket[9] / caskets[7]

**casket / ~ted** *v*
'kaskɪtɪd
**sp** casketted[1]

**casque** *n*
kask
**sp** caske[3]

**Cassado** *n*
kə'sɑ:do:
**sp** Cassado[1]

**Cassandra / ~'s** *n*
kə'sandrə / -z
**sp** Cassandra[8], Cassandra's [Cassandra is][1] / Cassandra's[1]

**Cassibulan** *n*
kə'sɪbjə,lan, -ələn
**sp** Cassibulan[4]

**Cassio / ~'s** *n*
'kasɪoː / -z
**sp** Cassio[136], Cassio's [Cassio is][4] / Cassio's[6]

**Cassius** *n*
'kasɪəs
**sp** Cassius[85]

**cassock / ~s** *n*
=
**sp** cassockes[1]

**cast** *adj / n*
kast
**sp** cast[1] / cast[4]
> countercaster; fore-, out-, over-, rough-, up-cast

**cast / ~s / ~ing** *v*
kast / -s / 'kast·ɪn, -ɪŋ
**sp** cast[91], cast-[him][1] / casts[2], cast's [casts][1] / casting[1]

**Castalion** *adj*
kəs'talɪən
**sp** Castalion-[king-vrinall][1]

**castaway / ~s** *n*
'kastə,wɛː / -z
**sp** castaway[1], cast-away[1] / castawayes[1]
**rh** day, lay *Luc 744*
> away

**casted** *adj*
'kastɪd
**sp** casted[1]

**castigate** *v*
'kastɪ,gɛːt
**sp** castigate[1]

**castigation** *n*
'kastɪ,gɛːsɪən
**sp** castigation[1]

**Castiliano** *n*
,kastɪlɪ'ɑːnoː
**sp** Castiliano[1]

**casting-forth** *n*
'kastɪn-'fɒɹθ, -ɪŋ-
**sp** casting forth[1]

**casting-up** *n*
'kastɪn-'ɤp, -ɪŋ-
**sp** casting vp[1]

**castle / ~'s / ~s** *n*
'kasəl / -z
**sp** castle[37], castle-[ditch][1], castles [castle is][1] / castles[2] / castles[9]

**casual** *adj*
'kazwɑl
**sp** casuall[1], casu-all[1]

**casually** *adv*
*m* 'kazwɑ,ləɪ
**sp** casually[1]

**casualty** *n*
*m* 'kazwɑl,təɪ
**sp** casualtie[1]

**cat / ~s** *n*
=
**sp** cat[38], [gyb]-cat[1], [wilde]-cat[2], catte[2] / cats[6], wilde-[cats][1]
> polecat

**catalogue** *n*
=
**sp** catalogue[4], cate-log[1]

**cataplasm** *n*
=
**sp** cataplasme[1]

**cataract / ~s** *n*
'katə,raks, -kts
**sp** cataracts[1]

**catarrh / ~s** *n*
kə'tɑːɹz
**sp** catarres[1]

**catastrophe** *n*
=
**sp** catastrophe[4]

**catch / ~es** *n*
=
**sp** catch[9] / catches[2]
**rh** snatch *MND 3.2.30*
> tallow catch

**catch / ~es / ~ing / ~ed / caught** *v*
= / = / 'katʃɪn, -ɪŋ / =
**sp** catch[54] / catches[2] / catching[4] / catcht[4] / caught[31]
**rh** match *TS 2.1.324*; dispatch *S 143.1*; hatch *KJ 1.1.173*; latch *Luc 360, S 113.8* / hatched *LLL 5.2.69* / caught her **rh** *1* daughter, slaughter *KL 1.4.314* / **rh** *2* after *KL 1.4.314* / **rh** *3* halter *KL 1.4.314*
> cony-catch, uncaught

**catcher** *n*
'katʃəɹ
**sp** catcher[1]
> gull-, rat-catcher

**catching** *adj / n*
'katʃɪn, -ɪŋ
**sp** catching[3] / catching[1]

**cate / ~s** *n*
kɛːts
**sp** cates[3]

**catechism** *n*
=
**sp** catechisme[2]

**catechize** *v*
'katə,kəɪz
**sp** catechize[3]

**catechizing** *n*
'katə,kəɪzɪn, -ɪŋ
**sp** catechizing[1]

**cater / ~s** *v*
'kɛːtəɹz
**sp** caters[1]

**cater-cousin / ~s** *n*
'kɛːtəɹ-,kɤzənz
**sp** catercosins[1]
> cousin

**caterpillar / ~s** *n*
'katəɹ,pɪləɹz

**sp** caterpillars[1], caterpillers[3], catterpillers[1]

**caterwauling** *n*
'katəɹˌwɑ:lɪn, -ɪŋ
**sp** catterwalling[2]

**Catesby** *n*
'kɛ:tsbəɪ
**sp** Catesby[36]

**Cathayan** *n*
kə'tɛ:ən
**sp** cataian[1], catayan[1]

**cathedral** *n*
kə'θi:drɑl
**sp** cathedrall[1]

**catlike** *adj*
'katləɪk
**sp** catlike[1]

**catling / ~s** *n*
'katlɪnz, -ɪŋz
**sp** catlings[1]

**Catling** [name] *n*
'katlɪn, -ɪŋ
**sp** Catling[1]

**Cato / ~'s** *n*
'kɛ:to: / -z
**sp** Cato[7] / Cato's[3], *emend of Cor 1.4.59* calues[1]

**cat o' mountain** *adj / n*
'katə'məʊntɪn
**sp** cat-a-moun-taine-[lookes][1] / cat o' mountaine[1]

**cattle** *n*
=
**sp** cattell[1], cattle[3]

**Caucasus** *n*
=
**sp** Caucasus[2]

**caudle** *n / v*
=
**sp** *emend of 2H6 4.7.83, LLL 4.3.172* candle[2] / cawdle[1]

**cauldron** *n*
'kɔ:ldrən, 'kɔ:d-
**sp** caldron[2], cauldron[5], cawdron[1]
**rh** chaudron *Mac 4.1.34*

**cause / ~s** *n*
=
**sp** cause[317] / causes[16]
**rh** clause *TN 3.1.151*; laws *S 49.14*; pause *CE 2.1.33, VA 220*
> love-cause

**cause / ~st / ~th / ~d** *v*
=
**sp** cause[5] / causest[1] / causeth[1] / caus'd[10], caused[1]

**causeless** *adj*
=
**sp** causelesse[2], causles[1]

**causer** *n*
'kɔ:zəɹ
**sp** causer[3]

**cautel** *n*
=
**sp** cautell[1]

**cautelous** *adj*
*m* 'kɔ:tləs, -təˌlɤs
**sp** cautelous[2]

**caution / ~s** *n*
'kɔ:sɪən / -z
**sp** caution[6] / cautions[1]

**cavaleiro** *adj*
ˌkavə'lɛ:ro:
**sp** caualeiro[1], caueleiro[1], caueleiro-[Iustice][1]

**cavaleiro / ~es** *n*
ˌkavə'lɛ:ro: / -z
**sp** [guest]-caualeire[1] / cauileroes[1]

**cavalery** *adj*
'kavələrəɪ
**sp** caualery[1]

**cavalier / ~s** *n*
ˌkavə'li:ɹz
**sp** caualiers[1]

**cave / ~s** *n*
kɛ:v, kav / -z
**sp** caue[24] / caues[5]
**rh** have *AY 5.4.193*

**cave** *v*
kɛ:v, kav
**sp** caue[1]

**cave-keeper** *n*
'kɛ:v-ˌki:pəɹ, 'kav-
**sp** caue-keeper[1]
> keep

**cavern / ~s** *n*
'kavəɹn / -z
**sp** cauerne[1] / cauernes[1]

**caveto** *Lat interj*
kə'vi:to:
**sp** caueto[1]

**caviary** *n*
'kavɪərəɪ
**sp** cauiarie[1]

**cavil** *n*
=
**sp** cauill[1]

**cavil / ~ling** *v*
= / 'kavɪlɪn, -ɪŋ, -vl-
**sp** cauill[4] / cauilling[1]

**caw / ~ing** *v*
'kɔ:ɪn, -ɪŋ
**sp** cawing[1]

**Cawdor** *n*
'kɔ:dəɹ
**sp** Cawdor[21]

**ce** *Fr det*
sə
**sp** ce[2]

*ces*
'se
**sp** ce[1]

*cette*
sɛt, st
**sp** [a]st[ure]

**cease / ~s / ~th / ~d** *v*
=
**sp** cease[48], cesse[1] / ceases[3] / ceaseth[1] / ceast[3]
**rh** increase *S 11.7*; peace *Cym 5.5.485*

**cedar / ~s** *n*
'si:dəɹ / -z
**sp** cedar[9] / cedars[3]

**Cedus** *n*
'si:dəs
**sp** Cedus[1]

**cein**
> ciel

**celebrate / ~s / ~d** *v*
'selɪˌbrɛ:t / -s / -ɪd
**sp** celebrate[5] / celebrates[1] / celebrated[2]
**rh** estate *Tem 4.1.84*; late *Tem 4.1.132*

**celebration** *n*
ˌselɪ'brɛ:sɪən
**sp** celebration[5]

**celerity** *n*
sə'lerɪtəɪ
**sp** celeritie[3], celerity[30]
**rh** authority *MM 4.2.107*

**celestial** *adj*
sə'lestɪɑl
**sp** celestiall[14], coelestiall[1]

**Celia** *n*
=
**sp** Celia[12], Cellia[2]

**Celius** *n*
'si:lɪəs
**sp** Celius[1]

**cell** *n*
=
**sp** cell[29], cell's [cell is][1]
**rh** farewell *RJ 2.5.77, 3.2.141*; tell *RJ 2.2.192*

**cellar** *n*
'seləɹ
**sp** cellar[1]

**cellarage** *n*
=
**sp** selleredge[1]

**cels·us / ~a** *Lat adj*
'selsa
**sp** celsa[3]

**cement** *n / v*
'sɪmənt
**sp** ciment[1], cyment[1] / ciment[1]

**censor** *n*
'sensəɹ
**sp** censor[3]

**censure / ~s** *n*
'sensjəɹ / -z
**sp** censure[18] / censures[3]

**censure / ~d** *v*
'sensjəɹ / *m* -d, -əˌrɪd
**sp** censure[9] / censur'd[3], censured[3]

**censurer / ~s** *n*
'sensjərəɹz
**sp** censurers[1]

**censuring** *adj*
'sensjərɪn, -ɪŋ
**sp** censuring[1]

**cent / ~s** *Fr n*
sɑ̃
**sp** cent[1]

**centaur / ~s / ~s'** *n*
'sentɔ:ɹ / -z
**sp** centaur[6], centaure[1] / centaures[1], centaurs[1] / centaures[1]

**centre** *n*
'sentəɹ
**sp** center[9], [th ']center[1], centre[1], centure[1], *emend of R3 5.2.11* centry[1]

**centurion / ~s** *n*
sen'tjʊrɪənz
**sp** centurions[1]

**century** *n*
*m* 'sentjəˌrəɪ
**sp** century[1]

**Cerberus** *n*
'sɐ:ɹbrəs, -bər-
**sp** Cerberus[3], Cer-berus[1]

**cerecloth** *n*
'si:ɹklɒθ
**sp** searecloath[1]

**cerements** *n*
'si:ɹmənts
**sp** cerments[1]

**ceremonial** *adj*
ˌserɪ'mo:nɪɑl
**sp** ceremoniall[1]

**ceremonious** *adj*
ˌserɪ'mo:nɪəs
**sp** ceremonious[7]

**ceremoniously** *adv*
*m* ˌserɪ'mo:nɪəsˌləɪ
**sp** ceremoniously[1]

**ceremon·y / ~ies** *n*
*m* 'serɪˌmo:nəɪ, -ɪmənəɪ / -z
**sp** ceremonie[13], ceremony[12], cerimony[2] / ceremonies[10]

**Ceres / ~'** *n*
'si:ri:z
**sp** Ceres[7] / Ceres[1]

**'cern**
> concern

**certain / ~er** *adj*
'sɐ:ɹt·ən / -nəɹ
**sp** certain[5], certaine[159], cer-taine[3] / certainer[1]
**rh** plain *MND 5.1.129*
> incertain

**certainly** *adv*
*m* 'sɐ:ɹtənˌləɪ
**sp** certainely[14], certainly[11]

**certaint·y / ~ies** *n*
'sɐ:ɹtənˌtəɪ, -nt- / 'sɐ:ɹtənˌtəɪz

**sp** certaintie[4], certainty[4] / certainties[3]
> uncertain; in-, un-certainty

**certes** *adv*
*m* 'sɐːɹtɪs, sɐːɹts
**sp** certes[4], certis[1]

**certificate** *n*
səɹ'tɪfɪˌkɛːt
**sp** certificate[1]

**certif·y / ~ies / ~ied** *v*
*m* 'sɐːɹtɪˌfəɪ / -z / -d
**sp** certifie[1] / certifies[1] / certified[2]

**ces** *Fr*
> ce

**Cesario** *n*
*m* sɪ'zarɪoː, -ɪˌoː
**sp** Cesario[18]

**cess** *n*
=
**sp** cesse[2]
**rh** bless *AW 5.3.72*

**c'est** *Fr pro + v*
sɛ
**sp** c'est
> est *Fr*

**cestern** *n*
'sestəɹn
**sp** cesterne[3]

**cestern / ~ed** *v*
'sestəɹnd
**sp** cestern'd[1]

**Cestos** *n*
'sestɒs
**sp** Cestos[1]

**cette** *Fr*
> ce

**chafe** *n*
ʧɛːf
**sp** chafe[1]

**chaf·e / ~es / ~ing / ~ed** *v*
ʧɛːf / -s / 'ʧɛːfɪn, -ɪŋ / *m* 'ʧɛːfɪd, ʧɛːft
**sp** chafe[4] / chafes[3] / chafing[1] / chaf 'd[2], chaft[2]

**chafed** *adj*
*m* 'ʧɛːfɪd, ʧɛːft
**sp** chafed[4], chaff 'd[1]
> enchafed

**chaff** *n*
=
**sp** chaffe[9]

**chaffless** *adj*
=
**sp** chaffelesse[1]

**chain / ~s** *n*
ʧɛːn / -z
**sp** chain[1], chaine[57] / chaines[8], chaynes[3]
**rh** detain *CE 2.1.106*; disdain *VA 110*; vain *CE 3.2.189*

**chain / ~s / ~ed** *v*
ʧɛːn / -z / -d
**sp** chaine[4], chayne[1] / chaines[1] / chain'd[3]
**rh** obtained, pained *Luc 900*
> unchain

**chair / ~s** *n*
ʧɛːɹ / -z
**sp** chaire[24], chayre[12] / chaires[5], chayres[1]

**chair-days** *n*
'ʧɛːɹ-ˌdɛːz
**sp** chaire-dayes[1]
> day

**Chalcas / ~'** *n*
'ʧalkəs
**sp** Chalcas[4] / Chalcas[1]

**chalice / ~s** *n*
=
**sp** challice[2] / challices[1]

**chaliced** *adj*
=
**sp** chalic'd[1]

**chalk / ~s / ~ed** *v*
=
**sp** chalkes[1] / chalk'd[1]

**chalky** *adj*
'ʧɔːkəɪ
**sp** chalky[1], chalkie[1], chalkle[1]

**challenge** *n*
=, *Caius MW 1.4.106* 'ʃalɪnʤ
**sp** challenge[21], *Caius* shallenge[1]

**challenge / ~s / ~ed** *v*
=
**sp** challenge[28] / challenges[1] / challeng'd[9], challenged[1]

**challenger / ~s** *n*
'ʧalɪnʤəɹ / -z
**sp** challenger[5] / challengers[1], challen-gers[1]

**Cham / ~'s** *n*
=
**sp** Chams[1]

**chamber** *adj*
'ʧambəɹ
**sp** chamber[12], chamber-[window][3]

**chamber / ~'s / ~s** *n*
'ʧambəɹ / -z
**sp** chamber[84], cham-ber[4] / chambers[1] / chambers[11], [charg'd]-chambers[1], cham-bers[1]
**rh** amber *WT 4.4.225*
> bed-, dining-, star-chamber

**chamber / ~ed** *v*
'ʧambəɹd
**sp** chamber'd[1]

**chamber-counsel / ~s** *n*
'ʧambəɹ-ˌkəʊnsɪls
**sp** chamber-councels[1]
> counsel

**chamberer / ~s** *n*
'ʧambrəɹz, -bər-
**sp** chamberers[1]

**chamber-hanging** *n*
'ʧambəɹ-ˌaŋɪn, -ɪŋ, -ˌhaŋ-
**sp** chamber-hanging[1]
> hang

**chamberlain / ~s** *n*
ˈʧambəɹˌlɛːn, -lɪn / -z
**sp** chamberlaine$^{23}$, cham-berlaine$^{2}$ / chamberlaines$^{1}$

**chamber-lye** *n*
ˈʧambəɹ-ˌləɪ
**sp** chamber-lye$^{1}$

**chambermaid / ~s** *n*
ˈʧambəɹ-ˌmɛːd / -z
**sp** chamber-maid$^{1}$ / chambermaides$^{1}$
> maid

**chamber-pot** *n*
ˈʧambəɹ-ˌpɒt
**sp** chamber-pot$^{1}$
> poy

**chamblet** *n*
ˈkamlət
**sp** chamblet$^{1}$

**chameleon / ~'s** *n*
kəˈmiːlɪən / -z
**sp** cameleon$^{1}$, camelion$^{2}$ / camelions$^{1}$

**Champ** [name] *n*
*Eng* ʃɒmp, *Fr* ʃɑ̃
**sp** Champ$^{1}$

**Champaigne** *n*
ʃamˈpɛːn, ʃɒm-, -ˈpen
**sp** Champaigne$^{1}$

**champain / ~s** *n*
ˈʃampɛːn / -z
**sp** champian$^{1}$ / champains$^{1}$

**champion** *adj*
=
**sp** champion$^{1}$

**champion / ~s** *n*
*m* =, ˈʧampɪˌɒn / -z
**sp** champion$^{10}$, champi-on$^{1}$ / champions$^{4}$

**champion** *v*
=
**sp** champion$^{1}$

**chance / ~'s / ~s** *n*
ʧɔːns, ʧans / ˈʧɔːnsɪz, ˈʧans-
**sp** chance$^{61}$, [main]-chance$^{1}$, chaunce$^{1}$ / chances$^{1}$ / chances$^{7}$, chaunces$^{1}$
**rh** advance, circumstance *Luc 1706*; dance *LLL 5.2.218*; France *KJ 1.1.151, 256, LLL 5.2.550*; trance *Luc 1596*
> be-, mis-, per-chance

**chance / ~s / ~d** *v*
ʧans, ʧɔː- / ˈʧans·ɪz, ˈʧɔː- / ʧanst, ʧɔː-
**sp** chance$^{37}$, chaunce$^{1}$ / chances$^{3}$, chaunces$^{1}$ / chanc'd$^{8}$, chanced$^{2}$, chanc't$^{1}$
**rh** dances *Per 5.Chorus.1*

**chancellor** *n*
ˈʧansləɹ, ˈʧɔː-, -səl-
**sp** chancellor$^{2}$, chancellour$^{2}$, chancelor$^{1}$

**chandler / ~'s** *n*
ˈʧandləɹz, ˈʧɔːn-
**sp** chandlers$^{1}$

**change / ~s** *n*
ʧɛːnʤ / ˈʧɛːnʤɪz
**sp** change$^{45}$, [long'd-for]-change$^{1}$ / changes$^{9}$
**rh** strange *LLL 5.2.209, S 76.2, 89.6, 93.6*
> counter-, exchange, inter-, sea-change

**chang·e / ~est / ~es / ~ing / ~ed** *v*
ʧɛːnʤ / ˈʧɛːnʤ·əst / -ɪz / -ɪn, -ɪŋ / *m* -ɪd, ʧɛːnʤd
**sp** change$^{99}$ / changest$^{1}$ / changes$^{8}$, chan-ges$^{1}$ / changing$^{4}$ / chang'd$^{32}$, changed$^{1}$, chaung'd$^{1}$
**rh** strange *Ham 3.2.211, S 123.1* / estranged *LLL 5.2.214*

**changeable** *adj*
ˈʧɛːnʤəbəl
**sp** changeable$^{3}$

**changed** *adj*
*m* ʧɛːnʤd, ˈʧɛːnʤɪd
**sp** chang'd$^{1}$, changed$^{2}$
> child-changed

**changeful** *adj*
ˈʧɛːnʤfʊl
**sp** changefull$^{1}$

**changeling / ~s** *n*
ˈʧɛːnʤlɪn, -ɪŋ / -z
**sp** changeling$^{7}$ / changelings$^{1}$
**rh** king *MND 2.1.23*

**changing** *adj / n*
ˈʧɛːnʤɪn, -ɪŋ
**sp** changing$^{2}$ / changing$^{3}$
**rh** ranging *TS 3.1.90*
> all-, near-, shallow-, un-, wind-changing

**channel / ~s** *n*
=
**sp** channel$^{1}$, channell$^{7}$ / channels$^{2}$

**channel** *v*
=
**sp** channell$^{1}$

**chanson** *n*
ˈʃansən, ˈʃɒn-
**sp** chanson$^{1}$

**Chanticleer** *n*
ˈʧɔːntɪˌkliːɹ, ˈʧan-
**sp** Chanticleere$^{1}$, Chanticlere$^{1}$
**rh** hear *Tem 1.2.386*

**chant / ~s / ~ing / ~ed** *v*
ʧɔːnt, ʧant / -s / ˈʧɔːnt·ɪn, -ɪŋ, ˈʧant- / -ɪd
**sp** chaunt$^{2}$ / chauntes$^{1}$, chaunts$^{2}$ / chanting$^{1}$ / chaunted$^{1}$
**rh** aunts *WT 4.3.9*

**chantr·y / ~ies** *n*
ˈʧɔːntrəɪ, ʧan-/ -z
**sp** chantry$^{1}$ / chauntries$^{1}$

**chaos** *n*
ˈkɛːɒs
**sp** chaos$^{4}$

**chape** *n*
ʧɛːp
**sp** chape$^{1}$

**chapel / ~s** *n*
=
**sp** chappell[9] / chappels[2]

**chapeless** *adj*
'ʧɛ:pləs
**sp** chapelesse[1]

**chaplain / ~s** *n*
=
**sp** chaplaine[4] / chaplaines[1]

**chapless** *adj*
=
**sp** chaplesse[1]

**chaplet** *n*
=
**sp** chaplet[1]

**chap·man / ~men / ~men's** *n*
=
**sp** chapmen[1] / chapmens[1]

**chaps** *n*
ʧaps, ʧɒps
**sp** chaps[5], chappes[1], chops[3]

**chapter** *n*
'ʧaptəɹ
**sp** chapter[1]

**charact / ~s** *n*
'karəks, -kts
**sp** caracts[1]

**character / ~s** *n*
*m* 'karək,tɛ:ɹ, -təɹ, kə'raktəɹ / -z
**sp** character[7], charracter[6] / characters[4], charracters[3], charrac-ters[1]
**rh** *1* bears *LC 16* / **rh** *2* tears [cry] *LC 16*

**character / ~ed** *v*
*m* 'karək,tɛ:ɹ, -təɹ, kə'raktəɹ / kə'raktəɹd
**sp** character[1], charracter[1] / character'd[2]
**rh** *1* register *S 108.1* / **rh** *2* every-where *AY 3.2.6*

**characterless** *adj*
*m* kə'raktəɹ,les
**sp** characterlesse[1]

**charactery** *n*
*m* kə'raktə,rəɪ
**sp** characterie[1], charractery[1]
**rh** embroidery, knee *MW 5.5.73*

**Charbon** *n*
'ʃaɹbɒn
**sp** Charbon[1]

**chare / ~s** *n*
ʧɑ:ɹ / -z
**sp** chare[1] / chares[1]

**charge / ~es** *n*
ʧɑ:ɹʤ / 'ʧɑ:ɹʤɪz
**sp** charge[108] / charges[9]
**rh** George *H5 3.1.33*; marriage *3H6 4.1.32*

**charg·e / ~es / ~eth / ~ing / ~ed** *v*
ʧɑ:ɹʤ / 'ʧɑ:ɹʤ·ɪz / -əθ / -ɪn, -ɪŋ / *m* -ɪd, ʧɑ:ɹʤd
**sp** charge[88] / charges[5] / chargeth[1] / charging[1] / charg'd[26], charged[2]
**rh** enlarged *S 70.10*; wide-enlarged *AY 3.2.137*
> double-, un-charge

**charged** *adj*
ʧɑ:ɹʤd
**sp** charg'd[2], charg'd-[chambers][1], charged[1]
> full-, over-charged

**chargeful** *adj*
'ʧɑ:ɹʤfʊl
**sp** chargefull[1]

**charge-house** *n*
'ʧɑ:ɹʤ-,əʊs, ,həʊs
**sp** charg-house[1]
> house

**chariness** *n*
'ʧarɪnəs
**sp** charinesse[1]

**Charing Cross** *n*
,ʧarɪn-'krɒs, -ɪŋ-
**sp** Charing-crosse[1]

**chariot / ~s** *n*
=
**sp** chariot[5] / chariots[3]

**chariot-wheel / ~s** *n*
'ʧarɪət-,ʍi:lz
**sp** chariot-wheeles[1], chariot wheeles[1]

**charitable** *adj*
*m* 'ʧarɪ,tabəl
**sp** charitable[17]
> uncharitable

**charitably** *adj*
*m* 'ʧarɪ,tabləɪ
**sp** charitably[1]
> uncharitably

**charit·y / ~ies** *n*
*m* 'ʧarɪ,təɪ, -ɪt- / -,təɪz
**sp** charitie[22], charity[31] / charities[1]
**rh** fee *Per 3.2.73*; society *LLL 4.3.125*
> self-charity

**Charlemaine** *n*
*m* 'ʃɑ:ɹlə,mɛ:n
**sp** Charlemaine[2]

**Charles** *n*
ʧɑ:ɹlz
**sp** Charles[60]

**charm / ~s** *n*
ʧɑ:ɹm / -z
**sp** charm[1], charme[16], [ayrie]-charme[1], charme's [charm is][1] / charmes[21]
**rh** arm, harm *Luc 173*; harm *MM 4.1.14, MND 2.2.17* / arms *PP 11.8*; harms *Mac 3.5.6*

**charm / ~s / ~eth / ~ing / ~ed** *v*
ʧɑ:ɹm / -z / 'ʧɑ:ɹm·əθ / -ɪn, -ɪŋ / *m* -ɪd, ʧɑ:ɹmd
**sp** charme[13] / charmes[1] / charmeth[1] / charming[3] / charm'd[6], charmed[1]
**rh** harm thee *Cym 4.2.277* / harmed, warmed *LC 193*

**charmed** *adj*
*m* ʧɑːɹmɪd
**sp** charmed[3]
> uncharmed

**charmer** *n*
'ʧɑːɹməɹ
**sp** charmer[1]

**Charmian** *n*
'ʧɑːɹmɪən
**sp** Charmian[36], Char-mian[1], Charmion[1]

**charming** *adj*
'ʧɑːɹmɪn, -ɪŋ
**sp** charming[3]

**charmingly** *adv*
*m* 'ʧɑːɹmɪn,ləɪ, -ɪŋ-
**sp** charmingly[1]

**charneco** *n*
'ʧɑːɹnɪkoː
**sp** charneco[1]

**charnel-house / ~s** *n*
'ʧɑːɹnəl-,əʊs, -,həʊ- / -zɪz
**sp** charnell house[1] / charnell houses[1]
> house

**Charolois** *n*
,ʃarə'lwɛ
**sp** Charaloyes[1]

**Charon** *n*
'karən
**sp** Charon[1]

**charter / ~s** *n*
'ʧɑːɹtəɹ / -z
**sp** charter[6] / charters[2]
> blank-charter

**chartered** *adj*
'ʧaɹtəɹd
**sp** charter'd[1]

**Chartham** *n*
'ʧɑːɹtəm
**sp** Chartam[1]

**Chartreux** *n*
ʃɑːɹ'trəː
**sp** Chartreux[2]

**char·y** *S* **/ ~iest** *adj*
'ʧarəɪ / -əst
**sp** chary[1] / chariest[1]
**rh** wary *S 22.11*
> unchary

**Charybdis** *n*
kə'rɪbdɪs
**sp** Charibdis[1]

**chase / ~s** *n*
ʧɛːs / 'ʧɛːsɪz
**sp** chase[10], chace[10] / chaces[1]
**rh** face *S 143.5, VA 3*; grace *MND 2.2.94*; place *Luc 1736, VA 883*

**chas·e / ~es / ~eth / ~ing / ~ed** *v*
ʧɛːs / 'ʧɛːs·ɪz / -əθ / -ɪn, -ɪŋ / ʧɛːst
**sp** chace[3], chase[8] / chases[1] / chaseth[1] / chasing[1] / chac'd[4], chas'd[4], chased[2]
**rh** chase it disgrace it *VA 410* / embracing *VA 561* / defaced, disgraced *Luc 716*; disgraced *Luc 1834*; embraced *MW 5.5.230*

**chaser** *n*
'ʧɛːsəɹ
**sp** chaser[1]

**chaste** *adj*
ʧast
**sp** chaste[27], chast[12]
**rh** haste *Luc 322*; waist *Luc 7*; waste *RJ 1.1.217*
> unchaste

**chastely** *adv*
'ʧastləɪ
**sp** chastly[3]

**chastise / ~d** *v*
'ʧastəɪz / *m* -d, -ɪd
**sp** chastise[5] / chastic'd[1], chasticed[1], chastis'd[1], chastised[1]

**chastised** *adj*
'ʧastəɪzd
**sp** chastiz'd[1]

**chastisement** *n*
*m* 'ʧastəɪz,ment
**sp** chasticement[8], chastisement[1]

**chastity** *n*
*m* 'ʧastɪ,təɪ
**sp** chastitie[8], chastities [chastity is][1], chastity[10]
**rh** *1* infirmity, posterity *PT 61*; luxury *LC 315*; scarcity *VA 751*; silently *MND 3.1.195*; **rh** *2* eye *MND 3.1.195, PP 4.8*

**chat** *n*
=
**sp** chat[8]
**rh** *1* that *LLL 5.2.228;* **rh** *2* gate *VA 422*

**chat / ~s** *v*
=
**sp** chat[4] / chats[1]

**Chatillon** *n*
ʃə'tɪlɪən
**sp** Chatilion[2], Chatillion[1], Chattilion[3], Chattillion[2], Chattylion[1], *abbr in s.d.* Chat[1]

**chattels** *n*
=
**sp** chattels[2]

**chatter** *v*
'ʧatəɹ
**sp** chatter[3]

**chattering** *adj*
'ʧatrɪn, -ɪŋ, -tər-
**sp** chattering[1], chatt'ring[1]

**chaud** *Fr adj*
ʃo
**sp** *emend of MW 1.4.49* ehando[1]

**chaudron** *n*
'ʧɔːdrən
**sp** chawdron[1]
**rh** cauldron *Mac 4.1.33*

**chawed** *adj*
ʧɔ:d
**sp** chaw'd-[grasse][1]

**che** [*dialect form of* I] *pro*
ʧə
**sp** che[1]

**cheap / ~er / ~est** *adj*
= / 'ʧi:pəɹ / =
**sp** cheap[1], cheape[13] / cheaper[1] / cheapest[1]

**cheapen** *v*
=
**sp** cheapen[1]

**cheaply** *adv*
'ʧi:pləɪ
**sp** cheapely[1]

**Cheapside** *n*
'ʧi:psəɪd
**sp** Cheapside[2]

**cheat** *n*
=
**sp** cheat[1], cheate[1]

**cheat / ~s / ~ed** *v*
=
**sp** cheat[1], cheate[1] / cheats[1] / cheated[3]

**cheater / ~s** *n*
'ʧi:təɹ / -z
**sp** cheater[5] / cheaters[2]

**cheating** *adj*
'ʧi:tɪn, -ɪŋ
**sp** cheating[1]

**check / ~s** *n*
=
**sp** checke[9] / checkes[4], checks[1]
> countercheck

**check / ~s / ~ing / ~ed** *v*
= / = / 'ʧekɪn, -ɪŋ / =
**sp** check[4], checke[9] / checkes[2] / checking[1] / check'd[4], checkt[2]
**rh** beck *S 58.7*
> half-, un-checked

**cheek / ~s** *n*
=
**sp** cheek[1], cheeke[65] / cheekes[67], cheeks[2]
**rh** meek *Luc 708*; seek *LLL 4.3.233, S 67.5*; speak *Per 5.1.94* / leeks *MND 5.1.324*; reeks *S 130.6*; seeks *VA 50, 475*; weeks *S 116.9*
> Aguecheek

**cheek-rose / ~s** *n*
*m* ˌʧi:k-'ro:zɪz
**sp** cheeke-roses[1]
> rose

**cheer** *n*
ʧi:ɹ
**sp** chear[1], cheare[6], cheer[1], cheere[39]
**rh** *1* dear *2H4 5.3.17, MND 3.2.96, 5.1.286, MV 3.2.312*; dear, here *CE 3.1.19*; fear *Luc 89*; fear, hear *Luc 264*; near *S 97.13*; year *2H4 5.3.17*; **rh** *2* there *2H4 5.3.17*; **rh** *3* worshipper *Luc 89* / tears [cry] *TNK 1.5.4*

**cheer / ~est / ~s / ~ing / ~ed** *v*
ʧi:ɹ / -st / -z / 'ʧi:ɹ·ɪn, -ɪŋ / *m* -ɪd, ʧi:ɹd
**sp** cheare[6], cheere[19] / cheer'st[1] / cheares[2], cheeres[2] / chearing[2] / chear'd[1], cheared[1], cheer'd[5]
**rh** cheer thee hear thee *PP 20.22*
> all-cheering

**cheerer** *n*
'ʧi:ɹəɹ
**sp** chearer[1]

**cheerful** *adj*
'ʧi:ɹfʊl
**sp** chearefull[8], cheerefull[8], cheerfull[1]

**cheerfully** *adv*
*m* 'ʧi:ɹfʊlˌəɪ, -fləɪ
**sp** chearefully[1], cheare-fully[1], chearfully[2], cheerefully[3], cheereful-ly[1], cheerfully[1]
**rh** victory *R3 5.3.270*

**cheerless** *adj*
'ʧi:ɹləs
**sp** cheerlesse[1]

**cheerly** *adv*
'ʧi:ɹləɪ
**sp** chearely[3], chearly[1], cheerely[9]

**cheese** *n*
=, *Evans MV 5.5.139f* tsi:z
**sp** cheese[13], *Evans MV 5.5.139f* seese[2]

**cheese-paring** *n*
'ʧi:z-ˌpɛ:rɪn, -ɪŋ
**sp** cheese-paring[1]

**chequer / ~ing** *v*
'ʧekrɪn, -ɪŋ
**sp** checkring[2]

**chequered** *adj*
'ʧekəɹd
**sp** checker'd[1], cheker'd[1]

**cher** *Fr adj*
ʃɛ:ɹ
**sp** [tres]cher[2]

**cherish / ~es / ~ing / ~ed** *v*
= / = / 'ʧerɪʃɪn, -ɪŋ / =
**sp** cherish[15], cherrish[2] / cherishes[1] / cherishing[1] / cherish'd[3], cherished[1], cherisht[5]
**rh** perish *Luc 1546, S 11.12*

**cherisher** *n*
'ʧerɪʃəɹ
**sp** cherisher[1]

**cherishing** *n*
*m* 'ʧerɪˌʃɪn, -ɪŋ
**sp** cherishing[1]

**cherr·y / ~ies** *n*
'ʧerəɪ / -z
**sp** cherry[7] / cherries[1]
**rh** berry *Per 5.Chorus.8* / berries *VA 1103*

**cherry-pit** *n*
'ʧerəɪ-ˌpɪt
**sp** cherrie-pit[1]

**cherry-stone** *n*
'ʧerəɪ-ˌsto:n
**sp** cherrie-stone[1]

**Chertsey** *n*
'ʧɐːɹtsəɪ
**sp** Chertsey[3]

**cherub / ~in / ~ins** *n*
= / *m* =, 'ʧerəˌbɪn / -z
**sp** cherube[1] / cherubin[4] / cherubins[4]

**Cheshu**
> Jesus

**chess** *n*
=
**sp** chesse[1]

**chest / ~s** *n*
=
**sp** chest[6] / chests[6]
**rh** breast *R2 1.1.180, S 48.9*; special-blest *S 52.9*; unrest *Tit 2.3.9*

**Chester** *n*
'ʧestəɹ
**sp** Chester[1]

**chestnut / ~s** *n*
'ʧesnət / -s
**sp** chessenut[1], chesse-nut[1], chestnuts[1]
> nut

**Chetas** *n*
'kiːtəs
**sp** Chetas[1]

**cheval** *Fr n*
ʃə'val
**sp** cheual[2]

**chevalier / ~s** *n*
*m* 'ʃevəˌliːɹ / -z
**sp** cheualier[1] / cheualiers[1]

**chevalier** *Fr n*
ʃəval'je
**sp** che-ualier[1]

**cheverel** *n*
'ʃevrəl, -vər-
**sp** cheuerell[1]
**pun** *RJ 2.4.82* ell

**cheveril** *adj*
'ʃevrəl, -vər-
**sp** cheu'rill[1], chiuerell[1]

**chew / ~ing / ~ed** *v*
= / 'ʧuːɪn, -ɪŋ / =
**sp** chew[2] / chewing[1] / chew'd[1], chewed[1]

**chewet** *n*
'ʧuːɪt
**sp** chewet[1]

**chez** *Fr prep*
ʃez
**sp** ches[1]

**chi** *Ital pro*
kiː
**sp** que[2]

**chick** *n*
=
**sp** chicke[1]

**chicken / ~s** *n*
=
**sp** chicken[2] / chickens[3], chic-kens[1]

**chicurmurco** *nonsense word*
ˌkiːkəɹ'mɐːɹkoː
**sp** chicurmurco[1]

**chidden** *adj*
=
**sp** chidden[3]

**chid·e / ~est / ~s / ~ing / chid / ~den** *v*
ʧəɪd / -st / -z / 'ʧəɪdɪn, -ɪŋ / =
**sp** chide[43] / chid'st[2] / chides[10] / chiding[1], chi-ding[1] / chid[15], chidde[2] / chidden[1]
**rh** abide *Luc 484*; dy'd, pride *S 99.1*; provide *S 111.1*

**chider / ~s** *n*
'ʧəɪdəɹz
**sp** chiders[1]

**chiding** *adj / n*
'ʧəɪdɪn, -ɪŋ
**sp** chiding[3] / chiding[5]

**chief / ~est** *adj*
=
**sp** cheefe[9], chiefe[2] / cheefest[8], chiefest[6]
**rh** grief *S 42.3, VA 970*

**chief** *n*
=
**sp** cheefe[2], cheff[1], chiefe[2]

**chiefest** *n*
=
**sp** cheefest[1]

**chiefly** *adv*
'ʧiːfləɪ
**sp** cheefely[3], chiefely[6], chieflie[1], chiefly[2]

**chien** *Fr n*
ʃjɛ̃
**sp** chien[1]

**child / ~'s / ~ren / ~'s** *n*
ʧəɪld / -z / =
**sp** child[62], male-[child][1], [with]-child[1], childe[146], male-[childe][1] / childes[3], childs[2] / children[104], chil-dren[1] / childrens[11]
**rh** *1* beguiled *MND 1.1.238, S 59.4*; beguiled, wild *Luc 954*; defiled *AW 5.3.299, Luc 785, MND 3.2.409*; mild *Luc 1094, Per 1.1.70*; [*following R2 1.3.239, Q*], *VA 1152*; wild *MND 2.1.24*; **rh** *2* spilled *RJ 3.1.146*
> unchilded

**child-bed** *n*
'ʧəɪld-ˌbed
**sp** child-bed[1]
> bed

**child-changed** *adj*
*m* ˌʧəɪld-'ʧɛːnʤɪd
**sp** childe-changed[1]
> changed

**Childeric** *n*
'ʧɪldəˌrɪk
**sp** Childerike[1]

**childhood / ~s** *n*
'ʧəɪldʊd, -hʊd / -z
**sp** childehood[1], childhood[2], child-hood[2], child-hoode[1] / child-hoods[1]

**childing** *adj*
'ʧəɪldɪn, -ɪŋ
**sp** childing[1]

**childish** *adj*
'ʧəɪldɪʃ
**sp** childish[9]

**childishness** *n*
*m* 'ʧəɪldɪʃˌnes
**sp** childishnesse[3]

**child-killer** *n*
*m* ˌʧəɪld-'kɪləɹ
**sp** child-killer[1]

**childlike** *adj*
'ʧəɪldləɪk
**sp** child-like[2]

**childness** *n*
'ʧəɪldnəs
**sp** child-nesse[1]

**chill** *adj*
=
**sp** chill[1]

**chill** [*dialect form of* I will] *pro + v*
ʧɪl
**sp** chill[3]

**chilling** *adj*
'ʧɪlɪn, -ɪŋ
**sp** chilling[1]

**chime / ~s** *n*
ʧəɪm / -z
**sp** chime[1] / chymes[1]
**rh** time *Per 1.1.86*

**chimney / ~s** *n*
'ʧɪmnəɪ / -z
**sp** chimney[7] / chimneys[1], chimnies[1], [Windsor]-chimnies[1]

**chimney-piece** *n*
'ʧɪmnəɪ-ˌpi:s
**sp** chimney-peece[1]
> piece

**chimney-sweeper / ~s** *n*
'ʧɪmnəɪ-ˌswi:pəɹz
**sp** chimney-sweepers[1], chimny-sweepers[1]

**chimurcho** *nonsense word*
ki:'mɐ:ɹko:
**sp** chimurcho[1]

**chin / ~s** *n*
=, *Katherine H5 3.4.33ff* sɪn / -z
**sp** chin[17], chinne[5], *Katherine* sin[4] / chinnes[2], chins[2]
**rh** begin *Luc 472, VA 59*; in *VA 85*; skin *LC 92, Luc 420*

**china** *adj*
'ʧəɪnə
**sp** china-[dishes][1]

**chine / ~s** *n*
ʧəɪn / -z
**sp** chine[2] / chines[1]

**chink / ~s** *n*
=
**sp** chink[1], chinke[4] / chincks[1]
**rh** think *MND 5.1.156, 189*

**chip / ~s** *S* *n*
=
**sp** chips[1]
**rh** lips *S 128.10*

**chip / ~ped** *v*
=
**sp** chipp'd[1]

**chipochia**
> capocchia

**chipped** *adj*
=
**sp** chipt[1]

**Chiron** *n*
'kəɪrən
**sp** Chiron[12]

**chirping** *n*
'ʧɐ:ɹpɪn, -ɪŋ
**sp** chirping[1]

**chirra** *interj*
'ʧɪrə
**sp** chirra[1]

**chirurgeonly** *adv*
*m* ʧɪ'rɐ:ɹʤɪənˌləɪ
**sp** chirurgeonly[1]

**chisel** *n*
=
**sp** chizzell[1]

**Chitopher** *n*
'ʧɪtəfəɹ
**sp** Chitopher[1]

**chivalrous** *adj*
*m* 'ʃɪvəlˌrɤs
**sp** chiualrous[1]

**chivalry** *n*
*m* 'ʃɪvəlˌrəɪ, -lr-
**sp** cheualrie[3], chiualrie[7], chiualry[1]
**rh** *1* fly *1H6 4.6.29*; lie *TC 4.4.147*;
**rh** *2* Jewry *R2 2.1.54*; see *R2 1.1.203*; Italy, victory *Luc 109*

**choice / ~est** *adj*
ʧəɪs / 'ʧəɪsəst
**sp** choise[6], chose[1], choyce[2] / choysest[1]

**choice** *n*
ʧəɪs
**sp** choice[30], choise[15], choyce[6], choyse[9]
**rh** voice *RJ 1.2.18*

**choice-drawn** *adj*
'ʧəɪs-ˌdrɔ:n
**sp** choyse-drawne[1]
> drawn

**choicely** *adv*
'ʧəɪsləɪ
**sp** choycely[1]

**choir** *n*
kwəɪɹ
**sp** quier[1], quire[4]

**choir / ~ing / ~ed** *v*
'kwəɪɹɪn, -ɪŋ / kwəɪɹd
**sp** quiring[1] / quier'd[1]

**chok·e / ~s / ~d** *v*
ʧo:k / -s / -t
**sp** choake[15], choke[1] / chokes[1] / choak'd[7], choaked[1], choakt[4]

**choking** *adj / n*
'ʧo:kɪn, -ɪŋ
**sp** choking[1] / choaking[1]

**Cholchos** *n*
'kɒlkəs
**sp** Cholchos[1]

**choler / ~s** *n*
'kɒləɹ / -z
**sp** choler[4], choller[22] / chollers[1], chollors[1]
**pun** *1H4 2.4.317* collar

**choleric** *adj*
*m* 'kɒlərɪk, -ˌrɪk
**sp** cholericke[1], chollericke[8]

**choos·e / ~s / ~eth / ~ing / chose / chosen** *v*
= / = / = / 'ʧu:zɪn, -ɪŋ / ʧo:z / 'ʧo:zən
**sp** choose[84], chuse[18] / chooses[3] / chooseth[11] / choosing[1], chusing[2] / chose[11] / chose[5], chosen[14]
**rh** lose *AW 1.3.209, CE 4.3.95, MV 2.9.80, R2 2.1.29, S 64.13*
> chosen, well-chosen

**chooser** *n*
'ʧu:zəɹ
**sp** chooser[1]

**choosing** *n*
'ʧu:zɪn, -ɪŋ
**sp** choosing[1]

**chop / ~ped** *v*
=
**sp** chop[8] / chop'd[1], chopt[1]
> wide-chopped

**chop-fallen** *adj*
'ʧɒp-ˌfɑ:ln
**sp** chopfalne[1]
> fallen

**chopine** *n*
ʧɒ'pi:n
**sp** choppine[1]

**chopped** *adj*
=
**sp** chopt[4]

**chopping** *adj*
'ʧɒpɪn, -ɪŋ
**sp** chopping[1]

**choppy** *adj*
'ʧɒpəɪ
**sp** choppie[1]

**chops**
> chaps

**chorister / ~s** *n*
'kwɪrɪstəɹz
**sp** quirristers[1]

**Chorus** *n*
=
**sp** Chorus[8]
**rh** morris *TNK 3.5.106*

**chosen** *adj / n*
'ʧo:zən
**sp** chosen[4] / chosen[1]

**chough / ~s** *n*
ʧɤf / -s
**sp** chough[1], chowgh[1] / choughes[3], choughs[1], chowghes[1], chuffes[1]

**Christ / ~'s** *n*
krəɪst, *Macmorris H5 3.2.85ff* krəɪʃ / -s
**sp** Christ[8], *Macmorris* Chrish[4] / Christs[1], *Macmorris* Chrish[1]

**christen / ~ed** *v*
=
**sp** christen[1] / christen'd[2], christned[1]
> new-christened

**christendom / ~s** *n*
*m* 'krɪsənˌdɤm, -ndəm / -ˌdɤmz
**sp** christendom[1], christendome[13], chri-stendome[2], christen-dome[1], christen dome[1] / christendomes[1]

**christening** *adj*
*m* 'krɪsnɪn, -ɪŋ
**sp** christening[1]

**christening / ~s** *n*
*m* 'krɪsnɪn, -ɪŋ, -səˌn- / -ɪnz, -ɪŋz
**sp** christening[3], christning[1] / christenings[1]

**Christian** *adj*
'krɪstɪən, *Evans MW 3.1.86* 'krɪstɪənz, *Quickly H5 2.3.11* 'krɪstəm
**sp** Christian[38], Chri-stian[1], *Evans* Christians-[soule][1], *Quickly* Christome[1]

**Christian / ~s** *n*
*m* 'krɪstɪən, -ɪˌan / -z
**sp** Christian[29], Christi-an[1], *Evans MW 1.1.95* Christians[1] / Christians[6], Christi-ans[1]

**Christian-like** *adj*
'krɪstɪən-ˌləɪk
**sp** Christian-like[4]

**Christmas** *n*
=
**sp** Christmas[3]

**Christopher** *n*
'krɪstəfəɹ, *Sly TS Induction 2.72* krɪs'tɒfəɹ
**sp** Christopher[3], Chri-stopher[1]

**Christophero** *n*
krɪs'tɒfəɹo:
**sp** Christophero[2]

**chronicle / ~s** *n*
=
**sp** chronicle[7] / chronicles[6]

**chronicle / ~ed** *v*
=
**sp** chronicle[1] / chronicled[3]

**chronicler / ~s** *v*
'krɒnɪkləɹ / -z
**sp** chronicler[1] / chronoclers[1]

**chrysolite** *n*
'krəɪsə,ləɪt
**sp** chrysolite[1]

**chuck / ~s** *n*
ʧɤk / -s
**sp** chuck[3], chucke[4] / chuckes[1]

**church / ~'s / ~es** *n*
ʧɐ:ɹʧ / 'ʧɐ:ɹʧɪz
**sp** church[62] / churches[1] / churches[5]

**churchlike** *adj*
'ʧɐ:ɹʧ-ləɪk
**sp** church-like[1]

**churchman / ~men / ~men's** *n*
'ʧɐ:ɹʧ·mən / -mən / -mənz
**sp** churchman[5], church-man[2] / church-men[6] / churchmens[1]

**churchway** *n*
'ʧɐ:ɹʧwɛ:
**sp** church-way[1]
> way

**churchyard / ~s** *n*
'ʧɐ:ɹʧjɑ:ɹd / -z
**sp** churchyard[5], church-yard[5] / churchyards[1], church-yards[1]
> yard

**churl / ~s** *n*
ʧɐ:ɹl / -z
**sp** churle[7] / churles[1]

**churlish** *adj*
'ʧɐɹlɪʃ
**sp** churlish[15]

**churlishly** *adv*
*m* 'ʧɐɹlɪʃ,ləɪ
**sp** churlishly[1]

**churn** *v*
ʧɐ:ɹn
**sp** cherne[1]
**rh** quern *MND 2.1.37*

**Chus** *n*
ʧu:s
**sp** Chus[1]

**cicatrice / ~s** *n*
'sɪkə,tri:s / -ɪz
**sp** cicatrice[2], sicatrice[1] / cicatrices[1]

**Cicely** *n*
'sɪsləɪ, -səl-
**sp** Cicely[1], Cisley[1]

**Cicero** *n*
*m* 'sɪsro:, 'sɪsə,ro:
**sp** Cicero[11]

**Cicester** *n*
'sɪsəstəɹ
**sp** Cicester[1]

**Cidrus**
> Cydnus

**ciel** *Fr n*
sjɛl
**sp** *emend of H5 4.2.4* cein

**Cimber** *n*
'sɪmbəɹ
**sp** Cimber[1], Cymber[9]

**Cimmerian** *n*
sɪ'mi:rɪən
**sp** Cymerion[1]

**cinder / ~s** *n*
'sɪndəɹz
**sp** cinders[1], cynders[3]

**Cinna** *n*
'sɪnə
**sp** Cinna[15], Cynna[4]

**cinquepace** *n*
'sɪŋkə,pɛ:s
**sp** cinque-pace[2], sinke-a-pace[1]

**Cinque Ports** *n*
'sɪŋk 'pɔɹts
**sp** Cinque-Ports[2]
> port

**cinque-spotted** *adj*
*m* ,sɪŋk-'spɒtɪd
**sp** cinque-spotted[1]

**cipher / ~s** *n*
'səɪfəɹ / -z
**sp** cipher[2], cypher[2] / cyphers[1]

**Circe / ~'s** *n*
'sɐ:ɹsi: / -z
**sp** Circe[1] / Circes[1]

**circle** *n*
'sɐ:ɹkəl
**sp** circle[12], cir-cle[1]

**circl·e / ~ing / ~ed** *v*
'sɐ:ɹkəl / 'sɐ:ɹklɪn, -ɪŋ / 'sɐ:ɹkəld
**sp** circle[1] / circling[1] / circled[2]
> encircle

**circled** *adj*
'sɐ:ɹkəld
**sp** circled[1]
> semi-circled

**circlet / ~s** *n*
'sɐ:ɹklɪts
**sp** circlets[1]

**circling** *adj*
'sɐɹklɪn, -ɪŋ
**sp** circkling[1]

**circuit** *n*
'sɐ:ɹkɪt
**sp** circuit[2]

**circumcised** *adj*
*m* 'sɐ:ɹkəm,səɪzɪd
**sp** circumcised[1]

**circumference** *n*
*m* səɹ'kɤmfə,rens, -frəns
**sp** circumference[2], circum-ference[1]

**circummure / ~d** *v*
'sɐ:ɹkəm,ju:ɹd
**sp** circummur'd[1]

**circumscribe / ~ed** *v*
*m* 'sɐːɹkəmˌskrəɪbɪd, -bd
**sp** circumscribed[1], circumscrib'd[1]

**circumscription** *n*
ˌsɐːɹkəm'skrɪpsɪən
**sp** circumscription[1]

**circumspect** *adj*
'sɐːɹkəmˌspekt
**sp** circumspect[2]

**circumstance / ~s** *n*
'sɐːɹkəmˌstans / -ɪz
**sp** circumstance[34] / circumstances[10], circumstan-ces[1]
**rh** advance, chance *Luc 1703*

**circumstanced** *adj*
'sɐːɹkəmˌstanst
**sp** circumstanc'd[1]

**circumstantial** *adj*
ˌsɐːɹkəm'stansɪɑl
**sp** circumstantial[1], circumstantiall[2]

**circumvent** *v*
'sɐːɹkəmˌvent
**sp** circumuent[1]

**circumvention** *n*
ˌsɐːɹkəm'vensɪən
**sp** circumuention[2]

**cita**
> citus

**citadel** *n*
=
**sp** citadell[1], cittadell[6]

**cital** *n*
'sɪtɑl
**sp** citall[1]

**cit·e / ~es / ~ing / ~ed** *v*
səɪt / -s / 'səɪt·ɪn, -ɪŋ / -ɪd
**sp** cite[3] / cites[2] / cyting[1] / cited[4], cyted[1]

**Citherea / ~'s** *n*
ˌsɪθə'riːə, ˌsɪt- / -z
**sp** Citherea[1], Cytherea[1] / Cytherea's[1]

**citizen / ~s** *n*
*m* 'sɪtɪˌzen, -ɪzən / -z
**sp** citizen[10] / citizens[48], [Sunday]-citizens[1], cittizens[6]
> Sunday-citizen

**cittern** *n*
'sɪtəɹn
**sp** citterne[1]

**cit·us / ~a** *Lat adj*
'sɪta
**sp** cita[1]

**city** *adj*
'sɪtəɪ
**sp** citie[6], city[5], city-[gate][1]

**cit·y / ~ies** *n*
'sɪtəɪ / -z
**sp** citie[48], cittie[5], citty[12], city[45] / cities[16], citties[8], cit-ties[1]
**rh** pity *LC 176, Luc 469, 1554*; witty *H8 Epil.5*

**civet** *n*
=
**sp** ciuet[3], ciuit[1]

**civil / ~est** *adj*
= / 'sɪvɪlst
**sp** ciuil[1], ciuill[46] / ciuel'st[1]
**pun** *MA 2.1.270* Seville
uncivil

**civility** *n*
*m* sɪ'vɪlɪˌtəɪ, -ɪt-
**sp** ciuilitie[1], ciuility[4], ciuillitie[1]

**civilly** *adv*
*m* 'sɪvɪˌləɪ
**sp** ciuilly[1]

**clack-dish** *n*
=
**sp** clack-dish[1]
> dish

**clad** *adj*
=
**sp** clad[5]

**claim** *n*
klɛːm
**sp** claim[1], claime[14], clayme[11]
**rh** aim CE *3.2.64*

**claim / ~s / ~ing / ~ed** *v*
klɛːm / -z / 'klɛːmɪn, -ɪŋ / klɛːmd
**sp** claim[1], claime[20], clayme[15] / claimes[8], claymes[1] / clayming[1] / claim'd[1], claym'd[1]
> reclaim, unclaimed

**clamber / ~ing** *v*
'klambəɹ / 'klambrɪn, -ɪŋ
**sp** clamber[1] / clambring[2]

**clamorous** *adj*
*m* 'klaməˌrɤs, -mrəs
**sp** clamorous[9], cla-morous[1]

**clamour / ~s** *n*
'klaməɹ / -z
**sp** clamor[7], clamour[7] / clamors[6], clamours[3]

**clamour / ~ed** *v*
'klaməɹ / -d
**sp** clamor[1] / clamor'd[1]

**clang** *v*
klaŋg
**sp** clangue[1]

**clangor** *n*
'klaŋgəɹ
**sp** clangor[1], clangour[1]

**clap / ~s** *n*
=
**sp** clap[2] / claps[1]
> hap *etc*

**clap / ~s / ~ping / ~ped** *v*
= / = / 'klapɪn, -ɪŋ / =
**sp** clap[12] / claps[4] / clapping[2] / clap'd[2], clapp'd[1], clapt[13], clap't[1]
**rh** hap *H8 Epil.14*

**clapper** *n*
'klapəɹ
**sp** clapper[1]

**clapper-claw / ~ing** *v*
'klapəɹ-ˌklɔ:, *Caius MW 2.3.60f* 'klapəɹ-də-ˌklɔ: / 'klapəɹ-ˌklɔ:ɪn, -ɪŋ
**sp** clapper-claw[1], *Caius* clapper-de-claw[2] / clapper-clawing[1]
> claw

**Clare** *n*
klɛ:ɹ
**sp** Clare[1]

**Clarence** *n*
=
**sp** Clarence[118], *abbr in s.d.* Clar[ence][2]

**claret** *n*
=
**sp** clarret[1]

**Claribel** *n*
=
**sp** Claribel[1], Claribell[3]

**clasp / ~s** *n*
klasps
**sp** claspes[2]
> unclasped

**clasp / ~ed** *v*
klasp / -t
**sp** claspe[2] / claspt[1]

**clatter** *n*
'klatəɹ
**sp** clatter[1]

**Claudio / ~'s** *n*
*m* 'klɔ:dɪo:, -ɪˌo: / -z
**sp** Claudio[113], Clau-dio[4], *abbr in s.d.* Clau.[1] / Claudios[1], Claudio's[5]

**Claudius** *n*
=
**sp** Claudius[1]

**clause** *n*
=
**sp** clause[1]
**rh** cause *TN 3.1.150*

**claw / ~s** *n*
=
**sp** claw[1] / clawes[2]
**rh** laws, pause *Luc 543*
> clapper-claw

**claw / ~s / ~ed** *v*
=
**sp** claw[1] / clawes[1] / claw'd[1]

**clay** *adj / n*
klɛ:
**sp** clay-[man][1] / clay[13]
**rh** away *Ham 5.1.209, Luc 609, R2 1.1.179*; decay *S 71.10*; stay *KJ 5.7.69*

**clay-brained** *adj*
'klɛ:-ˌbrɛ:nd
**sp** clay-brayn'd[1]

**clean** *adj / adv*
=
**sp** cleane[10] / clean[1], cleane[12]
> unclean

**cleanl·y / ~iest** *adj*
'klenləɪ / -əst
**sp** cleanly[2] / cleanliest[1]

**cleanly** *adv*
'klenləɪ
**sp** cleanly[2]

**cleans·e / ~ing / ~ed** *v*
= / 'klenzɪn, -ɪŋ / =
**sp** cleanse[2] / cleansing[1] / cleans'd[1]

**clear / ~er / ~est** *adj*
kli:ɹ /'kli:r·əɹ / -əst
**sp** cleare[19], cleere[19] / clearer[1], cleerer[1] / cleerest[1]
**rh** *1* fear *H8 Epil.4, Per 1.1.142*; here *Mac 5.3.61*; sphere *MND 3.2.60*; **rh** *2* bear *Tim 3.5.39*; every where *S 84.10*

**clear** *adv*
kli:ɹ
**sp** cleare[2], cleere[3]
**rh** dear *Per 1.1.100*; fear *Mac 1.5.69*

**clear / ~s / ~ed** *v*
kli:ɹ / -z / -d
**sp** cleare[10], cleere[4] / cleares[2], cleeres[2] / clear'd[3], cleerd[1], cleer'd[2]
**rh** clear her **rh** *1* hear her *Luc 1320*; **rh** *2* bear her *Luc 1320* / **rh** *1* ears *RJ 2.3.69*; tears [cry] *Luc 1710, S 148.12*; **rh** *2* bears *Luc 1710* / steered *Cym 4.3.45*

**clearer** *n*
'kli:ɹəɹ
**sp** cleerer[1]
**rh** dearer *S 115.4*

**clearly** *adv*
'kli:ɹləɪ
**sp** clearely[1], clearly[3], cleerely[1]

**clearness** *n*
'kli:ɹnəs
**sp** clearenesse[1], clearnesse[1], cleerenes[1]

**clear-shining** *adj*
*m* ˌkli:ɹ-'ʃəɪnɪn, -ɪŋ
**sp** cleare-shining[1]
> shine

**cleav·e / ~ing / cleft / clove / ~st / ~n** *v*
= / 'kli:vɪn, -ɪŋ / = / 'klo:v / -st / 'klo:vən
**sp** cleaue[11] / cleauing[2] / cleft[8] / clouest[1] / clouen[1]
> cloven *adj*

**clef** *n*
klɪf
**sp** cliffe[1]

**clemency** *n*
*m* 'klemənˌsəɪ
**sp** clemencie[1]
**rh** patiently, tragedy *Ham 3.2.159*

**clement** *adj*
=
**sp** clement[1], cle-ment[1]

**Clement's Inn** *n*
=
**sp** Clements Inne[4]
> inn

**Cleomines** *n*
kliːˈɒmiˌniːz
**sp** Cleomines[8]

**Cleon** *n*
ˈkliːoːn
**sp** Cleon[17]
**rh** full-grown [*emend of line-ending*] *Per 4.Chorus.15*

**Cleopatra / ~'s** *n*
ˌkliːoːˈpatrə / -z
**sp** Cleopater[3], Cleopatra[45], *abbr in s.d.* Cleo.[2] / Cleopatra's[4]

**clepe / ~th** *v*
kliːp / ˈkliːpəθ
**sp** cleape[1], cleep[1] / clepeth[1]

**clerestor·y / ~ies** *n*
ˈkliːɹˌstɔːrəɪz
**sp** cleer stores

**clergy / ~'s** *n*
ˈklɐːɹʤəɪ / -z
**sp** clergy[2], clergie[4] / clergies[1]

**clergyman / ~men** *n*
ˈklɐːɹʤəɪˌman / -ˌmen
**sp** clergie man[1], clergie-men[1]

**clerk / ~'s / ~s** *n*
klɐːɹk / -s
**sp** clark[2], clarke[10], clearke[10], clerke[1] / clarks[1] / clarks[1], clearkes[2], clerkes[1]
**rh** dark *MV 5.1.305*

**clerk-like** *adj*
*m* ˌklɐːɹk-ˈləɪk
**sp** clerke-like[1]

**clerkly** *adv*
ˈklɐːɹkləɪ
**sp** clarkely[1], clearkly[2], clerkly[1]

**client / ~s / ~s'** *n*
ˈkləɪənts
**sp** clients[1] / clients[1]

**cliff / ~s** *n*
=
**sp** cliffe[4] / cliffes[2]

**Clifford / ~'s / ~s** *n*
ˈklɪfəɹd / -z
**sp** Clifford[73] / Cliffords[5] / Cliffords[1]

**Clifton** *n*
=
**sp** Clifton[3]

**climate** *n*
ˈkləɪmət
**sp** climate[3], clymate[5], clymat's [climate is][1]

**climb / ~eth / ~ing / ~ed** *v*
kləɪm / ˈkləɪm·əθ / -ɪn, -ɪŋ / kləɪmd
**sp** climbe[15], clime[4], clymbe[1], clyme[1] / climbeth[1] / climbing[3], climing[1] / climb'd[3], climde[1]
**rh** crime, time *Luc 775*

**climber** *n*
ˈkləɪməɹ
**sp** climber[1]

**climbing** *adj / n*
ˈkləɪmɪn, -ɪŋ
**sp** climbing[1], climing[1] / climbing[1]

**clime** *n*
kləɪm
**sp** clime[3], clyme[3]
**rh** crime *Per 4.4.6*

**cling / clung** *n*
= / klɤŋ
**sp** cling[2] / clung[1]

**clink** *n / v*
=
**sp** clinke[1] / clinke[3]
**rh** drink *Oth 2.3.65*

**clinking** *n*
ˈklɪŋkɪn, -ɪŋ
**sp** clin-king[1]

**clinquant** *adj*
ˈklɪŋkənt
**sp** clinquant[1]

**clip / ~peth / ~ping / ~ped** *v*
= / = / ˈklɪpɪn, -ɪŋ / =
**sp** clip[4] / clippeth[1] / clipping[1] / clipt[6]
> pole-clipped

**clipper** *n*
ˈklɪpəɹ
**sp** clipper[1]

**clip-winged** *adj*
=
**sp** clip-wing'd[1]
> winged

**Clitus** *n*
ˈkləɪtəs
**sp** Clitus[5], Clytus[2]

**cloak / ~s** *n*
kloːk / -s
**sp** cloake[27] / cloakes[4], clokes[1]
**rh** smoke *Luc 801, S 34.2*

**cloak-bag** *n*
ˈkloːk-ˌbag
**sp** cloake-bagge[2]
> bag

**clock** *adj*
=
**sp** clocke[1]
> o'clock

**clock / ~'s / ~s** *n*
=
**sp** clock[5], clocke[22] / clocks[1] / clockes[2], clocks[3]
**rh** smocks *LLL 5.2.893*

**clock / ~ed** *v*
=
**sp** clock'd[1]

**clock-setter** *n*
ˈklɒk-ˌsetəɹ
**sp** clocke setter[1]

**clod** *n*
=
**sp** clod[3]

**cloddy** *adj*
ˈklɒdəɪ
**sp** cloddy[1]

**clodpole / ~s** *n*
'klɒd-ˌpoːl, 'klɒt- / -z
**sp** clodde-pole[1], clot-pole[2] / clotpoles[1]

**clog / ~s** *n*
=
**sp** clog[4] / clogges[1]
> unclog

**clog / ~s** *v*
=
**sp** clog[1] / clogges[1]

**clogging** *adj*
'klɒgɪn, -ɪŋ
**sp** clogging[1]

**cloister** *n / v*
'kləɪstəɹ
**sp** cloister[2], cloyster[2] / cloyster[1]

**cloistered** *adj*
'kləɪstəɹd
**sp** cloyster'd[1]

**cloistress** *n*
'kləɪstrəs
**sp** cloystresse[1]

**close / ~er** *adj*
kloːs / 'kloːsəɹ
**sp** close[22] / closer[1]

**close / ~er / ~est** *adv*
kloːs / 'kloːs·əɹ / -əst
**sp** close[50] / closer[1] / closest[1]

**close** *n*
kloːz
close[5], cloze[1]
**rh** foes *TG 5.4.118*; gloze *R2 2.1.12*

**clos·e / ~es / ~ing / ~ed** *v*
kloːz / 'kloːz·ɪz / -ɪn, -ɪŋ/ *m* -ɪd, kloːzd
**sp** close[25], cloze[1] / closes[4], clozes[1] / closing[1] / cloas'd[1], clos'd[5], closed[2]
> enclose, fast-closed

**closely** *adv*
'kloːsləɪ
**sp** closely[8]

**closeness** *n*
'kloːsnəs
**sp** closenes[1]

**close-stool** *n*
'kloːs-ˌstʊl, ˌstuːl
**sp** close stoole[1], close-stoole[1]
> stool

**closet / ~s** *n*
'klɒsɪt / -s
**sp** closet[4], closset[17] / clossets[1]

**closet-war** *n*
'klɒsɪt-ˌwɑːɹ
**sp** closset-warre[1]
> war

**closing** *adj*
'kloːzɪn, -ɪŋ
**sp** closing[1] / closing[2]
> still-closing

**closing-up** *n*
'kloːzɪn-'ɤp, -ɪŋ-
**sp** closing vp[1]

**closure** *n*
'kloːzjəɹ
**sp** closure[2]

**clot**
> clod

**Cloten / ~'s / ~s** *n*
'klɒtən / -z
**sp** Cloten[18], Clotten[6] / Clotens[5] / Clotens[1]

**cloth** *n*
=
**sp** cloth[10], cloath[3]
> bearing-, foot-, sack-cloth

**cloth·e / ~ing** *v*
kloːð / 'kloːðɪn, -ɪŋ
**sp** cloath[7] / cloathing[1]

**Clothair** *n*
klɒ'tɛːɹ
**sp** Clothair[1]

**Clotharius** *n*
klɒ'tarɪəs
**sp** Clotharius[1]

**clothes** *n*
kloːðz
**sp** cloathes[23], clothes[8], cloths[1]
**rh** rose *Ham 4.5.52*
> bed-, cradle-clothes

**clothier / ~'s / ~s** *n*
'kloːðɪəɹ / -z
**sp** cloathier[1] / cloathiers[1] / clothiers[1]

**cloud / ~s** *n*
kləʊd / -z
**sp** cloud[12], clow'd[1], clowd[9] / cloudes[11], clouds[40], clowds[5]
> encloud

**cloud / ~ed** *v*
kləʊd / 'kləʊdɪd
**sp** cloud[2] / clouded[2], clowded[1]

**cloud-capped** *adj*
'kləʊd-ˌkapt
**sp** clowd-capt[1]
> cap

**clouded** *adj*
'kləʊdɪd
**sp** clouded[1]

**cloudiness** *n*
'kləʊdɪnəs
**sp** clowdinesse[1]

**cloudy** *adj*
'kləʊdəɪ
**sp** cloudie[4], cloudy[5], clowdy[1], clowdy-[princes][1]

**clout / ~s** *n*
kləʊt / -s
**sp** clout[5], clowt[2] / clouts[1], clowts[2]
**rh** out *LLL 4.1.135*

**clouted** *adj*
'kləʊtɪd
**sp** clouted[1], clowted[1]

**clove / ~s** *n*
klo:vz
**sp** cloues[1]

**cloven** *adj*
'klo:vən
**sp** clouen[5]
> cleave

**clover** *n*
'klo:vəɹ
**sp** clouer[1]

**Clowder** *n*
'kləʊdəɹ
**sp** Clowder[1]

**clown / ~s** *n*
kləʊn / -z
**sp** clown[2], clowne[70] / clownes[4], *abbr in s.d.* clow[1], clo[2]
**rh** down *LLL 4.1.141, TNK 3.5.140*

**clownish** *adj*
'kləʊnɪʃ
**sp** clownish[1]

**cloy / ~s / ~ed** *v*
kləɪ / -z / kləɪd
**sp** cloy[3] / cloyes[1] / cloid[1], cloi'd[1], cloyd[1], cloy'd[2]
> overcloyed

**cloyed** *adj*
kləɪd
**sp** cloyed[1]

**cloyless** *adj*
'kləɪləs
**sp** cloylesse[1]

**cloyment** *n*
'kləɪmənt
**sp** cloyment[1]

**club / ~s** *n*
klɤb / -z
**sp** club[7], clubbe[1] / clubs[8], clubbes[2]

**clue** *n*
=
**sp** clewe[1]

**cluster / ~s** *n*
'klɤstəɹz
**sp** clusters[2]

**clustering** *adj*
'klɤstrɪn, -ɪŋ
**sp** clustring[3]

**cluster-pipe / ~s** *n*
'klɤstəɹ-ˌpəɪps
**sp** cluster-pipes[1]
> pipe

**clutch** *n*
klɤʧ
**sp** clutch[1]
**rh** such *Ham 5.1.72*

**clutch / ~ed** *v*
klɤʧ / -t
**sp** clutch[2] / clutch'd[1], clutcht[1]

**Clytus**
> Clitus

**coach / ~es** *n*
ko:ʧ / 'ko:ʧɪz
**sp** coach[7] / coaches[1]

**coach-fellow** *n*
'ko:ʧ-ˌfelə, -lo:
**sp** coach-fellow[1]
> fellow

**coach-maker / ~s** *n*
'ko:ʧ-ˌmɛ:kəɹz
**sp** coach-makers[1]
> make

**coact** *v*
ko:'akt
**sp** coact[1]

**coactive** *adj*
ko:'aktɪv
**sp** coactiue[1]

**coagulate** *adj*
ko:'agjələt
**sp** coagulate[1]

**coal / ~s** *n*
ko:l / -z
**sp** coale[6], cole[1] / coales[7], coles[1]
**rh** hole *Per 3.Chorus.5*
> sea-coal

**coal-black** *adj*
*m* 'ko:l-ˌblak, ˌko:l-'blak
**sp** coale-black[3], cole-blacke[2], cole-blacke-[calfe][1]
> black

**coarse** *adj*
kɔ:ɹs
**sp** course[1]

**coast / ~s** *n*
ko:st, kɒ- / -s
**sp** coast[14] / coasts[1]
**rh** lost *2H6 4.8.49, Per 5.Chorus.15* / ghosts *Cym 5.4.96*

**coast / ~s** *v*
ko:sts, kɒ-
**sp** coasts[1]

**coasting** *adj*
'ko:stɪn, -ɪŋ, kɒ-
**sp** coasting[1]

**coat / ~s** *n*
ko:t / -s
**sp** coat[16], coate[15] / coates[8], [tawney]-coates[1], coats[10], [tawney]-coats[1]
**rh** *1* dote, note *LC 236, Luc 205*; **rh** *2* got *2H6 4.10.68*
**pun** *TG 2.4.19* quote
> leather-, petti-, skin-, turn-coat; grey-, parti-coated

**coat-of-arms** *n*
ˌko:t-əv-'ɑ:ɹmz
**sp** coate of armes[1]
> arm

**cobble** *v*
=
**sp** cobble[1]

**cobbled** *adj*
=
**sp** cobled[1]

**cobbler** *n*
'kɒbləɹ
**sp** cobler[2]

**Cobham** *n*
'kɒbəm
**sp** Cobham[4]

**cobloaf** *n*
'kɒblo:f
**sp** coblofe[1]

**cobweb / ~s** *n*
=
**sp** cobwebs[2]

**Cobweb** [name] *n*
=
**sp** Cobweb[6]

**cock / ~s** *n*
=
**sp** cock[5], cocke[22], cocke's [cock is][1] / cockes[1], cocks[2]
> pea-, turkey-cock

**Cock** [*euphemism for God*] *n*
=
**sp** Cockes [Cock is][1], Cox [Cock is][1]

**cock-a-doodle-doo** *interj*
'kɒk-ə-dɪdl-'dəʊ
**sp** cockadidle-dowe[1]
**rh** bow-wow *Tem 1.2.382*

**cock-a-hoop** *n*
ˌkɒk-ə-'hu:p, -'u:p
**sp** cocke a hoope[1]

**cockatrice / ~s** *n*
'kɒkətri:s / -ɪz
**sp** cockatrice[2] / cockatrices[1]

**cockered** *adj*
'kɒkəɹd
**sp** cockred-[silken][1]

**cockerel / ~s** *n*
'kɒkrəl / -z
**sp** cockrell[1], cockrels[1]

**cockle** *n*
=
**sp** cockell[1], cockle[4]

**cockney** *n*
'kɒknəɪ
**sp** cockney[2]

**cock-pigeon** *n*
=
**sp** cocke-pidgeon[1]
> pigeon

**cockpit** *n*
=
**sp** cock-pit[1]
> pit

**cockshut** *n*
=
**sp** cockshut[1]

**cocksure** *adj*
'kɒkʃu:ɹ
**sp** cocksure[1]

**coctus** *Lat*
> coquo

**Cocytus** *n*
kə'səɪtəs
**sp** *emend of Tit 2.3.236* Ocitus[1]

**cod / ~s** *n*
=
**sp** cods[1]

**codding** *adj*
'kɒdɪn, -ɪŋ
**sp** codding[1]

**codling** *n*
'kɒdlɪn, -ɪŋ
**sp** codling[1]

**codpiece / ~s** *n*
=
**sp** cod-peece[5], codpiece[2] / codpeeces[1]
> piece

**codshead** *n*
'kɒdzed, -hed
**sp** cods-head[1]

**coelest·is / ~ibus** *Lat n*
si:'lestɪbʊs
**sp** coelestibus[1]

**co-equal** *adj*
ko:'ikwɑl
**sp** coequall[1]

**coffer / ~s** *n*
'kɒfəɹ / -z
**sp** coffer[7] / cofers[1], coffers[11]

**coffin / ~s** *n*
=
**sp** coffen[1], coffin[10] / coffins[3]
> custard-coffin

**coffin / ~ed** *v*
=
**sp** coffin'd[1]

**cog** *v*
=
**sp** cog[3], cogg[1], cogge[3]

**cogging** *adj*
'kɒgɪn, -ɪŋ
**sp** cogging[1], [scur-uy]-cogging-[companion][1], coging[1]

**cogitation / ~s** *n*
kɒʤɪ'tɛ:sɪən / -z
**sp** cogitation[1] / cogitations[1]

**cognition** *n*
kɒg'nɪsɪən
**sp** cognition[1]

**cognizance** *n*
*m* 'kɒgnɪˌzans
**sp** cognisance[2], cognizance[1]

**co-heir / s** *n*
ko:'ɛ:ɹz
**sp** co-heyres[1]
> heir

**cohere / ~d** *v*
ko:'i:ɹ, -'hi:ɹ / -d
**sp** co-here[1] / coheard[1]

**coherence** *n*
ko:'i:rəns, -'hi:-
**sp** coherence[1]

**coherent** *adj*
ko:'i:rənt, -'hi:-
**sp** coherent[1]

**coif / ~s** *n*
kəɪf / -s
**sp** quoife[1] / quoifes[1]

**coign / ~s** *n*
kəɪn / kəɪnz
**sp** coigne[1], coin[1] / *emend of Per Chorus.3.16* crignes
**rh** joins *Per 3.Chorus.17*

**coil / ~s** *n*
kəɪl / -z
**sp** coile[6], coyle[5] / coiles[1] [coil is]

**coin** *n*
kəɪn
**sp** coine[10], coyne[4]
**rh** join *Tim 3.3.27*

**coin / ~s / ~ing / ~ed** *v*
kəɪn / -z / 'kəɪnɪn, -ɪŋ / -d
**sp** coine[3], coyne[3] / coines[2] / coyning[1] / coyn'd[2]
**rh** joined *PP 7.9*
> uncoined

**coinage** *n*
'kəɪnɪʤ
**sp** coynage[2]

**coiner** *n*
'kəɪnəɹ
**sp** coyner[1]

**coistrel** *n*
'kəɪstrəl
**sp** coystrill[1]

**co-join** *v*
koː-'ʤəɪn
**sp** co-ioyne[1]
> join

**col** *Fr n*
kɔl
**sp** col[2]

**Colbrand**
> Colebrand

**cold / ~er / ~est** *adj*
koːld / 'koːld·əɹ / *m* -əst, -st
**sp** cold[155], cold-[spurre][1], colde[4] / colder[6] / coldest[3], cold'st[1]
**rh** *1* behold, bold, enfold, gold, inscrolled, old, sold, told *MV 2.7.73*; bold *VA 402*; old *S 2.14, 104.3, VA 135*; told *VA 1124*; **rh** *2* short *PP 12.7*
> a-, key-, scarce-cold

**cold** *n*
koːld
**sp** cold[17], colde[4]
**rh** behold *S 73.3*; behold, uphold *S 13.12*; bold, hold *Luc 1556*; old *Luc 48*; sold *CE 3.1.71*; unfold *Luc 1145*

**cold-blooded** *adj*
*m* ˌkoːld-'blɤdɪd
**sp** cold blooded[1]

**cold-hearted** *adj*
*m* ˌkoːld-'ɑːɹtɪd, -'hɑː-
**sp** cold-hearted[1]

**coldly** *adv*
'koːldləɪ
**sp** coldly[14]

**coldness** *n*
'koːldnəs
**sp** coldnesse[2]

**Colebrand** *n*
'koːlbrand
**sp** Colbrand[1], Colebrand[1]

**Colebrook** *n*
'koːlbrʊk
**sp** Cole-brooke[1]
> brook

**Colevile** *n*
'koːlvɪl
**sp** Coleuile[1], Colleuile[11]

**colic** *n*
=
**sp** collick[1], collicke[1], collike[1]

**collar / ~s** *n*
'kɒləɹ / -z
**sp** collar[1] / collars[2]

**collateral** *adj*
kə'latərɑl
**sp** colaterall[2]

**Collatine** *Luc* *n*
'kɒlətəɪn
**sp** Colatine[22]
**rh** design, mine *Luc 1689*; divine, incline *Luc 289*; divine, pine *Luc 1166*; line *Luc 819*; mine *Luc 826, 1177, 1799*

**colleague / ~d** *v*
*m* kɒ'liːgɪd
**sp** colleagued[1]

**collect / ~ed** *v*
=
**sp** collect[3] / collected[13]
**rh** infected *Ham 3.2.266*
> recollected

**collection** *n*
kə'leksɪən
**sp** collection[3]

**college / ~s** *n*
=
**sp** colledge[3] / colledges[1]

**collied** *adj*
'kɒləɪd
**sp** collied[1]

**collier / ~s** *n*
'kɒlɪəɹ / -z
**sp** colliar[1] / colliars[1], colliers[1]

**collop** *n*
'kɒləp
**sp** collop[2]

**collusion** *n*
kə'luːzɪən
**sp** collusion[1]

**colly / ~ied** *v*
'kɒləɪd
**sp** collied[1]

**Colme / ~'s** *n*
koːlmz
**sp** Colmes[1]

**Colmekill** *n*
'koːlmkɪl
**sp** Colmekill[1]

**coloquintida** *n*
ˌkɒlə'kɪntɪdə
**sp** coloquintida[1]

**colossus** *n*
=
**sp** colossus[2]

**colossus-wise** *adv*
kə'lɒsəs-ˌwəɪz
**sp** calossus-wise[1]

**colour / ~s** *n*
'kɤləɹ / -z
**sp** colour[67], co-lour[1], colour's [colour is][1] / colours[68], co-lours[1], coullers[1]
**pun** *2H4 5.5.90* collar
> water-colour

**colour / ~ing / ~ed** *v*
'kɤləɹ / -ɪn, -ɪŋ / *m* -d, -ed
**sp** co-lor[1], colour[5] / colouring[1] / colour'd[1], coloured[1]
**rh** dead *1H6 4.2.37*

**colourable** *adj*
'kɤlərəbəl
**sp** coloura-ble[1]

**coloured** *adj*
'kɤləɹd
**sp** coulord[3], coulour'd[2]
> amber-, cain-, dis-, dun-, ebon-, flame-, freestone-, French-crown-, high-, many-, parti-, peach-, raven-, sable-coloured; straw-colour

**colt / ~s** *n*
=
**sp** colt[3] / colts[4]

**colt / ~ed** *v*
=
**sp** colt[1] / colted[2]
> uncolted

**columbine / ~s** *n*
'kɤləmbəɪn / -z
**sp** cullambine[1] / columbines[1]

**Comagene** *n*
'kɒməˌʤi:n
**sp** *emend of AC 3.4.74* Comageat[1]

**co-mate / ~s** *n*
ko:-'mɛ:ts
**sp** coe-mates[1]
> mate

**comb** *n*
ko:m
**sp** combe[2]
> honeycomb

**comb / ~ed** *v*
ko:m / -d
**sp** combe[4] / comb'd[1]

**combat** *n*
=
**sp** combat[13], com-bat[1], combate[6]

**combat / ~ting / ~ed** *v*
= / 'kɒmbat·ɪn, -ɪŋ / -ɪd
**sp** combat[3], combate[2] / combating[2], combatting[1] / combatted[1]

**combatant / ~s** *n*
=
**sp** combatant[1] / combatants[4], combattants[1]

**combinate** *adj*
'kɒmbɪnət
**sp** combynate-[husband][1]

**combination** *n*
ˌkɒmbɪ'nɛ:sɪən
**sp** combination[3]

**combine / ~d** *v*
kəm'bəɪn / *m* -d, -ɪd
**sp** combine[6], combyne[1] / combin'd[4], combined[1]
**rh** mine *AY 5.4.147, RJ 2.3.56*

**combined** *adj*
*m* kəm'bəɪnɪd
**sp** combined[1]

**combless** *adj*
'ko:mləs
**sp** comblesse[1]

**combustion** *n*
kəm'bɤstɪən
**sp** combustion[2]

**com·e / ~est / ~es / ~eth / ~ing / came / ~est** *v*
kɤm / -st / -z / 'kɤm·əθ / -ɪn, -ɪŋ / kɛ:m / -st
**sp** com[3], come[2453], come-[on][10], *Caius MW 2.3.6ff* [no]-come[3] / commest[2], comm'st[3], comst[3], com'st[22] / comes[597], come's [comes][1], coms[3] / commeth[4] / coming[2], comming[103], com-ming[2] / came[327], cam't [came it][1] / camm'st[1], cam'st[29]
**rh** *1* drum *AW 2.5.90, 1H4 3.3.202, Mac 1.3.30*; dumb *TG 2.2.19*; masterdom *Mac 1.5.67*; some *LLL 5.2.818, Luc 1443*; sum *S 49.1*; thrum *MND 5.1.277*; thumb *LLL 5.2.112, Mac 1.3.28;* **rh** *2* doom *Luc 923, R2 3.2.188, S 107.2, 116.10, 145.5*; tomb *RJ 5.2.28, S 17.1* / **rh** *3* sung *Per Prol.2* / sums *LC 230*; thumbs *Mac 4.1.45* / roaming *TN 2.3.38* / dame, shame *Luc 1626*; tame *LC 309*
> be-, new-, non-, over-, wel-come; a-coming

**comedian / ~s** *n*
=
**sp** comedian[1] / comedians[1]

**comedy** *n*
*m* 'kɒməˌdəɪ, -əd-
**sp** comedie[6], comedy[3], come-dy[1], comon-tie[1]
**rh** courtesy *LLL 5.2.865*; perdy *Ham 3.2.301*; zany *LLL 5.2.462*

**comeliness** *n*
'kɤmlɪnəs
**sp** comelinesse[1]
> uncomeliness

**comely** *adj*
'kɤmləɪ
**sp** comely[5]

**comer** *n*
'kɤməɹ
**sp** commer[2]

**comet / ~s** *n*
=
**sp** comet[1], commet[2] / comets[2]

**comfect** *n*
'kɒmfekt
**sp** comfect[1]

**comfit / ~s** *n*
'kɤmfɪts
**sp** comfits[1]

**comfit-maker / ~s** *n*
'kɤmfɪt-ˌmɛ:kəɹz
**sp** comfit-makers[1]
> make

**comfort / ~s** *n*
'kɤmfəɹt / -s
**sp** comfort[140], com-fort[2], comfort's [comfort is][1], com-forts[1] / comforts[19], [smooth]-comforts-[false][1]
> dis-, widow-comfort

**comfort / ~s / ~ing / ~ed** *v*
'kɤmfəɹt / -s / -ɪn, -ɪŋ / -ɪd
**sp** comfort[40] / comforts[3] / comforting[2], com-forting[1] / comforted[6]
> recomforted

**comfortable** *adj*
*m* 'kɤmfəɹˌtabəl, -ɹtəb-
**sp** comfortable[11]
> uncomfortable

**comforter** *n*
'kɤmfəɹtəɹ
**sp** comforter[3]

**comforting** *adj*
'kɤmfəɹtɪn, -ɪŋ
**sp** comforting[1]

**comfortless** *adj*
*m* 'kɤmfəɹtˌles
**sp** comfortlesse[5]

**comic** *adj*
=
**sp** comick[1], comicke[1]

**comical** *adj*
'kɒmɪkɑl
**sp** [pastoricall]-comicall-[histori-call][1], [tragicall]-comicall-[historicall][1]

**coming** *adj*
'kɤmɪn, -ɪŋ
**sp** coming[1], comming[5]
> forth-, thick-, unbe-coming

**coming / ~s** *n*
'kɤmɪn, -ɪŋ / -z
**sp** coming[1], comming[23] / commings[1]

**coming-in / ~s ~** *n*
'kɤmɪn-'ɪn, -ɪŋ- / -z-'ɪn
**sp** comming in[2] / commings in[1]

**co-mingle / ~d** *v*
ko:'mɪŋgəld
**sp** co-mingled[1]
> mingle

**coming-on** *n*
'kɤmɪn-'ɒn, -ɪŋ-
**sp** comming-on[2]

**coming-out** *n*
'kɤmɪn-'əʊt, -ɪŋ-
**sp** comming out[1]

**coming-over,** *abbr* **o'er** *n*
'kɤmɪn-'o:ɹ, -ɪŋ-
**sp** comming ore[1]

**Cominius** *n*
*m* kə'mɪnɪəs, ˌ-ʊs
**sp** Cominius[33], Comi-nius[1]

**comma** *n*
=
**sp** comma[2]

**command / ~s** *n*
kə'mand / -z
**sp** command[61], com-mand[1], commaund[1] / commands[6], com-mands[1], commaunds[1]
**rh** hand *LC 227*

**command / ~est / ~s / ~ing / ~ed** *v*
kə'mand / -st, -nst / -z / -ɪn, -ɪŋ / -ɪd
**sp** command[101], com-mand[2], commaund[2] / command'st[3] / commands[17], co[m]mands[1], com-mands[3] / commanding[4] / commanded[37], com-manded[1]
**rh** hand *AW 2.1.194*; land *Tem 4.1.131*

**commanded** *adj*
kə'mandɪd
**sp** commanded[1]

**commander / ~s** *n*
kə'mandəɹ / -z
**sp** commander[10], com-mander[2] / commanders[5], com-manders[1]
**rh** Alexander *LLL 5.2.565*; Alisander *LLL 5.2.559*; slander *VA 1004*

**commander / commande** *Fr v*
kɔ'mɑ̃:d
**sp** commande[1]

**commanding** *adj / n*
kə'mandɪn, -ɪŋ
**sp** commanding[4] / commanding[1]

**commandment** *n*
*m* kə'mandmənt, -dəˌment / -mənts
**sp** commandement[6], commandment[3], command'ment[6] / commandements[2]
**rh** bent *PP 20.44*

**comme** *Fr conj*
kɔm
**sp** comme[1]

**commence / ~s / ~ing / ~ed** *v*
= / = / kə'mensɪn, -ɪŋ / =
**sp** commence[4] / commences[1] / commencing[1] / commenc'd[2], commenced[1]
**rh** hence *2H4 4.2.118, PT 21*; impa-tience *1H6 4.7.7*; offence *Per 2.5.51*; sense *S 35.11*

**commencement** *n*
=
**sp** commencement[1], commence-ment[1]

**commend / ~s** *n*
=
**sp** commends[3]

**commend / ~s / ~ing / ~ed** *v*
= / = / kə'mendɪn, -ɪŋ / =
**sp** commend[88], co[m]mend[1], com-mend[1] / commends[15] / commending[1] / commended[7], co[m]mended[1]
**rh** comprehend *LLL 4.2.112, PP 5.8*; mend *S 69.4*; commend her lend her *TG 4.2.39* / transcends *TC 1.3.243* / attended *LC 80*
> recommend

**commendable** *adj*
*m* 'kɒmən,dabəl, kə'mendəbəl
**sp** commendable[8], com-mendable[1]
**rh** vendible *MV 1.1.111*

**commendation / ~s** *n*
,kɒmən'dɛ:sɪən / -z
**sp** commendation[9] / commendations[13]

**commended** *adj*
=
**sp** commended[1]

**comment / ~s** *n*
=
**sp** comment[4] / comments[1]

**comment / ~s / ~ing** *v*
= / = / 'kɒmentɪn, -ɪŋ
**sp** comment[2] / comments[1] / commenting[1], commen-ting[1]
**rh** moment *S 15.4*

**comment** *Fr adv*
kɔ'mɑ̃
**sp** coment[3], comient[1], comment[1]

**commentar·y / ~ies** *n*
*m* 'kɒmən,tarəɪz
**sp** commentaries[1]

**commenting** *n*
'kɒməntɪn, -ɪŋ
**sp** commenting[1]

**commerce** *n*
'kɒməɹs
**sp** comerce[1], commerce[2], commerse[1]

**commiseration** *n*
kə,mɪsə'rɛ:sɪən
**sp** comiseration[1], commiseration[2], commisseration[1]

**commission / ~s** *n*
kə'mɪsɪən / -z
**sp** commission[45], commissi-on[1] / commissions[5]
**rh** impression *VA 568*

**commissioner / ~s** *n*
kə'mɪsɪənəɹz
**sp** commissioners[1]

**commit / ~est / ~s / ~ting / ~ted** *v*
= / kə'mɪts, -tst / -s / kə'mɪtɪn, -ɪŋ / =
**sp** commit[38] / commit'st[1], com-mitt'st[1] / commits[3] / committing[4] / commited[3], committed[31], com-mitted[1]
**rh** wit *TN 1.2.61* / befits *S 41.1*; sits *S 9.14* / fitted *S 119.5*

**commix / *LC* -ed** *v*
=
**sp** commix[1] / commxit[1]
**rh** fixed *LC 28*

**commixion** *n*
kə'mɪksɪən
**sp** commixion[1]

**commixture / ~s** *n*
kə'mɪkstəɹ / -z
**sp** commixture[1] / commixtures[1]

**commodious** *adj*
kə'mo:dɪəs
**sp** commodious[1]

**commodit·y / ~ies** *n*
*m* kə'mɒdɪ,təɪ, -ɪt- / -z
**sp** commoditie[12], commodity[6] / commodities[2], commodi-ties[1]
**rh** thee *KJ 2.1.597*

**common / ~est** *adj*
= / 'kɒmənst
**sp** common[130], co[m]mon[3], com-mon[1] / common'st[1]

**common** *adv*
=
**sp** common[1]

**common / ~s** *n*
=
**sp** common[8], com-mon[1] / commons[30]

**commonalty** *n*
'kɒmə,nɑltəɪ
**sp** commonalty[1], com-monalty[1]

**commoner / ~s** *n*
'kɒmənəɹ / -z
**sp** commoner[2] / commoners[5]

**common-hackneyed** *adj*
'kɒmən-'aknəɪd, -'hak
**sp** common hackney'd[1]
> hackney

**common-kissing** *adj*
'kɒmən-'kɪsɪn, -ɪŋ
**sp** common-kissing[1]
> kiss

**commonly** *adv*
'kɒmənləɪ
**sp** commonly[4]

**common sense** *n*
=
**sp** common sence[2], common sense[1], co[m]mon sense[1]

**commonweal / ~'s** *n*
=
**sp** commonweale[1], common-weale[8] / common weales[1]
**rh** appeal *2H6 2.1.186*
> weal

**commonwealth** *n*
=
**sp** commonwealth[9], common-wealth[18], common wealth[1], co[m]monwealth[1]

**commotion / ~s** *n*
*m* kə'mo:sɪən, -ˌɒn / -sɪənz
**sp** commotion[7] / commotions[1]

**commune** *v*
*m* 'kɒmjən, kə'mju:n
**sp** common[1], commune[4]

**communicate / ~st** *v*
kə'mju:nɪˌkɛ:t / -st
**sp** communicate[3] / communicat'st[1]
**rh** state *CE 2.2.185*
> excommunicate

**communication** *n*
kəmˌju:nɪ'kɛ:sɪən
**sp** communication[2]

**communit·y / ~ies** *n*
*m* kə'mju:nɪˌtəɪ / -z
**sp** communitie[1] / communities[1]

**commutual** *adj*
kə'mju:twɑl
**sp** comutuall[1]

**compact** *adj*
kəm'pakt
**sp** compact[4]

**compact** *n*
*m* kəm'pakt, 'kɒmpakt
**sp** compact[6], co[m]pact[1]

**compact / *Luc* ~ed** *v*
kəm'pakt / -ɪd
**sp** compact[4] / compacted[1]
**rh** enacted, unacted *Luc 530*

**companion / ~s** *n*
*m* kəm'panɪən, -ˌɒn / -z
**sp** companion[35], compa-nion[1], [scur-uy-cogging]-companion[1] / companions[16], compa-nions[1]

**companionship** *n*
=
**sp** companionship[2]

**compan·y / ~ies** *n*
*m* 'kɤmpnəɪ, -pəˌn- / -z
**sp** companie[60], com-panie[2], compa-nie[1], companie's [company is][1], company[137], com-pany[3] / companies[7], com-panies[1], compa-nies[1]
**rh** *1* be *LLL 5.2.224*; deity *Tem 4.1.90*; inconstancy *LLL 4.3.177*; melody, society *Luc 1110*; nobility *2H6 2.1.192*; policy *LLL 5.2.511*; see *Per 5.2.18* [*Chorus*]; society *Tem 4.1.90*; thee *3H6 5.2.4*; **rh** *2* eye *MND 3.2.436*; eye, sky *Luc 1584*; I *2H4 2.3.68, MND 3.2.341* / advise *TS 1.1.239*; eyes *MND 1.1.219* [*emend of F, Q* companions]

**comparative** *adj*
*m* kəm'pɑ:ɹtɪv, -'parəˌtɪv
**sp** comparatiue[3]

**compare** *n*
kəm'pɑ:ɹ, -ɛ:ɹ
**sp** compare[6]
**rh** are *S 35.6, TS 5.2.173, VA 8*; rare *S 21.5, 130.14*

**compar·e / ~ing / ~ed** *v*
kəm'pɑ:ɹ, -ɛ:ɹ / -ɪn, -ɪŋ / *m* -d, -ɪd
**sp** compare[12] / comparing[1] / compar'd[2], compared[1]
**rh** care *Luc 1102*

**comparison / ~s** *n*
*m* kəm'parɪsən, -ˌsɒn / -z
**sp** comparison[8] / comparisons[8]
> self-comparison

**compartner** *n*
kəm'pɑ:ɹtnəɹ
**sp** compartner[1]
> partner

**compass / ~es** *n*
'kɤmpəs / -ɪz
**sp** compasse[19], [garters]-compasse[1], com-passe[2] / compasses[1]
> encompass

**compass / ~ing / ~ed** *v*
'kɤmpəs / -ɪn, -ɪŋ / -t
**sp** compasse[10] / compassing[2] / compass'd[1], compast[3]

**compassed** *adj*
'kɤmpəst
**sp** compast[2]

**compassion** *n*
kəm'pasɪən
**sp** compassion[10]

**compassionate** *adj*
*m* kəm'pasɪənət -ˌnɛ:t
**sp** compassionate[2]
**rh** gate *Luc 594*; late *R2 1.3.174*
> uncompassionate

**compeer / ~s** *n*
kəm'pi:ɹz
**sp** compeeres[1]

**compel / ~s / ~led** *v*
=
**sp** compell[9] / compels[1] / compeld[1], compell'd[12]

**compelled** *adj*
=
**sp** compel'd[2], compell'd[1], compelled[1]

**compelling** *n*
kəm'pelɪn, -ɪŋ
**sp** compelling[1]

**compensation** *n*
ˌkɒmpən'sɛ:sɪən
**sp** compensation[1]

**competence** *n*
*m* 'kɒmpəˌtens
**sp** competence[1]

**competency** *n*
*m* 'kɒmptənˌsəɪ
**sp** competencie[2]

**competent** *adj*
*m* 'kɒmpəˌtent
**sp** competent[1]

**competitor / ~s** *n*
kəm'petɪˌtɒɹ / *m* -z, -tɪtəɹz
**sp** competitor[4] / competitors[5]

**compile / ~d** *v*
kəm'pəɪl / -d
**sp** compile[1] / compiled[2]
**rh** Longaville *LLL 4.3.132*; style *S 78.9* / filed *S 85.2*

**complain / ~est / ~s / ~ing / ~ed** *v*
kəm'plɛ:n / -st / -z / -ɪn, -ɪŋ / -d
**sp** complain[1], complaine[13] / complainest[1] / complaines[1] / complaining[1] / complain'd[1]
**rh** again *RJ 2.Chorus.7*; pain *CE 2.1.37*; refrain *PP 20.15*; reign *S 28.7*; **complain him** disdain him, entertain him *Luc 845*; **complain me** entertain thee *Luc 598* / maintained, stained *Luc 1839*

**complainer** *n*
kəm'plɛ:nəɹ
**sp** complayner[1]

**complaining** *adj*
kəm'plɛ:nɪn, -ɪŋ
**sp** complaining[3]

**complaining / ~s** *n*
kəm'plɛ:nɪn, -ɪŋ / -z
**sp** complaining[2] / complainings[1]
**rh** raining, sustaining *Luc 1269*; remaining, sustaining *Luc 1570*

**complaint / ~s** *n*
kəm'plɛ:nt / -s
**sp** complaint[14], com-plaint[1] / complaints[10]

**complement / ~s** *n*
*m* 'kɒmplɪˌment, -ɪmənt / -s
**sp** complement[14] / complements[4]

**complemental** *adj*
ˌkɒmplɪ'mentɑl
**sp** complementall[1]

**complete** *adj*
*m* kəm'pli:t, 'kɒmpli:t
**sp** compleat[13], compleate[6]

**complexion / ~s** *n*
kəm'pleksɪən / -z
**sp** complection[4], complexion[31], com-plexion[1] / complexions[6]
**rh** direction *VA 215*

**complice / ~s** *n*
'kɒmplɪsɪz, 'kɤm-
**sp** complices[5]

**complot / ~s** *n*
'kɒmplɒt / *m* 'kɒmplɒts, kɒm'plɒts
**sp** complot[3] / complots[3]

**complot / ~ted** *v*
'kɒmplɒt / *m* kɒm'plɒtɪd
**sp** complot[1] / complotted[1]

**comply** *v*
kəm'pləɪ
**sp** complie[1], comply[2]

**compose / *Per* ~s / ~d** *v*
kəm'po:z / -ɪz / -d
**sp** compose[2] / composes[1] / compos'd[9]
**rh** roses *Per 5.Chorus.5*
> ill-composed

**composed** *adj*
*m* kəm'po:zɪd
**sp** composed[1]

**composition** *n*
*m* ˌkɒmpə'zɪsɪən, -ɪˌɒn
**sp** composition[14], composion[1]

**compost** *n*
=
**sp** compost[1]

**composture** *n*
kəm'pɒstəɹ
**sp** composture[1]

**composure** *n*
kəm'po:zjəɹ
**sp** composure[2]

**compound** *adj*
'kɒmpəʊnd
**sp** compound[1]

**compound ~s** *n*
'kɒmpəʊnd / -z
**sp** compound[4] / compounds[3]

**compound / ~s / ~ed** *v*
kəm'pəʊnd / -z / -ɪd
**sp** compound[10], co[m]pound[1] / compounds[1] / compounded[6], com-pounded[1]

**compounded** *adj*
kəm'pəʊndɪd
**sp** compounded[2]
**rh** confounded *PT 44*

**comprehend / ~s / ~ed** *v*
ˌkɒmprɪ'end, -'he- / -z / -ɪd
**sp** comprehend[1], compre-hend[1] / comprehends[2] / comprehended[1]
**rh** commend *LLL 4.2.110, PP 5.6* / defends, friends *Luc 494*
> incomprehensible, uncomprehensive

**compris·e / ~ing / ~d** *v*
kəm'prəɪz·ɪn, -ɪŋ / -d
**sp** comprising[1] / compris'd[1]

**compromise / ~s** *n*
'kɒmprəˌməɪz / -ɪz
**sp** compremize[1], comprimise[1], comprimize[1] / compremises[1]

**compromise / ~d** *v*
'kɒmprəˌməɪzd
**sp** compremyz'd[1]

**compt** *n*
kɒmt, -mpt
**sp** compt[3]

**compter / ~s** *n*
'kɒmtəɹz, -mpt-
**sp** compters[1]

**comptible** *adj*
'kɒmtɪbəl, -mpt-
**sp** comptible[1]

**comptrol** *v*
kɒm'tro:l, -mpt-
**sp** comptroll[2]
> control

**comptroller / ~s** *n*
kɒm'tro:ləɹz, -mpt-
**sp** comptrollers[1]

**compulsative** *adj*
kəm'pɤlsətɪv
**sp** compulsatiue[1]

**compulsion** *n*
kəm'pɤlsɪən
**sp** compulsion[9], compulsi-on[1]

**compulsive** *adj*
kəm'pɤlsɪv
**sp** compulsiue[2]

**compunctious** *adj*
kəm'pɤŋksɪəs
**sp** compunctious[1]

**computation** *n*
ˌkɒmpjə'tɛ:sɪən
**sp** computation[2]

**computent** *adj*
'kɒmpjətənt
**sp** computent[1]

**comrade / ~s** *n*
*m* 'kɒmrɛ:d, kəm'rɛ:d / kəm'rɛ:dz
**sp** comrade[2] / cumrades[1]

**con / ~s / ~ned** *v*
=
**sp** con[5], conne[1] / cons[1] / cond[2], con'd[2], conn'd[1]

**con** *Ital prep*
kɒn
**sp** con[tutti][1]

**concave** *adj*
'kɒŋkɛ:v
**sp** concaue[2]

**concav·ity / ~ies** *n*
kəŋ'kavɪtəɪz
**sp** con-cauities[1]

**conceal / ~s / ~ing / ~ed** *v*
= / = / kən'si:l·ɪn, -ɪŋ / -d
**sp** conceale[14] / conceales[1] / concealing[2] / conceald[1], conceal'd[2]
**rh** steal *MND 1.1.212*

**concealed** *adj*
*m* kən'si:ld, -lɪd
**sp** conceal'd[3], concealed[2]

**concealing** *adj*
kən'si:lɪn, -ɪŋ
**sp** concealing[1]

**concealment / ~s** *n*
=
**sp** concealement[2], concealment[1] / concealements[1]

**conceit / ~s** *n*
kən'si:t, -'sɛ:t / -s
**sp** conceit[32], con-ceit[2], conceite[3] / conceites[1], conceits[4]
**rh** *1* deceit *CE 3.2.34*; receipt *Luc 701*; **rh** *2* bait *PP 4.9*; straight *CE 4.2.64*; wait *LLL 5.2.399*
> liberal-, odd-conceited

**conceit / ~s / ~ed** *v*
kən'si:t, -'sɛ:t / -s / -ɪd
**sp** conceit[1] / conceits[1] / conceited[3]

**conceited** *adj*
kən'si:tɪd, -'sɛ:-
**sp** conceited[2], co[n]ceited[1], con-ceited[1], conceyted[1]

**conceitless** *adj*
kən'si:tləs, -'sɛ:-
**sp** conceitlesse[1]

**conceiv·e / ~s / ~ing / ~d** *v*
kən'si:v, -'sɛ:v / -z / -ɪn, -ɪŋ / -d
**sp** conceiue[24], conceyue[1], concieue[1] / conceiues[3] / conceauing[1], conceiuing[1], conceyuing[1] / conceiu'd[5], conceiued[2], conceyu'd[2]
**rh** leave *LLL 5.2.340*
> misconceived

**conceiving** *adj / n*
kən'si:vɪn, -ɪŋ, -'sɛ:-
**sp** conceyuing[1] / conceyuing[1]

**conception / ~s** *n*
kən'sepsɪən / -z
**sp** conception[7], con-ception[1] / conceptions[1]

**conceptious** *adj*
kən'sepsɪəs
**sp** conceptious[1]

**concern / ~s,** ***abbr*** **cerns / ~eth / ~ing / ~ed** *v*
kən'sɐ:ɹn / -z, *abbr* sɐ:ɹnz / -əθ / -ɪn, -ɪŋ / -d
**sp** concerne[11] / concernes[21], *abbr* cernes[1] / concerneth[1] / concerning[12] / concern'd[1]

**concerning / ~s** *n*
kən'sɐ:ɹnɪnz, -ɪŋz
**sp** concernings[2]

**conclave** *n*
'kɒŋklɛ:v
**sp** conclaue[1]

**conclud·e / ~est / ~es / ~ing / ~ed** *v*
= / kəŋ'klu:d·st / = / -ɪn, -ɪŋ / =
**sp** conclude[27] / conclud'st[1] / concludes[6] / concluding[1] / concluded[16]
**rh** turpitude *TC 5.2.113*

**conclusion / ~s** *n*
kəŋ'klu:zɪən / -z
**sp** conclusion[25], con-clusion[1], conclu-sion[1] / conclusions[7]
**rh** *1* confusion *AY 5.4.123, Luc 1160*; **rh** *2* pollution *Luc 1160*

**concolinel** *n*
'kɒŋkɒlɪ'nel
**sp** concolinel[1]

**concord** *n*
'kɒŋkɔ:ɹd
**sp** concord[7]

**concubine** *n*
'kɒŋkjəˌbəɪn
**sp** concubine[1]

**concupiscible** *adj*
kɒŋ'kju:pɪsɪbəl
**sp** concupiscible[1]

**concupy** *n*
*m* 'kɒŋkjəˌpəɪ
**sp** concupie[1]

**concur / ~s / ~ring** *v*
kɒŋ'kɐ:ɹ / -z / -ɪn, -ɪŋ

**sp** concurre[1] / concurres[1] / concurring[1]

**condemn / ~s / ~ing / ~ed** *v*
= / = / kən'dem·ɪn, -ɪŋ / *m* -d, -nɪd
**sp** condemne[16], con-demne[1] / condemnes[3] / condemning[2] / condemnd[3], condemn'd[23], condemned[3]

**condemnation** *n*
ˌkɒndəm'nɛːsɪən
**sp** condemnation[2], con-demnation[1]

**condemned** *adj*
*m* kən'dem·d, -nɪd
**sp** condemn'd[5], condemned[6]

**condescend** *v*
=
**sp** condiscend[2]

**condign** *adj*
'kɒndəɪn
**sp** condigne[2]

**condition / ~s** *n*
*m* kən'dɪsɪən, -ˌɪɒn / -z
**sp** condition[55], con-dition[1], conditi-on[1] / conditions[25]
**rh** on *2H4 3.1.74*

**condition / ~ed** *v*
kən'dɪsɪənd
**sp** condition'd[2]
> best-conditioned

**conditionally** *adv*
*m* kən'dɪsɪənˌləɪ
**sp** conditionally[1]

**condole** *v*
kən'do:l
**sp** condole[2]

**condolement** *n*
kən'do:lmənt
**sp** condolement[1]

**condoling** *adj*
kən'do:lɪn, -ɪŋ
**sp** condo-ling[1]

**conduce** *v*
kən'dju:s
**sp** conduce[2]

**conduct** *n*
'kɒndəkt
**sp** conduct[26]
> safe-conducting

**conduct / ~ed** *v*
kən'dɤkt / -ɪd
**sp** conduct[22] / conducted[3]

**conduit / ~s** *n*
'kɒndɪt / -s
**sp** conduit[4] / conduits[2]

**confection / ~s** *n*
kən'feksɪən / -z
**sp** confection[1] / confections[1]

**confectionary** *n*
*m* kən'feksɪəˌnarəɪ
**sp** confectionarie[1]

**confederacy** *n*
*m* kən'fedrəˌsəɪ, -dər-
**sp** confederacy[1]
**rh** be *MND 3.2.192*

**confederate** *adj*
kən'fedrət, -dər-
**sp** confederate[8]

**confederate / ~s** *n*
*m* kən'fedrəts, -əˌrats
**sp** confederates[9], confedrates[1]

**confer / ~ring / ~red** *v*
kən'fɐ:ɹ / -ɪn, -ɪŋ / -d
**sp** confer[7], conferre[8] / conferring[2] / confer'd[2], conferr'd[1]

**conference** *n*
*m* 'kɒnfrəns, 'kɒnfəˌrens
**sp** conference[32]
**rh** innocence *MND 2.2.52*

**confess / ~es / ~eth / ~ing / ~ed** *v*
= / = / = / kən'fesɪn, -ɪŋ / =
**sp** confesse[122], con-fesse[3] / confesses[3] / confesseth[1] / confessing[2], con-fessing[1] / confes'd[2], confess'd[1], con-fess'd[1], confessed[1], confest[13]
**rh** bless *VA 1117*; decease *VA 1001*; gentleness *MND 2.2.137*; mess *LLL 4.3.203*

**confessed** *adj*
=
**sp** confess'd[1]

**confession / ~s** *n*
*m* kən'fesɪən, -ɪˌɒn / -ɪənz
**sp** confession[16], con-fession[1] / confessions[3]
**rh** transgression *LLL 5.2.432*

**confessor / ~s** *n*
*m* kən'fesəɹ, 'kɒnfeˌsɔ:ɹ / kən'fesəɹz
**sp** confessor[9] / confessors[1]

**confidence** *n*
*m* 'kɒnfɪˌdens, -ɪdəns
**sp** confidence[17]
**rh** impudence *AW 2.1.169*

**confident** *adj*
*m* 'kɒnfɪˌdent, -ɪdənt
**sp** confident[18], confi-dent[1]

**confidently** *adv*
'kɒnfɪdəntləɪ
**sp** confidently[2]

**confine / ~s** *n*
*m* 'kɒnfəɪn, kən'fəɪn / -z
**sp** confine[5] / confines[7], [neighbor]-confines[1], con-fines[1]
**rh** thine *LC 265*
> neighbour-confine

**confin·e / ~s / ~ing / ~ed** *v*
kən'fəɪn / -z / -ɪn, -ɪŋ / -d
**sp** confine[10] / confines[1] / confining[1] / confin'd[14], confinde[2]
**rh** crystalline, mine *Cym 5.4.110* / grind *S 110.12*; kind *S 105.7*
> unconfinable

**confined** *adj*
*m* kən'fəɪnɪd
**sp** confined[1]

**confineless** *adj*
kən'fəɪnləs
**sp** confinelesse[1]

**confiner / ~s** *n*
*m* 'kɒnfəɪnəɹz
**sp** confiners[1]

**confining** *adj*
kən'fəɪnɪn, -ɪŋ
**sp** confining[1]

**confirm / ~s / ~ed** *v*
kən'fɐːɹm / -z / -d
**sp** confirm[1], confirme[26] / confirmes[4] / confirm'd[9]
> soul-confirming, unconfirmed

**confirmation / ~s** *n*
'kɒnfəɹ,mɛːsɪən / -z
**sp** confirmation[6] / confirmations[2]

**confirmed** *adj*
*m* kən'fɐːɹmd, -mɪd
**sp** confirm'd[4], confirmed[1]

**confirmer / ~s** *n*
kən'fɐːɹməɹ / -z
**sp** confirmer[1] / confirmers[1]

**confirmit·y / ~ies** *n*
kən'fɐːɹmɪtəɪz
**sp** confirmities[1]

**confiscate** *adj*
*m* 'kɒnfɪs,kɛːt, kən'fɪskət
**sp** confiscate[6]

**confix / ~ed** *v*
*m* kən'fɪksɪd
**sp** confixed[1]

**conflict / ~s** *n*
'kɒnflɪkt / -s
**sp** conflict[8], con-flict[1] / conflicts[1]

**conflicting** *adj*
kən'flɪktɪn, -ɪŋ
**sp** conflicting[1]

**confluence** *n*
'kɒnfluːəns
**sp** confluence[1]

**conflux** *n*
kən'flɤks
**sp** conflux[1]

**conform** *v*
kən'fɔːɹm
**sp** conforme[1]

**conformable** *adj*
*m* kən'fɔːɹmə,bɤl
**sp** conformable[2]

**confound / ~ing / ~ed** *v*
kən'fəʊnd / -z / -ɪn, -ɪŋ / -ɪd
**sp** confound[32], counfound[1] / confoundes[1], confounds[6], 'confounds[1] / confounding[1] / confounded[6]
**rh** *1* bound *Per 5.2.14* [*Chorus*]; crowned *S 60.8, 69.7*; ground *Luc 1202, VA 1048*; sound *R2 5.3.85*; **rh** *2* wound *Luc 1202, MND 5.1.287* / hounds *VA 882*; sounds *S 8.7, 128.4*; swounds, wounds *Luc 1489*; wounds *TC 3.1.115* / compounded *PT 41*

**confounded** *adj*
kən'fəʊndɪd
**sp** confounded[2]

**confounding** *adj*
kən'fəʊndɪn, -ɪŋ
**sp** confounding[2]

**confront / ~ed** *v*
kən'frɤnt / -ɪd
**sp** confront[2] / confronted[4]
> front

**confused** *adj*
*m* kən'fjuːzɪd, -zd
**sp** confusd[1], confus'd[5], confused[4]
**rh** used *Oth 2.1.302*

**confusedly** *adv*
*m* kən'fjuːzɪd,ləɪ
**sp** confusedly[1]

**confusion / ~s** *n*
*m* kən'fjuːzɪən, -ɪ,ɒn / -ɪənz
**sp** confusion[29], confu-sion[1], confusions [confusion is][1] / confusions[3]
**rh** *1* conclusion *AY 5.4.122, Luc 1159*; illusion *Mac 3.5.29*; intrusion *CE 2.2.189*; **rh** *2* division *1H6 4.1.194*; **rh** *3* pollution *Luc 1159*; **rh** *4* Albion *KL 3.2.86*; **rh** *5* conjunction *MND 4.1.109*

**confutation** *n*
,kɒnfjə'tɛːsɪən
**sp** confutation[2]

**confute / ~s** *v*
kən'fjuːts
**sp** confutes[2]

**congeal / ~ed** *v*
kən'ʤiːl / *m* -d, -ɪd
**sp** congeale[1] / congeal'd[2], congealed[1]

**congealed** *adj*
*m* kɒn'ʤiːld, -lɪd
**sp** congeal'd[1], con-geal'd[1], congealed[2]

**congealment** *n*
kən'ʤiːlmənt
**sp** congealement[1]

**congee / ~d** *v*
kən'ʤiː / -d
**sp** conge[1] / congied[1]

**conger** *n*
'kɒŋgəɹ
**sp** conger[1]

**congest** *LC* *v*
kən'ʤest
**sp** congest[1]
**rh** breast *LC 258*

**congratulate** *v*
kəŋ'gratjə,lɛːt
**sp** congratulate[1]

**congree / ~ing** *v*
kəŋ'griːɪn, -ɪŋ
**sp** congreeing[1]

**congreet / ~ed** *v*
kəŋ'griːtɪd
**sp** congreeted[1]

**congregate** *vm*
'kɒŋgrɪ,gɛːt
**sp** congregate[1]

**congregated** *adj*
*m* 'kɒŋgrɪˌgɛ:tɪd
**sp** congregated[2]

**congregation / ~s** *n*
ˌkɒŋgrɪ'gɛ:sɪən / -z
**sp** congregation[3] / congregations[1]

**congruent** *adj*
=
**sp** congruent[2]

**conjectural** *adj*
kən'ʤektrɑl, -tər-
**sp** coniecturall[1], *emend of AW 5.3.114* connecturall[1]

**conjecture / ~s** *n*
kən'ʤektəɹ / -z
**sp** coniecture[5] / coniectures[3], con-iectures[1]

**conjoin / ~ed / ~s** *v*
kən'ʤəɪn / -z / -d
**sp** conioyne[1] / conioynes[1] / conioyn'd[4], conioyned[1]
> join

**conjointly** *adv*
kən'ʤəɪntləɪ
**sp** conioyntly[2]

**conjunction** *n*
*m* kən'ʤɤŋksɪən, -ɪˌɒn
**sp** coniunction[9]
**rh** confusion *MND 4.1.110*

**conjunctive** *adj*
kən'ʤɤŋktɪv
**sp** coniunctiue[2]

**conjuration / ~s** *n*
ˌkɒnʤə'rɛ:sɪən / -z
**sp** coniuration[4] / coniurations[1]

**conjur·e / ~es / ~ing / ~ed** *v*
'kɒnʤəɹ / -z / -ɪn, -ɪŋ / *m* -d, kən'ʤu:ɹd
**sp** coniure[29] / coniures[1] / coniuring[2] / coniur'd[6], coniured[2]

**conjuro** *Lat v*
kɒn'ʤu:ro:
**sp** coniuro[1]

**conjuror / ~s** *n*
'kɒnʤərəɹ / -z
**sp** coniurer[5] / coniurers[2]

**connive** *v*
kə'nəɪv
**sp** conniue[1]

**conquer / ~s / ~ed** *v*
'kɒŋkəɹ / -z / *m* -d, -əˌrɪd /
**sp** conquer[17] / conquers[3] / conquer'd[6], conquered[5]

**conquered** *adj*
'kɒŋkəɹd
**sp** conquer'd[4]
> half-, un-conquered

**conquered** *n*
*m* 'kɒŋkəˌrɪd
**sp** conquered[1]

**conquering** *adj*
'kɒŋkrɪn, -ɪŋ, -kər-
**sp** conquering[5], conqu'ring[3]

**conqueror / ~'s / ~s** *n*
*m* 'kɒŋkəˌrɔ:ɹ, -ərəɹ / 'kɒŋkərəɹz / 'kɒŋkəˌrɔ:ɹz
**sp** conqueror[20], con-queror[1], conquerour[1] / conquerors[1] / conquerors[5], conquerours[1]

**conquest / ~s** *n*
*m* 'kɒŋkwest, kəŋ'kwest / 'kɒŋkwests
**sp** conquest[28] / conquests[1]

**Conrade** *n*
'kɒnrad
**sp** Conrade[7]

**consanguineous** *adj*
=
**sp** consanguinious[1]

**consanguinity** *n*
*m* ˌkɒnsəŋ'gwɪnɪˌtəɪ
**sp** consanguinitie[1]

**conscience / ~s** *n*
*m* 'kɒnsɪəns, -ɪˌens / -ɪz
**sp** conscience[116], conscie[n]ce[1], con-science[2], consci-ence[1] / consciences[5]
**rh** dispense *Tim 3.2.89*

**conscionable** *adj*
'kɒnsɪənəbəl
**sp** conscionable[1]

**consecrate** *v*
*m* 'kɒnsɪˌkrɛ:t
**sp** consecrate[7]
**rh** gait *MND 5.1.405*

**consecrated** *adj*
*m* 'kɒnsɪˌkrɛ:tɪd
**sp** consecrated[4]

**consent / ~s** *n*
=
**sp** consent[61], con-sent[1] / consents[2]
**rh** banishment *Luc 1854*; experi-ment *AW 2.1.153*; merriment *LLL 5.2.460*

**consent / ~s / ~ing / ~ed** *v*
= / = / kən'sentɪn, -ɪŋ / =
**sp** consent[30] / consents[3] / consenting[3] / consented[8]
**rh** meant *Per Epil.15*; shent Ham *3.2.406*

**consenting** *n*
kən'sentɪn, -ɪŋ
**sp** consenting[1]

**consequence / ~s** *n*
*m* 'kɒnsɪˌkwens, -ɪkwəns / 'kɒnsɪˌkwensɪz
**sp** consequence[19] / consequences[1]
**rh** eloquence *MV 3.2.107*

**consequently** *adv*
*m* 'kɒnsɪˌkwentləɪ
**sp** consequently[3]

**conserve / ~s** *n*
*m* 'kɒnsɐ:ɹvz, kən'sɐ:ɹvz
**sp** conserues[2], con-serues[1]

**conserve / ~d** *v*
kən'sɐ:ɹv / -d
**sp** conserue[2] / conseru'd[1]

**consider / ~s / ~ing / ~ed** *v*
kən'sɪdəɹ / -z / *m* -ɪn, -ɪŋ, -drɪn, -drɪŋ / *m* -d, -əˌrɪd
**sp** consider[46], con-sider[1], consi-der[1] / considers[1] / considering[3] / consider'd[8], considered[8]

**considerance** *n*
kən'sɪdrəns, -dər-
**sp** considerance[1]

**considerate** *adj*
kən'sɪdrət, -dər-
**sp** considerate[2]
> inconsiderate

**consideration / ~s** *n*
*m* kən'sɪdəˌrɛ:sɪən, -ɪˌɒn / -ˌrɛ:sɪənz
**sp** consideration[8] / considerations[1], considera-tions[1]

**considered** *adj*
*m* kən'sɪdəɹd
**sp** consider'd[1]
> unconsidered

**considering / ~s** *n*
*m* kən'sɪdəˌrɪn, -ɪŋ / -z
**sp** considering[1] / considerings[1]

**consign / ~ing** *v*
kən'səɪn / -ɪn, -ɪŋ
**sp** consigne[3] / consigning[1]

**consigned** *adj*
'kɒnsəɪnd
**sp** consign'd[1]

**consist / ~s / ~eth / ~ing** *v*
= / = / = / kən'sɪstɪn, -ɪŋ
**sp** consist[4] / consists[3] / consisteth[1] / consisting[2]
**rh** resist *Per 1.4.83*

**consistory** *n*
'kɒnsɪsˌtrəɪ, -tər-
**sp** consistorie[2], consistory[2]

**consolation** *n*
ˌkɒnsə'lɛ:sɪən
**sp** consolation[1], conso-lation[1]

**consolate** *v*
*m* 'kɒnsəˌlɛ:t
**sp** consolate[1]
> disconsolate

**consonancy** *n*
'kɒnsnənsəɪ, -sən-
**sp** consonancy[2]

**consonant** *n*
'kɒnsnənt, sən-
**sp** consonant[1]

**consort** *n*
*m* kən'sɔ:ɹt, 'kɒnsɔ:ɹt
**sp** consort[4]

**consort / ~est / ~ed** *v*
*m* kən'sɔ:ɹt / -s, -st / -ɪd
**sp** consort[8] / consort'st[1] / consorted[5]

**consorted** *adj*
kən'sɔ:ɹtɪd
**sp** consorted[2]

**conspectuit·y / ~ies** *n*
ˌkɒnspɪk'tju:ɪtəɪz
**sp** conspectui-ties[1]

**conspiracy** *n*
*m* kən'spɪrəˌsəɪ, -rəs-
**sp** conspiracie[7], conspiracy[4]
**rh** lie *Tem 2.1.306*

**conspirant** *adj*
kən'spəɪrənt
**sp** conspirant[1]

**conspirator / ~s** *n*
*m* kən'spɪrəˌtɔɹ, -ɹtəɹ / -z
**sp** conspirator[5] / conspirators[6]
**rh** ravisher *Luc 769*

**conspir·e / ~s / ~ing / ~ed** *v*
kən'spəɪɹ / -z / -ɪn, -ɪŋ / *m* -d, -ɪd
**sp** conspire[7] / conspires[1] / conspiring[1] / conspir'd[4], conspired[2]
**rh** desire *S 10.6*

**conspirer / ~s** *n*
kən'spəɪɹəɹz
**sp** conspirers[1]

**constable / ~'s / ~s** *n*
=
**sp** constable[39], con-stable[3] / constables[1], con-stables[1] / constables[2]

**Constance** *n*
=
**sp** Constance[12]

**constanc·y / ~ies** *n*
*m* 'kɒnstənˌsəɪ, -ns- / -nˌsəɪz
**sp** constancie[11], constan-cie[1], constancy[2] / constancies[1]
**rh** see *S 152.10*
> inconstancy

**constant** *adj*
=
**sp** constant[43], con-stant[2]
> unconstant

**Constantine** *n*
'kɒnstənˌtəɪn
**sp** Constantine[1]

**Constantinople** *n*
'kɒnstantɪ'no:pəl
**sp** Constantinople[1]

**constantly** *adv*
*m* 'kɒnstəntˌləɪ, -tl-
**sp** constantly[6]

**constellation** *n*
ˌkɒnstə'lɛ:sɪən
**sp** constellation[1]

**conster** *v*
kən'stɐ:ɹ
**sp** conster[3]
> misconster

**constitution** *n*
*m* ˌkɒnstɪ'tju:sɪən, -sɪˌɒn
**sp** constitution[2]

**constrain / ~s / ~eth / ~ed** *v*
kən'strɛ:n / -z / -əθ / *m* -d, -ɪd
**sp** constraine[1] / constraines[2], con-strains / constraineth[1] / constrain'd[7], con-strain'd[1]

**constrained** *adj*
*m* kən'strɛ:nd, -nɪd

**sp** constrained[3]
> unconstrained

**constraint** *n*
kən'strɛ:nt
**sp** constraint[6]

**constring / ~ed** *v*
kən'strɪŋd
**sp** constring'd[1]

**construction** *n*
kən'strɤksɪən
**sp** construction[9]
> misconstruction

**construe** *v*
*m* kən'stru:, 'kɒnstru:
**sp** construe[7]
> misconstrue

**consul / ~'s / ~s** *n*
=
**sp** consul[1], consull[29] / consuls[2] / consuls[6]
> pro-consul

**consulship / ~s** *n*
=
**sp** consulship[1] / consulships[1]

**consult / ~ing** *v*
kən'sɤlt / -ɪn, -ɪŋ
**sp** consult[4] / consulting[1]

**consum·e / ~es / ~ing / ~ed** *v*
= / = / kən'sju:mɪn, -ɪŋ / =
**sp** consume[8] / consumes[1] / consuming[1] / consum'd[7]
**rh** fumes *Luc 1042*

**consumed** *adj*
*m* kən'sju:mɪd
**sp** consumed[1]

**consuming** *adj*
kən'sju:mɪn, -ɪŋ
**sp** consuming[3]
> blood-, sap-consuming

**consummate** *v*
'kɒnsjə,mɛ:t
**sp** consummate[3], consum-mate[1]

**consummation** *n*
'kɒnsjə,mɛ:sɪən
**sp** consumation[1], consummation[1]

**consumption / ~s** *n*
kən'sɤmpsɪən / -z
**sp** consumption[4] / consumptions[1]

**contagion** *n*
*m* kən'tɛ:ʤɪən, -ɪ,ɒn
**sp** contagion[7]

**contagious** *adj*
kən'tɛ:ʤɪəs
**sp** contagious[11]

**contain / ~s / ~ing / ~ed** *v*
kən'tɛ:n / -z / -ɪn, -ɪŋ / -d
**sp** contain[1], containe[12], contayn't[1] / containes[10] / containing[4], contayning[1] / contain'd[3]
**rh** brain *S 77.9* / remains *LC 189, S 74.13*

**containing** *n*
kən'tɛ:nɪn, -ɪŋ
**sp** containing[1]

**contaminate / ~d** *v*
kən'tamɪ,nɛ:t / -ɪd
**sp** contaminate[2] / contaminated[2]

**contaminated** *adj*
*m* kən'tamɪ,nɛ:tɪd, -ɪn-
**sp** contaminated[3]

**contemn / ~ing / ~ed** *v*
kən'tem / -ɪn, -ɪŋ / -d
**sp** contemne[2] / contemning[2], contenning[1] / contemn'd[2]
> uncontemn

**contemned** *adj*
*m* kən'temd, -mnɪd
**sp** contemn'd[1], contemned[1]

**contemplate** *v*
'kɒntəm,plɛ:t
**sp** contemplate[1]

**contemplation** *n*
*m* ,kɒntəm'plɛ:sɪən, -ɪ,ɒn
**sp** contemplation[1], con-templation[1]

**contemplative** *adj*
kən'templə,tɪv
**sp** contemplatiue[3]

**contempt / ~s** *n*
kən'temt, -mpt / -s
**sp** contempt[45] / contempts[3]
**rh** exempt *CE 2.2.181, Tim 4.2.32*
> court-contempt

**contemptible** *adj*
*m* kən'temtɪ,bɤl, -tɪbəl, -mpt-
**sp** contemptible[2]

**contemptuous** *adj*
kən'temtjəs, -mpt-
**sp** contemptuous[2]

**contemptuously** *adj*
*m* kən'temtjəs,ləɪ, -mpt-
**sp** contemptuously[1]

**contend / ~ing / ~ed** *v*
= / kən'tendɪn, -ɪŋ / =
**sp** contend[14] / contending[4] / contended[1]
**rh** end *S 60.4*; friend *VA 820*

**contending** *adj*
kən'tendɪn, -ɪŋ
**sp** contending[1]

**content** *adj*
= , *Caius MW 1.4.69*
kən'tent-ə
**sp** content[84], content-a[1]
**rh** banishment *AY 1.3.135*; present *MND 5.1.132*; repent, spent *MND 2.2.116*; spent *Cym 5.4.102*

**content / ~'s / ~s** *n*
*m* kən'tent, 'kɒntent / -s
**sp** content[34], con-tent[1] / contents[1] / contents[20]
**rh** event *Per 4.Chorus.46*; lament, lent *Luc 1503*; lineament *RJ 1.3.85*; ornament *S 1.11*; precedent *LC 157*; spent *AY 2.3.68, Mac 3.2.5, S 119.13* / events *AY 5.4.127*; monuments *Luc 948, S 55.3*; presents *LLL 5.2.515*; rents *LC 56*
> discontent

**content / ~s / ~eth** *v*
kən'tent / -s / -əθ
**sp** content[33] / contents[3], co[n]tents[1] / contenteth[1]
**rh** content ye meant ye *TNK Epil.13*; content you repent you *MND 5.1.113* / contents her sent her *TG 3.1.93*

**content** *Fr adj*
kɔ̃'tɑ̃
**sp** content[1]

**contente** [*Pistol H4 2.4.176*] *v*
kɒn'tente:
**sp** con-tente[1]

**contented** *adj*
=
**sp** contented[24], con-tented[1]
**rh** imprinted *VA 513*
dis-, well-contented

**contention** *n*
*m* kən'tensɪən, -ɪˌɒn
**sp** contention[9]

**contentious** *adj*
kən'tensɪəs
**sp** contentious[2]

**contentless** *adj*
=
**sp** contentlesse[1]

**contento** *Ital v*
kɒn'tento:
**sp** contento[1]

**contest** *v*
kən'test
**sp** contest[1]

**contestation** *n*
ˌkɒntəs'tɛ:sɪən
**sp** contestation[1]

**continence** *n*
*m* 'kɒntnəns, -tɪn-
**sp** continence[1]

**continency** *n*
'kɒntnənsəɪ, -tɪn-
**sp** continencie[1], continen-cie[1]
> incontinency

**continent** *adj*
*m* 'kɒntɪˌnent, -ɪnənt
**sp** continent[2]

**continent / ~s** *n*
*m* 'kɒntɪˌnent, -ɪnənt / -s
**sp** continent[8] / continents[3]

**continual** *adj*
kən'tɪnjɑl, -jʊɑl
**sp** continual[2], continuall[8], conti-nuall[1]
> long-continued

**continually** *adv*
*m* kən'tɪnjɑləɪ, -jʊɑ-, -ˌləɪ
**sp** continually[2], con-tinually[1]

**continuance** *n*
*m* kən'tɪnjəns, -jʊəns, -jʊˌans
**sp** continuance[7], con-tinuance[1]

**continuantly** *adv*
kən'tɪnjəntləɪ, jʊən-
**sp** continu-antly[1]

**continuate** *adj*
kən'tɪnjət, -jʊət
**sp** continuate[2]

**continu·e / ~s / ~ing / ~d** *v*
= / = / kən'tɪnju:·ɪn, -ɪŋ / *m* -d, -ɪd
**sp** continue[32] / continues[7] / conti-nuing[1] / continew'd[1], continued[5]

**continuer** *n*
kən'tɪnjʊəɹ
**sp** continuer[1]

**contract** *n*
kən'trakt, 'kɒntrakt
**sp** contract[21]
> pre-contract

**contract / ~ed** *v*
kən'trakt / =
**sp** contract[4] / contract[1], contracted[6]
> subcontract

**contracted** *adj*
=
**sp** contracted[3]

**contracting** *n*
kən'traktɪn, -ɪŋ
**sp** contracting[1]
**rh** exacting *MM 3.2.270*

**contraction** *n*
kən'traksɪən
**sp** contraction[1]

**contradict / ~s / ~ed** *v*
=
**sp** contradict[5] / contradicts[1] / contradicted[1]
**rh** inflict *Luc 1631*

**contradiction** *n*
ˌkɒntrə'dɪksɪən
**sp** contradiction[5]

**contrariet·y / ~ies** *n*
*m* ˌkɒntrə'rəɪəˌtəɪ / -z
**sp** contrariety[1] / contrarieties[1]

**contrarious** *adj*
kən'trarɪəs
**sp** contrarious[2]

**contrariously** *adv*
*m* kən'trarɪəsˌləɪ
**sp** contrariously[1]

**contrary** *adj*
*m* kən'trarəɪ, 'kɒntrəˌrəɪ
**sp** contrary[11], contrarie[3]

**contrar·y / ~ies** *n*
*m* 'kɒntrəˌrəɪ, -rərəɪ / -rəˌrəɪz
**sp** contrarie[9], contrary[16], con-trary[1] / contraries[4]
**rh** I *Per 2.Chorus.15*

**contrary** *v*
kən'trarəɪ
**sp** contrary[1]

**contrary to** *prep*
*m* 'kɒntrəɪ 'tʊ
**sp** contrary to[4], con-trary to[1]

**contre** *Fr prep*
'kɔ̃:trə
**sp** contra[1]

**contribution** *n*
*m* ˌkɒntrɪ'bju:sɪən, -ɪˌɒn
**sp** contribution[2]

**contributor / ~s** *n*
*m* kən'trɪbjəˌtɔ:ɹz
**sp** contributors[1]

**contrite** *adj*
'kɒntrəɪt
**sp** contrite[1]

**contrive / ~st / ~s / ~d** *v*
kən'trəɪv /-z / *m* -d, -ɪd / -st, -dst
**sp** contriue[8] / contriues[1] / contriu'd[7], contriued[1] / contriued'st[1]
**rh** survive *Luc 206*; live *v JC 2.3.15* / gyves, strives *LC 243*

**contrived** *adj*
*m* kən'trəɪvd, -vɪd
**sp** contriu'd[1], contriued[1]

**contriver** *n*
kən'trəɪvəɹ
**sp** contriuer[4]

**contriving** *adj / n*
kən'trəɪvɪn, -ɪŋ
**sp** contriuing[1] / contriuing[2]

**control / ~s** *n*
kən'tro:l / -z
**sp** controle[1], controll[3] / controules[1]
**rh** soul *S 125.14* / fowls *CE 2.1.19*
> comptrol

**control / ~led** *v*
kən'tro:l / kən'tro:ld
**sp** controle[1], controll[3], controule[2], controul't [control it][1] / control'd[1], controll'd[1], controul'd[1]
**rh** soul *Luc 500, 1781, S 107.3* / behold *Luc 448*; fold *Luc 678*
uncontrol

**controller** *n*
kən'tro:ləɹ
**sp** controller[1], controuler[1]

**controlling** *adj*
kən'tro:lɪn, -ɪŋ
**sp** controlling[3]
**rh** rolling *S 20.7*

**controlment** *n*
kən'tro:lmənt
**sp** controlement[2], controllment[1], controulement[1]

**controversy** *n*
ˌkɒntrə'vɐ:ɹsəɪ
**sp** controuersie[8], con-trouersie[2]

**contumelious** *adj*
ˌkɒntjə'mi:lɪəs
**sp** contumelious[3]

**contumeliously** *adv*
*m* ˌkɒntjə'mi:lɪəsˌləɪ
**sp** contumeliously[1]

**contumely** *n*
*m* 'kɒntjəmˌləɪ
**sp** contumely[1]

**contusion / ~s** *n*
kən'tu:zɪənz
**sp** contusions[1]

**contutti**
> con, tutto

**convenien·ce / ~s** *n*
=
**sp** conuenience[3], conueni-ence[1] / conueniences[2]
> inconvenience

**conveniency** *n*
*m* kən'vi:nɪənˌsəɪ, -ns-
**sp** conueniencie[2]

**convenient** *adj*
*m* kən'vi:nɪənt, -ɪˌent
**sp** conuenient[20]

**conveniently** *adv*
*m* kən'vi:nɪəntˌləɪ, -tl-
**sp** conueniently[4]

**convent / ~ed** *v*
kən'vent·s / -ɪd
**sp** conuents[1] / conuented[1]
> covent

**conventicle / ~s** *n*
*m* kən'ventɪˌkɤlz
**sp** conuenticles[1]

**conversant** *adj*
*m* 'kɒnvəɹˌsant, -sənt
**sp** conuersant[2]

**conversation / ~s** *n*
ˌkɒnvəɹ'sɛ:sɪən, -sɪˌɒn / -'sɛ:sɪənz
**sp** conuersation[7], conuer-sation[1] / conuersations[1]
**rh** benison *Per 2.Chorus.9*

**converse** *n*
kən'vɐ:ɹs
**sp** conuerse[3]

**convers·e / ~s / ~ing / ~d** *v*
kən'vɐ:ɹs / -ɪz / -ɪn, -ɪŋ / -ɪd
**sp** conuerse[10] / conuerses[1] / conuersing[2] / conuersed[1], conuerst[3], conuers't[1]

**conversion** *n*
kən'vɐ:ɹsɪən
**sp** conuersion[2]

**convert / *S* ~est / ~s / ~ing / ~ed** *v*
kən'vɐ:ɹt / -əst / -s / -ɪn, -ɪŋ / -ɪd
**sp** conuert[8] / conuertest[1] / conuerts[2] / conuerting[3] / conuerted[4], conuer-ted[1]
**rh** art *S 14.12*; art, heart *Luc 592* / departest *S 11.4*

**convertite / ~s** *n*
'kɒnvəɹˌtəɪt / -s
**sp** conuertite[1] / conuertites[1]
**rh** light *Luc 743*

**convey / ~ed** *v*
kən'vɛ: / -d
**sp** conuay[5], conuey[28] / conuaid[2], conuay'd[1], con-uay'd[1], conuei'd[2], conuey'd[10]
**rh** may *Per 3.Chorus.56*; way *Per 4 Chorus.49* / aid *VA 1192*

**conveyance / ~s** *n*
kən'vɛ:əns / -ɪz
**sp** conueiance[1], conueyance[6] / conueyances[2]

**conveyer / ~s** *n*
kən'vɛ:əɹz
**sp** conueyers[1]

**conveying** *adj*
kən'vɛ:ɪn, -ɪŋ
**sp** conueying[1]

**convict** *v*
=
**sp** conuict[1]

**convicted** *adj*
=
**sp** conuicted[1]

**convince / ~s / ~d** *v*
= / = / *m* kən'vɪnsɪd
**sp** conuince[5] / conuinces[1] / conuinced[1]
**rh** prince *Per 1.2.123*

**convive** *v*
kən'vəɪv
**sp** conuiue[1]

**convocation** *n*
*m* ˌkɒnvə'kɛ:sɪən, -ɪˌɒn
**sp** conuocation[2]

**convoy** *n*
'kɒnvəɪ
**sp** conuoy[6], con-uoy[1]

**convulsion / ~s** *n*
kən'vɤlsɪənz
**sp** convultions[1]

**con·y / ~ies** *n*
'ko:nəɪ, 'kɒ- / -z
**sp** conie[1], connie[1] / conies[1]

**cony-catch / ~ed** *v*
'ko:nəɪ-ˌkatʃ, 'kɒ- / -t
**sp** conicatch[1] / coni-catcht[1]
> catch

**cony-catching** *adj / n*
'ko:nəɪ-ˌkatʃɪn, -ɪŋ, 'kɒ-
**sp** cony-catching[1] / conicatching[1]

**cook / ~s** *n*
=
**sp** cooke[15] / cookes[3]

**cook / ~ed** *v*
=
**sp** cook'd[2]

**Cook** [name] *n*
=
**sp** Cook[1], Cooke[2]

**cookery** *n*
*m* 'kʊkəˌrəɪ, -krəɪ
**sp** cookerie[2]

**cool** *adj*
=
**sp** cool[1], coole[5]
> overcool

**cool / ~s / ~ing / ~ed** *v*
= / = / 'ku:lɪn, -ɪŋ / =
**sp** coole[25] / cooles[5] / cooling[3] / coold[1], cool'd[3], cooled[2]
**rh** fool *Mac 4.1.153* / should *VA 387*

**cooling** *adj / n*
'ku:lɪn, -ɪŋ
**sp** cooling[2] / cooling[1]

**coop / ~s / ~ed** *v*
=
**sp** coopes[1] / coop'd[1]

**copatain** *adj*
'kɒpətɛ:n
**sp** copataine[1]

**cope / ~st / ~d** *v*
ko:p / -st / -t
**sp** cope[9] / coap'st[2] / coap'd[2], cop'd[1]

**Cophetua** *n*
kə'fetə, -tjʊə
**sp** Cophetua[2], Couitha[1]

**copious** *adj*
'ko:pɪəs
**sp** copious[1]

**copper** *adj / n*
'kɒpəɹ
**sp** copper[3] / copper[4]

**Copperspur** *n*
'kɒpəɹˌspɐ:ɹ
**sp** Copperspurre[1]

**coppice** *n*
=
**sp** coppice[1]

**copulation** *n*
ˌkɒpjə'lɛ:sɪən
**sp** copulation[2]

**copulative / ~s** *n*
'kɒpjələtɪvz
**sp** copulatiues[1]

**cop·y / ~ies** *n*
'kɒpəɪ / -z
**sp** copie[5], coppie's [copy is][1], coppy[4], copy[1] / copies[2]

**cop·y / ~ied** *v*
'kɒpəɪd
**sp** coppied[3]

**copy-book** *n*
'kɒpəɪˌbʊk
**sp** coppie booke[1]

**coquo / coctus** *Lat v*
'kɒktʊs
**sp** coctus[1]

**coragio** *Ital n*
kɒ'radʒɪo:
**sp** coragio[3]

**coral** *adj / n*
=
**sp** corrall[1] / corrall[1]

**Coram,** *malap for Lat* quorum *n*
'kɔ:rəm
**sp** Coram[1]

**Corambus** *n*
kəˈrambəs
**sp** Corambus[1]

**coranto / ~s** *n*
kəˈranto: / -z
**sp** carranto[2] / carranto's[1]

**corbo** *nonsense word*
ˈkɒɹbo:
**sp** corbo[1]

**cord / ~s** *n*
ˈkɔ:ɹd / -z
**sp** cord[7], [penny]-cord[1] / cordes[1], cords[10]
> master-cord

**corded** *adj*
ˈkɔ:ɹdɪd
**sp** corded-[ladder][2]

**Cordelia** *n*
kɒɹˈdi:lɪə
**sp** Cordelia[25]

**Cordelion / ~'s** *n*
ˈkɔ:ɹdəˈli:ən / -z
**sp** Cordelion[3] / Cordelions[3]

**cordial** *adj / n*
ˈkɔ:ɹdɪɑl
**sp** cordiall[4] / cordiall[5]

**cordis**
> tremor cordis

**core** *n*
kɔ:ɹ
**sp** core[4]

**Corin** *n*
ˈkɒrɪn
**sp** Corin[8]

**Corinth** *n*
ˈkɒrɪnt, -nθ
**sp** Corinth[7]

**Corinthian** *n*
kəˈrɪntɪən, -nθɪ-
**sp** Corinthian[1]

**Coriolanus** *n*
ˌkɒrɪəˈlɛ:nəs
**sp** Coriolanus[52], Corio-lanus[1], *abbr in s.d.* Corio[1], Coriol[1]

**Corioles** *n*
*m* kəˈrəɪəˌles, -ələs
**sp** Carioles[5], Corialus[2], Corioles[13], Coriolus[1]

**co-rival / ~s** *n*
kɒˈrəɪvəl / -z
**sp** *n* co-riuall[1] / corriuals[1]

**co-rival / ~led** *v*
kɒˈrəɪvəld
**sp** co-riual'd[1]

**cork** *n*
kɒɹk
**sp** corke[2]

**corky** *adj*
ˈkɒɹkəɪ
**sp** corky[1]

**cormorant** *adj*
*m* ˈkɔ:ɹməˌrant, -mər-, -mrənt
**sp** comorant[1], cormorant[3]

**corn / ~s** *n*
kɔ:ɹn / -z
**sp** corn[2], corne[30], corne's [corn is][1] / cornes[2]
**rh** forsworn *LLL 4.3.359*
> peppercorn

**Cornelia** *n*
*m* kɔ:ɹˈni:lɪə, -lɪˌa
**sp** Cornelia[2]

**Cornelius** *n*
kɔ:ɹˈni:lɪəs
**sp** Cornelius[7]

**corner / ~s** *n*
ˈkɔ:ɹnəɹ / -z
**sp** corner[14], cor-ner[1], [Py]-Corner[1], [parke]-corner[1] / corners[9]

**corner-cap** *n*
ˈkɔ:ɹnəɹ-ˌkap
**sp** corner cap[1]
> cap

**cornerstone** *n*
ˈkɔ:ɹnəɹ-ˌsto:n
**sp** corner stone[1]
> stone

**cornet / ~s** *n*
ˈkɔ:ɹnəts
**sp** cornets[13]

**Cornish** *adj*
ˈkɔ:ɹnɪʃ
**sp** Cornish[2]

**cornuto** *n*
kɔ:ɹˈnu:to:
**sp** curnuto[1]

**Cornwall** *n*
ˈkɔ:ɹnwɑ:l
**sp** Cornewall[5], Cornwal[1], Cornwall[10], Cornwals [Cornwall is][1]

**corollary** *n*
*m* ˈkɒrəˌlarəɪ
**sp** corolary[1]

**coronal** *n*
ˈkɒrənɑl
**sp** coronall[2]
> demi-coronal

**coronation** *n*
*m* ˌkɒrəˈnɛ:sɪən, -ɪˌɒn
**sp** coronation[18], corronation[3]

**coroner**
> crowner

**coronet** *adj*
ˈkɒɹnət, -ɹən-
**sp** coronet[1]

**coronet / ~s** *n*
*m* ˈkɒrəˌnet, -nət, ˈkɒɹnət / -s
**sp** coronet[8] / coronets[3]

**corporal** *adj*
*m* ˈkɔ:ɹpəˌrɑl, -pərɑl, -prɑl
**sp** corporall[8]

**corporal / ~s** *n*
*m* 'kɔːɹpəˌrɑl, -pər-, -prɑl / -pərɑlz, -prɑlz
**sp** coporall[1], corporal[1], corporall[13], *Bullcalf malap 2H4 3.2.215* corporate / cor-porals[1]

**corporate** *adj*
'kɔːɹprət, -pər-
**sp** corporate[1]
> incorporate

**corpse / ~s** *n*
kɔːɹs, kɔːɹps / 'kɔːɹsɪz
**sp** coarse[28], corpes[7], corps[3], corse[1] / coarses[1]
**rh** nurse *RJ 3.2.128*

**corpulent** *adj*
'kɔːɹpjələnt
**sp** corpulent[1]

**correct / ~s / ~ing** *v*
= / = / kə'rektɪn, -ɪŋ
**sp** correct[6], cor-rect[1] / corrects[2] / correcting[1]
> incorrect

**corrected** *adj*
=
**sp** corrected[1]
> uncorrected

**correction** *n*
*m* kə'rɛksɪən, -ɪˌɒn
**sp** correction[19], correctio[n][1]
**rh** infection *S 111.12*

**correctioner** *n*
ˌkə'rɛksɪənəɹ
**sp** correctioner[1]

**correspond / ~ing** *v*
ˌkɒrə'spɒndɪn, -ɪŋ
**sp** corresponding[1]

**correspondent** *adj*
=
**sp** correspondent[1]

**corresponsive** *adj*
=
**sp** corresponsiue[1]

**corrigible** *adj*
=
**sp** corrigeable[1], corrigible[1]

**corroborate** *adj*
*m* kə'rɒbəˌret, -ərət
**sp** corroborate[1]

**corrosive** *adj*
'kɒrəˌsɪv
**sp** corosiue[1], corrosiue[1]

**corrupt** *adj*
kə'rɤpt
**sp** corrupt[11]

**corrupt / ~s / ~ing / ~ed** *v*
kə'rɤpt / -s / -ɪn, -ɪŋ / -ɪd
**sp** corrupt[15], cor-rupt[1] / corrupts[1] / corrupting[1] / corrupted[10]

**corrupted** *adj*
kə'rɤptɪd
**sp** corrupted[7]
**rh** interrupted *Luc 1172*

**corrupter / ~s** *n*
kə'rɤptəɹ / -z
**sp** corrupter[1], cor-rupter[1] / corrupters[1]

**corruptible** *Fr adj*
kɔryp'tiblə
**sp** corruptible[1]

**corruptibly** *adv*
*m* kə'rɤptɪˌbləɪ
**sp** corruptibly[1]

**corrupting** *adj*
kə'rɤptɪn, -ɪŋ
**sp** corrupting[1]

**corruption** *n*
*m* kə'rɤpsɪən, -ɪˌɒn
**sp** corruption[15]

**corruptly** *adv*
kə'rɤptləɪ
**sp** corruptly[1]

**corse**
> corpse

**corslet** *n*
'kɒɹslət
**sp** corslet[1]

**Cosmo** *n*
'kɒzmoː
**sp** Cosmo[1]

**cost / ~s** *n*
=
**sp** cost[22] / costs[1]
**rh** *1* lost *PP 13.12*; **rh** *2* boast *S 91.10*; host *TNK 3.5.127*

**cost / ~s** *v*
=
**sp** cost[20] / costs[1]
**rh** lost *Luc 146, Per 3.2.69*

**costard** *n*
'kɒstəɹd
**sp** costard[3]

**Costard** [name] *n*
'kɒstəɹd
**sp** Costard[15], Co-stard[2]

**costermonger / ~s** *n*
'kɒstəɹ-ˌmɤŋgəɹz
**sp** costor-mongers[1]

**costl·y / ~ier** *adj*
'kɒstləɪ / -əɹ
**sp** costly[10] / costlier[1]

**cote / ~d** *v*
'koːtɪd
**sp** coated[1], coted[1]

**cot-quean** *n*
'kɒt-ˌkwiːn
**sp** cot-queane[1]
> quean

**Cotswold** *adj*
'kɒtsəl, -soːld
**sp** Cot-sal-[man][1], Cotsall[1], Cottshold[1]

**cottage / ~s** *n*
=
**sp** cottage[4] / cottages[2]

**Cotus** *n*
'ko:təs
**sp** Cotus[2]

**couch / ~es** *n*
kəʊʧ / 'kəʊʧɪz
**sp** couch[5], cowch[1] / couches[1]

**couch / ~ing / ~ed** *v*
kəʊʧ / 'kəʊʧɪn, -ɪŋ / *m* kəʊʧt, 'kəʊʧɪd
**sp** couch[10], cowch[1] / couching[1], cowching[1] / couch'd[2], couched[5], coucht[2]

**couching** *adj*
'kəʊʧɪn, -ɪŋ
**sp** couching[1]

**couching / ~s** *n*
'kəʊʧɪnz, -ɪŋz
**sp** couchings[1]

**coude** *Fr n*
kud
**sp** coudee

**cough** *n*
=
**sp** coffe[1], cough[1]
**rh** laugh *MND 2.1.54*

**cough / ~ing** *v*
= / 'kɒfɪn, -ɪŋ
**sp** cough[3] / coffing[1]

**coughing** *n*
'kɒfɪn, -ɪŋ
**sp** coffing[1]

**could / ~est** *v*
=, kʊld / -st
**sp** could[603] / could'st[23], couldest[1], couldst[7]
**rh** should *Tim 1.2.159*
> can

**coulter**
> culter

**council / ~s** *n*
'kəʊnsəl / -z
**sp** councell[26], coun-cell[1], counsaile[2], counsell[7] / councels[3]
> counsel

**council-board** *n*
'kəʊnsəl-ˌbɔ:ɹd
**sp** councell boord[1], councell-boord[1]

**council-house** *n*
'kəʊnsəl-ˌəʊs, -ˌhəʊs
**sp** councell house[1], councell-house[1]
> house

**councillor / ~s** *n*
*m* 'kəʊnsəˌlɔ:ɹ, -sələɹ, -sləɹ / -səˌlɔ:ɹz
**sp** councellor[2], councellour[1], counsailor[1], counsellor[3], counsellour[1] / councellors[1], councellours[1], counsailors[1]

**council-table** *n*
'kəʊnsəl-ˌtɛ:bəl
**sp** councell table[2]

**counsel / ~'s / ~s** *n*
'kəʊnsəl / -z
**sp** councel[2], councell[11], counsaile[43], counsel[2], counsell[52] / counsailes[1], counsels[1] / councels[2], counsailes[9], counsels[5]
> council, chamber-counsel

**counsel / ~s / ~led** *v*
'kəʊnsəl / -z / -d
**sp** councell[1], counsaile[14], coun-saile[1], counsel[2], counsell[4] / counsels[2] / counsail'd[2]

**counsel-keeper** *n*
'kəʊnsəl-ˌki:pəɹ
**sp** councell-keeper[1]
> keep

**counsel-keeping** *adj*
'kəʊnsəl-ˌki:pɪn, -ɪŋ
**sp** counsaile-keeping[1]
> keep

**counsellor** *adj*
*m* 'kəʊnsləɹ, -səl-
**sp** counsailor[1]

**counsellor / ~s** *n*
*m* 'kəʊnsəˌlɔ:ɹ, -sələɹ, -sləɹ / -z
**sp** councellour[1], counsailor[3], counsailour[1], counseller[1], counsellor[2] / counsailers[1], counsailors[1], counsellors[2]
> councillor, fellow-counsellor

**count / ~s** *n*
kəʊnt / -s
**sp** count[6] / counts[1]

**count / ~s / ~ing / ~ed** *v*
kəʊnt / -s / 'kəʊnt·ɪn, -ɪŋ / -ɪd
**sp** count[23] / counts[5] / counting[1] / counted[8]
> overcount, uncounted

**count** [*Fr pron of* gown] *n*
kunt
**sp** count[4]

**Count / ~'s / ~s** [*title*] *n*
kəʊnt / -s
**sp** Count[79], Counte[1], Counts [Count is][2], / Countes[1], Counts[6] / Counts[1]

**count-cardinal** *n*
ˌkəʊnt-'kɑ:ɹdɪˌnɑl
**sp** count-cardinall[1]
> cardinal

**countenance / ~s** *n*
*m* 'kəʊntnəns, -tən-, -təˌnans / -təˌnansɪz
**sp** countenance[48], coun-tenance[2], counte-nance[1], countenaunce[1] count'nance[4] / countenances[1]

**countenance / ~d** *v*
*m* 'kəʊntnəns, -təˌnans / -t
**sp** countenance[3], coun-tenance[1] / countenanc'd[2], counte-nanc'd[1]

**counter / ~s** *n*
'kəʊntəɹ / -z
**sp** counter[3] / counters[3]

**countercaster** *n*
'kəʊntəɹ-ˌkastəɹ
**sp** counter-caster[1]
> cast

**counterchange** *n*
'kəʊntəɹ-ˌʧɛ:ndʒ
**sp** counter-change[1]
> change

**countercheck** *n*
'kəʊntəɹ-ˌʧek
**sp** counterchecke[1], counter-checke[2]
> check

**counterfeit** *adj*
*m* 'kəʊntəɹfet, -ˌfet
**sp** counterfeit[6], counterfet[3], counterfeyt[1]

**counterfeit / ~s** *n*
*m* 'kəʊntəɹfet, -ˌfet / -s
**sp** counterfait[1], counterfeit[16], coun-terfeit[1], counter-feit[1], counterfet[1], counterfeyt[1] / counterfeits[1], counterfeyts[1]
**rh** set *S 53.5*; unset *S 16.8*

**counterfeit / ~est / ~s / ~ed** *v*
*m* 'kəʊntəɹfet, -ˌfet / -s, -st / -s / -ˌfetɪd
**sp** counterfeit[15], counterfet[4], counter-fet[1] / counterfaits[1], counterfeit'st[1], counterfet'st[1] / counterfets[1] / counterfei-ted[2], counterfeyted[1]

**counterfeited** *adj*
'kəʊntəɹˌfetɪd
**sp** counterfeited[1], counterfetted[1]

**counterfeiting** *adj / n*
'kəʊntəɹˌfetɪn, -ɪŋ
**sp** counterfetting[1] / counterfeiting[2], counterfetting[1]
> death-counterfeiting

**counterfeitly** *adv*
'kəʊntəɹˌfetləɪ
**sp** counterfetly[1]

**countergate** *n*
'kəʊntəɹ-ˌgɛ:t
**sp** counter-gate[1]
> gate

**countermand** *n*
'kəʊntəɹˌmand
**sp** countermand[3]

**countermand / ~s** *v*
'kəʊntəɹˌmandz
**sp** counterma[n]ds[1]
**rh** lands *CE 4.2.37*

**countermine / ~s** *n*
'kəʊntəɹˌməɪnz
**sp** countermines[1]
> mine

**counterpoint / ~s** *n*
'kəʊntəɹˌpəɪnts
**sp** counterpoints[1]
> point

**counterpoise** *n*
'kəʊntəɹˌpəɪz
**sp** counterpoize[2]
> poise

**counterpoise / ~d** *v*
'kəʊntəɹˌpəɪz / -d
**sp** counterpoise[1], counterpoize[2] / counter-poys'd[3]

**counterseal / ~ed** *v*
'kəʊntəɹ-ˌsi:ld
**sp** counter-seal'd[1]
> seal

**countervail** *v*
'kəʊntəɹˌvɛ:l
**sp** counteruaile[1]

**Countess / ~es** *n*
kəʊn'tes / -ɪz
**sp** Countesse[9] / Countesses[2]

**countless** *adj*
'kəʊntləs
**sp** countlesse[1]

**country** *adj*
'kɤntrəɪ
**sp** countrey[4], countrie[2], country[7], country-[mistresses][1]

**countr·y / ~y's / ~ies** *n*
'kɤntrəɪ / -z
**sp** countrey[40], coun-trey[2], countrie[9], coun-trie[1], country[58], coun-try[1] / countreyes[3], countries[37], countryes[1] / countries[10]

**country·man / ~men** *n*
*m* 'kɤntrəɪ·mən, -ˌman / -mən, -ˌmen
**sp** countreyman[6], countrey-man[1], countriman[4], countryman[6], country-man[1] / countreymen[10], countrey-men[2], countrimen[11], countri-men[1], countrymen[13], country-men[3]
**rh** slaughtermen *1H6 3.3.74*

**countrywoman** *n*
'kɤntrəɪˌwʊmən
**sp** country-woman[1]
> woman

**count·y / ~ies** *n*
'kəʊntəɪ / -z
**sp** countie[2], county[3] / counties[4]

**Count·y / ~y's / ~ies** [*title*] *n*
'kəʊntəɪ / -z
**sp** Countie[20], County[2] / Counties[1] / Counties[1]

**couper** *Fr v*
ku'pe
**sp** couppes[1]

**couper la** *Fr v + det*
*Pistol H5 2.1.68, 4.4.37*
'ku:pələ
**sp** couple[1], cuppele[1]

**couple / ~s** *n*
'kɤpəl / -z
**sp** couple[10] / couples[4]
> uncouple

**couple / ~s / ~ed** *v*
'kɤpəl / -z / -d
**sp** couple[5] / couples[1] / coupled[6], cou-pled[1]

**couplement** *n*
'kɤpəlmənt
**sp** cupplement[1]

**couplet** *n*
'kɤplət
**sp** couplet[1]

**cour** *Fr n*
kuːɹ
**sp** court

**courage / ~s** *n*
ˈkɤrɪʤ / -ɪz
**sp** corage[1], courage[63], cou-rage[2] / courages[1]
**rh** forage *VA 556*

**couragious** *adj*
kəˈrɛːʤɪəs
**sp** coragious[1], coragi-ous[1], couragious[7], couragi-ous[1]

**couragiously** *adv*
*m* kəˈrɛːʤɪəsˌləɪ, -sl-
**sp** couragiously[2]

**courier** *n*
ˈkɤrɪəɹ
**sp** currier[1]
> currier

**couronner / couronne** *Fr v*
kuˈrɒn
**sp** corrone[1]

**course / ~s** *n*
kɔːɹs / ˈkɔːɹsɪz
**sp** course[150], [maine]-course[1] / courses[13]

**cours·e / ~es / ~ing / ~ed** *v*
kɔːɹs / ˈkɔːɹs·ɪz / -ɪn, -ɪŋ / kɔːɹst
**sp** course[6] / courses[2] / coursing[1] / cours'd[1], courst[1]

**coursely** *adv*
ˈkɔːɹsləɪ
**sp** coursely[1]

**courser / ~'s / ~s** *n*
ˈkɔːɹsəɹ / -z
**sp** courser[2] / coursers[2] / coursers[3]

**coursing** *adj*
ˈkɔːɹsɪn, -ɪŋ
**sp** coursing[1]

**court / ~s** *n*
kɔːɹt / -s
**sp** court[221], court-[gate][1], courts [court is][1] / courts[7]
**rh** report *Cym 4.2.33*; sport *LLL 4.1.99*
> Inns of Court

**court / ~s / ~ed** *v*
kɔːɹt / -s / ˈkɔːɹtɪd
**sp** court[11] / courts[1] / courted[1]

**court-contempt** *n*
ˈkɔːɹt-kənˈtemt, -mpt
**sp** court-contempt[1]

**court-cupboard** *n*
ˈkɔːɹt-ˈkɤbəɹd
**sp** court-cubbord[1]

**courteous** *adj*
ˈkɔːɹtjəs
**sp** courteous[13], curteous[8]
> uncourteous

**courteously** *adv*
*m* ˈkɔːɹtjəsˌləɪ, -sl-
**sp** curteously[2]

**courtesan / ~'s / ~s** *n*
*m* ˈkɔːɹtɪzən, -ˌzan / -ˌzanz
**sp** courtezan[1], courtizan[2], curtezan[1], curtizan[3] / courtizans[1] / curtezans[1], curtizans[1]

**courtes·y / ~ies** *n*
*m* ˈkɔːɹtəˌsəɪ, -tsəɪ / -z
**sp** courtesie[22], court'sie[1], curtesie[39] / courtesies[4], courte-sies[1], curtesies[4]
**rh** comedy *LLL 5.2.864*; he *LLL 5.2.324*; immediately *1H4 5.5.32*; injury *MND 3.2.147*; modesty *MND 2.2.62*; remedy *1H6 2.2.58* / **rh** *1* bees, dewberries, mulberries *MND 3.1.169*; **rh** *2* arise, butterflies, eyes, thighs *MND 3.1.169*
> dis-, kill-courtesy

**court-hand** *n*
ˈkɔːɹt-ˌand, -ˌha-
**sp** court hand[1]

**courtier / ~'s / ~s / ~s'** *n*
ˈkɔːɹtɪəɹ / -z
**sp** courtier[27] / courtiers[5] / courtiers[11] / courtiers[1]

**court-like** *adj*
ˈkɔːɹt-ləɪk
**sp** court-like[1]

**courtly** *adj*
ˈkɔːɹtləɪ
**sp** courtly[7]

**Courtney** *n*
ˈkɔːɹtnəɪ
**sp** Courtney[1]

**court-odour** *n*
ˈkɔːɹt-ˈoːdəɹ
**sp** court-odour[1]
> odour

**courtship** *n*
ˈkɔːɹtʃɪp
**sp** courtship[8]

**court-word** *n*
ˈkɔːɹt-ˈwɔːɹd
**sp** court-word[1]
> word

**cousin,** *abbr* **coz / ~'s / ~s** *n*
ˈkɤzən, ˈkʊz-, *abbr* kɤz, kʊz / -z
**sp** coosin[5], cosen[30], cosin[71], co-sin[1], cosine[12], cosin's [cousin is][1], cousen[1], cousin[101], couzen[1], cozen[23], cozin[12], *abbr* cooz[1], cooze[1], couze[3], coz[19], coze[10] / cosens[2], cosins[4], cousins[1] / coo-sins[1], cosens[2], cosins[5], co-sins[1], cousins[7], cozens[2], cozins[3]
**pun** *R3 4.4.223* cozen
> cater-cousin

**cousin-german / ~s** *n*
ˌkɤzən-ˈʤɐːɹmən, ˌkʊz- / -z
**sp** cousen german[1] / cozen-iermans[1]
> german

**cout**
> scout

**coutume** *Fr n*
kuˈtym
**sp** *emend of H5 5.2.256* costume[1]

**covenant / ~s** *n*
*m* 'kʏvnənt, -və,nant; kɒv- / -s
**sp** couenant[3], cou'nant[1] / couenants[4]

**covent** *n*
'kɒvənt
**sp** couent[2]
> convent

**Coventry** *n*
'kɒvən,tri:
**sp** Couentree[2], Couentrie[1], Couentry[7]
**rh** me *R2 1.2.56*

**cover** *n*
'kʏvəɹ
**sp** couer[7]
**rh** lover *RJ 1.3.89*

**cover / ~s / ~ing / ~ed** *v*
'kʏvəɹ / -z / -ɪn, -ɪŋ, 'kʏvr- / 'kʏvəɹd
**sp** couer[17]/ couers[4] / couering[2] couer'd[10] / couered[5]
**rh** lover *S 32.2* / lovers [*F at* LLL 2.1.113-129] / **rh** *1* lovered *LC 317*; **rh** *2* hovered *LC 317*
> overcovered, uncover

**covering** *adj / n*
'kʏvərɪn, -ɪŋ, -vr-
**sp** couering[2] / couering[1]

**coverlet** *n*
'kʏvəɹlət
**sp** couerlet[1]

**covert / ~est** *adj*
'kʏvəɹt / -st
**sp** couert[3] / couertst[1]

**covert** *n*
'kʏvəɹt
**sp** couert[4]

**covertly** *adv*
'kʏvəɹtləɪ
**sp** couertly[1]

**coverture** *n*
'kʏvəɹtəɹ
**sp** couerture[2]

**covet / ~s / ~ing / ~ed** *v*
'kʏvət / -s / -ɪn, -ɪŋ / -ɪd
**sp** couet[3] / couets[1] / coueting[1] / coueted[1]

**coveting / ~s** *n*
'kʏvətɪnz, -ɪŋz
**sp** couetings[1]

**covetous** *adj*
*m* 'kʏvə,tʏs, -ətəs
**sp** couetous[7], co-uetous[1]

**covetously** *adv*
'kʏvtəsləɪ, -vət-
**sp** couetously[1]

**covetousness** *n*
*m* 'kʏvtəsnəs, -,nes, -vət-
**sp** couetousnesse[4]

**cow / ~'s** *n*
kəʊ, ko: / -z
**sp** cow[7] / cowes[1]
**rh** low *MA 5.4.49*

**cow / ~ed** *v*
kəʊd, ko:d
**sp** cow'd[1]

**coward / ~'s / ~s** *n*
*m* 'kəʊəɹd, ko:ɹd / -z
**sp** coward[82], coward-[iack-priest] / cowards[1] / cowards[29]
**rh** froward VA 569; toward *VA 1158*

**coward / ~ed** *v*
*m* 'kəʊəɹdɪd, ko:ɹ-
**sp** cowarded[1]

**cowardice** *n*
*m* 'kəʊɹdɪs, 'ko:ɹ-
**sp** cowardice[5], cowardise[4], cow-ardise[1], cowardize[5], cowar-dize[1]

**cowardly** *adj / adv*
*m* 'kəʊəɹd,ləɪ, -dl-, 'ko:ɹd-
**sp** cowardly[13] / cowardly[4]

**cowardship** *n*
'kəʊɹdʃɪp, 'ko:ɹ-
**sp** coward-ship[1]

**cow-dung** *n*
'kəʊ-,dʏŋ, 'ko:-
**sp** cow-dung[1]
> dung

**cower / ~ed** *v*
kəʊɹd, ko:ɹd
**sp** cowr'd[1]

**cowish** *adj*
'kəʊɪʃ, 'ko:-
**sp** cowish[1]

**cowl-staff** *n*
'kəʊl-,staf, 'ko:l-
**sp** cowle-staffe[1]

**cowslip / ~'s / ~s** *n*
'kəʊslɪp, 'ko:- / -s
**sp** cowslip[2], cowslippe[1] / cowslips[2] / cowslippes[1], cowslips[1]

**coxcomb / ~s** *n*
'kɒkskəm, *Evans MW 3.1.81* 'kɒgzkəm / -z
**sp** coxcombe[17], cox-combe[1], coxecombe[1], coxe-combe[1], *Evans* cogs-combe[1] / coxcombes[2], cox-combes[1], coxcombs[1]

**coy** *adj*
kəɪ
**sp** coy[4]
**rh** boy *VA 96*

**coy / ~ed** *v*
kəɪ / -d
**sp** coy[1] / coy'd[1]
**rh** joy *MND 4.1.2*

**coying** *n*
'kəɪɪn, -ɪŋ
**sp** coying[1]

**cozen / ~ing / ~ed** *v*
'kʏzən, 'kʊz- / -ɪn, -ɪŋ, -zn- / -d
**sp** cosen[3], cousen[1], cozen[1] / cozening[1] / cosen'd[1], cousend[1], cousen'd[1], couzend[1], cozend[2], cozen'd[1], cozened[1], cozond[2], cozon'd[1], cozoned[2]
**pun** *R3 4.4.223* cousin

**cozenage** *n*
*m* 'kɤzənɪʤ, 'kʊz-, -zn-, -nɑ:ʤ
**sp** coozenage[1], cosenage[1], cozonage[2]

**cozened** *adj*
'kɤzənd, 'kʊz-
**sp** cosin'd[1]

**cozener / ~s** *n*
'kɤzənəɹ, 'kʊz-, -zn- / -z
**sp** cozener[1] / couzeners[1], cozeners[1], cozoners[1]

**cozening** *adj*
'kɤzənɪn, -ɪŋ, 'kʊz-, -zn-
**sp** couzening[2], cozening[1]

**cozier / ~s'** *n*
'ko:zɪəɹz
**sp** cozi-ers[1]

**crab / ~s** *n*
=
**sp** crab[6], crabbe[1], crabbe's [crab is][1] / crabs[2]
**rh** bob *MND 2.1.48*

**Crab** [name] *n*
=
**sp** Crab[3]

**crabbed** *adj*
*m* krabd, 'krabɪd
**sp** crabbed[3]

**crab-tree / ~s** *n*
=
**sp** crab-tree[2] / crab-trees[1]
> tree

**crack / ~s** *n*
=
**sp** crack[2], cracke[9] / cracks[2]

**crack / ~s / ~ing / ~ed** *v*
= / = / 'krakɪn, -ɪŋ / =
**sp** crack[4], cracke[13], crake[1] / cracks[1] / cracking[5] / crack'd[11], crackt[2], crak'd[1]
**rh** back *KJ 2.1.146*; black *LLL 4.3.266*

**cracked** *adj*
=
**sp** crack'd[4]

**cracker** *n*
'krakəɹ
**sp** cracker[1]
> wit-cracker

**crackhemp** *n*
'krakˌemp, -ˌhemp
**sp** crackhempe[1]

**cradle / ~'s / ~s** *n*
'krɛ:dl / -z
**sp** cradle[12] / cradles[1] / cradles[2]

**cradle / ~d** *v*
'krɛ:dld
**sp** cradled

**cradle-babe** *n*
'krɛ:dl-ˌbɛ:b
**sp** cradle-babe[1]
> babe

**cradle-clothes** *n*
'krɛ:dl-ˌklo:ðz
**sp** cradle-clothes[1]
> clothes

**craft / ~s** *n*
kraft / -s
**sp** craft[17] / crafts[2]
**rh** daffed, daft *LC 295*
> handi-, witch-craft

**craft / ~ed** *v*
'kraftɪd
**sp** crafted[1]

**craftily** *adv*
'kraftɪləɪ
**sp** craftily[1]

**crafts·man / ~men** *n*
'kraftsmən
**sp** craftes-men[1]

**crafts-master** *n*
'krafts-ˌmastəɹ
**sp** crafts-master[1]
> master

**craft·y / ~ier** *adj*
'kraftəɪ / -əɹ
**sp** craftie[8], crafty[5] / craftier[1]
> outcrafty

**cram / ~s / ~med** *v*
=
**sp** *v* cram[3], cramme[2], cram's [cram us][1] / crams[1] / cram'd[5], cramm'd[2]

**crammed** *adj*
=
**sp** cramm'd[1]
> news-, promise-crammed

**cramp / ~s** *n*
=
**sp** cramp[1], crampe[2] / crampes[1], cramps[2]

**crank / ~s** *n*
=
**sp** crankes[1]

**crank / ~ing** *v*
'kraŋkɪn, -ɪŋ
**sp** cranking[1]

**Cranmer** *n*
'kranməɹ
**sp** Cranmer[12], Cranmer's [Cranmer is][1]

**crannied** *adj*
'kranəɪd
**sp** crannied[1]

**crann·y / ~ies** *n*
'kranəɪ / -z
**sp** cranny[2] / crannies[1]

**crash** *n*
=
**sp** crash[1]

**crasing** *n*
'krɛ:zɪn, -ɪŋ
**sp** crasing[1]

**Crassus / ~'** *n*
'krasəs
**sp** Crassus[2] / Crassus[1]

**crav·e / ~s / ~eth / ~ing / ~ed** *v*
krɛ:v, krav / -z / ˈkrɛ:v·əθ, ˈkrav- / -ɪn, -ɪŋ / *m* -d, -ɪd
**sp** craue[41] / craues[22] / craueth[1] / crauing[4] / crau'd[2], craued[1]
**rh** *1* grave *Per 2.1.11, 2.3.47*; rave, slave *Luc 985*; slave *S 58.3*; wave *VA 88*; **rh** *2* have *PP 10.9*; crave her have her *MW 4.4.88*

**craven** *adj*
ˈkrɛ:vən, ˈkrav-
**sp** crauen[1]

**craven / ~'s** *n*
ˈkrɛ:vən, ˈkrav- / -z
**sp** crauen[2] / cravens[1]

**craven / ~s** *v*
ˈkrɛ:vənz, ˈkrav-
**sp** crauens[1]

**crawl / ~ing / ~ed** *v*
= / ˈkrɔ:lɪn, -ɪŋ / =
**sp** crawle[2] / crawling[1] / crawl'd[1]

**crawling** *adj*
ˈkrɔ:lɪn, -ɪŋ
**sp** crawling[1]

**craze / ~d** *v*
*m* ˈkrɛ:zd
**sp** craz'd[2]

**crazed** *adj*
*m* krɛ:zd, ˈkrɛ:zɪd
**sp** craz'd[1], crazed[1]

**crazy** *adj*
ˈkrɛ:zəɪ
**sp** crasie[1]

**creak / ~ing** *v*
ˈkri:kɪn, -ɪŋ
**sp** creeking[1]

**creaking** *n*
ˈkri:kɪn, -ɪŋ
**sp** creaking[1]

**cream** *n / v*
=
**sp** creame[4] / creame[1]

**cream-faced** *adj*
ˈkri:m-ˌfɛ:st
**sp** cream-fac'd[1]
> face

**creat·e / ~es / ~ing / ~ed** *v*
kri:ˈɛ:t / -s / -ɪn, -ɪŋ / -ɪd
**sp** create[18], create [created][3] / creates[1] / creating[1] / created[16]
**rh** *1* fortunate *MND 5.1.395* / **rh** *2* hate *RJ 1.1.177* / defeated *S 20.9*
> miscreate, part-created

**creating** *adj / n*
kri:ˈɛ:tɪn, -ɪŋ
**sp** creating-[nature][1] / creating[2]

**creation** *n*
kri:ˈɛ:sɪən
**sp** creation[8]

**creator / ~'s** *n*
kri:ˈɛ:təɹ / -z
**sp** creator[1] / creators[1]

**creature / ~'s / ~s** *n*
ˈkrɛ:təɹ, ˈkri:- / -z
**sp** creature[64], cre-ature[2], creature's [creature is][2], [good]-creature[1] / creatures[1] / creatures[37]
**rh** feature *S 113.10*

**Crécy** *n*
ˈkresi:
**sp** Cressy[1]

**credence** *n*
=
**sp** credence[3]

**credent** *adj*
=
**sp** credent[3]

**credible** *adj*
=
**sp** credible[1]

**credit** *n / v*
=
**sp** credit[30], credite[10] / creadit[1], credit[6], cre-dit[1], credite[1]
> discredit

**creditor / ~s** *n*
*m* ˈkredɪtəɹ, -ˌtɔ:ɹ / -z
**sp** creditor[5], creditour[1] / creditors[6], credi-tors[1]

**credo** *Lat v*
ˈkrɛ:do:
**sp** credo[4]

**credulity** *n*
*m* kreˈdju:lɪˌtəɪ
**sp** credulitie[1]

**credulous** *adj*
*m* ˈkredjəˌlɤs, -jələs, -dləs
**sp** creadulous[1], credulous[7]
**rh** ridiculous *VA 986*
> overcredulous

**creed** *n*
=
**sp** creede[1]

**creek / ~s** *n*
=
**sp** creeke[1], creekes[1]

**creep / ~s / ~ing / crept** *v*
= / = / ˈkri:pɪn, -ɪŋ / =
**sp** creep[1], creepe[24] / creepes[5] / creeping[2] / crept[16]
**rh** peep, sleep *Luc 1248*; sleep *MND 3.2.365* / sleeps *Luc 1575* / kept *Luc 839*; slept *TC 2.2.213*

**creeping** *adj*
ˈkri:pɪn, -ɪŋ
**sp** creeping[6]

**crescent** *adj / n*
ˈkresənt
**sp** cressant[1], cressent[2] / crescent[1]

**crescive** *adj*
=
**sp** cressiue[1]

**cresset / ~s** *n*
=
**sp** cressets[1]

**Cressid / ~'s / ~s / -a / ~a's** *n*
'kresɪd / -z / -z / 'kresɪdə / -z
**sp** Cressed[2], Cressid[34] / Cresseds[1], Cressids[4] / Cressids[1] / Cressida[15] / Cressidas[1]

**crest / ~s** *n*
=
**sp** crest[21] / crests[3]
**rh** blest *MW 5.5.63*; breast *VA 395*; jest *VA 104*
> under-crest

**crest / ~ed** *v*
=
**sp** crested[1]

**crestfallen** *adj*
'krestfɑ:ln
**sp** crest-falne[3]
> fallen

**crestless** *adj*
=
**sp** crestlesse[1]

**Cretan** *adj*
=
**sp** Cretan[1]

**Crete** *n*
=
**sp** Creet[3], Creete[2]
**rh** sweet *1H6 4.6.54*

**crevice** *n*
=
**sp** creuice[1]

**crew / ~s** *n*
=
**sp** crew[8] / crewes[1]
**rh** drew, threw *Luc 1731*

**crew** *v*
=
**sp** crew[2]

**crib / ~s** *n*
=
**sp** crib[1] / cribs[1]

**crib / ~bed** *v*
=
**sp** crib'd[1]

**cricket / ~'s / ~s** *n*
=
**sp** cricket[2] / crickets[1] / crickets[4]

**crier** *n*
'krəɪəɹ
**sp** crier[1], cryer[1]
> cry

**crime / ~s** *n*
krəɪm / -z
**sp** crime[7], cryme[1] / crimes[15], crymes[2]
**rh** climb, time *Luc 772*; clime *Per 4.4.5*; time *Luc 931, 993, S 19.8, 58.12, 120.8, 124.14, WT 4.1.4* / sometimes *LLL 4.1.31*; times *MM 3.2.261*

**crimeful** *adj*
'krəɪmfʊl
**sp** crimefull[1]

**crimeless** *adj*
'krəɪmləs
**sp** crimelesse[1]

**criminal** *adj*
'krɪmɪˌnɑl
**sp** criminall[3]

**crimson** *adj / n*
=
**sp** crimson[10] / crimson[1], crymson[1]

**crimson / ~ed** *v*
=
**sp** crimson'd[1]

**cringe** *v*
=
**sp** crindge[1]

**cripple** *adj / n / v*
=
**sp** creeple-[tardy-gated][1] / cripple[3] / cripple[2]

**crisp** *adj*
=
**sp** crispe[2], crispe-[head][1]

**Crispian** *n*
*m* 'krɪspɪˌan
**sp** Crispian[4]

**Crispianus** *n*
ˌkrɪspɪ'anəs
**sp** Crispianus[1]

**Crispin / ~'s** *n*
=
**sp** Crispin[1], Crispine[1] / Crispines[1]

**critic / ~s** *n*
=
**sp** criticke[1], critticke[1] / criticks[1]

**critical** *adj*
*m* 'krɪtɪˌkɑl
**sp** criticall[2]

**croak / ~s** *v*
kro:k / -s
**sp** croke[1] / croakes[1]

**croaking** *adj*
'kro:kɪn, -ɪŋ
**sp** croaking[1]

**crocodile** *n*
*m* 'krɒkəˌdəɪl, -kəd-
**sp** crocodile[5]

**Cromer** *n*
'kro:məɹ
**sp** Cromer[1]

**Cromwell** *n*
=
**sp** Cromwel[9], Cromwell[13]

**crone** *n*
kro:n
**sp** croane[1]

**crook** *v*
=
**sp** crooke[1]

**crook-back** *adj / n*
=
**sp** crook-back[1] / crooke-back[1], crooke-backe[1]
> back

**crooked** *adj*
*m* krʊkt, 'krʊkɪd
**sp** crook'd[2], crook'd-[wayes][1], crooked[10]
> low-crooked

**crooked-pated** *adj*
'krʊkɪd-'pɛ:tɪd
**sp** crooked-pated[1]

**crook-kneed** *adj*
=
**sp** crooke kneed[1]
> knee

**crop / *Luc* ~s** *n*
=
**sp** crop[5] / crops[1]
**rh** water-drops *Luc 958*

**crop / ~ped** *v*
=
**sp** crop[4] / cropt[7]
> uncropped

**crop-ear** *n*
'krɒp-ˌi:ɹ
**sp** crop eare[1]
> ear

**Crosby** *n*
'krɒzbəɪ
**sp** Crosbie[1], Crosby[2]

**cross** *adj / adv*
=
**sp** crosse[5] / crosse[1]

**cross / ~es** *n*
=
**sp** crosse[15] / crosses[7]
**rh** loss *S 34.12, 42.12*

**cross / ~est / ~ing / ~ed** *v*
= / = / 'krɒsɪn, -ɪŋ / =
**sp** crosse[37] / crossest[1] / crossing[5] / cross'd[4], crossed[1], crost[19]
**rh** after-loss *S 90.2*; loss *1H6 4.3.52* / **rh** *1* lost *MV 2.5.54*; **rh** *2* engrossed *S 133.8*
> uncrossed

**crossbow / ~s** *n*
*m* krɒs'bo: / 'krɒsbo:z
**sp** crosse-bow[1] / crosse-bowes[2]

**cross-gartered** *adj*
ˌkrɒs-'gɑ:ɹtəɹd
**sp** crosse garter'd[6], crosse-garter'd[2]
> garter

**cross-gartering** *n*
ˌkrɒs-'gɑ:ɹtrɪn, -ɪŋ, -tər-
**sp** crosse-gartering[1]

**crossing / ~s** *n*
'krɒsɪnz, -ɪŋz
**sp** crossings[1]

**crossly** *adv*
'krɒsləɪ
**sp** crossely[1]

**crossness** *n*
=
**sp** crosseness[1]

**cross-row** *n*
'krɒs-ˌro:
**sp** crosse-row[1]

**crossway / ~s** *n*
*m* ˌkrɒs'wɛ:z
**sp** crosse-waies[1]

**crotchet / ~s** *n*
=
**sp** crochets[3], crotchets[1]

**crouch** *v*
krəʊtʃ
**sp** crouch[2], crowch[1]

**crouching** *adj*
'krəʊtʃɪn, -ɪŋ
**sp** crouching[1]

**crow / ~s** *n*
kro: / -z
**sp** crow[18] / crowes[15], crows[1]
**rh** go *PT 17*; show *RJ 1.2.86*; snow *MND 3.2.142, WT 4.4.221*; so *CE 3.1.80, 84, MND 2.1.267, Per 4. Chorus.32* / shows *RJ 1.5.48*
> night-, scare-crow

**crow / ~ing / ~ed** *v*
kro: / 'kro:ɪn, -ɪŋ / kro:d
**sp** crow[8] / crowing[1] / crow'd[1]
> overcrow

**crowd** *n*
krəʊd
**sp** crowd[1]

**crowd / ~ing / ~ed** *v*
krəʊd / 'krəʊd·ɪn, -ɪŋ / -ɪd
**sp** crowd[3] / crowding[2] / crowded[1]

**crow-flower / ~s** *n*
'kro:-ˌflo:ɹz
**sp** crow-flowers[1]
> flower

**crowing** *n*
'kro:ɪn, -ɪŋ
**sp** crowing[1]

**crow-keeper** *n*
'kro:-ˌki:pəɹ
**sp** crow-keeper[2]
> keep

**crown / ~s** *n*
krəʊn / -z
**sp** crown[5], crowne[225], [French]-crowne[1] / crownes[55], crowns[2]
**rh** down *Cym 3.5.66, 2H4 3.1.31, 2H6 1.1.256, 3H6 3.2.194, 4.6.99, Luc 216, R2 3.4.65, 4.1.193, 5.1.24*; down, lown, renown *Oth 2.3.85*; drown *3H6 4.4.24*; frown *3H6 4.5.29*; renown *AW 4.4.35*; town *AY 5.4.138*
> French-crown-coloured

**crown / ~s / ~ed** *v*
krəʊn / -z / *m* -d, 'krəʊnɪd
**sp** crown[2], crowne[19] / crownes[5] / crownd[1], crown'd[39], crowned[13]
**rh** down *Tem 4.1.80* / confound *S 60.6, 69.5*; drowned, round *AC 2.7.114*
> uncrown

**crowned** *adj*
*m* krəʊnd, 'krəʊnɪd
**sp** crown'd[3], crowned[1]
> new-, thrice-crowned

**crowner / ~'s** *n*
'krəʊnəɹ / -z
**sp** crowner[2] / crowners[1]

**crownet / ~s** *n*
'krəʊnət / -s
**sp** crownet[1] / crownets[2]

**crowning** *n*
'krəʊnɪn, -ɪŋ
**sp** crowning[1]

**crown's-worth** *n*
'krəʊnz-ˌwɔːɹθ
**sp** crownes-worth[1]
> worth

**crudy** *adj*
'krɤdəɪ
**sp** cruddie[1]

**cruel / ~ler / ~lest** *adj*
'kruːəl / -əɹ / -st
**sp** cruell[62] / crueller[3] / cruell'st[1]
**rh** fuel *S 1.8*; jewel *S 131.2*

**cruel / ~s** *n*
'kruːəlz
**sp** cruels[1]

**cruel-hearted** *adj*
'kruːəl-ˌɑːɹtɪd, -ˌhɑː-
**sp** cruell-hearted[1]

**cruelly** *adv*
'kruːələɪ
**sp** cruelly[3], cruel-ly[1]

**cruelty** *n*
*m* 'kruːəlˌtəɪ, -ltəɪ
**sp** crueltie[9], cruelty[11]
**rh** *1* be *TN 1.5.277*; **rh** *2* I *MND 3.2.59*

**crumb / ~s** *n*
krɤm / -z
**sp** crum[1] / crums[1]
**rh** mum, some *KL 1.4.193*

**crumble** *v*
'krɤmbəl
**sp** crumble[1]

**crupper** *n*
'krɤpəɹ
**sp** crupper[3]

**crusado / ~s** *n*
krʊ'zadoːz
**sp** cruzadoes[1]

**crush / ~est / ~ed** *v*
krɤʃ / 'krɤʃəst / krɤʃt
**sp** crush[12] / cru-shest[1] / crush'd[1], crusht[2]

**crushed** *adj*
krɤʃt
**sp** crush'd[1]

**crushing** *adj*
'krɤʃɪn, -ɪŋ
**sp** crushing[1]

**crust / ~s** *n*
krɤst / -s
**sp** crust[3] / crusts[1]

**crust** *v*
krɤst
**sp** crust[1]

**crusty** *adj*
'krɤstəɪ
**sp** crusty[1]

**crutch / ~es** *n*
krɤʧ / 'krɤʧɪz
**sp** crutch[11] / crutches[4]

**cry / cries** *n*
krəɪ / -z
**sp** crie[2], cry[22] / cries[41], cryes[1]
**rh** *1* lustily *VA 870*; **rh** *2* I *R2 5.3.74* / eyes *Luc 1459, S 29.3*; eyes, lies *Luc 445*; eyes, surprise *Luc 165*
> outcry; crier, town-crier

**cry / ~est / ~cries / ~ing / cried / criedest** *v*
krəɪ / -st / -z / 'krəɪɪn, -ɪŋ / krəɪd / -st
**sp** crie[14], cry[169], crye[1] / cri'st[1] / cries[7], cryes[8] / crying[26] / cride[17], cride-[game][1], cri'de[3], cried[13], cry'd[13], cryde[1], cry'de[8], cryed[10] / cried'st[1], cryedst[1]
**rh** *1* adversity *CE 2.1.35*; deity *Cym 5.4.88*; jollity *S 66.1*; merrily *Tem 5.1.90*; patiently *Luc 1639* / **rh** *2* by *PP 20.13*; die *LLL 5.2.255, TC 3.1.118*; fly *Cym 5.4.88*; fly, I, lie *Tem 5.1.90* / **rh** *1* enemies *Luc 677* / **rh** *2* eyes *LLL 4.3.139*; lies *Luc 1751*; tyrannize *Luc 677*

**crying** *adj / n*
'krəɪɪn, -ɪŋ
**sp** crying[3] / crying[5]

**crystal** *adj*
=
**sp** crystall[1], christall[7]

**crystal / ~s** *n*
=
**sp** christall[3] / chrystalls[1]

**crystalline** *adj*
*m* 'krɪstəˌləɪn
**sp** christalline[1]
**rh** confine, mine *Cym 5.4.113*

**cub / ~s** *n*
kɤb / -z
**sp** cub[1] / cubs[1]

**cubiculo** *n*
kjʊ'bɪkjʊloː
**sp** cubiculo[1]

**cubit** *n*
=
**sp** cubit[1]

**cuckold / ~'s / ~s** *n*
'kɤkəld / -z
**sp** cuckold[26] / cuckolds[2], cuck-olds[1] / cuckolds[4]

**cuckold** *v*
'kɤkəld
**sp** cuckold[3]
> uncuckold

**cuckoldly** *adj*
'kɤkəldləɪ
**sp** cuckoldly[3], cuckoldly-[rogues][1]

**cuckold-mad** *adj*
'kɤkəld-ˌmad
**sp** cuckold mad[1]
> mad

**cuckold-maker** *n*
'kɤkəld-ˌmɛːkəɹ
**sp** cuckold-maker[1], cuckold maker[1]
> make

**cuckoo / ~'s** *n*
'kɤkuː / -z
**sp** cuckoe[1], cuckoo[3], cuckow[15] / cuckowes[1]

**cuckoo-bird / ~s** *n*
'kɤkuː-ˌbɐːɹdz
**sp** cuckoo-birds[1]

**cuckoo-bud / ~s** *n*
'kɤkuː-ˌbɤdz
**sp** cuckow-buds[1]

**cucullus** *Lat n*
kʊ'kʊlʊs
**sp** cucullus[2]

**cudgel / ~s** *n*
'kɤʤəl / -z
**sp** cudgell[8], cud-gell[2] / cudgels[1], cud-gels[1]

**cudgel / ~led** *v*
'kɤʤəl / -d
**sp** cudgell[6] / cudgeld[2], cudgel'd[2], cudgell'd[1]

**cudgelled** *adj*
'kɤʤəld
**sp** cudgeld[1]

**cudgelling** *n*
'kɤʤəlɪn, -ɪŋ, -ʤl-
**sp** cudgelling[1]

**cue / ~s** *n*
=
**sp** cue[7] / cues[1]

**cuff / ~s** *n*
kɤf / -s
**sp** cuffe[2] / cuffes[2]

**cuff** *v*
kɤf
**sp** cuffe[3]

**cuique** *Lat pro*
'kuːiːkwe, -ke
**sp** *emend of Tit 1.1.283* cuiquam[1]

**cuishes** *n*
'kwɪʃɪz
**sp** cushes[1]

**cull / ~ing / ~ed** *v*
kɤl / 'kɤlɪn, -ɪŋ / kɤld
**sp** cull[5] / culling[3] / culd[2], cul'd[1], cull'd[2]

**culled** *adj*
kɤld
**sp** cul'd[1], cull'd[1]

**cullion / ~s** *n*
'kɤlɪən / -z
**sp** cullion[1] / cullions[2]

**cullionly** *adv*
'kɤlɪənləɪ
**sp** cullyenly[1]

**culpable** *adj*
*m* 'kɤlpəˌbɤl
**sp** culpable[1]

**culter** *n*
'kɤltəɹ
**sp** culter[1]

**culverin** *n*
*m* 'kɤlvəˌrɪn
**sp** culuerin[1]

**cum** *Lat prep*
kʊm
**sp** cum[3], cum[alijs][1]

**cumber** *v*
'kɤmbəɹ
**sp** cumber[2]

**Cumberland** *n*
*m* 'kɤmbəɹˌland
**sp** Cumberland[4]

**cunning / ~est** *adj*
'kɤnɪn, -ɪŋ / -st
**sp** cunning[36] / cunning'st[1]

**cunning** *n*
'kɤnɪn, -ɪŋ
**sp** cunning[32], cun-ning[1], *emend of TC 3.2.130* comming[1]
**rh** wooing *TS 2.1.404*

**cunningly** *adv*
'kɤnɪnˌləɪ, -ɪŋ-
**sp** cunningly[4]

**cuore** *Ital n*
'kwɔːreː
**sp** core[1]

**cup / ~s** *n*
kɤp / -s
**sp** cup[41], cuppe[3] / cuppes[1], cups[8]
**rh** up *S 114.12*
> sneak-cup

**cup** *v*
kɤp
**sp** cup[2]

**cup-bearer** *n*
'kɤp-ˌbɛːrəɹ
**sp** cup-bearer[2]
> bearer

**cupboard / ~ing** *v*
'kɤbəɹˌdɪn, -ɪŋ
**sp** cubbording[1]

**Cupid / ~'s / ~s** *n*
'kjɤpɪd / -z
**sp** Cupid[33], Cupid's [Cupid is][1] / Cupids[17] / Cupids[2]

**cuplet** *n*
'kɤplət
**sp** cuplet[1]

**cur / ~s** *n*
kɐːɹ / -z
**sp** cur[8], curre[24] / curres[11], curs[3]

**Curan** *n*
'kɤrən
**sp** Curan[2]

**curate** *n*
=
**sp** curate[6]

**curb / ~s** *n*
kɐ:ɹb / -z
**sp** curbe[3] / curbes[2]

**curb / ~s / ~ing / ~ed** *v*
kɐ:ɹb / -z / 'kɐ:ɹbɪn, -ɪŋ / kɐ:ɹbd
**sp** courb[1], curb[1], curbe[4] / curbes[2] / curbing[1] / curb'd[2]
> uncurbable

**curbed** *adj*
*m* kɐ:ɹbd, 'kɐ:ɹbɪd
**sp** curb'd[1], curbed[1]
> uncurbed

**curd / ~s** *n*
kɐ:ɹdz
**sp** curds[3]

**curd** *v*
kɐ:ɹd
**sp** curd[2]

**curd·y / ~ied** *v*
'kɐ:ɹdəɪd
**sp** curdied[1]

**cure** *n*
kju:ɹ
**sp** cure[24]
**rh** endure *MA 4.1.250, S 153.8, VA 505*; sure *AW 2.1.158*
> past-cure

**cur·e / ~es / ~ing / ~ed** *v*
kju:ɹ / -z / 'kju:rɪn, -ɪŋ / kju:ɹd
**sp** cure[23] / cures[7] / curing[1] / cur'd[10], cured[2]
**rh** cure thee assure thee *VA 372* / assured *S 118.12*; endured *Luc 1581*
> uncurable

**cureless** *adj*
'kju:ɹləs
**sp** curelesse[1]

**curer** *n*
'kju:rəɹ
**sp** curer[3]
> body-, soul-curer

**curfew** *adj / n*
'kɐ:ɹfju:
**sp** curphew[1] / curfew[1], curfewe[1], curphew[1]

**curing** *n*
'kju:rɪn, -ɪŋ
**sp** curing[1]

**Curio** *n*
'kju:rɪo:
**sp** Curio[6]

**curiosity** *n*
*m* ˌkju:rɪ'ɒsɪˌtəɪ, -ɪt-
**sp** curiositie[1], curio-sitie[1], curiosity[2]

**curious** *adj*
*m* 'kju:rɪəs, -ɪˌɤs
**sp** curious[11]

**curiously** *adv*
'kju:rɪəsləɪ
**sp** curiously[3], cu-riously[1]

**curl / ~s** *n*
kɐ:ɹlz
**sp** curls[2]
**rh** hurls *LC 85*
> uncurl

**curl / ~ed / ~ing** *v*
'kɐ:ɹlɪn, -ɪŋ / kɐ:ɹld
**sp** curling[1] / curl'd[1]

**curled** *adj*
*m* kɐ:ɹld, 'kɐ:ɹlɪd
**sp** curld[1], curl'd[1], curled[3]

**curled-pate** *adj*
'kɐ:ɹld-ˌpɛ:t
**sp** curl'd pate[1]
> pate

**currance** *n*
'kɤrəns
**sp** currance[1]

**currant** *adj*
'kɤɹənt
**sp** currant[11], cur-rant[1]
> uncurrant

**currant / ~s** *n*
'kɤɹənt / -s, 'kɤɹəns
**sp** currant[5], current[8] / currence[1], currants[2], currents[3]

**currier / ~s** *n*
'kɤrɪəɹz
**sp** curriors[1]
> courier, vaunt-currier

**currish** *adj*
'kɐ:rɪʃ
**sp** currish[5]

**curry** *v*
'kɤrəɪ
**sp** currie[1]

**curs·e / ~es** *n*
kɐ:ɹs / 'kɐ:ɹsɪz
**sp** curse[49], cursse[2] / curses[28], cursses[1]
**rh** worse *R2 3.4.103, S 84.13*

**curs·e / ~es / ~ing / ~ed** *v*
kɐ:ɹs / 'kɐ:ɹs·ɪz / -ɪn, -ɪŋ / kɐ:ɹst
**sp** curse[47], cursse[1] / curses[1] / cursing[4] / curs'd[5], curst[5], cur'st[1]
**rh** worse *CE 4.2.28, MND 3.2.46, R3 4.4.123*
> a-cursing, uncurse

**cursed / ~est** *adj*
*m* 'kɐ:ɹsɪd / -st
**sp** cursed[33] / cursed'st[1]

**curselary** *adj*
'kɐ:ɹsəˌlarəɪ
**sp** curselarie[1]

**cursing** *adj*
'kɐ:ɹsɪn, -ɪŋ
**sp** cursing[2]

**curst / ~er / ~est** *adj*
kɐːɹst / ˈkɐːɹst·əɹ / -əst
**sp** curst[27] / curster[1] / curstest[1]
**rh** first *VA 887*

**curst** *n*
kɐːɹst
**sp** curst[3]
**rh** worst *TS 1.2.127*

**curstness** *n*
ˈkɐːɹstnəs
**sp** curstnesse[1]

**curtail / ~ed** *v*
kəɹˈtɛːl / -d
**sp** curtall[1] / curtail'd[1]

**curtain / ~s** *n*
ˈkɐːɹtən / -z
**sp** curtain[2], curtaine[12] / curtaines[6], cur-taines[1]

**curtain / ~ed** *v*
ˈkɐːɹtənd
**sp** curtain'd[1]

**curtained** *adj*
ˈkɐːɹtənd
**sp** curtain'd[1]

**curtal** *adj*
ˈkɐːɹtl
**sp** curtall[1], curtall-[dog][1], curtull[1]

**Curtis** *n*
ˈkɐːɹtɪs
**sp** Curtis[8]

**curtle-axe** *n*
ˈkɐːɹtl-ˌaks
**sp** curtelax[1], curtleax[1]

**curts·y / ~ies** *n*
ˈkɐːɹtsəɪ / -z
**sp** cursie[3], curtsie[5], curt'sie[3], curt-sie[2] / cursies[2], curtsies[3], [low-crooked]-curtsies[1]

**curts·y / ~ies / ~ied** *v*
ˈkɐːɹtsəɪ / -z / -d
**sp** cursie[2], curtsie[4], curt'sie[2] / curtsies[2] / curtsied[1]

**curvet** *n*
ˈkɐːɹvət
**sp** curuet[1]

**curvet / ~s** *v*
ˈkɐːɹvəts
**sp** curuettes[1]

**cushion / ~s** *n*
ˈkʊʃɪən / -z
**sp** cushion[7] / cushions[6]

**custalorum** *Lat n*
ˌkʊstəˈlɔːrʊm
**sp** cust-alorum[1]

**custard** *n*
ˈkɤstəɹd
**sp** custard[1]

**custard-coffin** *n*
ˈkɤstəɹd-ˌkɒfɪn
**sp** custard coffen[1]
> coffin

**custody** *n*
*m* ˈkɤstəˌdəɪ
**sp** custodie[3]
**rh** die *CE 1.1.156*

**custom / ~s** *n*
ˈkɤstəm / -z
**sp** custome[42] / customes[3], customs[1]

**customary** *adj*
*m* ˈkɤstəˌmarəɪ, -əmərəɪ, -əmrəɪ
**sp** customarie[4], customary[2]

**customed** *adj*
*m* ˈkɤstəmd, -mɪd
**sp** custom'd[1], customed[1]
> accustomed, unac-customed

**customer / ~s** *n*
ˈkɤstəməɹ / -z
**sp** customer[2] / customers[3]

**custom-shrunk** *adj*
ˈkɤstəm-ˌʃrɤŋk
**sp** custom-shrunke[1]
> shrink

**custure** [*mock French by Pistol*]
kʊˈstuːreː
**sp** custure[1]

**cut** *adj*
kɤt
**sp** cut[1]

**cut / ~s** *n*
kɤt / -s
**sp** cut[9] / cuts[2]

**cut / ~test / ~s / ~ting** *v*
kɤt / -st / -s / ˈkɤtɪn, -ɪŋ
**sp** cut[160] / cut'st[1] / cuts[12] / cutting[5]

**Cut / ~'s** [name] *n*
kɤts
**sp** Cuts[1]

**cutler / ~'s** *n*
ˈkɤtləɹz
**sp** cutlers[1]

**cutpurse / ~s** *n*
ˈkɤtˌpɐːɹs / -ɪz
**sp** cutpurse[1], cut-purse[4] / cut-purses[1]
> purse

**cutter** *n*
ˈkɤtəɹ
**sp** cutter[1]
> stone-cutter

**cutter-off** *n*
ˌkɤtəɹ-ˈɒf
**sp** cutter off[1]

**cut-throat** *adj*
ˈkɤt-ˌθroːt
**sp** cut-throate[1]

**cut-throat / ~s** *n*
ˈkɤt-ˌθroːts
**sp** cut-throats[1]
> throat

**cutting** *n*
ˈkɤtɪn, -ɪŋ
**sp** cutting[2]

**cutting-short** *n*
'kɤtɪn-'ʃɔ:ɹt, -ɪŋ-
**sp** cutting short[1]

**cuttle** *n*
'kɤtl
**sp** cuttle[1]

**Cyclops / ~'** *n*
'sɪklɒps
**sp** Cyclops[2]

**Cydnus** *n*
'sɪdnəs
**sp** Sidnis[1], Sidnus[1], *emend of AC 5.2.228* Cidrus[1]

**cygnet / ~s** *n*
=
**sp** *emend of KJ 5.7.21* symet[1] / cignets[1], signets[1]

**cymbal / ~ s** *n*
'sɪmbɑlz
**sp** symboles[1]

**Cymbeline** *n*
'sɪmbəli:n
**sp** Cymbaline[1], Cymbeline[19]

**cyme** *n*
sɪm
**sp** cyme[1], *often emend to* senna

**cynic** *n*
'sɪnɪk
**sp** cynicke[1]

**Cynthia** *n*
'sɪntɪəz, -nθɪ-
**sp** Cinthias[1]

**cypress** *adj / n*
'sɪprəs
**sp** cyprus[1] / cipresse[1], cypres[1], cypresse[2]

**cypress tree / ~s** *n*
'sɪprəs ˌtri:z
**sp** cypresse trees[1]

**Cyprus** *adj / n*
'sɪprəs
**sp** Cyprus[3] / Ciprus[1], Cyprus[20]

**Cyrus / ~'** *n*
'sɪrəs
**sp** Cyrus[1]

# D

**d,** *abbr for* penny / pence *n*
'penəɪ / pens
**sp** [i].d[1] / [ii].d[1], [iv].d[1], [vi].d[1], [viii].d[1], [xiiii].d[1]
> pence, penny

**D** [music] *n*
=
**sp** D[1]

**d'** *Fr*
> de

**dabble / ~d** *v*
=
**sp** dabbel'd[1]

**dace** *n*
dɛ:s
**sp** dace[1]

**dad** *n*
=
**sp** dad[3]
**rh** lad *TN 4.2.128*

**Daedalus** *n*
*m* 'dedə,lɤs
**sp** Dedalus[1]

**daemon** *n*
'di:mən
**sp** daemon[2]

**daff / ~est / ~ed** *v*
= / dafts / =
**sp** daffe[1] / dafts[1] / daft[3]
**rh** craft *LC 297*

**daffodil / ~s** *n*
=
**sp** daffadils[2]

**dagger / ~s** *n*
'dagəɹ / -z
**sp** dagger[35], dag-ger[2], [ayre-drawne]-dagger[1] / daggers[15]

**Dagonet** *n*
'dagə,net
**sp** Dagonet[1]

**daily** *adj*
'dɛ:ləɪ
**sp** daily[2], dayly[7]

**daily** *adv*
'dɛ:ləɪ
**sp** daily[9], dayly[11]

**daintiest** *n*
'dɛ:ntəɪəst
**sp** daintiest[2]

**daintily** *adv*
*m* 'dɛ:ntɪ,ləɪ
**sp** daintily[2]

**daintiness** *n*
*m* 'dɛ:ntɪ,nes
**sp** daintinesse[1]

**daint·y / ~ier** *adj*
'dɛ:ntəɪ / -əɹ
**sp** daintie[3], dainty[17] / daintier[1]
> super-dainty

**daint·y / ~ies** *n*
'dɛ:ntəɪz
**sp** dainties[3]

**daisied** *adj*
'dɛ:zəɪd
**sp** dazied-[plot][1]

**dais·y / ~ies** *n*
'dɛ:zəɪ / -z
**sp** daysie[1] / dasies[1], daysies[1]

**dale** *n*
dɛ:l
**sp** dale[3]
**rh** pale *MND 2.1.2, VA 232, WT 4.3.2*; tale *Luc 1077*

**Dale** [name] *n*
dɛ:l
**sp** Dale[4]

**dalliance** *n*
=
**sp** dalliance[7]
**rh** France *1H6 5.2.5*

**dall·y / ~ies / ~ying / ~ied** *v*
'daləɪ / -z / -ɪn, -ɪŋ / -d
**sp** dallie[3], dally[7] / dallies[2] / dallying[2] / dallied[1]
**rh** folly *Luc 554*

**Dalmatian / ~s** *n*
*m* dal'mɛ:sɪənz, -ɪ,anz
**sp** Dalmatians[2]

**dam / ~'s** *n*
= , *Evans MW 1.1.139* tam / -z
**sp** dam[21], damme[6], *Evans* tam[1] / dams[2]
**rh** am *MND 5.1.220*
**pun** *MV 3.1.28* damn

**damage** *n*
=
**sp** damage[2], dammage[1]

**Damascus** *n*
=
**sp** Damascus[1]

**damask** *adj / n*
=
**sp** damaske[3] / damaske[2]

**dame / ~'s / ~s** *n*
dɛ:m / -z
**sp** dame[16] / dames[1] / dames[7]
**rh** *1* blame *PP 18.1*; came, shame *Luc 1628*; defame, shame *Luc 1034*; fame *Luc 21*; fame, shame *Luc 51*; frame *MND 5.1.285, Per Prol.31*;
**rh** *2* remain *PP 17.10*
> step-dame, troll-my-dames

**Dame** [*title*] *n*
dɛ:m
**sp** Dame[8], dame[1]

**dame / ~s** *Fr n*
dam
**sp** dames[2]

**damn / ~est** *adj*
=
**sp** damnest[1]
**pun** *MV 3.1.29* dam

**damn / ~est / ~s / ~ed** *v*
= / -st / =
**sp** dam[2], damne[14] / dam'st[1] / damnes[1] / dam'd[1], damm'd[1], damnd[1] damn'd[38]
> land-damn

**damnable** *adj*
*m* =, 'damnə,bɤl
**sp** damnable[11]

**damnably** *adv*
'damnəbləɪ
**sp** dam-nably[1]

**damnation** *n*
dam'nɛ:sɪən
**sp** damnation[14]

**damned** *adj / n*
*m* damd, 'damnɪd
**sp** damn'd[24], damned[39] / damn'd[1], damned[1]
> double-, drug-damned

**Damon** *n*
'dɛ:mən
**sp** Damon[1]

**damp** *n*
=
**sp** dampe[2]
**rh** lamp *AW 2.1.163*

**dam·sel / ~osel / ~osella** *n*
dam'zel / ,damə'zel / ,damə'zelə
**sp** damsell[3] / damosell[3] / damosella[1]

**damson / ~s** *n*
=
**sp** damsons[1]

**dance / ~s** *n*
dans, dɔ:ns / 'dansɪz, 'dɔ:-
**sp** dance[14], daunce[2] / dances[4]
**rh** advance *TNK 3.5.132*

**danc·e / ~es / ~ing / ~ed** *v*
dans, dɔ:ns / 'dans·ɪz, 'dɔ:- / -ɪn, -ɪŋ / danst, dɔ:-
**sp** dance[45], daunce[5] / dances[4], daunces[1] / dancing[2], dauncing[3] / danc'd[2], danc't[1], dan'st[1], daunst[2]
**rh** advance *LLL 5.2.122*; chance *LLL 5.2.219*; ignorance *LLL 5.2.400*; lance *VA 105* / chances *Per 5.Chorus.3*

**dancer** *n*
'dansəɹ, 'dɔ:-
**sp** dancer[1], dauncer[1]

**dancing** *adj / n*
'dansɪn, -ɪŋ, 'dɔ:-
**sp** dancing[4], dauncing[1], daunsing[1] / dancing[5]

**dancing-school / ~s** *n*
'dansɪn-,sku:lz, -ɪŋ-, 'dɔ:-
**sp** dancing-schooles[1]
> school

**dancing-shoe / ~s** *n*
'dansɪn-,ʃu:z, -ɪŋ-, 'dɔ:-
**sp** dancing shooes[1]
> shoe

**dandl·e / ~ing** *v*
= / 'dandlɪn, -ɪŋ
**sp** dandle[2] / dandling[1]
**rh** handling *VA 562*

**Dane** *n*
dɛ:n
**sp** Dane[9]

**danger / ~s** *n*
'dɛ:nʤəɹ / -z
**sp** danger[96], danger's [danger is][1], daunger[1] / dangers[17]
**rh** stranger *VA 788*
> self-danger

**dangerous** *adj*
*m* 'dɛ:nʤə,rɤs, -ʤər-, -ʤrəs
**sp** dangerous[97], danger-ous[2], dang'rous[2], daungerous[1]
**rh** us *Tim 3.5.75*

**dangerously** *adv*
*m* 'dɛ:nʤrəs,ləɪ, -ʤər-
**sp** dangerously[3]

**dangling** *adj*
'daŋglɪn, -ɪŋ
**sp** dangling[1]

**Daniel** *n*
=
**sp** Daniel[6]

**Danish** *adj / n*
'dɛ:nɪʃ
**sp** Danish[5] / Danish[1]

**dank** *adj*
=
**sp** danke[4]

**dankish** *adj*
=
**sp** dankish[1]

**Dansker / ~s** *n*
'danskəɹz
**sp** Danskers[1]

**Daphne / ~'s** *n*
=
**sp** Daphne[2] / Daphnes[1]

**dapple / ~s** *v*
=
**sp** dapples[1]

**dappled** *adj*
=
**sp** dapled[1]

**Dardan** *adj*
'dɑ:ɹdən
**sp** Dardan[1]

**Dardanian** *adj*
dɑ:ɹ'dɛ:nɪən
**sp** Dardanian[1]

**Dardanius** *n*
dɑ:ɹ'dɛ:nɪəs
**sp** Dardenius[3]

**dare** *n*
dɛ:ɹ
**sp** dare[2]

**dar·e / ~est / ~es / ~ing / ~ed / durst** *v*
dɛ:ɹ / -st / -z / 'dɛ:rɪn, -ɪŋ / dɛ:ɹd / dɐ:ɹst
**sp** dare[198] / darest[1], dar'st[47] / dares[44] / daring[5] / dar'd[8], dared[1] / durst[51]
**rh** *1* fair *Tim 1.2.11*; hare *VA 676;* dare not spare not *TN 2.3.109*;
**rh** *2* are *Mac 3.5.3*
> outdare

**dareful** *adj*
'dɛ:ɹfʊl
**sp** darefull[1]

**daring / ~est** *adj*
'dɛ:rɪn, -ɪŋ / -st
**sp** daring[7] / daringst[1]
> overdaring

**daring-hardy** *adj*
'dɛ:rɪn-'ɑ:ɹdəɪ, -ɪŋ-, -'hɑ:-
**sp** daring hardie[1]
> hardy

**Darius** *n*
'darɪəs
**sp** Darius[1]

**dark / ~er / ~est** *adj*
dɑ:ɹk / 'dɑ:ɹk·əɹ / -əst
**sp** dark[1], dark-[backward][1], darke[50] / darker[2] / darkest[2]
**rh** clerk *MV 5.1.304*

**dark** *adv / n*
dɑ:ɹk
**sp** darke[2] / dark[3], darke[16]
**rh** *n* mark *RJ 2.1.32*; shark *Mac 4.1.25*

**dark / *Per* ~s** *v*
dɑ:ɹks
**sp** darkes[1]
**rh** marks *Per 4.Chorus.35*

**darken / ~s / ~ing / ~ened** *v*
'dɑ:ɹkən / -z / -ɪn, -ɪŋ, 'dɑ:ɹk·nɪn, -ɪŋ / -ənd
**sp** darken[3] / darkens[1] / darkning[1] / darkned[2]

**dark-eyed** *adj*
'dɑ:ɹk-ˌəɪd
**sp** darke ey'd[1]
> eye

**darking** *n*
'dɑ:ɹkɪn, -ɪŋ
**sp** darking[1]

**darkling** *adv*
dɑ:ɹklɪn, -ɪŋ
**sp** darkling[2], dark-ling[1]

**darkly** *adv*
'dɑ:ɹkləɪ
**sp** darkelie[1], darkely[4], darkly[2]

**darkness** *n*
'dɑ:ɹknəs
**sp** darkenesse[14], darke-nes[1], darke-nesse[2], darknes[1], darkness[1], darknesse[20]

**dark-seated** *adj*
ˌdɑ:ɹk-'si:tɪd
**sp** darke seated[1]

**dark-working** *adj*
ˌdɑ:ɹk-'wɔ:ɹkɪn, -ɪŋ
**sp** darke working[1]

**darling / ~'s** *n*
'dɑ:ɹlɪn, -ɪŋ / -z
**sp** darling[4], dearling[1] / darlings[1]

**darnel** *n*
'dɑ:ɹnəl
**sp** darnell[3]

**darraign** *v*
da'rɛ:n
**sp** darraigne[1]
> arraign

**dart / ~s** *n*
dɑ:ɹt / -s
**sp** dart[3] / darts[5]
**rh** heart *VA 941*
> thunder-darter

**dart / ~s / ~ed** *v*
dɑ:ɹt / -s / 'dɑ:ɹtɪd
**sp** dart[3] / darts[2] / darted[3]

**darting** *adj*
'dɑ:ɹtɪn, -ɪŋ
**sp** darting[1]
> death-darting

**dash** *n*
=
**sp** dash[2]

**dash / ~es / ~ing / ~ed** *v*
= / = / 'daʃɪn, -ɪŋ / =
**sp** dash[8] / dashes[1] / dashing[1] / dash'd[4], dasht[3]
> bedash

**dashing** *adj*
'daʃɪn, -ɪŋ
**sp** dashing[1]

**dastard** *adj*
'dastəɹd
**sp** dastard[2]

**dastard / ~s** *n*
'dastəɹd / -z
**sp** dastard[4] / dastards[2]

**Datchet** *n*
=
**sp** Dat-chet[1], Datchet-[lane][1], Datchet-[Meade][1], Dotchet[1]

**date / ~s** *n*
dɛ:t / -s
**sp** date[13] / dates[5]
**rh** *1* expiate *S 22.2*; fate *1H6 4.6.9*; invocate *S 38.12*; prognosticate *S 14.14*; **rh** *2* temperate *S 18.4*
> new-dated

**dateless** *adj*
ˈdɛ:tləs
**sp** datelesse[2]

**daub / ~ed** *v*
=
**sp** daub[1], daube[2] / dawb'd[1]
> bedaub

**daubery** *n*
ˈdɔ:brəɪ, -bər-
**sp** dawbry[1]

**daughter / ~'s / ~s / ~s'** *n*
ˈdɔ:təɹ, ˈdɑ:- / -z
**sp** daughter[367], [baby]-daughter[1], daugh-ter[12], daughter's [daughter is][1] / daughters[20] / daughters[45], daugh-ters[1] / daughters[6]
**rh** *1* brought her *AY 5.4.108*; caught her, slaughter *KL 1.4.315*; slaughter *Luc 953, Per 4.4.36, R3 4.4.211*; **rh** *2* after *KL 1.4.315, TS 1.1.237, WT 4.1.27*; **rh** *3* halter *KL 1.4.315*
> god-daughter

**daughter-beamed** *adj*
ˈdɔ:təɹ-ˌbi:mɪd, ˈdɑ:-
**sp** daughter beamed[1]
> beam

**daughter-in-law** *n*
ˈdɔ:tər-ɪn-ˈlɔ:, ˈdɑ:-
**sp** daughter-in-law[2], daughter in law[1]
> law

**daunt / ~ed** *v*
=
**sp** daunt[2] / danted[1], daunted[2]
> never-, un-daunted

**dauntless** *adj*
=
**sp** dauntlesse[4]

**Dauphin / ~'s** *n*
ˈdɒlfɪn / -z
**sp** Daulphin[1], Daul-phin[1], Dolphin[71], Dolphine[3] / Dolphines[1], Dolphins[9]
> dolphin

**Daventry** *n*
ˈdɛ:ntrəɪ
**sp** Daintry[1], Dauintry[1]

**Davy / ~'s** *n*
ˈdɛ:vəɪ / -z, *Fluellen H5 4.7.101* ˈtɛ:vəɪz
**sp** Dauie[7], Dauy[15] / Dauies[2], *Fluellen* Tauies[1]

**daw / ~s** *n*
=
**sp** daw[2] / dawes[6]
**rh** law *1H6 2.4.18* / straws *LLL 5.2.894*

**dawn** *n*
=
**sp** dawne[2]

**dawning** *adj / n*
ˈdɔ:nɪn, -ɪŋ
**sp** dawning[1] / dawning[5]

**day / ~'s / ~s / ~s'** *n*
dɛ: / -z
**sp** daie[3], day[695] / daies[9], dayes[20] / daies[31], dayes[145] / daies[1], dayes[6]
**rh** affray *RJ 3.5.34*; array *VA 481*; away *AW 3.2.128, 1H4 4.1.132, H5 4.2.61, 4.3.132, JC 5.5.81, KJ 1.1.165, LLL 4.1.108, Luc 1280, MA 4.1.251, MM 4.1.3, MND 3.2.50, MV 3.2.311, PP 18.29, R2 3.2.218, RJ 3.5.25, S 73.5, 75.13, 145.10, TG 1.3.85, TNK 1.5.2*; away, gay *PP 15.13*; away, stay *Luc 1013*; castaway, lay *Luc 746*; decay *Luc 806, R2 3.2.103, S 13.11*; decay, may *3H6 4.4.15*; delay *MND 3.2.395, R3 5.3.18, RJ 1.4.45*; dismay *MV 1.3.178*; display *Luc 119*; fray *MND 3.2.446*; grey, way *MA 5.3.25*; hay *Mac 1.3.19*; lay *Luc 399, R2 4.1.333*; may *Cym 3.5.70, Ham 5.1.288, LLL 5.2.339, Mac 1.3.147, 4.3.239*; May *LLL 4.3.99, PP 16.1, 20.1, R2 5.1.80, S 18.1*; pay *AW 5.3.335, 3H6 4.7.86*; play *LLL 5.2.866, MND 3.2.12, TNK Prol.4*; pray *R2 1.1.151*; prey *VA 1098*; repay *S 117.4*; re-survey *S 32.1*; say *CE 4.2.59, Ham 2.1.56, 2H4 5.2.145, 1H6 2.4.134, H8 Prol.32, LLL 1.1.115, 4.3.88, 5.2.816, R2 3.2.195, TS 4.4.93*; stay *AW 5.3.70, 1H6 4.6.37, 3H6 2.1.186, 2.2.177, MND 2.1.139, 5.1.412, MV 5.1.303, S 43.10*; stray *MND 5.1.391*; sway *S 150.4*; way *CE 4.2.61, 1H4 5.5.42, Luc 1142, MND 2.2.44, 3.2.418, S 7.10, 34.1, WT 4.3.123* / betrays *Luc 161*; decays *S 65.6*; dispraise *LLL 4.3.260*; praise *3H6 4.6.43, LLL 4.1.22, 5.2.365, S 2.6, 38.13, 59.13, 62.14, 70.9, 82.8, 95.5, 106.13, Tit 1.1.170*; lays *S 102.8*; raise *1H6 1.2.131*; says *R2 4.1.220*; sprays *2H6 2.3.46*; stays *Ham 3.3.96, RJ 1.3.106*
> All Souls'-, good-, high-, love-, marriage-, to-, working-, worky-day; a-, chair-, dog-, law-, school-days

**day-bed** *n*
ˈdɛ:-ˌbed
**sp** day bedde[1]
> bed

**daylight** *n*
*m* ˈdɛ:ləɪt, dɛ:ˈləɪt
**sp** day-light[6], daylight[4]
**rh** night *MND 3.2.433*

**day-wearied** *adj*
ˌdɛ:ˈwi:rəɪd
**sp** day-wearied[1]
> weary

**day-woman** *n*
ˈdɛ:-ˌwʊmən
**sp** day-woman[1]
> woman

**dazzl·e / ~ing / ~ed** *v*
= / ˈdazlɪn, -ɪŋ / =
**sp** dazell[1], dazle[1] / dazling[1] / dazel'd[1], dazled[1]
> bedazzle

**de,** *abbr* **d'** *Fr / [in Fr name] prep*
də, *abbr* d
**sp** de[24], *abbr* d'[19] / de[20]
> flower-de-luce, viol-de-gamboys

*des*
de

*du* [de + le]
dy
**sp** du[4]

**de** *[in Sp name] prep*
de:
**sp** de[4]

**de** *nonsense syll*
de:
**sp** de[6]

**dead** *adj / adv / n*
=
**sp** dead[460], dead[mans][1], dead-[mans][1], dead[men][1], dead-[mens][3], deade[1] / dead[2] / dead[41]
**rh** *adj 1* astonished *S 86.6*; bed *Ham 3.2.194*; bread *Per 1.4.96*; bred *Luc 489, S 108.14, 112.14, VA 212*; bred, dishonoured *Luc 1187*; buried *Per 2.1.76, RJ 4.5.63, S 31.2, TG 4.2.109*; death-bed *Ham 4.5.192*; fed *Luc 1456, VA 172*; fled *1H6 4.7.50, MND 5.1.293, PP 17.32, PT 22, R2 2.4.17, 3.2.73, 79, S 71.1, Tim 3.3.37, VA 948*; head *3H6 1.4.108, MND 4.1.80, Per 1.1.170, 3.Chorus.25, R3 3.4.107, VA 1060*; lead [mineral] *PP 20.23, RJ 2.5.16, VA 1070*; murdered *R2 5.6.39*; ordered *Per 4.4.46*; red *VA 467*; remembered *S 74.10*; shed *R2 1.3.58*; spread *Luc 1267*; stead *1H6 4.6.30, Per 4.Chorus.42*; unbred *S 104.14*; wed *Ham 3.2.225*; well-coloured *1H6 4.2.38*; **rh** *2* shall o'er-read *S 81.12*; **rh** *n* bed *Cym 4.2.358*; head *S 68.5*; uttered *MA 5.3.19*
> die; half-, pale-dead

**dead-killing** *adj*
*m* ˌded-ˈkɪlɪn, -ɪŋ
**sp** dead-killing[1]
> kill

**deadly** *adj / adv*
ˈdedləɪ
**sp** deadly[40] / deadlie[1], deadly[5]

**deadly-handed** *adj*
ˈdedləɪ-ˌandɪd, -ˌha-
**sp** deadly handed[1]
> handed

**deadly-standing** *adj*
ˈdedləɪ-ˌstandɪn, -ɪŋ
**sp** deadly standing[1]

**deaf** *adj*
=
**sp** deafe[23]
> ear-deafening, undeaf

**deaf / ~s / ~ed** *v*
=
**sp** deafes[1] / deaft[1]

**deafening** *adj*
ˈdefnɪn, -ɪŋ
**sp** deaff'ning[1]

**deafness** *n*
=
**sp** deafenesse[2]

**deal** *n*
dɛ:l
**sp** deale[24]
**rh** knell *PP 17.17*

**deal / ~est / ~s / ~ing / ~t** *v*
dɛ:l / -st / -z / ˈdɛ:lɪn, -ɪŋ / =
**sp** deale[26] / deal'st[1] / deales[1] / dealing[2] / dealt[7]

**dealer / ~s** *n*
ˈdɛ:ləɹ / -z
**sp** dealer[1] / dea-lers[1]

**dealing / ~s** *n*
ˈdɛ:lɪn, -ɪŋ / -z
**sp** dealing[10] / dealings[3]
**rh** sealing *VA 514*
> double-, plain-, well-dealing

**deanery** *n*
ˈdi:nrəɪ, ˈden-, -nər-
**sp** deanerie[1], deanrie[1], deanry[1]

**dear / ~er / ~est** *adj*
di:ɹ / ˈdi:r·əɹ / *m* -əst, di:ɹst
**sp** deare[118], deer[3], deere[252], deere-deere [dear, dear][2], *emend of TN 2.5.170* deero[1] / dearer[4], deerer[11] / dearest[21], deerest[25], deer'st[6]
**rh** *1* appear, here *MND 3.1.78*; cheer, here *CE 3.1.21*; cheer, year *2H4 5.3.19*; ear *LLL 5.2.444, RJ 1.5.47*; fear *S 48.14*; here *Ham 3.2.290, R2 2.1.143*; peer *R2 5.5.68*; year *KJ 1.1.153*; **rh** *2* there *2H4 5.3.19, S 110.3*
**pun** *1H4 5.4.107* deer
> heart-dear

**dear / ~er / ~est** *adv*
di:ɹ / ˈdi:r·əɹ / *m* -əst, di:ɹst
**sp** deare[11], deere[13], [heart]-deere[1] / deerer[2] / deerest[1]
**rh** *1* appear *LC 96*; cheer *MND 3.2.97, MV 3.2.313*; clear *Per 1.1.99*; dear *n MND 3.2.175*; here *H8 3.1.184, LLL 4.3.274, MND 3.2.426, RJ 2.3.62*; peer *Oth 2.3.86*; **rh** *2* wear *LC 96* / clearer *S 115.2*

**dear / ~s** *n*
di:ɹ / -z
**sp** deare[8], deere[10], [*song*] deere-a[1] / deers[1]
**rh** *1* appear, near *MND 2.2.39*; cheer *MND 5.1.284*; dear *adv MND 3.2.176*; here *Luc 1293, MND 5.1.273*; near *MND 2.2.49*; **rh** *2* bear *Luc 1293*; there *WT 4.3.15*; wear *Cor 2.1.170, LLL 5.2.131, 457*; wear-a, ware-a *WT 4.4.315* [*song*] / stomachers *WT 4.4.227*

**dear-beloved** *n*
ˌdi:ɹ-bɪˈlʏvd, *m emend of Tem 5.1.310* bɪˈlʏvɪd
**sp** deere-belou'd[1]
> beloved

**dear-bought** *adj*
ˈdi:ɹ-ˌbɔ:t
**sp** deere bought[1]

**dearer** *adv / n*
ˈdi:rəɹ

**sp** dearer[1] / dearer[1]
**rh** *n* nearer *Luc 1163*

**dearest** *n*
*m* 'di:rəst, di:ɹst
**sp** dearest[1], dear'st[1], deerest[3], dee-rest[1]

**dearest-valued** *adj*
'di:rəst-'valju:d
**sp** deerest valued
> valued

**dearly** *adv*
'di:ɹləɪ
**sp** dearely[12], dearly[2], deerelie[2], deerely[23], deerly[3]
**rh** clearly *AW 5.3.314*; nearly *S 42.2*

**dearness** *n*
'di:ɹnəs
**sp** dearenesse[2]

**dearth** *n*
dɐ:ɹθ
**sp** dearth[7]
**rh** earth *S 146.3, VA 545*

**death / ~'s / ~s** *n*
=
**sp** death[833], deaths [death is][1], death's [death is][5], [s]death [God's death][1], / deaths[17], death's[1] / deaths[19], death's[1]
**rh** *1* breath *2H4 4.2.122, 1H6 4.3.42, 4.6.5, 4.7.23, KJ 4.2.248, LLL 4.3.105, Luc 402, 1178, 1778, Mac 5.6.10, MND 3.2.167, PP 16.7, R2 1.3.65, 172, 231, 3.2.184, 5.3.72, R3 5.3.172, S 99.13, TC 4.1.75, 5.8.4, TN 2.4.50, VA 413, 509, 930, 932, 1174*; breath, vanisheth *Luc 1038*; Macbeth *Mac 1.2.67, 3.5.5*; **rh** *2* bequeath *Luc 1178, MND 3.2.167*; **rh** *3* wrath *TG 5.4.127*

**death-bed,** *Evans MW 1.1.48*
**death's-bed** *n*
=
**sp** death-bed[7], *Evans* deaths-bed[1]
**rh** dead *Ham 4.5.193*
> bed

**death-counterfeiting** *adj*
*m* ˌdeθ-'kəʊntəɹˌfetɪn, -ɪŋ
**sp** death-counterfeiting[1]
> counterfeiting

**death-darting** *adj*
*m* ˌdeθ-'daɹtɪn, -ɪŋ
**sp** death-darting[1]
> darting

**deathful** *adj*
=
**sp** deathfull[1]

**death-practised** *adj*
*m* ˌdeθ-'praktɪst
**sp** death-practis'd[1]
> practice

**death's-head** *n*
'deθs-ˌed, -ˌhed
**sp** deaths head[1], deaths-head[2]
> head

**deaths·man / ~men** *n*
=
**sp** deathsman[1], deaths-man[1], deathsmen[1]

**death-token / ~s** *n*
'deθ-ˌto:kənz
**sp** death tokens[1]

**debase** *v*
dɪ'bɛ:s
**sp** debase[3]

**debate** *n*
dɪ'bɛ:t
**sp** debate[5]
**rh** hate *S 89.13*; relate *LLL 1.1.171*

**debat·e / ~ing / ~ed** *v*
dɪ'bɛ:t / -ɪn, -ɪŋ / -ɪd
**sp** debate[8] / debating[3] / debated[3]
**rh** premeditate *Luc 185*; state *KL 5.1.69*

**debatement** *n*
dɪ'bɛ:tmənt
**sp** debatement[2]

**debater / *Luc* ~s** *n*
dɪ'bɛ:təɹz
**sp** debators[1]
**rh** arbitrators, mediators *Luc 1019*

**debating** *n*
dɪ'bɛ:tɪn, -ɪŋ
**sp** debating[2]

**debile** *adj*
'debɪl
**sp** debile[2]

**debility** *n*
*m* dɪ'bɪlɪˌtəɪ
**sp** debilitie[1]

**debitor** *n*
'debɪtəɹ
**sp** debitor[2]

**debonair** *adj*
ˌdebə'nɛ:ɹ
**sp** debonnaire[1]

**Debora** *n*
*m* 'debəˌra
**sp** Debora[1]

**deboshed** *adj*
dɪ'bɒʃt
**sp** debosh'd[4]

**debt / ~s** *n*
=, *Holofernes LLL 5.1.21*
debt / -s
**sp** debt[43], *Holofernes describing Armado* det[1] / debts[16]
**rh** Boyet *LLL 5.2.333*; Capulet *RJ 1.5.118*; forget *Ham 3.2.203, RJ 1.1.238*; fret, let *Luc 649*; let *Luc 329*; Plantagenet *R3 4.4.21*; set *S 83.4*; wet *VA 84* / gets *Per 4.Chorus.34*
> after-debt

**debted** *adj*
=
**sp** debted[1]

**debtor / ~s** *n*
'detəɹ / -z
**sp** debter[4], debtor[5] / debtors[2]
**rh** better *AY 2.3.76, Luc 1155, Per 2.1.144*; letter *LLL 5.2.43*

**decay** *n*
dɪ'kɛ:
**sp** decay[13]
**rh** away *PP 14.4, S 11.6, 80.14*; day *3H6 4.4.16, Luc 808, R2 3.2.102, S 13.9*; may *3H6 4.4.16*; slay, way *Luc 516*; stay *S 15.11*; way *S 16.3*

**decay / ~s / ~ed** *v*
dɪ'kɛ: / -z / -d
**sp** decay[3] / decaies[2], decayes[1] / decay'd[1]
**rh** away *Luc 1168, S 64.10*; clay *S 71.12*; say *S 23.7*; survey *S 100.11* / days *S 65.8*; prays *Luc 713* / aid *S 79.3*; prayed *1H6 1.1.34*

**decayed** *adj*
*m* dɪ'kɛ:d, dɪ'kɛ:ɪd
**sp** decaied[1], de-cay'd[1], decayed[2]

**decayer** *n*
dɪ'kɛ:əɹ
**sp** decayer[1]

**decaying** *adj*
dɪ'kɛ:ɪn, -ɪŋ
**sp** decaying[1]

**decease** *n*
dɪ'sɛ:s
**sp** decease[3]
**rh** *1* increase *S 1.3, 97.8*; lease *S 13.7*; **rh** *2* confess *VA 1002*
> **predeceased**

**decease / ~d** *v*
dɪ'sɛ:s / -t
**sp** deceas'd[1]

**deceased** *adj*
*m* dɪ'sɛ:sɪd, dɪ'sɛ:st, *TS 1.2.101* 'dɪsɛ:st
**sp** deceas'd[2], deceased[4], deceast[6]

**deceit / ~s** *n*
=
**sp** deceit[16], deceite[3] / deceits[1], de-ceits[1]
**rh** conceit *CE 3.2.36*; repeat *Per 1.4.75*

**deceitful** *adj*
=
**sp** deceitfull[7]

**deceivable** *adj*
*m* dɪ'si:və,bɤl
**sp** deceiuable[1], deceiueable[1]

**deceiv·e / *S* ~est / ~es / ~ing / ~ed** *v*
= / dɪ'si:vəst / = / dɪ'si:vɪn, -ɪŋ / =
**sp** deceiue[26] / deceauest[1] / deceaues[1], deceiues[2] / deceiuing[2] / deceau'd[1], deceiu'd[42], deceiued[10], deceyu'd[2]
**rh** leave *MND 2.2.146, S 4.10, 39.12, TC 5.3.90*; **deceive me** heave thee, leave me *Luc 585*; leave me *AW 1.1.224* / receivest *S 40.7* / leaves, receives *LC 306* / perceived *S 104.12*

**deceiver / ~s** *n*
dɪ'si:vəɹ / -z
**sp** deceiuer[1] / deceiuers[1]

**deceiving** *adj / n*
dɪ'si:vɪn, -ɪŋ
**sp** deceiuing[1], de-ceyuing[1] / deceiuing[1]

**December** *n*
dɪ'sembəɹ
**sp** December[6]

**decent** *adj*
=
**sp** decent[1]

**deceptious** *adj*
dɪ'sepsɪəs
**sp** deceptious[1]

**decide / ~s** *v*
dɪ'səɪd / -z
**sp** decide[2] / decides[1]

**decimation** *n*
desɪ'mɛ:sɪən
**sp** decimation[1]

**decipher / ~s / ~ed** *v*
dɪ'səɪfəɹ / -z / -d
**sp** decipher[1] / deciphers[1] / decipher'd[1]

**decision** *n*
dɪ'sɪzɪən
**sp** decision[3]

**Decius** *n*
'desɪəs
**sp** Decius[13], De-cius[1]

**deck** *n*
=
**sp** decke[4]
**rh** speak *Per 3.Chorus.59*

**deck / ~s / ~ing / ~ed** *v*
= / = / 'dekɪn, -ɪŋ / =
**sp** deck[2], decke[6] / deckes[1] / decking[1] / deck'd[4], deckt[4]
**rh** aspect *LLL 4.3.256*
> **undeck**

**declare / ~s** *v*
dɪ'klɛ:ɹ / -z
**sp** declare[7] / declares[1]

**declension / ~s** *n*
dɪ'klensɪən / -z
**sp** declension[3] / declensions[1]

**declin·e / ~s / ~ing / ~ed** *v*
dɪ'kləɪn / -z / -ɪn, -ɪŋ / -d
**sp** declin[1], decline[8] / declines[3] / declining[2] / declin'd[6], declined[1]
**rh** mine *CE 3.2.44* / shines *S 18.7*

**declined** *n*
dɪ'kləɪnd
**sp** declin'd[1], declined[1]

**declining** *adj*
dɪ'kləɪnɪn, -ɪŋ
**sp** declining[4]

**decoct** *v*
=
**sp** decoct[1]

**decorum** *n*
=
**sp** decorum[2], de-corum[1]

**decrease / ~d** *v*
dɪ'krɛ:s / -t
**sp** decrease[1], decreast[1]
**rh** increase *S 15.7*

**decreasing** *adj*
dɪ'krɛ:sɪn, -ɪŋ
**sp** decreasing[1]

**decree / ~s** *n*
=
**sp** decree[8] / decrees[11]
**rh** be *LLL 4.3.215*; necessity *LLL 1.1.145*; thee *Luc 1030*

**decree / ~d** *v*
=
**sp** decree[2] / decreed[7]
**rh** be *S 93.9* / bleed *Per 1.1.58*; exceed *Per 2.3.15*

**decrepit** *adj*
=
**sp** decrepit[2]

**Decretas** *n*
dɪ'krɛ:təs
**sp** Decretas[2]

**dedicat·e / ~s / ~ed** *v*
'dedɪˌkɛ:t / -s / -ɪd
**sp** dedicate[6] / dedicates[2] / dedicate [dedicated][2], dedicated[1]

**dedicated** *adj*
'dedɪˌkɛ:tɪd
**sp** dedicated[1]

**dedication** *n*
'dedɪˌkɛ:sɪən
**sp** dedication[2], dedica-tion[1]

**deed / ~s** *n*
=
**sp** deed[105], deede[41], deed's [deed is][1], [good]-deed[1] / deedes[25], deeds[83]
**rh** bleed *Luc 1730, Tit 5.3.63*; bleed, exceed *Luc 226*; breed, speed *Luc 502*; feed *Tit 5.3.52*; meed *Tit 5.3.65*; need *R2 5.6.37*; proceed *AW 2.1.210, 2.3.125, Luc 252*; speed *AW 3.7.45*; steed *LC 111*; weed *Luc 195* / bleeds, proceeds *Luc 1822*; breeds *S 111.2*; breeds, feeds *Luc 908*; exceeds *S 150.6*; feeds *TC 5.3.111*; proceeds *AW 4.2.63, S 131.13*; sheeds *S 34.14*; weeds *S 69.10, 94.13*
**pun** *Mardian AC 1.5.15* in deed
> alms-, mis-deed; undeeded

**deed-achieving** *adj*
'di:d-əˌʧi:vɪn, -ɪŋ, -'ʧɪv-
**sp** deed-atchieuing[1]
> achieve

**deedless** *adj*
=
**sp** deedelesse[1]

**deem** *n*
=
**sp** deeme[1]

**deem / *Luc* ~s / ~ed** *v*
=
**sp** deeme[9] / deems[1] / deem'd[2]
**rh** esteem *AW 2.1.124*; seem *S 54.3* / extremes *Luc 1336* / esteemed *S 96.8, 121.3*

**deep / ~er / ~est** *adj*
= / 'di:pəɹ / =
**sp** deep[1], deepe[94] / deeper[6] / deepest[5]
**rh** keep *Per 4.2.140*; sleep, weep *LC 121*
> breast-, knee-, pottle-deep

**deep / ~er** *adv*
= / 'di:pəɹ
**sp** deepe[12] / deeper[6]
**rh** sleep *TC 2.3.263*; weep *Per 1.4.13*

**deep / ~s** *n*
=
**sp** deepe[15], deepes[2]
**rh** sleep *MND 3.1.149, 3.2.48*; weep *LLL 4.3.29*

**deep-damned** *adj*
'di:p-ˌdamd
**sp** deepe damn'd[1]
> damned

**deep-divorcing** *adj*
'di:p-dɪˌvɔ:ɹsɪn, -ɪŋ
**sp** deepe-diuorcing[1]

**deep-drawing** *adj*
*m* ˌdi:p-'drɔ:ɪn, -ɪŋ
**sp** deepe-drawing[1]
> drawing

**deep-fet** *adj*
'di:p-ˌfet
**sp** deepe-fet[1]
> fet

**deeply** *adv*
'di:pləɪ
**sp** deepely[10], deeply[5]

**deep-mouthed** *adj*
'di:p-ˌməʊðd
**sp** deep-mouth'd[1], deepe mouth'd[1], deepe-mouth'd[1]
> mouth

**deep-revolving** *adj*
'di:p-rɪˌvɒlvɪn, -ɪŋ, -ˌvo:
**sp** deepe reuoluing[1]
> revolve

**deep-searched** *adj*
*m* ˌdi:p-'sɐ:ɹʧt
**sp** deepe search'd[1]

**deep-sworn** *adj*
'di:p-ˌswɔ:ɹn
**sp** deepe-sworne[1]

**Deep-vow** [name] *n*
'di:p-ˌvəʊ
**sp** Deepe-vow[1]

**deer / ~'s** *n*
di:ɹ, dɛ:ɹ / -z
**sp** deare[13], deares [deer's][1], deere[24], [male]-deere[1] / deeres[1]
**rh** *1* fear *VA 689*; here *VA 231*; near *LLL 4.1.115*; year *KL 3.4.132*;
**rh** *2* bear, wear *AY 4.2.10*; wear *KL 3.4.132*
**pun** *1H4 5.4.106* dear

**déesse** *Fr n*
de'ɛs
**sp** deesse[1]

**defac·e / ~ing / ~ed** *v*
dɪ'fɛ:s / -ɪn, -ɪŋ / -t
**sp** deface[3] / defacing[1] / defac'd[3], defac't[1]
**rh** place *S 6.1*; **deface her** grace her *PP 7.6* / **rh** *1* chased, disgraced *Luc 719*; **rh** *2* down-razed *S 64.1*
> face

**defacer / ~s** *n*
dɪ'fɛ:səɹ / -z
**sp** defacer[1] / defacers[1]

**defame / ~d** *v*
dɪ'fɛ:md
**sp** defam'd[1]
**rh** blame, shame *Luc 768*; dame, shame *Luc 1033*; name, shame *Luc 817*
> fame

**default** *n*
dɪ'fɔ:t, -fɑ:lt
**sp** default[4]
> fault

**defeat** *n*
dɪ'fɛ:t
**sp** defeat[3], defeate[1]

**defeat / ~est / ~s / ~ed** *v*
dɪ'fɛ:t / -st / -s / -ɪd
**sp** defeat[3], defeate[4] / defeat'st[1] / defeats[1] / defeated[2]
**rh** great *S 61.11* / created *S 20.11*

**defeated** *adj*
dɪ'fɛ:tɪd
**sp** defeated[1]

**defeature** *VA* **/ ~s** *n*
dɪ'fɛ:təɹ / -z
**sp** defeature[1] / defeatures[2]
**rh** nature *VA 736*

**defect / ~s** *n*
dɪ'fekt / -s
**sp** defect[7] / defects[5]
**rh** effect *Ham 2.2.102*; expect, neglect *Luc 151*; respect *Luc 1345, S 149.11*; suspect *S 70.1* / respects *S 49.2*

**defect** *v*
dɪ'fekt
**sp** defect[1]

**defective** *adj*
=
**sp** defectiue[5]

**defence / ~s** *n*
=
**sp** defence[38] / defences[4]
**rh** hence *LLL 5.2.85, S 12.13*; offence *KJ 1.1.258, S 89.4*; sense *PP 8.8*

**defend / ~s / ~ing / ~ed** *v*
= / = / dɪ'fendɪn, -ɪŋ / =
**sp** defend[62], de-fend[2] / defends[2] / defending[2] / defended[6]
**rh** **defend her** reprehend her *VA 472*; **defend me** attend me, lend me *Luc 1684* / comprehends, friends *Luc 492*

**defendant** *n*
=
**sp** defendant[3]

**defended** *adj*
=
**sp** defended[1]

**defender / ~s** *n*
dɪ'fendəɹ / -z
**sp** defender[2] / defenders[1]

**defensible** *adj*
=
**sp** defensible[2]

**defensive** *adj*
=
**sp** defensiue[2]

**defer / ~red** *v*
dɪ'fɐ:ɹ / -d
**sp** deferre[2] / deferr'd[1]

**defiance** *n*
dɪ'fəɪəns
**sp** defiance[12]
> defy

**deficient** *adj*
dɪ'fɪsɪənt
**sp** deficient[2]

**defil·e / ~es /** *LC* **~ing / ~ed** *v*
dɪ'fəɪl / -z / -ɪn, -ɪŋ / -d
**sp** defile[4] / defiles[2] / defiling[1] / defil'd[4]
**rh** vile *MW 1.3.91*; **defile thee** reconciles thee *KL 3.6.110* [*Q*] / beguiling, smiling *LC 173* / beguild, mild *Luc 1545*; child *AW 5.3.298, Luc 787, MND 3.2.410*

**defiled** *adj*
dɪ'fəɪld
**sp** defil'd[1]

**defiler** *n*
dɪ'fəɪləɹ
**sp** defiler[1]

**define** *v*
dɪ'fəɪn
**sp** define[4]
**rh** mine *S 62.7*

**definite** *adj*
*m* 'defɪˌnɪt
**sp** definit[1]

**definitive** *adj*
*m* dɪ'fɪnɪˌtɪv
**sp** definitiue[1]

**definitively** *adv*
*m* dɪ'fɪnɪˌtɪvləɪ
**sp** definitiuely[1]

**deflower / ~ed** *v*
di:'flo:ɹ, -u:ɹ / *m* di:'flo:ɹd, -rɪd, -lu:-
**sp** defloure[1] / deflour'd[1], defloured[1], deflowr'd[1], deflowred[2]
**rh** *1* hour, power *Luc 348*; **rh** *2* Moor *Tit 2.3.191*
> flower

**deform** *v*
dɪ'fɔ:ɹm
**sp** deforme[1]

**deformed** *adj / n*
*m* dɪ'fɔːɹmɪd, -md / dɪ'fɔːɹmd
**sp** deform'd[4], deformed[7] / deformed[3], defor-med[1]

**deform·ity / ~ities** *n*
*m* dɪ'fɔːɹmɪˌtəɪ, -ɪt- / -ɪˌtəɪz
**sp** deformitie[3], de-formitie[1], deformity[1] / deformities[1]

**deftly** *adv*
'deftləɪ
**sp** deaftly[1]

**defunct** *adj / n*
dɪ'fɤŋkt
**sp** defunct[1] / defunct[2]
> function

**defunction** *n*
dɪ'fɤŋksɪən
**sp** defunction[1]

**defuse / ~ed** *v*
=
**sp** defuse[1] / defus'd[2]

**def·y / ~ies / ~ying / ~ied** *v*
dɪ'fəɪ / -z / -ɪn, -ɪŋ / -d
**sp** defie[25], defye[1] / defies[1] / defying[2] / defide[3], defi'de[1]
**rh** lie *S 123.9*; **defy thee** hie thee *PP 12.11*

**degenerate** *adj*
*m* dɪ'ʤenəˌrɛːt, -nərət, -nrət
**sp** degenerate[10]
**rh** hate, state *Luc 1003*

**degrade / ~d** *v*
dɪ'grɛːdɪd
**sp** degraded[2]

**degree / ~s** *n*
=
**sp** degree[47] / degrees[16], de-grees[2]
**rh** me *AY 5.4.145, LLL 1.1.154*; thee *Oth 2.3.89*

**deif·y / *LC* ~ied** *v*
*m* 'dɛːɪˌfəɪd
**sp** 'deified[1]
**rh** abide *LC 84*

**deign / ~ed** *v*
dɛːn / *m* 'dɛːnɪd
**sp** deigne[1], deine[1] / deigned[1]

**Deiphobus** *n*
*m* dɛː'ɪfəˌbɤs, -əbəs
**sp** Deiphebus[1], Deiphoebus[3], Diephoebus[1], Doephobus[1]

**deit·y / ~ies** *n*
*m* 'dɛːɪˌtəɪ, 'dɛːtəɪ / -z
**sp** deitie[2], deity[5] / deities[4]
**rh** *1* company, society *Tem 4.1.92*; idolatry *LLL 4.3.72*; liberty *R3 1.1.76*;
**rh** *2* cry, fly *Cym 5.4.90*

**déjà** *Fr adv*
de'ʒa
**sp** desia[1]

**deject** *adj / v*
=
**sp** deiect[3] / deiect[1]
**rh** *adj* respect *TC 2.2.50*

**dejected** *adj*
=
**sp** deiected[4], deie-cted[1]

**Delabreth** *n*
ˌdelə'bret
**sp** Delabreth[2]

**delay / ~s** *n*
dɪ'lɛː / -z
**sp** delay[23] / delayes[1]
**rh** away *1H6 4.3.46*; day *MND 3.2.394, R3 5.3.17, RJ 1.4.44*; hay *3H6 4.8.60*; say *R2 5.1.101*; way *MND 5.1.200, Oth 2.3.377* / assays, says *Luc 1719*; ways *VA 909*

**delay / ~s / ~ing / ~ed** *v*
dɪ'lɛː / -z / -ɪn, -ɪŋ / -d
**sp** delay[10], de-lay[1] / delayes[5] / delaying[1] / delaid[1], delayd[1]
**rh** away *1H4 3.2.180*; **delay him** stay him *Luc 325* / plays *Luc 552*

**Delay** [*ship name*] *n*
dɪ'lɛː
**sp** Delay[1]

**delayed** *adj*
dɪ'lɛːd
**sp** delay'd[1]

**delaying** *n*
dɪ'lɛːɪn, -ɪŋ
**sp** delaying[1]

**delectable** *adj*
*m* 'delɪkˌtabəl
**sp** delectable[2]

**deliberate** *adj / v*
*m* dɪ'lɪbəˌrɛːt, -brət
**sp** deliberate[4] / deliberate[2]

**delicate** *adj*
*m* 'delɪˌkɛːt, -ɪkət
**sp** delicate[27]

**delicate / ~s** *n*
*m* 'delɪˌkɛːts
**sp** delicates[1]

**delicious** *adj*
dɪ'lɪsɪəs
**sp** delicious[3]

**deliciousness** *n*
*m* dɪ'lɪsɪəsˌnes
**sp** deliciousnesse[3]

**delight / ~s** *n*
dɪ'ləɪt / -s
**sp** delight[33] / delights[10]
**rh** appetite, white *Luc 12*; despite *MND 5.1.114*; knight *Per 4.4.12*; light *VA 1030*; might, night *Luc 487*; night *Luc 357, 697, 742, 927, MND 2.1.254, PP 18.28, RJ 1.2.28, 2.5.75, S 102.12, VA 843*; quite *LLL 1.1.71*; sight *Luc 385, MND 3.2.455, Per 1.4.29, S 47.14, 75.11*; silver-white *LLL 5.2.886*; spite *S 36.8, 37.1*; tonight *MV 2.6.67*; white *S 98.11, 130.7, VA 78, 400* / rites *AY 5.4.195*; sprites *Mac 4.1.127*

**delight / ~s / *Luc* ~ing / ~ed** *v*
dɪ'ləɪt / -s / -ɪn, -ɪŋ / -ɪd
**sp** delight[15] / delights[8] / delighting[1] / delighted[2]
**rh** flight *Luc 697* / fighting *Luc 430* / invited *S 141.5*

**delighted** *adj*
dɪˈləɪtɪd
**sp** delighted[3]

**delightful** *adj*
dɪˈləɪtfʊl
**sp** delightfull[3]

**delinquent / ~s** *n*
=
**sp** delinquents[1]

**deliver / ~s / ~ing / ~ed** *v*
dɪˈlɪvəɹ / -z / -ɪn, -ɪŋ, -vr- / dɪˈlɪvəɹd
**sp** deliuer[98], de-liuer[2], deliuer't [deliver it][1], deli-uer[1] / deliuers[8] / deliuering[4] / deliuerd[1], deliuer'd[40], de-liuer'd[1], deliuered[23], deliu'red[1]
> ditch-, new-delivered

**deliverance** *n*
*m* dɪˈlɪvəˌrans, -vərəns, -vrəns
**sp** deliuerance[8], deliu'rance[1]

**delivered** *adj*
dɪˈlɪvəɹd
**sp** diliuered[1]

**delivery** *n*
*m* dɪˈlɪvəˌrəɪ, -vərəɪ, -vrəɪ
**sp** deliuerie[2], deliuery[2]

**Delphos** *n*
=
**sp** Delphos[3]

**delud·e / ~ing / ~ed** *v*
dɪˈlju:dɪn, -ɪŋ / -ɪd
**sp** deluding[1] / deluded[1]

**deluding** *adj*
dɪˈlju:dɪn, -ɪŋ
**sp** deluding[1]

**deluge** *n*
ˈdelju:ʤ
**sp** deluge[2]

**delve** *v*
=
**sp** delue[1]

**delver** *n*
ˈdelvəɹ
**sp** deluer[1]

**demand / ~s** *n*
dɪˈmand, -ˈmɔ:nd / -z
**sp** demand[19] / demands[17]

**demand / ~s / ~ing / ~ed** *v*
dɪˈmand, -ˈmɔ:nd / -z / -ɪn, -ɪŋ / -ɪd
**sp** demand[36], demaund[4] / demands[2] / demanding[2] / demanded[8]

**demean / ~ed** *v*
=
**sp** demeane[2] / demean'd[2]

**demeanor** *n*
dɪˈmi:nəɹ
**sp** demeanor[3], demeanure[1]
> misdemeanour

**demerit / ~s** *n*
*m* dɪˈmerɪt, -ˈmeɹt / -s
**sp** demerite[1] / demerits[2]
> merit

**demesne / ~s** *n*
dɪˈmi:nz
**sp** demeanes[2], demesnes[1]

**Demetrius / ~'** *n*
*m* dɪˈmi:trɪəs, -ɪˌɤs / dɪˈmi:trɪəs
**sp** Demetrius[60], De-metrius[1] / Demetrius[2]
**rh** thus *MND 2.2.90, 102, 3.2.362*; us *MND 1.1.221*

**demi-atlas** *n*
ˈdeməɪ-ˈatləs
**sp** demy atlas[1]
> Atlas

**demi-cannon** *n*
ˈdeməɪ-ˈkanən
**sp** demi cannon[1]

**demi-coronal** *n*
ˈdeməɪ-ˈkɒrənɑl
**sp** demy coronall[1]

**demi-devil** *n*
ˈdeməɪ-ˈdɪvəl
**sp** demy-diuell[2]
> devil

**demi-God** *n*
ˈdeməɪ-ˈgɒd
**sp** demie God[2], demy-god[1]
> God

**demi-natured** *adj*
ˈdemɪ-ˈnɛ:təɹd
**sp** demy-natur'd[1]
> nature

**demi-paradise** *n*
ˈdeməɪ-ˈparəˌdəɪs
**sp** demy paradise[1]
> paradise

**demi-puppet / ~s** *n*
ˈdeməɪ-ˈpɤpɪts
**sp** demy-puppets[1]
> puppet

**demise** *n*
dɪˈməɪz
**sp** demise[1]

**demi-wol·f / ~ves** *n*
ˈdeməɪ-ˈwʊlvz
**sp** demi-wolues[1]
> wolf

**demoiselle / ~s** *Fr n*
dəmwɛˈzɛl / -z
**sp** damoiseil[1] / damoisels[1]

**demonstrable** *adj*
*m* ˈdemənˌstrabəl
**sp** demonstrable[1]

**demonstr·ate / ~ating** *v*
*m* dɪˈmɒnstrɛ:t, ˈdemənˌstrɛ:t / ˈdemənˌstrɛ:tɪn, -ɪŋ
**sp** demonstrate[5] / demonstrating[1]

**demonstration** *n*
ˌdemənˈstrɛ:sɪən
**sp** demonstration[1]

**demonstrative** *adj*
*m* dɪ'mɒnstrəˌtɪv
**sp** demonstratiue[1]

**demure** *adj*
dɪ'mjuːɹ
**sp** demure[3]

**demur·e / ~ing** *v*
dɪ'mjuːrɪn, -ɪŋ
**sp** demuring[1]

**demurely** *adv*
dɪ'mjuːɹləɪ
**sp** demurely[3]

**den / ~s** *n*
=
**sp** den[7], denne[1] / dennes[2]
**rh** then *LLL 4.1.94*

**denay** *n*
dɪ'nɛː
**sp** denay[1]
**rh** say *TN 2.4.123*
> deny

**denay / ~ed** *v*
dɪ'nɛːd
**sp** denay'd[1]

**denial / ~s** *n*
dɪ'nəɪɑl / -z
**sp** denial[1], deniall[7], denyall[1] / denials[2]
**rh** dial, trial *Luc 324*
> deny

**denier** *n*
də'nəɪəɹ
**sp** denier[2], deniere[1]

**Denmark / ~'s** *n*
'denmɑːɹk / -s
**sp** Denmark[1], Denmark's [Denmark is][1], Denmarke[19] / Denmarkes[1], Denmarks[1]

**Dennis** *n*
=
**sp** Dennis[7]

**Denny** *n*
'denəɪ
**sp** Denny[4]

**denote / ~d** *v*
dɪ'noːt / -ɪd
**sp** denote[3] / denoted[1]
**rh** dote *S 148.7*

**denounc·e / ~ing / ~ed** *v*
dɪ'nəʊns / -ɪn, -ɪŋ / -t
**sp** denounce[1] / denouncing[1] / denounc'd[2]

**denunciation** *n*
dɪˌnɤnsɪ'ɛːsɪən
**sp** denunciation[1]

**den·y / ~iest / ~ies / ~ing / ~ied / ~iedest** *v*
dɪ'nəɪ / -st / -z / -ɪn, -ɪŋ / -d / -dst
**sp** denie[46], deny[83], denye[1], deny't [deny it][4] / deniest[1], denyest[1], deny'st[1] / denies[12] / denying[6] / deni'd[3], denide[4], deni'de[5], denied[18], deny'd[14], denyde[1], deny'de[9], denyed[1] / denied'st[1]
**rh** *1* die *AY 4.3.63*; eye *LLL 5.2.808*; I *TN 5.1.142*; lie *Cym 2.4.145, MND 2.2.57, S 46.7*; **rh** *2* prettily *MND 2.2.57* / aside *RJ 1.1.157*; beside *R2 5.3.102*; dried *AW 2.1.141*; hide *S 142.14*
> denay

**deo** *Lat*
> deus

**depart** *n*
dɪ'pɑːɹt
**sp** depart[4]
> part

**depart / ~est / ~ed / ~edest** *v*
dɪ'pɑːɹt / -əst, -st / -ɪd / -ɪdst
**sp** depart[60] / departest[1] *S*, depart'st[1] / departed[4] / departedst[1]
**rh** art *S 6.11*; heart *Mac 4.1.110, S 109.3, VA 578* / convertest *S 11.2*

**departed** *adj*
dɪ'pɑːɹtɪd
**sp** departed[2]

**departing** *adj / n*
dɪ'pɑɹtɪn, -ɪŋ
**sp** departing[1] / departing[3]

**departure** *n*
dɪ'pɑːɹtəɹ
**sp** departure[18], de-parture[2]
**rh** shorter *KL 1.5.48*

**dépêcher / dépêche** *Fr v*
de'pɛʃ
**sp** de-peech[1]

**depend / ~s / ~ing / ~ed** *v*
= / = / dɪ'pendɪn, -ɪŋ / =
**sp** depend[11] / dipends[9] / dipending[7] / depended[1]
**rh** end *S 92.8*; extend *LC 274* / amends *S 101.3* / amending, ending *Luc 1615* / ended *Oth 1.3.201*

**dependant / ~s** *n*
=
**sp** dependant[1] / dependants[4]

**dependence** *n*
=
**sp** dependance[1]
> by-dependence

**dependency** *n*
*m* dɪ'pendənˌsəɪ
**sp** dependancie[2], dependancy[1]

**dependent** *adj*
=
**sp** dependant[2]

**depender** *n*
dɪ'pendəɹ
**sp** depender[1]

**deplore** *v*
dɪ'plɔːɹ
**sp** deplore[1]
**rh** more *TN 3.1.159*

**deploring** *adj*
dɪ'plɔːrɪn, -ɪŋ
**sp** deploring[1]

**depopulate** *v*
dɪ'pɒpjəˌlɛ:t
**sp** depopulate[1]

**depos·e / ~ing / ~ed** *v*
dɪ'po:z / -ɪn, -ɪŋ / *m* -ɪd
**sp** depose[10] / deposing[1] / depos'd[20], deposed[2]
**rh** those *R2 4.1.191*

**deposed** *adj*
*m* dɪ'po:zɪd
**sp** deposed[1]

**deposing** *n*
dɪ'po:zɪn, -ɪŋ
**sp** deposing[2]

**depositar·y / ~ies** *n*
*m* dɪ'pɒzɪˌtrəɪz
**sp** depositaries[1]

**deprave / ~s / ~d** *v*
dɪ'prɛ:v / -z / -d
**sp** depraue[1] / deprausn[1] / deprаued[1]
**rh** graves *Tim 1.2.137*

**depraved** *adj*
dɪ'prɛ:vd
**sp** deprau'd[1]

**depress / ~ed** *v*
=
**sp** deprest[1]

**deprivation** *n*
ˌdeprɪ'vɛ:sɪən
**sp** deprauation[1]

**deprive / ~d** *v*
dɪ'prəɪv / -d
**sp** depriue[2] / depriu'd[6]
**rh** derived, unlived *Luc 1752*

**depth / ~s** *n*
=
**sp** depth[8] / depths[1]

**deputation** *n*
*m* ˌdepjə'tɛ:sɪən, -ɪˌɒn
**sp** deputation[4]

**deput·e / ~ing** *v*
= / dɪ'pju:tɪn, -ɪŋ
**sp** depute[1] / deputing[1]

**deputed** *adj*
=
**sp** deputed[1]

**deput·y / ~ies** *n*
*m* 'depjəˌtəɪ, -ətəɪ / 'depjətəɪz / 'depjəˌtəɪz
**sp** deputie[17], de-putie[1], deputy[6] / deputies[1] / deputies[1]

**deracinate** *v*
dɪ'rasɪˌnɛ:t
**sp** deracinate[2]

**Derby** *n*
'dɐ:ɹbəɪ
**sp** Darby[1], Derbie[3], Derby[12]

**deride / ~s** *v*
dɪ'rəɪdz
**sp** derides[1]
**rh** hides *KL 1.1.281*

**derision** *n*
*m* dɪ'rɪzɪən, -ɪˌɒn
**sp** derision[5]
**rh** vision *MND 3.2.370*

**derivation** *n*
ˌderɪ'vɛ:sɪən
**sp** deriuation[1]

**derivative** *adj*
=
**sp** deriuative[1]

**deriv·e / ~s / ~ed** *v*
dɪ'rəɪv / -z / *m* -d, -ɪd
**sp** deriue[10] / deriues[5] / deriu'd[14], deriued[2]
**rh** thrive *AW 2.3.135, S 14.9* / deprived, unlived *Luc 1755*
> false-, true-, well-derived

**derogate** *adj / v*
*m* 'derəgət / *m* 'derəˌgɛ:t
**sp** derogate[1] / derogate[2]

**derogately** *adv*
'derəgətləɪ, 'dɛ:ɹg-
**sp** derogately[1]

**derogation** *n*
ˌderə'gɛ:sɪən
**sp** derogation[1]

**derry** *interj*
'derəɪ
**sp** derry[2]
**rh** merry *TNK 3.5.138*

**des** *Fr*
> de

**dès** *Fr prep*
dɛ
**sp** des[2]

**descant** *n / v*
=
**sp** descant[2] / descant[1]

**descend / ~s / ~ing / ~ed** *v*
= / dɪ'sendɪn, -ɪŋ / =
**sp** descend[19], discend[2] / descends[7] / descending[1] / descended[10]
**rh** finger-end *MW 5.5.85*; friend *RJ 3.5.42* / ended *Luc 1081*

**descent / ~s** *n*
=
**sp** descent[8], discent[8] / discents[1]
**rh** spent *R2 1.1.107*

**describe / ~s / ~ed** *v*
dɪ'skrəɪb / -z / -d
**sp** describe[1] / describes[2] / describ'd[1]

**description** *n*
*m* dɪ'skrɪpsɪən, -ɪˌɒn
**sp** description[15], descrip-tion[1], descripti-on[1], discription[1]

**descry** *n*
dɪ'skrəɪ
**sp** descry[1]
> undescry

**descr·y / ~ied** *v*
dɪ'skrəɪ / -d

**sp** descry[4] / descried[3], discried[1]
**rh** loyalty *Per Epil.7*

**Desdemona / ~'s / Desdemon** *n*
ˌdezdɪˈmoːnə / -z / ˌdezdɪˈmɒn
**sp** Desdemona[46], Desdemona's [Desdemona is][1] / Desdemonaes[1] / Desdemon[7]

**desert** [place] *adj*
ˈdezəɹt
**sp** desart[1], desert[5]

**desert / ~s** [place] *n*
ˈdezəɹt / -s
**sp** desart[2], de-sart[1], desert[4], de-sert[1] / desarts[2], deserts[1]

**desert / ~s** [due] *n*
dɪˈzɐːɹt / -s
**sp** desart[1], desert[25] / deserts[16]
**rh** impart *S 72.6*; part *S 49.10* / parts *S 17.2*

**desertless** *adj*
dɪˈzɐːɹtləs
**sp** desartlesse[1]

**deserv·e / ~est / ~es / ~ing / ~ed** *v*
dɪˈzɐːɹv / -st / -z / -ɪn, -ɪŋ / *m* -ɪd, -d
**sp** deserue[62] / deser-uest[1], deseru'st[2] / deserues[35], de-serues[1] / deseruing[2] / deseru'd[43], deserued[11], deser-ued[1]
**rh** *1* starve *Cor 2.3.113*; **rh** *2* swerve *Cym 5.4.130*

**deserved** *adj*
*m* dɪˈzɐːɹvɪd, -vd
**sp** deseru'd[1], deserued[3]
> un-, well-deserved

**deservedly** *adv*
*m* dɪˈzɐɹvɪdˌləɪ
**sp** deseruedly[1]

**deserver / ~s** *n*
dɪˈzɐːɹvəɹ / -z
**sp** deseruer[2] / deseruers[1]
> undeserver

**deserving** *adj*
dɪˈzɐːɹvɪn, -ɪŋ
**sp** deser-uing[1]

**deserving / ~s** *n*
dɪˈzɐːɹvɪn, -ɪŋ / -z
**sp** deseruing[9], de-seruing[1], deser-uing[1] / deseruings[6]
**rh** swerving *S 87.6*

**design / ~s** *n*
dɪˈzəɪn / -z
**sp** designe[19] / designes[11]
**rh** Collatine, mine *Luc 1692*; mine, pine *LC 278*

**designment / ~s** *n*
dɪˈzəɪnmənt / -s
**sp** designement[1] / designements[1]

**desire / ~s** *n*
dɪˈzəɪɹ / -z
**sp** desire[59] / desires[48], de-sires[1]
**rh** admire *S 123.7*; aspire, fire *Luc 2*; conspire *S 10.8*; fire *1H6 4.6.11, Luc 182, 1490, 1606, MW 5.5.90, 96, S 45.3, 154.7, VA 36, 276, 386, 653, 1074*; relier, retire *Luc 642*; require *S 57.2*; retire *LLL 2.1.221, Luc 175, 574*; sire *Luc 234, VA 1180*; squire *KJ 1.1.176*; tire *Luc 706*; Tyre *Per 2. Chorus.21, 3.Chorus.40, 4.Chorus.2* / briars *MND 3.2.445*; fires *Mac 1.4.52*

**desir·e / ~est / ~es / ~ing / ~ed** *v*
dɪˈzəɪɹ / -st / -z / -ɪn, -ɪŋ / -d
**sp** desire[145], de-sire[2] / desirest[2], desir'st[4] / desires[28], *Evans MW 3.1.73, 3.3.208* desires [desire][3] / desiring[4] / desir'd[22], desired[3]
**rh** fire *VA 496*; mire *Luc 1011*; Tyre *Per 1.3.38* / admired, tired *Luc 415*; new-fired *S 153.11*

**desired** *adj*
*m* dɪˈzəɪɹd, -rɪd
**sp** desir'd[2], desired[3]

**desirer / ~s** *n*
dɪˈzəɪɹəɹz
**sp** desirers[1]

**desiring** *adj*
dɪˈzəɪɹɪn, -ɪŋ
**sp** desiring[1]

**desirous** *adj*
dɪˈzəɪɹəs
**sp** desirous[5], desi-rous[1]

**desist** *v*
=
**sp** desist[2]
**rh** resist *Per 1.1.40*

**desk** *n*
=
**sp** deske[4]

**desolate** *adj*
*m* ˈdesələt, -ˌlɛːt
**sp** desolate[6], de-solate[1]

**desolation** *n*
*m* ˌdesəˈlɛːsɪən, -ɪˌɒn
**sp** desolation[9], deso-lation[1]

**despair / ~s** *n*
dɪˈspɛːɹ / -z
**sp** despaire[7], dispaire[22] / despaires[2]
**rh** air *MV 3.2.109*; fair *PP 2.1, S 144.1, VA 743, 955*; hair *Luc 983, S 99.9*; prayer *RJ 1.5.104, Tem Epil.15*

**despair / ~ing** *v*
dɪˈspɛːɹ / -ɪn, -ɪŋ
**sp** despaire[3], dispaire[19], dis-paire[1] / dispairing[3], dispayring[1]
**rh** fair *RJ 1.1.222*

**despairing** *adj*
dɪˈspɛːrɪn, -ɪŋ
**sp** despairing[1], despayring[1]

**desperate** *adj*
*m* ˈdesprət, -pər-, -pəˌrɛːt
**sp** desparate[1], desperate[49], despe-rate[1], desp'rate[7], disperate[1]
**rh** intimate *AW 2.1.184*

**desperately** *adv*
*m* ˈdesprətˌləɪ, -pər-, -tl-
**sp** desperately[4], desp'rately[1]

**desperation** *n*
ˌdespəˈrɛːsɪən
**sp** desperation[2]

**despis·e / ~eth / ~ing / ~ed** *v*
dɪˈspəɪz / -əθ / -ɪn, -ɪŋ / *m* -d, -ɪd
**sp** despise[15] / despiseth[2] / despising[1] / despis'd[8], de-spis'd[1], despised[4], dispisde[1]
**rh** arise, enterprise *Luc 187*; eyes *Per 2.3.26, S 141.3, 149.10* / arising *S 29.9*

**despised** *adj / n*
*m* dɪˈspəɪzd, -ɪd
**sp** despis'd[1], despised[5], dispis'd[1], dispised[1] / despis'd[1]
**rh** *1* disguised *MM 3.2.267*; **rh** *2* sufficed *S 37.9*

**despiser** *n*
dɪˈspəɪzəɹ
**sp** despiser[1]

**despite** *n / prep / v*
dɪˈspəɪt
**sp** despight[17], de-spight[1], despite[2], dispight[1] / despight[2], despite[1] / despight[1]
**rh** *n* delight *MND 5.1.112*; night, right *Luc 1026*; night *VA 731*; white *Luc 55*

**despiteful / ~est** *adj*
dɪˈspəɪtfʊl / -st
**sp** despightful[1], despightfull[5] / despightful'st[1]

**despite of / in ~** *prep*
dɪˈspəɪt əv / ˌɪn-
**sp** despight of[5], despite of[1] / in despight of[15], in dispight of[1]
> spite of

**despiteous** *adj*
dɪsˈpɪtɪəs
**sp** dispitious[1]

**despoiled** *adj*
*m* dɪˈspəɪlɪd
**sp** despoyled[1]

**destine / ~d** *v*
=
**sp** destin'd[2]

**destined** *adj*
=
**sp** destin'd[2]

**destin·y / ~ies** *n*
*m* ˈdestnəɪ, -tɪn-, -tɪˌnəɪ / -z
**sp** destenie[1], destinie[7], desti-nie[1], destiny[11] / destinies[4]
**rh** *1* fly *Luc 1729*; **rh** *2* he *Mac 3.5.17*; heresy *MV 2.9.83*; quality *MW 5.5.39* / infirmities *VA 733*

**destitute** *adj*
ˈdestɪˌtjuːt
**sp** destitute[1]

**destroy / ~s / ~ing / ~ed,** *abbr* **stroyed** *v*
dɪˈstrəɪ / -z / -ɪn, -ɪŋ / -d, *abbr* strəɪd
**sp** destroy[20] / distroyes[1] / destroying[2] / destroy'd[8], destroyed[2], *abbr* stroy'd[1]
**rh** annoy, Troy *Luc 1369*; boy *1H6 4.6.25, VA 346*; enjoy *VA 1163*; joy *Ham 3.2.207, 231, Mac 3.2.6, Per 2.5.88*; joy, toy *Luc 215*; pardonnez-moi *R2 5.3.119*; destroy thee enjoy thee *Luc 514* / destroys it enjoys it *S 9.12* / avoid *H5 3.3.43, R2 1.3.242*

**destroyer / ~s** *n*
dɪˈstrəɪəɹ / -z
**sp** destroyer[1] / destroyers[1]

**destroying** *adj*
dɪˈstrəɪɪn, -ɪŋ
**sp** destroying[1]

**destruction / ~s** *n*
*m* dɪˈstrɤksɪən, -ɪˌɒn / -z
**sp** destruction[27], distruction[1] / destructions[1]

**detain / ~ed** *v*
dɪˈtɛːn / -d
**sp** detaine[6], de-taine[1] / detain'd[3], detayn'd[1]
**rh** chain *CE 2.1.107*; detain him restrain him *VA 577*

**detect / ~s / ~ed** *v*
=
**sp** detect[5] / detects[1] / detected[3]
**rh** recollect *Per 2.1.51*

**detecting** *n*
dɪˈtektɪn, -ɪŋ
**sp** detecting[1]

**detection** *n*
dɪˈteksɪən
**sp** detection[1]

**detector** *n*
dɪˈtektəɹ
**sp** detector[1]

**detention** *n*
dɪˈtensɪən
**sp** detention[1]

**determinate** *adj*
*m* dɪˈtɐːɹmɪnət, -mn-, -mɪˌnɛːt
**sp** determinate[4]
**rh** estimate *S 87.4*

**determination / ~s** *n*
dɪˌtɐɹmɪˈnɛːsɪən / -z
**sp** determination[5] / deter-minations[1]

**determine / ~s / ~d** *v*
dɪˈtɐːɹmɪn / -z / *m* -d, -ɪˌnɪd
**sp** determine[25] / determines[3] / determin'd[15], determined[4]
**rh** impannelled *S 46.11*
> undetermined

**detest / ~s / ~ed** *v*
=
**sp** detest[9] / detests[2] / detested[1]
**rh** *1* breast, guest *Luc 1566*;
**rh** *2* east *MND 3.2.434*

**detestable** *adj*
*m* ˈdetɪsˌtabəl
**sp** detestable[6]

**detested** *adj*
=
**sp** detested[14]

**detesting** *adj*
dɪ'testɪn, -ɪŋ
**sp** detesting[1]

**detract** *v*
=
**sp** detract[2]

**detraction / ~s** *n*
dɪ'traksɪən / -z
**sp** detraction[3] / detractions[1]

**detriment** *Luc* *n*
*m* 'detrɪˌment
**sp** detriment[1]
**rh** discontent, spent *Luc 1579*

**Deucalion** *n*
dju:'kɛ:lɪən
**sp** Deucalion[2]

**deuce-ace** *n*
'dju:s-ˌas
**sp** deus-ace[1]
> ace

**deum**
> Te Deum

**de·us / ~o / dii** *Lat n*
'de:o: / di:
**sp** deo[1] / dij[1]

**deux** *Fr adj*
dø
**sp** deux[1], diux[1]

**devant** *Fr prep*
də'vɑ̃
**sp** deuant[2]

**device / ~s** *n*
dɪ'vəɪs / -ɪz
**sp** deuice[31], deuise[11] / deuices[3], deuises[2], deui-ses[1]
> point-device

**devil** *adj*
*m* 'dɪvəl, dɛ:l
**sp** diuell[6]

**devil / ~'s / ~s / ~s'** *n*
*m* 'dɪvəl, dɛ:l, *Evans MW 1.1.139* 'tevɪl / -z
**sp** deuil[1], deuill[60], [borne]-deuill[1], deule[2], deu'le[1], diuel[9], diuell[133], di-uell[1], diu'll[1], *Evans* teuill[1] / deuills[3], deuils[7], diuels[8] / deuills[1], deuils[3] deules[1], diuelles[1], diuells[1], diuels[29], [germane]-diuels[1] / deuils[1]
**rh** evil *LLL 4.3.286, 5.2.106, Luc 85, 847, 973, 1246, 1513, PP 2.7, S 144.7, TN 3.4.361*
> demi-, yoke-devil

**devilish** *adj*
'dɪvlɪʃ, -vəl-
**sp** diuelish[2], diuellish[12]
**rh** womanish *R3 1.4.266*

**devil-porter** *v*
'dɪvɪl-'pɔ:ɹtəɹ
**sp** deuill-porter[1]

**devise / ~s / ~ing / ~d** *v*
dɪ'vəɪz / -ɪz / -ɪn, -ɪŋ / *m* -ɪd, -d
**sp** deuise[43], de-uise[2] / deuises[1] / deuising[1] / deuis'd[15], de-uis'd[1], deuised[4]
**rh** eyes *MND 3.2.35, S 83.14* / prized *AY 3.2.146*; sympathized *S 82.9*
> new-devised

**devoid** *adj*
dɪ'vəɪd
**sp** deuoid[1]

**Devonshire** *n*
*m* 'devənˌʃəɪɹ
**sp** Deuonshire[1]

**devote / ~d** *v*
dɪ'vo:t / -ɪd
**sp** deuote[2] / deuoted[2]
> true-devoted

**devoted** *adj*
dɪ'vo:tɪd
**sp** deuoted[4]

**devotement** *n*
dɪ'vo:tmənt
**sp** deuotement[1]

**devotion / ~'s** *n*
*m* dɪ'vo:sɪən, -ɪˌɒn / -ɪənz
**sp** deuotion[18] / deuotions[1]

**devour / ~s / ~ing / ~ed** *v*
dɪ'vo:ɹ / -z / -ɪn, -ɪŋ / *m* -d, -ɪd
**sp** deuour[1], deuoure[9] / deuoures[1], deuours[1] / deuouring[2] / deuour'd[3], deuoured[3]
**rh** flower *Luc 1256* / flowers, ours *Luc 872* / o'ershowered *Per 4.4.25*

**devourer / ~s** *n*
dɪ'vo:rəɹz
**sp** deuourers[1]

**devouring** *adj / n*
dɪ'vo:ɹɪn, -ɪŋ
**sp** deuouring[2] / deuouring[1]
**rh** *n* souring *Luc 700*
> fell-, love-devouring

**devout** *adj*
dɪ'vəʊt
**sp** deuout[8]

**devoutly** *adv*
dɪ'vəʊtləɪ
**sp** deuoutly[3]

**dew / ~s** *n*
dju: / -z
**sp** deaw[3], dew[21], [hony-heauy-] dew[1], dewe[4], dewe's [dew is][1] / dewes[5]
**rh** few *Luc 24*
> morn-dew

**dew** *v*
dju:
**sp** dew[4], dewe[1]
**rh** strew *RJ 5.3.14*

**dewberr·y / ~ies** *n*
*m* 'dju:bəˌrəɪz
**sp** dewberries[1]
**rh** *1* bees, courtesies, mulberries *MND 3.1.161*; *rh 2* arise, butterflies, eyes, thighs *MND 3.1.161*

**dew-drop / ~s** *n*
'dju:ˌdrɒp / -s
**sp** dew drop[1] / dew drops[1]
> drop

**dew-dropping** *adj*
'dju:ˌdrɒpɪn, -ɪŋ
**sp** dew dropping[1]

**dewlap** *n*
'dju:lap
**sp** dewlop[1]

**dewlap / ~ped** *v*
'dju:lapt
**sp** dew-lapt[2]

**dewy** *adj*
'dju:əɪ
**sp** dewy[1]

**dexter** *adj*
'dekstəɹ
**sp** dexter[1]

**dexteriously** *adv*
dek'sterɪəsləɪ
**sp** dexteriously[1]

**dexterity** *n*
*m* dek'sterɪ,təɪ, -ɪt-, -'steɹtəɪ
**sp** dexteritie[3], dexterity[2]
**rh** majesty *Luc 1389*

**di** *Lat*
> deus

**diable** *Fr interj*
'djablə
**sp** diable[4]

**diablo** *Sp interj*
dɪ'ablo:
**sp** diablo[1]

**diadem** *n*
*m* 'dəɪə,dem, 'dəɪd-
**sp** diadem[10], diademe[3]

**dial / ~'s / ~s** *n*
*m* 'dəɪɑl, dəɪl / -z
**sp** diall[5], dyall[1] / dialls[1], dials[2] / dialls[2]
**rh** denial, trial *Luc 327*

**dialect** *n*
*m* 'dəɪə,lekt, 'dəɪl-
**sp** dialect[2]

**dial-hand** *S* *n*
'dəɪɑl-'and, -'hand
**sp** dyall hand[1]
**rh** stand *S 104.9*

**dialogue** *n*
*m* 'dəɪə,lɒg, 'dəɪl-
**sp** dialogue[7]

**diamond / ~s** *n*
*m* 'dəɪə,mɒnd, 'dəɪmənd / -z
**sp** diamond[13] / diamonds[4]

**Dian / ~'s** *n*
'dəɪən / -z
**sp** Dian[12], Diane[1], Dyan[1] / Dians[5]

**Diana / ~'s** *n*
dəɪ'anə, dɪ- / -z
**sp** Diana[15] / Dianaes[2], dianas[2], Diana's[2]

**diaper** *n*
'dəɪpəɹ
**sp** diaper[1]

**dibble** *n*
=
**sp** dible[1]

**dice** *n*
dəɪs
**sp** dice[10]
**rh** nice *LLL 5.2.233, 326*

**dice / ~d** *v*
dəɪst
**sp** dic'd[1]

**dicer / ~s'** *n*
'dəɪsəɹz
**sp** dicers[1]

**dich** [do it] *v*
dɪʧ
**sp** dich[1]

**Dick** *n*
=
**sp** Dick[1], Dicke[8]
**rh** trick *LLL 5.2.464*

**dickens** *n*
=
**sp** dickens[1]

**Dickie** *n*
'dɪkəɪ
**sp** Dickie[1]

**Dickon** *n*
'dɪkən
**sp** Dickon[1]

**dictator** *n*
dɪk'tɛ:təɹ
**sp** dictator[1]

**Dictynna** *n*
dɪk'tɪnə
**sp** *LLL 4.2.36 emend of* dictisima[2], *Dull's* dictima[1]

**did, didst**
> do

**Dido / ~'s** *n*
'dəɪdo: / -z
**sp** Dido[11] / Didoes[1], Dido's[1]

**die** *n*
dəɪ
**sp** dye[1]
**pun** *KJ 2.1.323* dye

**die / ~est / ~s / dying / died / ~est** *v*
dəɪ / -st, 'dəɪəst / -z / 'dəɪɪn, -ɪŋ / dəɪd / -st
**sp** die[184], dye[271] / diest[8], di'st[1], dyest[10], dy'st[2] / dies[47], dyes[31] / dying[20] / di'd[4], dide[8], di'de[6], died[25], dy'd[9], dyde[1], dy'de[17], dyed[31], dy-ed[2] / dyed'st[1]
**rh** *1* ay *R2 3.3.174*; by *H8 3.1.14*; cry *LLL 5.2.254, TC 3.1.118*; deny *AY 4.3.64*; eye *CE 2.1.115, Luc 274, 1477, MW 5.5.47, Per 1.1.34, R2 1.2.73, RJ 1.2.50, 89, S 9.3, 25.8, TC 5.7.8*; eye, I *Luc 1139*; fly *AW 2.1.168, 1H6 4.5.20, 45, 54, 4.6.47, 3H6 4.4.35, Luc 231, RJ 3.1.175*; high *Per 1.1.149, R2 5.5.112*; I *AW 1.3.154, 1H6 4.5.51, LLL 4.3.207, MM 4.3.79, RJ 3.5.11, TS 3.1.76, VA 1017*; lie *CE 3.2.51, Cym 4.4.51, 2H4 4.2.239, MA 4.1.152, RJ 2. Chorus.3, S 81.6, 92.12, TN 2.3.103, VA 246*; sky *MND 5.1.298*; testify *Per Prol.39*; thereby *S 11.14*; try *AW 2.1.186, R2 1.1.185;* **rh** *2* custody,

jealousy *CE 1.1.155*; dignity *S 94.10*; eternity *Ham 1.2.72*; infamy, livery *Luc 1052*; iniquity *Luc 1686*; jealousy *CE 2.1.115*; loyalty *R3 3.3.2*; memory *S 1.2*; misery *1H6 3.2.136*; philosophy *LLL 1.1.31*; presently *Tit 5.1.145*; property *AW 2.1.188*; remedy *RJ 3.5.243, 4.1.66*; willingly *TN 5.1.131* / eyes *Luc 1652*; eyes, lies *MV 3.2.68*; implies *AW 1.3.212*; lies *KJ 3.1.338, Luc 1485, MA 5.3.6, R2 5.3.69, VA 803*; lies, skies *Luc 508* / flying *TNK 1.5.3* / pride *1H6 4.7.15*; side *Luc 379*
> a-dying, dead

**dies** *mock Lat TN 4.2.12*
'di:ez
**sp** dies[1]

**diet** *n*
'dəɪət
**sp** diet[9], dyet[4]

**diet / ~ed** *v*
'dəɪət / -ɪd
**sp** diet[2], dyet[3] / dieted[3], dyeted[1]
> lust-dieted

**dieter** *n*
'dəɪətəɹ
**sp** dieter[1]

**Dieu** *Fr n*
djø, *Pistol H5 4.4.7ff* dju:
**sp** Dieu[11], Du[1], *Pistol* Dewe[3]

**differ / ~s / ~ing** *v*
'dɪfəɹ / -z / 'dɪfrɪn, -ɪŋ, -fər-
**sp** differ[2] / differs[3], dif-fers[1] / differing[1], diffring[1]

**difference / ~s** *n*
*m* 'dɪfəˌrens, -fərəns, -frəns / -ɪz
**sp** difference[32], dif-ference[2], diffe-rence[1], diff'rence[1] / differences[6], differe[n]ces[1]
**rh** excellence *S 105.8*

**differency** *n*
'dɪfrənsəɪ
**sp** differency[1]

**different** *adj*
*m* 'dɪfəˌrent, -fərənt, -frənt
**sp** different[9]
**rh** excellent *RJ 2.3.10*
> indifferent

**differing** *adj*
'dɪfrɪn, -ɪŋ, -fər-
**sp** differing[1]

**difficile** *Fr adj*
difi'sil
**sp** difficile[1]

**difficult** *adj*
'dɪfkəlt, -fɪk-
**sp** difficult[1]

**difficult·y / ~ies** *n*
*m* 'dɪfkəltəɪ, -ˌtəɪ, -fɪk- / -z
**sp** difficultie[1], difficulty[2] / difficulties[2]

**diffidence** *n*
*m* 'dɪfɪˌdens
**sp** diffidence[2]

**diffuse / ~est** *v*
=
**sp** diffusest[1]

**diffused** *adj*
*m* dɪ'fju:zɪd
**sp** diffused[1]

**dig / ~ging / ~ged** *v*
= / dɪgɪn, -ɪŋ / *Fluellen H5 3.2.60* dɪgt
**sp** dig[2], digge[7] / digging[1] / dig'd[2], digg'd[6], *Fluellen* digt[1]

**digest / ~ed** *v*
dɪ'ʤest / -ɪd
**sp** digest[12] / digested[5]
> disgest

**digestion / ~s** *n*
*m* dɪ'ʤestɪən, -ɪˌɒn / -tɪˌɒnz
**sp** digestion[6] / digestions[1]
> disgestion

**Dighton** *n*
'dəɪtən
**sp** Dighton[3]

**dignif·y / ~ies / ~ied** *v*
*m* 'dɪgnɪˌfəɪ / -z / -d
**sp** dignifie[2] / dignifies[2] / dignified[4]
**rh** dyed *S 101.4*; hide, pride *Luc 660*; misapplied *RJ 2.3.18*

**dignit·y / ~ies** *n*
*m* 'dɪgnɪˌtəɪ, -nɪt- / -z
**sp** dignitie[16], dignity[19] / dignities[14]
**rh** *1* be *Cym 4.2.4*; be, he *Cym 5.4.57*; mutiny *RJ Prol.1*; quantity *MND 1.1.233*; revelry *AY 5.4.173*; sover-eignty *LLL 4.3.234*; **rh** *2* die *S 94.12*; eye *Luc 437*

**digress / ~ing** *v*
dɪ'gres / -ɪn, -ɪŋ
**sp** digresse[2] / digressing[1]

**digressing** *adj*
dɪ'gresɪn, -ɪŋ
**sp** digressing[1]

**digression** *n*
dɪ'gresɪən
**sp** digression[2]

**dig-you-den** *greeting*
ˌdɪgjə'den
**sp** dig-you-den[1]

**dii** *Lat*
> deus

**dilate** *v*
dɪ'lɛ:t
**sp** dilate[2]

**dilated** *adj*
dɪ'lɛ:tɪd
**sp** dilated[3]

**dilation / ~s** *n*
dɪ'lɛ:sɪənz
**sp** dilations[1]

**dilatory** *adj*
'dɪləˌtɒrəɪ
**sp** dilatory[2]

**dildo / ~s** *n*
'dɪldo:z
**sp** dil-do's[1]

**dilemma / ~s** *n*
dɪ'lemə / -z
**sp** delemma[1] / dilemma's[1]

**diligence** *n*
*m* 'dɪlɪˌʤens, -ʤəns
**sp** diligence[7], dilligence[2]
**rh** expense *Per 3.Chorus.19*; offence, thence *Luc 1853*

**diligent** *adj*
*m* 'dɪlɪˌʤent, -ʤənt
**sp** diligent[5], dilligent[1]

**diluculum / ~o** *Lat n*
*Lat* dɪ'lʊkjʊlo:
**sp** deliculo[1]

**dim** *adj*
=
**sp** dim[4], dimme[5], dimne[1], dym[1]
**rh** trim *TNK 1.1.9*

**dim / ~s / ~med** *v*
=
**sp** dim[1], dimme[3] / dims[1] / dim'd[4]
**rh** untrimmed *S 18.6*

**dimension / ~s** *n*
dɪ'mɛ:nsɪən / -z
**sp** dimension[2] / dimensions[2], dementions[1]

**diminish / ~ed** *v*
=
**sp** diminish[2] / diminish'd[1]
**rh** finish *AY 5.4.136* / unfinished *VA 417*

**diminishing** *n*
*m* dɪ'mɪnɪˌʃɪn, -ɪŋ
**sp** diminishing[1]

**diminution** *n*
ˌdɪmɪ'nju:sɪən
**sp** diminution[2]

**diminutive** *adj*
dɪ'mɪnɪˌtɪv, -ɪnjə-
**sp** diminitiue[1], diminutiue[1]

**diminutive / ~s** *n*
dɪ'mɪnɪˌtɪvz, -ɪnjə-
**sp** diminitiues[1], diminutiues[1]

**dimmed** *adj*
=
**sp** dimn'd[1]

**dimming** *n*
'dɪmɪn, -ɪŋ
**sp** dimming[1]

**dimple / ~d** *adj*
=
**sp** dimpled[3]

**dimple** *VA* **/ ~s** *n*
=
**sp** dimple[1] / dimples[1]
**rh** simple *VA 242*

**din** *n*
=
**sp** din[2], dinne[5], dyn[1]
**rh** Mytilene *Per 5.2.7* [*Chorus*]; wherein *Cym 5.4.111*

**dine / ~s / ~d** *v*
dəɪn / -z / -d
**sp** dine[25] / dines[2] / din'd[13], din'de[1], dined[2], dyn'd[1]
**rh** fine *LLL 1.1.61*
> half-dine

**dîner** *Fr v*
di'ne
**sp** diner[1]

**ding-a-ding-ding** *interj*
=
**sp** ding a ding, ding[1]
**rh** sing, spring *AY 5.3.19, 25, 31, 37*

**ding-dong** *interj*
=
**sp** ding dong[1]; ding, dong[2]; ding-dong[1]

**dining-chamber / ~s** *n*
'dəɪnɪn-ˌʧambəɹ, -ɪŋ- / -z
**sp** dyning-chamber[1] / dy-ning chambers[1]
> chamber

**dinner / ~s** *n*
'dɪnəɹ / -z
**sp** dinner[82], dinners [dinner is][2] / dinners[2]
**rh** sinner *CE 2.2.196*; win her *TS 1.2.215*
> after-dinner

**dinner-time** *n*
'dɪnəɹ-ˌtəɪm
**sp** dinner time[10]
> time

**dint** *n*
=
**sp** dint[2]
**rh** print *VA 354*
> undinted

**Diomedes / Diomed / ~'s** *n*
dəɪ'ɒmɪˌdi:z / 'dəɪə-ˌmed / -z
**sp** Diomedes[5], Diome-des[1] / Diomed[41], Diomede[1], Dio-mede[1], Diomed's [Diomed is][1] / Diomeds[2]
**rh** head *TC 4.4.135, 5.2.189*

**Dion** *n*
'dəɪən
**sp** Dion[6]

**dip / ~s / ~ping / ~ped / ~pedest** *v*
= / = / 'dɪpɪn, -ɪŋ / = / dɪpst, -pdst
**sp** dip[2] / dips[1] / dipping[1] / dipt[1] / dipd'st[1]

**dire / ~est** *adj*
dəɪɹ / *m* -st, 'dəɪrəst
**sp** dire[13], dyre[3] / dyr'st[1], direst[1]

**dire / dis / dit / dites** *Fr v*
di:ɹ / di / di, dit *when followed by* il / dit
**sp** dire[1] / de / dict[1], dit[4] / dites[2]

**direct** *adj*
=
**sp** direct[15]
> indirect

**direct / ~s / ~ing / ~ed** *v*
= / = / dɪ'rektɪn, -ɪŋ / =
**sp** direct[19] / directs[1] / directing[1] / directed[12]
**rh** unrespected *S 43.4*

**direction / ~s** *n*
dɪ'reksɪən / -z
**sp** direction[23] / directions[5], directi-ons[1]
**rh** complexion *VA 216*

**direction-giver** *n*
dɪ'reksɪən-ˌgɪvəɹ
**sp** direction-giuer[1]
> giver

**directitude** *n*
dɪ'rektɪˌtju:d
**sp** directitude[2]

**directive** *n*
=
**sp** directiue[1]

**directly** *adv*
dɪ'rekləɪ, -ktləɪ
**sp** directly[27], di-rectly[2], direct-ly[1]

**direful** *adj*
'dəɪɹfʊl
**sp** direfull[7]

**dire-lamenting** *adj*
'dəɪɹ-ləˌmentɪn, -ɪŋ
**sp** dire-lamenting[1]
> lament

**direness** *n*
'dəɪɹnəs
**sp** direnesse[1]

**dirge / ~s** *n*
dɐ:ɹʤ / 'dɐ:ɹʤɪz
**sp** dirge[1] / dyrges[1]

**dirt** *n*
dɐ:ɹt
**sp** dirt[3], durt[7]

**dirty** *adj*
'dɐ:ɹtəɪ
**sp** dirtie[1], dirty[1], durtie[2], durty[3]

**Dis / ~'s** *n*
dɪs / 'dɪsɪz
**sp** Dis[1] / Dysses[1]

**disability** *n*
*m* ˌdɪsə'bɪlɪˌtəɪ
**sp** disabilitie[1]

**disab·le / ~led** *v*
dɪs'ɛ:bəl / *m* dɪs'ɛ:bəld, -lɪd
**sp** disable[2] / disabled[1], *S* disabled[1]
**rh** strumpeted *S 66.8*

**disabling** *n*
dɪs'ɛ:blɪn, -ɪŋ
**sp** disabling[1]

**disadvantage** *n*
ˌdɪsəd'vantɪʤ
**sp** disaduantage[1], dis-aduantage[1]
> advantage

**disagree** *v*
=
**sp** disagree[1]
> agree

**disallow** *v*
ˌdɪsə'ləʊ
**sp** disallow[1]

**disanimate / ~s** *v*
dɪs'anɪˌmɛ:ts
**sp** dis-animates[1]

**disannul / ~s** *v*
ˌdɪsə'nɤl / -z
**sp** disanull[1] /disanulls[1]

**disappointed** *adj*
ˌdɪsə'pəɪntɪd
**sp** disappointed[1]

**disarm / ~eth / ~ed** *v*
dɪs'ɑ:ɹm / -əθ / -d
**sp** disarme[3] / disarmeth[1] / disarm'd[1]
**rh** warmed *S 154.8*

**disaster / ~s** *n*
dɪs'astəɹ / -z
**sp** disaster[4] / disasters[5]

**disaster** *v*
dɪs'astəɹ
**sp** disaster[1]

**disastrous** *adj*
dɪs'astrəs
**sp** disastrous[1]

**disbench / ~ed** *v*
dɪs'benʃt
**sp** disbench'd[1], dis-bench'd[1]
> bench

**disburse / ~d** *v*
dɪs'bɐ:ɹs / *m* -ɪd, -t
**sp** disburse[1] / disbursed[2], disburst[1]

**disburthen / ~ed** *v*
dɪs'bɐ:ɹðənd
**sp** disburthen'd[1]

**discandering** *n*
dɪs'kandrɪn, -ɪŋ, -dər-
**sp** discandering[1]

**discandy** *v*
dɪs'kandəɪ
**sp** dis-candie[1]

**discard / ~ed** *v*
dɪs'kɑ:ɹd / -ɪd
**sp** discard[3] / discarded[5], dis-carded[1]

**discase** *v*
dɪs'kɛ:s
**sp** discase[1], dis-case[1]
> case

**discern / ~est / ~s / ~ing / ~ed** *v*
dɪ'sɐ:ɹn / -st / -z / -ɪn, -ɪŋ / -d
**sp** discerne[7] / discern'st[1] / decernes[1], discernes[1] / [eye]-discerning[1] / discern'd[1]
**rh** learn *Luc 619*
> undiscernable

**discerner** *n*
dɪ'sɐ:ɹnəɹ
**sp** discerner[1]

**discerning / ~s** *n*
dɪˈsɐːɹnɪnz, -ɪŋz
**sp** discernings[1]

**discharge** *n*
dɪsˈʧɑːɹʤ
**sp** discharge[6], dis-charge[1]

**discharg·e / ~ed / ~ing** *v*
dɪsˈʧɐːɹʤ / -ɪn, -ɪŋ / *m* -d, -ɪd
**sp** discharge[24] / discharging[1] / dischargd[1], discharg'd[12], discharged[4]

**disciple / ~s** *n*
dɪˈsəɪpəl / -z
**sp** disciples[1]

**disciple / ~d** *v*
dɪˈsəɪpəld
**sp** discipled[1]

**discipline / ~s** *n*
*m* ˈdɪsɪplɪn, -ˌplɪn / -ɪplɪnz
**sp** discipline[14], dis-cipline[1] / disciplines[7]

**discipline / ~d** *v*
*m* ˈdɪsɪplɪnd, -ˌplɪnd
**sp** disciplin'd[2]

**disclaim / ~est / ~s / ~ing / ~ed** *v*
dɪsˈklɛːm / -st / -z / -ɪn, -ɪŋ / -d
**sp** disclaim[1], disclaime[1] / disclaim'st[1] / disclaimes[1] / disclaiming[1] / disclaim'd[1]

**disclaiming** *n*
dɪsˈklɛːmɪn, -ɪŋ
**sp** disclaiming[1]

**disclose** *n*
dɪsˈkloːz
**sp** disclose[1]

**disclose / ~s / ~d** *v*
dɪsˈkloːz / -ɪz / -d
**sp** disclose[3] / discloses[1] / disclos'd[7], disclosed[1]
**rh** roses *S 54.8* / disposed *LLL 2.1.237, 5.2.467*

**discolour / ~s** *v*
dɪsˈkɤləɹ / -z
**sp** discolour[1] / discolours[1]
> colour

**discoloured** *adj*
dɪsˈkɤləɹd
**sp** discolour'd[1], discoloured[2]

**discomfit / ~ed** *v*
dɪsˈkɤmfɪt / -ɪd
**sp** discomfite[1] / discomfited[4]

**discomfiture** *n*
dɪsˈkɤmfɪtəɹ
**sp** discomfiture[1]

**discomfort** *n / v*
dɪsˈkɤmfəɹt
**sp** discomfort[5] / discomfort[3]

**discomfortable** *adj*
*m* dɪsˈkɤmfəɹˌtabəl
**sp** discomfortable[1]

**discommend** *v*
=
**sp** discom-mend[1]

**disconsolate** *adj*
*m* dɪsˈkɒnsəˌlɛːt
**sp** disconsolate[1]
> consolate

**discontent / ~s** *n*
=
**sp** discontent[13] / discontents[6]
**rh** accident *S 124.7*; bent *S 143.8*; detriment, spent *Luc 1580*; event, spent *Luc 1601* / events *VA 1161*
> content

**discontented** *adj*
=
**sp** discontented[13]

**discontentedly** *adv*
ˌdɪskənˈtentɪdləɪ
**sp** discontentedly[1]

**discontenting** *adj*
ˌdɪskənˈtentɪn, -ɪŋ
**sp** discontenting[1]

**discontinue / ~d** *v*
=
**sp** discontinue[1] / discontinued[1]

**discord / ~s** *n*
ˈdɪskɔːɹd / -z
**sp** discord[16], dis-cord[1] / discords[4], dis-cords[1]

**discordant** *adj*
dɪsˈkɔːɹdənt
**sp** discordant[1]
> still-discordant

**discourse / ~s** *n*
dɪsˈkɔːɹs / -ɪz
**sp** discourse[44] / discourses[2]
> love-discourse

**discourse / ~s / ~d** *v*
dɪsˈkɔːɹs / -ɪz / *m* -ɪd
**sp** discourse[13] / discourses[2] / discoursed[2]
> dumb-discoursive

**discourser** *n*
dɪsˈkɔːɹsəɹ
**sp** discourser[1]

**discourtesy** *n*
*m* dɪsˈkɔːɹtəˌsəɪ
**sp** discourtesie[1]
> courtesy

**discover / ~s / ~ed** *v*
dɪsˈkɤvəɹ / -z / *m* -ɪd, -d
**sp** discouer[33], disco-uer[1] / discouers[3], dis-couers[1] / discouerd[1], discouer'd[6], discouered[8], dis-couered[1]
**rh** lover *TG 2.1.158*
> undiscovered

**discoverer / ~s** *n*
dɪsˈkɤvrəɹz, -vər-
**sp** discouerers[1]

**discover·y / ~ies** *n*
*m* dɪsˈkɤvrəɪ, -vər-, əˌrəɪ / -vrəɪz
**sp** discouerie[4], discouery[8], discou'rie[1] / discoueries[1], discoue-ries[2]
**rh** quality, uncertainly *Luc 1314*

**discredit / ~s** *n*
=
**sp** discredits[1]
> credit

**discredit / ~ed** *v*
=
**sp** discredit[4], discredite[1] / discredited[2]

**discreet** *adj*
=
**sp** discreet[6], discreete[1]
**rh** sweet *RJ 1.1.193*
> indiscreet

**discreetly** *adv*
dɪs'kri:tləɪ
**sp** discreetly[2]

**discretion / ~s** *n*
dɪs'kresɪən / -z
**sp** discretion[31] / discretions[3]

**discretion-answer** *n*
dɪs'kresɪən-'ansəɹ
**sp** discretion-answere[1]
> answer

**discuss** *v*
dɪs'kɤs
**sp** discusse[6]

**disdain** *n*
dɪs'dɛ:n
**sp** disdain[17]

**disdain / ~est / ~s / ~eth / ~ing/ ~ed** *v*
dɪs'dɛ:n / -st / -z / -əθ / -ɪn, -ɪŋ / *m* -d, -ɪd
**sp** disdain[12] / disdainst[1] / disdaines[4], dis-daines[1] / disdaineth[1] / disdaining[3], disdayning[1] / disdain'd[1], disdained[2]
**rh** again *VA 501*; again, pain *Luc 691*; chain *VA 112*; gain, pain *PP 15.11*; pain *3H6 3.3.127, S 132.2, 140.2*; rein *VA 33, 394*; remain *Luc 521*; slain *VA 241, 761*; **disdain him** complain him, entertain him *Luc 844*; **disdain me** entertain me *CE 3.1.121* / staineth *S 33.13*

**disdainful** *adj*
dɪs'dɛ:nfʊl
**sp** disdainefull[2], disdainful[1], disdainfull[6]

**disdainfully** *adv*
dɪs'dɛ:nfləɪ, -fəl-
**sp** disdainfully[1]

**disease / ~d** *adj*
*m* dɪs'i:zd, -zɪd
**sp** dis-eas'd[5], diseased[2]

**disease / ~s** *n*
dɪs'i:z / dɪs'i:zɪz
**sp** disease[29] / diseases[20], dis-eases[1]
**rh** please *S 147.2* / eases *TC 5.10.57*

**disedge / ~d** *v*
=
**sp** disedg'd[1]

**disembark** *v*
ˌdɪsɪm'bɑ:ɹk
**sp** dis-embarque[1], disimbarke[1]

**disfigure / ~d** *v*
dɪs'fɪgəɹ / -d, -ɪd
**sp** disfigure[5] / disfigur'd[1], disfigured[1]
> figure

**disfurnish** *v*
dɪs'fɐ:ɹnɪʃ
**sp** disfurnish[2]
> furnish

**disgest / ~ed** *v*
dɪs'ʤest / -ɪd
**sp** disgest[2] / disgested[1]
> digest

**disgestion / ~s** *n*
dɪs'ʤestɪənz
**sp** disgestions[1]
> digestion

**disgorge** *v*
dɪs'gɔ:ɹʤ
**sp** disgorge[3]
> gorge

**disgrace / ~'s / ~s** *n*
dɪs'grɛ:s / -ɪz
**sp** disgrace[31] / disgraces[1] / disgraces[5]
**rh** base *1H6 4.6.20*; case *R2 1.1.133*; face *Luc 479, 827, R2 1.1.194, 2.1.168, S 33.8, 34.8, 103.8, 127.8*; face, place *Luc 802*

**disgrac·e / ~ing / ~ed** *v*
dɪs'grɛ:s / -ɪn, -ɪŋ / *m* -t, -ɪd
**sp** disgrace[9] / disgracing[1] / disgrac'd[9], dis-grac'd[1], disgraced[1]
**rh** **disgrace it** chase it *VA 412* / chased *Luc 1833*; chased, defaced *Luc 718*; misplaced *S 66.7*
> all-disgraced, grace

**disgraced** *adj*
*m* dɪs'grɛ:st
**sp** disgrac'd[3]

**disgraceful** *adj*
dɪs'grɛ:sfʊl
**sp** disgracefull[1]

**disgracious** *adj*
dɪs'grɛ:sɪəs
**sp** disgracious[2]

**disguise / ~s** *n*
dɪs'gəɪz / -ɪz
**sp** disguise[11] / disguises[2]

**disguis·e / ~ing / ~ed** *v*
dɪs'gəɪz / -ɪn, -ɪŋ / -d
**sp** disguise[6] / disguising[1] / disguis'd[1]
**rh** arise, eyes *Luc 1815*

**disguised** *adj*
dɪs'gəɪzd
**sp** disguis'd[12], dis-guisd[1], disguisde[1], disguised[5]
**rh** advised *LLL 5.2.301, 433*; anatomized *Luc 1452*; surprised *LLL 5.2.83*; well-advised *CE 2.2.224*

**disguised** *n*
dɪs'gəɪzd
**sp** disguised[1]
**rh** despised *MM 3.2.268*

**disguiser** *n*
dɪs'gəɪzəɹ
**sp** disguiser[1]

**disguising** *adj*
dɪsˈɡəɪzɪn, -ɪŋ
**sp** disguising[1]

**dish / ~es** *n*
=
**sp** dish[34], [Dutch]-dish[1] / dishes[9], [china]-dishes[1]
**rh** fish *CE 3.1.23, Cym 4.2.35, Tem 2.2.179*; wish *LLL 4.3.80*
> clack-, tun-dish

**dish / ~ed** *v*
=
**sp** dish'd[1]

**dishabit / ~ed** *v*
dɪsˈabɪtɪd, -ˈha-
**sp** dishabited[1]

**dish-clout** *n*
ˈdɪʃ-ˌkləʊt
**sp** dish-clout[1], dishclout[1]

**dishearten / ~s** *v*
dɪsˈɑːɹtən, -ˈhɑː- / -z
**sp** dis-hearten[1] / dis-heartens[1]
> hearten

**dishonest** *adj*
=
**sp** dishonest[10], dis-honest[1]
> honest

**dishonestly** *adv*
*m* dɪsˈɒnɪstˌləɪ
**sp** dishonestly[2]

**dishonesty** *n*
*m* dɪsˈɒnɪsˌtəɪ, -st-
**sp** dishonestie[1], dishonesty[3]

**dishonour / ~'s / ~s** *n*
dɪsˈɒnəɹ / -z
**sp** dishonor[17], dis-honor[3], dishonour[8], dis-honour[1] / dishonours[1] / dishonors[1]
> honour

**dishonour / ~s / ~ed** *v*
dɪsˈɒnəɹ / -z / -d
**sp** dishonor[3], dishonour[8] / dishonors[2] / dishonor'd[3], dis-honor'd[1], dishonored[2], dis-honored[2], dishonour'd[3], dishonoured[5]
**rh** bred, dead *Luc 1185*

**dishonourable** *adj*
*m* dɪsˈɒnəˌrabəl, -ərəb-
**sp** dis-honorable[2], dishonourable[4]

**dishonoured** *adj*
*m* dɪsˈɒnəɹd, -əˌrɪd
**sp** dishonor'd[2], dishonour'd[1], dishonoured[2]
> undishonoured

**dis-horn** *v*
dɪsˈɔːɹn, -ˈhɔː-
**sp** dis-horne[1]
> horn

**disinherit / ~ed** *v*
ˌdɪsɪnˈerɪt, -ˈhe- / -ɪd
**sp** disinherit[1], dis-inherite[2] / disinherited[1], dis-inherited[2]
> inherit

**disjoin / ~s / ~ing / ~ed** *v*
dɪsˈdʒəɪn / -z / -ɪn, -ɪŋ / -d
**sp** dis-ioyne[1] / dis-ioynes[1] / disioyning[1] / dis-ioyn'd[1]
> join

**disjoint** *adj*
dɪsˈdʒəɪnt
**sp** disioynt[1], dis-ioynt[1]

**disjunction** *n*
dɪsˈdʒɤŋksɪən
**sp** disiunction[1]

**dislike / ~s** *n*
dɪsˈləɪk / -s
**sp** dislike[7] / dislikes[1]
> like

**dislike / ~est / ~s / ~n** *v*
dɪsˈləɪk / -st / -s / -ən
**sp** dislike[8] / dislik'st[2] / dislikes[2] / disliken[1]

**dislimn / ~s** *v*
dɪsˈlɪmz
**sp** dislimes[1]

**dislodge / ~d** *v*
=
**sp** dislodg'd[1]
> lodge

**disloyal** *adj*
dɪsˈləɪəl
**sp** disloyall[12]
> loyal

**disloyalty** *n*
*m* dɪsˈləɪəlˌtəɪ
**sp** disloyaltie[1]
**rh** eye *CE 3.2.11*

**dismal / ~lest** *adj*
ˈdɪzmɑl / -st
**sp** dismall[19] / dismall'st[1], dismal'st[1]

**dismantle / ~d** *v*
=
**sp** dismantle[1], dis-mantle[1] / dismantled[1]
> mantle

**dismask / ~ed** *v*
dɪsˈmaskt
**sp** dismaskt[1]
> mask

**dismay / ~ed** *adj*
dɪsˈmɛːd
**sp** dismaid[5], dismay'd[2], dismayde[1], dismayed[1]
**rh** afraid *VA 896*; aid *R3 5.3.175*; displayed *Luc 273*

**dismay** *n*
dɪsˈmɛː
**sp** dismaie[1], dismay[3]
**rh** away *Ham 4.1.45*; day *MV 1.3.177*; fray *MV 3.2.61*

**dismay / ~ed** *v*
dɪsˈmɛː / -d
**sp** dismay[2] / dismay'd[1]

**disme / ~s** *n*
dəɪmz
**sp** dismes[1]

**dismember / ~ed** *v*
dɪs'membəɹ / -d
**sp** dismember[2] / dismembred[1]

**dismiss / ~ing / ~ed** *v*
= / dɪs'mɪsɪn, -ɪŋ / =
**sp** dismisse[23] / dismissing[1] / dismiss'd[5], dismist[2]

**dismissed** *adj*
*m* dɪs'mɪst, -sɪd
**sp** dismis'd[1], dismissed[1]

**dismission** *n*
dɪs'mɪsɪən
**sp** dismission[2]

**dismount / ~ed** *v*
dɪs'məʊnt / -ɪd
**sp** dismount[2] / dismounted[1], dismoun-ted[1]
**rh** fount *LC 281*

**disnatured** *adj*
dɪs'nɛ:təɹd
**sp** disnatur'd[1]
> nature

**disobedience** *n*
=
**sp** disobedience[7], diso-bedience[1]

**disobedient** *adj*
=
**sp** disobedient[1]

**disobey / ~s** *v*
ˌdɪsə'bɛ: / -z
**sp** disobey[3] / disobeyes[1]
> obey

**disorbed** *adj*
dɪs'ɔ:ɹbd
**sp** disorb'd[1]

**disorder / ~s** *n*
dɪs'ɔ:ɹdəɹ / -z
**sp** disorder[7], diorder's [disorder is][1] / disorders[3]
> order

**disordered** *adj*
dɪs'ɔ:ɹdəɹd
**sp** disorder'd[6], disordered[1]

**disorderly** *adv*
dɪs'ɔ:ɹdəɹləɪ
**sp** disorderly[1]

**disparage** *v*
=
**sp** disparage[2]

**disparagement / ~s** *n*
=
**sp** disparagement[2] / disparagements[1]

**dispark / ~ed** *v*
dɪs'pɑ:ɹkt
**sp** dis-park'd[1]

**dispatch / ~ed** *v*
=
**sp** dispach[1], dispatch[68] / dispatch'd[11], dispatcht[9]
**rh** catch *S 143.3*

**dispensation** *n*
ˌdɪspən'sɛ:sɪən
**sp** dispensation[2]
**rh** disputation *Luc 248*

**dispense / ~s** *v*
=
**sp** dispence[4], dispense[3] / dispenses[1]
**rh** conscience *Tim 3.2.88*; hence *CE 2.1.103*; hence, negligence *Luc 1279*; offence *Luc 1070, 1704*; sense *S 112.12*

**disperse / ~d** *v*
dɪs'pɐ:ɹs / *m* -t, -ɪd
**sp** disperse[10] / disperc't[1], dispersd[1], dispers'd[5], dispersed[1], disperst[3], dispierc'd[1], dis-pursed[1]
**rh** verse *S 78.4* / hearsed *Luc 658*
> ill-dispersing

**dispersedly** *adv*
dɪs'pɐ:ɹsɪdləɪ
**sp** dispersedly[1]

**dispiteous**
> despiteous

**displace / ~d** *v*
dɪs'plɛ:s / -t
**sp** displace[2] / displac'd[3]
> place

**displant** *v*
dɪs'plant
**sp** displant[1]
> plant

**displanting** *n*
dɪs'plantɪn, -ɪŋ
**sp** displanting[1]

**display / ~ed** *v*
dɪs'plɛ: / -d
**sp** display[3] / displaid[2], displaied[1], displayd[2], display'd[2], displayed[1]
**rh** day *Luc 118* / dismayed *Luc 272*

**displease / ~d** *v*
=
**sp** displease[4] / displeas'd[8], dis-pleas'd[1]
**rh** Antipodes *MND 3.2.54*
> pleasure

**displeasing** *adj*
dɪs'pli:zɪn, -ɪŋ
**sp** displeasing[2]

**displeasure / ~s** *n*
dɪs'plezəɹ / -z
**sp** displeasure[39], dis-pleasure[1] / displeasures[3]

**disport / ~s** *n*
dɪs'pɔ:ɹts
**sp** disports[1]

**disport** *v*
dɪs'pɔ:ɹt
**sp** disport[2]
> sport

**dispose** *n*
dɪs'po:z
**sp** dispose[6]

**dispose / ~d** *v*
*m* dɪs'po:z / -d, -ɪd
**sp** dispose[16] / disposd[2], dispos'd[16], disposde[1], disposed[1]
**rh** disclosed *LLL 2.1.236, 5.2.466*

**disposed** *adj*
*m* dɪs'po:zɪd
**sp** disposed[1]
> ill-, un-, well-disposed

**disposer** *n*
dɪs'po:zəɹ
**sp** disposer[2], disposer's [disposer is][1]

**dispos·er / ~é** *Fr v*
dispo'ze
**sp** disposee[1]

**disposing** *n*
dɪs'po:zɪn, -ɪŋ
**sp** disposing[4]
> true-disposing

**disposition / ~s** *n*
ˌdɪspə'zɪsɪən / -z
**sp** disposition[40], dis-position[2], dispo-sition[1], dispositi-on[1] / dispositions[4], *Evans MW 3.1.21* dispositions [disposition][1]
**rh** imposition *Luc 1695*
> indisposition

**dispossess / ~ing / ~ed** *v*
ˌdɪspə'zes / -ɪn, -ɪŋ / -t
**sp** dispossesse[3], dis-possesse[1] / dispossessing[1] / dispossest[1]
> possess

**dispraise** *n*
dɪs'prɛ:z
**sp** dispraise[4]
**rh** days *LLL 4.3.262*
> praise

**disprais·e / ~ing / ~ed** *v*
dɪs'prɛ:z / -ɪn, -ɪŋ / -d
**sp** dispraise[3], disprayse[2] / dispraising[2] / disprais'd[2], disprays'd[1]

**dispraisingly** *adv*
dɪs'prɛ:zɪnˌləɪ, -ɪŋ-
**sp** dispraisingly[1]

**disprize / ~ing** *v*
dɪs'prəɪzɪn, -ɪŋ
**sp** disprising[1]
> prize

**disprized** *adj*
'dɪsprəɪzd
**sp** dispriz'd[1]

**dispropert·y / ~ied** *v*
dɪs'prɒpəɹtəɪd
**sp** dispropertied[1]
> property

**disproportion / ~s** *n*
ˌdɪsprə'pɔ:ɹsɪən / -z
**sp** dis-proportion[1] / disproportions[1]
> proportion

**disproportion / ~ed** *v*
ˌdɪsprə'pɔ:ɹsɪən / -d
**sp** disproportioned[1]

**disproportioned** *adj*
ˌdɪsprə'pɔ:ɹsɪənd
**sp** disproportion'd[1]

**disprove / ~st / ~d** *v*
dɪs'prɤv, -u:v / -st / *m* -ɪd
**sp** disprooue[1], disproue[3] / disproou'st[1] / disproued[1]
> prove

**dispunge** *v*
dɪs'pɤnʤ
**sp** dispunge[1]

**disputable** *adj*
*m* 'dɪspjəˌtabəl
**sp** disputeable[1]

**disputation / ~s** *n*
*m* ˌdɪspjə'tɛ:sɪən, -ɪˌɒn / -ɪənz
**sp** disputation[2] / disputations[1]
**rh** dispensation *Luc 246*; reputation *Luc 822*

**disput·e / ~est / ~s / ~ing / ~d** *v*
= / dɪs'pju:ts, -tst / = / dɪs'pju:tɪn, -ɪŋ / =
**sp** dispute[4] / disputes[1] / disputes[1] / disputing[1] / disputed[1]

**disquantity** *v*
*m* dɪs'kwɒntɪˌtəɪ
**sp** disquantity[1]
> quantity

**disquiet** *n*
dɪs'kwəɪət
**sp** disquiet[3]
> quiet

**disquietly** *adv*
dɪs'kwəɪətləɪ
**sp** disquietly[1]

**disrelish** *v*
=
**sp** disrellish[1]
> relish

**disrobe** *v*
dɪs'ro:b
**sp** disrobe[3]
> robe

**dis-seat** *v*
=
**sp** dis-eate[1]
> seat

**dissemble / ~d** *v*
=
**sp** dissemble[11] / dissembled[2]
**rh** tremble *VA 641*

**dissembler / ~s** *n*
dɪ'sembləɹ / -z
**sp** dissembler[2] / dissemblers[1]

**dissembling** *adj / n*
dɪ'semblɪn, -ɪŋ
**sp** dissembling[12] / dissembling[2]

**dissembly** *n*
dɪ'sembləɪ
**sp** dissembly[1]

**dissension / ~s** *n*
dɪ'sensɪən / -z
**sp** dissention[9] / dissentions[1]

**dissentious** *adj*
dɪ'sensɪəs
**sp** dissentious[4]

**dissever / ~ed** *v*
dɪ'sevəɹ / -d
**sp** disseuer[2] / disseuer'd[1]

**dissolute** *adj*
'dɪsəˌluːt
**sp** dissolute[3]

**dissolutely** *adv*
ˌdɪsə'luːtləɪ
**sp** dissolutely[3]

**dissolution** *n*
ˌdɪsə'luːsɪən
**sp** dissolution[3]
**rh** absolution, resolution *Luc 355*

**dissolve / ~s / ~ed** *v*
dɪ'sɒlv, -'zɒ- / -z / *m* -d, -ɪd
**sp** dissolue[8] / dissolues[2] / dissolu'd[4], dissolued[2]

**dissuade / ~d** *v*
dɪ'swɛːd / -ɪd
**sp** disswade[6] / disswaded[2]

**distaff / ~s** *n*
'dɪstaf / -s
**sp** distaffe[3] / distaffes[1]

**distaff-women** *n*
'dɪstaf-'wɪmɪn
**sp** distaffe-women[1]

**distain / ~s** *v*
dɪ'stɛːn / -z
**sp** distaine[1] / distaines[1]
**rh** again, pain *Luc 786*

**distained** *adj*
dɪ'stɛːnd
**sp** distain'd[1]

**distance** *n*
=
**sp** distance[14], di-stance[2]

**distant** *adj*
=
**sp** distant[3]

**distast·e / ~ing** *v*
dɪs'tast / -ɪn, -ɪŋ
**sp** distaste[4] / distasting[1]

**distasteful** *adj*
dɪs'tastfʊl
**sp** distastefull[1]

**distemper** *n*
dɪs'tempəɹ
**sp** distemper[8], di-stemper[1], distem-per[1]

**distemperature / ~s** *n*
*m* dɪs'temprətəɹ, -ˌtuːɹ, -pər- / -prəˌtuːɹz, -pər-
**sp** distemperature[3], distemprature[1] / distemperatures[1]
**rh** assure *RJ 2.3.36*

**distempered** *adj*
dɪs'tempəɹd
**sp** distemp'red[7], distempered[2]

**distempering** *adj*
dɪs'temprɪn, -ɪŋ, -pər-
**sp** distempring[1]

**distil / ~led** *v*
= / dɪs'tɪld
**sp** distill[4] / destil'd[1], distil'd[1], distill'd[3], *Ham 1.2.204 emend of* bestil'd[1]
**rh** filled *AY 3.2.140*; self-killed *S 6.2*

**distillation** *n*
ˌdɪstɪ'lɛːsɪən
**sp** distillation[1]

**distilled** *adj*
*m* dɪs'tɪld, -lɪd
**sp** distil'd[1], distill'd[1], distilled[1]

**distilling** *adj*
dɪs'tɪlɪn, -ɪŋ
**sp** distilling[1]

**distilment** *n*
=
**sp** distilment[1]

**distinct** *adj*
*m* 'dɪstɪŋkt, dɪs'tɪŋkt
**sp** distinct[3]

**distinction** *n*
dɪs'tɪŋksɪən
**sp** distinction[10]

**distinctly** *adv*
dɪs'tɪŋkləɪ, -ktl-
**sp** distinctly[6], di-stinctly[1]

**distingué** *Fr adj*
distɛ̃'ge
**sp** distime[1]

**distinguish / ~es / ~ed** *v*
=
**sp** distinguish[8] / distinguishes[1] / distinguish'd[2], distinguisht[1]
> **indistinguished, undistinguishable**

**distinguishment** *n*
=
**sp** distinguishment[1]

**distract** *adj*
=
**sp** distract[7]

**distract / ~s / ~ed** *v*
=
**sp** distract[2] / distracts[1] / distracted[1], distra-cted[1]

**distracted** *adj*
=
**sp** distracted[12], distra-cted[1]

**distractedly** *adv*
*m* dɪs'traktɪdˌləɪ
**sp** distractedly[1]

**distraction / ~s** *n*
dɪs'traksɪən, -ɪˌɒn / -z
**sp** distraction[11] / distractions[2]

**distrain / ~ed** *v*
dɪs'trɛːnd
**sp** distraynd[1], distrayn'd[1]

**distraught** *adj*
dɪs'trɔːt
**sp** distraught[2]

**distress / ~es** *n*
=
**sp** distres[1], distresse[12] / distresses[2]

**distressed** *adj*
*m* dɪs'tresɪd, dɪs'trest, 'dɪstrest
**sp** distressed[7], distrest[5]
**rh** breast *Luc 465, VA 814*

**distressful** *adj*
=
**sp** distressefull[4]

**distribute / ~d** *v*
=
**sp** distribute[2] / distributed[1]

**distribution** *n*
*m* ˌdɪstrɪ'bju:sɪən, -ɪˌɒn
**sp** distribution[2]

**distrust** *n / v*
dɪs'trɤst
**sp** distrust[3] / distrust[3]
**rh** *v* must *Ham 3.2.174*

**distrustful** *adj*
dɪs'trɤstfʊl
**sp** distrustfull[1]

**disturb / ~ing / ~ed** *v*
dɪs'tɐ:ɹb / -ɪn, -ɪŋ / -d
**sp** disturb[1], disturbe[9] / disturbing[1] / disturb'd[7], disturbed[1]

**disturbed** *adj*
dɪs'tɐ:ɹbd
**sp** disturbed[1]
> late-disturbed

**disturber / ~s** *n*
dɪs'tɐ:ɹbəɹz
**sp** disturbers[2]

**disunite** *v*
ˌdɪsjə'nəɪt
**sp** disunite[1]

**disvalue / ~d** *v*
=
**sp** dis-valued[1]
> value

**disvouch / ~ed** *v*
dɪs'vəʊʧt
**sp** disuouch'd[1]

**dit** *Fr*
> dire

**ditch / ~es** *n*
=
**sp** ditch[5], [castle]-ditch[1] / ditches[2]
> Moorditch

**ditch / ~ed** *v*
=
**sp** ditch'd[1]

**ditch-deliver / ~ed** *v*
'dɪʧ-dɪ'lɪvəɹd
**sp** ditch-deliuer'd[1]
> deliver

**ditch-dog** *n*
=
**sp** ditch-dogge[1]
> dog

**ditcher / ~s** *n*
'dɪʧəɹz
**sp** ditchers[1]

**dites** *Fr*
> dire

**ditt·y / ~ies** *n*
'dɪtəɪ / -z
**sp** dittie[2], ditty[2] / ditties[2]
**rh** pity *PP 20.11*; pretty *PP 14.19*; witty *VA 836*

**diurnal** *adj*
dɪ'u:ɹnɑl
**sp** diurnall[1]

**dive / ~s / ~d** *v*
dəɪv / -z / -d
**sp** diue[7] / diues[1] / diu'd[1]
**rh** drives *Per 3.Chorus.49*

**diver** *n*
'dəɪvəɹ
**sp** diuer[1]

**divers** [several] *adj*
'dəɪvəɹz
**sp** diuers[24]

**diversely** *adv*
dɪ'vɐ:ɹsləɪ
**sp** diuersly[1]

**diversity** *n*
*m* dɪ'vɐ:ɹsɪˌtəɪ
**sp** diuersitie[1]

**divert / ~s / ~ed** *v*
dɪ'vɐ:ɹt / -s / -ɪd
**sp** diuert[2] / diuerts[2] / diuerted[1]

**diverted** *adj*
dɪ'vɐ:ɹtɪd
**sp** diuerted[1]

**Dives** *n*
'di:vɛ:z
**sp** Diues[1]

**divest / ~ing** *v*
dɪ'vest / -ɪn, -ɪŋ
**sp** deuest[1], diuest[1] / deuesting[1]

**dividable** *adj*
dɪ'vəɪdəbəl
**sp** diuidable[1]
> in-, un-dividable

**dividant** *adj*
dɪ'vəɪdənt
**sp** diuidant[1]

**divide / ~s / ~th / *Luc* ~ing / ~d** *v*
dɪ'vəɪd / -z / -əθ / -ɪn, -ɪŋ / -ɪd
**sp** deuide[2], diuide[22] / diuides[3] / diuideth[1] / deuiding[1] / deuided[1], diuided[12]
**rh** applied, side *LC 67*; side *1H6 4.5.49, Luc 1737* / biding, hiding *Luc 551*

**divided** *adj*
dɪ'vəɪdɪd
**sp** diuided[4]
> well-divided

**divin** *Fr adj*
dɪ'vɛ̃
**sp** deuin[1]

**divination** *n*
ˌdɪvɪˈnɛːsɪən
**sp** diuination[3]
**rh** imagination *VA 670*

**divine / ~st** *adj*
dɪˈvəɪn / -əst
**sp** diuine[39] / diuinest[2]
**rh** Collatine, incline *Luc 291*; Collatine, pine *Luc 1164*; eyne *MND 3.2.137*; mine *CE 3.2.32, TG 2.1.4*; shine *LLL 4.3.246, VA 730*; shrine, thine *Luc 193*; thine *S 108.5*

**divine / ~s** *n*
dɪˈvəɪn / -z
**sp** diuine[4] / diuines[3]

**divine / ~s** *v*
dɪˈvəɪn / -z
**sp** diuine[3] / diuines[1]

**divinely** *adv*
dɪˈvəɪnləɪ
**sp** diuinely[2]

**divineness** *n*
dɪˈvəɪnəs
**sp** diuinenesse[1]

**diviner** *n*
dɪˈvəɪnəɹ
**sp** diuiner[1]

**divining** *adj*
dɪˈvəɪnɪn, -ɪŋ
**sp** diuining[1]
> ill-, true-divining

**divinity** *n*
*m* dɪˈvɪnɪˌtəɪ, -ɪt-
**sp** diuinitie[4], diuinity[4], di-uinity[1]

**division / ~s** *n*
*m* dɪˈvɪzɪən, -ɪˌɒn / dɪˈvɪzɪənz
**sp** deuision[5], diuision[16] / diuisions[2], diui-sions[1]
**rh** confusion *1H6 4.1.193*

**divorce** *n*
dɪˈvɔːɹs
**sp** diuorce[13]

**divorce / ~d** *v*
dɪˈvɔːɹs / *m* -ɪd, -t
**sp** diuorce[8] / diuorced[1], diuorc'd[4]

**divorcement** *n*
dɪˈvɔːɹsmənt
**sp** diuorcement[1]

**divulg·e / ~ing / ~ed** *v*
dɪˈvɤldʒ / -ɪn, -ɪŋ / *m* -d, -ɪd
**sp** divulge[1] / divulging[1] / divulg'd[1], divulged[1]
> un-, well-divulged

**divulged** *adj*
*m* dɪˈvɤldʒɪd
**sp** divulged[1]

**dizzy** *adj / n*
ˈdɪzəɪ
**sp** dizie[1] / dizzie[1]

**Dizzy** [name] *n*
ˈdɪzəɪ
**sp** dizie[1]

**dizzy-eyed** *adj*
ˈdɪzəɪ-ˌəɪd
**sp** dizzie-ey'd[1]
> eye

**do** *v*
*str* =, *unstr* də, d
**sp** do[2371], doe[1398], doe't [do it][2], doo[7], doo't [do it][53], do't [do it][23], *informal* de['ye][1] [do ye], *Scots* de[1]
**rh** *1* thereunto *Oth 2.1.140*; through *Cor 2.3.123*; to *R2 5.5.99, WT 4.1.12*; too *Cym 5.3.61, Ham 3.2.184, LLL 1.1.22, 5.2.204, MND 3.2.37, 149, 254, R2 3.3.207, RJ 1.5.103, S 88.11, TNK 3.5.142, TS 1.2.223*; woo *LLL 5.2.298, MND 2.1.241, 2.2.135, Tim 4.3.471*; you *Mac 3.5.12, Per 1.1.52, 2.5.26*; **do** it to it *LLL 5.2.217*; **do't** shoot *LLL 4.1.27*; to't *Cor 2.3.117, Ham 4.5.61*; **rh** *2* go *TN 2.3.107*
> out-, un-do

***doest***
*str* ˈduːəst, duːst, dɤst, *unstr* dəst
**sp** doest[25], dooest[2], doost[8], doo'st[10], dost[240], do'st[114], dos't[1]

***does***
*str* dɤz, duːz, *unstr* dəz
**sp** does[148], doe's[13], dooes[4], doo's[2], dos[1], do's[154]
**rh** glorious *Per 2.Chorus.13*

***doeth, doth***
*str* ˈduːəθ, duːθ, dɤθ, *unstr* dəθ
**sp** doeth[2], dooth[2], doth[847]
**rh** tooth *TC 4.5.292*

***doing***
ˈduːɪn, -ɪŋ
**sp** doing[43], dooing[4]
**rh** wooing *TC 1.2.287, TS 2.1.74*
> doing *n*; a-, harm-, ill-, over-doing

***did***
=
**sp** did[1569], did't [did it][1]
**rh** forbid *LC 148*

***diddest***
dɪds, -t
**sp** diddest[1], didd'st[11], didst[111], did'st[56]

***done***
dɤn
**sp** done[635], don[1], done't [done it][6], don't [done it][6]
**rh** *1* begun *Ham 4.3.69, R2 1.2.61, TN 5.1.403* [*F sp* begon], *TS 1.1.251, VA 846*; begun, sun *LC 11, Luc 23*; one *R2 1.1.183*; run *LLL 5.2.483*; son *1H6 4.3.38, 4.6.7, Mac 3.5.10, R2 1.3.223, 5.2.103, R3 4.4.24, Tem 2.1.331, 4.1.94, Tit 1.1.344*; sun *CE 1.1.27, Cym 4.2.260, Ham 4.5.66, Mac 1.1.3, S 24.9, 35.1, 59.8, TC 5.8.8, Tim 1.2.141, VA 197, 749, 802*; won *AW 4.2.65, 5.3.311, 332, 1H4 5.5.43, 1H6 4.5.27, Mac 1.1.3, 1.2.69, R2 4.1.195*; **rh** *2* Amazon *3H6 4.1.104*; gone *JC 5.3.64, TN 2.3.101*; on *3H6 4.1.104, KL 1.4.202, MM 4.3.77, RJ 1.4.39*; **rh** *3* afternoon *AW 5.3.65*; moon *Ham 3.2.171*; **rh** *4* sum *S 24.9*
**pun** done *RJ 1.4.39* dun, Dun

**do** *nonsense syll*
do:
**sp** do[4]

**Dobbin / ~'s** *n*
=
**sp** Dobbin[1] / Dobbins[1]

**dock / ~s** *n*
=
**sp** docke[1] / docks[1]

**dock / ~s** *v*
=
**sp** docks[1]

**doctor / ~'s / ~s** *n*
'dɒktəɹ / -z
**sp** docter[1], doctor[69], do-ctor[1], [bully]-doctor[1], doctour[1], *abbr* doct[1] / doctors[3] / doctors[7]

**doctrine** *n*
=
**sp** doctrine[8]

**document** *n*
=
**sp** document[1]

**dodge** *v*
=
**sp** dodge[1]

**doe** [animal] *n*
do:
**sp** doe[2]
**rh** bow [weapon] *Luc 581, TC 3.1.114*

**doer / ~'s / ~s** *n*
'du:əɹ / -z
**sp** doer[1] / doers[1] / doers[3], dooers[2]

**does**
> do

**doff** *v*
=
**sp** doff[2], doffe[4]

**dog / ~'s / ~s** *n*
=
**sp** dog[42], [curtall]-dog[1], dogge[85], dogg's [dog is][1] / dogges[3], dogs[1] / dogs[13], [gentleman-like]-dogs[1]
**rh** frog *Mac 4.1.15*
> ditch-, Jack-, night-, puppy-, watch-dog

**dog / ~s / ~ged** *v*
=
**sp** dogge[3] / dogges[2] / dog'd[2], dogg'd[3]

**dog-ape / ~s** *n*
'dɒg-ˌɛ:ps
**sp** dog-apes[1]
> ape

**Dogberry** *n*
'dɒgbrəɪ, -bər-
**sp** Dogbery[2]

**dog-days** *n*
'dɒg-ˌdɛ:z
**sp** dog-dayes[1]
> day

**dog-fish** *n*
=
**sp** dog-fish[1]
> fish

**dog-fox** *n*
=
**sp** dog-foxe[1]
> fox

**dogged** *adj*
'dɒgɪd
**sp** dogged[3]

**dog-hole** *n*
'dɒg-ˌo:l, -ˌho:l
**sp** dog-hole[1]
> hole

**dog-weary** *adj*
'dɒg-ˌwɛ:rəɪ
**sp** dogge-wearie[1]
> weary

**doigt / ~s** *Fr n*
dwɛ
**sp** doyt[1], doyts[4]

**doing / ~s** *n*
'du:ɪn, -ɪŋ / -z
**sp** doing[21] / doings[5]
> do

**doit** *n*
dəɪt
**sp** doit[5], doite[1], doyt[1]

**Doit** [name] *n*
dəɪt
**sp** Doit[1]

**Dolabella** *n*
ˌdɒlə'belə
**sp** Dolabella[11], Dollabella[3], Dollabello[1]

**dole** *n*
do:l
**sp** dole[9]

**doleful** *adj*
'do:lfʊl
**sp** dolefull[4]

**Doll** [name] *n*
=
**sp** Dol[15], Doll[5]

**dollar / ~s** *n*
'dɒləɹ / -z
**sp** dollor[1] / dollars[1]
**pun** *KJ 2.1.20, Tem 2.1.21* dolour

**dolorous** *adj*
*m* 'dɒləˌrɤs
**sp** dolorous[1]

**dolour / ~s** *n*
'dɒləɹ / -z
**sp** dolor[1], dolour[5] / dollours[1], dolors[2]
**pun** *KJ 2.1.21, Tem 2.1.20* dollar

**dolphin** *adj*
'dɒlfɪn
**sp** dolphin[1]

**dolphin / ~'s** *n*
'dɒlfɪnz
**sp** dolphines[1], dolphins[1]
> Dauphin

**dolphin-chamber** *n*
'dɒlfɪn-ˌʧambəɹ
**sp** dolphin-chamber[1]

**dolphin-like** *adj*
'dɒlfɪn-ˌləɪk
**sp** dolphin-like[1]

**dolt / ~s** *n*
do:lt / -s
**sp** dolt[1] / dolts[2]

**Dombe** *n*
dʊm
**sp** Dombe[1]

**Dombledon** *n*
'dʊmbəldən
**sp** Dombledon[1]

**domestic** *adj*
=
**sp** domesticke[7], domestique[1]

**domestic / ~s** *n*
=
**sp** domestickes[1]

**domination / ~s** *n*
ˌdɒmɪ'nɛ:sɪənz
**sp** dominations[1]

**dominator** *n*
'dɒmɪˌnɛ:təɹ
**sp** dominator[1], domi-nator[1]

**dominator** *Lat n*
ˌdɒmɪ'nɑ:tɔ:ɹ
**sp** dominator[1]

**domineer** *v*
ˌdɒmɪ'ni:ɹ
**sp** domineere[1]

**domineering** *adj*
ˌdɒmɪ'ni:rɪn, -ɪŋ
**sp** domineering[1]

**dominical** *n*
də'mɪnɪˌkɑl
**sp** dominicall[1]

**dominion / ~s** *n*
də'mɪnɪən / *m* də'mɪnɪənz, -ɪˌɒnz /
**sp** dominion[1] / dominions[6]

**domin·us / ~e** *Lat n*
'dɒmɪnɛ:
**sp** domine[1], do-mine[1], domi-ne[1]

**Domitian** *n*
də'mɪsɪən
**sp** Domitian[1]

**Domitius** *n*
də'mɪsɪəs
**sp** Domitius[1]

**don / ~ned** *v*
=
**sp** don[1] / don'd[1], donn'd[1]

**Don** [*title*] *v*
=
**sp** Do[20], don[4], Dun[2]

**Donalbaine** *n*
'dɒnəlˌbɛ:n
**sp** Donalbaine[6], Donal-baine[1], Donalbane[2]

**donation** *n*
də'nɛ:sɪən
**sp** donation[4]

**donc** *Fr adv*
dɔ̃:k
**sp** donc[1]

**Doncaster** *n*
'dɒnkastəɹ
**sp** Doncaster[2]

**done**
> do

**dong**
> ding-dong

**donner / donne / ~rai** *Fr v*
dɔ'ne / dɔn / dɔnə'rɛ
**sp** donnes / donnes / donneray

**doom / ~'s** *n*
dɤm, du:m / -z
**sp** dombe[1], doom[1], doombe[1], doome[35] / doomes[1]
**rh** *1* groom *Luc 672*; room *3H6 5.6.93, MW 5.5.58, R2 5.6.24, S 55.12*; *rh 2* come *Luc 924, R2 3.2.189, S 107.4, 116.12, 145.7*; **rh** *3* Rome *Luc 717, 1849*; **rh** *4* soon *Per 5.2.20* [*Chorus*] / moons *Per 3. Chorus.32*

**doom / ~ed** *v*
dɤm, du:m / -d
**sp** doome[5], doom'd[5]

**doomsday** *n*
'dɤmzdɛ:, 'du:-
**sp** doomesday[8], doomsday[1], dooms-day[1]

**door / ~s** *n*
dɔ:ɹ / -z
**sp** doore[113], dore[25], [without]-dore-[forme][1] / doores[54], dores[6]
**rh** before *H5 1.2.309, Luc 1301, MND 5.1.380, R2 5.3.76*; before, sore *CE 3.1.64*; four *LLL 3.1.89,95, VA 448*; more *CE 2.1.11, Ham 4.5.53, LLL 3.1.89, 95, Luc 337*; more, score, whore *KL 1.4.124*; store *CE 3.1.35*; wherefore *CE 3.1.38*
> hold-door

**door-nail** *n*
'dɔ:ɹ-ˌnɛ:l
**sp** doore nail[1]
> nail

**Dorcas** *n*
'dɒɹkəs
**sp** Dorcas[2]

**Doreus** *n*
'dɒɹɪəs
**sp** Doreus[1]

**Doricles** *n*
'dɒɹɪˌkli:z
**sp** Doricles[4]

**dormouse** *n*
'dɔ:ɹməʊs
**sp** dormouse[1]

**Dorothy** *n*
'dɒrətəɪ
**sp** Dorothie[2], Dorothy[1]

**Dorset** *n*
'dɔ:ɹsət
**sp** Dorset[23]

**Dorsetshire** *n*
*m* 'dɔ:ɹsət,ʃəɪɹ
**sp** Dorsetshire[1]

**dost**
> do

**dotage** *n*
'do:tɪʤ
**sp** dotage[10]

**dotant** *n*
'do:tənt
**sp** dotant[1]

**dotard / ~s** *n*
'do:təɹd / -z
**sp** dotard[3] / dotards[1]

**dot·e / ~s / ~eth / ~ing / ~ed** *v*
do:t / -s / 'do:t·əθ / -ɪn, -ɪŋ / -ɪd
**sp** doat[3], doate[10], dote[12] / doates[1], dotes[8] / doteth[1] / doting[3] / doted[1]
**rh** coat, note *LC 235, Luc 207*; denote *S 148.5*; note *CE 3.2.47, LLL 4.3.124, 5.2.76, S 141.4, VA 837* / noteth *VA 1059* / noted *Luc 416*
> a-doting

**doter / ~s** *n*
'do:təɹ / -z
**sp** doters[1]

**doth**
> do

**doting** *adj / n*
'do:tɪn, -ɪŋ
**sp** doating[1], doting[6] / doting[2]

**double / ~r** *adj*
'dɤbəl / -bləɹ
**sp** double[68], double-[beere][1], dou-ble[1] / doubler[1]

**double / ~s** *VA* *n*
'dɤbəlz
**sp** doubles[1]
**rh** troubles *VA 682*

**Double** [name] *n*
'dɤbəl
**sp** Double[2]

**doubl·e / ~ing / ~ed** *v*
'dɤbəl / 'dɤblɪn, -ɪŋ / 'dɤbəld
**sp** double[6] / doubling[1] / doubled[3]
**rh** trouble *VA 521*
> redouble

**double-charge** *v*
'dɤbəl-,ʧɑ:ɹʤ
**sp** double charge[1]
> charge

**doubled** *adj*
'dɤbəld
**sp** doubled[2]
**rh** troubled *VA 1067*

**double-damned** *adj*
'dɤbəl-,damd
**sp** double damn'd[1]
> damned

**double-dealer** *n*
,dɤbəl-'di:ləɹ
**sp** double dealer[1]
> deal

**double-dealing** *n*
,dɤbəl-'di:lɪn, -ɪŋ
**sp** double dealing[1]
> deal

**double-fatal** *adj*
'dɤbəl-,fɛ:tɑl
**sp** double fatall[1]
> fatal

**double-horned** *adj*
'dɤbəl-,ɔ:ɹnd, -,hɔ:-
**sp** *TC 5.7.11 emend of* dou-ble hen'd[1]
> horn

**double-man** *n*
'dɤbəl-,man
**sp** double man[1]
> man

**double-meaning** *adj*
'dɤbəl-,mi:nɪn, -ɪŋ
**sp** double-meaning[1]
> mean

**doubleness** *n*
'dɤbəlnəs
**sp** doublenes[1]

**doublet / ~s** *n*
'dɤblɪt / -s
**sp** doublet[18], dou-blet[1], doub-let[2], dub-let[1] / doublets[2], doub-lets[1], dublets[1]

**doubling** *n*
'dɤblɪn, -ɪŋ
**sp** doubling[1]

**doubly** *adv*
'dɤbləɪ
**sp** doubly[9]

**doubt / ~s** *n*
dəʊt, *Holofernes LLL 5.1.20*
dəʊbt / -s
**sp** doubt[73], *Holofernes describing Armado* dout[1] / doubts[8]
**rh** lout *KJ 3.1.219*; out *LLL 5.2.101, 151, PP 2.13, S 144.13, VA 692*; shout *MV 3.2.144*; without *LC 97*

**doubt / ~est / ~s / ~ing / ~ed** *v*
dəʊt / -st / -s / 'dəʊt·ɪn, -ɪŋ / -ɪd
**sp** doubt[96] / doubtst[1] / doubts[3] / doubting[5] / doubted[9]
**rh** hereabout *RJ 5.3.44*; out *KJ 4.2.102, 5.2.180*
> misdoubt; re-, un-doubted

**doubtful** *adj*
'dəʊtfʊl
**sp** doubtfull[21], doubt-full[1]
> undoubtful

**doubtfully** *adv*
*m* 'dəʊtfʊ,ləɪ, -fl-
**sp** doubtfully[4]

**doubtless** *adj*
'dəʊtləs
**sp** doubtlesse[8], doubt-lesse[1]

**dough** *n*
do:
**sp** dough[2]

**doughty-handed** *adj*
'dəʊtəɪ-ˌandɪd, -ˌha-
**sp** doughty handed[1]
> handed

**doughy** *adj*
'do:əɪ
**sp** dowy[1]

**Douglas** *n*
'do:gləs
**sp** Dowglas[38]

**doute** *Fr n*
dut
**sp** doute[1]

**dove / ~'s / ~s** *n*
dɤv / -z
**sp** doue[18] / doues[1], doues-[downe][1] / doues[7]
**rh** love *MND 2.2.120, 5.1.317, PP 9.3, PT 50, TN 5.1.129* / loves *MND 1.1.171*
> turtle-dove

**dovecote** *n*
'dɤv-ˌko:t
**sp** doue-coat[1]

**dove-drawn** *adj*
*m* ˌdɤv-'drɔ:n
**sp** doue-drawn[1]
> draw

**dove-feathered** *adj*
'dɤv-ˌfeðəɹd
**sp** doue-feather'd[1]
> feathered

**dove-house** *n*
'dɤvˌəʊs, -ˌhəʊs
**sp** douehouse[1], doue-house[1]
> house

**Dover** *n*
'do:vəɹ
**sp** Douer[13]

**dowager** *n*
'dəʊədʒəɹ
**sp** dowager[6]

**dowdy** *n*
'dəʊdəɪ
**sp** dowdie[1]

**dower / ~s** *n*
do:ɹ, dəʊɹ / -z
**sp** dower[11], dowre[6] / dowers[1], dowres[1]
**rh** flower AW *5.3.325*

**dower / ~ed** *v*
do:ɹd, dəʊɹd
**sp** dow'rd[1]

**dowerless** *adj*
'do:ɹləs, dəʊɹ-
**sp** dowerlesse[1], dowrelesse[1]

**dowlas** *n*
'dəʊləs
**sp** doulas[2]

**dowle** *n*
dəʊl
**sp** dowle[1]

**down** *adj / adv, prep / n / v / nonsense word in song*
dəʊn
**sp** downe[4] / down[38], downe[551] / dowlne[1], downe[4], [doues]-downe[1] / down[1], downe[2] / downe[3]
**rh** *1 adv, prep* clown *LLL 4.1.142*; crown *Cym 3.5.65, 2H4 3.1.30, 2H6 1.1.257, 3H6 3.2.195, 4.6.100, Luc 217, R2 3.4.66, 4.1.194, 5.1.25, Tem 4.1.81*; crown, lown, renown *Oth 2.3.90*; frown *KL 5.3.5, S 117.9, VA 43, 463*; town *CE 3.1.59, MND 3.2.396, PP 18.18*; **rh** *2* bone *TC 5.8.11* / **rh** *in song* clown *TNK 3.5.139*
> a-, setting-, steep-down

**downfall** *n*
'dəʊnfɑ:l
**sp** downefall[2], downe-fall[2], downfall[4]
> fall

**down-gyved** *adj*
*m* ˌdəʊn-'dʒəɪvɪd
**sp** downe giued[1]

**down-pillow** *n*
*m* ˌdəʊn-'pɪlə, -lo:
**sp** downe-pillow[1]
> pillow

**down-razed** *S* *adj*
*m* ˌdəʊn-'rɛ:st
**sp** downe rased[1]
**rh** defaced *S 64.3*
> raze

**downright** *adv*
*m* 'dəʊnrəɪt, dəʊn'rəɪt
**sp** downeright[1], downe-right[6], downe right[1], downright[2], down-right[2],
**rh** white *VA 645*
> right

**down-rop·e / ~ing** *v*
*m* ˌdəʊn-'ro:pɪn, -ɪŋ
**sp** downe roping[1]
> rope

**Downs** *n*
dəʊnz
**sp** Downes[1] / downes[1]
**rh** hounds *VA 677*

**downstairs** *adv*
ˌdəʊn'stɛ:ɹz, 'dəʊnˌstɛ:ɹz
**sp** down-staires[1], downe stayres[4]
> stair

**downtrodden** *adj*
ˌdəʊn'trɒdən
**sp** downe-troden[1]
> tread

**downward / ~s** *adv*
'dəʊnwəɹd / -z
**sp** downward[3] / downewards[1]

**downy** *adj*
'dəʊnəɪ
**sp** dowlney[1], downey[1], downie[2]

**dowr·y / ~ies** *n*
'dəʊrəɪ / -z
**sp** dowrie[16], dowry[7] / dowries[1]

**Dowsabell** *n*
*m* 'dəʊzəˌbel
**sp** Dowsabell[1]

**dowset / ~s** *TNK* *n*
'dəʊsets
**sp** dowsets[1]
**rh** lcts *TNK 3.5.156*

**doxy** *n*
'dɒksəɪ
**sp** doxy[1]

**dozen** *adj*
'dɤzən
**sp** dosen[1], dozen[22]
> half-a-dozen

**dozen / ~s** *n*
'dɤzən / -z
**sp** dozen[11] / dozens[1]

**drab / ~s** *n*
=
**sp** drab[7], drabbe[1] / drabs[1]
**rh** *1* slab *Mac 4.1.31*; **rh** *2* babe *Mac 4.1.31*

**drab / ~bing** *n*
'drabɪn, -ɪŋ
**sp** drabbing[1]

**drachma / ~s** *n*
'drakmə / -z
**sp** drachme[1] / drachmaes[2]

**draff** *n*
=
**sp** draffe[1], draugh[1]

**drag / ~ged** *v*
=
**sp** drag[7], dragge[3] / drag'd[2], dragg'd[1]

**dragon / ~'s / ~s / ~s'** *n*
=
**sp** dragon[8] / dragons[1], dra-gons[1] / dragons[6] / dragons[1]
> flap-dragon

**dragonish** *adj*
=
**sp** dragonish[1]

**dragon-like** *adj*
'dragən-ˌləɪk
**sp** dragon-like[1]

**drain / ~s / ~ed** *v*
drɛ:n / -z / -d
**sp** draine[1], drayne[1], dreyne[2] / dreines[1] / drained[1]

**dram** *n*
=
**sp** dram[10], dramme[5]

**drank**
> drink

**draught / ~s** *n*
draft / -s
**sp** draught[8] / draughtes[1], draughts[2]

**draught-oxen** *n*
'draft-ˌɒksən
**sp** draft-oxen[1]
> ox

**drave**
> drive

**draw / ~est / ~s / ~eth / ~ing / ~n / drew / ~est** *v*
= / drɔ:st / = / = / 'drɔ:ɪn, -ɪŋ / = / = / dru:st
**sp** draw[193], drawe[3] / draw'st[2] / drawes[28], drawes-[on][2], draws[1] / draweth[2] / drawing[8] / drawn[2], drawne[72] / drew[32] / drew'st[1]
**rh** saw *Luc 1673* / sawn *LC 90* / crew, threw *Luc 1734*; flew, knew *LC 61*; knew *VA 541*; slew *Luc 1520*; threw *LC 36*
> withdraw

**drawbridge** *n*
=
**sp** draw-bridge[1]

**drawer / ~s** *n*
'drɔ:əɹ / -z
**sp** drawer[7], draw-er[1] / drawers[3]
> tooth-drawer

**drawing** *adj*
'drɔ:ɪn, -ɪŋ
**sp** drawing[1]
> deep-, self-drawing

**drawling-affecting** *adj*
'drɔ:lɪn-ə'fektɪn, -ɪŋ-, -ɪŋ
**sp** drawling-affecting[1]
> affecting

**drawn** *adj*
=
**sp** drawn[1], drawne[2]
> air-, choice-, dove-drawn

**dray·man / ~men** *n*
'drɛ:-mən
**sp** dray-man[1], dray-men[1]

**dread** *adj / n*
=
**sp** dread[35] / dread[6]
**rh** *n 1* bed *Luc 171*; **rh** *2* mead *VA 635*

**dread / ~s / ~eth / ~ing / ~ed** *v*
= / = / = / 'dredɪn, -ɪŋ / =
**sp** dread[4] / dreads[2] / dreadeth[1] / dreading[2] / dreaded[2]
**rh** leadeth, pleadeth *Luc 270*

**dreaded** *adj*
=
**sp** dreaded[3]
> all-dreaded

**dreadful** *adj*
=
**sp** dreadful[1], dreadfull[58]

**dreadfully** *adv*
'dredfləɪ, -fʊl-
**sp** dreadfully[1], dread-fully[1]

**dream / ~s** *n*
=
**sp** dream[2], dreame[68], dreame's [dream is][1] / dreames[35]
**rh** extreme *S 129.12*; stream *Luc 1772, Oth 2.3.58, TN 4.1.60*; team *MND 5.1.376*; theme *CE 2.2.191, MND 5.1.418*
> John-a-dreams

**dream / ~est / ~s / ~ing / ~ed / -t** *v*
= / driːmst / = / ˈdriːmɪn, -ɪŋ / =
**sp** dream[1], dreame[43] / dream'st[3] / dreames[8] / dreaming[3] / dream'd[11] / dreampt[8], dreamt[9], dream't[1]
> undreamed

**dreamer / ~s** *n*
ˈdriːməɹ / -z
**sp** dreamer[3] / dreamers[1]

**dreaming** *adj / n*
ˈdriːmɪn, -ɪŋ
**sp** dreaming[3] / dreaming[2]

**dreamt**
> dream *v*

**dreg / ~s** *n*
=
**sp** dreg[1] / dregges[3], dregs[3]
**rh** legs *Tim 1.2.238*

**drench** *n*
=
**sp** drench[2]
> horse-drench

**drench / ~ed** *v*
=
**sp** drench[3] / drench'd[2], drencht[1]
**rh** French *1H6 4.7.14* / trenched *VA 1054*
> bedrench

**drenched** *adj*
*m* ˈdrenʃɪd
**sp** drenched[1]
> indrenched

**dress** *n*
=
**sp** dresse[1]

**dress / ~ed** *v*
=
**sp** dresse[18] / dress'd[1], drest[15]
> undress

**dresser** *n*
ˈdresəɹ
**sp** dresser[1]

**dressing / ~s** *n*
ˈdresɪnz, -ɪŋz
**sp** dressings[1]

**drew**
> draw

**dribbling** *adj*
ˈdrɪblɪn, -ɪŋ
**sp** dribling[1]

**dried** *adj*
drəɪd
**sp** dride[1], dried[2], dride-[peare][1], dry'de[1], dryed[1]
> dry

**drift** *n*
=
**sp** drift[19]
**rh** shrift *RJ 2.3.51*; swift *TG 2.6.43*

**drily** *adv*
ˈdrəɪləɪ
**sp** drily[1]
> dry

**drink / ~s** *n*
=
**sp** drink[3], drinke[42] / drinkes[1]
**rh** think *LLL 5.2.372*
> alms-drink

**drink / ~est / ~s / ~ing / drank / drunk / ~est** *v*
= / drɪnkst / = / ˈdrɪnkɪn, -ɪŋ / = / drɤŋk / -st
**sp** drink[5], drinke[105] / drink'st[2] / drinkes[19], drinks[1] / drinking[11] / drank[1], dranke[1] / drunk[2], drunke[21], drunke [drank][3] / drunk'st[1]
**rh** clink *Oth 2.3.68*; think *S 111.9*

**drinking / ~s** *n*
ˈdrɪnkɪn, -ɪŋ / -z
**sp** drinking[13], drin-king[1], drink-ing[1] / drinkings[1]
> blood-, by-drinking

**driv·e / ~est / ~s / ~eth / ~ing / drave / driven / drove / droven** *v*
drəɪv / -st / -z / -əθ / ˈdrəɪvɪn, -ɪŋ / drɛːv / = / droːv / ˈdroːvən
**sp** driue[34] / driu'st[1] / driues[12] / driueth[2] / driuing[3] / draue[4] / droue[7] / driuen[12] / drouen[1]
**rh** dives *Per 3.Chorus.50*
> thrice-driuen

**drivelling** *adj*
ˈdrɪvlɪn, -ɪŋ, -vəl-
**sp** driueling[1]

**driven** *adj*
=
**sp** driuen[1]

**driving** *adj*
ˈdrəɪvɪn, -ɪŋ
**sp** driuing[1]

**drizzle / ~s** *v*
=
**sp** drizzle[1] / drissels[1]

**drizzled** *adj*
=
**sp** drizel'd[1], drizled[1]

**droit** *Fr* *adv*
drwɛ
**sp** droict[1]

**drollery** *n*
ˈdrɒlrəɪ, -lər-
**sp** drolerie[1], drollery[1]

**Dromio / ~s** *n*
*m* ˈdroːmɪoː, -ɪˌoː / ˈdroːmɪoːz
**sp** Dromio[51], *in s.d.* Dro[1], [S.]Dromio[1] / Dromio's[2]
**rh** owe *CE 3.1.43*

**drone / ~s** *n*
droːn / -z
**sp** drone[2] / drones[2]
**rh** home *Per 2.Chorus.18*

**droop / ~s / ~eth / ~ing / ~ed** *v*
= / = / = / 'dru:pɪn, -ɪŋ / =
**sp** droop[1], droope[5] / droopes[1], droupes[2] / droopeth[1] / drooping[2] / droop'd[1]

**drooping** *adj*
'dru:pɪn, -ɪŋ
**sp** drooping[5], droo-ping[1], drouping[1]

**drop / ~s** *n*
=
**sp** drop[38] / droppes[4], drops[39]
> dew-, eye-, water-drop

**drop / ~s / ~eth / ~ping / ~ped** *v*
= / = / = / 'drɒpɪn, -ɪŋ / =
**sp** drop[37] / droppes[1], drops[5] / droppeth[1] /dropping[3] / drop'd[2], dropp'd[1], dropt[10]
**rh** stopped *VA 958*

**Drop-heir** [name] *n*
'drɒp-ˌɛ:ɹ
**sp** Drop-heire[1]

**droplet / ~s** *n*
=
**sp** droplets[1]

**dropped** *adj*
=
**sp** drop'd[1]

**dropping** *adj*
'drɒpɪn, -ɪŋ
**sp** dropping[1]
> tempest-dropping

**dropping / ~s** *n*
'drɒpɪnz, -ɪŋz
**sp** droppings[1]

**dropsied** *adj*
'drɒpsəɪd
**sp** dropsied[1]

**drops·y / ~ies** *n*
'drɒpsəɪ / -z
**sp** dropsie[1] / dropsies[1]

**dross** *n*
=
**sp** drosse[3]
**rh** loss *S 146.11, TC 4.4.9*; moss *CE 2.2.186*

**drossy** *adj*
'drɒsəɪ
**sp** drossie[1]

**drove, droven**
> drive

**drought / *Per, VA* drouth** *n*
drəʊt / drəʊθ
**sp** drought[1] / drouth[2]
**rh** mouth *Per 3.Chorus.8, VA 544*

**drovier** *n*
'dro:vɪəɹ
**sp** drouier[1]

**drown / ~s / ~ing / ~ed** *v*
drəʊn / -z / 'drəʊn·ɪn, -ɪŋ / *m* -ɪd, drəʊnd
**sp** drown[2], drowne[41] / drownes[2] / drow-ning[2] / dround[5], droun'd[3], drown'd[32], drown'de[1], drowned[2]
**rh** crown *3H6 4.4.23* / crowned, round *AC 2.7.113*; ground *VA 984*; sound *PP 8.11*

**drowned** *adj*
*m* drəʊnd, 'drəʊnɪd
**sp** drown'd[2], drownde[1], drowned[4]
> undrowned

**drowning** *n*
'drəʊnɪn, -ɪŋ
**sp** drowning[4], drow-ning[1]

**drowning-mark** *n*
'drəʊnɪn-ˌmɑ:ɹk, -ɪŋ-
**sp** drowning marke[1]
> mark

**drowse / ~d** *v*
drəʊz / -d
**sp** drowse[1] / drowz'd[1]
**rh** rouse *Mac 3.2.52*

**drowsily** *adv*
'drəʊzɪləɪ
**sp** drowsily[1]

**drowsiness** *n*
'drəʊzɪnəs
**sp** drowsines[1]

**drowsy** *adj*
'drəʊzəɪ
**sp** drowsie[15], drowzie[2]

**drudge / ~'s / ~s** *n*
drɤʤ / 'drɤʤɪz
**sp** drudg[1], drudge[5] / drudges[1] / drudges[1]

**drudgery** *n*
'drɤʤrəɪ, -ʤər-
**sp** drudgery[1]

**drug / ~s** *n*
drɤg / -z
**sp** *n* drugge[5] / drugges[6], drugs[4]

**drug / ~ged** *v*
drɤgd
**sp** drugg'd[1]

**drug-damned** *adj*
'drɤg-ˌdamd
**sp** drug-damn'd[1]
> damned

**drum / ~s** *n*
drɤm / -z
**sp** drum[47], drumme[62] / drummes[26], drums[11]
**rh** come *AW 2.5.91, 1H4 3.3.203, Mac 1.3.29*
> kettle-drum

**drum / ~s** *v*
drɤmz
**sp** drummes[1], drums[1]

**Drum / ~'s** [name] *n*
drɤmz
**sp** drummes[1]

**drumble** *v*
'drɤmbəl
**sp** drumble[1]

**drummer** *n*
'drɤməɹ
**sp** drummer[1]

**drumming** *n*
'drʏmɪn, -ɪŋ
**sp** drumming[1]

**drunk** *adj*
drʏŋk
**sp** drunk[4], drunke[33]
> drink, half-, swine-drunk

**drunkard / ~s** *n*
'drʏŋkəɹd / -z
**sp** drunkard[13], drun-kard[1] / drunkards[6]

**drunken** *adj*
'drʏŋkən
**sp** drunken[18]

**drunkenly** *adv*
*m* 'drʏŋkənləɪ, -ˌləɪ
**sp** drunkenly[2]

**drunkenness** *n*
*m* 'drʏŋkənˌnes, -ənəs
**sp** drunkennesse[4]

**dr·y / ~ier** *adj*
drəɪ / -əɹ
**sp** drie[16], dry[31] / drier[2]
**rh** fly *R2 2.2.145*; high *VA 552*; lie *VA 233*

**dr·y / ~ies / ~ied** *v*
drəɪ / -z / -d
**sp** drie[8], dry[8] / dries[1], dryes[2] / dri'd[1], dride[1], dri'de[1], dried[5], dry'd[1]
**rh** eye *RJ 2.3.2, VA 964* / denied *AW 2.1.140*
> oil-dried

**dry-beat** *v*
ˌdrəɪ-'biːt
**sp** drie-beate[1], dry beate[1]

**dry-beaten** *adj*
ˌdrəɪ-'biːtən
**sp** drie beaten[1]

**dryfoot** *n*
'drəɪfʊt
**sp** drifoot[1]
> foot

**dryness** *n*
'drəɪnəs
**sp** drinesse[1]

**dry-nurse** *n*
'drəɪ-ˌnɐːɹs
**sp** dry-nurse[1]
> nurse

**du** *Fr*
> de

**dualist** *n*
'djuːəlɪst
**sp** dualist[2]

**dub / ~bed** *v*
dʏb / -d
**sp** dub[3] / dubb'd[2], dub'd[2]

**ducat / ~s** *n*
'dʏkət / -s
**sp** ducat[2], ducate[2], ducket[2] / ducates[10], ducats[23], du-cats[1], du-kates[1], duckets[16]

**ducdame** *interj*
ˌdʏk'damiː
**sp** ducdame[4]
**rh** me *AY 2.5.51*

**Duchess / ~'** *n*
'dʏʧes
**sp** Duchesse[16], Dutches[2], Dutchesse[18] / Duchesse[2]

**Duchy** *n*
'dʏʧəɪ
**sp** Dutchy[2]

**duck / ~s** *n*
dʏk / -s
**sp** duck[1], [wilde]-ducke[1], ducke[8] / ducks[1]

**duck / ~s** *v*
dʏk / -s
**sp** ducke[1] / duckes[1]
> a-, silly-ducking

**dudgeon** *n*
'dʏʤən, -ɪən
**sp** dudgeon[1]

**due** *adj*
djuː
**sp** due[49]
**rh** true *LLL 4.1.19*; you *CE 4.1.1, TC 4.5.51*

**due / ~r** *adv*
'djuːəɹ
**sp** duer[1]

**due / ~s** *n*
djuː / -z
**sp** deaw[1], dew[1], due[18] / dues[6]
**rh** review *S 74.7*; view *S 69.3*

**duello** *n*
djʊ'eloː
**sp** duello[2]

**Duff** [name] *n*
dʏf
**sp** Duff[1]

**dug / ~s** *n*
dʏg / -z
**sp** dug[1], dugge[4] / dugges[2], dugs[1]

**Duke / ~'s / ~s** [*title*] *n*
djuːk / -s
**sp** Duke[557], Dukes [Duke is][1], Duke's [Duke is][3], *abbr* D[uke][5], Du[ke][1] / Dukes[33] / Dukes[25]

**duke / ~s** *v*
djuːks
**sp** dukes[1]

**dukedom / ~s** *n*
'djuːkdəm / -z
**sp** dukdome[1], dukedom[1], dukedome[22] / dukedomes[8]

**dulcet** *adj*
'dʏlsɪt
**sp** dulcet[6]

**dulche** *nonsense word*
'dʊlkeː
**sp** dulche[1]

**dull / ~er / ~est** *adj*
dʏl / 'dʏl·əɹ / -əst
**sp** dull[71] / duller[5] / dullest[3]
**rh** pull *AW 1.1.215*

**dull / ~s / ~ed** *v*
dɤl / -z / -d
**sp** dull[3] / duls[1] / dull'd[1]

**Dull** [name] *n*
dɤl
**sp** Dull[9]

**dullard** *n*
'dɤləɹd
**sp** dullard[2]

**dull-brained** *adj*
'dɤl-ˌbrɛ:nd
**sp** dull-brain'd[1]
> brain

**dull-eyed** *adj*
'dɤl-ˌəɪd
**sp** dull ey'd[1]
> eye

**dulling** *n*
'dɤlɪn, -ɪŋ
**sp** dulling[1]

**dullness** *n*
'dɤlnəs
**sp** dulnesse[5]
**rh** fullness *S 56.8*

**dully** *adv*
'dɤləɪ
**sp** dully[2]

**duly** *adv*
'dju:ləɪ
**sp** duely[2], duly[5]
**rh** truly *H5 3.2.17*

**Dumaine** *n*
du:'mɛ:n
**sp** Dumain[1], Dumaine[13], Dumane[5]
**rh** pain *LLL 4.3.169*; twain *LLL 5.2.47*

**dumb** *adj*
dɤm
**sp** dombe[1], dum[1], dumb[1], dumbe[27]
**rh** *1* entomb *Luc 1123*; tomb *AW 2.3.138, MA 5.3.10, MND 5.1.319, S 101.9, 83.10*; **rh** *2* come *TG 2.2.20*; **rh** *3* run *Per 5.2.2* [*Chorus*]

**dumb-discoursive** *adj*
'dɤm-dɪs'kɔ:ɹsɪv
**sp** dumb-discoursiue[1]

**dumbly** *adv*
'dɤmləɪ
**sp** dumbely[1], dumbly[1]

**dumbness** *n*
'dɤmnəs
**sp** dumbenesse[1], dumbnesse[3]

**dumb-show / ~s** *n*
'dɤm-ˌʃo: / -z
**sp** dumbe shew[2], dumbe show[1] / dumbe shewes[2]
> show

**dump / ~s** *n*
dɤmp / -s
**sp** dump[1], dumpe[1] / dumps[3]

**dun / ~nest** *adj*
dɤn / 'dɤnəst
**sp** dun[1], duns [dun is][1] / dunnest[1]
**rh** sun *S 130.3*
**pun** *RJ 1.4.40* done, Dun

**Dun** [name] *n*
dɤn
**sp** dun[1]
**pun** *RJ 1.4.41* done, dun

**Duncan / ~'s** *n*
'dɤŋkən / -z
**sp** Duncan[10], Duncane[1] / Duncans[1]

**dun-coloured** *adj*
'dɤn-ˌkɤləɹd
**sp** *emend of TN 1.3.128* dam'd colour'd[1]
> colour

**dung** *n*
dɤŋ
**sp** dung[1]
> cow-dung

**dungeon / ~s** *n*
'dɤnʤən / -z
**sp** dungeon[5], dun-geon[1], dunge-on[1] / dungeons[2]

**dunghill / ~s** *n*
'dɤŋ-ˌɪl, -ˌhɪl / -z
**sp** dunghill[7], dung-hill[1] / dunghills[1], dunghils[1]
> hill

**dungy** *adj*
'dɤnʤəɪ
**sp** dungie[1], dungy-[earth][1]

**Dunsinane** *n*
*m* 'dɤnsɪˌnɛ:n, dɤn'sɪnən
**sp** Dunsinane[8], Dunsmane[1]
**rh** bane *Mac 5.3.60*

**Dunsmore** *n*
'dɤnzmɔ:ɹ
**sp** Dunsmore[1]

**Dunstable** *n*
*m* 'dɤnsbəl, -stəb-
**sp** Dunstable[1]

**dup / ~ped** *v*
'dɤpt
**sp** dupt[1]

**durance** *n*
'dju:rəns
**sp** durance[7]
> endurance

**during** *prep*
'dju:rɪn, -ɪŋ
**sp** during[13], du-ring[1]
> long-during

**durst**
> dare

**dusky** *adj*
'dɤskəɪ
**sp** duskie[5], dusky[1]

**dust** *n*
dɤst
**sp** dust[56]
**rh** lust, thrust *Luc 1381*; must *Cym 4.2.269, 275, 263, 3H6 5.2.27*; rust *Per 2.2.54*; unjust *AW 5.3.64*
> overdusted

**dusty** *adj*
'dɤstəɪ
**sp** dustie[1], dusty[1]

**Dutch** *adj / n*
dɤʧ
**sp** Dutch-[dish][1] / Dutch[1]

**Dutchman / ~'s** *n*
'dɤʧmən / -z
**sp** Dutchman[2], Dutch-man[2] / Dutchmans[1]

**duteous** *adj*
'dju:tɪəs
**sp** duteous[3], dutious[7]
> unduteous

**dutiful** *adj*
'dju:tɪfʊl
**sp** dutifull[2]
> undutiful

**dut·y / ~y's / ~ies** *n*
'dju:təɪ / -z
**sp** duetie[4], dutie[90], duty[55] / duties[1] / duties[19]
**rh** beauty *Luc 497, VA 168* / beauties *Luc 14*

**dwarf** *n*
dwɑ:ɹf
**sp** dwarfe[5]

**dwarfish** *adj*
'dwɑ:ɹfɪʃ
**sp** dwarfish[5]

**dwell / ~est / ~s / ~ing / ~ed / dwelt** *v*
= / dwelst / = / 'dwelɪn, -ɪŋ / =
**sp** dwel[1], dwell[31] / dwel'st[2] / dwells[4], dwels[12] / dwelling[4] / dwelled / dwelt[2]
**rh** bell *S 71.4*; excel *S 5.2*; farewell *H8 3.2.459*; hell *Luc 1557, MND 1.1.206*; smell *VA 1173*; spell *Tem Epil.7*; tell *S 84.5, 89.10, 93.10* / smells *S 99.4* / bring, excelling, sing, thing *TG 4.2.51* / beheld, stelled *Luc 1446*
> outdwell

**dwelling** *n*
'dwelɪn, -ɪŋ
**sp** dwelling[5], dwel-ling[1]

**dwelling-house** *n*
'dwelɪn-ˌəʊs, -ɪŋ-, -ˌhəʊs
**sp** dwelling house[1]
> house

**dwelling-place / ~es** *n*
'dwelɪn-ˌplɛ:s, -ɪŋ- / -ɪz
**sp** dwelling place[1] / dwel-ling places[1]
> place

**dwindle** *v*
=
**sp** dwindle[2]

**dye** *n*
dəɪ
**sp** die[1], dye[1]
**rh** *1* archery *MND 3.2.102*; fearfully *PP 17.26*; wantonly *S 54.5*; **rh** *2* espy *MND 3.2.102*
**pun** *KJ 2.1.323* die

**dye / ~ing / ~d** *v*
dəɪ / 'dəɪɪn, -ɪŋ / dəɪd
**sp** dye[1] / dy-ing[1] / dide[1], died[1], dyde[1], dy'de[1]
**rh** chide, pride *S 99.5*; dignified *S 101.2*
> new-, over-dyed

**dying** *adj / n*
'dəɪɪn, -ɪŋ
**sp** dying[18] / dying[5]
> die; never-, tender-dying

# E

**E** [music] *n*
=
**sp** e[la][1]

**each** *pro*
=
**sp** each[216]
**rh** leech *Tim 5.4.83*

**eager** *adj*
'i:gəɹ
**sp** eager[7]

**eagerly** *adv*
*m* 'i:gəɹləɪ, -ˌləɪ
**sp** eagerly[3]

**eagerness** *n*
'*m* 'i:gəɹˌnes
**sp** eagernesse[1]

**eagle** *adj*
=
**sp** eagle[1]

**eagle / ~'s / ~s** *n*
=
**sp** eagle[21] / eagles[4] / eagles[8]

**eagle-sighted** *adj*
'i:gl-ˌsəɪtɪd
**sp** eagle-sighted[1]
> sight

**ean** *v*
i:n
**sp** eane[1]

**eaning** *adj*
'i:nɪn, -ɪŋ
**sp** eaning[1]

**eanling / ~s** *n*
'i:nlɪnz, -ɪŋz
**sp** eanelings[1]

**ear / ~s** *n*
i:ɹ, ɛ:ɹ / -z
**sp** eare[184], ere[1] / eares[161], ears[3]
**rh** *1* appear *LLL 4.3.42, MND 1.1.184*; dear *LLL 5.2.443, RJ 1.5.46*; fear *LLL 5.2.891, 900, Luc 283, PP 18.51, VA 659, 889, 1023*; hear *KJ 1.1.42, Luc 1325, R2 2.1.16, VA 698*; here *LLL 5.2.286, 436, MND 2.1.15, Oth 1.3.217*; **rh** 2 bear *Luc 1325, S 8.6*; bear, swear *Luc 1416*; hair *VA 145*; swear *LLL 4.1.62*; there *PP 4.5, 18.16, R2 5.3.125, VA 779* / clears *RJ 2.3.70*; tears [cry] *Luc 1126*
> crop-ear, overears

**ear / ~s** *v*
i:ɹ, ɛ:ɹ / -z
**sp** eare[2] / eres[1]
> shag-eared

**ear-deafening** *adj*
'i:ɹ-ˌdefnɪn, -ɪŋ, ɛ:ɹ-
**sp** eare-deaff'ning[1]
> deafening

**earing** *n*
'i:rɪn, -ɪŋ, ɛ:r-
**sp** earing[1]

**ear-kissing** *adj*
'i:ɹ-ˌkɪsɪn, -ɪŋ, ɛ:ɹ-
**sp** ear-kissing[1]
> kiss

**Earl / ~'s / ~s** [*title*] *n*
ɐ:ɹl / -z
**sp** Earle[99], earle[1] / Earles[1] / Earles[11]

**earldom** *n*
'ɐ:ɹldəm
**sp** earledome[4]

**earliness** *n*
*m* 'ɐ:ɹlɪˌnes
**sp** earlinesse[1]

**earl·y / ~ier / ~iest** *adj*
'ɐ:ɹləɪ / -əɹ / -əst
**sp** earely[7], early[40] / earlyer[1] / earliest[3]

**earn / ~s / ~ed** [gain] *v*
ɐ:ɹn / -z / -d
**sp** earne[6] / earnes[2] / earn'd[5], earned[2]
> unearned

**earn / ~s** [yearn] *v*
ɐ:ɹn / -z
**sp** erne[2] / earnes[1]

**earnest** *adj / n*
'ɐ:ɹnɪst
**sp** earnest[11] / earnest[26], ear-nest[2]
> overearnest

**earnest-gaping** *adj*
'ɐ:ɹnɪst-'gɛ:pɪn, -ɪŋ
**sp** earnest-gaping-[sight][1]
> gaping

**earnestly** *adv*
'ɐɹnɪstləɪ
**sp** earnestly[9]

**earnestness** *n*
*m* 'ɐ:ɹnɪstˌnes, -tnəs
**sp** earnestnesse[4]

**ear-piercing** *adj*
'i:ɹ-ˌpɛ:ɹsɪn, -ɪŋ, 'ɛ:ɹ-

**sp** eare-piercing[1]
> piercing

**earth / ~'s** *n*
ɐ:ɹθ / -s
**sp** earth[285], [dungy]-earth[1], earth's [earth is][1] / earths[10], earth's[1]
**rh** birth *1H4 3.1.14, MW 5.5.80* [middle-earth], *Per 1.2.113, 4.4.39*; dearth *S 146.1, VA 546*

**earth / ~ed** *v*
ɐ:ɹθt
**sp** earth'd[1]

**earth-bound** *adj*
'ɐ:ɹθ-ˌbəʊnd
**sp** earth-bound[1]
> bound

**earthen** *adj*
'ɐ:ɹθən
**sp** earthen[1]

**earthl·y / ~ier** *adj*
'ɐ:ɹθləɪ / -əɹ
**sp** earthly[28], earth-ly[1] / earthlier[1]
> unearthly

**earthquake / ~s** *n*
'ɐ:ɹθˌkwɛ:k / -s
**sp** earthquake[3], earth-quake[3] / earth-quakes[1]
> quake

**earth-treading** *adj*
*m* ˌɐ:ɹθ-'tredɪn, -ɪŋ
**sp** earth-treading[1]
> tread

**earth-vexing** *adj*
*m* ˌɐ:ɹθ-'veksɪn, -ɪŋ
**sp** earth-vexing[1]
> vex

**earthy** *adj*
'ɐ:ɹθəɪ
**sp** earthie[3], earthy[4]

**ear-wax** *n*
'i:ɹ-ˌwaks, 'ɛ:ɹ-
**sp** eare-wax[1]
> wax

**ease / ~s** *n*
=
**sp** ease[35], eases[1]
**rh** please *AY 2.5.49, H8 Epil.2, TS 5.2.178*; seas *Per 2.4.44, 2.Chorus.28* / diseases *TC 5.10.56*
> heart's ease

**eas·e / ~ing / ~ed** *v*
= / 'i:zɪn, -ɪŋ / =
**sp** ease[18] / easing[1] / eas'd[2], eased[1]

**easeful** *adj*
=
**sp** easefull[1]

**easil·y / ~iest** *adv*
*m* 'i:zləɪ, -zɪl-, 'i:zɪˌləɪ / 'i:zɪləst
**sp** easilie[1], easily[27], easlie[2] / easilest[1]

**easiness** *n*
*m* 'i:zɪˌnes, -ɪnəs
**sp** easinesse[2], ea-sinesse[1]
> uneasiness

**east** *adj / adv / n*
est
**sp** east[3] / east[32] / east[32]
**rh** *n* breast *LLL 4.3.221*; detest *MND 3.2.432*; rest *PP 14.13*; west *S 132.6*

**Eastcheap** *n*
'estʧi:p
**sp** Eastcheap[1], Eastcheape[3], East-cheape[3]

**Easter** *n*
'estəɹ
**sp** Easter[1]

**eastern** *adj*
'estəɹn
**sp** easterne[8]

**eas·y / ~ier / ~iest** *adj*
'i:zəɪ / -əɹ / -əst
**sp** easie[58], easy[2] / easier[9] / easiest[1]
> uneasy

**easy-borrowed** *adj*
'i:zəɪ-ˌbɒrəd, -ro:d
**sp** easie borrowed[1]

**easy-melting** *adj*
'i:zəɪ-ˌmeltɪn, -ɪŋ
**sp** easie-melting[1]
> melt

**easy-yielding** *adj*
'i:zəɪ-ˌji:ldɪn, -ɪŋ
**sp** easie-yeelding[1]

**eat / ~s / ~ing / ate / eaten** *v*
i:t / -s / 'i:tɪn, -ɪŋ / ɛ:t, et / 'etən
**sp** eat[20], eate[108] / eates[14], eats[5] / eating[6] / eate [ate][2] / eate [eaten][6], eaten[18]
**rh** great *Cym 4.2.266* / gets *AY 2.5.37* / sweaten *Mac 4.1.63*
**pun** *Tim 4.3.307* hate
> mouse-, over-, worm-eaten

**eater** *n*
'i:təɹ
**sp** eater[2]

**eating** *adj / n*
'i:tɪn, -ɪŋ
**sp** eating[2] / eating[4]

**eaux** *Fr n*
o
**sp** ewes[1]

**eaves** *n*
=
**sp** eaues[1], eeues[1]

**eavesdropper** *n*
'i:z-ˌdrɒpəɹ, 'i:vz-
**sp** ease-dropper[1]

**ebb / ~s /** *n*
=
**sp** ebbe[7] / ebs[1]

**ebb / ~s / ~ed** *v*
=
**sp** ebbe[8] / ebbes[1], ebs[1] / ebb'd[1]

**ebbed** *adj*
=
**sp** ebb'd[1]

**ebbing** *adj*
'ebɪn, -ɪŋ
**sp** ebbing[1], ebbing-[Neptune][1]

**ebon** *n*
'ebən
**sp** ebon[1]

**ebon-coloured** *adj*
'ebən-ˌkɤləɹd
**sp** ebon coloured[1]
> colour

**ebony** *n*
*m* 'ebənəɪ, -ˌnəɪ
**sp** ebonie[2], ebony[1]
**rh** felicity *LLL 4.3.245*

**ecce** *Lat interj*
'etʃe:
**sp** ecce[1]

**échapper** *Fr v*
eʃa'pe
**sp** eschapper[1]

**eche** *v*
i:tʃ
**sp** ich[1], *Per* each[1]
**rh** speech *Per 3.Chorus.13*

**echo / ~es** *n*
'eko: / -z
**sp** eccho[7] / ecchoes[1]

**echo / ~est** *v*
'eko: / -st
**sp** eccho[3] / ecchos't[1]

**eclipse / ~s** *n*
=
**sp** ecclipse[1], eclipse[1] / eclipses[3]
**rh** lips *Mac 4.1.28*

**eclipse / ~ed** *v*
=
**sp** eclipse[1] / eclipst[1]
> half-eclipsed

**écolier** *Fr n*
ekɔl'je
**sp** escholier[1]

**écouter / écoutez** *Fr v*
eku'tez
**sp** escoute[3]

**ecstas·y / ~ies** *n*
*m* 'ekstəsəɪ, -ˌsəɪ / 'ekstəˌsəɪz
**sp** extasie[12] / extasies[1]
**rh** fantasy *VA 895*; jealousy *MV 3.2.111*

**écu / ~s** *Fr n*
e'ky
**sp** escues[1], escus[1]

**Eden** *n*
=
**sp** Eden[1]

**Edgar** *n*
'edgəɹ
**sp** Edgar[21]

**edge / ~s** *n*
=
**sp** edge[38] / edges[3]
**rh** *1* hedge *WT 4.3.7*; **rh** *2* privilege *S 95.14*

**edge / ~d** *v*
edʒd
**sp** edged[1]

**edged** *adj*
*m* 'edʒɪd
**sp** edged[1]

**edgeless** *adj*
=
**sp** edgelesse[2]

**edict / ~s** *n*
*m* e'dɪkt, 'edɪkt / 'edɪkts
**sp** edict[7] / edicts[2]

**edifice / ~s** *n*
*m* 'edɪfɪs, -ˌfɪs / 'edɪˌfɪsɪz
**sp** edifice[2] / edifices[1]

**edif·y / ~ies / ~ied** *v*
'edɪfəɪ·z / -d
**sp** edifies[1] / edified[2]

**edition** *n*
e'dɪsɪən
**sp** edition[1]

**Edmondsbury** *n*
*m* 'edmənzˌbrəɪ, -ndz-
**sp** Edmondsbury[1]

**Edmund** *n*
'edmənd
**sp** Edmond[20], Edmund[31]

**educate** *v*
'edjəkɛ:t
**sp** educate[1]
> un-, well-educated

**education** *n*
ˌedjə'kɛ:sɪən
**sp** education[7], educati-on[1]

**Edward / ~'s** *n*
'edwəɹd / -z
**sp** Edward[156] / Edwards[52]
> Yedward

**eel / ~s** *n*
=
**sp** eele[4], eeles[1]

**eelskin / ~s** *n*
=
**sp** eele-skinne[1] / eele skins[1]
> skin

**e'en**
> even

**e'er**
> ever

**effect / ~s** *n*
=
**sp** effect[42] / effects[26]
**rh** aspect *AY 4.3.53*; defect *Ham 2.2.101*; reflect *VA 1132*; respect *S 36.7, 85.14*

**effect / ~s / *Luc, VA* ~ing / ~ed** *v*
= / = / ɪ'fektɪn, -ɪŋ / =
**sp** effect[24] / effects[1] / effecting[3] / effected[8]

**rh** expecting, respecting *Luc 429*; respecting *VA 912*

**effectless** *adj*
=
**sp** effectlesse[1]

**effectual** *adj*
*m* ɪ'fektjʊˌɑl, -jɑl
**sp** effectuall[4]
> uneffectual

**effectually** *adv*
*m* ɪ'fektjɑˌləɪ
**sp** effectually[1]

**effeminate** *adj*
*m* ɪ'femnət, -mɪn-, -mɪˌnɛ:t
**sp** effeminate[7]

**effig·y / ~ies** *n*
e'fɪʤəɪz
**sp** effigies[1]

**effuse** *n*
=
**sp** effuse[1]

**effuse / ~d** *v*
=
**sp** effus'd[1]

**effusion** *n*
ɪ'fju:zɪən
**sp** effusion[4]

**eft / ~est** *adj*
=
**sp** eftest[1]

**egal** *adj*
'ɛ:gɑl
**sp** egal[1], egall[1]

**egally** *adv*
*m* 'ɛ:gɑˌləɪ
**sp** egally[1]

**eg·eo / ~et** *Lat v*
'eget
**sp** egit[1]

**Egeon** *n*
ɪ'ʤi:ən
**sp** Egean[1], Egeon[4]

**Egeus** *n*
ɪ'ʤi:əs
**sp** Egeus[10]

**egg / ~s** *n*
=
**sp** egge[13] / egges[6]
> finch-, pigeon-egg

**eggshell / ~s** *n*
=
**sp** egge-shels[1]

**Eglamour** *n*
'egləˌmo:ɹ
**sp** Eglamore[2], Eglamoure[11]

**eglantine** *n*
'eglənˌtəɪn
**sp** eglantine[2]
**rh** woodbine *MND 2.1.252*

**egma** [enigma] *n*
=
**sp** egma[1]

**ego** *Lat pro*
'ego:
**sp** ego[1]

*meus det*
'me:ʊs
**sp** meus[1]

**egregious** *adj*
e'gri:ʤəs, -ɪəs
**sp** egregious[4]

**egregiously** *adv*
*m* e'gri:ʤəsˌləɪ, -ɪəs-
**sp** egregiously[1]

**egress** *n*
'i:gres
**sp** egresse[1]
> regress

**Egypt / ~'s** *n*
=
**sp** Aegypt[1], Egipt[1], Egypt[41], Egypte[1] / Egypts[3]

**Egyptian / ~s** *n*
ɪ'ʤɪpsɪən / -z
**sp** Aegyptian[2], Egiptian[1], Egyptian[9] / Aegyptians[1], Egyptians[2]

**eight** *adj / n*
ɛ:t
**sp** eight[20], *abbr* viii.[1] / eight[17]

**eighteen** *adj / n*
*m* ɛ:'ti:n, 'ɛ:ti:n / ɛ:'ti:n
**sp** eighteene[4], eigh-teene[1] / eighteene[1]

**eighth** *n*
ɛ:t
**sp** eight[1], Eight [*in* Henry the Eight][1], eighth[1]

**eightpenny** *adj*
'ɛ:tpnəɪ, -pən-
**sp** eight-penny[1]
> penny

**eighty** *adj*
'ɛ:təɪ
**sp** eightie[1]

**eight-year-old** *adj*
'ɛ:t-jɪr-ˌo:ld
**sp** eight yeare old[1]

**eisel** *n*
'esɪl
**sp** esile[1]

**either** *adj / conj*
'ɛðəɹ, 'ɛ:-
**sp** either[12], eyther[4] / either[109], eyther[15]
> neither

**either / ~'s** *pro*
'ɛðəɹ, 'ɛ:- / -z
**sp** either[20], ei-ther[1], eyther[1] / eithers[1], eythers[2]
**rh** *1* neither *CE 3.1.66*; **rh** *2* hither *CE 3.1.66*
> neither

**eject** *v*
=
**sp** eiect[1]

**eke** *adv / v*
i:k
**sp** eeke[1], eke[2] / eech[1], eeke[2]

**Elbe** *n*
elb
**sp** Elue[2]

**elbow / ~s** *n*
=, *Katherine H5 3.4.26ff*
'bɪlbo:, 'ɪlbo: / -z
**sp** elboe[1], elbow[17], *Katherine* bilbow[1], ilbow[1] / elbowes[1], elbows[1]

**Elbow / ~'s** [name] *n*
=
**sp** Elbow[7] / Elbowes[2]

**elbow-room** *n*
=
**sp** elbow roome[1]

**eld** *n*
=
**sp** [idle-headed]-eld[1], [palsied]-eld[1]

**elder** *adj*
'eldəɹ
**sp** elder[21], el-der[1]

**elder / ~s** [old] *n*
'eldəɹ / -z
**sp** elder[12] / elders[4]

**elder** [tree] *n*
'eldəɹ
**sp** [stinking]-elder[1]

**elder-gun** *n*
'eldəɹ-ˌgɤn
**sp** elder gunne[1]
> gun

**elder tree** *n*
'eldəɹ ˌtri:
**sp** elder tree[2]

**eldest** *adj / n*
*m* 'eldəst, eldst
**sp** eldest[22], eld'st[1] / eldest[4]

**eldest-born** *adj*
'eldəst-ˌbɔ:ɹn
**sp** eldest borne[1]
> born

**Eleanor / ~'s** *n*
*m* 'elɪˌnɔ:ɹ, -lɪn-, -lnəɹ / -z, el'nɔ:ɹz
**sp** Eleanor[1], Elianor[16], Elinor[3] / Elianors[2]

**elect** *adj / n*
=
**sp** elect[1] / elect[1]

**elect / ~ed** *v*
=
**sp** elect[2] / elected[4]

**elected** *adj*
=
**sp** elected[1]
> unelected

**election** *n*
*m* ɪ'leksɪən, -sɪˌɒn
**sp** election[21], electio[n][1]

**elegancy** *n*
'elɪgənsəɪ
**sp** elegancy[1]

**eleg·y / ~ies** *n*
*m* 'elɪʤəɪz, -ˌʤəɪz
**sp** elegies[2]

**element / ~s** *n*
*m* 'elɪˌment, 'elmənt / -s
**sp** element[9], ele-ment[2] / elements[20], ele-ments[2]
**rh** spent *Luc 1588*

**elephant / ~s** *n*
*m* 'elɪfənt, -ˌfant / 'elɪˌfants
**sp** elephant[6] / elephants[1]

**elevated** *adj*
'elɪvɛ:tɪd
**sp** eleuated[1]

**eleven,** *abbr* **leven** *adj / n*
*m* ɪ'lɛ:n, ɪ'levən, *abbr* lɛ:n, 'levən
**sp** a leuen[1], eleuen[6], *abbr* leauen-[weather][1] / eleuen[15]

**elevenpence,** *abbr* **leven~** *n*
ɪ'lɛ:npəns, -'levən-
**sp** a leuenpence-[farthing][1]

**eleventh** *adj / n*
ɪ'lɛ:nθ, ɪ'levənθ
**sp** eleue[n]th[1] / eleuenth[1]

**elf / elves** *n*
=
**sp** elfe[1] / elues[8]

**elfskin** *n*
=
**sp** elfe-skin[1]
> skin

**Elizabeth** *n*
ə'lɪzəˌbet, -eθ
**sp** Elizabeth[6]

**elk-lock / ~s** *n*
=
**sp** elk-locks[1]

**ell** *n*
=
**sp** ell[3]

**elle** *Fr pro*
ɛl
**sp** il

**Ellen** *n*
=
**sp** Ellen[1]

**elm** *n*
=
**sp** elme[3]

**eloquence** *n*
*m* 'eləˌkwens, 'elkwəns
**sp** eloquence[11]
**rh** *1* consequence *MV 3.2.106*; **rh** *2* recompense *S 23.9*

**eloquent** *adj*
*m* 'elə,kwent, 'elkwənt
**sp** eloquent[3]

**else** *adv*
=
**sp** els[19], else[382]

**Elsinore** *n*
'elsɪ,nɔ:ɹ
**sp** Elsenour[1], Elsonower[3]

**elsewhere** *adv*
*m* els'ʍɛ:ɹ, 'elsʍɛ:ɹ
**sp** elsewhere[5], else-where[2]
**rh** near *S 61.13*

**Eltham** *n*
'eltəm
**sp** Eltam[3]

**elvish-marked** *adj*
'elvɪʃ-,mɑ:ɹkt
**sp** eluish mark'd[1]
> mark

**Ely** *n*
'i:ləɪ
**sp** Ely[8]

**Elysium** *n*
*m* ə'lɪzɪʊm, -ɪ,ʊm
**sp** Elyzium[6]

**em-**
> *also* im-

**emballing** *n*
em'bɑ:lɪn, -ɪŋ
**sp** emballing[1]

**embalm / ~s** *v*
em'bɔ:m / -z
**sp** embalme[1] / embalmes[1]
> balm

**embar** *v*
em'bɑ:ɹ
**sp** imbarre[1]
> bar

**embark / ~ed** *v*
em'bɑ:ɹk / *m* -t, -ɪd
**sp** embarke[1], embarque[1] / embark'd[3], embarked[1], imbarkt[1], imbark't[1]

**embarkment / ~s** *n*
em'bɑ:ɹkmənts
**sp** embarquements[1]

**embassade** *n*
,embə'sɑ:d
**sp** embassade[1]

**embassador**
> ambassador

**embassage** *n*
,embə'sɛ:ʤ
**sp** embassage[4], em-bassage[1]
**rh** page *LLL 5.2.98*; vassalage *S 26.3*

**embass·y / ~ies** *n*
*m* 'embə,səɪ / -z
**sp** ambassie[1] / embasses[1], embassies[1]
**rh** majesty *LLL 1.1.132*

**embattaile / ~d** *v*
em'batl / *m* -tld, -tə,lɪd
**sp** embattaile[1] / embattaild[1], embattail'd[1], embattailed[1]

**embay / ~ed** *v*
em'bɛ:d
**sp** embay'd[1]

**embellish / ~ed** *v*
=
**sp** embellished[1]

**ember / ~s** *n*
'embəɹz
**sp** embers[1]

**emblaze** *v*
'emblɛ:z
**sp** emblaze[1]
> blaze

**emblem / ~s** *n*
=
**sp** embleme[1] / emblemes[1]

**embod·y / ~ied** *v*
em'bɒdəɪd
**sp** embodied[1]
> body

**embolden / ~s / ~ed** *v*
em'bo:ldən·z / -d
**sp** imboldens[1] / emboldned[1]

**emboss / ~ed** *v*
em'bɒst
**sp** imbost[3]

**embossed** *adj*
*m* em'bɒsɪd, em'bɒst
**sp** embossed[1], imbossed[2], imbost[1]

**embound / ~ed** *v*
em'bəʊndɪd
**sp** embounded[1]

**embowel / ~ed** *v*
em'bəʊəl / em'bəʊəld
**sp** imbowell[1] / embowel'd[1], imbowell'd[2]

**emboweled** *adj*
em'bəʊəld
**sp** embowel'd[1]

**embrace / ~s** *n*
em'brɛ:s / -ɪz
**sp** embrace[2] / embraces[1]
**rh** apace *VA 811*

**embrac·e / ~es / ~ing / ~ed** *v*
em'brɛ:s / -ɪz / -ɪn, -ɪŋ / *m* -t, -ɪd
**sp** embrace[50], em-brace[2], imbrace[13] / embraces[3] / embracing[1] / embrac'd[7], embraced[1], embrast[1], imbrac'd[2]
**rh** face *LLL 4.3.212, VA 539, 874*; **embrace him** place him *Luc 518* / chased *MW 5.5.229*; **embraced me** unlaced me *PP 11.5*

**embraced** *adj*
*m* em'brɛ:sɪd, -st
**sp** embraced[1], imbrac'd[1]

**embracement / ~s** *n*
em'brɛ:smənt / -s
**sp** embracement[3], imbracement[1] / embracements[5]

**embracing** *n*
em'brɛ:sɪn, -ɪŋ
**sp** embracing[1]
**rh** chasing *VA 559*

**embrasure / ~s** *n*
em'brɛ:zəɹz
**sp** embrasures[1]

**embrew / ~ed** *v*
em'bru: / -d
em-brew[1], imbrue[1] / embrewed[1]
> imbrue

**embroidered** *adj*
em'brəɪdəɹd
**sp** imbroider'd[1]

**embroidery** *n*
*m* em'brəɪdə,rəɪ
**sp** embroiderie[1]
**rh** charactery, knee *MW 5.5.71*

**embrue**
> imbrue

**emerald** *adj*
'emrɑld
**sp** emrold-[tuffes][1]

**Emilia** *n*
*m* e'mɪlɪə [*3 sylls*], -lɪ,a
**sp** Aemilia[28], Ae-milia[2], Aemillia[1], Emilia[5]

**Emillius** *n*
e'mɪlɪəs [*3 sylls*]
**sp** Emillius[6]

**eminence** *n*
*m* 'emɪ,nens
**sp** eminence[1]
> pre-eminence

**eminent** *adj*
*m* 'emɪ,nent, -mɪn-, 'emnənt
**sp** eminent[6]

**Emmanuel** *n*
=
**sp** Emanuell[1]

**emmew** *v*
em'ju:
**sp** emmew[1]

**empale**
> impale

**empannel**
> impannel

**emperator**
> imperator

**emperial**
> imperial

**empericutic** *n*
,emperɪ'kju:tɪk
**sp** emperickqutique[1]

**emperious**
> imperious

**Emperor / ~'s** *n*
*m* 'empə,rɔ:ɹ, -prəɹ, -pər- / -z
**sp** Emperor[27], Emperour[61], Em-perour[1], Emperour's [Emperor is][1] / Emperors[7], Emperours[12], Em-perours[1], *abbr* Emp[1]

**empery** *n*
*m* 'empə,rəɪ
**sp** emperie[4], empery[1], empyrie[1]

**emphasis** *n*
*m* 'emfə,sɪs
**sp** emphasis[2]

**empire** *n*
'empəɪɹ
**sp** empire[14]

**empiric / ~s** *n*
*m* 'empɪ,rɪks
**sp** empericks[1]

**empleached** *LC* *adj*
em'pli:ʧt
**sp** empleacht[1]
**rh** beseeched, enriched *LC 205*

**employ / ~ed** *v*
em'pləɪ / -d
**sp** employ[11], imploy[11] / employd[3], employ'd[5], employed[1], imploid[1], imployd[4], imploy'd[13]
**rh** boy *MND 3.2.374*
> pre-employ

**employer** *n*
em'pləɪəɹ
**sp** imploier[1]

**employment / ~s** *n*
em'pləɪmənt / -s
**sp** employment[11], imployement[1], imployment[9] / employments[1], imployments[1]

**empoison / ~ed** *v*
em'pəɪzən / -d
**sp** impoison[1] / im-poyson'd[1]

**Empress / ~'** [*title*] *n*
=
**sp** Empresse[40] / Empresse[13]

**emptiness** *n*
*m* 'emtɪ,nes, -mpt-
**sp** emptinesse[3]

**empt·y / ~ier** *adj*
'emtəɪ, -mpt- / -əɹ
**sp** emptie[17], empty[27] / emptier[2]

**empt·y / ~ies / ~ying / ~ied** *v*
'emtəɪ, -mpt- / -z / -ɪn, -ɪŋ / -d
**sp** emptie[1], empty[4] / empties[2] / emptying[1] / emptied[1]
**rh** plenty *Tem 4.1.111*

**empty-hearted** *adj*
'emtəɪ-'ɑ:ɹtɪd, -mpt-, -'hɑ:
**sp** empty hearted[1]
> heart

**emptying** *n*
'emtəɪɪn, -ɪŋ, -mpt-
**sp** emptying[2]

**emulate** *adj / v*
*m* 'emlət, -jələt / 'emjə,lɛ:t
**sp** emulate[1] / emulate[1]

**emulation / ~s** *n*
*m* 'emjə,lɛ:sɪən, -sɪ,ɒn / -z
**sp** emulation[10] / aemulations[1], emulations[1]

**emulator** *n*
'emjə,lɛ:təɹ
**sp** emulator[1]

**emulous** *adj*
'emjələs, -ml-
**sp** emulous[3]

**emure, emured**
> immure, immured

**en** *Fr prep / pro*
ɑ̃
**sp** en[7] / [m]an[1], en [m]en[2]

**enact / ~s** *n*
=
**sp** enacts[1]

**enact / ~s / ~ed** *v*
=
**sp** enact[3] / enacts[1] / enacted[4]
**rh** compacted, unacted *Luc 529*

**enactor / ~s** *n*
en'aktəɹz
**sp** ennactors[1]

**enamelled** *adj*
*m* =, e'namə,led
**sp** enamaled[1], enameld[1], enammel'd[1]
**rh** bed *CE 2.1.109*

**enamoured** *adj*
e'naməɹd
**sp** enamor'd[2], enamored[2], enamour'd[1], enamoured[1]

**encamp / ~ed** *v*
=
**sp** encampe[3] / encamp'd[2]
> camp

**encave** *v*
en'kɛ:v
**sp** encaue[1]

**Enceladus** *n*
*m* en'sɛlə,dɤs
**sp** Enceladus[1]

**enchafed** *adj*
*m* en'ʧɛ:ft, -fɪd
**sp** enchaf'd[1], enchafed[1]
> chafed

**enchange** *n*
en'ʧɛ:nʤ
**sp** enchange[1]

**enchant / ~s / ~ing / ~ed** *v*
en'ʧant, -'ʧɔ:nt / -s / -ɪn, -ɪŋ / -ɪd
**sp** enchaunt[2], inchant[1] / enchants[1], inchants[1] / inchanting[2] / enchaunted[1], inchanted[1]
**rh** want *Tem Epil.14* / **rh** *1* granted *LC 128*; **rh** *2* haunted *LC 128*

**enchanted** *adj*
en'ʧantɪd, -'ʧɔ:n-
**sp** inchanted[2]

**enchanting** *adj*
en'ʧantɪn, -ɪŋ, -'ʧɔ:n-
**sp** enchanting[2], inchanting[2]

**enchantingly** *adv*
en'ʧantɪnləɪ, -ɪŋ-, -'ʧɔ:n-
**sp** enchantingly[1]

**enchantment** *n*
en'ʧantmənt, -'ʧɔ:n-
**sp** enchantment[2]

**enchantress** *n*
en'ʧantrəs, -'ʧɔ:n-
**sp** inchantresse[1]

**enchased** *adj*
en'ʧɛ:st
**sp** inchac'd[1]

**encircle / ~d** *v*
en'sɐ:ɹkəl / -d
**sp** encircle[1] / encircled[1]
> circle

**encline**
> incline

**enclip / ~s** *v*
=
**sp** inclippes[1]

**enclog** *v*
=
**sp** enclogge[1]

**enclos·e** *S / LC, Luc* **~es / ~eth / ~ing / ~ed** *v*
en'klo:z / -ɪz / -əθ / -ɪn, -ɪŋ / -d
**sp** inclose[1] / incloses[1] / incloseth[1] / enclosing[1] / enclos'd[1], enclosed[3], inclos'd[1]
**rh** rose *S 95.4* / roses *LC 287, Luc 73* / supposed *Luc 378*
> close

**enclosed** *adj*
*m* en'klo:zɪd
**sp** inclosed[1]

**encloud / ~ed** *v*
en'kləʊdɪd
**sp** enclowded[1]
> cloud

**encompass / ~eth / ~ed** *v*
en'kɤmpə·səθ / *m* -st, -,sɪd
**sp** incompasseth[1] / encompass'd[2], incompass'd[1], incompassed[1], incompast[2]
> compass

**encompassment** *n*
*m* en'kɤmpəs,ment
**sp** encompassement[1]

**encore** *Fr adv*
ɑ̃'kɔ:ɹ
**sp** encore[1]

**encorpse / ~d** *v*
en'kɔ:ɹpst
**sp** encorps't[1]

**encounter / ~s** *n*
en'kəʊntəɹ / -z
**sp** encounter[23], en-counter[1], incounter[2] / encounters[5], incounters[1]
**rh** mount her *VA 596*

**encounter / ~ing / ~ed** *v*
en'kəʊntəɹ / en'kəʊntrɪn, -ɪŋ / *m* en'kəʊntəɹd, -əˌred
**sp** encounter[24], incounter[2] / encountring[1] / encounter'd[1], encountred[13], en-countred[2], incountred[1]
**rh** shed *1H6 4.6.18*

**encounterer / ~s** *n*
en'kəʊntrəɹz, -tər-
**sp** encounterers[1]

**encourage / ~ed** *v*
en'kɤrɪʤ / -d
**sp** encourage[4] / encourag'd[1]

**encouragement** *n*
*m* en'kɤrɪʤˌment
**sp** encouragement[2]

**encrease**
> increase

**encroaching** *adj*
en'kro:ʧɪn, -ɪŋ
**sp** incroaching[1]

**encumber** *v*
en'kɤmbəɹ
**sp** encombred[1]

**end / ~s** *n*
=
**sp** end[222], [figges]-end[1], lagge-[end][1], [Mile]-end[1], [Mile]-end-[Greene][1], [world-without]-end[1] / ends[31]
**rh** attend *R3 4.4.195, VA 1138*; contend *S 60.2*; depend *S 92.6*; friend *AC 4.15.90, AY 3.2.132, Cym 5.3.59, LLL 5.2.822, Luc 238, 528, S 50.2, 110.9, TG 2.1.153*; intend *LLL 5.2.430*; lend *TNK 1.5.14*; offend *MND 5.1.111*; penned *LLL 5.2.304*; send *VA 272*; spend *Mac 3.5.21, S 9.11, 146.8, Tim 3.4.56*; wend *CE 1.1.159* / friends *Tim 4.3.467*
> butt-, finger-, fore-, lag-end

**end / ~s / ~ing / ~ed** *v*
= / = / 'endɪn, -ɪŋ / =
**sp** end[71] / endes[1], ends[15] /ending[5] / ended[29]
**rh** *1* friend *Luc 899, MND 2.2.67, RJ 3.1.185, S 30.14*; mend *Tim 5.1.218*; wend *MND 3.2.373*; **rh** *2* fiend *PT 7, S 145.9* / friends *LLL 5.2.221, MND 5.1.338, VA 716* / amended, pretended *Luc 579*; befriended *TC 5.9.10*; depended *Oth 1.3.200*; descended *Luc 1079*; extended *AW 2.1.174*; offended *LLL 2.1.192*

**endamage** *v*
=
**sp** endamage[1], endammage[1]

**endamagement** *n*
=
**sp** endamagement[1]

**endanger** *v*
en'dɛ:nʤəɹ
**sp** endanger[1], en-danger[1]

**endart** *v*
en'dɑ:ɹt
**sp** endart[1]

**endear / ~ed** *v*
*m* en'di:ɹd, -i:rɪd
**sp** endeer'd[2], endeered[2]
> self-endeared

**endeavour / ~s** *n*
en'devəɹ / -z
**sp** endeauour[2], endeuour[6], indeauor[1], indeauour[1], indeuor[1], indeuour[1] / endeauors[3], endeuors[2], endeuours[3]

**endeavour / ~s / ~ed** *v*
en'devəɹ / -z / -d
**sp** endeauour[2], en-deauour[1], endeuour[1] / endeuours[1] / endeuour'd[1]

**ended** *adj*
=
**sp** ended[1]

**ender** *LC* *adj*
'endəɹ
**sp** ender[2]
**rh** render, tender *LC 222*

**ending** *adj*
'endɪn, -ɪŋ
**sp** ending[3]

**ending / ~s** *n*
'endɪn, -ɪŋ / -z
**sp** ending[3] / endings[2]
**rh** amending, depending *Luc 1612*; attending *Per Epil.18*

**endite** *v*
en'dəɪt
**sp** endite[1]

**endless** *adj*
=
**sp** endles[1], endlesse[8]

**endow / ~s / ~ed** *v*
en'dəʊ / -z / -d
**sp** indow[1] / endowes[1] / endow'd[2], endowed[1], indowed[1]

**endowment / ~s** *n*
en'dəʊmənt / -s
**sp** endowments[2]

**endue / ~s / ~d** *v*
en'dju: / -z / -d
**sp** endue[1], indue[2] / endues[1] / endu'd[1], indued[4]

**endurance** *n*
en'dju:rəns
**sp** indurance[2]

**endur·e / ~st / ~s / ~ing / ~ed** *v*
en'dju:ɹ / -st / -z / -ɪn, -ɪŋ / -d
**sp** endure[61], indure[13], in-dure[1] / endur'st[1] / endures[1] / enduring[1] / endur'd[8], en-dur'd[1], endured[1], indur'd[4], indured[1]
**rh** cure *MA 4.1.252, S 153.6, VA 507*; pure *LLL 5.2.353, Luc 1659*; sure *JC 1.2.319*; unsure *TN 2.3.50* / assured *S 107.5*; cured *Luc 1582*

**Endymion** *n*
*m* en'dɪmɪˌɒn
**sp** Endimion[1]

**enem·y / ~y's / ~ies / ~ies'** *n*
*m* 'enəˌməɪ, -nm- / -z
**sp** enemie[66], ene-mie[1], enemy[84], ene-my[1], enemy's [enemy is][1] / enemies[16] / enemies[94], enemyes[1] / enemies[9]
**rh** *1* impiety, infamy *Luc 1171*; me *Per 2.5.65, RJ 1.5.141, 2.3.45*; security *Mac 3.5.33*; see *AY 2.5.7, 41*; **rh** *2* fly *JC 5.3.2*; try *Ham 3.2.219* / **rh** *1* injuries *S 139.10*; **rh** *2* cries, tyrannize *Luc 674*; eyes *Luc 1470*; flies *Ham 3.2.215*; guise *Tim 4.3.469*; lies *R2 5.6.32*
> arch-enemy, ennemi

**enfeeble / ~s / ~d** *v*
=
**sp** enfeebles[1] / enfeebled[2]
> feeble

**enfeoff / ~ed** *v*
en'fi:ft
**sp** enfeoff 'd[1]

**enfetter / ~ed** *v*
en'fetəɹd
**sp** enfetter'd[1]

**enfix / ~ing** *v*
en'fɪksɪn, -ɪŋ
**sp** enfixing[1]

**enflame / ~d** *v*
en'flɛ:m / -d
**sp** enflame[2] / enflam'd[1]

**enflamed** *adj*
en'flɛ:md
**sp** enflam'd[1]

**enfold** *v*
en'fo:ld
**sp** enfold[1], infold[2]
**rh** behold, bold, cold, gold, inscrolled, old, sold, told *MV 2.7.69*
> fold

**enfolding / ~s** *n*
en'fo:ldɪnz, -ɪŋz
**sp** enfoldings[1]

**enforce / ~st / ~s / ~d** *v*
en'fɔ:ɹs / -əst / -ɪz / *m* -t, -ɪd
**sp** enforce[21], inforce[13] / inforcest[1] / enforces[2] / enforc'd[6], en-forc'd[1], enforced[3], enforc't[2], enforst[1], enfor'st[1], inforced[2], in-forced[1], infor'd[1]
> force

**enforced** *adj*
*m* en'fɔ:ɹst, -sɪd
**sp** enforced[4], inforc'd[1], inforced[2]

**enforcedly** *adv*
*m* en'fɔ:ɹsɪdˌləɪ
**sp** enforcedly[1]

**enforcement** *n*
en'fɔ:ɹsmənt
**sp** enforcement[5], inforcement[1]
> reinforcement

**enform**
> inform

**enfranched** *adj*
*m* en'franʧɪd
**sp** enfranched[1]

**enfranchise / ~d** *v*
en'franʧəɪz / -d
**sp** enfranchise[1], infranchise[3] / enfranchis'd[2], enfranchisde[1], enfranchized[1], infranchised[1]
> franchise

**enfranchisement** *n*
*m* en'franʧəɪzˌment
**sp** enfranchisement[2], infranchisement[4]

**enfreed** *adj*
=
**sp** enfreed

**enfreedom / ~ing** *v*
en'fri:dəmɪn, -ɪŋ
**sp** enfreedoming[1]
> freedom

**engag·e / ~ing / ~ed** *v*
en'gɛ:ʤ / -ɪn, -ɪŋ / *m* -ɪd, -d
**sp** engage[4] / engaging[1] / engag'd[5], engagde[1], engaged[2], ingag'd[9], ingaged[1]

**engagement / ~s** *n*
en'gɛ:ʤmənts
**sp** engagements[1]

**engaol / ~ed** *v*
en'ʤɛ:ld
**sp** engaol'd[1]

**engender / ~s / ~ed** *v*
en'ʤendəɹ / -z / -d
**sp** ingender[1] / engenders[5], ingenders[1] / engendred[4]
> high-engendered

**engendering** *n*
en'ʤendrɪn, -ɪŋ
**sp** ingendring[1]

**engild / ~s** *v*
en'gɪldz
**sp** engilds[1]

**engine / ~s** *n*
=
**sp** engin[1], engine[7] / engines[4]

**enginer** *n*
'enʤɪnəɹ
**sp** enginer[1]

**engirt** *v*
en'gɐ:ɹt
**sp** engirt[1], engyrt[1]

**England / ~'s** *n*
=
**sp** England[241], Eng-land[4], [Mother]-England[1] / Englands[64]

**English** *adj / n*
=, *Fr pron H5 5.2.259* 'ɒŋglɪʃ
**sp** English[83], Eng-lish[1] / English[64], *Fr* Anglish[1]

**English / ~d** *v*
=
**sp** english'd[1]

**English·man / ~man's / ~men** *n*
=
**sp** Englishman[8], English man[1] / Englishmans[1] / Englishmen[6], English men[1]
**rh** can *R2 1.3.309* / Amen *H5 5.2.359*; ten *H5 3.7.153*

**Englishwoman** *n*
=
**sp** English-woman[1]
> woman

**englut / ~s / ~ted** *v*
eŋ'glɤts / -ɪd
**sp** engluts[1] / englutted[2]

**engraffed**
> ingraffed, long-engraffed

**engrave / ~d, *abbr* graved** *v*
eŋ'grɛ:v / -d, *abbr* grɛ:vd
**sp** ingraue[1] / engrau'd[2], *abbr* grau'd[1]

**engross / ~est / ~ed** *v*
eŋ'grɒs / -əst / *m* -ɪd, -t
**sp** engrosse[2] / engrossest[1] / engross'd[1], ingross'd[1], ingrossed[1], ingrost[1]
**rh** crossed *S 133.6*

**engrossing** *adj*
eŋ'grɒsɪn, -ɪŋ
**sp** ingrossing[1]

**engrossment / ~s** *n*
eŋ'grɒsmənts
**sp** engrossements[1]

**enguard** *v*
eŋ'gɑ:ɹd
**sp** enguard[1]

**enigma** *n*
e'nɪgmə
**sp** aenigma[1], enigma[1]

**enigmatical** *adj*
*m* ˌenɪg'matɪˌkal
**sp** enigmaticall[1]

**enjoin / ~ed** *v*
en'ʤəɪn / -d
**sp** enioyne[2] / enioynd[2], enioyn'd[3], inioynd[1], inioyn'd[1], inioyned[1]

**enjoy / ~s / ~ing / ~ed** *v*
en'ʤəɪ / -z / -ɪn, -ɪŋ / -d
**sp** enioy[43], inioy[1] / enioyes[7] / enioying[2] / enioy'd[7], enioyed[1], inioy'd[2]
**rh** destroy *VA 1164*; enjoy thee destroy thee *Luc 512* / enjoys it destroys it *S 9.10*

**enjoying** *n*
en'ʤəɪɪn, -ɪŋ
**sp** enioying[3]

**enkindle / ~d** *v*
=
**sp** enkindle[2] / enkindled[2]
> kindle

**enkindled** *adj*
=
**sp** enkindled[1], inkindled[1]

**enlard** *v*
en'lɑ:ɹd
**sp** enlard[1]

**enlarge / ~th / ~d** *v*
en'lɑ:ɹʤ / -əθ / *m* -ɪd, -d
**sp** enlarge[5], inlarge[3] / enlargeth[1] / enlarged[1], inlarg'd[1]
**rh** charged *S 70.12*
> wide-enlarged

**enlargement** *n*
en'lɑ:ɹʤmənt
**sp** enlargement[5]

**enlink / ~ed** *v*
=
**sp** enlynckt[1]

**enmash** *v*
=
**sp** en-mash[1]

**enmit·y / ~ies** *n*
*m* 'enmɪˌtəɪ / -z
**sp** enmitie[5], enmity[14] / enmities[2]
**rh** *1* Brittany *3H6 4.6.98*; infamy *Luc 503*; posterity *S 55.9*; **rh** *2* lie *RJ 5.3.304*

**ennemi** *Fr n*
ɛn'mi
**sp** ennemie[1]
> enemy

**ennoble / ~d** *v*
e'no:bəl / -d
**sp** ennoble[1] / ennobled[1]
> noble

**Enobarbus** *n*
ˌi:nə'bɑ:ɹbəs, -no:-
**sp** Enobarbe[1], Enobarbus[31], *abbr in s.d.* Enob[3]

**enormity** *n*
*m* ɪ'nɔ:ɹmɪˌtəɪ
**sp** enormity[1]

**enormous** *adj*
ɪ'nɔ:ɹməs
**sp** enormous[1]

**enough** *adv*
ɪ'nɤf, ɪ'nɒf
**sp** enough[285], e-nough[8], inough[11], ynough[1]
**rh** *1* Macduff *Mac 4.1.71, 5.6.73*; rough *VA 235*; **rh** *2* off *TG 5.1.12*

**enow** *adv*
ɪ'nəʊ
**sp** enow[10]

**enpearce / ~d** *v*
*m* en'pɛ:ɹsɪd
**sp** enpearced[1]

**enquire / ~d** *v*
ɪn'kwəɪɹ / -d
**sp** enquier[1], enquire[16], en-quire[1], inquire[4] / enquir'd[3], enquired[2]
**rh** Tyre *Per 3.Chorus.22*

**enquiry** *n*
ɪn'kwəɪɹəɪ
**sp** enquiry[1], inquiry[1]
> after-enquiry

**enrage / ~s / ~d** *v*
en'rɛ:ʤ / -ɪz / *m* -d, -ɪd
**sp** enrage[2] /enrages[1] / enrag'd[7], enraged[4], inrag'd[2], inraged[1]

**rh** assuaged *VA 317*
> threat-enraged

**enrank** *v*
=
**sp** enranke[1]

**enrapt** *v*
=
**sp** enrapt[1]

**enrich / ~es / ~ed** *v*
= / = / *m* en'rɪʧt, -ʧɪd
**sp** enrich[7], inrich[1] / enriches[1] / enrich'd[6], enricht[1], inrich'd[1], inriched[1], inricht[1]
**rh** beseeched, empleached *LC 208*
> rich

**enring / ~s** *v*
=
**sp** enrings[1]

**enrobe / ~d** *v*
en'ro:b / -d
**sp** enrobe[1] / en-roab'd[1]

**enrol / ~led** *v*
en'ro:l / *m* -d, -ɪd
**sp** enrold[1] / enroll'd[1], enrolled[4], inroll'd[1]

**enrolled** *adj*
*m* en'ro:lɪd
**sp** inrolled[1]

**enroot / ~ed** *v*
=
**sp** en-rooted[1]
> root

**enround / ~ed** *v*
en'rəʊndɪd
**sp** enrounded[1]

**enschedule / ~d** *v*
en'sedju:ld
**sp** enschedul'd[1]
> schedule

**ensconc·e / ~ing** *v*
= / en'skɒnsɪn, -ɪŋ
**sp** ensconce[1], en-sconce[1], insconce[1] / ensconcing[1]
> sconce

**enscroll**
> inscroll

**enseamed** *adj*
*m* en'sɛ:mɪd
**sp** enseamed[1]

**ensear** *v*
en'si:ɹ
**sp** enseare[1]
> sear

**enseign·er / ~ez / ~é** *Fr v*
ɑ̃nsɛ'ɲe
**sp** ensigniez[1] / ensignie[1]

**ensemble** *Fr adv*
ɑ̃n'sɑ̃:blə
**sp** ensembe[1]

**enshelter / ~ed** *v*
en'ʃeltəɹd
**sp** enshelter'd[1]
> shelter

**enshield** *adj*
'enʃi:ld
**sp** en-shield[1]

**enshrine / ~s** *v*
en'ʃrəɪnz
**sp** inshrines[1]
> shrine

**ensign / ~s** *v*
'ensəɪn / -z
**sp** ensigne[5] / ensignes[2]

**enskied** *adj*
en'skəɪd
**sp** en-skied[1]

**ensnare / ~th / ~ed** *v*
en'snɛ:ɹ / -əθ / -d
**sp** ensnare[1] / ensnareth[1] / ensnar'd[1]
**rh** spare me *Luc 584*
> snare

**enstate** *n*
en'stɛ:t
**sp** en-state[1]
> state

**ensteeped** *adj*
=
**sp** ensteep'd[1]

**ensue / ~s / ~d** *v*
en'sju: / -z / -d
**sp** ensue[10], insue[2] / ensues[2], insues[2] / ensu'de[1], ensued[1]
**rh** blue *CE 2.2.200*; true *MND 3.2.90*; view *Luc 1263*; you *Oth 2.3.9* / news *WT 4.1.25*; renews, views *Luc 1104*

**ensuing** *adj*
en'sju:ɪn, -ɪŋ
**sp** ensuing[7], insuing[1]
**rh** viewing *VA 1078*

**entail** *n*
en'tɛ:l
**sp** intaile[1]

**entail** *v*
*m* en'tɛ:l, 'entɛ:l
**sp** entayle[2]

**entame** *v*
en'tɛ:m
**sp** entame[1]

**entangle / ~s / ~d** *v*
=
**sp** entangles[1] / entangled[1], intangled[1]

**entend**
> intend

**entendre** *Fr v*
ɑ̃n'tɑ̃:drə
**sp** entendre[1]

**entent**
> intend

**enter / ~s / ~eth / ~ing / ~ed** *v*
'entəɹ / -z / 'entr·əθ, -tər- / -ɪn, -ɪŋ / 'entəɹd
**sp** enter[2204] / enters[13] / entereth[1], entreth[1] / entering[2], entring[4] / enter'd[10], entred[18], en-tred[1]
**rh** venture *VA 626*

**entered** *adj*
'entəɹd
**sp** entred[1]
> man-, well-entered

**entering** *n*
'entrɪn, -ɪŋ
**sp** entring[1]

**enterprise / ~s** *n*
'entəɹˌprəɪz / -ɪz
**sp** enterprise[5], enterprize[26] / enterprises[2], enterprizes[1]
**rh** *1* arise, despise *Luc 184*; eyes *MND 3.2.157, 350*; **rh** *2* sacrifice *TC 1.2.283*

**entertain / ~est / ~ing / ~ed** *v*
ˌentəɹ'tɛ:n / -st / -ɪn, -ɪŋ / *m* -d, -ɪd
**sp** entertaine[37], enter-taine[1] / entertainst[1], entertain'st[1] / entertaining[1] / entertaind[1], entertain'd[9], enter-tain'd[1], entertained[5]
**rh** again *Luc 1361*; amain *Tem 4.1.75*; **entertain him** complain him, disdain him *Luc 842*; **entertain me** disdain me *CE 3.1.120*; **entertain thee** complain me *Luc 596*

**entertainer** *n*
ˌentəɹ'tɛ:nəɹ
**sp** entertainer[1]

**entertainment / ~s** *n*
ˌentəɹ'tɛ:nmənt / -s
**sp** entertainement[2], entertainment[32], enter-tainment[1] / entertainments[1]

**enthralled** *adj*
*m* en'θrɑ:ld, -lɪd
**sp** enthral'd[1], enthrall'd[1], enthralled[2], inthral'd[1]

**enthrone / ~d** *v*
*m* en'θro:nd, -nɪd
**sp** enthroaned[1], enthron'd[3], enthroned[1]

**entice / ~d, *abbr* ticed** *v*
en'təɪs / *abbr* təɪst
**sp** entice[2] / *abbr* tic'd[1]
**rh** advice, nice *Luc 1411*; vice *PP 20.42*

**enticement / ~s** *n*
en'təɪsmənts
**sp** entise-ments[1]

**enticing** *adj*
en'təɪsɪn, -ɪŋ
**sp** enticing[1], inticing[1]

**entire** *adj*
en'təɪɹ
**sp** entire[3], entyre[1], intire[4]

**entirely** *adv*
en'təɪɹləɪ
**sp** entirely[1], intirely[7]

**entit·le / ~ling / ~led /** *v*
en'təɪtl, -'tɪt- / -ɪn, -ɪŋ / -d
**sp** intitle[3] / entit'ling[1] / intitled[1]
> title

**entitule / ~d** *v*
*m* en'təɪtjəˌled, -jəld, -'tɪt-
**sp** intituled[1], *Luc* entituled[1]
**rh** red *Luc 57*

**entomb / ~ed** *v*
en'tɤm, -'tu:m / -d
**sp** entombe[1], intombe[2] / entomb'd[1], intomb'd[1]
**rh** dumb *Luc 1121*

**entrails** *n*
'entrɛ:lz
**sp** entrailes[3], en-trailes[1], entrayles[2], intrailes[4], intrals[1]

**entrance / ~s** *n*
=
**sp** entrance[18], entrances[1]

**entrap / ~ped** *v*
=
**sp** entrap[1], intrap[3] / intrapt[1]

**entre** *Fr prep*
'ɑ̃:ntrə
**sp** entre[1]

**entreasured** *adj*
*m* en'trezəˌred
**sp** entreasured[1]
> treasure

**entreat / ~s** *n*
en'trɛ:ts, -rets
**sp** entreats[1], intreats[2]

**entreat / ~s / ~ing / ~ed** *v*
en'trɛ:t, -ret / -s / -ɪn, -ɪŋ / -ɪd
**sp** entreat[36], entreate[14], intreat[43], intreate[18] / entreats[6], en-treats[1], intreats[2] / intreating[1] / entreated[8], intreated[4]
**rh** frets *VA 73*

**entreatment / ~s** *n*
en'trɛ:tmənts, -ret-
**sp** entreatments[1]

**entreat·y / ~ies** *n*
en'trɛ:təɪ, -ret- / -z
**sp** entreatie[4], entreaty[2], intreatie[2], intreaty[4] / entreaties[8], intreaties[3]

**entrench / ~ed** *v*
=
**sp** entrench'd[1], entrencht[1]

**entry** *n*
'entrəɪ
**sp** entry[1]

**entwist** *v*
=
**sp** entwist[1]
> twist

**enurn / ~ed** *v*
en'ɐ:ɹnd
**sp** enurn'd[1]

**envelop** *v*
=
**sp** inuellop[1], inuelop[1]

**envenom / ~s / ~ed** *v*
=
**sp** envenom[2] / enuenoms[1] / envenom'd[2]
> venom

**envenomed** *adj*
*m* en'venə,mɪd
**sp** inuenomed[2]

**envious** *adj*
=
**sp** enuious[35]
> envy

**enviously** *adv*
*m* 'envɪəs,ləɪ
**sp** enuiously[1]
> envy

**environ / ~ed** *v*
en'vəɪrən / *m* en'vəɪrə,nɪd, -rənd
**sp** enuiron[2], inuiron[1] / enuironed[1], inuiron'd[3], inuironed[1], inuironned[1]

**envy / ~s** *n*
'envəɪ / -z
**sp** enuie[9], enuy[30] / enuies[3]

**env·y / ~ies / ~ing / ~ied** *v*
'envəɪ / -z / -ɪn, -ɪŋ / -d
**sp** enuie[5], enuy[4] / enuies[1] / enuying[2] / enui'd[1], enuide[1], enuied[2]

**enwheel** *v*
en'ʍi:l
**sp** enwheele[1]
> wheel

**enwomb / ~ed** *v*
*m* en'wʊmɪd
**sp** enwombed[1]
> womb

**enwrap / ~s** *v*
=
**sp** enwraps[1]

**eo / ibat** *Lat v*
'i:bat
**sp** ibat[3]

**Ephesian / ~s** *n*
e'fi:zɪən / -z
**sp** Ephesian[1] / Ephesians[1]

**Ephesus** *n*
'efesəs
**sp** Ephesus[13], *abbr* Eph[2], Ephes[2], *CE 2.1.1. s.d. emend of* Sereptus[1]
**rh** votaress *Per 4.Chorus.3*

**epicure / ~s** *n*
'epɪkju:ɹ / -z
**sp** epicure[1] / epicures[1]

**epicurean** *adj*
=
**sp** epicurean[1], epicurian-[rascall][1]

**epicurism** *n*
=
**sp** epicurisme[1]

**Epicurus** *n*
,epɪ'kju:rəs
**sp** Epicurus[1]

**Epidamium** *n*
,epɪ'damɪəm
**sp** Epidamium[7]

**Epidarus** *n*
,epɪ'darəs
**sp** Epidarus[1]

**epigram** *n*
=
**sp** epigram[1]

**epilepsy** *n*
'epɪlepsəɪ
**sp** epilepsie[1]

**epileptic** *adj*
=
**sp** epilepticke[1]

**epilogue / ~s** *n*
=
**sp** epilogue[5], epi-logue[2], epilogve[3] / epilogues[1]

**epistle / ~s** *n*
=
**sp** epistles[2]

**Epistrophus** *n*
e'pɪstrə,pʊs
**sp** Epistropus[1]

**epitaph / ~s** *n*
=
**sp** epitaph[12], epytaph[1] / epitaphes[1], epitaphs[1]

**epithet / ~s** *n*
=
**sp** epithat[1], epithite[1], epythite[1] / epithites[1], epythithes[1]

**epitheton** *n*
ə'pɪθətən
**sp** apa-thaton[1]

**epitome** *n*
=
**sp** epitome[1]

**equal** *adj / adv*
'i:kwɑl
**sp** equal[1], equall[29] / equall[1]
> unequal

**equal / ~s** *n*
'i:kwɑl / -z
**sp** equall[3] / equals[1]
> inequality

**equal / ~s / ~led** *v*
'i:kwɑl / -z / -d
**sp** equall[8] / equals[2] / equall'd[2]

**equality** *n*
*m* ɪ'kwɑlɪ,təɪ
**sp** equality[2]

**equally** *adv*
*m* 'i:kwɑ,ləɪ, -ɑləɪ
**sp** equallie[1], equally[7]

**equalness** *n*
*m* 'i:kwɑl,nes
**sp** equalnesse[1]

**equinoctial** *n*
,ekwɪ'nɒksɪəl
**sp** equinoctial[1]

**equinox** *n*
*m* 'ekwɪ,nɒks
**sp** equinox[1]

**equipage** *S* *n*
*m* 'ekwɪˌpɛːdʒ
**sp** equipage[1]
**rh** age *S 32.12*

**equity** *n*
*m* 'ekwɪˌtəɪ
**sp** equitie[1], equity[2]

**equivocal** *adj*
*m* e'kwɪvəˌkɑl
**sp** equiuocall[1], equi-uocall[1]
**rh** gall *Oth 1.3.215*

**equivocate / ~s** *v*
e'kwɪvəˌkɛːt / -s
**sp** equiuocate[1] / equiuocates[1]

**equivocation** *n*
e'kwɪvəˌkɛːsɪən
**sp** equiuocation[2]

**equivocator** *n*
e'kwɪvəˌkɛːtəɹ
**sp** equiuocator[3]

**Ercles**
> Hercules

**ere** *conj / prep*
ɛːɹ
**sp** ere[340], er['t] [ere it][5] / ere[65]
> ever

**Erebus** *n*
*m* 'erəˌbʏs, -əbəs
**sp** Erebus[2], Erobus[1]

**erect / ~s / ~ing / ~ed** *v*
= / = / ɪ'rektɪn, -ɪŋ / =
**sp** erect[4] / erects[1] / erecting[1] / erected[2]
> ill-erected

**erection** *n*
ɪ'reksɪən
**sp** erection[3]

**erewhile** *adv*
ɛːɹ'ʍəɪl
**sp** erewhile[1], ere-while[1], yerewhile[1]
**rh** style *LLL 4.1.98*

**erga** *Lat prep*
'eɹga
**sp** erga[1]

**ergo** *adv*
ɐːɹ'goː
**sp** argo[1], ergo[7]
> argal

**Ermengare** *n*
*m* 'ɐːɹmɪŋˌgɑːɹ
**sp** Ermengare[1]

**Eros** *n*
'iːrɒs
**sp** Eros[34]

**Erotes** *n*
e'roːtiːz
**sp** Erotes[1], Errotis[1]

**Erpingham** *n*
*m* 'ɐːɹpɪŋˌam, -ŋəm
**sp** Erpingham[6]

**err / ~est / ~s / ~ing / ~ed** *v*
ɐːɹ / -st / -z / 'ɐːɹɪn, -ɪŋ / ɐːɹd
**sp** erre[12] / errest[1] / erres[3] / erring[1] / er'd[1], err'd[1]
**rh** her *AW 2.3.182* / transferred *S 137.13*

**errand / ~s** *n*
=
**sp** arrand[1], errand[13] / errands[2]

**errant** *adj / n*
=
**sp** erant[1] / errant[1]

**erring** *adj*
'ɐːɹɪn, -ɪŋ
**sp** erring[4]

**erroneous** *adj*
e'roːnɪəs
**sp** erreoneous[1], erroneous[1]

**error / ~s** *n*
'erəɹ / -z
**sp** error[25], errour[4] / errors[7]
**rh** 1 terror *LLL 5.2.471, WT 4.1.2;*
**rh** 2 mirror *Per 1.1.47*

**erst** *adv*
ɐːɹst
**sp** erst[4], er'st[1]

**erudition** *n*
ˌerə'dɪsɪən
**sp** erudition[1]

**eruption / ~s** *n*
ɪ'rʏpsɪən / -z
**sp** erruption[1] / eruptions[3]

**eryngo / ~es** *n*
ɪ'rɪŋgoː / -z
**sp** eringoes[1]

**Escalus** *n*
*m* 'eskəˌlʏs, -ləs
**sp** Escalus[12], Esculus[1], Eskales[1]

**escape,** ***abbr*** **scape / ~s** *n*
ɪ'skɛːp, *abbr* skɛːp / -s
**sp** escape[10], *abbr* scape[2] / escapes[1], *abbr* scapes[3]

**escape,** ***abbr*** **scape / ~s / ~d / ~dest** *v*
ɪ'skɛːp, *abbr* skɛːp / -s / *m* -t, -ɪd / -st, -tst
**sp** escape[9], *MW 3.3.155 emend of* uncape[1], *abbr* scape[34] / escapes[3], *abbr* scapes[3] / escap'd[5], escaped[2], escap't[1], *abbr* scap'd[8], scaped[2], scap't[3] / escap'dst[1]

**eschew / ~ed** *v*
es'tʃuːd
**sp** eschew'd[1]

**escot / ~ed** *v*
e'skɒtɪd
**sp** escorted[1]

**especial** *adj*
*m* e'spesɪɑl, -ɪˌɑl
**sp** especial[1], especiall[3]
> special

**especially** *adv*
e'spesɪɑˌləɪ
**sp** especially[16], espe-cially[1]

**esperance** *n*
'espəˌrans
**sp** esperance[4]

**espial / ~s** *n*
*m* ɪ'spəɪəlz
**sp** espials[1], espyals[2]

**espouse** *n*
ɪ'spəʊz
**sp** espouse[2]

**espouse / ~d** *v*
ɪ'spəʊz / -d
**sp** espouse[2] / espous'd[3]

**esp·y / ~ies / ~ied** *v*
ɪ'spəɪ / -z / -d
**sp** espie[2], espy[1] / espies[2] / espied[2]
**rh** *1* by *VA 261*; by, dye, eye, sky *MND 3.2.105*; eye *KJ 2.1.506, R2 1.3.97*; **rh** *2* archery, gloriously, remedy *MND 3.2.105* / eyes *MND 2.1.262*; hies *Per 5.Chorus.18* / aside, wide *Luc 361*

**esquire / ~s** *n*
ɪ'skwəɪɹ / -z
**sp** esquire[7] / esquires[2]

**ess / ~es** *n*
=
**sp** esses[2]

**essay** *n*
'esɛː
**sp** essay[1]

**esse** *Lat v*

*est*
est
**sp** est[6]

*sit*
sɪt
**sp** sit[2]

**essence** *n*
=
**sp** essence[3]

**essential** *adj*
ɪ'sensɪɑl
**sp** essentiall[1]

**essentially** *adv*
ɪ'sensɪɑləɪ
**sp** essentially[3]

**Essex** *n*
=
**sp** Essex[2]

**est** *Fr*
> c'est, être

**est** *Lat*
> esse

**establish,** *abbr* **stablish / ~ed** *v*
=, *abbr* 'stablɪʃ / *m* -t, -ˌɪd
**sp** establish[5], *abbr* stablish[1] / establish'd[2], established[2], establisht[1]

**established** *adj*
*m* ɪ'stablɪʃt, -ɪˌʃɪd
**sp** established[1], e-stablished[1]

**establishment**
> stablishment

**estate / ~s** *n*
ɪ'stɛːt / -s
**sp** estate[44], e-state[1] / estates[8]
**rh** gate *TN 5.1.390*; late *Per 4.4.16, Tim 5.1.39*

**estate** *v*
ɪ'stɛːt
**sp** estate[3]
**rh** *1* celebrate *Tem 4.1.85*; **rh** *2* inordinate *Luc 92*

**esteem** *n*
=
**sp** esteeme[16]
**rh** seem *S 127.12*

**esteem / ~est / ~s / ~eth / ~ing / ~ed** *v*
= / ɪ'stiːm·st / = / -ɪn, -ɪŋ / *m* -d, -ɪd
**sp** esteeme[9], e-steeme[1] / esteem'st[2] / esteemes[5] / esteemeth[1] / *S* esteeming[1] / esteem'd[7], esteemed[3]
**rh** deem *AW 2.1.123*; redeem *S 100.7* / seeming *S 102.3* / deemed *S 96.6, 121.1*

**esteemed** *adj*
*m* ɪ'stiːmd
**sp** esteemed[1], estee-med[2]
> best-, ever-esteemed

**estimable** *adj*
*m* 'estɪˌmabəl
**sp** estimable[2]
> inestimable

**estimate** *n*
*m* 'estɪˌmɛːt
**sp** estimate[5]
**rh** determinate *S 87.2*; rate *AW 2.1.180*

**estimation / ~s** *n*
ˌestɪ'mɛːsɪən / -z
**sp** estimation[20], estima-tion[1] / estimations[1]

**estimer / estime** *Fr v*
ɛ'stim
**sp** estime[1]

**estranged** *adj*
*m* ɪ'strɛːndʒd, -dʒɪd
**sp** estranged[1], e-stranged[1]
**rh** changed *LLL 5.2.213*

**estridge / ~s** *n*
=
**sp** estridge[1] / estridges[1]

**et** *Fr conj*
e
**sp** e[4], et[3], &[20]

**et** *Lat conj*
et
**sp** et[1], &[3]

**etcetera / ~s** *n*
=
**sp** &c.[38], et cetera's[1]

**été** *Fr n*
> être

**eternal** *adj*
ɪˈtɐːɹnɑl
**sp** eternall[30]

**eternal / ~'s** *n*
ɪˈtɐːɹnɑlz
**sp** eternalls[1]

**eternally** *adv*
*m* ɪˈtɐːɹnɑˌləɪ
**sp** eternally[1]

**eterne** *adj*
ɪˈtɐːɹn
**sp** eterne[2]

**eternity** *n*
*m* ɪˈtɐɹnɪtəɪ, -ɪˌtəɪ
**sp** eternitie[2], eter-nitie[1], eternity[4]
**rh** *1* canopy *S 125.3*; extremity *Luc 967*; memory *S 77.8, 122.4*; **rh** *2* die *Ham 1.2.73*

**eternize / ~d** *v*
ɪˈtɐːɹnəɪzd
**sp** eterniz'd[1]

**êtes** *Fr*
> être

**Ethiop / ~'s / ~s** *n*
ˈiːtɪəp / -s
**sp** Aethiop[1], Ethiop[1], Ethiope[3] / Aethiops[1] / Aethiops[1]

**Ethiopian / ~'s** *n*
ˌiːtɪˈoːpɪən / -z
**sp** Ethiopian[1], Ethyopians[1]

**Etna** *n*
=
**sp** Aetna[1], Etna[1]

**Eton** *n*
=
**sp** Eaton[4]

**être** *v*
ˈɛːtrə
**sp** estre[1]

***est***
e
**sp** est[6], et[3], [n]et[1], &[4]
> c'est

***été***
eˈte
**sp** este[1]

***êtes***
ɛt
**sp** estes[3]

***soit***
swɛ
**sp** soit[1]

***sont***
sũ
**sp** sont[2] / ont[1]

***suis***
swi
**sp** suis[3], *emend of H5 4.4.55* in[tombe][1]

**eunuch / ~s** *n*
=
**sp** eunuch[15] / eunuches[1], eunuchs[1]

**Euphrates** *n*
jʊˈfrɛːtiːz
**sp** euphrates[1]

**Euriphile** *n*
jʊˈrɪfɪˌliː
**sp** Euriphile[4]

**Europa** *n*
jʊˈroːpə
**sp** Europa[3]

**Europe** *n*
ˈjuːrəp
**sp** Europe[10]

**evade / ~s** *v*
ɪˈvɛːd / -z
**sp** euade[1] / euades[1]

**Evans** *n*
=
**sp** Euans[12]

**evasion / ~s** *n*
ɪˈvɛːzɪən / -z
**sp** euasion[4] / euasions[1]

**Eve / ~'s** *n*
=
**sp** Eue[3] / Eues[3]
**rh** sleeve *LLL 5.2.322*
> All-Hallond Eve, Lammas Eve

**even** *adj / adv*
=, ˈevən
**sp** eauen[1], eeuen[2], euen[31], e-uen[1] / euen[6]
**rh** *adj* heaven *AW 2.1.191, AY 5.4.106*
> odd-, un-even

**even** *adv intensifier*
=, ˈevən
**sp** ee'n[3], eene[1], e'ene[7], eeuen[1], e'n[1], e'ne[18], euen[484], e-uen[1], eu'n[13], ev'n[2]

**even [evening]** *n*
=, ˈevən
**sp** euen[3], eu'n[5], ev'n[2]
**rh** *S 28.12, 132.7, VA 495*
> good-even

**even / ~ed** *v*
=, ˈevən / -d
**sp** euen[2] / eeuen'd[1]

**even-handed** *adj*
ˈiːvən-ˌandɪd, -han-, ˈevən-
**sp** euen-handed[1]

**evening** *adj / n*
ˈiːvnɪn, -ɪŋ, ˈevən-
**sp** euening[3] / euening[15], eue-ning[1]

**evenly** *adv*
*m* ˈiːvənləɪ, -ˌləɪ, ˈevən-
**sp** euenly[3]

**event / ~s** *n*
=
**sp** euent[23] / euents[15]
**rh** content *Per 4.Chorus.45*; discontent, spent *Luc 1598*; spent *2H6 3.1.326* / contents *AY 5.4.124*; discontents *VA 1159*

**eventful** *adj*
=
**sp** euentfull[1]

**ever**, *abbr* **e'er** *adv*
*m* 'evəɹ, *abbr* ɛ:ɹ
**sp** euer[624], e-uer[3], *abbr* e'er[1], ere[35], e're[4]
**rh** never *MA 2.3.61, R2 2.2.147*; per-sever *AW 4.2.36*
> ere; how-, howsom-, so-, what-, whatso-, when-, wher-, whereso-, who-, whoso-ever

**ever-angry** *adj*
'evəɹ-'aŋgrəɪ
**sp** euer-angry[1]
> angry

**ever-burning** *adj*
'evəɹ-'bɐ:ɹnɪn, -ɪŋ
**sp** euer-burning[2]

**ever-esteemed** *adj*
=
**sp** euer esteemed[1]

**ever-fixed** *adj*
*m* 'evəɹ-'fɪksɪd
**sp** euer-fixed[1]
> fixed

**ever-harmless** *adj*
'evəɹ-'ɑ:ɹmləs, -'hɑ-
**sp** euer-harmelesse[1]

**everlasting** *adj / n*
'evəɹ'lastɪn, -ɪŋ
**sp** euerlasting[17], euer-lasting[2], euerla-sting[1] / euerlasting[1]
> last

**everlastingly** *adv*
'evəɹ'lastɪn,ləɪ, -ɪŋ-
**sp** euerlastingly[4]
**rh** knee *KJ 5.7.105*

**ever-living** *adj*
'evəɹ-'lɪvɪn, -ɪŋ
**sp** euer-liuing[1]
> live

**evermore** *adv*
'evəɹ'mɔ:ɹ
**sp** euermore[22], euer more[1]
> more

**ever-preserved** *adj*
'evəɹ-prɪ'zɐ:ɹvd, -vɪd
**sp** euer-preserued[1]
> preserve

**ever-running** *adj*
'evəɹ-'rɤnɪn, -ɪŋ
**sp** euer-running[1]
> run

**ever-valiant** *adj*
'evəɹ-'valɪənt
**sp** euer-valiant[1]
> valiant

**every** *adj*
'evrəɪ
**sp** euerie[56], eue-rie[1], euery[456], e-uery[4], eu'rie[1], eu'ry[10]

**everyone, every one / ~'s** *pro*
'evrəɪ,ɤn, -,wɒn / -z
**sp** euerie one[7], euery one[44] / euery ones[1]

**everything, every thing** *pro*
'evrəɪ,θɪŋ
**sp** euerie thing[2], euery thing[46], eu'ry thing[1]
**rh** spring *TN 3.1.147*

**everywhere** *adv*
'evrəɪ,ʍɛ:ɹ
**sp** euerie where[2], euery where[17]
**rh** character *AY 3.2.8*; forswear *MND 1.1.241*; sere *CE 4.2.20*
> where

**evidence / ~s** *n*
*m* 'evɪ,dens, -ɪdəns / -ɪdənsɪz
**sp** euidence[9] / euidences[1]

**evident** *adj*
*m* 'evɪ,dent, -ɪdənt
**sp** euident[6]
**rh** unprovident *S 10.4*

**evil** *adj*
'evɪl
**sp** euill[21]
**rh** devil *LLL 5.2.105, Luc 1245*

**evil / ~s** *n*
'evɪl / -z
**sp** euil[1], euill[37] / euilles[2], euills[3], [past]-euills[1], euils[18]
**rh** devil *LLL 4.3.284, Luc 87, 846, 972, 1515, PP 2.5, S 144.5, TN 3.4.360*

**evil-eyed** *adj*
'evɪl-,əɪd
**sp** euill-ey'd[1]
> eye

**evilly** *adv*
*m* 'evləɪ, -vɪl-, ev'ləɪ
**sp** euilly[2]

**evitate** *v*
'evɪ,tɛ:t
**sp** euitate[1]

**ewe / ~s** *n*
=
**sp** ewe[4] / ewes[10]
**pun** *LLL 5.1.54* you

**ewer / ~s** *n*
'ju:əɹ / -z
**sp** ewer[2], ewre[1] / ewers[1]

**exact / ~est** *adj*
= / ɪg'zaktəst, eg-
**sp** exact[6] / exactest[1]

**exact / ~est / ~ed** *v*
= / ɪg'zakst, -tst, eg- / =
**sp** exact[2] / exact'st[1] / exacted[1]

**exacting** *n*
ɪg'zaktɪn, -ɪŋ, eg-
**sp** exacting[1]
**rh** contracting *MM 3.2.269*

**exaction / ~s** *n*
ɪg'zaksɪən, eg- / -z
**sp** exaction[3] / exactions[3]

**exactly** *adv*
ɪg'zakləɪ, eg-, -ktl-
**sp** exactly[6]

**exalt / ~ed** *v*
ɪg'zɑ:lt, eg- / -ɪd
**sp** exalt[1] / exalted[1]

**exalted** *adj*
ɪg'zɑ:ltɪd, eg-
**sp** exalted[1], ex-alted[1]

**examination / ~s** *n*
ɪg,zamɪ'nɛ:sɪən, eg- / -z
**sp** examination[4] / examinations[1]
> unexamined

**examine / ~s / ~d** *v*
= / = / *m* ɪg'zamɪnd, -,nɪd, eg-
**sp** examine[12], ex-amine[1] / examines[1] / examind[1], examin'd[1], examined[2], ex-amined[1]

**example / ~s** *n*
ɪg'zampl, eg- / -z
**sp** example[24], ex-ample[1] / examples[3]

**example / ~d** *v*
ɪg'zampl, eg- / -d
**sp** example[3] / exampl'd[1], exampled[2]

**exasperate / ~s** *v*
ɪg'zaspə,rɛ:t, eg- / -s
**sp** exasperate[3] / exasperates[1]

**exceed / ~s / ~eth / ~ing / ~ed** *v*
= / = / = / ɪk'si:dɪn, -ɪŋ, ek- / =
**sp** exceed[9], exceede[4] / exceedes[6], exceeds[3] / exceedeth[1] / exceeding[4] / exceeded[2]
**rh** bleed, deed *Luc 229*; decreed *Per 2.3.16*; feed *Tim 1.2.203*; need *S 83.3*; steed *VA 292* / deeds *S 150.8*

**exceeding** *adj / adv*
ɪk'si:dɪn, -ɪŋ, ek-
**sp** exceeding[4] / exceeding[20]

**exceedingly** *adv*
ɪk'si:dɪn,ləɪ, -ɪŋ-, ek-
**sp** exceedingly[4]

**excel / ~s / ~ling / ~led** *v*
= / = / ɪk'selɪn, -ɪŋ, ek- / =
**sp** excell[5] / excells[1], excels[6] / excelling[1] / excelled[1]
**rh** dwell *S 5.4*; tell *LLL 4.3.38* / bring, dwelling, sing, thing *TG 4.2.49* / beheld *VA 1131*

**excellence** *n*
*m* 'eksə,lens, -sələns, -sləns
**sp** excellence[17]
**rh** difference *S 105.6*; expense *S 94.8*

**excellenc·y / ~ies** *n*
*m* 'eksə,lensəɪ, -sələn-, -slən- / 'ekslənsəɪz, -səl-
**sp** excellencie[1], excellency[3] / excellencies[1]

**excellent** *adj / adv*
*m* 'eksə,lent, -sələnt, -slənt
**sp** excellant[1], excellent[100], ex-cellent[3], excel-lent[2] / excellent[9], ex-cellent[1], excel-lent[1]
**rh** *adj* different *RJ 2.3.9*; invent *S 38.3*

**excellent** *Fr adj*
ɛksɛ'lɑ̃
**sp** excellent[1]

**excellently** *adv*
'ekslәntləɪ, -səl-, -,ləɪ
**sp** excellently[6]

**excelling** *adj*
ɪk'selɪn, -ɪŋ, ek-
**sp** excelling[2]
**rh** smelling *VA 443*

**except** *conj / prep*
=
**sp** except[19], *emend of TS 4.4.88* expect[1] / except[11]

**except / ~ed** *v*
=
**sp** except[3] / excepted[6]
**rh** kept *S 147.8*

**excepting** *prep*
ɪk'septɪn, -ɪŋ, ek-
**sp** excepting[4]

**exception / ~s** *n*
*m* ɪk'sepsɪən, -ɪ,ɒn, ek- / -z
**sp** exception[4], excepti-on[1] / exceptions[6]

**exceptless** *adj*
=
**sp** exceptlesse[1]

**excess** *n*
=
**sp** excesse[12]
**rh** *1* less *MV 3.2.112*; less, possess *Luc 138*; wantonness *LLL 5.2.73*; **rh** *2* lease *S 146.7*

**excessive** *adj*
=
**sp** excessiue[1]

**exchange** *n*
ɪks'ʧɛ:nʤ, ek-
**sp** exchange[19]
> change

**exchange / ~d** *v*
ɪks'ʧɛ:nʤ, ek- / -d
**sp** exchange[9], ex-change[2] / exchang'd[2]
**rh** ranged *S 109.7*

**exchequer / ~s** *n*
ɪks'ʧekəɹ, ek- / -z
**sp** exchequer[6] / exchequers[1]

**excite / ~s / ~d** *v*
ɪk'səɪt, ek- / -s / -ɪd
**sp** excite[2] / excites[1] / excited[1]

**excitement / ~s** *n*
ɪk'səɪtmənts, ek-
**sp** excitements[1]

**exclaim / ~s** *n*
ɪks'klɛ:m, ek- / -s
**sp** exclaime[1] / exclaimes[4]

**exclaim / ~s / ~ed** *v*
ɪks'klɛ:m, ek- / -s / -d
**sp** exclaim[1], exclaime[7] / exclaimes[2] / exclaim'd[1], exclaym'd[1]
**rh** aim, maim *LC 313*

**exclamation / ~s** *n*
*m* ,eksklə'mɛ:sɪən, -ɪ,ɒn / -ɪ,ɒnz

**sp** exclamation[4] / exclamations[1]
**rh** abomination, imagination *Luc 705*

**exclude / ~s** *v*
=
**sp** excludes[1]

**excommunicate** *adj*
ˌekskəˈmjuːnɪˌkɛːt
**sp** excommunicate[2]

**excommunication** *n*
ˌekskəˌmjuːnɪˈkɛːsɪən
**sp** excommuni-cation[1]
> communicate

**excrement / ~s** *n*
*m* ˈekskrəmənt, -ˌment / ˈekskrəˌments
**sp** excrement[4], excre-ment[1] / excrements[1]

**excursion / ~s** *n*
ɪksˈkɐːɹsɪən, ek- / -z
**sp** excursion[2] / excursions[19]

**excusable** *adj*
=
**sp** excusable[1]

**excuse,** *abbr* **scuse / ~s** *n*
=, *abbr* skjuːs / =, *abbr* ˈskjuːsɪz
**sp** excuse[31], *abbr* scuse[1] / excuses[4], *abbr* scuses[1]
**rh** abuse *Luc 1316, 1653, VA 791*; use *n S 2.11* / abuses *Luc 267, RJ 3.1.192*; abuses, sluices *Luc 1073*

**excuse / ~ing / ~d** *v*
= / ɪksˈkjuːzɪn, -ɪŋ, ek- / =
**sp** excuse[40] / excusing[1] / excus'd[10], excused[2]
**rh** accused *MA 4.1.214*

**excuser / excusez** *Fr v*
ɛksˈkyzez
**sp** excuse[2]

**execrable** *adj*
*m* ˈeksɪˌkrabəl
**sp** execrable[1]
> inexecrable

**execration / ~s** *n*
*m* ˌeksɪˈkrɛːsɪənz, -ɪˌɒnz
**sp** execrations[2]

**execut·e / ~ing / ~ed** *v*
= / ˈeksɪˌkjuːtɪn, -ɪŋ / =
**sp** execute[21] / executing[2] / executed[15], ex-ecuted[2], exe-cuted[1], execu-ted[1]
> thought-executing, unexecuted

**execution** *n*
*m* ˌeksɪˈkjuːsɪən, -ɪˌɒn
**sp** execution[47], execu-tion[1]

**executioner / ~s** *n*
ˌeksɪˈkjuːsɪənəɹ / -z
**sp** executioner[11], exe-cutioner[1] / executioners[2]

**executor / ~s** *n*
ɪgˈzekjətəɹ, eg- / *m* -z, ˌeksɪˈkjuːtəɹz
**sp** executor[1] / executors[3]

**exempt / ~ed** *v*
ɪgˈzemt, eg-, -mpt / -ɪd
**sp** exempt[9] / exempted[1]
**rh** contempt *CE 2.2.180, Tim 4.2.31*

**exe·o / ~unt** *Lat* *v*
ˈegzɪʊnt
*sp in s.d.* exeunt[676]

**exequies** *n*
ˈeksəˌkwəɪz
**sp** exequies[1]

**exercise / ~s** *n*
ˈeksəɹˌsəɪz / -ɪz
**sp** exercise[16], ex-ercise[1] / exercises[4]

**exercise** *v*
ˈeksəɹˌsəɪz
**sp** exercise[2]
**rh** injuries, miseries *Cym 5.4.82*

**Exeter** *n*
*m* ˈeksɪtəɹ
**sp** Exeter[44], *abbr in s.d.* Exe[1]

**exhalation / ~s** *n*
ˌeksəˈlɛːsɪən, -shə- / -z
**sp** exhalation[2] / exhalations[2]

**exhale / ~st / ~s** *v*
ekˈsɛːl, eksˈhɛːl / -st / -z
**sp** exhale[2] / exhalest[1] / exhales[2]

**exhaled** *adj*
ˈeksɛːld, -shɛː-
**sp** exhall'd[1]

**exhaust** *v*
=
**sp** exhaust[1]

**exhibit** *v*
=
**sp** exhibit[3], exhibite[1]

**exhibiter / ~s** *n*
*m* egˈzɪbɪˌtɐːɹz
**sp** exhibiters[1]

**exhibition** *n*
ˌeksɪˈbɪsɪən
**sp** exhibition[6]

**exhort** *v*
ɪgˈzɔːɹt, eg-
**sp** exhort[1]

**exhortation** *n*
ˌegzɔːɹˈtɛːsɪən
**sp** exhortation[1]

**exigent** *n*
*m* ˈeksɪˌʤent
**sp** exigent[3]
**rh** spent *1H6 2.5.9*

**exile** *n*
ˈegzəɪl
**sp** exile[23]
**rh** smile *PP 14.9*

**exile / ~d** *v*
ˈegzəɪl / -d
**sp** exile[2] / exild[1], exil'd[3]
**rh** beguiled *RJ 3.2.133*

**exiled** *adj*
'egzəɪld
**sp** exil'd[1]

**exist / ~est** *v*
=
**sp** exist[2] / exists[1]

**exit / ~s** *n*
=
**sp** exit[2] / exits[2]

**exit** *v*
=
**sp** exit[788], *abbr in s.d.* ex[it][1]

**exorcism / ~s** *n*
'eksəɹˌsɪzəmz, -sɔːɹ-
**sp** exorcismes[1]

**exorcisor** *n*
'eksəɹˌsəɪzəɹ, -sɔːɹ-
**sp** exorcisor[1]

**exorcist** *n*
'eksəɹˌsɪst, -sɔːɹ-
**sp** exorcist[2]

**expect** *n*
=
**sp** expect[1]

**expect / ~est / ~s / ~ing / ~ed** *v*
= / ɪk'speks, -kts, ek- / ɪk'speks, -kts, ek- / ɪk'spektɪn, -ɪŋ, ek- / =
**sp** expect[31] / expects[1] / expects[2], ex-pects[1] / expecting[5] / expected[9]
**rh** defect, neglect *Luc 149* / effect-ing, respecting *Luc 432*

**expectance** *n*
=
**sp** expectance[1]

**expectancy** *n*
*m* ɪk'spektənˌsəɪ, ek-
**sp** expectancie[1], expectansie[1]

**expectation / ~s** *n*
*m* ˌekspek'tɛːsɪən, -ɪˌɒn / -ɪənz
**sp** expectation[23], expecta-tion[1] / expectations[1]

**expected** *adj*
=
**sp** expected[1]
> unexpected

**expecter / ~s** *n*
ɪk'spektəɹz, ek-
**sp** expecters[1]

**expedience** *n*
*m* ɪk'spiːdɪəns, -ɪˌens, ek-
**sp** expedience[4]

**expedient** *adj*
ɪk'spiːdɪənt, ek-
**sp** expedient[8]

**expediently** *adv*
*m* ɪk'spiːdɪəntˌləɪ, ek-
**sp** expediently[1]

**expedition / ~'s** *n*
*m* ˌekspɪ'dɪsɪən, -sɪˌɒn / -sɪənz
**sp** expedition[23], expidition[1] / expeditions[1]

**expeditious** *adj*
ˌekspɪ'dɪsɪəs
**sp** expeditious[1]

**expel / ~s / ~led** *v*
*m* ɪk'spel, ek-, 'ekspel / ɪk'spel·s, ek- / -d, ek-
**sp** expell[5] / expels[1] / expelld[1]
**rh** well *VA 976*

**expend** *v*
=
**sp** expend[3]

**expense / ~s** *n*
=
**sp** expence[13] / expences[2]
**rh** diligence *Per 3.Chorus.20*; excellence *S 94.6*; hence *CE 3.1.123*; intelligence *MND 1.1.249*; whence *Per 5.Chorus.19*

**experience / ~s** *n*
=
**sp** experience[19] / experiences[1]

**experienced** *adj*
=
**sp** experienc'd[3], experien'st[1]
> long-, un-experienced

**experiment / ~s** *n*
=
**sp** experiment[2] / experiments[2]
**rh** consent *AW 2.1.154*

**experimental** *adj*
ɪkˌsperɪ'mentɑl, ek-
**sp** experimental[1]

**expert** *n*
'ekspəɹt
**sp** expert[3]

**expertness** *n*
'ekspəɹtnəs
**sp** expertnesse[2]

**expiate** *v*
*m* 'ekspɪˌɛːt
**sp** expiate[1]
**rh** date *S 22.4*

**expiration** *n*
ˌekspɪ'rɛːsɪən
**sp** expiration[3]

**expir·e / ~s / ~ing / ~ed** *v*
ɪk'spəɪɹ, ek- / -z / -ɪn, -ɪŋ / -d
**sp** expire[5] / expires[1] / expiring[1] / expir'd[1], expyr'd[1]
**rh** fire *2H4 5.5.108, S 73.11* / tired *S 27.4*

**explication** *n*
ˌekspliˈkɛːsɪən
**sp** explication[1]
> inexplicable, self-explication

**exploit / ~s** *n*
ɪk'spləɪt, ek- / -s
**sp** exploit[13], ex-ploit[2], exploit's [exploit is][1], exployt[1] / exploits[5], ex-ploits[1]

**expos·e / ~ing / ~ed** *v*
ɪk'spoːz, ek- / -ɪn, -ɪŋ / -d
**sp** expose[5] / exposing[1] / expos'd[6]

**exposition** *n*
*m* ˌekspəˈzɪsɪən, -sɪˌɒn
**sp** exposition[4]

**expositor** *n*
ɪkˈspɒzɪˌtɔːɹ, ek-
**sp** expositor[1]

**expostulate** *v*
ɪkˈspɒstjəˌlɛːt, ek-
**sp** expostulate[5]

**expostulation** *n*
ɪkˈspɒstjəˌlɛːsɪən, ek-
**sp** expostulation[1]

**exposture** *n*
ɪkˈspɒstəɹ, ek-
**sp** exposture[1]

**exposure** *n*
ɪkˈspoːzəɹ, ek-
**sp** exposure[2]

**expound / ~ed** *v*
ɪkˈspəʊnd, ek- / -ɪd
**sp** expound[4] / expounded[1]

**express** *adj*
*m* ɪkˈspres, ek-, ˈekspres
**sp** expresse[7]

**express / ~eth / ~ing / ~ed** *v*
*m* ɪkˈspres, ek-, ˈekspres / ɪkˈspres·əθ, ek- / -ɪn, -ɪŋ, ek- / -t, ek-
**sp** expresse[25] / expresseth[1] / expressing[1] / express'd[1], expressed[1], exprest[9], expre'st[1]
**rh** heaviness, less *Luc 1286*; less *AW 5.3.329, Per 2.2.8*; press *S 140.3*; success *Luc 111* / best *S 106.7*; breast *S 23.12*; guest *Luc 91*; impressed *LLL 2.1.223*; protest *LLL 5.2.412*; unrest *S 147.12*

**expressing** *n*
ɪkˈspresɪn, -ɪŋ, ek-
**sp** expressing[1]

**expressive** *adj*
ɪkˈspresɪv, ek-
**sp** expressiue[1]

**expressly** *adv*
ɪkˈspresləɪ, ek-
**sp** expresly[3], expressely[7]

**expressure** *n*
ɪkˈspresəɹ, ek-
**sp** expressure[3]
> pressure

**expulse / ~d** *v*
ɪkˈspɤlst, ek-
**sp** expuls'd[1]

**expulsion** *n*
ɪkˈspɤlsɪən, ek-
**sp** expulsion[2]

**exquisite** *adj*
*m* ˈekskwɪzɪt, -kɪz-
**sp** exquisit[1], exquisite[12]

**exsufflicate** *adj*
ɪkˈsɤflɪˌkɛːt, ek-
**sp** exufflicate[1]

**extant** *adj*
=
**sp** extant[3], ex-tant[1]

**extemporal** *adj*
ɪkˈstemprɑl, ek-, -pər-
**sp** extemporall[3]

**extemporally** *adv*
*m* ɪkˈstemprɑˌləɪ, -pər-, ek-
**sp** extemporally[1]

**extempore** *adv*
*m* ɪkˈstemprəɪ, ek-, -pər-
**sp** extempore[3], extemporie[1], extempory[1]

**extend / ~s / ~ed** *v*
=
**sp** extend[15] / extends[1] / extended[6]
**rh** depend *LC 276*; intend, lend *LC 25* / ended *AW 2.1.173*; friended *MM 4.2.109*

**extent** *n*
=
**sp** extent[5]

**extenuate / ~s / ~d** *v*
*m* ɪkˈstenjuː·ɛt, -ˌɛːt, ek- / -ˌɛːts, ek- / -ɛtɪd, ek-
**sp** extenuate[5] / extenuates[1] / extenuated[1]
**rh** insinuate *VA 1010*; relate *Oth 5.2.338*

**extenuation** *n*
ɪkˌstenjuːˈɛsɪən, ek-
**sp** extenuation[1]

**exterior** *adj*
ɪkˈstiːrɪəɹ, ek-
**sp** exterior[3], exteriour[1]

**exterior / ~s** *n*
ɪkˈstiːrɪəɹz, ek-
**sp** exteriors[1]

**exteriorly** *adv*
*m* ɪkˈstiːrɪəɹˌləɪ, ek-
**sp** exteriorly[1]

**extermine / ~d** *v*
ɪkˈstɐːɹmɪnd, ek-
**sp** extermin'd[1]

**external** *adj*
ɪkˈstɐːɹnɑl, ek-
**sp** externall[7]

**externe** *adj*
ɪkˈstɐːɹn, ek-
**sp** externe[1]

**extinct** *adj*
=
**sp** extinct[2]

**extincted** *adj*
=
**sp** extincted[1]

**extinguish** *v*
=
**sp** extinguish[1]

**extirp / ~ed** *v*
ɪkˈstɐːɹp, ek- / *m* -ɪd
**sp** extirpe[1] / extirped[1]

**extirpate** *v*
ɪk'stɐːɹpɪt, ek-
**sp** extirpate[1]

**extol / ~led** *v*
ɪk'stoːl, ek- / -d
**sp** extoll[4] / extold[1]

**Exton** *n*
=
**sp** Exton[6]

**extort** *v*
ɪk'stɔːɹt, ek-
**sp** extort[5]
**rh** sort, sport *MND 3.2.160*

**extorted** *adj*
ɪk'stɔːɹtɪd, ek-
**sp** extorted[2]

**extortion / ~s** *n*
*m* ɪk'stɔːɹsɪən, ek- / -sɪˌɒnz, ek-
**sp** extortion[1] / extortions[1]

**extract / ~ing / ~ed** *v*
= / ɪk'straktɪn, -ɪŋ, ek- / =
**sp** extract[1] / extracting[1] / extracted[1]

**extracting** *adj*
ɪk'straktɪn, -ɪŋ, ek-
**sp** extracting[1]

**extraordinarily** *adv*
ˌekstra'ɔːɹdɪˌnarɪləɪ
**sp** ex-traordinarily[2]

**extraordinary** *adj*
*m* ˌekstra'ɔːɹdɪˌnarəɪ
**sp** extraordinarie[3], extraordinary[2]
> ordinary

**extraught** *adj*
=
**sp** extraught[1]

**extravagancy** *n*
ɪk'stravəˌgansəɪ, ek-
**sp** extrauagancie[1]

**extravagant** *adj*
*m* ɪk'stravəgənt, -ˌgant, ek-
**sp** extrauagant[3]

**extreme / ~st** *adj*
*m* ɪk'striːm, ek-, 'ekstriːm / ɪk'striːməst, ek-
**sp** extreame[5], extreme[8] / extreamest[6], extremest[4]
**rh** dream *S 129.10*

**extreme / ~s** *n*
*m* ɪk'striːm, ek- / -z
**sp** extreame[1] / extreames[9], extremes[4]
**rh** deems *Luc 1337*; seems *VA 987*

**extremely** *adv*
ɪk'striːmləɪ, ek-
**sp** extreamely[1], extreamly[3], extremelie[1]

**extremit·y / ~ies** *n*
*m* ɪk'stremɪtəɪ, -ˌtəɪ, ek- / -z
**sp** extreamitie[1], extreamity[1], extremitie[12], extremity[12] / extreamities[1], extremities[4]
**rh** *1* eye *MND 3.2.3*; **rh** *2* eternity *Luc 969*; quantity *Ham 3.2.177*; she *R3 1.1.65*

**exult** *v*
ɪg'zɤlt, eg-
**sp** exult[2]

**exultation** *n*
ˌegzɤl'tɛːsɪən
**sp** exultation[1]

**eyas** *n*
'əɪəs
**sp** yases[1]

**eyas-musket** *n*
'əɪəs-ˌmɤskɪt
**sp** eyas-musket[1]

**eye / ~'s / ~s / ~s' / eyne** *n*
əɪ / -z / əɪn
**sp** eie[43], eye[325], eye-[discerning][1], [water-standing]-eye[1] / eies[1] / eies[65], eyes[546], [baby]-eyes[1], [glasse]-eyes[1], / eies[1], eyes[2] / eine[3], eyne[5]
**rh** *1* apply *MND 3.2.451*; ay *LLL 2.1.124*; buy *LLL 2.1.228*; by *CE 3.2.55, LLL 1.1.81, MV 2.5.41, PP 6.11, RJ 1.2.94, VA 281*; by, dye, espy, sky *MND 3.2.104*; deny *LLL 5.2.810*; die *CE 2.1.114, Luc 276, 1476, Per 1.1.33, R2 1.2.74, RJ 1.2.49, 87, S 9.1, 25.6*; die, I *Luc 1138*; dry *RJ 2.3.1, VA 962*; espy *KJ 2.1.504, R2 1.3.98*; fly *LC 323, 179, 1015, RJ 1.3.99*; hie, lie *Luc 1339*; high *AW 1.1.217*; I *LLL 4.3.182*; justify *Per Prol.41*; lie *LLL 2.1.238, 4.3.83, RJ 2.3.31, S 31.6, 152.13, VA 644, 661*; nigh *VA 342*; satisfy *Luc 95*; sky *CE 2.1.16, Luc 1227, 1586, R2 3.2.196, VA 182, 486, 816, S 121.5*; spy *TG 5.4.116*; her eye fly, religion's eye *LC 247*; **rh** *2* advisedly *Luc 179*; alchemy *S 33.2*; archery, gloriously, remedy *MND 3.2.105*; bastardy, obloquy *Luc 520*; be *VA 1065*; capacity *LLL 5.2.375*; chastity *MND 3.1.193, PP 4.6*; company *Luc 1586, MND 3.2.435*; dignity *Luc 435*; disloyalty *CE 3.2.9*; extremity *MND 3.2.2*; gravity *S 49.6*; history *S 93.5*; imaginary *R2 2.2.26*; infancy *LLL 4.3.241*; insufficiency *MND 2.2.133*; jealousy *CE 2.1.114*; knee *TNK 3.4.20*; majesty *LLL 4.3.224, Luc 95, S 7.2*; melody *MND 1.1.188*; merrily *CE 4.2.2, LLL 5.2.475, 480*; perjury *LLL 4.3.58, PP 3.1*; piety *Luc 540*; poverty *LLL 5.2.379*; property MND *3.2.366*; remedy *MND 3.2.451, S 62.1*; skilfully *LLL 2.1.238*; sympathy *Luc 1227* / **rh** *1* arise *Cym 2.3.23, 4.2.402, MND 5.1.321, S 55.14*; arise, butterflies, thighs *MND 3.1.160*; arise, disguise *Luc 1817*; cries *LLL 4.3.140, Luc 163, 1457, S 29.1*; cries, lies *Luc 446*; despise *Per 2.3.25, S 141.1, 149.12*; devise *MND 3.2.36, S 83.13*; dies *Luc 1651*; dies, lies *MV 3.2.67*; enterprise *MND 3.2.158, 351*; espies *MND 2.1.261*; flies, hies *Luc 1213*; guise *VA 1179*; lies *LC 50, 290, LLL 1.1.79, 2.1.215, 4.3.276, 5.2.421, Luc 392, 459, 1448, MND 2.2.97, R2 3.3.169, RJ 1.3.87, 2.3.64, S 1.5, 17.5, 24.8, 46.6, 137.1, 153.14, Tem 1.2.399, VA 70, 120, 1127*; lies, rise *Luc 254*; prize *MV 3.2.142*; replies *AW 2.3.79*; rise *Ham 1.2.258, Per 1.4.8, PP 14.16, Tim 1.2.125*; sighs *RJ 1.1.191, TG 2.4.132*; spies *Luc 1088, S 121.5*; surmise *Luc 84*;

surprise *Luc 163, VA 1050*; wise *Luc 1548*; **rh** *2* suffice *LLL 4.2.109, Luc 1680, PP 5.5*; **rh** *3* bees, courtesies, dewberries, mulberries *MND 3.1.160*; companies *MND 1.1.218* [*emend*]; enemies *Luc 1469*; fantasies *MND 2.1.257*; forgeries *Luc 459*; gravities *LLL 5.2.762*; infamies *Luc 637*; infirmities *Per Prol.4*; miseries *1H6 1.1.87*; prophecies *S 106.11*; qualities *MND 1.1.230*; remedies *R2 3.3.202*; secrecies *Luc 99* / brine *LC 15*; divine *MND 3.2.138*; mine *AY 4.3.51, Luc 643, MND 1.1.242, 2.2.105, 5.1.174, TS 5.1.106*; shine *LLL 5.2.206*; thine *VA 633*; vine *AC 2.7.112*
**pun** *RJ 3.2.45ff* I, ay
> blue-, dark-, dizzy-, dull-, evil-, fire-, green-, grey-, hollow-, onion-, open-, sad-, sour-, thick-, wall-, young-eyed

**eye / ~st / ~s / ~d** *v*
 əɪ / -st / -z / -d
**sp** eie[1], eye[5] / ey'st[1] / eyes[2] / ey'd[2], eyde[1], eyed[1]
**rh** die *MW 5.5.48, TC 5.7.7*; spy *MND 3.2.20* / pride *S 104.2*; side *MND 3.2.40*
**pun** *RJ 3.2.47* I
> after-, over-eye

**eyeball / ~s** *n*
ˈəɪ-ˌbɑ:l / -z
**sp** eye-ball[1] / eie-bals[1], eye-balles[3], eye-balls[3], eye-bals[1]

**eyebrow / ~s** *n*
ˈəɪ-ˌbrəʊ, -ˌbro: / -z
**sp** eye-brow[1] / eye-browes[2]
> brow

**eye-drop / ~s** *n*
ˈəɪ-ˌdrɒps
**sp** eye-drops[1]
> drop

**eyeglass** *n*
*m* ˌəɪ-ˈglas
**sp** eye-glasse[1]
> glass

**eyeless** *adj*
ˈəɪləs
**sp** eyelesse[4]

**eyelid / ~s** *n*
*m* ˈəɪ-ˌlɪd, ˌəɪ-ˈlɪd / -z
**sp** eye-lid[1] / eielids[1], eie-lids[1], eye-lids[7]
**rh** forbid *MND 2.2.87*
> lid

**eye-offending** *adj*
ˈəɪ-əˌfendɪn, -ɪŋ
**sp** eye-offending[2]
> offend

**eyesight** *n*
ˈəɪ-ˌsəɪt
**sp** eie-sight[1], eye-sight[6]
> sight

**eyesore** *n*
ˈəɪ-ˌsɔ:ɹ
**sp** eye-sore[1]
> sore

**eye-string / ~s** *n*
ˈəɪ-ˌstrɪŋz
**sp** eye-strings[1]
> string

**eye-wink** *n*
ˈəɪ-ˌwɪŋk
**sp** eye-winke[1]
> wink

**eyne**
> eye

**eyrie / ~'s** *n*
ˈɛ:rəɪ / -z
**sp** ayerie[2], ayery[1] / ayeries[1]

# F

**fa** [music] *n*
=
**sp** Cfavt [C fa ut][1]

**Fabian** *n*
'fɛ:bɪən
**sp** Fabian[15]

**fable / ~s** *n*
'fabəl / -z
**sp** fable[3] / fables[1]

**fable / ~s** *v*
'fabəl / -z
**sp** fable[1] / fables[1]
**rh** rabble *TNK 3.5.104*

**fabric** *n*
=
**sp** fabrick[2], fabricke[2]

**fabulous** *adj*
'fabjələs
**sp** fabulous[2]

**face / ~'s / ~s** *n*
fɛ:s / 'fɛ:sɪz
**sp** face[382], [brazon-, no-, wee]-face[3] / faces[1] / faces[47], fa-ces[1]
**rh** *1* apace *LC 282*; base *Luc 203*; case *CE 4.2.6, LLL 5.2.388*; case, place *KJ 1.1.146, Luc 312*; chase *S 143.7, VA1*; disgrace *Luc 477, 829, R2 1.1.195, 2.1.170, S 33.6, 34.6, 103.6, 127.6*; disgrace, place *Luc 800*; embrace *LLL 4.3.214, VA 540, 872*; grace *CE 2.1.86, LC 282, LLL 3.1.65, 5.2.79, 129, 148, MND 5.1.190, Per Prol.23, R2 5.3.99, S 132.9, Tit 3.1.204, VA 62*; grace, place *LC 81, Luc 562*; place *1H6 1.3.44, 45, KJ 1.1.146, LLL 3.1.65, Luc 1744, MND 1.1.202, 3.2.424, S 93.2, 131.10, 137.12*; place, space *Luc 1775*; **rh** *2* has *TNK Epil.6* / cases *LLL 5.2.271*; graces *Luc 1408, S 17.8, 94.7, TG 3.1.103*; interlaces, paces *Luc 1388*; places *Luc 1526*
> ague-, half-, whey-face; bare-, black-, bloody-, bold-, brazen-, cream-, fair-, false-, foul-, glass-, good-, ill-, lean-, old-, pale-, paper-, red-, sad-, shame-, smooth-, sweet-, thin-, white-faced

**face / ~s / ~d** *v*
fɛ:s / 'fɛ:sɪz / fɛ:st
**sp** face[10] / faces[1] / fac'd[2], fac't[1]
> deface, out-face

**facere / facit / faciant** *Lat v*
'fakəre / 'fakɪt / 'fakɪant
**sp** facere[1] / facit[2] / faciant[1]

**face-royal** *n*
'fɛ:s-'rəɪəl
**sp** face-royall[2]

**facile** *adj*
'fasəɪl
**sp** facile[1]

**facile** *Lat adv*
'fasɪlɛ
**sp** facile[1]

**facility** *n*
fa'sɪlɪtəɪ
**sp** facilitie[1], facility[1], facillitie[1]
**rh** scurrility *LLL 4.2.56*

**facinerious** *adj*
fasɪ'nerɪəs
**sp** facineri-ous[1]

**facing** *n*
'fɛ:sɪn, -ɪŋ
**sp** facing[1]

**fact** *n*
=
**sp** fact[11]
**rh** act *AW 3.7.47, Luc 349*

**faction / ~s** *n*
*m* 'faksɪən, -ɪˌɒn / -z
**sp** faction[21] / factions[7]

**factionary** *n*
'faksɪəˌnarəɪ, -ənrəɪ
**sp** factionary[1]

**factious** *adj*
'faksɪəs
**sp** factious[10]

**factor / ~'s / ~s** *n*
'faktəɹ / -z
**sp** factor[4] / factors[1] / factors[1]

**facult·y / ~ies** *n*
*m* 'fakəltəɪ, -ˌtəɪ / -z
**sp** facultie[1], faculty[2] / faculties[5]

**fad·e / ~ing / ~ed** *v*
fɛ:d / 'fɛ:d·ɪn, -ɪŋ / -ɪd
**sp** fade[4] / fading[1] / faded[1]
**rh** made *Cym 5.4.106, S 54.10, Tem 1.2.400*; shade *S 18.9*

**faded** *adj*
'fɛ:dɪd
**sp** faded[2]

**fadge** *v*
=
**sp** fadge[2]

**fading** *adj / n*
'fɛ:dɪn, -ɪŋ
**sp** fading[3] / fading[1]

**faggot / ~s** *n*
=
**sp** faggot[1] / faggots[1]

**fail** *n*
fɛ:l
**sp** faile[3]

**fail / ~est / ~s / ~ing / ~ed** *v*
fɛ:l / -st / -z / 'fɛ:lɪn, -ɪŋ / fɛ:ld
**sp** faile[52], fayle[7] / failst[1] / failes[5], fayles[4] / failing[2], fayling[3] / faild[3], fail'd[1], fayl'd[2]
**rh** nail *Cor 4.7.55*; tail *TC 5.10.45, TNK 3.5.51*; **fail with me** prevail with me *H5 3.2.15* / sails *Tem Epil.12*

**failing** *n*
'fɛ:lɪn, -ɪŋ
**sp** fayling[1]

**fain** *adj / adv*
fɛ:n
**sp** faine[7] / fain[1], faine[62], fayne[1], feine[1]

**faint / ~er** *adj*
fɛ:nt / 'fɛ:ntəɹ
**sp** faint[26], faint-[puling, slumbers][2] / fainter[1]
**rh** attaint *VA 739*; quaint *TNK 1.1.4*

**faint / ~s / ~ing / ~ed** *v*
fɛ:nt / -s / 'fɛ:nt·ɪn, -ɪŋ / -ɪd
**sp** faint[13] / faints[6] / fainting[2] / fainted[2]
**rh** painted *Luc 1543*

**faint-hearted** *adj*
ˌfɛ:nt-'ɑ:ɹtɪd, -'hɑ:-
**sp** faint-harted[1], faint-hearted[2]

**fainting** *adj*
'fɛ:ntɪn, -ɪŋ
**sp** fainting[5]

**faintly** *adv*
'fɛ:ntləɪ
**sp** faintly[8]

**faintness** *n*
*m* 'fɛ:ntnəs, fɛ:nt'nes
**sp** faintnesse[2]

**fair / ~er / ~est** *adj*
fɛ:ɹ / 'fɛ:ɹəɹ / *m* -əst, fɛ:ɹst
**sp** fair[2], faire[645], faire-[play][1], fayre[10] / fairer[26], fayrer[5] / fairest[28], fairst[1], fayrest[5], fayr'st[1]
**rh** air *LLL 4.3.101, Mac 1.1.9, PP 16.3, S 21.10, TNK 1.1.17*; dare *Tim 1.2.12*; despair *PP 2.3, RJ 1.1.221, S 144.3, VA 744, 957*; hair *LLL 4.3.259*; heir *AW 2.3.130, Oth 2.1.134, RJ 2.Chorus.4, S 6.13, 127.1*; prayer, repair *PT 66*; repair, there *TG 4.2.43*
**pun** *VA 1083* fear

**fair / ~er** *adv*
fɛ:ɹ / 'fɛ:ɹəɹ
**sp** fair[1], faire[42], fayre[2] / fairer[2]
**rh** heir *Cym 5.4.49*

**fair / ~s** *n*
fɛ:ɹ / -z
**sp** faire[10], fayre[1] / faires[2], fairs[1], fayres[2]
**rh** air *Luc 780, MND 1.1.182, S 70.2, VA 1086*; hair *LC 206*; prayer *Luc 346*; repair *CE 2.1.98, LLL 2.1.227, S 16.11* / wares *LLL 5.2.318*

**faire / fais / fait / faites** *Fr v*
fɛ / fɛ / fɛt
**sp** fay / fait / faite

**fairer** *n*
'fɛ:ɹəɹ
**sp** fairer[1]

**fairest** *n*
'fɛ:ɹəst
**sp** fairest[4], fayrest[1]

**fair-faced** *adj*
*m* 'fɛ:ɹ-ˌfɛ:st, ˌfɛ:ɹ-'fɛ:st
**sp** faire-fac'd[1], faire fac'd[1]
> face

**fairing / ~s** *n*
'fɛ:rɪnz, -ɪŋz
**sp** fairings[1]

**fairly** *adj*
'fɛ:ɹləɪ
**sp** fairely[45]

**fairness** *n*
'fɛ:ɹnəs
**sp** fairenesse[4]

**fair-play** *adj*
'fɛ:ɹ-ˌplɛ:
**sp** fayre-play-[orders][1]

**fair-shining** *adj*
ˌfɛ:ɹ-'ʃəɪnɪn, -ɪŋ
**sp** faire shining[1]
> shine

**fairy** *adj*
'fɛ:rəɪ
**sp** faiery[1], fairie[5], fairy[11]
> meadow-fairies

**fair·y / ~ies / ~'** *n*
'fɛ:rəɪ / -z
**sp** faiery[3], [night-tripping]-faiery[1], fairie[2], fairy[11] / fairies[30], fai-ries[1], fayeries[1], fayries[4], pharies[1] / fairies[1], faries[1]

**fairy-like** *adj*
'fɛ:ɹəɪ-ˌləɪk
**sp** fairy-like[1]

**Fairy Queen** *n*
'fɛ:rəɪ-'kwi:n
**sp** Faerie-Queene[1], Faierie Queene[1], Fairy Queene[3]

**fais, fait, faites**
> faire *Fr*

**faith / ~s** *n*
fɛ:θ, *Jamie H5 3.2.99* fi:θ / -s
**sp** faith[267], 'faith[19], [good]faith[1], [good]-faith[1], [in]faith[17], [y]faith[27], [y']faith[2], fayth[1], *Jamie* feith[1] / faithes[1], faiths[5]
> fay, i'faith, unfaithful

**faith-breach** *n*
'fɛ:θ-ˌbri:ʧ
**sp** faith-breach[1]
> breach

**faithed** *adj*
fɛ:θt
**sp** faith'd[1]

**faithful / ~est** *adj*
'fɛ:θfʊl / -st
**sp** faithful[2], faithfull[31] / faithfull'st[1]

**faithfully** *adv*
*m* 'fɛ:θfʊˌləɪ, -fl-
**sp** faithfully[11]

**faithless** *adj*
'fɛ:θləs
**sp** faithlesse[4]

**falchion** *n*
'fɔ:ʃɪən
**sp** faulchion[4]

**Falconbridge** *n*
'fɔ:kənˌbrɪʤ
**sp** Falconbridge[5], Fauconbridge[3], Faulconbridge[11]

**falcon / ~'s** *n*
'fɔ:kən / -z
**sp** falcon[3], faulcon[4] / faulcons[2]

**falconer / ~'s / -s** *n*
'fɔ:knəɹ, -kən- / -z
**sp** falkners[1] / faulconers[1], faulkners[1]

**fall / ~s** *n*
fɑ:l / -z
**sp** fall[48] / falles[1], falls[1], fals[1]
**rh** *1* all *CE 1.1.1, H5 3.5.68, 2H6 1.2.106, R2 4.1.317*; hall *TC 5.10.49*; **rh** *2* burial *Per 2.4.11*; madrigals *MW 3.1.16, PP 19.7*
> down-, foot-fall

**fall / ~est / ~s / ~eth / ~ing / fell / ~est / fallen** *v*
fɑ:l / -st / -z / 'fɑ:l·əθ / -ɪn, -ɪŋ / = / felst / *m* 'fɑ:l·ən, 'fɑ:ln
**sp** fall[242] / fall'st[4] / falles[15], falls[17], falls-[off][1], fals[23] / falleth[1] / falling[14] / fel[3], fell[73] / fell'st[1] / fallen[4], falne[41]
**rh** *1* all *AY 5.4.176, KL 3.3.23, LC 41, TNK 3.5.109, VA 719*; call *S 151.14*; tall *MND 5.1.141*; wall, withal *Luc 466*; **rh** *2* burial *Per 1.4.48*; general *Luc 1483*; **rh** *3* shall *Ham 4.5.218, Tit 5.3.135* / calls *MND 3.2.25, S 124.6*
> befall

**fallacy** *n*
'faləˌsəɪ
**sp** fallacie[1]
**rh** uncertainty *CE 2.2.195*

**fallen** *adj*
fɑ:ln
**sp** falne[3]
> chop-, crest-, folly-, new-, sick-fallen

**fallen-off** *adj*
'fɑ:ln-ˌɒf
**sp** falne-off[1]

**fallible** *adj*
'falɪbəl
**sp** falliable[1], fallible[1]
> in-, un-fallible

**falling** *adj / n*
'fɑ:lɪn, -ɪŋ
**sp** falling[6] / falling[7]
> fast-, tear-falling

**falling-off** *n*
'fɑ:lɪn-'ɒf, -ɪŋ-
**sp** falling off[1]

**falloir / faut** *Fr v*
fo
**sp** faut[1]

**fallow** *adj*
'falə, -o:
**sp** fallow[2]

**fallow / ~s** *n*
'falə, -o: / -z
**sp** fallow[1] / fallowes[1]

**false / ~r** *adj*
fɑls / 'fɑlsəɹ
**sp** falce[2], false[242], [smooth-comforts]-false[1] / falser[2]

**false** *adv / n*
fɑls
**sp** false[17] / false[4]

**false-boding** *adj*
*m* ˌfɑls-'bo:dɪn, -ɪŋ
**sp** false boding[1]
> boding

**false-derived** *adj*
*m* 'fɑls-dɪˌrəɪvɪd
**sp** false-deriued[1]
> derive

**false-faced** *adj*
'fɑls-ˌfɛ:st
**sp** false-fac'd[1]
> face

**false-heart** *adj*
'fɑls-ˌɑ:ɹt, -ˌhɑ:-
**sp** false-heart[1]

**false-hearted** *adj*
'fɑls-ˌɑ:ɹtɪd, -ˌhɑ:-
**sp** false-hearted[1]

**falsehood** *n*
'fɑlsʊd, -hʊd
**sp** falsehood[12], falshood[21]

**falsely** *adv*
'fɑlsləɪ
**sp** falselie[1], falsely[15], falsly[1]

**falseness** *n*
'fɑlsnəs
**sp** falsenesse[1]

**falsify** *v*
*m* 'fɑlsɪˌfəɪ
**sp** falsifie[1]

**falsing** *adj*
'fɑlsɪn, -ɪŋ
**sp** falsing[1]

**Falstaff / ~'s / ~s** *n*
'fɑlstaf / -s
**sp** Falstaffe[93], Fal-staffe[6], Fal-staffes [Falstaff is][1], Falstoffe[3] / Falstaffes[4], Fal-staffes[1], Falstaffs[1], Falstafs[2] / Falstoffs[1]

**falter** *v*
'fɑltəɹ
**sp** falter[1]

**fame / ~'s** *n*
fɛ:m / -z
**sp** fame[63] / fames[2]
**rh** dame *Luc 20*; dame, shame *Luc 53*; frame *TNK 3.5.113*; inflame, shame *LC 270*; name *1H6 4.6.39, LLL 1.1.92, Luc 106, Per Epil.11, R3 1.4.83, S 80.4*; shame *1H6 4.6.45, MA 5.3.8*

**fame / ~d** *v*
fɛ:md
**sp** fam'd[6]
> defame

**famed** *adj*
fɛ:md
**sp** fam'd[2]
> thrice-, un-, well-famed

**familiar** *adj*
fə'mɪlɪəɹ
**sp** familiar[32], familier[1]

**familiar / ~s** *n*
fə'mɪlɪəɹ / -z
**sp** familiar[2], fa-miliar[2] / familiars[2]

**familiarity** *n*
*m* fəˌmɪlɪ'arɪtəɪ, -ˌtəɪ
**sp** familiaritie[1], familiarity[2]

**familiarly** *adv*
*m* fə'mɪlɪəɹləɪ, -ˌləɪ
**sp** familiarlie[1], familiarly[3]

**famil·y / ~ies** *n*
*m* 'famɪˌləɪ, -mɪl-, -ml- / 'famɪˌləɪz
**sp** familie[3], family[3] / families[1]

**famine** *n*
=
**sp** famine[10], fa-mine[1]

**famish** *v*
=
**sp** famish[8]

**famished** *adj*
=
**sp** famish'd[2], famisht[8]

**famous** *adj*
'fɛ:məs
**sp** famous[30]

**famously** *adv*
*m* 'fɛ:məsləɪ, -ˌləɪ
**sp** famouslie[1], famously[1]

**fan / ~s** *n*
=
**sp** fan[7], fanne[2], fans [fan is][1] / fannes
**rh** man *LLL 4.1.146*

**fan / ~ning / ~ned** *v*
= / 'fanɪn, -ɪŋ / =
**sp** fan[4], fanne[1] / fanning[2], fayning[1] / fan'd[1]
**rh** man *TNK Prol.18*

**fanatical** *adj*
fə'natɪkɑl
**sp** pha-naticall[1]

**fanc·y / ~'s / ~ies** *n*
'fansəɪ / -z
**sp** fancie[27], fancies [fancy is][1], fancie's [fancy is][1], fancy[12] / fancies[5] / fancies[11]

**fancy** *v*
'fansəɪ
**sp** fancie[6], fancy[1]

**fancy-free** *adj*
'fansəɪ-'fri:
**sp** fancy free[1]
> free

**fancy-monger** *n*
'fansəɪ-ˌmɤŋgəɹ
**sp** fancie-monger[1]

**fancy-sick** *adj*
'fansəɪ-'sɪk
**sp** fancy sicke[1]
> sick

**fane / ~s** *n*
fɛ:n / -z
**sp** phane[1] / phanes[1]

**fang / ~s** *n*
=
**sp** phang[2], phange[1] / phangs[4]

**Fang [name]** *n*
=
**sp** Fang[4]

**fangled** *adj*
=
**sp** fangled[1]
> new-fangled

**fangless** *adj*
=
**sp** fanglesse[1]

**fanned** *adj*
=
**sp** fan'd[1]

**fantastic** *adj*
=
**sp** fanasticke[1], fantasticke[2], fantastique[1], phantastique[1]

**fantastical** *adj*
*m* fan'tastɪkɑl, -ɪˌk-
**sp** fantastical[2], fan-tastical[1], fantasticall[10], fanta-sticall[1]

**fantastically** *adv*
*m* fan'tastɪkləɪ, -ˌkaləɪ
**sp** fantastically[1], phantastically[1]

**fantas·y / ~ies** *n*
*m* 'fantəsəɪ, -əˌs- / -z
**sp** fantasie[11], phantasie[2] / fantasies[3], phan-tacies[1], phantasies[1]
**rh** ecstasy *VA 897*; infancy *MW 5.5.51*; luxury *MW 5.5.93* / eyes *MND 2.1.258*

**fantas·y / ~ied** *v*
*m* 'fantəˌsəɪd
**sp** fantasied[1]

**fap** *adj*
=
**sp** fap[1]

**far / ~ther / ~thest** *adv*
fɑːɹ / ˈfɑːɹðəɹ, *Edgar's assumed dialect KL 4.6.235* ˈvɑːɹðəɹ / ˈfɑːɹðəst
**sp** far[16], farre[244], farre-[forth][1], farre-[vnworthie][1], [too]-farre[1] / farther[43], further[180], fur-ther[3], *Edgar* vurther[1] / farthest[12], furthest[2]
**rh** *1* car, mar *MND 1.2.32*; **rh** *2* war *AW 3.4.10* / murther *VA 905* / harvest *Tem 4.1.114*
> a-, over-far; far-fet, further

**fardel / ~s** *n*
ˈfɑːɹdəl, -ɹð- / -z
**sp** farthell[7] / fardles[1]

**fare / ~s / ~d** *v*
fɛːɹ / -st / -z / -d
**sp** faire[1], far[10], far[thee][2], far[thee-well][2], far-[thee-well][1], far[thewell][1], far[yewell][2], far[youwell][1], fare[111], fare[thee][1], fare[thee-well][1], fare[youwel][1], fare [youwell][4] / far'st[2] / fares[25], fare's[3] / far'd[1]
**rh** care *1H6 4.6.27* / cares, stares *Luc 1594*
> seafaring

**farewell / ~s** *n*
fɛːɹˈwel / -z
**sp** farewel[4], farewell[289], fare-well[7], far-well[2], farwel[3], farwell[45] / farewels[1], farwels[2]
**rh** cell *RJ 2.5.78, 3.2.143*; dwell *H8 3.2.458*; tell *R2 2.1.211*; well *R3 4.1.103*
> well

**far-fet** *adj*
ˈfɑːɹ-ˌfet
**sp** farre-fet[1]
> fet

**farm / ~s** *n*
fɑːɹm / -z
**sp** farme[6] / farmes[1]
> fee-farm

**farm** *v*
fɑːɹm
**sp** farme[1]

**farmer / ~'s / ~s** *n*
ˈfɑːɹməɹ / -z
**sp** farmer[1] / farmers[2] / far-mers[1]

**farmhouse** *n*
ˈfɑːɹm-ˌəʊs, -ˌhəʊs
**sp** farm-house[1]
> house

**far-off** *adj*
ˈfɑːɹ-ˌɒf
**sp** farre-off[2], farre off[1]
> far

**farrow** *n*
ˈfarə, -oː
**sp** farrow[1]

**farsed** *adj*
*m* ˈfɑːɹsɪd
**sp** farsed[1]

**farther, farthest**
> far

**farthing / ~s** *n*
ˈfɑːɹðɪŋ / -z
**sp** farthing[1], [leuenpence]-farthing[1], [three]farthing[1] / farthings[1], [three]-farthings[1], [three]-far-things[1]

**farthingale / ~s** *n*
*m* ˈfɑːɹdɪŋgɛːl, -ŋˌg-, -ɹðɪ- / -z
**sp** farthingale[3] / fardingales[1]

**fas** *Lat adj*
fas
**sp** fas[1]

**fashion / ~'s / ~s** *n*
ˈfaʃɪən, *French Lady H5 5.2.258* ˈfaʃɒn / -z
**sp** fashion[81], fa-shion[1], *French Lady* fashon[1] / fashions[1] / fashions[8]
**rh** passion *AY 2.4.56, LLL 4.3.137, Luc 1319, S 20.4*
> Newgate-fashion

**fashion / ~ing / ~ed** *v*
ˈfaʃɪən / -ɪn, -ɪŋ / *m* -d, -ˈɪd
**sp** fashion[14] / fashioning[2] / fashion'd[8], fashioned[1]

**fashionable** *adj*
*m* ˈfaʃɪənˌabəl
**sp** fashionable[2]
> unfashionable

**fashioned** *adj*
ˈfaʃɪənd
**sp** fashion'd[1]

**fashion-monger / ~s** *n*
ˈfaʃɪən-ˌmɤŋgəɹz
**sp** fashion mongers[1]

**fashion-monging** *adj*
ˈfaʃɪən-ˌmɤŋgrɪn, -ɪŋ
**sp** fashion-monging[1]

**fast** *adj*
fast
**sp** fast[7]

**fast / ~er / ~est** *adv*
fast / ˈfast·əɹ / -əst
*hsp* fast[92], fast-[by][1], feast[1] / faster[15] / fastest[2]
**rh** *1* blast *Luc 1334*; last *VA 575*; past *Luc 1670*; **rh** *2* haste *CE 4.2.30, KJ 4.2.269, Luc 1334, 1670, MND 3.2.379, R3 2.4.14, RJ 2.3.90*; taste *VA 527*; waist *LLL 4.3.184*

**fast / ~s** *n*
fast / -s
**sp** fast[7] / fasts[4]
**rh** *1* last *Luc 891*; **rh** *2* haste *VA 55*; taste *Luc 891*

**fast / ~ing / ~ed** *v*
fast / ˈfast·ɪn, -ɪŋ / -ɪd
**sp** fast[20] / fasting[5] / fasted[1]

**fast-closed** *adj*
*m* ˌfast-ˈkloːzɪd
**sp** fast closed[1]
> close

**fasten / ~ed** *v*
ˈfasən / -d
**sp** fasten[4] / fasten'd[3], fastened[1], fastned[2], fast'ned[1]
> unfasten

**fastened** *adj*
ˈfasənd
**sp** fastned[1]

**fast-falling** *adj*
*m* ˌfast-ˈfɑːlɪn, -ɪŋ
**sp** fast-falling[1]
> fall

**fast-growing** *adj*
*m* ˌfast-ˈgroːɪn, -ɪŋ
**sp** fast growing[1]
> grow

**fasting** *adj / n*
ˈfastɪn, -ɪŋ
**sp** fasting[6] / fasting[1]

**fat / ~ter / ~test** *adj*
= / ˈfatəɹ / =
**sp** fat[59], fat-[fellow][1], fat-[woman][1], [old]-fat-[woman][1] / fatter[1] / fattest[2]
**rh** at *LLL 5.2.268*; flat *LLL 3.1.100*

**fat / ~s** *n*
=
**sp** fat[1] / fattes[1]

**fat / ~ting / ~ted** *v*
= / ˈfatɪn, -ɪŋ / =
**sp** fat[5] / fatting[1] / fatted[2]

**fatal** *adj*
ˈfɛːtl
**sp** fatall[43]
> double-fatal

**fatally** *adv*
*m* ˈfɛːtɑˌləɪ
**sp** fatally[1]

**fatal-plotted** *adj*
ˈfɛːtl-ˌplɒtɪd
**sp** fatall plotted[1]

**fat-brained** *adj*
ˈfat-ˌbrɛːnd
**sp** fat-brain'd[1]
> brain

**fate / ~s** *n*
fɛːt / -s
**sp** fate[43] / fates[14]
**rh** date *1H6 4.6.8*; gate, state *Luc 1069*; late *H8 2.3.85*; state *LLL 5.2.68, MW 5.5.225, S 29.4* / gates *MND 1.2.34*

**fate / ~d** *v*
ˈfɛːtɪd
**sp** fated[3]

**fated** *adj*
ˈfɛːtɪd
**sp** fated[2]

**fat-guts** *n*
ˈfat-ˌgɤts
**sp** fat guttes[1]

**father / ~'s / ~s / ~s'** *n*
ˈfaðəɹ / -z
**sp** father[805], fa-ther[9], fathers [father][1], fathers [father is][4], father's [father is][4] / fathers[211], fa-thers[2] / fathers[60] / fathers[1]
**rh** *1* rather *R2 1.3.238*; **rh** *2* hither *LLL 1.1.136*; **rh** *3* labour *Per 1.1.68*
> fore-, grand-father

**father / ~s / ~ed** *v*
ˈfaðəɹ·z / -d
**sp** fathers[1] / father'd[2]
> unfathered

**father-in-law** *n*
ˈfaðrɪnˌlɔː, -ðər-
**sp** father-in-law[3]
> law

**fatherless** *adj*
*m* ˈfaðəɹˌles
**sp** fatherlesse[1], father-lesse[1]

**fatherly** *adv*
*m* ˈfaðəɹˌləɪ
**sp** fatherly[3]

**fathom / ~s** *n*
ˈfadəm, -að- / -z
**sp** faddom[1], fadom[2], fadome[3], fathom[2], fathome[2] / fadomes[3]

**fathomless** *adj*
*m* ˈfadəmˌles, -að-
**sp** fathomlesse[1]

**fathom-line** *n*
ˈfadəm-ˌləɪn, -að-
**sp** fadome-line[1]
> line

**fatigate** *adj*
*m* ˈfatɪˌgɛːt
**sp** fatigate[1]

**fat-kidneyed** *adj*
ˈfat-ˌkɪdnəɪd
**sp** fat-kidney'd[1]

**fatness** *n*
=
**sp** fatnesse[1]

**fatuus**
> ignis fatuus

**fat-witted** *adj*
ˈfat-ˈwɪtɪd
**sp** fat-witted[1]
> wit

**fault / ~'s / ~s** *n*
fɔːt, fɑlt / -s
**sp** falt[1], fault[153], [fowle]-fault[1], faults [fault is][2], fault's [fault is][2] / faults[1] / faults[91]
**rh** halt *S 89.1* / assaults *Tem Epil.18*
> default, fellow-, find-fault

**faultiness** *n*
ˈfɔːtɪnəs, fɑlt-
**sp** faultinesse[1]

**faultless** *adj*
ˈfɔːtləs, fɑlt-
**sp** faultlesse[3]

**faulty** *adj*
ˈfɔːtəɪ, fɑlt-
**sp** faultie[2], faulty[1]

**fausse** *Fr adj*
fos
**sp** fause[1]

**Faust·us / ~es / ~e** *n*
ˈfɔːstəsɪz / ˈfɔːste
**sp** Fau-stasses[1] / *emend of LLL 4.3.92* facile

**faut** *Fr*
> falloir

**favour / ~s** *n*
'fɛ:vəɹ / -z
**sp** fauor[16], fauour[100], fa-uour[1] / fauors[6], fauours[32]

**favour / ~s / ~ing / ~ed** *v*
'fɛ:vəɹ / -z / -ɪn, -ɪŋ, 'fɛ:vr- / -d
**sp** fauour[8] / fauours[3] / fauou-ring[1] / fauour'd[1]
**rh** labour *R2 5.6.42*; savour *S 125.5* / savours *MND 2.1.12*
> hard-, ill-, well-favoured

**favourable** *adj*
*m* 'fɛ:və,rabəl, 'fɛ:vrə,bɤl
**sp** fauorable[1], fauourable[4]

**favourably** *adv*
'fɛ:və,rabləɪ, -rəbləɪ
**sp** fauorably[1]

**favourer / ~s** *n*
'fɛ:vrəɹ, -vər- / -z
**sp** fauourer[2] / fauourers[1]

**favouring** *adj*
'fɛ:vrɪn, -ɪŋ, -ər-
**sp** fauouring[1]

**favourite / ~s** *n*
'fɛ:vrɪt, -vər- / *m* 'fɛ:vrɪts, -ə,rɪts
**sp** fauorite[1] / fauorites[3], fauourites[3]

**fawn** *n*
=
**sp** fawne[2]

**fawn / ~s / ~eth / ~ed** *v*
=
**sp** fawne[10] / fawnes[2] / fawneth[1] / fawn'd[1]

**fawning** *adj / n*
'fɔ:nɪn, -ɪŋ
**sp** fawning[4] / fawning[1]

**fay** *n*
fɛ:
**sp** faie[1], fay[1], fey[1]
> faith

**fe** *Fr interj*
fɛ
**sp** fe[4]

**fealty** *n*
'fi:əltəɪ, -l,t-
**sp** fealtie[3], fealty[2]

**fear / ~s** *n*
fi:ɹ, fɛ:ɹ / -z
**sp** fear[3], feare[232], feare's [fear is][1], feere[1] / feares[48], fears[1]
**rh** *1* appear *Luc 117, 1435*; cheer, hear *Luc 261*; deer *VA 690*; ear *LLL 5.2.890, 899, Luc 281, VA 891, 1021*; hear *CE 4.2.55, MND 2.2.160*; here *Cym 2.2.49, MND 2.2.154*; near *Ham 1.3.43, Per 3.Chorus.52*; severe *VA 998, 1153*; year *1H4 4.1.135*; **rh** *2* bear *Luc 610, Mac 3.5.31, 5.3.10, MND 2.2.101, 5.1.21*; swear *1H6 4.5.29, Luc 1647, TN 5.1.169*; tear [rip] *Luc 740, R2 1.1.193*; there *Ham 3.2.181* [*Q2*], *Luc 117, 308, 740, 1647, MND 2.1.30, 3.2.31, VA 320* / **rh** *1* appears *LC 298, Luc 456*; tears [cry] *LC 298, S 119.3*; years *Per 1.2.84*; **rh** *2* bears *LC 273*
**pun** *VA 1083* fair
> beggar-fear

**fear / ~est / ~s / ~ing / ~ed** *v*
fi:ɹ, fɛ:ɹ / -st / -z / 'fi:ɹɪn, -ɪŋ, 'fɛ:ɹ- / fi:ɹd, fɛ:ɹd
**sp** fear[5], feare[373] / fearst[1], fear'st[3] / feares[18] / fearing[23] / feard[3], fear'd[36], feared[5]
**rh** *1* cheer *Luc 88*; clear *H8 Epil.3, Mac 1.5.70, Per 1.1.143*; dear *S 48.13*; ear *PP 18.49, VA 660*; hear *H8 Epil.7*; here *1H6 1.2.14, MND 5.1.215*; fear him **hear him** *VA 1094;* **fear it rh** *1* hear it *LLL 4.3.199*; **rh** *2* tear it *LLL 4.3.199* / **rh** *1* tears [cry] *LC 295*; **rh** *2* forbear *AC 1.3.12*; there *1H6 5.2.17, R2 2.1.299*; wear *VA 1083*; **rh** *3* worshipper *Luc 88* / swearing *PP 7.10*
> not-, soul-fearing; afeared

**feared** *adj / n*
fi:ɹd, fɛ:ɹd
**sp** feard[1], fear'd[2] / feared[1]

**fearful / ~lest** *adj*
'fi:ɹfʊl, 'fɛ:ɹ- / -st
**sp** fearefull[66], fearful[1], fearfull[20] / fearefull'st[1]

**fearfully** *adv*
*m* 'fi:ɹfʊ,ləɪ, 'fɛ:ɹ-
**sp** fearefully[5], fearfully[1]
**rh** dye *PP 17.28*

**fearfulness** *n*
*m* 'fi:ɹfʊl,nes, 'fɛ:ɹ-
**sp** fearefulnesse[1]

**fearless** *adj*
'fi:ɹləs, 'fɛ:ɹ-
**sp** fearelesse[3]

**fear-surprised** *adj*
*m* 'fi:ɹ-səɹ'prəɪzɪd, 'fɛ:ɹ-
**sp** feare-surprized[1]
> surprise

**feast / ~s** *n*
fest / -s
**sp** feast[69], sheepe-shearing-[feast][1] / feasts[13]
**rh** best *RJ 1.2.97*; breast *Per 3. Chorus.4*; guest *CE 3.1.26, RJ 1.2.20, 1.5.74, S 47.5, VA 450*; rest *TS 5.1.129* / guests *Per 2.3.7*

**feast / ~s / ~ing / ~ed** *v*
fest / -s / 'fest·ɪn, -ɪŋ / -ɪd
**sp** feast[26] / feasts[3] / feasting[4] / feasted[4]
**rh** *1* guest *Tim 3.6.102*; **rh** *2* least *Tim 4.3.516*
> a-feasting

**feasted** *adj*
'festɪd
**sp** feasted[1]

**feasting** *adj / n*
'festɪn, -ɪŋ
**sp** feasting[1] / feasting[2], fea-sting[1]

**feat / ~er** *adj*
fi:t / 'fi:təɹ
**sp** feate[1] / feater[1]
> love-feat

**feat / ~s** *n*
fi:t / -s
**sp** feat[3] / feates[3], feats[10]
**rh** bleat *MA 5.4.50*

**feat / ~ed** *v*
'fi:tɪd
**sp** feated[1]

**feather / ~s** *n*
'feðəɹ / -z
**sp** feather[22], fether[1] / feathers[12]
**rh** together *CE 3.1.82*; whether *VA 302*

**featherbed** *n*
'feðəɹ,bed
**sp** featherbed[1]

**feathered** *adj*
'feðəɹd
**sp** feather'd[1], feathered[1]
> dove-feathered

**featly** *adv*
'fi:tləɪ
**sp** featly[2]

**feature / ~s** *n*
'fɛ:təɹ / -z
**sp** feature[13] / features[3]
**rh** creature *S 113.12*

**featured** *adj*
'fɛ:təɹd
**sp** featur'd[1]

**February** *adj*
'febrʊ,arəɪ
**sp** Februarie[1]

**fecks**
> i'fecks

**fed**
> feed

**fedary / federary** *n*
'fedə,rəɪ / 'fedə,rarəɪ
**sp** fedarie[1] / federarie[1]

**fee / ~s** *n*
=
**sp** fee[18] / fees[5]
**rh** be *VA 609*; charity *Per 3.2.72*; me *AW 2.1.189, MND 3.2.113, S 120.13*; thee *2H6 3.2.217, Luc 913, Tit 2.3.179*; tree *VA 393* / knees *TC 3.3.49*

**fee / ~d** *v*
=
**sp** fee[1] / fee'd[2]

**feeble** *adj / n*
=
**sp** feeble[19] / feeble[1]

**feebl·e / ~ing / ~ed** *v*
'fi:blɪn, -ɪŋ / =
**sp** feebling[1] / feebled[1]
> enfeeble

**Feeble** [name] *n*
=
**sp** Feeble[8]

**feebleness** *n*
=
**sp** feeblenesse[1]

**feebly** *adv*
'fi:bləɪ
**sp** feebly[1]

**feed / ~est / ~s / ~eth / ~ing / fed** *v*
= / fi:dst / = / = / 'fi:dɪn, -ɪŋ / =
**sp** feed[32], feede[44] / feed'st[2] / feedes[6], feeds[7] / feedeth[1] / feeding[4] / fed[29]
**rh** breed *Per 1.1.133, 65, VA 169*; deed *Tit 5.3.53*; exceed Tim *1.2.202*; need *AY 2.7.169* / breeds, deeds *Luc 905*; deeds *TC 5.3.110* / bed *TC 5.8.19, VA 399*; bred *Tit 5.3.60*; dead *Luc 1455, VA 170*; fled *VA 795*
> unfeed; bacon-, bean-, rump-fed

**fee'd** *adj*
=
**sp** feed[1], feede[1]

**feeder / ~s** *n*
'fi:dəɹ / -z
**sp** feeder[5] / feeders[3]

**feeding** *n*
'fi:dɪn, -ɪŋ
**sp** feeding[9]
**rh** needing *S 118.6*

**fee-farm** *n*
'fi:-,fɑ:ɹm
**sp** fee-farme[1]
> farm

**fee-grief** *n*
=
**sp** fee-griefe[1]
> grief

**feel / ~s / ~ing / felt / ~est** *v*
= / = / 'fi:lɪn, -ɪŋ / = / felst, -ltst
**sp** feele[100], feele't[1], feel't[3] / feeles[7] / feeling[4] / felt[32] / feltst[1]
**rh** heel *RJ 1.2.26*; steel *Luc 756, S 120.2, VA 201*; **feel it** steel it *VA 373* / heels *VA 311*; kneels *VA 352* / melt *MND 1.1.244, VA 143*

**feeler / ~'s** *n*
'fi:ləɹz
**sp** feelers[1]

**feeling** *adj / n*
'fi:lɪn, -ɪŋ
**sp** feeling[5] / feeling[17]
> tender-, un-feeling

**feelingly** *adv*
*m* 'fi:lɪnləɪ, -ɪŋ-, -,ləɪ
**sp** feelingly[4]

**fee-simple** *n*
=
**sp** fee-simple[5]
> simple

**feet**
> foot

**feeze**
> pheeze

**feign / ~ing / ~ed** *v*
fɛ:n / 'fɛ:nɪn, -ɪŋ / fɛ:nd
**sp** faigne[1], feigne[3] / faining[1] / feign'd[2]
**rh** remain *PP 8.13*

**feigned** *adj*
*m* 'fɛ:nɪd, fɛ:nd
**sp** fained[4], feign'd[1], feigned[2]
> unfeigned

**feigning** *adj / n*
'fɛ:nɪn, -ɪŋ
**sp** faining[2], fai-ning[1], fayning[1] / feigning[1]

**felicitate** *adj*
*m* fe'lɪsɪˌtɛ:t
**sp** felicitate[1]

**felicity** *n*
*m* fe'lɪsɪˌtəɪ
**sp** felicite[1], felicitie[1]
**rh** ebony *LLL 4.3.247*

**fell / ~est** *adj*
= / 'feləst
**sp** fell[40] / fellest[2]

**fell / ~s** *n*
=
**sp** fell[2] / fels[1]
**rh** hell *Luc 766*; quell *MND 5.1.276*

**fell / ~s / ~ed** *v*
=
**sp** fell[2] / fells[1] / fell'd[2]
**rh** well *AW 3.1.22, LLL 5.2.114*

**fell** *past tense*
> fall

**fell-devouring** *adj*
'fel-dɪ'vo:rɪn, -ɪŋ
**sp** fell deuouring[1]
> devour

**fell-lurking** *adj*
*m* ˌfel-'lɐ:ɹkɪn, -ɪŋ
**sp** fell-lurking[1]
> lurk

**fellow / ~'s / ~s / ~s'** *n*
'felə, -lo: / -z
**sp** fellow[285], fel-low[8], [fat]-fellow[1], [good]fellow[1], [good]-fellow[2], fellowe[1], fellowes [fellow is][1], fellow's [fellow is][2] / fellowes[3] / fellowes[67], [good]fellowes[1], [good]-fellowes[1], [tall]-fellowes[1], fellows[1] fellow's[1] / fellowes[1]
**rh** yellow *H8 Prol.15*
> bed-, coach-, Good-, play-, pew-, vow-, yoke-fellow

**fellow / ~est** *v*
'feləst, -lo:st
**sp** fellow'st[1]

**fellow-counsellor** *n*
ˌfelə-'kəʊnsələɹ, ˌfelo:-
**sp** fellow councellor[1]

**fellow-fault** *n*
'felə-ˌfɔ:t, 'felo:-, -ˌfɑ:lt,
**sp** fellow-fault[1]
> fault

**fellow-king / ~s** *n*
ˌfelə-'kɪŋz, ˌfelo:-
**sp** fellow-kings[1]
> king

**fellowly** *adv*
'feləlaɪ, -lo:l-
**sp** fellowly[1]

**fellow-minister / ~s** *n*
ˌfelə-'mɪnɪstəɹz, ˌfelo:-
**sp** fellow ministers[1]
> minister

**fellow-partner** *n*
ˌfelə-'pɑ:ɹtnəɹ, ˌfelo:-
**sp** fellow partner[1]
> partner

**fellow-scholar / ~s** *n*
ˌfelə-'skɒləɹz, ˌfelo:-
**sp** fellow schollers[1]
> scholar

**fellow-schoolmaster** *n*
ˌfelə-'sku:lmastəɹ, ˌfelo:-
**sp** fellow schoolemaster[1]
> schoolmaster

**fellow-servant** *n*
ˌfelə-'sɐ:ɹvənt, ˌfelo:-
**sp** fellow-seruant[1]
> servant

**fellowship / ~s** *n*
'feləʃɪp, 'felo:- / -s
**sp** fellowship[15], fel-lowship[2] / fellowships[1]
**rh** o'erskip *KL 3.6.105* [*Q*]

**fellow-soldier** *n*
ˌfelə-'so:djəɹ, ˌfelo:-
**sp** fellow souldior[1]
> soldier

**fellow-student** *n*
ˌfelə-'stju:dənt, ˌfelo:-
**sp** fellow student[1]
> student

**fellow-tribune** *n*
ˌfelə-'trɪbju:n, ˌfelo:-
**sp** fellow tribune[1]
> tribune

**fell·y / ~ies** *n*
'feləɪz
**sp** fallies[1]

**felon** *n*
=
**sp** fellon[1], felon[1]

**felony** *n*
'felənəɪ
**sp** fellony[2]

**felonious** *adj*
fe'lo:nɪəs
**sp** felonious[1]

**felt** *adj / n*
=
**sp** felt-[absence][1] / felt[1]

**felt** *v*
> feel

**female** *adj*
'fi:mɛ:l
**sp** female[6], femall[1]

**female / ~s** *n*
'fi:mɛ:l / -z
**sp** female[7], fe-male[1] / females[3]

**feminine** *adj*
=
**sp** feminine[1]

**fen / ~s** *n*
=
**sp** fen[2], fenne[2] / fennes[1], fens[1]

**fence** *n*
=
**sp** fence[7]

**fence / ~d** *v*
=
**sp** fence[5] / fenc'd[1]
> unfenced

**fencer / ~s** *n*
'fensəɹ / -z
**sp** fencer[1] / fencers[1]

**fencing** *adj / n*
'fensɪn, -ɪŋ
**sp** fencing[1] / fencing[2]

**fennel** *adj / n*
=
**sp** fennell[1] / fennell[2]

**fenny** *adj*
'fenəɪ
**sp** fenny[1]

**fen-sucked** *adj*
'fen-ˌsɤkt
**sp** fen-suck'd[1]

**Fenton** *n*
=
**sp** Fenton[21], Fenten[1]

**feodary** *n*
'fju:dərəɪ
**sp** foedarie[1]

**fer** *v*
fɐ:ɹ
**sp** fer[2]
**pun** *H5 4.4.29f* Fer

**Fer** [name] *Fr n*
fɛ:ɹ
**sp** Fer[2]

**Ferdinand / ~o** *n*
*m* 'fɐ:ɹdɪˌnand, -ɪnənd / ˌfɐ:ɹdɪ'nando:
**sp** Ferdinand[13] / Ferdinando[1]

**fernseed** *n*
'fɐ:ɹnˌsi:d
**sp** fernseed[1], fern-seede[1]
> seed

**Ferrara** *n*
fe'rɑ:rə
**sp** Ferrara[1]

**ferret** *adj / v*
=
**sp** ferret[1] / ferret[2]

**Ferris** *n*
=
**sp** Ferris[1]

**ferry** *n*
'ferəɪ
**sp** ferrie[1]

**ferryman** *n*
'ferəɪˌman
**sp** ferry-man[1]

**fertile** *n*
'fɐ:ɹtl
**sp** fertile[11], fertill[3]

**fertile-fresh** *adj*
'fɐ:ɹtl-'freʃ
**sp** fertile-fresh[1]

**fertility** *n*
*m* fəɹ'tɪlɪˌtəɪ
**sp** fertilitie[2]

**fervency** *n*
*m* 'fɐɹvənˌsəɪ
**sp** feruencie[1]

**fervour** *n*
'fɐ:ɹvəɹ
**sp** feruour[3]

**Feste** *n*
'festə
**sp** Feste[1]

**fester / ~ing** *v*
'festəɹ / 'festrɪn, -ɪŋ
**sp** fester[2] / festring[1]

**festered** *adj*
'festəɹd
**sp** fester'd[1], festred[1]

**festinate** *adj*
'festɪnət
**sp** festinate[1]

**festinately** *adv*
'festɪnətləɪ
**sp** fe-stinatly[1]

**festival** *adj*
'festɪvɑl
**sp** festiuall[2]

**festival / ~s** *n*
*m* 'festɪˌvɑl / -z
**sp** festiuall[4] / festiuals[1]
**rh** funeral *RJ 4.5.84*

**fet** *v*
=
**sp** fet[1]
> deep-, far-fet

**fetch / ~es** *n*
=
**sp** fetch[1] / fetches[2]

**fetch / ~es / ~ing / ~ed** *v*
=, *Caius MW 1.4.44* veʧ / = / 'feʧɪn, -ɪŋ / =
**sp** fetch[119], fetcht [fetch it][1], *Caius* vetch[1] / fetches[3] / fetching[1] / fetch'd[1], fetcht[1]

**fetlock / ~s** *n*
=
**sp** fet-locke[1] / fetlockes[1]

**fetter / ~s** *n*
'fetəɹz
**sp** fetters[2]

**fetter / ~ed** *v*
'fetəɹ / -d
**sp** fetter[4] / fetter'd[2], fettred[2]
**rh** better *TN 3.1.152*

**fettering** *n*
'fetrɪn, -ɪŋ, -tər-
**sp** fettering[1]

**fettle** *v*
=
**sp** fettle[1]

**feu** *Fr n*
fø
**sp** feu[2]

**feud** *n*
=
**sp** feud[1]

**fever / ~s** *n*
'fɛ:vəɹ, 'fevəɹ / -z
**sp** feauer[10], feauor[4], feauour[1], feuer[6] / feauors[1]
**rh** never *S 119.8*

**fever** *v*
'fɛ:vəɹ, 'fevəɹ
**sp** feauer[1]

**feverous** *adj*
'fɛ:vrəs, 'fevrəs, -vər-
**sp** feauorous[3], feuorous[1]

**fever-weakened** *adj*
'fɛ:vəɹ-ˌwi:kənd, 'fev-
**sp** feauer-weakned[1]

**few / ~er / est** *adj*
= / 'fju:əɹ / =
**sp** few[33] / fewer[4] / fewest[2]

**few** *n*
=
**sp** few[31]
**rh** dew *Luc 22*

**fewness** *n*
=
**sp** fewnes[1]

**fickle** *adj*
=
**sp** fickle[7]
**rh** brittle *PP 7.1*

**fickleness** *n*
=
**sp** ficklenesse[1]

**fico** *interj*
'fɪko:
**sp** fico[1]
> figo

**fiction** *n*
'fɪksɪən
**sp** fiction[2], fixion[1]

**fiddious**
> Aufidius

**fiddle** *n / v*
=
**sp** fiddle[1] / fiddle[1]

**fiddler** *n*
'fɪdləɹ
**sp** fidler[3]

**fiddlestick** *n*
=
**sp** fiddlesticke[1], fiddle-sticke[1]

**Fidele / ~'s** *n*
fɪ'dɛ:li: / -z
**sp** Fidele[9] / Fideles[1]

**fidelicet**
> videlicet

**fidelity** *n*
fɪ'delɪtəɪ
**sp** fidelity[1]

**fie** *interj*
fəɪ
**sp** fie[124], fye[26]

**field / ~s** *n*
=
**sp** feild[1], field[153], fielde[1] / fields[29]
**rh** *1* shield *H5 3.2.9, LLL 5.2.549* [*F end line*], *Luc 58, R3 4.3.57*; yield *CE 3.2.38, H5 4.2.34, Luc 72, PP 19.3* [fields: yields *in another version*], *VA 454, 894*; yield, wield *Luc 1430*; **rh** *2* build *KL 3.2.91*; gild *Luc 58*; killed *Luc 72*; **rh** *3* held *S 2.2*
> afield

**field-bed** *n*
=
**sp** field-bed[1]
> bed

**fielded** *adj*
=
**sp** fielded[1]

**fiend / ~'s / ~s** *n*
=, fend / -z
**sp** feend[1], feind[1], fiend[54], fiends[1] / fiends[15]
**rh** end *PT 6, S 145.11*; friend *PP 2.9, S 144.9*; friends *VA 638*
> under-fiend

**fiend-like** *adj*
'fi:nd-ləɪk, 'fend-
**sp** fiend-like[2]

**fierce** *adj*
fi:ɹs
**sp** fierce[37]

**fiercely** *adv*
'fi:ɹsləɪ
**sp** fiercely[1]

**fierceness** *n*
'fi:ɹsnəs
**sp** fiercenesse[3]

**fiery** *adj*
'fəɪrəɪ
**sp** fierie[23], fierie-[glow-wormes][1], fiery[20], firie[1]

**fiery-footed** *adj*
'fəɪrəɪ-ˌfʊtɪd
**sp** fiery footed[1]
> foot

**fiery-kindled** *adj*
'fəɪrəɪ-ˌkɪndəld
**sp** fierie kindled[1]
> kindle

**fife / ~s** *n*
fəɪf / -s
**sp** fife[5] / fifes[1]

**Fife** [name] *n*
fəɪf
**sp** Fife[6], Fiffe[1]

**fifteen** *adj*
*m* 'fɪfti:n
**sp** fifteene[14], fif-teene[1]

**fifteen / ~s** *n*
*m* 'fɪfti:n / -z
**sp** fifteene[1] / fifteenes[1]

**fifteenth** *adj*
*m* fɪf'ti:nt, -nθ
**sp** fifteenth[1]

**fifth** *adj*
fɪft
**sp** fift[28], fift's [fifth is][1]

**fifty** *adj / n*
'fɪftəɪ
**sp** fiftie[12], fifty[7] / fiftie[8], fifty[3]

**fifty-five** *n*
ˌfɪftəɪ-'fəɪv
**sp** fiftie fiue[1]

**fifty-fold** *n*
'fɪftəɪ-ˌfo:ld
**sp** fifty-fold[1]
> fold

**fig / ~s** *n*
=
**sp** figge[4] / figges[1], figs[3]

**fig** *v*
=
**sp** figge[-me][1]

**fight / ~s** *n*
fəɪt / -s
**sp** fight[53], [sea]-fight[1] / fights[3]
**rh** knight *1H6 4.7.43, TC 4.5.90*; might *AC 4.4.37, VA 114*; night *JC 5.3.110*; plight *PP 17.24*; right *1H6 4.2.56, 3H6 4.7.74, R2 1.3.56, TC 3.2.169*; white *Luc 62*
> sea-fight

**fight / ~est / ~s / ~eth / ~ing / fought / ~est** *v*
fəɪt / *m* -st, 'fəɪtəst / -s / 'fəɪt·əθ / -ɪn, -ɪŋ / = / fɔ:tst
**sp** fight[205] / fightest[1], fightst[1], fight'st[1] / fights[11] / fighteth[1] / fighting[8] / fought[63] / fought'st[1]
**rh** fight, night, sprite *Luc 124*; flight *R2 1.3.62*; knight *PP 15.5*; knight, light, might, night *MW 2.1.17*; light *R2 1.1.83, S 60.7, 88.3*; night *MND 3.2.354, TC 5.3.92*; right, *R2 3.2.61*; right, sight, white *Luc 1402*; spite *PP 15.5*; tonight *Mac 5.6.8*; white *Luc 68*; write *Luc 1298*; **fight, yea** almighty *LLL 5.2.651* [*recitation*] / delighting, effecting *Luc 428* / sought *Luc 1436*; wrought *KL 4.7.97*
> unfought, well-foughten

**fighter** *n*
'fəɪtəɹ
**sp** fighter[4]

**fighting** *adj / n*
'fəɪtɪn, -ɪŋ
**sp** fighting[3] / fighting[2]

**fig-leaf / ~leaves** *n*
=
**sp** figge-leaues[1]
> leaf

**figo** *interj*
'fɪgo:
**sp** figo[1]
> fico

**fig's-end** *n*
=
**sp** figges-end[1]

**figure / ~s** *n*
'fɪgəɹ / -z
**sp** figure[38], figures [figure is][1] / figures[12]

**figur·e / ~s / ~ing / ~ed** *v*
'fɪgəɹ / -z / -ɪn, -ɪŋ, 'fɪgrɪn, -ɪŋ / -d
**sp** figure[1] / figures[1] / figuring[2] / figur'd[2]
> disfigure

**figured** *adj*
'fɪgəɹd
**sp** figur'd[1]
> self-figured

**filbert / ~s** *n*
'fɪlbəɹts
**sp** philbirts[1]

**filch / ~es / ~ed** *v*
=
**sp** filch[1] / filches[1] / filch'd[1]

**filching** *n*
'fɪlʧɪn, -ɪŋ
**sp** filching[2]

**file / ~s** *n*
fəɪl / -z
**sp** file[14] / files[5]
> muster-file

**file / ~d** *v*
fəɪl / fəɪld
**sp** file[1] / fil'd[1]
**rh** compiled *S 85.4*

**filed** *adj*
fəɪld
**sp** filed[2]

**filial** *adj*
'fɪlɪɑl
**sp** filiall[2], filliall[1]
> unfilial

**filius** *Lat n*
'fɪlɪʊs
**sp** filius[1]

**fill / ~s** *n*
=
**sp** fill[7] / fils[1]

**fill / ~s / *VA* ~eth / ~ing / ~ed** *v*
= / = / = / 'fɪlɪn, -ɪŋ / =
**sp** fil[1], fill[59] / filles[5], fills[4], fils[3] / filleth[1] / filling[8] / fild[2], fill'd[24]
**rh** ill *S 112.1*; kill *S 56.5* / distilled *AY 3.2.138*; killed, spilled *Luc 1804*; willed *Per 5.2.15* [*Chorus*] / willeth *VA 548* / spilling, willing *Luc 1234*
> mouth-filling, unfilled, upfill

**fillet** *n*
=
**sp** fillet[1]

**fill-horse** *n*
'fɪl-ˌɔːɹs, -ˌhɔː-
**sp** philhorse[1]

**fillip** *v*
=
**sp** fillip[1], fillop[2]

**film** *n / v*
'fɪləm, =
**sp** philome[1] / filme[1]

**fils** *Fr n*
fis, fiz
**sp** filz[1]

**filth / ~s** *n*
=
**sp** filth[8] / filthes[1]

**filthy** *adj*
'fɪlθəɪ
**sp** filthie[3], filthy[18]

**fin / ~s** *n*
=
**sp** fin[1], finne[1] / finnes[2]
**rh** in *CE 3.1.79*

**fin** *Fr n*
fɛ̃
**sp** fin[1]

**finally** *adv*
'fəɪnələɪ
**sp** fi-nally[1]

**finch** *n*
=
**sp** finch[1]

**finch-egg** *n*
=
**sp** finch egge[1]
> egg

**find / ~est / ~s / ~eth / ~ing / found / ~est** *v*
fəɪnd / 'fəɪnd·əst / -z / -əθ / -ɪn, -ɪŋ / fəʊnd / -st, fəʊnst
**sp** find[78], finde[427] / findst[1], find'st[4] / findes[29], finds[11] / findeth[1] / finding[11] / found[214] / found'st[1]
**rh** *1* assigned, mind *LC 137*; blind *S 148.14*; blind, mind *Luc 760*; inclined, mind *Luc 1654*; kind *AW 1.3.60, RJ 2.3.8*; kind, mind *LC 187*; mankind *Tim 4.1.35*; mind *LC 88, Luc 1539, MV 2.5.52, Per 4.Chorus.6, S 27.14, 77.10, 92.11, TC 5.2.111, TN 1.5.298*; Rosalind *AY 3.2.107*; unkind *KL 1.1.261*; **rh** *2* wind *LC 88, LLL 4.3.104, MND 3.2.95, PP 16.6, 20.32, S 14.8, 51.5* / minds *S 116.3, TG 5.4.109* / **rh** *1* ground *CE 2.1.96, MND 4.1.100, PP 13.7, S 75.4, 153.2*; sound *MND 3.2.181, R2 2.1.18*; **rh** *2* wound *RJ 2.1.42* [*rh with RJ 2.2.1*]
> new-, well-found; founder

**finder** *n*
'fəɪndəɹ
**sp** finder[2]
> hare-finder

**finder-out** *n*
'fəɪndəɹ-'əʊt
**sp** finder-out[1]
> out

**find-fault / ~s** *n*
'fəɪnd-ˌfɔːts, -ˌfɑːlts
**sp** finde-faults[1]
> fault

**finding / ~s** *n*
'fəɪndɪnz, -ɪŋz
**sp** findings[1]

**fine / ~r / ~st** *adj*
fəɪn / 'fəɪn·əɹ / *m* -əst, fəɪnst
**sp** fine[67] / finer[4], fi-ner[1] / finest[3], fin'st[1], fins't[2]
**rh** dine *LLL 1.1.63*; mine *2H4 5.3.45, TG 1.2.10*; nine *LLL 5.2.487*; wine *2H4 5.3.45*
> confineless

**fine / ~s** *n*
fəɪn / -z
**sp** fine[22], fines [fine is][1] / fines[5]
**rh** mine *RJ 3.1.190*

**fine / ~ed** *v*
fəɪn / -d
**sp** fine[2] / fined[1], fin'de[1]

**fine-baited** *adj*
'fəɪn-ˌbɛːtɪd
**sp** fine baited[1]

**fineless** *adj*
'fəɪnləs
**sp** finelesse[1]

**finely** *adv*
'fəɪnləɪ
**sp** finely[10]

**finem** *Lat*
> finis

**fineness** *n*
'fəɪnəs
**sp** finenesse[3]

**finer** *n*
'fəɪnəɹ
**sp** finer[1]

**finger / ~'s / ~s / ~s'** *n*
'fɪŋgəɹ / -z, *Katherine, Lady H5 3.4.10ff* 'fiːŋgrə, 'fɛ̃ŋgrə
**sp** finger[60], [lazie]-finger[1] / fingers[1] / fingers[31], fin-gers[4] / fingers[2], fin-gers[1], *Katherine, Lady* fingre[3], fingres[4]
> forefinger

**finger ~ed** *v*
'fɪŋgəɹd
**sp** finger'd[2]

**finger-end** *n*
'fɪŋgəɹ-ˌend
**sp** finger end[1]
**rh** descend *MW 5.5.84*
> end

**fingering** *n*
*m* 'fɪŋgəˌrɪn, -grɪn, -ɪŋ
**sp** fingering[2], fin-gering[1], fingring[1]

**finical** *adj*
'fɪnɪkɑl
**sp** finicall[1]

**fin·is / ~em** *Lat n*
'fi:nem
**sp** finem[1]

**finish / ~ed** *v*
= / *m* 'fɪnɪʃt, -ʃɪd
**sp** finish[9] / finish'd[3], finished[3], finisht[2]
**rh** diminish *AY 5.4.137*
> unfinished

**finisher** *n*
'fɪnɪʃəɹ
**sp** finisher[1]
**rh** minister *AW 2.1.136*

**finless** *adj*
=
**sp** finne-lesse[1]

**Finsbury** *n*
*m* 'fɪnzbəˌrəɪ
**sp** Finsbury[1]

**fire / ~'s / ~s** *n*
fəɪɹ / -z
**sp** fier[2], fire[245], [sea-cole]-fire[1], [tempest-dropping]-fire[1], [triall]-fire[1], fire's [fire is][1] / fires[1] / fiers[1], [reioycing]-fires[1], fires[16]
**rh** admire *LLL 4.2.116, PP 5.12*; aspire *VA 149*; aspire, desire *Luc 4*; briar *MND 5.1.382*; briar *MND 2.1.5, 3.1.103*; desire *1H6 4.6.10, Luc 181, 1491, 1604, MW 5.5.88, 95, S 45.1, 154.5, VA 35, 275, 388, 494, 654, 1073*; expire *2H4 5.5.109, S 73.9*; ire *R2 1.1.19*; liar *Ham 2.2.115*; sire *VA 1162*; squier [square] *LLL 5.2.476* / desires *Mac 1.4.51*; liars *RJ 1.2.88*
> a-, bon-, cannon-, hell-, rejoicing-, wild-fire

**fir·e / ~s / ~ing / ~ed** *v*
fəɪɹ / -z / 'fəɪɹɪn, -ɪŋ / fəɪɹd
**sp** fire[6] / fires[2] / fiering[1] / fier'd[1], fir'd[1]
> new-fired

**firebrand / ~s** *n*
'fəɪɹˌbrand / -z
**sp** firebrand[1], fire-brand[2] / firebrands[1]
> brand

**fire-drake** *n*
'fəɪɹ-ˌdrɛ:k
**sp** fire-drake[1]

**fire-eyed** *adj*
'fəɪɹ-ˌəɪd
**sp** fire-ey'd[1]
> eye

**fire-new** *adj*
'fəɪɹ-ˌnju:
**sp** fire-new[2], fire new[1]
> new

**fire-robed** *adj*
'fəɪɹ-ˌro:bd
**sp** fire-roab'd-[god][1]
> robe

**fire-shovel** *n*
'fəɪɹ-ˌʃɤvəl
**sp** fire-shouell[1]
> shovel

**firework / ~s** *n*
'fəɪɹˌwɔ:ɹk / -s
**sp** fire-worke[1] / fire-workes[1]
> work

**firing** *n*
'fəɪɹɪn, -ɪŋ
**sp** firing[1]
**rh** requiring *Tem 2.2.177*

**firk** *v*
fɐ:ɹk
**sp** firke[2]

**firm** *adj*
fɐ:ɹm
**sp** firme[40]
> unfirm

**firmament** *n*
*m* 'fɐ:ɹməˌment, -əmə-
**sp** firemament[1], firmament[3], fir-mament[1]

**firmly** *adv*
'fɐ:ɹmləɪ
**sp** firmely[7], firmly[2]

**firmness** *n*
'fɐ:ɹmnəs
**sp** firmenesse[2]

**firm-set** *adj*
'fɐ:ɹm-ˌset
**sp** firme-set[1]
> set

**first** *adj / adv / n*
'fɐ:ɹst
**sp** first[115] / first[311] / first[96], first's [first is][1]
**rh** accurst *Ham 3.2.190, VA 1118*; curst *VA 888*; worst *KL 5.3.3, TS 1.2.13, 34*

**first-begotten** *adj*
'fɐ:ɹst-bɪˌgɒtən
**sp** first begotten[1]

**first-born** *adj*
'fɐ:ɹst-ˌbɔ:ɹn
**sp** first borne[5], first-borne[1]
> born

**first-conceived** *adj*
*m* 'fɐ:ɹst-kənˌsi:vɪd
**sp** first-conceiued[1]

**firstling / ~s** *n*
'fɐ:ɹstlɪnz, -ɪŋz
**sp** firstlings[3]

**fish / ~es** *n*
=
**sp** fish[35], fish-[meales][1], Fish-[streete][1], [fresh]-fish[1], [salt]-fish[1] / fishes[8]
> dog-, land-, stock-fish

**fish / ~es / ~ed** *v*
=
**sp** fish[3] / fishes[1] / fish'd[2]
**rh** dish *CE 3.1.22, Cym 4.2.36, Tem 2.2.176*

**fisher / ~s** *n*
'fɪʃəɹ / -z
**sp** fisher[1] / fishers[1]

**fisher·man / ~men / ~s** *n*
'fɪʃəɹˌmen / -z
**sp** fishermen[3] / fishermens-[boots][1]

**fishif·y / ~ied** *v*
'fɪʃɪfəɪd
**sp** fishified[1]

**fish-like** *adj*
'fɪʃ-ləɪk
**sp** fish-like[1]

**fishmonger** *n*
'fɪʃˌmɤŋgəɹ
**sp** fishmonger[1], fishmon-ger[1]

**fishpond** *n*
=
**sp** fish-pond[1]
> pond

**fisnomy** *n*
*Clown's pron of physiognomy AW 4.5.38* 'fɪznəməɪ
**sp** fisno-mie[1]

**fist / ~s** *n*
=
**sp** fist[9] / fists[1]

**fist / ~ing** *v*
'fɪstɪn, -ɪŋ
**sp** fisting[1]

**fistula** *n*
'fɪstjələ
**sp** fistula[1]

**fit / ~er / ~est** *adj*
= / 'fɪtəɹ / =, fɪtst
**sp** fit[101] / fitter[8] / fit'st[1], fittest[4]
**rh** it *MW 5.5.59, Per 1.1.106*; wit *KL 1.2.180, 3.2.76, LLL 4.1.51, 144, TN 3.1.65*[F], *emend as* hits
> unfit

**fit** *adv*
=
**sp** fit[5]

**fit / ~s** *n*
=
**sp** fit[21], fitte[1] / fits[12]
**rh** sits, wits *Luc 856*; wits *CE 5.1.85*

**fit / ~s / ~eth / ~ting / ~ted** *v*
= / = / = / 'fɪtɪn, -ɪŋ / =
**sp** fit[33] / fits[29] / fitteth[2] / fitting[4] / fitted[13]
**rh** wit *KL 3.2.76, Oth 2.1.132*; fit it hit it *LLL 4.1.130* / hits *AW 2.1.144* [*emend of* shifts], *S 120.12*; sits *VA 327* / committed *S 119.7*; omitted *LLL 4.3.358*

**fitchew** *n*
'fɪʧu:
**sp** fitchew[3]

**fitful** *adj*
=
**sp** fitfull[1]

**fitly** *adv*
'fɪtləɪ
**sp** fitly[5]

**fitment** *n*
=
**sp** fitment[1]

**fitness** *n*
=
**sp** fitnesse[7]

**fitting** *adj*
'fɪtɪn, -ɪŋ
**sp** fitting[4]

**Fitzwater / ~s** *n*
fɪtz'wɑ:təɹ / -z
**sp** Fitz-water[2] / *in s.d.* Fitz-waters[1]

**five** *adj*
fəɪv
**sp** fiue[96], fiue-[weekes][1], *abbr* v.[1]
> seventy-five

**five / ~s** *n*
fəɪv / -z
**sp** fiue[32] / fiues[1]
**rh** thrive *LLL 5.2.535*

**five-finger-tied** *adj*
*m* ˌfəɪv-'fɪŋgəɹ-ˌtəɪd
**sp** fiue finger tied[1]

**five-fold** *adj*
'fəɪv-ˌfo:ld
**sp** fiue-fold[1]
> fold

**fivescore** *n*
*m* 'fəɪvˌskɔ:ɹ, ˌfəɪv'skɔ:ɹ
**sp** fiuescore[2]
**rh** more *LLL 4.2.41*
> score

**fix / ~s / ~eth / ~ing / ~ed** *v*
= / = / = / 'fɪks·ɪn, -ɪŋ / *m* -ɪd, fɪkst
**sp** fix[1], fixe[2] / fixes[1] / fixeth[1] / fixing[2] / fix'd[3], fixed[3], fixt[12]
**rh** commixed *LC 27*; intermixed *S 101.6*; mixed *Luc 561, VA 487*
> unfix

**fixed** *adj*
*m* 'fɪksɪd, fɪkst
**sp** fix'd[1], fixed[11], fixt[9]
> ever-fixed

**fixture** *n*
'fɪkstəɹ
**sp** fixture[1]

**fixure** *n*
'fɪksəɹ
**sp** fixure[2]

**flag / ~s** *n*
=
**sp** flag[2], flagge[5] / flagges[2]

**flagging** *adj*
'flagɪn, -ɪŋ
**sp** flagging[1]

**flagon / ~s** *n*
=
**sp** flaggon[1] / flagons[1]

**flail** *n*
flɛ:l
**sp** flaile[1]

**flake / ~s** *n*
flɛ:ks
**sp** flakes[1]

**flaky** *adj*
'flɛ:kəɪ
**sp** flakie[1]

**flam·e / ~s** *n*
flɛ:m / -z
**sp** flame[14] / flames[9]

**flam·e / ~s / ~eth / ~ed** *v*
flɛ:m / -z / 'flɛ:məθ / flɛ:md
**sp** flame[4] / flames[2] / flameth[1] / flam'd[1]
**rh** out-burneth *PP 7.13*

**flame-coloured** *adj*
'flɛ:m-ˌkɤləɹd
**sp** flame-coloured[1]
> colour

**flamen / ~s** *n*
'flamɪn / -z
**sp** flamen[1] / flamins[1]

**flaming** *adj*
'flɛ:mɪn, -ɪŋ
**sp** flaming[5]

**Flaminius** *n*
flə'mɪnɪəs
**sp** Flaminius[9]

**Flanders** *n*
'flandəɹz
**sp** Flanders[2]

**flannel** *n*
=
**sp** flannell[1]

**flap** *n*
=
**sp** flap[1]

**flap-dragon / ~s** *n*
=
**sp** flapdra-gon[1] / flap-dragons[1]
> dragon

**flap-dragon / ~ed** *v*
=
**sp** flap-dragon'd[1]

**flap-eared** *adj*
'flap-ˌi:ɹd
**sp** flap-ear'd[1]

**flar·e / ~ing** *v*
'flɛ:rɪn, -ɪŋ
**sp** flaring[1]

**flash / ~es** *n*
=
**sp** flash[4] / flashes[3]
**rh** rash *Cym 4.2.270*

**flashing** *adj*
'flaʃɪn, -ɪŋ
**sp** flashing[1]

**flask** *n*
=
**sp** flaske[2]

**flat** *adj / adv*
=
**sp** flat[21] / flat[2]
**rh** fat *LLL 3.1.99*

**flat / ~s** *n*
=
**sp** flat[2] / flats[5]

**flatlong** *adv*
=
**sp** flat-long[1]
> long

**flatly** *adv*
'flatləɪ
**sp** flatly[4]

**flatness** *n*
=
**sp** flatnesse[1]

**flatter / ~est / ~s / ~ing / ~ed** *v*
'flatəɹ / -st / -z / *m* -ɪn, -ɪŋ, 'flatrɪn / -d
**sp** flatter[39], flat-ter[1] / flatter'st[2] / flatters / flattering[3], flatt'ring[1] / flatter'd[10], flattered[4], flattred[1]
**rh** *1* matter *S 87.13*; **rh** *2* water *Luc 1560*

**flatterer / ~'s / ~s** *n*
*m* 'flatrəɹ, -tər-, -təˌrɐ:ɹ / -z
**sp** flatterer[12], flat-terer[1] / flatterers[2] / flatterers[12]

**flattering** *adj / n*
*m* 'flatrɪn, -ɪŋ, -tər-
**sp** flatt'ring[4], flattering[11] / flattering[1]
**rh** *n* king *PP 20.39*

**flattering-sweet** *adj*
'flatrɪn-'swi:t, -ɪŋ-, -tər-
**sp** flattering sweet[1]
> sweet

**flatter·y / ~ies** *n*
*m* 'flatrəɪ, -tər-, -təˌr- / -z
**sp** flatterie[9], flattery[11] / flatteries[5]
**rh** alchemy *S 114.2*; battery *VA 425*; be *Tim 1.2.254*; villainy *Per 4.4.45*

**flaunt / ~s** *n*
=
**sp** flaunts[1]

**Flavia / ~'s** *n*
'flavɪəz
**sp** Flauia's[1]

**Flavio** *n*
'flavɪo:
**sp** Flauio[1]

**Flavius** *n*
'flavɪəs
**sp** Flauius[8]

**flaw / ~s** *n*
=
**sp** flaw[4], flawe[1] / flawes[4]
**rh** awe *Ham 5.1.212*; law *LLL 5.2.415*

**flaw / ~ing / ~ed** *v*
'flɔ:ɪn, -ɪŋ / =
**sp** flawing[1] / flaw'd[2]

**flawed** *adj*
=
**sp** flaw'd[1]
> honour-flawed

**flax** *n*
=
**sp** flax[3]

**flaxen** *adj*
=
**sp** flaxen[1]

**flax-wench** *n*
=
**sp** flax-wench[1]
> wench

**flay / ~ed** *v*
flɛ:d
**sp** flayd[2], flay'd[1], flead[1], fled[1]

**flaying** *n*
'flɛ:ɪn, -ɪŋ
**sp** flaying[1], fleaing[1]

**flea / ~'s / ~s** *n*
=
**sp** flea[5] / fleas[1] / fleas[2]

**Fleance** *n*
'fli:əns
**sp** Fleance[2], Fleans[9]

**fleckled** *adj*
=
**sp** fleckel'd[1], fleckled[1]

**fled**
> flee

**fledge / ~d** *v*
=
**sp** fledg'd[2]
> unfledged

**flee / fled** *v*
=
**sp** flea[1], flee[1] / fled[86], fledde[1]
**rh** he *LLL 3.1.63* / dead *1H6 4.7.49, MND 5.1.294, PP 17.31, PT 23, R2 2.4.16, 3.2.74, 77, S 71.3, Tim 3.3.36, VA 947*; fed *VA 793*; head *KL 3.6.72, MND 3.2.405, S 148.3, VA 1037*

**fleece / ~s** *n*
=
**sp** fleece[7] / fleeces[1]

**fleece / ~d** *v*
=
**sp** fleece[1] / fleec'd[1]

**fleer / ~s** *n*
fli:ɹz
**sp** fleeres[1]

**fleer / ~ed** *v*
fli:ɹ / -d
**sp** fleere[2] / fleer'd[1]

**fleering** *adj*
'fli:rɪn, -ɪŋ
**sp** flearing[1]

**fleet / ~er** *adj*
= / 'fli:təɹ
**sp** fleete[1] / fleeter[2]

**fleet** *n*
=
**sp** fleet[6], fleete[10]
> after-fleet

**fleet / ~est / ~ing** *v*
= / fli:tst / 'fli:tɪn, -ɪŋ
**sp** fleet[4], fleete[3] / fleet'st[1] / fleeting[1]
**rh** sweets *S 19.5*

**fleeting** *adj*
'fli:tɪn, -ɪŋ
**sp** fleeting[2]

**Fleming** *n*
=
**sp** Fleming[1]

**Flemish** *adj*
=
**sp** Flemish[1]

**flesh** *n*
=
**sp** flesh[123]

**flesh / ~es / ~ed** *v*
=
**sp** flesh[4] / fleshes[1] / flesh'd[1], flesht[2]

**fleshed** *adj*
=
**sp** flesh'd[2], flesht[1]

**flesh-fly** *n*
'fleʃ-ˌfləɪ
**sp** flesh-flie[1]

**fleshly** *adj*
'fleʃləɪ
**sp** fleshly[1]

**fleshment** *n*
=
**sp** fleshment[1]

**fleshmonger** *n*
'fleʃˌmɤŋgəɹ
**sp** flesh-mon-ger[1]

**fleur-de-luce**
> flower-de-luce

**flew**
> fly

**flewed** *adj*
=
**sp** flew'd[1]

**flexible** *adj*
=
**sp** flexible[2]

**flexure** *n*
'fleksəɹ
**sp** flexure[1]

**Flibbertigibbet** *n*
ˌflɪbəɹtɪ'ʤɪbɪt
**sp** Flibbertigibbet[1]

**flickering** *adj*
'flɪkrɪn, -ɪŋ, -kər-
**sp** flickring[1]

**flier / ~s** *n*
'fləɪəɹz
**sp** fliers[1]

**flight / ~s** *n*
fləɪt / -s
**sp** flight[53] / flights[2]
**rh** affright, night *Luc 968*; delight, night *Luc 695*; fight *R2 1.3.61*; light

*MND 5.1.297*; might *LC 244*; night *MND 1.1.246, 4.1.98*; plight *3H6 3.3.36*; right *KJ 5.4.60*; tonight *Mac 3.1.140*

**flighty** *adj*
'flǝɪtǝɪ
**sp** flighty[1]

**flinch** *v*
=
**sp** flinch[2]

**fling** *n*
=
**sp** fling[1]

**fling / flong / flung** *v*
= / = / flɤŋ
**sp** fling[5] / flong[2] / flung[3]

**flint / ~s** *n*
=
**sp** flint[18] / flints[2]
**rh** stint *Per 4.4.43*

**Flint** [name] *n*
=
**sp** Flint[1]

**flinty** *adj*
'flɪntǝɪ
**sp** flintie[5], flinty[5]

**flirt-gill / ~s** *n*
'flɐːɹt-ˌʤɪlz
**sp** flurt-gils[1]
> Gill

**float** *n*
flo:t
**sp** flote[1]
> afloat

**float / ~ing / ~ed** *v*
flo:t / 'flo:t·ɪn, -ɪŋ / -ɪd
**sp** floate[1], flote[1] / floating[1] / floated[1]

**floating** *n*
'flo:tɪn, -ɪŋ
**sp** floating[1]

**flock / ~s** *n*
=
**sp** flock[2], flocke[12] / flockes[4]
**rh** rocks *PP 19.6*

**flock** *v*
=
**sp** flock[1], flocke[4]

**flood / ~s** *n*
flɤd / -z
**sp** flood[39], floud[6] / floods[7], flouds[4]
**rh** *1* blood *Luc 653, 1741, TC 1.3.300*; blood, mud *LC 44* / **rh** *2* good *Luc 653, 1118*; stood *Luc 266, 1741, PP 6.14*; wood *VA 824* / **rh** *3* food *Luc 1118*; **rh** *4* moved [*also emend* mood] *Per 3.Chorus.45*

**floodgate / ~s** *n*
'flɤd-ˌgɛːt / -s
**sp** flood-gate[1] / floud-gates[1]

**floor** *n*
flɔːɹ
**sp** floore[4]
**rh** roar *MND 5.1.216*

**Flora** *n*
=
**sp** Flora[1]

**Florence / ~'s** *n*
=
**sp** Florence[13], Flo-rence[1] / Florences[1]

**Florentine / ~s** *n*
'flɒrǝnˌtǝɪn / -z
**sp** Florentine[1] / Florentines[2]

**Florentius / ~'** *n*
flɒ'rensɪǝs
**sp** Florentius[1]

**Florizel** *n*
'flɒrɪˌzel
**sp** Florizel[1], Florizell[7]
**rh** well *WT 4.1.22*

**flourish / ~es** *n*
'flɤrɪʃ / -ɪz
**sp** florish[6], flourish[109], *abbr in s.d.* flo[2], flor[2] / flourishes[1]
> overflourish

**flourish / ~es / ~eth / ~ed** *v*
'flɤrɪʃ / -ɪz / -ǝθ / -t
**sp** flourish[12] / flourishes[2], flou-rishes[1] / florisheth[1] / flourish'd[3], flourisht[1]
**rh** nourisheth *TS 2.1.333*

**flourishing** *adj*
'flɤrɪʃɪn, -ɪŋ
**sp** flourishing[3]

**flout / ~s** *n*
flǝʊt / -s
**sp** flout[3] / floutes[1]
**rh** out *LLL* 5.2.269, 397

**flout / ~s / ~ing / ~ed** *v*
flǝʊt / -s / 'flǝʊt·ɪn, -ɪŋ / ɪd
**sp** flout[15], floute[1], flowt[2] / flouts[1] / flouting[1], flowting[1] / flouted[1], flowted[3]
**rh** flout 'em scout 'em *Tem 3.2.122*

**flouting** *adj*
'flǝʊtɪn, -ɪŋ
**sp** flowting[1]

**flouting-stock** *n*
*Evans MW 3.1.108* 'vlǝʊtɪn-ˌstɒg, -ɪŋ- / *MW 4.5.74* -ˌstɒks
**sp** vlowting-stog[1], vlouting stocks[1]
> stock

**flow / ~s** *n*
flo: / flo:z
**sp** flow[8] / flowes[2]

**flow / ~s / ~ing / ~ed / ~n** *v*
flo: / -z / 'flo:ɪn, -ɪŋ / flo:d / flo:n
**sp** flow[19], flowe[1] / flowes[5] / flowing[1] / flow'd[4], flowed[1] / flowne[6]
**rh** go *Cym 3.5.161*; know *AW 5.3.323*; woe *H8 Prol.4, S 30.5* / rose *LLL 4.3.27, TNK 5.1.163* / shown *AW 2.1.139*
> overflow

**flower / ~'s / ~s** *n*
flo:ɹ / flo:ɹz
**sp** flower[35], flowre[8] / flowers[1] / flours[1], flowers[31], flowres[22]
**rh** bower *MND 3.1.194*; devour *Luc 1254*; dower *AW 5.3.324*; hour *AY 5.3.29, PP 13.5, TN 2.4.38, VA 1188*; hour, power *LC 75*; power *LC 147, MND 4.1.72, RJ 2.3.19, S 65.4, VA 946*; scour *MW 5.5.62* / bowers *TN 1.1.41*; devours, ours *Luc 870*; hours *LLL 4.3.356, PP 14.28, S 16.7*; ours *Cym 5.4.98, RJ 2.3.4*; showers *Ham 4.5.38, H8 3.1.6, Tem 4.1.78, VA 65*
> crow-, de-flower

**flower-de-luce / ~s** *n*
'flo:ɹ-də-'lu:s / -ɪz
**sp** fleure-de-luce[1], flower-de-luce[1], flowre-de-luce[1] / flower-de-luces[2]
> luce

**flowered** *adj*
*m* flo:ɹd, 'flo:ɹɪd
**sp** flowr'd[1], flowred[1]

**floweret / ~s** *n*
'flo:ɹəts
**sp** flouriets[1], flowrets[1]

**flowering** *adj*
'flo:rɪn, -ɪŋ
**sp** flowring[4]

**flower-soft** *adj*
'flo:ɹ-ˌsɒft
**sp** flower-soft[1]
> soft

**flowery** *adj*
'flo:ɹəɪ
**sp** flowrie[2], flowry[2]

**flowing** *adj*
flo:ɪn, -ɪŋ
**sp** flowing[3]
> water-flowing

**Fluellen** *n*
flu:'elən
**sp** Fluellen[18]

**fluent** *adj*
=
**sp** fluent[1]

**flung**
> fling

**flush** *adj*
flɤʃ
**sp** flush[2]

**flushing** *n*
'flɤʃɪn, -ɪŋ
**sp** flushing[1]

**fluster / ~ed** *v*
'flɤstəɹd
**sp** fluster'd[1]

**flute / ~s** *n*
=
**sp** flutes[2]

**Flute** [name] *n*
=
**sp** Flute[5]

**flux** *n*
flɤks
**sp** fluxe[2]

**fly / flies** *n*
fləɪ / -z
**sp** flie[3], fly[8], flye[3] / flies[11], flyes[6]
> butter-, water-fly

**fl·y / ~ies / ~eth / ~ing / flew** *v*
fləɪ / -z / 'fləɪ·əθ / -ɪn, -ɪŋ / =
**sp** flie[34], fly[31], flye[158] / flies[16], flyes[19] / flyeth[2] / flying[13] / flew[5]
**rh** *1* cry *Cym 5.4.92, Tem 5.1.91*; die *AW 2.1.167, 1H6 4.5.21, 44, 55, 4.6.46, 3H6 4.4.34, Luc 230, RJ 3.1.174*; dry *R2 2.2.146*; eye *LC 249, 325, Luc 177, 1014, RJ 1.3.100*; high *AW 2.3.73*; I *2H6 2.1.159, MND 3.2.416, TN 3.4.364*; I, lie *Tem 5.1.91*; nigh *Oth 2.1.150*; pie *TNK 1.1.24*; sky *Luc 1406*; *MND 3.2.24, R2 1.1.42*;
**rh** *2* advisedly *Luc 177*; chivalry *1H6 4.6.28*; deity *Cym 5.4.92*; destiny *Luc 1728*; enemy *JC 5.3.1*; majesty *S 78.6*; merrily *Tem 5.1.91*; mutiny, readily *Luc 1150*; perdy *KL 2.4.79* / **rh** *1* advise *Per 4.3.50*; eyes, hies *Luc 1216*; spies *VA 1027*; **rh** *2* adulteries *Cym 5.4.31*; enemies *Ham 3.2.214*; **rh** *3* precise *LLL 5.2.408* / dying *TNK 1.5.6*; lying *TG 3.1.141* / drew, knew *LC 60*
> overfly

**fly-bitten** *adj*
'fləɪ-ˌbɪtən
**sp** fly-bitten[1]
> bitten

**fly-blowing** *n*
'fləɪ-ˌblo:ɪn, -ɪŋ
**sp** fly-blowing[1]
> blow

**fly-blown** *adj*
'fləɪ-ˌblo:n
**sp** fly-blowne[1]

**flyer / ~s** *n*
'fləɪəɹz
**sp** flyers[3]

**flying** *adj*
'fləɪɪn, -ɪŋ
**sp** flying[3]

**foal** *n*
fo:l
**sp** foale[1]
**rh** bowl *MND 2.1.46*

**foal / ~s** *v*
fo:lz
**sp** foles[1]

**foam** *n*
fo:m
**sp** fome[2]

**foam / ~s / ~ed** *v*
fo:m / -z / -d
**sp** foame[1] / foames[2], fomes[1] / foam'd[1]

**foaming** *adj*
'fo:mɪn, -ɪŋ
**sp** foaming[4], foming[1]

**foamy** *adj*
'fo:məɪ
**sp** foamy[1]

**fob / ~bed** *v*
=
**sp** fobbe[2] / fobb'd[1]

**fodder** *n*
'fɒdəɹ
**sp** fodder[1]

**foe / ~'s / ~s** *n*
fo: / -z
**sp** foe[61], foes [foe is][1] / foes[1] / foes[66]
**rh** go *1H6 4.5.37, Luc 77, R2 5.4.11, RJ 1.1.80, TC 1.3.309*; know *KJ 5.1.79, PP 20.56*; lo *RJ 2.3.50*; know, show *Luc 471*; know, woe *Luc 1608*; no *1H6 4.7.26*; snow *VA 364*; so *Luc 1035, 1196, 1683, 1827, MND 3.2.44, RJ 1.5.61, Tim 2.2.238* / close *TG 5.4.119*; goes *1H6 3.1.187, Luc 988, R2 2.4.23, Tit 5.2.147, VA 620, 684*; knows *S 139.11*; oppose *KJ 3.1.171*; overthrows *RJ Prol.5*; repose, woes *Luc 936*; shows *S 40.14*; shows, woes *TNK 1.5.8*; those *Mac 2.4.41*; those, woes *Luc 1460*; throes *Cym 5.4.46*; woes *KL 3.6.101 [Q]*
> night-foe

**foeman / ~'s / foemen / ~'s** *n*
'fo:mən / -z
**sp** foe-man[1] / foe-mans[1] / foe-men[2] / foe-mens[1]

**fog / ~s** *n*
=
**sp** fog[1], [south]-fog[1], fogge[5] / fogges[3]

**foggy** *adj*
'fɒgəɪ
**sp** foggy[3]

**foh** *interj*
fɔ:
**sp** foh[6]

**foh** *Fr interj*
fo
**sp** fo

**foi** *Fr n*
fwɛ
**sp** foy[3]

**foil / ~s** *n*
fəɪl / -z
**sp** foile[2], foyle[4] / foiles[2], foyles[7]
**rh** spoil *LC 153*

**foil / ~ed** *v*
fəɪl / fəɪld
**sp** foile[1], foyle[3] / foil'd[1], foyld[1], foyl'd[1]
**rh** toiled *S 25.10*

**foin / ~s** *n*
fəɪnz
**sp** foynes[1]

**foin / ~ing** *v*
fəɪn / 'fəɪnɪn, -ɪŋ
**sp** foigne[1], foyne[1] / foyning[1]

**foining** *adj*
'fəɪnɪn, -ɪŋ
**sp** foyning[1]

**fois** *Fr n*
fwɛ
**sp** [autre]foys, foyes[1]

**foison / ~s** *n*
'fəɪzən / -z
**sp** foizon[1], foyson[1], foyzon[2] / foysons[1]

**Foix** *n*
fwɛ
**sp** Foyes[1]

**fold / ~s** *n*
fo:ld / -z
**sp** fold[2], foulde[1] / folds[1]
**rh** controlled *Luc 679*
> fifty-, five-, nine-, seven-, ten-, thousand-, three-, two-fold

**fold / ~s / ~ed** *v*
fo:ld / -z / 'fo:ldɪd
**sp** fold[11], folde[1], foulde[1] / folds[1] / folded[3]
> blind-, en-, un-fold

**folded** *adj*
'fo:ldɪd
**sp** folded[1], foulded[2]

**folio** *n*
'fo:lɪo:
**sp** folio[1]

**folk / ~s** *n*
fo:k, *Edgar's assumed dialect KL 4.6.237* vo:k / -s
**sp** folke[3], *Edgar* volke[1] / folkes[11], folks[1], [olde]-folkes[1]

**follow / ~est / ~s / ~ing / ~ed / ~est** *v*
'fɒlə, -lo: / -st / -z / -wɪn, -ɪŋ / -d / -dst
**sp** follow[293], fol-low[5], followe[1], folow[1] / followest[1], follow'st[1] / followes[65], fol-lowes[1], follows[1] / following[21] / follow'd[26], followed[34], fol-lowed[1] / followd'st[1]
**rh** hollow *VA 975*

**follower / ~s** *n*
'fɒləwəɹ / -z
**sp** follower[10] / followers[43], fol-lowers[2], followres[1], folowers[1]

**following** *adj / n*
'fɒləwɪn, -ɪŋ
**sp** following[7] / following[2]

**foll·y / ~ies** *n*
'fɒləɪ / -z
**sp** follie[5], folly[71], fol-ly[1] / follies[9], follyes[3]
**rh** dally *Luc 556*; holly *AY 2.7.182, 192*

**folly-fallen** *adj*
'fɒləɪ-ˌfa:ln
**sp** folly falne[1]
> fall

**fond / ~er** *adj*
= / 'fɒndəɹ
**sp** fond[53] / fonder[1]
**rh** bond *Luc 134, Tim 1.2.63*
> overfond

**fondly** *adv*
'fɒndləɪ
**sp** fondly[9]

**fondness** *n*
=
**sp** fondnesse[3]

**font** *n*
=
**sp** font[2]

**Fontybell** *n*
=
**sp** Fontybell[1]

**food** *n*
=, fʊd
**sp** food[42], foode[21], *emend of TS 4.1.128* soud[4]
**rh** good, flood *Luc 1115*

**fool** *adj*
fʊl, =
**sp** foole[1]
**pun** *TC 5.1.9* full

**fool / ~'s / ~s / ~s'** *n*
fʊl, = / -z
**sp** fool[3], foole[417], 'foole[1], [holiday]-foole[1], [struck]-foole[1], foole's [fool is][1] / fooles[12], [an]-fooles[1] / fooles[93], fools[3] / fooles[3]
**rh** cool *Mac 4.1.152*; school *LLL 4.2.30, 5.2.72, Luc 1819*; stool *TS 1.1.65*; tool *TNK 3.5.130* / schools *Luc 1016*

**fool / ~ing / ~ed** *v*
fʊl, = / 'fʊlɪn, -ɪŋ, 'fu:l- / fʊld, =
**sp** foole[7] / fooling[1] / fool'd[3]
> unfool

**fool-begged** *adj*
'fʊl-ˌbegd, 'fu:l-
**sp** foole-beg'd[1]
> beg

**fool-born** *adj*
'fʊl-ˌbɔ:ɹn, 'fu:l-
**sp** foole-borne[1]

**fooler·y / ~ies** *n*
'fʊlrəɪ, 'fu:l-, -lər- / -z
**sp** foolerie[8], foo-lerie[1], foolery[4], foolrie[1], fool'rie[1], fool'ry[2] / fooleries[1]

**foolhardiness** *n*
'fʊl-ˌɑ:ɹdɪnəs, -ˌhɑ:-, 'fu:l-
**sp** foole-hardinesse[1]
> hardiness

**foolhardy** *adj*
*m* 'fʊl-ˌɑ:ɹdəɪ, 'fu:l-, -ˌhɑ:-, ˌfʊl-'ɑ:-, ˌfu:l-, -'hɑ:-
**sp** foole-hardie[1], foole-hardy[1]

**fooling** *n*
'fʊlɪn, -ɪŋ, 'fu:l-
**sp** fooling[9]

**foolish** *adj*
'fʊlɪʃ, 'fu:l-
**sp** foolish[90], foo-lish[2], *emend of MW 3.3.181* foolishion[1]
> fool

**foolishly** *adv*
*m* 'fʊlɪʃləɪ, -ˌləɪ, 'fu:l-
**sp** foolishly[5]

**foolishness** *n*
*m* 'fʊlɪʃˌnes, 'fu:l-
**sp** foolishnes[1]

**foot / feet** *n*
=
**sp** foot[89], foote[68], [on]-foot[1], [s]foote [God's foot] [1] / feet[24], feete[32]
**rh** boot *1H6 4.6.53, R2 1.1.165, TS 5.2.176*; root *Luc 664*; to't *LLL 5.2.146* / meet *TN 5.1.166*; see't *KL 3.2.94*; street *CE 3.1.37*; sweet *LLL 5.2.330, TNK 1.1.14*
> a-, bare-, dry-, fore-, light-, three-, under-foot

**foot / ~ed** *v*
=
**sp** foot[2], foote[4] / footed[4]
> fiery-, free-, hasty-, nimble-, tiger-footed

**football** *n*
'fʊtbɑ:l
**sp** foot-ball[2]
> ball

**footboy / ~s** *n*
'fʊtbəɪ / -z
**sp** foot-boy[2], foot-boyes[2]

**foot-cloth** *n*
=
**sp** foot-cloth[2], foot-cloth-[horse][1]
> cloth

**footfall** *n*
'fʊtfɑ:l
**sp** foot fall[1], foot-fall[1]
> fall

**footing** *n*
'fʊtɪn, -ɪŋ
**sp** footing[14]

**foot-landraker / ~s** *n*
'fʊt-landˌrɛ:kəɹz
**sp** foot-land-rakers[1]

**foot-licker** *n*
'fʊt-ˌlɪkəɹ
**sp** foot-licker[1]
> lick

**foot·man / ~men** *n*
=
**sp** footeman[1], footman[3], foot-man[1] / [warre-markt]-footmen

**footpath** *n*
'fʊtpaθ
**sp** foot-path[2]
> path

**footsteps** *n*
=
**sp** footsteps[1]

**footstool** *n*
'fʊtstʊl, -stu:l
**sp** footstoole[1]
> stool

**fop / ~s** *n*
=
**sp** fops[1]

**fopped** *adj*
=
**sp** fopt[1]

**foppery** *n*
'fɒprəɪ, -pər-
**sp** fopperie[1], foppery[2], fop-pery[1]

**foppish** *adj*
=
**sp** foppish[1]
**rh** apish *KL 1.4.164*

**for** *prep*
*str* fɔːɹ, *unstr* fəɹ, *Edgar's assumed dialect KL 4.6.244, Caius MW 2.3.82* vɔːɹ
**sp** for[7343], for's [for his][9], for't [for it][77], *Edgar, Caius* vor[2]
**rh** short *Per 4.4.2*

**forage** *n*
=
**sp** forrage[1]
**rh** courage *VA 554*

**forager / ~s** *n*
'fɒrɪʤəɹz
**sp** forragers[1]

**forbear / ~s / forborn** *v*
fəɹ'bɛːɹ / -z / fəɹ'bɔːɹn
**sp** forbeare[54], forbear't [forbear it][1] / forbeares[1] / forborne[1]
**rh** *1* forswear *LLL 5.2.439*; there *S 41.9*; where *CE 2.1.31* [*also as* other-where]; **rh** *2* fear *AC 1.3.11*; **forbear thee** near thee *Cym 4.2.278* / years *VA 526*

**forbearance** *n*
fəɹ'bɛːɹəns
**sp** forbearance[6]

**for·bid / ~s / ~bad / ~bidden** *v*
fəɹ'bɪd / -z / fəɹ'bad / fəɹ'bɪdən
**sp** forbid[70] / forbids[6] / forbad[3] / forbidden[3]
**rh** did *LC 150*; eyelid *MND 2.2.86*; hid *LLL 1.1.62, S 65.12*; lid *Mac 1.3.21*

**forbidden** *adj*
fəɹ'bɪdən
**sp** forbidden[2]

**forbiddenly** *adv*
*m* fəɹ'bɪdən,ləɪ
**sp** forbiddenly[1]

**force / ~s** *n*
fɔːɹs / 'fɔːɹsɪz
**sp** force[76] / forces[20]
**rh** horse *S 91.2, VA 29*

**forc·e / ~ing / ~ed** *v*
fɔːɹs / 'fɔːɹsɪn, -ɪŋ / fɔːɹst
**sp** force[25] / forcing[2] / forc;d[20], forced[1], forc;t[1], forst[2]
> enforce

**force** *Fr n*
fɔɹs
**sp** force[1]

**forced** *adj*
*m* 'fɔːɹsɪd, fɔːɹst
**sp** forc'd[5], forced[6], forc't[1], for'st[1]
> unforced

**forceful** *adj*
'fɔːɹsfʊl
**sp** forcefull[1]

**forceless** *adj*
'fɔːɹsləs
**sp** forcelesse[1]

**forcible** *adj*
*m* 'fɔːɹsɪbəl, -,bɤl
**sp** forceable[1], forcible[2]

**forcibly** *adv*
*m* 'fɔːɹsɪbləɪ, -,ləɪ,
**sp** forcibly[3]

**forcing** *adj*
'fɔːɹsɪn, -ɪŋ
**sp** forcing[1]

**ford / ~s** *Luc* *n*
fɔːɹdz
**sp** foords[1]
**rh** words *Luc 1329*

**Ford / ~'s** [name] *n*
fɔːɹd / -z
**sp** Ford[77], Ford's [Ford is][1] / Fords[11]
**rh** word *MW 5.5.237*

**for·do / ~does / ~did / ~done** *v*
fəɹ'duː / -'dɤz / -'dɪd / -'dɤn
**sp** fore do[1] / foredoes[2] / for-did[1] / fore-done[2]
**rh** moon *MND 5.1.364*

**fore** *prep*
fɔːɹ
**sp** 'fore[17], fore[10], 'fore-[noone][1]

**fore-advised** *adj*
'fɔːɹ-əd'vəɪzd
**sp** fore-aduis'd[1]
> advise

**forecast** *n*
*m* fɔːɹ'kast
**sp** fore-cast[1]
> cast

**fore-end** *n*
'fɔːɹ-,end
**sp** fore-end[1]
> end

**forefather / ~s / ~s'** *n*
*m* ,fɔːɹ'faðəɹ / -z
**sp** fore-father[1] / fore-fathers[1] / forefathers[1], fore-fathers[1]
> father

**forefinger** *n*
'fɔːɹ,fɪŋgəɹ
**sp** fore-finger[2]
> finger

**forefoot** *n*
'fɔːɹ,fʊt
**sp** fore-foote[1]
> foot

**forego / ~ne** *v*
fəɹ'goː, ,fɔːɹ- / fəɹ'goːn, -gɒn, ,fɔːɹ-
**sp** forgo[2], forgoe[6] / forgone[1]
**rh** *1* none *AW 1.3.129*; **rh** *2* moan *S 30.9*
> go

**foregoer / ~s** *n*
ˌfɔːɹˈgoːəɹz
**sp** fore-goers[1]

**foregone** *adj*
fəɹˈgoːn, -gɒn, ˌfɔːɹ-
**sp** fore-gone[1], forgon[1]

**forehand** *adj / n*
*m* ˌfɔːɹˈand, -ˈha-, ˈfɔːɹˌand, -ˌha-
**sp** forehand[1], fore-hand[1] / fore-hand[2]
> aforehand, hand

**forehead / ~s** *n*
ˈfɔːɹˌed, -ˌhe- / -z
**sp** forehead[11], fore-head[5], fore-head's [forehead is][1], forhead[5], for-head[1] / foreheads[1]
> head

**forehorse** *n*
ˈfɔːɹˌɔːɹs, -ˌhɔː-
**sp** for-horse[1]
> horse

**foreign** *adj*
=
**sp** forraigne[12], forraine[10], forreigne[1], forreine[2], forren[1]

**foreigner / ~s** *n*
ˈfɒrɪnəɹ / -z
**sp** forreyner[1] / forreyners[1]

**foreknowing** *n*
ˌfɔːɹˈnoːɪn, -ɪŋ
**sp** foreknowing[1], fore-knowing[1]
> know

**foreknowledge** *n*
ˌfɔːɹˈnɒlɪʤ
**sp** fore knowledge[1]

**foremost** *adj / adv*
ˈfɔːɹmoːst
**sp** formost[2] / formost[3]
> most

**forenamed** *adj*
ˈfɔːɹˌnɛːmd
**sp** fore-named[1]
> name

**forenoon** *n*
ˈfɔːɹˌnuːn, -ˌnʊn
**sp** forenoone[2]
> noon

**fore-past** *adj*
ˈfɔːɹ-ˌpast
**sp** fore-past[1]
> past

**fore-rank** *n*
ˈfɔːɹ-ˌraŋk
**sp** fore-ranke[1]
> rank

**fore-recited** *adj*
ˈfɔːɹ-rɪˌsəɪtɪd
**sp** fore-recited[1]

**fore-run / ~s / ~ning** *v*
ˌfɔːɹ-ˈrɤn / -z / -ɪn, -ɪŋ
**sp** fore-run[2], fore-runne[2] / fore-runnes[1] / forerunning[1]
> run

**fore-runner** *n*
ˌfɔːɹ-ˈrɤnəɹ
**sp** fore-runner[3]

**foresaid** *adj*
ˈfɔːɹˌsed
**sp** foresaid[6]
> aforesaid

**fore·say** *v*
ˌfɔːɹ-ˈsɛː
**sp** fore-say[1]
> say

**foresee / ~s / ~ing / foresaw** *v*
ˌfɔːɹˈsiː / -z / -ɪn, -ɪŋ / fɔːɹˈsɔː
**sp** foresee[5], fore-see[1] / foresees[1] / fore-seeing[1] / forsaw[1]
> see

**fore-show / ~ed** *v*
ˌfɔːɹ-ˈʃoːd
**sp** fore-shew'd[1]
> show

**fore-skirt** *n*
ˈfɔːɹ-ˌskɐːɹt
**sp** fore-skirt[1]
> skirt

**foreslow** *v*
ˌfɔːɹ-ˈsloː
**sp** foreslow[1]
> slow

**fore·speak / ~spoke** *v*
ˌfɔːɹ-ˈspoːk
**sp** forespoke[1]
> speak

**forespen·d / ~t** *v*
ˌfɔːɹ-ˈspent
**sp** fore-spent[4]
> spend

**fore-spurrer** *n*
ˌfɔːɹ-ˈspɐːɹəɹ
**sp** fore-spurrer[1]
> spur

**forest** *adj*
=
**sp** forrest[4]

**forest / ~s** *n*
=
**sp** forest[1], forrest[39], for-rest[1] / forrests[2]

**forestall / ~ed** *v*
ˌfɔːɹ-ˈstɑːl / *m* -d, -ɪd
**sp** forestall[2], fore-stall[3] / fore-stall'd[1], fore-stalled[1]

**forestalled** *adj*
ˌfɔːɹ-ˈstɑːld
**sp** fore-stall'd[1]

**forest-born** *adj*
ˈfɒrɪst-ˌbɔːɹn
**sp** forrest borne[1]
> born

**forester / ~s** *n*
ˈfɒrɪstəɹ / -z
**sp** forrester[7] / forresters[2], forre-sters[1]

**foretell / ~s / ~ing / ~foretold** *v*
ˌfɔːɹ-ˈtel / -z / -ɪn, -ɪŋ / ˌfɔːɹ-ˈtoːld

**sp** foretell[2], fore-tell[3] / fore-tells[1], fore-tels[1], fortels[1] / fore-telling[1] / foretold[3], fore-told[1]
> tell

**forethink / ~ing / forethought** *v*
ˌfɔːɹ-ˈθɪŋk / -ɪn, -ɪŋ / ˌfɔːɹ-ˈθɔːt
**sp** fore-thinke[1] / fore-thinking[1] / fore-thought[1]
> think

**foretold**
> foretell

**fore-vouched** *adj*
ˌfɔːɹ-ˈvəʊʧt
**sp** fore-voucht[1]
> vouch

**forewarn / ~ed** *v*
ˌfɔːɹ-ˈwɑːɹn / *m* -d, -ɪd
**sp** forewarne[1] / fore-warn'd[1], fore-warned[1]
> warn

**forewarning** *adj*
ˌfɔːɹ-ˈwɑːɹnɪn, -ɪŋ
**sp** fore-warning[1]

**fore-wearied** *adj*
ˌfɔːɹ-ˈwiːrəɪd, -ˈwe-
**sp** fore-wearied[1]
> weary

**forfeit** *adj*
ˈfɔːɹfɪt
**sp** forfeit[6], forfeite[1]

**forfeit / ~s** *n*
ˈfɔːɹfɪt / -s
**sp** forfeit[10], forfeite[3], forfeyt[1] / forfeites[1], forfeits[2]

**forfeit / ~s / ~ing / ~ed** *v*
ˈfɔːɹfɪt / -s / -ɪn, -ɪŋ / -ɪd
**sp** forfaite[2], forfeit[2], forfeite[1], for-feite[1] / forfeits[1] /forfeyting[2] / forfeited[3], forfeyted[2]
**rh** bring *H8 Prol.19*
> unforfeited

**forfeiter / ~s** *n*
ˈfɔːɹfɪtəɹz
**sp** forfeytours[1]

**forfeit-seller** *n*
ˈfɔːɹfɪt-ˌseləɹ
**sp** forfet-seller[1]

**forfeiture / ~s** *n*
ˈfɔːɹfɪˌtuːɹ / -z
**sp** forfeiture[7], forfeyture[1] / forfeitures[1]

**forfend** *v*
fəɹˈfend, ˈfɔːɹ-
**sp** forefend[4], fore-fend[2], forfend[2]

**forfended** *adj*
fəɹˈfendɪd, ˈfɔːɹ-
**sp** fore-fended[1]

**forge / ~s** *n*
fɔːɹʤ / ˈfɔːɹʤɪz
**sp** forge[3] / forges[1]

**forge / ~s / ~ed** *v*
fɔːɹʤ / ˈfɔːɹʤ·ɪz / *m* -ɪd, ˈfɔːɹʤd
**sp** forge[2] / forges[3] / forged[1], forg'd[6]

**forged** *adj*
*m* ˈfɔːɹʤd, -ʤɪd
**sp** forg'd[2], forged[3]

**forger·y / ~ies** *n*
*m* ˈfɔːɹʤəˌrəɪ / -z
**sp** forgery[2] / forgeries[2]
**rh** eyes, lies *Luc 460*; lies *PP 1.4*

**forget / ~test / ~s / ~ting / forgot / ~ten** *v*
fəɹˈget / -st / -s / -ɪn, -ɪŋ / fəɹˈgɒt / fəɹˈgɒtən
**sp** forget[89], for-get[1] / forgetst[2] / forgets[3] / forgetting[5] / forgot[81], for-got[2], forgott[1] / forgotten[9]
**rh** debt Ham *3.2.202, RJ 1.1.237*; set *MW 5.5.76* / blot, lot *Luc 536*; not *AY 2.7.187, MM 4.4.31, MND 5.1.170, S 71.7 149.3*; overshot *LLL 1.1.139*; rot *CE 3.2.1*; wot *PP 17.5, R2 5.6.17* / rotten *S 81.4*

**forgetful** *adj*
fəɹˈgetfʊl
**sp** forgetfull[4]

**forgetfulness** *n*
*m* fəɹˈgetfʊlˌnes
**sp** forgetfulnesse[5]

**forgetive** *adj*
ˈfɔːɹʤɪtɪv
**sp** forge-tiue[1]

**for·give / ~gave / ~given** *v*
fəɹˈgɪv / fəɹˈgɛːv / fəɹˈgɪvən
**sp** forgiue[73], for-giue[1] / forgaue[2] / forgiuen[4]
**rh** live *AW 3.4.12, 2H4 4.5.218*

**forgiven** *adj*
fəɹˈgɪvən
**sp** forgiuen[1]

**forgiveness** *n*
fəɹˈgɪvnəs
**sp** forgiuenesse[9]

**forgo**
> forego

**forgot** *adj*
fəɹˈgɒt
**sp** forgot[1]

**forgotten** *adj*
fəɹˈgɒtən
**sp** forgotten[5]

**fork / ~s** *n*
fɔːɹk / -s
**sp** forke[3] / forkes[1]

**forked** *adj*
*m* ˈfɔːɹkt, -kɪd
**sp** fork'd[1], forked[6], for-ked[1]

**forlorn** *adj*
*m* ˈfɔːɹlɔːɹn, fəɹˈlɔːɹn
**sp** forlorn[1], forlorne[15], for-lorne[1]
**rh** forsworn *VA 725*; horn *VA 1026*; morn *PP 6.3*; scorn *VA 251*; thorn *PP 20.9*

**form / ~s** *n*
fɔ:ɹm / -z
**sp** form[1], forme[89] / formes[22], forms[1]
**rh** storm *KL 2.4.75, LC 99* / storms *Luc 1519*
> new-form

**form / ~s / ~ed** *v*
fɔ:ɹm / -z / *m* -d, 'fɔ:ɹmɪd
**sp** forme[3], [without-dore]-forme[1] / formes[1] / form'd[3], formed[1]
> pre-formed

**formal** *adj*
'fɔ:ɹmɑl
**sp** formall[10]
> informal

**formally** *adv*
*m* 'fɔ:ɹmɑˌləɪ
**sp** formally[1]

**former** *adj / n*
'fɔ:ɹməɹ
**sp** former[5] / former[51]

**formerly** *adv*
*m* 'fɔ:ɹməɹˌləɪ, -ləɪ
**sp** formerly[7]

**formless** *adj*
'fɔ:ɹmləs
**sp** formelesse[2]

**fornication / ~s** *n*
ˌfɔ:ɹnɪ'kɛ:sɪən / -z
**sp** fornication[3], forni-cation[1] / fornications[1]

**fornicatress** *n*
ˌfɔ:ɹnɪ'kɛ:trəs
**sp** fornicatresse[1]

**Forres** *n*
'fɒrɪs
**sp** *emend of Mac 1.3.38* Soris[1]

**Forrest** *n*
=
**sp** Forrest[3]

**forsake / ~eth / ~n / forsook** *v*
fəɹ'sɛ:k / -əθ / -ən / fəɹ'sʊk
**sp** forsake[22], for-sake[1] / forsaketh[1] / forsaken[4] / forsook[2], forsooke[6]
**rh** make *Luc 157, S 12.11*; forsake him take him *VA 321* / taken *S 133.7* / brook *VA 161*; look, took *Luc 1538*; forsook them overlook them *VA 176*

**forsaken** *n*
fəɹ'sɛ:kən
**sp** forsaken[1]

**forsooth** *adv*
fəɹ'su:θ, -'sʊθ
**sp** forsooth[46], for-sooth[1], [rascally-yea]-forsooth-[knaue][1]
> sooth

**forswear / ~ing / forswor·e / ~n** *v*
fəɹ'swɛ:r / -ɪn, -ɪŋ / fəɹ'swɔ:ɹ / -n
**sp** forswear[3], forsweare[22], for-sweare[3], forsweare't [forswear it][1], forswear't [forswear it][1] / forswearing[1] / forswore[9] / forsworn[4], forsworne[52], for-sworne[2]
**rh** everywhere *MND 1.1.240*; forbear *LLL 5.2.440* / born *LLL 1.1.147, 4.3.217, S 66.4*; corn *LLL 4.3.361*; forlorn *VA 726*; morn *MM 4.1.2*; scorn *S 88.4*; torn *LLL 4.3.281, S 152.1*
> swear

**forswearing** *n*
fəɹ'swɛ:rɪn, -ɪŋ
**sp** forswearing[2]

**fort / ~s** *n*
fɔ:ɹts
**sp** forts[1]
> fortify, fortress, unfortified

**fort** *Fr adv*
fɔ:ɹ
**sp** for[1], fort[1]

**forted** *adj*
'fɔ:ɹtɪd
**sp** forted[1]

**forth** *adv*
'fɔ:ɹθ
**sp** forth[339], foorth[14], [farre]-forth[1]
**rh** *1* north *Per 3.Chorus.48*; **rh** *2* worth *AW 3.4.13, Ham 4.4.65* [*Q2*], *LC 269, S 25.11, 38.11, 72.13, 103.1, VA 416, TC 1.3.242*
> bringing-, casting-, hence-, so-forth

**forthcom·e / ~ing** *v*
fɔ:ɹθ'kɤm / -ɪn, -ɪŋ
**sp** forth comming[1], forth-comming[2]

**Forthlight** [name] *n*
'fɔ:ɹθləɪt
**sp** forthlight[1]

**forthright / ~s** *n*
*m* fɔ:ɹθ'rəɪt / 'fɔ:ɹθrəɪts
**sp** forth right[1] / fourth-rights[1]
> right

**forthwith** *adv*
*m* fɔ:ɹθ'wɪθ, 'fɔ:ɹθwɪθ
**sp** forthwith[22], forth-with[1]

**fortification** *n*
ˌfɔ:ɹtfɪ'kɛ:sɪən
**sp** fortification[1]
> unfortified

**fortif·y / ~ies / ~ied** *v*
*m* 'fɔ:ɹtɪˌfəɪ, -ɪf- / 'fɔ:ɹtɪˌfəɪz / 'fɔ:ɹtɪˌfəɪd, -ɪf-
**sp** fortifie[5] / fortifies[1] / fortified[4]
**rh** memory *S 63.9*

**Fortinbras** *n*
'fɔ:ɹtɪnˌbras
**sp** Fortinbras[13]

**fortitude** *n*
'fɔ:ɹtɪˌtju:d
**sp** fortitude[5]

**fortnight** *n*
'fɔ:ɹtnəɪt, *Edgar's assumed dialect KL 4.6.239* 'vɔ:ɹtnəɪt
**sp** fortnight[7], fort-night[2], *Edgar* vortnight[1]
> night

**fortress / ~es** *n*
'fɔːɹtrəs / -ɪz
**sp** fortresse[3] / fortresses[1]

**fortuna** *Pistol's* *Ital/Span n*
fɔːɹ'tuːnə
**sp** *Pistol 2H4 2.4.176* fortuna[1], *2H4 5.5.99* fortune[1]

**Fortuna** [name] *n*
fɔːɹ'tuːnə
**sp** Fortuna[1]

**fortunate** *adj*
*m attributive* 'fɔːɹtnət, *predicative* 'fɔːɹtən,ɛːt
**sp** fortunate[19]
**rh** create *MND 5.1.396*; mate *1H6 1.2.91*
> in-, un-fortunate

**fortunately** *adv*
*m* 'fɔːɹtən,ɛːtləɪ
**sp** fortunately[3]

**fortune / ~'s / ~s** *n*
'fɔːɹtən / -z
**sp** fortune[300], for-tune[4], [infant]-fortune[1], [strumpet]-fortune[1] / fortunes[37], for-tunes[1] / fortunes[110]
**rh** importune *TG 3.1.147*
> misfortune

**fortune** *Fr n*
fɔɹ'tyn
**sp** fortune

**fortune / ~d** *v*
'fɔːɹtən / *m* 'fɔːɹtə,nɪd
**sp** fortune[1] / fortuned[1]
> full-fortuned

**fortune-tell** *v*
'fɔːɹtən-,tel
**sp** fortune-tell[1]

**fortune-teller** *n*
'fɔːɹtən-,teləɹ
**sp** fortune-teller[1]

**fortune-telling** *n*
'fɔːɹtən-,telɪn, -ɪŋ
**sp** fortune-telling[1]

**forty** *adj / n*
'fɔːɹtəɪ
**sp** fortie[11], forty[14] / fortie[4], forty[1]

**forty-eight** *adj*
,fɔːɹtəɪ-'ɛːt
**sp** forty eight[1]

**forward** *adj / adv / n*
'fɔːɹwəɹd
**sp** forward[30] / forward[37] / foreward[1]
> henceforward

**forward / ~ing** *v*
'fɔːɹwəɹdɪn, -ɪŋ
**sp** forwarding[1]

**forwardness** *n*
*m* 'fɔːɹwəɹd,nes, -nəs
**sp** forwardnesse[5]
**rh** readiness *3H6 5.4.65*

**forwards** *adv*
'fɔːɹwəɹdz
**sp** forwards[3]

**foster / ~ed** *v*
'fɒstəɹ / *m* 'fɒstəɹd, 'fɒstə,rɪd
**sp** foster[1] / foster'd[2], fostered[2]

**fostering** *adj*
'fɒstrɪn, -ɪŋ
**sp** fo-string[1]

**foster-nurse** *n*
'fɒstəɹ-,nɐːɹs
**sp** foster nurse[2]
> nurse

**fought**
> fight

**foul / ~er / ~est** *adj*
fəʊl, foːl / 'fəʊl·əɹ, 'foː- / *m* -əst, fəʊlst, foːlst
**sp** foul[1], foule[186], foule-[play][1], fowle[21], fowle-[fault][1], fowle-[play][1] / fouler[7], fowler[2] / foulest[2], foul'st[1], fowlest[1], fowl'st[1]
**rh** *1* bowl *LLL 4.1.138*; **rh** *2* bowl, owl *LLL 4.1.138, 5.2.905*
**pun** *MW 5.5.10* fowl

**fouled** *adj*
fəʊld
**sp** foul'd[1]

**foul-faced** *adj*
*m* ,fəʊl-'fɛːst
**sp** foule-fac'd[1]
> face

**foully** *adv*
'fəʊləɪ
**sp** fouly[1], fowly[3]

**foul-mouthed / ~est** *adj*
'fəʊl-,məʊθt, -ðd / -θst, -ðst
**sp** foule mouth'd[1], foule-mouth'd[1] / foule-mouth'dst[1]
> mouth

**foulness** *n*
'fəʊlnəs
**sp** foulenesse[1], foulnesse[3], fowlenesse[1]

**foul-spoken** *adj*
*m* ,fəʊl-'spoːkən
**sp** foule spoken[1]
> speak

**found,** *past tense*
> find

**found / ~ed** *v*
'fəʊndɪd
**sp** founded[2]
> find

**foundation / ~s** *n*
*m* fəʊn'dɛːsɪən, -sɪ,ɒn / -sɪənz
**sp** foundation[6] / foundations[3]

**founder** *n*
'fəʊndəɹ
**sp** founder[2]

**founder / ~ed** *v*
'fəʊndəɹ / -d
**sp** founder[1] / founderd[1], fowndred[1]

**fount / ~s** *n*
faʊnt / -s
**sp** fount[2] / founts[1]
**rh** dismount *LC 283*

**fountain / ~s** *n*
'faʊntɪn / -z
**sp** fountaine[13], foun-taine[1] / fountaines[2]

**four** *adj / n*
fɔːɹ
**sp** four[4], foure[74], foure-[threes][1], fowre[2], *abbr* iiii.[1] / four[2], foure[59] fowre[2]
**rh** *1* door *VA 446*; door, more *LLL 3.1.96*; more *LLL 4.3.209; MND 3.2.438*; **rh** *2* hour *LLL 5.2.367*

**four-inched** *adj*
'fɔːɹ-ˌɪnʃt
**sp** foure incht[1]
> inch

**fourscore** *adj*
*m* 'fɔːɹˌskɔːɹ, ˌfɔːɹ'skɔːɹ
**sp** fourescore[12], foure-score[2]
**rh** more *AY 2.3.71*
> score

**fourteen** *adj / n*
*m* 'fɔːɹtiːn, fɔːɹ'tiːn
**sp** foureteene[4], fourteene[6], *abbr* xiiii.[d][1] / foureteene[2], foure-teene[1], fourteene[8]

**fourth** *adj*
fɔːɹθ
**sp** fourth[20]

**foutre** *n*
'fuːtrə, -təɹ
**sp** footra[2]

**fowl / ~s** *n*
faʊl, foːl / -z
**sp** foule[2], fowl[7], fowle[2], [wilde]-fowle[1] / fowles[3]
**rh** controls *CE 2.1.18*; souls *CE 2.1.23*
**pun** *MW 5.5.10* foul
> a-bat-fowling, wildfowl

**fowler** *n*
'faʊləɹ, 'foː-
**sp** fowler[1]

**fox / ~es** *n*
=
**sp** fox[20], foxe[12], kid-foxe[1] / foxes[2]
> dog-, kid-fox

**foxship** *n*
=
**sp** foxship[1]

**fracted** *adj*
=
**sp** fracted[1], fra-cted[1]

**fraction / ~s** *n*
'fraksɪən / -z
**sp** fraction[1] / fractions[2]

**fragile** *adj*
'fradʒɪl
**sp** fragile[1]

**fragment / ~s** *n*
=
**sp** fragment[3] / fragments[4]

**fragrant** *adj*
'frɛːgrənt
**sp** fragrant[4]

**frail / ~est** *adj*
frɛːl / -st
**sp** fraile[15], frayle[2] / frailst[1]
**rh** tail *Oth 2.1.151*

**frailt·y / ~ies** *n*
'frɛːltəɪ / -z
**sp** frailety[2], frailtie[2], frailty[8] / frailties[2]

**frame / ~s** *n*
frɛːm / -z
**sp** frame[18] / frames[1]
**rh** fame *TNK 3.5.112*; same v *S 59.10*

**fram·e / ~es / ~ing / ~ed** *v*
frɛːm / -z / 'frɛːm·ɪn, -ɪŋ / *m* -d, -ɪd
**sp** frame[24] / frames[2] / framing[1] / fram'd[16], framed[4]
**rh** dame *MND 5.1.283, Per Prol.32*; same *S 5.1* / a-turning *PP 7.15*
> strong-framed

**frampold** *adj*
'frampoːld
**sp** 'frampold[1]

**français** *Fr n*
frɑ̃'sɛ
**sp** Francois[1]

**France / ~'s** *n*
frans, *Fr accent in English by Katherine, Lady H5 5.2.169, 258, Frenchman Cym 1.5.59, ?Henry H5 5.2.262* frɔːns / 'fransɪz
**sp** France[369], Fraunce[6] / France's[1]

**France** *Fr n*
frɑ̃ːs
**sp** France[2], Fraunce[6]
**rh** advance *H5 2.2.193, 5.2.347, 5. Chorus.45*; arrogance *AW 2.1.196*; chance *KJ 1.1.150, KL 1.1.257, LLL 5.2.551*; dalliance *1H6 5.2.4*; ignorance *H8 1.3.25*; mischance *1H6 4.6.48, 3H6 3.3.255, R3 4.4.115*

**franchise / ~s** *n*
'frantʃəɪz / -ɪz
**sp** franchise[1] / franchises[1]
> enfranchise

**franchised** *adj*
'frantʃəɪzd
**sp** franchis'd[1]

**franchisement** *Fr n*
frɑ̃ʃiz'mɑ̃
**sp** franchisement[1]

**Franci·a / ~ae** *Lat n*
'fransɪe
**sp** Franciae[1]

**Francis** *n*
=
**sp** Francis[33], Fran-cis[1], *abbr* Fran[1]

**Francisca** *n*
fran'sɪskə
**sp** Francisca[1]

**Franciscan** *adj*
=
**sp** Franciscan[1]

**Francisco** *n*
fran'sɪsko:
**sp** Francisco[5], Fran-cisco[1]

**frank / ~er** *adj*
= / 'fraŋkəɹ
**sp** frank[1], franke[7] / franker[1]

**frank** *n*
=
**sp** frank[1]

**frank / ~ed** *v*
=
**sp** frank'd[1], frankt[1]

**Frankfurt** *n*
'fraŋkfɔ:ɹt
**sp** Franckford[1]

**franklin / ~'s / ~s** *n*
=
**sp** franklin[1] / franklins[1] / francklins[1]

**frankly** *adv*
'fraŋkləɪ
**sp** frankely[5], frankly[5]

**frankness** *n*
=
**sp** franknesse[1]

**frantic** *adj*
=
**sp** frantick[2], franticke[11], frantike[1]

**franticly** *adv*
*m* 'frantɪkˌləɪ
**sp** frantiquely[1]

**frat·er / ~rum** *Lat n*
'fratrʊm
**sp** fratrum[1]

**Fraterretto** *n*
ˌfratə'reto:
**sp** Fraterretto[1]

**fraud** *n*
=
**sp** fraud[4]
**rh** o'erstrawed *VA 1141*

**fraudful** *adj*
=
**sp** fraudfull[1]

**fraught** *n / v*
=
**sp** fraught[3] / fraught[5]
> full-, over-fraught

**fraughtage** *n*
'frɔ:tɪʤ
**sp** fraughtage[1], frautage[1]

**fraughting** *adj*
'frɔ:tɪn, -ɪŋ
**sp** fraughting[1]

**fray / ~s / ~ed** *v*
frɛ: / -z / -d
**sp** fray[16] / frayes[1] / fraid[1]
**rh** away, say *MND 3.2.342*; day *MND 3.2.447*; dismay *MV 3.2.62*; obey *RJ 3.1.141*; say *TS 1.2.23*; slay *RJ 3.1.151*; today *1H4 5.4.107, RJ 1.1.117*; weigh *MND 3.2.129*

**freckle / ~s** *n*
=
**sp** freckles[1]

**freckled** *adj*
=
**sp** freckled[1], frekelld[1]

**Frederic** *n*
*m* 'fredəˌrɪk, -drɪk
**sp** Frederick[1], Fredericke[2], Fre-dericke[1], Fredricke[1]

**free / ~r** *adj*
= / 'fri:əɹ
**sp** free[158], free-[men][1], free-[will][1] / freer[5]
**rh** be *LC 100, MM 3.2.37, Oth 1.2.98, Tem Epil.20*; legacy *S 4.4*; me *AW 3.4.17, 1H6 5.3.115, Luc 1624, Per 2.4.2, S 134.5, 134.14*; monarchy *LC 195*; see *LC 100, LLL 5.2.422*; she *TS 1.2.230*; thee *3H6 4.6.16, S 125.10, TG 5.4.82, Tim 4.3.539*; **free it** be it, see it *Luc 1208*
> fancy-, shot-free

**free** *n*
=
**sp** free[1]

**free / ~s / ~d** *v*
=
**sp** free[18], free't [free it][1] / frees[1] / freed[2], free'd[1]

**freed** *adj*
=
**sp** free'd[1]

**freedom / ~s** *n*
=
**sp** freedom[1], freedome[29] / freedomes[1]
**rh** need 'em *Tim 1.2.67*
> enfreedom

**free-footed** *adj*
ˌfri:-'fʊtɪd
**sp** free-footed[1]
> foot

**free-hearted** *adj*
ˌfri:-'ɑ:ɹtɪd, -'hɑ:-
**sp** free-hearted[1]

**freel·y / ~ier** *adv*
'fri:ləɪ / -əɹ
**sp** freely[55] / freelier[1]

**freeman** *n*
=
**sp** free-man[1]

**freeness** *n*
=
**sp** freenesse[1]

**freestone-coloured** *adj*
'fri:sto:n-ˌkɤləɹd
**sp** freestone coloured[1]
> colour

**Free-town** *n*
*m* ˌfriːˈtəʊn
**sp** Free-towne[1]

**freez·e / ~s / froze** *v*
= / = / froːz
**sp** freeze[7], frieze[2] / freezes[2] / froze[3]
**rh** trees *H8 3.1.4*

**freezing** *adj*
ˈfriːzɪn, -ɪŋ
**sp** freezing[1]

**French** *adj / n*
=
**sp** French[62], Fench-[crowne][1], French-[thrift][1] / French[96], Frenche[1]
**rh** drench *1H6 4.7.13*; wench *1H6 4.7.42*

**French-crown-coloured** *adj*
ˈfrenʃ-ˈkrəʊn-ˌkɤləɹd
**sp** French-crowne colour'd[1]
> colour, crown

**French·man / ~man's / ~men / ~men's** *n*
=
**sp** Frenchman[13], French-man[1] / Frenchmans[1] / Frenchmen[15], French men[1] / Frenchmens[4], French-mens[1]

**Frenchwoman** *n*
=
**sp** French-woman[2]
> woman

**frenz·y / ~'s** *n*
ˈfrenzəɪ / -z
**sp** frensie[3], frenzie[7], frenzy[1] / frensies[1]

**frequent** *adj*
=
**sp** frequent[1]

**frequent / ~s** *v*
=
**sp** frequent[1] / frequents[1]
> unfrequented

**fresh / ~er / ~est** *adj*
= / freʃəɹ / =
**sp** fresh[79], fresh-[fish][1] / fresher[7] / freshest[3]
> afresh

**fresh / ~es** *n*
=
**sp** freshes[1]
> refresh

**fresh-brook** *adj*
=
**sp** fresh-brooke[1]
> brook

**freshly** *adv*
ˈfreʃləɪ
**sp** freshly[8]

**freshness** *n*
=
**sp** freshnesse[2]

**fret / ~s** *n*
=
**sp** frets[2]

**fret / ~s / ~ting / ~ted** *v*
= / = / ˈfretɪn, -ɪŋ / =
**sp** fret[12] / frets[4] / fretting[1] / fretted[5]
**rh** debt, let *Luc 648*; net *VA 69*; set *VA 621* / **rh** *1* begets *VA 767*; **rh** *2* entreats VA 75

**fretful** *adj*
=
**sp** fretfull[4]

**fretted** *adj*
=
**sp** fretted[1]

**fretting** *adj / n*
ˈfretɪn, -ɪŋ
**sp** fretting[2] / fretting[1]

**friar / ~'s / ~s** *n*
ˈfrəɪəɹ, frəɪɹ / -z
**sp** friar[12], frier[69], fri-er[1], fryar[1], fryer[11] / friers[3] / fryers[1]
> Whitefriars

**Friday / ~s** *n*
ˈfrəɪdɛː / -z
**sp** Friday[1] / Fridaies[2]
> Good Friday

**friend / ~'s / ~s / ~s'** *n*
=
**sp** freind[2], frend[3], friend[395], friend's [friend is][1] / friends[7] / freinds[2], frends[7], friendes[3], friends[451] / friends[2]
**rh** *1* contend *VA 818*; descend *RJ 3.5.43*; end *AC 4.15.89, AY 3.2.130, Cym 5.3.60, LLL 5.2.823, Luc 237, 526, 897, MND 2.2.66, RJ 3.1.184, S 30.13, 50.4, 110.11, TG 2.1.151*; intend *H8 Prol.22*; lend *S 82.12*; offend *1H6 5.3.59*; penned *LLL 5.2.404*; spend *PP 20.33, S 149.5*; tend *Ham 3.2.217*; **rh** *2* fiend *PP 2.11, S 144.11* / **rh** *1* amends *MND 5.1.427*; amends, lends *Luc 963*; comprehends, defends *Luc 495*; ends *LLL 5.2.220, MND 5.1.337, Tim 4.3.466, VA 718*; intends *VA 588*; **rh** *2* fiends *VA 640*
> mouth-, trencher-friend

**friend / ~ed** *v*
=
**sp** friend[1] / frended[1], friended[2]
**rh** extended *MM 4.2.110*
> befriend, unfriended

**friending** *n*
ˈfrendɪn, -ɪŋ
**sp** friending[1]

**friendless** *adj*
ˈfrenləs, -dl-
**sp** frendlesse[1]

**friendliness** *n*
ˈfrenləɪnəs, -dl-
**sp** friendlinesse[1]

**friendly** *adj / adv*
ˈfrenləɪ, -dl-
**sp** friendly[27] / friendly[9]

**friendship / ~s** *n*
ˈfrenʃɪp, -nd- / ~s
**sp** frendship[2], friendship[39], friendshippe[2] / friendshippes[1], friendships[1]

**frieze** *n*
=
**sp** freeze[1], frieze[1], frize[1]

**fright / ~s** *n*
frəɪt / -s
**sp** fright[2] / frights[3]

**fright / ~s / ~ing / ~ed** *v*
frəɪt / -s / 'frəɪt·ɪn, -ɪŋ / -ɪd
**sp** fright[30] / frights[4] / frighting[3] / frighted[13]
> affright

**frighted** *adj*
'frəɪtɪd
**sp** frighted[2]
> self-affrighted

**frightful** *adj*
'frəɪtfʊl
**sp** frightfull[2]

**fringe** *n*
=
**sp** fringe[1]

**fringed** *adj*
*m* 'frɪndʒɪd
**sp** fringed[1]

**frippery** *n*
'frɪprəɪ, -pər-
**sp** frippery[1]

**frisk** *v*
=
**sp** frisk[1]

**fritter / ~s** *n*
'frɪtəɹz
**sp** fritters[1]

**frivolous** *adj*
=
**sp** friuolous[3]

**fro**
> to and fro

**frog** *n*
=
**sp** frog[1], frogge[1]
**rh** dog *Mac 4.1.14*
> leapfrog

**Frogmore** *n*
'frɒgmɔːɹ
**sp** Frogmore[3]

**Froissart** *n*
'frwɛsɑːɹ
**sp** Froysard[1]

**frolic** *adj / v*
=
**sp** frollicke[1] / frolicke[1]

**from** *prep*
=
**sp** fro[1], fro[m] [23], from[2498], from's [from his][2], from's [from us][2], from't [from it][4]

**front / ~s** *n*
frɤnt / -s
**sp** front[13] / fronts[3]

**front / ~s / ~ed** *v*
frɤnt / -s / 'frɤntɪd
**sp** front[8] / fronts[1] / fronted[1]
> a-, con-front; broad-fronted

**frontier / ~s** *n*
'frɤntiːɹ / -z
**sp** frontier[1] / frontiers[1]

**fronting** *adj*
'frɤntɪn, -ɪŋ
**sp** fronting[1]

**frontlet** *n*
'frɤntlət
**sp** frontlet[1]

**frost / ~s** *n*
=
**sp** frost[11] / frosts[4]
**rh** *1* lost *MV 2.7.75*; **rh** *2* boast *LLL 1.1.100*

**frosty** *adj*
'frɒstəɪ
**sp** frostie[6], frosty[2]

**frosty-spirited** *adj*
'frɒstəɪ-ˌspɪɹɪtɪd
**sp** frosty-spirited[1]

**froth** *n / v*
=
**sp** froth[3] / froth[2]

**Froth** [name] *n*
=
**sp** Froth[10]

**froward** *adj*
*m* froːɹd, 'froːəɹd
**sp** froward[12]
**rh** coward *VA 570*; toward *PP 4.14, TS 1.1.69, 5.2.182*; untoward *TS 4.5.78*

**frown / ~s** *n*
frəʊn / -z
**sp** frowne[17] / frownes[8]
**rh** crown *3H6 4.5.28*; down *KL 5.3.6, S 117.11, VA 465*

**frown / ~s / ~ing / ~ed** *v*
frəʊn / -z / 'frəʊnɪn, -ɪŋ / frəʊnd
**sp** frown[2], frowne[24] / frownes[10] / frowning[8] / frown'd[5]
**rh** down *VA 45* renown v *PP 20.45*
> outfrown

**frowning** *adj / n*
'frəʊnɪn, -ɪŋ
**sp** frowning[6] / frowning[2]

**frowningly** *adv*
'frəʊnɪnləɪ, -ɪŋ-
**sp** frowningly[1]

**froze, frozen**
> freeze

**frozen** *adj*
'froːzən
**sp** frozen[11]

**fructify** *v*
'frɤktɪfəɪ
**sp** fructifie[1]

**frugal** *adj*
'fruːgɑl
**sp** frugal[1], frugall[1]

**fruit** *adj*
=
**sp** fruit[1]

**fruit / ~s** *n*
=
**sp** fruit[13], fruite[17] / fruites[5], fruits[5]
**rh** mute *S 97.10*; pollute *Luc 1064*

**fruiterer** *n*
'fru:trəɹ, -ərəɹ
**sp** fruiterer[1]

**fruitful** *adj*
=
**sp** fruitefull[2], fruitful[1], fruitfull[12]

**fruitfully** *adv*
'fru:tfləɪ, -fʊləɪ
**sp** fruitfully[2]

**fruitfulness** *n*
*m* 'fru:tfʊlˌnes
**sp** fruitfulnesse[1]

**fruition** *n*
fru:'ɪsɪən
**sp** fruition[1]

**fruitless** *adj*
=
**sp** fruitless[1], fruitlesse[3]

**fruit-tree / ~s** *n*
'fru:t-ˌtri: / *m* -z, ˌfru:t-'tri:z
**sp** fruite tree[1] / fruit-trees[2]
> tree

**frush** *v*
frɤʃ
**sp** frush[1]

**frustrate** *adj / v*
*m* 'frɤstrɛ:t, frɤ'strɛ:t
**sp** frustrate[2] / frustrate[3]

**frutify** *v*
'fru:tɪfəɪ
**sp** frutifie[1]
> fruit

**fry** *n / v*
frəɪ
**sp** fry[3] / frie[1], frye[2]

**fub / ~bed** *v*
fɤbd
**sp** fub'd[1], fub'd-[off][1]

**fubfast** *n*
'fɤbfast
**sp** fubfast[1]

**fuel** *n*
=
**sp** fewell[1], fuell[3]
**rh** cruel *S 1.6*

**fugitive** *adj / n*
=
**sp** fugitiue[1] / fugitiue[2]

**fulfil / ~s / ~led** *v*
=
**sp** fulfill[4] / fulfills[1] / fulfill'd[7]
**rh** will *CE 4.1.114*; Will *S 136.4*; will, kill *Luc 628, 1635* / hild [held], killed *Luc 1258*

**fulfilling** *adj*
fʊl'fɪlɪn, -ɪŋ
**sp** fulfilling[1]

**full / ~er / ~est** *adj*
= / -əɹ / =
**sp** ful[9], full[301] / fuller[2] / fullest[1]
**pun** *TC 5.1.9* full
> overfull

**full** *adv / n*
=
**sp** full[85] / full[17]

**full-acorned** *adj*
*m* ˌfʊl-'ɛ:ko:ɹnd
**sp** full acorn'd[1]
> acorn

**fullam** *n*
=
**sp** fullam[1]

**full-charged** *adj*
*m* ˌfʊl-'ʧɑ:ɹʤd
**sp** full-charg'd[1]
> charged

**fuller / ~s** *n*
'fʊləɹz
**sp** fullers[1]

**full-flowing** *adj*
*m* ˌfʊl-'flo:ɪn, -ɪŋ
**sp** full flowing[1]
> flowing

**full-fortuned** *adj*
*m* ˌfʊl-'fɔ:ɹtənd
**sp** full-fortun'd[1]
> fortune

**full-fraught** *adj*
*m* ˌfʊl-'frɔ:t, 'fʊl-ˌfrɔ:t
**sp** full fraught[2]
> fraught

**full-grown** *adj*
*m* 'fʊl-ˌgro:n
**sp** full growne[1]
**rh** Cleon *emend of line-ending* 4.Chorus.16

**full-hearted** *adj*
*m* ˌfʊl-'ɑ:ɹtɪd, -'hɑ:-
**sp** full-heart'd[1]

**fullness** *n*
=
**sp** fulnesse[5]
**rh** dullness *S 56.6*

**full-winged** *adj*
*m* 'fʊl-ˌwɪŋd
**sp** full-wing'd[1]
> winged

**fully** *adv*
'fʊləɪ
**sp** fully[13]

**fulsome** *adj*
=
**sp** fullsome[1]

**Fulvia / ~'s** *n*
=
**sp** fuluia[14] / fuluias[3], fuluia's[1]

**fum** *interj*
fɤm
**sp** fumme[1]

**fumbl·e / ~est / ~s / ~ing** *v*
'fɤm·bəl / -bləst / -bəlz / -blɪn, -ɪŋ
**sp** fumble[2] / fumblest[1] / fumbles[1] / fumbling[1]

**fume / ~s** *n*
=
**sp** fume[3] / fumes[2]
**rh** plume *VA 316*

**fum·e / *Luc* ~es / ~ing** *v*
= / = / 'fju:mɪn, -ɪŋ
**sp** fume[1] / fumes[1] / fuming[1]
**rh** consumes *Luc 1043*

**fumiter** *n*
'femɪˌtɐ:ɹ
**sp** fenitar[1]

**fumitory** *n*
'femɪˌtrəɪ
**sp** femetary[1]
**rh** savagery *H5 5.2.45*

**function / ~s** *n*
'fɤŋksɪən / -z
**sp** function[16] / functions[8]
> defunction

**fundamental** *adj*
ˌfɤndə'mentɑl
**sp** fundamentall[2]

**funeral / ~s** *n*
*m* 'fju:nəˌrɑl, -nrɑl / -nəˌrɑlz
**sp** funerall[20] / funerals[3]
**rh** *1* festival *RJ 4.5.85*; **rh** *2* shall *AC 5.2.362*

**fur / ~red /** *v*
fɐ:ɹ / -d
**sp** furre[1] / furd[1]
> furred

**furbished** *adj*
'fɐ:ɹbɪʃt
**sp** furbusht[1]

**furious** *adj*
=
**sp** furious[15]
**rh** venturous *R3 4.4.170*

**furlong / ~s** *n*
'fɐ:ɹlɒŋz
**sp** furlongs[2]

**furnace** *n*
'fɐ:ɹnəs
**sp** furnace[2]

**furnace / ~s** *v*
'fɐ:ɹnəsɪz
**sp** furnaces[1]

**furnace-burning** *adj*
'fɐ:ɹnəs-'bɐ:ɹnɪn, -ɪŋ
**sp** furnace-burning[1]

**furnish / ~ed** *v*
'fɐ:ɹnɪʃ / *m* 'fɐ:ɹnɪʃt, -nɪʃɪd
**sp** furnish[22] / furnishd[1], furnish'd[14], furnished[2], furnisht[3]
> dis-, un-, well-furnished

**furnishing / ~s** *n*
'fɐ:ɹnɪʃɪnz, -ɪŋz
**sp** furnishings[1]

**furniture** *n*
'fɐ:ɹnɪtjəɹ
**sp** furniture[5]

**Furnivall** *n*
'fɐ:ɹnɪvɑl
**sp** Furniuall[1]

**furor** *Lat n*
fjʊ'rɔ:ɹ
**sp** furor[1]

**furred** *adj*
fɐ:ɹd
**sp** fur'd[1], furr'd[3]
> fur

**furrow** *adj / n / v*
'fɤrə, -o:
**sp** furrow[1] / furrow[1] / furrow[1]

**furrowed** *adj*
'fɤrəd, -ro:d
**sp** furrowed[1]

**further** *adj, adv*
> far

**further** *v*
'fɐ:ɹðəɹ
**sp** further[1]

**furtherance** *n*
*m* 'fɐ:ɹðrəns, -ðər-
**sp** furth'rance[1], furtherance[1]

**furtherer** *n*
*m* 'fɐ:ɹðrəɹ, -ðər-
**sp** furtherer[1]

**furthermore** *adv*
ˌfɐ:ɹðəɹ'mɔ:ɹ
**sp** furthermore[2]

**furthest**
> far

**fur·y / ~'s / ~ies** *n*
'fju:rəɪ / -z
**sp** furie[32], fury[32] / furies[1] / furies[4]

**furze / ~s** *n*
fɐ:ɹz / 'fɐ:ɹzɪz
**sp** firrs[1] / firzes[1]

**fustian** *adj / n*
'fɤstɪən
**sp** fustian[2] / fustian[2]

**fustilarian** *n*
ˌfɤstɪ'larɪən
**sp** fustil-lirian[1], *2H4 2.1.57* [Q] fustilarian

**fusty** *adj*
'fɤstəɪ
**sp** fustie[2], fusty[1]

**future** *adj / n*
'fju:təɹ
**sp** future[8] / future[6]

**futurity** *n*
*m* fjʊ'tʊrɪˌtəɪ
**sp** futurity[1]

# G

**G** *n*
=
**sp** G[4]
**rh** be *R3 1.1.39, 1.1.56*; he *R3 1.1.58*

**gabble** *v*
=
**sp** gabble[3]

**gaberdine** *n*
*m* 'gabəɹdi:n, -ˌdi:n
**sp** gaberdine[3]

**Gabriel / ~'s** *n*
'gɛ:brəl, -rɪəl [2 *sylls*] / -z
**sp** Gabriel[1] / Gabrels[1]

**gad** *n*
=
**sp** gad[2]

**gad / ~ding** *v*
'gadɪn, -ɪŋ
**sp** gadding[1]

**Gadshill** [person] *n*
'gadzɪl
**sp** Gads-hill[4], Gads hill[1]

**Gadshill** [place] *n*
'gadz'ɪl, -'hɪl
**sp** Gads-hill[2], Gads-Hill[2], Gads hill[3]
> hill

**gage** *n*
gɛ:ʤ
**sp** gage[15]
**rh** age *R2 1.1.161*

**gag·e / ~ing / ~ed** *v*
gɛ:ʤ / 'gɛ:ʤ·ɪn, -ɪŋ / *m* -ɪd, gɛ:ʤd
**sp** gage[1] / gaging[1] / gag'd[3], gaged[1]
**rh** age *Luc 1351*; age, rage *Luc 144*

**gagner / gagné** *Fr v*
ga'ɲe
**sp** gaynie[1]

**gain / ~s** *n*
gɛ:n / -z
**sp** gaine[24], gayne[1] / gaines[4]
**rh** again *Per 5.Chorus.10*; disdain *PP 15.10*; pain *Luc 860, PP 15.10, S 141.13*; pain, remain *Luc 730*; reign *Tim 5.1.220*; sustain *Luc 140*; twain *S 42.9*; pains *Mac 4.1.40, R2 5.6.12*; reigns *R3 1.1.162*; veins *S 67.12*

**gain / ~s / ~ed** *v*
gɛ:n / -z / -d
**sp** gaine[21], gayne[3] / gaines[2] / gain'd[6], gained[1], gayned[1]
**rh** main *S 64.5*; rain *KL 2.4.74*; reign *Per 2.Chorus.8*; remain *H8 5.3.181* / abstaining, obtaining *Luc 131* / trained *Per 4.Chorus.8*

**gained** *adj*
gɛ:nd
**sp** gain'd[1]
> ungained

**gainer** *n*
'gɛ:nəɹ
**sp** gainer[1]

**gain-giving** *n*
'gɛ:n-ˌgɪvɪn, -ɪŋ
**sp** gain-giuing[1]
> giving

**gain·say / ~says / ~said** *v*
*m* 'gɛ:n-ˌsɛ:, ˌgɛ:n-'sɛ: / ˌgɛ:n-'sɛ:z / ˌgɛ:n-'sed
**sp** gaine-say[2], gainsay[2] / gainsayes[1] / gainsaid[1]

**gainsaying** *n*
ˌgɛ:n-'sɛɪn, -ɪŋ
**sp** gaine-saying[1]

**gainst**
> against

**gait** *n*
gɛ:t
**sp** gate[29], [lyon]-gate[1]
**rh** consecrate *MND 5.1.406*; hate *Tim 5.4.73*; late *VA 529*; state *S 128.11, Tem 4.1.102*
**pun** *TN 3.1.80* gate
> heavy-, slow-, tardy-gaited

**Galathe** *n*
'galəˌtɛ:
**sp** Galathe[1]

**gale / ~s** *n*
gɛ:l / -z
**sp** gale[2] / gales[1]

**Galen** *n*
'gɛ:lən
**sp** Galen[4], Galien[1]

**gall / ~s** *n*
gɑ:l / -z
**sp** gall[20], gaulle[1] / galles[2], gals[1], gauls[1]
**rh** 1 all *TC 2.2.145*; thrall *PP 17.16*; **rh** 2 equivocal *Oth 1.3.214*; **rh** 3 shall *RJ 1.5.92*

**gall / ~s / ~ing / ~ed** *v*
gɑ:l / -z / 'gɑ:l·ɪn, -ɪŋ / *m* -ɪd, gɑ:ld

**sp** gall[6], gaul[2], gaule[2] / galles[1], galls[2] / galling[2] / gal'd[1], gald[1], gall'd[4], galled[1]
> over-, spur-gall

**gallant / ~est** *adj*
= / 'galənst, -ntst
**sp** gallant[39], gal-lant[1] / gallant'st[1]

**gallant / ~s** *n*
=
**sp** gallant[13] / gallants[11], gal-lants[1]
> topgallant

**gallantly** *adv*
*m* 'galəntləɪ, gə'lantləɪ
**sp** gallantly[4]

**gallantry** *n*
'galəntrəɪ
**sp** gallantry[1]

**gallant-springing** *adj*
'galənt-'sprɪŋɪn, -ɪŋ
**sp** gallant springing[1]

**galled** *adj*
*m* gɑ:ld, 'gɑ:lɪd
**sp** gall'd[1], galled[2], gauled[3]
> ungalled

**gallery** *n*
'galəˌrəɪ
**sp** gallerie[1], gallery[2]

**gall·ey / ~ies** *n*
'galəɪ / -z
**sp** gally[1] / gallies[6]

**Gallia** *adj*
'galɪə
**sp** Gallia[1]

**Gallia / ~'s** *n*
'galɪə / -z
**sp** Gallia[11] / Gallia's[1]

**Gallian** *adj*
'galɪən
**sp** Gallian[1], Gallian-[girle][1]

**galliard** *n*
'galɪɑ:ɹd
**sp** galliard[4]

**galliass / ~es** *n*
'galɪasɪz
**sp** galliasses[1]

**gallimaufry** *n*
ˌgalɪ'mɔ:frəɪ
**sp** gal-ly-maufrey[1], gally-mawfry[1]

**gallon / ~s** *n*
=
**sp** gallons[1]

**gallop** *n*
=
**sp** gallop[2]

**gallop / ~s** *v*
=
**sp** gallop[4] / gallops[4], gal-lops[1]

**galloping** *n*
'galəpɪn, -ɪŋ
**sp** gallopping[1]

**gallow** *v*
'galə, -lo:
**sp** gallow[1]

**Galloway** *adj*
'galəwɛ:
**sp** Gallo-way[1]

**gallowglass / ~es** *n*
'galə-ˌglasɪz
**sp** gallow-glasses[1], gallowgrosses[1]

**gallows / ~'** *n*
'galəz, -lo:z, *Gaoler Cym 5.4.207* 'galəzɪz
**sp** gallowes[20], *Gaoler* gallowses[1] / gallowes[1]

**gallows-maker** *n*
'galəz-ˌmɛ:kəɹ
**sp** gallowes maker[1]
> make

**Gallus** *n*
'galəs
**sp** Gallus[2]

**Gam** [name] *n*
=
**sp** Gam[1]

**gambol** *adj / v*
=
**sp** gamboll[1] / gambole[1], gamboll[1]

**gambol / ~s** *n*
=
**sp** gambals[1], gambols[2]

**gambold** *n*
'gambɔ:ld
**sp** gambold[1]

**gam·e / ~s** *n*
gɛ:m / -z
**sp** game[23], [cride]-game[1], game's [game is][2] / games[3]
**rh** shame *LLL 5.2.155, 360*
> game

**gamesome** *adj*
'gɛ:msəm
**sp** gamesom[1], gamesome[2]

**gamester** *n*
'gɛ:mstəɹ
**sp** game-ster[1], gamester[5], gamster[1]

**gaming** *n / v*
'gɛ:mɪn, -ɪŋ
**sp** gaming[2] / gaming[1]

**gammon** *n*
=
**sp** gammon[1]

**gamut** *n*
=
**sp** gamoth[1], gamouth[4]

**gan**
> begin

**gangrene / ~d** *v*
gaŋ'gri:nd
**sp** gangren'd[1]

**Ganymede** *n*
'ganɪˌmɛ:d
**sp** Ganimed[9]

**gaol / ~s** *n*
ʤɛ:l / -z
**sp** gaole[3], iaile[5] / gaoles[1]
**rh** bail *S 133.12*

**gaoler / ~s** *n*
'ʤɛ:ləɹ / -z
**sp** gaoler[10], iailor[3], iaylor[8] / gaolers[1], iaylors[1]

**gap** *n*
=
**sp** gap[11]

**gape / ~s** *v*
gɛ:p / -s
**sp** gape[11] / gapes[2]

**gaping** *adj / n / v*
'gɛ:pɪn, -ɪŋ
**sp** gaping[6] / gaping[1] / gaping[1]
> earnest-gaping

**Gar**
> God

**garb** *n*
gɑ:ɹb
**sp** garb[2], garbe[3]

**garbage** *n*
'gɑ:ɹbɪʤ
**sp** garbage[2]

**garboil / ~s** *n*
'gɑ:ɹbəɪlz
**sp** garboiles[1], garboyles[1]

**garçon** *Fr n*
gaɹ'sɔ̃
**sp** garsoon[1]

**garden** *adj*
'gɑ:ɹdən
**sp** garden[2]

**garden / ~s** *n*
'gɑ:ɹdən / -z
**sp** garden[29] / gardens[2]

**gardener / ~s** *n*
'gɑ:ɹdnəɹ / -z
**sp** gardiner[2], gard'ner[1] / gardeners[1], gardiners[3]

**garden-house** *n*
'gɑ:ɹdən-ˌəʊs, -ˌhəʊs
**sp** garden-house[1], garden house[1]
> house

**garder / garde / ~z** *Fr v*
gaɹd / gaɹ'dez
**sp** guard[1] / garde[1]

**Gardiner** *n*
'gɑ:ɹdnəɹ, -dɪn-
**sp** Gardiner[9]

**Gargantua / ~'s** *n*
gɑ:ɹ'gantjʊəz
**sp** Gargantuas[1]

**Gargrave** *n*
'gɑ:ɹgrɛ:v
**sp** Gargraue[2]

**garish** *adj*
'garɪʃ
**sp** garish[2]

**garland / ~s** *n*
'gɑ:ɹlənd / -z
**sp** garland[24], gar-land[1] / garlands[8]

**garlic** *n*
'gɑ:ɹlɪk
**sp** garlick[2], garlicke[2]

**garlic-eater / ~s** *n*
'gɑ:ɹlɪk-ˌi:təɹz
**sp** garlicke-eaters[1]

**garment / ~s** *n*
'gɑ:ɹmənt / -s
**sp** garment[18] / garments[43], gar-ments[2]

**garner / ~s** *n*
'gɑ:ɹnəɹz
**sp** garners[2]

**garner / ~ed** *v*
'gɑ:ɹnəɹd
**sp** garnerd[1]

**garnish** *n*
'gɑ:ɹnɪʃ
**sp** garnish[1]

**garnish / ~ed** *v*
'gɑ:ɹnɪʃ / *m* -t, -ɪd
**sp** garnish[1] / garnish'd[1], garnished[1], garnisht[1]

**garret** *n*
=
**sp** garret[1]

**garrison / ~s** *n*
*m* 'garɪˌsɒn / -z
**sp** garrison[1] / garrisons[1]

**garrison / ~ed** *v*
*m* 'garɪˌsɒnd
**sp** garrison'd[1]

**garter / ~'s / ~s** *n*
'gɑ:ɹtəɹ / -z
**sp** garter[7], gar-ter[1] / garters-[compasse][1] / garters[2], [heire-apparant]-garters[1]
> caddis-garter

**Garter** [name] *n*
'gɑ:ɹtəɹ, *Caius MW 1.4.115* 'ʤɑ:ɹti:ɹ
**sp** Garter[11], *Caius* larteer[2], larteere[1]

**garter / ~ed** *v*
'gɑ:ɹtəɹ / -d
**sp** garter[2] / gartred[1]
> cross-, un-gartered

**gash / ~es** *n*
=
**sp** gash[4] / gashes[4], [honour'd]-gashes[1]

**gashed** *adj*
=
**sp** gash'd[1]

**gaskins** *n*
=
**sp** gaskins[1]

**gasp** *n*
gasp
**sp** gasp[6]

**gasp / ~ing** *v*
gasp / 'gaspɪn, -ɪŋ
**sp** gasp[2] / gasping[2]

**gasping** *adj*
'gaspɪn, -ɪŋ
**sp** gasping[1]

**gast / ~ed** *v*
gastɪd
**sp** gasted[1]

**gastness** *n*
'gastnəs
**sp** gastnesse[1]

**gat**
> beget

**gate / ~s** *n*
gɛ:t / gɛ:ts
**sp** gate[53], [city]-gate[1], [court]-gate[1], [north]-gate[1] / gates[92], [towne]-gates, *in s.d.* gati[1]
**rh** *1* estate *TN 5.1.392*; fate, state *Luc 1068*; late *CE 3.1.48, LLL 1.1.109*; late, pate *CE 2.2.227*; pate *CE 3.1.73, TS 1.2.11*; state *2H6 4.10.22, S 29.12*; straight *Tim 2.1.10*; wait *Per 1.1.81*; **rh** *2* compassionate *Luc 595*; **rh** *3* chat *VA 424* / fates *MND 1.2.30*
**pun** *TN 3.1.80* gait
> counter-, flood-, hell-gate; six-gated

**gather / ~s / ~ing / ~ed** *v*
'gaðəɹ / -z / 'gaðrɪn, -ɪŋ, -ðər- / 'gaðəɹd
**sp** gather[23] / gathers[1] / gathering[2] / gather'd[4], gathered[4]
**rh** unfathered *S 124.4*

**gathered** *adj*
'gaðəɹd
**sp** gathred[1]

**gaud / ~s** *n*
=
**sp** gaude[1] / gaudes[1], gawdes[2]

**gauded** *adj*
=
**sp** gawded[1]

**gaudeo** *Lat v*
'gɔ:dɪo:
**sp** gaudio[1]

**gaudy** *adj*
'gɔ:dəɪ
**sp** gaudie[2], gaudy[1], gawdie[1], gawdy[1]

**gauge** *v*
gɔ:ʤ
**sp** gage[1]

**Gaul** *n*
=
**sp** Gaule[1]

**Gaultier**
> Walter

**Gaultree** *n*
'gɔ:ltri:
**sp** Gaultree[1]

**gaunt** *adj*
=
**sp** gaunt[6]
**pun** *R2 2.1.74ff* Gaunt

**Gaunt / ~'s [name]** *n*
=
**sp** Gaunt[29] / Gauntes[1]
**pun** *R2 2.1.74ff* gaunt

**gauntlet / ~s** *n*
=
**sp** gantlets[1], gauntlet[4] / gauntlets[1]

**gave**
> give

**Gawsey** *n*
'gɔ:zəɪ
**sp** Gausey[1], Gawsey[1]

**gay** *adj*
gɛ:
**sp** gay[7]
**rh** array *S 146.4*; away *S 68.8*; away, day *PP 15.15*; may *Oth 2.1.147*; say *VA 286*

**gayness** *n*
'gɛ:nəs
**sp** gaynesse[1]

**gaze / ~s** *n*
gɛ:z / 'gɛ:zɪz
**sp** gaze[4] / gazes[2]

**gaz·e / ~s / *S* ~eth / ~ing / ~ed** *v*
gɛ:z / 'gɛ:z·ɪz / -əθ / -ɪn, -ɪŋ / gɛ:zd
**sp** gaze[21] / gazes[1]/ gazeth[1] / gazing[9] / gaz'd[2]
**rh** maze *Luc 1149* / amazes *LLL 2.1.233, VA 632* / amazeth *S 20.6* / amazed *VA 927*; amazed, blazed *Luc 1355*
> agazed

**gazer / ~s** *n*
'gɛ:zəɹ / -z
**sp** gazer[1] / gazers[1]

**gazing** *adj / n*
'gɛ:zɪn, -ɪŋ
**sp** gazing[2] / gazing[3]
> glass-gazing

**gear** *n*
gi:ɹ
**sp** geare[6], geere[3], gere[1]
**rh** here *LLL 5.2.303, TC 3.2.209*

**geck** *n*
=
**sp** gecke[1], geeke[1]

**geese**
> goose

**geld / ~ing / ~ed / gelt** *v*
= / 'geldɪn, -ɪŋ / =
**sp** geld[1], gell'd[1], gueld[1]/ gelding[1] / gelded[2], guelded[1] / gelt[1]

**gelding** *n*
'geldɪn, -ɪŋ
**sp** gelding[2], gel-ding[1]

**gelidus / ~a** *Lat adj*
'ʤelɪd·ʊs / -a
**sp** gelidus[1] / gellida[1]

**gem / ~s** *n*
=
**sp** iem[2], iemme[3] / gemmes[1], iems[1]
**rh** hems *S 21.6*

**geminy** *n*
'ʤemɪnəɪ
**sp** geminy[1]

**gender / ~s** *n*
'ʤendəɹ / -z
**sp** gender[2] / gen-ders[1]

**gender** *v*
'ʤendəɹ
**sp** gender[1]

**general** *adj*
*m* 'ʤenrɑl, -nər-, -nəˌr-
**sp** general[5], generall[76], gen'rall[1]
> heir general

**general / ~'s / ~s** *n*
*m* 'ʤenrɑl, -nər-, -nəˌr- / -z
**sp** general[5], generall[100], ge-nerall[3], generall's [general is][1] / generalls[1], generall's[1], generals[3], general's[1], / generals[9]
**rh** fall *Luc 1484*

**generally** *adv*
*m* 'ʤenrələɪ, -ˌləɪ
**sp** generally[12]

**generation / ~s** *n*
ˌʤenə'rɛ:sɪən / -z
**sp** generation[10] / generations[1]

**generative** *adj*
=
**sp** generatiue[1]

**generosity** *n*
*m* ˌʤenə'rɒsɪˌtəɪ
**sp** generosity[1]

**generous** *adj*
*m* 'ʤenrəs, -nər-, -nəˌrɤs
**sp** generous[10]

**genitive** *n*
=
**sp** genitiue[3]

**genitiv·us / ~o** *Lat n*
ˌʤenɪ'ti:vo:
**sp** geni-tiuo[1]

**genius** *n*
=
**sp** genius[7]

**gennet / ~s** *n*
=
**sp** gennets[1]

**Genoa** *n*
=
**sp** Genoa[1], Genowa[4]

**genou / ~x** *Fr n*
ʒnu, ʒə'nu
**sp** genoux[1]

**gens** *Fr n*
ʒɑ̃
**sp** gens[1]

**gens** *Lat n*
ʤenz
**sp** gens[1]

**gentilhomme** *Fr n*
ʒɑ̃ti'jɔm
**sp** gentilhome[2]

**gentility** *n*
*m* ˌʤen'tɪlɪˌtəɪ, -ɪtəɪ
**sp** gentilitie[1], gentility[1]
**rh** penalty *LLL 1.1.127*

**gentle / ~r** *adj*
= / 'ʤentləɹ
**sp** gentle[348], gen-tle[2] / gentler[10]
> thrice-, un-gentle

**gentle / ~s** *n*
=
**sp** gentle[3] / gentles[8]
**pun** *MV 2.6.51* Gentile

**gentle** *v*
=
**sp** gentle[1]

**gentle-hearted** *adj*
'ʤentl-ˌɑ:ɹtɪd, -ˌhɑ:-
**sp** gentle-hearted[1]

**gentle·man / ~man's / ~men** *n*
=
**sp** gentleman[276], gentlema[n][1], gen-tleman[5], gentle-man[9], ientleman[1], *abbr AW 5.3.245* Gent.[1], *abbr in s.d.* Gent.[1] / gentlemans[3], gentle-mans[1] / gentlemen[188], gentleme[n][1], gen-tlemen[1], gentle-men[2]

**gentleman-like** *adj*
'ʤentlmən-ləɪk
**sp** gentleman-like[4], gentleman-like-[dogs][1]

**gentleness** *n*
*m* 'ʤentlˌnes, -nəs
**sp** gentlenesse[16], gen-tlenesse[1]
**rh** confess *MND 2.2.138*

**gentlewo·man / ~man's / ~men** *n*
=
**sp** gentlewoman[47], gen-tlewoman[1], gentle-woman[3] / gentlewomans[2] / gentlewomen[6], gen-tlewomen[1]
> waiting-gentlewoman, woman

**gently** *adj*
'ʤentləɪ
**sp** gently[30]

**gentry** *n*
'ʤentrəɪ
**sp** gentrie[2], gentry[12]

**Geoffrey / ~'s** *n*
'ʤefrəɪ / -z
**sp** Geffrey[3] / Geffreyes[5], Geffreys[1]

**George / ~'s** *n*
ʤɑ:ɹʤ / 'ʤɑ:ɹʤɪz
**sp** George[42] / Georges[6]
**rh** charge *H5 3.1.34*

**Gerard** *n*
'ʤerəɹd
**sp** Gerard[3]

**Germaine** *n*
ʤəɹ'mɛ:n
**sp** Germaine[1]

**German** *adj*
'ʤɐːɹmən
**sp** German[1], Germane[1], Germane-[diuels][1], Iarmen[1]

**german / ~s** *n*
'ʤɐːɹmən / -z
**sp** germane[1] / germaines[1]
> cousin-german

**German / ~s** *n*
'ʤɐːɹmən / -z
**sp** Germaine[1], German[1], Germane[2] / Germanes[2]

**germane** *adj*
ʤəɹ'mɛːn
**sp** germaine[1], iermaine[1]

**Germany** *n*
*m* 'ʤɐːɹməˌnəɪ, -ənəɪ, *Caius MW 4.5.80* 'ʤamənəɪ
**sp** Germanie[3], Germany[2], *Caius* Iamanie[1]

**germen / ~s** *n*
'ʤɐːɹmən / -z
**sp** germaine[1] / germaines[1]

**Gertrude** *n*
'gɑːɹtrʊd
**sp** Gertrude[13]

**gest** *n*
ʤest
**sp** gest[1]

**gesture / ~s** *n*
'ʤestəɹ / -z
**sp** gesture[6], ge-sture[1], iesture[1] / gestures[2]

**get / ~test / ~s / got / ~test / ~ten** *v*
= / getst / = / gɒt·s, -st / =
**sp** get[285], gette[1] / getst[1], get'st[1] / gets[11] / got[65] / got's[1], got'st[2] / gotten[4]
**rh** *1* set *LC 134*; Somerset *1H6 4.3.32*; threat *Luc 549*; **rh** *2* heat *VA 93*; *rh 3* great *Luc 878* / **rh** *1* debts *Per 4.Chorus.33*; **rh** *2* eats *AY 2.5.38* / **rh** *1* blot *S 95.9*; not *Tem Epil.6*; plot *Tem 4.1.89*; pot *Mac 4.1.8*; **rh** *2* coat *2H6 4.10.69*

**get** [beget]
> beget

**getter** *n*
'getəɹ
**sp** getter[1]

**getting** *n*
> begetting

**ghastly** *adj / adv*
'gastləɪ
**sp** gastly[3], ghastly[1] / gastly[1]

**ghost / ~'s / ~s** *n*
goːst / -s
**sp** ghost[50] / ghosts[1] / ghostes[3], ghosts[11]
**rh** boast *S 86.9* / coasts *Cym 5.4.94*

**ghost / ~ed** *v*
'goːstɪd
**sp** ghosted[1]

**ghostly** *adv*
'goːstləɪ
**sp** ghostly[7]

**giant** *adj*
'ʤəɪənt
**sp** giant[1], gyant-[masse][1], giant-[world][1], gyant[3]

**giant / ~'s / ~s** *n*
'ʤəɪənt / -s
**sp** giant[5], gyant[3]/ giants[2] / giants[1]

**giantess** *n*
'ʤəɪənˌtes
**sp** giantesse[1]

**giant-like** *adj*
'ʤəɪənt-ləɪk
**sp** gyant-like[2]

**gib** *n*
gɪb
**sp** gibbe[1], gyb-[cat][1]

**gibbet / ~s** *n*
=
**sp** gibbet[3] / gibbets[2]

**gibbet / ~s** *v*
=
**sp** gibbets[1]

**gibbet-maker** *n*
'ʤɪbɪt-ˌmɛːkəɹ
**sp** iibbetmaker[1]
> make

**gibe / ~s** *n*
ʤəɪb / -z, *Fluellen H5 4.7.47* ʤəɪps
**sp** gibes[2] / gybes[2], *Fluellen* gypes[1]

**gibe** *v*
ʤəɪb
**sp** gibe[1]

**giber** *n*
ʤəɪbəɹ
**sp** gyber[1]

**gibing** *adj*
'ʤəɪbɪn, -ɪŋ
**sp** gibing[1], gybing[1]

**gibingly** *adv*
'ʤəɪbɪnləɪ, -ɪŋ-
**sp** gibingly[1]

**giddily** *adv*
*m* 'gɪdɪləɪ, -ɪˌləɪ
**sp** giddily[2]

**giddiness** *n*
'gɪdəɪnəs
**sp** giddinesse[1]

**giddy** *adj*
'gɪdəɪ
**sp** giddie[14], giddy[14], giddy-[goose][1]

**giddy-paced** *adj*
*m* 'gɪdəɪ-ˌpɛːsɪd
**sp** giddy-paced[1]

**gift / ~s** *n*
=
**sp** gift[38], guift[22] / gifts[34], guifts[12]
**rh** uplift *Cym 5.4.101* / shifts *CE 3.2.191*
> nothing-gift

**gig** *n*
gɪg
**sp** gigge[3]
**rh** jig *LLL 4.3.165*

**giglet / ~s** *n*
'gɪglət / -s
**sp** giglet[1], giglot[1] / giglets[1]

**Gilbert** *n*
'gɪlbəɹt
**sp** Gilbert[3]

**gild / ~ed** *v*
=
**sp** gild[4], gil'd[1], gilde[2], gill'd[1], guild[4] / gilded[3], guilded[2]
**rh** field, shield *Luc 60*
> engild

**gilded** *adj*
=
**sp** gilded[9], guilded[3]

**Gill**
> Jill

**Gilliams** *n*
'gɪlɪəmz
**sp** Gilliams[1]

**Gillian** *n*
=
**sp** Gillian[1]

**gills** *VA* *n*
=
**sp** *VA* gils[1]
**rh** bills *VA 1100*

**gillyvor / ~s** *n*
'ʤɪləɪˌvɔːɹz
**sp** gilly-vors[1], gilly' vors[1]

**gilt** *adj / n / v*
=
**sp** gilt[5], guilt[1] / gilt[5] / gilt[3]
**pun** *n H5 2.Chorus.26* guilt

**gimmaled** *adj*
'ʤɪməld
**sp** iymold[1]

**gimmer / ~s** *n*
'ʤɪməɹz
**sp** gimmors[1]

**gin / ~s** *n*
=
**sp** gin[3], gynne[1] / gynnes[1]

**ginger** *n*
'ʤɪnʤəɹ
**sp** ginger[7]

**gingerbread** *n*
'ʤɪnʤəɹ-ˌbred
**sp** ginger bread[1], ginger-bread[1]
> bread

**gingerly** *adj*
'ʤɪnʤəɹləɪ
**sp** gingerly[1]

**Ginn** [name] *n*
ʤɪn
**sp** Ginn[1]
**rh** in *CE 3.1.31*

**gips·y / ~y's / ~ies** *n*
'ʤɪpsəɪ / -z
**sp** gipsie[1], gypsie[1] / gypsies[1] / gipsies[1]

**gird / ~ing** *v*
gɐːɹd / 'gɐːɹd·ɪn, -ɪŋ
**sp** gird[3], gyrd[1] / girding[1]
> ungird

**girded** *adj*
'gɐːɹdɪd
**sp** girded[1]

**girdle / ~s** *n*
'gɐːɹdl / -z
**sp** girdle[8], [salt-water]-girdle[1] / girdles[2]

**girdl·e / ~es / ~ing / ~ed** *v*
'gɐːɹdl / -z / 'gɐːɹdlɪn, -ɪŋ / 'gɐːɹdld
**sp** girdle[1] / girdles[1] / girdling[1] / girdled[1], gyrdled[1]

**girl / ~s** *n*
gɐːɹl / -z
**sp** girle[39], [Gallian]-girle[1], gyrle[11] / girles[9], gyrles[4]

**girt** *adj*
gɐːɹt
**sp** girt[1], gyrt[2]

**girth** *n*
gɐːɹθ
**sp** girth[1]

**Gis** *n*
ʤɪs
**sp** gis[1]

**Gisors** *n*
ʒiː'zɔːɹ
**sp** Guysors[1]

**giv·e / ~est / ~s / ~eth / ~ing / gave / given** *v*
= / gɪvst / = / = / 'gɪvɪn, -ɪŋ / gɛːv / =, gɪən
**sp** giue[1289], 'giue[2], giue-[o're][1], *Caius MW 1.4.105* giue-'a[1], giue't [give it][5], giu't [give it][8] / giuest[1], gi-uest[1], giu'st[5] / giues[117] / giueth[2] / giuing[29], gi-uing[1] / gaue[218], gaue't [gave it][1], gau't [gave it][2] / gauest[1], gau'st[14] / giuen[179], gi-uen[3], giuen't [given it][1], giu'n[4]
**rh** live *AW 2.1.130, 2.3.101, 2H6 5.2.89, Luc 987, 1053, R2 1.3.226, RJ 2.3.14, 3.1.180, S 4.6, 13.4, 31.11, 37.10, 39.7, 54.2, 79.10, TC 4.5.38, WT 4.3.21*; **give me** relieve me *Per 5.2.3 [Chorus]*; believe *H8 Prol.7*; sleeve *LLL 5.2.454* / lives [*v*] *Mac 2.1.61, TNK Prol.13* / living *Luc 1715* / **rh** *1* grave *VA 1108*; **rh** *2* have *Luc 1511* / akin *TNK Prol.2*
> misgive

**giver / ~s** *n*
=
**sp** giuer[3] / giuers[1]
> direction-, lie-giver

**giving** *adj / n*
'gɪvɪn, -ɪŋ
**sp** giuing[1] / giuing[1]
> gain-, health-, honour-, thanks-giving

**giving-out** *n*
'gɪvɪn-'əʊt, -ɪŋ-
**sp** giuing-out[1], giuing out[2]
> out

**giving-up** *n*
'gɪvɪn-'ɤp, -ɪŋ-
**sp** giuing vp[1]

**glad** *adj / Per n*
=
**sp** glad[120], gladde[1] / glad[1]
**rh** had Per 2.5.73 [*emend as end of line*]; sad *S 45.13* / bad *Per 2. Chorus.38*

**glad / ~ded** *v*
=
**sp** glad[2] / gladded[1]

**gladding** *n*
'gladɪn, -ɪŋ
**sp** gladding[1]

**gladly** *adv*
'gladləɪ
**sp** gladly[15]
**rh** sadly *S 8.3*

**gladness** *n*
=
**sp** gladnesse[3]
**rh** sadness *TC 1.1.41*

**Glamis** *n*
*m* 'glamɪs, glɑ:mz
**sp** Glamis[4], Glamys[4]

**glanc·e / ~s** *n*
glans, glɔ:ns / 'glansɪz, 'glɔ:-
**sp** glance[3], glances[2] / glaunces[1]
> overglance

**glanc·e / ~ing / ~ed** *v*
glans, glɔ:ns / 'glans·ɪn, -ɪŋ, 'glɔ:- / *m* -ɪd, -t
**sp** glance[5], glaunce[1] / glancing[1] / glanc'd[1], glanced[2]

**glanders** *n*
'glandəɹz
**sp** glanders[1]

**Glansdale** *n*
'glanzdɛ:l
**sp** Glansdale[1]

**glare / ~s** *v*
glɛ:ɹ / -z
**sp** glare[1] / glares[1]

**glass** *adj*
glas
glasse-[eyes][1]

**glass / ~es** *n*
glas / -ɪz
**sp** glasse[43] / glasses[10]
**rh** *1* grass *MND 1.1.210*; pass *AW 2.1.165, Per 2.3.36, R3 1.2.262, VA 980*; **rh** *2* was *Luc 1763, S 5.10*
> burning-, eye-, hour-, looking-glass

**glass / ~ed** *v*
glast
**sp** glast[1]
**rh** passed *LLL 2.1.230*

**glass-faced** *adj*
'glas-ˌfɛ:st
**sp** glasse-fac'd[1]
> face

**glass-gazing** *adj*
'glas-ˌgɛ:zɪn, -ɪŋ
**sp** glasse-gazing[1]

**glassy** *adj*
'glasəɪ
**sp** glassie[3]

**glaze / ~ed** *v*
*m* glɛ:zd, 'glɛ:zɪd
**sp** glaz'd[1] / glazed[1]

**gleam / ~s** *n*
=
**sp** *emend of MND 5.1.266* beams[1]
**rh** beams *MND 5.1.266*

**glean / ~ing / ~ed** *v*
= / 'gli:nɪn, -ɪŋ / gli:nd
**sp** gleane[4] / gleaning[1] / glean'd[1], gleaned[2]

**gleaned** *adj*
*m* 'gli:nɪd
**sp** gleaned[1]

**gleeful** *adj*
=
**sp** gleefull[1]

**gleek / ~s** *n*
=
**sp** gleeke[1] / glikes[1]

**gleek / ~ing** *v*
= / 'gli:kɪn, -ɪŋ
**sp** gleeke[1] / gleeking[1]

**Glendower / ~'s** *n*
*m* glen'do:ɹ, 'glendo:ɹ / 'glendo:ɹz
**sp** Glendour[3], Glendoure[1], Glendower[18], Glen-dower[1] / Glendowers[1]
**rh** hour *1H4 1.3.100*

**glib** *adj / v*
=
**sp** glib[3] / glib[1]

**glide / ~s** *n*
gləɪdz
**sp** glides[1]

**glid·e / ~s / ~eth / ~ed** *v*
gləɪd / -z / 'gləɪd·əθ / -ɪd
**sp** glide[2] / glides[2] / glideth[1] / glyded[1]
**rh** wide *MND 5.1.372*

**gliding** *adj*
'gləɪdɪn, -ɪŋ
**sp** gliding[1]

**glimmer** *n*
'glɪməɹ
**sp** glimmer[1]

**glimmer / ~s** *v*
'glɪməɹ / -z
**sp** glimmer[1] / glimmers[1]

**glimmering** *adj*
'glɪmrɪn, -ɪŋ, -mər-
**sp** glimmering[3]

**glimpse / ~s** *n*
=
**sp** glimpse[2] / glimpses[1]

**glister / ~s** *v*
'glɪstəɹ / -z
**sp** glister[1] / glisters[2]

**glistering** *adj / n*
'glɪstrɪn, -ɪŋ, -tər-
**sp** glistering[2], glistring[1], glist'ring[2] / glistering[1]

**glitter / ~ing** *v*
'glɪtrɪn, -ɪŋ, -tər-
**sp** glittering[2]

**glittering** *adj*
'glɪtrɪn, -ɪŋ, -tər-
**sp** glittering[5]

**globe / ~s** *n*
glo:b / -z
**sp** globe[10] / globes[1]
> under-globe

**glooming** *adj*
'glu:mɪn, -ɪŋ
**sp** glooming[1]

**gloomy** *adj*
'glu:məɪ
**sp** gloomy[2]

**glorif·y / ~ied** *v*
'glɔ:rɪˌfəɪ / -d
**sp** glorifie[3] / glorified[1]

**glorious** *adj*
=
**sp** glorious[40]
**rh** *1* does *Per 2.Chorus.14* /
**rh** *2* melius [*Latin*] *Per Prol.9*
> in-, self-glorious

**gloriously** *adv*
*m* 'glɔ:rɪəsˌləɪ
**sp** gloriously[1]
**rh** *1* by, dye, espy, eye, sky *MND 3.2.106*; **rh** *2* archery, remedy *MND 3.2.106*

**glor·y / ~ies** *n*
'glɔ:rəɪ / -z
**sp** glorie[7], glory[69] / glories[12]
**rh** *1* story *H5 Epil.4, Luc 1523, RJ 1.3.92, S 84.6, 88.8*; **rh** *2* sorry *Luc 1523* / stories *VA 1014*
> vainglory

**glory** *v*
'glɔ:rəɪ
**sp** glory[2]

**glose**
> gloze

**gloss / ~es** *n*
=
**sp** glosse[12] / glosses[1]

**Gloucester / ~'s** *n*
'glɒstəɹ / -z
**sp** Glocester[8], Gloster[93], Gloster's [Gloucester is][1], Gloucester[30], Glou-cester[1], Glouster[26], *abbr in s.d.* Glou[1] / Glosters[12], Gloucesters[1], Glousters[12]

**Gloucestershire** *n*
*m* 'glɒstəɹˌʃəɪɹ, -ɹʃəɹ
**sp** Glocestershire[1], Glo-cestershire[1], Glostershire[1], Gloucestershire[3], Gloustershire[2]

**glove / ~s** *n*
glɤv / -z
**sp** gloue[33] / gloues[17]

**glove** *v*
glɤv
**sp** gloue[2]

**glover / ~'s** *n*
'glɤvəɹz
**sp** glouers[1]

**glow** *n*
glo:
**sp** glowe[1]

**glow / *Luc* ~s / ~ing / ~ed** *v*
glo: / -z / 'glo:ɪn, -ɪŋ / glo:d
**sp** glow[4] / glowes[1] / glowing[1], glowing-[hot][1] / glow'd[1]
**rh** *1* woe *MND 5.1.365*; **rh** *2* brow *VA 337* / goes, those *Luc 47* / bestowed, owed *LC 324*

**glow-worm / ~s / ~s'** *n*
'glo:-ˌwɔ:ɹm / -z
**sp** glow-worme[1] / glow-wormes[1] / [fierie]-glow-wormes[1]
> worm

**glose / ~s** *n*
'glo:zɪz
**sp** glozes[1]

**gloze / ~d** *v*
glo:z / -d
**sp** glose[2], gloze[1] / gloz'd[1]
**rh** close *R2 2.1.10*

**glue / ~s / ~d** *v*
=
**sp** glew[1] / glewes[1] / glew'd[1], glued[1]

**glut** *v*
glɤt
**sp** glut[1]

**glutted** *adj*
'glɤtɪd
**sp** glutted[1]

**glutton** *adj*
'glɤtən
**sp** glutton-[bosome][1]

**glutton / ~'s** *n*
'glɤtən / -z
**sp** glutton[1] / glut-tons[1]

**gluttonous** *adj*
'glɤtnəs
**sp** glutt'nous[1]

**gluttony** *n*
'glɤtnəɪ, -tən-
**sp** gluttonie[2]

**gnarl / ~ing** *v*
'nɑ:ɹlɪn, -ɪŋ, gn-
**sp** gnarling[1]

**gnarled** *adj*
*m* 'nɑ:ɹlɪd, gn-
**sp** gnarled[1]

**gnat / ~s** *n*
=, gn- / -s
**sp** gnat[4] / gnats[5]
**rh** sat *LLL 4.3.164*

**gnaw / ~s / ~ing / ~ed / ~n** *v*
=, gnɔ: / -z / 'nɔ:ɪn, -ɪŋ, 'gn- / =, gnɔ:d / =, gnɔ:n
**sp** gnaw[7] / gnawes[2] / gnawing[2] / gnaw'd[2] / gnawne[1]
> bare-gnawn, begnaw

**gnaw / ~ing** *adj*
'nɔ:ɪn, -ɪŋ, 'gn-
**sp** gnawing[1]

**Gneius** *n*
'nɛ:əs, gn-
**sp** Gneius[1]

**go / ~est / ~es / ~ing / went / ~est / gone** *v*
go: / -st, 'go:əst / -z / 'go:ɪn, -ɪŋ / = / wenst, -ntst / go:n, gɒn
**sp** go[968], go-[too][6], goe[762], goe-[by][1] / goest[10], go'st[3] / goes[166], goe's[2], go's[1], gos't [goes it][1] / going[82], go-ing[2] / went[97] / wentst[1], went'st[2] / gon[33], [be]gon[2], gone[421], [be]gone[1]
**rh** *1* below *Ham 3.3.98, VA 924*; bow [weapon] *MND 3.2.100*; crow *PT 20*; flow *Cym 3.5.160*; foe *1H6 4.5.36, Luc 76, R2 5.4.10, RJ 1.1.79, TC 1.3.308*; grow *R2 3.2.211, S 12.10*; ho *KJ 3.3.71*; know *CE 4.3.79, MM 3.2.252, S 130.11, WT 4.4.295*; no *KJ 3.4.182, KL 5.3.319, MND 3.1.143, TG 1.3.89, TS 1.2.226*; slow *1H4 3.1.257*; snow *Ham 4.5.39*; so *AW 2.3.129, 2.3.297, CE 2.2.226, 4.3.79, Cor 2.3.121, Ham 3.1.189, LLL 2.1.35, 4.3.186, 5.2.60, 622, MND 1.1.187, 2.2.93, 3.1.152, 3.2.184, 5.1.202, MV 2.7.78, R2 1.2.64, 1.3.248, 2.1.298, RJ 3.5.23, Tem 4.1.44, TN 2.1.43, VA 379, 611*; sow [*v*] *MM 4.1.74*; throw *Mac 4.1.4*; wilful-slow *S 51.14*; woe *MA 2.3.64, 5.3.15, 31, MND 3.2.444, Per 3. Chorus.41, R2 3.4.96, 5.1.85, TC 2.2.113, 5.10.30*; **rh** *2* do *TN 2.3.106* / knowest, owest, showest, throwest, trowest *KL 1.4.120* / foes *1H6 3.1.186, Luc 990, R2 2.4.24, Tit 5.2.146, VA 622, 683*; glows, those *Luc 46*; rose *KJ 1.1.143*; shows, woes *Luc 1745*; woes *Luc 1494, 1504* / ornament *LC 113, TN 3.4.372*; Trent *TNK Prol.11* / **rh** *1* Acheron *Mac 3.5.14*; anon *MND 2.1.16, RJ 1.5.144*; benison *KL 1.1.264*; John *1H6 4.7.1*; Oberon *MND 2.1.59, 2.2.88*; on *AC 1.2.127, 2H4 1.3.110, MND 3.2.414, Oth 1.3.202, Per 4.4.20, R3 4.2.120, S 5.7, VA 1089*; Timon *Tim 4.3.97*; upon *AW 3.4.4, MND 3.2.384*; gone, sir anon, sir *TN 4.2.122*; **rh** *2* alone *KJ 3.1.63, S 4.11, 31.10, 45.5, 66.13, TG 3.1.98, TNK 1.1.1, VA 380*; bone *VA 58*; groan *R2 5.1.99*; groan, moan *Luc 1360*; moan *Ham 4.5.197, MND 5.1.325, S 44.10, 71.14*; stone *Ham 4.5.30*; throne *2H6 2.3.37*; **rh** *3* done *JC 5.3.63, TN 2.3.99*; none *CE 3.2.161, [F, at LLL 2.1.113–129], MND 2.2.72, 3.2.170, VA 390*; one *CE 4.2.24, 52, Tit 1.1.370, VA 227, 520, 1071*; son *R3 1.3.10*; sun *VA 188*
> out-, over-, under-go; a-, hence-going; by-, fore-gone

**goad / ~s** *n*
go:dz
**sp** goades[1]

**goad / ~ed** *v*
go:d / 'go:dɪd
**sp** goad[1] / goaded[2]

**goal** *n*
go:l
**sp** goale[1], gole[2]

**goat / ~s** *n*
go:t / -s
**sp** goat[4], goate[3] / goates[6], goats[3]
**pun** goats *AY 3.3.5* Goths

**goatish** *adj*
'go:tɪʃ
**sp** goatish[1]

**gobbet / ~s** *n*
=
**sp** gobbets[1], gobbits[1]

**Gobbo** *n*
'gɒbə, -bo:, 'ʤɒ-
**sp** Iobbe[6], *s.d.* Gobbe[1], *Q* Gobbo

**go-between** *n*
'go:-bɪˌtwi:n
**sp** goe-betweene[1]

**goblet / ~s** *n*
=
**sp** goblet[2] / goblets[1]

**goblin / ~s** *n*
=
**sp** goblin[2] / goblins[5]
> hobgoblin

**God, god,** *abbr* **'od / ~'s / ~s / ~s'** *n*
=, *abbr* ɒd, *MW Evans* gɒt, *Caius* gɑ:ɹ / =, *abbr* ɒdz
**sp** God[645], [fire-roab'd]-God[1], God [sheild][1], Gods [God is][3], God's [God is][2]; *Evans* Got[4], Got-[plesse][1], got-[udge][1], got's[1], go't's[1], Got's-[will][1]; *Caius* gar[21], [be]-gar[1], [by]-gar[6] / Gods[92], God's[1], goggs[1] / Goddes[8], Gods[282], [hot-bloodied]-Gods[1] / gods[1]
**rh** odds *Cym 5.2.10, Tim 1.2.60, 3.5.118*
> demi-, love-god

***God's*** [*in swearing*]
odd's-[hart-lings][1], od's-[me][1], 'ods [my litle life][1], 'od's [my will][1], od's-[nownes] [wounds][1], 'ods [pittikins][1], 's[blud] [God's blood][1], s[death] [God's death][1], s[foote] [God's foot][1], s[lid] [God's lid][1], s[light][1], s'[light] [God's light][1]

***God give good day***
ˌgɒdɪgə'den
**sp** *abbr* Godgigoden[1], Godigoden[1]

***God have mercy***
ˌgɒdə'mɐ:ɹsəɪ, 'gɒdəˌmɐ:ɹsəɪ
**sp** *abbr* God-a-mercie[1], Godamercy[1], God-a-mercy[1]

***God yield***
gə'dɪld, gɒ-
**sp** *abbr* goddild[1], God dil'd[1], God-eyld[1], God'ild[1]

**god / ~ed** *v*
=
**sp** godded[1]

**god-daughter** *n*
'gɒd-ˌdɔ:təɹ, -ˌdɑ:-
**sp** god-daughter[1]

**goddess / ~es** *n*
*m* 'gɒdes / -ɪz
**sp** goddesse[23], god-desse[1] / goddesses[4]

**goddess-like** *adj*
'gɒdes-ləɪk
**sp** goddesse-like[2]

**godfather / ~s** *n*
'gɒdfaðəɹ / -z
**sp** godfather[2], god-father[1] / godfathers[3]

**godhead / ~s** *n*
'gɒdˌed, -ˌhed /
**sp** godhead[2], god-head[1] / godheads[1]

**godlike** *adj*
'gɒdləɪk
**sp** god-like[2]

**godliness** *n*
'gɒdləɪnəs
**sp** godlinesse[1], godly-nesse[1]

**godly** *adv*
'gɒdləɪ
**sp** godly[5]
> ungodly

**godmother** *n*
'gɒdmɤðəɹ
**sp** godmother[2]
> mother

**godson** *n*
'gɒdsɤn
**sp** godsonne[1]

**goer / ~s** *n*
'go:əɹ / -z
**sp** goer[1] / goers[1]

**goer-between / goers-~** *n*
'go:əɹz-bɪˌtwi:n
**sp** goers betweene[1]
> between

**going** *n*
'go:ɪn, -ɪŋ
**sp** going[16]

**gold / ~'s** *n*
go:ld / -z
**sp** gold[209], [tested]-gold[1], golde[3] / golds[2]
**rh** behold *2H6 4.7.92, Luc 855, VA 858*; behold, bold, cold, enfold, inscrolled, old, sold, told *MV 2.7.65*

**gold-bound** *adj*
'go:l-ˌbəʊnd, -ld-
**sp** gold-bound-[brow][1]
> bound

**golden** *adj*
'go:ldən
**sp** golden[82], gol-den[2]

**goldenly** *adv*
'go:ldənləɪ
**sp** goldenly[1]

**goldsmith / ~'s / ~s'** *n*
'go:lsmɪθ, -ld- / -s
**sp** goldsmith[11], gold-smith[1] / goldsmiths[1] /goldsmiths[1]

**Golgotha** *n*
'gɒlgətə, -əθə
**sp** Golgotha[2]

**Golia·th / ~sses** *n*
gə'ləɪəθ / *m* gə'ləɪəˌsɪz
**sp** Goliath[1] / Goliasses[1]

**gondola** *n*
'gɒndələ, -lo:
**sp** gondilo[1], gundello[1]

**gondolier** *n*
ˌgɒndə'li:ɹ
**sp** gundelier[1]

**Goneril** *n*
*m* 'gɒnərɪl, -nr-
**sp** Generill[18]

**Gonzago / ~'s** *n*
gən'zɑ:go: / -z
**sp** Gonzago[2], Gon-zago[1] / Gonzago's[1]

**Gonzalo / ~s** *n*
gən'zɑ:lo: / -z
**sp** Gonzallo[6], Gonzalo[8] / Gonzaloes[1]

**good** *adj / adv*
=, *Evans MW 1.1.41ff* gʊt, *Macmorris H5 3.2.99ff* gyd
**sp** good[2589], 'good[1], good'[2], good-[creature][1], good-[deed][1], [good]faith[1], good-[faith][1], good[fellow][1], good-[fellow][2], good-[fellowes][1], good-[heart][1], good-[hearts][1], good-[lucke][1], good-[manners][1], [good]-morrowes[1], good[sooth][1], good-[sooth][2], good-[wife][1], *Evans* goot[3], goo't[1], *Macmorris* gud[5] / *sp* good[3]
**rh** *adj 1* blood *AW 2.3.95, LC 164, LLL 2.1.122, Luc 1028, Mac 3.4.134, 4.1.38, MND 5.1.274, R2 2.1.130, 5.5.114, S 121.8, Tim 3.5.53, 4.2.39, Tit 5.1.50, VA 1181*; flood *Luc 1117*;
**rh** *2* food *Luc 1117*; mood *Luc 1274*;
**rh** *3* livelihood *VA 28*; stood *AW 1.3.75, 76*; understood *R2 2.1.214*; wood *Mac 4.1.95, MND 2.2.43*
> good-day, -even, -morrow, -night

**good / ~s** *n*
=
**sp** good[127] / goodes[1], goods[23]
**rh** blood *1H6 2.5.129, S 109.12*; blood, flood *Luc 656*; bud *PP 13.1*

**good-day** *n*
gʊ'dɛ:, ˌgʊd- *Macmorris H5 3.2.80* gyd'dɛ:
**sp** good day[15], *Macmorris* gudday[1]
> day

**good-even** *n*
gʊd'i:vn, 'i:n, -'en
**sp** [dig-you]-den[1], godden[3], good den[6], gooden[3], good euen[6], good'-euen[1], good-euen[1], [ye]-good-ev'n[1]
> even

**good-faced** *adj*
'gʊd-ˌfɛ:st
**sp** good fac'd[1]
> face

**Goodfellow** [name] *n*
'gʊdfelə, -lo:
**sp** good-fellow[1], Good-fellow[1]
> fellow

**Good Friday** *n*
ˌgʊd 'frəɪdɛ:
**sp** Good-Friday[1], good Friday[1]
> Friday

**good-limbed** *adj*
'gʊd-ˌlɪmd
**sp** good limb'd[1]
> limb

**goodl·y / ~ier / ~iest** *adj*
'gʊdləɪ / -əɹ / -əst
**sp** goodlie[1], goodly[69] / goodlier[2] / goodliest[2]

**goodly** *adv*
'gʊdləɪ
**sp** goodly[2]

**goodman / ~'s** *n*
=
**sp** goodman[14], good-man[2] / goodmans[1]

**good-morrow / ~s** *n*
gʊd'mɒrə, -ro: / -z
**sp** god morrow[1], good morow[1], good morrow[92], good mor-row[2], goodmorrow[4], good-morrow[8] / good-morrowes[1], good morrowes[2], good-morrows[1]
**rh** borrow *VA 859*; sorrow *Luc 1219*

**goodness** *n*
=
**sp** goodnes[3], goodnesse[49]

**good-night / ~s** *n*
ˌgʊd'nəɪt / -s
**sp** godnight[1], goodnight[42], good-night[3], good night[59] / good nights[1]
**rh** might *TNK Epil.18*; sight *Mac 5.1.73*
> night

**Goodrig** *n*
'gʊdrɪg
**sp** Goodrig[1]

**goodwife** *adj*
'gʊdwəɪf
**sp** goodwife[1]
> wife

**Goodwin / ~s** *n*
=
**sp** Goodwin[2] / Goodwins[1]

**goodyear** *n*
'gʊdjəɹ, -ji:ɹ
**sp** good-ier[1], good yeere[1], good-yere[2]
> year

**goose** *adj*
=
**sp** goose-[looke][1]

**goose / geese** *n*
=
**sp** goose[24], [giddy]-goose[1], [sweet]-goose[1], [wild]-goose[2] / geese[7], [wilde]-geese[3], geesse[1]
**rh** loose *LLL 3.1.102*

**gooseberry** *n*
'gu:zbrəɪ, -bər-
**sp** gooseberry[1]

**goose-pen** *n*
=
**sp** goose-pen[1]
> pen

**goose-quill / ~s** *n*
=
**sp** goose-quils[1]
> quill

**gorbellied** *adj*
'gɔ:ɹˌbeləɪd
**sp** gorbellied[1]
> belly

**Gorboduc** *n*
'gɔ:ɹbəˌdɤk
**sp** Gorbodacke[1]

**Gordian** *adj*
'gɔ:ɹdɪən
**sp** Gordian[1], Gordian-[knot][1]

**gore** *adj / n*
gɔ:ɹ
**sp** gore[1] / gore[7]
**rh** *n* more *Tim 3.5.85*; shore *MND 5.1.331*

**gore / ~d** *v*
gɔ:ɹ / gɔ:ɹd
**sp** gore[1] / goard[1], gor'd[2], gored[1], go-red[1]
**rh** adore *TN 2.5.105*; boar *VA 616, 664*

**gored** *adj*
gɔ:ɹd
**sp** gor'd[1]

**gorge** *n*
gɔ:ɹʤ
**sp** gorge[4]

**gorg·e / ~ing / ~ed** *v*
gɔ:ɹʤ / 'gɔ:ɹʤɪn, -ɪŋ / gɔ:ɹʤd
**sp** gorge[1] / gorging[1] / gorg'd[3]
> dis-, over-gorge; shrill-, un-gorged

**gorge** *Fr n*
gɔɹʒ, *Pistol H5 2.1.68, 4.4.37*
gɔ:ɹʤ, gɔ:ɹʒ
**sp** gorge[1], *Pistol* gorge[2]

**gorgeous** *adj*
*m* 'gɔ:ɹʤəs, -ɪəs, -ɪˌɤs
**sp** gorgeous[9]
> thrice-gorgeous

**gorget** *n*
'gɔ:ɹʤɪt
**sp** gorget[1]

**Gorgon** *n*
'gɔ:ɹgən
**sp** Gorgon[2]

**gormandiz·e / ~ing** *v*
'gu:ɹmənˌdəɪz / -ɪn, -ɪŋ
**sp** gurmandize[1] / gourmandizing[1]

**gorse** *n*
gɒs, gɔːs
**sp** gosse[1]

**gory** *adj*
ˈgɔːrəɪ
**sp** goarie[1], goary[1], gorie[1]

**gosling** *n*
=
**sp** gosling[1]

**gospel / ~s** *n*
=
**sp** gospels[1]

**gospel / ~led** *v*
=
**sp** gospell'd[1]

**gossamer / ~s** *n*
*m* ˈgɒsəˌmoːɹ, ˈgɒz- / -z
**sp** gozemore[1] / gossamours[1]

**gossip / ~'s / ~s** *n*
=
**sp** goship[1], gossip[6] / gossips[4] / gossips[4]

**gossip / ~s / ~ped** *v*
=
**sp** gossip[1] / gossips[1] / gossipt[1]

**gossip-like** *adj*
ˈgɒsɪp-ləɪk
**sp** gossep-like[1]

**gossipping** *n*
ˈgɒsɪpɪn, -ɪŋ
**sp** gossipping[2]

**got**
> get

**Goth / ~s** *n*
goːt / -s
**sp** Goth[5] / Gothes[30], Goths[1]
**pun** *AY 3.3.5* goats

**Gough** *n*
gɒf
**sp** Goffe[2]

**gourd** *n*
guːɹd
**sp** gourd[1]

**gout** [disease] *n*
gəʊt
**sp** gowt[6]

**gout / ~s** [stream] *n*
gəʊts
**sp** gouts[1]

**gouty** *adj*
ˈgəʊtəɪ
**sp** gowtie[1], gowty[1]

**govern / ~s / ~ed** *v*
ˈgɤvəɹn / -z / -d
**sp** gouern[2], gouerne[21], go-uerne[1] / gouernes[2] / gouern'd[14], gouerned[4]
> best-, hell-, mis-, un-, well-governed

**governance** *n*
*m* ˈgɤvəɹˌnans
**sp** gouernance[1]

**governess** *n*
*m* ˈgɤvəɹˌnes
**sp** gouernesse[1]

**government** *n*
*m* ˈgɤvəɹˌment, -ɹmənt
**sp** gouernment[24], go-uernment[1]
**rh** lent *Luc 1400*

**governor / ~s** *n*
*m* ˈgɤvəɹˌnɔːɹ, ˈgɤvnəɹ / -əɹˌnɔːɹz
**sp** gouernor[7], gouernour[8] / gouernors[2]

**Gower** *n*
ˈgoːɹ
**sp** Gower[16], Gowre[3]

**gown / ~s** *n*
gəʊn / -z
**sp** gown[1], gowne[48], [blacke]-gowne[1], gown's [gown is][1] / gownes[6]
> night-, sea-gown

**grace / ~'s / ~s** *n*
grɛːs / ˈgrɛːsɪz
**sp** grace[526] / graces[19] / graces[44]
**rh** apace, face *LC 285*; base *Cym 4.2.27, R2 3.3.181, Tim 3.5.95*; case *TS 4.2.44*; case, pace *Luc 712*; case, place *LC 114*; chase *MND 2.2.95*; face *CE 2.1.87, LLL 3.1.64, 5.2.80, 128, 147, MND 5.1.192, Per Prol.24, R2 5.3.98, S 132.11, Tit 3.1.203, VA 64*; face, place *LC 79, Luc 564*; pace *WT 4.1.24*; place *3H6 4.6.30, KL 1.1.273, LC 316, LLL 2.1.178, 3.1.64, Mac 5.6.111, MND 5.1.389, Per 2.3.19, 4.Chorus.9, R2 3.4.105, S 79.2, Tem 4.1.72*; place, space *LC 261*; space *AW 2.1.160, LLL 1.1.51, 150*; grace her deface her *PP 7.5* / faces *Luc 1410, TG 3.1.102, S 17.6, 94.5*
> herb-grace

**grac·e / ~ing / ~ed** *v*
grɛːs / ˈgrɛːs·ɪn, -ɪŋ / *m* -ɪd, grɛːst
**sp** grace[32] / gracing[1] / grac'd[9], graced[2]

**grâce** *Fr n*
grɑːs
**sp** grace[1]

**graced** *adj*
grɛːst
**sp** grac'd[2]
> well-graced

**graceful** *adj*
ˈgrɛːsfʊl
**sp** graceful[1], gracefull[3], grace-full[1]
> disgraceful

**gracefully** *adv*
ˈgrɛːsfləɪ, -fʊl-
**sp** gracefully[1]

**graceless** *adj*
ˈgrɛːsləs
**sp** gracelesse[5]

**gracious** *adj*
ˈgrɛːsɪəs
**sp** gracious[184], gra-cious[1], gratious[5]
**rh** spacious *S 135.7*
> thrice-, un-gracious

**graciously** *adv*
*m* 'grɛ:sɪəs,ləɪ
**sp** graciously[4]

**gradation** *n*
grə'dɛ:sɪən
**sp** gradation[2]

**graff** *v*
graf
**sp** graffe[2]
graf
> in-, long-in-, mis-graffed

**graffing** *n*
'grafɪn, -ɪŋ
**sp** graf-fing[1]

**graft / ~est / graft / ~ed** *v*
grafst, -tst / graft / 'graftɪd
**sp** graft'st[1] / grafft[1], graft[1] / grafted[5]

**grafter / ~s** *n*
'graftəɹz
**sp** grafters[1]

**grain / ~s** *n*
grɛ:n / -z
**sp** grain[1], graine[17] / graines[3]
> purple-in-grain

**grained** *adj*
*m* 'grɛ:nɪd
**sp** grained[3]

**gramerc·y / ~ies** *n*
grə'mɐ:ɹsəɪ / -z
**sp** gramercie[3], gramercy[3] / gramercies[3]

**grammar** *n*
'graməɹ
**sp** grammar[1], grammer[1]

**grand** *adj*
=
**sp** grand[11]

**grand / ~e** *Fr adj*
grɑ̃ / grɑ̃:d
**sp** grand[3] / grand[1]

**grandam / ~'s** *n*
'gran,dam / -z
**sp** grandam[18], grandame[10] / grandames[1], grandams[2]

**grandchild** *n*
'gran,ʧəɪld
**sp** grandchilde[1]

**grandeur** *Fr n*
grɑ̃'dœ:ɹ
**sp** *emend of H5 5.2.251* grandeus

**grandfather / ~'s** *n*
'gran,faðəɹ / -z
**sp** grandfather[14], grand-father[1] / grand-fathers[2]
> father, great-grandfather

**grandjuror / ~s** *n*
'gran,ʤu:rəɹz
**sp** grand iurers[1]

**grand-jury** *adj*
,gran-'ʤu:rəɪ
**sp** grand iurie[1]
> jury

**grandmother** *n*
'gran,mɤðəɹ
**sp** grandmother[2], grand-mother[2]

**Grandpre** *n*
grɔ:n'pri:
**sp** Grandpree[2], Grand Pree[1], Graundpree[1]

**grandsire** *adj*
'gran,səɪɹ
**sp** grandsier[1]
> great-grandsire

**grandsire / ~'s / ~s** *n*
'gran,səɪɹ / -z
**sp** grandsier[1], grandsire[17], grand-sire[4], gransier[2] / grandsires[3] / grandsires[2]

**grange** *n*
grɛ:nʤ
**sp** grange[2], [moated]-grange[1]

**grant** *n*
grɔ:nt, grant
**sp** graunt[7]

**grant / ~s / *Luc* ~eth / ~ing / ~ed** *v*
grɔ:nt, grant / -s / 'grɔ:nt·əθ, -ran- / -ɪn, -ɪŋ / -ɪd
**sp** grant[69], graunt[28] / grants[1], graunts[2] / granteth[1] / granting[2] / granted[18], graunted[11]
**rh** *1* panteth *Luc 558*; **rh** *2* wanteth *Luc 558* / wanting *S 87.5* / **rh** *1* enchanted *LC 131*; planted *LLL 1.1.159*; **rh** *2* haunted *LC 131, LLL 1.1.159*

**grape / ~s** *n*
grap / -s
**sp** grape[4] / grapes[8]
**rh** mishaps *VA 601*

**grapple** *n*
'grapəl
**sp** grapple[2]

**grapple / ~s** *v*
'grapəl / -z
**sp** grapple[6] / grapples[1]

**grappling** *adj*
'graplɪn, -ɪŋ
**sp** grapling[1]

**grasp / ~s** *n*
grasp / -s
**sp** graspe[1] / graspes[1]

**grasp / ~s / ~ed** *v*
grasp / -s / *m* -t, 'graspɪd
**sp** graspe[1] / graspes[1] / grasped[1], graspt[3]

**grass** *n*
gras
**sp** grasse[16], [chaw'd]-grasse[1]
**rh** *1* ass *CE 2.2.210*; glass *MND 1.1.211*; **rh** *2* was *Luc 395*
> knot-, spear-grass; short-grassed

**grass-green** *n*
'gras-,gri:n
**sp** grasse-greene[1]

**grasshopper / ~s** *n*
'grasɒpəɹz, -hɒ-
**sp** grashoppers[1]

**grass-plot** *n*
'gras-ˌplɒt
**sp** grasse-plot[1]

**grassy** *adj*
'grasəɪ
**sp** grassie[1]

**grate** *n*
grɛ:t
**sp** grate[3]

**grat·e / ~s / ~ing / ~ed** *v*
grɛ:t / -s / 'grɛ:t·ɪn, -ɪŋ / -ɪd
**sp** grate[2] / grates[1] / grating[2] / grated[2]

**grateful** *adj*
'grɛ:tfʊl
**sp** gratefull[4]
> ungrateful

**Gratiano / ~'s** *n*
*m* ˌgratsɪ'ɑ:no:, -'sjɑ:- / -z
**sp** Gratiano[26], *abbr in s.d.* Grati[1] / Gratianos[1]

**gratify** *v*
*m* 'gratɪˌfəɪ, -tɪf-
**sp** gratifie[8]

**Gratii** *n*
'gratɪi: [*3 sylls*]
**sp** Gratij[1]

**gratility** *n*
grə'tɪlɪtəɪ
**sp** gratillity[1]

**grating** *adj*
'grɛ:tɪn, -ɪŋ
**sp** grating[1]

**gratis** *adv*
'gratɪs
**sp** gratis[8]

**gratitude** *n*
*m* 'gratɪˌtju:d, -ɪt-
**sp** gratitude[3], grati-tude[1]

**gratulate** *v*
*m* 'gratjəˌlɛ:t, -əl-
**sp** gratulate[4]

**grave / ~er / ~est** *adj*
grɛ:v, grav / 'grɛ:v·əɹ, 'grav- / -əst
**sp** graue[35] / grauer[5] / grauest[1]
**rh** knave *Ham 3.4.215*

**grave / ~s** *n*
grɛ:v, grav / -z
**sp** graue[140], graue's [grave is][1] / graues[30]
**rh** *1* crave *Per 2.1.10, 2.3.46*; gave *VA 1106*; save *TN 2.4.64*; slave *AW 2.3.137, Luc 198, 661*; wave *3H6 2.2.174* ; **rh** *2* have *AW 5.3.62, Cym 4.2.281, 1H6 4.3.40, 4.7.32, Luc 198, R2 1.1.168, 2.1.137, 140, RJ 2.3.79, S 81.7, VA 757* / depraves *Tim 1.2.138*

**grave / ~ed** *v*
grɛ:v, grav / -d
**sp** graue[1] / grau'd[1]
**rh** grave it have it *VA 376*

**gravel** *adj / n*
=
**sp** grauell[1] / grauell[2]

**gravel / ~led** *v*
=
**sp** grauel'd[1]

**gravel-blind** *adj*
'gravəl-ˌbləɪnd
**sp** grauel blinde[1]
> blind

**graveless** *adj*
'grɛ:vləs, 'grav-
**sp** grauelesse[1]

**gravely** *adv*
'grɛ:vləɪ, 'grav-
**sp** grauely[1]

**grave-maker / ~s** *n*
'grɛ:v-ˌmɛ:kəɹ, 'grav- / -z
**sp** graue-maker[2] / graue-makers[1]
> make

**grave-making** *n*
'grɛ:v-ˌmɛ:kɪn, -ɪŋ, 'grav-
**sp** graue-making[1]

**graver** *n*
'grɛ:vəɹ, 'grav-
**sp** grauer[1]

**gravestone** *n*
'grɛ:vsto:n, 'grav-
**sp** grauestone[1], graue-stone[1], graue stone[1]
> stone

**gravit·y / ~y's / ~ies** *n*
*m* 'gravɪˌtəɪ, -vɪt-, -vt- / 'gravɪˌtəɪz
**sp** grauitie[5], grauity[7] / grauities[1] / grauities[1]
**rh** eye *S 49.8* / eyes *LLL 5.2.763*

**gravy** *n*
'gravəɪ
**sp** grauy[3]
**pun** *2H4 1.2.164* gravity

**gray, Grey**
> grey, Grey

**Gray's Inn** *n*
ˌgrɛ:z 'ɪn
**sp** Greyes-Inne[1]

**graze / ~d** *v*
grɛ:z / -d
**sp** grase[1], graze[6] / graz'd[1]

**grazing** *n*
'grɛ:zɪn, -ɪŋ
**sp** grasing[1]

**grease** *n*
gri:s, gri:z
**sp** greace[1], grease[4], greaze[1]

**grease / ~s** *v*
'gri:sɪz, -i:z-
**sp** greases[1]

**greasely** *adv*
'gri:sləɪ, -i:z-
**sp** greasely[1]

**greasy** *adj*
'gri:səɪ, -i:z-
**sp** greasie[7], greazie[3]

**great / ~er / ~est** *adj*
gret, grɛ:t / 'gret·əɹ, 'grɛ:- / *m* -əst, gretst, grɛ:-
**sp** great[854], great-[ones][2] / greater[75] / greatest[49], great'st[8]
**rh** *1* get *Luc 876*; Plantagenet *KJ 1.1.161*; sweat *H8 Prol.27*; **rh** *2* defeat *S 61.9*; repeat *Per 1.4.30*; seat *Luc 69* / better *S 119.12*
> overgreat

**great** *n*
gret, grɛ:t
**sp** great[22]
**rh** *1* eat *Cym 4.2.264*; seat *Per Prol.17*; **rh** *2* sweat *LLL 5.2.548*

**great-bellied** *adj*
*m* ˌgret-'beləɪd, ˌgrɛ:t-
**sp** great bellied[1], great belly'd[1]

**great-belly** *adj*
'gret-ˌbeləɪ, 'grɛ:t-
**sp** great belly[1]
> belly

**greater** *n*
'gretəɹ, 'grɛ:-
**sp** greater[7]

**greatest** *n*
*m* gretəst, -tst, grɛ:-
**sp** greatest[8], great'st[3]

**great-grandfather** *n*
ˌgret-'granfaðəɹ, ˌgrɛ:t-
**sp** great grandfather[3]
> grandfather

**great-grandsire / ~'s** *n*
ˌgret-'gransəɪɹ, ˌgrɛ:t- / -z
**sp** great grand-sire[1] / great grandsires[1]
> grandsire

**great-grown** *adj*
'gret-ˌgro:n, 'grɛ:t-
**sp** great-growne[1]
> grow

**greatly** *adv*
'gretləɪ, 'grɛ:t-
**sp** greatly[11]

**greatness** *n*
'gretnəs, 'grɛ:t-
**sp** greatnes[3], greatnesse[73], great-nesse[1]

**great-sized** *adj*
'gret-ˌsəɪzd, 'grɛ:t-
**sp** great siz'd[2]
> size

**great-uncle / ~s** *n*
ˌgret-'ɤŋkəl, ˌgrɛ:t- / -z
**sp** great vncle[1] / great vnckles[1]
> uncle

**Grecian** *adj*
'gri:sɪən
**sp** Grecian[16]

**Grecian** *n*
'gri:sɪən / -z
**sp** Grecian[8] / Grecians[1] / Grecians[7]

**Greece** *n*
=
**sp** Greece[19]
**rh** piece *Luc 1368*

**greedily** *adv*
*m* 'gri:dɪˌləɪ
**sp** greedily[1]
> overgreedy

**greediness** *n*
*m* 'gri:dɪˌnes, -nəs
**sp** greedinesse[4]

**greedy** *adj*
'gri:dəɪ
**sp** greedie[1], greedy[5]

**Greek** *adj*
=
**sp** Greeke[2]

**Greek / ~s / ~s'** *n*
=
**sp** Greek[4], Greeke[20], greke[1] / Greekes[23], Greeks[3] / Greekes[2], Greeks[1]
**rh** seek *TC 4.5.86, 5.8.9*

**Greekish** *adj*
=
**sp** greekish[8]

**green / ~er** *adj*
= / 'gri:nəɹ
**sp** green[2], green-[land][1], greene[60], greene-[a-box][2], greene-[sicknesse][2] / greener[1]
**rh** queen *PP 4.2*; seen *S 33.3, 63.14, 104.8*; teen *VA 806*

**green / ~s** *n*
=
**sp** green[2], greene[8], [Mile-end]-Greene[1] / greenes[1]
**rh** queen *MND 2.1.9, Tem 4.1.83*; seen *S 68.11, VA 146*; sheen *MND 2.1.28*

**Green** [name] *n*
=
**sp** Greene[12]

**green-eyed** *adj*
'gri:n-ˌəɪd
**sp** greene-eyed[1], greene-ey'd[1]
> eye

**greenly** *adv*
'gri:nləɪ
**sp** greenely[1], greenly[1]

**Greensleeves** *n*
=
**sp** Greene-sleeues[1]

**greensward** *n*
'gri:n-ˌsɔ:ɹd
**sp** greene-sord[1]

**Greenwich** *n*
'gri:nɪʧ
**sp** Greenwich[1]

**greenwood** *n*
=
**sp** greene wood[1]
> wood

**greet / ~s / ~ed** *v*
=
**sp** greet[29], greete[11] / greetes[4], greets[7] / greeted[1]
**rh** meet *LLL 5.2.144*; sweet *LLL 5.2.374, S 145.8, TN 2.4.60*
> regreet

**greeting / ~s** *n*
'gri:tɪn, -ɪŋ / -z
**sp** greeting[24] / greetings[8]
**rh** meeting *RJ 1.5.90*

**Gregory / ~'s** *n*
'gregrəɪ, -gər- / -z
**sp** Gregory[7] / Gregories[1]

**Gremio** *n*
*m* 'gremɪo:, -ɪ,o:
**sp** Gremio[31]
**rh** Hortensio, know *TS 1.2.233*

**grew**
> grow

**grey** *adj*
grɛ:
**sp** gray[13], gray-[beard][2], grey[6]
**rh** day, way *MA 5.3.27*; nay *MND 3.1.124*; way *TS 4.1.131*

**Grey** [name] *n*
grɛ:
**sp** Gray[11], Grey[13]
**rh** play *R3 4.4.69*

**greybeard / ~s** *n*
*m* 'grɛ:,bɛ:ɹd, ,grɛ:'bɛ:ɹd, -bɐ:ɹd / -z
**sp** gray-beard[2], grey-beard[1] / gray-beards[2]
> beard

**grey-coated** *adj*
,grɛ:-'ko:tɪd
**sp** gray-coated[1]
> coat

**grey-eyed** *adj*
'grɛ:-,əɪd
**sp** gray ey'd[2]
> eye

**greyhound / ~'s / ~s** *n*
'grɛ:,əʊnd, -,həʊ- / -z
**sp** gray-hound[1], grey-hound[5] / grey-hounds[1] / gray-hounds[1], greyhounds[1], grey-hounds[3]

**Grey-Malkin** *n*
,grɛ:-'mɔ:kɪn
**sp** Gray-Malkin[1]

**grief / ~s** *n*
=
**sp** greefe[102], griefe[98], greefe's [grief is][1] / greefes[23], griefes[34], griefs[1]
**rh** brief *Luc 1308, R2 5.1.94*; chief *S 42.1, VA 968*; relief *3H6 3.3.19, S 34.9*; thief *Luc 889, Oth 1.3.207, S 40.11, 48.6*
> fee-, heart-grief

**grief-shot** *adj*
=
**sp** greefe-shot[1]
> shot

**grievance / ~s** *n*
=
**sp** greeuance[2], grieuance[3] / greeuances[2], grieuances[4]

**griev·e / ~est / ~s / ~ing / ~ed** *v*
= / gri:vst / = / 'gri:vɪn, -ɪŋ / =
**sp** greeue[19], grieue[19] / greeu'st[1] / greeues[12], grieues[9] / greeuing[2] / greeu'd[5], greeued[1], grieu'd[6], grieued[1]
**rh** **grieve for them** relieve them *Per 1.2.100* / thieves *VA 1024* / leaving *WT 4.1.18* / achieved *R2 4.1.215*

**grieved** *adj*
*m* 'gri:vɪd
**sp** greeued[4], grieued[2]

**grieving** *n*
'gri:vɪn, -ɪŋ
**sp** greeuing[3], grieuing[2]

**grievingly** *adv*
*m* 'gri:vɪn,ləɪ, -ɪŋ
**sp** greeuingly[1]

**grievous** *adj*
=
**sp** greeuous[15], grieuous[9]

**grievously** *adv*
*m* 'gri:vəs,ləɪ, -sl-
**sp** greeuously[5], grieuously[1]

**griffin** *n*
=
**sp** griffin[2]

**Griffith** *n*
=
**sp** Griffith[11]

**grim** *adj*
=
**sp** grim[15]
**rh** him *LLL 2.1.242, MND 3.2.57, VA 920*; lym *KL 3.6.67* [*emend*]

**grime** *n / v*
grəɪm
**sp** grime[1] / grime[1]

**grim-looked** *adj*
=
**sp** grim lookt[1]
> look

**grimly** *adv*
'grimləɪ
**sp** grimly[2]

**grim-visaged** *adj*
=
**sp** grim-visag'd[1]
> visage

**grin / ~ning** *v*
= / 'grɪnɪn, -ɪŋ
**sp** grin[4], grinne[1], grynne[1] / grinning[1]

**grind** *n*
grəɪnd
**sp** grin'd[2], grinde[3]
**rh** confined *S 110.10*

**grinding** *n*
'grəɪndɪn, -ɪŋ
**sp** grinding[3]

**grindstone** *n*
'grəɪnsto:n, -nds-
**sp** grindstone[1]
> stone

**grinning** *adj*
'grɪnɪn, -ɪŋ
**sp** grinning[1]

**grip / ~s** *n*
=
**sp** gripe[2] / gripes[2]

**grip** *v*
=
**sp** grip[2]

**gripe / ~s / ~ped** *v*
grəɪp / -s / -t
**sp** gripe[5] / gripes[1] / grip'd[1]

**griping** *adj*
'grəɪpɪn, -ɪŋ
**sp** griping[1]

**grise** *n*
gri:z
**sp** grise[1], grize[2]

**grisly** *adj*
'grɪzləɪ
**sp** grisly[2], grizly[1]

**Grissel** *n*
=
**sp** Grissell[1]

**grizzle** *n*
=
**sp** grizzle[1]

**grizzled** *adj*
=
**sp** grizled[1]

**groan / ~s** *n*
'gro:n / -z
**sp** groane[5], grone[3] / groanes[16], grones[15]
**rh** *1* alone *Ham 3.3.23*; throne *VA 1044*; **rh** *2* gone *Luc 1362, R2 5.1.100*; on *S 50.11*; **rh** *3* none *2H6 3.1.221* / bones *TC 5.10.50*; moans *Luc 588, 797, R2 5.1.89*; moans, stones *Luc 975*; stones *R2 1.2.70*

**groan / ~s / ~ing / ~ed** *v*
gro:n / -z / 'gro:nɪn, -ɪŋ / gro:nd
**sp** groane[9], grone[13] / grones[3] / groaning[3], groning[1] / groan'd[2], gron'd[1]
**rh** alone *S 131.6, 133.1, VA 785*; Joan *LLL 3.1.201*; moan *Luc 1362, MA 5.3.17* / moans *VA 829*

**groaning** *adj / n*
'gro:nɪn, -ɪŋ
**sp** groaning[4] / groaning[1]

**groat / ~s** *n*
'gro:t / -s
**sp** groat[5] / groates[2], groats[3]
> shove-groat

**groin** *n*
grəɪn
**sp** groyne[1]
**rh** swine *VA 1116*

**groom / ~s** *n*
gru:m, grʊm / -z
**sp** groome[15] / groomes[8]
**rh** *1* doom *Luc 671*; **rh** *2* Rome *Luc 1645*
> bridegroom

**grop·e / ~ing / ~ed** *v*
'gro:pɪn, -ɪŋ / gro:pt
**sp** groping[1] / grop'd[1]

**gros** *Fr adj*
gro:s
**sp** grosse[1]

**gross / ~er** *adj*
gro:s, grɒs / 'gro:səɹ, 'grɒs-
**sp** grose[1], grosse[47], grosse-[selues][1], grosse-[watry][1] / grosser[5]

**gross** *n*
gro:s, grɒs
**sp** grosse[4]

**grossly** *adv*
'gro:sləɪ, 'grɒs-
**sp** grosely[2], grosly[1], grosselie[2], grossely[13]

**grossness** *n*
'gro:snəs, 'grɒs-
**sp** grosenesse[1], grossenesse[5]

**ground / ~s** *n*
grəʊnd, *Macmorris H5 3.2.112* grʏnd / -z
**sp** ground[157], grownd[2], *Macmorris* grund[1] / grounds[8]
**rh** *1* bound *VA 224*; confound *Luc 1199, VA 1046*; drowned *VA 983*; found *CE 2.1.97, MND 4.1.101, PP 13.9, S 75.2, 153.4*; hound *Tit 2.2.26*; profound *LLL 5.2.115, Mac 3.5.25*; round *Ham 3.2.165*; sound *MND 2.2.81, 3.2.448, S 130.12*; **rh** *2* wound *Luc 1199, MND 2.2.106, R2 3.2.140* / hounds *PP 9.8*
> sharp-, winter-ground

**ground / ~ed** *v*
'grəʊndɪd
**sp** grounded[2]

**grounded** *adj*
'grəʊndɪd
**sp** grounded[1]

**groundling / ~s** *n*
'grəʊndlɪnz, -ɪŋz
**sp** groundlings[1]

**grove / ~s** *n*
grɤv, gro:v / -z
**sp** groue[14] / groues[5]
**rh** love *MND 2.1.245, 259, 3.2.5, VA 865*
> broom-, lime-grove

**grovel / ~ling** *v*
= / 'grovlɪn, -ɪŋ, -vəl-
**sp** grouell[2] / groueling[1]

**grow / ~est / ~s / ~eth / ~ing / grew / ~est / grown** *v*
gro: / -st / -z / 'gro:·əθ / -ɪn, -ɪŋ / = / gru:st / gro:n
**sp** grow[129], growe[1] / grow'st[3] / growes[69], grows[2] / groweth[1] / growing[14] / grew[27] / grew'st[2] / grown[1], growne[49]
**rh** *1* Angelo *MM 3.2.258*; go *R2 3.2.212, S 12.12*; know *LLL 2.1.54, R2 5.3.105, RJ 1.1.154*; low *Tim 4.1.39*; overthrow *TN 5.1.164*; owe *MND 3.2.84*; owe, show *Luc 298*; show *MND 3.2.140, S 69.14, 83.8, 93.13*; so *LLL 3.1.54, 5.2.253, R3 2.4.9, S 115.14, TN 2.4.41*; woe *R2 3.4.101, 5.6.46*; **rh** *2* brow *VA 141* / bestow'st *S 11.1*; ow'st *S 18.12*; show'st *S 126.4* / blows *MND 2.1.250*; rose, shows *LLL 1.1.107*; shows *S 15.1*; those *S 142.11*; woes *RJ 3.5.35* / **rh** *1* blowing *TNK 1.1.10*; knowing *S 87.11*; **rh** *2* bowing [head] *Tem 4.1.112* / hue *S 98.8*; untrue *LC 171*; you *S 84.4, 86.4*
> a-growing, overgrow

**growing** *adj / n*
'gro:ɪn, -ɪŋ
**sp** growing[6] / growing[4]
**rh** *n* allowing *WT 4.1.16*

**grown** *adj*
gro:n
**sp** growne[1]
> full-, great-, high-, long-, moss-, out-, thick-, un-grown

**growth** *n*
gro:θ
**sp** growth[13]
**rh** both *S 99.12*; oath, troth *Luc 1062*

**grub / ~s** *n*
grɤb / -z
**sp** grub[3] / grubs[1]

**grub / ~bed** *v*
grɤbd
**sp** grubb'd[1]

**grudge / ~s** *n*
grɤʤ / 'grɤʤɪz
**sp** grudge[7] / grudges[2]

**grudge / ~d** *v*
grɤʤ / -d
**sp** grudge[2] / grug'd[1]

**grudging** *adj / n*
'grɤʤɪn, -ɪŋ
**sp** grudging[3] / grudging[1]

**gruel** *n*
=
**sp** grewell[1]

**grumble / ~st** *v*
'grɤm·bəl / -bləst
**sp** grumble[2] / grumblest[1]

**grumbling** *adj*
'grɤmblɪn, -ɪŋ, -ml-
**sp** grumbling[2], grumlling[1]

**grumbling / ~s** *n*
'grɤmblɪnz, -ɪŋz, -ml-
**sp** grumblings[1]

**Grumio / ~'s** *n*
*m* 'gru:mɪo: [*2 sylls*], 'gru:mɪˌo: / 'gru:mɪo:z [*2 sylls*]
**sp** Grumio[28] / Grumio's[1]

**grunt / ~est** *v*
grɤnt / grɤnst, -ntst
**sp** grunt[2] / grunt'st[1]

**Gualtier** *n*
'wɑltəɹ
**sp** Gualtier[2]

**guard / ~s** *n*
gɑ:ɹd / -z
**sp** gard[3], guard[60], guarde[1] / gardes[1], gards[1], guardes[1], guards[2]
**rh** reward *Per 2.4.14*; ward *S 133.11*
> velvet-guard

**guard / ~s / ~ed** *v*
gɑ:ɹd / -z / 'gɑ:ɹdɪd
**sp** guard[38] / guards[2] / garded[2], guarded[11]
> safeguard, unguarded

**guardage** *n*
'gɑ:ɹdɪʤ
**sp** guardage[1]

**guardant** *adj*
'gɑ:ɹdənt
**sp** gardant[1], guardant[1]

**guardian / ~s** *n*
'gɑ:ɹdɪən / -z
**sp** gardian[2], guardian[3] / guardians[1]

**guardsman** *n*
'gɑ:ɹdzmən
**sp** guardsman[4]

**gudgeon** *n*
'gɤʤɪn
**sp** gudgin[1]

**guerdon** *n*
'gɐ:ɹdən
**sp** gardon[3], gar-don[1], guerdon[2]
> reguerdon

**guerdon / ~ned** *v*
'gɐ:ɹdənd
**sp** guerdon'd[2]

**guerra, de la** *Sp prep phrase*
ˌdela'gɛra
**sp** delaguar[1]

**guess / ~es** *n*
=
**sp** gesse[2], guesse[8], ghesse[1] / gesses[1]

**guess / ~ed** *v*
=
**sp** gesse[4], ghesse[6], guesse[27] / guesd[1], guest[2]
**rh** thus, us *LLL 5.2.121*

**guessingly** *adv*
*m* 'gesɪnˌləɪ, -ɪŋ-
**sp** guessingly[1]

**guest / ~s** *n*
=
**sp** ghuest[1], guest[34], guest-[caualeire][1], guest-[iustice][1] / ghests[1], guests[20]
**rh** *1* addressed *H5 3.3.57*; breast *S 153.12*; breast, detest *Luc 1565*; expressed *Luc 90*; protest *LLL 5.2.354*; **rh** *2* feast *CE 3.1.27, RJ 1.2.21, 1.5.75, S 47.7, Tim 3.6.103, VA 449* /

**rh** *1* breasts, rests *Luc 1125*; **rh** *2* feast *Per 2.3.8*

**guestwise** *adv*
*m* ˌgest'wəɪz
**sp** guest-wise[1]

**Guiana** *n*
gəɪ'ana
**sp** Guiana[1]

**Guichard** *n*
'giːʃɑːɹd
**sp** Guichard[1]

**guide / ~s** *n*
gəɪd / -z
**sp** guide[7] / guides[2]
**rh** tried *Luc 351*
> misguide

**guid·e / ~es / ~ing / ~ed** *v*
gəɪd / -z / 'gəɪd·ɪn, -ɪŋ / -ɪd
**sp** guide[17] / guides[6] / guiding[3] / guided[5]
**rh** side *VA 179*; **guide thee** possess thee, tend thee, with me *R3 4.1.91*

**guider** *n*
'gəɪdəɹ
**sp** guider[1]

**Guiderius** *n*
gɪ'derɪəs
**sp** Guidereus[1], Guiderius[11]

**guiding** *adj*
'gəɪdɪn, -ɪŋ
**sp** guiding[2]

**Guienne** *n*
giː'en
**sp** Guyen[1]

**Guildenstern** *n*
'gɪldənˌstɐːɹn
**sp** Guildenstern[2], Guildensterne[16], Guilden-sterne[1], *abbr in s.d.* Guild[1]

**guilder / ~s** *n*
'gɪldəɹz
**sp** gilders[2]

**Guildhall** *n*
'gɪldˌɑːl, -ˌhɑːl
**sp** Guild-Hall[2]
> hall

**guile** *n*
gəɪl
**sp** guile[3]
**rh** while *Luc 1534*

**guiled** *adj*
*m* 'gəɪlɪd
**sp** guiled[1]

**guileful** *adj*
'gəɪlfʊl
**sp** guilefull[2]

**Guilford / ~s** *n*
'gɪlfəɹd / -z
**sp** Guilford[3] / Guilfords[1]

**guilt / ~s** *n*
=
**sp** gilt[1], guilt[29] / guilts[1]
**rh** spilt *Ham 4.5.19*
**pun** *H5 2.Chorus.26* gilt

**Guiltian** *n*
'gɪltɪən
**sp** Guiltian[1]

**guiltily** *adv*
*m* 'gɪltɪˌləɪ
**sp** guiltily[1]

**guiltiness** *n*
*m* 'gɪltɪˌnes, -ɪnəs
**sp** guiltinesse[9]

**guiltless** *n*
'gɪltləs
**sp** guiltlesse[20]

**guilt·y / ~ier** *adj*
'gɪltəɪ / -əɹ
**sp** guiltie[30], guilty[37] / guiltier[2]

**guilty-like** *adj*
'gɪltəɪ-ləɪk
**sp** guilty-like[1]

**guinea-hen** *n*
'gɪnəɪ-ˌen, -ˌhen
**sp** gynney hen[1]

**Guinevere** *n*
'gwɪnəvəɹ
**sp** Guinouer[1]

**guise** *n*
gəɪz
**sp** guise[3], guize[1]
**rh** *1* eyes *VA 1177*; **rh** *2* enemies *Tim 4.3.468*

**gules** *n*
gjuːlz
**sp** geulles[1], gules[2]

**gulf / ~s** *n*
gɤlf / -s
**sp** gulfe[9] / gulfes[1]
**rh** wolf *Mac 4.1.23*

**gull / ~s** *n*
gɤl / -z
**sp** gull[10] / gulles[1]

**gull / ~ed** *v*
gɤl / -d
**sp** gull[1] / gull'd[1]

**gull-catcher** *n*
'gɤl-ˌkaʧəɹ
**sp** gull catcher[1]

**gum / ~s** *n*
gɤm / -z
**sp** gumme[3] / gummes[1]

**gummed** *adj*
gɤmd
**sp** gum'd[1]

**gun / ~'s / ~s** *n*
gɤn / -z
**sp** gun[3], gunne[2] / guns[1] / gunnes[1], guns[1]
**rh** begun *VA 461*
> elder-gun

**gunner** *n*
'gɤnəɹ
**sp** gunner[4]

**gunpowder** *n*
'gɤnpəʊdəɹ
**sp** gunpowder[1], gun-powder[2]
> powder

**gunstone / ~s** *n*
'gɤnsto:nz
**sp** gun-stones[1]
> stone

**gurnet** *n*
'gɐ:ɹnət
**sp** [sowc't]-gurnet[1]

**Gurney** *n*
'gu:ɹnəɪ
**sp** Gournie[1], Gurney[1]

**gust / ~s** *n*
gɤst / -s
**sp** gust[4] / gustes[1], gusts[5]
**rh** just *Tim 3.5.55*

**gust** *v*
gɤst
**sp** gust[1]

**gusty** *adj*
'gɤstəɪ
**sp** gustie[1]

**guts** *n*
gɤts
**sp** guts[9], guttes[4]
> calves'-guts

**guts-griping** *adj*
'gɤts-ˌgrəɪpɪn, -ɪŋ
**sp** guts-griping[1]

**guttered** *adj*
'gɤtəɹd
**sp** gutter'd-[rockes][1]

**Guy** *n*
gəɪ
**sp** Guy[1]

**Guynes** *n*
gi:n
**sp** Guynes[1]

**gypsy**
> gipsy

**gyves** *n*
ʤəɪvz
**sp** gyues[5]
**rh** contrives, strives *LC 242*

# H

**H** [letter] *n*
ɛ:ʧ
**sp** H[2]
**pun** ache *AC 4.7.8*

**ha** *interj*
=
**sp** ha[179], ha'[1]

**ha / ~s** *n*
a, = / -z
**sp** ha[1] / ha's[1]

**haberdasher / ~'s** *n*
'abəɹˌdaʃəɹ, 'hab- / -z
**sp** haberdasher[1] / habberda-shers[1]

**haber-de-pois**
> avoirdupois

**habiliment / ~s** *n*
*m* a'bɪlɪˌment, ha- / -s
**sp** habilliament[1] / habiliments[3]

**habit / ~s** *n*
'abɪt, = / -s
**sp** habit[25], habite[8] / habites[3], habits[7]

**habit / ~ed** *v*
'abɪtɪd, =
**sp** habited[5]

**habitation** *n*
abɪ'tɛ:sɪən, ha-
**sp** habitation[4]

**hac** [*from Lat*] *v*
ak, hak
**sp** hac[1]
> hic

**hack / ~s** *n*
aks, =
**sp** hacks[2]
**pun** *Quickly MW 4.1.61 Lat* haec
> unhacked

**hack / ~ed** *v*
ak, = / -t
**sp** hack[2], hacke[3] / hackt[7]

**hacked** *adj*
akt, =
**sp** hackt[7]

**Hacket** *n*
'akɪt, =
**sp** Hacket[2]

**hackney** *n*
'aknəɪ, 'hak-
**sp** hacknie[1]
> common-hackneyed

**had**
> have

**haec** *Lat*
> hic

**haeres** *Lat n*
'heres
**sp** heres[1]

**hag / -s** *n*
ag, = / -z
**sp** hag[3], hagge[4] / hagges[2], hags[2]

**Hagar / ~'s** *n*
'ɛ:gəɹz / 'hɛ:-
**sp** Hagars[1]

**hag-born** *adj*
'ag-'bɔ:ɹn, 'hag-
**sp** hag-borne[1]
> born

**haggard / ~s** *n*
'agəɹd, 'hag- / -z
**sp** haggard[4] / haggerds[1]

**haggish** *adj*
'agɪʃ, =
**sp** haggish[1]

**haggled** *adj*
'agəld, =
**sp** hagled[1]

**hag-seed** *n*
'ag-ˌsi:d, =
**sp** hag-seed[1]
> seed

**hah** *interj*
=
**sp** hah[14]

**hail** *interj / n*
ɛ:l, hɛ:l
**sp** haile[52], hayle[9] / haile[3]
> all-hail

**hail / ~ed** [greeting] *v*
ɛ:ld, hɛ:ld
**sp** haild[1], hail'd[1]

**hail** [rain] *v*
ɛ:l, hɛ:l
**sp** haile[1]

**hail-kissing** *adj*
'ɛ:l-ˌkɪsɪn, -ɪŋ, 'hɛ:-
**sp** haile-kissing[1]
> kiss

**hailstone / ~s** *n*
'ɛ:lsto:n, 'hɛ:- / -z
**sp** hailstone[1] / haile-stones[1]
> stone

**hair / ~'s / ~s** *n*
ɛ:ɹ, hɛ:ɹ / -z
**sp** haire[90], hayre[17], heire[5] / haires[1] / haires[24], hayres[4], heires[1]
**rh** *1* bear *Luc 1129, MND 2.2.37*; despair *Luc 981, S 99.7*; fair *LC 204 LLL 4.3.257*; **rh** *2* ear *VA 147*; tear [cry] *Luc 1129* / **rh** *1* swears *Per 4.4.28*; **rh** *2* tears [cry] *CE 3.2.48, VA 51, 191*
**pun** *CE 3.2.131* heir; *TG 3.1.191* hare
> horse-hair, shag-haired

**hairbreadth** *adj*
'ɛ:ɹbretθ, 'hɛ:-
**sp** haire-breadth[1]
> breadth

**hairless** *adj*
'ɛ:ɹləs, 'hɛ:-
**sp** hairelesse[1]

**hairy** *adj*
'ɛ:ɹəɪ, 'hɛ:-
**sp** hairie[1], hayrie[1], hairy[3]

**Hal** *n*
al, =
**sp** Hal[36], Hall[6]

**halberd / ~s** *n*
'ɔ:lbəɹd, 'hɔ:l- / -z
**sp** halbert[1] / halberds[6]

**halcyon / ~s** *adj*
'alsɪən, = / -z
**sp** halcion[1] / halcyons[1]

**hale / ~s / ~ed** *v*
ɛ:l, hɛ:l / -z / -d
**sp** hale[9] / hales[2] / hal'd[1], hall'd[1]
> new-haled

**half / halves** *n*
ɔ:f, hɔ:f, *Holofernes LLL 5.1.22* half / ɔ:vz, hɔ:-
**sp** halfe[195], *Holofernes describing Armado* haufe[1] / halues[1]
**rh** calf *LLL* 5.2.246, 249

**half-achieved** *adj*
'ɔ:f-ə'ʧɪvd, 'hɔ:-
**sp** halfe-atchieued[1]
> achieve

**half-a-dozen** *adj*
'ɔ:f-ə-'dɤzn, 'hɔ:-
**sp** halfe a dozen[6]
> dozen

**half-blasted** *adj*
*m* ˌɔ:f-'blastɪd, ˌhɔ:-
**sp** halfe blasted[1]
> blast

**half-blooded** *adj*
*m* ˌɔ:f-'blɤdɪd, ˌhɔ:-
**sp** halfe-blooded[1]
> blood

**half-blown** *adj*
'ɔ:f-ˌblo:n, 'hɔ:-
**sp** halfe-blowne[1]
> blown

**Half-Can** [name] *n*
'ɔ:f-ˌkan, ˌhɔ:-
**sp** Halfe-Canne[1]
> can

**half-cap / ~s** *n*
'ɔ:f-ˌkaps, ˌhɔ:-
**sp** halfe-caps[1]
> cap

**half-checked** *adj*
'ɔ:f-ˌʧekt, ˌhɔ:-
**sp** halfe-chekt[1]
> check

**half-conquered** *adj*
*m* ˌɔ:f-'kɒŋkəɹd, ˌhɔ:-
**sp** halfe conquer'd[1]
> conquer

**half-dead** *adj*
*m* ˌɔ:f-'ded, ˌhɔ:-
**sp** halfe dead[2]
> dead

**half-dined** *adj*
*m* ˌɔ:f-'dəɪnd, ˌhɔ:-
**sp** halfe din'd[1]
> dine

**half-drunk** *adj*
*m* ˌɔ:f-'drɤŋk, ˌhɔ:-
**sp** halfe drunke[1]
> drunk

**half-eclipsed** *adj*
*m* ˌɔ:f-ɪ'klɪpst, ˌhɔ:-
**sp** halfe eclips'd[1]
> eclipse

**half-face** *n*
'ɔ:f-ˌfɛ:s, ˌhɔ:-
**sp** half-face[1]
> face

**half-faced** *adj*
'ɔ:f-ˌfɛ:st, ˌhɔ:-
**sp** halfe-fac'd[4]

**half-hour** *n*
'ɔ:f-ˌo:ɹ, ˌhɔ:-
**sp** halfe houre[4]
> hour

**half-kirtle / ~s** *n*
'ɔ:f-ˌkɐ:ɹtlz, ˌhɔ:-
**sp** halfe kirtles[1]
> kirtle

**half-malcontent** *adj*
*m* ˌɔ:f-'malkənˌtent, ˌhɔ:-
**sp** halfe malecontent[1]
> malcontent

**half-moon** *n*
*m* ˌɔ:f-'mu:n, ˌhɔ:-, -'mʊn
**sp** halfe-moone[1], halfe moone
> moon

**Half Moon** [name] *n*
*m* ˌɔ:f-'mu:n, ˌhɔ:-, -'mʊn
**sp** Halfe Moone[1]

**halfpence** *n*
'ɔ:pəns, 'hɔ:-
**sp** halfepence[2], halfpence[1]

**halfpenny** *n*
'ɔ:pnəɪ, 'hɔ:-
**sp** halfe-penie[1], halfe pennie[1], halfe-penny[1], halfepeny[1], halfe peny[1], halfpenny[1]
> penny

**halfpennyworth** *n*
'ɔ:pnəɪˌwɔ:ɹθ, 'hɔ:-
**sp** halfe penny-worth[1]
> worth

**half-pint** *n*
'ɔ:f-ˌpəɪnt, ˌhɔ:-
**sp** halfe pinte[1]
> pint

**half-supped** *adj*
'ɔ:f-ˌsɤpt, ˌhɔ:-
**sp** halfe supt[1]
> sup

**half-sword** *n*
'ɔ:f-ˌsɔ:ɹd, ˌhɔ:-
**sp** halfe sword[1]
> sword

**half-tale / ~s** *n*
*m* ˌɔ:f-'tɛ:lz, ˌhɔ:-
**sp** halfe tales[1]
> tale

**halfway** *adv*
'ɔ:fwɛ:, ˌhɔ:-
**sp** halfe way[2]
> way

**half-worker / ~s** *n*
*m* ˌɔ:f-'wɔ:ɹkəɹz, ˌhɔ:-
**sp** halfe-workers[1]
> work

**half-world** *n*
*m* ˌɔ:f-'wɔ:ɹld, ˌhɔ:-
**sp** halfe world[1]
> world

**halidom** *n*
'ɑlɪdəm, 'hɑl-, 'ɒ-, 'hɒ-
**sp** hallidome[1], hollidam[1], holy-dam[1], holydame[1]

**hall** *n*
ɑ:l, hɑ:l
**sp** hall[14], [Kate]-hall[1]
**rh** all *2H4 5.3.34*; fall *TC 5.10.48*; wall *LLL 5.2.903*
> Guild-, White-hall

**hallow** [call] **/ ~ing / ~ed** *v*
'ɑlə, 'ɑlo:, 'hɑ- / -wɪn, -ɪŋ / -d
**sp** hallow[1] / hallowing[1] / hallow'd[1], hallowed[1]
> alow *interj*

**hallow** [holy] **/ ~ed** *v*
'ɑlə, 'ɑlo:, 'hɑ- / -d
**sp** hallow[1] / hallow'd[1]

**hallowed** *adj*
'ɑləd, 'ɑlo:d, 'hɑ-
**sp** hallow'd[2], hallowed[4]
> un-, well-hallowed

**hallowing** *n*
'ɑləwɪn, -ɪŋ, 'hɑ-
**sp** hallowing[1], hal-lowing[1]

**Hallowmass** *n*
'ɑləˌmas, -lo:-, 'hɑ-
**sp** Hallowmas[2], Hal-low-Masse[1], Hollowmas[1]
> All-Hallowmas

**halt / ~s / ~ing** *v*
ɔ:t, hɔ:t / -s / 'ɔ:tɪn, -ɪŋ, 'hɔ:-
**sp** halt[8] / halts[3] / halting[3]
**rh** *1* fault *S 89.3*; **rh** *2* talk *PP 18.10*
> springhalt

**halter / ~s** *n*
'ɔ:təɹ, 'hɔ:- / -z
**sp** halter[7] / halters[3]
**rh** after, caught her, daughter, slaughter *KL 1.4.317*

**haltered** *adj*
'ɔ:təɹd, 'hɔ:-
**sp** halter'd[1]

**halting** *adj / n*
'ɔ:tɪn, -ɪŋ, 'hɔ:-
**sp** halting[2] / halting[1]

**halves**
> half

**ham / ~s** *n*
amz, =
**sp** hammes[1], hams[1]

**Hames** *n*
ɛ:mz, hɛ:-
**sp** Hames[1]

**Hamlet / ~'s** *n*
'amlət, = / -s
**sp** Hamlet[97] / Hamlets[7]

**hammer / ~s** *n*
'aməɹ, 'ha- / -z
**sp** hammer[2], ham-mer[1] / hammers[3]

**hammer / ~ing / ~ed** *v*
'aməɹ, 'ha- / 'amrɪn, -ɪŋ, -məɹ-, 'ha- / 'aməɹd, 'ha-
**sp** hammer't [hammer it][1] / hamering[1], hammering[2] / hammered[1]

**hammered** *adj*
'aməɹd, 'ha-
**sp** hammer'd[1]

**hamper** *v*
'ampəɹ, 'ha-
**sp** hamper[1]

**Hampton**
> Southampton

**hamstring** *n*
'amstrɪŋ, =
**sp** ham-string[1]
> string

**hand / ~s** *n*
and, = / -z
**sp** hand[823], [honor-giuing]-hand[1], [selfe]-hand[1] / hands[305], ha[n]ds[1]
**rh** band *Luc 253, MA 3.1.112, MND 3.2.111, VA 223, 361*; brand *S 111.7, 154.4*; command *AW 2.1.193, LC 225*; land *2H4 3.1.103, KJ 1.1.163, 4.3.158, LLL 5.2.308, Mac 1.3.31, R2 5.5.109, 5.6.35, 50*; land, stand *Luc 436*; scanned *Mac 3.4.138*; stand *2H6 2.3.44, LC 141, Luc 1235, 1403, 1597, MND 5.1.399, R2 5.3.129, RJ 1.5.51, 93, S 60.14, 99.6, 128.6*; strand *TS 1.1.166*; understand *AY 2.7.203* / bands *AY 5.4.125, Ham 3.2.168, Tem Epil.10*; lands *R2 2.1.209*; sands *Tem 1.2.376*; stands *AC 2.1.51, Per 2.4.57*
> afore-, behind-, fore-, sleeve-, two-, under-hand

**hand / ~ed** *v*
and, = / 'andɪd, =
**sp** hand[2] / handed[1]
> unhand

**handed** *adj*
'andɪd, =
**sp** handed[1]
> deadly-, doughty-, even-, hard-, large-, white-handed

**handfast** *adj*
'anfast, 'ha-, -ndf-
**sp** hand-fast[2]

**handful** *n*
'anfʊl, 'ha-, -ndf-
**sp** handfull[2]

**handicraft / ~s** *n*
'andəɪˌkraft, 'ha- / -s
**sp** handy-craft[1] / handy-crafts[1]
> craft

**handiwork** *n*
'andəɪˌwɔ:ɹk, 'ha-
**sp** handy-worke[2], handy worke[1]
> work

**handkercher / ~s** *n*
'aŋkəɹʧəɹ, 'ha- / -z
**sp** handkercher[3], hand-kercher[1] / handkerchers[1], hand-kerchers[1]
> kerchief

**handkerchief** *n*
'aŋkəɹˌʧɪf, 'ha-, -ˌʧi:f
**sp** hand-kercheefe[1], hand-kerchief[1], handkerchiefe[27], hand-kerchiefe[1], handkerchife[1]

**handle** *n*
'andl, =
**sp** handle[3]
> unhandled

**handl·e / ~est / ~s / ~ing / ~d** *v*
'andl-, = / -st / -z / -ɪn, -ɪŋ / -d
**sp** handle[9] / handlest[1] / handles[1] / handling[1] / handled[4]

**handless** *adj*
'andləs, =
**sp** handlesse[2]

**handling** *n*
'andlɪn, -ɪŋ, 'ha-
**sp** handling[3]
**rh** dandling *VA 560*

**handmaid / ~s** *n*
'andmɛ:d, 'ha- / -z
**sp** handmaid[2], hand-maid[2] / handmaides[1]

**handsaw** *n*
'andsɔ:, =
**sp** handsaw[1], hand-saw[1]

**handsome** *adj*
'ansəm-, =
**sp** handsom[1], handsome[10], hand-some[1]
> unhandsome

**handsomely** *adv*
*m* 'ansəmˌləɪ, 'ha-, -ml-
**sp** handsomely[2], hansomely[1]

**handsomeness** *n*
*m* 'ansəmˌnes, 'ha-
**sp** handsomnesse[1]

**handwriting** *n*
'andˌrəɪtɪn, -ɪŋ, 'ha-
**sp** hand-writing[1]

**handy-dandy** *interj*
ˌandəɪ-'dandəɪ, ˌha-
**sp** handy-dandy[1]

**hang / ~est / ~s / ~eth / ~ing / ~ed / hung** *v*
aŋ, = / -st / -z / 'aŋg·əθ, 'ha- / -ɪn, -ɪŋ / aŋd, = / ɤŋ, hɤŋ
**sp** hang[161] / hang'st[1] / hangs[36] / hangeth[2] / hanging[13], hang-ing[1] / handg'd[1], hangd[1], hang'd[73], hang'de[1], hanged[2] / hung[23]
**rh** sang *S 73.2*; tang *Tem 2.2.50*
> a-hanging, unhanged

**hanger / ~s** *n*
'aŋgəɹz, 'ha-
**sp** hangers[3]

**hang-hog** *n*
*Quickly version of Evans' 'hanc hoc' MW 3.1.44* 'aŋ-'ɒg, 'haŋ-'hɒg
**sp** hang-hog[1]

**hanging** *adj*
'aŋgɪn, -ɪŋ, 'ha-
**sp** hanging[2]
> overhanging

**hanging / ~s** *n*
'aŋgɪn, -ɪŋ, 'ha- / -z
**sp** hanging[19], han-ging[1], hanging's [hanging is][1] / hangings[3]
> bed-, chamber-hanging

**hangman / ~man's / ~men** *n*
'aŋ·mən, 'ha- / -mənz / -mən
**sp** hangman[11], hang-man[5] / hangmans[3] / hangmen[1], hang-men[1]
> under-hangman

**Hannibal** *n*
'anɪˌbɑl, 'ha-
**sp** Hannibal[1], Hanniball[3]

**hap / ~s** *n*
ap, = / -s
**sp** hap[17], happe[1] / happes[2], haps[1]
**rh** cap *LLL 2.1.196*; clap *H8 Epil.13* / traps *MA 3.1.105*
> mishap

**hap / ~s / ~ped** *v*
ap, = / -s / -t
**sp** hap[6] / haps[2] / happ'd[1]

**hapless** *adj*
'apləs, =
**sp** haplesse[7]

**haply** *adv*
'apləɪ, 'ha-
**sp** haplie[1], haply[27], hap'ly[4], happely[4]

**happen / ~ed** *v*
'apən, = / -d
**sp** happen[7] / happened[1], hapned[2], happend[1], happen'd[2]

**happily** *adv*
*m* 'apɪˌləɪ, -pɪl-, -pl-, 'ha-
**sp** happilie[3], happily[30], happlie[1]
> unhappily

**happiness** *n*
*m* 'apɪˌnes, -ɪnəs, 'ha-

**sp** happines[8], happinesse[47], happi-nesse[2]
> unhappiness

**happ·y / ~ier / ~iest** *adj*
'apəɪ, 'ha- / -əɹ / -əst
**sp** happie[40], hap-pie[1], happy[148] / happier[13], happyer[1] / happiest[4]
> over-, un-happy

**harbinger / ~s** *n*
*m* 'ɑ:ɹbɪndʒəɹ, -ˌdʒɛɹ, 'hɑ:- / -z
**sp** harbenger[1], harbinger[1], herbenger[1] / harbingers[1]
**rh** *1* there *MND 3.2.380*; Ver *TNK 1.1.8*; **rh** *2* orator *CE 3.2.12*; **rh** *3* near *PT 5*

**harbour** *n*
'ɑ:ɹbəɹ, 'hɑ:-
**sp** harbor[1], harbour[9]

**harbour / ~s / ~ing / ~ed** *v*
'ɑ:ɹbəɹ, 'hɑ:- / -z / -ɪn, -ɪŋ, 'ɑ:ɹbrɪn, -ɪŋ, 'hɑ:- / -d
**sp** harbor[1], harbour[9] / harbors[1], harbours[2] / harbouring[1] / harbour'd[1]

**harbourage** *n*
'ɑ:ɹbəˌrɪdʒ, 'hɑ:-
**sp** harbourage[1]

**Harcourt** *n*
'ɑ:ɹkəɹt, 'hɑ:-
**sp** Harcourt[1]

**hard / ~er / ~est** *adj*
ɑ:ɹd, hɑ:- / 'ɑ:ɹd·əɹ, 'hɑ:- / -əst
**sp** hard[107], harde[1], hard-[hearts][1] / harder[8] / hardest[1]
**rh** marred *AW 2.3.295, CE 2.1.93*; regard *LC 211, VA 378*
**pun** *TS 2.1.183* heard

**hard / ~er** *adv*
ɑ:ɹd, hɑ:- / 'ɑ:ɹdəɹ, 'hɑ:-
**sp** hard[48], hard-[by][1] / harder[2]
**rh** marred *VA 476*

**harden / ~ing / ~ed** *v*
'ɑ:ɹdnɪn, -ɪŋ, 'hɑ:- / 'ɑ:ɹdənd, 'hɑ:-
**sp** hardning[1] / hardned[1]
> heart-hardening, unhardened

**hardest-timbered** *adj*
'ɑ:ɹdəs-ˌtɪmbəɹd, ˌhɑ:-
**sp** hardest-tymber'd[1]
> timber

**hard-favoured** *adj*
*m* ˌɑ:ɹd-'fɛ:vəɹd, ˌhɑ:-
**sp** hard fauor'd[1], hard-fauor'd[1], hard fauour'd[1], hard-fauour'd[2], hard fauoured[1]
> favour

**hard-handed** *adj*
*m* ˌɑ:ɹd-'andɪd, ˌhɑ:-, -'ha-
**sp** hard handed[1]
> hand

**hard-hearted** *adj*
*m* ˌɑ:ɹd-'ɑ:ɹtɪd, ˌhɑ:-, -'hɑ:-
**sp** hard-harted[2], hard-hearted[5]
> heart

**hardiment** *n*
*m* 'ɑ:ɹdɪˌment, 'hɑ:-
**sp** hardiment[3]
**rh** argument *TC 4.5.28*

**hardiness** *n*
*m* 'ɑ:ɹdɪˌnes, 'hɑ:-
**sp** hardinesse[2]
> foolhardy

**hardly** *adv*
'ɑ:ɹdləɪ, 'hɑ:-
**sp** hardly[38], hard-ly[1], hardly-[off][1]

**hardness** *n*
'ɑ:ɹdnəs, 'hɑ:-
**sp** hardnes[1], hardnesse[5]

**hardock** *n*
'ɑ:ɹdəks, 'hɑ:-
**sp** hardokes[1]

**hard-ruled** *adj*
'ɑ:ɹd-ˌru:ld, 'hɑ:-
**sp** hard rul'd[1]
> rule

**hard·y / ~iest** *adj*
'ɑ:ɹdəɪ, 'hɑ:- / -əst
**sp** hardie[4], hardy[4] / hardyest[1]
**pun** *TS 2.1.183* heard
> daring-hardy

**hare / ~s** *n*
ɛ:ɹ, hɛ:ɹ / -z
**sp** hare[15] / hares[4]
**rh** care *VA 679*; dare *VA 674*
**pun** *TG 3.1.191* hair

**harebell** *n*
'ɛ:ɹ-ˌbel, 'hɛ:-
**sp** hare-bell[1]

**hare-brained** *adj*
'ɛ:ɹ-ˌbrɛ:nd, 'hɛ:-
**sp** haire-brain'd[1], hayre-brayn'd[1]
> brain

**hare-finder** *n*
'ɛ:ɹ-ˌfəɪndəɹ, 'hɛ:-
**sp** hare-finder[1]
> finder

**harelip** *n*
*m* 'ɛ:ɹ-ˌlɪp, ˌɛ:ɹ-'lɪp, 'hɛ:-, ˌhɛ:-
**sp** harelip[1], hare-lippe[1]
> lip

**Harflew** [Harfleur] *n*
*m* 'ɑ:ɹflo:, ɑ:ɹ'flo:
**sp** Harflew[8], Harflewe[1]

**hark** *v*
ɑ:ɹk, hɑ:-
**sp** hark[5], harke[76], heark[1], hearke[66]
**rh** bark *Per 5.Chorus.24, Tem 1.2.381*

**harken / ~s / ~ing / ~ed** *v*
'ɑ:ɹkən, 'hɑ:- / -z / 'ɑ:ɹknɪn, -ɪŋ, 'hɑ:- / 'ɑ:ɹkənd, 'hɑ:-
**sp** harken[2], hearken[5] / hearkens[2] / harkning[1] / hearkned[1]

**harlot / ~'s / ~s** *n*
'ɑ:ɹlət, 'hɑ:- / -s
**sp** harlot[6] / harlots[2] / harlots[3]

**harlot-king** *n*
'ɑ:ɹlət-'kɪŋ, 'hɑ:-
**sp** harlot-king[1]

**harlotry** *n*
*m* 'ɑːɹlətrəɪ, -ˌtrəɪ, 'hɑː-
**sp** harlotry[4]

**harm / ~s** *n*
ɑːɹm, hɑː- / -z
**sp** harm[1], harme[80] / harmes[15], harme's[1]
**rh** *1* arm, charm *Luc 172*; barm *MND 2.1.39*; charm *Luc 172, MM 4.1.15, MND 2.2.16*; **rh** *2* warm *VA 195* / arms *1H6 4.7.30, 46, Luc 28, 199, 1694*; charms *Mac 3.5.7*
> self-harming

**harm / ~ed** *v*
ɑːɹm, hɑː- / -d
**sp** harme[9] / harm'd[4]
**rh** harm thee charm thee *Cym 4.2.276* / **rh** *1* armed *VA 627*; charmed *LC 194*; **rh** *2* warmed *LC 194*

**harm-doing** *n*
*m* ˌɑːɹm-'duːɪn, -ɪŋ, ˌhɑː-
**sp** harme-doing[1]

**harmful** *adj*
'ɑːɹmfʊl, 'hɑː-
**sp** harmefull[6], harmfull[2]

**harmless** *adj*
'ɑːɹmləs, 'hɑː-
**sp** harmelesse[7], harmles[1], harmlesse[6]

**harmonious** *adj*
ɑːɹ'moːnɪəs, hɑː-
**sp** harmonious[2]

**harmony** *n*
*m* 'ɑːɹməˌnəɪ, -mnəɪ, 'hɑː-
**sp** harmonie[6], harmony[11], hermony[1]
**rh** liberty *3H6 4.6.14*; mutiny *LLL 1.1.165*; philosophy *TS 3.1.14*

**harness** *n*
'ɑːɹnəs, 'hɑː-
**sp** harneis[1], harnesse[5]

**harness / ~ed** *v*
'ɑːɹnəs, 'hɑː- / 'ɑːɹnəst, 'hɑː-
**sp** harnest[1]

**harnessed** *adj*
'ɑːɹnəst, 'hɑː-
**sp** harneis'd[1], harness'd[1]

**Harold** *n*
'arəld, 'ha-
**sp** Harold[1], Harrold[1]

**harp** *n*
ɑːɹp, hɑː-
**sp** harpe[4]

**harp / ~ing / ~ed** *v*
ɑːɹp, hɑː- / 'ɑːɹpɪn, -ɪŋ, 'hɑː- / ɑːɹpt, hɑː-
**sp** harpe[4] / harping[2] / harp'd[1]

**harper / ~s** *n*
'ɑːɹpəɹz, 'hɑː
**sp** [blind]-harpers[1]

**Harpier** *n*
'ɑːɹpɪəɹ, 'hɑː- [2 *sylls*]
**sp** Harpier[1]

**harpy** *n*
'ɑːɹpəɪ, 'hɑː-
**sp** harpie[1], harpey[1], harpy[1]

**harrow / ~s** *v*
'arə, 'aroː, 'ha- / -z
**sp** harrow[2] / harrowes[1]

**harr·y / ~ied** *v*
'arəɪd, 'ha-
**sp** harried[1]

**Harry / ~'s** *n*
'arəɪ, 'har- / -z
**sp** Harrie[14], Harrie's [Harry is][1], Harry[93], Har-ry[1], *abbr in s.d.* H[arry][1] / Harries[4], Harryes[3]

**harsh** *adj*
ɑːɹʃ, hɑː-
**sp** harsh[26]

**harshly** *adv*
'ɑːɹʃləɪ, 'hɑː-
**sp** harshly[3]

**harshness** *n*
'ɑːɹʃnəs, 'hɑː-
**sp** harshnesse[3]

**harsh-resounding** *adj*
'ɑːɹʃ-rɪ'səʊndɪn, -ɪŋ, 'hɑː-
**sp** harsh resounding[1]

**hart / ~s** *n*
ɑːɹt, hɑː- / -s
**sp** hart[8], harts[1]
**pun** *JC 3.1.207, TN 1.1.18* heart

**hartlings** *n*
'ɑːɹtlɪnz, -ɪŋz, 'hɑː-
**sp** [odd's]-hart-lings[1]

**harum** *Lat*
> hic

**harvest** *n*
'ɑːɹvɪst, 'hɑː-
**sp** haruest[15]
**rh** farthest *Tem 4.1.115*

**harvest-home** *n*
'ɑːɹvɪst-ˌoːm, 'hɑː-, -ˌhoː-
**sp** haruest-home[1], haruest home[1]
> home

**harvest-man** *n*
'ɑːɹvɪst-ˌman, 'hɑː-
**sp** haruest man[1]

**Harvey** *n*
'ɑːɹvəɪ, 'hɑː-
**sp** Haruey[1]

**has, hast**
> have

**haste** *n*
ast, hast
**sp** haste[69]
**rh** *1* blast, fast *Luc 1332*; fast *CE 4.2.29, KJ 4.2.268, MND 3.2.378, R3 2.4.15, RJ 2.3.89, VA 57*; fast, past *Luc 1668*; last *RJ 3.1.194*; past *S 123.12*; **rh** *2* chaste *Luc 321*; taste *Luc 650, MND 1.1.237*
> post-haste

**hast·e / ~es / ~ing / ~ed** *v*
ast, ha- / -s / 'ast·ɪn, -ɪŋ, 'ha- / -ɪd
**sp** haste[15] / hasts[1] / hasting[1] / hasted[1]

**hasten / ~ing** *v*
'astən, 'ha- / 'astnɪn, -ɪŋ, 'ha-
**sp** hasten[7] / hastning[1]

**hastily** *adv*
*m* 'astɪ,ləɪ, -ləɪ, 'ha-
**sp** hastily[5]

**Hastings / ~'** *n*
'astɪŋz, 'has-
**sp** Hastings[66], Ha-stings[1] / Hastings[3]

**hasty** *adj*
'astəɪ, 'ha-
**sp** hastie[10], hasty[11]
> overhasty

**hasty-footed** *adj*
'astəɪ-,fʊtɪd, 'ha-
**sp** hasty footed[1]
> foot

**hasty-witted** *adj*
'astəɪ-,wɪtɪd, 'ha-
**sp** hastie witted[1]
> wit

**hat / ~s** *n*
at, = / -s
**sp** hat[32], [holy]-hat[1] / hats[6]
**rh** plait *LC 31*; sat *VA 351*; that *LLL 1.1.295*

**hatch / ~es** *n*
aʧ, = / 'aʧɪz, =
**sp** hatch[6] / hatches[7]
**rh** catch *KJ 1.1.171*; patch *CE 3.1.33*

**hatch / ~ed** *v*
aʧ, = / aʧt, =
**sp** hatch[2], hatch'd[5], hatcht[1]
**rh** catched *LLL 5.2.70*
> new-, un-hatched

**hatchet** *n*
'aʧɪt, =
**sp** hatchet[1]

**hatching** *n*
'aʧɪn, -ɪŋ, 'ha-
**sp** hatching[1]

**hatchment** *n*
'aʧmənt, =
**sp** hatchment[1]

**hate / ~'s / ~s** *n*
ɛ:t, hɛ:- / -s
**sp** hate[73] / *emend of RJ 3.1.188* hearts / hates[2]
**rh** accumulate *S 117.12*; advocate *S 35.12*; arbitrate *R2 1.1.201*; create *RJ 1.1.176*; degenerate, state *Luc 1005*; late *RJ 1.5.138*; ruinate *S 10.5*; ruminate *TG 1.2.48*; state *Luc 668, S 124.3, 142.1, 150.10*
**pun** *Tim 4.3.308* eat

**hat·e / ~est / ~s / ~eth / ~ing / ~ed** *v*
ɛ:t, hɛ:- / -s, -st / -s / 'ɛ:t·əθ, hɛ:- / -ɪn, -ɪŋ / -ɪd
**sp** hate[85] / hat'st[1] / hates[17] / hateth[4] / hating[2] / hated[22]
**rh** debate *S 89.14*; gait *Tim 5.4.72*; state *S 145.2*
> all-hating

**hated** *adj / n*
'ɛ:tɪd, 'hɛ:-
**sp** hated[4] / hated[1]
> hell-hated

**hateful** *adj*
'ɛ:tfʊl, 'hɛ:-
**sp** hateful[2], hatefull[37]

**hater / ~s** *n*
'ɛ:tə.ɪ, 'hɛ:- / -z
**sp** hater[1] / haters[1]

**Hatfield** *n*
'atfi:ld, =
**sp** Hatfield[2]

**hath**
> have

**hatred** *n*
'ɛ:trəd, 'hɛ:-
**sp** hatred[16]

**haud** *Lat adv*
hɔ:d
**sp** haud[4]

**haught** *adj*
ɔ:t, =
**sp** haught[2], haught-[insulting][1]

**haughtiness** *n*
'ɔ:tɪ,nes, 'hɔ:-
**sp** haughtinesse[1]

**haughty** *adj*
'ɔ:təɪ, 'hɔ:-
**sp** haughtie[11], haughty[4]

**haunch / ~es** *n*
ɔ:nʧ, = / -ɪz
**sp** haunch[2] / hanches[1]

**haunt / ~s** *n*
ɔ:nt, = / -s
**sp** haunt[4] / haunts[2]
> temple-haunting

**haunt / ~s / ~ing / ~ed** *v*
ɔ:nt, = / -s / 'ɔ:nt·ɪn, -ɪŋ, 'hɔ:- / -ɪd, =
**sp** haunt[13] / haunts[6] / haunting[1] / hanted[2], haunted[3]
**rh** enchanted, granted *LC 130*; granted, planted *LLL 1.1.160*

**haunted** *adj*
'ɔ:ntɪd, =
**sp** haunted[1]

**haunting** *n*
'ɔ:ntɪn, -ɪŋ, 'hɔ:-
**sp** haunting[1]

**hautbois / *plural* hautbois** *n*
'o:bəɪ, 'ho:- / -z
**sp** hoe-boy[1] / hoboies[1], hoboyes[11], ho-boyes[2]

**have,** *abbr* **ha, a, ve / hast / has / hath / having / had / ~dest** *v*
av, =, *Fr H5 5.2.216* av, *abbr str* a, ha, *unstr* ə, v
**sp** haue[5750], have[1], [a']haue[1], [I']haue[1], [they]'aue[1], haue's [have is][1], *Fr* 'aue[1], *abbr* ha[16], ha'[9]
**rh** cave *AY 5.4.192*; crave *PP 10.7*; gave *Luc 1512*; grave *AW 5.3.61, Cym 4.2.280, 1H6 4.3.39, 4.7.31, R2 1.1.169, 2.1.138, 139, RJ 2.3.80, S 81.5, VA 759*; grave, slave *Luc 201*; slave *AY 3.2.149, Luc 1000, VA 102*; **have her** crave her *MW 4.4.87*; **have it** grave it *VA 374* / glad *Per 2.5.72* [had *emend as end of line*]

***God have mercy*** *abbr*
ˌgɒdəˈmɐːɹsəɪ, ˈgɒdəˌmɐːɹsəɪ
**sp** God-a-mercie[1], Godamercy[1], God-a-mercy[1]

***have it*** *abbr*
avt, at, ha-
**sp** haue't[8], hau't[2], ha't[9]
**rh** Kate *TS 5.2.180*

***I have*** *abbr*
*unstr* əɪv, əv
**sp** I'ue[3]

***hast***
*str* ast, =, *unstr* əst
**sp** hast[701], [th']hast[4], has't[3], ha'st[5]
**rh** repast *R3 4.4.395*
> overpass

***has***
*str* az, =, *unstr* əz, z
**sp** has[164], ha's[199], 'has [he has][1], h'as [he has][1], haz[2]
**rh** face *TNK Epil.5*

***it has*** *abbr*
təz
**sp** 'tas[2], t'has[1]

***hath***
*str* aθ, =, *unstr* əθ
**sp** hath[1891]
**rh** wrath *LC 294, MND 2.1.21, Per 4.Chorus.43*

***having***
ˈavɪn, -ɪŋ, ˈha-
**sp** hauing[131], ha-uing[2]

***had***
*str* ad, =, *unstr* əd, d
**sp** had[1398], hadde[1]
**rh** bad *S 67.13*; glad *Per 2.5.74*; mad *1H6 5.3.86, S 129.6*; sad *3H6 3.2.109, Luc 1385*

***haddest***
*str* ads, hads, -st, *unstr* əds, -st
**sp** hadd'st[2], had'st[45], hadst[53]

**haven** *n*
ˈavən, ˈha-
**sp** hauen[6]
**pun** *R2 1.3.275* heaven
> Milford Haven

**haver** *n*
ˈavəɹ, ˈha-
**sp** hauer[1]

**having / ~s** *n*
ˈavɪn, -ɪŋ, ˈha- / -z
**sp** hauing[14] / hauings[1]
> more-having

**haviour** *n*
ˈɛːvɪəɹ, ˈhɛː- [*2 sylls*]
**sp** hauior[1], hauiour[4]
> behaviour

**havoc** *n / v*
ˈavək, =
**sp** hauocke[8] / hauocke[1]

**hawk / ~s** *n*
ɔːk, = / -s
**sp** hauke[1], hawke[4] / hawkes[2], hawks[1]
**rh** balk *Luc 694*

**hawk / ~ed** *v*
ɔːk, = / -t
**sp** hawke[1] / hawkt[1]

**hawking** *adj*
ˈɔːkɪn, -ɪŋ, ˈhɔː-
**sp** hawking[1]

**hawking** [bird] **/** [throat] *n*
ˈɔːkɪn, -ɪŋ, ˈhɔː-
**sp** hawking[2] / hauking[1]

**hawthorn / ~s** *n*
ˈɔːθɔːɹn, ˈhɔː- / -z
**sp** hauthorne[4], hawthorne[1] / hauthornes[1]

**hay** [fencing] *n*
aɪ, haɪ
**sp** hay[1]

**hay** [grass] *n*
ɛː, hɛː
**sp** hay[7]
**rh** away, play *LLL 5.1.148*; day *Mac 1.3.18*; delay *3H6 4.8.61*; jay *WT 4.3.12*

**haystack / ~s** *n*
ˈɛːstaks, ˈhɛː-
**sp** haystackes[1]

**hazard** *n*
ˈazəɹd, ˈha-
**sp** hazard[22]

**hazard / ~s / ~ed** *v*
ˈazəɹd, ˈha- / -z / -ɪd
**sp** hazard[18], hazzard[1] / hazards[4] / hazarded[2]

**hazel** *adj*
ˈazəl, ˈasəl, ˈha-
**sp** hasell[1], hazle[2]

**hazelnut** *n*
ˈazəlˌnɤt, ˈas-, ˈha-
**sp** haselnut[1]
> nut

**he,** *abbr* **a / him / himself / his** *pro*
iː, =, *unstr* ɪ, ə
**sp** he[5724], hee[659], *abbr* 'a[1], a'[haue][1], h'[as][1]
**rh** be *KJ 2.1.509, LLL 4.2.29, R2 2.1.153, TC 1.3.290, 5.9.6, TN 3.4.14*;

be, dignity *Cym 5.4.53*; courtesy *LLL 5.2.323*; destiny *Mac 3.5.16*; flee *LLL 3.1.62*; G *R3 1.1.59*; knee, thee *LLL 5.2.543*; me *AY 2.5.53, CE 4.2.11, 3H6 4.6.75, Luc 1721, MND 3.2.62, R2 4.1.174, RJ 3.1.138*; pedigree *1H6 2.5.76*; see *AY 2.5.53, 3.5.79*; she *AY 5.4.120, VA 715*; thee *Luc 1632*; tree *LLL 5.2.888, 897, VA 264*; villagery *MND 2.1.34*

***he has** abbr*

*unstr* əz, həz

**sp** h'as[1]

***he is** abbr*

*str* iːz, =, *unstr* ɪz

**sp** hees [he is][2], hee's[137], hes[1], he's[166]

***he will** abbr*

*str* iːl, hiːl, *unstr* ɪl

**sp** heele[13], hee'l[57], hee'le[19], hee'll[4], he'l[4], he'le[5], he'll[6]

***he would** abbr*

*str* iːd, =, iːld, hiːld, *unstr* ɪd

**sp** hee'd[1], heel'd[4], hee'ld[4]

***him***

*str* ɪm, hɪm, *unstr* ɪm

**sp** him[5069], [awe]-him[1], [cast]-him[1]
**rh** *1* brim *PP 6.12*; grim *LLL 2.1.241, MND 3.2.56, VA 922*; limb *R2 3.2.186*; swim *TNK Prol.23*; trim *LC 119, S 98.4, TC 4.5.34, VA 1080*; **rh** *2* sin *Per 2. Chorus.24*; win *TC 3.3.213*

***himself** str*

ɪm'self, hɪm-

**sp** himself[5], himselfe[426], him-selfe[7], him selfe[1]
**rh** pelf *Per 2.Chorus.36*

***his***

*str* ɪz, hɪz, *unstr* ɪz, z

**sp** his[6550], 's[43], [and]'s[3] , at's [at his][3]
**rh** *1* is *AY 5.4.111, Luc 1793, R2 2.1.145, S 67.11, 80.7*; **rh** *2* kiss *LLL 2.1.234, TC 4.5.50*; this *TC 5.10.55*

**head / ~'s / ~s** *n*

ed, = / -z

**sp** head[496], [bare]-head[1], [crispe]-head[1], [hold-vp]-head[1], head's [head is][1] / heads [head's][1] / heades[3], heads[102], [pinnes]-heads[1]
**rh** answered *MND 3.2.17*; bed *Luc 777, MND 2.2.46, 4.1.3, RJ 2.3.29, S 27.3*; bed, imagined *Luc 1621*; bed, misled *Luc 368*; bed, shed *Luc 681*; bed, sped *MV 2.9.71*; bred *Per 1.1.109*; bred, nourished *MV 3.2.64*; dead *3H6 1.4.107, MND 4.1.79, Per 1.1.171, 3.Chorus.26, R3 3.4.106, S 68.7, VA 1058*; Diomed *TC 4.4.136, 5.2.190*; fled *KL 3.6.71, MND 3.2.406, S 148.1, VA 1038*; imagined *Luc 1427*; punished *RJ 5.3.306*; red *Luc 1415, S 130.4, VA 118*; shed *VA 666*; thread *WT 4.4.317*; unwed *PP 18.5* / beds *Per 2.3.97, TN 5.1.400*
> block-, death's-, fore-, jolt-, over-, ox-head; bare-, beetle-, hoary-, Hydra-, ill-, mad-, many-, puppy-, rug-, sleek-, three-, two-, waspish-headed

**head** *v*

ed, =

**sp** head[1]
> behead

**headborough** *n*

'edbrə, 'he-

**sp** headborough[1], head-borough[1]

**heading** *n*

'edɪn, -ɪŋ, 'he-

**sp** heading[1]

**headland** *n*

'edlənd, =

**sp** head-land[1]

**headless** *adj*

'edləs, =

**sp** headlesse[5]

**headlong** *adv*

'edlɒŋ, =

**sp** headlong[6]

**headpiece / ~s** *n*

'edpiːs, = / -ɪz

**sp** head-peece[2] / head-pieces[1]
> piece

**headsman** *n*

'edzmən, =

**sp** heades-man[1], headsman[1]

**headstall** *n*

'edstɑːl, 'he-

**sp** headstall[1]

**headstrong** *adj*

'edstrɒŋ, 'he-

**sp** headstrong[4], head-strong[6]

**head·y / ~ier** *adj*

'edəɪ, 'he- / -əɹ

**sp** headdy[1], heady[2] / headier[1]

**heady-rash** *adj*

'edəɪ-'raʃ, 'he-

**sp** headie-rash[1]
> rash

**heal / *Luc* ~eth / ~ed** *v*

iːl, = / 'iːləθ, 'hiː- / iːld, =

**sp** heale[13] / healeth[1] / heal'd[1], healed[1]
**rh** stealeth *Luc 731*
> new-healed

**healing** *adj*

'iːlɪn, -ɪŋ, hiː-

**sp** healing[2]

**health / ~s** *n*

elθ, = / -s

**sp** health[99] / healths[4]

**healthful** *adj*

'elθfʊl, =

**sp** healthfull[8]

**health-giving** *adj*

'elθ-'gɪvɪn, -ɪŋ, 'he-

**sp** health-giuing[1]
> giving

**healthsome** *adj*

'elθsəm, =

**sp** healthsome[1]

**healthy** *adj*

'elθəɪ, 'he-

**sp** healthy[2]

**heap / ~s** *n*
iːp, = / -s
**sp** heape[6] / heapes[7]

**heap / ~est / ~ing / ~ed** *v*
iːp, = / -st / ˈiːpɪn, -ɪŋ, ˈhiː- / iːpt, hiː-, ept, he-
**sp** heap[1], heape[2] / heap'st[1] / heaping[1] / heap'd[6], heapt[2]
**rh** unswept *Cor 2.3.119*

**heaping** *adj*
ˈiːpɪn, -ɪŋ, ˈhiː-
**sp** heaping[1]

**hear / ~est / ~s / ~eth / ~ing / ~d / ~dest** *v*
iːɹ, hiːɹ, ɛːɹ, hɛːɹ / -st / -z / ˈiːr·əθ, ˈhiː-, ˈɛːɹ-, ˈhɛː- / -ɪn, -ɪŋ / ɛːɹd, hɛː-, ɐːɹd, hɐː- / -st
**sp** hear[6], heare[852], heare'm [hear them][1], hear't [hear it][1], heare't [hear it][2] / hearest[2], hear'st[8] / heares[27] / heareth[1] / hearing[36], hea-ring[2] / hard[1], heard[351] / heardst[1], heard'st[2]
**rh** *1* appear *TNK Prol.27*; chanticleer *Tem 1.2.385*; cheer, fear *Luc 263*; ear *KJ 1.1.43, Luc 1328, Oth 1.3.216* [*F* ears], *R2 2.1.15, VA 700*; fear *CE 4.2.54, H8 Epil.8, MND 2.2.159*; **hear her** clear her *Luc 1318*; **hear him** fear him *VA 1096*; **hear it** fear it *LLL 4.3.200*; **hear thee** cheer thee *PP 20.21*; **rh** *2* bear *Luc 1328*; swear *LLL 4.3.143*; **hear her** bear her *Luc 1318*; **hear it** tear it [rip] *LLL 4.3.200*; **hear thee** bear thee, tear thee [rip] *Luc 667* / bears *Oth 1.3.211* / bearing *VA 428* / **rh** *1* beard *LLL 2.1.188*; **rh** *2* regard *Luc 306, R2 2.1.27*; **rh** *3* reward *Per Epil.1*; ward *Luc 306*
**pun** *heard TS 2.1.183* hard
> mis-, over-hear; never-heard-of, unheard

**hearer / ~s** *n*
ˈiːrəɹ, ˈhiː-, ˈɛːr-, ˈhɛː- / -z
**sp** hearer[5] / hearers[11]

**hearing** *adj*
ˈiːrɪn, -ɪŋ, ˈhiː-, ˈɛːr-, ˈhɛː-
**sp** hearing[1]

**hearing / ~s** *n*
ˈiːrɪn, -ɪŋ, ˈhiː-, ˈɛːr-, ˈhɛː- / -z
**sp** hearing[48] / hearings[1]

**hearsay** *n*
ˈiːɹˌsɛː, ˈhiː-, ˈɛːɹ-, ˈhɛː-
**sp** heare-say[1]

**hearse** *n*
ɛːɹs, hɛːɹs
**sp** hearse[3], herse[1]

**hearse / ~d** *v*
*m* ˈɛːɹsɪd, ɛːɹst, hɛː-
**sp** hearsed[1], hearst[1]
**rh** dispersed *Luc 657*

**heart / ~'s / ~s / ~s'** *n*
ɑːɹt, hɑː- / -s
**sp** hart[62], heart[874], [good]-heart[1], [sweet]-heart[5], [White]-heart[1], hearts [heart is][1], heart's [heart is][5] / harts[2], hearts[30], hearts-[sorrow][1], [sweet]-heart's[1] / harts[8], hearts[192], [good]-hearts[1], [hard]-hearts[1] / harts[1], hearts[1]
**rh** *1* apart *AY 4.3.46*; art *H8 3.1.13, LC 175, LLL 5.2.278, Luc 590, 1396, Mac 4.1.99, MND 1.1.193, 2.2.111, R2 5.3.134, S 22.6, 24.2, 24.14, 41.2, 125.9, 131.3, 139.2, TS 4.2.10*; art, part *LC 142*; dart *VA 942*; depart *Mac 4.1.109, S 109.1, VA 580*; impart *R3 4.4.131*; part *AY 3.2.141, 5.4.129, CE 3.1.29, 3.2.62, JC 5.3.90, LLL 4.1.33, 5.2.55, 149, 335, 807, Luc 293, 1137, 1828, MND 3.2.164, MV 2.7.76, PP 20.53, R2 5.1.82, 96, 98, RJ 1.2.16, 2.3.22, S 23.4, 46.10, 46.14, 47.6, 53.14, 62.4, 113.5, 122.5, 132.10, VA 423, 890*; smart *1H6 4.6.43, TC 4.4.15*; start *1H6 4.7.11, MW 5.5.87*; **rh** *2* athwart *LLL 4.3.134*; short *AY 3.5.137, LLL 5.2.55, R2 5.1.92*; **rh** *3* convert *Luc 590* / parts *AW 5.3.337, AY 3.2.147, MND 3.2.154, S 31.1, TS 5.2.166*; smarts *Luc 1239*
**pun** *JC 3.1.208, TN 1.1.18* hart
> unheart

**heartache** *n*
ˈɑːɹt-ˌɛːʧ, ˈhɑː-
**sp** heart-ake[1]
> ache

**heart-blood** *n*
*m* ˈɑːɹt-ˌblɤd, ˌɑːɹt-ˈblɤd, ˈhɑː-, ˌhɑː-
**sp** heart-blood[3], heart blood[3]
**rh** withstood *R2 1.1.172*
> blood

**heartbreak** *n*
ˈɑːɹt-ˌbrɛːk, ˈhɑː-
**sp** heart-breake[1]
> break

**heartbreaking** *n*
ˈɑːɹt-ˌbrɛːkɪn, -ɪŋ, ˈhɑː-
**sp** heart-breaking[1]

**heart-burn / ~ed** *v*
ˈɑːɹt-ˌbɐːɹnd, ˈhɑː-
**sp** heart-burn'd[2]
> burn

**heart-burning** *adj*
ˈɑːɹt-ˌbɐːɹnɪn, -ɪŋ, ˈhɑː-
**sp** heart-burning[1]

**heart-dear** *adj*
ˈɑːɹt-ˌdiːɹ, ˈhɑː-
**sp** heart-deere-[1]
> dear

**hearted** *adj*
ˈɑːɹtɪd, ˈhɑː-
**sp** hearted[3]
> empty-, hard-, honest-, pale-, pitiful-, shallow-, soft-, tender-, true-hearted

**hearten** *v*
ˈɑːɹtən, ˈhɑː-
**sp** hearten[1]
> dishearten

**heart-grief** *n*
ˈɑːɹt-ˌgriːf, ˈhɑː-
**sp** heart-greefe[1]
> grief

**hearth / ~s** *n*
ˈɑːɹθ, ˈhɑː- / -s
**sp** harth[3] / hearths[1]

**heart-hardening** *adj*
*m* ˌɑːɹt-ˈɑːɹdnɪn, -ɪŋ, ˌhɑː-, -ˈhɑː-
**sp** heart-hardning[1]
> harden

**heartily** *adj*
*m* ˈɑːɹtɪˌləɪ, -tɪləɪ, -tləɪ, ˈhɑː-
**sp** hartely[1], hartily[6], hartly[1], heartyly[1]

**heartiness** *n*
*m* ˈɑːɹtɪˌnes, ˈhɑː-
**sp** heartinesse[1]

**heartless** *adj*
ˈɑːɹtləs, ˈhɑː-
**sp** heartlesse[1]

**heart-offending** *adj*
ˈɑːɹt-əˌfendɪn, -ɪŋ, ˈhɑː-
**sp** heart-offending[1]
> offend

**heart's ease** *n*
*m* ˌɑːɹts-ˈiːz, ˌhɑː-
**sp** hearts-ease[1], hearts ease[5]
> ease

**heartsick** *adj*
*m* ˈɑːɹt-ˌsɪk, ˌɑːɹt-ˈsɪk, ˈhɑː-, ˌhɑː-
**sp** hart sick[1], hartsicke[1], heart-sicke[1]
> sick

**heartsore** *adj*
ˈɑːɹt-ˌsɔːɹ, ˈhɑː-
**sp** hart-sore[2]
> sore

**heart-sorrowing** *adj*
ˌɑːɹt-ˈsɒrəwɪn, -ɪŋ, ˌhɑː-
**sp** hart-sorowing-[Peeres][1]
> sorrow

**heartstring / ~s** *n*
*m* ˈɑːɹt-ˌstrɪŋ, ˌɑːɹt-ˈstrɪŋ, ˈhɑː-, ˌhɑː- / -z
**sp** heart-string[1] / heart-strings[3]
> string

**heart-struck** *adj*
ˈɑːɹt-ˌstrɤk, ˈhɑː-
**sp** heart-strooke[1]
> strike

**heart-whole** *adj*
ˈɑːɹt-ˌoːl, ˈhɑː-, ˌhoː-
**sp** heart hole[1]

**hearty** *adj*
ˈɑːɹtəɪ, ˈhɑː-
**sp** harty[1], heartie[4], hearty[4]

**heat** *n*
iːt, =, ɛːt, hɛː-
**sp** heat[18], heate[31]
**rh** get *VA 91*; sweat *VA 177*

**heat / ~est / ~s / ~ed** *v*
iːt, =, ɛːt, hɛː- / -s, -st / -s / ˈiːtɪd, =, ˈɛːtɪd, ˈhɛː-
**sp** heat[5], heate[7] / heat'st[1] / heates[1] / heated[1]

**heated** *adj*
ˈiːtɪd, =, ˈɛːt-, ˈhɛː-
**sp** heated[3]

**heath** *n*
ɛːθ, hɛːθ, iːθ, =
**sp** heath[3]
**rh** Macbeth *Mac 1.1.6*
> Black-, Burton-heath

**heathen** *adj / n*
ˈiːðən, =
**sp** heathen[2] / heathen[3]

**heathenish** *adj*
ˈiːðnɪʃ, -ðən-, =
**sp** heathenish[1]

**heating** *n*
ˈiːtɪn, -ɪŋ, ˈhiː-, ˈɛːt-, ˈhɛː-
**sp** heating[1]

**heat-oppressed** *adj*
*m* ˈiːt-əˌpresɪd, ˈhiː-, ˈɛːt-, ˈhɛː-
**sp** heat-oppressed[1]
> oppress

**heave / ~s / ~d** *v*
iːv, = / -z / *m* iːvd, =, ˈiːvɪd, ˈhiː-
**sp** heaue[10] / heaues[2] / heau'd[5], heaued[2]
**rh** heave thee deceive me, leave me *Luc 586*
> upheave

**heaven / ~'s / ~s / ~s'** *n*
*m* ˈevən, ˈhe-, ɛːn, hɛːn, evn, he- / -z
**sp** heauen[662], heauen-[blesse][1], hea-uen[2], heau'n[9], heuen[1] / heauen's[2], heauens[33], heau'ns[1] / heauens[144], heaue[n]s[1], heauen's[1], heau'ns[5], heuens[1] / heauens[1], heau'ns[1]
**rh** burden *H8 3.2.385*; even *AW 2.1.192, AY 5.4.105, S 28.10, 132.5, VA 493*
**pun** *R2 1.3.276* havens

**heaven-bred** *adj*
*m* ˈevn-ˌbred, ˈhe-, ˈɛːn-, ˈhɛːn-
**sp** heauen-bred[1]

**heaven-kissing** *adj*
*m* ˈevən-ˌkɪsɪn, -ɪŋ, ˈhe-
**sp** heauen-kissing[1]
> kiss

**heavenly** *adv*
*m* ˈevnləɪ, ˈhev-, ˈɛːn-, ˈhɛːn-
**sp** heauenlie[1], heauenly[54], heau'nly[1]

**heaven-moving** *adj*
ˈevən-ˌmɤvɪn, -ɪŋ, ˈhe-
**sp** heauen-mouing[1]
> move

**heavily** *adv*
*m* ˈevɪləɪ, -ˌləɪ, ˈhe-
**sp** heauily[8]

**heaviness** *n*
*m* ˈevɪnəs, -ˌnes, ˈhe-
**sp** heauinesse[16]
**rh** express, less *Luc 1283*; redress *Luc 1602*

**heaving** *adj*
ˈiːvɪn, -ɪŋ, ˈhiː-
**sp** heauing[1]

**heaving / ~s** *n*
'i:vɪn, -ɪŋ, 'hi:- / -z
**sp** heauing[1] / heauings[1]

**heav·y / ~ier / ~iest** *adj*
'evəɪ, 'he- / -əɹ / -əst
**sp** heauie[67], hea-uie[1], heauy[88], hea-uy[2] / heauier[13] / heauiest[6]
**rh** leavy *MA 2.3.69*
> honey-heavy

**heavy-gaited** *adj*
'evəɪ-ˌgɛ:tɪd, 'he-
**sp** heauie-gated[1]
> gait

**heavy-sad** *adj*
'evəɪ-ˌsad, 'he-
**sp** heauy sad[1]
> sad

**hebenon** *n*
'ebənən, 'he-
**sp** hebenon[1]

**Hebrew** *adj*
'i:bru:, 'hi:-
**sp** Ebrew[1], Hebrew[3]

**Hecat, Hecate / ~'s** *n*
'ekət, *1H6 3.2.64* 'ekəˌti:, 'hek- / -s
**sp** Hecat[3], Hecate[1], Heccat[1] / Hecates[1], Hecats[1], Heccats[2]

**hectic** *n*
'ektɪk, =
**sp** hecticke[1]

**Hector / ~'s / ~s** *n*
'ektəɹ, 'he- / -z
**sp** Hecter[1], Hector[134], Hectors [Hector is][2], Hector's [Hector is][4] / Hectors[17] / Hectors[2]

**Hecuba** *n*
*m* 'ekjəˌba, -əbə, 'he-
**sp** Hecuba[13]

**hedge** *adj*
edʒ, =
**sp** hedge[1]

**hedge / ~s** *n*
edʒ, = / 'edʒɪz, =
**sp** hedg[1], hedge[7] / hedges[4]
**rh** edge *WT 4.3.5*

**hedge / ~s / ~d** *v*
edʒ, = / 'edʒɪz, = / edʒd, =
**sp** hedge[6] / hedges[4] / hedg'd[2]

**hedge-born** *adj*
'edʒ-ˌbɔ:ɹn, 'he-
**sp** hedge-borne[1]
> born

**hedgehog / ~s** *n*
'edʒɒg, 'he-, -hɒg / -z
**sp** hedge-hogge[1] / hedgehogges[1], hedg-hogs[1]

**hedge-pig** *n*
'edʒ-ˌpɪg, =
**sp** hedge-pigge[1]
> pig

**hedge-priest** *n*
'edʒ-ˌpri:st, =
**sp** hedge-priest[1]
> priest

**hedge-sparrow** *n*
'edʒ-ˌsparə, -ro:, 'he-
**sp** hedge-sparrow[1]
> sparrow

**heed** *n*
i:d, =
**sp** heed[30], heede[20]
**rh** indeed *LLL 1.1.82*
> unheedy

**heed / ~ed** *v*
i:d, = / 'i:dɪd, =
**sp** heed[1] / heeded[1]

**heedful / ~est** *adj*
'i:dfʊl, = / -st
**sp** heedfull[4] / heedefull'st[1]

**heedfully** *adv*
*m* 'i:dfʊˌləɪ, -fʊl-, -fləɪ, 'hi:-
**sp** heedefully[1], heedfully[2]

**heedless** *adj*
'i:dləs, =
**sp** heedlesse[2]

**heel / ~s** *n*
i:l, = / -z
**sp** heele[14] / heeles[73]
**rh** feel *RJ 1.2.27*; steel *WT 4.4.229* / feels *VA 312*
> lighter-heeled

**heel** *v*
i:l, =
**sp** heele[1]

**heft / ~s** *n*
efts, =
**sp** hefts[1]
> tender-hefted

**heifer / ~'s / ~s** *n*
'efəɹ, 'he- / -z
**sp** heycfer[1], heyfer[1] / heifers[1] / heyfors[1]

**heigh, hey** *interj*
ɛ:, hɛ:
**sp** heigh[5], hey[20]

**heigh, hey / ~-ho** *interj*
'ɛ:-'o:, 'hɛ:-'ho:
**sp** heigh-ho[3], heigh ho[5], hey ho[7]

**height** *n*
əɪt, həɪt
**sp** height[26], hight[2]
**rh** night *H8 1.2.214*; sight *R2 1.1.189*; tonight *TC 5.1.3*
> a-height

**heightened** *adj*
'əɪtənd, 'həɪ-
**sp** heighten'd[1]

**heighth** *n*
əɪt, həɪt, -tθ
**sp** heighth[2]

**heinous** *adj*
'ɛ:nəs, 'hɛ:-
**sp** hainous[5], heinous[1], haynous[1], heynous[10]

**heinously** *adv*
'ɛ:nəsləɪ, 'hɛ:-
**sp** heynously[1]

**heir / ~s** *n*
ɛ:ɹ / -z
**sp** heire[74], heyre[29] / heires[15], heyres[6], [rich-left]-heyres[1]
**rh** 1 fair *AW 2.3.131, Cym 5.4.51, Oth 2.1.135, RJ 2.Chorus.2, S 6.14, 127.3*;
**rh** 2 peer *Per Prol.22*
**pun** *CE 3.2.131* hair; *1H4 1.2.57* here
> co-heir

**heir-apparent** *adj / n*
*m* 'ɛ:ɹ-ə,parənt, ,ɛ:ɹ-ə'parənt
**sp** heire-apparant-[garters][1] / heire apparant[3], heyre apparant[1]
**pun** *1H4 1.2.57* here apparent
> apparent

**heir general** *n*
,ɛ:ɹ-'ʤenrɑl, -nər-
**sp** heire generall[1]
> general

**heirless** *adj*
'ɛ:ɹləs
**sp** heire-lesse[1]

**held**
> hold

**Helen / ~'s** *n*
'elən, = / -z
**sp** Helen[30], Helene[1], Hellen[31] / Helens[6], Hellens[2]

**Helena** *n*
*m* 'elənə, -,na, 'he-
**sp** Helena[35]
**rh** Hermia *MND 3.2.156*

**Helenus** *n*
'elənəs, 'he-
**sp** Helenus[5], Hellenus[5], Hel-lenus[1]

**Helias** *n*
'elɪəs, 'he-
**sp** Helias[1]

**Helicon / ~s** *n*
'elɪ,kɒnz, 'he-
**sp** Hellicons[1]

**hell / ~'s** *n*
el, = / -z
**sp** hel[1], hell[156], hell's [hell is][1] / hels[1]
**rh** dwell *Luc 1555, MND 1.1.207*; fell *Luc 764*; knell *Mac 2.1.64*; pell-mell *KJ 2.1.407, R3 5.3.314*; tell *2H6 5.1.216, Luc 1287, PP 2.12, S 144.12*; well *CE 2.2.222, 4.2.32, 40, KJ 1.1.272, LLL 4.3.252, MND 2.1.243, R2 5.5.116, R3 4.4.167, S 58.13, 129.14, TN 3.4.213*

**hell-black** *adj*
'el-,blak, =
**sp** hell-blacke-[night][1]
> black

**hell-broth** *n*
'el-,brɒθ, =
**sp** hell-broth[1]
> broth

**Hellespont** *n*
'elɪs,pɒnt, 'he-
**sp** Hellespont[3], Hel-lespont[1]

**hell-fire** *n*
'el-,fəɪɹ, 'he-
**sp** hell fire[1]
> fire

**hell-gate** *n*
'el-,gɛ:t, 'he-
**sp** hell gate[1]
> gate

**hell-governed** *adj*
*m* ,el-'gɤvəɹnd, ,he-
**sp** hell-gouern'd[1]
> govern

**hell-hated** *adj*
*m* ,el-'ɛ:tɪd, ,hel-'hɛ:-
**sp** hell-hated[1]
> hate

**hell-hound / ~s** *n*
'el-,əʊnd, 'hel-,həʊnd / -z
**sp** hell-hound[2] / hell-hounds[1]
> hound

**hellish** *adj*
'elɪʃ, =
**sp** hellish[8]

**hell-kite** *n*
'el-,kəɪt, 'he-
**sp** hell-kite[1]
> kite

**hell-pains** *n*
*m* 'el-,pɛ:nz, ,el-'pɛ:nz, 'he-, ,he-
**sp** hell paines[2]
> pain

**helm / ~s** *n*
elm, = / -z
**sp** helme[16] / helmes[3]

**helm / ~ed** *v*
elmd, =
**sp** helmed[1]

**helmet / ~s** *n*
'elmət, = / -s
**sp** helmet[6] / helmets[4]

**help / ~s** *n*
elp, = / -s
**sp** help[5], helpe[83] / helpes[6]
> unhelpful

**help / ~est / ~s / ~ing / ~ed / holp / ~est** *v*
elp, = / -st / -s / 'elpɪn, -ɪŋ, 'he- / elpt, = / ɒlp, hɒ- / -st
**sp** help[10], helpe[212] / help'st[1] / helpes[7] / helping[4], hel-ping[1] / help'd[5], helpt[1] / holp[2], holpe[14] / holp'st[1]

**helper / ~s** *n*
'elpəɹ, 'he- / -z
**sp** helper[2] / helpers[1]

**helpful** *adj*
'elpfʊl, =
**sp** helpeful[1], helpefull[12], helpfull[1]

**helping** *adj*
'elpɪn, -ɪŋ, 'he-
**sp** helping[1]

**helpless** *adj*
'elpləs, =
**sp** helpelesse[2], helplesse[1]

**helter-skelter** *adv*
ˌeltəɹ-ˈskeltəɹ, ˌhe-
**sp** helter skelter[1]

**hem** *interj / n*
em, =
**sp** hem[6], hem-[boyes][1] / hemme[1]

**hem / ~s / ~med** *v*
em, = / -z / -d
**sp** hem[1] / hems[1] / hem'd[2], hemm'd[1]
**rh** gems *S 21.8*

**hemlock** *n*
ˈemlɒk, =
**sp** hemlock[1], hemlocke[2]

**hemp** *n*
emp, =
**sp** hempe[1]

**hempen** *adj*
ˈempən, =
**sp** hempen[3]

**hempseed** *n*
ˈempsiːd, =
**sp** hempseed[1]

**hen / ~s** *n*
en, = / -z
**sp** hen[7], henne[1] / hennes[1]
> guinea-hen

**hence** *adv*
ens, =
**sp** hence[359]
**rh** commence *2H4 4.2.119, PT 24*; defence *LLL 5.2.86, S 12.14*; dispense *CE 2.1.102*; dispense, negligence *Luc 1276*; expense *CE 3.1.122*; offence *MND 2.2.21, Oth 3.3.376, RJ 3.1.187, TS 1.2.229*; recompense *1H6 1.2.115*; sense *TNK 1.1.18*

**henceforth** *adv*
*m* ˌensˈfɔːɹθ, ˈensˌfɔːɹθ, ˌhe-, ˈhe-
**sp** hencefoorth[1], hence foorth[1], henceforth[39]
> forth

**henceforward** *adv*
ˌens-ˈfɔːɹwəɹd, ˌhe-
**sp** hence-forward[3], henceforward[3]
> forward

**hencegoing** *n*
ˌens-ˈgoːɪn, -ɪŋ, ˌhe-
**sp** hence-going[1]
> go

**henchman** *n*
ˈentʃmən, =
**sp** henchman[1]

**Henricus** *Lat n*
ˌhenˈriːkʊs
**sp** Henricus[1]

**Henry / ~'s** *n*
ˈenrəɪ, ˈhe- / -z
**sp** Henrie[21], Henry[173], Hen-ry[1], Henry's [Henry is][1] / Henries[44], Henryes[1], Henry's[1]

**hent** *n / v*
ˈent, =
**sp** hent[1] / hent[3]

**Henton** *n*
ˈentən, ˈhe-
**sp** Henton[2]

**her / ~s / herself** *pro*
*str* ɐːɹ, hɐːɹ, ɛːɹ, hɛːɹ, *unstr* əɹ
**sp** her[3639], [be-lye]-her[1], [carry]-her[1], [iump]-her[1], [mary]-her[2], [thump]-her[1], hir[19]
**rh** err *AW 2.3.181*; love her, approve her *S 42.6, 8*; stir *TNK Prol.5*
> she

***hers***
ɐːɹz, hɐːɹz, ɛːɹz, hɛːɹz
**sp** hers[48], her's[1]
**rh** tears [cry] *MND 2.2.99*

***herself***
əɹˈself, hə-
**sp** her self[3], herselfe[10], her selfe[77], her selfe's [self is][1]

**herald / ~'s / ~s** *n*
ˈerəld, = / -z
**sp** herald[28], herauld[10], herault[1] / heralds[2] / heralds[6], heraulds[1]

**herald** *v*
ˈerəld, =
**sp** harrold[1]

**heraldry** *n*
ˈerəldrəɪ, ˈhe-
**sp** heraldrie[1], heraldry[4]

**herb / ~s** *n*
ɛːɹb / -z
**sp** hearb[1], hearbe[5] / hearbes[5], hearbs[3], herbes[2]
> nose-herb

**Herbert** *n*
ˈɐːɹbəɹt, ˈhɐː-
**sp** Herbert[3]

**herb-grace, herb of grace** *n*
ˈɛːɹb-ˌgrɛːs, ˈɛːɹbəˌgrɛːs
**sp** herbe-grace[1], hearbe of grace[1], herbe of grace[1]
> grace

**herblet / ~s** *n*
ˈɛːɹbləts
**sp** herbelets[1]

**Herculean** *adj*
əɹˈkjuːlɪən, həɹ-
**sp** Herculean[1]

**Hercules** *n*
ˈɐːɹkjəˌliːz, ˈhɐː-, *Bottom MND 1.2.26* ˈɐːɹkliːz
**sp** Hercules[33], Her-cules[2], Hercu-les[1], *Bottom* Ercles[2]
**rh** Hesperides *LLL 4.3.316*

**herd / ~s** *n*
ɐːɹd, hɐː-, ɛːɹd, hɛː- / -z
**sp** heard[2], herd[1] / heards[1]
**rh** beard *S 12.6* / birds *VA 456*
> neat-, shep-, swine-herd

**herds·man / ~men** *n*
ˈɐːɹdzmən, ˈhɐː-, ˈɛːɹ-, ˈhɛː-
**sp** heardsman[1] / heardsmen[2]

**here** *adv*
iːɹ, hiː-, ɛːɹ, hɛː-

**sp** heere[1267], here[844]
**rh** *1* appear *Cor 2.3.114, KL 1.1.181, 1.4.144* [Q], *Mac 5.5.48, MND 3.2.98, 5.1.415, MV 2.9.74, R2 5.6.10*; appear, dear *MND 3.1.81*; bier *R2 5.6.51, RJ 3.2.59, TNK 3.6.307*; cheer, dear *CE 3.1.20*; clear *Mac 5.3.62*; dear *H8 3.1.183, Ham 3.2.292, LLL 4.3.272, Luc 1290, MND 3.2.425, 5.1.270, R2 2.1.144, RJ 2.3.61*; deer *VA 229*; ear *LLL 5.2.287, 435, MND 2.1.14*; fear *Cym 2.2.50, 1H6 1.2.13, MND 2.2.153, 5.1.217*; gear *LLL 5.2.302, TC 3.2.208*; nea'er [nearer] *R2 5.1.87*; near *MND 2.2.20*; overhear *LLL 5.2.96*; rear *R2 5.3.88*; spear *R2 1.1.170*; tear [cry] *H8 Prol.5, LC 54, 291*; year *Per 4.4.34*;
**rh** *2* bear *LC 54, Luc 1290, 1475, R2 5.5.118*; otherwhere *CE 2.1.105*; swear *LLL 5.2.357*; tear [rip] *Luc 1475*; there *KL 1.4.144* [Q], *LLL 4.3.188, MND 3.2.412, MV 2.9.52, Per 1.4.79*; uprear *S 49.9*; tear [cry], wear *LC 292, MND 2.2.76*; where *RJ 1.1.197*;
**rh** *3* villager *TNK 3.5.102*; **rh** *4* were *CE 4.2.9*
**pun** *1H4 1.2.56* heir

**here is** *abbr*
iːɹz, hiː-, ɛːɹz, hɛː-
**sp** heeres[11], heere's[80], heers[1], heer's[8], heres[6], here's[101], her's[1]

**hereabout / ~s** *adv*
'iːɹəˌbəʊt, 'hiː-, 'ɛːɹ-, 'hɛː- / -s
**sp** heereabout[1], heere about[1], here about[1], herea-bout[1] / here abouts[1]
**rh** doubt *RJ 5.3.43*

**hereafter** *adv*
ˌiːɹ'ɑːtəɹ, -'aftəɹ, ˌhiː-, ˌɛːɹ-, ˌhɛː-
**sp** heareafter[1], heereafter[27], heere-after[2], hereafter[17], here-after[1]
**rh** laughter *TN 2.3.45*

**hereby** *adv*
ˌiːɹ'bəɪ, ˌhiː-, ˌɛːɹ-, ˌhɛː-
**sp** heereby[1], hereby[1]

**hereditary** *adj*
*m* ə'redɪˌtarəɪ, -ɪtər-, -ɪtr-, hə-
**sp** hereditarie[4], hereditary[4]

**Hereford / ~'s** *n*
'ɐːɹfəɹd, 'hɐː- / -z
**sp** Hereford[11], Herford[18] / Here-fords[1], Herfords[6]

**Herefordshire** *n*
*m* 'ɐːɹfəɹdˌʃəɪɹ, 'hɐː-
**sp** Herefordshire[1]

**herein** *adv*
*m* ˌiːɹ'ɪn, 'iːɹɪn, ˌhiː-, 'hiː-, ˌɛːɹ'ɪn, 'ɛːɹɪn, ˌhɛː-, 'hɛː-
**sp** heerein[13], herein[14]

**hereof** *adv*
ˌiːɹ'ɒv, ˌhiː-, ˌɛːɹ-, ˌhɛː-
**sp** heereof[2], hereof[3]

**here·sy / ~ies** *n*
'erəˌsəɪ, 'he- / -z
**sp** heresie[6] / heresies[2]
**rh** destiny *MV 2.9.82*; me *MND 2.2.147*

**heretic / ~s** *n*
'erɪˌtɪk, 'he- / -s
**sp** heretike[1], heretique[4] / heretiques[2]
**rh** politic *S 124.9*
> arch-heretic

**hereto** *adv*
'iːɹˌtuː, 'hiː-, 'ɛːɹ-, 'hɛː-
**sp** hereto[1]

**hereupon** *adv*
'iːɹəˌpɒn, 'hiː-, 'ɛːɹ-, 'hɛː-
**sp** heereupon[1]

**heritage** *n*
'erɪtɪʤ, =
**sp** heri-tage[1]

**héritier** *Fr n*
erɪt'je
**sp** heretere[1]

**Hermes** *n*
'ɐːɹmiːz, 'hɐː-
**sp** Hermes[1]

**Hermia / ~'s** *n*
*m* 'ɐːɹmɪə, -mɪˌa, 'hɐː- / -z
**sp** Hermia[44] / Hermiaes[1], Hermias[6]
**rh** Helena *MND 3.2.155*

**Hermione / ~'s** *n*
*m* əɹ'məɪəˌniː, -əniː, həɹ- / əɹ'məɪəniːz, həɹ-
**sp** Hermione[20] / Hermiones[1]

**hermit / ~s / ~s'** *n*
'ɐːɹmɪt, 'hɐː- / -s
**sp** hermit[3], hermite[2] / ermites[1], hermits[1] / hermites[1]

**hermitage** *n*
'ɐːɹmɪˌtɪʤ, 'hɐːɹ-
**sp** hermitage[2]

**Herne / ~'s** *n*
ɐːɹn, hɐːɹn / -z
**sp** Herne[6] / Hernes[2], Hernes-[oake, -oke][2]

**hero / ~es** *n*
'iːroːz, 'hiː-
**sp** heroes[2]

**Hero / ~'s** [name] *n*
'iːroː, 'hiː- / -z
**sp** Hero[65], He-ro[2] / Heroes[7], Hero's[1]

**Herod / ~s** *n*
'erəd, 'he- / -z
**sp** Herod[5], Herode[1] / Herods[2]
> out-Herod

**heroic** *adj*
e'roːɪk, he-
**sp** heroick[1]

**heroical** *adj*
e'roːɪkal, he-
**sp** heroicall[2], heroi-call[1], heroycall[1]

**herring / ~s** *n*
'erɪn, -ɪŋ, 'he- / -z
**sp** hering[1], herring[4] / herrings[2]

**hers, herself**
> her

**Hertford** *n*
'ɐːɹtfəɹd, 'hɐː-
**sp** Hertford[3]

**Hesperides** *n*
e'sperɪˌdiːz, he-
**sp** Hesperides[1]
**rh** Hercules *LLL 4.3.317*

**Hesperus** *n*
*m* 'espəˌrɤs, he-
**sp** Hesperus[1]

**hest / ~s** *n*
est, = / -s
**sp** hest[2] / hests[1]
**rh** jests *emend of LLL 5.2.65* devices

**heure** *Fr n*
œːɹ
**sp** [ast]ure

**heureux** *Fr adj*
œ'rø
**sp** heurex[1]

**hew** *n*
juː, =
**sp** hew[4]

**hew / ~s / ~ing / ~ed / ~n** *v*
juː, = / -z / 'juːɪn, -ɪŋ, 'hjuː- / juːd, = / juːn, =
**sp** hew[9] / hewes[2] / hewing[1] / hew'd[1] / hewne[2], hew'ne[1]
> rough-hew

**hewgh** *interj*
hjuː, ʍjuː
**sp** hewgh[1]

**hey** *interj*
> heigh

**hey** *n*
'ɛː, 'hɛː-
**sp** hey[1]

**heyday** *n*
'ɛːdɛː, 'hɛː-
**sp** hey-day[1]

**hic** *Lat det / Eng [from Lat]* *v*
hɪk, *Evans MW 4.1.39* hɪg / hɪk
**sp** hic[12], *Evans* hig[1] / hic[1]
**pun** *MW 4.1.61* hick

**haec** *nominative feminine singular*
hek, *Evans MW 4.1.39* hag
**sp** haec[1], *Evans* hag[1]
**pun** *MW 4.1.61* hack

**harum** *genitive feminine plural*
'hɑːɹʊm
**sp** harum[1]

**hoc** *nominative neuter singular*
hɒk, *Evans MW 4.1.39* hɒg
**sp** hoc[2], *Evans* hog[2]

**horum** *genitive masculine or neuter plural*
'hɔːrʊm
**sp** horum[3]
**pun** *MW 4.1.62* whore

**huius** *genitive singular*
'huːɪʊs
**sp** huius[1]

**hunc** *accusative masculine singular*
*William MW 4.1.41* hɪŋk, *Evans MW 4.1.43* hʊŋg
**sp** *William* hinc[1], *Evans* hing[1]

**hidden** *adj*
'ɪdn, =
**sp** hidden[7]

**hide / ~s** *n*
əɪd, həɪd / -z
**sp** hide[8] / hides[2]
**rh** abide *TC 5.6.31*; side *S 50.10*; wide *VA 298*

**hid·e / ~est / ~es / ~ing / hid** *v*
əɪd, həɪd / -st / -z / 'əɪdɪn, -ɪŋ, 'həɪ- / ɪd, =
**sp** hide[95] / hid'st[2] / hides[11] / hiding[8] / hid[43]
**rh** denied *S 142.13*; dignified, pride *Luc 663*; pride *RJ 1.3.91, S 52.10, TN 3.1.149*; ride *S 33.7*; side MM *3.2.259* / derides *KL 1.1.280* / biding, dividing *Luc 548* / forbid *LLL 1.1.64, S 65.10*

**hideous** *adj*
'ɪdɪəs, =
**sp** hiddeous[3], hideous[15], hidious[2]

**hideously** *adv*
*m* 'ɪdɪəsˌləɪ, 'hɪ-
**sp** hideously[1], hidiously[1]

**hideousness** *n*
*m* 'ɪdɪəsˌnes, 'hɪ-
**sp** hidiousnesse[1]

**hiding** *n*
'əɪdɪn, -ɪŋ, 'həɪ-
**sp** hiding[1]

**hie / ~s** *v*
əɪ, həɪ / -z
**sp** hie[30], high[7], hye[9] / hies[1], highes[1], hyes[2]
**rh** *1* eye, lie *Luc 1341*; sanctify *AW 3.4.9*; hie them overfly them *VA 323*; **rh** *2* jeopardy *KJ 3.1.347*; **rh** *3* hie thee abhore thee *pp 12.9*, defy thee *PP 12.11* / espies *Per 5.Chorus.20*; eyes, flies *Luc 1215*; skies *VA 1189*
**pun** *RJ 2.5.78* high

**Hiems** *n*
'əɪəmz, 'həɪ-
**sp** Hiems[1], Hyems[1]

**high / ~er / ~est** *adj*
əɪ, həɪ / 'əɪ·əɹ, 'həɪ- / *m* -əst, -st
**sp** hie[3], high[195] / higher[11] / highest[8]
**rh** die *Per 1.1.150*; dry *VA 551*; fly *AW 2.3.74*
**pun** *RJ 2.5.78* hie
> a-high

**high** *adv*
əɪ, həɪ / 'əɪ·əɹ, 'həɪ- / *m* -əst, -st
**sp** high[17], hye[3] / higher[18] / highest[2]
**rh** eye *AW 1.1.216* / aspire *MW 5.5.98*

**high** *n*
əɪ, həɪ
**sp** high[5], hye[1]
**rh** *1* die *R2 5.5.111*; I *R2 4.1.188*; lie *1H4 3.3.200*; **rh** *2* majesty *VA 854*

**high-battled** *adj*
*m* ˌəɪ-ˈbatld, ˌhəɪ-
**sp** hye battel'd[1]
> battle

**high-blown** *adj*
ˈəɪ-ˌbloːn, ˈhəɪ-
**sp** high-blowne[1]
> blown

**high-born** *adj*
ˈəɪ-ˌbɔːɹn, ˈhəɪ-
**sp** high-borne[2]
> born

**high-coloured** *adj*
*m* ˌəɪ-ˈkɤləɹd, ˌhəɪ-
**sp** high coulord[1]
> colour

**high-day** *n*
ˈəɪ-ˌdɛː, ˈhəɪ-
**sp** high-day[4]
> day

**high-engendered** *adj*
ˈəɪ-enˌʤendəɹd, ˈhəɪ-
**sp** high-engender'd[1]
> engender

**higher** *n*
ˈəɪəɹ, ˈhəɪ-
**sp** higher[3]
**rh** aspire *Per 1.4.6*

**highest** *n*
*m* ˈəɪəst, ˈhəɪ-, əɪst, həɪst
**sp** highest[8], high'st[1]

**highest-peering** *adj*
ˈəɪəst-ˌpiːrɪn, -ɪŋ, ˈhəɪ-
**sp** highest piering[1]
> peer

**high-grown** *adj*
ˈəɪ-ˌgroːn, ˈhəɪ-
**sp** high-growne[1]
> grow

**high-judging** *adj*
*m* ˌəɪ-ˈʤɤʤɪn, -ɪŋ, ˌhəɪ-
**sp** high-iudging[1]
> judge

**highly** *adv*
ˈəɪləɪ, ˈhəɪ-
**sp** highly[15]

**high-minded** *adj*
*m* ˌəɪ-ˈməɪndɪd, ˌhəɪ-
**sp** high-minded[1]
> mind

**highmost** *adj*
ˈəɪmoːst, ˈhəɪ-
**sp** highmost[1]

**highness / ~'** *n*
ˈəɪnəs, ˈhəɪ-
**sp** Highnes[25], Highnesse[117], High-nesse[1] / Highnes[2], Highnesse[44]
> high

**high-placed** *adj*
*m* ˌəɪ-ˈplɛːst, ˌhəɪ-
**sp** high plac'd[1]
> place

**high-proof** *adj*
ˈəɪ-ˌprɤf, ˈhəɪ-, -ruːf
**sp** high proofe[1]
> proof

**high-reaching** *adj*
*m* ˌəɪ-ˈriːʧɪn, -ɪŋ, ˌhəɪ-
**sp** high-reaching[1]
> reach

**high-reared** *adj*
ˈəɪ-ˌriːɹd, ˈhəɪ-
**sp** high rear'd[1]
> rear

**high-repented** *adj*
ˈəɪ-rɪˌpentɪd, ˈhəɪ-
**sp** high repented[1]
> repent

**high-resolved** *adj*
*m* ˈəɪ-rɪˌsɒlvɪd, ˈhəɪ-, -ˌzɒ-
**sp** high resolued[1]
> resolve

**high-sighted** *adj*
*m* ˌəɪ-ˈsəɪtɪd, ˌhəɪ-
**sp** high-sighted-[tyranny][1]
> sight

**high-soaring** *adj*
*m* ˌəɪ-ˈsɔːrɪn, -ɪŋ, ˌhəɪ-
**sp** high soaring[1]
> soar

**high-stomached** *adj*
*m* ˌəɪ-ˈstɒməkt, ˌhəɪ-
**sp** high stomack'd[1]
> stomach

**high-swollen** *adj*
ˈəɪ-ˌswoːln, ˈhəɪ-
**sp** high-swolne[1]
> swell

**hight** *v*
əɪt, həɪt
**sp** hight[3]
**rh** knight *LLL 1.1.168*

**high-viced** *adj*
ˈəɪ-ˌvəɪst, ˈhəɪ-
**sp** high-vic'd[1]
> vice

**highway / ~s** *n*
*m* ˈəɪwɛː, əɪˈwɛː, ˈhəɪ-, həɪ- / -z
**sp** highway[1], high-way[3], high way[1] / highwayes[1], high waies[1]
> way

**high-witted** *adj*
*m* ˌəɪ-ˈwɪtɪd, ˌhəɪ-
**sp** high witted[1]
> wit

**high-wrought** *adj*
ˈəɪ-ˌrɔːt, ˈhəɪ-
**sp** high wrought[1]
> wrought

**hilding / ~s** *n*
ˈɪldɪn, -ɪŋ, ˈhɪ- / -z
**sp** hielding[1], hilding[5] / hildings[1]

**hill / ~s** *n*
ɪl, = / -z
**sp** hil[2], hill[37] / hilles[6], hills[3], hils[2]
**rh** still *S 7.5, VA 697*; until *Mac 4.1.92*; will *PP 9.5*
> dung-, mole-hill; Gad's Hill

**hillo, illo / ~a** *interj*
ɪ'lo:, hɪ- / ɪ'lo:ə, hɪ-
**sp** hillo[1], illo[1] / hilloa[1]

**hilt / ~s** *n*
ɪlt, = / -s
**sp** hilt[3] / hiltes[1], hilts[5]
> basket-, sword-hilt

**him / himself**
> he

**hinc** *Lat*
> hic

**Hinckley** *n*
'ɪŋkləɪ, 'hɪ-
**sp** Hinckley[1]

**hind / ~s** *n*
əɪnd, həɪ- / -z
**sp** hind[1], hinde[8] / hindes[6], hinds[1]
**rh** *1* behind *CE 3.1.77*; Rosalind *AY 3.2.97*; **rh** *2* wind *CE 3.1.77*

**hinder / ~s / ed** *v*
'ɪndəɹ, 'hɪ- / -z / -d
**sp** hinder[14] / hinders[1] / hindered[1], hindred[7]

**hindering** *adj*
'ɪndrɪn, -ɪŋ, 'hɪ-
**sp** hindring[1]

**hindmost** *adj / adv*
'əɪndmo:st, 'həɪ-
**sp** hindmost[1] / hindmost[1]

**hinge / ~s** *n*
ɪnʤ, = / 'ɪnʤɪz, =
**sp** hindge[1] / hindges[2]

**hinge** *v*
ɪnʤ, =
**sp** hindge[1]

**hint** *n*
ɪnt, =
**sp** hint[8]

**hip / ~s** *n*
ɪp, = / -s
**sp** hip[3], hippe[2] / heps[1], hippes[1], hips[3]
**rh** lips *VA 44*
> red-hipped

**hip / ~ped** *v*
ɪpt, =
**sp** hip'd[1]

**Hipparchus** *n*
ɪ'pɑ:ɹkəs, hɪ-
**sp** Hiparchus[1]

**Hippocrates** *n*
*Evans MW 3.1.61* ɪ'bɒkrəti:z, hɪ-
**sp** Hibocrates[1]

**Hippolita** *n*
*m* ɪ'pɒlɪtə, -ˌta, hɪ-
**sp** Hippolita[9]

**hire** *n*
əɪɹ, həɪɹ
**sp** hier[1], hire[2], hyer[1]

**hire / ~d** *v*
əɪɹ, həɪɹ / *m* əɪɹd, 'əɪrɪd, həɪ-, 'həɪ-
**sp** hier[1], hyre[5] / hir'd[1], hired[1], hyr'd[4], hyred[1]

**hired** *adj*
*m* əɪɹd, 'əɪrɪd, həɪ-, 'həɪ-
**sp** hyred[2]

**Hiren** *n*
'əɪrən, 'həɪ-
**sp** Hiren[2]

**Hirsius** *n*
'ɐ:ɹsɪəs, 'hɐ:-
**sp** Hirsius[1]

**his**
> he

**Hisperia** *n*
ɪs'pi:rɪə, hɪ-
**sp** Hisperia[1]

**hiss** *TNK* *n*
ɪs, =
**sp** hisse[1]
**rh** this *TNK Prol.16*

**hiss / ~es / ~ing / ~ed** *v*
ɪs, = / 'ɪs·ɪz, 'hɪ- / -ɪn, -ɪŋ / ɪst, =
**sp** hisse[10] / hisses[1] / hizzing[1] / hist[1]
**rh** this *TC 5.10.55*; **hiss you** kiss you *VA 1084* / kisses *VA 17*

**hissing** *adj / adv*
'ɪsɪn, -ɪŋ, 'hɪ-
**sp** hissing[1] / hissing[1]

**hist** *interj*
=
**sp** hist[2]

**historical** *adj*
ɪs'tɒrɪkɑl, hɪ-
**sp** [pastoricall-comicall]-historicall-[pastorall][1], [tragicall-comicall]-historicall-[pastorall][1]

**history** *n*
*m* 'ɪstəˌrəɪ, -tər-, -tr-, 'hɪ-
**sp** historie[10], history[10]
**rh** eye *S 93.7*

**hit / ~s** *n*
ɪt, = / -s
**sp** hit[10] / hits[2]

**hit / ~s / ~ting** *v*
ɪt, = / -s / 'ɪtɪn, -ɪŋ, 'hɪ-
**sp** hit[49] / hits[6], hit's[1] / hitting[2]
**rh** it *VA 940*; sit *VA 1033*; wit *RJ 1.1.208*; **hit it** fit it *LLL 4.1.131* / fits *S 120.10*; shifts *AW 2.1.143* [F], *emend as* hits

**hither** *adv*
'ɪðəɹ, 'hɪ-
**sp** hether[21], hither[269], hi-ther[2]
**rh** *1* either, neither *CE 3.1.68*; **rh** *2* father *LLL 1.1.138*; **rh** *3* leather *CE 2.1.84*; together *AY 5.4.110, TNK 3.5.119*; weather *AY 2.5.5, 39*

**hitherto** *adv*
'ɪðəɹ'tu:, 'hɪ-
**sp** hitherto[9]

**hitherward / ~s** *adv*
ˈɪðəɹˌwɑːɹd, ˈhɪ- / -z
**sp** hitherward[4], hither-ward[1] / hither-wards[2]

**hive / ~s** *n*
əɪv, həɪv / -z
**sp** hiue[4] / hyues[1]
**rh** alive, survive *Luc 1769*

**hive** *v*
əɪv, həɪv
**sp** hiue[1]

**ho** *interj*
oː, hoː
**sp** ho[69], [whoa]-ho-[hoa][1], hoe[19]
**rh** go *KJ 3.3.73*; nonino *AY 5.3.16, 22, 28, 34*
> heigh-, what ho

**hoa** *interj*
ˈoːə, ˈhoːə
**sp** hoa[61], [whoa-ho]-hoa[1]

**hoar** *adj*
oːɹ, hoːɹ
**sp** hoare[5], hore[1]
**rh** nor *TNK 1.1.20*; score *RJ 2.4.134*

**hoar / ~s** *v*
oːɹ, hoːɹ / -z
**sp** hoare[1] / hoares[1]

**hoard** *n*
oːɹd, hoː-
**sp** hoard[1], hoord[1]
> uphoard

**hoard / ~ed** *v*
oːɹd, hoː- / ˈoːɹdɪd, ˈhoː-
**sp** hord[1] / hoorded[1]

**hoarded** *adj*
ˈoːɹdɪd, ˈhoː-
**sp** hoorded[1]

**hoarding** *adj / n*
ˈoːɹdɪn, -ɪŋ, ˈhoː-
**sp** hoording[1] / hoording[1]

**hoarse** *adj*
oːɹs, hoːɹs
**sp** hoarse[5]

**hoary-headed** *adj*
ˈoːɹəɪ-ˌedɪd, ˈhoː-, -ˌhe-
**sp** *emend of MND 2.1.107* hoared headed[1]
> head

**Hob** [name] *n*
ɒb, hɒb
**sp** hob[1]

**hobby-horse / ~s** *n*
ˈɒbəɪ-ˌɔːɹs, ˈhɒ-, -ˌhɔː- / -ɪz
**sp** hobbey-horse[1], hobbie-horse[2], hobbi-horse[1], hoby-horse[1], hoby-horsse[1], *emend of WT 1.2.276* holy-horse[1] / hobby-horses[1]
> horse

**hobgoblin** *n*
ɒbˈgɒblɪn, hɒb-
**sp** hobgoblin[1], hob-goblyn[1]
> goblin

**hobnail / ~s** *n*
ˈɒbnɛːlz, ˈhɒ-
**sp** hobnailes[1], hob-nayles[1]
> nail

**hob-nob** *interj*
ˈɒb-ˈnɒb, ˈhɒ-
**sp** hob nob[1]

**hoc** *Lat*
> hic

**hodge-pudding** *n*
ˈɒʤ-ˌpʊdɪn, -ɪŋ, ˈhɒ-
**sp** hodge-pudding[1]
> pudding

**hog / ~s** *n*
ɒg, hɒg / -z
**sp** hog[2], hogge[2] / hogs[2]

**hogshead / ~s** *n*
ˈɒgzed, -ˌed, ˈhɒ-, -ˌhe- / -z
**sp** hogshead[3], hogs-head[2] / hogsheads[1]

**hoise / ~d** *v*
əɪz, həɪz / -d
**sp** hoyse[1] / hoys'd[1]

**hoist / ~s / ~ed** *v*
əɪst, həɪst / -s / ˈəɪstɪd, ˈhəɪ-
**sp** hoist[1], hoyst[3] / hoists[1] / hoisted[1]

**hola**
> holla

**Holborn** *n*
ˈoːlˌbɔːɹn, ˈhoːl-
**sp** Holborne[1]

**hold / ~s** *n*
oːld, hoː- / -z
**sp** hold[20] / holds[1]

**hold / ~est / ~s / ~eth / ~ing / ~en / held / *Luc* hild** *v*
oːld, hoː- / -st / -z / ˈoːld·əθ, hoː- / -ɪn, -ɪŋ / -ən / eld, held / ɪld, hɪld
**sp** hold[412], hold-[vp-head][1], holde[7], hould[1] / hold'st[1], holdst[2] / holdes[3], holds[70] / holdeth[2] / holding[15], hol-ding[1] / holden[1] / held[81] / hild[1]
**rh** bold *S 122.9*; bold, cold *Luc 1558*; told *Per 3.Chorus.58*; unfold *MW 1.3.90*; untold *S 136.11* / field *S 2.4*; steeled *S 24.3* / fulfilled, killed *Luc 1257*
> a-, over-, with-hold

**hold-door** *adj*
ˈoːld-ˌdɔːɹ, ˈhoː-
**sp** hold-dore[1]
> door

**Holdfast** [name] *n*
ˈoːld-ˌfast, ˈhoː-
**sp** hold-fast[1]

**holding** *n*
ˈoːldɪn, -ɪŋ, hoː-
**sp** holding[5]

**holding-anchor** *n*
ˈoːldɪn-ˌaŋkəɹ, -ɪŋ, ˈhoː-
**sp** holding-anchor[1]
> anchor

**hole / ~s** *n*
o:l, ho:l / -z
**sp** hole[28], [worme-eaten]-hole[1] / holes[7]
**rh** coal *Per 3.Chorus.6*; soul *Luc 1175*
**pun** *RJ 2.4.90* whole; *CE 2.1.80* holy
> augur-, button-, dog-, key-, kiln-, starting-hole

**holidam**
> halidom

**holiday** *adj*
'ɒlɪˌdɛ:, 'hɒ-
**sp** holiday[2], holiday-[foole][1], holly-day-[time][1], holy-day[1]

**holiday / ~s** *n*
'ɒlɪˌdɛ:, 'hɒ- / -z
**sp** holiday[1], holliday[2], holly day[1], holyday[1], holy-day[2], holy day[4] / holidaies[1]
**rh** stay *H8 5.5.76*

**holily** *adv*
'o:lɪləɪ, 'ho:-
**sp** holily[3]
> holy

**holiness** *n*
'o:lɪnəs, 'ho:-
**sp** holinesse[12], holynesse[1]
> holy

**holla, hola** *interj / v*
*m* 'ɒlə, ɒ'lɑ:, 'hɒ-, hɒ-
**sp** hola[2], holla[8] / holla[2]

**holland / Holland** *n*
'ɒlənd, 'hɒ-
**sp** holland[1] / Holland[2]

**Hollander / ~s** *n*
'ɒləndəɹ, 'hɒ- / -z
**sp** Hollander[2] / Hollanders[1]

**hollo** *interj*
ə'lo:, hə-
**sp** hollo[1]

**hollow** *adj / n / v*
'ɒlə, -o:, 'hɒ-
**sp** hollow[44] / hollow[3] / hollow[1]
**rh** *v* follow *VA 973*

**hollow-eyed** *adj*
'ɒlə-ˌəɪd, -lo:-, 'hɒ-
**sp** [needy]-hollow-ey'd-[sharp][1]

**hollow-hearted** *adj*
'ɒlə-'ɑ:ɹtɪd, -lo:-, 'hɒ-, -'hɑ:-
**sp** hollow-hearted[1]

**hollowing** *n*
'ɒləwɪn, -ɪŋ, 'ɒlo:-, 'hɒ-
**sp** hollowing[1]

**hollowly** *adv*
*m* 'ɒləˌləɪ, 'ɒlo:-, 'hɒ-
**sp** hollowly[2]

**hollowness** *n*
*m* 'ɒlənəs, -ˌnes, 'ɒlo:-, 'hɒ-
**sp** hollownes[1], hollownesse[2]

**hollow-pampered** *adj*
'ɒlə-'pampəɹd, -lo:-, 'hɒ-
**sp** hollow-pamper'd[1]

**holly** *n*
'ɒləɪ, 'hɒ-
**sp** holly[2]
**rh** folly *AY 2.7.181, 191*; jolly *AY 2.7.183, 193*

**Holmedon / ~'s** *n*
'ɒlmdən, 'hɒ- / -z
**sp** Holmeden[1], Holmedon[3] / Holmedons[1]

**Holofernes** *n*
'ɒləˌfɐ:ɹni:z, 'hɒ-
**sp** Holofernes[5]

**holp**
> help

**hol·y / ~ier** *adj*
'o:ləɪ, 'ho:- / -əɹ
**sp** holie[9], holy[170], holy-[hat][1], holy-[water][3] / holier[1], holyer[1]
**pun** *CE 2.1.80* hole
> unholy

**Holy Land** *n*
'o:ləɪ ˌland, 'ho:-
**sp** Holy-Land[2], Holy-land[1], Holy Land[2]
> land

**Holy-rood** *adj*
'o:ləɪ-'ru:d, 'ho:-
**sp** Holy-roode[1]
> rood

**homage** *n*
'ɒmɪʤ, 'hɒ-
**sp** homage[16]

**homager** *n*
'ɒmɪʤəɹ, 'hɒ-
**sp** homager[1]

**home** *adj*
o:m, ho:m
**sp** home[1]

**home / ~s** *n*
o:m, ho:m / -z
**sp** home[328] / homes[2]
**rh** 1 Rome *JC 1.1.32*; **rh** 2 drone *Per 2.Chorus.17*

**home-bred** *adj*
'o:m-ˌbred, 'ho:-
**sp** home-bred[2]

**home-keeping** *adj*
*m* ˌo:m-'ki:pɪn, -ɪŋ, 'ho:-
**sp** home-keeping[1]
> keep

**homely** *adj*
'o:mləɪ, 'ho:-
**sp** homelie[1], homely[14]

**homespun / ~s** *n*
'o:m-ˌspɤnz, 'ho:-
**sp** home-spuns[1]

**homeward / ~s** *adv*
'o:mwəɹd, 'ho:- / -z
**sp** homeward[4], home-ward[1] / homewards[1]

**homicide / ~s** *n*
'ɒmɪˌsəɪd, 'hɒ- / -z
**sp** homicide[4] / homicides[1]

**homily** *n*
'ɒmɪləɪ, 'hɒ-
**sp** homilie[1]

**hominem** *Lat*
> homo

**homme / ~s** *Fr n*
ɔm
**sp** hommes[1]

**hom·o / ~inem** *Lat n*
'hɒm·o: / -ɪnem
**sp** homo[1] / *emend of LLL 5.1.9* hominum[1]

**honest / ~er / ~est** *adj*
'ɒnɪst / -əɹ / -əst
**sp** honest[284], ho-nest[4] / honester[5] / honestest[1]
> dis-, under-honest

**honest-hearted** *adj*
'ɒnɪst-ˌɑ:ɹtɪd, -ˌhɑ:-
**sp** honest hearted[1]
> heart

**honestly** *adv*
*m* 'ɒnɪstˌləɪ, -tl-
**sp** honestlie[1], honestly[6]

**honest-natured** *adj*
'ɒnɪst-ˌnɛ:təɹd
**sp** honest natur'd[1]
> nature

**honesty** *n*
*m* 'ɒnɪsˌtəɪ, -st-
**sp** honestie[40], ho-nestie[1], honestie's [honesty is][1], honesty[45]
**rh** me, three *LLL 5.2.813*; thee *KJ 1.1.181*

**honey** *adj / n*
'ɤnəɪ, 'hɤ-
**sp** honey[1], honie[2], hony[6] / honey[7], honie[3], hony[11]

**honey / ~ing** *v*
'ɤnəɪɪn, -ɪŋ, 'hɤ-
**sp** honying[1]

**honey-bag / ~s** *n*
'ɤnəɪ-ˌbag, 'hɤ- / -z
**sp** hony-bag[1], hony bag[2] / honie-bags[1]
> bag

**honey-bee / ~s** *n*
'ɤnəɪ-ˌbi:z, 'hɤ-
**sp** hony bees[1]
> bee

**honeycomb** *n*
'ɤnəɪ-ˌko:m, 'hɤ-
**sp** hony-combe[1]
> comb

**honeyed** *adj*
'ɤnəɪd, 'hɤ-
**sp** honyed[1]

**honey-heavy** *adj*
'ɤnəɪ-ˌevəɪ, 'hɤ-, -'he-
**sp** hony-heauy-[dew][1]
> heavy

**honeyless** *adj*
'ɤnəɪˌles, 'hɤ-
**sp** hony-lesse[1]

**honey-mouthed** *adj*
'ɤnəɪ-ˌməʊðd, 'hɤ-
**sp** hony-mouth'd[1]
> mouth

**honeyseed** *adj / n*
'ɤnəɪ-ˌsi:d, 'hɤ-
**sp** hony-seed[1] / honyseed[1]
> seed

**honey-stalk / ~s** *n*
'ɤnəɪ-ˌstɔ:ks, 'hɤ-
**sp** hony stalkes[1]

**honeysuckle / ~s** *n*
'ɤnəɪ-ˌsɤkl, 'hɤ- / -z
**sp** honisuckle[1], hony-suckle[1] / hony-suckles[1]
> suckle

**honey-sweet** *adj*
'ɤnəɪ-ˌswi:t, 'hɤ-
**sp** honey sweete[1], hony sweete[2]
> sweet

**honey-tongued** *adj*
'ɤnəɪ-ˌtɒŋd, 'hɤ-, -ˌtʊ-
**sp** honie-tongued[1]
> tongue

**honi** *Fr v*
'ɔni
**sp** hony[1]

**honneur** *Fr n*
ɔ'nœ:ɹ
**sp** honeur[3], honneur[1], *emend of H5 3.4.44* honeus[1]

**honorato** *Ital adj*
ˌɒnə'rɑ:ta
**sp** honorata[1]

**honorificabilitudinitatibus**
*supposed longest word in Lat*
ˌɒnəˌrɪfɪkabɪlɪˌtju:dɪnɪ'tɑ:tɪbʊs
**sp** honorificabilitu-dinitatibus[1]

**honour / ~'s / ~s / ~s'** *n*
'ɒnəɹ / -z
**sp** honor[370], ho-nor[4], honour[189], ho-nour[2], honors [honour is][1], honor's [honour is][1], honour's [honour is][1] / honors[8], honours[9] / honors[56], honours[24] / honors[1]
> dishonour

**honour / ~est / ~s / *S* ~ing / ~ed** *v*
'ɒnəɹ / -əst / -z / 'ɒnəˌrɪn, -ɪŋ / *m* 'ɒnəɹd, -əˌred
**sp** honor[13], honour[16] / honorest[1] / honors[4], honours[1] / honor'd[2], honored[2], honourd[1], honour'd[12], honoured[1]
**rh** ruining *S 125.2* / *rh* bed *AY 5.4.141*; bred, unconquered *Luc 410*

**honourable** *adj*
*m* 'ɒnəˌrabəl, 'ɒnrəbəl
**sp** honorable[26], hono-rable[1], honora-ble[1], honourable[94]

**honourably** *adv*
*m* 'ɒnrəbˌləɪ, 'ɒnəˌrabləɪ
**sp** honorably[1], honourably[5]
**rh** lie *JC 5.5.79*

**honoured** *adj*
'ɒnəɹd
**sp** honor'd[7], honored[2], honour'd[16], honourd[1], honour'd-[gashes][1], honoured[1]
> all-, time-honoured

**honour-flawed** *adj*
'ɒnəɹ-'flɔ:d
**sp** honor-flaw'd[1]
> flaw

**honour-giving** *adj*
'ɒnəɹ-'gɪvɪn, -ɪŋ
**sp** honor-giuing-[hand][1]
> give

**honour-owing** *adj*
'ɒnəɹ-'o:ɪn, -ɪŋ
**sp** honour-owing-[wounds][1]
> owe

**hoo** *interj*
hu:, ho:
**sp** hoo[6]

**hood / ~s** *n*
ʊd, = / -z
**sp** hood[3] / hoods[1]
> Robin Hood

**hood / ~ed** *v*
ʊd, = / 'ʊdɪd, =
**sp** hood[2] / hooded[1]

**hooded** *adj*
'ʊdɪd, =
**sp** hooded[1]

**hoodman** *n*
'ʊdmən, =
**sp** hoodman[1]

**hoodman-blind** *n*
'ʊdmən-'bləɪnd, 'hʊ-
**sp** hoodman-blinde[1]
> blind

**hoodwink / ~ed** *v*
'ʊdwɪŋk, = / -t
**sp** hoodwinke[2], hudwinke[1] / hood-wink'd[1], hoodwinkt[1], hood winkt[1]
> wink

**hoof,** *plural* **hooves** *n*
u:f, ʊf, = / u:fs, u:vz, ʊ-, =
**sp** hoofe[2] / hoofes[3], hooues[1]

**hook / ~s** *n*
ʊk, = / -s
**sp** hooke[6], [Welch]-hooke[1] / hookes[2]
**rh** books, looks *Luc 103*; looks *RJ 2. Chorus.8, S 137.7*
> nut-, sheep-hook

**hook / ~ing** *v*
ʊk, = / 'ʊkɪn, -ɪŋ , 'hʊ-
**sp** hooke[1], hooke-[on][2] / hooking[1]

**hook-nosed** *adj*
'ʊk-ˌno:zd, 'hʊk-
**sp** hooke-nos'd[1]

**hoop / ~s** *n*
u:p, = / -s
**sp** hoope[5] / hoopes[2]

**hoop / ~ed** *v*
u:p, = / -t
**sp** hoope[1] / hoop'd[1]
> three-hooped

**hooping** *n*
'u:pɪn, -ɪŋ, 'hu:-
**sp** hooping[1]

**hoot / ~s / ~ing / ~ed** *v*
u:t, = / -s / 'u:t·ɪn, -ɪŋ, 'hu:- / -ɪd
**sp** hoote[1] / hoots[1] / hooting[1], howting[1] / hooted[1], howted[1]
> a-hooting

**hooves**
> hoof

**hop** *v*
ɒp, =
**sp** hop[8]
**rh** pap *MND 5.1.291*

**hope / ~'s / ~s** *n*
o:p, ho:p / -s
**sp** hope[167] / hope's[1] / hopes[48]
**rh** scope *Ham 3.2.228* [Q2], *S 29.5, 52.14*

**hop·e / ~est / ~es / ~ing / ~ed** *v*
o:p, ho:p / -st / -s / 'o:pɪn, -ɪŋ, ho:- / o:pt, ho:pt
**sp** hope[182] / hop'st[4] / hopes[6] / hoping[6] / hop'd[4]

**hoped-for** *adj*
'o:pt-ˌfɔ:ɹ, 'ho:-
**sp** hop'd-for[2]

**hopeful** *adj*
'o:pfʊl, 'ho:-
**sp** hopefull[9]

**hopeless** *adj*
'o:pləs, 'ho:-
**sp** hopelesse[7]

**Hopkins** *n*
'ɒpkɪnz, =
**sp** Hopkins[2]

**Horace** *n*
'ɒrɪs, =
**sp** Horace[2], Horrace[1]

**Horatio** *n*
ə'rɛ:sɪo:, hə-
**sp** Horatio[39], Ho-ratio[1]

**horizon** *n*
'ɒrɪˌzɒn, 'hɒ-
**sp** horizon[1]

**horn / ~s** *n*
ɔ:ɹn, hɔ:- / -z
**sp** horn[2], horne[33] / horns[4], hornes[48], [rag'd]-hornes[1], [tun'd]-hornes[1]
**rh** born *AY 4.2.14*; forlorn *VA 1025*; o'erworn *VA 868*; scorn *AY 4.2.18, TC 1.1.114*; sworn *TC 4.5.46* / scorns *TC 4.5.31*
> dis-, ink-, shoeing-horn

**horn-beast / ~s** *n*
'ɔ:ɹn-ˌbi:sts, 'hɔ:-, -ˌbests
**sp** horne-beasts[1]
> beast

**horn-book** *n*
'ɔ:ɹn-ˌbʊk, 'hɔ:-

**sp** horne-booke[1]
> book

**horned** *adj*
*m* 'ɔ:ɹnɪd, 'hɔ:-
**sp** horned[4]
> double-horned

**Horner** *n*
'ɔ:ɹnəɹ, 'hɔ:-
**sp** horner[2]

**horning** *n*
'ɔ:ɹnɪn, -ɪŋ, 'hɔ:-
**sp** horning[1]

**horn-mad** *adj*
'ɔ:ɹn-'mad, 'hɔ:-
**sp** horne-mad[2], horne mad[3]
> mad

**hornmaker** *n*
'ɔ:ɹn,mɛ:kəɹ, 'hɔ:-
**sp** horne-maker[1]
> make

**hornpipe / ~s** *n*
'ɔ:ɹn,pəɪps, 'hɔ:-
**sp** horne-pipes[1]
> pipe

**horn-ring** *n*
'ɔ:ɹn-,rɪŋ, 'hɔ:-
**sp** horne-ring[1]
> ring

**horologe** *n*
'ɒrəlɒʤ, 'hɒ-
**sp** horologe[1]

**horrible** *adj*
'ɒrɪbəl, =
**sp** horrible[28]

**horribly** *adv*
*m* 'ɒrɪb,ləɪ, -bləɪ, 'hɒ-
**sp** horribly[4]

**horrid / ~er** *adj*
'ɒrɪd, = / -əɹ
**sp** horrid[13], horride[3] / horrider[1]

**horridly** *adv*
*m* 'ɒrɪd,ləɪ, -dləɪ, 'hɒ-
**sp** horridly[2]

**horror / ~s** *n*
'ɒrəɹ, 'hɒ- / -z
**sp** horror[15] / horrors[5]

**horse / ~'s / ~s / ~s'** *n*
ɔ:ɹs, hɔ:ɹs / 'ɔ:ɹsɪz, 'hɔ:-
**sp** horse[213], [foot-cloth]-horse[1], horsse[1] / horses[3] / horses[50], hor-ses[2], horsses[4] / horses[4]
**rh** force *S 91.4, VA 30*; remorse *VA 258*
> fore-, hobby-, malt-, pack-, post-, stalking-, un-horse

**horse / ~ing / ~ed** *v*
'ɔ:ɹsɪn, -ɪŋ, 'hɔ:- / ɔ:ɹst, hɔ:-
**sp** horsing[1] / hors'd[4]

**horseback** *n*
'ɔ:ɹsbak, 'hɔ:-
**sp** horsebacke[3]
> a-horseback

**horseback-breaker** *n*
'ɔ:ɹsbak-,brɛ:kəɹ, 'hɔ:-
**sp** hors-back-breaker[1]
> break

**horse-drench** *n*
'ɔ:ɹs-,drenʧ, 'hɔ:-
**sp** horse-drench[1]
> drench

**horsehair / ~s** *n*
'ɔ:ɹs-,ɛ:ɹz, 'hɔ:-, -hɛ:-
**sp** horse-haires[1]
> hair

**horse-leech / ~es** *n*
'ɔ:ɹs-,li:ʧɪz, 'hɔ:-
**sp** horse-leeches[1]

**horse·man / ~man's / ~men** *n*
'ɔ:ɹs·mən, 'hɔ:- / -mənz / -mən
**sp** horse-man[1] / horsemans[1] / horsemen[10], horsmen[1]

**horsemanship** *n*
'ɔ:ɹsmən,ʃɪp, 'hɔ:-
**sp** horsemanship[1], horseman-ship[1]

**horse-piss** *n*
'ɔ:ɹs-,pɪs, 'hɔ:-
**sp** horse-pisse[1]

**horseshoe** *n*
'ɔ:ɹs,ʃu:, 'hɔ:-
**sp** horse-shoo[1]

**horse-stealer** *n*
'ɔ:ɹs-,sti:ləɹ, 'hɔ:-
**sp** horse-stealer[1]
> steal

**horsetail** *n*
'ɔ:ɹs,tɛ:l, 'hɔ:-
**sp** horse-taile[1]
> tail

**horseway** *n*
'ɔ:ɹs,wɛ: , 'hɔ:-
**sp** horseway[1]

**Hortensio / ~'s** *n*
*m* ɔ:ɹ'tensɪo:, -ɪ,o:, hɔ:ɹ- / -z
**sp** Hortensio[28], Hortentio[10] / Hortensios[1], Hortensio's[1]
**rh** ago *TS 3.1.70*; Gremio, know *TS 1.2.234*

**Hortensius** *n*
ɔ:ɹ'tensɪəs, hɔ:ɹ-
**sp** Hortensius[2]

**horum** *Lat*
> hic

**hose** *n*
o:z, =
**sp** hose[22]
**rh** prose *LLL 4.3.56*
> boot-hose

**hospitable** *adj*
'ɒspɪ,tabəl, 'hɒ-
**sp** hospitable[3]
> unhospitable

**hospital** *n*
'ɒspɪˌtal, 'hɒ-
**sp** hospitall[1]
**rh** befall *LLL 5.2.860*

**hospitality** *n*
*m* ˌɒspɪ'talɪˌtəɪ, 'hɒ-
**sp** hospitalitie[1]
**rh** to thee *Luc 575*

**host / ~'s / ~s** *n*
o:st, ho:- / -s
**sp** hoast[19], hoaste[1], host[49], [ranting]-host[1], hoste[5] / hosts[1] / hostes[1], hosts[2]
**rh** *1* post *Luc 3* / **rh** *2* cost *TNK 3.5.126*

**host** *v*
o:st, ho:-
**sp** host[1]

**hostage / ~s** *n*
'ɒstɪʤ, 'hɒ- / -ɪz
**sp** hostage[2] / hostages[4]

**hostess** *n*
'o:stes, 'ho:-
**sp** hostesse[38], ho-stesse[1]

**hostess-ship** *n*
*m* 'o:stesˌʃɪp, 'ho:-
**sp** hostesseship[1]

**hostile** *adj*
'ɒstəɪl, 'hɒ-
**sp** hostile[4]

**hostility** *n*
ɒs'tɪlɪˌtəɪ, hɒ-
**sp** hostility[1], hostilitie[3]

**Hostilius** *n*
ɒs'tɪlɪəs, hɒ-
**sp** Hostilius[2]

**hostler**
> ostler

**hot / ~ter / ~test** *adj*
ɒt, hɒt / 'ɒt·əɹ, 'hɒ- / -əst
**sp** hot[139], hot-[blood][1], hot-[blouds][1], [glowing]-hot[1], hotte[3] / hoter[1], hotter[4] / hotest[1], hottest[1]
**rh** not *LC 218*
> red-hot

**hot-bloodied** *adj*
ˌɒt-'blɤdəɪd, ˌhɒ-
**sp** hot-bloodied[1], hot-bloodied-[Gods][1]
> blood

**hot-house** *n*
'ɒt-ˌəʊs, 'hɒ-, -ˌhəʊ-
**sp** hot-house[1]
> house

**hotly** *adv*
'ɒtləɪ, 'hɒ-
**sp** hotly[4]

**Hotspur / ~'s** *n*
'ɒtspəɹ, 'hɒ- / -z
**sp** Hotspur[5], Hotspurre[12], Hot-spurre[2] / Hotspurres[4], Hotspurs[2]
> spur

**hound / ~s** *n*
əʊnd, həʊnd / -z, -nz
**sp** hound[12] / houndes[1], hounds[20]
**rh** *1* ground *Tit 2.2.25*; round *MND 3.1.102*; **rh** *2* wound *VA 913* / **rh** *1* bounds *MND 3.2.64*; confounds *VA 881*; grounds *PP 9.6*; **rh** *2* downs *VA 678*
> blood-, grey-, hell-hound

**hour / ~'s / ~s / ~s'** *n*
o:ɹ, o:əɹ [*1 syll*] / -z
**sp** houre[245], hower[8], howre[43], howr's [hour is][1] / houres[9], howres[2] / houres[97], hours[3], howers[1], howres[23] / houres[2]
**rh** bower *MND 3.2.8*; deflower, power *Luc 347*; flower, power *LC 72*; flower *AY 5.3.27, PP 13.6, TN 2.4.39, VA 1187*; Glendower *1H4 1.3.99*; power *3H6 4.1.147, S 126.2, Tim 3.1.63, WT 4.1.8*; sour *S 57.5*; four *LLL 5.2.368*; sycamore *LLL 5.2.90* / flowers *LLL 4.3.355, PP 14.26, S 16.5*; powers *Luc 297*; showers *S 124.10*; towers *Luc 944*
**pun** *AY 2.7.24ff* whore
> half-, marriage-hour; after-hours

**hour-glass** *n*
'o:ɹ-ˌglas, 'o:əɹ-
**sp** houre-glasse[1], howre-glasse[1]
> glass

**hourly** *adj / adv*
'o:ɹləɪ, 'o:əɹ-
**sp** hourely[8] / hourely[12], hourly[1], howrely[1]

**house** *adj*
əʊs, həʊs
**sp** house[1]

**house / ~'s / ~s** *n*
əʊs, həʊs / 'əʊsɪz, 'həʊ- / 'əʊzɪz, 'həʊ-
**sp** house[394], [prison]-house[1], [senate]-house[4], howse[1] / houses[5] / houses[20], howses[1]
**rh** *1* mouse *MND 5.1.378*; **rh** *2* allows *Tim 3.3.42*; rouse [*emend of* rout] *Per 3.Chorus.2*
> ale-, alms-, bawdy-, brew-, brothel-, charge-, charnel-, council-, dove-, dwelling-, farm-, garden-, hot-, jewel-, leaping-, manor-, pent-, play-, prison-, senate-, slaughter-, spital-, store-, summer-, tap-, tiring-, working-house

**house / ~d** *v*
əʊz, həʊz / *m* -d, 'əʊzɪd, 'həʊ-
**sp** house[3] / hous'd[3], hows'd[1]
**rh** louse *KL 3.2.27*
> unhoused

**housed** *adj*
*m* 'əʊzɪd, 'həʊ-
**sp** housed[1]

**house-eaves** *n*
'əʊs-ˌi:vz, 'həʊs-
**sp** house-eeues[1]

**household** *adj*
'əʊsˌo:ld, 'həʊs-, -ˌho:-
**sp** household[2], house-hold[1], hous-hold[6], houshold-[stuffe][1], houshould[1]

**household / ~'s** *n*
'əʊsˌo:ld, 'həʊs-, -ˌho:- / -z
**sp** household[2], houshold[2] / households[1], housholds[1]

**householder / ~s** *n*
ˈəʊsˌoːldəɹ, ˈhəʊs-, -ˌhoː- / -z
**sp** houshoul-der[1] / house-holders[1]

**housekeeper / ~s** *n*
ˈəʊsˌkiːpəɹ, ˈhəʊs- / -z
**sp** house-keeper[1], hous-keeper[1] / house-kee-pers[1]
> keep

**housekeeping** *n*
ˈəʊsˌkiːpɪn, -ɪŋ, ˈhəʊs-
**sp** house-keeping[3]

**houseless** *adj*
ˈəʊsləs, ˈhəʊs-
**sp** house-lesse[1], houselesse[1]

**house·wife / ~wife's / ~wives** *n*
ˈɤzɪf, ˈhɤ- / -s / ˈɤzɪvz, ˈhɤ-
**sp** houswife[2], huswife[11] / huswiues[1] / house-wiues[1], huswiues[1]
> wife

**housewifery** *n*
ˈɤzɪfrəɪ, ˈhɤ-
**sp** huswiferie[2]

**hovel** *n / v*
ˈɒvəl, ˈhɒ-
**sp** houel[2], houell[2] / houell[1]

**hovel-post** *n*
ˈɒvəl-ˌpoːst, ˈhɒ-
**sp** houell-post[1]

**hover / ~s / ~ed** *v*
ˈɒvəɹ, ˈhɒ- / -z / -d
**sp** houer[5] / houers[1] / houerd[1]
**rh** covered, lovered *LC 319*

**hovering** *adj*
ˈɒvrɪn, -ɪŋ, ˈɒvər-, ˈhɒ-
**sp** houering[1]

**how** *adv*
əʊ, həʊ
**sp** how[2139], howe[1], how's [how is][2]
**rh** brow *Luc 748*; brow, vow *Luc 810*; now *LLL 5.2.514, MM 2.2.187, R2 5.3.115, S 101.13*; vow *RJ 2.3.57*

**howbeit** *adv*
əʊˈbiːt, həʊ-
**sp** howbeit[3]

**Hower** [name] *n*
oːɹ, ˈoːəɹ
**sp** Hower[1]
**pun** hour *R3 4.4.176*

**however, *abbr* ~e'er** *adv*
*m* əʊˈevəɹ, *abbr* əʊˈɛːɹ, həʊ-
**sp** howeuer[1], how-euer[1], *abbr* how ere[10], how e're[2]
> ever

**howl / ~s** *n*
əʊlz, həʊlz
**sp** howles[1], howle's [howl is][1]

**howl / ~est / ~ing / ~ed** *v*
əʊl, həʊl / -st / ˈəʊlɪn, -ɪŋ, ˈhəʊ- / *m* əʊld, ˈəʊlɪd, həʊ-, ˈhəʊ-
**sp** howle[9] / howl'st[1] / howling[2] / howld[1], howl'd[4], howled[1]
**rh** scowling *VA 918*

**howlet / ~'s** *n*
ˈəʊlɪts, ˈhəʊ-
**sp** howlets[1]

**howling** *adj*
ˈəʊlɪn, -ɪŋ, ˈhəʊ-
**sp** houling[1], howling[3]

**howling / ~s** *n*
ˈəʊlɪn, -ɪŋ, ˈhəʊ- / -z
**sp** howling[5] / howlings[1]

**howsoever, *abbr* ~e'er** *adv*
ˌəʊsoːˈevəɹ, ˌhəʊ-, *abbr* ˌəʊsoːˈɛːɹ, ˌhəʊ-
**sp** howsoeuer[8], howso-euer[1], howsoeu'r[1], *abbr* howsoere[5]
> ever

**howsomever, *abbr* ~e'er** *adv*
*abbr* ˌəʊsəmˈɛːɹ, ˌhəʊ-
**sp** how somere[1], how som ere[1]
> ever, somever

**hox / ~es** *v*
ˈɒksɪz, hɒ-
**sp** hoxes[1]

**hoy** *adj*
əɪ, həɪ
**sp** hoy[1]

**hoyday** *n*
ˈəɪdɛː, ˈhəɪ-
**sp** hoyday[2], hoy-day[1]

**hubbub** *n*
ˈuːbəb, ˈhuː-
**sp** whoo-bub[1]

**Hubert / ~s** *n*
ˈjuːbəɹt, ˈhjuː / -s
**sp** Hubert[40] / Huberts[2]

**huddl·e / ~ing / ~ed** *v*
ˈɤdl·ɪn, -ɪŋ, ˈhɤ- / -d
**sp** hudling[1] / hudled[1]

**hue** *n*
juː, hj-
**sp** hue[15], huy[2]
**rh** anew *S 82.5, Tit 1.1.264*; blue *LLL 5.2.885*; grew *S 98.6*; Jew *MND 3.1.86*; true *MND 3.1.118, S 67.6, TNK 1.1.3*; view *VA 345*

**hug / ~s / ~ged** *v*
ɤg, hɤg / -z / -d
**sp** hug[2], hugge[4] / hugges[1] / hudg'd[1] hugg'd[1]

**huge** *adj*
juːʤ, hj-
**sp** huge[31]

**hugely** *adv*
ˈjuːʤləɪ, ˈhj-
**sp** hugely[1]

**hugeness** *n*
ˈjuːʤnəs, ˈhj-
**sp** hugenesse[1]

**hugger-mugger** *n*
ˈɤgəɹ-ˈmɤgəɹ, ˈhɤ-
**sp** hugger mugger[1]

**Hugh** *n*
juː, hj-
**sp** Hugh[25]

**huius** *Lat*
> hic

**hulk** *n*
ɤlk, hɤ-
**sp** hulke[3]

**hull / ~ing** *v*
ɤl, hɤl / ˈɤlɪn, -ɪŋ, ˈhɤ-
**sp** hull[2] / hulling[1]

**hum** *interj*
ɤm, hɤm
**sp** hum[4], humh[6]

**hum / ~s** *n*
ɤm, hɤm / -z
**sp** hum[3], humme[2] / hums[1], hum's[1]

**hum / ~s** *v*
ɤm, hɤm / -z
**sp** hum[2], humme[1] / hums[1]

**human** *adj*
*m* ˈjuːmən, ˈhj-
**sp** humaine[1], humane[24]
> inhuman

**humane** *adj*
juːˈmɛːn, hj-
**sp** humaine[2], humane[3]

**humanely** *adv*
juːˈmɛːnləɪ, hj-
**sp** humanely[1], hu-manely[1]

**humanity** *n*
*m* juːˈmanɪˌtəɪ, -ɪt-, hj-
**sp** humanitie[1], humanity[8]
**rh** be *Tim 3.6.105*

**humble / ~er / ~st** *adj*
ˈɤmbəl, ˈhɤ- / -əɹ / -əst
**sp** humble[60] / humbler[3] / humblest[2]
**rh** stumble *LLL 5.2.626*

**humbl·e / ~es / ~ing / ~ed** *v*
ˈɤmbəl, ˈhɤ- / -z / -ɪn, -ɪŋ / -d
**sp** humble[2] / humbles[1] / humbling[1] / humbled[8]

**humble-bee / ~s** *n*
ˈɤmbəl-ˌbiː, ˈhɤ- / -z
**sp** humble-bee[2], humble bee[2] / humble bees[1]
**rh** three *LLL 3.1.83, 87, 93*

**humbled** *adj*
ˈɤmbəld, ˈhɤ-
**sp** humbled[1]

**humble-mouthed** *adj*
ˈɤmbəl-ˌməʊðd, ˈhɤ-
**sp** humble-mouth'd[1]
> mouth

**humbleness** *n*
ˈɤmbəlˌnes, ˈhɤ-
**sp** humblenesse[7]

**humble-visaged** *adj*
ˈɤmbəl-ˌvɪzɪʤd, ˈhɤ-
**sp** humble visag'd[1]

**humbly** *adv*
ˈɤmbləɪ, ˈhɤ-
**sp** humblie[2], humbly[58]

**Hume / ~'s** *n*
juːm, hjuːm / -z
**sp** Hume[9] / Humes[2]

**humidity** *n*
*m* jʊˈmɪdɪˌtəɪ, -ɪt-, hj-
**sp** humidity[2]

**humility** *n*
*m* jʊˈmɪlɪˌtəɪ, -ɪt-, hj-
**sp** humilitie[10], humility[7]

**humming** *n*
ˈɤmɪn, -ɪŋ, ˈhɤ-
**sp** humming[1]

**humorous** *adj*
*m* ˈjuːmrəs, -mər-, -məˌrɤs, hj-
**sp** humerous[2], humorous[8], humo-rous[1], humourous[1]

**humour / ~s / ~s'** *n*
ˈjuːməɹ, ˈhj- / -z
**sp** humor[48], hu-mor[1], humour[36], hu-mour[1] / humors[28], humours[4] / humours[1]

**humour / ~s / ~ed** *v*
ˈjuːməɹ, ˈhj- / -z / -d
**sp** humor[2], humour[4] / humors[1] / humor'd[1]

**humoured** *adj*
ˈjuːməɹd, ˈhj-
**sp** humour'd[1]

**humour-letter** *n*
ˈjuːməɹ-ˌletəɹ, ˈhj-
**sp** humor-letter[1]

**Humphrey / ~'s** *n*
ˈɤmfrəɪ, ˈhɤ- / -z
**sp** Humfrey[47], Humphrey[2], Vmpheir[1], *abbr in s.d.* Hum[frey] / Humfreyes[5], Humfries[7], Humphreyes[2]

**hunc** *Lat*
> hic

**hundred** *adj*
ˈɤndrəd, ˈhɤ-
**sp** hundred[88], [three-suited]-hundred pound, hun-dred[3], hundreth[1]

**hundred / ~s** *n*
ˈɤndrəd, ˈhɤ- / -z
**sp** hundred[19] / hundreds[3]

**hung**
> hang

**Hungarian** *adj*
ɤŋˈgɛːrɪən, hɤ-
**sp** Hungarian[1]

**Hungar·y / ~'s** *n*
ˈɤŋgərəɪ, ˈhɤ- / -z
**sp** Hungary[1] / Hungaries[1]

**hunger** *n / v*
ˈɤŋgəɹ, ˈhɤ-
**sp** hunger[9], hunger-[broke][1], hunger's [hunger is][1] / hunger[3]

**Hungerford** *n*
'ɤŋgəɹˌfɔːɹd, 'hɤ-
**sp** Hungerford[2]

**hungerly** *adv*
*m* 'ɤŋgəɹˌləɪ, -ləɪ, 'hɤ-
**sp** hungerly[3]

**hunger-starved** *adj*
'ɤŋgəɹ-ˌstɑːɹvɪd, 'hɤ-
**sp** hunger-starued[1]
> starve

**hungry** *adj*
'ɤŋgrəɪ, 'hɤ-
**sp** hungrie[1], hungry[21]
> a-hungry

**hungry-starved** *adj*
'ɤŋgrəɪ-ˌstɑːɹvɪd, 'hɤ-
**sp** hungry-starued[1]
> starve

**hunt** *n*
ɤnt, hɤ-
**sp** hunt[4]
> mouse-hunt

**hunt / ~s / ~eth / ~ing / ~ed** *v*
ɤnt, hɤ- / -s / 'ɤnt·əθ, 'hɤ- / -ɪn, -ɪŋ / -ɪd
**sp** hunt[27] / hunts[3] / hunteth[1] / hunting[6] / hunted[5]
> bloody-hunting

**hunt-counter** *n*
'ɤnt-ˌkəʊntəɹ, 'hɤ-
**sp** hunt-counter[1]

**hunter / ~'s / ~s** *n*
'ɤntəɹ, 'hɤ- / -z
**sp** hunter[8], hun-ter[1] / hunters[4] / hunters[3]

**hunting** *n*
'ɤntɪn, -ɪŋ
**sp** hunting[12]

**Huntington** *n*
'ɤntɪŋtən, 'hɤ-
**sp** Huntington[1]

**huntress / ~'** *n*
'ɤntrəs, 'hɤ-
**sp** huntresse[1]

**hunts·man, ~men** *n*
'ɤntsmən, 'hɤ-
**sp** huntsman[7], huntsmen[3], hunts-men[1]

**hunts-up** *n*
'ɤnts-ˌɤp, 'hɤ-
**sp** hunts-vp[1]

**hurdle** *n*
'ɐːɹdl, 'hɐː-
**sp** hurdle[1]

**hurl / *LC* ~s / ~ing / ~ed** *v*
ɐːɹl, hɐːɹl / -z / 'ɐːɹlɪn, -ɪŋ, 'hɐː- / ɐːɹld, hɐː-
**sp** hurle[9] / hurles[1] / hurling[1] / hurld[1], hurl'd[1]
**rh** curls *LC 87*

**hurling** *adj*
'ɐːɹlɪn, -ɪŋ, 'hɐː-
**sp** hurling[1]

**hurly** *n*
'ɐːɹləɪ, 'hɐː-
**sp** hurlie[1], hurley[2]

**hurly-burly** *n*
'ɐːɹləɪ-'bɐːɹləɪ, 'hɐː-
**sp** hurley-burley's [burley is][1], hurly-burly[1], hurly burly[1]

**hurricano / ~es** *n*
ˌɤrɪ'kɛːnoː, ˌhɤ- / -z
**sp** hurricano[1] / hyrricano's[1]

**hurry** *n*
'ɤrəɪ, 'hɤ-
**sp** hurry[1]

**hurr·y / ~ies / ~ied** *v*
'ɤrəɪ, 'hɤ- / -z / -d
**sp** hurrie[1], hurry[1] / hurries[1], hurryes[1] / hurried[5]

**hurt** *adj*
ɐːɹt, 'hɐː-
**sp** hurt[3]

**hurt / ~s** *n*
ɐːɹt, hɐːɹt / -s
**sp** hurt[20] / hurts[5]

**hurt / ~s** *v*
ɐːɹt, hɐːɹt / -s
**sp** hurt[65] / hurts[8]

**hurtle / ~d** *v*
'ɐːɹtld, 'hɐː-
**sp** hurtled[1]

**hurtless** *adj*
'ɐːɹtləs, 'hɐː-
**sp** hurtlesse[1]

**hurtling** *n*
'ɐːɹtlɪn, -ɪŋ, 'hɐː-
**sp** hurtling[1]

**husband / ~'s / ~s / ~s'** *n*
'ɤzbənd, 'hɤ- / -z
**sp** housband[1], husband[275], husba[n]d[1], hus-band[7], [combynate]-husband[1], husband's [husband is][4] / husbands[30] / husbands[24], hus-bands[2] / husbands[2]

**husband / ~ed** *v*
'ɤzbənd, 'hɤ- / -ɪd
**sp** husband[3] / husbanded[4]

**husbandless** *adj*
*m* 'ɤzbəndˌles, 'hɤ-
**sp** husbandles[1]

**husbandry** *n*
*m* 'ɤzbəndˌrəɪ, -dr-, 'hɤ-
**sp** husbandrie[1], husbandry[11]
**rh** posterity *S 3.6*

**hush** *adj / interj*
ɤʃ, hɤʃ
**sp** hush[1] / hush[10]

**hush / ~es / ~ed** *v*
ɤʃ, hɤʃ / 'ɤʃɪz, 'hɤ- / ɤʃt, hɤ-
**sp** hush[1] / hushes[1] / hush'd[1], huisht[1], husht[2]

**hushed** *adj*
ɤʃt, hɤ-
**sp** husht[2]

**husht** *interj*
ɤʃt, hɤ-
**sp** husht[1]

**husk / ~s** *n*
ɤsks, hɤ-
**sp** huskes[5]

**Hybla** *n*
'əɪblə, 'həɪ-
**sp** Hibla[1]

**Hydra / ~'s** *n*
'əɪdrə, 'həɪ- / -z
**sp** Hidra[1], Hydra[1], Hydra-[sonne][1] / Hydra's[1]

**Hydra-headed** *adj*
'əɪdrə-ˌedɪd, 'həɪ-, -ˌhed-
**sp** Hidra-headed[1]
> **head**

**hyena** *n*
əɪ'en, həɪ-
**sp** hyen[1]

**Hymen / ~s** *n*
'əɪmən, həɪ- / -z
**sp** Hymen[7] / Himens[1], Hymens[3]

**Hymeneus / ~'** *n*
ˌəɪmə'nɛːəs, ˌhəɪ-
**sp** Hymeneus[1]

**hymn / ~s** *n*
ɪm, = / -z
**sp** hymne[5] / hymnes[2]

**hyperbole / ~s** *n*
əɪ'pɐːɹbliːz, -bəl-, həɪ-
**sp** hyperboles[2]

**hyperbolical** *adj*
ˌəɪpəɹ'bɒlɪkɑl, ˌhəɪ-
**sp** hyperbolicall[2]

**Hyperion / ~'s** *n*
əɪ'piːrɪən, həɪ- / -z
**sp** Hiperion[2], Hiperio[n][1] / Hyperions[2], *emend of Tit 5.2.56* Eptons[1]

**hypocrisy** *n*
*m* ɪ'pɒkrɪˌsəɪ, hɪ-
**sp** hipocrisie[1], hypocrisie[4]
**rh** integrity *R2 5.3.106*; me *LLL 4.3.149*; simplicity *LLL 5.2.51*

**hypocrite / ~s** *n*
'ɪpəˌkrɪt, 'hɪ- / -s
**sp** hypocrite[7] / hypocrites[1]

**Hyrcan** *n*
'ɐːɹkən, 'hɐː-
**sp** Hircan[1]

**Hyrcania** *n*
ɐːɹ'kɛːnɪə, hɐː-
**sp** Hyrcania[1]

**Hyrcanian** *adj*
ɐːɹ'kɛːnɪən, hɐː-
**sp** Hircanion[1], Hyrcanian[1]

**hyssop** *n*
'ɪsəp, 'hɪ-
**sp** hisope[1]

**hysterica** *Lat adj*
hɪs'terɪkɑː
**sp** historica[1]

# I

**I** [letter] *n*
əɪ
**sp** I[6], [M.O.A.]I.[4]
**pun** *RJ 3.2.45ff* ay, eye, I [*pro*], *TN 2.5.118* ay

**I** *pro*
*str* əɪ, *unstr* ə
**sp** I[19743], i[2], I['haue][1], [nod]-I[1]
**rh** *1* ay *RJ 1.3.59*; by *R3 5.3.184*; cry *R2 5.3.75*; cry, fly, lie *Tem 5.1.88*; deny *TN 5.1.143*; die *AW 1.3.153, 1H6 4.5.50, LLL 4.3.206, MM 4.3.78, RJ 3.5.12, TS 3.1.75, VA 1015*; die, eye *Luc 1136*; eye *LLL 4.3.181*; fly *2H6 2.1.158, MND 3.2.415, TN 3.4.365*; high *R2 4.1.187*; lie *LLL 1.1.172, MND 1.1.214, RJ 1.4.50, S 72.7* [*emend of* eye], *152.13*; rely *AW 2.1.203*; sky *Tem 4.1.71*; untie *TN 2.2.40*; why *Cym 5.4.131*; **rh** *2* company *2H4 2.3.67, MND 3.2.340*; contrary *Per 2. Chorus.16*; cruelty *MND 3.2.58*; loyalty *MND 2.2.68*; majesty *2H6 1.2.69, R3 1.3.31*; Margery *Tem 2.2.45*; melancholy *Cym 4.2.207*; merrily *Tem 5.1.88*; minstrelsy *LLL 1.1.172*; reportingly *MA 3.1.115*
**pun** *RJ 3.2.45ff* ay, eye, I [letter], *TG 1.1.113* noddy
> iwis, me

*I am* *abbr*
*str* əɪm, *unstr* əm
**sp** I'am[1], I'm[8], I'me[7]

*I have* *abbr*
*unstr* əɪv, əv
**sp** I'ue[3]

*I should* *abbr*
*Edgar's assumed dialect KL 4.6.238* ʧʊd
**sp** 'chud[1]

*I will* *abbr*
*str* əɪl, *unstr* əl, *Jamy H5 3.2.111* aɪl
**sp** Ile[1701], I'le[27], I'll[3], *Jamy* ayle[1]

*I would abbr*
*str* əɪd, əɪld, *unstr* əd
**sp** Ide[1], I'de[24], Il'd[11], I'ld[23]

**iac·eo / ~et** *Lat v*
'jaset
**sp** ia-cet[1]

**Iachimo** *n*
*m* 'jakɪmo:, -ˌmo:
**sp** Iachimo[16]

**iacul·um / ~is** *Lat n*
'jakʊli:s
**sp** iaculis[1]

**Iago** *n*
i:'ɑ:go:
**sp** Iago[76]

**ibat** *Lat*
> eo

**Icarus** *n*
*m* 'ɪkəˌrɤs
**sp** Icarus[3]

**ice** *n*
əɪs
**sp** ice[15], yce[3]

**ice-brook / ~'s** *n*
'əɪs-ˌbrʊks
**sp** ice brookes[1]
> brook

**Iceland** *n*
'əɪslənd
**sp** Island[2]

**ici** *Fr adv*
i'si
**sp** icy[1]

**icicle / ~s** *n*
'əɪsɪkəl / -z
**sp** isicle[1], ysickle[1] / isicles[1], isyckles[1], ysicles[1]

**icy** *adj*
'əɪsəɪ
**sp** icie[4], ycie[2]

**idea / ~s** *n*
əɪ'di:ə / -z
**sp** idea[2] / ideas[1]

**idem** *Lat pro*
'ɪdem
**sp** idem[1]

**Iden** *n*
'əɪdən
**sp** Iden[6]

**Ides** *n*
əɪdz
**sp** Ides[6]

**idiot** *adj*
=
**sp** idiot[1]

**idiot / ~s** *n*
=
**sp** ideot[5], idiot[1], idi-ot[1] / ideots[1], idiots[1]

**idiot-worshipper / ~s** *n*
'ɪdɪət-ˌwɔːɹʃɪpəɹz
**sp** ideot-worshippers[1]
> worshipper

**idle** *adj / adv*
'əɪdl
**sp** idle[60], ydle[3] / idle[1]

**idle / ~s** *v*
'əɪdlz
**sp** ydles[1]

**idle-headed** *adj*
'əɪdl-ˌedɪd, -ˌhe-
**sp** idle-headed-[eld][1]

**idleness** *n*
*m* 'əɪdlnəs, -ˌnes
**sp** idlenesse[15]

**idly** *adv*
'əɪdləɪ
**sp** idely[3], idlely[5], idly[8]

**idol** *adj / n*
'əɪdl
**sp** idoll[1] / idoll[6]

**idolatrous** *adj*
əɪ'dɒlətrəs
**sp** idolatrous[1]

**idolatry** *n*
*m* əɪ'dɒləˌtrəɪ
**sp** idolatrie[1], idolatry[4]
**rh** be *S 105.1*; deity *LLL 4.3.73*

**if** *conj*
=
**sp** if[3461], if['t] [if it][11]

**if / ~s** *n*
=
**sp** ifs[1]

**i'faith** *prep phrase*
ɪ'fɛːθ
**sp** ifaith[15], i'faith[5]

**i'fecks** *prep phrase*
ɪ'feks
**sp** i'fecks[1]

**ignis fatuus** *Lat n + adj*
'ɪgnɪs 'fatjuːʊs
**sp** ignis fatuus[1]

**ignoble** *adj*
ɪg'noːbəl
**sp** ignoble[9]
> noble

**ignobly** *adv*
ɪg'noːbləɪ
**sp** ignobly[4]

**ignominious** *adj*
ˌɪgnə'mɪnɪəs
**sp** ignominious[3]

**ignominy** *n*
*m* 'ɪgnəˌmɪnəɪ
**sp** ignominie[1]

**ignomy** *n*
*m* 'ɪgnəˌməɪ
**sp** ignomie[2], ignomy[2]

**ignorance** *n*
*m* 'ɪgnərəns, -ˌrans
**sp** ignorance[37], ig-norance[1]
**rh** advance *S 78.14*; dance *LLL 5.2.398*; France *H8 1.3.26*

**ignorant** *adj*
*m* 'ɪgnərənt, -ˌrant
**sp** ignorant[46], ig-norant[1]

**il** *Fr pro*
il
**sp** il[14]

*son* *det*
sɔ̃
**sp** son[2]

**il** *Ital det*
iːl
**sp** *emend of TS 1.2.24* le[1]

**Ilion** *n*
'ɪlɪən
**sp** Illion[6]
**rh** pavilion *LLL 5.2.650*

**Ilium** *n*
'ɪlɪəm
**sp** Ilium[1], Illium[4]

**ill** *adj / adv*
=
**sp** ill[112], ill-[spirit][1], ill-[tydings][1] / ill[61], ill-[school'd][1]
**rh** *adj 1* fill *S 112.3*; Jill *MND 3.2.462*; kill *LLL 4.1.25*; quill, will *Luc 1300*; skill *Luc 1530, S 66.12, 150.5*; *still Luc 1530, Mac 3.2.55, PP 2.4, S 144.4*; will *CE 2.1.12, KJ 4.1.55, Per 1.1.105, RJ 1.1.203, S 22.12, 89.5*; **rh** *2* well *KJ 3.4.5, MND 3.2.462, RJ 4.5.75*

**ill / ~s** *n*
=
**sp** ill[26] / illes[7]
**rh** kill, spill *Luc 996, Tim 3.5.38*; kill, still *Luc 380*; Longaville *LLL 4.3.122*; mill *WT 4.4.302*; skill *S 91.3*; skill, will *Luc 1244*; spill *LLL 4.1.35*; still *Luc 476, Per 1.1.78, S 147.3*; will *Luc 304, 1207, Per 2.1.134, 167, RJ 4.5.94, S 57.14*

**ill-beseeming** *adj*
'ɪl-bɪ'siːmɪn, -ɪŋ
**sp** ill-beseeming[2], ill beseeming[3]
> beseem

**ill-boding** *adj*
*m* ˌɪl-'boːdɪn, -ɪŋ
**sp** ill-boading[2]
> bode

**ill-breeding** *adj*
*m* ˌɪl-'briːdɪn, -ɪŋ
**sp** ill breeding[1]
> breed

**ill-composed** *adj*
'ɪl-kəm'poːzd
**sp** ill-composd[1]
> compose

**ill-dispersing** *adj*
'ɪl-dɪs'pɐːɹsɪn, -ɪŋ
**sp** ill dispersing[1]
> disperse

**ill-disposed** *adj*
'ɪl-dɪs'poːzd

**sp** ill dispos'd[2]
> disposed

**ill-divining** *adj*
'ɪl-dɪ'vəɪnɪn, -ɪŋ
**sp** ill diuining[1]
> divining

**ill-doing** *n*
*m* ˌɪl-'du:ɪn, -ɪŋ
**sp** ill-doing[1]
> do

**illegitimate** *adj*
ˌɪlə'dʒɪtɪmət
**sp** illegitimate[2]
> legitimate

**ill-erected** *adj*
'ɪl-ə'rektɪd
**sp** ill-erected[1]
> erect

**ill-faced** *adj*
*m* ˌɪl-'fɛ:st
**sp** ill-fac'd[1]
> face

**ill-favoured** *adj*
*m* ˌɪl-'fɛ:vəɹd
**sp** il-fauor'd[1], illfauourd[1], illfauour'd[1], ill-fauourd[1], ill-fauour'd[3], ill-fauoured[1]
> favour

**ill-favouredly** *adv*
*m* ˌɪl-'fɛ:vəɹdˌləɪ
**sp** ill-fauoredly[1], illfauouredly[1], ill-fauouredly[2]

**ill-inhabited** *adj*
'ɪl-ɪn'abɪtɪd, -'ha-
**sp** ill inhabited[1]
> inhabit

**ill-headed** *adj*
'ɪl-'edɪd, 'he-
**sp** ill headed[1]
> head

**illiterate** *adj*
ɪ'lɪtrət, -tər-
**sp** illiterate[1]

**illness** *n*
=
**sp** illnesse[1]

**ill-nurtered** *adj*
*m* ˌɪl-'nɐ:ɹtəɹd
**sp** ill-nurter'd[1]

**illo**
> hillo

**ill-roasted** *adj*
'ɪl-ˌro:stɪd
**sp** ill roasted[1]
> roast

**ill-rooted** *adj*
'ɪl-'ru:tɪd, -'rʊt-
**sp** ill rooted[1]
> root

**ill-seeming** *adj*
*m* ˌɪl-'si:mɪn, -ɪŋ
**sp** ill seeming[1]
> seem

**ill-shaped** *adj*
'ɪl-ˌʃɛ:pt
**sp** ill shap'd[1]
> shape

**ill-sheathed** *adj*
*m* ˌɪl-'ʃi:ðɪd
**sp** ill-sheathed[1]
> sheathe

**ill-spirited** *adj*
*m* ˌɪl-'spɪɹɪtɪd
**sp** ill-spirited[1]
> spirit

**ill-starred** *adj*
'ɪl-ˌstɑ:ɹd
**sp** ill-starr'd[1]
> star

**ill-taken,** *abbr* **-ta'ne** *adj*
*m* ˌɪl-'tɛ:n
**sp** ill-ta'ne[1]
> take

**ill-tempered** *adj*
*m* ˌɪl-'tempəɹd
**sp** ill temper'd[2]
> temper

**ill-thinking** *n*
*m* ˌɪl-'θɪnkɪn, -ɪŋ
**sp** ill-thinking[1]
> think

**ill-tuned** *adj*
*m* ˌɪl-'tju:nɪd
**sp** ill-tuned[1]
> tune

**illume** *v*
ɪl'ju:m
**sp** illume[1]

**illuminate / ~th** *v*
*m* ɪl'ju:mɪˌnɛ:t / -əθ
**sp** illuminate[1] / illuminateth[1]

**illumine / ~d** *v*
ɪl'ju:mɪnd
**sp** illumin'd[1]

**ill-urged** *adj*
*m* ˌɪl-'ɐ:ɹdʒd
**sp** ill vrg'd[1]
> urge

**ill-used** *adj*
*m* ˌɪl-'ju:zd
**sp** ill-vs'd[1]
> use

**illusion / ~s** *n*
ɪ'lu:zɪən / -z
**sp** illusion[3] / illusions[2]
**rh** confusion *Mac 3.5.28*

**illustrate** *adj*
*m* ɪ'lɤstrɛ:t
**sp** illustrate[2]

**illustrate / ~d** *v*
*m* ɪ'lɤstrɛ:ˌtɪd
**sp** illustrated[1]

**illustrious** *adj*
ɪ'lɤstrɪəs
**sp** illustrious[5]

**ill-uttering** *adj*
*m* ˌɪl-ˈɤtrɪn, -ɪŋ, -tər-
**sp** ill vttering[1]
> utter

**ill-weaved** *adj*
*m* ˌɪl-ˈwiːvd
**sp** ill-weau'd[1]
> weave

**Illyria** *n*
ɪˈlɪrɪə
**sp** Illyria[11]

**Illyrian** *adj*
ɪˈlɪrɪən
**sp** Illyrian[1]

**ils** *Fr pro*
il
**sp** il[1], ils[1]

**im-**
> *also* em-

**image / ~s** *n*
=
**sp** image[42] / images[10]

**imagery** *n*
*m* ˈɪmɪʤˌrəɪ
**sp** imagery[1]

**imaginary** *adj*
*m* ɪˈmaʤɪˌnarəɪ, -ɪnˌrəɪ
**sp** imaginarie[4], imaginary[2], immaginarie[1]
**rh** eye *R2 2.2.27*

**imagination / ~s** *n*
ɪˌmaʤɪˈnɛːsɪən / -z
**sp** imagination[23], imagi-nation[1], immagination[1] / imaginations[4]
**rh** *1* abomination, exclamation *Luc 702*; divination *VA 668*; **rh** *2* region *Per 4.4.3*

**imagin·e / ~ing / ~ed** *v*
ɪˈmaʤɪn / -ɪn, -ɪŋ / *m* -d, -ed
**sp** imagine[21], ima-gine[1] / imagining[1] / imagin'd[2], imagined[2]
**rh** bed, head *Luc 1622*; head *Luc 1428*

**imagined** *adj*
ɪˈmaʤɪnd
**sp** imagin'd[5]

**imagining / ~s** *n*
ɪˈmaʤɪnɪnz, -ɪŋz
**sp** imaginings[1]

**imbecility** *n*
*m* ˌɪmbəˈsɪlɪˌtəɪ
**sp** imbecility[1]

**imbrue** *v*
ɪmˈbruː
**sp** em-brew, imbrue
**rh** adieu *MND 5.1.336*

**imitate / ~d** *v*
*m* ˈɪmɪˌtɛːt, -ɪt- / ˈɪmɪtɛːtɪd
**sp** imitate[10] / imitated[1]

**imitation / ~s** *n*
ˌɪmɪˈtɛːsɪən / -z
**sp** imitation[4] / imitations[1]
**rh** nation *R2 2.1.23*

**imit·or / ~ari** *Lat v*
ɪmɪˈtɑːriː
**sp** imitarie[1]

**immaculate** *adj*
*m* ɪˈmakjəˌlɛːt
**sp** immaculate[7]

**immanity** *n*
*m* ɪˈmanɪˌtəɪ
**sp** immanity[1]

**immask** *v*
ɪˈmask
**sp** immaske[1]

**immaterial** *adj*
ˌɪməˈtiːrɪɑl
**sp** immateriall[1]

**immediacy** *n*
*m* ɪˈmiːdɪəˌsəɪ
**sp** immediacie[1]

**immediate** *adj*
ɪˈmiːdɪət
**sp** imediate[1], immediate[14]

**immediately** *adv*
*m* ɪˈmiːdɪətˌləɪ, -tl-
**sp** imediately[1], immediately[18]
**rh** *1* courtesy *1H4 5.5.33*; injury *CE 4.2.63*; property *Ham 3.2.269*; **rh** *2* nigh *MND 2.2.162*

**imminence** *n*
*m* ˈɪmɪˌnens
**sp** imminence[1]

**imminent** *adj*
*m* ˈɪmɪˌnent, -ɪnənt
**sp** iminent[1], imminent[5]

**immoderate** *adj*
ɪˈmɒdrət, -dər-
**sp** immoderate[1]
> moderate

**immoderately** *adv*
*m* ɪˈmɒdrətˌləɪ, -dər-
**sp** immoderately[1]

**immodest** *adj*
ɪˈmɒdəst
**sp** immodest[5]
> modest

**immoment** *adj*
ɪˈmoːmənt
**sp** immoment[1]

**immortal** *adj*
ɪˈmɔːɹtl
**sp** immortall[21], im-mortall[1], immor-tall[1], imortall[1]

**immortalized** *adj*
*m* ɪˈmɔːɹtəˌləɪzd
**sp** immortaliz'd[1]

**immortally** *adv*
*m* ɪˈmɔːɹtəˌləɪ
**sp** immortally[1]

**immure / ~s** *n*
ɪmˈjuːɹz
**sp** emures[1]

**immure /~d** *v*
*m* ɪmˈjuːɹd, -ɹɪd
**sp** emured[2], immur'd[2]

**Imogen / ~'s** *n*
*m* 'ɪmə,ʤen, -əʤən / 'ɪmə,ʤenz
**sp** Imogen[39] / Imogens[1]
**rh** *1* again *Cym 3.5.105, 5.3.83*; **rh** *2* in *Cym 5.4.107*
> Innogen

**imp** *n / v*
=
**sp** impe[4] / impe[1]
**rh** *n* shrimp *LLL 5.2.584*

**impaint** *v*
ɪm'pɛ:nt
**sp** impaint[1]

**impair / ~ing** *v*
ɪm'pɛ:ɹ / -ɪn, -ɪŋ
**sp** impaire[2] / impairing[1]

**impaired** *adj*
'ɪmpɛ:ɹd
**sp** impaired[1]

**impale / ~d** *v*
ɪm'pɛ:l / *m* ɪm'pɛ:lɪd
**sp** empale[1], impale[1] / impaled[1]

**impannel / *S* ~led** *v*
ɪm'panə,lɪd
**sp** impannelled[1]
**rh** determined *S 46.9*

**impart / ~s / *Luc* ~eth / ~ed** *v*
ɪm'pɑ:ɹt / -s / -əθ / -ɪd
**sp** impart[10] / imparts[1] / imparteth[1] / imparted[1]
**rh** *1* heart *R3 4.4.130*; **rh** *2* desert *S 72.8* / starteth *Luc 1039*
> part

**impartial** *adj*
ɪm'pɑ:ɹsɪɑl
**sp** impartiall[3]
> partial

**impartment** *n*
ɪm'pɑ:ɹtmənt
**sp** impartment[1]

**impaste / ~d** *v*
ɪm'pastɪd
**sp** impasted[1]

**impatience** *n*
*m* ɪm'pɛ:sɪəns, -ɪ,ens
**sp** impatience[18]
**rh** commence *1H6 4.7.8*
> patience

**impatient** *adj*
*m* ɪm'pɛ:sɪənt, -ɪ,ent
**sp** impatient[19]

**impatiently** *adv*
*m* ɪm'pɛ:sɪənt,ləɪ
**sp** impatiently[3]

**impawn / ~ed** *v*
=
**sp** impawne[1] / impawnd[1], impawn'd[1]

**impeach** *n*
=
**sp** impeach[2]

**impeach / ~ed** *v*
=
**sp** impeach[8] / impeach'd[1]

**impeachment / ~s** *n*
=
**sp** impeachment[2] / impeachments[1]

**impede / ~s** *v*
=
**sp** impeides[1]

**impediment / ~s** *n*
*m* ɪm'pedɪmənt, -,ment / -s
**sp** impediment[15] / impediments[5]

**impenetrable** *adj*
*m* ɪm'penɪ,trabəl
**sp** impenetrable[1]

**imperator** *n*
,ɪmpə'rɑ:tɔ:ɹ
**sp** emperator[1]

**imperfect** *adj*
ɪm'pɐ:ɹfɪt
**sp** imperfect[4]
> perfect

**imperfection / ~s** *n*
,ɪmpəɹ'feksɪən / -z
**sp** imperfection[1], im-perfection[1] / imperfections[4]

**imperfectly** *adj*
*m* ɪm'pɐ:ɹfɪt,ləɪ
**sp** imperfectly[1]

**imperial** *adj*
*m* ɪm'perɪɑl, -,ɑl
**sp** emperiall[2], imperial[1], imperiall[24], im-periall[1]

**imperial / ~'s** *n*
ɪm'perɪɑlz
**sp** emperialls[1], imperialls[1]

**imperious** *adj*
ɪm'perɪəs
**sp** emperious[2], imperious[10]

**imperiously** *adv*
ɪm'perɪəsləɪ
**sp** imperiously[1]

**imperseverant** *adj*
,ɪmpəɹ'sevrənt, -vər-
**sp** imperseuerant[1]

**impertinency** *n*
*m* ɪm'pɐ:ɹtɪ,nensəɪ
**sp** impertinency[1]

**impertinent** *adj*
ɪm'pɐ:ɹtɪnənt
**sp** impertinent[2]

**impeticos / *emend***
**impetticoat** *v*
ɪm'petɪkɒs / -ko:t
**sp** impeticos[1]

**impetuosity** *n*
ɪm,petju:'ɒsɪtəɪ
**sp** impetuositie[1]

**impiet·y / ~ies** *n*
*m* ɪm'pəɪə,təɪ / -ətəɪz
**sp** impietie[2], impiety[3] / impieties[1]
**rh** angry [*3 sylls*] *Tim 3.5.57*; enemy, infamy *Luc 1174*; society *S 67.2*

**impious** *adj*
=
**sp** impious[6]
> pious

**impitious** *adj*
ɪm'pɪtɪəs
**sp** impittious[1]

**implacable** *adj*
=
**sp** implacable[1]

**implement / ~s** *n*
*m* 'ɪmplɪmənts, -ˌments
**sp** implements[2]

**implorator / ~s** *n*
*m* ɪm'plɒrəˌtɔːɹz
**sp** implorators[1]

**implor·e / ~ing / ~ed** *v*
ɪm'plɔːɹ / -ɪn, -ɪŋ / -d
**sp** implore[6] / imploring[1] / implor'd[2]

**impl·y / ~ies** *v*
ɪm'pləɪz
**sp** implies[1]
**rh** dies *AW 1.3.211*

**impone / ~d** *v*
ɪm'poːnd
**sp** impon'd[2]

**import** *n*
ɪm'pɔːɹt
**sp** import[7], im-port[1]

**import / ~s / ~eth / ~ing / ~ed** *v*
ɪm'pɔːɹt / -s / -əθ / -ɪn, -ɪŋ / -ɪd
**sp** import[10] / imports[6], im-ports[1] / importeth[2] / importing[6] / imported[1]

**importance** *n*
ɪm'pɔːɹtəns
**sp** importance[5]

**importancy** *n*
*m* ɪm'pɔːɹtənˌsəɪ
**sp** importancie[1]

**important** *adj*
ɪm'pɔːɹtənt
**sp** important[6], impor-tant[1]

**importantly** *adv*
*m* ɪm'pɔːɹtəntˌləɪ
**sp** importantly[1]

**importing** *prep*
ɪm'pɔːɹtɪn, -ɪŋ
**sp** importing[1]

**importless** *adj*
ɪm'pɔːɹtləs
**sp** importlesse[1]

**importunacy** *n*
*m* ˌɪmpɒɹ'tjuːnəsəɪ, -ˌsəɪ
**sp** importunacie[1], importunacy[1]

**importunate** *adj*
*m* ɪm'pɔːɹtənət, -ˌnɛːt
**sp** importunat[1], importunate[4], importu-nate[1]

**importune / ~s / ~d** *v*
ɪm'pɔːɹtən / -z / -d
**sp** importune[11], impor-tune[1] / importunes[3], im-portunes[1] / importun'd[7]
**rh** fortune *TG 3.1.145*

**importuned** *adj*
ɪm'pɔːɹtjənd
**sp** importun'd[1]

**importunity** *n*
*m* ˌɪmpɒɹ'tjuːnɪtəɪ, -ˌtəɪ
**sp** importunitie[1], importunity[2]

**impose** *n*
ɪm'poːz
**sp** impose[1]

**impose / ~d** *v*
ɪm'poːz / -d
**sp** impose[9] / impos'd[2], imposed[1], im-posed[1]

**imposition / ~s** *n*
*m* ˌɪmpə'zɪsɪən, -sɪˌɒn / -sɪənz
**sp** imposition[5], im-position[1], impositi-on[1] / impositions[1]
**rh** disposition *Luc 1697*

**impossibility** *n*
*m* ɪmˌpɒsɪ'bɪlɪˌtəɪ, -təɪ / -z
**sp** impossibility[4] / impossibilities[3]

**impossible** *adj*
=
**sp** impossible[39], im-possible[1]

**impossible** *Fr adj*
ɛ̃pɔ'siblə
**sp** impossible[1]

**impostor / ~s** *n*
ɪm'pɒstəɹ / -z
**sp** impostor[1], imposture[1] / impostors[1]

**impotence** *n*
*m* 'ɪmpəˌtens
**sp** impotence[1]
> potency

**impotent** *adj*
*m* 'ɪmpəˌtent, -tənt
**sp** impotent[4]

**impound / ~ed** *v*
ɪm'pəʊndɪd
**sp** impounded[1]

**impregnable** *adj*
=
**sp** impregnable[3]

**impress** *n*
*m* 'ɪmpres, ɪm'pres
**sp** impresse[5]

**impress / ~ed** *v*
ɪm'pres / *m* -t, -ɪd
**sp** impresse[2] / impressed[2], imprest[2]
**rh** expressed *LLL 2.1.222*

**impressed** *adj*
ɪm'prest
**sp** imprest[1]

**impression** *n*
ɪm'presɪən
**sp** impression[9]
**rh** commission *VA 566*

**impressure** *n*
ɪm'presəɹ
**sp** impressure[2], im-pressure[1]
> pressure

**imprimis** *Lat adv*
ɪm'pri:mɪs
**sp** inprimis[5]

**imprim·o / ~endum** *Lat v*
ˌɪmprɪ'mendʊm
**sp** impremendum[1]

**imprint / ~ed** *v*
ɪm'prɪntɪd
**sp** imprinted[1]
**rh** contented *VA 511*

**imprison / ~ed** *v*
=
**sp** imprison[3], imprison't [imprison it][1] / imprison'd[9], imprisoned[1]

**imprisoned** *adj*
*m* =, ˌɪmprɪ'zɒnɪd
**sp** imprisoned[2]
> long-imprisoned

**imprisoning** *n*
*m* ɪm'prɪzəˌnɪn, -ɪŋ
**sp** imprisoning[1]

**imprisonment** *n*
*m* ɪm'prɪzənˌment, -mənt
**sp** imprisonment[15], imprison-ment[1]

**improbable** *adj*
=
**sp** improbable[1]

**improve** *v*
ɪm'prɤv, -ru:v
**sp** improue[1]
> prove, unimproved

**improvident** *adj*
ɪm'prɒvdənt, -vɪd-
**sp** improuident[2]

**impudence** *n*
*m* 'ɪmpjʊˌdens
**sp** impudence[3]
**rh** confidence *AW 2.1.170*; offence *Per 2.3.69*

**impudency** *n*
*m* 'ɪmpjʊˌdensəɪ
**sp** im-pudency[1]

**impudent** *adj*
*m* 'ɪmpjʊdənt, -ˌdent
**sp** impudent[8]

**impudently** *adv*
*m* 'ɪmpjʊˌdentləɪ
**sp** impudently[1]

**impudique** *Fr adj*
ɛ̃py'dik
**sp** impudique[1]

**impugn / ~s** *v*
=
**sp** impugne[1] / impugnes[1]

**impure** *adj*
*m* 'ɪmpju:ɹ
**sp** impure[1]
> pure

**imputation** *n*
ˌɪmpjʊ'tɛ:sɪən
**sp** imputation[5], im-putation[1]

**impute** *v*
=
**sp** impute[3]
**rh** mute *S 83.9*

**in,** ***abbr*** **i** *adv, prep*
=, *abbr* ɪ
**sp** in[10522], [shouels]-in, [take]-in[1], [*without following space, eg* infaith][32], y[faith][27], y'[faith][2]
**rh** begin *LLL 3.1.105* [*F line ending*]; chin *VA 87*; fin *CE 3.1.78*; Ginn *CE 3.1.30*; Innogen *Cym 5.4.105*; pin *LLL 4.1.136*; shin *LLL 3.1.105*; sin *LLL 4.3.176, MM 4.2.106, R2 5.3.80, R3 4.2.62*; skin *MND 2.1.256*; thin *CE 3.1.69*; women *H8 Epil.9*

***in his abbr***
ɪns
**sp** in's[36]

***in it abbr***
ɪnt
**sp** in't[87]

***in the abbr***
ɪθ
**sp** ith[3], i'th [85], ith'[19], i'th'[184], i'the[3], y'th[1]

***in thy abbr***
ɪðɪ
**sp** i'thy[1]

**in** *v*
=
**sp** inne[1]

**in** *Lat prep*
ɪn
**sp** in[3]

**inaccessible** *adj*
=
**sp** inaccessible[2]

**inaidible** *adj*
ɪn'ɛ:dɪbəl
**sp** inaydible[1]
> aid

**inaudible** *adj*
=
**sp** inaudible[1]
> audible

**inauspicious** *adj*
ˌɪnɒ'spɪsɪəs
**sp** inauspicious[1]
> auspicious, unauspicious

**incaged** *adj*
*m* ɪn'kɛ:ʤɪd
**sp** incaged[2]
> cage

**incantation / ~s** *n*
ˌɪŋkən'tɛ:sɪənz
**sp** incantations[1]

**incapable** *adj*
*m* ɪn'kɛ:pəbəl, -əˌbɤl
**sp** incapable[2], incapeable[3]
> capable

**incardinate** *adj*
ɪn'kɑːɹdɪnət
**sp** incardinate[1]

**incarnardine** *v*
*m* ɪn'kɑːɹnəɹˌdəɪn
**sp** incarnardine[1]

**incarnate** *adj*
ɪn'kɑːɹnət
**sp** incarnate[1], incar-nate[1]

**incarnation** *n*
ˌɪnkəɹ'nɛːsɪən
**sp** incarnation[1]

**incense** *n*
'ɪnsens
**sp** incense[4]
> wrong-incensed

**incense / ~s / ~ed** *v*
ɪn'sens / -ɪz / *m* -ɪd, -t
**sp** incense[6] / incenses[1] / incensed[2], incenst[4]

**incensed** *adj*
*m* ɪn'sensɪd
**sp** incensed[6]

**incensement** *n*
ɪn'sensmənt
**sp** incense-ment[1]

**incensing** *adj*
ɪn'sensɪn, -ɪŋ
**sp** incensing[1]

**incertain** *adj*
ɪn'sɐːɹtən
**sp** incertaine[6]
> certain, uncertain

**incertaint·y** *S* **/ ~ies** *n*
ɪn'sɐːɹtənˌtəɪ / -z
**sp** in-certainty[1] / incertainties[1]
**rh** tyranny *S 115.11*
> certainty, uncertainty

**incessant** *adj*
=
**sp** incessant[5]

**incessantly** *adv*
*m* ɪn'sesəntˌləɪ
**sp** incessantly[1]

**incest** *n*
'ɪnsest
**sp** incest[2]

**incestuous** *adj*
ɪn'sestjəs
**sp** incestuous[5]

**inch / ~es** *n*
=
**sp** inch[10], ynch[7] / inches[11]
> four-inched, three-inch

**incharitable** *adj*
ɪn'ʧarɪtəbəl
**sp** incharitable[1]
> charitable

**inch-meal** *n*
=
**sp** ynch-meale[1]
> meal

**inch-thick** *adj*
=
**sp** ynch-thick[1]

**incidency** *n*
'ɪnsɪˌdensəɪ
**sp** incidencie[1]

**incident** *adj*
*m* 'ɪnsɪdənt, -ˌdent
**sp** incident[3]

**incision** *n*
*m* ɪn'sɪzɪən, -zɪˌɒn
**sp** incision[6]
**rh** *1* misprision *LLL 4.3.95*; **rh** *2* physician *R2 1.1.155*

**incite / ~s** *v*
ɪn'səɪt / -s
**sp** incite[5] / incites[1]
**rh** right *KL 4.4.27*; incite thee requite thee *MA 3.1.113*

**incivil** *adj*
=
**sp** inciuill[1]

**incivility** *n*
*m* ˌɪnsɪ'vɪlɪˌtəɪ
**sp** inciuility[1]

**inclinable** *adj*
ɪn'kləɪnəbəl
**sp** inclinable[1], inclineable[1]

**inclination** *n*
*m* ˌɪnklɪ'nɛːsɪən, -sɪˌɒn
**sp** inclination[11]
**rh** abomination, subornation *Luc 922*

**inclin·e / ~est / ~s / ~ing / ~ed** *v*
ɪn'kləɪn / -st / -z / -ɪn, -ɪŋ / -d
**sp** incline[9] / inclin'st[1] / inclines[1] / enclining[1], inclining[2] / enclin'd[6], inclin'd[8], inclinde[2]
**rh** Collatine, divine *Luc 292* / find, mind *Luc 1657*

**inclining** *adj / n*
ɪn'kləɪnɪn, -ɪŋ
**sp** inclyning[1] / inclining[3]

**inclose**
> enclose

**include / ~s / ~d** *v*
=
**sp** include[1] / includes[2] / included[1]

**inclusive** *adj*
=
**sp** inclusiue[2]

**incomparable** *adj*
*m* ɪn'kɒmpəˌrabəl, -prəbəl
**sp** incomparable[3], incompareable[1]

**incompass**
> encompass

**incomprehensible** *adj*
ɪnˌkɒmprɪ'ensɪbəl, -'he-
**sp** incomprehensible[1]
> comprehend

**inconsiderate** *adj*
ˌɪnkən'sɪdrət, -dər-
**sp** inconsiderate[2]
> considerate

**inconstancy** *n*
*m* ɪn'kɒnstən,səɪ
**sp** inconstancie[2], inconstancy[2], in-constancy[1]
**rh** company *LLL 4.3.178*; majesty *KJ 3.1.322*
> constancy

**inconstant** *adj*
ɪn'kɒnstənt
**sp** inconstant[9]
> unconstant

**incontinency** *n*
*m* ɪn'kɒntɪ,nensəɪ
**sp** incontinencie[3]
> continence

**incontinent** *adj*
*m* ɪn'kɒntɪ,nent, -ɪnənt
**sp** incontinent[5], inconti-nent[1]
**rh** lament *R2 5.6.48*

**incontinently** *adv*
*m* ɪn'kɒntɪ,nentləɪ
**sp** incontinently[1]

**inconvenience / ~s** *n*
*m* ,ɪnkən'vi:nɪ,ens / ,ɪnkən'vi:nɪən,sɪz
**sp** inconuenience[1] / inconueniences[1]
> convenience

**inconvenient** *adj*
,ɪnkən'vi:nɪənt
**sp** inconuenient[1]

**incony** *adj*
ɪn'ko:nəɪ, -'kɤ-
**sp** inconie[1], in-conie[1]

**incorporate** *adj / n / v*
*m* ɪn'kɔ:ɹprət, -ə,rɛ:t /
*m* ɪn'kɔ:ɹpə,rɛ:t /
*m* ɪn'kɔ:ɹprət, -ə,rɛ:t
**sp** incorparate[1], incorporate[5] / incorporate[1] / incorporate[2]

**incorrect** *adj*
=
**sp** incorrect[1]
> correct

**incounter**
> encounter

**increase** *n*
ɪn'kri:s, -'kres
**sp** encrease[7], in-crease[1]
**rh** cease *S 11.5*; decease *S 1.1, 97.6*; peace *R3 5.5.38*

**increas·e / ~eth / ~ing / ~ed** *v*
ɪn'kri:s, -'kres / -əθ / -ɪn, -ɪŋ / -t
**sp** encrease[9] / encreaseth[2] / encreasing[1], encrea-sing[1], increasing[1] / increast[1]
**rh** decease *S 15.5* / releasing *VA 254*

**increasing** *adj / n*
ɪn'kri:sɪn, -ɪŋ, -'kres-
**sp** encreasing[1], incresing[1] / encreasing[1]
**rh** *n* blessing *Tem 4.1.107*

**incredible** *adj*
ɪn'kredɪbəl
**sp** incredible[1]

**incredulous** *adj*
ɪn'kredləs, -djəl-
**sp** incredulous[2]

**incroaching**
> encroaching

**incur / ~red** *v*
ɪn'kɐ:ɹ / -d
**sp** encurre[2], incurre[4] / incur'd[2], incurr'd[1], incurred[1]
**rh** stir *Luc 1473*

**incurable** *adj*
=
**sp** incureable[3]

**incursion / ~s** *n*
ɪn'kɐ:ɹsɪənz
**sp** incursions[1]

**Inde** *n*
əɪnd
**sp** Inde[3]
**rh** blind *LLL 4.3.220*; Rosalind *AY 3.2.84*

**indeavour**
> endeavour

**indebted** *adj*
=
**sp** indebted[2]

**indeed** *adv*
=
**sp** indeed[287], in-deed[3], in deed[1], indeede[141], in-deede[6], indeede-[la][2]
**rh** bleed *VA 667*; heed *LLL 1.1.80*; need *PP 20.49*; read *S 62.9*; speed *Tim 3.2.62*
**pun** *AC 1.5.15* in deed

**indent** *n*
ɪn'dent
**sp** indent[1]

**indent / ~ed** *v*
=
**sp** indent[1] / indented[1]

**indenture / ~s** *n*
ɪn'dentəɹ / -z
**sp** indenture[2] / indentures[4]

**in despite of**
> despite of, in

**index / ~es** *n*
=
**sp** index[4] / indexes[1]

**India** *n*
*m* =, 'ɪndɪ,a
**sp** India[7]

**Indian** *adj / n*
=
**sp** Indian[5] / Indian[2]

**Indian-like** *adj*
'ɪndɪən-,ləɪk
**sp** Indian like[1]

**indictment** *n*
ɪn'dəɪtmənt
**sp** indictment[4]

**Indies** *n*
'ɪndəɪz
**sp** Indies[5]

**indifferency** *n*
*m* ɪn'dɪfrənsəɪ, -ˌsəɪ
**sp** indiffe-rencie[1], indifferency[1]
> differ

**indifferent** *adj*
*m* ɪn'dɪfrənt, -fəˌrent
**sp** indifferent[14], indiffe-rent[1]

**indifferently** *adv*
*m* ɪn'dɪfrəntləɪ, -ˌləɪ
**sp** indifferently[5]

**indigent** *adj*
=
**sp** indigent[1]

**indigest** *n*
*m* 'ɪndɪˌʤest
**sp** indigest[1]
**rh** best *S 114.5*

**indigested** *adj*
*m* 'ɪndɪˌʤestɪd
**sp** indigested[2]

**indign** *adj*
ɪn'dəɪn
**sp** indigne[1]

**indignation / ~s** *n*
*m* ˌɪndɪg'nɛ:sɪən, -sɪˌɒn / ˌɪndɪg'nɛ:sɪənz
**sp** indignation[11] / indignations[1]

**indigne** *Fr adj*
ɛ̃'diɲ
**sp** indignie[1]

**indignit·y / ~ies** *n*
*m* ɪn'dɪgnɪˌtəɪ, -ɪtəɪ / -ɪˌtəɪz
**sp** indignitie[3], indignity[3] / indignities[4]
**rh** be *LLL 5.2.289*; me *Tit 1.1.8*

**indirect** *adj*
=
**sp** indirect[8]
> direct

**indirection / ~s** *n*
ˌɪndɪ'reksɪən / -z
**sp** indirection[2] / indirections[1]

**indirectly** *adv*
ˌɪndɪ'rekləɪ, -ktləɪ
**sp** indirectlie[1], indirectly[6]

**indiscreet** *adj*
=
**sp** indiscreet[2]
> discretion

**indiscretion** *n*
ˌɪndɪ'skresɪən
**sp** indiscretion[2]

**indisposed** *adj*
ˌɪndɪ'spo:zd
**sp** indispos'd[1]

**indisposition** *n*
ɪnˌdɪspə'zɪsɪən
**sp** indisposition[1]
> disposition

**indissoluble** *adj*
*m* ɪn'dɪsələbəl
**sp** indissoluble[1]

**indistinct** *adj*
=
**sp** indistinct[2]

**indistinguishable** *adj*
=
**sp** indi-stinguishable[1]
> distinguish

**indistinguished** *adj*
=
**sp** indistinguish'd[1]

**indite / ~d** *v*
ɪn'dəɪt / -ɪd
**sp** indite[1] / indited[3]

**individible** *adj*
ˌɪndɪ'vəɪdbəl, -dəb-
**sp** indiuidible[1]
> divide

**indrenched** *adj*
=
**sp** indrench'd[1]
> drench

**indubitate** *adj*
ɪn'dju:bɪtət
**sp** indubitate[1]

**induce / ~d** *v*
=
**sp** induce[4] / induc'd[3], induced[2]

**inducement** *n*
=
**sp** inducement[3]

**induction / ~s** *n*
ɪn'dɤksɪən / -z
**sp** induction[2] / inductions[1]

**indue**
> endue

**indulgence / ~s** *n*
ɪn'dɤlʤəns / -ɪz
**sp** indulgence[2] / indulgences[1]

**indulgent** *adj*
ɪn'dɤlʤənt
**sp** indulgent[1]

**indurance**
> endurance

**industrious** *adj*
ɪn'dɤstrɪəs
**sp** industrious[4]

**industriously** *adv*
*m* ɪn'dɤstrɪəsˌləɪ
**sp** industriously[1]

**industry** *n*
*m* 'ɪndɤstrəɪ, -ˌtrəɪ
**sp** industrie[2], industry[5], indu-stry[1]

**inequality** *n*
*m* ˌɪnɪ'kwɑlɪˌtəɪ
**sp** inequality[1]
> equal

**inestimable** *adj*
*m* ɪn'estɪˌmabəl
**sp** inestimable[2]
> estimable

**inevitable** *adj*
*m* ɪn'evɪˌtabəl, -ɪt-
**sp** ineuitable[4]

**inexecrable** *adj*
*m* ɪn'eksɪˌkrabəl
**sp** inexecrable[1]

**inexorable** *adj*
*m* ɪn'eksəˌrabəl
**sp** inexorable[2]

**inexplicable** *adj*
=
**sp** inexplicable[1]
> explication

**infallible** *adj*
=
**sp** infallible[5]
> fallible, unfallible

**infallibly** *adv*
ɪn'falɪbləɪ
**sp** infallibly[1]

**infamonize** *v*
ɪn'famənəɪz
**sp** infamonize[1]

**infamous** *adj*
=
**sp** infamous[2]

**infamy** *n*
*m* 'ɪnfəˌməɪ, -əm-
**sp** infamie[8], infamy[4], in-famy[1]
**rh** *1* be *Luc 1638*; enemy, impiety *Luc 1173*; enmity *Luc 504*; livery *Luc 1055*; me *Luc 794*; mortality *1H6 4.5.33*; nativity *Luc 539*; opportunity *Luc 1025*; **rh** *2* die *Luc 1055* / eyes *Luc 636*

**infancy** *n*
'ɪnfənˌsəɪ
**sp** infancie[11], infancy[1]
**rh** *1* fantasy *MW 5.5.52*; me *R3 4.4.169*; thee *[F] at Tit 5.3.163*; **rh** *2* eye *LLL 4.3.243*

**infant** *adj*
=
**sp** infant[7]

**infant / ~'s / ~s** *n*
=
**sp** infant[10], infant-[fortune][1] / infants[1] / infants[11]

**infant-like** *adj*
'ɪnfənt-ˌləɪk
**sp** infant-like[1]

**infect / ~s / ~ing / ~ed** *v*
= / = / ɪn'fektɪn, -ɪŋ / =
**sp** infect[20], infect [infected][1], in-fect[1] / infects[4] / infecting[1] / infected[15]
**rh** affected *LLL 2.1.216*; collected *Ham 3.2.267*

**infected** *adj / n*
=
**sp** infected[3] / infected[1]

**infection / ~s** *n*
*m* ɪn'feksɪən, -ɪˌɒn / ɪn'feksɪənz
**sp** infection[17], infectio[n][1] / infections[1]
**rh** correction *S 111.10*

**infectious** *adj*
ɪn'feksɪəs
**sp** infectious[7]

**infectiously** *adv*
*m* ɪn'feksɪəsˌləɪ
**sp** infectiously[1]

**infer / ~reth / ~ring / ~red** *v*
ɪn'fɐːɹ / -əθ / -ɪn, -ɪŋ / -d
**sp** inferre[6] / inferreth[1] / inferring[1] / inferr'd[3]

**inference** *n*
*m* 'ɪnfəˌrens
**sp** inference[1]

**inferior** *adj*
ɪn'ferɪəɹ
**sp** inferior[4], inferiour[5]

**inferior / ~s** *n*
ɪn'ferɪəɹz
**sp** inferiors[1]

**infernal** *adj*
ɪn'fɐːɹnəl
**sp** infernall[3]

**infest** *v*
=
**sp** infest[1]

**infidel / ~s** *n*
*m* 'ɪnfɪdəl, -ɪˌdel / 'ɪnfɪˌdelz
**sp** infidell[3] / infidels[2]

**infinite** *adj / n*
*m* 'ɪnfɪnɪt, -ˌnɪt
**sp** infinit[2], infinite[32], infinite[1], in-finite[1], infi-nite[1], *emend of AC 5.3.216* insuite / infinite[3]

**infinitely** *adv*
*m* 'ɪnfɪˌnɪtləɪ
**sp** infinitely[4], in-finitely[1]

**infinitive** *n*
=
**sp** infinitiue[1]

**infirm** *adj*
ɪn'fɐːɹm
**sp** infirme[4]

**infirmit·y / ~ies** *n*
*m* ɪn'fɐːɹmɪˌtəɪ, -ɪt- / ɪn'fɐːɹmɪˌtəɪz
**sp** infirmity[9], infirmitie[7] / infirmities[4]
**rh** be *Luc 150*; chastity, posterity *PT 60* / **rh** *1* destinies *VA 735* / **rh** *2* eyes *Per Prol.3*

**infixed** *adj*
*m* ɪn'fɪksɪd
**sp** infixed[1]

**inflame / ~ed** *v*
ɪn'flɛːm / -d
**sp** inflame[1] / inflam'd[1]
**rh** fame, shame *LC 268*

**inflaming** *adj*
ɪn'flɛːmɪn, -ɪŋ
**sp** inflaming[2]

**inflammation** *n*
ˌɪnflə'mɛːsɪən
**sp** inflamation[1]

**inflict** *v*
=
**sp** inflict[1]
**rh** contradict *Luc 1630*

**infliction** *n*
ɪn'flɪksɪən
**sp** infliction[1]

**influence / ~s** *n*
*m* =, 'ɪnflʊˌens / -ɪz
**sp** influence[7] / influences[1], [skyie]-influences[1]

**infold, inforce**
> enfold, enforce

**inform / ~s / ~ed** *v*
ɪn'fɔːɹm / -z / -d
**sp** enforme[1], informe[21] / informes[1] / enformed[1], inform'd[17], informed[2]

**informal** *adj*
ɪn'fɔːɹmɑl
**sp** informall[1]
> form

**information / ~s** *n*
ˌɪnfəɹ'mɛːsɪən / -z
**sp** information[2] / informations[1]

**infortunate** *adj*
*m* ɪn'fɔːɹtəˌnɛːt
**sp** infortunate[3]
> fortune, unfortunate

**infranchise**
> enfranchise

**infringe / ~d** *v*
= / *m* ɪn'frɪnʤd, -ˌʤɪd
**sp** infringe[5] / infring'd[1], infringed[1]

**infus·e / ~ing / ~ed** *v*
= / ɪn'fjuːz·ɪn, -ɪŋ / *m* -d, -ɪd
**sp** infuse[3] / infusing[1] / infus'd[3], infused[2]

**infusion** *n*
ɪn'fjuːzɪən
**sp** infusion[1]

**ingaged**
> engage

**ingender**
> engender

**ingener** *n*
ɪn'ʤenəɹ
**sp** ingeniuer[1]

**ingenious** *adj*
ɪn'ʤenɪəs
**sp** ingenious[7]

**ingeniously** *adv*
*m* ɪn'ʤenɪəsˌləɪ
**sp** ingeniously[1]

**ingenuous** *adj*
=
**sp** ingenuous[3]

**inglorious** *adj*
=
**sp** inglorious[1]
> glory

**ingot / ~s** *n*
=
**sp** ingots[1]

**ingraffed / ingraft** *adj*
ɪn'graft
**sp** ingraffed[1] / ingraft[1]

**ingrafted** *adj*
ɪn'graftɪd
**sp** ingrafted[1]

**ingrate** *adj*
ɪn'grɛːt
**sp** ingrate[5]

**ingrateful** *adj*
ɪn'grɛːtfʊl
ingratefull[13]
> ungrateful

**ingratitude / ~s** *n*
ɪn'gratɪˌtjuːd / -z
**sp** ingratitude[21] / ingratitudes[1]
**rh** rude *AY 2.7.177*

**ingrave**
> engrave

**ingredience** *n*
ɪn'gredɪəns
**sp** ingredience[2]

**ingredient** *n*
ɪn'gredɪənt
**sp** ingredient[1], ingre-dient[1]

**ingross**
> engross

**inhabit / ~s / ~ed** *v*
ɪn'abɪt, -'ha- / -s / -ɪd
**sp** inhabit[4], inhabite[5] / inhabites[1], inhabits[3] / inhabited[1]
> ill-inhabited

**inhabitable** *adj*
*m* ɪn'abɪˌtabəl, -'ha-
**sp** inhabitable[1]
> uninhabitable

**inhabitant / ~s** *n*
*m* ɪn'abɪˌtants, -'ha-
**sp** inhabitants[2]

**inhearse** *S* **/ ~d** *v*
ɪn'ɐːɹs, -'hɐː- / *m* ɪn'ɐːɹsɪd, -'hɐː-
**sp** inhearce[1] / inherced[1]
**rh** verse *S 86.3*

**inherent** *adj*
ɪn'erənt, -'he-
**sp** inherent[1]

**inherit / ~s / ~ed** *v*
ɪn'erɪt, -'he- / -s / -ɪd
**sp** inherit[10], inhe-rit[1], inherite[3] / inherits[2] / inherited[3]
**rh** merit *LLL 4.1.20*
> disinherit, trunk-inheriting

**inheritance** *n*
*m* ɪn'erɪˌtans, -təns, -'he-
**sp** inheritance[12]

**inheritor / ~s** *n*
*m* ɪn'erɪˌtɔːɹ, -ɪtəɹ, -'he- / -ɪˌtɔːɹz, -'he-
**sp** inheritor[3], inheritour[1] / inheritors[1]

**inheritrix** *n*
*m* ɪn'erɪˌtrɪks, -'he-
**sp** inheritrix[1]

**inhibited** *adj*
ɪn'ɪbɪtɪd, -'hɪ-
**sp** inhibited[2]

**inhibition** *n*
ˌɪnɪ'bɪsɪən, ˌɪnhɪ-
**sp** inhibition[1]

**inhooped** *adj*
ɪn'uːpt, -'huː-
**sp** in hoopt[1]

**inhuman** *adj*
ɪn'juːmən, -'hj-
**sp** inhumaine[2], inhumane[6]
> human

**iniquit·y / ~y's / ~ies** *n*
*m* ɪ'nɪkwɪˌtəɪ, -ɪt- / -ɪtəɪz
**sp** iniquitie[5], ini-quitie[1] / ini-quities[1] / iniquities[1]
**rh** *1* antiquity *S 62.12*; thee *Luc 626*; **rh** *2* die *Luc 1687*

**initiate** *adj*
ɪ'nɪsɪət
**sp** initiate[1]

**injoin**
> enjoin

**injointed** *adj*
ɪn'ʤəɪntɪd
**sp** inioynted[1]

**injoy**
> enjoy

**injunction / ~s** *n*
ɪn'ʤɤŋksɪən / -z
**sp** iniunction[3] / iniunctions[2]

**injure / ~d** *v*
'ɪnʤəɹ / -d
**sp** iniure[1] / iniur'd[4]

**injurer** *n*
'ɪnʤərəɹ
**sp** iniurer[1]

**injurious** *adj*
ɪn'ʤuːrɪəs
**sp** iniurious[12], iniurous[1]

**injur·y / ~ies** *n*
*m* 'ɪnʤəˌrəɪ, -ər- / -z
**sp** iniurie[17], iniury[9] / iniuries[21]
**rh** courtesy *MND 3.2.148*; immediately *CE 4.2.65*; liberty *S 58.8*; memory *Cor 5.6.154*; poverty *S 40.12* / **rh** *1* enemies *S 139.12*; miseries *Cym 5.4.84*; **rh** *2* exercise *Cym 5.4.84*

**injustice** *n*
ɪn'ʤɤstɪs
**sp** iniustice[9]
> justice

**ink** *n*
=
**sp** incke[1], ink[1], inke[24]
**rh** think *CE 3.1.13*

**ink-horn** *adj / n*
'ɪŋk-ˌɔːɹn, -ˌhɔː-
**sp** inke-horne[1] / inke-horne[1], inkehorne[1]
> horn

**inkindled**
> enkindled

**inkle / ~s** *n*
=
**sp** yncle[1] / inckles[1]

**inkling** *n*
=
**sp** inckling[1], inkling[1]

**inky** *adj*
'ɪŋkəɪ
**sp** inkie[1], inky[2]

**inland** *adj*
=
**sp** inland[2], in-land[3]

**inlarge**
> enlarge

**inlay / ~ed** *v*
'ɪnlɛː / -d
**sp** in-lay[1] / inlayed[1]

**inly** *adj / adv*
'ɪnləɪ
**sp** inly[2] / inly[2]

**inmost** *adj*
'ɪnmoːst
**sp** inmost[2]

**inn** *n*
=
**sp** inne[7]
> Clement's Inn, Inns of Court

**innkeeper** *n*
'ɪn-ˌkiːpəɹ
**sp** inne-keeper[1]
> keep

**innocence** *n*
*m* 'ɪnəˌsens, -səns
**sp** innocence[21]
**rh** conference *MND 2.2.51*; offence *Per 1.2.93*

**innocency** *n*
*m* 'ɪnəˌsensəɪ, -sənsəɪ
**sp** innocencie[3], innocency[3]

**innocent** *adj*
*m* 'ɪnəˌsent, -sənt
**sp** innocent[41]

**innocent / ~s** *n*
*m* 'ɪnəˌsent, -sənt / 'ɪnəˌsents
**sp** innocent[9] / innocents[4]

**Innocent** [name] *n*
'ɪnəˌsent
**sp** innocent[2]

**innoculate** *v*
ɪ'nɒkjəˌlɛːt
**sp** innocculate[1]

**Innogen** *n*
ˈɪnəʤən
**sp** Innogen[1]
> Imogen

**innovation** *n*
*m* ˌɪnəˈvɛːsɪən, -sɪˌɒn
**sp** innouation[2], inouation[1]

**innovator** *n*
ˈɪnəˌvɛːtəɹ
**sp** innouator[1]

**Inns of Court** *n phrase*
ˈɪnz ə ˈkɔːɹt
**sp** Innes of Court[3]
> court, inn

**innumerable** *adj*
*m* ɪˈnjuːməˌrabəl
**sp** inumerable[1]

**inordinate** *adj*
*m* ɪnˈɔːɹdɪnət, -ɪˌnet
**sp** inordinate[2]
**rh** estate *Luc 94*
> ordinate

**inquire, inquiry**
> enquire, enquiry

**inquisition** *n*
ˌɪnkwɪˈzɪsɪən
**sp** inquisition[2]

**inquisitive** *adj*
*m* ˌɪnˈkwɪzɪˌtɪv
**sp** inquisitiue[2]

**inraged**
> enrage

**inrich**
> enrich

**inroads** *n*
*m* ɪnˈroːdz
**sp** inrodes[1]

**inrolled**
> enrol

**insane** *adj*
*m* ˈɪnsɛːn
**sp** insane[1]

**insatiate** *adj*
*m* ɪnˈsɛːsɪət, -ɪˌet
**sp** insatiate[3]

**insconce**
> ensconce

**inscri·be / ~d** *v*
ɪnˈskrəɪbd
**sp** inscrib'd[1]

**inscription / ~s** *n*
ɪnˈskrɪpsɪən / -z
**sp** inscription[1] / inscriptions[1]

**inscrol / ~led** *v*
ɪnˈskroːld
**sp** inscrold[1]
**rh** behold, bold, cold, enfold, gold, old, sold, told *MV 2.7.72*

**inscrutible** *adj*
=
**sp** inscrutible[1]

**insculp / ~ed** *v*
ɪnˈskɤlpt
**sp** insculpt[1]

**insculpture** *n*
ɪnˈskɤlptəɹ
**sp** insculpture[1]

**insensible** *adj*
=
**sp** insensible[3]
> sensible

**inseparable** *adj*
*m* ɪnˈsepəˌrabəl
**sp** inseparable[1], inseperable[1]
> separate

**inseparate** *adj*
ɪnˈseprət, -pər-
**sp** inseperate[1]

**insert / ~ed** *v*
ɪnˈsɐːɹt / -ɪd
**sp** insert[2] / inserted[1]

**inshell / ~ed** *v*
=
**sp** in-shell'd[1]
> shell

**inshrine**
> enshrine

**inside** *adj / n*
ˈɪnsəɪd
**sp** in-side[1] / in-side[4], inside[1]
> side

**insinewed** *adj*
ɪnˈsɪnjuːd
**sp** insinewed[1]
> sinew

**insinuate / ~th** *v*
*m* ɪnˈsɪnjʊˌɛːt, -ʊɛːt / ɪnˈsɪnjʊɛːtəθ
**sp** insinuate[5] / insinuateth[1]
**rh** extenuate *VA 1012*

**insinuating** *adj*
*m* ɪnˈsɪnjʊˌɛːtɪn, -ɪŋ, -ʊɛː-
**sp** insinuating[4]

**insinuation** *n*
ɪnˌsɪnjʊˈɛːsɪən
**sp** insinuation[2], insi-nuation[1]

**insist / ~ing / ~ed** *v*
ɪnˈsɪstɪn, -ɪŋ / =
**sp** insisting[1] / insisted[1]

**insisture** *n*
ɪnˈsɪstəɹ
**sp** insisture[1]

**insociable** *adj*
*m* ɪnˈsoːsɪəbəl, -ɪˌabəl
**sp** insociable[2]
> sociable

**insolence** *n*
*m* ˈɪnsəˌlens, -ləns
**sp** insolence[13], in-solence[1]

**insolent** *adj*
*m* ˈɪnsəˌlent, -lənt
**sp** insolent[9]

**insomuch** *adv*
ˌɪnsə'mɤʧ
**sp** insomuch[1]

**inspiration / ~s** *n*
*m* ˌɪnspɪ'rɛːsɪən, -sɪˌɒn / ˌɪnspɪ'rɛːsɪənz
**sp** inspiration[3] / inspirations[1]
> new-inspired

**inspire / ~d** *v*
ɪn'spəɪɹ / *m* ɪn'spəɪɹɪd, -ɹd
**sp** inspire[2] / inspir'd[4], inspired[2]

**inspired** *adj*
*m* ɪn'spəɪɹɪd, -ɹd
**sp** inspir'd[1], inspired[1]

**instal / ~led** *v*
ɪn'stɑːl, -tɔːl / *m* ɪn'stɑːlɪd, -ld, -tɔːl-
**sp** install'd[3], installed[1], instaul'd[1]

**instalment** *n*
ɪn'stɑːlmənt, -tɔːl-
**sp** installment[1], instalment[1]

**instance / ~s** *n*
=
**sp** instance[25] / instances[7]

**instant** *adj / n*
=
**sp** instant[17] / instant[43]

**instantly** *adv*
*m* 'ɪnstəntˌləɪ, -ləɪ
**sp** instantly[24]

**instead** *adv*
=
**sp** instead[3], in stead[9], insted[1], insteed[1], in steed[1], insteede[1]
> stead

**insteeped** *adj*
=
**sp** insteeped[1]

**instigate / ~d** *v*
'ɪnstɪˌgɛːt / -ɪd
**sp** instigate[1] / instigated[1]
**rh** state *Luc 43*

**instigation / ~s** *n*
*m* ˌɪnstɪ'gɛːsɪən, -sɪˌɒn / ˌɪnstɪ'gɛːsɪənz
**sp** instigation[3] / instigations[1]

**instinct** *n*
ɪn'stɪŋt, -ŋkt
**sp** instinct[14], in-stinct[1]

**instinctively** *adv*
*m* ɪn'stɪŋtɪvˌləɪ, -ŋkt-
**sp** instinctiuely[2]

**institute** *v*
'ɪnstɪˌtjuːt
**sp** institute[2]

**institution / ~s** *n*
ˌɪnstɪ'tjuːsɪənz
**sp** institutions[1]

**instruct / ~s / ~ed** *v*
ɪn'strɤkt/ -s / -ɪd /
**sp** instruct[25] / instructs[3], in-structs[1] / instructed[5], in-structed[1]
**rh** instruct you becomes you *TS 4.2.120*

**instruction / ~s** *n*
*m* ɪn'strɤksɪən, -sɪˌɒn / -z
**sp** instruction[16] / instructions[7]

**instrument / ~s** *n*
*m* 'ɪnstrəˌment, -əmənt /
**sp** instrument[36], in-strument[1], instrument's [instrument is][1] / instruments[26]
**rh** languishment *Luc 1140*; spent *R2 2.1.149*

**instrumental** *adj*
ˌɪnstrə'mentɑl
**sp** instrumentall[1]

**insubstantial** *adj*
ˌɪnsəb'stansɪɑl
**sp** insubstantiall[1]

**insue**
> ensue

**insufficience** *n*
ˌɪnsə'fɪsɪəns
**sp** insuffi-cience[1]

**insufficiency** *n*
*m* ˌɪnsə'fɪsɪənˌsəɪ
**sp** insufficiency[1]
**rh** eye *MND 2.2.134*

**insult / ~ing / ~ed** *v*
= / ɪn'sɤltɪn, -ɪŋ / =
**sp** insult[4] / insulting[1] / insulted[1]

**insulting** *adj*
ɪn'sɤltɪn, -ɪŋ
**sp** insulting[7], [haught]-insulting[1]

**insultment** *n*
ɪn'sɤltmənt
**sp** insulment[1]

**insupportable** *adj*
ˌɪnsə'pɔːɹtəbəl
**sp** insupportable[3]
> supportable

**insuppressive** *adj*
=
**sp** insuppressiue[1]

**insurrection / ~'s / ~s** *n*
ˌɪnsə'reksɪən, -sɪˌɒn / ˌɪnsə'reksɪənz / ˌɪnsə'reksɪˌɒnz
**sp** insurrection[4] / insurrections[1] / insurrecti-ons[1]
**rh** subjection *Luc 722*

**intail**
> entail

**intangled**
> entangled

**integer** *Lat adj*
'ɪnteʤeɹ
**sp** integer[1]

**integritas** *Lat n*
ɪn'tegrɪˌtas
**sp** integritas[1]

**integrity** *n*
*m* ɪn'tegrɪˌtəɪ, -ɪtəɪ
**sp** integritie[8], integrity[11]
**rh** affy *Tit 1.1.51*; be *LLL 5.2.356*; hypocrisy *R2 5.3.107*

**intellect / ~s** *n*
=
**sp** intellect[4] / intellects[1]

**intellectual** *adj*
ˌɪntəˈlektjʊɑl
**sp** intellectuall[1], in-tellectuall[1]

**intelligence** *n*
*m* ɪnˈtelɪˌʤens, -ɪʤəns
**sp** intelligence[25], intel-ligence[1]
**rh** expense *MND 1.1.248*; thence *S 86.10*

**intelligencer** *n*
*m* ɪnˈtelɪˌʤensəɹ
**sp** intelligencer[2]

**intelligencing** *adj*
*m* ɪnˈtelɪˌʤensɪn, -ɪŋ
**sp** intelligencing[1]

**intelligent** *adj*
*m* ɪnˈtelɪˌʤent, -ɪʤənt
**sp** intelligent[4]

**intellig·o / ~is** *Lat v*
ɪnˈtelɪg·oː / -is
**sp** intelligo[1] / inteligis[1]

**intemperance** *n*
ɪnˈtemprəns, -pər-
**sp** intemperance[1]

**intemperate** *adj*
ɪnˈtemprət, -pər-
**sp** intemperate[2]

**intemperature** *n*
ɪnˈtemprətəɹ
**sp** intemperature[1]

**intenable** *adj*
=
**sp** intemible[1]

**intend / ~est / ~s / ~eth /~ing / ~ed** *v*
= / ɪnˈtenst, -ndst / = / = / ɪnˈtendɪn, -ɪŋ / =
**sp** entend[1], intend[50] / intend'st[1] / intends[16] / intendeth[1] / intending[2] / intended[13]
**rh** end *LLL 5.2.429*; extend, lend *LC 23*; friend *H8 Prol.21* / friends *VA 587*

**intended** *adj*
=
**sp** entended[1], intended[4]

**intendment** *n*
=
**sp** intendment[2], intend-ment[1]

**intent / ~s** *n*
=
**sp** intent[49] / entents[2], intents[17]
**rh** merriment *LLL 5.2.140*; prevent *Luc 218, VA 469*; tent *TC 1.3.306* / accidents *S 115.7*

**intent** *v*
=
**sp** intent[1]

**intention** *n*
ɪnˈtensɪən
**sp** intention[2]

**inter / ~red** *v*
ɪnˈtɐːɹ / *m* -d, -ɪd
**sp** enterre[1], interre[4] / enterred[1], inter'd[1], interr'd[4], interred[2]
**rh** preferred *Cym 4.2.401*

**intercept / ~s / ~ed** *v*
ˌɪntəɹˈsept / -s / -ɪd
**sp** intercept[4] / intercepts[1] / intercepted[3]

**intercepted** *adj*
ˌɪntəɹˈseptɪd
**sp** intercepted[1]

**intercepter** *n*
ˌɪntəɹˈseptəɹ
**sp** intercepter[1]

**interception** *n*
ˌɪntəɹˈsepsɪən
**sp** interception[1]

**intercession** *n*
ˌɪntəɹˈsesɪən
**sp** intercession[6]

**intercessor / ~s** *n*
ˌɪntəɹˈsesəɹz
**sp** intercessors[1]

**interchange** *n*
ˈɪntəɹˌʧɛːnʤ
**sp** enterchange[2], enter-change[1], interchange[1]
> change

**interchange / ~ing / ~ed** *v*
ˈɪntəɹˌʧɛːnʤ / -ɪn, -ɪŋ / *m* -d, -ɪd
**sp** enterchange[1] / enterchanging[1], interchanging[1] / interchang'd[1], interchanged[1]

**interchangeably** *adv*
*m* ˌɪntəɹˈʧɛːnʤəˌbləɪ
**sp** enterchangeably[1], interchangeably[3]

**interchangement** *n*
ˌɪntəɹˈʧɛːnʤmənt
**sp** enterchangement[1]

**interdict** *PT* *v*
ˈɪntəɹˌdɪkt
**sp** interdict[1]
**rh** strict *PT 9*

**interdiction** *n*
ˌɪntəɹˈdɪksɪən
**sp** interdiction[1]

**interess / ~ed** *v*
*m* ˈɪntəˌrest, ˈɪntrəst
**sp** interest[1]

**interest** *n*
*m* ˈɪntəˌrest, -trəst
**sp** interest[25], interrest[3], intrest[1]
**rh** arrest *S 74.3*

**intergator·y / ~ies** *n*
ɪnˈtɛːɹgətrəɪ / -z
**sp** intergatory[1] / intergatories[2]

**interim / ~s** *n*
ˈɪntrɪm, -tər- / -z
**sp** interim[9], interim's [interim is][1], intrim[1] / interims[1]

**interior** *adj / n*
ɪn'terɪəɹ
**sp** interiour[2] / interior[1]

**interjection / ~s** *n*
ˌɪntəɹ'ʤeksɪənz
**sp** interiections[1]

**interjoin** *v*
ˌɪntəɹ'ʤəɪn
**sp** inter-ioyne[1]
> join

**interlace / ~s** *Luc* *v*
'ɪntəɹˌlɛ:sɪz
**sp** interlaces[1]
**rh** faces, paces *Luc 1390*

**interlude** *n*
'ɪntəɹˌlu:d
**sp** enterlude[2], enter-lude[1], interlude[1]

**intermingle** *v*
ˌɪntəɹ'mɪŋgəl
**sp** intermingle[2]
> mingle

**intermission** *n*
*m* ˌɪntəɹ'mɪsɪən, -sɪˌɒn
**sp** intermission[4]

**intermissive** *adj*
ˌɪntəɹ'mɪsɪv
**sp** intermissiue[1]

**intermit** *v*
ˌɪntəɹ'mɪt
**sp** intermit[1]

**intermix / ~ed** *v*
*m* 'ɪntəɹˌmɪkst
**sp** intermixt[1]
**rh** fixed *S 101.8*
> mix

**interpose** *v*
*m* ˌɪntəɹ'po:z
**sp** interpose[2]

**interposer** *n*
*m* ˌɪntəɹ'po:zəɹ
**sp** interposer[1]

**interpret / ~s / ~ed** *v*
ɪn'tɐ:ɹprɪt / -s / -ɪd
**sp** interpret[5], interprete[1] / interprets[2] / interpreted[2]
> misinterpret

**interpretation** *n*
ɪnˌtɐ:ɹprɪ'tɛ:sɪən
**sp** interpretation[5]

**interpreter / ~s** *n*
ɪn'tɐ:ɹprɪtəɹ / -z
**sp** interpreter[9] / interpreters[2]

**interrogator·y / ~ies** *n*
*m* ɪn'terəˌgɛ:trəɪz
**sp** interrogatories[2]

**interrupt / ~est / ~s / ~ed** *v*
ˌɪntə'rɤpt / -pst, -ptst / -s / -ɪd
**sp** interrupt[4] / interruptest[1] / interrupts[1] / interrupted[2]
**rh** corrupted *Luc 1170*

**interrupted** *adj*
ˌɪntə'rɤptɪd
**sp** interrupted[1]

**interrupter** *n*
*m* ɪn'trɤptəɹ, ɪntə'r-
**sp** interrupter[1]

**interruption** *n*
*m* ˌɪntə'rɤpsɪən, -sɪˌɒn
**sp** interruption[3]

**intertissued** *adj*
ˌɪntəɹ'tɪsju:d, -ɪʃu:-
**sp** enter-tissued[1]
> tissue

**intervallum / ~s** *n*
ˌɪntəɹ'valəmz
**sp** interuallums[1]

**interview** *n*
*m* 'ɪntəɹˌvju:
**sp** enteruiew[1], enterview[3], interview[1]

**intestine** *adj*
ɪn'testɪn
**sp** intestine[3]

**inthralled**
> enthralled

**inticing**
> enticing

**intimate** *v*
*m* 'ɪntɪˌmɛ:t
**sp** intimate[3]
**rh** desperate *AW 2.1.183*

**intimation** *n*
ˌɪntɪ'mɛ:sɪən
**sp** intimation[1]

**intire, intirely**
> entire, entirely

**intitle, intituled**
> entitle, entituled

**into** *prep*
=
**sp** into[618], in-to[3], into't [into it][3], intoo't [into it][3], *emend of Ham 5.1.73* intill[1]

**intolerable** *adj*
*m* ɪn'tɒlrəbəl, -ləˌrabəl
**sp** intollerable[9]
> tolerable

**intomb**
> entomb

**intoxicates** *adj*
*Fluellen H5 4.7.35*
ɪn'tɒksɪkəts
**sp** intoxicates[1]

**intrap**
> entrap

**intreat, intreaty**
> entreat, entreaty

**intrenchant** *adj*
ɪn'trenʧənt
**sp** intrenchant[1]

**intricate** *adj*
=
**sp** intricate[1]

**intrince** *v*
ɪn'trɪns
**sp** intrince[1]

**intrinsicate** *adj*
*m* ɪn'trɪnsɪˌkɛ:t
**sp** intrinsicate[1]

**intrude** *v*
=
**sp** intru'd[1], intrude[1]

**intruder** *n*
ɪn'tru:dəɹ
**sp** intruder[2]

**intruding** *adj*
ɪn'tru:dɪn, -ɪŋ
**sp** intruding[1]

**intrusion** *n*
ɪn'tru:zɪən
**sp** intrusion[4]
**rh** confusion *CE 2.2.188*

**inundation** *n*
*m* ˌɪnən'dɛ:sɪən, -sɪˌɒn
**sp** inundation[3]

**inure** *v*
ɪn'ju:ɹ
**sp** in-vre[1]
**rh** procured *LC 251*

**invade / ~s** *v*
ɪn'vɛ:d / -z
**sp** inuade[2] / inuades[1]

**invasion** *n*
*m* ɪn'vɛ:zɪən, -zɪˌɒn
**sp** inuasion[1]
**rh** persuasion *Luc 287*

**invasive** *adj*
ɪn'vɛ:zɪv
**sp** inuasiue[1]

**invective / ~s** *n*
=
**sp** inuectiues[1]

**invectively** *adv*
*m* ɪn'vektɪvˌləɪ
**sp** inuectiuely[1]

**inveigle / ~d** *v*
ɪn'vɛ:gəld
**sp** inueigled[1]

**invelop**
> envelop

**invenom**
> envenom

**invent / ~ed** *v*
=
**sp** inuent[5] / inuented[2]
**rh** argument *S 79.7*; excellent *S 38.1*

**invention / ~s** *n*
*m* ɪn'vensɪən, -sɪˌɒn / -z
**sp** inuention[24], in-uention[1] / inuentions[2]

**inventor / ~'s** *n*
ɪn'ventəɹ / -z
**sp** inuenter[1], inuentors[1]

**inventory** *n*
*m* 'ɪnvəntrəɪ, -ˌtɒrəɪ
**sp** inuentorie[2], inuentory[3], inuentory[1]

**inventor·y / ~ied** *v*
*m* 'ɪnvəntrəɪd
**sp** inuentoried[1]

**Inverness** *n*
=
**sp** Envernes[1]

**invert** *v*
ɪn'vɐ:ɹt
**sp** inuert[2]

**invest / ~ing / ~ed** *v*
= / ɪn'vestɪn, -ɪŋ / =
**sp** inuest[8] / inuesting[1] / inuested[4]

**investment / ~s** *n*
=
**sp** inuestments[2]

**inveterate** *adj*
ɪn'vetrət
**sp** inueterate[4]

**invincible** *adj*
=
**sp** inuincible[5]

**inviolable** *adj*
*m* ɪn'vəɪəˌlabəl
**sp** inuiolable[3]

**inviron**
> environ

**invisible** *adj*
=
**sp** inuisible[23], in-uisible[1], invisible[1]
**rh** *1* sensible *LLL 5.2.257, VA 434*;
**rh** *2* steeple *TG 2.1.128*

**invitation** *n*
ˌɪnvɪ'tɛ:sɪən
**sp** inuitation[1]

**invit·e / ~s / ~ing / ~ed** *v*
ɪn'vəɪt / -s / -ɪn, -ɪŋ / -ɪd
**sp** enuite[1], inuite[18] / inuites[6] / inuiting[2] / inuited[8]
**rh** delighted *S 141.7*

**inviting** *adj / n*
ɪn'vəɪtɪn, -ɪŋ
**sp** inuiting[1] / in-uiting[1]

**invitus / ~is** *Lat adj*
ɪn'vi:tis
**sp** inuitis[1]

**invocate** *v*
*m* 'ɪnvəˌkɛ:t
**sp** inuocate[2]
**rh** date *S 38.10*

**invocation / *Luc* ~s** *n*
*m* ˌɪnvə'kɛ:sɪən, -sɪˌɒn / -sɪənz
**sp** inuocation[4]
**rh** abominations, lamentations *Luc 1831*

**invoke** *v*
ɪn'vo:k
**sp** inuoke[1]

**invulnerable** *adj*
*gm* ɪn'vɤlnəˌrabəl, -nrəˌbɤl

**sp** involnerable[1], invulnerable[1], [like]-invulnerable[1], vnvulnerable[1]
> unvulnerable, vulnerable

**inward** *adj / adv*
'ɪnwəɹd
**sp** inward[20] / inward[1], in-ward[1]

**inward / ~s** *n*
'ɪnwəɹd / -z
**sp** inward[1] / inwardes[1], inwards[1]

**inwardly** *adv*
*m* 'ɪnwəɹd,ləɪ
**sp** inwardly[2], inward-ly[1]

**inwardness** *n*
*m* 'ɪnwəɹd,nes
**sp** inwardnesse[1]

**io** *Ital pro*

*mi*
mi:
**sp** me

*mio*
'mi:o:
**sp** mio[1]

**Ionia** *n*
əɪ'o:nɪə
**sp** Ionia[1]

**Ionian** *adj*
əɪ'o:nɪən
**sp** Ionian[1]

**ipse** *Lat pro*
'ɪpse:
**sp** ipse[2]

**Ipswich** *adj / n*
=
**sp** Ipswich[1] / Ipswich[1]

**ir·a / ~ae** *Lat n*
'i:rɑ: / 'i:re
**sp** ira[1] / irae[1]

**Iras** *n*
'əɪrəs
**sp** Iras[19]

**ire** *n*
əɪɹ
**sp** ire[4]
**rh** fire *R2 1.1.18*

**ireful** *adj*
'əɪɹfʊl
**sp** irefull[3], yrefull[1]

**Ireland** *n*
'əɪɹlənd
**sp** Ireland[31]

**Iris** *n*
'əɪrɪs
**sp** Iris[5]

**Irish** *adj / n*
'əɪrɪʃ
**sp** Irish[8] / Irish[2]

**Irishman** *n*
'əɪrɪʃmən
**sp** Irish-man[1], Irish man[1], Irishmen[1]

**irk / ~s** *v*
ɐ:ɹks
**sp** irkes[3]

**irksome** *adj*
'ɐ:ɹksəm
**sp** irkesome[3]

**iron** *adj*
'əɪrən
**sp** iron[10], yron[4]
> plough-irons, toasting-iron

**iron / ~s** *n*
'əɪrən / -z
**sp** iron[26], yron[3] / irons[7]

**iron-witted** *adj*
'əɪrən-,wɪtɪd
**sp** iron-witted[1]
> wit

**irreconciled** *adj*
ɪ'rekənsəɪld
**sp** irreconcil'd[1]
> reconcile

**irrecoverable** *adj*
,ɪrə'kɤvrəbəl
**sp** irrecoue-rable[1]
> recover

**irregular** *adj*
*m* ɪ'regələɹ, -gl-, -,lɐ:ɹ
**sp** irregular[3]
> regular

**irregulous** *adj*
ɪ'regləs, -gjəl-
**sp** irregulous[1]

**irreligious** *adj*
,ɪrə'lɪʤɪəs
**sp** irreligious[3]
> religion

**irremovable** *adj*
,ɪrə'mɤvəbəl, -mu:v-
**sp** irremoueable[1]
> remove

**irreparable** *adj*
ɪ'reprəbəl
**sp** irreparable[1]

**irresolute** *adj*
ɪ'rezlət, -zəl-
**sp** irresolute[1]

**irrevocable** *adj*
*m* ɪ'revə,kabəl
**sp** irreuocable[3]

**is,** *abbr* **s** *v*
ɪz, ɪʀ, *Macmorris H5 3.2.85ff*
ɪʃ, *abbr* s
**sp** is[9037], 'is[1], *abbr* 's[230], s [*without preceding apostrophe, e.g. counts, fancies*][22], *Macmorris* ish[7]
**rh** *1* his *AY 5.4.112, Luc 1795, R2 2.1.146, S 67.9, 80.5*; thee it is *LLL 4.3.66*; vapour is *LLL 4.3.68*; **rh** *2* amiss *Ham 4.5.17, S 59.1, 151.1*; amiss, bliss, iwis, kiss, this *MV 2.9.64*; bliss, kiss *Luc 390*; kiss *MV 3.2.137, VA 538*; this *R3 2.1.83, RJ 1.1.181, S 72.11, TC 1.2.289, Tim 1.2.194, 5.3.10, VA 615*
> be

***is it** abbr*
ɪzt, ɪst
**sp** ist[33], 'ist[2], i'st[2], is't[146]

***it is** abbr*
ɪts, ts, tɪz, tɪs, *Macmorris 3.2.85ff* tɪʃ
it's[45], 'tis[1289], tis[93], 'ts[1], *Macmorris* tish[4]

***who is** abbr*
u:z, hu:z
**sp** who's[75]

**Isabel / ~'s** *n*
*m* 'ɪzbel, 'ɪzə,bel / -z
**sp** Isabel[4], Isabell[24], Isbell[2] / Isabels[1], Isbels[3]

**Isabella** *n*
'ɪzə,belə
**sp** Isabella[13]

**Iscariot** *n*
ɪs'karɪət
**sp** Iscariot[1]

**ish**
> is

**Isidore** *n*
'ɪzɪ,dɔ:ɹ
**sp** Isidore[4]

**Isis** *n*
'əɪsɪs
**sp** Isis[8]

**island** *adj*
'əɪlənd
**sp** iland[2]

**island / ~s** *n*
'əɪlənd / -z
**sp** iland[8], island[18], island's [island is][1] / islands[4]

**islander / ~s** *n*
'əɪləndəɹ / -z
**sp** islan-der[1] / ilanders[1], islanders[3]

**isle / ~s** *n*
əɪl / -z
**sp** ile[7], isle[28] / iles[1], isles[1]
**rh** while *KJ 4.2.99*

**Isle of Man** *n*
'əɪl ə 'man
**sp** Ile of Man[3]

**Israel** *n*
=
**sp** Israel[1]

**issue / ~s** *n*
'ɪsju:, 'ɪʃu: / -z
**sp** issue[91] / issues[6]

**issu·e / ~es / ~ing / ~ed** *v*
'ɪsju:, 'ɪʃu: / -z / -ɪn, -ɪŋ / -d
**sp** issue[10], yssue[6] / issues[3], yssues[1] / issuing[2] / issu'd[1], issued[4], yssued[1]

**issueless** *adj*
*m* 'ɪsju:,les, 'ɪʃu:-
**sp** issue-lesse[1]

**issuing** *adj*
'ɪsju:ɪn, -ɪŋ, 'ɪʃu:-
**sp** issuing[2]

**iste / ista** *Lat pro*
'ɪstɑ:
**sp** ista[1]

**it,** *abbr* **t / its / itself** *pro*
=
**sp** it[7732], *emend of Mac 1.5.45* hit[1], *abbr* t [*without preceding apostrophe, eg fort*][2], 't[206], -t[1]
**rh** fit *MW 5.5.60, Per 1.1.107*; hit *VA 938*; knit *MND 2.2.54*; sit *KJ 3.1.74, S 103.14*; wit *CE 2.1.90, H5 1.2.297, LLL 4.3.146, Luc 154, Oth 2.1.129, TC 4.4.107*; writ *Luc 1294, 1333*

***and it** abbr*
*str* ant, *unstr* ənt
**sp** ant[1], an't[10]

***as it** abbr*
azt
**sp** as't[4]

***in it** abbr*
ɪnt
**sp** in't[87]

***is it** abbr*
ɪzt, ɪst
**sp** ist[33], 'ist[2], i'st[2], is't[146]

***of it** abbr*
ɒvt
**sp** of't[2]

***was it** abbr*
wɑst
**sp** wast[39], was't[60]

***it had** abbr*
təd
**sp** t'had[1]

***it has** abbr*
təz
**sp** 'tas[2], t'has[1]

***it is,** abbr* its / tis
ɪts, ts / tɪz, tɪs, *Macmorris 3.2.85ff* tɪʃ
**sp** it's[45], 'ts[1] / 'tis[1289], tis[93], *Macmorris* tish[4]

***it was** abbr*
twəz
**sp** twas[7], 'twas[144], t'was[1]

***it were** abbr*
twəɹ
**sp** 'twer[8], 'twere[108], t'were[2]

***it will** abbr*
twɪl
**sp** 'twil[2], twill[3], 'twill[56], 'twill[be][1]

***it would** abbr*
*str* twʊd, twʊld, *unstr* twəd
**sp** 'twold[1], twoo'd[1], 'twould[21], t'would[2]

***its***
=
**sp** its[1]

***itself***
=
**sp** it selfe[234]
**rh** myself *R3 1.3.66*

**Italian** *adj / n*
=
**sp** italian[14] / Italian[6]

**Italy** *n*
'ɪtələɪ
**sp** Italie[6], Italy[28]
**rh** chivalry, victory *Luc 107*; jealousy, villainy *Cym 5.4.64*

**itch / ~es** *n*
=
**sp** itch[2], itches[1]

**itch / ~es / ~ed** *v*
=
**sp** itch[5] / itches[1] / itcht[1]
**rh** pitch *Tem 2.2.52*

**itching** *adj*
'ɪʧɪn, -ɪŋ
**sp** itching[2]

**item / ~s** *n*
'əɪtəm / -z
**sp** item[31] / items[1]

**iterance** *n*
=
**sp** itterance[1]

**iteration** *n*
'ɪtəˌrɛːsɪən
**sp** iteration[2]

**Ithaca** *n*
'ɪθəkə
**sp** Ithaca[1]

**itself**
> it

**ivory** *adj / n*
*m* 'əɪvrəɪ, -vəˌrəɪ
**sp** iuory[2] / iuorie[1]

**ivy** *n*
'əɪvəɪ
**sp** iuie[1], iuy[3]

**iwis** *adv*
ə'wɪs
**sp** iwis[2], i-wis[1]
**rh** *1* amiss, bliss, kiss, this *MV 2.9.68*;
**rh** *2* is *MV 2.9.68*
> I

# J

**Jack / ~s** *n*
=
**sp** Iack[18], Iacke[63], iacke[1] / Iackes[4], Iacks[2]

**Jack-a-lent** *n*
'ʤakəˌlent
**sp** Iack-a-lent[1], Iacke-a-Lent[1]
> Lent

**Jackanape** *adj*
'ʤakəˌnɛ:p, -kˌn-
**sp** Iack-a-nape[1]

**Jackanape / ~s** *n*
'ʤakəˌnɛ:p, -kˌn- / -s
**sp** Iack-an-ape[1], Iack'nape[1] / Iack an Apes[1], Iacke-an-apes[3]

**Jack-dog** *n*
=
**sp** [scuruy]-Iack-dog-[Priest][1]
> dog

**Jack-priest** *n*
=
**sp** Iack-priest[1], [coward]-Iack-priest[1]
> priest

**Jack-sauce** *n*
=
**sp** Iacke sawce[1]
> sauce

**Jack-slave** *n*
'ʤakˌslɛ:v
**sp** Iacke-slaue[1]
> slave

**Jacob / ~'s** *n*
'ʤɛ:kəb / -z
**sp** Iacob[4], Ia-cob[1] / Iacobs[3]

**jade / ~'s / ~s** *n*
ʤɛ:d / -z
**sp** iade[9] / iades[3] / iades[11]
**rh** made *S 51.12*

**jade / ~d** *v*
ʤɛ:d / 'ʤɛ:dɪd
**sp** iade[1] / iaded[2]

**jaded** *adj*
'ʤɛ:dɪd
**sp** iaded[1]

**jail, jailor**
> gaol, gaoler

**jakes** *n*
ʤɛ:ks
**sp** iakes[1]

**James** *n*
ʤɛ:ms
**sp** Iames[9]

**Jamy** *n*
'ʤɛ:məɪ
**sp** Iamy[4]

**Jane** *n*
ʤɛ:n
**sp** Iane[2]

**jangle / ~ing / ~d** *v*
'ʤaŋglɪn, -ɪŋ / =
**sp** iangling[1] / iangled[1]

**jangling** *n*
'ʤaŋglɪn, -ɪŋ
**sp** iangling[1]

**January** *n*
*m* 'ʤanjəˌrəɪ, -ər-
**sp** Ianuary[2]

**Janus** *n*
'ʤɛ:nəs
**sp** Ianus[2]

**Japhet** *n*
'ʤafet
**sp** Iaphet[1]

**Jaquenetta / ~'s** *n*
ˌʤakə'netə / -z
**sp** Iaquenetta[11] / Iaquenettas[1]

**Jaques** *n*
*m* ʤɛ:ks, 'ʤɛ:kəɪz, *Fr* ʒɛ:ks, ʒɛ:'ki:z
**sp** Iaques[22], Ia-ques[1]

**jar / ~s** *n*
ʤɑ:ɹ / -z
**sp** iarre[3] / iarres[5]
**rh** war *VA 100*

**jar / ~s / ~ring** *v*
ʤɑ:ɹ / -z / 'ʤɑ:ɹɪn, -ɪŋ
**sp** iar[1], iarre[3] / iarres[1], iars[2] / iarring[4]

**jarring** *n*
'ʤɑ:ɹɪn, -ɪŋ
**sp** iarring[1]

**Jason / ~s** *n*
'ʤɛ:sənz
**sp** Iasons[2]

**jauncing** *adj*
'ʤɑ:nsɪn, -ɪŋ, 'ʤɔ:-
**sp** iauncing[1]

**jaundice** *n*
'ʤɑ:ndəɪz, 'ʤɔ:-
**sp** iaundies[2]

**jaunt** *n*
ʤɑ:nt, 'ʤɔ:-
**sp** iaunt[1]

**jaunting** *v*
'ʤɑ:ntɪn, -ɪŋ, 'ʤɔ:-
**sp** iaunting[1]

**jaw / ~s** *n*
=
**sp** iaw[1] / iawes[10]
**rh** paws *S 19.3*

**jawbone** *n*
'ʤɔ:ˌbo:n
**sp** iaw-bone[1]

**jay / ~'s / ~s** *n*
ʤɛ: / -z
**sp** iay[3] / iayes[1] / iayes[1]
**rh** hay *WT 4.3.10*

**je** *Fr pro*
ʒə, *abbr* ʒ
**sp** ie[31], i'[ay][1], *emend of H5 4.4.54* se[1]

*ma det singular feminine*
ma
**sp** ma[5], mai[1], may[1]

*me, abbr* m *pro*
mə, *abbr* m
**sp** ma[1], me[2], *abbr* m'[1], m[an][1], m[aves][1], m[e][1], m[en][2]

*mes det plural*
me
**sp** mes[1]

*mienne pro*
mjɛn
**sp** mienne[1]

*moi pro*
*Fr* mwɛ, *Eng* məɪ
**sp** moy[10]
**rh** destroy *R2 5.3.118*

*mon det singular masculine*
mɔ̃
**sp** mon[5]

**jealous** *adj*
=
**sp** iealous[30], iealious[17], iealious-[rascally-knaue][1], ielous[1]

**jealousy** *adj*
'ʤeləsəɪ
**sp** iealousie-[man][1]

**jealous·y / ~ies** *n*
*m* 'ʤeləsəɪ, -ˌsəɪ / -z
**sp** iealousie[28], ielousie[2], ielou-sie[1], ielousy[1], ielouzie[1] / iealousies[8], iealouzies[1], ielousies[2]
**rh** *1* ecstasy *MV 3.2.110*; Italy, villainy *Cym 5.4.66*; mutiny *VA 649*; **rh** *2* die, eye *CE 2.1.116*; prophesy *VA 1137*; pry *S 61.8*; spy *VA 657*

**jeer** *v*
ʤi:ɹ
**sp** ieere[1]

**jeering** *adj / n*
'ʤi:rɪn, -ɪŋ
**sp** geering[1] / ieering[1]

**jelly** *n*
'ʤeləɪ
**sp** gelly[2], ielly[1]

**jem**
> gem

**Jenny / ~'s** *n*
'ʤenəɪz
**sp** Ginyes[1]

**jeopardy** *n*
*m* 'ʤepəɹˌdəɪ
**sp** ieopardie[1]
**rh** hie *KJ 3.1.346*

**Jephthah** *n*
'ʤeftə
**sp** Iephah[1], Iephta[3]

**jerk / ~s** *n*
ʤɐ:ɹks
**sp** ierkes[1]

**jerkin / ~s** *n*
'ʤɐ:ɹkɪn / -z
**sp** ierkin[10], [buffe]-ierkin[1], ier-kin[1] / ierkins[2]

**Jeronimy** *n*
ʤə'rɒnɪməɪ
**sp** Ieronimie[1]

**Jerusalem** *n*
=
**sp** Ierusalem[10]

**Jeshu**
> Jesu

**jess / ~es** *n*
=
**sp** iesses[1]

**Jessica** *n*
=
**sp** Iessica[29]

**jest / ~'s / ~s** *n*
=
**sp** ieast[6], iest[67] / iests[1] / ieasts[1], iests[13]
**rh** *1* breast *LLL 4.3.172, R2 5.3.100*; rest *LLL 1.1.54*; **rh** *2* beast *LLL 2.1.207*

**jest / ~s / ~ing / ~ed** *v*
= / = / 'ʤestɪn, -ɪŋ / =
**sp** ieast[3], iest[27] / ieasts[1], iests[2] / iesting[1] / iested[1]
**rh** *1* breast *R2 1.3.95*; crest *VA 106*; **rh** *2* beast *VA 997* / hests *LLL 5.2.66* [*emend of* device]
> outjest

**jester / ~s** *n*
'ʤestəɹ / -z
**sp** ieaster[1], iester[5] / iesters[2]

**jesting** *adj*
'ʤestɪn, -ɪŋ
**sp** iesting[2] / ieasting[1], iesting[1]

**jesting / *PP* ~s** *n*
'ʤestɪn, -ɪŋ / -z
**sp** ieasting[1], iesting[1] / ieastings[1]
**rh** protestings *PP 7.12*

**Jesu** *n*
'ʤi:zju:, *Fluellen H5 3.2.61ff* 'ʧeʃu:
**sp** Iesu[12], *Fluellen* Cheshu[3], Ieshu[1]

**Jesus** *n*
=
**sp** Iesus[2]

**jet** *n*
=
**sp** iet[5]
**rh** set, wet *LC 37*

**jet / ~s** *v*
=
**sp** iet[1] / iets[1]

**Jew / ~'s / ~s** *n*
=
**sp** Iew[63], Iewe[3] / Iewes[11] / Iewes[1]
**rh** adieu *LLL 3.1.133*; hue *MND 3.1.88*; yew *Mac 4.1.26*

**jewel / ~s** *n*
=
**sp** iewel[3], iewell[48] / iewels[24]
**rh** cruel *S 131.4*
> rich-jewelled

**jewel-house** *n*
'ʤu:əl-ˌəʊs, -ˌhəʊs
**sp** iewell-house[1], iewell house[1]
> house

**jeweller** *n*
'ʤu:ələɹ
**sp** ieweller[3]

**Jewish** *adj*
=
**sp** Iewish[2]

**Jewry** *n*
'ʤu:rəɪ
**sp** Iewry[4], Iurie[1], Iury[2]
**rh** chivalry *R2 2.1.55*

**Jezabel** *n*
=
**sp** Iezabel[1]

**jibe / ~s** *n*
ʤəɪbz
**sp** iibes[1]

**jig** *n / v*
=
**sp** iigge[2], iygge[1], jigge[2] / gidge[1], iigge[1]
**rh** gig *LLL 4.3.166*

**jigging** *adj*
=
**sp** iigging[1]

**jig-maker** *n*
'ʤɪg-ˌmɛ:kəɹ
**sp** iigge-maker[1]
> make

**Jill / ~s** *n*
=
**sp** Gill[1], Iill[1] / Gils[1]
**rh** *1* ill *MND 3.2.461*; **rh** *2* well *MND 3.2.461*
> flirt-gill

**jingling** *adj*
'ʤɪŋglɪn, -ɪŋ
**sp** gingling[1]

**Joan** *n*
ʤo:n
**sp** Ioane[14], Ione[13]
**rh** groan *LLL 3.1.202*

**Job** *n*
ʤo:b
**sp** Iob[2]

**jockey** *n*
'ʤɒkəɪ
**sp** iockey[1]

**jocund** *adj*
'ʤɒkənd
**sp** iocond[5], iocund[3]

**jog / ~ging** *v*
= / 'ʤɒgɪn, -ɪŋ
**sp** iog-[on][2] / iogging[1]

**John / ~'s / ~s** *n*
=
**sp** Iohn[303] / Iohns[4] / Iohns[1]
**rh** gone *1H6 4.7.2*
> apple-john

**John-a-dreams** *n*
'ʤɒn-ə-ˌdri:mz
**sp** Iohn a-dreames[1]
> dream

**join / ~est / ~s / ~eth / ~ed** *v*
ʤəɪn / -st / -z / 'ʤəɪn·əθ / *m* -ɪd, ʤəɪnd
**sp** ioyn[1], ioyne[56] / ioyn'st[2] / ioynes[1] / ioyneth[1] / ioynd[1], ioyn'd[25], ioyned[2]
**rh** coin *Tim 3.3.26* / coigns *Per 3. Chorus.18* / coined *PP 7.7*
> ad-, co-, con-, dis-, inter-join

**joinder** *n*
'ʤəɪndəɹ
**sp** ioynder[1]

**joiner** *adj / n*
'ʤəɪnəɹ
**sp** ioyner[1] / ioyner[5]

**joint** *adj*
ʤəɪnt
**sp** ioynt[3]

**joint / ~s** *n*
ʤəɪnt / -s
**sp** ioynt[17] / ioints[2], ioynts[16]

**joint / ~ing / ~ed** *v*
'ʤəɪnt·ɪn, -ɪŋ / -ɪd
**sp** ioynting[1] / ioynted[2]
> strong-, un-jointed

**joint-labourer** *n*
ˌʤəɪnt-'lɛ:brəɹ
**sp** ioynt-labourer[1]
> labour

**jointly** *adv*
'ʤəɪntləɪ
**sp** ioyntly[4]

**jointress** *n*
'ʤəɪntrəs
**sp** ioyntresse[1]

**joint-ring** *n*
ˈʤəɪnt-ˌrɪŋ
**sp** ioynt ring[1]

**joint-servant** *n*
*m* ˌʤəɪnt-ˈsɐːɹvənt
**sp** ioynt-seruant[1]
> servant

**joint-stool / ~s** *n*
ˈʤəɪn-ˌstʊl, -ˌstuːl, -nd- / -z
**sp** ioyn'd-stoole[1], ioyn'd stoole[1] / ioyn'd-stooles[1], ioynstooles[1]
> stool

**jointure** *n*
ˈʤəɪntəɹ
**sp** ioyncture[1], ioynter[1], ioynture[3]

**jollity** *n*
*m* ˈʤɒlɪˌtəɪ, -ɪtəɪ
**sp** iollitie[2], iollity[3]
**rh** *1* amity, be, me, prosperity, solemnly, triumphantly *MND 4.1.91*; solemnity *MND 5.1.360*; **rh** *2* cry *S 66.3*

**jolly** *adj*
ˈʤɒləɪ
**sp** iolly[8]
**rh** holly *AY 2.7.184,194*

**jolt-head / ~s** *n*
ˈʤɒlt-ˌed, -ˌhed / -z
**sp** iolt-head[1] / iolt-heads[1]
> head

**jordan** *n*
ˈʤɔːɹdən
**sp** iordan[1], iourden[1]

**Jordan** [name] *n*
ʤɔːɹˈdɛːn
**sp** Iordan[1], Iordane[1]

**Joseph** *n*
ˈʤoːsəf
**sp** Ioseph[1]

**Joshua** *n*
=
**sp** Iosua[1]

**jot** *n*
=
**sp** iot[21]

**jour** *Fr n*
ʒuːɹ
**sp** iour[1]
> bonjour

**journal** *n*
ˈʤɐːɹnɑl
**sp** iournall[2]

**journey / ~'s / ~s** *n*
ˈʤɔːɹnəɪ / -z
**sp** iourney[21], iournie[2] / iourneys[1], iournies[2] / iournies[1]

**journey / ~s / ~ing** *v*
ˈʤɔːɹnəɪ / -z / -ɪn, -ɪŋ
**sp** iourney[1] / iournies[1] / iournying[1]

**journey-bated** *adj*
ˈʤɔːɹnəɪ-ˌbɛːtɪd
**sp** iourney bated[1]

**journey·man, ~men** *n*
ˈʤɔːɹnəɪ-ˌmen
**sp** iouerney-men[1]

**joust / ~s** *n*
ʤɤst / -s
**sp** iust[1] / iusts[1]

**Jove / ~'s** *n*
ʤoːv, ʤɤv / -z
**sp** Ioue[71] / Ioues[17]
**rh** love *LLL 4.3.117, Luc 568, MA 5.4.46, PP 16.17*

**Jovem** *Lat*
> Juppiter

**jovial** *adj*
ˈʤoːvɪɑl
**sp** iouiall[4]

**jowl** *n*
ʤəʊl
**sp** iowle[1]

**jowl / ~s** *v*
ʤəʊl / -z
**sp** ioule[1] / iowles[1]

**joy / ~'s / ~s** *n*
ʤəɪ / -z
**sp** ioy[172] / ioyes[1] / ioyes[25]
**rh** annoy *3H6 5.7.46, Luc 1107, R3 5.3.156, S 8.2, VA 498, 600*; boy *MND 2.1.27, VA 405*; coy *MND 4.1.4*; destroy *Ham 3.2.206, 230, Mac 3.2.7, Per 2.5.89*; destroy, toy *Luc 212*; Troy *AW 1.3.71, Luc 1431* / boys *Cym 5.5.106*

**joy / ~s / ~ed** *v*
ʤəɪ / -z / -d
**sp** ioy[10] / ioyes[2] / ioy'd[3]
**rh** boy *R2 5.3.94*
> overjoyed

**joyful** *adj*
ˈʤəɪfʊl
**sp** ioyful[1], ioyfull[30]

**joyfully** *adv*
*m* ˈʤəɪfʊˌləɪ
**sp** ioyfully[3]

**joyless** *adj*
ˈʤəɪləs
**sp** ioylesse[2]

**joyous** *adj*
ˈʤəɪəs
**sp** ioyous[2]

**Judas / ~'s / ~es** *n*
=
**sp** Iudas[17], Iud-as[1] / Iudasses[2] / Iudasses[1]

**Jude** *n*
=
**sp** Iude[2]

**Judean** *n*
=
**sp** Iudean[1]

**judge / ~'s / ~s** *n*
ʤɤʤ / ˈʤɤʤɪz
**sp** iudge[52] / iudges[4] / iudges[9]

**judge / ~est / ~d** *v*
ʤɤʤ / 'ʤɤʤ·əst / *m* -ɪd, ʤɤʤd
**sp** iudge[35] *Evans MW 1.1.171* [got]-udge[1] / iudgest[2] / iudg'd[7], iudged[1]

**judgement / ~s** *n*
'ʤɤʤmənt / -s
**sp** iudgement[103], iudge-ment[3], iudgment[5], iudgme[n]t[1] / iudgements[10], iudgments[1]

**Judgement Day** *n*
'ʤɤʤmənt,dɛ:
**sp** Iudgement-Day[1]

**judgement-place** *n*
'ʤɤʤmənt-,plɛ:s
**sp** iudgement place[1]
> place

**judging** *n*
'ʤɤʤɪn, -ɪŋ
**sp** iudging[1]
> high-judging

**judicious** *adj / n*
ʤʊ'dɪsɪəs
**sp** iudicious[4] / iudicious[1]

**Jug** [name] *n*
ʤɤg
**sp** Iugge[1]

**juggl·e / ~ing / ~ed** *v*
'ʤɤg·əl / -lɪn, -lɪŋ / -əld
**sp** iuggle[1] / iugling[1] / iuggel'd[1]

**juggler / ~s** *n*
'ʤɤglə.ɪ / -z
**sp** iugler[3] / iuglers[1]

**juggling** *adj / n*
'ʤɤglɪn, -ɪŋ
**sp** iugling[3] / iugling[1]

**juice** *n*
ʤəɪs
**sp** iuyce[6]
**rh** voice *VA 136*
> love-, precious-juiced

**Jule** [Juliet] *n*
=
**sp** Iule[3]

**Julia / ~'s** *n*
=
**sp** Iulia[34] / Iulia's[3], Iulias[2]

**Juliana** *n*
ʤʊlɪ'anə
**sp** Iuliana[1]

**Juliet / ~'s** *n*
*m* 'ʤu:lɪət, -ɪ,et / 'ʤu:lɪəts
**sp** Iuliet[58] / Iuliets[4]
**rh** set *RJ 5.3.302*

**Julietta / ~s** *n*
ʤʊlɪ'eta / -z
**sp** iulietta[2] / Iulietas[1]

**Julio** *n*
'ʤu:lɪo:
**sp** Iulio[1]

**Julius** *n*
=
**sp** Iulius[16]

**July / ~s** *n*
'ʤu:ləɪ / -z
**sp** Iuly[2] / Iulyes[1]

**jump** *adv / n*
ʤɤmp
**sp** iumpe[2] / iumpe[1]

**jump / ~s / ~eth / ~ing** *v*
ʤɤmp / -s / 'ʤɤmp·əθ / -ɪn, -ɪŋ
**sp** iump[1], iump-[her][1], iumpe[6] / iumpes[3], iumps[2] / iumpeth[1] / iumping[1]

**June** *n*
=
**sp** Iune[2]

**junior** *n*
'ʤu:nɪə.ɪ
**sp** *emend of LLL 3.1.177* Iunios[1]

**Junius** *n*
=
**sp** Iunius[2]

**junket / ~s** *n*
'ʤɤŋkɪts
**sp** iunkets[1]

**Juno / ~'s** *n*
'ʤu:no: / -z
**sp** Iuno[15] / Iuno's[2], Iunos[2]

**Juno-like** *adj*
'ʤu:no:-,ləɪk
**sp** Iuno-like[1]

**Jupiter** *n*
*m* 'ʤu:pɪtə.ɪ, -,tɛ:.ɪ
**sp** Iupiter[36]
**rh** ne'er *Tem 4.1.77*

**Juppiter** *Lat n*

***Jovem accusative***
'ʤo:vem
**sp** Iouem[1]

**jure** *v*
ʤu:.ɪ
**sp** iure[1]

**jurement** *Fr n*
ʒy.ɪ'mɛ̃
**sp** 'iurement'[1]

**jurisdiction** *n*
,ʤʊrɪs'dɪksɪən
**sp** iurisdiction[2]

**juror / ~s** *n*
'ʤu:rə.ɪ / -z
**sp** iuror[1] / iurers[1], iurors[1]

**jury** *n*
'ʤu:rəɪ
**sp** iurie[1], iury[1]
> grand-jury

**just / ~est** *adj*
ʤɤst / 'ʤɤstəst
**sp** iust[78] / iustest[1]

**rh** gust *Tim 3.5.56*; lust, self-trust *Luc 159*; mistrust *VA 1156*; mistrust, thrust *Luc 1514*
> unjust

**just** *adv*
ʤɤst
**sp** iust[27]

**just** *n*
> joust

**just-borne** *adj*
'ʤɤst-ˌbɔːɹn
**sp** iust-borne[1]

**Justeus** *n*
ʤə'stɛːəs
**sp** Iusteus[1]

**justice / ~'s / ~s / ~s'** *n*
'ʤɤstɪs / -ɪz
**sp** iustice[138], iustice [justice's][1], iu-stice[2] / iustices[9] / iustices[1]
> brother-, in-justice

**Justice / ~s** [*title*] *n*
'ʤɤstɪs
**sp** Iustice[27], Iu-stice[1], [Caueleiro]-Iustice[1], [Guest]-Iustice[1]

**justice-like** *adj*
'ʤɤstɪs-ˌləɪk
**sp** iustice-like[1]

**justicer** *n*
'ʤɤstɪsəɹ
**sp** iusticer[1]

**justification** *n*
ˌʤɤstɪfɪ'kɛːsɪən
**sp** iustification[1]

**justif·y / ~ied** *v*
'ʤɤstɪfəɪ / -d
**sp** iustifie[6], iustify't [justify it][1] / iustifi'de[1], iustified[3]
**rh** eye *Per Prol.42*

**justle / ~s / ~d** *v*
'ʤɤsəl / -z / -d
**sp** iustle[2] / iustles[1] / iustled[1]

**justling** *adj*
'ʤɤslɪn, -ɪŋ
**sp** iustling[1]

**justly** *adv*
'ʤɤsləɪ, -stl-
**sp** iustlie[1], iustly[23]

**justness** *n*
'ʤɤsnəs, -stn-
**sp** iustnesse[1]

**jut / ~ting** *v*
ʤɤt / 'ʤɤtɪn, -ɪŋ
**sp** iutt[1] / iut-ting[1]

**jutty** *adj / v*
'ʤɤtəɪ
**sp** iutty[1] / iutty[1]

**juvenal** *n*
'ʤuːvənɑl
**sp** iuuenall[7]

# K

**kam** *adj*
kam
**sp** kamme[1]

**Kate / ~s** *n*
kɛ:t, kat / -s
**sp** Kate[111], Kate-[hall][1] / Kates[2]
**rh** *1* late *TS 5.1.140*; mate *Tem 2.2.48*; **rh** *2* ha't *TS 5.2.179*
**pun** *TS 2.1.189* cate

**Kate / ~d** *v*
'kɛ:tɪd, 'ka-
**sp** Kated[1]
**rh** mated *TS 3.2.244*

**Katherina** *n*
ˌkatə'ri:nə
**sp** Katerina[7], Katherina[6]

**Katherine / ~'s** *n*
*m* 'katrin, -əˌrɪn / 'katrinz
**sp** Katerine[3], Katherine[40], Ka-therine[1] / Katherines[1]

**kecks·y / ~ies** *n*
'keksəɪz
**sp** keksyes[1]

**keech / Keech** *n*
=
**sp** keech[1] / Keech[1]

**keel / ~s** *n*
=
**sp** keele[1] / keeles[1]

**keel** *v*
=
**sp** keele[2]

**keen** *adj*
=
**sp** keen[1], keene[19]
**rh** seen *AY 2.7.178, LC 161, LLL 5.2.256, Per Epil.4*; unseen *S 118.1*

**keen-edged** *adj*
=
**sp** keene-edg'd[1]

**keenness** *n*
=
**sp** keennesse[1]

**keep / ~est / ~s / ~ing / kept / ~est** *v*
= / -st / -s / 'ki:pɪn, -ɪŋ / = / kepst, -tst
**sp** keep[21], keepe[442] / keepest[1], keepst[1], keep'st[5], keept'st[1] / keeps[4], keepes[72] / keeping[15] / kept[93] / keptst[1], kept'st[1]
**rh** asleep *S 154.3*; deep *Per 4.2.141*; sheep *Tem 4.1.63, VA 687*; sleep *LLL 1.1.47, TNK Prol.30*; weep *LLL 4.3.36, RJ 5.3.16, S 9.7* / crept *Luc 840*; except *S 147.6*
> unkept

**Keepdown** [name] *n*
'ki:pdəʊn
**sp** Keepe-downe[1]

**keeper / ~'s / ~s** *n*
'ki:pəɹ / -z
**sp** keeper[17], [tennis-court]-keeper[1] / keepers[5] / keepers[7]
> counsel-, home-, house-, inn-keeper

**keeping** *adj / n*
'ki:pɪn, -ɪŋ
**sp** keeping[1] / keeping[4]
> cave-, counsel-, crow-, promise-, swine-keeping

**keisar** *n*
'kəɪzəɹ
**sp** keiser[1]

**ken** *n / v*
=
**sp** ken[2] / ken[3], kenne[1]

**Kendal** *n*
'kendɑl
**sp** Kendall[2]

**kennel** *n*
=
**sp** kennell[6]
> unkennel

**Kent / ~'s** *n*
=
**sp** Kent[40] / Kents[1]
**rh** sent *R2 5.6.8*

**Kentish** *adj*
=
**sp** Kentish[2]

**Kentish·man / ~men** *n*
=
**sp** Kentishman[1] / Kentishmen[1]

**kept**
> keep

**kerchief** *n*
'kɐ:ɹʧɪf
**sp** kerchiefe[3]
> handkerchief

**kerelybonto** *nonsense word*
ˌkerelɪ'bɒnto:
**sp** kerelybonto[1]

**kern / ~s** *n*
'kɐːɹn / -z
**sp** kerne[2] / kernes[7]

**kernel / ~s** *n*
'kɐːɹnəl / -z
**sp** kernell[4] / kernels[2]

**kersey** *adj / n*
'kɐːɹzəɪ
**sp** kersie[1], kersey[1] / kersey[1]

**Ketly** *n*
'ketləɪ
**sp** Ketly[1]

**kettle** *n*
'ketl
**sp** kettle[1]

**kettle-drum** *n*
'ketl-ˌdrɤm
**sp** kettle drum[1]
> drum

**key / ~s** *n*
kɛː / -z
**sp** key[28] / keies[1], keyes[14]
**rh** survey *S 52.1*

**key-cold** *adj*
'kɛː-ˌkoːld
**sp** key-cold[1]
> cold

**key-hole** *n*
'kɛː-ˌoːl, -ˌhoːl
**sp** key-hole[1]
> hole

**kibe / ~s** *n*
kəɪb / -z
**sp** kibe[1], kybe[1] / kibes[1], kybes[1]

**kick / ~ed** *v*
=
**sp** kicke[3] / kickt[2]
**rh** quick *AW 5.3.300*

**kickie-wickie** *n*
ˌkɪkəɪ-'wɪkəɪ
**sp** kickie wickie[1]

**kickshaws / ~es** *n*
'kɪkʃɔːz / -ɪz
**sp** kickshawes[1] / kicke-chawses[1]

**kid-fox** *n*
=
**sp** kid-foxe[1]
> fox

**kidney** *n*
'kɪdnəɪ
**sp** kidney[1]

**kill / ~est / ~s / ~eth / ~ing / ~ed / ~edest** *v*
= / -st / = / 'kɪl·əθ / -ɪn, -ɪŋ / = / kɪldst
**sp** kil[5], kill[186] / kill'st[1], kilst[2], kil'st[3] / killes[11], kills[4], kils[13] / killeth[2] / killing[14], kil-ling[1] / kild[13], kil'd[24], killd[1], kill'd[81], killed[1] / killd'st[1]
**rh** *1* fill *S 56.7*; fulfil, will *Luc 627, 1636*; ill *LLL 4.1.24, Tim 3.5.37*; ill, spill *Luc 998*; ill, still *Luc 383*; skill *LLL 4.1.29, S 126.8*; still *2H6 5.2.71, Luc 168, MND 5.1.194, TC 3.1.119, VA 618*; still, will *Luc 250*; will *3H6 2.5.122, Per 2.2.35, RJ 3.1.197, TNK Epil.8*; Will *S 135.13*; **rh** *2* sentinel *VA 652* / **rh** *1* filled, spilled *Luc 1803*; fulfilled, hild [held] *Luc 1255*; spilled *VA 1165*; **rh** *2* field, yield *Luc 74*
> a-killing, king-killer, self-killed

**Kildare / ~'s** *n*
kɪl'dɛːɹz
**sp** Kildares[1]

**kill-courtesy** *n*
*m* 'kɪl-kəɹtˌsəɪ
**sp** kill-curtesie[1]
**rh** lie *MND 2.2.83*
> courtesy

**killing** *adj / n*
'kɪlɪn, -ɪŋ
**sp** killing[3] / killing[5]
> dead-, soul-killing

**Killingworth** *n*
'kɪlɪŋˌwɔːɹθ
**sp** Killingworth[2]

**kiln-hole** *n*
'kɪl-ˌoːl, -ˌhoːl
**sp** kill-hole[2]
> lime-kiln

**Kimbolton** *n*
*m* 'kɪməlˌtɤn
**sp** Kymmalton[1]

**kin** *n*
=
**sp** kin[24], kinne[10]
**rh** begin *TC 4.5.92*; sin *KJ 1.1.273, RJ 1.5.58*

**kind / ~er / ~est** *adj*
kəɪnd / 'kəɪnd·əɹ / *m* -əst, kəɪnst, -ndst
**sp** kind[29], kinde[94] / kinder[6] / kindest[3], kind'st[1]
**rh** behind *Ham 3.2.186, 3.4.179, S 143.12*; behind, mind *Luc 1423*; bind *S 134.6*; blind *KL 2.4.49*; confined *S 105.5*; find, mind *LC 186*; mind *H5 3.Chorus.34, MV 1.3.175, S 10.11, 69.11, Tim 2.2.6*
> over-, un-kind

**kind / ~s** *n*
kəɪnd / kəɪnz, -ndz
**sp** kind[30], kinde[112] / kindes[3], kinds[1]
**rh** find *AW 1.3.62, RJ 2.3.7*; mind *AY 4.3.60, MA 4.1.195, TG 3.1.90, VA 1018*; Rosalind *AY 3.2.99* / minds *Luc 1147, 1242*

**kindl·e / ~ing / ~ed** *v*
= / 'kɪndlɪn, -ɪŋ / =
**sp** kindle[8] / kindling[2] / kindled[6]
> enkindle; fiery-, wrath-kindled

**kindless** *adj*
'kəɪnləs, -ndl-
**sp** kindles[1]

**kindly** *adj*
'kəɪnləɪ, -ndl-
**sp** kindely[2], kindly[4]

**kindl·y / ~ier** *adv*
'kəɪnləɪ, -ndl- / -əɹ
**sp** kindely[7], kindly[21], kind-ly[1] / kindlier[1]

**kindness / ~es** *n*
'kəɪnnəs, -ndn- / -ɪz
**sp** kindenesse[1], kindnes[2], kindnesse[46] / kindnesses[4]
**rh** blindness *CE 3.2.6, S 152.9, TG 4.2.44*

**kindred / ~'s** *n*
'kɪnrəd, = / -z
**sp** kindred[24], kindred-[action][1], kinred[1] / kindreds[5]

**kine** *n*
kəɪn
**sp** kine[1]
> milch-kine

**king / ~'s / ~s / ~s'** *n*
=
**sp** king[1410], [castalion]-king-[vrinall][1], [sainted]-king[1], kings [king is][2], king's [king is][3], *emend of R2 1.3.86, TN 3.1.8* kings[2], *abbr* K[ing][8] / kings[140] / kings[112], [fellow]-kings[1] / kings[1]
**rh** bring *Per 2.Chorus.1*; burying *Per 3.2.71*; changeling *MND 2.1.22*; flattering *PP 20.40*; managing *H5 Epil.9*; misgoverning *Luc 652*; sing *2H4 5.5.111, R2 2.1.262, 3.3.182, WT 4.3.8*; spring *Per 1.1.14, R2 5.2.45, S 63.6*; spring, thing *Luc 606*; sting, thing *Luc 37*; thing *Ham 2.2.603, Luc 601, 1002, Per 3.Chorus.37, R2 5.3.79*; wing *PT 11, R3 4.3.55* / brings *S 29.14*; springs *R2 1.3.215*; things *Luc 939, 1812, S 115.6, VA 995*; wings *R3 5.2.24*
> fellow-king

**king / ~ed** *v*
=
**sp** king'd[2]
> unking

**king-becoming** *adj*
'kɪŋ-bɪˌkʏmɪn, -ɪŋ
**sp** king-becoming[1]
> become

**king-cardinal** *n*
'kɪŋ-ˌkɑːɹdɪnɑl
**sp** king-cardinall[1]
> cardinal

**kingdom / ~'s / ~s** *n*
=
**sp** kingdome[86], kingdomes[22] / kingdomes[10] / kingdoms[2]

**kingdomed** *adj*
=
**sp** kingdom'd[1]

**king-killer** *n*
'kɪŋ-ˌkɪləɹ
**sp** king-killer[1]
> king

**kingly** *adj*
'kɪŋləɪ
**sp** kingly[24], kinglye[1]

**kins·man / ~man's / ~men** *n*
=
**sp** kinsman[44], kins-man[1] / kinsmans[3] / kinsmen[18]

**kinswoman** *n*
=
**sp** kinswoman[2], kinswo-man[1]
> woman

**kirtle / ~s** *n*
'kɐːɹtl / -z
**sp** kirtle[1] / kirtles[1]
**rh** myrtle *PP 19.11*
> half-kirtle

**kiss / ~es** *n*
=
**sp** kisse[59] / kisses[21]
**rh** *1* bliss *Luc 387*; miss *VA 54*; this *Oth 5.2.355, RJ 1.5.96, 100, VA 207, 723*; **rh** *2* his *LLL 2.1.235, TC 4.5.49*; is Luc *387, MV 3.2.138, VA 536*

**kiss / ~es / ~ing / ~ed** *v*
= / = / 'kɪsɪn, -ɪŋ / =
**sp** kis[2], kisse[124] / kisses[10] / kissing[9] / kiss'd[6], kist[20]
**rh** *1* amiss, bliss, iwis, this *MV 2.9.66*; bliss *MND 3.2.143*; this *AW 4.3.223, Per 1.2.79, S 128.14*; kiss you hiss you *VA 1082*; **rh** *2* is *MV 2.9.66* / hisses *VA 18* / missing *VA 606* / whist *Tem 1.2.377*
> unkiss

**kissing** *adj / n*
'kɪsɪn, -ɪŋ
**sp** kissing[3] / kissing[8], kis-sing[1]
> common-, ear-, hail-, heaven-kissing

**kitchen** *adj*
=
**sp** kitchen[2], kitchin[3], kitchin-[trulles][1]

**kitchen / ~s** *n*
=
**sp** kit-chens[1], kitchins[1]
> privy-kitchen

**kitchen / ~ed** *v*
=
**sp** kitchin'd[1]

**kite / ~s** *n*
kəɪt / -s
**sp** kite[4], kyte[3] / kites[6], kytes[3]
> hell-kite

**kitten** *n*
=
**sp** kitten[1]

**kitten / ~ed** *v*
=
**sp** kitten'd[1]

**knack / ~s** *n*
=, knak / -s
**sp** knacke[2] / knackes[2]

**knap / ~ped** *v*
=, knapt
**sp** knapt[2]

**knav·e / ~'s / ~s / ~s'** *n*
nɛːv, kn- / -z
**sp** knaue[162], [iealious-rascally]-knaue[1], [rascally-yea-forsooth]-knaue[1], [wittolly]-knaue[1] / knaues[8] / knaues[41] / knaues[1]
**rh** grave *Ham 3.4.216*
**pun** *2H4 2.4.250* nave

**knaver·y / ~ies** *n*
*m* 'nɛːvrəɪ, - vər-, -vəˌrəɪ, 'kn- / -z

**sp** knauerie[7], kna-uerie[1], knauery[7], knaue-ry[1], knau'ry[1] / knaueries[5]
**rh** bravery *TS 4.3.58*

**knavish** *adj*
'nɛ:vɪʃ, 'kn-
**sp** knauish[7]

**knead / ~ing** *v*
=, kni:d / 'ni:dɪn, -ɪŋ, 'kn-
**sp** knede[1] / kneading[1]

**kneaded** *adj*
=, 'kni:dɪd
**sp** kneaded[1]

**kneading** *n*
'ni:dɪn, -ɪŋ, 'kn-
**sp** kneading[1]

**knee / ~s** *n*
=, kni: / =, kni:z
**sp** knee[62] / knees[50]
**rh** *1* be *R2 5.3.96*; ee [eye] *TNK 3.4.19*; he, thee *LLL 5.2.544*; me *1H6 4.7.5, R2 5.3.131*; thee *KJ 1.1.82, R3 1.2.178*; tree *Oth 4.3.40*; **rh** *2* charactery, embroidery *MW 5.5.72*; everlastingly *KJ 5.7.103*; mutiny *1H6 5.1.61* / fees *TC 3.3.48*; please *Per 1.2.47*; sees *R2 5.3.92*

**knee** *v*
=, kni:
**sp** knee[1]

**knee-crooking** *adj*
'ni:-ˌkrʊkɪn, -ɪŋ, 'kn-
**sp** knee-crooking[1]

**knee-deep** *adj*
=, 'kni:-ˌdi:p
**sp** knee-deepe[1]
> deep

**kneel / ~s / ~ing / ~ed** *v*
=, kni:l / -z / 'ni:lɪn, -ɪŋ, 'kn- / =, kni:ld
**sp** kneel[3], kneele[62] / kneeles[8], kneels[1] / kneeling[3] / kneel'd[10]
**rh** feels *VA 350*

**kneeling** *adj / n*
'ni:lɪn, -ɪŋ, 'kn-
**sp** kneeling[1] / kneeling[1]

**knell** *n*
=, knel
**sp** knell[11]
**rh** *1* bell *MV 3.2.70, Tem 1.2.403*; bell, tell *Luc 1495*; hell *Mac 2.1.63*; **rh** *2* deal *PP 17.18*

**knew**
> know

**knife / ~'s / knives** *n*
nəɪf, kn- / -s / nəɪvz, kn-
**sp** knife[47], knife's [knife is][1] / kniues[2] / kniues[9]
**rh** life *LLL 2.1.125, Luc 1184, Per 4. Chorus.14, S 63.10, 74.11, 100.14, TN 2.5.104*; life, wife *Luc 1047*; wife *Luc 1840* / lives [*n*] *Tim 1.2.43*
> paring-, pen-knife

**knight / ~'s / ~s** *n*
nəɪt, kn- / -s
**sp** knight[120], [bully]-knight[1], knights [knight is][1] / knights[2] / knights[29]
**rh** delight Per 4.4.11; fight *1H6 4.7.44, TC 4.5.88*; fight, light, might, night *MW 2.1.13*; fight, spite *PP 15.6*; hight *LLL 1.1.170*; light *Per 2.5.16*; might *LLL 5.2.563, MND 2.2.150*; night *MA 5.3.13, RJ 3.2.142*; right *2H4 5.3.74, 3H6 2.2.61, KL 3.2.88, LLL 5.2.563*; spite *MND 5.1.269*; wight *LLL 1.1.176* / wights *S 106.4*
> trencher-knight

**knight / ~ed** *v*
nəɪt, kn- / 'nəɪtɪd, kn-
**sp** knight[1] / knighted[5]

**knight-errant** *n*
ˌnəɪt-'erənt, ˌkn-
**sp** [shee]-knight-arrant[1]

**knighthood / ~s** *n*
'nəɪtʊd, -hʊd, 'kn- / -z
**sp** knighthood[6], knight-hood[4] / knighthoods[1], knight-hoods[1]

**knightly** *adv*
'nəɪtləɪ, 'kn-
**sp** knightly[5]

**knit** *n*
=, knɪt
**sp** knit[1]

**knit / ~s / ~teth** *v*
=, knɪt / -s / =, 'knɪtəθ
**sp** knit[32] / knits[4] / knitteth[1]
**rh** it *MND 2.2.53*; my wit *S 26.2*
> strong-, un-, well-knit

**knitter / ~s** *n*
'nɪtəɹz, kn-
**sp** knitters[1]

**knob / ~s** *n*
=, knɒbz
**sp** knobs[1]

**knock / ~s** *n*
=, knɒk / -s
**sp** knock[3], knocke[18], knocks[2]

**knock / ~s / ~ing / ~ed** *v*
=, knɒk, *Evans MW 3.1.13ff* nɒg, knɒg / -s / 'nɒkɪn, -ɪŋ, 'kn- / =, knɒkt
**sp** knock[24], knocke[40], *Evans* knog[3] / knockes[11], knocks[8] / knocking[3] / knock'd[4], knockt[6]
**rh** locks *Mac 4.1.46*

**knocking** *n*
'nɒkɪn, -ɪŋ, 'kn-
**sp** knocking[11]

**knoll / ~ing / ~ed** *v*
no:l, kn- / 'no:lɪn, -ɪŋ, 'kn- / no:ld, kn-
**sp** knolling[1] / knoll'd[2], knowld[1]

**knot / ~s** *n*
=, knɒt / -s
**sp** knot[24], [Gordian]-knot[1], [virgin]-knot[1], knotte[1] / knots[8]

**knot** *v*
=, knɒt
**sp** knot[1]

**knot-grass** *n*
ˈnɒt-ˌgras, ˈkn-
**sp** knot-grasse[1]
> grass

**knot-pated** *adj*
ˈnɒt-ˌpɛ:tɪd, ˈkn-
**sp** not-pated[1]
> pate

**knotted** *adj*
=, ˈknɒtɪd
**sp** knotted[2]

**knotty** *adj*
ˈnɒtəɪ, ˈkn-
**sp** knottie[1], knotty[2]

**knotty-pated** *adj*
ˈnɒtəɪ-ˌpɛ:tɪd, ˈkn-
**sp** knotty-pated[1]

**know / ~est / ~s / ~ing / ~n / knew / ~est / known** *v*
no:, kno: / ˈno:əst, ˈkn- / no:z, kn- / ˈno:ɪn, -ɪŋ, ˈkn- / nju:, kn- / -st / no:n, kn-
**sp** kno[3], know[1614], ˈknow[1], knowe[8], know't [know it][18] / knowest[13], knowst[12], know'st[67] / knowes[195], knows[6] / knowing[33], know-ing[1] / knew[149], knewe[3] / knewest[1], knew'st[7] / known[16], knowne[160]
**rh** *1* bestow *AW 2.1.199, LLL 5.2.124*; blow *Mac 1.3.16, TC 4.5.276*; bow [weapon] *LLL 4.1.109, Tem 4.1.87*; flow *AW 5.3.322*; foe *KJ 5.1.78, PP 20.55*; foe, show *Luc 473*; foe, woe Luc *1607*; go *MM 3.2.251, S 130.9, WT 4.4.296*; go, so *CE 4.3.80*; Gremio, Hortensio *TS 1.2.232*; grow *R2 5.3.104, RJ 1.1.155*; grow, so *LLL 2.1.53*; know *LLL 1.1.55, 56*; low *Cym 5.4.95, R2 3.3.194, TN 2.3.42*; no *LLL 5.2.485*; no, so *LLL 1.1.68*; owe *CE 3.2.41, LLL 1.2.99, Mac 5.4.17, TN 2.4.103*; saddle-bow *VA 16*; show *AY 3.2.134, CE 3.1.11, Cym 5.1.29, H8 Prol.17, LLL 5.2.319, Mac 1.7.82, MM 5.1.536, MND 5.1.117, 128, PP 18.40, R2 1.3.249, 5.3.48, S 53.12, 77.7*; slow *S 51.8*; so *CE 3.2.54, Ham 3.2.179, LLL 1.1.60, 4.3.50, 127, 5.2.490, Luc 1058, MND 1.1.229, 3.2.163, 174, 189, Oth 4.3.101, R2 3.4.91, S 13.13, 140.8, Tit 5.3.138, TN 3.4.370, VA 1109*; woe *LC 62, Luc 1312, S 50.7*; know it owe it *AW 4.3.224, VA 409*; know me owe me *VA 525*; know not show not *CE 3.2.29*; know their love show their love *TG 1.2.32*; **rh** *2* who *TN 2.5.98*; woo *MND 5.1.135* / goest, owest, showest, throwest, trowest *KL 1.4.118* / blows *AC 3.11.73, LLL 5.2.290, Luc 833*; foes *S 139.9*; noes *LLL 5.2.411*; o'erflows Luc *1120*; shows *AW 2.1.149* / growing *S 87.9* / blue *Luc 409*; drew *VA 543*; drew, flew *LC 58*; sue *TC 1.2.290* / **rh** *1* own *Luc 239*; own, shown *MND 3.2.458*; shown *LLL 1.2.95*; **rh** *2* town *H8 Prol.23*
> acknow; un-, well-known

**knower** *n*
ˈno:əɹ, ˈkn-
**sp** knower[1], know-er[1]

**knowing** *adj*
ˈno:ɪn, -ɪŋ, ˈkn-
**sp** knowing[3]

**knowing / ~s** *n*
ˈno:ɪn, -ɪŋ, ˈkn- / -z
**sp** knowing[4] / knowings[1]
> fore-ˌ small-, un-knowing

**knowingly** *adv*
ˈno:ɪnləɪ, -ɪŋ-, ˈkn-
**sp** knowingly[2]

**knowledge** *n*
ˈno:lɪʤ, ˈkn-
**sp** knowledge[67], know-ledge[7]

**known** *adj*
no:n, kn-
**sp** known[1], knowne[6]

**known** *v*
> know

**L** [letter] *n*
=
**sp** ell[2]

**la** *interj*
=
**sp** la[15], [indeede]-la[2], [truely]-la[1], la-[you][1], *Fluellen* law[2], [sooth]-law[1]

**la** [music] *n*
=
**sp** la[2], [e]la[1]

**la** *Fr*
> le

**là** *Fr adv*
la
**sp** la[2]

**Laban / ~'s** *n*
'lɛ:bən / -z
**sp** Laban[1] / Labans[1]

**label** *n*
'lɛ:bəl
**sp** labell[2]

**label / ~led** *v*
'lɛ:bəld
**sp** labell'd[1]

**Labienus** *n*
ˌlabɪ'ɛ:nəs
**sp** Labienus[1]

**Labio** *n*
'labɪo:
**sp** Labio[1]

**labour / ~'s / ~s** *n*
'lɛ:bəɹ / -z
**sp** labor[7], labour[62] / labors[1], labours[1] / labors[1], labours[8]
**rh** *1* father Per 1.1.67; **rh** *2* favour *R2 5.6.41*
> joint-labourer, overlaboured, well-labouring

**labour / ~est / ~s / ~ing / ~ed** *v*
'lɛ:bəɹ / -st / -z / -ɪn, -ɪŋ / *m* -d, -ɪd
**sp** labor[3], labour[14] / labourst[1] / labours[2] / labouring[5] / labour'd[11], la-bour'd[1], laboured[4]

**laboured** *adj*
*m* 'lɛ:bəɹd
**sp** labour'd[1]

**labourer / ~s** *n*
'lɛ:brəɹ, -bər- / -z
**sp** labourer[1], labourers[1]

**labouring** *adj / n*
'lɛ:brɪn, -ɪŋ, -bər-
**sp** laboring[2], labouring[4], la-bouring[1] / labouring[2]

**laboursome** *adj*
*m* 'lɛ:bəɹˌsɤm
**sp** laboursome[1]

**labras,** *anglicized plural of Lat* **labra** *n*
*Pistol MW 1.1.151* 'labras
**sp** labras[1]

**labyrinth** *n*
*m* 'labrɪnθ, -bɪˌr-
**sp** labyrinth[2]

**lace / ~s** *n*
lɛ:s / -ɪz
**sp** lace[4] / laces[1]
> tawdry-, un-lace

**lace / ~d** *v*
lɛ:s / lɛ:st
**sp** lace[1] / lac'd[4]

**laced** *adj*
lɛ:st
**sp** lac'd-[mutton][2]

**Lacedemon** *n*
lasɪ'di:mən
**sp** Lacedemon[2]

**lack** *n*
=
**sp** lack[3], lacke[18]

**lack / ~est / ~s / ~ing / ~ed** *v*
= / lakst / = / 'lakɪn, -ɪŋ / =
**sp** lack[6], lacke[63] / lackst[1], lack'st[2] / lackes[5], lacks[9], lack's[1] / lacking[7] / lack'd[9], lackt[4], lack't[1]
**rh** back *AC 4.14.59, VA 299*; black *LLL 4.3.249*, Oth *1.3.286, S 127.11, 132.14*

**lackbeard** *n*
'lak-ˌbɛ:ɹd, -ˌbɐ:ɹd
**sp** lacke-beard[1]
> beard

**lack-brain** *n*
'lak-ˌbrɛ:n
**sp** lacke-braine[1]
> brain

**lackey** *adj*
'lakəɪ
**sp** lackey[1]

**lackey / ~s** *n*
'lakəɪ / -z
**sp** lackey[2], lackie[2], lacky[2], lacquay[1], lacquey[2] / lackeyes[1], lackies[1], lacqueyes[1], lacquies[1]
> Starve-lackey

**lack-linen** *adj*
=
**sp** lacke-linnen-[mate][1]

**lack-love** *n*
*m* ˌlak-'lɤv
**sp** lacke-loue[1]
> love

**lack-lustre** *adj*
*m* ˌlak-'lɤstəɹ
**sp** lacke-lustre[1]
> lustre

**Lac·y / ~ies** [name] *n*
'lɛ:səɪz
**sp** Lacies[1]

**lad / ~s** *n*
=
**sp** lad[23] / laddes[2], lads[19]
**rh** dad *TN 4.2.128*; mad, sad *MND 3.2.440*

**ladder / ~s** *n*
'ladəɹ / -z
**sp** ladder[15], [corded]-ladder[2] / ladders[3]

**lade** *v*
lɛ:d
**sp** lade[1]

**lading** *n*
'lɛ:dɪn, -ɪŋ
**sp** lading[2]

**laden** *adj*
'lɛ:dən
**sp** laden[3]

**lady** *adj*
'lɛ:dəɪ
**sp** lady[1]
> by Our Lady

**lad·y / ~'s / ~ies / ~ies'** *n*
'lɛ:dəɪ / -z
**sp** ladie[94], [sweet]-ladie[1], la-die[2], ladies [lady is][1], ladie's [lady is][1], lady[530], [wedded]-lady[1], la-dy[2], ladyes [lady is][1], lady's [lady is][1] / ladies[50] ladyes[4] / ladies[113], la-dies[2], ladyes[4] / ladies[10] ladyes[1]
**rh** be *LLL 2.1.193, 4.1.132*

**ladybird** *n*
'lɛ:dəɪˌbɐ:ɹd
**sp** ladi-bird[1]

**ladyship / ~'s / ~s** *n*
'lɛ:dəɪʃɪp / -s
**sp** ladie-ship[1], ladiship[21], ladyship[14], la-dyship[1], lady-ship[1] / ladiships[1], ladyships[1] / ladiships[5]

**lady-smock / ~s** *n*
'lɛ:dəɪ-ˌsmɒks
**sp** ladie-smockes[1]

**Laertes** *n*
lɛ:'ɐ:ɹti:z
**sp** Laertes[36], *abbr in s.d.* Laer[1]

**Lafew** *n*
la'fju:
**sp** Lafew[15]

**lag** *adj / v*
=
**sp** lag[2], lagge[1], lagge-[end][1] / lagge[1]

**lagging** *adj*
'lagɪn, -ɪŋ
**sp** lagging[1]

**laid, lain**
> lay

**laisser / laissez** *Fr v*
lɛ'sez
**sp** laisse[3]

**lake / ~s** *n*
lɛ:k / -s
**sp** lake[5] / lakes[1]

**lakin**
> by Our Lady

**lamb / ~s** *n*
=
**sp** lamb[3], lambe[31] / lambes[7], lambs[5]
> she-lamb

**Lambert / ~'s** *n*
'lambəɹts
**sp** Lamberts[1]

**lambkin / ~s** *n*
=
**sp** lamb-kinne[1] / lambekins[1]

**lambskin / ~s** *n*
=
**sp** lamb-skins[1]
> skin

**lam-damn** *v*
*m* ˌlam-'dam
**sp** *emend of WT 2.1.143* land-damne
> damn

**lame** *adj*
lɛ:m
**sp** lame[12]
**rh** tame *PP 12.6*

**lame / ~s / ~ing / ~ed** *v*
lɛ:m / -z / 'lɛ:mɪn, -ɪŋ / lɛ:md
**sp** lame[1] / lames[1] / laming[1] / lam'd[2]

**lamely** *adv*
'lɛ:mləɪ
**sp** lamely[3], lame-ly[1]

**lameness** *n*
'lɛ:mnəs
**sp** lamenesse[1]

**lament** *n*
lə'ment
**sp** lament[1]
> dire-lamenting

**lament / ~est / ~s / ~ing / ~ed** *v*
lə'ment / -st, lə'menst / -s / -ɪn, -ɪŋ / -ɪd
**sp** lament[23] / lament'st[1] / laments[3] / lamenting[4] / lamented[6]

**rh** accident *Ham 3.2.208*; content, lent *Luc 1500*; incontinent *R2 5.6.47*; merriment *RJ 4.5.82*

**lamentable** *adj*
*m* 'lamən,tabl
**sp** lamentable[13], la-mentable[1], lamenta-ble[1]

**lamentably** *adv*
*m* 'lamən,tabləɪ
**sp** lamentably[2]

**lamentation / ~s** *n*
*m* ,lamən'tɛːsɪən, -sɪ,ɒn / -sɪənz
**sp** lamentation[9], *emend of Cor 4.6.34* lamention[1] / lamentations[1]
**rh** abominations, invocations *Luc 1829*

**lamenting** *adj*
lə'mentɪn, -ɪŋ
**sp** lamenting[3]

**lamenting / ~s** *n*
lə'mentɪnz, -ɪŋz
**sp** lamentings[1]

**Lammas Eve** *n*
'laməs 'iːv
**sp** Lammas Eue[1], La-mas Eue[1]
> Eve

**Lammastide** *n*
'laməs,təɪd
**sp** Lammas tide[1]
> tide

**Lamord** *n*
la'mɔːɹ
**sp** *emend of Ham 4.7.91* Lamound[1]

**lamp / ~s** *n*
=
**sp** lampe[9] / lampes[3], lamps[1]
**rh** damp *AW 2.1.164*

**lampas** *n*
'lampəs
**sp** lampasse[1]

**Lamprius** *n*
'lamprɪəs
**sp** Lamprius[1]

**Lancaster** *n*
'laŋkastəɹ
**sp** Lancaster[74]

**lance / ~'s / ~s** *n*
lans, lɔːns / -ɪz
**sp** lance[7], launce[5] / lances[1] / lances[2], launces[7]
**rh** dance *VA 103*

**lance / ~th** *v*
lansəθ, lɔːns-
**sp** lanceth[1]

**lanch / ~ed** *v*
lanʃt
**sp** lanch'd[1]

**land** *adj*
=
**sp** land[4]
> a-land, Holy Land

**land / ~'s / ~s** *n*
=
**sp** land[191], [green]-land[1], land's [land is][1] / lands[4] / lands[53]
**rh** command *Tem 4.1.130*; hand *2H4 3.1.104, KJ 1.1.164, 4.3.159, LLL 5.2.309, Mac 1.3.32, R2 5.5.110, 5.6.36, 49*; hand, stand *Luc 439*; stand *Cym 2.1.64, KL 1.4.139* [Q], *S 44.7*; understand *R2 5.3.122* / counter-mands *CE 4.2.38*; hands *R2 2.1.210*

**land / ~ing / ~ed** *v*
= / 'landɪn, -ɪŋ / =
**sp** land[3] / landing[1] / landed[14]
**rh** sands *Luc 336*

**land-damn** *v*
*m* ,lan-'dam
**sp** land-damne[1]
> damn

**landed** *adj*
=
**sp** landed[1]

**land-fish** *n*
=
**sp** land-fish[1]
> fish

**landless** *adj*
=
**sp** landlesse[2]

**landlord** *n*
'landlɔːɹd
**sp** landlord[2]

**landman / ~men** *n*
=
**sp** land·men[1]

**land-service** *n*
'land-,sɐːɹvɪs
**sp** land-seruice[2], land seruice[1]
> service

**lane / ~'s / ~s** *n*
lɛːn / -z
**sp** lane[9], [Datchet]-lane[1] / lanes[2] / lanes[2]
**rh** bane *Cym 5.3.57*
> Long-lane

**langage** *Fr n*
lɑ̃'gaːʒ
**sp** langage[1], language[1]

**Langley** *n*
'laŋləɪ
**sp** Langley[3]

**Langton** *n*
=
**sp** Langton[1]

**language / ~s** *n*
'laŋgwɪʤ, -gɪʤ / -ɪz
**sp** language[37] / languages[4]

**languageless** *adj*
'laŋgwɪʤ,les, -gɪʤ-
**sp** languagelesse[1]

**langue / ~s** *Fr n*
lɑ̃ːg
**sp** langues[1]

**languish** *n*
=
**sp** languish[2]
**rh** anguish *RJ 1.2.48*

**languish / ~s / ~ed** *v*
=
**sp** languish[4] / languishes[2] / languish'd[1]
**rh** punish *Per 1.2.32*

**languishing** *adj*
'laŋgwɪʃɪn, -ɪŋ
**sp** languishing[1]

**languishing / ~s** *n*
'laŋgwɪʃɪnz, -ɪŋz
**sp** languishings[1]

**languishment** *n*
*m* 'laŋgwɪʃˌment
**sp** languishment[1]
**rh** instrument *Luc 1141*; ravishment *Luc 1130*

**languor** *n*
'laŋgəɹ
**sp** languor[1]

**lank** *adj*
=
**sp** lanke[2]

**lank / ~ed** *v*
=
**sp** lank'd[1]

**lank-lean** *adj*
=
**sp** lanke-leane[1]

**lantern, lanthorn / ~s** *n*
'lantəɹn, -tɔ:ɹn / -z
**sp** lanterne[2], lanthorne[13], lan-thorne[1] / lanthornes[1]

**lap / ~s** *n*
=
**sp** lap[11], lappe[6] / laps[2]

**lap / ~s / ~ped** *v*
=
**sp** lap[3] / laps[2] / lapt[2]

**lapis** *Lat n*
'lapi:s
**sp** lapis[3]

**Lapland** *n*
=
**sp** Lapland[1]

**lapse** *n*
=
**sp** lapse[1]

**lapse / ~d** *v*
= / *m* 'lapsɪd, lapst
**sp** lapse[1] / lapsed[1], laps't[1]

**lapsing** *n*
'lapsɪn, -ɪŋ
**sp** lapsing[1]

**lapwing** *n*
=
**sp** lapwing[4]

**lard / ~s / ~ing / ~ed** *v*
lɑ:ɹdz / 'lɑ:ɹdɪn, -ɪŋ / 'lɑ:ɹdɪd
**sp** lards[2] / larding[1] / larded[4]

**larder** *n*
'lɑ:ɹdəɹ
**sp** larder[1]

**large / ~r / ~st** *adj*
lɑ:ɹʤ / 'lɑ:ɹʤ·əɹ / -əst
**sp** large[46] / larger[5] / largest[1]

**large** *n*
lɑ:ɹʤ
**sp** large[19]

**large-handed** *adj*
*m* ˌlɑ:ɹʤ-'andɪd, -'ha-
**sp** large-handed[1]

**largely** *adv*
'lɑ:ɹʤləɪ
**sp** largely[3]

**largeness** *n*
'lɑ:ɹʤnəs
**sp** largenesse[1]

**largesse** *n*
*m* 'lɑ:ɹʤes
**sp** largesse[4]

**lark / ~s** *n*
lɑ:ɹk / -s
**sp** larke[23] / larkes[2], larks[1]
**rh** mark *MND 3.1.123, 4.1.93, PP 14.18*

**larron** *Fr n*
la'rɔ̃
**sp** la-roone[1]

**Lartius** *n*
'lɑ:ɹsɪəs
**sp** Lartius[12], Latius[2]

**larum**
> alarum

**lascivious** *adj*
=
**sp** lasciuious[13]

**lash** *n*
=
**sp** lash[2]

**lash / ~ed** *v*
=
**sp** lash[3] / lasht[1]

**lass / ~es** *n*
=
**sp** lasse[7] / lasses[1]
**rh** pass *AY 5.3.15*

**lasslorn** *adj*
'laslɔ:ɹn
**sp** lasse-lorne[1]

**last** *adj / adv / n*
last
**sp** last[112] / last[46] / last[87]
**rh** *1* blast *Per Epil.6*; fast *VA 576*; past *R2 2.1.13*; **rh** *2* haste *RJ 3.1.195*; taste *LC 168, S 90.9*
> ever-, still-lasting

**last / ~s / ~ed** *v*
last / =
**sp** last[19] / lasts[5] / lasted[2]

**rh** *1* fast *Luc 894*; **rh** *2* taste *Luc 894, VA 447*

**lasting** *adj*
'lastɪn, -ɪŋ
**sp** lasting[12]

**lastly** *adv*
'lastləɪ
**sp** lastlie[1], lastly[7]

**latch / ~es** *n*
=
**sp** latch[1] / latches[1]
**rh** catch *Luc 358*

**latch / ~ed** *v*
=
**sp** latch[1] / lacht[1], latch'd[1]
**rh** catch *S 113.6*

**late / ~er / ~est** *adj*
lɛ:t / 'lɛ:t·əɹ / -əst
**sp** late[63] / later[2] / latest[13]
**rh** celebrate *Tem 4.1.133*; gait *VA 531*; gate *LLL 1.1.108*

**late** *adv / n*
lɛ:t
**sp** late[83] / late[42]
**rh** *adv* compassionate *R2 1.3.175*; estate *Per 4.4.15, Tim 5.1.40*; fate *H8 2.3.84*; gate *CE 3.1.49*; gate, pate *CE 2.2.229*; hate *RJ 1.5.139*; Kate *TS 5.1.141*; state *Ham 3.2.172, LLL 5.2.361, R2 3.2.71*

**late / ~d** *v*
'lɛ:tɪd
**sp** lated[1]

**lated** *adj*
'lɛ:tɪd
**sp** lated[1]

**late-disturbed** *adj*
*m* 'lɛ:t-dɪs,tɐ:ɹbɪd
**sp** late-disturbed[1]
> disturbed

**lately** *adv*
'lɛ:tləɪ
**sp** latelie[1], lately[30]

**latest** *adv / n*
'lɛ:təst
**sp** latest[1] / latest[1]

**late-walking** *adj*
'lɛ:t-,wɔ:kɪn, -ɪŋ
**sp** late-walking[1]
> walk

**lath** *n*
laθ
**sp** lath[5]
**rh** wrath *TN 4.2.126*

**Latin** *adj / n*
=
**sp** Latine[3] / Latin[1], Latine[6], La-tine[1], Latten[2]

**latter** *adj*
'latəɹ
**sp** latter[17]

**lattice** *n*
=
**sp** lattice[1], lettice[2]

**laud** *n / v*
=
**sp** laud[2] / laud[2]
**rh** *n* bawd *Luc 622*; bawd, thawed *Luc 887*

**laudable** *adj*
=
**sp** laudable[2]

**laudis** *Lat*
> laus

**laugh / ~est / ~s / ~ing / ~ed** *v*
laf / -st / -s / 'lafɪn, -ɪŋ / laft
**sp** laugh[81], laughe[1], loffe[1] / laughest[1], laugh'st[1] / laughes[6], laughs[1] / laughing[10] / laugh'd[12], laughed[1], laught[17], laugh't[1]
**rh** *1* staff *CE 3.1.50*; **rh** *2* cough *MND 2.1.55*

**laughable** *adj*
'lafəbəl
**sp** laughable[1]

**laughing** *n*
'lafɪn, -ɪŋ
**sp** laughing[4]

**laughing-stock / ~s** *n*
'lafɪn-,stɒks, -ɪŋ-
**sp** laughing-stocks[1]

**laughter** *n*
'laftəɹ
**sp** laughter[30]
**rh** hereafter *TN 2.3.46*

**Launce** *n*
lɔ:ns, lɑ:ns
**sp** Launce[11]

**Launcelot** *n*
'lɔ:nslət, 'lɑ:n-, -səl-
**sp** Lancelet[12], Lance-let[1], Launcelet[15]

**launch / ~ed** *v*
lɔ:nʃ, lɑ:nʃ / -t
**sp** launch[1] / launch'd[1]

**laund** *n*
lɔ:nd
**sp** laund[1]

**laundress** *n*
'lɔ:ndrəs, 'lɑ:n-
**sp** landresse[2]

**laundry** *n*
'lɔ:ndrəɪ, 'lɑ:n-
**sp** laundry[1]

**Laura** *n*
=
**sp** Laura[1]

**laurel** *adj*
=
**sp** lawrell[3]

**laurel / ~s** *n*
=
**sp** lawrels[1]

**Laurence**
> Lawrence

**lau·s / ~dis** *Lat n*
lɔ:s / 'lɔ:dis
**sp** laus[1] / laudis[1]

**Lavatch** *n*
la'vatʃ
**sp** Lauatch[1]

**lave** *v*
lɛ:v
**sp** laue[3]

**lavender** *n*
'lavəndəɹ
**sp** lauender[1]

**laver / lavée** *Fr v*
la've
**sp** lauee[1], leuye[1]

**Lavinia / ~'s** *n*
=
**sp** Lauinia[50] / Lauinia's[3]

**lavish** *adj*
=
**sp** lauish[5]

**lavishly** *adv*
*m* 'lavɪʃ,ləɪ
**sp** lauishly[1]

**lavolt,** *anglicized* **lavolta / ~s** *n*
lə'vɒlt / -əz
**sp** lauolt[1] / lauolta's[1]

**law / ~'s / ~s** *n*
=
**sp** law[202], [all-building]-law[1] / lawes[3] / lawes[36], laws[1]
**rh** awe *Per Prol.35, R3 5.3.312*; daw *1H6 2.4.17*; flaw *LLL 5.2.414*; saw *Cym 5.4.38*; straw *Luc 1022* / cause *S 49.13*; claws, pause *Luc 544*; pause *R2 2.3.168*
> brother-, daughter-, father-, son-in-, out-law, unlawful

**law-breaker** *n*
'lɔ:-,brɛ:kəɹ
**sp** law-breaker[1]

**law-day / ~s** *n*
'lɔ:-,dɛ:z
**sp** law-dayes[1]
> day

**lawful** *adj*
=
**sp** lawful[3], lawfull[55]

**lawfully** *adv*
*m* 'lɔ:fʊ,ləɪ
**sp** lawful-lie[1], lawfully[1]

**lawless** *adj*
=
**sp** lawlesse[6]

**lawlessly** *adv*
*m* 'lɔ:ləs,ləɪ
**sp** lawlesly[1]
**rh** thee *TG 5.3.14*

**lawn / ~s** *n*
=
**sp** lawne[2] / lawnes[1]

**Lawrence / ~'s** *n*
= / 'lɒrəns
**sp** Laurence[2], Lawrence[3] / Lawrence[6]

**lawyer / ~'s / ~s ~s'** *n*
'lɔ:jəɹ / -z
**sp** lawyer[4] / lawyers[1] / lawiers[2], lawyers[3] / lawyers[1]

**lay** *adj*
lɛ:
**sp** lay[1], lay-[thoughts][1]

**lay / ~s** *n*
lɛ: / lɛ:z
**sp** lay[3] / layes[1]
**rh** obey *PT 1* / says *Per 5.Chorus.4*

**lay / ~est / ~s / ~ing / lay / laid / laidest** *v*
lɛ: / -st / -z / 'lɛ:ɪn, -ɪŋ / lɛ: / -d / -dst
**sp** laie[1], lay [*non-past*][228], lay't [lay it][2] / lai'st[1], layest[2], lay'st[2] / laies[3], layes[15] / laying[9] / lay [*past*][44] / laid[48], laide[12], layd[19], lay'd[6], lay'd-[on][1], layde[2] / layd'st[1]
**rh** away *Luc 258, 1057*; away, say *Luc 1794*; castaway, day *Luc 747*; day *Luc 398, R2 4.1.332*; say *Luc 1620, Mac 2.3.51, S 101.7*; way *VA 827* / days *S 102.6* / maid *Luc 1212, TN 2.4.51*
> lie; low-, un-laid

**layer-up** *n*
'lɛ:əɹ-'ɤp
**sp** layer vp[1]

**laying in** *n*
'lɛ:ɪn-'ɪn, -ɪŋ-
**sp** laying in[1]

**lazar** *adj*
'lazəɹ
**sp** lazar[1]

**lazar / ~s** *n*
'lazəɹ / -z
**sp** lazar[1] / lazars[2]

**lazar-like** *adj*
'lazəɹ-,ləɪk
**sp** lazar-like[1]

**Lazarus** *n*
'lazrəs, -zər-
**sp** Lazarus[1]

**lazy** *adj*
'lɛ:zəɪ
**sp** lazie[8], lazie-[finger][1], lazy[3]

**le** *Fr det masculine*
lə, *abbr* l
**sp** le[30], *emend of* de[1] *H5 3.4.36*, *abbr* l[4], l[ayt][1]

***la*** *det feminine*
la
**sp** la[5], *emend of* le[14]

***les*** *det plural*
le
**sp** les[12], *emend of* la[1], le[12], e[1]

**le** *Ital*
> il *Ital*

**lea / ~s** *n*
=
**sp** leas[3]
**rh** peas *Tem 4.1.60*

**lead** [mineral] **/ ~s** *n*
=
**sp** lead[23], leade[2] / leads[2], leades[1]
**rh** dead *PP 20.24, RJ 2.5.17*

**lead** [bring] **/ ~est / ~s / ~eth / ~ing / led** *v*
=, lɛ:d / -st / -z / ˈli:d·əθ, ˈlɛ:- / -ɪn, -ɪŋ / =
**sp** lead[57], leade[63] / leadest[1], lead'st[3] / leadeth[1] / leades[12], leads[14], leds[1] / leading[5], lead [led][2], led[58]
**rh** dreadeth, pleadeth *Luc 271* / bed *Luc 300*
> mislead, ringleader, wing-led

**leaden** *adj*
=
**sp** leaden[15]

**leader / ~s** *n*
ˈli:dəɹ, ˈlɛ:- / -z
**sp** leader[12] / leaders[3]

**leading** *n*
ˈli:dɪn, -ɪŋ, ˈlɛ:-
**sp** leading[5]

**leaf / leaves** *n*
=
**sp** leafe[13], leaffe's [leaf is][1] / leafes[1], leaues[25]
**rh** bereaves *VA 798*; sheaves *S 12.5*
> fig-, title-, wood-leaf

**leafy**
> leavy

**league** [compact] **/ ~s** *n*
=
**sp** league[30] / leagues[1]

**league** [distance] **/ ~s** *n*
=
**sp** league[4] / leagues[10]

**league / ~d** *v*
=
**sp** leagu'd[1]

**leaguer** *n*
ˈli:gəɹ
**sp** leager[1]

**Leah** *n*
ˈlɛ:ə
**sp** Leah[1]

**leak / ~ed** *v*
=
**sp** leake[2] / leak'd[1]
**rh** speak *KL 3.6.26* [*Q*]

**leaky** *adj*
ˈli:kəɪ
**sp** leakie[1], leaky[1]

**lean / ~er** *adj*
= / ˈli:nəɹ
**sp** leane[37] / leaner[1]
**rh** mean *VA 931*

**lean / ~s / ~ing / ~ed** *v*
= / -z / ˈli:nɪn, -ɪŋ / li:nd
**sp** leane[13], leane-[on][1] / leanes[5] / leaning[5] / leand[1], lean'd[1]
**rh** mean *VA 125*

**Leander** *n*
lɪˈandəɹ
**sp** Leander[3], Lean-der[1]

**lean-faced** *adj*
ˈli:n-ˌfɛ:st
**sp** leane-fac'd[2]
> face

**lean-looked** *adj*
ˈli:n-ˌlʊkt
**sp** leane-look'd[1]
> look

**leanness** *n*
=
**sp** leannesse[4]

**lean-witted** *adj*
=
**sp** leane-witted[1]
> wit

**leap** *n*
=, lep
**sp** leap[1], leape[1]
**rh** reap *S 128.5*

**leap / ~s / ~ing / leapt** *v*
=, lep / -s / ˈli:pɪn, -ɪŋ, ˈlep- / li:pt, lept
**sp** leape[21] / leapes[3], leaps[1] / leaping[1] / leap'd[4], leapt[7]
**rh** steps *VA 279* / unswept *MW 5.5.43*
> overleap

**leapfrog** *n*
=, ˈlepfrɒg
**sp** leape-frogge[1]

**leaping** *adj*
ˈli:pɪn, -ɪŋ, ˈlep-
**sp** leaping[1]

**leaping-house / ~s** *n*
ˈli:pɪn-ˌəʊzɪz, -ɪŋ-, ˈlep-, -ˌhəʊ-
**sp** leaping-houses[1]
> house

**Lear / ~'s** *n*
li:ɹ / -z
**sp** Lear[27] / Lears[127]

**learn / ~s / ~ing / ~ed / learnt** *v*
lɐ:ɹn / -z / ˈlɐ:ɹn·ɪn, -ɪŋ / *m* -ɪd, lɐ:ɹnd / lɐ:ɹnt
**sp** learn[3], learne[84] / learnes[3] / learning[2] / learn'd[26], learned[4], lear-ned[1] / learnt[4]
**rh** discern *Luc 617*
> un-, well-learned

**learned** *adj / n*
*m* lɐ:ɹnd, ˈlɐ:ɹnɪd / ˈlɐ:ɹnɪd
**sp** learn'd[9], learned[35], lerned[1] / learned[2]

**learnedly** *adv*
*m* ˈlɐ:ɹnɪdˌləɪ
**sp** learnedly[3]

**learning / ~s** *n*
'lɐːɹnɪn, -ɪŋ / -z
**sp** learning[25], lear-ning[2] / learnings[1]

**learning-place** *n*
'lɐːɹnɪn-ˌplɛːs, -ɪŋ-
**sp** learning place[1]
> place

**leas·e / ~es** *n*
liːs, les / 'liːsɪz, 'les-
**sp** lease[5] / leases[1]
**rh** *1* decease *S 13.5*; **rh** *2* excess *S 146.5*

**lease / ~d** *v*
liːst, lest
**sp** leas'd[1]
> releasing

**leash** *n*
=
**sp** leash[3]

**leash / ~ed** *v*
=
**sp** leasht[1]

**leasing** *n*
'liːsɪn, -ɪŋ, 'les-
**sp** leasing[2]

**least** *adj / adv / n*
lest
**sp** least[20], lest[2] / least[9] / least[63], lest[1]
**rh** *adj* feast *Tim 4.3.517* / *adv* possessed *S 29.8*
> less, little

**leather** *adj / n*
'leðəɹ
**sp** leather[6] / leather[5]
**rh** *n* hither *CE 2.1.85*
> overleather

**leather-coat / ~s** *n*
'leðəɹ-ˌkoːts
**sp** lether-coats[1]
> coat

**leathern** *adj*
'leðəɹn
**sp** leathern[1], leatherne[3]

**leave / ~s** *n*
=, *Macmorris H5 3.2.100* lev
**sp** leaue[247], *Macmorris* leue[1] / leaues[2]
**rh** deceive *TC 5.3.89*; receive *AW 2.3.84, MV 3.2.139, TC 4.5.35*

**leav·e / ~est / ~es / ~ing / left** *v*
= / liːvst / = / 'liːvɪn, -ɪŋ / =
**sp** leaue[392], leaue't [leave it][1] / leau'st[1] / leaues[30] / leauing[22] / left[218], lefte[1]
**rh** conceive *LLL 5.2.342*; deceive *MND 2.2.145, S 4.12, 39.10*; perceive *TNK Prol.32*; receive *LC 239*; **leave it** receive it *2H6 2.3.35*; **leave me** deceive me *AW 1.1.225*; deceive me, heave thee *Luc 583* / bereaves *VA 798*; deceives, receives *LC 305*; sheaves *S 12.5* / grieving *WT 4.1.17* / bereft *CE 2.1.41, S 5.9, Tim 5.4.71*; bereft, theft *Luc 837*; theft *Mac 2.3.143, VA 158*; **left me** bereft me *VA 441*

**leaven** *n*
'levən
**sp** leauen[2]

**leavened** *adj*
'levənd
**sp** leauen'd[1]

**leavening** *n*
'levnɪn, -ɪŋ, -vən-
**sp** leauening[1], leau'ning[1]

**leaver** *n*
'liːvəɹ
**sp** leauer[1]

**leaves** *n*
> leaf

**leave-taking** *n*
*m* ˌliːv-'tɛːkɪn, -ɪŋ
**sp** leaue-taking[5]

**leaving** *n*
'liːvɪn, -ɪŋ
**sp** leauing[1]

**leavy** *adj*
'liːvəɪ
**sp** leauy[2]
**rh** heavy *MA 2.3.71*
> leaf

**Le Beau** *n*
lə 'boː
**sp** Le Beau[1], Le Beu[3]

**le Bon** *n*
lə 'bɔ̃, *Eng version* -boːn
**sp** Le Boune[1]

**lecher / ~'s / ~s** *n*
'letʃəɹ / -z
**sp** leacher[1], letcher[1] / letchers[1] / letchers[1]

**lecher** *v*
'letʃəɹ
**sp** letcher[1]

**lecherous** *adj*
'letʃrəs, -tʃər-
**sp** leacherous[1], lecherous[1], letcherous[1]

**lechery** *n*
*m* 'letʃrəɪ, -tʃər-
**sp** leacherie[1], lecherie[5], le-cherie[1], lechery[7], letcherie[2], letchery[2]
**rh** treachery *MW 5.3.21*

**leçon** *Fr n*
lə'sɔ̃
**sp** lecon[1]

**lecture / ~s** *n*
'lektəɹ / -z
**sp** lecture[5], lectors[1] / lectures[2]

**led**
> lead *v*

**Leda / ~'s** *n*
'liːdə / -z
**sp** Leda[1] / Laedaes[1]

**leech** *n*
=
**sp** leach[1]
**rh** each *Tim 5.4.84*

**leek / ~s** *n*
=
**sp** leeke[13] / leekes[5]
**rh** cheeks *MND 5.1.327*

**leer** *n*
liːɹ
**sp** leere[3]

**leer / ~s** *v*
liːɹ / -z
**sp** leere[2] / leeres[1]

**lees** *n*
=
**sp** lees[2]

**leet / ~s** *n*
=
**sp** leete[1] / leetes[1]

**left** *adj*
=
**sp** left[18]
**rh** VA *158*
> rich-left

**left** *v*
> leave *v*

**leg / ~s** *n*
=
**sp** leg[7], [capons]-leg[1], legge[29] / legges[45], leggs[1], legs[23]
**rh** dregs *Tim 1.2.239*

**leg / ~ged** *v*
=
**sp** leg'd[1]
> long-, near-, short-, three-legged

**legac·y / ~ies** *n*
*m* 'legəˌsəɪ, -əs- / -əˌsəɪz
**sp** legacie[4] / legacies[1]
**rh** free *S 4.2*

**legate** *n*
'legət
**sp** legat[2], legate[5]

**legatine** *adj*
'legəˌtəɪn
**sp** legatine[1]

**lege** *Lat*
> lego

**'lege**
> allege

**legend**
> legion

**legerity** *n*
*m* lə'dʒerɪˌtəɪ
**sp** legeritie[1]

**legion / ~s** *n*
'liːdʒɪən / -z
**sp** legion[3] / legions[17], *emend of MW 1.3.49* legend[1]

**legitimate** *adj*
*m* lə'dʒɪtmət, -tɪm-, -tɪˌmɛːt
**sp** legitimate[6], legittimate[2]
> illegitimate

**legitimation** *n*
ləˌdʒɪtɪ'mɛːsɪən
**sp** legitimation[1]

**leg·o / ~e** *Lat v*
'lege
**sp** lege[1]

**Leicester** *n*
'lestəɹ
**sp** Leicester[3]

**Leicestershire** *n*
*m* 'lestəɹˌʃəɪɹ
**sp** Leicestershire[1]

**leisure / ~s** *n*
'lezəɹ / -z
**sp** leasure[5], leisure[22], leysure[31], ley-sure[1] / leysures[2]
**rh** measure *MM 5.1.407*; pleasure *S 58.4*; treasure *TS 4.3.59*

**leisurely** *adv*
*m* 'lezəɹˌləɪ
**sp** leysurely[2]
**rh** audacity, saucily *Luc 1349*

**leman** *n*
'lemən
**sp** leman[1], lemman[1], lemon[1]

**lemon** *n*
=
**sp** lemmon[1]

**Lena** *n*
'liːnə
**sp** Lena[2]

**lend / ~s / ~eth / ~ing / lent** *v*
= / = / = / 'lendɪn, -ɪŋ / =
**sp** lend[88] / lends[9] / lendeth[1] / lending[2] / lent[24]
**rh** end *TNK 1.5.13*; extend, intend *LC 26*; friend *S 82.10*; spend *S 4.3*; tend *S 53.4*; **lend her** commend her *TG 4.2.41*; **lend me** attend me, defend me *Luc 1685* / amends, friends *Luc 964* / attendeth *Luc 1676* / banishment *R2 1.3.146*; content, lament *Luc 1502*; government *Luc 1399*; malcontent *VA 315*; tent *Luc 17*; **lent me** sent me *LC 199*

**lender / ~s'** *n*
'lendəɹ / -z
**sp** lender[2] / lenders[1]

**lending / ~s** *n*
'lendɪnz, -ɪŋz
**sp** lendings[2]

**length / ~s** *n*
=
**sp** length[33] / lengths[1]
**rh** strength *PP 18.33, TC 1.3.136*

**lengthen / ~s / ~ing / ~ed** *v*
= / = / 'leŋθnɪn, -ɪŋ / =
**sp** lengthen[2] / lengthens[3] / length'ning[1] / lengthen'd[2], length'ned[2]

**lenity** *n*
*m* 'lenɪˌtəɪ, -ɪt-
**sp** lenitie[3], lenity[4]

**Lennox** *n*
'lenəks
**sp** Lenox[11]

**lent**
> lend

**Lent** *n*
=
**sp** Lent[3]
**rh** spent *RJ 2.4.133*
> Jack-a-lent

**Lenten** *adj*
=
**sp** Lenten[1], Lenton[1], lenton[1]

**lentus** *Lat adj*
'lentʊs
**sp** lentus[2]

**lenvoy** *n*
'lenvəɪ
**sp** lenuoy[12], len-uoy[2]

**Leonardo** *n*
lɪə'nɑ:ɹdo:
**sp** Leonardo[1], *abbr in s.d.* Le[1]

**Leonati** *n*
lɪə'nɑ:ti:
**sp** Leonati[3]

**Leonato / ~'s** *n*
lɪə'nɑ:to: / -z
**sp** Leonato[35], Leo-nato[1] / Leonatoes[5], Leo-natoes[1]

**Leonatus / ~'** *n*
lɪə'nɑ:təs, ˌli:o:-
**sp** Leonatus[18], Leo-natus[1] / Leonatus[2]
**pun** *Cym 5.5.446 Lat* leo [lion]

**Leontes** *n*
lɪ'ɒnti:z
**sp** Leontes[15]

**leopard / ~'s / ~s** *n*
'lepəɹd / -z
**sp** leopard[2], leo-pard[1] / libbards[1] / leopards[1]

**leper** *n*
'lepəɹ
**sp** leaper[1]

**leperous** *adj*
*m* 'lepəˌrɤs
**sp** leaperous[1]

**Lepidus** *n*
*m* 'lepɪdəs, -ˌdʊs
**sp** Lepidus[33]

**Le Port Blanc** *Fr n*
lə 'pɔ:ɹ 'blɑ̃
**sp** *emend of R2 2.1.277* Port le Blan[1]

**leprosy** *n*
*m* 'leprəsəɪ, -ˌsəɪ
**sp** leprosie[4]

**lequel** *Fr pro*
lə'kɛl
**sp** le quel[1]

**les** *Fr*
> le

**less** *adj, n*
=
**sp** lesse[210]
**rh** access *RJ 2.Chorus.11*; excess *MV 3.2.113*; excess, possess *Luc 137*; express *AW 5.3.328, Per 2.2.9*; express, heaviness *Luc 1285*; possess *LLL 5.2.384, RJ 1.3.95*; wantonness *S 96.3*
> least, little, nevertheless

**lessen / ~s / ~ed** *v*
=
**sp** lessen[3] / lessen's[1] / lesned[2], lessen'd[2]

**lesser** *adj / adv / n*
'lesəɹ
**sp** lesser[17] / lesser[4] / lesser[4]

**lesson / ~s** *n*
=
**sp** lesson[4] / lessons[2]

**lesson / ~s / ~ed** *v*
=
**sp** lesson[1] / lessons[1] / lesson'd[2], lessoned[1]
> unlessoned

**lest** *conj*
=
**sp** least[14], lest[28]

**Lestrale** *n*
lə'stral
**sp** Lestrale[2]

**let** *n*
=
**sp** let[1]

**let / ~test / ~s / ~ting** *v*
= / lets, -tst / = / 'letɪn, -ɪŋ
**sp** let[2061], le't [let it][1], lets [let us][14], let's [let us][243], let't [let it][3], lett's [let us][1], *Caius* let-a-[mee][1] / let'st[3] / lets[15], letts[1] / letting[7]
**rh** debt *Luc 328*; debt, fret *Luc 646*; set *Luc 10* / dowsets *TNK 3.5.155*

**letharg·y / ~ies** *n*
'letəɹʤəɪ / -z
**sp** lethargie[4], lethar-gie[1] / lethargies[1]

**letharg·y / ~ied** *v*
'letəɹʤəɪd
**sp** lethargied[1]

**Lethe** *n*
'li:θi:
**sp** Lethe[5], Lethee[1]

**Lethied** *adj*
'li:θi:d
**sp** Lethied[1]

**letter / ~s** *n*
'letəɹ / -z
**sp** leter[1], letter[222], let-ter[4] / letters[120], let-ters[3]
**rh** better *LLL 4.1.95, Luc 1322, TG 2.1.133*; debtor *LLL 5.2.44*
> love-letter

**lettered** *adj*
'letəɹd
**sp** lettred[1]
> unlettered

**letters patent** *n*
'letəɹz 'patənt
**sp** latters patents[3]

**leur** *Fr det*
lœ:ɹ
**sp** leur[1]

**level** *adj / n*
=
**sp** leuell[8] / leuell[7], leuill[1]

**level / ~s / ~led** *v*
=
**sp** leuell[5] / leuels[1] / leuelld[1], leuell'd[1]
**rh** bevel *S 121.9*

**levelled** *adj*
=
**sp** leuell'd[1]

**lever / ~s** *n*
'levəɹz
**sp** leauers[1]

**Leviathan / ~s** *n*
lɪ'vəɪətən / -z
**sp** Leuiathan[2] / Leuiathans[1]

**levied** *adj*
'levəɪd
**sp** leuied[2]

**levity** *n*
*m* 'levɪ,təɪ, -ɪt-
**sp** leuitie[5], leuities [levity is][1], leuity[1]

**lev·y / ~ies** *n*
'levəɪ / -z
**sp** leuie[2], leuy[1] / leuies[3]

**lev·y / ~ying / ~ied** *v*
'levəɪ / -ɪn, -ɪŋ / -d
**sp** leuie[6], leuy[1] / leuying[2] / leuied[10], leuyed[1]

**lewd** *adj*
lu:d
**sp** lewd[9], lewde[2]

**lewdly** *adv*
'lu:dləɪ
**sp** lewdly[2]

**lewdness** *n*
'lu:dnəs
**sp** lewdnesse[2]

**lewdster / ~s** *n*
'lu:dstəɹz
**sp** lewdsters[1]

**lewd-tongued** *adj*
'lu:d-,tɒŋd, -,tʊ-
**sp** lewd-tongu'd[1]

**Lewis** *n*
'lu:i:
**sp** Lewes[6], Lewis[30]

**liable** *adj*
*m* 'ləɪə,bɤl, 'ləɪəbəl, 'ləɪbəl
**sp** liable[4], lia-ble[1], lyable[1]

**liar / ~s** *n*
'ləɪəɹ / -z
**sp** liar[3], lier[2], lyar[7], lyer[1] / liars[2], liers[1], lyars[2], ly-ars[1], lyers[1]
**rh** fire *Ham 2.2.117* / fires *RJ 1.2.90* [*F* fire]

**libel / ~s** *n*
'ləɪbəlz
**sp** libels[1]

**libel / ~ling** *v*
*m* 'ləɪbə,lɪn, -ɪŋ
**sp** libelling[1]

**liberal** *adj*
*m* 'lɪbə,rɑl, -bər-, -br-
**sp** liberal[1], liberall[27], li-berall[1]

**liberal-conceited** *adj*
'lɪbrɑl-kən,si:tɪd, -bər-
**sp** liberall conceited[1]
> conceit

**liberality** *n*
*m* ,lɪbə'rɑlɪ,təɪ
**sp** liberalitie[1], liberality[2]

**liberté** *Fr n*
libɛɹ'te
**sp** liberte[1]

**libertine / ~s** *n*
'lɪbəɹ,ti:n / -ɹti:nz
**sp** libertine[4] / libertines[1]

**libert·y / ~ies** *n*
*m* 'lɪbəɹ,təɪ, -ɹt- / 'lɪbəɹ,təɪz
**sp** libertie[34], li-bertie[1], liber-tie[1], liberty[34], li-berty[1] / liberties[6]
**rh** deity *R3 1.1.77*; harmony *3H6 4.6.15*; injury *S 58.6*

**library** *n*
*m* 'ləɪbrə,rəɪ
**sp** librarie[1], library[2]

**Libya** *n*
=
**sp** Libia[2], Lybia[2]

**licence** *n*
'ləɪsəns
**sp** licence[1], license[9]
> all-licensed

**license** *v*
'ləɪsəns
**sp** license

**licentious** *adj*
*m* ləɪ'sensɪəs, -ɪ,ɤs
**sp** licencious[1], licentious[2]

**Lichas** *n*
'ləɪkəs
**sp** Licas[1], Lychas[1]

**lick / ~ed** *v*
=
**sp** licke[7] / licked[1]
> foot-licker, unlicked

**lictor / ~s** *n*
'lɪktəɹz
**sp** lictors[2]

**lid / ~s** *n*
=
**sp** lid[2], [s]lid [God's lid][2] / lids[4]
**rh** forbid *Mac 1.3.20*
> eyelid

**lie / ~s** *n*
ləɪ / -z
**sp** lie[6], lye[41] / lies[7], lyes[7]
**rh** eye *S 152.14* / dies *VA 804*; eyes *LC 52*

**lie / ~est / ~s / ~th / lying / ~d / lain** *v*
ləɪ, *Jamy H5 3.2.111* liː / -st, ˈləɪəst / ləɪz / ˈləɪ·əθ / -ɪn, -ɪŋ / ləɪd / lɛːn, ˈləɪən
**sp** lie[58], lye[202], *Jamy* ligge[1] / liest[12], lyest[27], lye'st[1], ly'st[5] / lies[122], lyes[90] / lyeth[3] / lying[10] / lied[1], lyed[2] / laine[4], lyen[1]
**rh** *1* apply *MM 3.2.266*; by *1H4 5.4.109, S 73.10*; cry, fly, I *Tem 5.1.89*; defy *S 123.11*; deny *Cym 2.4.144, MND 2.2.58, S 46.5*; die *CE 3.2.49, Cym 4.4.52, 2H4 4.5.238, MA 4.1.150, RJ 2.Chorus.1, S 81.8, 92.10, TN 2.3.104, VA 245*; dry *VA 234*; eye *LLL 2.1.239, 4.3.84, RJ 2.3.32, S 31.8, 152.14* [*also emend* I], *VA 646, 663*; eye, hie *Luc 1342*; I *LLL 1.1.173, MND 1.1.215, RJ 1.4.51, S 72.5*; high *1H4 3.3.201*; qualify *S 109.4*; rye *AY 5.3.23*; sky *AW 1.1.212, VA 151*; thigh *RJ 2.1.20*; why *S 115.1*; **rh** *2* chivalry *TC 4.4.146*; conspiracy *Tem 2.1.305*; enmity *RJ 5.3.303*; prettily *MND 2.2.58*; skilfully *LLL 2.1.239*; honourably *JC 5.5.78*; kill-courtesy *MND 2.2.82*; loyalty *R2 1.1.68*; merrily *Tem 5.1.89*; minstrelsy *LLL 1.1.173*; rarity, simplicity *PT 55* / **rh** *1* arise *Cym 2.3.22*; cries *Luc 1753*; cries, eyes *Luc 443*; dies *KJ 3.1.337, Luc 1487, MA 5.3.4, MV 3.2.69, R2 5.3.70*; dies, skies *Luc 509*; eyes *LC 288, LLL 1.1.78, 2.1.214, 4.3.278, 5.2.420, Luc 391, 457, 1449, MND 2.2.96, MV 3.2.69, R2 3.3.168, RJ 1.3.86, 2.3.63, S 1.7, 2.5, 17.7, 24.6, 46.8, 137.3, 153.13, Tem 1.2.397, VA 68, 119, 1128*; eyes, rise *Luc 256*; prize *Luc 280*; spies *Luc 318*; **rh** *2* enemies *R2 5.6.31*; forgeries *Luc 457, PP 1.2*; qualities *RJ 2.3.11*; remedies *RJ 2.3.48*; subtleties *S 138.2* / flying *TG 3.1.143* / pride *MND 2.2.61*
> lay

**lief / ~est** *adj*
liːv / ˈliːvəst
**sp** leeue[1], lief[4], liefe[10], lieue[2] / liefest[1]
> alderliefest

**liege / ~'s** *n*
=
**sp** leege[1], leige[4], liedge[10], liege[123] / liedges[1], lieges[1]
**rh** beseech *R2 5.3.90*

**liege·man / ~men** *n*
=
**sp** liege-man[2] / leige-men[1], liegemen[1]

**lieger / ~s** *n*
ˈliːʤəɹ / -z
**sp** leiger[1] / leidgers[1]

**lie-giver** *n*
ˈləɪ-ˌgɪvəɹ
**sp** lye-giuer[1]
> giver

**lieu** *n*
luː, ljuː
**sp** lieu[7], liew[1]

**lieutenant / ~'s / ~s** *n*
lɪfˈtenənt, ljuː- / -s
**sp** lieutenant[54], lieu-tenant[1] / lieutenants[1] / lieutenants[1]

**lieutenantry** *n*
*m* lɪfˈtenəntrəɪ, -ˌtrəɪ, ljuː-
**sp** lieutenan-trie[1], lieutenantry[1]

**life / ~'s / lives / ~'** *n*
ləɪf / -s / ləɪvz
**sp** life[804], life's [life is][6] / lifes[3], life's[1], liues[8] / liues[79] / liues[1]
**rh** knife *LLL 2.1.126, Luc 1186, Per 4.Chorus.13, S 63.12, 74.9, 100.13, TN 2.5.106*; knife, wife *Luc 1045*; strife *1H6 4.4.38, Luc 141, 406, 687, MND 5.1.222, Oth 2.3.250, R2 5.6.26, RJ Prol.6, 3.1.179, S 75.1, Tim 1.1.39, VA 12, 289, 766*; strife, wife *Luc 233, 1374*; wife *AW 5.3.290, CE 3.2.67, 162, Luc 1800, 1805, Per Prol.38, 1.4.46, 5.1.245, R2 1.2.55, S 9.2, TN 5.1.133* / **rh** *1* knives *Tim 1.2.44*; **rh** *2* restoratives *Per Prol.7*

**life-blood** *n*
ˈləɪf-ˌblɤd
**sp** life-blood[3], life blood[3]
> blood

**lifeless** *adj*
ˈləɪfləs
**sp** liuelesse[4]

**lifeling / ~s** *n*
ˈləɪflɪnz, -ɪŋz
**sp** lifelings[1]

**life-preserving** *adj*
ˈləɪf-prɪˌzɐːɹvɪn, -ɪŋ
**sp** life-preseruing[1]
> preserve

**life-rendering** *adj*
*m* ˌləɪf-ˈrendrɪn, -ɪŋ
**sp** life-rend'ring[1]
> render

**lifetime** *n*
ˈləɪftəɪm
**sp** life time[1]
> time

**life-weary** *adj*
*m* ˌləɪf-ˈwɛːrəɪ, -ˈwe-
**sp** life-wearie-[taker][1]
> weary

**lift / ~s / ~eth / ~ing / ~ed** *v*
= / = / ˈlɪft·əθ / -ɪn, -ɪŋ / -ɪd
**sp** lift[24] / lifts[3] / lifteth[1] / lifting[2] / lifted[3]
> uplifted

**lifter** *n*
ˈlɪftəɹ
**sp** lifter[1]

**lifting-up** *n*
ˈlɪftɪn-ˈɤp, -ɪŋ-
**sp** lifting vp[1]

**Ligarius** *n*
lɪˈgarɪəs
**sp** Ligarius[9]

**light / ~er / ~est** *adj*
ləɪt / ˈləɪt·əɹ / -əst
**sp** light[75] / lighter[2] / lightest[2]
**rh** bite *R2 1.3.293* [*Q*]; night *RJ 1.2.25* / writer *TNK Prol.20*
> alight; day-, moon-, star-, taper-, torch-light

**light** *adv*
ləɪt
**sp** light[2], lyte[1]
**rh** delight *VA 1028*

**light / ~s** *n*
ləɪt / -s
**sp** light[137], [bone-fire]-light[1], [s]light[1], [s']light[1] / lights[21]
**rh** bright *LLL 4.3.30, 267, S 43.7, VA 860*; bright, sight *Luc 375*; convertite *Luc 745*; fight *R2 1.1.82, S 60.5, 88.1*; fight, knight, might, night *MW 2.1.15*; flight *MND 5.1.296*; knight *Per 2.5.17*; lily-white *VA 1051*; midnight *Luc 1627*; might *Per Prol.16, S 100.4*; night *Ham 3.2.226, 3H6 2.5.2, LLL 4.3.229, 255, Luc 164, 673, 773, 783, 1091, 1231, MND 3.2.188, 386, Oth 1.3.398, Per 1.1.137, 2.3.44, R2 1.3.176, 221, 5.6.44, RJ 2.2.189, Tim 5.1.43, VA 491, 533, 756, 1039*; night, right *Luc 940*; night, white *Luc 397*; sight *Luc 105, S 7.1, 38.8*; spite *MND 3.2.419, VA 1134*; sprite *MND 5.1.381*; white *LLL 2.1.184* / nights *LLL 1.1.88, Luc 1378*; sights *Luc 461*

**light / ~s / *Luc* ~eth / ~ed** *v*
ləɪt / -s / 'ləɪt·əθ / -ɪd
**sp** light[33] / lights[7] / lighteth[1] / lighted[10]
**rh** smiteth *Luc 178*

**lighten / ~s / ~ing** *v*
'ləɪtən / -z / 'ləɪtnɪn, -ɪŋ
**sp** lighten[3] / lightens[7] / lightning[2]

**lighter-heeled** *adj*
'ləɪtəɹ-ˌi:ld, -ˌhi:-
**sp** lighter heel'd[1]
> heel

**lightfoot** *adj*
'ləɪtˌfʊt
**sp** light-foot[1]
> foot

**lightly** *adv*
'ləɪtləɪ
**sp** lightly[12]
**rh** nightly *TG 3.1.142*

**lightness** *n*
'ləɪtnəs
**sp** lightnesse[8]

**lightning** *adj*
'ləɪtnɪn, -ɪŋ
**sp** lightning[1]

**lightning / ~s** *n*
'ləɪtnɪn, -ɪŋ / -z
**sp** lightning[23] / lightnings[1]

**light-winged** *adj*
'ləɪt-ˌwɪŋd
**sp** light wing'd[1]
> winged

**like / ~r / ~st** *adj*
ləɪk / 'ləɪk·əɹ / -əst
**sp** like[74] / liker[2] / likest[1]
> be-, dis-, mis-, sea-, un-, war-like; unlikely, well-liking

**like** *adv*
ləɪk
**sp** like[89], like-[invulnerable][1]

**like / ~s** *n*
ləɪk / -s
**sp** like[45] / likes[2]

**like / ~st** *prep*
ləɪk / -s, -st
**sp** like[1230], *emend of Tit 2.2.24* likes[1] / likest[1]
> like to

**lik·e / ~est / ~s / ~ing / ~ed** *v*
ləɪk / -s, -st / -s / 'ləɪkɪn, -ɪŋ / ləɪkt
**sp** like[146] / lik'st[4] / likes[26] / liking[2] / lik'd[7], likt[1], like'd[1], lyk'd[1]

**likelihood / ~s** *n*
'ləɪklɪˌʊd, -ˌhʊd / -z
**sp** likeliehood[1], likelihood[4], likelyhood[4], likely-hood[2], liklyhood[1] / likelihoods[3], likely-hoods[2]

**like·ly / ~liest** *adj*
'ləɪkləɪ / -əst
**sp** likely[25] / likelyest[1]

**liken / ~ing / ~ed** *v*
'ləɪknɪn, -ɪŋ / 'ləɪkənd
**sp** lik'ning[1] / lik'ned[1]

**likeness** *n*
'ləɪknəs
**sp** likenes[3], likenesse[19]

**like to** *prep*
'ləɪk tə, -tʊ
**sp** like to[69]
> like prep

**likewise** *adv*
'ləɪkwəɪz
**sp** likewise[24]

**liking / ~s** *n*
'ləɪkɪn, -ɪŋ / -z
**sp** liking[24] / likings[2]
**rh** *1* striking *Luc 434, MM 3.2.256, VA 248*; **rh** *2* respecting *Luc 434*

**lil·y / ~ies** *n*
'lɪləɪ / -z
**sp** lillie[1], lilly[9] / lillies[2]

**lily-bed / ~s** *n*
'lɪləɪ-ˌbedz
**sp** lilly beds[1]
> bed

**lily-livered** *adj*
'lɪləɪ-ˌlɪvəɹd
**sp** lilly-liuer'd[1], lilly-liuered[1]
> liver

**lily-tincture** *n*
ˌlɪləɪ-'tɪŋktəɹ
**sp** lilly-tincture[1]
> tincture

**lily-white** *adj*
'lɪləɪ-ˌʍəɪt
**sp** lilly white[1]
**rh** light *VA 1053*
> white

**Limander** *n*
lɪ'mandəɹ
**sp** Limander[1]

**limb / ~s** *n*
=
**sp** limbe[13], limme[3] / limbes[30], limbs[11], limmes[2], lims[1], lyms[1]
**rh** him *R2 3.2.187*
> good-, white-limbed

**limbeck** *n*
=
**sp** lymbeck[1]

**limber** *adj*
'lɪmbəɹ
**sp** limber[1]

**limb-meal** *n*
=
**sp** limb-meale[1]
> meal

**limb·us / ~o** *Lat n*
'lɪmbo:
**sp** limbo[4]

**lime** *n*
ləɪm
**sp** lime[10], lyme[1]

**lime / ~d** *v*
ləɪm / *m* -d, 'ləɪmɪd
**sp** lyme[1] / lim'd[1], limed[3], lym'd[2], lymde[1]

**lime-grove** *n*
'ləɪm-ˌgrʏv, -ˌgro:v
*sp emend of Tem 5.1.10* line-groue[1]
> grove

**Limehouse** *n*
'ləɪməʊs, -həʊs
**sp** Limehouse[1]

**lime-kiln** *n*
'ləɪm-ˌkɪl
**sp** lime-kill[1]
> kiln-hole

**lime-twig / ~s** *n*
'ləɪm-ˌtwɪgz
**sp** lime-twigs[1]
> twig

**limit / ~s** *n*
=
**sp** limit[16] / limits[8]
> unlimited

**limit / ~ed** *v*
=
**sp** limit[1] / limited[1], li-mited[1]

**limitation** *n*
*m* ˌlɪmɪ'tɛ:sɪən, -sɪˌɒn
**sp** limitation[2]

**limited** *adj*
=
**sp** limited[1], limitted[1]

**limn / ~ed** *v*
lɪmd
**sp** limn'd[1]

**Limoges** *n*
*m KJ 3.1.114* 'lɪmədʒɪz [*Fr* lɪ'mo:ʒ]
**sp** Lymoges[1]

**limp / ~s / ~ed** *v*
=
**sp** limpe[3] / limpes[1] / limpt[1]

**limping** *adj*
'lɪmpɪn, -ɪŋ
**sp** limping[2]

**Lincoln** *n*
=
**sp** Lincolne[2], Lincolne-[Washes][1]

**Lincolnshire** *n*
'lɪŋkənʃəɹ
**sp** Lincolnshire[1]

**line / ~s** *n*
ləɪn / -z
**sp** line[27], lyne[5] / lines[24], lynes[3]
**rh** Collatine *Luc 818*; mine *S 86.13*
**pun** lines *RJ Prol.5* loins
> fathom-, love-line

**line / ~d** *v*
ləɪn / ləɪnd
**sp** line[3], lyne[3] / lin'd[3], linde[2]
**rh** Rosalind *AY 3.2.88, 101*

**lineal** *adj*
*m* 'lɪnɪɑl, -ɪˌɑl
**sp** lineall[8]
> unlineal

**lineally** *adv*
*m* 'lɪnɪɑˌləɪ
**sp** lineally[1]

**lineament / ~s** *n*
*m* 'lɪnɪəˌment / -s, -əmən-
**sp** lineament[1], liniament[1] / lineaments[5], lyniaments[1]
**rh** content *RJ 1.3.84*

**lined** *adj*
ləɪnd
**sp** lyn'd[1]

**line-grove**
> lime-grove

**linen** *adj*
=
**sp** linnen[13]

**linen / ~s** *n*
=
**sp** linnen[11], lynnen[1] / linnens[1]

**ling / ~s** *n*
=
**sp** ling[1] / lings[1]

**Lingare** *n*
'lɪŋgəɹ
**sp** Lingare[1]

**linger / ~s / ~ing / ~ed** *v*
'lɪŋgəɹ / -z / 'lɪŋgrɪn, -ɪŋ / 'lɪŋgəɹd
**sp** linger[11] / lingers[3] / ling'ring[1] / lingerd[1], linger'd[1], lingred[1]

**lingering** *adj*
'lɪŋgrɪn, -ɪŋ
**sp** lingring[9], ling'ring[2]

**linguist** *n*
=
**sp** linguist[2]

**lining** *n*
'ləɪnɪn, -ɪŋ
**sp** lining[2]

**link** *n*
=
**sp** linke[3]

**link / ~s / ~ed** *v*
=
**sp** linke[2] / linkes[2] / link'd[5]
> unlink

**linsey-woolsey** *adj*
'lɪnsəɪ-'wʊlsəɪ
**sp** linsie wolsy[1]

**linstock** *n*
=
**sp** linstock[1], lynstock[1]

**linta** *nonsense word*
'lɪnta
**sp** linta[1]

**lion** *adj*
'ləɪən
**sp** lyon-[gate][1]

**lion / ~'s / ~s / ~s'** *n*
'ləɪən / -z
**sp** lion[37], lyon[49] / lions[5], lyons[13] / lions[4], lyons[21] / lyons[1]

**Lionel / ~'s** *n*
'ləɪənəl / -z
**sp** Lionel[3], Lyonel[1] / Lionels[1]

**lioness** *n*
ˌləɪə'nes
**sp** lionnesse[2], lyonesse[1], lyonnesse[4]

**lion-mettled** *adj*
'ləɪən-ˌmetld
**sp** lyon metled[1]

**lip / ~s** *n*
=
**sp** lip[21], [nether]-lip[1], lippe[11] / lippes[47], lipps[1], lips[79]
**rh** slip *VA 127* / chips *S 128.12*; eclipse *Mac 4.1.29*; hips *VA 46*; ships *LLL 2.1.206*; skips *PP 11.9*; slips *VA 516*; trips *VA 724*
> harelip, thick-lips

**lip / ~ped** *v*
=
**sp** lip[1] / lipt[1]
> thick-lipped

**Lipsbury** *n*
'lɪpsbrəɪ, -bər-
**sp** Lipsbury[1]

**liquid** *adj*
=
**sp** liquid[8]

**liquor / ~s** *n*
'lɪkəɹ / -z
**sp** licquor[1], liquor[17] / liquors[2]

**liquor / ~ed** *v*
'lɪkəɹd
**sp** liquor'd[1]

**liquorish** *adj*
'lɪkrɪʃ, -kər-
**sp** licourish[1]

**Lisbon** *n*
=
**sp** Lisbon[1]

**Lisio** *n*
'lɪsɪoː
**sp** Lisio[4], Litio[3]

**lisp / ~ing** *v*
= / 'lɪspɪn, -ɪŋ
**sp** lispe[3] / lisping[1]

**lisping** *adj*
'lɪspɪn, -ɪŋ
**sp** lisping[1], lisping-[hauthorne][1]

**list / ~s** *n*
=
**sp** list[11], lyst[3] / listes[2], lists[9], lysts[1]

**list** [listen] **/ ~eth** *v*
=
**sp** list[22], list[-me][1]

**list** [please, list] **/** *VA* **~eth** *v*
=
**sp** list[17] / listeth[1]
**rh** *1* missed *Luc 1008*; **rh** *2* priest *TS 3.2.164* / resisteth *VA 564*

**listen / ~ing / ~ed** *v*
= / 'lɪsnɪn, -ɪŋ / =
**sp** listen[13] / listning[1] / listen'd[1]

**listening** *n*
'lɪsnɪn, -ɪŋ
**sp** listning[3], list-ning[1]

**literatured** *adj*
'lɪtrətəɹd
**sp** literatured[1]

**lither** *adj*
'ləɪðəɹ
**sp** lither[1]

**litter** *n*
'lɪtəɹ
**sp** litter[6]

**litter / ~ed** *v*
'lɪtəɹ / -d
**sp** littour[1] / litter'd[2], lytter'd[1]

**little** *adj / adv / n*
=
**sp** litle[7], littell-[a-while][1], little[291], little-[one][1], little-[tyne][1] / little[73] / litle[2], li-tle[1], little[94], lit-tle[1]
> least, less

**liv·e / ~est / ~es / ~eth / ~ing / ~ed / ~edest** *v*
= / lɪvst / = / = / 'lɪvɪn, -ɪŋ / *m* lɪvd, 'lɪvɪd / lɪvdst
**sp** liue[487] / lives[113] / liuest[1], liu'st[11] / liueth[3] / liuing[14] / liu'd[66], liued[16] / liu'dst[1]
**rh** *1* forgive *AW 3.4.14, 2H4 4.5.219*; give *AW 2.1.131, 2.3.102, 2H6 5.2.88, Luc 986, 1051, R2 1.3.225, RJ 2.3.13, 3.1.181, S 4.8, 13.2, 31.9, 37.12, 39.5, 54.4, 79.12, TC 4.5.37, WT 4.3.19*; **rh** *2* contrive *JC 2.3.14*; thrive *R2 1.3.83*; **rh** *3* achieve *S 67.1* / gives *Mac 2.1.60, TNK Prol.14* / giving *Luc 1714*; thanksgiving *LLL 2.1.127* / achieved *H5 Epil.5*
> out-, over-live; short-lived

**livelihood** *n*
ˈləɪvləɪˌʊd, -ˌhʊd
**sp** liuelihood[1], liuelyhood[1]
**rh** good *VA 26*

**livelong** *adj*
ˈləɪvlɒŋ
**sp** liue-long[3]

**livel·y / ~ier** *adj*
ˈləɪvləɪ / -əɹ
**sp** liuely[7] / liuelier[1]

**lively** *adv*
ˈləɪvləɪ
**sp** liuelie[1], liuely[2]

**liver** *adj*
ˈlɪvəɹ
**sp** liuer[1]
> lily-, milk-, pigeon-, white-livered

**liver / ~s** *n*
ˈlɪvəɹ / -z
**sp** liuer[16], li-uer[1] / liuers[6], li-uers[1], lyuers[1]

**liver·y / ~ies** *n*
*m* ˈlɪvrəɪ, -vər-, -vəˌrəɪ / -z
**sp** liuerie[8], liuery[7], liuorie[1], liu'rie[1] / liueries[4], liuories[1]
**rh** *1* audaciously, modesty *Luc 1222*; infamy *Luc 1054*; **rh** *2* die *Luc 1054*

**lives** *n*
> life

**Livia** *n*
=
**sp** Liuia[2]

**living** *adj*
ˈlɪvɪn, -ɪŋ
**sp** liuing[72]
> ever-living

**living / ~s** *n*
ˈlɪvɪn, -ɪŋ / -z
**sp** liuing[21], li-uing[3] / liuings[1]
> live

**lizard / ~'s / ~s'** *n*
ˈlɪzəɹd / -z
**sp** li-zard[1] / lizards[1] / lizards[1], lyzards[1]

**lo** *interj*
lo:
**sp** lo[18], lo-[you][1], loe[60]
**rh** foe *RJ 2.3.49*

**loa** *interj*
ˈlo:ə
**sp** loa[1]

**loach** *n*
lo:ʧ
**sp** loach[1]

**load / ~s** *n*
lo:d / -z
**sp** load[9], loade[3], lode[1] / loades[1], loads[1]
> unload

**load / ~s / ~en** *v*
lo:d / -z / ˈlo:dən
**sp** load[3], loade[4] / loades[1] / loaden[5], loden[1]

**loaden** *adj*
ˈlo:dən
**sp** loaden[1]

**loading** *n*
ˈlo:dɪn, -ɪŋ
**sp** loading[1]

**loaf / loaves** *n*
lo:f / lo:vz
**sp** loafe[1] / loaues[1]

**loam** *n*
lo:m
**sp** loame[2], lome[3]

**loan** *n*
lo:n
**sp** lone[1]
**rh** one *S 6.6*

**loath / ~er** *adj*
lo:θ / ˈlo:θəɹ
**sp** loath[16], loth[15] / loather[1]
**rh** oath *LLL 1.1.157*

**loath·e / ~s / ~ed** *v*
lo:ð / -z / -d
**sp** loath[4], loathe[1] / loathes[3], loaths[1], lothes[1] / loath'd[1], loth'd[1]

**loathed** *adj*
*m* lo:ðd, ˈlo:ðɪd
**sp** loath'd[2], loathed[9]

**loathing** *n*
ˈlo:ðɪn, -ɪŋ
**sp** loathing[2]

**loathly** *adv*
ˈlo:ðləɪ
**sp** loathly[2], lothly[1]

**loathness** *n*
ˈlo:ðnəs
**sp** loathnesse[3]

**loathsome / ~st** *adj*
ˈlo:ðsəm / -st
**sp** loathsome[14], lothsome[1] / loth-som'st[1]

**loathsomeness** *n*
ˈlo:ðsəmnəs
**sp** loathsomnesse[1]

**lob** *n / v*
=
**sp** lob[1] / lob[1]

**lobb·y / ~ies** *n*
ˈlɒbəɪ / -z
**sp** lobby[3] / lobbies[1]

**local** *adj*
ˈlo:kɑl
**sp** locall[2]

**lock / ~s** *n*
=
**sp** lock[2], locke[3] / lockes[9], locks[5]
**rh** knocks *Mac 4.1.46*; rocks, shocks *MND 1.2.29*
> elk-locks, picklock

**lock / ~s / ~ing / ~ed** *v*
= / = / ˈlɒkɪn, -ɪŋ / =
**sp** lock[2], locke[14] / lockes[2], locks[1] / locking[1] / lock'd[11], lockt[15]

**rh** rocked *Luc 260*
> unlock

**locked** *adj*
=
**sp** lockt[1]

**locking-up** *n*
'lɒkɪn-'ɤp, -ɪŋ-
**sp** locking vp[1]

**lockram** *n*
'lɒkrəm
**sp** lockram[1]

**locust / ~s** *n*
'lo:kəsts
**sp** locusts[1]

**lodestar / ~s** *n*
'lo:dstɑ:ɹz
**sp** loadstarres[1]
> star

**lodge** *n*
=
**sp** lodge[4]

**lodge / ~es / ~ed** *v*
=
**sp** lodge[19] / lodges[5] / lodg'd[11], lodged[1]
> dislodge

**lodged** *adj*
=
**sp** lodg'd[1]

**lodger / ~s** *n*
'lɒʤəɹz
**sp** lodgers[2]

**lodging / ~s** *n*
'lɒʤɪn, -ɪŋ / -z
**sp** lodging[23], lodg-ing[1] / lodgings[1]

**Lodovico** *n*
ˌlɒdə'vi:ko:
**sp** Lodouico[8]

**Lodowick** *n*
*m* 'lɒdwɪk, dəˌw-
**sp** Lodowick[3], Lodowicke[2]

**lofty** *adj*
lɒftəɪ
**sp** loftie[6], lofty[10]

**log / ~s** *n*
=
**sp** log[2], logge[1] / logges[2], logs[5]

**loggerhead / ~s** *n*
'lɒgəɹˌed, -ˌhed / -z
**sp** loggerhead[2] / logger-heads[1]

**loggerheaded** *adj*
'lɒgəɹˌedɪd, -ˌhed-
**sp** logger-headed[1]

**loggets** *n*
'lɒgəts
**sp** loggets[1]

**logic** *n*
=
**sp** lodgicke[1], logicke[1]

**log-man** *n*
=
**sp** logge-man[1]

**loins** *n*
ləɪnz
**sp** loines[5], loynes[6]
**pun** *RJ Prol.5* lines

**loiter / ~ing** *v*
'ləɪtəɹ / -ɪn, -ɪŋ, 'ləɪtrɪn, -ɪŋ
**sp** loyter[1] / loytering[1]

**loiterer / ~s** *n*
'ləɪtrəɹ, -tər- / -z
**sp** loyterer[1] / loyterers[1]

**loll / ~s / ~ing** *v*
= / 'lɒlɪn, -ɪŋ
**sp** lolls[1] / lolling[3]

**Lombard** *n*
'lɤmbəɹd
**sp** Lombard[1]

**Lombardy** *n*
*m* 'lɤmbəɹˌdəɪ
**sp** Lumbardie[1]

**London / ~'s** *n*
'lɤndən / -z
**sp** London[65], Lon-don[2] / Londons[1]

**London Bridge** *n*
ˌlɤndən 'brɪʤ
**sp** London-bridge[1], London Bridge[2]
> bridge

**Londoner / ~s** *n*
'lɤndənəɹz
**sp** Londoners[1]

**lone** *adj*
'lo:n
**sp** lone[1]

**loneliness** *n*
*m* 'lo:nləɪˌnes
**sp** lonelinesse[1]

**lonely** *adv*
'lo:nləɪ
**sp** lonely[1]

**long / ~er / ~est** *adj*
= / 'lɒŋg·əɹ / -əst
**sp** long[81], [too]-long[1] / longer[13], lon-ger[1] / longest[4]
**rh** *1* song *PP 18.52*; strong *VA 295*; throng *H5 4.5.23*; wrong *TN 5.1.139*; **rh** *2* tongue *TS 4.2.57*; young *LLL 5.2.824, RJ 1.1.161*
> be-, flat-, over-long

**long / ~er / ~est** *adv*
= / 'lɒŋg·əɹ / -əst
**sp** long[311], [*song*] long-a[1] / longer[90] / longest[1]
**rh** *1* song *S 100.1*; strong *Luc 866, S 73.14, TNK 3.5.153*; throng *Luc 1782*; wrong *3H6 3.3.232, 4.1.111, Luc 1468, R2 2.1.163*; **rh** *2* tongue *Luc 1468, 1616, 1782, MND 5.1.424*; young *Luc 866, KL 1.4.211, 5.3.324, PP 12.12, RJ 4.5.77* / stronger *Luc 1765, S 28.13*

**long** *conj*
=
**sp** long[1]

**long / ~er** *n*
= / ˈlɒŋgəɹ
**sp** long[5] / longer[1]
**rh** prolong *TNK Epil.15*

**long / est / ~s / ~ing / ~ed** *v*
= / lɒŋst / = / ˈlɒŋɪn, -ɪŋ / *m* lɒŋd, ˈlɒŋɪd
**sp** long[25] / long'st[3] / longs[9] / longing[5] / long'd[5], longed[1]
**rh** tongue *LLL 5.2.244*

**Longaville** *n*
ˈlɒŋgəˌvɪl, -vəɪl
**sp** Longauile[3], Longauill[12], *abbr in s.d.* Long[1]
**rh** *1* compile *LLL 4.3.131*; half a mile *LLL 5.2.53*; **rh** *2* ill *LLL 4.3.121*

**longboat / ~'s** *n*
ˈlɒŋbo:ts
**sp** long boats[1]

**long-continued** *adj*
=
**sp** long-continew'd[1]
> continue

**long-during** *adj*
*m* ˌlɒŋ-ˈdju:rɪn, -ɪŋ
**sp** long during[1]

**longed-for** *adj*
ˈlɒŋd-ˌfɔ:ɹ
**sp** long'd-for-[change][1]

**long-experienced** *adj*
=
**sp** long experien'st[1]
> experience

**long-grown** *adj*
ˈlɒŋ-ˌgro:n
**sp** long-growne[1]
> grow

**long-imprisoned** *adj*
=
**sp** long imprisoned[1]
> imprison

**longing** *adj*
ˈlɒŋgɪn, -ɪŋ
**sp** longing[3]

**longing / ~s** *n*
ˈlɒŋgɪn, -ɪŋ / -z
**sp** longing[5], [nice]-longing[1] / longings[1]

**long-ingraffed** *adj*
ˈlɒŋ-ɪnˌgraft
**sp** long ingraffed[1]
> engraffed, graff

**Long Lane** *n*
*m* ˈlɒŋ ˌlɛ:n
**sp** Long-lane[1]
> lane

**long-legged** *adj*
=
**sp** long leg'd[1]
> leg

**longly** *adv*
ˈlɒŋləɪ
**sp** longly[1]

**long of** *prep*
ˈlɒŋə, -əv
**sp** long of[6]

**long-parted** *adj*
*m* ˌlɒŋ-ˈpɑ:ɹtɪd
**sp** long parted[1]
> part

**long-since-due** *adj*
*m* ˌlɒŋ-ˈsɪns-ˌdju:
**sp** long since due[1]
> due

**long-staff** *adj*
ˈlɒŋ-ˌstaf
**sp** long-staffe[1]
> staff

**long-sword** *n*
=
**sp** long-sword[1], long sword[1]
> sword

**long-tail** *n*
ˈlɒŋ-ˌtɛ:l
**sp** long-taile[1]
> tail

**long-tongued** *adj*
ˈlɒŋ-ˌtɒŋd, -ˌtʊ-
**sp** long-tongu'd[1]
> tongue

**long-usurped** *adj*
*m* ˈlɒŋ-jʊˌzɐ:ɹpɪd
**sp** long vsurped[1]
> usurp

**long-vanished** *adj*
*m* ˌlɒŋ-ˈvanɪʃt
**sp** long-vanisht[1]
> vanish

**long-winded** *adj*
*m* ˌlɒŋ-ˈwəɪndɪd
**sp** long-winded[1]
> wind

**loo** *interj*
lo:
**sp** loo[2], lowe[4]

**loof**
> luff

**look / ~s** *n*
=
**sp** look[1], looke[26], [goose]-looke[1] / lookes[88], [cat-a-moun-taine]-lookes[1], looks[6]
**rh** book *LLL 1.1.76, S 59.5*; brook *PP 4.3*; Bullingbrook *R2 3.4.98*; forsook, took *Luc 1535*; took *CE 2.1.88, S 47.3, 75.10* / books *AY 3.2.7, LLL 1.1.85, Luc 812, 1252, RJ 2.2.157*; books, hooks *Luc 100*; brooks *Tem 4.1.129*; hooks *RJ 2.Chorus.6, S 137.5*

**look / ~est / ~s / ~ing / ~ed / ~edest** *v*
= / lʊkst, ˈlʊkəst / = / ˈlʊkɪn, -ɪŋ / *m* lʊkt, ˈlʊkɪd / lʊktst, -kst
**sp** look[32], looke[744], look't [look it][1] / lookest[2], look'st[11] / lookes[98], looks[5] / looking[22] / look'd[80], looked[2], lookt[12], look't[1] / look'dst[1]

**rh** book *LLL 4.2.23, 4.3.250, Luc 616, S 77.13*; brook *PP 6.7*
> out-, over-look; grim-, lean-looked; sharp-looking, unlooked-for

**looker-on / ~s-on** *n*
'lʊkəɹ-'ɒn / -əɹz-
**sp** looker-on[1], looker on[1] / lookers on[1]

**looking** *n*
'lʊkɪn, -ɪŋ
**sp** looking[2]

**looking-glass** *n*
'lʊkɪn-ˌglas, -ɪŋ-
**sp** looking-glasse[6]
> glass

**looking-on** *n*
'lʊkɪn-'ɒn, -ɪŋ-
**sp** looking on[2]

**loon** *n*
=
**sp** loone[1]

**loop** *n*
=
**sp** loope[2]

**loose** *adj / adv / n*
=
**sp** loose[32] / loose[6] / loose[1]
**rh** goose *LLL 3.1.101*

**loose / ~ing / ~d** *v*
= / 'lu:s·ɪn, -ɪŋ / *m* -ɪd, lu:st
**sp** loose[4], lose[1] / loosing[1] / loos'd[3], loosed[2]

**loose-bodied** *adj*
'lu:s-ˌbɒdəɪd
**sp** loose-bodied[1], loose bodied[1]
> body

**loosely** *adv*
'lu:sləɪ
**sp** loosely[2]

**loose-wived** *adj*
*m* ˌlu:s-'wəɪvd
**sp** loose-wiu'd[1]
> wive

**lop** *n*
=
**sp** lop[1]

**lop / ~ped** *v*
=
**sp** lop[2] / lopp'd[1], lopt[6]

**lopped** *adj*
=
**sp** lop'd[1], lopt[1]

**loqu·or / ~itur** *Lat*
'lɒkwɪtʊɹ
**sp** loquitur[1]

**lord** *interj*
lɔ:ɹd
**sp** lord[66]

**lord / ~'s / ~s / ~s'** *n*
lɔ:ɹd / -z
**sp** lord[2594], lords [lord is][1], lord's [lord is][1], *emend of 1H4 1.3.289* loe[1], L[ord] *in s.d*[27] / lords[23] / lordes[2], lords[409] / lords[1]
**rh** *1* accord *AY 5.4.131, TS 3.1.73*; afford *LLL 4.1.40, Luc 1303, R2 1.1.176, RJ 4.1.124*; sword *H5 Epil.8, TNK 3.1.41*; **rh** *2* word *2H4 5.5.73, 1H6 4.3.30, LLL 2.1.201, 4.1.102, 4.3.91, 5.2.239, 314, 5.2.369, 5.2.448, MND 2.2.157, Per 2.Chorus.3, R2 5.3.120, R3 3.7.2* / **rh** *1* accords *CE 2.1.24*; **rh** *2* words *Luc 1609*

**lord / ~ing / ~ed** *v*
'lɔ:ɹd·ɪn, -ɪŋ / -ɪd
**sp** lording[1] / lorded[1]

**lording / ~s** *n*
'lɔ:ɹdɪnz, -ɪŋz
**sp** lordings[2]

**lordliness** *n*
*m* 'lɔ:ɹdlɪˌnes
**sp** lordlinesse[1]

**lordly** *adj*
'lɔ:ɹdləɪ
**sp** lordly[6]

**lordship / ~'s / ~s / ~s'** *n*
'lɔ:ɹdʃɪp / -s
**sp** lordship[98], lord-ship[2], lordshippe[8], lordships [lordship is][1] / lordshippes[1], lordships[8] / lordships[3] / lordships[1]

**Lorenzo** *n*
lɒ'renzo:
**sp** Lorenso[4], Lorenzo[27]

**Lorraine** *n*
'lɒrən
**sp** Loraine[2]

**lose / ~st / ~s / ~eth / ~ing / lost** *v*
= / 'lu:zəst / = / = / 'lu:zɪn, -ɪŋ / =
**sp** loose[149], loose't[1], lose[49] / loosest[3] / looses[8], loses[1] / loo-seth[1], loseth[1] / loosing[13], losing[2] / lost[249]
**rh** *1* choose *AW 1.3.210, CE 4.3.96, MV 2.9.81, R2 2.1.30, S 64.14*; **lose it** abuse it *1H6 4.5.40*; **rh** *2* propose *Ham 3.2.205* / **rh** *1* boast *1H6 4.5.25, Luc 1191, VA 1075*; coast *2H6 4.8.48, Per 5.Chorus.13*; most *LLL 1.1.144, S 152.8*; **rh** *2* cost *Luc 147, Per 3.2.68, PP 13.11*; crost *MV 2.5.55*; frost *MV 2.7.74*; tempest-tossed *Mac 1.3.24*; tossed *Per 2.Chorus.33*
> lost *adj*, well-lost

**losel** *n*
'lɒzəl
**sp** lozell[1]

**loser / ~s** *n*
'lu:zəɹ / -z
**sp** looser[3], loser[1] / loosers[2], losers[2]

**losing** *adj / n*
'lu:sɪn, -ɪŋ
**sp** loosing[3] / loosing[1]

**loss / ~es** *n*
=
**sp** losse[115] / losses[14]
**rh** across *Luc 1660*; cross *1H6 4.3.53, S 34.10, 42.10*; dross *S 146.9, TC 4.4.10*

**lost** *adj*
=
**sp** lost[6], lost-[mutton] [2]
> lose

**lot / ~s** *n*
=
**sp** lot[4] / lots[3]
**rh** blot, forgot *Luc 534*; wot *Ham 2.2.415*

**lottery** *n*
'lɒtrəɪ, -tər-
**sp** lotterie[1], lot-terie[1], lottery[2], lottrie[1], lottry[1], lott'ry[1]
> allottery

**loud / ~er / ~est** *adj*
ləʊd / 'ləʊd·əɹ / -st
**sp** loud[16], lowd[20], low'd[1] / louder[1], lowder[1] / lowd'st[1]
**rh** proud *Oth 2.1.146*

**loud / ~er** *adv*
ləʊd / 'ləʊdəɹ
**sp** loud[16], lowd[10], low'd[2] / louder[1], lowder[5]
**rh** shroud *MND 5.1.366*

**loud** *n*
ləʊd
**sp** loud[1]

**loudest** *n*
ləʊdst
**sp** lowd'st[1]

**loudly** *adv*
'ləʊdləɪ
**sp** lowdly[1]

**lour / ~eth / ~ing / ~ed** *v*
ləʊɹ / 'ləʊr·əθ / -ɪn, -ɪŋ / ləʊɹd
**sp** lowre[3] / lowreth[1] / lowring[1] / lowr'd[1]
**rh** sour *R2 1.3.235*

**louring** *adj*
'ləʊrɪn, -ɪŋ
**sp** lowring[3]

**louse** *n / v*
ləʊs / ləʊz
**sp** lowse[1] / lowse[1]
**rh** *v* house *KL 3.2.29*

**lousy** *adj*
'ləʊzəɪ, -səɪ
**sp** lowsie[8], low-sie[1]

**lout / ~s** *n*
ləʊt / -s
**sp** lout[2], lowt[3] / lowts[1]
**rh** doubt *KJ 3.1.220*

**lout / ~ed** *v*
'ləʊtɪd
**sp** lowted[1]

**Louvre** *n*
'lu:vrə, *Exeter H5 2.4.132* 'lu:vəɹ
**sp** Louure[1], *Exeter* Louer[1]

**love / ~'s / ~s** *n*
lɤv / -z
**sp** loue[1299], [a]loue [of love][1], [noble-ending]-loue[1], [true]-loue[1], loue's [love is][4] / loues[55], [true]-loues[1], loue's[1] / loues[49]
**rh** *1* above *AW 2.3.82, AY 3.2.1, 1H6 1.2.113, MA 5.2.26, S 110.8, TN 5.1.136*; dove *MND 5.1.316, PP 9.1, PT 51*; **rh** *2* approve *KL 1.1.185, MND 2.2.75, S 147.5, Tit 2.1.36*; move *CE 4.2.13, Ham 2.1.119, 3.2.193, LLL 4.3.54, MND 1.1.196, PP 19.16, 19.20, RJ 1.3.97, S 47.9, TN 3.1.161*; prove *AW 3.3.11, Ham 3.2.213, LLL 4.3.64, 280, MND 2.1.266, PP 3.7, 19.1, RJ 2.3.88, S 10.10, 32.14, 39.11, 117.14, 136.5, 151.2, 153.5, 154.14, TC 1.3.288, TG 1.1.38, TN 2.4.117, 3.3.11, 3.4.375, VA 595*; remove *AY 3.4.52, LC 238, Luc 611, PP 17.7, RJ Prol.9, S 116.2, VA 185*; reprove *LLL 4.3.152, VA 789*; **rh** *3* grove *MND 2.1.246, 260, 3.2.6, VA 867*; Jove *LLL 4.3.118, Luc 570, MA 5.4.47, PP 16.18*; strove *AW 1.1.223* / **rh** *1* doves *MND 1.1.172*; **rh** *2* removes *LLL 5.2.134*
> after-, lack-, self-love

**lov·e / ~est / ~es / ~eth / ~ing / ~ed / ~edest** *v*
lɤv / *m* -st, 'lɤvəst / lɤvz / 'lɤv·əθ / -ɪn, -ɪŋ / lɤvd / -st, 'lɤvdəst
**sp** loue[576], *Caius* loue[-a-me][1] / louest[7], lou'st[22] / loues[139] / loueth[3] / louing[18] / lou'd[148], loued[25], lo-ued[1], lov'd[1] / lou'dst[2], loued'st[2]
**rh** *1* above *Per 2.3.21, TC 3.2.154*; dove *MND 2.2.119, TN 5.1.128*; **rh** *2* approve *S 70.7*; move *AY 4.3.55, Ham 2.2.118, TN 2.5.95, VA 433*; prove *LLL 4.2.105, PP 5.1, S 72.2, TS 1.2.176, VA 38*; remove *LLL 4.3.152; VA 79*; **love her** approve her *S 42.6*; **love thee** move me *MND 3.1.134*; prove me *S 26.13*; **love us** move us *CE 3.2.22* / proved *S 116.1*; **rh** *3* behove *Ham 5.1.61* / broom-groves *Tem 4.1.67*

**love-affair / ~s** *n*
'lɤv-əˌfɛ:ɹz
**sp** loue-affaires[1]
> affair

**love-bed** *n*
*m* ˌlɤv-'bed
**sp** loue-bed[1]
> bed

**love-book** *n*
'lɤv-ˌbʊk
**sp** loue-booke[1]
> book

**love-broker** *n*
'lɤv-ˌbro:kəɹ
**sp** loue-broker[1]
> broke

**love-cause** *n*
'lɤv-ˌkɔ:z
**sp** loue cause[1]
> cause

**loved** *adj*
lɤvd
**sp** loued[3]

**love-day** *n*
'lɤv-ˌdɛ:
**sp** loue-day[1]

**love-devouring** *adj*
'lɤv-dɪˌvo:rɪn, -ɪŋ
**sp** loue-deuouring[1]
> devour

**love-discourse** *n*
'lɤv-dɪsˌkɔ:ɹs
**sp** loue-discourse[1]
> discourse

**love-feat** *n*
'lɤv-ˌfi:t
**sp** loue-feat[1]
> feat

**love-god / ~s** *n*
'lɤv-ˌgɒdz
**sp** loue-gods[1]
> God

**love-juice** *n*
'lɤv-ˌʤəɪs
**sp** loue iuyce[2]
> juice

**love-letter / ~s** *n*
'lɤv-ˌletəɹz
**sp** loue-letters[1], loue letters[1]
> letter

**love-line** *n*
'lɤv-ˌləɪn
**sp** loue-line[1]
> line

**loveliness** *n*
'lɤvlɪnəs
**sp** louelinesse[2]

**Lovell / ~'s** *n*
'lɤvəl / -z
**sp** Louel[3], Louell[20] / Louels[1]

**lovel·y / ~ier** *adj*
'lɤvləɪ / -əɹ
**sp** louelie[2], louely[41] / louelier[2]

**lovely** *adv*
'lɤvləɪ
**sp** louely[3]

**love-monger** *n*
'lɤv-ˌmɤŋgəɹ
**sp** loue-monger[1]

**love-performing** *adj*
'lɤv-pəɹˌfɔ:ɹmɪn, -ɪŋ
**sp** loue-performing[1]
> perform

**love-prate** *n*
'lɤv-ˌprɛ:t
**sp** loue-prate[1]
> prate

**lover / ~'s / ~s / ~s'** *n*
'lɤvəɹ / -z
**sp** louer[49], lo-uer[2] / louers[11] / louers[51], lo-uers[1] / louers[7]
**rh** *1* cover *RJ 1.3.88, S 32.4*; discover *TG 2.1.159*; **rh** *2* moreover *LLL 5.2.50, 447*; over *TG 1.1.109, VA 573* / covers [*F, at* LLL 2.1.113-129]

**lovered** *adj*
'lɤvəɹd
**sp** louerd[1]
**rh** *1* covered *LC 320*; **rh** *2* hovered *LC 320*

**love-rhyme / ~s** *n*
'lɤv-ˌrəɪmz
**sp** loue-rimes[1]
> rhyme

**love-shaft** *n*
'lɤv-ˌʃaft
**sp** loue-shaft[1]
> shaft

**love-shaked** *adj*
'lɤv-ˌʃɛ:kt
**sp** loue-shak'd[1]
> shake

**lovesick** *n*
'lɤv-ˌsɪk
**sp** loue-sicke[2]
> sick

**love-song / ~s** *n*
'lɤv-ˌsɒŋ / -z
**sp** loue-song[2], loue song[3] / loue-songs[2]
> song

**love-spring / ~s** *n*
'lɤv-ˌsprɪŋz
**sp** loue-springs[1]
> spring

**love-suit** *n*
'lɤv-ˌʃu:t, -ˌsju:t
**sp** loue-suit[1], loue-suite[1]
> suit

**love-thought / ~s** *n*
*m* ˌlɤv-'θɔ:ts
**sp** loue-thoughts[1]
> thought

**love-token / ~s** *n*
*m* ˌlɤv-'to:kənz
**sp** loue-tokens[1]
> token

**love-wounded** *adj*
*m* ˌlɤv-'wəʊndɪd
**sp** loue wounded[1]
> wound

**loving** *adj / n*
'lɤvɪn, -ɪŋ
**sp** louing[84] / louing[5]
**rh** moving *S 26.11*; removing, reproving *Luc 240*; reproving *S 142.2*
> unloving

**lovingly** *adv*
*m* 'lɤvɪnˌləɪ, -ɪŋ-
**sp** louingly[2]

**low / ~er / ~est** *adj*
lo: / 'lo:·əɹ / -əst
**sp** low[52], lowe[7] / lower[15] / lowest[6]
**rh** grow *Tim 4.1.40*; know *Cym 5.4.93, R2 3.3.195*; woe *LC 21*

**low / ~er** *adv*
lo: / 'lo:·əɹ
**sp** low[21], lowe[7] / lower[9]
**rh** know *TN 2.3.39*; no *Luc 1338*; show, throw *Mac 4.1.66*; woe *VA 1139*

**low / ~est** *n*
lo: / 'lo:əst
**sp** low[6], low's [low is][1], lowe[1] / lowest[1]
**rh** cow *MA 5.4.48*

**low / ~ing** *v*
'lo:ɪn, -ɪŋ
**sp** lowing[1]

**low-born** *adj*
'lo:-ˌbɔ:ɹn
**sp** low-borne[1]
> born

**low-crooked** *adj*
*m* ˌlo:-'krʊkɪd
**sp** low-crooked-[curtsies][1]
> crook

**lower** *v*
> lour

**lowing** *n*
'lo:ɪn, -ɪŋ
**sp** lowing[1]

**low-laid** *adj*
'lo:-ˌlɛ:d
**sp** low-laide[1]
> lay

**lowliness** *n*
*m* 'lo:lɪnəs, -ˌnes
**sp** lowlinesse[4], lowlynesse[1]

**lowly** *adj / adv*
'lo:ləɪ
**sp** lowlie[1], lowly[10] / lowly[1]

**lown / ~s** *n*
ləʊn / -z
**sp** lowne[1] / lownes[1]
**rh** crown, down, renown *Oth 2.3.87*

**lowness** *n*
'lo:nəs
**sp** lownesse[2]

**low-rated** *adj*
*m* ˌlo:-'rɛ:tɪd
**sp** low-rated[1]
> rate

**low-spirited** *adj*
'lo:-ˌspɪɹtɪd
**sp** low spiri-ted[1]
> spirit

**low-voiced** *adj*
*m* ˌlo:-'vəɪst
**sp** low voic'd[1]
> voice

**loyal / ~est** *adj*
'ləɪəl / -st
**sp** loyall[29] / loyall'st[1]
**rh** royal *R3 1.4.169*
> disloyal

**loyal** *n*
'ləɪəl
**sp** loyall[1]

**loyally** *adv*
*m* 'ləɪəˌləɪ
**sp** loyally[1]

**loyal·ty / ~ties** *n*
*m* 'ləɪəlˌtəɪ, -lt- / 'ləɪəlˌtəɪz
**sp** loyaltie[13], loyalty[11] / loyalties[1]
**rh** *1* thee *AY 2.3.70*; **rh** *2* descry *Per Epil.8*; I *MND 2.2.69*; die *R3 3.3.3*; lie *R2 1.1.67*

**Loys** *n*
lwɛ
**sp** Loys[1]

**lubber / ~'s / ~s** *n*
'lɤbəɹ / -z
**sp** lubber[3] / lubbers[1] / lubbars[1]

**lubberly** *adj*
'lɤbəɹləɪ
**sp** lubberly[1]

**Luccicos** *n*
'lu:ʧɪkəs
**sp** Luccicos[1]

**luce / ~s** *n*
lu:s / 'lu:sɪz, *Evans MW 1.1.17* 'ləʊsɪz
**sp** luse[1] / luces[1], *Evans* lowses[1]
> flower-de-luce

**Luce** [name] *n*
lu:s
**sp** Luce[4]

**Lucentio / ~'s** *n*
lʊ'sensɪo:, -ˌo: / lʊ'sensɪo:z
**sp** Lucentio[45], Lu-centio[2], *abbr in s.d.* Lucen[1] / Lucentios[3]
**rh** Tranio *TS 1.1.241*

**Lucetta** *n*
lʊ'ʧetə
**sp** Lucetta[12]

**Luciana** *n*
lʊsɪ'anə
**sp** Luciana[9], *abbr in s.d.* Luci[1]

**Lucianus** *n*
lʊsɪ'anəs
**sp** Lucianus[2]

**Lucifer / ~'s** *n*
'lu:sɪfəɹ / -z
**sp** Lucifer[6] / Lucifers[1]

**Lucilius** *n*
lʊ'sɪlɪəs
**sp** Lucilius[1], Lucillius[15], Lucilli-us[1]

**Lucina** *n*
lʊ'səɪnə
**sp** Lucina[1]

**Lucio / ~s** *n*
'lu:sɪo: / -z
**sp** Lucio[15], Lu-cio[1] / Lucio's[1]

**Lucius** *n*
'lu:sɪəs
**sp** Lucius[108]

**luck** *n*
lɤk
**sp** luck[4], lucke[20], [good]-lucke[1]
**rh** pluck *S 14.3*; Puck *MND 2.1.41, 5.1.422*

**luckily** *adv*
*m* 'lɤkɪˌləɪ
**sp** luckily[1]

**luckless** *adj*
'lɤkləs
**sp** lucklesse[2]

**luck·y / ~ier / ~iest** *adj*
'lɤkəɪ / -əɹ / -əst
**sp** luckie[4], lucky[2] / luckier[1] / luckiest[1]
> unlucky

**lucre** *n*
ˈluːkəɹ
**sp** lucre[2]

**Lucrece / ~'** *n*
*m* lʊˈkriːs, ˈluːkriːs
**sp** Lucrece[3], Lu-cresse[1] / Lucrece[2]

**Lucrecia / ~'s** *n*
lʊˈkriːsɪəz
**sp** Lucrecia's[1]

**Lucullus** *n*
lʊˈkɤləs
**sp** Lucullus[8], *abbr in s.d.* L[1]

**Lucy** *n*
ˈluːsəɪ
**sp** Lucie[4], Lucy[1]

**Ludlow** *n*
ˈlɤdloː
**sp** Ludlow[1]

**Lud's-town** *n*
*m* ˈlɤdzˌtəʊn, ˌlɤdzˈtəʊn
**sp** Luds-Towne[4]

**luff / ~ed** *v*
lʊft
**sp** looft[1]

**lug** *v*
lɤg
**sp** lugge[2]

**luggage** *n*
ˈlɤgɪʤ
**sp** luggage[5]

**lugged** *adj*
lɤgd
**sp** lugg'd[1]

**lukewarm** *adj*
ˈluːkwɑːɹm
**sp** lukewarm[1], luke-warme[1]

**Luke / ~'s** *n*
=
**sp** Lukes[3]

**lull / ~s / ~ing / ~ed** *v*
lɤl / -z / ˈlɤlɪn, -ɪŋ / lɤld
**sp** lull[1] / lulls[1] / lulling[1] / lul'd[1], lull'd[1]

**lulla** *interj*
ˈlɤlə
**sp** lulla[4]

**lullaby** *n*
*m* ˈlɤləˌbəɪ, -əb-
**sp** lullabie[2], lullaby[5]
**rh** *1* nigh *MND 2.2.19*; *rh 2* melody *MND 2.2.14, 25*

**lump** *n*
ˈlɤmp
**sp** lump[1], lumpe[5]

**lumpish** *adj*
ˈlɤmpɪʃ
**sp** lumpish[1]

**Luna** *n*
ˈluːnə
**sp** Luna[1]

**luna·cy / ~cies** *n*
*m* ˈluːnəˌsəɪ, -əs- / -əˌsəɪz
**sp** lunacie[4], lunacy[1] / lunacies[1]
**rh** by *Tit 5.2.70*

**lunatic** *adj*
*m* ˈluːnəˌtɪk, -ət- / *Evans MW 4.1.64, 4.2.117* ˈluːnətɪks
**sp** lunaticke[8], lunatique[1], *Evans* lunaticks[1], lunatics[1]

**lunatic** *n*
*m* ˈluːnəˌtɪk, -ət-
**sp** lunaticke[3]

**lune / ~s** *n*
luːnz
**sp** lunes[1]

**lung / ~s** *n*
lɤŋz
**sp** lunges[1], lungs[15]

**Lupercal** *n*
ˈluːpəɹˌkɑl
**sp** Lupercall[2]

**lurch / ~ed** *v*
lɐːɹʧ / -t
**sp** lurch[1] / lurcht[1]

**lure** *n / v*
luːɹ
**sp** lure[1] / lure[1]

**lurk / ~s / ~eth / ~ing / ~ed** *v*
lɐːɹk / -s / ˈlɐːɹk·əθ / -ɪn, -ɪŋ / lɐːɹkt
**sp** lurke[3] / lurkes[2], lurks[1] / lurketh[1] / lurking[2] / lurk'd[1], lurkt[1]
**rh** work *PP 18.39*

**lurking** *adj*
ˈlɐːɹkɪn, -ɪŋ
**sp** lurking[3]
> fell-lurking

**luscious** *adj*
ˈlɤʃɪəs
**sp** luscious[1], lushious[1]

**lush** *adj*
lɤʃ
**sp** lush[1]

**lust / ~'s / ~s** *n*
lɤst / -s
**sp** lust[41] / lusts[1] / lustes[1], lusts[5]
**rh** dust, thrust *Luc 1384*; just, self-trust *Luc 156*; mistrust *Luc 1354*; mistrust, unjust *Luc 282*; thrust *VA 42*; trust *S 129.2*; unjust *Luc 188*

**lust / ~s / ~ed** *v*
lɤsts / ˈlɤstɪd
**sp** lusts[1] / lusted[1]

**lust-dieted** *adj*
*m* ˌlɤst-ˈdəɪətɪd
**sp** lust-dieted[1]
> diet

**lustful** *adj*
ˈlɤstfʊl
**sp** lustfull[4]

**lustihood** *n*
ˈlɤstəɪˌʊd, -ˌhʊd
**sp** lustihood[1], lustyhood[1]

**lustily** *adv*
*m* ˈlɤstɪləɪ, -ˌləɪ
**sp** lustily[3]
**rh** cry *VA 869*

**lustique** *adj*
ˈlɤstɪk
**sp** lustique[1]

**lustre** *n*
ˈlɤstəɹ
**sp** luster[6], lustre[7]
> lack-, out-lustre

**lustrous** *adj*
ˈlɤstrəs
**sp** lustrous[2]

**lust-stained** *adj*
ˌlɤst-ˈstɛːnd
**sp** lust-stain'd[1]
> stain

**lust-wearied** *adj*
ˌlɤst-ˈwiːrəɪd, -ˈwe-
**sp** lust-wearied[1]
> weary

**lust·y / ~ier / ~iest** *adj*
ˈlɤstəɪ / -əɹ / -əst
**sp** lustie[18], lu-stie[1], lusty[13] / lustier[3] / lustiest[1]
> overlusty

**lusty** *adv*
ˈlɤstəɪ
**sp** lustie[1]

**lute / ~s** *n*
ljuːt / -s
**sp** lute[15] / lutes[2]
**rh** mute *Per 4.Chorus.25*

**lute-case** *n*
ˈljuːt-ˌkɛːs
**sp** lute-case[1]
> case

**lute-string** *n*
ˈljuːt-ˌstrɪŋ
**sp** lute-string[1]
> string

**Lutheran** *n*
ˈluːθrən, -θər-
**sp** Lutheran[1]

**luxurious** *adj*
ləkˈsjuːrɪəs
**sp** luxurious[5]

**luxuriously** *adv*
*m* ləkˈsjuːrɪəsˌləɪ
**sp** luxuriously[1]

**luxury** *n*
*m* ˈlɤksərəɪ, -əˌr-
**sp** luxurie[4], luxury[3]
**rh** chastity *LC 314*; fantasy *MW 5.5.94*

**Lycaonia** *n*
lɪkəɪˈoːnɪə
**sp** Licoania[1]

**Lycurgus / ~es** *n*
ləɪˈkɐːɹgəsɪz
**sp** Licurgusses[1]

**Lydia** *n*
ˈlɪdɪə
**sp** Lydia[2]

**lying / ~est** *adj*
ˈləɪɪn, -ɪŋ / -st
**sp** lying[6] / lying'st[1], lyingst[1]
> lie

**lying** *n*
ˈləɪɪn, -ɪŋ
**sp** lying[8], ly-ing[1]
> lie

**lym** *n*
lɪm
**sp** *emend of KL 3.6.68* hym[1]
**rh** grim *KL 3.6.68*

**Lysander / ~'s** *n*
lɪˈsandəɹ, ləɪ- / -z
**sp** Lisander[1], Lysander[44] / Lysanders[3]

# M

**M** [letter] *n*
'em
**sp** M.[O.A.I.][4]

**ma** *Fr*
> je

**Mab** *n*
=
**sp** Mab[3]

**Macbeth / ~'s** *n*
=
**sp** Macbeth[60] / Macbeths[4]
**rh** *1* breath *Mac 4.1.97*; death *Mac 1.2.68, 3.5.4*; **rh** *2* heath *Mac 1.1.7*

**Maccabeus** *n*
ˌmakə'bɛːəs
**sp** Machabeus[5]

**Macdonwald** *n*
mək'dɒnəld
**sp** Macdonwald[1]

**Macduff / ~'s** *n*
=
**sp** Macduff[9], Macduffe[18] / Macduffes[1]
**rh** enough *Mac 4.1.70, 5.6.72*

**mace / ~s** *n*
mɛːs / 'mɛːsɪz
**sp** mace[7], mase[1] / maces[1]

**Macedon** *n*
'masɪdən
**sp** Macedon[5]

**Machiavel** *n*
*m* 'matʃəˌvɪl
**sp** Macheuile[1], Macheuill[1], Machiuell[1]

**machination / ~s** *n*
ˌmatʃɪ'nɛːsɪən / -z
**sp** machination[1] / machinations[1]

**machine** *n*
'maʃiːn
**sp** machine[1]

**mackerel** *n*
'makrəl
**sp** mackrell[1]

**Macmorris** *n*
=
**sp** Mackmorrice[5], Makmorrice[2]

**maculation** *n*
ˌmakjə'lɛːsɪən
**sp** maculation[1]

**mad** *adj*
=
**sp** mad[219], [starke]-mad[1], madde[10]
**rh** bad *CE 5.1.68, Luc 997, S 140.9*; had *1H6 5.3.85, S 129.8*; lad, sad *MND 3.2.441*
> cuckold-, horn-mad

**mad** *n*
=
**sp** madde[1]

**mad / ~s / ~ding / ~ded** *v*
= / = / 'madɪn, -ɪŋ / =
**sp** mad[2] / maddes[1], mads[1] / madding[1] / madded[1]

**madam / ~'s / ~s** *n*
=
**sp** madam[428], ma-dam[1], madame[75], madam's [madam is][1], maddam[4] / madams[1] / madames[1], madams[1]

**madame** *Fr n*
ma'dam
**sp** madame[9]

**mad-brain / ~ed** *adj*
'mad-ˌbrɛːn / -d
**sp** mad-braine[1] / mad-brain'd[2], mad-brayn'd[1]
> brain

**mad-bred** *adj*
=
**sp** mad-bred[1]
> breed

**madcap** *adj / n*
=
**sp** madcap[1], mad-cap[2] / mad-cap[4]
> cap

**madded** *adj*
=
**sp** madded[1]

**madding** *adj / n*
'madɪn, -ɪŋ
**sp** madding[1] / madding[1]

**made** *adj*
mɛːd
**sp** made[3]

**made** *v*
> make

**Madeira** *n*
mə'derə
**sp** Madera[1]

**made-up** *adj*
'mɛːd-ˌɤp
**sp** made-vp-[villaine][1]

**mad-headed** *adj*
'mad-ˌedɪd, -ˌhe-
**sp** mad-headed[1]
> head

**madly** *adv*
'madləɪ
**sp** madlie[1], madly[12]

**madly-used** *adv*
'madləɪ-ˌju:zd
**sp** madly vs'd[1]
> use

**mad·man / ~man's / ~men** *n*
=
**sp** madman[15], mad man[6] / madmans[1], mad-mans[2], mad mans[1] / madmen[8], mad men[3]

**madness** *n*
=
**sp** madnes[2], madnesse[63]

**Madonna** *n*
=
**sp** Madona[10]

**madrigal / ~s** *n*
'madrɪˌgɑlz
**sp** madrigalls[2]
**rh** falls *MW 3.1.17, PP 19.8*

**madwom·an / ~en** *n*
=
**sp** mad woman[2] / madwomen[1]
> woman

**Maecenas** *n*
mə'si:nəs
**sp** Mecenas[10], Me-cenas[1]

**maggot** *adj*
=
**sp** maggot[2]

**maggot / ~s** *n*
=
**sp** magots[2]

**magic** *adj / n*
=
**sp** magick[2], magicke[2] / magick[3], magicke[6]

**magical** *adj*
'madʒɪkɑl
**sp** magicall[1]

**magician** *n*
mə'dʒɪsɪən
**sp** magitian[5]

**magistrate / ~s** *n*
*m* 'madʒɪˌstrɛ:t, -ɪstrət / -s
**sp** magistrate[3] / magistrates[6]

**magnanimity** *n*
ˌmagnə'nɪmɪtəɪ
**sp** magnanimitie[1]

**magnanimous** *adj*
=
**sp** magnanimious[2], magnanimous[4], magnani-mous[1]

**magni** *Lat*
> magnus

**magnificence** *n*
=
**sp** magnificence[1]

**magnificent** *adj*
=
**sp** magnificent[2]

**magnifico / ~s** *n*
məg'nɪfɪˌko: / -z
**sp** magnifico[1] / magnificoes[2]

**magnif·y / ~iest** *v*
'magnɪˌfəɪst
**sp** magnifi'st[1]

**magn·us / ~i** *Lat adj*
'magni:
**sp** magni[1]

**Magnus** *n*
'magnəs
**sp** Magnes[1]

**Mahomet** *n*
*m* 'mɑ:əˌmet, -hə-
**sp** Mahomet[1]

**Mahu** *n*
'mɑ:u:, -hu:
**sp** Mahu[1]

**maid / ~'s / ~s / ~s'** *n*
mɛ:d / -z
**sp** made[1], maid[119], maide[48], mayd[3] / maides[3], maids[7] / maides[23], maids[29] / maids[1]
**rh** *1* afraid *LC 177*; aid *AW 5.3.327*; braid *AW 4.2.74*; laid *Luc 1214, TN 2.4.53*; paid *AW 2.1.145, Tem 4.1.95*; sore-betrayed *LC 329*; stayed *Luc 1277*; swayed *MND 2.2.122*; weighed *RJ 1.2.96*; **rh** *2* said *AW 2.3.141, 1H6 4.7.38, KL 1.1.182, LC 177, MND 2.2.65, 79, MW 5.5.49, Per 4. Chorus.17*
**pun** *TN 3.4.53* made
> beggar-, chamber-, hand-, market-, mermaid, milk-, school-, sea-maid

**maiden** *adj*
'mɛ:dən
**sp** maiden[24], mayden[1]

**maiden / ~'s / ~s / ~s'** *n*
'mɛ:dən / -z
**sp** maiden[14], maiden-[bed][1], maiden-[blood][1] / maidens[6] / maidens[12], maydens[1] / maidens[1]

**maidenhead / ~s** *n*
'mɛ:dənˌed, -ˌhed / -z
**sp** maidenhead[4], maiden-head[3], maiden head[1], maydenhead[1], mayden-head[1] / maiden-heads[4]
**rh** bed *Per 3.Chorus.10*; wedding-bed *RJ 3.2.137*

**maidenhood / ~s** *n*
'mɛ:dənˌʊd, -ˌhʊd / -z
**sp** maidenhood[1], maiden-hood[1] / maidenhoods[1]
**rh** blood *1H6 4.6.17*

**maiden·ly / ~liest** *adj*
'mɛ:dənləst
**sp** maidenlest[1]

**maidenly** *adv*
*m* 'mɛ:dənləɪ, -dənˌləɪ
**sp** maidenly[2]

**maidhood** *n*
'mɛ:d,ʊd, -,hʊd
**sp** maidhood[1], maid-hood[1]
**pun** *TN 3.4.54* made

**Maid Marian** *n*
,mɛ:d 'marɪən
**sp** Maid-marian[1]

**maid-pale** *adj*
'mɛ:d-,pɛ:l
**sp** maid-pale[1]
> pale

**mail** *n*
mɛ:l
**sp** male[2]

**mail / ~ed** *v*
*m* mɛ:ld
**sp** mayl''d[1]

**mailed** *adj*
*m* mɛ:ld, 'mɛ:lɪd
**sp** mail'd[1], mayled[1]

**maim / ~s** *n*
mɛ:m / -z
**sp** maime[1], mayme[2] / maimes[1]

**maim** *LC* **/ ~ed** *v*
mɛ:m / *m* mɛ:md
**sp** maime[1] / maim'd[2], maym'd[1]
**rh** aim, exclaim *LC 312*

**maimed** *adj*
*m* 'mɛ:mɪd
**sp** maimed[1]

**main** *adj*
mɛ:n
**sp** main-[chance][1], maine[29], maine-[course][1]
**rh** gain *S 64.7*
**pun** *2H6 1.1.208ff* Maine

**main** *n*
mɛ:n
**sp** maine[11], mayne[1]

**main / ~ed** *v*
mɛ:nd
**sp** main'd[2]

**main / ~s** *Fr n*
mɛ̃
**sp** main[4] / main[1]

**Maine** *n*
mɛ:n
**sp** Main[1], Maine[16], Mayne[2]
**rh** slain *2H6 1.1.210*
**pun** *2H6 1.1.208ff* main

**mainly** *adv*
'mɛ:nləɪ
**sp** mainely[3], mainly[1]

**mainmast** *n*
'mɛ:nmast
**sp** maine mast[1]
> mast

**maintain / ~s / ~ed** *v*
*m* mən'tɛ:n, 'mentɛ:n / mən'tɛ:nz / mən'tɛ:nd
**sp** maintaine[40], main-taine[1] / maintaines[2], maintains[1] / maintain'd[12], maintained[1]
**rh** pain *2H4 4.5.223*; reign *S 121.13*; slain, twain *Cym 5.4.74* / complained, stained *Luc 1838*

**maintenance** *n*
*m* 'mɛ:ntə,nans
**sp** maintenance[3]

**mais** *Fr conj*
mɛ
**sp** mays[1]

**maison** *Fr n*
mɛ'zɔ̃
**sp** maison[1]

**majestas** *Lat n*
'majestas
**sp** maiestas[1]

**majestic** *adj*
=
**sp** maiesticke[3]

**majestical** *adj*
*m* mə'ʤestɪ,kɑl, -ɪk-
**sp** maiesticall[8]

**majestically** *adv*
mə'ʤestɪkləɪ
**sp** maiestically[1]

**majest·y / ~'s / ~ies** *n*
*m* 'maʤɪs,təɪ, -stəɪ / -z
**sp** maiestee[2], maiestie[136], ma-iestie[2], maie-stie[1], maiesty[113], ma-iesty[1], *Fluellen* maiesties [majesty][1], *emend of H5 1.2.197* maiesties[1] / maiesties[10], maie-sties[2] / maiesties[17]
**rh** *1* calamity *1H6 1.2.79*; dexterity *Luc 1387*; embassy *LLL 1.1.134*; inconstancy *KJ 3.1.321*; modesty *AY 3.2.142*; willingly *2H6 1.3.209*; **rh** *2* awry *R2 2.2.20*; eye *LLL 4.3.226, S 7.4*; eye, satisfy *Luc 93*; fly *S 78.8*; high *VA 856*; I *2H6 1.2.70, R3 1.3.32*

**major** *adj / n*
'mɛ:ʤəɹ
**sp** maior[2] / maior[1]

**majority** *n*
*m* mə'ʤɒrɪ,təɪ
**sp** maioritie[1]

**mak·e / ~est / ~es / ~eth / ~ing / made / ~'st** *v*
mɛ:k / -st / -s / 'mɛ:k·əθ / -ɪn, -ɪŋ / mɛ:d / -st
**sp** make[1565], make's [make his][1], make's [make us][1], make't[3], mak't[1], make-[a-de-sot][1], make[-a-the][1] / makest[1], mak'st[22] / makes[348] / maketh[2] / making[59] / mad[1], made[792], made[-me][1] / mad'st[7]
**rh** awake *MND 3.2.116*; forsake *Luc 155, S 12.9*; sake *LC 321, MV 1.1.184, S 145.1*; shake *Luc 225*; take *AY 4.3.62, Luc 1198, S 81.1, 91.14*; wake *KL 3.2.32*; **make it** take it *AW 4.3.220* / tak'st *PT 18* / betakes *PP 8.10*; takes *LC 109, MND 3.2.178, Oth 1.3.205* / awaketh, slaketh *Luc 1678* / mistaking *S 87.12* / fade *Cym 5.4.108, S 54.12, Tem 1.2.398*; jade *S 51.10*; persuade *Luc 31*; shade *Luc 804, PP 6.4, 20.4, S 43.9, 53.1*; spade *Ham 5.1.94*; trade *TC 5.10.53*
**pun** made *TN 3.4.54* maid
> unmake; a-making; mouth-, new-made

**makepeace** *n*
'mɛːkpiːs
**sp** make-peace[1]

**maker / ~s** *n*
'mɛːkəɹ / -z
**sp** maker[6] / ma-kers[1]
> ballad-, card-, coach-, comfit-, cuckold-, gallows-, gibbet-, grave-, horn-, jig-, noise-, peace-, rope-, sail-, shoe-, widow-maker

**making / ~s** *n*
'mɛːkɪn, -ɪŋ / -z
**sp** making[10], mak-ing[1] / makings[1]

**mal** *Fr n*
mal
**sp** mal-[y-pence][1]

**mala** *Lat*
'mɑːlə
**sp** mala[1]

**malad·y / ~ies** *n*
*m* 'maləˌdəɪ, -ədəɪ / 'maləˌdəɪz
**sp** maladie[3], malady[5], mala-dy[1], malladie[1], mallady[1] / maladies[1]
**rh** qualities *VA 745*

**malapert** *adj*
*m* 'maləˌpɐːɹt, -əpəɹt
**sp** malapert[3]

**Malcolm / ~'s** *n*
=
**sp** Malcolm[2], Malcolme[13], Malcome[1] / Malcolmes[1]

**malcontent** *adj*
=
**sp** malecontent[1]
**rh** lent *VA 313*
> half-malcontent

**malcontent / ~s** *n*
=
**sp** male-content[1] / malecontents[2]

**male** *adj*
mɛːl
**sp** male[7], male-[child][1], male-[childe][1], male-[deere][1], male-[tyger][1]

**male / ~s** *n*
mɛːl / -z
**sp** male[3] / males[2]

**malefaction / ~s** *n*
*m* ˌmalɪ'faksɪˌɒnz
**sp** malefactions[1]

**malefactor / ~s** *n*
ˌmalɪ'faktəɹ / -z
**sp** malefactor[1] / malefactors[2]

**malevolence** *n*
*m* mə'levəˌlens
**sp** maleuolence[1]

**malevolent** *adj*
*m* mə'levəˌlent
**sp** maleuolent[1]

**malice** *n*
=
**sp** malice[56], mallice[16]

**malicho** *n*
mə'lɪkoː, -'ləɪ-
**sp** malicho[1]

**malicious** *adj*
mə'lɪsɪəs
**sp** malicious[11], malitious[1]

**maliciously** *adv*
*m* mə'lɪsɪəsˌləɪ
**sp** maliciously[3]

**malign** *adj*
mə'ləɪn
**sp** maligne[1]

**malignancy** *n*
mə'lɪgnənsəɪ
**sp** malignancie[1]

**malignant** *adj*
mə'lɪgnənt
**sp** malignant[7]

**malignantly** *adv*
*m* mə'lɪgnəntˌləɪ
**sp** malignantly[1]

**malkin** *n*
'mɔːkɪn
**sp** malkin[1]

**Mall / ~'s** *n*
mɒl / -z
**sp** Mall[1] / Mals[1]

**mallard** *n*
'maləɹd
**sp** mallard[1]

**mallet** *n*
=
**sp** mallet[1]

**mallicholie**
> melancholy

**mallow / ~s** *n*
'maləz, -loːz
**sp** mallowes[1]

**Malmsey** *n*
'mɔːmzəɪ
**sp** Malmsey[1]

**malmsey-butt** *n*
'mɔːmzəɪ-ˌbɤt
**sp** malmesey-but[1], malmesey-butte[1]
> butt

**malmsey-nose** *n*
'mɔːmzəɪ-ˌnoːz
**sp** malmesey-nose[1]
> nose

**malt** *n*
mɔːt, mɔːlt
**sp** malt[1]

**malthorse** *n*
'mɔːt-ˌɔːɹs, mɔːlt, -ˌhɔːɹs
**sp** malthorse[1], malt-horse[1],
> horse

**maltworm / ~s** *n*
'mɔːt-ˌwɔːɹmz, mɔːlt-

**sp** [mustachio-purple-hu'd]-maltwormes[1], mault-wormes[1]
> worm

**Malvolio / ~'s** *n*
*m* mal'vo:lɪo:, -ɪˌo: / mal'vo:lɪo:z
**sp** Maluolio[38], Maluo-lio[1], Maluolios [Malvolio is][1], Maluolio's [Malvolio is][1] / Maluolios[1], Maluolio's[1]

**Mamilius** *n*
mə'mɪlɪəs
**sp** Mamillius[5]

**mammer / ~ing** *v*
'mamrɪn, -ɪŋ
**sp** mam'ring[1]

**mammet / ~s** *n*
'mamɪt / -s
**sp** mammet[1] / mammets[1]

**mammock / ~ed** *v*
=
**sp** mammockt[1]

**man / ~'s / ~s / men / ~'s** *n*
=
**sp** man[1774], ma[n][1], [back-sword]-man[1], [clay]-man[1], [cot-sal]-man[1], [iealousie]-man[1], [o']-man[1], [old]-man[2], [poore-old]-man[1], [slaue]-man[1], [true]-man[3], [whore-master]-man[1], [wise]man[4], [yong]-man[3], mans [man is][4], man's [man is][2], / mans[139], [blind]-mans[1], [dead]mans[1], [dead]-mans[1], [sick]mans[1], [wise]-mans[2], man's[1] / *Fr Lady H5 5.2.119* mans[1] / men[892], me[n][1], [big-bon'd]-men[1], [dead]men[1], [free]-men[1], [rich]men[2], [sad-hearted]-men[1], true-[men][1], [wise]men[6], [wise]-men[2], [yong] men[1] / mens [men's][82], [dead]-mens [men's][3], [wise]mens[1]
**rh** *1* Athenian *MND 3.2.42*; began *VA 9, 369*; Caliban *Tem 2.2.181*; can *AC 4.8.22, 1H6 4.3.44, LLL 4.1.127, MND 2.2.131, Per 2.Chorus.11, R2 5.3.86, S 141.11*; fan *LLL 4.1.145, TNK Prol.17*; scan *Per 2.2.56*; span *AY 3.2.125, Oth 2.3.66, Tim 5.3.4*; no man woman *TG 3.1.104*; **rh** *2* on *MND 2.1.263, 3.2.348*; **rh** *3* one *TS 3.2.81* / again *R2 3.2.76, Tim 4.2.41*; pen *H5 Epil.3, Luc 1291, S 16.12, 19.12, 32.8, 81.14*; then *H5 4.8.125, LLL 5.2.346, MND 3.2.67, MV 2.1.46, Oth 4.3.54, PP 18.35, 18.43, RJ 2.3.76, S 146.13*; when *AW 2.1.152, H8 1.1.6, MM 4.2.84*
> alms-, apron-, beggar-, church-, clergy-, country-, deaths-, double-, foe-, French-, gentle-, hang-, harvest-, heads-, liege-, market-, sea-, slaughter-, three-, work-man

**man / ~ned** *v*
=
**sp** man[2] / mans[1] / mann'd[6]
> unmanned

**manacle / ~s** *n*
=
**sp** manacle[1] / manacles[4]

**manacle** *v*
=
**sp** manacle[2]

**manage** *n*
=
**sp** manage[3], mannage[7]

**manage / ~d** *v*
= / *m* 'manɪˌʤed
**sp** manage[9], mannage[1], man-nage[1] / managed[2]
**rh** bed *CE 3.2.19*

**manager** *n*
'manɪʤəɹ
**sp** manager[3]

**managing** *n*
'manɪʤɪn, -ɪŋ
**sp** managing[2]
**rh** king *H5 Epil.11*

**man-at-arms / ~-of-** *n*
ˌman ət 'ɑ:ɹmz / -əv-
**sp** man at armes[2] / man of armes[2]

**man-child** *n*
'man-ˌʧəɪld
**sp** man-child[1]

**Manchus** *n*
'maŋkəs
**sp** Manchus[1]

**mandate** *n*
'mandɛ:t
**sp** mandate[3]

**mandragora** *n*
man'dragrə, -gər-
**sp** mandragora[2]

**mandrake / ~'s / ~s** *n*
'mandrɛ:k / -s
**sp** mandrake[1] / mandrakes[1] / mandrakes[1]

**mane / ~s** *n*
mɛ:n / -z
**sp** mane[1] / manes[1]
**rh** again *VA 271*

**man-entered** *adj*
*m* ˌman-'entəɹd
**sp** man-entred[1]

**man·eo / ~et / ~ent** *Lat v*
'manet / 'manent
**sp** manet[40] / manent[1]

**manes** *Lat n*
'manez
**sp** manes[1]

**manfully** *adv*
*m* 'manfʊˌləɪ
**sp** manfully[2]

**mangl·e / ~es / ~ing /~ed** *v*
= / = / 'maŋglɪn, -ɪŋ / =
**sp** mangle[2] / mangles[1] / mangling[1] / mangled[4]

**mangled** *adj*
=
**sp** mangled[9]

**mangy** *adj*
'mɛ:nʤəɪ
**sp** mangie[1]

**manhood / ~s** *n*
'manʊd, -hʊd / -z
**sp** manhood[23], man-hood[1], manhoode[1] / manhoods[2]

**manifest** *adj*
=
**sp** manifest[10]

**manifest / ~s / ~ed** *v*
=
**sp** manifest[2], ma-nifest[1] / manifests[2] / manifested[3]

**manifested** *adj*
=
**sp** manifested[1]

**manifold** *adj*
*m* 'manɪˌfo:ld, -ɪf-
**sp** manifold[6]

**manifoldly** *adv*
*m* 'manɪˌfo:ldləɪ
**sp** manifoldlie[1]

**manka** *nonsense word*
'maŋka
**sp** manka[1]

**mankind** *n*
man'kəɪnd
**sp** mankind[1], mankinde[18]
**rh** find *Tim 4.1.36*

**manlike** *adj*
'manləɪk
**sp** manlike[1]

**manly** *adj / adv*
'manləɪ
**sp** manlie[1], manly[16] / manly[1]
**rh** *adj* victory *2H6 4.8.50*
> unmanly

**man-monster** *n*
'man-ˌmɒnstəɹ
**sp** man-monster[1]

**manna** *n*
=
**sp** manna[1]

**manner / ~s** *n*
'manəɹ / -z
**sp** maner[1], manner[79] / maners[1], ma-ners[1], manners[64], [good]-manners[1], man-ners[2]
**pun** *LLL 1.1.202* manor

**mannered** *adj*
'manəɹd
**sp** manner'd[1]
> unmannered

**mannerly** *adj / adv*
*m* 'manəɹˌləɪ
**sp** mannerly[4] / manerly[1], mannerly[2]
**rh** *adv* be, see *MV 2.9.100*
> unmannerly

**mannikin** *n*
=
**sp** manakin[1]

**Manningtree** *adj*
=
**sp** Manning Tree[1]

**man of arms**
> man-at-arms

**manor / ~s** *n*
'manəɹ / -z
**sp** mannor[3] / mannors[2], manors[1]

**manor-house** *n*
'manəɹ-ˌəʊs, -ˌhəʊs
**sp** mannor house[1]
**pun** *LLL 1.1.203* manner
> house

**man-queller** *n*
'man-ˌkweləɹ
**sp** man-queller[1]
> quell

**mansion** *n*
'mansɪən
**sp** mansion[11]

**manslaughter** *n*
*m* ˌman'slɑ:təɹ, -lɔ:t-
**sp** man-slaughter[1]

**mansonry** *n*
*m* 'mansənˌrəɪ
**sp** mansonry[1]

**mantle** *adj*
=
**sp** mantled[1]

**mantle / ~s** *n*
=
**sp** mantle[13] / mantles[1]

**mantle / ~d** *v*
=
**sp** mantle[2] / mantled[1]
> dismantle

**Mantua / ~'s** *n*
*m* 'mantjʊə, -ʊˌa / 'mantjʊəz
**sp** Mantua[20] / Mantuas[1]

**Mantuan** *n*
'mantjʊən
**sp** Mantuan[2], Man-tuan[1]

**manu** *Lat*
> manus

**manual** *adj*
'manjʊal
**sp** manuall[1]

**manure / ~d** *v*
mən'ju:ɹ / -d
**sp** manure[1] / manured[1], manu-red[1]

**manus / manu** *Lat* *n*
'manʊs / 'manu:
**sp** manus[2] / *Lat emend of LLL 5.1.65* vnum[1]
**rh** canus *LLL 5.2.587* [*Lat*]

**many** *adj*
'manəɪ
**sp** manie[25], [a]-manie[1], many[443], ma-ny[7]

**many / ~'s** *n*
'manəɪ / -z
**sp** manie[2], ma-nie[1], many[65], ma-ny[2], meynie[1] / manies[1]
**rh** any *KL 3.2.30, S 10.3, VA 707*; penny *TS 3.2.83*

**many-coloured** *adj*
'manəɪ-ˌkɤləɹd
**sp** manie colour'd[1], many-coloured[1]
> colour

**many-headed** *adj*
'manəɪ-ˌedɪd, -ˌhe-
**sp** many-headed[1]
> head

**map / ~s** *n*
=
**sp** map[5], mappe[4] / maps[2]

**map / ~ped** *v*
=
**sp** mapp'd[1]

**mappery** *n*
'maprəɪ
**sp** mapp'ry[1]

**mar / ~s / ~ring / ~red** *v*
mɑːɹ / -z / 'mɑːrɪn, -ɪŋ / mɑːɹd
**sp** mar[5], marre[21] / marres[5] / marring[2] / mard[1], mar'd[5], marr'd[6]
**rh** car, far *MND 1.2.33* / hard *AW 2.3.296, CE 2.1.92, VA 478*

**marble** *adj / adv / n*
'mɑːɹbəl
**sp** marble[7] / marble[2] / marble[5]

**marble-breasted** *adj*
'mɑːɹbəl-ˌbrestɪd
**sp** marble-brested[1]

**marbled** *adj*
'mɑːɹbəld
**sp** marbled[1]

**marble-hearted** *adj*
'mɑːɹbəl-ˌɑːɹtɪd, -ˌhɑː
**sp** marble-hearted[1]

**Marcade** *n*
mɑːɹ'kad
**sp** Marcade[2]

**marcantant** *n*
'mɑːɹkəntənt
**sp** marcantant[1]

**Marcellae** *n*
mɑːɹ'sele
**sp** Marcellae[1]

**Marcellus** *n*
mɑːɹ'seləs
**sp** Marcellus[13], *abbr in s.d.* Mar[1]

**march** *n*
mɑːɹʧ
**sp** march[35]

**march / ~eth / ~ing / ~ed** *v*
mɑːɹʧ / 'mɑːɹʧ·əθ / -ɪn, -ɪŋ / mɑːɹʧt
**sp** march[61] / marcheth[3] / marching[21], mar-ching[1] / march'd[5], marcht[4]

**March / ~es** [location, title] *n*
mɑːɹʧ / 'mɑːɹʧɪz
**sp** March[10] / Marches[2]

**March** [month] *n*
mɑːɹʧ
**sp** March[11]

**March-chick** *n*
'mɑːɹʧ-'ʧɪk
**sp** March-chicke[1]

**marchioness** *n*
*m* 'mɑːɹʃɪəˌnes, -ən-
**sp** Marchionesse[4]

**marchpane** *n*
'mɑːɹʃpɛːn
**sp** marchpane[1]

**Marcus** *n*
'mɑːɹkəs
**sp** Marcus[66]

**Mardian** *n*
'mɑːɹdɪən
**sp** Mardian[11]

**mare / ~s** *n*
mɛːɹ / -z
**sp** mare[3], [wilde]-mare[1], mare's [mare is][1] / mares[2]
**rh** care *VA 384*

**Margarelon** *n*
ˌmɑːɹgə'relən
**sp** Margarelon[1]

**Margaret / ~'s** *n*
*m* 'mɑːɹgrɪt, -gəˌrɪt / -s
**sp** Margaret[77], Margarite[1], Marg'ret[1], *abbr in s.d.* Marg[1] / Margarets[5]

**margent** *n*
'mɑːɹʤənt
**sp** margent[4]

**Margery** *n*
*m* 'mɑːɹʤəˌrəɪ, -ʤər-, -ʤr-
**sp** Margerie[5]
**rh** I *Tem 2.2.47*

**Maria / ~'s** *n*
mə'rəɪə / -z
**sp** Maria[21] / Marias[1]

**Marian / ~'s** *n*
=
**sp** Marian[2], Marrian[2] / Marrians[1]
> Maid Marian

**Mariana / ~'s** *n*
ˌmarɪ'anə / -z
**sp** Mariana[12] / Mariana's[2]

**marigold** *n*
'marɪˌgoːld
**sp** mary-gold[1]

**mariner / ~s** *n*
'marɪnəɹ / -z
**sp** marriner[1] / mariners[4], marriners[4]

**maritime** *adj*
'marɪˌtəɪm
**sp** maritime[1]

**marjoram** *n*
'mɑːɹʤərəm
**sp** margerom[1], mariorum[2]

**mark / ~s** *n*
mɑːɹk / -s
**sp** mark[3], marke[33] / markes[31], marks[2]
**rh** barque *S 116.5*; dark *RJ 2.1.33* / darks *Per 4.Chorus.36*
> drowning-, sea-mark

**mark / ~s / *VA* ~eth / ~ing / ~ed** *v*
mɑːɹk / -s / ˈmɑːɹk·əθ / -ɪn, -ɪŋ / *m* -ɪd, mɑːɹkt
**sp** mark[5], marke[131] / markes[3] / marketh[1] / marking[2] / mark'd[14], marked[2], markt[13]
**rh** lark *MND 3.1.125, 4.1.92, PP 14.17* / barketh *VA 457*
> elvish-, war-marked

**Mark** [name] *n*
mɑːɹk
**sp** Mark[17], Marke[28]

**market** *adj*
ˈmɑːɹkɪt
**sp** market[9]

**market / ~s** *n*
ˈmɑːɹkɪt / -s
**sp** market[4] / markets[3]

**marketable** *adj*
ˈmɑːɹkɪtəbəl
**sp** marketable[2]

**market-maid** *n*
ˈmɑːɹkɪt-ˌmɛːd
**sp** market-maid[1]
> maid

**market-man / ~men** *n*
ˈmɑːɹkɪt-ˌmen
**sp** market men[2]
> man

**market-place** *n*
ˈmɑːɹkɪt-ˌplɛːs
**sp** market-place[9], market place[14]
> place

**marking** *n*
ˈmɑːɹkɪn, -ɪŋ
**sp** marking[2]

**markman** *n*
ˈmɑːɹkmən
**sp** marke man[1]

**marl** *n*
mɑːɹl
**sp** marle[1]

**Marle** [name] *n*
mɑːɹl
**sp** marle[1]

**marmoset** *n*
ˈmɑːɹməˌzet
**sp** marmazet[1]

**marquess** *n*
ˈmɑːɹkɪs, -kw-
**sp** marques[1], marquesse[14], mar-quesse[1]

**marriage / ~s** *n*
*m* ˈmarɪʤ, -ɪˌɑːʤ, -ɪɑːʤ / -ɪz
**sp** mariage[4], marriage[103], mar-riage[2], marri-age[1], mar-ryage[1] / marriages[3]
**rh** charge *3H6 4.1.33*; rage, sage *Luc 221*

**marriage-bed** *n*
ˈmarɪʤ-ˌbed, -ɪɑːʤ-
**sp** marriage bed[3]
> bed

**marriage-day** *n*
ˈmarɪʤ-ˌdɛː, -ɪɑːʤ-
**sp** marriage day[2]
> day

**marriage-hour** *n*
ˈmarɪʤ-ˌoːɹ, -ɪɑːʤ-
**sp** mariage howre[1]
> hour

**marriage-vow / ~s** *n*
ˈmarɪʤ-ˌvəʊ, -ɪɑːʤ- / -z
**sp** marriage-vow[1] / marriage vowes[1]
> vow

**married** *adj*
*m* ˈmarəɪd, -əɪˌed
**sp** married[17], marryed[1]

**marring** *n*
ˈmɑːrɪn, -ɪŋ
**sp** marring[1]

**marrow / ~s** *n*
ˈmarə, -roː / -z
**sp** marrow[3] / marrowes[2]

**marrowless** *adj*
*m* ˈmarəˌles, -roː-
**sp** marrowlesse[1]

**marry** *interj*
ˈmarəɪ
**sp** marie[3], ma-rie[1], marrie[44], mar-rie[1], marry[182], 'marry[1], mar-ry[1], mary[11]

**marr·y / ~ies / ~ing / ~ied** *v*
ˈmarəɪ / -z / -ɪn, -ɪŋ / *m* -d, -ˌed
**sp** marrie[44], mar-rie[3], marry[70], mary[1], mary-[her][2] / maries[2], marries[2], marryes[1] / marrying[10] / maried[4], married[128], mar-ried[2], marri-ed[1], marryed[10]
**rh** miscarry *LLL 4.1.112* / bed *RJ 1.5.134*
> new-, un-married

**marrying** *n*
ˈmarəɪɪn, -ɪŋ
**sp** marrying[1]

**Mars / ~'s** *n*
mɑːɹz / ˈmɑːɹzɪz
**sp** Mars[38] / Marses[2]

**Mar·s / ~tem** *Lat n*
ˈmɑːɹtem
**sp** Martem[1]

**marsh** *n*
mɑːɹʃ
**sp** marsh[1]

**marshal / ~'s** *n*
ˈmɑːɹʃal / -z
**sp** marshal[1], marshall[14] / marshalls[1], marshals[2]

**marshal / ~lest** *v*
ˈmɑːɹʃal / -st
**sp** marshall[1] / marshall'st[1]

**Marshalsea** *n*
*m* ˈmɑːɹʃalˌsiː
**sp** Marshallsey[1]

**marshalship** *n*
ˈmɑːɹʃalʃɪp
**sp** marshalship[1]

**Marsham** *n*
'mɑːɹʃəm
**sp** Marsham[1], Masham[3]

**mart / ~s** *n*
mɑːɹt / -s
**sp** mart[13] / marts[1]
**rh** part *TS 2.1.320*

**mart / ~ed** *v*
mɑːɹt / 'mɑːɹtɪd
**sp** mart[2] / marted[1]

**Martem** *Lat*
> Mars

**Martext** *n*
'mɑːɹtekst
**sp** Mar-text[4]

**martial** *adj*
'mɑːɹsɪɑl, -ɹʃɑl
**sp** marshall[2], martial[1], martiall[7]

**Martian / ~s** *n*
'mɑːɹsɪənz
**sp** Martians[1]

**Martin / ~'s** *n*
'mɑːɹtɪnz
**sp** Martins[1]

**Martino** *n*
mɑːɹ'tiːnoː
**sp** Martino[1]

**Martius** *n*
'mɑːɹsɪəs
**sp** Martius[96], Mar-tius[1]

**Martlemass** *n*
'mɑːɹtlməs
**sp** Martlemas[1]

**martlet** *n*
'mɑːɹlət, -ɹtl-
**sp** martlet[1], *emend of Mac 1.6.4* barlet[1]

**martyr / ~s** *n*
'mɑːɹtəɹ / -z
**sp** martyr[2] / martyrs[1]

**martyr / ~ed** *v*
'mɑːɹtəɹ / -d
**sp** martyr[1] / martir'd[1], martyr'd[2]

**martyred** *adj*
'mɑːɹtəɹd
**sp** martir'd[1]

**Marullus** *n*
mə'rɤləs
**sp** Murellus[2], Murrellus[1]

**marvel / ~s** *n*
'mɑːɹvəl / -z
**sp** maruaile[3], maruel[2], maruell[6], meruaile[5] / maruels[1]

**marvel / ~est / ~s / ~led** *v*
'mɑːɹvəl / -st / -z / -d
**sp** maruaile[2], maruell[10], meruaile[3], meruell[2] / maruell'st[1] / maruels[1] / marueyl'd[1]

**marvellous** *adj / adv*
'mɑːɹvləs, -vəl-
**sp** maruellous[1], meruailous[1] / maruailous[3], marueilous[3], maruellous[9], marue'lous[1], maruel's[1], maru'llous[2], meruay-lous[1]

**marvellously** *adv*
'mɑːɹvləsləɪ, -vəl-
**sp** maruellously[2]

**Mary** *n*
'mɛːrəɪ
**sp** Mary[6]

**Mary-bud / ~s** *n*
'mɛːrəɪ-ˌbɤdz
**sp** Mary-buds[1]

**masculine** *adj*
*m* 'maskjəˌlɪn, -kl-
**sp** masculine[3]

**Masham**
> Marsham

**mask, masqu·e / ~s** *n*
mask / -s
**sp** mask[2], maske[16], masque[1] / maskes[4], masks[3], masques[1]
**rh** ask *LLL 5.2.245; RJ 1.4.48*

**mask, masqu·e / ~ing / ~ed** *v*
mask / 'maskɪn, -ɪŋ / maskt
**sp** maske[1] / masking[1] / mask'd[4], maskt[5]
**rh** ask [*F, at LLL 2.1.113–29*] / tasked *LLL 5.2.127*
> dis-, un-mask

**masker, masquer / ~s** *n*
'maskəɹ / -z
**sp** masker[1] / maskers[9]

**masking, masquing** *adj*
'maskɪn, -ɪŋ
**sp** masking[2]

**mason / ~s** *n*
'mɛːsən / -z
**sp** mason[2] / masons[1]

**masonry** *n*
*m* 'mɛːsənˌrəɪ
**sp** masonry[1]
**rh** memory *S 55.6*

**mass / ~es** *n*
mas / 'masɪz
**sp** masse[8], [gyant]-masse[1] / masses[1]

**Mass** *n*
mas
**sp** Masse[1]

**Mass / by the ~** *interj*
mas / bɪθ 'mas, ˌbəɪðə-, *Jamie H5 3.2.110* bɪθ 'mes
**sp** Mas[1], Masse[3], 'Masse[1] / by'th' Masse[2], by th' masse[1], by th' Masse[1], by the Masse[2], *Jamie* by the Mes[1]

**massacre / ~s** *n*
'masakəɹ / -z
**sp** massacre[6] / massacres[2]

**massy** *adj*
'masəɪ
**sp** massie[5]

**mast / ~s** *n*
mast / -s
**sp** mast[8], maste[1] / masts[1]
> main-, top-mast

**master / ~'s / ~s / ~s'** *n*
'mastəɹ / -z
**sp** maister[47], mai-ster[1], maister's [master is][1], master[631], ma-ster[8], masters [master is][1], masters [*emend to AY 2.7.202* master][1], mayster[3], may-ster[2], *abbr* M[93], Mast[er][1] / maisters[2], masters[44], ma-sters[1] / maisters[8], mai-sters[1], masters[108] / masters[3]
**rh** plaster *VA 914*
> crafts-, over-, post-, school-, ship-, thunder-, whore-master; unmastered

**master / ~s / ~ed** *v*
'mastəɹ / -z / -d
**sp** maister[1], master[3] / masters[4] / master'd[1], mastred[2]

**master-cord** *n*
'mastəɹ-ˌkɔ:ɹd
**sp** master-cord[1]
> cord

**masterdom** *n*
*m* 'mastəɹˌdɤm
**sp** masterdome[1]
**rh** come *Mac 1.5.68*

**master-leaver** *n*
'mastəɹ-ˌli:vəɹ
**sp** master leauer[1]

**masterless** *adj*
*m* 'mastəɹˌles
**sp** masterlesse[2]

**masterly** *adv*
*m* 'mastəɹˌləɪ, -ləɪ
**sp** masterly[3], 'masterly[1]

**masterpiece** *n*
*m* 'mastəɹˌpi:s
**sp** master-peece[1]
> piece

**mastership** *n*
*m* 'mastəɹˌʃɪp
**sp** maistership[1], mastership[3]

**mastic** *adj*
=
**sp** masticke[1]

**mastiff / ~s** *n*
=
**sp** mastiffe[1] / mastiffes[3]

**match / ~es** *n*
=
**sp** match[59] / matches[3]
**rh** *1* catch *TS 2.1.323*; **rh** *2* watch *VA 586*

**match / ~es / ~ing / ~ed** *v*
= / = / 'maʧɪn, -ɪŋ / =
**sp** match[23] / matches[1] / matching[3] / match'd[3], matcht[12]
> overmatched, unmatchable, unmatched

**matchless** *adj*
=
**sp** matchlesse[2]

**mate / ~s** *n*
mɛ:t / -s
**sp** mate[9], [lacke-linnen]-mate[1] / mates[10]
**rh** fortunate *1H6 1.2.92*; Kate *Tem 2.2.46*; rate, state *Luc 18*
> bed-, book-, co-, skaines-mate

**mate / ~s / ~d** *v*
mɛ:t / -s / 'mɛ:tɪd
**sp** mate[1] / mates[1] / mated[3]
**rh** Kated *TS 3.2.243*

**mated** *adj*
'mɛ:tɪd
**sp** mated[3]

**material** *adj*
mə'ti:rɪɑl
**sp** materiall[4]

**mathematics** *n*
=, ˌmatə'matɪks
**sp** mathematickes[3]

**matine** *n*
'matɪn
**sp** matine[1]

**matron / ~'s / ~s** *n*
'mɛ:trən / -z
**sp** matron[4] / matrons[1] / matrons[4]

**matter / ~s** *n*
'matəɹ / -z
**sp** matter[348], mat-ter[5], matter's [matter is][1] / matters[25], mat-ters[1]
**rh** *1* flatter *S 87.14*; **rh** *2* water *KL 3.2.81, LC 302, LLL 5.2.207*

**Matthew** *n*
=
**sp** Mathew[2]

**mattock** *n*
=
**sp** mattocke[3]

**mattress** *n*
=
**sp** matris[1]

**mature** *adj*
mə'tju:ɹ
**sp** mature[7]

**maturity** *n*
*m* mə'tju:rɪˌtəɪ
**sp** maturity[1]

**Maud** *n*
=
**sp** Maud[1]

**Maudlin** *n*
=
**sp** Maudlin[1]

**mauger** *n*
'mɔ:gəɹ
**sp** mauger[1]

**maugre** *prep*
'mɔ:gəɹ
**sp** maugre[2]

**maul** *v*
=
**sp** maul[1], maule[1]

**Mauritania** *n*
ˌmɒrɪ'tɛ:nɪə
**sp** Mauritania[1]

**Maur·us / ~i** *Lat n*
'mɔ:ri
**sp** maury[1]

**mauvais** *Fr adj*
mɔ'vɛ
**sp** mauvais[1]

**maw / ~s** *n*
=
**sp** maw[5], mawe[1] / mawes[2]
**rh** saw *VA 602*

**maxim** *n*
=
**sp** maxime[1]

**may / ~est** *v*
mɛ: / mɛ:st, mɛst, [*also, followed by consonant*] mɛ:s, mɛs
**sp** may[1574], 'may[1], may't [may it][5] / maiest[3], maist[30], mayest[6], mayst[10], may'st[14]
**rh** away *Tit 1.1.288*; away, stay *LLL 2.1.111*; betray *S 151.7*; convey *Per 3. Chorus.55*; day *Cym 3.5.69, 3H6 4.4.14, Ham 5.1.287, LLL 5.2.341, Mac 1.3.146, 4.3.238*; decay *3H6 4.4.14*; gay *Oth 2.1.148*; play *H5 2.Chorus.39*; pray *R2 5.3.83*; say *WT 4.1.32*; stay *2H6 4.4.48*; today *CE 3.1.41, TC 1.1.116*; **may do** they do *MA 4.1.17*

**May / ~'s** *n*
mɛ: / -z
**sp** Maie[2], May[12] / Mayes[1]
**rh** day *LLL 4.3.100, PP 16.2, 20.2, R2 5.1.79, S 18.3*

**maybe** *adv*
mɛ:'bi:
**sp** maybe[1], may be[7]

**May-day** *n*
'mɛ:-ˌdɛ:
**sp** May-day[2]

**May-morn** *n*
'mɛ:-ˌmɔ:ɹn
**sp** May-morne[1]
> morn

**mayor / ~'s** *n*
'mɛ:əɹ, mɛ:ɹ / -z
**sp** maior[9], mayor[1] / maiors[1]

**maypole** *n*
'mɛ:-ˌpo:l
**sp** may-pole[1]
> pole

**maze / ~s** *n*
mɛ:z / 'mɛ:zɪz
**sp** maze[3] / mazes[1]
**rh** gaze *Luc 1151*

**maze** *adj, v*
> amaze

**mazzard** *n*
'mazəɹd
**sp** mazard[2]

**me / mine / my / myself** *det, pro*
*str* mi:, *unstr* mɪ
**sp** me[7167], [ay-]me[1], [figge-]me[1], [loue-a-]me[1], [list-]me[1], [made-]me[1], [od's-]me[1], [sty-]me[1], [tell-a-]me[2], mee[474], [let-a-]mee[1]
**rh** agree *PP 8.3*; agree, be *LLL 2.1.210*; amity, be, jollity, prosperity, solemnly, triumphantly *MND 4.1.84*; be *CE 2.2.212, Cym 4.2.29, H5 5.2.365, 1H6 4.5.23, 2H4 4.5.220, 2H6 3.1.383, LC 224, Luc 1050, 1204, PP 1.13, Per 1.2.109, R2 1.3.145, 2.1.90, RJ 2.3.85, S 35.14, 91.9, 132.1, 133.2, 138.13, Tem 4.1.103, TG 3.1.148, Tim 3.5.91, TN 4.1.63, TNK 3.5.10, WT 4.1.19, 4.4.305*; be, thee *Luc 1195*; bee *Luc 834*; benedicite *RJ 2.3.28*; Burgundy *KL 1.1.259*; Coventry *R2 1.2.57*; degree *AY 5.4.144, LLL 1.1.156*; ducdame *AY 2.5.54*; enemy *Per 2.5.64, RJ 1.5.140, 2.3.46*; fee *AW 2.1.190, MND 3.2.112, S 120.14*; free *AW 3.4.16, 1H6 5.3.116, Luc 1623, Per 2.4.1, S 134.13, 134.7*; he *AY 2.5.54, CE 4.2.12, 3H6 4.6.76, Luc 1722, MND 3.2.63, R2 4.1.175, RJ 3.1.139*; heresy *MND 2.2.148*; honesty *LLL 5.2.812*; hypocrisy *LLL 4.3.150*; indignity *Tit 1.1.7*; infamy *Luc 792*; infancy *R3 4.4.168*; knee *1H6 4.7.6, R2 5.3.130*; Muscovy *LLL 5.2.396*; necessity *LLL 1.1.151, MV 1.3.151*; opportunity *Luc 934*; perjury *LLL 5.2.396*; policy *R2 5.1.83*; preposterously *MND 3.2.120*; see *AW 2.3.72, AY 2.5.54, Ham 3.1.161, 1H6 1.2.85, LLL 2.1.244, 4.3.148, Mac 3.5.35, MND 1.1.205, 3.2.428, 5.1.178, R2 1.2.66, 3.3.171, TS 1.2.189*; see, thee *Luc 1307*; she *AW 2.3.143, Ham 4.5.63, 1H6 5.5.77, Luc 1690, 1701, MND 2.1.52*; subtlety *VA 673*; thee *AC 1.3.103, AW 4.2.67, AY 4.3.58, CE 1.2.71, 2.1.39, 2H4 4.5.48, H5 4.1.301, 1H6 4.5.39, 2H6 3.2.298, 4.4.24, 3H6 4.7.39, 5.1.97, KJ 4.1.132, KL 1.4.140, LLL 4.3.34, 65, 113, Luc 916, Mac 2.1.33, MND 1.1.177, 3.1.147, 5.1.186, PP 3.8, 10.12, R2 2.1.86, 4.1.213, RJ 3.3.173, 5.1.85, S 10.13, 22.7, 24.10, 28.6, 31.14, 36.11, 37.14, 38.5, 39.2, 41.14, 43.14, 45.12, 47.10, 50.6, 61.7, 74.8, 88.12, 97.9, 122.14, 133.14, 143.11, 150.13, Tit 1.1.63, 111, 3.2.81, 5.2.43, TN 4.1.57, VA 138, 196, 517*; three *MND 3.2.194, 5.1.329, LLL 5.2.812*; tree *AY 2.5.2, LLL 5.2.283*; trippingly *MND 5.1.385*; usury *Tim 3.5.98*; we *2H6 3.2.412, S 42.7*; ye *S 111.14*; **follows me** hateth me *MND 1.1.198*; **moved me** loves ye *TG 1.2.27*
> I, pardon-me

***mine*** *det, pro*
məɪn, *unstr* mɪn
**sp** min[1], mine[1108], mine's [mine is][5]
**rh** brine, pine *Luc 793*; Collatine *Luc 825, 1179, 1798*; Collatine, design *Luc 1691*; combine *AY 5.4.146, RJ 2.3.55*; confine, crystalline *Cym 5.4.112*; decline *CE 3.2.42*; define *S 62.5*; design, pine *LC 277*; divine *CE 3.2.30, TG 2.1.3*; eyne *AY 4.3.52, Luc 644, MND 1.1.243, 2.2.104, 5.1.172, TS 5.1.105*; fine *2H4 5.3.46, RJ 3.1.191, TG 1.2.11*; line *S 86.14*; nine *Mac 1.3.34*; resign *2H6 2.3.34, R2 4.1.190*; Rosaline *LLL 4.1.57, 105, 5.2.441, RJ 2.3.39, 2.3.78*; shine *LLL 4.3.69, 90, PP 3.12, PT 36, S 33.11, TN 4.3.35*; thine *Cor 4.7.57, 1H6 4.6.23, Luc 483, R3 4.4.125, S 2.10, 26.5, 92.2, 134.3, 142.7, VA 117, 502*;

Valentine *TG 5.4.126*; wine *2H4 5.3.46*; of mine were mine *MND 1.1.200*

***my*** *det*
maɪ, *unstr also* mɪ
**sp** my[12528], [a']my[1]

***myself*** *pro*
mɪ'self, məɪ-
**sp** my self[2], myselfe[2], my selfe[547]
**rh** itself *R3 1.3.67*; pelf *PP 14.11, Tim 1.2.62*; thyself *R3 1.2.85, Tim 4.3.220*; yourself *R3 4.4.420*

**me** *Fr*
> je

**meacock** *n*
'mi:kɒk
**sp** meacocke[1]

**mead / ~s** *n*
=, mɛ:d / -z
**sp** mead[3], meade[1], [Datchet]-Meade[1] / meades[3], meads[1], medes[1]
**rh** dread *VA 636*

**meadow / ~s** *n*
'medəz, -do:z
**sp** meadowes[1], medowes[1]

**meadow-fair·y / ~ies** *n*
'medə-ˌfɛ:rəɪz, -do:-
**sp** [nightly]-meadow-fairies[1]
> fairy

**meager** *adj*
'mi:gəɹ
**sp** meager[5]

**meal / ~s** *n*
=
**sp** meale[9] / meales[6], [fish]-meales[1]
> inch-, limb-meal

**meal / ~ed** *v*
=
**sp** meal'd[1]

**mealy** *adj*
'mi:ləɪ
**sp** mealie[1]

**mean / ~er / ~est** *adj*
= / 'mi:n·əɹ / -əst, mi:nst
**sp** mean[3], meane[62] / meaner[13] / meanest[7], mean'st[2]

**mean / ~s** *n*
=
**sp** meane[24] / meanes[162], means[5]

**mean / ~est / ~s / ~eth / ~ing / ~t / ~'st** *v*
= / mi:nst / = / 'mi:n·əθ / -ɪn, -ɪŋ / = / menst, -ntst
**sp** mean[5], meane[220] / meanest[4], meanst[1], mean'st[9], means't[1] / meanes[90], means[2] / meaneth[1] / meaning[11] / meant[48] / meant'st[1]
**rh** lean *VA 126, 933* / *rh* consent *Per Epil.16*; meant ye content ye *TNK Epil.14*
> well-meant

**mean-born** *adj*
'mi:n-ˌbɔ:ɹn
**sp** meane-borne[1]
> born

**meander / ~s** *n*
mɪ'andəɹz
**sp** meanders[1]

**meanest** *n*
'mi:nəst
**sp** meanest[2]

**meaning / ~s** *n*
'mi:nɪn, -ɪŋ / -z
**sp** meaning[46], mea-ning[2] / meanings[3]
> double-, well-meaning

**meanly** *adv*
'mi:nləɪ
**sp** meanely[2], meanly[2]

**meantime** *n*
'mi:nˌtəɪm
**sp** meane time[30]

**meanwhile** *adv*
'mi:nˌʍəɪl
**sp** meane while[4]

**measles** *n*
=
**sp** meazels[1]

**measurable** *adj*
'mezəɹəbəl
**sp** measurable[1]
> unmeasurable

**measure / ~s** *n*
'mezəɹ / -z
**sp** measure[70], mea-sure[2] / measures[7], meazures[1]
**rh** leisure *MM 5.1.408*; pleasure *S 91.7*; treasure *LLL 4.3.360* / pleasures *AY 5.4.190*; treasures *VA 1148*
> overmeasure, passy-measures

**measur·e / ~es / ~ing / ~ed** *v*
'mezəɹ / -z / -ɪn, -ɪŋ / -d
**sp** measure[18] / measures[1] / measuring[2] / measur'd[10], mea-sur'd[1]

**measureless** *adj*
*m* 'mezəɹləs, -ˌles
**sp** measurelesse[2]

**measuring** *n*
'mezəɹɪn, -ɪŋ
**sp** measuring[1]

**meat / ~s** *n*
=
**sp** meat[21], [wormes]meat[1], meate[46] / meates[1], meats[2]
> spoon-, sweet-meat; baked-meats

**meatyard** *n*
'mi:tˌjɑ:ɹd
**sp** meat-yard[1]
> yard

**mechanic** *adj*
mə'kanɪk
**sp** mechanicke[3]

**mechanic / ~s** *n*
mə'kanɪks
**sp** mechanickes[1]

**mechanical** *adj*
*m* mə'kanɪkal, -ˌkɑ:l

**sp** mechanicall[2], mechanicall-[salt-butter][1]

**mechanical / ~s** *n*
*m* mə'kanɪˌkɑ:l / -z
**sp** mechanicall[1] / mechanicals[1]
**rh** stalls *MND 3.2.9*

**méchante** *Fr adj*
mɛ'ʃɑ̃:t
**sp** meschante[1]

**medal** *n*
=
**sp** medull[1]

**meddle** *v*
=
**sp** meddle[19], medle[1]

**meddler** *n*
'medləɹ
**sp** medler[2]
**rh** pedlar *WT 4.4.320*
**pun** *Tim 4.3.311* medlar

**meddling** *adj*
'medlɪn, -ɪŋ
**sp** medling[4]

**Mede** *n*
mi:d
**sp** Mede[1]

**Medea** *n*
mə'di:ə
**sp** Medea[2]

**Media** *n*
'mi:diə
**sp** Media[2]

**mediation** *n*
ˌmi:dɪ'ɛ:sɪən
**sp** mediation[2]

**mediator / ~s** *n*
*m* ˌmi:dɪ'ɛ:təɹz
**sp** mediators[1]
**rh** arbitrators, debaters *Luc 1020*

**medice** *Lat n*
'medɪse
**sp** medice[1]

**medicinable** *adj*
*m* 'medsɪˌnabəl, med'sɪnəbəl
**sp** med'cinable[1], medcinable[1], medicinable[3]

**medicinal** *adj*
*m* 'medsɪˌnɑl
**sp** medicinall[1]

**medicine / ~s** *n*
*m* 'medsɪn, -dɪˌs- / 'medsɪnz
**sp** medcine[2], med'cine[5], medicine[15], me-dicine[1] / med'cines[1], medicines[3]

**medicine** *v*
*m* 'medsɪn, -dɪs-
**sp** med'cine[1], medicine[1]

**meditat·e / ~s / ~ing** *v*
'medɪˌtɛ:t / -s / -ɪn, -ɪŋ
**sp** meditate[2] / meditates[1] / meditating[5]
> premeditated

**meditation / ~s** *n*
ˌmedɪ'tɛ:sɪən / -z
**sp** meditation[5] / meditations[4]

**Mediterranean** *adj*
ˌmedɪ'trɛ:nɪən, -ɪtə'r-
**sp** Mediterranian[1]

**Mediterraneum** *n*
*Don Armado LLL 5.1.55*
ˌmedɪ'trɛ:nɪəm
**sp** Mediteranium[1]

**medlar / ~s** *n*
'medləɹ / -z
**sp** medler[5] / medlers[2]
**pun** *Tim 4.3.309* meddler

**medlar tree** *n*
'medləɹ ˌtri:
**sp** medler tree[1]
> tree

**meed / ~s** *n*
=
**sp** meed[6], meede[9] / meedes[1]
**rh** deed *Tit 5.3.65*; speed *Cym 3.5.163*; steed *VA 15*

**meek** *adj*
=
**sp** meek[1], meeke[6]
**rh** cheek *Luc 710*

**meekly** *adv*
'mi:kləɪ
**sp** meekely[1]

**meekness** *n*
=
**sp** meekenesse[2], meeknes[1], meeknesse[1]

**meet / ~er / ~est** *adj*
= / 'mi:təɹ / =
**sp** meet[31], meete[29] / meeter[2] / meetest[3]
**rh** sheet *Ham 5.1.95*; sweet *AW 5.3.330, Ham 5.1.64, LLL 5.2.237, R2 5.3.117*
> unmeet

**meet / ~est / ~s / ~ing / met / ~test** *v*
= / mi:tst / = / 'mi:tɪn, -ɪŋ / = / metst
**sp** meat[1], meet[118], meete[142], *Caius MW 3.1.73* meet-a[1] / meet'st[1] / meetes[7], meets[8] / meating[1], meeting[14] / met[134] / met'st[3]
**rh** feet *TN 5.1.167*; greet *LLL 5.2.143*; sweet *Ham 3.4.211* [Q2], *MND 1.1.217, RJ 2.Chorus.13, S 5.13, 94.11* / streets *TNK 1.5.16*
> bemeet

**meeting / ~s** *n*
'mi:tɪn, -ɪŋ / -z
**sp** mee-ting[1], meeting[26] / meetings[2]
**rh** greeting *RJ 1.5.89*; sweeting *TN 2.3.41*
> after-meeting

**meeting-place** *n*
'mi:tɪn-ˌplɛ:s, -ɪŋ-
**sp** meeting place[1]
> place

**meetly** *adv*
'mi:tləɪ
**sp** meetly[1]

**meetness** *S* *n*
=
**sp** meetnesse[1]
**rh** sweetness *S 118.7*

**Meg** *n*
=
**sp** Meg[4]

**mehercle** *Lat interj*
me'hɛ:ɹkle
**sp** me hercle[1]

**meilleur** *Fr*
mɛ'jœ:ɹ
**sp** melieus[1]

**meiny** *n*
'mɛ:nəɪ
**sp** meiney[1]

**Meisen** *n*
'məɪsən
**sp** Meisen[1]

**melancholy / ~'s** *n*
*m* 'melən,kɒləɪ, -nkəl-, -nkl- / -z
**sp** mallicholie[2], melancholie[4], *Evans MW 3.1.13* melancholies[1], melancholly[39], me-lancholly[1], melancholy[20], me-lancholy[1], mellancholly[1] / melancholies[1]
**rh** *1* thee *S 45.8*; **rh** *2* I *Cym 4.2.208*

**Melford** *n*
'melfəɹd
**sp** Melforde[1]

**melius** *Lat*
> bonus

**mell** *v*
=
**sp** mell[1]

**mellifluous** *adj*
=
**sp** mellifluous[1]

**mellow** *adj*
'melə, -lo:
**sp** mellow[3]

**mellow / ~ed** *v*
'melə, -lo: / -d
**sp** mellow[2] / mellow'd[1]

**mellowed** *adj*
'meləd, -lo:d
**sp** mellow'd[1]
> unmellowed

**mellowing** *n*
'meləwɪn, -ɪŋ, -lo:ɪ-
**sp** mellowing[1]

**melodious** *adj*
mɪ'lo:dɪəs
**sp** melodious[5], mellodius[1]

**melody** *n*
*m* 'melə,dəɪ, -əd-
**sp** melodie[4], melody[4]
**rh** *1* company, society *Luc 1108*; lullaby *MND 2.2.13, 24*; **rh** *2* eye *MND 1.1.189*

**melt / ~s / ~eth / ~ing / ~ed** *v*
= / = / = / 'meltɪn, -ɪŋ / =
**sp** melt[27] / melts[3] / melteth[2] / melting[1] / melted[13], mel-ted[2]
**rh** felt *MND 1.1.245, VA 144*

**melted** *adj*
=
**sp** melted[1]

**melting** *adj*
'meltɪn, -ɪŋ
**sp** melting[7]
> easy-melting

**Melun** *n*
me'lu:n
**sp** Melloone[1], Meloon[1], Meloone[4]

**member / ~s** *n*
'membəɹ / -z
**sp** member[10] / members[10]

**memento mori** *n phrase*
mɪ,mento: 'mɔ:rəɪ
**sp** memento mori[1]

**memorable** *adj*
*m* 'memərəbəl, -,rabəl
**sp** memorable[4]

**memorandum / ~s** *n*
=
**sp** memorandums[1]

**memorial / ~s** *n*
mɪ'mɔ:rɪɑl / -z
**sp** memoriall[2] / memorials[1]

**memorize / ~d** *v*
'memə,rəɪz / -d
**sp** memorize[1] / memoriz'd[1]

**memor·y / ~ies** *n*
*m* 'memə,rəɪ, -mər-, -mr- / -z
**sp** memorie[23], memory[25], [sprag]-memory[1] / memories[3]
**rh** *1* eternity *S 77.6, 122.2*; injury *Cor 5.6.155*; masonry *S 55.8*; validity *Ham 3.2.198*; **rh** *2* die *S 1.4*; fortify *S 63.11*; sky *S 15.8*

**Memphis** *n*
'memfɪs
**sp** Memphis[1]

**men**
> man

**menace / ~d** *v*
=
**sp** menace[3] / menac'd[2]

**Menaphon** *n*
'menə,fɒn
**sp** Menaphon[1]

**Menas** *n*
'menəs
**sp** Menas[13], Menes[1]

**men-children** *n*
=
**sp** men-children[1]

**mend / ~s** *n*
=
**sp** mends[1]

**mend / ~s / ~ed** *v*
=
**sp** mend[56] / mends[1] / mended[10], men-ded[1]
**rh** attend *RJ Prol.14*; commend *S 69.2*; end *Tim 5.1.219*; reprehend *MND 5.1.420*; send *Oth 4.3.104*; tend *S 103.9* / offended *MND 5.1.414*

**mended** *adj*
=
**sp** mended[2]

**mender** *n*
'mendəɹ
**sp** mender[1]
> bellows-mender

**mending** *n*
'mendɪn, -ɪŋ
**sp** mending[2]
> a-mending

**Menecrates** *n*
mə'nekrəˌti:z
**sp** Menacrates[1], Menecrates[1]

**Menelaus / ~'** *n*
ˌmenə'lɛ:əs
**sp** Menelaus[15] / Menelaus[3]

**Menenius** *n*
mə'ni:nɪəs
**sp** Menenius[29], Mene-nius[1], *abbr in s.d.* Mene[1]

**Menon** *n*
'menən
**sp** Menon[1]

**men·s / ~tis** *Lat n*
'mentɪs
**sp** mentis[1]

**mental** *adj*
'mentɑl
**sp** mentall[3]

**Menteith** *n*
men'ti:θ
**sp** Menteith[1], Menteth[2]

**mention** *n*
'mensɪən
**sp** mention[1]

**mention / ~ed** *v*
'mensɪən / -d
**sp** mention[1] / mentioned[1]

**mentioned** *adj*
'mensɪənd
**sp** mention'd[1]

**mentis** *Lat*
> mens

**menton** *Fr n*
mɑ̃'tɔ̃
**sp** menton[2]

**Mephistophilus** *n*
ˌmefɪ'stɒfɪləs
**sp** Mephostophilus[1]

**Mercatio** *n*
*m* məɹ'kɛ:sɪˌo:
**sp** Mercatio[1]
**rh** so so *TG 1.2.12*

**mercenary** *adj*
*m* 'mɐ:ɹsəˌnarəɪ, -ənrəɪ
**sp** mercenary[1], mercinarie[1]

**mercenar·y / ~ies** *n*
*m* 'mɐ:ɹsəˌnarəɪ, -ənrəɪ / 'mɐ:ɹsənˌrəɪz
**sp** mercenary[1] / mercenaries[1]

**mercer** *n*
'mɐ:ɹsəɹ
**sp** mercer[2]

**merchandise** *n*
*m* 'mɐ:ɹʧənˌdəɪz
**sp** marchandise[1], marchandize[1], merchandize[5]

**merchant / ~'s / ~s / ~s'** *n*
'mɐ:ɹʧənt / -s
**sp** marchant[3], merchant[26] / marchants[3], merchants[1] / marchants[1], merchants[9] / merchants[1]

**merchant-like** *adj*
'mɐ:ɹʧənt-ˌləɪk
**sp** merchant-like[1]

**merchant-marring** *adj*
'mɐ:ɹʧənt-ˌmɑ:rɪn, -ɪŋ
**sp** merchant-marring[1]

**merciful** *adj*
*m* 'mɐ:ɹsɪˌfʊl, -fəl
**sp** merciful[1], mercifull[18]

**mercifully** *adv*
'mɐ:ɹsɪfləɪ, -fʊl-
**sp** mercifully[1]

**merciless** *adj*
*m* 'mɐ:ɹsɪˌles, -ɪləs
**sp** merciles[1], mercilesse[5]

**mercurial** *adj*
*m* məɹ'kju:rɪˌɑl
**sp** mercuriall[1]

**Mercury / ~s** *n*
*m* 'mɐ:ɹkjəˌrəɪ, -ər- / 'mɐ:ɹkjəˌrəɪz
**sp** Mercurie[7], Mercury[8] / Mercuries[1]
> she-Mercury

**Mercutio / ~'s** *n*
*m* məɹ'kju:sɪo:, -ɪˌo: / məɹ'kju:sɪo:z
**sp** Mercutio[19], Mercutio's [*emend of RJ 3.1.116* Mercutio's is][1] / Mercutio's[1], Mercutios[2], Mercutius[1]
**rh** owe *RJ 3.1.182*; Romeo *RJ 3.1.145*

**merc·y / ~ies** *n*
'mɐ:ɹsəɪ / -z
**sp** mercie[41], 'mercie[2], [God-a]-mercie[1], mer-cie[1], mercie's [mercy is][1], mercy[128], mer-cy[1], [Goda]mercy[1], [God-a]-mercy[1], mercy-[sake][1] / mercies[3]
**rh** miscarry *2H6 4.8.47*
> unmerciful

**mere / ~st** *adj*
miːɹ / ˈmiːrəst
**sp** meere[56] / meerest[1]

**mered** *adj*
ˈmiːrɪd
**sp** meered[1]

**merely** *adv*
ˈmiːɹləɪ
**sp** meerely[20], meerly[6]

**meridian** *n*
=
**sp** meridian[1]

**Meriman** *n*
=
**sp** Meriman[1]

**merit / ~s** *n*
=
**sp** merit[36], merite[1], merrit[2], merit's [merit is][1] / merites[2], merits[6]
**rh** inherit *LLL 4.1.21*; spirit *S 108.4*

**merit / ~s / ~ed** *v*
=
**sp** merit[6] / merites[1], merits[3] / merited[6]
> demerit, unmeritable, unmeriting

**merited** *adj*
=
**sp** me-rited[1]

**meritorious** *adj*
=
**sp** meritorious[3]

**Merlin** *n*
ˈmɐːɹlɪn
**sp** Merlin[2]

**mermaid / ~'s / ~s** *n*
ˈmɐːɹmɛːd / -z
**sp** meare-maide[1], mermaid[1], mermaide[1], mer-maide[1] / mermaids[1] / mer-maides[1]

**mermaid-like** *adj*
ˈmɐːɹmɛːd-ˌləɪk
**sp** mermaid-like[1]

**Mermidon**
> Myrmidon

**Merops / ~'** *n*
ˈmerɒps
**sp** Merops[1]

**merrily** *adv*
*m* ˈmerəɪləɪ, -ˌləɪ
**sp** merily[1], merrilie[1], merrily[21]
**rh** *1* cry, fly, I, lie *Tem 5.1.92*; eye *CE 4.2.4, LLL 5.2.477, 481*; **rh** *2* speedily *1H4 4.1.134*

**merriment / ~s** *n*
*m* ˈmerəɪmənt, -ɪˌment / -ɪˌments
**sp** merriment[12], merryment[1] / merriments[1]
**rh** bent *MND 3.2.146*; consent *LLL 5.2.461*; intent *LLL 5.2.139*; lament *RJ 4.5.83*

**merriness** *n*
ˈmerəɪnəs
**sp** merrinesse[1]

**merr·y / ~ier / ~iest** *adj*
ˈmerəɪ / -əɹ / -əst
**sp** merrie[42], mer-rie[3], merry[120], mer-ry[1], mery[1] / merrier[7] / merriest[2], merryest[1]
**rh** *1* derry *TNK 3.5.137*; **rh** *2* weary *Tem 4.1.135*
> overmerry

**mes** *Fr*
> je

**Mesapotamia** *n*
ˌmesəpəˈtɛːmɪə
**sp** Mesapotamia[1]

**mesh / ~es** *n*
=
**sp** mesh[1] / meshes[1]

**mesh / ~ed** *v*
=
**sp** mesh'd[1]

**mess / ~es** *n*
=
**sp** messe[10] / messes[3]
**rh** confess *LLL 4.3.205*

**message / ~s** *n*
=
**sp** message[31] / messages[2]

**Messala** *n*
məˈsɑːlə
**sp** Messala[25]

**Messaline** *n*
ˈmesəlɪn
**sp** Messaline[2]

**messenger / ~s** *n*
ˈmesənʤəɹ / -z
**sp** messenger[133], messe[n]ger[1], mes-senger[1], messen-ger[2], *abbr in s.d.* mes[1], messeng[1] / messengers[20]

**Messina** *n*
məˈsiːnə
**sp** Messina[10]

**met**
> meet

**metal / ~s** *n*
=
**sp** mettall[13], met-tall[1], mettle[5], [base]-mettle[1], [selfe]-mettle[1] / mettals[1], mettels[1]

**metamorphose / ~d** *v*
ˌmetəˈmɔːɹfɪst
**sp** metamorphis'd[2]

**metamorphosis** *n*
ˌmetəməɹˈfoːsɪs
**sp** metamorphosis[1]

**metaphor** *n*
ˈmetəfəɹ
**sp** metaphor[3], meta-phor[1]

**metaphysical** *adj*
ˌmetəˈfɪzkɑl, -zɪk-
**sp** metaphysicall[1]

**metaphysics** *n*
=
**sp** metaphysickes[1]

**mete** *v*
mi:t
**sp** mete[1]
> bemete

**Metellus** *n*
mə'teləs
**sp** Metellus[13]

**meteor / ~s** *n*
*m* 'mi:tjəɹ, -tɪ,ɔ:ɹ / -z
**sp** meteor[4] / meteors[6]

**meter** [verse]
> metre

**metheglin / ~s** *n*
mə'teglɪn, -'θe- / -z
**sp** metheglne[1], metheglins[1]

**methink·s / ~est / methought** *v*
mɪ'θɪŋks / -t / mɪ'θɔ:t
**sp** methinkes[11], me-thinkes[10], me thinkes[104], methinks[3], me thinks[14], me think's[1] / mee-think'st[1] / methought[1], me-thought[6]
> think

**method** *n*
=
**sp** method[7], methode[1]

**methought**
> methinks

**metre, meter / ~s** *n*
'mi:təɹ / -z
**sp** meeter[2] / meeters[1]

**metropolis** *n*
=
**sp** metropolis[1]

**mettle** *n*
=
**sp** mettal[1], mettall[1], met-tall[1], mettell[3], met-tell[1], mettle[23]
> self-mettle

**mettled** *adj*
=
**sp** metled[1]
> muddy-mettled, self-mettle

**mettre / mette** *Fr v*
mɛt
**sp** mette[1]

**meus** *Lat*
> ego

**mew** *n*
mju:
**sp** mew[1]

**mew / ~ed** *v*
mju: / -d
**sp** mew[3] / meu'd[1], mew'd[4], mewed[2]

**mewling** *n*
mju:lɪn, -ɪŋ
**sp** mewling[1]

**Mexico** *n*
'meksɪko:
**sp** Mexico[1], Mexi-co[1]

**mi** [music] *n*
=
**sp** [bee]me[1], me[1]

**mi** *Ital*
> io

**mice**
> mouse

**Michael** *n*
'məɪkəl
**sp** Michael[11], Michaell[4], Michell[6]

**Michaelmas** *n*
'mɪkəlməs
**sp** Michaelmas[2]

**micher** *n*
'mɪʧəɹ
**sp** micher[1]

**miching** *adj*
'mɪʧɪn, -ɪŋ
**sp** miching[1]

**mickle** *adj*
=
**sp** mickle[5]

**microcosm** *n*
'məɪkrə,kɒzəm
**sp** microcosme[1]

**mid** *adj / n*
=
**sp** mid[1] / mid[1]

**mid-age** *n*
*m* ,mɪd-'ɛ:ʤ
**sp** mid-age[1]

**Midas** *n*
'məɪdəs
**sp** Midas[1]

**mid-day** *adj*
'mɪd-,dɛ:
**sp** mid-day[2]

**middle** *adj / n*
=
**sp** middle[5] / middle[12], mid-dle[1], midle[1]

**middle-earth**
> earth

**midnight** *adj / n*
*m* 'mɪdnəɪt, mɪd'nəɪt
**sp** midnight[5], midnight-[mushrumps][1], mid-night[1] / midnight[27], mid-night[7]
**rh** *n* light *Luc 1625*; sight *MND 1.1.223*
> night

**midriff** *n*
=
**sp** midriffe[1]

**midst** *n*
=
**sp** middest[1], midd'st[3], midst[5], mid'st[2]

**midsummer** *adj / n*
'mɪdsəməɹ
**sp** midsomer-[night][1], midsommer[1] / mid-summer[1]
> summer

**midway** *adj / n*
mɪd'wɛ:
**sp** midway[1] / midway[2], mid-way[1]

**midwife / ~'s** *n*
'mɪdwəɪf / -s
**sp** midwife[9], mid-wife[1] / midwiues[1]
> wife

**mienne** *Fr*
> je

**might** *n*
məɪt
**sp** might[21]
**rh** *1* appetite *S 56.4*; bright *S 65.13*; delight, night *Luc 488*; fight *VA 113*; flight *LC 245*; flight, light, night *MW 2.1.16*; goodnight *TNK Epil.17*; knight *MND 2.2.149, MW 2.1.16*; knight, right *LLL 5.2.560*; light *S 100.2*; rite *S 23.8*; sight *AY 3.5.81, MND 3.2.368, S 123.2, 139.7, 150.1*; spite *S 90.12*; write *S 80.3*; **rh** *2* strike *PP.18.4*

**might / ~est** *v*
məɪt / -s, -st
**sp** might[446] / mightest[2], mightst[6], might'st[21],
**rh** fight *AC 4.4.36*; light *Per Prol.15*; sight *Per 5.Chorus.23*

**mightful** *adj*
'məɪtfʊl
**sp** mightfull[1]

**mightier** *adj*
'məɪtɪəɹ
**sp** mightier[1]

**mightiest** *n*
'məɪtɪəst
**sp** mightiest[2]

**mightily** *adv*
'məɪtɪləɪ
**sp** mightilie[3], mightily[11]

**mightiness** *n*
*m* 'məɪtɪnəs, -ˌnes
**sp** mightinesse[5]

**might·y / ~ier / ~iest** *adj*
'məɪtəɪ / -əɹ / -əst
**sp** mightie[41], mighty[69] / mightier[5] / mightiest[4]

**Milan / ~'s** *n*
'mɪlən / -z
**sp** Millain[1], Millaine[23], Millane[2] / Millaines[1]

**milch** *adj*
=
**sp** milche[1]

**milch-kine** *n*
'mɪlʧ-ˌkəɪn
**sp** milch-kine[2]
> kine

**mild / ~er / ~est** *adj*
məɪld / 'məɪld·əɹ / -əst
**sp** mild[2], milde[24] / milder[4] / mildest[2]
**rh** beguild, defiled *Luc 1542*; child [*following* R2 1.3.240 [*Q*], *Per 1.1.69, VA 1151*; child, wild *Luc 1096*

**mildew / ~s** *v*
=
**sp** mildewes[1]

**mildewed** *adj*
=
**sp** mildew'd[1]

**mildly** *adv*
'məɪldləɪ
**sp** mildely[6], mildly[3]
**rh** wildly *CE 5.1.87*

**mildness** *n*
'məɪldnəs
**sp** mildnesse[7]
**rh** wildness *Luc 979*

**mile / ~s** *n*
məɪl / -z
**sp** mile[29], [*song*] mile-a[1] / miles[20]
**rh** stile-a *WT 4.3.124*; half a mile Longaville *LLL 5.2.54*

**Mile End** *n*
ˌməɪl 'end
**sp** Mile-end[1]

**Mile End Green** *n*
ˌməɪl end 'gri:n
**sp** Mile-end-Greene[1]

**Milford** *n*
'mɪlfəɹd
**sp** Milford[9]

**Milford Haven** *n*
ˌmɪlfəɹd 'avən, -'ha-
**sp** Milford-Hauen[9], Milford Hauen[1]
> haven

**militarist** *n*
'mɪlɪtrɪst, -tər-
**sp** militarist[1]

**military** *adjm*
'mɪlɪtrəɪ, -ˌtarəɪ
**sp** militarie[5], military[2], millitarie[1]

**milk** *adj / n*
=
**sp** milke[1] / milk[1], milke[18]
**rh** *n* silk *MND 5.1.330, Per 4. Chorus.22*

**milk / ~s / ~ed** *v*
=
**sp** milke[3] / milkes[2] / milk'd[1]

**milking-time** *n*
'mɪlkɪn-ˌtəɪm, -ɪŋ-
**sp** milking-time[1]
> time

**milk-livered** *adj*
*m* ˌmɪlk-'lɪvəɹd
**sp** milke-liuer'd[1]
> liver

**milkmaid** *n*
'mɪlkˌmɛ:d
**sp** milke-maid[2]

**milksop / ~s** *n*
=
**sp** milke-sop[1] / milke-sops[1]
> sop

**milk-white** *adj*
*m* 'mɪlk,ʍəɪt, ,mɪlk'ʍəɪt
**sp** milk-white[1], milke-white[3], milke-white-[rose][1]
> white

**milky** *adj*
'mɪlkəɪ
**sp** milkie[2], milky[1]

**mill / ~s** *n*
=
**sp** mill[2], myll[1] / milles[1], mils[1]
**rh** ill *WT 4.4.301*
> paper-mill

**mille / ~s** *Fr adj*
mil
**sp** milles[1]

**miller / Miller** *n*
'mɪləɹ
**sp** miller[1] / Miller[1]

**milliner** *n*
'mɪlɪnəɹ
**sp** milliner[2]

**million / ~s** *n*
=
**sp** million[14] / millions[7]

**mill-sixpence / ~s** *n*
=
**sp** mill-sixpences[1]
> sixpence

**millstone / ~s** *n*
'mɪlsto:nz
**sp** mill-stones[1], milstones[2]
> stone

**millwheel / ~s** *n*
'mɪl,ʍi:lz
**sp** mill-wheeles[1]
> wheel

**Milo** *n*
'məɪlo:
**sp** Milo[1]

**mimic** *n*
=
**sp** mimmick[1]

**minc·e / ~es / ~ing** *v*
= / = / 'mɪnsɪn, -ɪŋ
**sp** mince[5] / minces[1] / mincing[1]

**minced** *adj*
=
**sp** minc'd[1]

**mincing** *adj / n*
'mɪnsɪn, -ɪŋ
**sp** mincing[1], minsing[1] / mincing[1]

**mind / ~'s / ~s** *n*
məɪnd / -z
**sp** mind[62], mind [mind's][1], minde[262], mindes [mind is][1], mind's [mind is][1] / mindes[2] / mindes[34], minds[17]
**rh** *1* assigned, find *LC 135*; behind *KL 3.6.102 [Q], Luc 735, 1414, 1426, Oth 2.1.153, Per 4.4.14, S 9.8, 50.13, Tim 1.2.161*; blind *MND 1.1.234, S 113.1, 149.13*; blind, find *Luc 761*; find *LC 89, Luc 1540, MV 2.5.53, Per 4.Chorus.5, S 27.13, 77.12, 92.9, TC 5.2.112, TN 1.5.299*; find, inclined *Luc 1656*; find, kind *LC 184*; kind *AY 4.3.59, H5 3.Chorus.35, Luc 1426, MA 4.1.196, MV 1.3.176, S 10.9, 69.9, TG 3.1.91, VA 1016*; Rosalind *AY 3.2.90*; unkind *CE 4.2.22, Ham 3.1.100, TN 3.4.358, VA 203, 308*; **rh** *2* wind *LC 86, LLL 4.2.32, VA 340* / **rh** *1* finds *S 116.1, TG 5.4.110*; kinds *Luc 1148, 1240*; **rh** *2* winds *S 117.5*

**mind / ~s / ~ing / ~ed** *v*
məɪnd / -z / 'məɪndɪn, -ɪŋ / -ed
**sp** mind[2], minde[6] / minds[1] / minding[2] / minded[7]
**rh** kind *Tim 2.2.5*
> bloody-, high-, motley-, noble-, proud-, tender-, un-, well-minded

**mindless** *adj*
'məɪnləs, -ndl-
**sp** mindelesse[1], mindlesse[1]

**mine** *det, pro*
> I

**mine / ~s** *n*
məɪn / -z
**sp** mine[2], mines[1], myne[1] / mynes[6]
> countermine

**min·e / ~s / ~ing** *v*
məɪnz / 'məɪnɪn, -ɪŋ
**sp** mines[1] / mining[1]
> undermine

**mineral / ~s** *n*
*m* 'mɪnrɑl, -nər-, -nə'rɑl / 'mɪnrɑlz, -nər-
**sp** minerall[3] / minerals[1]

**Minerva** *n*
mɪ'nɐ:ɹvə
**sp** Minerua[2]

**mingle** *n*
=
**sp** mingle[2]

**mingl·e / ~ing / ~ed** *v*
= / 'mɪŋglɪn, -ɪŋ / =
**sp** mingle[10] / mingling[2] / mingled[7]
**rh** singled *VA 691*
> co-, inter-mingle

**mingled** *adj*
=
**sp** mingled[5]
> unmingled

**minim** *n*
=
**sp** minum[1]

**minime** *Lat adv*
'mɪnɪme
**sp** minnime[1]

**minimus** *n*
*m* 'mɪnɪ,mɤs
**sp** minimus[1]

**minim·us / ~o** *Lat adj*
'mɪnɪmo:
**sp** minimo[1]
**rh** so *TS 1.1.159*

**minion / ~s** *n*
=
**sp** minion[15], mynion[1] / minions[5]

**minister / ~s** *n*
'mɪnɪstəɹ / -z
**sp** minister[19] / ministers[20], mini-sters[1]
**rh** finisher *AW 2.1.137*
> fellow-minister

**minister / ~s / ~ed** *v*
'mɪnɪstəɹ / -z / -d
**sp** minister[17], mi-nister[1] / ministers[2] / ministred[5]

**ministering** *adj*
'mɪnstrɪn, -ɪŋ
**sp** ministring[1]

**ministration** *n*
ˌmɪnɪs'trɛ:sɪən
**sp** ministration[1]

**minnow / ~s** *n*
'mɪnə, -no: / -z
**sp** minow[1] / minnoues[1]

**Minola** *n*
'mɪnəˌla
**sp** Minola[6]

**minority** *n*
*m* mɪ'nɒrɪˌtəɪ, -təɪ
**sp** minoritie[3] , minority[1]
**rh** apology *LLL 5.2.588*

**Minos** *n*
'mɪnɒs
**sp** Minos[1]

**Minotaur / ~s** *n*
*m* 'mɪnəˌtɔ:ɹz
**sp** Minotaurs[1]

**minstrel / ~s** *n*
=
**sp** minstrell[1] / minstrels[3], min-strels[2]

**minstrelsy** *n*
*m* 'mɪnstrəlˌsəɪ
**sp** minstrelsie[2]
**rh** I, lie *LLL 1.1.174*

**mint / ~s** *n*
=
**sp** mint[4] / mints[1]

**minute / ~'s / ~s** *n*
=
**sp** minute[32], mi-nute[1], my-nute[1] / minutes[4] / minutes[11], mi-nutes[1]

**minutely** *adv*
*m* 'mɪnɪtˌləɪ
**sp** minutely[1]

**minx / ~'s** *n*
=
**sp** minx[2] / minxes[1]

**mio** *Ital*
> io

**mirable** *adj*
*m* 'mɪrəˌbɤl
**sp** mirable[1]

**miracle / ~s** *n*
*m* 'mɪrəˌkɤl, -əkəl / -z
**sp** miracle[20], mi-racle[1], mira-cle[1], myracle[3] / miracles[6], myracles[1]

**miraculous** *adj*
mɪ'rakləs, -kjəl-
**sp** miraculous[1], myraculous[2]

**Miranda** *n*
=
**sp** Miranda[9]

**mire** *n*
məɪɹ
**sp** mire[4], myre[4]
**rh** desire *Luc 1009*; tire [*F, at LLL 2.1.113-129*]

**mire / ~d** *v*
məɪɹ / -d
**sp** myre[1] / mir'd[1]

**mirror / ~s** *n*
'mɪrəɹ / -z
**sp** mirror[6], mirror's [mirror is][1], mirrour[1] / mirrors[2]
**rh** error *Per 1.1.46*

**mirth** *n*
mɐ:ɹθ
**sp** mirth[47], myrth[4]
**rh** birth *LLL 5.2.517*

**mirthful** *adj*
'mɐ:ɹθfʊl
**sp** mirthfull[1]

**mirth-moving** *adj*
*m* ˌmɐ:ɹθ-'mɤvɪn, -ɪŋ, -'mu:-
**sp** mirth-mouing[1]
> move

**miry** *adj*
'məɪɹəɪ
**sp** miery[2]

**misadventure** *n*
ˌmɪsəd'ventəɹ
**sp** misaduenture[2]
> adventure

**misanthropos** *n*
mɪs'antrəˌpɒs
**sp** misantropos[1]

**misapplied** *adj*
ˌmɪsə'pləɪd
**sp** misapplied[1]
**rh** dignified *RJ 2.3.17*
> apply

**misbe·come / ~d / ~came** *v*
ˌmɪsbɪ'kɤm / -d / ˌmɪsbɪ'kɛ:m
**sp** mis-become[1] / misbecom'd[1] / misbecame[1]
> become

**misbegot / ~ten** *adj*
ˌmɪsbɪ'gɒt / -ən
**sp** mis-begot[1] / misbegotten[2], mis-begotten[1], mis-be-gotten[1]
> begotten

**misbeliever** *n*
ˌmɪsbɪ'li:vəɹ
**sp** misbeleeuer[1]
> believe

**misbelieving** *adj*
ˌmɪsbɪ'li:vɪn, -ɪŋ
**sp** misbelieuing[1]

**miscall** *v*
mɪs'kɑ:l
**sp** miscall[2]
> call

**miscarr·y / ~ies / ~ying / ~ied** *v*
mɪs'karəɪ / -z / -ɪn, -ɪŋ / -d
**sp** miscarrie[3], miscarry[9], mis-carry[1] / miscarries[1] / miscarrying[1] / miscaried[1], miscarried[8], mis-carryed[1]
**rh** *1* marry *LLL 4.1.113*; **rh** *2* mercy *2H6 4.8.46*
> carry

**mischance / ~s** *n*
mɪs'ʧans / -ɪz
**sp** mischance[21] / mischances[1]
**rh** France *1H6 4.6.49, 3H6 3.3.254, R3 4.4.114* / trances *Luc 976*
> chance

**mischief / ~s** *n*
=
**sp** mischeefe[11], mischefe[1], mischeife[1], mischiefe[26], mis-chiefe[1] / mischeefes[2], mischiefes[6]

**mischief** *v*
=
**sp** mischeefe[1]

**mischievous** *adj*
=
**sp** mischeeuous[1], mischieuous[1]

**misconceived** *adj*
*m* ˌmɪskən'si:vɪd
**sp** misconceyued[1]
> conceive

**misconster / ~s / ~ed** *v*
*m* mɪs'kɒnstəɹ / -z / -d
**sp** misconster[2] / misconsters[1] / misconsterd[1]
> conster

**misconstruction** *n*
ˌmɪskən'strɤksɪən
**sp** misconstruction[1]
> construction

**misconstrue / ~d** *v*
*m* mɪs'kɒnstru:d
**sp** misconstrued[2]
> construe

**miscreant** *n*
*m* 'mɪskrɪənt, -ɪˌant
**sp** miscreant[4]

**miscreate** *adj*
ˌmɪskri:'ɛ:t
**sp** miscreate[1]
> create

**misdeed / ~s** *n*
=
**sp** misdeed[1] / misdeeds[1]
> deed

**misdemean / ~ed** *v*
ˌmɪsdɪ'mi:nd
**sp** misdemean'd[1]
> demean

**misdemeanour / ~s** *n*
ˌmɪsdɪ'mi:nəɹz
**sp** misdemeanors[1]

**misdoubt / ~s** *n*
mɪs'dəʊt / -s
**sp** misdoubt[1] / mis-doubts[1]
> doubt

**misdoubt / ~s / ~eth** *v*
mɪs'dəʊt / -s / -əθ
**sp** misdoubt[5] / mis-doubts[1] / misdoubteth[1]

**Misena** *n*
mɪ'si:nə
**sp** [Mount]-Misena[1]

**miser / ~s** *n*
'məɪzəɹ / -z
**sp** miser[2], mi-ser[1] / mysers[1]

**miserable** *adj*
*m* 'mɪzəˌrabəl, -zərəbəl, -zrəbəl
**sp** miserable[34]

**miserably** *adv*
*m* 'mɪzəˌrabləɪ
**sp** miserably[1]

**miséricorde** *Fr n*
mizeri'kɔɹd
**sp** miserecordie

**miser·y / ~'s / ~ies** *n*
*m* 'mɪzəˌrəɪ, -zər-, -zr- / -z
**sp** miserie[16], misery[21] / miseries[1] / miseries[20], mi-series[1]
**rh** *1* mockery *3H6 3.3.264*; see *H8 Prol.30*; thee *PP 20.30*, *Tit 2.4.57*; tyranny *VA 738*; **rh** *2* die *1H6 3.2.137* / **rh** *1* injuries *Cym 5.4.86*; **rh** *2* exercise *Cym 5.4.86*; eyes *1H6 1.1.88*

**misfortune / ~'s / ~s** *n*
mɪs'fɔ:ɹtən / -z
**sp** misfortune[8] / misfortunes[2] / misfortunes[2]
> fortune

**misgive / ~s** *v*
=
**sp** mis-giue[1] / misgiues[2], mis-giues[1]
> give

**misgiving** *n*
mɪs'gɪvɪn, -ɪŋ
**sp** misgiuing[1]

**misgovern / ~ing** *v*
mɪs'gɤvəɹnɪn, -ɪŋ
**sp** mis-gouerning[1]
**rh** king *Luc 654*
> govern

**misgoverned** *adj*
mɪs'gɤvəɹnd
**sp** mis-gouern'd[1]
> govern

**misgovernment** *n*
*m* mɪs'gɤvəɹnˌment
**sp** misgouernment[1]

**misgraffed** *adj*
*m* mɪs'grafɪd
**sp** misgraffed[1]
> graff

**misguide** *v*
mɪs'gəɪd
**sp** misguide[1]
> guide

**mishap / ~s** *n*
mɪs'ap, -'hap / -s
**sp** mishap[2] / mishaps[2]
**rh** grapes *VA 603*

**mishear / ~d** *v*
mɪs'ɛ:ɹd, -'hɛ:-, -'ɐ:ɹ-, -'hɐ:-
**sp** misheard[1]
> hear

**misinterpret** *v*
ˌmɪsɪn'tɐ:ɹprɪt
**sp** mis-interprete[1]
> interpret

**mislead / misled** *v*
=, mɪs'lɛ:d / =
**sp** mislead[1], misleade[1] / misled[6], mis-led[3]
**rh** bed, head *Luc 369*
> lead

**misleader / ~s** *n*
mɪs'li:dəɹ, -'lɛ:d- / -z
**sp** misleader[1], mis-leader[1] / misleaders[1]

**misleading** *n*
mɪs'li:dɪn, -ɪŋ, -'lɛ:d-
**sp** mis-leading[1]

**mislike** *v*
mɪs'ləɪk
**sp** mislike[4]
> like

**misordered** *adj*
mɪs'ɔ:ɹdəɹd
**sp** mis-order'd[1]
> order

**misplace / ~d** *v*
mɪs'plɛ:s·ɪz / -t
**sp** misplaces[1] / misplaced[1]
**rh** disgraced *S 66.5*
> place

**misplaced** *adj*
*m* 'mɪsplɛ:st
**sp** mis-plac'd-[1]

**mispris·e / ~ing / ~ed** *v*
mɪs'prəɪz·ɪn, -ɪŋ / -d
**sp** mis-prizing[1] / misprised[2]

**misprised** *adj*
'mɪsprəɪzd
**sp** mispris'd[1]

**misprising** *n*
mɪs'prəɪzɪn, -ɪŋ
**sp** misprising[1]

**misprision** *n*
*m* mɪs'prɪzɪən, -zɪˌɒn
**sp** misprision[6]
**rh** incision *LLL 4.3.96*

**misproud** *adj*
'mɪsprəʊd
**sp** misproud[1]
> proud

**misquote** *v*
mɪs'ko:t, -'kw-
**sp** misquote[1]
> quote

**misreport** *v*
ˌmɪsrɪ'pɔ:ɹt
**sp** mis-report[1]
> report

**miss** *n*
=
**sp** misse[2]
**rh** kiss *VA 53*

**miss / ~es / ~ing / ~ed** *v*
= / = / 'mɪsɪn, -ɪŋ / =
**sp** misse[20], misse't [miss it][1] / misses[1] / missing[5] / miss'd[3], mist[6]
**rh** this *AW 1.3.251* / list *Luc 1007*; subsist *S 122.8* / kissing *VA 605*

**mis-shaped** *adj*
*m* 'mɪsʃɛ:ˌpɪd, -ɛ:pt
**sp** mishaped[1], mis-shap'd[1]
> shape

**mis-shapen** *adj*
mɪs'ʃɛ:pən
**sp** mishapen[5], mis-shapen[1]

**mis-sheathed** *adj*
*m* mɪs'ʃi:ðɪd
**sp** misheathed[1]
> sheathe

**missing** *n*
'mɪsɪn, -ɪŋ
**sp** missing[1]

**missingly** *adv*
'mɪsɪnləɪ, -ɪŋ-
**sp** missingly[1]

**mission / ~s** *n*
'mɪsɪənz
**sp** missions[1]

**missive / ~s** *n*
=
**sp** misiue[1] / missiues[1]

**mis-speak / ~spoke** *v*
mɪ'spo:k
**sp** mispoke[1]
> speak

**mist / ~s** *n*
=
**sp** mist[1] / mists[1]

**mist** *v*
=
**sp** mist[1]

**mistak·e / ~est / ~s / ~eth / ~ing / ~en, *abbr* mista'en, mistook** *v*
mɪs'tɛ:k / -s, -st / -s / -əθ / -ɪn, -ɪŋ / -ən, *abbr* mɪs'tɛ:n / =
**sp** mistake[40] / mistakes[1], mistak'st[2] / mistakes[2] / mistaketh[1] / mistaking[4] / mistaken[9], *abbr* mistaine[1], mistane[1] / mistook[1], mistooke[17], mi-stooke[2]
**rh** making *S 87.10*

**mistaking** *adj*
mɪs'tɛ:kɪn, -ɪŋ
**sp** mistaking[2]

**mistaking / ~s** *n*
mɪs'tɛ:kɪn, -ɪŋ / -z
**sp** mistaking[2], mista-king[1] / mistakings[1]

**mistempered** *adj*
mɪs'tempəɹd
**sp** mistemper'd[1], mistempred[1]
> temper

**misterm / ~ed** *v*
mɪs'tɐ:ɹmd

**sp** mistearm'd[1]
> term

**mistership** *n*
'mɪstəɹʃɪp
**sp** mistership[1]

**mis·think / ~thought** *v*
mɪs'θɪŋk / mɪs'θɔ:t
**sp** mis-thinke[1] / mis-thoght[1]
> think

**mistletoe** *n*
'mɪsəl,to:
**sp** misselto[1]

**mist-like** *adj*
*m* ,mɪst'ləɪk
**sp** mist-like[1]

**mistook**
> mistake

**mistreading / ~s** *n*
mɪs'tredɪnz, -ɪŋz
**sp** mistreadings[1]
> tread

**mistress / ~'s / ~es** *n*
=
**sp** mistres[4], mistresse[84], mi-stresse[4], mistris[278], mi-stris[6], *abbr* Mist.[7], M[istris][5], Mi[stris][3], Mis[tris][1], Mist[ris][13] / mistresse[5], mistresses[1], mistris[21], mistris-ses[1] / mistresses[5], [country]-mistresses[1]

**mistrust / ~ing / ~ed** *v*
mɪs'trɤst / -ɪn, -ɪŋ / -ɪd
**sp** mistrust[15] / mistrusting[1] / mistrusted[3]
**rh** just *VA 1154*; just, thrust *Luc 1516*; lust *Luc 284, 1352*; unjust *Luc 284* / mistrusting them Buckingham *R3 4.4.526*

**mistrustful** *adj*
mɪs'trɤstfʊl
**sp** mistrustfull[1]

**misty** *adj*
'mɪstəɪ
**sp** mistie[2], misty[2]

**misuse** *n*
=
**sp** misuse[1], misvse[1]
> use

**misuse / ~s / ~d** *v*
=
**sp** misuse[3], misvse[1], mis-vse[1] / misuses[1] / misus'd[1], misusde[1], misvs'd[1], mis-vs'd[1]
**rh** misuse thee accuse thee *S 152.7*
> self-misused

**mite / ~s** *n*
məɪts
**sp** mites[1]

**Mithridates** *n*
,mɪtrɪ'dɑ:ti:z, -ɪθr-
**sp** Mithridates[1]

**mitigate** *v*
'mɪtɪ,gɛ:t
**sp** mittigate[3]
> unmitigable, unmitigated

**mitigation** *n*
,mɪtɪ'gɛ:sɪən
**sp** mitigation[2], mittigation[1]

**mix / ~ed** *v*
=
**sp** mixe[1] / mixt[6]
**rh** fixed *Luc 563, VA 489*
> inter-, un-mix

**mixtful** *adj*
=
**sp** mixtfull[1]

**mixture / ~s** *n*
'mɪkstəɹ / -z
**sp** mixture[3] / mixtures[1]

**mo, moe** [more] *adj / adv / n*
mo:
**sp** mo[10], moe[19] / mo[1], moe[2]/ moe[8]
**rh** go, so, woe *MA 2.3.68*; so, woe *Luc 1479*

**moan / ~s** *n*
mo:n / -z
**sp** moane[7], mone[6] / moanes[2], mones[2]
**rh** *1* alone *PP 20.7*; groan *Luc 1363, MA 5.3.16*; stone *LC 217*; thunder-stone *Cym 4.2.273*; **rh** *2* foregone *Ham 4.5.198, S 30.11*; gone *Luc 1363, MND 5.1.326, S 44.12, 71.13*; upon *S 149.8* / groans *Luc 587, 798, R2 5.1.90, VA 831*; groans, stones *Luc 977*; stones *MND 5.1.185, Oth 4.3.42, RJ 5.3.15*
> unmoaned

**moan** *v*
mo:n
**sp** mone[1]

**moat** *n*
mo:t
**sp** moate[1]

**moated** *adj*
'mo:tɪd
**sp** moated-[grange][1]

**mobled** *adj*
'mɒbəld
**sp** *emend of Ham 2.2.500ff* inobled[3]

**mock / ~s** *n*
=
**sp** mock[3], mocke[11], mockes[8]
**rh** ox *LLL 5.2.251*
> arch-mock

**mock / ~est / ~s / ~ing / ~ed** *v*
= / mɒkst / = / 'mɒkɪn, -ɪŋ / =
**sp** mock[18], mocke[51] / mock'st[1] / mockes[6], mocks[4], mock's[1] / mocking[9] / mock'd[19], mockt[9], mock't[1]

**mockable** *adj*
=
**sp** mockeable[1]

**mocker / ~s** *n*
'mɒkəɹ / -z
**sp** mocker[4] / mockers[2]

**mockery / ~ies** *n*
*m* 'mɒkrəɪ, -kəˌrəɪ / -z
**sp** mockerie[4], mockery[4], mockrie[1], mock'rie[1], mockry[1], mock'ry[3] / moc-keries[1], mock'ries[1]
**rh** misery *3H6 3.3.265*

**mocking** *adj / n*
'mɒkɪn, -ɪŋ
**sp** mocking[4] / mocking[4]

**Mockwater** *n*
'mɒkwɑ:təɹ, *Caius MW 2.3.54* 'mɒkvɑtəɹ
**sp** Mocke-water[1], Mock-water[1], *Caius* Mock-vater[2]

**model** *n*
=
**sp** modell[13]

**Modena** *n*
mə'di:nə
**sp** Medena[1]

**moderate** *adj*
'mɒdrət, -dər-
**sp** moderate[7], mo-derate[1]
> immoderate

**moderately** *adv*
*m* 'mɒdrətˌləɪ, -dər-
**sp** moderately[2]

**moderation** *n*
*m* ˌmɒdə'rɛ:sɪən, -sɪˌɒn
**sp** moderation[1]

**modern** *adj*
'mɒdəɹn
**sp** moderne[8], mo-derne[1]

**modest** *adj*
=
**sp** modest[37], [quip]-modest[1]
> immodest

**modestly** *adv*
*m* 'mɒdəstˌləɪ, -tl-
**sp** modestly[4]

**modest·y / ~ies** *n*
*m* 'mɒdəsˌtəɪ, -dəst-, -dst- / -z
**sp** modestie[35], modesty[14] / modesties[2]
**rh** *1* audaciously, livery *Luc 1220*; courtesy *MND 2.2.63*; majesty *AY 3.2.144*; mortality *Luc 401*; outwardly *LC 202*; **rh** *2* beautify *Luc 401*; reply *TG 2.1.156*

**modicum / ~s** *n*
=
**sp** modicums[1]

**Modo** *n*
'mo:do:
**sp** Modo[1]

**module** *n*
'mɒdjəl
**sp** module[2]

**moe**
> mo

**moi** *Fr*
> je

**moist** *adj / v*
məɪst
**sp** moist[3], moyst[3] / moist[1], moyst[1]

**moistened** *adj*
'məɪstənd
**sp** moistned[1]

**moisture** *n*
'məɪstəɹ
**sp** moysture[1]

**moity** *n*
'məɪtəɪ
**sp** moitie[2], moity[9], moytie[4]

**moldwarp** *n*
'mo:ldwɑ:ɹp
**sp** moldwarpe[1]

**mole / ~s** *n*
mo:l / -z
**sp** moale[1], mole[7] / moales[1] moles[1]

**molehill** *n*
'mo:lˌɪl, -ˌhɪl
**sp** mole-hill[3]
> hill

**molest** *v*
=
**sp** mollest[2]

**molestation** *n*
ˌmɒləs'tɛ:sɪən
**sp** mollestation[1]

**mollification** *n*
ˌmɒlɪfɪ'kɛ:sɪən
**sp** mollification[1]

**mollis** *Lat adj*
'mɒlɪs
**sp** mollis[2]

**molten** *adj*
'mo:ltən
**sp** molten[2], moulten[1]

**molto** *Ital adv*
'mɒlto:
**sp** multo[1]

**Mome** *n*
mo:m
**sp** Mome[1]

**moment / ~'s** *n*
'mɒmənt / -s
**sp** moment[29] / moments[1]
**rh** comment *S 15.2*

**momentary** *adj*
*m* 'mɒmənˌtarəɪ, -ntərəɪ, -ntrəɪ
**sp** momentarie[4], momentary[2]

**momentary-swift** *adj*
'mɒmənˌtarəɪ-'swɪft, -ntərəɪ-
**sp** momentary, swift[1]

**mon** *Fr*
> je

**monachus / ~um** *Lat n*
'mɒnakʊm
**sp** monachum[2]

**monarch / ~'s / ~s** *n*
'mɒnəɹk / -s

**sp** monarch[16], monarke[1] / monarches[1], monarkes[1] / monarches[1], monarchs[3], mo-narchs[1]

**monarchize** *v*
*m* 'mɒnəɹˌkəɪz
**sp** monarchize[1]

**monarcho** *n*
'mɒnəɹko:
**sp** monarcho[1]

**monarch·y / ~ies** *n*
'mɒnəɹˌkəɪ / -z
**sp** monarchie[1], monarchy[4] / monarchies[1]
**rh** free *LC 196*

**monastery** *n*
*m* 'mɒnəsˌterəɪ, - strəɪ
**sp** monasterie[1], mo-nasterie[1], monastery[1], monast'ry[1]

**monastic** *adj*
=
**sp** monastick[1]

**Monday** *n*
'mʏndɛ:
**sp** Monday[6], Munday[1]

**monde** *Fr n*
mɔ̃:d
**sp** monde[2]

**money / ~'s / ~s** *n*
'mʏnəɪ / -z
**sp** monie[22], money[129], mo-ney[5], money's [money is][1], mony[18] / moneys[1] / moneyes[6], monies[1]

**money-bag / ~s** *n*
'mʏnəɪ-ˌbagz
**sp** money bags[1]
> bag, press-money

**mongrel** *adj*
'mʏŋgrəl
**sp** mungrel[1], mungrill[2]

**mongrel / ~s** *n*
'mʏŋgrəl / -z
**sp** mongrill[1], mungrell[1] / mungrels[1]

**mongst**
> amongst

**monied** *adj*
'mʏnəɪd
**sp** monied[1]

**monk / ~s** *n*
mʏŋk / -s
**sp** monke[6] / monkes[1]

**monkey / ~'s / ~s** *n*
'mʏŋkəɪ / -z
**sp** monkey[3], mon-key[1], monkie[2] / monkeys[1] / monkeyes[1], monkeys[2], monkies[2]

**Monmouth** *adj*
'mɒnməθ
**sp** Monmouth[1]

**Monmouth / ~'s** *n*
'mɒnməθ / -s
**sp** Monmouth[13] / Monmouthes[1], Monmouth's[2]

**mons** *Lat n*
mɒnz
**sp** mons[1]

**monsieur / ~s** *n*
*Fr* m'sjœ, mə'-, *Eng* 'mo:nsjəɹ, mo:n'sjɐ:ɹ / -z
**sp** *in French conversation* monsieur[3], mounsieur[2], *in English conversation* monsier[1], monsieuer[1], monsieur[21], mon-sieur[3], mounseur[1], mounsier[7], moun-sieuer[1], mounsieur[12] / monsieurs[1]

**monster** *adj*
'mɒnstəɹ
**sp** monster[1]
> sea-monster

**monster / ~'s / ~s** *n*
'mɒnstəɹ / -z
**sp** monster[68], mon-ster[2], [bully]-monster[1], monster's [monster is][1], mon-ster's [monster is][1] / monsters[2] / monsters[9]

**monster / ~s / ~ed** *v*
'mɒnstəɹ·z / -d
**sp** monsters[1] / monster'd[1]

**monster-like** *adj*
'mɒnstəɹ-ˌləɪk
**sp** monster-like[1]

**monstrous** *adj*
'mɒnstrəs
**sp** monstrous[63], mon-strous[1]

**monstrously** *adv*
*m* 'mɒnstrəsˌləɪ
**sp** monstrously[1]

**monstrousness** *n*
*m* 'mɒnstrəsˌnes
**sp** monstrousnesse[1]

**monstruosity** *n*
*m* ˌmɒnstrʊ'ɒsɪˌtəɪ
**sp** monstruositie[1]

**Montacute** *n*
'mɒntəˌkju:t
**sp** Mountacute[2]

**Montague / ~'s / ~s** *n*
'mɒnt·əˌgju:, -əg- / -əgju:z / -əˌgju:z, -əg-
**sp** Montague[5], Mountague[47], Mount-ague[1] / Mountagues[2] / Mountagues[5]
**rh** true *RJ 3.1.149, 176*

**Montano** *n*
mɒn'tɑ:no:
**sp** Montano[9]

**montant** *adj / n*
'mɒntənt
**sp** mountant[1] / montant[1]

**monter / montez** *Fr v*
mɔ̃'tez
**sp** monte[1]

**Montferrat** *n*
ˌmɒntfə'rat
**sp** Mount-ferrat[1]

**Montgomery** *n*
*m* mɒnt'gɒmə,rəɪ
**sp** Mountgomerie[3], Mountgomery[1]

**month / ~'s / ~s** *n*
mɤnθ / -s
**sp** moneth[23], mo-neth[1], month[14] / moneths[1], months[1] / moneths[14], mo-neths[1], monthes[7], months[16]
> twelvemonth

**monthly** *adv*
'mɤnθləɪ
**sp** monethly[1], monthly[1]

**Montjoy** *n*
*Fr* mɔ̃'ʤwɛ, *Eng* mɒnt'ʤəɪ
**sp** Montioy[4], Mountioy[5]

**monument / ~s** *n*
*m* 'mɒnjə,ment, -əmənt / -s
**sp** monument[28] / monuments[6]
**rh** spent *S 107.13* / contents *Luc 946, S 55.1*

**monumental** *adj*
,mɒnjə'mentɑl
**sp** monumentall[3]

**mood / ~s** *n*
=
**sp** mood[9], moode[10] / moodes[2], moods[2]
**rh** *1* blood *LC 201, MND 3.2.74*; flood *Per 3.Chorus.46* [*emend of* moved]; **rh** *2* good *Luc 1273*; understood *LC 201*

**moody** *adj*
'mu:dəɪ
**sp** moodie[7], moody[6]

**moon / ~'s / ~s** *n*
=, mʊn
**sp** moon[4], moone[117], moone's [moon is][1], moones [moon is][1] / moones[2], moons[1] / moones[10]
**rh** *1* Berowne *LLL 4.3.228*; noon *Mac 3.5.23*; soon *LLL 5.2.212, Luc 371, MND 3.2.53, 4.1.97, PP 14.27*; **rh** *2* done *Ham 3.2.170*; foredone *MND 5.1.362* / dooms *Per 3.Chorus.31*

**moonbeam / ~s** *n*
=, 'mʊnbi:mz
**sp** moone-beames[1]

**mooncalf / ~'s** *n*
'mu:n,kɔ:f, 'mʊn- / -s
**sp** moone-calfe[4] / moone-calfes[1]
> calf

**moonish** *adj*
=, 'mʊnɪʃ
**sp** moonish[1]

**moonlight** *n*
'mu:nləɪt, 'mʊn-
**sp** moonelight[1], moone-light[7]
> light

**moonshine / ~'s** *n*
'mu:nʃəɪn, 'mʊn- / -z
**sp** mooneshine[2], moone-shine[13], moonshine[1] / moonshines[2]
> shine

**Moor / ~s** *n*
mo:ɹ / -z
**sp** Moor[1], Moore[83], Moore's [Moor is][1] / Moores[2]
**rh** deflower *Tit 2.3.190*
**pun** *MV 3.5.37* more

**Moorditch** *n*
'mo:ɹdɪʧ
**sp** Moore Ditch[1]

**Moore** [name] *n*
mo:ɹ
**sp** Moore[1]

**Moorship / ~'s** *n*
'mo:ɹʃɪps
**sp** Mooreships[1]

**mop** *n*
=
**sp** mop[1]

**mop·e / ~ing** *v*
mo:p / 'mo:pɪn, -ɪŋ
**sp** mope[1] / moaping[1]

**Mopsa** *n*
'mɒpsə
**sp** Mopsa[3]

**moral** *adj / n / v*
'mɒrɑl
**sp** morall[8] / morall[8], mo-rall[1], morrall[3] / morall[1]

**moralize** *v*
'mɒrɑ,ləɪz
**sp** moralize[2], morallize[1]
**rh** rise *VA 712*

**moraller** *n*
'mɒrɑləɹ
**sp** moraller[1]

**Mordake** *n*
'mɔ:ɹdɛ:k
**sp** Mordake[4]

**more / ~s** *adj, adv, n*
mɔ:ɹ / -z
**sp** more[2208], more's [more is][1] / mores[1]
**rh** *1* abhor *S 150.9*; before *CE 1.1.95, PP 20.48, R2 2.1.9, S 40.4, 85.10, TN 1.1.7*; boar *VA 709, 899*; deplore *TN 3.1.158*; door *CE 2.1.10, Ham 4.5.55, Luc 339*; door, four *LLL 3.1.98*; door, score *KL 1.4.125*; fivescore *LLL 4.2.40*; four *LLL 4.3.208, MND 3.2.437*; fourscore *AY 2.3.72*; gore *Tim 3.5.86*; o'er *Mac 3.4.136, MND 3.2.128, TG 3.1.95*; o'er, tore *Luc 1789*; roar *KJ 2.1.293*; score *Mac 5.6.90, S 122.12*; shore *Luc 1116, MA 2.3.60, VA 819*; sore *R2 1.3.302, TC 3.1.112*; store *Luc 98, RJ 1.2.23, S 11.11, 37.6, 84.1, 135.12, 146.12, Tit 1.1.98*; therefore *MND 3.2.79*; whore *KL 1.4.125, TC 4.1.66, 5.2.115*; more 'L' sorrel *LLL 4.2.62*; **rh** *2* sworn *LLL 1.1.112*
**pun** *MV 3.5.37* Moor
> evermore

**more-having** *n*
*m* ,mɔ:ɹ-'avɪn, -ɪŋ, -'ha-
**sp** more-hauing[1]
> have

**moreover** *adv*
ˌmɔːɹ'oːvəɹ, mɒ-
**sp** moreouer[18], more ouer[1], moreour[1]
**rh** lover *LLL 5.2.49, 446*

**Morgan** *n*
'mɔːɹgən
**sp** Mergan[1], Morgan[2]

**mori** *Lat*
> memento mori

**Morisco** *n*
mə'rɪskoː
**sp** Morisco[1]

**morn** *adj / n*
mɔːɹn
**sp** morne-[praier][1] / morne[32]
**rh** *n* forlorn *PP 6.1*; forsworn *MM 4.1.4*; o'erworn *S 63.4*; scorn *VA 2*
**pun** *S 132.5* mourning
> May-morn

**morn-dew** *n*
'mɔːɹn-ˌdjuː
**sp** morne-dew[1]

**morning** *adj*
'mɔːɹnɪn, -ɪŋ
**sp** morning[10]

**morning / ~'s / ~s** *n*
'mɔːɹnɪn, -ɪŋ / -z
**sp** morning[106], mor-ning[3] / mornings[12] / mornings[2]
**pun** *S 132.5* mourning

**Morocco** *n*
mə'rɒkoː
**sp** Morocho[1], Morochus[1], Moroco[1], Morrocho[1]

**morris** *n*
=
**sp** morris[2]
**rh** chorus *TNK 3.5.107*

**morris-dance** *n*
'mɒrɪs-ˌdans
**sp** Morris-dance[1]

**morris-pike** *n*
'mɒrɪs-ˌpəɪk
**sp** moris pike[1]

**morrow** *n*
'mɒrə, -roː
**sp** morow[1], morrow[5]
**rh** borrow, sorrow *Luc 1082*; sorrow *Luc 1571, R2 1.3.228, RJ 2.2.185, S 90.7*
> good-, to-morrow

**morsel / ~s** *n*
'mɔːɹsəl / -z
**sp** morcell[1], morsell[7] / morsels[1]

**mort** *n*
mɔːɹt
**sp** mort[1]

**mort** *Fr n*
mɔːɹ
**sp** mor[2], mort[2]

**mortal** *adj*
'mɔːɹtal
**sp** mortal[2], mortall[83], mor-tall[2]
> immortal

**mortal / ~s** *n*
'mɔːɹtal / -z
**sp** mortall[6] / mortalls[2], mortals[5]

**mortality / ~'s** *n*
*m* mɔːɹ'talɪˌtəɪ, -ɪt- / mɔːɹ'talɪˌtəɪz
**sp** mortalitie[6], mortality[5], mortallitie[2] / mortalities[1]
**rh** *1* calumny *MM 3.2.175*; infamy *1H6 4.5.32*; modesty *Luc 403*; **rh** *2* beautify *Luc 403*; sky *1H6 4.7.22*

**mortally** *adv*
*m* 'mɔːɹtəˌləɪ
**sp** mortally[1]

**mortal-staring** *adj*
'mɔːɹtal-ˌstɛːrɪn, -ɪŋ
**sp** mortall staring[1]

**mortar** *n*
'mɔːɹtəɹ
**sp** morter[1]

**mortar-piece** *n*
'mɔːɹtəɹ-ˌpiːs
**sp** morter-piece[1]
> piece

**mortified** *adj*
*m* 'mɔːɹtɪˌfəɪd, -ˌfəɪɪd
**sp** mortified[4]

**mortify / ~ing** *adj*
'mɔːɹtɪˌfəɪɪn, -ɪŋ
**sp** mortifying[2]

**mortif·y / ~ied** *v*
*m* 'mɔːɹtɪˌfəɪd
**sp** mortify'd[1]

**Mortimer / ~s** *n*
'mɔːɹtɪməɹ / -z
**sp** Mortimer[46] / Mortimers[1]

**mortise** *n*
'mɔːɹtɪs
**sp** morties[1]

**mortise / ~d** *v*
'mɔːɹtɔɪzd
**sp** mortiz'd[1]

**Morton** *n*
'mɔːɹtən
**sp** Morton[4], Mourton[1]

**mose** *v*
moːz
**sp** mose[1]

**moss** *n*
=
**sp** mosse[3]
**rh** dross *CE 2.2.187*

**moss / ~ed** *v*
=
**sp** moss'd[1]

**moss-grown** *adj*
'mɒs-ˌgroːn
**sp** mosse-growne[1]
> grow

**most** *adj, adv, n*
mo:st
**sp** most[1131]
**rh** *1* boast *S 25.4*; **rh** *2* lost *LLL 1.1.143, S 152.6*
> foremost

**mot / ~s** *Fr n*
mo
**sp** mots[5]

**mote** *n*
mo:t
**sp** moth[5]

**moth / ~s** *n*
mo:θ / -s
**sp** moath[1], moth[2] / mothes[1]
**rh** oath, wrath *MV 2.9.79*

**Moth** [name] *n*
mo:θ, mo:t
**sp** Moth[5]

**mother / ~'s / ~s / ~s'** *n*
'mɤðəɹ / -z
**sp** mother[336], Mother-[England] [1], mo-ther[2], mothers [mother is][2] / mo-thers[1], mothers[62] / mothers[20] / mothers[4]
**rh** another *S 3.4, 8.11*; brother *Ham 3.4.29*; other *VA 863*
> aunt-, god-, step-mother

**mother-bleeding** *adj*
'mɤðəɹ-ˌbli:dɪn, -ɪŋ
**sp** mother-bleeding[1]
> bleed

**mother-queen** *n*
'mɤðəɹ-ˌkwi:n
**sp** mother queene[1]
> queen

**mother-wit** *n*
'mɤðəɹ-ˌwɪt
**sp** mother wit[1]
> wit

**mothy** *adj*
'mo:θəɪ, -o:t-
**sp** mo-thy[1]

**motion / ~s** *n*
'mo:sɪən / -z
**sp** motion[71], motions [motion is][1] / motions[12]
**rh** ocean *Luc 591*

**motion / ~s** *v*
'mo:sɪənz
**sp** motions[1]

**motionless** *adj*
*m* 'mo:sɪənˌles
**sp** motionlesse[1]

**motive / ~s** *n*
'mo:tɪv / -z
**sp** motiue[15] / motiues[5]

**motley** *adj / n*
'mɒtləɪ
**sp** motley[5] / motley[3], motley's [motley is][1]

**motley-minded** *adj*
'mɒtləɪ-ˌməɪndɪd
**sp** motley-minded[1]
> mind

**mought** *v*
mɔ:t
**sp** mought[1]

**mould** *n*
mo:ld
**sp** mold[1], mould[7]
> self-mould

**mould / ~s / ~eth / ~ed** *v*
mo:ld / -z / 'mo:ld·əθ / -ɪd
**sp** mould[1] / moulds[1] / mouldeth[1] / molded[2], moulded[6]

**mouldy** *adj*
'mo:ldəɪ
**sp** mouldie[3], moul-die[1], mouldy[1]

**Mouldy** [name] *n*
'mo:ldəɪ
**sp** Mouldie[10]

**moult** *v*
mo:lt
**sp** moult[1]

**moulten** *adj*
'mo:ltən
**sp** moulten[1]

**mount** *n*
məʊnt
**sp** mount[6], Mount-[Mesena][1]

**mount / ~s / ~eth / ~ing / ~ed** *v*
məʊnt / -s / 'məʊnt·əθ / -ɪn, -ɪŋ / -ɪd
**sp** mount[26] / mounts[6] / mounteth[1] / mounting[4] / mounted[14]
**rh** mount her encounter *VA 598*
> overmounting, surmount

**mountain** *adj*
'məʊntɪn
**sp** mountaine[14], moun-taine[1], *emend of RJ 3.5.10* mountaines[1]

**mountain / ~'s / ~s** *n*
'məʊntɪn / -z
**sp** mountaine[17] / mountaines[2], mountains[1] / mountaines[19], [turphie]-mountaines[1]

**mountaineer / ~s** *n*
ˌməʊntɪ'ni:ɹ / -z
**sp** mountaineer[2] / mountaineers[1], mountayneeres[1], [villaine]-mountainers[1]

**mountainous** *adj*
'məʊntnəs, -tɪn-
**sp** mountainous[1]

**mountain-squire** *n*
'məʊntɪn-ˌskwəɪɹ
**sp** mountaine-squier[1]

**Mountanto** *n*
mɒn'tanto:
**sp** Mountanto[1]

**mountebank / ~s** *n*
'mɒntɪˌbaŋk / -s
**sp** mountebanke[2] / mountebankes[1], mountebanks[1]

**mountebank** *v*
'mɒntɪˌbaŋk
**sp** mountebanke[1]

**mounted** *adj*
'məʊntɪd
**sp** mounted[2]

**mounting** *adj*
'məʊntɪn, -ɪŋ
**sp** mounting[3], mou[n]ting[1]

**mourn / ~est / ~s / ~ing / ~ed** *v*
mu:ɹn / -st / -z / 'mu:ɹnɪn, -ɪŋ / mu:ɹnd
**sp** mourn[1], mourne[22] / mournst[1] / mournes[2] / mourning[19] / mourn'd[5]
**pun** mourning *S 132.9* morning

**mourner / ~s** *n*
'mu:ɹnəɹ / -z
**sp** mourner[3] / mourners[1]

**mournful** *adj*
'mu:ɹnfʊl
**sp** mournefull[2], mournfull[4]

**mournfully** *adv*
*m* 'mu:ɹnfʊˌləɪ
**sp** mournfully[1]

**mourning** *adj / n*
'mu:ɹnɪn, -ɪŋ
**sp** mourning[7] / mourning[2]
**pun** *n S 132.9* morning

**mourningly** *adv*
'mu:ɹnɪnləɪ, -ɪŋ-
**sp** mourningly[1]

**mouse / mice** *n*
məʊs / məɪs
**sp** mouse[13] / mice[3], myce[1]
**rh** house *MND 5.1.377*

**mous·e / ~ing / ~ed** *v*
'məʊzɪn, -ɪŋ / məʊzd
**sp** mousing[1] / mouz'd[1]

**mouse-eaten** *adj*
'məʊs-ˌi:tən
**sp** mouse-eaten[1]
> eat

**mouse-hunt** *n*
'məʊs-ˌɤnt, -ˌhɤ-
**sp** mouse-hunt[1]
> hunt

**mousetrap** *n*
'məʊs-ˌtrap
**sp** mouse-trap[1]
> trap

**mousing** *adj*
'məʊsɪn, -ɪŋ, -əʊzɪ-
**sp** mowsing[1]

**mouth / ~s** *n*
məʊθ / -s
**sp** mouth[127] / mouthes[24], mouths[9], mouth's[1]
**rh** drouth *Per 3.Chorus.7, VA 542*; south *KJ 2.1.414*

**mouth / ~ed** *v*
məʊð / -d
**sp** mouth[3] / mouth'd[1]

**mouthed** *adj*
*m* 'məʊðɪd
**sp** mouthed[1]
> deep-, foul-, honey-, humble-, narrow-, stretch-, venom-mouthed

**mouth-filling** *adj*
*m* ˌməʊθ-'fɪlɪn, -ɪŋ
**sp** mouth-filling[1]
> fill

**mouth-friend / ~s** *n*
'məʊθ-ˌfrenz, -ndz
**sp** mouth-friends[1]
> friend

**mouth-honour** *n*
'məʊθ-ˌɒnəɹ
**sp** mouth-honor[1]

**mouth-made** *adj*
'məʊθ-ˌmɛ:d
**sp** mouth-made[1]
> make

**movable / ~s** *n*
'mɤvəbəl, 'mu:v- / -z
**sp** mouable[2] / moueables[5]

**mov·e / ~est / ~s / ~eth / ~ing / ~ed** *v*
mɤv, mu:v / -st / -z / 'mɤv·əθ, 'mu:- / -ɪn, -ɪŋ / *m* -ɪd, mɤvd, mu:-
**sp** mooue[6], moue[90] / moou'st[1], mou'st[2] / mooues[3], moues[20] / moueth[1] / moouing[1], mouing[3] / moou'd[6], moud[1], mou'd[50], moued[15]
**rh** *1* prove *R2 1.1.45*; **rh** *2* love *AY 4.3.56, CE 4.2.14, Ham 2.1.118, 2.2.116, 3.2.192, LLL 4.3.53, MND 1.1.197, PP 19.15, 19.19, RJ 1.3.98, S 47.11, TN 2.5.97, 3.1.160, VA 435*; move me love thee *MND 3.1.133*; move us love us *CE 3.2.24* / loving *S 26.9* / flood *Per 3.Chorus.46*
> remove

**moved** *adj*
*m* mɤvd, mu:-, 'mɤvɪd, 'mu:-
**sp** mooued[1], moued[3]
> unmoved

**mover / ~s** *n*
'mɤvəɹ, 'mu:- / -z
**sp** mouer[1] / moouers[1], mouers[1]

**moving** *adj / n*
'mɤvɪn, -ɪŋ, 'mu:-
**sp** mouing[10] / moouing[1], mouing[4]
> best-, heaven-, mirth-moving

**moving** *adv*
'mɤvɪnləɪ, -ɪŋ-, 'mu:-
**sp** mouingly[1]

**movousus** *nonsense word*
mə'vu:səs
**sp** movousus[1]

**mow [grimace] / ~s** *n*
mo: / -z
**sp** mow[1], mowe[1] / mowes[3]
**rh** no, toe *Tem 4.1.47*

**mow [grimace]** *v*
mo:
**sp** moe[1]

**mow** [grass] **/ ~ing / ~ed** *v*
moː / ˈmoːɪn, -ɪŋ / moːd
**sp** mow[1], mowe[3] / mowing[1] / mow'd[1]
**rh** brow *S 60.12*

**Mowbray / ~'s** *n*
ˈmoːbrɛː / -z
**sp** Mowbray[26] / Mowbraies[1], Mowbrayes[5]

**mower / ~'s** *n*
ˈmoːəɹz
**sp** mowers[1]

**moy / ~s** [*Pistol misunderstanding of* moi, *H5 4.4.13ff*] *n*
məɪ / -z
**sp** moy[1] / moyes[2]

**Moyses** *n*
ˈməɪzɪz
**sp** Moyses[1]

**much** *adj, adv, n*
mɤʧ, *Caius MW 3.2.59* mɤʃ
**sp** much[1000], [as]much[1], [too]-much[1], *Caius* mush[1]
**rh** such *LLL 4.3.130, MA 3.1.108*; touch *MND 3.2.71, RJ 1.5.97, VA 442*
> overmuch

**muck** *n*
mɤk
**sp** muck[1]

**mud** *n*
mɤd
**sp** mud[4], mudde[2]
**rh** blood, flood *LC 46*; bud *Luc 850, S 35.2*

**mud / ~ded** *v*
ˈmɤdɪd
**sp** mudded[2]

**muddy** *adj*
ˈmɤdəɪ
**sp** muddie[3], muddy[7]
**rh** study *TNK 3.5.121*

**mudd·y / ~ied** *v*
ˈmɤdəɪd
**sp** muddied[3]

**muddy-mettled** *adj*
ˈmɤdəɪ-ˌmetld
**sp** muddy-metled

**muffin / ~s** *n*
ˈmɤfɪnz
**sp** muffins[1]

**muffl·e / ~ing / ~ed** *v*
ˈmɤfəl / ˈmɤflɪn, -ɪŋ / ˈmɤfəld
**sp** muffle[3] / muffling[1] / muffled[1]

**muffled** *adj*
ˈmɤfəld
**sp** muffeld[2], muffled[4], mufled[1]

**muffler** *n*
ˈmɤfləɹ
**sp** muffler[4]

**Mugges** *n*
mɤgz
**sp** Mugges[1]

**mulberr·y / ~ies** *n*
*m* ˈmɤlbəˌrəɪ, -brəɪ / ˈmɤlbəˌrəɪz
**sp** mulberry[2] / mulberries[1]
**rh** *1* bees, courtesies, dewberries *MND 3.1.162*; **rh** *2* arise, butterflies, eyes, thighs *MND 3.1.162*

**mule / ~s** *n*
=
**sp** mule[4] / mules[4]

**muleter / ~s** *n*
ˈmjuːlətəɹz
**sp** muleters[1], *emend of AC 3.7.35* militers[1]

**mulier / ~es** *Lat n*
ˈmuːlɪɛːɹ / mʊlɪˈɛːrez
**sp** mulier[2] / mulieres[1]

**mulled** *adj*
mɤld
**sp** mull'd[1]

**Mulmutius** *n*
məlˈmjuːsɪʊs
**sp** Mulmutius[2]

**multipl·y / ~ied** *v*
ˈmɤltɪˌpləɪ / -d
**sp** multiply[1] / multiplied[1], [bosome]-multiplied[1], multiplyed[1]

**multiplying** *adj*
ˈmɤltɪˌpləɪɪn, -ɪŋ
**sp** multiplying[4]

**multipotent** *adj*
*m* məlˈtɪpəˌtent
**sp** multipotent[1]

**multitude / ~s** *n*
ˈmɤltɪˌtjuːd / -z
**sp** multitude[17], multi-tude[1] / multitudes[7]

**multitudinous** *adj*
ˌmɤltɪˈtjuːdnəs, -dɪn-
**sp** multitudinous[2]

**Muly** *n*
ˈmjuːləɪ
**sp** *emend of* Muliteus[1]

**mum** *interj*
mɤm
**sp** mum[11], mumme[1]
**rh** crumb, some *KL 1.4.192*

**mumbl·e / ~ing** *v*
ˈmɤmblɪn, -ɪŋ
**sp** mumbling[1]

**mumble-news** *n*
ˈmɤmbəl-ˌnjuːz
**sp** mumble-newes[1]

**mumbling** *adj*
ˈmɤmblɪn, -ɪŋ
**sp** mumbling[1]

**mummer / ~s** *n*
ˈmɤməɹz
**sp** mum-mers[1]

**mummy** *n*
ˈmɤməɪ
**sp** mummey[2], mummie[1]

**mun** *nonsense word*
mɤn
**sp** mun[1]

**munch / ~ed** *v*
mɤnʧ / -t
**sp** munch[1] / mouncht[3]

**muniment / ~s** *n*
*m* ˈmɤnɪˌments
**sp** muniments[1]

**munition** *n*
*m* məˈnɪsɪən, -sɪˌɒn
**sp** munition[2]

**murder / ~'s / ~s** *n*
ˈmɐːɹðəɹ / -z
**sp** murder[18], mur-der[1], murther[62], mur-ther[1], murther's [murder is][1] / murders[1] murthers[2] / murthers[11]
**rh** further *VA 906*

**murder / ~s / ~ing / ~ed** *v*
ˈmɐːɹðəɹ / -z / -ɪn, -ɪŋ, -ðr- / *m* -d, -ˌed
**sp** murder[4], mur-der[1], murther[26] / murders[1], murthers[1] / murd'ring[2], murthering[1] / murder'd[2], murdered[3], murdred[11], murther'd[10], murthered[9]
**rh** dead *R2 5.6.40*

**murdered** *adj*
ˈmɐːɹðəɹd
**sp** murther'd[1], murthered[1]

**murdered** *n*
*m* ˈmɐːɹðəˌred
**sp** murthered[1]

**murderer / ~'s / ~s** *n*
*m* ˈmɐːɹðrəɹ, -ðər-, -ðəˌrɛːɹ / -z
**sp** murderer[7], murderour[1], murtherer[22], murthe-rer[1], murth'rer[1] / murderers[1], murtherers[2] / murderers[2], murderors[1], murtherers[12]
**rh** appear *Per 4.Chorus.52*

**murdering** *adj*
ˈmɐːɹðrɪn, -ɪŋ, -ðər-
**sp** murd'ring[1], murthering[1], murth'ring[2]

**murdering piece** *n*
ˈmɐːɹðrɪn ˌpiːs, -ɪŋ, -ðər-
**sp** murdering peece[1]

**murderous** *adj*
*m* ˈmɐːɹðrəs, -ərəs, -əˌrɤs
**sp** murderous[4], murdrous[2], murd'rous[8], murtherous[6], murth'rous[1]

**mure** *n*
mjuːɹ
**sp** mure[1]

**Murellus**
> Marullus

**murk** *n*
mɐːɹk
**sp** murke[1]

**murk·y / ~iest** *adj*
ˈmɐːɹkəɪ / -əst
**sp** murky[1] / murkiest[1]

**murmur** *n*
ˈmɐːɹməɹ
**sp** murmure[3]

**murmur / ~est / ~ing / ~ed** *v*
ˈmɐːɹməɹ / -st / -ɪn, -ɪŋ, -mr- / -d
**sp** murmore[1] / murmur'st[1] / murmuring[1] / murmur'd[1]

**murmurer / ~s** *n*
ˈmɐːɹmərəɹz
**sp** murmurers[1]

**murmuring** *adj*
ˈmɐːɹmrɪn, -ɪŋ, -mər-
**sp** murmuring[3]

**murrain** *n*
ˈmɤrən
**sp** murrain[1], murren[2]

**Murray** *n*
ˈmɤrɛː
**sp** Murry[1]

**murrion** *adj*
ˈmɤrɪən
**sp** murrion[1]

**Muscadel** *n*
ˌmɤskəˈdel
**sp** Muscadell[1]

**Muscovite / ~s** *n*
*m* ˈmɤskəˌvɪts
**sp** Muscouites[2], Muscouits[1]
**rh** wits *LLL 5.2.265*

**Muscovy** *n*
*m* ˈmɤskəˌvəɪ
**sp** Muscouie[1]
**rh** me, perjury *LLL 5.2.393*

**Muse / ~s** *n*
=
**sp** Muse[2] / Muses[1]
**rh** use *S 21.1, 78.1, 82.1*

**muse / ~d** *v*
=
**sp** muse[13] / mus'd[1]

**music / ~'s / ~s** *n*
=
**sp** musick[21], musicke[148], mu-sicke[3], musique[19] / musickes[1] / musickes[2]

**musical** *adj*
ˈmjuːzɪˌkɑl, -ɪk-
**sp** musicall[7]
> unmusical

**musician / ~s** *n*
mjuːˈzɪsɪən, -sɪˌɒn / -z
**sp** musician[1], musitian[9], musiti-an[1] / musitians[8], musitions[5]

**musing / ~s** *n*
ˈmjuːzɪn, -ɪŋ / -z
**sp** musing[4] / musings[1]

**musk** *n*
mɤsk
**sp** muske[1]

**musk-cat** *n*
'mɤsˌkat
**sp** muscat[1]

**musket / ~s** *n*
'mɤskɪts
**sp** muskets[1]

**Muskos** *adj*
'mɤskɒs
**sp** Muskos[1]

**muskrose / ~s** *n*
*m* 'mɤskˌro:z / ˌmɤsk'ro:zɪz
**sp** muske rose[1] / muske roses[2]
> rose

**muss** *n*
mɤs
**sp** musse[1]

**mussel / ~s** *n*
'mɤsəlz
**sp** mussels[1]

**mussel-shell** *n*
'mɤsəl-ˌʃel
**sp** mussel-shell[1]
> shell

**must** *v*
mɤst
**sp** must[1451]
**rh** distrust *Ham 3.2.175*; dust *Cym 4.2.262, 268, 274, 3H6 5.2.28*; trust *AW 2.1.205*

**mustachio** *n*
mɤs'taʃɪo:
**sp** mustachio[1], mustachio-[purple-hu'd-maltwormes][1]

**mustard** *n*
'mɤstəɹd
**sp** mustard[9]

**Mustardseed** [name] *n*
'mɤstəɹdˌsi:d
**sp** Mustardseed[2], Mustard-seede[3], Mustard seede[1]
> seed

**muster / ~s** *n*
'mɤstəɹ / -z
**sp** muster[2] / musters[5]

**muster / ~ing / ~ed** *v*
'mɤstəɹ / -ɪn, -ɪŋ, -tr- / -d
**sp** muster[13] / mustring[1] / muster'd[4]

**muster-book** *n*
'mɤstəɹ-ˌbʊk
**sp** muster-booke[1]
> book

**muster-file** *n*
'mɤstəɹ-ˌfəɪl
**sp** muster file[1]
> file

**musty** *adj*
'mɤstəɪ
**sp** mustie[2], musty[6]

**mutabilit·y / ~ies** *n*
*m* ˌmju:tə'bɪlɪˌtəɪ, -ɪt- / -ɪtəɪz
**sp** mutabilitie[1], mutability[1] / mutabilities[1]

**mutable** *adj*
=
**sp** mutable[1]

**mutation / ~s** *n*
mju:'tɛ:sɪən / -z
**sp** mutation[1] / mutations[1]

**mute / ~est** *adj*
=
**sp** mute[9] / mutest[1]
**rh** fruit *S 97.12*; impute *S 83.11*; lute *Per 4.Chorus.26*; suit *AW 2.3.76, LLL 5.2.277, VA 208, 335*

**mute / ~s** *n*
=
**sp** mute[3] / mutes[2]

**mutine / ~s** *n*
'mju:tɪnz
**sp** mutines[2]

**mutine** *v*
'mju:tɪn
**sp** mutine[1]

**mutineer / ~s** *n*
*m* 'mju:tɪˌni:ɹ / -z
**sp** mutineere[1] / mutiners[1]

**mutinous** *adj*
*m* 'mju:tɪˌnɤs, -tnəs
**sp** mutenous[1], mutinous[7]

**mutin·y / ~ies** *n*
*m* 'mju:tɪˌnəɪ, -tnəɪ / -z
**sp** mutinie[9], mutiny[7] / mutinies[3]
**rh** *1* dignity *RJ Prol.3*; harmony *LLL 1.1.167*; jealousy *VA 651*; knee *1H6 5.1.62*; readily *Luc 1153*; **rh** *2* fly *Luc 1153*; supply *1H6 1.1.160*

**mutin·y / ~ies** *v*
*m* 'mju:tɪˌnəɪ, -tɪn-, -tn- / 'mju:tnəɪz, -tɪn-
**sp** mutinie[1], mutiny[5] / mutinies[1]

**Mutius** *n*
'mju:tɪəs
**sp** Mutius[7]

**mutter / ~ed** *v*
'mɤtəɹ / *m* 'mɤtəˌrɪd
**sp** mutter[4] / muttered[1]

**mutton / ~s** *n*
'mɤtən / -z
**sp** mutton[7], [lac'd]-mutton[2], [lost]-mutton[2] / muttons[2]

**mutual** *adj*
'mju:twɑl
**sp** mutuall[13]

**mutually** *adj*
*m* 'mju:twɑˌləɪ
**sp** mutually[5]
**rh** villainy *MW 5.5.99*

**muzzle** *n*
'mɤzəl
**sp** mussell[1], muzzle[1]

**muzzle / ~d** *v*
'mɤzəl / -d
**sp** muzzle[1] / muzzel'd[1]

**muzzled** *adj*
'mɤzəld

**sp** muzled[1]
> unmuzzle

## my
> I

## Myrmidon / ~s *n*
*m* 'mɐːɹmɪˌdɤn / -z, -ɪdənz

**sp** Myrmidon[1] / Mermidons[1], Myrmidons[5]

## myrtle *PP* *n*
'mɐːɹtl

**sp** mertill[1], mertle[1]
**rh** kirtle *PP 19.12*

## myself
> I

## myster·y / ~ies *n*
*m* 'mɪstəˌrəɪ, -tər-, -tr- / -z

**sp** misterie[5], mistrie[1], mysterie[7], mystery[4], my-stery[1] / misteries[1], mysteries[3]

## Mytilene *Per* *n*
*m* 'mɪtəˌlɪn, -lɪn

**sp** Metalin[1], Metaline[5], Meteline[1], Metiliue[1], Mettelyne[1], Mittelin[1]
**rh** *1* din *Per 5.2.8* [*Chorus*]; **rh** *2* then *Per 4.4.51*

# N

**nag / ~s** *n*
=
**sp** nagge[2] / nagges[1]

**Naiades** *n*
'nəɪəˌdiːz
**sp** Nayades[1]

**nail / ~s** *n*
nɛːl / -z, *mispronunciation by Katherine H5 3.4.41* 'mɛːliːz
**sp** naile[11], nayle[1] / nailes[11], nails[2], nayles[15], *Katherine* maylees[1]
**rh** fail *Cor 4.7.54*; pail *LLL 5.2.902* / assails *Luc 1564*
> door-, hob-nail

**nail / ~ed** *v*
nɛːld
**sp** nail'd[1]

**naked** *adj*
'nɛːkɪd
**sp** naked[50], [starke]-nak'd[1]

**nakedness** *n*
*m* 'nɛːkɪdˌnes
**sp** nakednesse[3], na-kednesse[1]

**name / ~'s / ~s** *n*
nɛːm / -z
**sp** name[569], names [name is][2], names [name, *emend of RJ 2.2.43, 3.1.150*][2] / names[2], name's[4] / names[46]
**rh** blame *CE 3.1.44, VA 794, 994*; blame, shame *Luc 621*; defame, shame *Luc 814*; fame *1H6 4.6.38, LLL 1.1.93, Luc 108, Per Epil.12, R3 1.4.82, S 80.2*; same *Cym 4.2.381, LLL 2.1.181, PT 39, S 76.7, 108.8*; same, shame *LLL 1.1.117, Luc 599*; shame *AW 2.1.172, CE 2.1.112, 1H6 4.4.9, 2H6 2.1.194, LLL 1.1.153, 2.1.185, 4.3.48, 201, Luc 892, R2 1.1.167, S 36.12, 95.3, 127.2, TC 5.3.124 [Q], 5.10.34, TG 1.2.16*
> surname

**name / ~st / ~s / ~d** *v*
nɛːm / -st / -z / -d
**sp** name[60] / namest[1] / names[2] / nam'd[18], named[3], na-med[1]
> forenamed, overname

**nameless** *adj*
'nɛːmləs
**sp** nameles[1], namelesse[2]

**namely** *adv*
'nɛːmləɪ
**sp** namely[6]

**naming** *n*
'nɛːmɪn, -ɪŋ
**sp** naming[4]

**Nan** *n*
=
**sp** Nan[11]

**nap** *n*
=
**sp** nap[3], nappe[1]

**nap / ~ping** *v*
'napɪn, -ɪŋ
**sp** napping[2]

**nape / ~s** *n*
nɛːps
**sp** napes[1]

**napkin / ~s** *n*
=
**sp** napkin[13] / napkins[5]

**Naples** *n*
'nɛːpəlz
**sp** Naples[30], Na-ples[1]

**Naps** [name] *n*
=
**sp** Naps[1]

**Narbon** *n*
'nɑːɹbən, nɑːɹˌbɒn
**sp** Narbon[3]

**Narcissus** *n*
nɑːɹ'sɪsəs
**sp** Narcissus[1]

**narine / ~s** *Fr n*
na'rin
**sp** narines[1]

**narrow** *adj*
'narə, -roː
**sp** narrow[19]

**narrowly** *adv*
*m* 'narəˌləɪ, -roː-
**sp** narrowly[2]

**narrow-mouthed** *adj*
'narə-ˌməʊðd, -roː-
**sp** narrow-mouth'd[1]
> mouth

**Naso** *n*
'nɑːsoː
**sp** Naso[2]

**nasty** *adj*
'nastəɪ
**sp** nastie[1], nasty[1]

**Nathaniel / ~'s** *n*
nə'tanɪəl, = / -z
**sp** Nathaniel[6] / Nathaniels[1]

**natif / ~s** *Fr*
na'tif
**sp** natifs[1]

**nation / ~'s / ~s** *n*
'nɛːsɪən / -z
**sp** nation[26], natio[n][1], na-tion[1] / nations[2] / nations[7]
**rh** imitation *R2 2.1.22*

**native** *adj / n*
'nɛːtɪv
**sp** natiue[41] / natiue[2]

**nativity** *n*
*m* nə'tɪvɪˌtəɪ, -ɪt-
**sp** natiuitie[9], natiuity[4]
**rh** be *MND 5.1.403*; infamy *Luc 538*

**natural** *adj / n*
*m* 'natrɑl, -tər-, -tjər-, -təˌrɑl
**sp** natural[1], naturall[55] / naturall[2]
> super-, un-natural

**naturalize** *v*
'natrəˌləɪz, -tjər-
**sp** naturalize[1]

**naturally** *adv*
*m* 'natəɹˌləɪ, 'natəˌrɑləɪ, -tjəɹ-
**sp** naturally[4]
> unnaturally

**nature / ~'s / ~s** *n*
'nɛːtəɹ / -z
**sp** nature[325], [creating]-nature[1], na-ture[3], nature's [nature is][2] / natures[30] / natures[25], na-tures[1]
**rh** defeature *VA 734*
> demi-, dis-, honest-, sourest-natured

**naught, nought** *n*
=
**sp** naught[42], nought[33], nought's [nought is][1]
**rh** *1* thought *Mac 4.1.69, R3 3.6.13, S 57.11, TG 1.1.68*; wrought *VA 993*; **rh** *2* oft *PP 18.42*

**naughtily** *adv*
*m* 'nɔːtɪˌləɪ
**sp** naughtily[1]

**naughty** *adj*
'nɔːtəɪ
**sp** naughtie[6], naughty[9]

**Navarre** *n*
nə'vɑːɹ
**sp** Nauar[9], Nauarre[2]

**nave** *n*
nɛːv
**sp** naue[3]
**pun** *2H4 2.4.250* knave

**navel** *n*
'nɛːvəl
**sp** nauell[1]

**navigation** *n*
ˌnavɪ'gɛːsɪən
**sp** nauigation[1]

**navy** *n*
'nɛːvəɪ
**sp** nauie[7], nauies [navy is][1], nauy[2]

**nay** *adv*
nɛː
**sp** naie[1], nay[588]
**rh** away *TNK 3.5.70*; grey *MND 3.1.126*; say *PP 18.32*; way *MV 3.2.229*

**nayword** *n*
'nɛːˌwɔːɹd
**sp** nay-ward[1], nayword[1], nay-word[2]
> word

**Nazarite** *n*
'nazəˌrəɪt
**sp** Nazarite[1]

**ne,** *abbr* **n** *Fr adv*
nə, *abbr* n
**sp** ne[3], *abbr* n'[1], n[et][1]

**ne** *Lat particle*
ne
**sp** ne[2]

**neaf** *n*
niːf
**sp** neafe[1], neaffe[1]

**néanmoins** *Fr adv*
neɑ̃'mwɛ̃
**sp** neant-mons[1], neant moys[1]

**Neapolitan** *adj*
=
**sp** Neopolitane[1]

**Neapolitan / ~'s / ~s** *n*
=
**sp** Neapolitan[1], Neopolitan[2] / Neopolitans[1] / Neapolitanes[1]

**near** *adj*
niːɹ / 'niːr·əɹ / -əst, niːɹst
**sp** neare[1], neere[41], neere's [near is][1] / nearer[1], neerer[3] / neerest[4], neer'st[1]
**rh** *1* appear, dear *MND 2.2.40*; cheer *S 97.14*; fear *Ham 1.3.44*; **rh** *2* were *S 140.7*; **rh** *3* elsewhere *S 61.14* / dearer *Luc 1165*

**near** *adv*
niːɹ / 'niːr·əɹ / -əst, niːɹst
**sp** neare[3], neere[56], nere[1] / nearer[1], neerer[7] / neerest[2]
**rh** *1* dear *MND 2.2.50*; deer *LLL 4.1.116*; fear *Per 3.Chorus.51*; here *MND 2.2.22*; **rh** *2* harbinger *PT 8*; **rh** *3* there *MND 2.2.142, S 136.1*
> well-a-near

**near** *n*
niːɹ
**sp** neere[2]

**near / ~er / ~est** *prep*
niːɹ / 'niːr·əɹ / -əst
**sp** neare[1], neer[1], neere[89], nere[1], ne're[1] / neerer[6] / neerest[4]
**rh** near thee forbear thee *Cym 4.2.279*

**near-bred** *adj*
*m* ˌniːɹ-'bred
**sp** neere bred[1]
> breed

**near-changing** *adj*
*m* ˌniːɹ-ˈʧɛːndʒɪn, -ɪŋ
**sp** nere-changing[1]
> change

**nearer** *n*
ˈniːɹəɹ
**rh** here *R2 5.1.88*
**sp** neerer[1]

**nearest** *n*
ˈniːrəst, -niːɹst
**sp** nearest[1], neerest[1], neer'st[2]

**near-legged** *adj*
*m* ˌniːɹ-ˈlegd
**sp** neere leg'd[1]
> leg

**nearly** *adv*
ˈniːɹləɪ
**sp** nearely[1], neerely[4]
**rh** dearly *S 42.4*

**nearness** *n*
ˈniːɹnəs
**sp** neerenesse[1]

**near to / ~er ~ / ~est ~** *prep*
ˈniːɹ tə, -tʊ / -əɹ- / -əst-
**sp** neere to[11] / neerer to[2] / neerest to[1]

**neat** *adj*
=
**sp** neat[6], neate[3]

**neat / ~'s** *n*
=
**sp** neat[2] / neates-[lea-ther][1], neats[4]

**neat-herd / ~s** *n*
ˈniːt-ˌɐːɹdz, -ˌhɐː-
**sp** neat-heards[1]

**neatly** *adv*
ˈniːtləɪ
**sp** neatly[1]

**neb** *n*
=
**sp** neb[1]

**Nebuchadnezzar** *n*
nəˌbʊkədˈnezəɹ
**sp** Nabuchadnezar[1]

**nec** *Lat conj*
nek
**sp** nec[1]

**necessarily** *adv*
ˌnesɪˈsarɪləɪ
**sp** necessarilie[1]

**necessar·y / ~ies** *n*
*m* ˈnesɪˌsarəɪ, -ɪsrəɪ / -z
**sp** necessarie[4], neces-sarie[1], necessary[13] / necessaries[6]
> unnecessary

**necessit·y / ~y's / ~ies** *n*
*m* nəˈsesɪˌtəɪ, -ɪtəɪ / -z
**sp** necessitie[20], necessity[14] / necessities[1] / necessities[12]
**rh** be *Per 2.Chorus.6*; decree *LLL 1.1.146*; me *LLL 1.1.152, MV 1.3.152*

**necessit·y / ~ied** *v*
*m* nəˈsesɪˌtəɪd
**sp** necessitied[1]

**neck / ~s** *n*
=, *Katherine H5 2.4.30ff* nɪk / -s
**sp** neck[13], necke[56], *Katherine* nick[5] / neckes[9], necks[2]
**rh** back *VA 593*
> break-neck, wry-necked

**necklace** *n*
=
**sp** necke-lace[1]

**nectar** *n*
ˈnektəɹ
**sp** nectar[2]

**Ned** *n*
=
**sp** Ned[20]

**Nedar / ~'s** *n*
ˈniːdəɹz
**sp** Nedars[2]

**need / ~s** *n*
=
**sp** need[40], neede[32] / needs[2]
**rh** feed *AY 2.7.170*; indeed *PP 20.50*; proceed *LLL 4.3.287*; speed *2H4 1.1.215, KJ 1.1.179, S 51.4*

**need / ~est / ~s / *PP* ~ing / ~ed** *v*
= / niːdst / = / ˈniːdɪn, -ɪŋ / =
**sp** need[49], neede[53] / need'st[5] / needes[40], needs[97] / needing[1] / needed[3]
**rh** deed *R2 5.6.38*; exceed *S 83.1*; need 'em freedom *Tim 1.2.68* / weeds *Mac 5.2.29* / bleeding *PP 17.15*
> never-needed

**needer** *n*
ˈniːdəɹ
**sp** needer[1]

**needful** *adj*
=
**sp** needefull[2], needful[1], needfull[26]

**needing *S*** *n*
ˈniːdɪn, -ɪŋ
**sp** needing[1]
**rh** feeding *S 118.8*

**needle / ~'s / ~s** *n*
=
**sp** needle[6] / needles[1] / needles[3], needl's[1]

**needless** *adj*
=
**sp** needlesse[10]

**needlework** *n*
ˈniːdlˌwɔːɹk
**sp** needle worke[1]
> work

**needly** *adv*
ˈniːdləɪ
**sp** needly[1]

**needy** *adj*
ˈniːdəɪ

**sp** needie[3], needy[1], needy-[hollow-ey'd][1]

**ne'er, ne'ertheless**
> never, nevertheless

**neeze** *v*
=
**sp** neeze[1]

**nefas** *Lat adj*
'nefas
**sp** nefas[1]

**negation** *n*
nɪ'gɛːsɪən
**sp** negation[1]

**negative** *adj*
*m* 'negəˌtɪv
**sp** negatiue[1]

**negative / ~s** *n*
'negətɪvz
**sp** negatiues[1]

**neglect** *n*
=
**sp** neglect[8]
**rh** respect *KL 1.1.254*

**neglect / ~est / ~ing / ~ed** *v*
= / nɪ'glekst, -ktst / nɪ'glektɪn, -ɪŋ / =
**sp** neglect[13] / neglectst[1] / neglecting[2] / neglected[7]
**rh** defect, expect *Luc 152* / respected *Per 2.2.12*

**neglected** *adj*
=
**sp** neglected[5]

**neglecting** *n*
nɪ'glektɪn, -ɪŋ
**sp** neglecting[1]
> self-neglecting

**neglectingly** *adv*
*m* nɪ'glektɪnˌləɪ, -ɪŋ-
**sp** neglectingly[1]

**neglection** *n*
nɪ'gleksɪən
**sp** neglection[2]

**negligence** *n*
*m* 'neglɪˌʤens, -ʤəns
**sp** negligence[12]
**rh** dispense, hence *Luc 1278*; thence *LC 35*

**negligent** *adj*
*m* 'neglɪˌʤent, -ʤənt
**sp** negligent[7]
> wilful-negligent

**negotiate** *v*
nɪ'goːsɪət
**sp** negotiate[2]

**negotiation / ~s** *n*
nɪˌgoːsɪ'ɛːsɪənz
**sp** negotiations[1]

**negro / ~'s** *n*
'niːgroːz
**sp** negroes[1]

**neigh / ~s** *n*
nɛː / -z
**sp** neigh[2] / neighes[1], neighs[1]

**neigh / ~ing / ~ed** *v*
nɛː, *Holofernes LLL 5.1.24* nɛːx / 'nɛːɪn, -ɪŋ / nɛːd
**sp** neigh[5], *Holofernes describing Armado* ne[1] / neighing[3] / neigh'd[1]

**neighing** *adj*
'nɛːɪn, -ɪŋ
**sp** neighing[2]

**neighbour** *adj*
'nɛːbəɹ
**sp** neighbor[2], neighbor-[confines][1], neighbour[3], neighbour-[neerenesse][1]

**neighbour / ~'s / ~s / ~s'** *n*
'nɛːbəɹ, *Holofernes LLL 5.1.24* 'nɛːxbəɹ / -z
**sp** neighbor[5], neighbour[25], neigh-bour[3], *Holofernes describing Armado* nebour[1] / neighbours[2] / neighbors[8], neighbours[16] / neighbors[1]

**neighbour / ~ed** *v*
'nɛːbəɹd
**sp** neighbour'd[3]

**neighbourhood** *n*
*m* 'nɛːbəɹˌʊd, -ˌhʊd
**sp** neighbourhood[1], neighbour-hood[2]

**neighbouring** *adj*
'nɛːbrɪn, -ɪŋ, -bər-
**sp** neighbouring[3]

**neighbourly** *adj*
*m* 'nɛːbəɹˌləɪ, -ɹl-
**sp** neighbourly[2]
> unneighbourly

**neighbour-shepherd / ~s** *n*
'nɛːbəɹ-ˌʃepəɹdz
**sp** neighbour-shepheards[1]
> shepherd

**neighbour-stained** *adj*
*m* 'nɛːbəɹ-ˌstɛːnɪd
**sp** neighbor-stained[1]
> stain

**neither** *adj / adv / conj / pro*
'nɛðəɹ, 'nɛː-, 'niː-
**sp** neither[5], neyther[1] / neither[47], nei-ther[1], neyther[10], ney-ther[1] / neither[69], neyther[21] / neither[22], nei-ther[1], neyther[3]
**rh** *adv* together *LLL 4.3.189* / *pro*
**rh** *1* either *CE 3.1.67*; **rh** *2* hither *CE 3.1.67*; whither *WT 4.4.303*; **rh** *3* together *PT 43*; whether *PP 7.18*

**Nell** *n*
=
**sp** Nel[3], Nell[13]

**Nemean** *adj*
'niːmɪən
**sp** Nemean[1], Nemian[1]

**nemesis** *n*
'nemɪˌsɪs
**sp** nemesis[1]

**Neoptolymus** *n*
ˌniːəpˈtɒlɪməs
**sp** Neoptolymus[1]

**nephew / ~'s / ~s** *n*
ˈnefjuː, -ev-
**sp** nephew[27], nephewe[1] / nephewes[4] / nephewes[1], ne-phewes[1], nephews[2]

**Neptune / ~'s** *n*
ˈneptjən / -z
**sp** Neptune[10] / Neptunes[8]

**Nereides** *n*
ˈnerɪˌdiːz
**sp** Nereides[1]

**Nerissa / ~'s** *n*
nəˈrɪsə / -z
**sp** Nerissa[2], Nerrissa[19], Ner-rissa[1], Nerryssa[2] / Nerrissas[1]

**Nero / ~'s** *n*
ˈneroː / -z
**sp** Nero[3] / Nero's[1]

**nerve / ~s** *n*
ˈnɐːɹv / -z
**sp** nerue[2] / nerues[6]
unnerved

**Nervii** *n*
ˈnɐːɹvɪˌəɪ
**sp** Neruij[1]

**nervy** *adj*
ˈnɐːɹvəɪ
**sp** neruie[1]

**Nessus** *n*
=
**sp** Nessus[2]

**nest / ~s** *n*
=
**sp** neast[1], nest[22], [swannes]-nest[1] / nests[2]
**rh** best *2H6 2.1.183, Luc 1611*; breast, rest *PT 56*; west *VA 532* / behests, breasts *Luc 849*

**Nestor** *n*
ˈnestəɹ
**sp** Nester[1], Nestor[23], Ne-stor[1]

**Nestor-like** *adj*
ˈnestəɹ-ˌləɪk
**sp** Nestor-like[1]

**net / ~s** *n*
=
**sp** net[6] / nets[2]
**rh** fret *VA 67*

**nether** *adj*
ˈneðəɹ
**sp** neather[1], nether[2], nether-[lip][1]

**Netherlands** *n*
*m* ˈneðəɹˌlands
**sp** Netherlands[1]

**nether-stocks** *n*
ˈneðəɹ-ˌstɒks
**sp** nether-stocks[1], nether stockes[1]
> stock

**nettle / ~s** *n*
=
**sp** nettle[5] / net-tels[1], nettles[5]

**nettle / ~d** *v*
=
**sp** netled[2]

**nettle-seed** *n*
=
**sp** nettle-seed[1]
> seed

**neuter** *n*
ˈnjuːtəɹ
**sp** neuter[1]

**neutral** *adj / n*
ˈnjuːtrɑl
**sp** neutrall[1], newtrall[1] / newtrall[1]

**never,** *abbr* **ne'er** *adv*
ˈnevəɹ, *abbr* nɛːɹ
**sp** neuer[977], ne-uer[10], neuer's [never is][1], *abbr* ne'r[2], nere[75], ne're[121], neu'r[11]
**rh** *1* ever *MA 2.3.63, R2 2.2.148*; **rh** *2* fever *S 119.6*; *abbr* Jupiter *Tem 4.1.76*

**never-daunted** *adj*
ˈnevəɹ-ˈdɔːntɪd
**sp** neuer-daunted[1]
> daunt

**never-dying** *adj*
ˈnevəɹ-ˈdəɪɪn, -ɪŋ
**sp** neuer-dying[1]
> die

**never-heard-of** *adj*
ˈnevəɹ-ˈɐːɹd-əv, -hɐː-
**sp** neuer heard-of[1]
> hear

**never-needed** *adj*
ˈnevəɹ-ˈniːdɪd
**sp** neuer-needed[1]
> need

**never-quenching** *adj*
ˈnevəɹ-ˈkwenʧɪn, -ɪŋ
**sp** neuer-quenching[1]
> quench

**never-surfeited** *adj*
ˈnevəɹ-ˈsɐːɹfɪtɪd
**sp** neuer surfeited[1]

**nevertheless,** *abbr* **ne'er~** *adv*
ˌnɛːɹðəˈles
**sp** nere the lesse[2]

**never-touched,** *abbr* **ne'er--** *adj*
ˈnɛːɹ-ˌtɤʧt
**sp** ne're touch'd[1]
> touch

**never-withering** *adj*
ˈnevəɹ-ˈwɪðrɪn, -ɪŋ, -ðər-
**sp** neuer-withering[1]
> wither

**never-yet** *adj*
ˈnɛːɹ-jɪt
**sp** nere-yet[1]
> yet

**Neville / ~'s / ~s / ~s'** *n*
=
**sp** Neuil[1], Neuill[1] / Neuils[1] / Neuills[1], Neuils[2] / Neuils[2]

**new** *adj*
= / 'nju:·əɹ / -əst, 'nju:st
**sp** new[175], new-[spring][1] / newer[4] / newest[5], news't[1]
**rh** adieu *KL 1.1.187, Mac 2.4.38*; adieu, true *R2 5.3.145*; true *S 93.3*; view *S 27.12, 56.10, 110.4*; you *CE 3.2.39, MV 3.2.134, S 15.14, 53.8, 76.11*

**new** *adv / n*
=
**sp** new[35] / new[1]
**rh** *adv* true *S 68.12*; *n* true *PP 18.22*; view *S 56.10*
> a-, fire-new; news

**new-apparelled** *adj*
=
**sp** new apparel'd[1]
> apparel

**new-appearing** *adj*
'nju:-ə'pi:rɪn, -ɪŋ
**sp** new appearing[1]
> appear

**new-beaten** *adj*
ˌnju:-'bi:tən, -'bɛ:-
**sp** new beaten[1]
> beat

**new-born** *adj*
*m* 'nju:-ˌbɔ:ɹn, ˌnju:-'bɔ:ɹn
**sp** new-borne[2], new-borne-[babe][1], new borne[3], now borne[1]
**rh** outworn, torn *Luc 1759*; worn *LLL 4.3.242*
> born

**new-built** *adj*
*m* 'nju:-ˌbɪlt, ˌnju:-'bɪlt
**sp** new-built[1], new built[1]
> build

**new-christened** *adj*
*m* ˌnju:-'krɪsənd
**sp** new christned[1]
> christen

**new-come** *adj*
'nju:-ˌkɤm
**sp** new-come[2]
> come

**new-crowned** *adj*
*m* ˌnju:-'krəʊnɪd
**sp** new crowned[1]
> crown

**new-dated** *adj*
*m* ˌnju:-'dɛ:tɪd
**sp** new-dated[1]
> date

**new-delivered** *adj*
'nju:-dɪ'lɪvəɹd
**sp** new deliuered[2]
> deliver

**new-devised** *adj*
'nju:-dɪˌvəɪzd
**sp** new deuis'd[1]
> devise

**new-dyed** *adj*
'nju:-'dəɪd
**sp** new dy'de[1]
> dye

**new-fallen** *adj*
'nju:-ˌfɑln
**sp** new-falne[2]
> fall

**new-fangled** *adj*
*m* ˌnju:-'faŋgəld
**sp** new fangled[1], new-fang-led[1]
> fangled

**new-fired** *adj*
*m* ˌnju:-'fəɪɹd
**sp** new-fir'd[1]
**rh** desired *S 153.9*
> fire

**new-formed** *adj*
*m* ˌnju:-'fɔ:ɹmd
**sp** new form'd[1]
> form

**new-found** *adj*
'nju:-ˌfəʊnd
**sp** new-found[1]
> find

**Newgate-fashion** *adv*
'njugɛ:t-ˌfaʃɪən
**sp** Newgate fashion[1]
> fashion

**new-haled** *adj*
*m* ˌnju:-'ɛ:lɪd, -'hɛ-
**sp** new haled[1]
> hale

**new-hatched** *adj*
*m* ˌnju:-'atʃt, -'ha-
**sp** new hatch'd[1]
> hatch

**new-healed** *adj*
'nju:-ˌi:ld, -ˌhi:-
**sp** new-heal'd[2]
> heal

**new-inspired** *adj*
*m* ˌnju:-ɪn'spəɪɹd
**sp** new inspir'd[1]
> inspire

**newly** *adv*
'nju:ləɪ
**sp** newly[28], newly [borne][1]

**newly-born** *adj*
'nju:ləɪ-'bɔ:ɹn
**sp** newly borne[1]
> born

**new-made** *adj*
*m* 'nju:-ˌmɛ:d, ˌnju:-'mɛ:d
**sp** new-made[4], new made[4]
> make

**new-married** *adj*
*m* ˌnju:-'marəɪd
**sp** new-maried[1], new-married[1], new married[1]
> marry

**newness** *n*
=
**sp** newnes[1], newnesse[2]

**new-planted** *adj*
*m* ˌnjuː-ˈplɔːntɪd, -lan-
**sp** new-planted[1]
> plant

**new-risen** *adj*
ˈnjuː-ˈrɪzən
**sp** new risen[1]
> rise

**news** *n*
=
**sp** newes[305], [stiffe]-newes[1], news[7]
**rh** ensues *WT 4.1.26*

**new-sad** *adj*
=
**sp** new sad-[soule][1]

**news-crammed** *adj*
ˈnjuz-ˌkramd
**sp** newes-cram'd[1]
> cram

**new-shed** *adj*
ˈnjuː-ˌʃed
**sp** new-shed-[blood][1]
> shed

**newsmonger / ~s** *n*
ˈnjuz-ˌmɤŋgəɹz
**sp** newes-mongers[1]

**new-store** *v*
ˈnjuː-ˌstɔːɹ
**sp** new-store[1]
> store

**newt / ~s** *n*
=
**sp** newt[2] / newts[1]

**new-taken,** *abbr* **ta'n** *adj*
ˈnjuː-ˌtɛːn
**sp** new tane[1]
> take

**new-transformed** *adj*
ˈnjuː-transˈfɔːɹmɪd
**sp** new transformed[1]
> transform

**new-trimmed** *adj*
ˈnjuː-ˈtrɪmd
**sp** new trim'd[1]
> trim

**new-trothed** *adj*
ˈnjuː-ˌtroːðd
**sp** new trothed[1]
> troth

**new-tuned** *adj*
ˈnjuː-ˌtjuːnd
**sp** new-tuned[1]
> tune

**new-year's** *adj*
ˈnjuː-ˌjiːɹz
**sp** new-yeares[1]
> year

**next** *adj / adv / n / prep*
=
**sp** next[97] / next[30] / next[21] / next[10]
**rh** *adj* text *Per 2.Chorus.39, RJ 4.1.20*

**next to** *prep*
=
**sp** next to[3]

**nibbl·e / ~ing** *v*
ˈnɪblɪn, -ɪŋ
**sp** nibling[1]

**nibling** *adj*
ˈnɪblɪn, -ɪŋ
**sp** nibling[1]

**Nicanor** *n*
nɪˈkɛːnəɹ
**sp** Nicanor[1], Ni-canor[1]

**nice / ~r** *adj*
nəɪs / ˈnəɪsəɹ
**sp** nice[27], nice-[longing][1] / nicer[1]
**rh** advice, entice *Luc 1412*; dice *LLL 5.2.232;* price *LLL 5.2.222*

**nice** *n*
nəɪs
**sp** nice[1]
**rh** dice *LLL 5.2.325*

**nicely** *adv*
ˈnəɪsləɪ
**sp** nicely[8]

**niceness** *n*
ˈnəɪsnəs
**sp** nicenesse[1]

**nice-preserved** *adj*
*m* ˈnəɪs-prɪˈzɐːɹvɪd
**sp** nice-preserued[1]
> preserve

**nicety** *n*
ˈnəɪstəɪ, -sət-
**sp** nicetie[1]

**Nicholas** *n*
ˈnɪkləs, -kəl-
**sp** Nicholas[9], Nicolas[1]

**nick** *n*
=
**sp** nicke[1]

**nick / ~s / ~ed** *v*
=
**sp** nickes[1] / nickt[1]

**Nick** [name] *n*
=
**sp** Nick[1], Nicke[1]

**nickname** *n / v*
ˈnɪknɛːm
**sp** nickname[3] / nickname[2]

**niece / ~'s / ~s** *n*
=
**sp** neece[57], neice[1], niece[5] / neeces[1] / neeces[1]

**niggard** *adj / n / v*
ˈnɪgəɹd
**sp** niggard[2] / niggard[3] / niggard[1]

**niggarding** *n*
ˈnɪgəɹdɪn, -ɪŋ
**sp** niggarding[1]
**rh** spring *S 1.12*

**niggardly** *adj / adv*
*m* 'nɪgəɹdləɪ, -d,l- / 'nɪgəɹdləɪ
**sp** niggardly[2], niggard-ly[1] / nigardly[1]

**nigh** *adj / adv / prep*
nəɪ
**sp** nye[2] / nie[4], nigh[6], nye[3] / nie[1], nye[1]
**rh** *1 adv* by *LC 57*; eye *VA 341*; fly *Oth 2.1.149*; lullaby *MND 2.2.18*; sky *AY 2.7.186*; try *CE 2.1.43*; **rh** *2* immediately *MND 2.2.161*
> well-nigh

**night / ~'s / ~s / ~s'** *n*
nəɪt / -s
**sp** night[507], [blacke]-night[1], [hell-blacke]-night[1], [midsomer]-night[1] / night's[3], nights[20] / nights[30], [a]-nights[2] / nights[1]
**rh** affright *MND 5.1.139*; affright, flight *Luc 970*; aright *MND 2.1.43*; bright *RJ 1.5.45, 2.2.22, S 28.11, 147.14, TNK 3.5.125*; daylight MND *3.2.431*; delight *Luc 356, 741, 925, MND 2.1.253, PP 18.26, RJ 1.2.29, 2.5.76, S 102.10, VA 841*; delight, flight *Luc 698*; delight, might *Luc 485*; despite *VA 732*; despite, right *Luc 1024*; fight *JC 5.3.109, MND 3.2.355, TC 5.3.93*; fight, light *MW 2.1.14*; fight, sprite *Luc 123*; flight *MND 1.1.247, 4.1.99*; height *H8 1.2.213*; knight *MA 5.3.12; RJ 3.2.140*; knight, might *MW 2.1.14*; light *Ham 3.2.227, 3H6 2.5.3, LLL 4.3.231, 253, Luc 162, 675, 771, 784, 1092, 1232, MND 3.2.187, 387, Oth 1.3.397, Per 1.1.136, 2.3.43, R2 1.3.177, 222, 5.6.43, RJ 1.2.24, 2.2.188, Tim 5.1.42, VA 492, 534, 755, 1041*; light, right *Luc 942*; light, white *Luc 396*; plight *S 28.3*; quite *Oth 5.1.128*; right *KJ 1.1.172, R3 4.4.16, VA 1186, WT 4.3.16*; rite *MA 5.3.22*; sight *CE 3.2.58, PP 14.20, RJ 1.5.53, S 15.12, 27.11, 30.6, 61.2, 63.5, 113.11, VA 122, 821*; spite *Luc 763, RJ 1.5.63*; sprite *Luc 449, MND 5.1.369*; white *1H6 2.4.127, MW 5.5.38, S 12.2, TS 5.2.186*; write *S 86.7* / lights *LLL 1.1.90, Luc 1379*
> a-nights, fort-, good-, mid-, out-, over-, sennight, to-, yester-night

**night-alarm** *n*
'nəɪt-ə,lɑ:ɹm
**sp** night-alarme[1]
> alarm

**night-brawler** *n*
'nəɪt-,brɔ:ləɹ
**sp** night-brawler[1]
> brawl

**nightcap / ~s** *n*
'nəɪt-,kaps
**sp** night-cape[1] / night-cappes[1]
> cap

**night-crow** *n*
'nəɪt-,kro:
**sp** night-crow[1]
> crow

**night-dog / ~s** *n*
'nəɪt-,dɒgz
**sp** night-dogges[1]
> dog

**nighted** *adj*
'nəɪtɪd
**sp** nighted[1]

**night-foe / ~s** *n*
*m* ,nəɪt-'fo:z
**sp** night-foes[1]
> foe

**nightgown** *n*
'nəɪt-,gəʊn
**sp** night-gown[1], night-gowne[5]
> gown

**nightingale / ~'s / ~s** *n*
'nəɪtɪŋ,gɛ:l / -z
**sp** nightingale[6], nightin-gale[1], nightinghale[1] / nightingales[1] / nightingales[2]

**nightly** *adj / adv*
'nəɪtləɪ
**sp** nightly[6], nightly-[meadow-fairies][1] / nightly[14]
**rh** lightly *TG 3.1.140*

**nightmare** *n*
'nəɪtmɛ:ɹ
**sp** night-mare[1]

**night-owl / ~'s / ~s** *n*
'nəɪt-,əʊl / -z
**sp** night-owle[1] / night-owles[1] / night-owls[1]
> owl

**night-raven** *n*
'nəɪt-,rɛ:vən
**sp** night-rauen[1]
> raven

**night-rest** *n*
*m* ,nəɪt-'rest
**sp** night-rest[1]
> rest

**night-rule** *n*
'nəɪt-,ru:l
**sp** night-rule[1]
> rule

**night-shriek** *n*
'nəɪt-,ʃri:k
**sp** night-shrieke[1]
> shriek

**night-swift** *adj*
'nəɪt-,swɪft
**sp** night-swift[1]
> swift

**night-taper / ~s** *n*
'nəɪt-,tɛ:pəɹz
**sp** night-tapers[1]
> taper

**night-tripping** *adj*
*m* ,nəɪt-'trɪpɪn, -ɪŋ
**sp** night-tripping-[faiery][1]
> trip

**night-walking** *adj*
*m* ,nəɪt-'wɔ:kɪn, -ɪŋ
**sp** night-walking[1]
> walk

**night-wanderer / ~s** *n*
*m* ,nəɪt-'wɒndrəɹz, -dər-
**sp** night-wanderers[1]
> wander

**night-watch** *n*
ˈnəɪt-ˌwɒʧ
**sp** night-watch[1]
> watch

**Nightwork** [name] *n*
ˈnəɪtwɔːɹk
**sp** Night-worke[3]

**nihil** *Lat n*
ˈnɪhɪl
**sp** nihil[1]

**Nile** *n*
nəɪl
**sp** Nyle[6]

**nill** *v*
=
**sp** nill[2]

**Nilus** *n*
ˈnəɪləs
**sp** Nilus[1], Nylus[5]

**nimble / ~r** *adj*
= / ˈnɪmbləɹ
**sp** nimble[21] / nimbler[1]

**nimble-footed** *adj*
=
**sp** nimble footed[1], nimble-footed[1]
> foot

**nimbleness** *n*
=
**sp** nimblenesse[1]

**nimble-pinioned** *adj*
=
**sp** nimble pinion'd[1]
> pinion

**nimbly** *adv*
ˈnɪmbləɪ
**sp** nimbly[4]

**nine** *adj / n*
nəɪn
**sp** nine[28] / nine[28]
**rh** fine *LLL 5.2.488*; mine *Mac 1.3.35*; pine *Mac 1.3.22*

**nine-fold** *adj*
*m* ˌnəɪn-ˈfoːld
**sp** nine-fold[1]
**rh** old *KL 3.4.116*
> fold

**nineteen** *adj / n*
ˈnəɪntiːn
**sp** nineteene[2], ninteene[1] / nineteene[2]

**ninny** *n*
ˈnɪnəɪ
**sp** ninnie's [ninny is][1]

**Ninny** [name] **/ ~'s** *n*
ˈnɪnəɪz
**sp** Ninnies [Ninus's][3]
> Ninus

**ninth** *adj / n*
nəɪnt, -nθ
**sp** ninth[6] / ninth[1]

**Ninus / ~'** *n*
ˈnəɪnəs
**sp** Ninus[2]

**Niobe / ~s** *n*
*m* ˈnəɪəˌbiː / ˈnəɪəbiːz
**sp** Niobe[1], / Niobes[1]

**nip / ~s / ~ped** *v*
=
**sp** nip[3] / nippes[1], nips[1] / nipt[1]

**nipping** *adj*
ˈnɪpɪn, -ɪŋ
**sp** nipping[2]

**nipple** *n*
=
**sp** nipple[2]

**nit** *n*
=
**sp** nit[2]
**rh** wit *LLL 4.1.149*

**no** *adv*
noː
**sp** no[3707], noe[1], *Caius MW 2.3.6ff* no-[come][3], no-[face][1], no-[the][1]
**rh** blow *CE 3.1.55*; foe *1H6 4.7.25*; go *KJ 3.4.183, KL 5.3.320, MND 3.1.144, TG 1.3.91, TS 1.2.227*; know *LLL 5.2.486*; know, so *LLL 1.1.69*; low *Luc 1340*; mow [*n*] *Tem 4.1.48*; show *AY 3.2.122*; slow *LLL 3.1.58*; slow, woe *LLL 4.1.14*; so *CE 3.2.60, 4.2.3, LLL 2.1.197, MND 3.2.81, MV 3.2.145, R2 3.3.209, S 148.8, TC 4.4.134, VA 852*; toe *Tem 4.1.48*; trow *CE 3.1.55*; woe *RJ 2.3.41, 3.2.50*

**no / ~es** *n*
noːz
**sp** noes[1]
**rh** knows *LLL 5.2.413*

**Noah / ~'s** *n*
ˈnoːə / -z
**sp** Noah[1] / Noahs[1]

**Nob** [name] *n*
=
**sp** nobbe[1]

**nobility / ~'s** *n*
*m* nəˈbɪlɪˌtəɪ, -ɪt- / nəˈbɪlɪˌtəɪz
**sp** nobilitie[14], no-bilitie[1], nobility[20], nobi-lity[1] / nobilities[1]
**rh** company *2H6 2.1.191*

**nobis** *Lat*
> nos

**noble / ~r / ~st** *adj*
ˈnoːbəl / ˈnoːbl·əɹ / -əst
**sp** noble[585], noble [borne][1], noble-[youth][1], no-ble[2] / nobler[19] / noblest[17]
> all-, ignoble, thrice-, un-noble

**noble** *adv*
ˈnoːbəl
**sp** noble[1]

**noble / ~s** *n*
ˈnoːbəl / -z
**sp** noble[7] / nobles[40]
> ennoble

**noble-ending** *adj*
ˈnoːbəl-ˌendɪn, -ɪŋ
**sp** noble-ending-[loue][1]

**noble·man / ~men** *n*
'no:bəlmən
**sp** nobleman[9], noble man[4], no-ble man[1] / noblemen[4], noble-men[1]

**noble-minded / noblest-~** *adj*
'no:bəl-ˌməɪndɪd / 'no:bləst-
**sp** noble-minded[1], noble minded[1] / noblest minded[1]
> mind

**nobleness** *n*
'no:bəlnəs
**sp** noblenesse[16]

**nobler** *n*
'no:bləɹ
**sp** nobler[1]

**noblest** *n*
'no:bləst
**sp** noblest[5]

**noblish** *adj*
'no:blɪʃ
**sp** noblish[1]

**nobly** *adv*
'no:bləɪ
**sp** noblie[1], nobly[34]

**nobody** *pro*
*m* 'no:bədəɪ, ˌno:'bɒdəɪ, *Caius MW 3.3.201* 'no:bədəɪz
**sp** no-bodie[2], nobody[1], no-body[1], no body[15], *Caius* no-bodies[1]
> body

**noce / ~s** *Fr n*
nɔs
**sp** nopcese[1]

**nod / ~s** *n*
=
**sp** nod[6] / nods[4]

**nod / ~s / ~ded** *v*
=
**sp** nod[10], nodde[2] / noddes[1] / nodded[2]

**nodding** *adj / n*
'nɒd-ɪn, -ɪŋ
**sp** nodding[1] / nodding[1]

**noddle / ~s** *n*
=
**sp** noddle[1] / *Evans MW 3.1.114* noddles[1]

**noddy** *n*
'nɒdəɪ
**sp** noddy[3]
**pun** *TG 1.1.113* nod-I[1]

**nointed**
> anoint

**noise** *n*
nəɪz / 'nəɪzɪz
**sp** noise[48], noyse[57] / noyses[2]
**rh** *1* boys *CE 3.1.61*; **rh** *2* voice VA 919

**noise** *v*
nəɪz / 'nəɪzɪz / nəɪzd
**sp** noyse[2] / noyses[1] / nois'd[2]

**noiseless** *adv*
'nəɪzləs
**sp** noiselesse[1]

**noise-maker** *n*
'nəɪz-ˌmɛ:kəɹ
**sp** noyse-maker[1]
> make

**noisome** *adj*
'nəɪsəm
**sp** noisome[1], noysome[4]

**nole** *n*
no:l
**sp** nole[1]

**nominate / ~d** *v*
*m* 'nɒmɪˌnɛ:t, -ɪn- / -ɪd
**sp** nominate[3] / nominated[3]
> prenominate

**nomination** *n*
*m* ˌnɒmɪ'nɛ:sɪən, -sɪˌɒn
**sp** nomination[2]

**nominativ·us / ~o** *Lat n*
ˌnɒmɪnə'ti:vo:
**sp** nominatiuo[2]

**non** *Fr adv*
nɔ̃
**sp** non[1], *H5 3.4.40 emend of* nome[1]

**non** *Ital adv / Lat adv / nonsense word in song*
nɒn
**sp** non[2] / non[4] / non[1]

**nonage** *n*
'no:nɪʤ
**sp** nonage[1]

**nonce** *n*
no:ns
**sp** nonce[3]

**noncome** *n*
'nɒnkəm
**sp** non-come[1]
> come

**none** *pro*
no:n, nɒn
**sp** none[455]
**rh** *1* alone *AW 2.3.126, 1H6 4.7.10, MM 2.1.39, PP 17.36, TN 3.1.156*; bone *Tim 4.3.530*; groan *2H6 3.1.222*; own *Per Prol.28*; stone *S 94.1*; **rh** *2* one *Luc 1162, Mac 5.6.14, PT 27, 47, R3 4.4.104, RJ 1.2.33, S 8.14, 136.8, TC 4.5.41, TG 5.4.51*; **rh** *3* foregone *AW 1.3.130*; gone *CE 3.2.160*, [*F, at* LLL 2.1.113-129], *MND 2.2.73, 3.2.169, VA 389*; on *Per 3.Chorus.28*

**none-sparing** *adj*
*m* ˌno:n-'spɛ:rɪn, -ɪŋ, ˌnɒn-
**sp** none-sparing[1]
> sparing *adj*

**nonny** *nonsense word in song*
'nɒnəɪ
**sp** nonny[1], nony[5]
**rh** bonny *MA 2.3.67*

**nonny-no, nonino** *nonsense word in song*
'nɒnəɪ'no:
**sp** nonino[4]
**rh** ho *AY 5.3.16, 22, 28, 34*

**nonpareil** *n*
*m* 'nɒnpə,rɪl
**sp** non-pareil[1], non-pareill[4]

**non-performance** *n*
,nɒnpəɹ'fɔ:ɹməns
**sp** non-performance[1]
> perform

**non-regardance** *n*
,nɒnrɪ'gɑ:ɹdəns
**sp** non-regardance[1]
> regard

**nonsuit / ~s** *v*
nɒn'ʃu:ts, -'sju:
**sp** non-suites[1]
> suit

**nook / ~s** *n*
nu:k, nʊk / -s
**sp** nooke[2] / nookes[1]

**nook-shotten** *adj*
'nu:k-,ʃɒtən, nʊk-
**sp** nooke-shotten[1]
> shot

**noon** *n*
=, nʊn
**sp** noone[14], '[fore]-noone[1]
**rh** *1* moon *Mac 3.5.22*; soon *TN 3.1.145*; **rh** *2* son *S 7.13*
> after-, fore-noon

**noonday** *adj*
'nu:ndɛ:, 'nʊn-
**sp** noone-day[1]

**no-one** *pro*
*m* ,no:-'o:n, -'wɒn, 'no:wən
**sp** no one[5]

**noontide** *adj*
'nu:ntəɪd, 'nʊn-
**sp** noonetide[1], noone-tide[2], noon-tide[1]

**nor** *conj*
*str* nɔ:ɹ, *unstr* nɒɹ
**sp** nor[894], nor's [nor his][1]
**rh** hoar *TNK 1.1.19*

**Norbery** *n*
'nɔ:ɹbrəɪ, -bər-
**sp** Norberie[1]

**Norfolk / ~'s** *n*
'nɔ:ɹfək / -s
**sp** Norfolk[4], Norfolke[58], Nor-folke[2] / Norfolkes[2]

**Norman** *adj*
'nɔ:ɹmən
**sp** Norman[1]

**Norman / ~s** *n*
'nɔ:ɹmən / -z
**sp** Norman[3] / Normans[3]

**Normandy** *n*
*m* 'nɔ:ɹmən,dəɪ, -ndəɪ
**sp** Normandie[6], Normandy[1]

**north** *adj / adv / n*
nɔ:ɹθ
**sp** north[4], north-[gate][1], north-[pole][1], north-[side][1] / north[3] / north[25]
**rh** forth *Per 3.Chorus.47*

**Northampton** *n*
nɔ:ɹ'θamtən, -mpt-
**sp** Northampton[3]

**Northamptonshire** *n*
*m* nɔ:ɹ'θamtən,ʃəɪɹ, -mpt-
**sp** Northamptonshire[1]

**north-east** *adj*
*m* 'nɔ:ɹθ-,est
**sp** northeast[1]

**northerly** *adv*
'nɔ:ɹðəɹləɪ
**sp** northerly[1]

**northern** *adj*
'nɔ:ɹðəɹn
**sp** northern[1], northerne[9]

**north-north-east** *adv*
'nɔ:ɹθ-nɔ:ɹθ-'est, 'nɔ:ɹ-nɔ:ɹ-
**sp** north north-east[3]

**north-north-west** *adv*
'nɔ:ɹθ-nɔ:ɹθ-'west, 'nɔ:ɹ-nɔ:ɹ-
**sp** north, north-west[1]
> west

**Northumberland / ~'s / ~s** *n*
*m* nɔ:ɹ'θɤmbəɹ·,land, -lənd / -,landz
**sp** Northumberland[60], Nor-thumberland[1], Northum-berland[2], *abbr in s.d.* North.[1] / Northumberlands[1] / Northumberlands[1]

**northward** *adv*
'nɔ:ɹθwəɹd
**sp** northward[2], north-ward[1]

**Norway / ~'s** *n*
'nɔ:ɹwɛ: / -z
**sp** Norway[6], Norwey[5] / Norwayes[1]

**Norwayan** *adj*
nɔ:ɹ'wɛ:ən
**sp** Norweyan[3]

**nos** *Lat pro*

***nobis*** *pro*
'no:bɪs
**sp** nobis[1]

***noster*** *det*
'nɒstəɹ
**sp** noster[1]

**nosco / ~vi** *Lat v*
'no:vi:
**sp** noui[1]

**nose / ~s** *n*
no:z / 'no:zɪz
**sp** nose[62] / noses[14]
**rh** roses *WT 4.4.223*
> malmsey-, red-nose

**nose** *v*
no:z
**sp** nose[2]

**nosegay / ~s** *n*
'no:zgɛ:z
**sp** nose-gaies[1], nose-gayes[1]

**nose-herb / ~s** *n*
'no:z-ˌɛ:ɹbz
**sp** nose-hearbes[1]
> herb

**noseless** *adj*
'no:zləs
**sp** noselesse[1]

**nose-painting** *n*
'no:z-ˌpɛ:ntɪn, -ɪŋ
**sp** nose-painting[1]
> paint

**noster** *Lat*
> nos

**nostra** *Ital det*
'nɒstra
**sp** nostra[1]

**nostril / ~s** *n*
=
**sp** nosthrill[2], no-strill[1] / nostrils[3]

**not** *adv*
=
**sp** not[8248]
**rh** *1* begot *KJ 1.1.276*; blot *LLL 4.3.237, Luc 190, S 92.14*; forgot *AY 2.7.190, MM 4.4.32, MND 5.1.168, S 71.5, 149.1*; got *Tem Epil.5*; hot *LC 220*; o'ershot *LLL 4.3.157*; plot *S 137.11*; sot *CE 2.2.202*; wot *MND 3.2.421*; **rh** *2* smote *LLL 4.3.24*

**notable** *adj*
'no:təbəl
**sp** notable[13]

**notably** *adv*
'no:təbləɪ
**sp** notably[1]

**notary / ~'s** *n*
*m* 'no:trəɪ, -tər- / 'no:təˌrəɪz
**sp** notarie[1] / notaries[1]

**notch /~ed** *v*
=
**sp** notcht[1]

**note / ~s** *n*
no:t / -s
**sp** note[105] / noates[2], notes[20]
**rh** *1* coat, dote *LC 233, Luc 208*; dote *CE 3.2.45, LLL 4.3.123, 5.2.75, VA 835*; rote *MND 5.1.388*; throat *AY 2.5.3, R2 1.1.43*; **rh** *2* pot *LLL 5.2.908, 917* / throats *Tim 1.2.50*

**not·e / ~est / *VA* ~eth / ~ing / ~ed** *v*
no:t / -st / 'no:t·əθ / -ɪn, -ɪŋ / -ɪd
**sp** note[40] / not'st[1] / noteth[1] / noting[2], no-ting[1] / noted[18]
**rh** dote *S 141.2* / doteth *VA 1057* / doted *Luc 414*; quoted *LLL 4.3.86*
**pun** noting *MA 2.3.53* nothing
> un-, well-noted

**notebook** *n*
'no:tbʊk
**sp** note-booke[3]
> book

**noted** *adj*
'no:tɪd
**sp** noted[1]

**notedly** *adv*
'no:tɪdləɪ
**sp** notedly[1]

**noteworthy** *adj*
*m* ˌno:t'wɔ:ɹðəɪ
**sp** note-worthy[1]

**not-fearing** *adj*
*m* ˌnɒt'fi:rɪn, -ɪŋ
**sp** not-fearing-[Britaine][1]
> fear

**nothing / ~s** *n*
'no:tɪn, -ɪŋ
**sp** nothing[596], no-thing[14], no thing[2], nothings [nothing is][1] / nothings[3]
**rh** a-doting *S 20.12*
**pun** *MA 2.3.55* noting
> thing

**nothing-gift** *n*
'no:tɪn-ˌgɪft, -ɪŋ-
**sp** nothing-guift[1]
> gift

**notice** *n*
'no:tɪs
**sp** notice[30]

**notify** *v*
'no:tɪfəɪ
**sp** notifie[2]

**noting** *n*
'no:tɪn, -ɪŋ
**sp** noting[1]

**notion** *n*
'no:sɪən
**sp** notion[3]

**notorious** *adj*
nə'tɔ:rɪəs, no:-
**sp** notorious[14]

**notoriously** *adv*
nə'tɔ:rɪəsləɪ, no:-
**sp** notoriouslie[1], notoriously[1]

**notre** *Fr det*
'nɔtrə
**sp** nostre[2]

**notwithstanding** *prep*
ˌnɒtwɪθ'standɪn, -ɪŋ
**sp** notwithstanding[17], not-withstanding[1], notwith-standing[1], not withstanding[3], not with-standing[1]

**nought**
> naught

**noun / ~s** *n*
nəʊn / -z
**sp** nowne[1] / nownes[1], [od's]-nownes [wounds][1]

**nourish** *n*
'nɤrɪʃ
**sp** nourish[1]

**nourish / ~es / ~eth / ~ing / ~ed** *v*
ˈnɤrɪʃ / -ɪz / -əθ / -ɪn, -ɪŋ / *m* -t, -ed
**sp** nourish[7] / nourishes[1] / nourisheth[2] / nourishing[1] / norisht[1], nourish'd[1], nourished[1], nourisht[5]
**rh** flourisheth *TS 2.1.332* / bred, head *MV 3.2.65*

**nourisher** *n*
ˈnɤrɪʃəɹ
**sp** nourisher[1]

**nourishment** *n*
*m* ˈnɤrɪʃˌment
**sp** nourishment[2]

**nous** *Fr pro*
nu
**sp** nous[1]

**novelt·y / ~ies** *n*
ˈnɒvəltəɪ / *m* ˈnɒvəlˌtəɪz
**sp** noueltie[1], no-ueltie[1] / nouelties[1]

**no-verb / ~s** *n*
ˈnoːˌvɐːɹbz
**sp** no-verbes[1]

**novi** *Lat*
> nosco

**novice / ~s** *n*
=
**sp** nouice[3] / nouices[2]

**novum** *n*
ˈnoːvʊm
**sp** novum[1]

**now** *adv*
nəʊ
**sp** now[2715], nowes [now is][1], now's [now is][2]
**rh** allow *R2 5.2.39, RJ 2.3.81, WT 4.1.30*; bough *S 102.9, Tem 5.1.93, VA 39*; bow [head] *KL 3.6.106* [Q], *S 120.1, 90.1, VA 97, 1062*; brow *H8 Prol.1, KJ 2.1.507, LLL 4.1.16, 119, 4.3.227, 261, S 2.3, 33.12, 63.1, 68.2, 106.8*; how *LLL 5.2.513, MM 2.2.186, R2 5.3.114, S 101.14*; thou *LLL 5.2.338, MND 3.2.401*; vow *LLL 5.2.343, RJ 1.1.224*

**nowadays** *adv*
ˈnəʊəˌdɛːz
**sp** now adaies[1], now-adayes[1]

**nowhere** *adv*
ˈnoːʍɛːɹ
**sp** no where[2]

**noyance**
> annoyance

**nub·es / ~ibus** *Lat n*
ˈnuːbɪbʊs
**sp** nubibus[1]

**Numa / ~'s** *n*
ˈnuːməz
**sp** Numaes[1]

**numb** *adj*
nɤm
**sp** numbe[1], numme[2]

**numbed** *adj*
nɤmd
**sp** num'd[1]

**number / ~s** *n*
ˈnɤmbəɹ, -z
**sp** number[45], numbers [number is][1] / numbers[37]

**number / ~ing / ~ed** *v*
ˈnɤmbəɹ / ˈnɤmbrɪn, -ɪŋ / ˈnɤmbəɹd
**sp** number[3] / numbring[1], numb'ring[1] / number'd[1], numbred[6]

**numbered** *adj*
ˈnɤmbəɹd
**sp** number'd[1]
> unnumbered

**numbering** *adj / n*
ˈnɤmbrɪn, -ɪŋ
**sp** numbring[1] / numbring[1]

**numberless** *adj*
*m* ˈnɤmbəɹˌles
**sp** numberlesse[2]

**numbness** *n*
ˈnɤmnəs
**sp** numnesse[1]

**nun / ~'s / ~s** *n*
nɤn / -z
**sp** nun[3], nunne[1] / nuns[1] / nunnes[2], nuns[1]
**rh** shun *LC 232* [nun *emend of* sunne] / sons *VA 752*

**nuncle** *n*
ˈnɤŋkəl
**sp** nunckle[9], nuncle[3], nunkle[5]
> uncle

**nunnery** *n*
ˈnɤnrəɪ, -nər-
**sp** nunnerie[1], nunnery[4]

**nuntio / ~'s** *n*
ˈnɤnsɪoːz
**sp** nuntio's[1]

**Nuntius** *n*
ˈnɤnsɪəs
**sp** Nuntius[1]

**nuptial** *adj / n*
ˈnɤpsɪɑl
**sp** nuptiall[8] / nuptiall[12]

**nurse / ~'s / ~s** *n*
nɐːɹs, nɔːɹs, *Caius MW 3.2.58* nɐːɹʃ / -ɪz
**sp** nourse[1], nurse[89], nursse[1], *Caius* nursh-[a-Quickly][1] / nurses[3] / nurses[1]
**rh** *1* corse *RJ 3.2.127*; **rh** *2* worse *VA 773*
> dry-, foster-nurse

**nurs·e / ~ing / ~ed** *v*
nɐːɹs, nɔːɹs / ˈnɐːɹsɪn, -ɪŋ, ˈnɔː- / nɐːɹst, ˈnɔː-
**sp** nurse[4] / nursing[1] / nurst[3], nur'st[2]

**nurse-like** *adj*
ˈnɐːɹs-ləɪk, ˈnɔː-
**sp** nurse-like[1]

**nurser** *n*
'nɐːɹsəɹ, 'nɔː-
**sp** nursser[1]

**nursery** *n*
*m* 'nɐːɹsrəɪ, -sə,rəɪ, 'nɔː-
**sp** nurserie[1], nursery[3], nursserie[1]

**nursing** *n*
'nɐːɹsɪn, -ɪŋ, 'nɔː-
**sp** nursing[3]

**nurture** *n*
'nɐːɹtəɹ
**sp** nourture[1], nurture[1]

**nut** *n*
nɤt / -s
**sp** nut[6] / nuts[3]
> chest-, hazel-, pig-nut

**nuthook / ~s** *n*
'nɤt,ʊk, -,hʊk / -s
**sp** nut-hooke[2] / nut-hooks[1]
> hook

**nutmeg / ~s** *n*
'nɤtmeg / -z
**sp** nutmeg[1], nutmegge[1] / nutmegges[1]

**nutriment** *n*
*m* 'njuːtrɪ,ment
**sp** nutriment[1]

**nutshell** *n*
'nɤʧel
**sp** nutshell[1], nutt-shell[1]
> shell

**Nym** *n*
=
**sp** Nim[11], Nym[10], Nymme[2]

**nymph / ~s** *n*
=
**sp** nimph[4], nymph[3] / nimphes[4], nimphs[3], nymphes[1], nymphs[1]
> sea-nymph

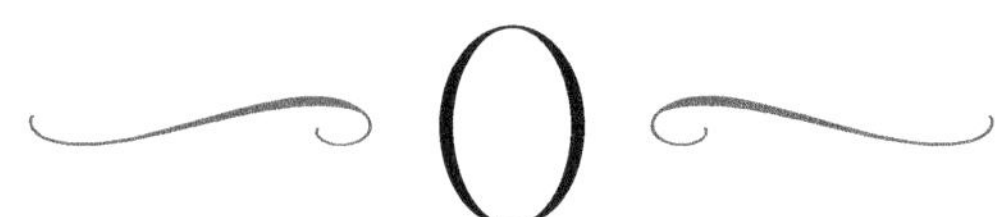

**O** *interj*
oː
**sp** O[1338], Oh[764], oh[125]

**O / ~s** *n*
oː / oːz
**sp** [M.]O.[A.I.][4] / oes[2]
**rh** shrews *LLL 5.2.45*

**oak / ~s** *n*
oːk / -s
**sp** oake[21], [Hernes]-oake[1], oke[3], [Hernes]-oke[1] / oakes[5], okes[1]
**rh** *1* stroke *Cym 4.2.267*; **rh** *2* o'clock *MW 5.5.75*

**oak-cleaving** *adj*
*m* ˌoːk-ˈkliːvɪn, -ɪŋ
**sp** oake-cleauing[1]

**oaken** *adj*
ˈoːkən
**sp** oaken[2]

**oar / ~s** *n*
ɔːɹz
**sp** oares[1], ores[1], owers[1]

**oar / ~ed** *v*
ɔːɹd
**sp** oared[1]

**Oatcake** [name] *n*
ˈoːtkɛːk
**sp** Ote-cake[1]

**oaten** *adj*
ˈoːtən
**sp** oaten[1]

**oath / ~s** *n*
oːθ / -s
**sp** oath[136] / oathes[56], [bold-beating]-oathes[1], oaths[8]
**rh** *1* both *Per 1.2.120*; both, troth *Luc 569*; growth, troth *Luc 1061*; loath *LLL 1.1.158*; troth *LC 279, LLL 1.1.65, 4.3.142, 5.2.348, 5.2.451, Luc 883, MND 2.2.55, 3.2.93*; **rh** *2* moth, wrath *MV 2.9.77*
> book-oath

**oathable** *adj*
ˈoːθəbəl
**sp** othable[1]

**oath-breaking** *n*
*m* ˌoːθ-ˈbrɛːkɪn, -ɪŋ
**sp** oath-breaking[1]
> break

**oats** *n*
oːts
**sp** oates[3], oats[1]

**ob** [obolus] *n*
ɒb
**sp** ob[1]

**obduracy** *n*
ɒbˈdjuːrəsəɪ
**sp** obduracie[1]

**obdurate** *adj*
ɒbˈdjuːrət
**sp** obdurate[7]

**obedience** *n*
*m* əˈbiːdɪəns, -ɪˌens, oː-
**sp** obedience[52]

**obedient** *adj*
əˈbiːdɪənt, oː-
**sp** obedient[27]

**obeisance** *n*
ˈɒbɪsɔːns
**sp** obeisance[1]

**Oberon** *n*
ˈoːbəˌrɒn
**sp** Oberon[11]
**rh** gone *MND 2.1.58, 2.2.89*

**obey / ~s / ~ing / ~ed / ~edest** *v*
əˈbɛː, oː- / -st / -ɪn, -ɪŋ / -d / -dst
**sp** obay[4], obey[68], o-bey[2] / obeyes[2] / obaying[1], obeying[2] / obeyd[1], obey'd[8] / obeyd'st[1]
**rh** away *R2 3.2.210*; aye *Tim 5.1.51*; fray *RJ 3.1.140*; lay *PT 4*; prey *VA 61, 549*; say *KL 5.3.321, LC 133*; sway *CE 2.1.29, TS 5.2.163* / praise, raise *LC 229* / overswayed *VA 111*
> disobey; all-, wind-obeying

**object / ~s** *n*
ˈɒbʤɪkt /-s
**sp** obiect[32] / obiects[7], ob-iects[1]

**object** *v*
əbˈʤekt / -ɪd
**sp** obiect[6] / obiected[1]

**objection / ~s** *n*
*m* əbˈʤeksɪənz, -ɪˌɒnz
**sp** obiections[3]

**obligation / ~s** *n*
ˌɒblɪˈgɛːsɪən / -z
**sp** obligation[6] / obligations[1]

**obliged** *adj*
*m* əˈbləɪʤɪd
**sp** obliged[1]

**oblique** *adj*
=
**sp** oblique[1]

**oblivion** *n*
*m* ə'blɪvɪən, -ɪˌɒn
**sp** obliuion[12], obli-uion[1]

**oblivious** *adj*
=
**sp** obliuious[1]

**obloquy** *n*
*m* 'ɒbləˌkwəɪ
**sp** obliquie[1], obloquie[3]
**rh** *1* bastardy *Luc 523*; **rh** *2* eye *Luc 523*

**obscene** *adj*
=
**sp** obscene[2], ob-scene[1]

**obscenely** *adv*
əb'si:nləɪ
**sp** obscenely[2]

**obscure** *adj*
əb'skju:ɹ
**sp** obscure[10]

**obscur·e / ~es / ~ing / ~ed** *v*
əb'skju:ɹ / -z / -ɪn, -ɪŋ / -d
**sp** obscure[1] / obscures[1] / obscuring[1] / obscur'd[6], obscured[1]

**obscured** *adj*
*m* əb'skju:ɹd, -u:rɪd
**sp** obscur'd[1], obscured[2]

**obscurely** *adv*
əb'skju:ɹləɪ
**sp** obscurely[1]

**obscurity** *n*
*m* əb'skju:rɪˌtəɪ
**sp** obscurity[1]
**rh** posterity *VA 760*

**obsequious** *adj*
=
**sp** obsequious[6]

**obsequiously** *adv*
*m* əb'si:kwɪəsˌləɪ
**sp** obsequiously[1]

**obsequ·y / ~ies** *n*
*m* 'ɒbsɪˌkwəɪz
**sp** obsequies[7]

**observance / ~s** *n*
əb'zɐ:ɹvəns / -ɪz
**sp** oberuance[1], obseruance[13], ob-seruance[1], obser-uance[1] / obseruances[2]

**observancy** *n*
*m* əb'zɐ:ɹvənˌsəɪ
**sp** obseruancie[1]

**observant** *adj*
əb'zɐ:ɹvənt
**sp** obseruant[2]

**observant / ~s** *n*
*m* 'ɒbzəɹˌvants
**sp** obseruants[1]

**observation / ~s** *n*
*m* ˌɒbzəɹ'vɛ:sɪən, -sɪˌɒn / ˌɒbzəɹ'vɛ:sɪənz
**sp** obseruation[9], ob-seruation[1] / obseruations[1]
**rh** possession *3H6 2.6.108*

**observ·e / ~ing / ~ed** *v*
əb'zɐ:ɹv / -ɪn, -ɪŋ / -d
**sp** obserue[34] / obseruing[3] / obseru'd[11], obserued[1]
**rh** served *AW 2.1.201*

**observed** *n*
əb'zɐ:ɹvd
**sp** obseru'd[1]

**observer / ~s** *n*
əb'zɐ:ɹvəɹ / -z
**sp** obseruer[2] / obseruers[1]

**observing** *adj / n*
əb'zɐ:ɹvɪn, -ɪŋ
**sp** obseruing[1] / obseruing[1]

**observingly** *adv*
əb'zɐ:ɹvɪnləɪ, -ɪŋ-
**sp** obseruingly[1]

**obsque** *Lat prep*
'ɒbskwe, -ke
**sp** obsque[1]

**obstacle / ~s** *n*
=
**sp** obstacle[2] / obstacles[2]

**obstinacy** *n*
*m* 'ɒbstɪˌnasəɪ
**sp** obstinacie[1], obstinacy[1]

**obstinate** *adj*
*m* 'ɒbstɪˌnɛ:t
**sp** obstinate[6]

**obstinately** *adv*
*m* 'ɒbstɪˌnɛ:tləɪ
**sp** obstinately[1]

**obstruction / ~s** *n*
əb'strɤksɪən / -z
**sp** obstruction[3], ob-struction[1] / obstructions[1]

**obtain / ~ing / ~ed** *v*
əb'tɛ:n / -ɪn, -ɪŋ / -d
**sp** obtaine[6] / obtaining[1] / obtain'd[7], obtained[2], obtayn'd[2]
**rh** chained, pained *Luc 898*

**obtaining** *n*
əb'tɛ:nɪn, -ɪŋ
**sp** obtaining[2]
**rh** abstaining, gaining *Luc 128*

**occasion,** *abbr* **casion / ~s** *n*
ə'kɛ:zɪən, *abbr* 'kɛ:zɪən / -z
**sp** occasion[67], oc-casion[2], occa-sion[2], *abbr* 'casion[1] / occasions[16]

**occident** *n*
*m* 'ɒksɪˌdent
**sp** occident[2]
**rh** bent *R2 3.3.67*

**occidental** *adj*
ˌɒksɪ'dentɑl
**sp** occidentall[1]

**occulted** *adj*
ə'kʏltɪd
**sp** occulted[1]

**occupation / ~s** *n*
ˌɒkjə'pɛ:sɪən / -z
**sp** occupation[8], oc-cupation[1], occupation's [occupation is][1] / occupations[1]

**occupo / ~at** *Lat v*
'ɒkjʊpat
**sp** occupat[1]

**occupy** *v*
*m* 'ɒkjəˌpəɪ
**sp** occupie[1]
> pre-occupy

**occurrence / ~s** *n*
ə'kʏrəns / -ɪz
**sp** occurrence[1] / occurrences[1]

**occurrent / ~s** *n*
ə'kʏrənts
**sp** occurrents[1]

**ocean / ~'s / ~s** *n*
*m* 'o:sɪən, -sɪˌan / 'o:sɪənz
**sp** ocean[24] / oceans[1] / oceans[2]
**rh** motion *Luc 589*

**o'clock / of the clock,** *abbr* **o'th' clock** *prep + n*
ə'klɒk / əðə'klɒk, *abbr* əθ'klɒk
**sp** a clock[9], a clocke[31], a' clocke[1], o' clocke[1], of clock[1] / of the clocke[3] / o'th' clock[1], o'th' clocke[1]
**rh** oak *MW 5.5.74*

**Octavia** *n*
ɒk'tɛ:vɪə
**sp** Octauia[28]

**Octavius / ~'** *n*
ɒk'tɛ:vɪəs
**sp** Octauius[26] / Octauio's[2]

**ocular** *adj*
'ɒkjələɹ
**sp** occular[1]

**'od**
> God

**odd / ~est** *adj*
=
**sp** odde[31] / oddest[1]

**odd-conceited** *adj*
'ɒd-kən'si:tɪd, -'sɛ:t-
**sp** od-conceited[1]
> conceit

**odd-even** *adj*
=, ɒd-'evən
**sp** odde euen[1]
> even

**oddly** *adv*
'ɒdləɪ
**sp** oddely[1], odly[3]

**odds** *n*
=
**sp** oddes[32], odds[1], odd's[1], ods[6]
**rh** gods *Cym 5.2.9, Tim 1.2.59, 3.5.117*

**ode / ~s** *n*
o:d / -z
**sp** ode[1] / oades[1]

**odious** *adj*
*m* 'o:dɪəs, -ɪˌʏs
**sp** odious[9]

**odoriferous** *adj*
ˌo:də'rɪfrəs, -fər-
**sp** odoriferous[2]

**odorous** *adj*
'o:drəs, -dər-
**sp** odorous[2]

**odour / ~s** *n*
'o:dəɹ / -z
**sp** odour[1] / odours[5], o-dours[1]
> court-odour

**oeillade / ~s** *n*
'ɪlɪadz
**sp** eliads[1], illiads[1]

**o'er**
> over

**oeuvre / ~s** *Fr n*
'œ:vrə
**sp** *emend of 2H6 5.2.28* eumenes[1]

**of,** *abbr* **a, o** *prep*
*str* ɒv, *unstr* əv, ə
**sp** of[15826], talk'd-[of][1], *abbr* a'[1], a [doore][1], a [dore][2], a [dores][1], a'[my][1], a'[that][1], o'[16], o'[that][10], o'[their][1], o'[these][1], o'[this][1], o'[th's] [of these][1], o'[thy][1], o'[your][4]

*of it* *abbr*
ɒvt
**sp** of't[2]

*of the* *abbr*
əθ, ɒθ, -ð
**sp** ath'[2], a'th[19], a'th'[24], o't[201], oth'[8], o'th[27], o'th'[173], o'the[4]

**off** *adv*
=
**sp** off[460], [a farre]-off[2], [cutter] off[1], [falls]-off[1], [fub'd]-off[1], [take]-off[1], [threw]-off[1], off 's [off his][2]
**rh** *1* scoff *LLL 5.2.262*; **rh** *2* enough *TG 5.1.11*

**offal** *n*
'ɒfal
**sp** offall[3]

**off-cap / ~ped** *v*
=
**sp** off-capt[1]
> cap

**offence / ~s** *n*
=
**sp** offence[102], of-fence[3] / offences[22]
**rh** commence *Per 2.5.50*; defence *KJ 1.1.257, S 89.2*; diligence, thence *Luc 1852*; dispense *Luc 1071, 1702*; hence *MND 2.2.23, Oth 3.3.377, RJ 3.1.186, TS 1.2.228*; impudence *Per 2.3.68*; innocence *Per 1.2.92*; thence *Luc 738, S 51.1*
> self-offence

**offenceless** *adj*
=
**sp** of-fencelesse[1]

**offend / ~est / ~s / ~eth / ~ing / ~ed** *v*
= / -st, ə'fenst / = / = / ə'fendɪn, -ɪŋ / =
**sp** offend[56], of-fend[1] / offend'st[1] / offends[7] / offendeth[1] / offending[4] / offended[42], offen-ded[1]
**rh** end *MND 5.1.109*; friend *1H6 5.3.58* / amended *AW 3.4.5*; attended *VA 810*; ended *LLL 2.1.190*; mended *MND 5.1.413*

**offended** *adj*
=
**sp** offended[1]

**offendendo** [*malap for* defendendo] *Lat v*
ˌɒfən'dendo:
**sp** offendendo[1]

**offender / ~s** *n*
ə'fendəɹ / -z
**sp** offender[7], offendor[2], offendour[1] / offenders[8], offendors[7]

**offending** *adj / n*
ə'fendɪn, -ɪŋ
**sp** offending[2] / offending[2]
> eye-, heart-offending

**offendress** *n*
=
**sp** offendresse[1]

**offensive** *adj*
=
**sp** offensiue[2]

**offer / ~s** *n*
'ɒfəɹ / -z
**sp** offer[36] / offers[8]
**rh** proffer *PP 4.12*; scoffer *AY 3.5.61*

**offer / ~est / ~s / ~ing / ~ed** *v*
'ɒfəɹ / -st, 'ɒfrəst / -z / -ɪn, -ɪŋ, -fr- / 'ɒfəɹd, *Fluellen H5 4.7.3* 'ɒfəɹt
**sp** offer[49] / offer'st[2], offrest[1] / offers[8] / offering[2], offring[1] / offer'd[17], offered[10], of-fered[1], offred[2], *Fluellen* offert[1]

**offered** *adj*
'ɒfəɹd
**sp** offer'd[4]

**offering** *adj*
'ɒfrɪn, -ɪŋ
**sp** offring[3]

**offering / ~s** *n*
'ɒfrɪn, -ɪŋ, -fər- / -z
**sp** offering[1], offring[1] / offerings[1], offrings[3]

**office / ~s** *n*
=
**sp** office[125] / offices[28], offi-ces[1]

**office / ~d** *v*
=
**sp** offic'd[2]
> overoffices

**office-badge** *n*
=
**sp** office-badge[1]
> badge

**officed** *adj*
=
**sp** offic'd[1]

**officer / ~s** *n*
'ɒfɪsəɹ / -z
**sp** officer[48], offi-cer[2] / officers[45], of-ficers[1]

**officer-at-arms / ~s ~** *n*
'ɒfɪsəɹz-ət-'ɑːɹmz
**sp** officers at armes[1]
**rh** alarms *R2 1.1.204*

**official** *adj*
ə'fɪsɪɑl
**sp** officiall[1]

**officious** *adj*
*m* ə'fɪsɪəs, -ɪˌɤs
**sp** officious[6]

**offspring** *n*
=
**sp** off-spring[6]

**oft** *adv*
=
**sp** oft[134], ofte[1]
**rh** naught *PP 18.51*

**often / ~er** *adv*
= ['ɒfən, 'ɒftən] / 'ɒfnəɹ, 'ɒftnəɹ
**sp** often[113], of-ten[1] / oftner[4]

**oftentimes** *adv*
'ɒfəntəɪmz, 'ɒftən-
**sp** oftentimes[7], often-times[1]
> time

**oft-subdued** *adj*
*m* 'ɒft-səb'djuːɪd
**sp** oft-subdued[1]

**oil / -s** *n*
əɪl / -z
**sp** oile[1], oyle[12] / oyles[1]

**oil-dried** *adj*
'əɪl-ˌdrəɪd
**sp** oyle-dride[1]
> dried

**oily** *adj*
'əɪləɪ
**sp** oylie[1], oyly[3]

**old / ~er / ~est** *adj*
oːld / 'oːld·əɹ / -əst
**sp** old[537], old-[age][1], old-[fat-woman][1], old[man][3], old-[man][2], old-[wither'd][1], [poor]-old-[man][1], [poor]-old-[woman][1], olde[72], olde-[folkes][1], *emend of TG 2.3.26* would-[woman][1] / older[4] / oldest[2]
**rh** behold, bold, cold, enfold, gold, inscrolled, sold, told *MV 2.7.71*; behold *LC 73, 1760, S 22.1*; cold *Luc 49, S 2.13, 104.1, VA 133*; nine-fold *KL 3.4.115*; told *PP 1.10, S 76.13, 123.6, 138.10*
> wit-old

**old** *n*
oːld
**sp** old[7]

**Oldcastle** *n*
'o:ldkasəl
**sp** Old-Castle[1]

**olden** *adj*
'o:ldən
**sp** olden[1]

**oldest** *n*
'o:ldəst
**sp** oldest[1]

**old-faced** *adj*
'o:ld-ˌfɛ:st
**sp** old-fac'd[2]
> face

**oldness** *n*
'o:ldnəs
**sp** oldnesse[1]

**olive / ~s** *n*
'ɒlɪv, -ɪf / -z
**sp** oliue[4], olyffe[1] / oliues[1]

**Oliver / ~s** *n*
'ɒlɪvəɹ / -z
**sp** Oliuer[13] / Oliuers[1]

**olive-tree / ~s** *n*
=
**sp** oliue-trees[1]
> tree

**Olivia / ~'s** *n*
=
**sp** Oliuia[19], O-liuia[1] / Oliuia's[1], Oliuiaes[1]

**Olympian** *adj / n*
=
**sp** Olympian[1] / Olympian[1]

**Olympus** *n*
=
**sp** Olympus[7]

**'oman**
> woman

**ominous** *adj*
*m* 'ɒmɪˌnɤs, -mnəs
**sp** ominous[10]

**omission** *n*
ə'mɪsɪən
**sp** omission[1]

**omit / ~test / ~ting / ~ted** *v*
ə'mɪt, o:'mɪt / -st / -ɪn, -ɪŋ / -ɪd
**sp** omit[12] / omitst[1] / omitting[2] / omitted[3]
**rh** fitted *LLL 4.3.357*

**omittance** *n*
ə'mɪtəns, o:-
**sp** omittance[1]

**omnipotent** *adj*
=
**sp** omnipotent[2], omni-potent[1]

**omn·is / ~e / ~es / ~ia** *Lat adj, pro*
'ɒmne / 'ɒmnez / 'ɒmnɪɑ:
**sp** omne[1] / omnes[28], *abbr* omn[1] / omnia[1]

**on,** *abbr* **a, o** *adv, prep*
=, *abbr* ə
**sp** on[2992], [come]-on[10], [drawes]-on[2], [hooke]-on[2], [iog]-on[2], [lay'd]-on[1], [leane]-on[1], [push]-on[2], [rode]-on[1], [sway]-on[1], *abbr* a[7], o'[8]
**rh** *1* Amazon *3H6 4.1.105*; condition [*4 sylls*] *2H4 3.1.73*; gone *AC 1.2.128, 2H4 1.3.109, MND 3.2.413, Oth 1.3.203, Per 4.4.19, R3 4.2.121, S 5.5, VA 1087*; on you upon you *Tem 4.1.109*; **rh** *2* done *3H6 4.1.105, KL 1.4.203, MM 4.3.76, RJ 1.4.38*; none *Per 3.Chorus.27*; one *Tem 4.1.136, TG 2.1.1*; on you shun you *Tem 4.1.117*; **rh** *3* groan *S 50.9*; **rh** *4* man *MND 2.1.264, 3.2.349*
> upon

**once** *adv*
o:ns, ɒns, wɒns
**sp** once[403]

**one / ~'s / ~s** *adj, n, pro*
*str* o:n, wɒn, *unstr* ən / -z
**sp** one[1654], 'ton [the one][1] *abbr* [money] i.[d] / ones [one is][1], one's [one is][1] / ones[12], one's[1] / ones[54], [blind]-ones[1], [great]-ones[2], [rich]-ones[1], [wise]-ones[1], [yong]-ones[1], [young]-ones[1]
**rh** *1* alone *Luc 1478, MND 3.2.118, PP 9.13, R3 1.1.99, RJ 2.6.37, S 36.2, 39.6, 42.13, 105.14, TS 1.2.243*; bone *LC 43, LLL 5.2.331, VA 293*; loan *S 6.8*; Scone *Mac 5.6.113*; throne *Cym 5.4.61*; **rh** *2* gone *CE 4.2.23, 53, Tit 1.1.369, VA 228, 518, 1069*; on *Tem 4.1.137, TG 2.1.2*; **rh** *3* man *TS 3.2.82*; **rh** *4* done *R2 1.1.182*; none *Luc 1161, Mac 5.6.13, PT 26, 46, R3 4.4.103, RJ 1.2.32, S 8.13, 136.6, TC 4.5.40, TG 5.4.52*; **rh** *5* shoon *Ham 4.5.24*
> any-, every-, no-, some-, thirty-one

**oneyer / ~s** *n*
'o:nɪəɹz
**sp** oneyers[1]

**ongle / ~s** *Fr n*
'ɔ̃:glə
**sp** ongles[2]

**onion / ~s** *n*
'ɤnɪən / -z
**sp** onion[2] / onions[2]

**onion-eyed** *adj*
'ɤnɪən-ˌəɪd
**sp** onyon-ey'd[1]
> eye

**only** *adv*
'o:nləɪ
**sp** onelie[8], onely[278], onlie[1], only[17], on-ly[2]

**onset** *n*
=
**sp** onset[1], on-set[2]
> set

**onward** *adv*
'ɒnwɑɹd
**sp** onward[1], on-ward[1]

**ooze** *n*
=
**sp** ooze[4], owse[1]

**oozy** *adj*
'u:zəɪ
**sp** oo-zie[1]

**opal** *n*
'o:pɑl
**sp** opall[1]

**ope** *adj*
o:p
**sp** ope[5]

**ope / ~s / ~d** *v*
o:p / -s / -t
**sp** ope[22] / opes[2] / op'd[3]

**open** *adj*
'o:pən
**sp** open[135], o-pen[1]
**rh** broken *S 61.1*

**open / ~s / ~ing / ~ed** *v*
'o:pən / -z / -ɪn, -ɪŋ, -pn- / -d
**sp** open[56], open't[4] / opens[7] / opening[4] / opend[1], open'd[8], opened[1]
**rh** broken *VA 48* / betokened *VA 451*

**opener** *n*
'o:pnəɹ, -pən-
**sp** opener[1]

**open-eyed** *adj*
'o:pən-ˌəɪd
**sp** open-ey'd[1]
> eye

**opening** *adj*
'o:pnɪn, -ɪŋ, -pən-
**sp** opening[1] / opening[5]

**openly** *adv*
*m* 'o:pənˌləɪ
**sp** openly[8]

**openness** *n*
*m* 'o:pəˌnes
**sp** opennesse[1]

**operant** *adj*
'ɒprənt, -pər-
**sp** operant[2]

**operate** *v*
*m* 'ɒpəˌrɛ:t
**sp** operate[2]

**operation / ~s** *n*
ˌɒpə'rɛ:sɪən / -z
**sp** operation[6] / opperations[1]

**operative** *adj*
*m* 'ɒprəˌtɪv, -pər-
**sp** operatiue[1]

**Ophelia** *n*
=
**sp** Ophelia[26], O-phelia[2]

**opinion / ~s** *n*
=
**sp** opinion[78], o-pinion[4] / opinions[13]

**opinion / ~ed** *v*
=
**sp** *malap for* pinioned *MA 4.2.65* opinion'd[1]

**opportune** *adj*
*m* ə'pɔ:ɹtən
**sp** opportune[2]

**opportunit·y / ~ies** *n*
*m* ˌɒpəɹ'tju:n·ɪˌtəɪ, -ɪtəɪ / -ɪtəɪz
**sp** oportunitie[2], opportunitie[6], oppor-tunitie[1], opportunity[5], oppor-tunity[1] / *Evans MW 3.1.14* oportunities [opportunity][1], opportunities[2]
**rh** infamy *Luc 1023*; me *Luc 932*; quality *Luc 874*; thee *Luc 895, 903*

**oppos·e / ~es / ~ing / ~ed** *v*
ə'po:z / -ɪz / -ɪn, -ɪŋ / -d
**sp** oppose[17] / opposes[1] / opposing[3] / oppos'd[17], opposed[7]
**rh** foes *KJ 3.1.170*

**opposed** *adj*
*m* ə'po:zd, -zɪd
**sp** oppos'd[1], opposed[7]

**opposed** *n*
*m* ə'po:zɪd
**sp** opposed[1]

**opposeless** *adj*
ə'po:zləs
**sp** opposelesse[1]

**opposer / ~'s / ~s** *n*
ə'po:zəɹ / -z
**sp** opposer[2] / opposers[1] / opposers[1]

**opposite** *adj*
=
**sp** opposite[12], oppo-site[1]
> wilful-opposite

**opposite / ~s** *n*
=
**sp** opposit[1], opposite[10] / opposites[3]

**opposition / ~s** *n*
*m* ˌɒpə'zɪsɪən, -sɪˌɒn / ˌɒpə'zɪsɪənz
**sp** opposition[8] / oppositions[1]

**oppress / ~es / ~eth / ~ing / ~ed** *v*
= / = / = / ə'presɪn, -ɪŋ / =
**sp** oppresse[2] / oppresses[1] / oppresseth[1] / oppressing[1] / oppress'd[1], oppressed[1], opprest[7]
**rh** rest *Cym 5.4.99, S 28.4*

**oppressed** *adj*
*m* ə'pres·ɪd, -t
**sp** oppressed[3], opprest[1]
> heat-oppressed

**oppressing** *adj*
ə'presɪn, -ɪŋ
**sp** oppressing[1]

**oppression** *n*
ə'presɪən
**sp** oppression[13], opression[1]
**rh** transgression *RJ 1.1.184*

**oppressor / ~'s** *n*
ə'presəɹz
**sp** oppressors[1]

**opprobriously** *adj*
*m* ə'pro:brɪəsˌləɪ
**sp** opprobriously[1]

**oppugnancy** *n*
*m* ə'pɤgnən,səɪ
**sp** oppugnancie[1]

**opulency** *n*
*m* 'ɒpjə,lensəɪ
**sp** opulencie[1]

**opulent** *adj*
'ɒpələnt
**sp** opilent[1], opulent[1]

**or** *conj*
*str* ɔːɹ, *unstr* əɹ
**sp** or[2314]

**oracle / ~s** *n*
=
**sp** oracle[27] / oracles[3]

**orange** *adj / n*
=
**sp** orendge[1] / orange[1], orenge[1]

**orange-tawny** *adj*
'ɒrɪnʤ-,tɔːnəɪ
**sp** orange tawnie[1], orenge-tawny[1]
> tawny

**oration** *n*
*m* ə'rɛːsɪən, -sɪ,ɒn
**sp** oration[8]

**orator / ~s** *n*
*m* 'ɒrə,tɔːɹ, -təɹ / -z
**sp** orator[10], oratour[1] / orators[3], oratours[1]
**rh** *1* harbinger *CE 3.2.10*; **rh** *2* publisher *Luc 30*; **rh** *3* singular *Luc 30*

**oratory** *n*
*m* 'ɒrə,trəɪ, -,tɒrəɪ
**sp** oratorie[4]
**rh** story *Luc 815*

**orb / ~s** *n*
ɔːɹb / -z
**sp** orbe[9] / orbes[4], orbs[1]

**orbed** *adj*
'ɔːɹbɪd
**sp** orbed[2]

**orchard** *adj*
'ɔːɹʧəɹd
**sp** orchard[3]

**orchard / ~s** *n*
'ɔːɹʧəɹd / -z
**sp** orchard[15], [ith ']orchard[1] / orchards[1]

**'ord**
> word

**ordain / ~ing / ~ed** *v*
ɔːɹ'dɛːn / -ɪn, -ɪŋ / *m* -d, -ɪd
**sp** ordaine[1] / ordaining[1] / ordain'd[6], ordained[2], ordayn'd[1], ordayned[1]

**order / ~s** *n*
'ɔːɹdəɹ / -z
**sp** order[82], or-der[1] / [fayre-play]-orders[1], orders[4]
> disorder

**order / ~ed** *v*
'ɔːɹdəɹ / *m* 'ɔːɹdəɹd, -əred
**sp** order[10] / order'd[1], ordered[3], ordred[2]
**rh** dead *Per 4.4.47*
> mis-, well-ordered

**ordering** *n*
'ɔːɹdrɪn, -ɪŋ, -dər-
**sp** ordering[2], ord'ring[2]
**rh** sing *S 8.10*

**orderless** *adj*
*m* 'ɔːɹdəɹ,les
**sp** orderlesse[1]

**orderly** *adv*
*m* 'ɔːɹdəɹ,ləɪ
**sp** orderlie[1], orderly[7]

**ordinance** *n*
*m* 'ɔːɹdɪ,nans, -,ɔːns, -dnəns
**sp** ordinance[8], ord'nance[1]
> pre-ordinance

**ordinary** *adj*
*m* 'ɔːɹdɪ,narəɪ, -ɪn,r-
**sp** ordinarie[2], ordinary[8]
> extraordinary

**ordinar·y / ~ies** *n*
*m* 'ɔːɹdɪ,narəɪ, -ɪn,r- / 'ɔːɹdɪn,rəɪz
**sp** ordinary[2] / ordinaries[1]

**ordinate** *adj*
*m* 'ɔːɹdɪ,nɛːt
**sp** ordinate[1]
> inordinate

**ordnance** *n*
*m* 'ɔːɹdɪ,nans, -,ɔːns, -dnəns
**sp** ordenance[3], ordinance[1], ordnance[3]

**ordure** *n*
'ɔːɹdjəɹ
**sp** ordure[1]

**ore** *n*
ɔːɹ
**sp** oare[1]

**ore-, o're-**
> over-

**organ / ~s** *n*
'ɔːɹgən / -z
**sp** organ[4], organe[1] / organs[7]

**organ-pipe** *n*
'ɔːɹgən-,pəɪp
**sp** organ-pipe[2]

**orgillous** *adj*
'ɔːɹgɪləs
**sp** orgillous[1]

**orient** *adj / n*
=
**sp** orient[3] / orient[1]

**orifex** *n*
'ɒrɪfeks
**sp** orifex[1]

**origin** *n*
=
**sp** origin[1]

**original** *n*
*m* ə'rɪʤɪ,nɑl
**sp** originall[2]

**Orion** *n*
ə'rəɪən
**sp** Orion[1]

**orison / ~s** *n*
'ɒrɪzənz
**sp** orisons[2], orizons[2], orysons[1]

**Orlando** *n*
ɔ:ɹ'lando:
**sp** Orlando[36], Orlan-do[1]

**'orld**
> world

**Orleans** *n*
*m* 'ɔ:ɹlɪ,ɔ:ns, -ɪəns, ɔ:ɹ'lɪəns
**sp** Orleance[33]

**ornament / ~s** *n*
*m* 'ɔ:ɹnə,ment, -mənt / -s
**sp** ornament[12] / ornaments[10]
**rh** content *S 1.9*; went *LC 115, TN 3.4.373* / rents *S 142.6*

**Orodes** *n*
'ɒrə,di:z
**sp** *emend of AC 3.1.4* Orades[1]

**orphan** *adj*
'ɔ:ɹfən
**sp** orphan[1]

**orphan / ~'s / ~s / ~s'** *n*
'ɔ:ɹfən / -z
**sp** orphan[1] / orphans[2] / orphans[4] / orphanes[1], orphants[1]

**Orpheus / ~'** *n*
'ɔ:ɹfɪəs
**sp** Orpheus[2] / Orpheus[1]

**Orsino / ~'s** *n*
ɔ:ɹ'si:no: / -z
**sp** Orsino[8] / Orsinoes[1], Orsinos[1], Orsino's[6]

**ort / ~s** *n*
ɔ:ɹt / -s
**sp** ort[1] / orts[1]

**'ort**
> word

**orthography** *n*
ɔ:ɹ'tɒgrəfəɪ
**sp** ortagriphie[1], ortho-graphy[1]

**oscorbidulchos** *nonsense word*
,ɒskɔ:ɹbɪ'dɤlkɒs
**sp** oscorbidulchos[1]

**osier** *adj*
'o:zɪəɹ
**sp** osier[1]

**osier / ~s** *n*
'o:zɪəɹz
**sp** osiers[1]

**osprey** *n*
'ɒsprɛ:
**sp** aspray[1]

**Osric** *n*
=
**sp** Osricke[4]

**Ossa** *n*
=
**sp** Ossa[1]

**ostent / ~s** *n*
=
**sp** ostent[2] / ostents[1]

**ostentare** *Lat v*
,ɒsten'tɑ:re
**sp** ostentare[1]

**ostentation** *n*
*m* ,ɒstən'tɛ:sɪən, -sɪ,ɒn
**sp** ostentation[6], osten-tation[1], ostenta-tion[1]
**rh** affection *LLL 5.2.409*

**ostler / ~s** *n*
'ɒsləɹ / -z
**sp** hostler[1], ostler[6] / ostlers[1]

**ostrich** *n*
'ɒstrɪʤ, -ɪʧ
**sp** ostridge[1]

**Oswald** *n*
=
**sp** Oswald[3]

**Othello / ~'s** *n*
ə'θelo:, ə't- / -z
**sp** Othello[40], Othel-lo[1] / Othello's[11]

**other** *adj / adv*
'ɤðəɹ
**sp** other[391], [at]other[1], [a t]other[1], [t]other[2], other[some][1], other-[some][1], o-ther[3] / other[3]

**other / ~'s / ~s / ~s'** *pro*
'ɤðəɹ / -z
**sp** other[202], o-ther[2], [t]other[1], others [other is][3] / others[24] / others[112], o-thers[2] / others[13]
**rh** another *Mac 1.3.14*; brother *AW 1.3.160, MM 4.2.58, PP 8.4*; mother *VA 864*; smother *S 47.2*

**othergates** *adv*
'ɤðəɹ,gɛ:ts
**sp** other gates[1]

**otherwhere** *adv*
'ɤðəɹ,ʍɛ:ɹ
**sp** otherwhere[1], other-where[1], other where[2]
**rh** forbear *CE 2.1.30*; here *CE 2.1.104*

**otherwhiles** *adv*
*m* o:ɹ'ʍəɪlz
**sp** otherwhiles[1]
> whiles

**otherwise** *adv*
*m* 'ɤðəɹ,wəɪz, -ɹw-
**sp** otherwise[32], o-therwise[1], other-wise[2]

**Ottamite / ~s** *n*
*m* 'ɒtə,mɪts
**sp** Ottamites[2], Ottamittes[1]

**otter** *n*
'ɒtəɹ
**sp** otter[3]

**Ottoman** *adj*
*m* 'ɒtəˌman
**sp** Ottoman[1]

**où** *Fr adv*
u
**sp** ou

**oublier / oubli·e / ~é** *Fr v*
u'bli / ubli'je
**sp** oublie[2] / oublie[2]

**ouche / ~s** *n*
'əʊʧɪz
**sp** owches[1]

**ought** *n*
=
**sp** ought[64]

**ought / ~est** *v*
= / ɔ:tst
**sp** ought[19] / ought'st[1]

**oui** *Fr adv*
wi
**sp** ouy[5], *Pistol H5 4.4.37* owy[1]

**ounce / ~s** *n*
əʊns / 'əʊnsɪz
**sp** ounce[6] / ounces[1]

**ouph / ~s** *n*
əʊfs
**sp** ouphes[2]

**our / ~s** *det / pro*
o:ɹ, *unstr* əɹ / o:ɹz
**sp** our[3149] / ours[87], our's[1]
**rh** devours, flowers *Luc 873*; flowers *Cym 5.4.100, RJ 2.3.3*; sours *Luc 868*; none of ours progenitors *Luc 1757*

**ousel** *n*
u:zəl
woosell[1]

**out** *adv*
əʊt
**sp** out[885], [peere]-out[2], [throw]-out[2]
**rh** about *Luc 413, MA 5.3.24, MW 5.5.56, 102, RJ 1.2.35, 3.5.41, S 113.4, TNK Prol.25*; clout *LLL 4.1.134*; doubt *KJ 4.2.101, 5.2.179, LLL 5.2.102, 152, PP 2.14, S 144.14, VA 694*; flout *LLL 5.2.267, 395*; rout *TNK 3.5.145*; stout *S 65.5*
> finder-, giving-, stretched-, thrower-, weeder-, where-out

***out of*** *prep*
'əʊt əv, -ə
**sp** out of[457]

**outbid / ~s** *v*
əʊt'bɪdz
**sp** out-bids[1]
> bid

**outbrave** *v*
əʊt'brɛ:v
**sp** out-braue[1]
> brave

**outbreak** *n*
'əʊtbrɛ:k
**sp** out-breake[1]
> break

**outbreath / ~ed** *v*
əʊt'breθt, -ri:ðd
**sp** out-breath'd[1]
> breath

**outburn / *PP* ~ eth** *v*
əʊt'bɐ:ɹnəθ
**sp** out burneth[1]
**rh** flameth *PP 7.14*
> breath

**outcast** *n*
'əʊtkast
**sp** out-cast[2]
> cast

**outcraft·y / ~ied** *v*
əʊt'kraftəɪd
**sp** out-craftied[1]
> crafty

**outcr·y / ~ies** *v*
'əʊtkrəɪ / -z
**sp** outcry[1] / outcries[1]
> cry

**outdare / ~s** *v*
əʊt'dɛ:ɹ / -z
**sp** out-dare[1] / out-dares[1]
> dare

**outdared** *adj*
əʊt'dɛ:ɹd
**sp** out-dar'd[1]

**outdo / ~ne** *v*
əʊt'dɤn
**sp** out-done[1]
> do

**outdwell / ~s** *v*
əʊt'dwelz
**sp** out-dwels[1]
> dwell

**outfac·e / ~ing / ~ed** *v*
*m* əʊt'fɛ:s, 'əʊtfɛ:s / əʊt'fɛ:s·ɪn, -ɪŋ / *m* -t, -ɪd
**sp** outface[2], out-face[4] / out-facing[1] / outfac'd[1], out-fac'd[2], out-faced[1]
> face

**outfacing** *adj*
*m* 'əʊtfɛ:sɪn, -ɪŋ
**sp** out-facing[1]

**outfrown** *v*
əʊt'frəʊn
**sp** out-frowne[1]
> frown

**out·go / ~goes / ~went** *v*
əʊt'go: / -z / əʊt'went
**sp** out-go[1], outgoe[1] / out-goes[1] / out-went[1]
> go

**outgrow / ~n** *v*
əʊt'gro:n
**sp** out-growne[1]
> grow

**out-Herod / ~s** *v*
əʊt-'erədz, -'he-
**sp** out- Herod's[1]
> Herod

**outjest** *v*
əʊt'ʤest
**sp** out-iest[1]
> jest

**outlaw / ~s** *n*
'əʊtlɔ: / -z
**sp** out-law[2] / out-lawes[6]
> law

**outlaw / ~ed** *v*
'əʊtlɔ:d
**sp** out-law'd[1]

**outlawry** *n*
*m* 'əʊtlə,rəɪ
**sp** outlarie[1]

**outliv·e / ~es / ~ing / ~ed** *v*
*m* əʊt'lɪv, 'əʊtlɪv / əʊt'lɪv·z / -ɪn, -ɪŋ / -d
**sp** out-liue[14] / outliues[1], out-liues[2] / out-liuing[1] / out-liu'd[1]
> live

**outlook** *v*
*m* 'əʊt,lʊk
**sp** out-looke[1]
> look

**outlustre / ~s** *v*
əʊt'lɤstəɹz
**sp** out-lusters[1]
> lustre

**outnight** *v*
əʊt'nəɪt
**sp** out-night[1]
> night

**outparamour / ~ed** *v*
*m* əʊt'parə,mɔ:ɹd
**sp** out-paramour'd[1]
> paramour

**outpeer** *v*
əʊt'pi:ɹ
**sp** out-peere[1]
> peer

**outpray** *v*
*m* 'əʊtprɛ:
**sp** out-pray[1]
> pray

**outprize / ~d** *v*
*m* 'əʊtprəɪzd
**sp** out-priz'd[1]
> prize

**outrage / ~s** *n*
'əʊtrɛ:ʤ / -ɪz
**sp** outrage[9], out-rage[3] / outrages[5]
**rh** age *Luc 605*

**outragious** *adj*
əʊt'rɛ:ʤɪəs
**sp** outragious[4], out-ragious[1], [with]out ragious[1]

**outran**
> outrun

**outride / outrod** *v*
əʊt'rɒd
**sp** out-rod[1]
> ride

**outright** *adv*
əʊt'rəɪt
**sp** outright[1], out-right[2], out right[1]
> right

**outroar** *v*
əʊt'rɔ:ɹ
**sp** out-roare[1]
> roar

**outrun / ~nest / ~s / ~ning / outran** *v*
əʊt'rɤn / -st / -z / -ɪn, -ɪŋ / əʊt'ran
**sp** outrun[1], out-run[3], out-runne[3] / out-runst[1] / out-runnes[1] / out-running[1] / out-ran[1]
> run

**outscold** *v*
əʊt'sko:ld
**sp** out-scold[1]
> scold

**outsell / ~s** *v*
əʊt'sel / -z
**sp** out-sell[1] / out-selles[1]
> sell

**outshining** *adj*
əʊt'ʃəɪnɪn, -ɪŋ
**sp** out-shining[1]
> shine

**outside / ~s** *n*
əʊt'səɪd / -z
**sp** outside[3], out-side[9] / out-sides[1]
> side

**outsleep** *v*
əʊt'sli:p
**sp** out-sleepe[1]
> sleep

**outspeak / ~s** *v*
əʊt'spi:ks, -pɛ:ks
**sp** out-speakes[1]
> speak

**outsport** *v*
əʊt'spɔ:ɹt
**sp** out-sport[1]
> sport

**out·stand / ~stood** *v*
əʊt'stʊd
**sp** out-stood[1]
> stand

**outstare** *v*
əʊt'stɛ:ɹ
**sp** out-stare[2]
> stare

**outstay** *v*
əʊt'stɛ:
**sp** out-stay[1]
> stay

**outstretch / ~ed** *v*
'əʊtstreʧt
**sp** out-stretcht[2]
> stretch

**outstretched** *adj*
*m* əʊt'streʧt, -ʧɪd, 'əʊtstreʧt
**sp** out-stretched[1], out-stretcht[2]

**outstrike** *v*
*m* 'əʊtstrəɪk
**sp** out-strike[1]
> strike

**outstrip** *v*
*m* 'əʊtstrɪp, əʊt'strɪp
**sp** out-strip[3]
> strip

**outswear** *v*
*m* 'əʊtswɛ:ɹ, əʊt'swɛ:ɹ
**sp** out-sweare[2]
> swear

**outsweeten / ~ed** *v*
əʊt'swi:tənd
**sp** out-sweetned[1]
> sweet

**outswell** *v*
əʊt'swel
**sp** out-swell[1]
> swell

**out-talk** *v*
əʊt-'tɔ:k
**sp** out-talke[1]
> talk

**out-tongue** *v*
'əʊt-ˌtɒŋ, -ˌtʊ-
**sp** out-tongue[1]
> tongue

**outvenom / ~s** *v*
əʊt'venəmz
**sp** out-venomes[1]
> venom

**outvie / ~d** *v*
əʊt'vəɪd
**sp** out-vied[1]
> vie

**outvillain / ~ed** *v*
əʊt'vɪlənd
**sp** out-villain'd[1]
> villain

**outvoice** *v*
əʊt'vəɪs
**sp** out-voyce[1]
> voice

**outwall** *v*
əʊt'wɑ:l
**sp** out-wall[1]
> wall

**outward** *adj / adv / n*
'əʊtwəɹd
**sp** outward[40] / outward[2] / outward[1]

**outwardly** *adv*
*m* 'əʊtwəɹdˌləɪ
**sp** outwardly[4]
**rh** modesty *LC 203*

**outward-sainted** *adj*
'əʊtwəɹd-ˌsɛ:ntɪd
**sp** outward sainted[1]
> saint

**out·wear / ~worn** *v*
əʊt'wɛ:ɹ / əʊt'wɔ:ɹn
**sp** out-weare[2] / out-worne[1]
**rh** born *S 68.1*; new-born, torn *Luc 1761*
> wear

**outweigh / ~s** *v*
əʊt'wɛ:z
**sp** out-weighes[2]
> weigh

**outwent**
> outgo

**outwork** *v*
'əʊtwɔ:ɹk
**sp** out-worke[1]
> work

**outworn**
> outwear

**outworth / ~s** *v*
əʊt'wɔ:ɹθs
**sp** out-worths[1]
> worth

**ouzel** *n*
'u:zəl
**sp** ouzell[1]

**oven** *n*
'ɒvən
**sp** ouen[2]

**over, *abbr* o'er** *adv / prep*
'o:vəɹ, *abbr* o:ɹ
**sp** ouer[65], o-uer[2], *abbr* ore[44], o're[34], [giue]-o're[1] / ouer[85], o-uer[1], *abbr* ore[53], o're[53]
**rh** lover *TG 1.1.108, VA 571* / before *S 30.10*; more, tore *Luc 1790, Mac 3.4.137, MND 3.2.130, TG 3.1.94*; sore *Luc 1567*; swore *MND 3.2.135*

**overawe** *v*
'o:vəɹ'ɔ:
**sp** ouer-awe[1]
> awe

**overbear, *abbr* o'er / ~s / overborne** *v*
'o:vəɹ'bɛ:ɹ, *abbr* *m* ˌo:ɹ'bɛ:ɹ, 'o:ɹˌbɛ:ɹ / -z / 'o:vəɹ'bɔ:ɹn, *abbr* ˌo:ɹ'bɔ:ɹn
**sp** ouer-beare , *abbr* ore-beare[1], o're-beare[2] / ouer-beares[1], *abbr* ore-beares[2] / ouerborne[2], ouer-borne[4], *abbr* ore-borne[1], o're-borne[1]
> bear *v*

**overbearing** *n*
ˌo:ɹ'bɛ:rɪn, -ɪŋ
**sp** ore-bearing[2]
> bear *v*

**overbeat, *abbr* o'er** *v*
ˌo:ɹ'bi:t
**sp** o're-beate[1]
> beat

**overblow, *abbr* o'er / ~s / ~n** *v*
ˌo:ɹ'blo:z / 'o:vəɹ'blo:n
**sp** o're-blowes[1] / ouerblowne[1], ouer-blowne[4]
**rh** own *R2 3.2.190*
> blow

**overboard, *abbr* o'er** *adv*
'o:vəɹ'bɔ:ɹd, *abbr* ˌo:ɹ-
**sp** ouer-boord[2], *abbr* ore-boord[1], o're-boord[1]
> board

**overbold** *adj*
'o:vəɹ'bo:ld
**sp** ouer-bold[1]
> bold

**overboldly** *adv*
'o:vəɹ'bo:ldləɪ
**sp** ouer-boldly[1]
> bold

**overboots** *adv*
'o:vəɹ'bu:ts, -'bʊts
**sp** ouer-bootes[1]
> boot

**overborne**
> overbear

**overbulk** *v*
'o:vəɹ'bɤlk
**sp** ouer-bulke[1]
> bulk

**overbuy / ~s** *v*
'o:vəɹ'bəɪz
**sp** ouer-buyes[1]
> buy

**overcame**
> overcome

**overcanopied** *adj*
*m* 'o:vəɹ'kanə,pɪd
**sp** ouer-cannoped[1]
> canopy

**overcareful** *adj*
'o:vəɹ'kɛ:ɹfʊl
**sp** ouer-carefull[1]
> care

**overcast,** *abbr* **o'er** *v*
'o:vəɹ'kast, *abbr* ,o:ɹ-
**sp** ouercast[1], *abbr* orecast[1], o're-cast[1]
> cast

**overcharg·e / ~ing / ~ed,** *abbr* **o'er** *v*
,o:ɹ-'ʧɑ:ɹʤɪn, -ɪŋ /
'o:vəɹ'ʧɑ:ɹʤd, *abbr* ,o:ɹ-
**sp** o're-charging[1] / ouer-charg'd[2], *abbr* ore-charg'd[1], orecharged[1]
> charge

**overcharged** *adj*
'o:vəɹ'ʧɑ:ɹʤɪd
ouer-charged[2], o're-charg'd[1]
> charge

**overcloyed,** *abbr* **o'er** *adj*
,o:ɹ'kləɪɪd
**sp** o're-cloyed[1]
> cloy

**over·come / ~comes / ~came,** *abbr* **o'er** *v*
'o:vəɹ'kɤm, *abbr* ,o:ɹ- / -z /
'o:vəɹ'kɛ:m, *abbr* ,o:ɹ-
**sp** ouercome[8], *abbr* orecome[1], ore-come[1], o'recome[2] / ouercomes[1] / ouercame[5], o-uercame[1], ouer-came[2], *abbr* o'recame[2]
> come

**overcool** *v*
'o:vəɹ'ku:l
**sp** ouer-coole[1]
> cool

**overcount,** *abbr* **o'er** *v*
,o:ɹ'kəʊnt
**sp** orecount[1], o're-count[1]
> count

**overcover / ~ed,** *abbr* **o'er** *v*
,o:ɹ'kɤvəɹd
**sp** orecouered[1]
> cover

**overcredulous** *adj*
'o:vəɹ'kredləs, -djəl-
**sp** ouer-credulous[1]
> credulity

**overcrow / ~s,** *abbr* **o'er** *v*
,o:ɹ'kro:z
**sp** ore-crowes[1]
> crow

**overdaring** *adj*
'o:vəɹ'dɛ:rɪn, -ɪŋ
**sp** ouer-daring[1]
> dare

**over·doing,** *abbr* **o'er / ~done** *v*
'o:ɹdu:ɪn, -ɪŋ, o:ɹ'du:- /
'o:vəɹ'dɤn
**sp** o're-doing[1] / ouer-done[2]

**Overdone / ~'s** [name] *n*
'o:vəɹdən, *MM 2.1.192*
'o:vəɹ'dɤn / -z
**sp** Ouer-don[2] / Ouer-dons[2]
**pun** *MM 2.1.192* over done

**overdusted,** *abbr* **o'er** *adj*
,o:ɹ'dɤstɪd
**sp** oredusted[1]
> dust

**overdyed,** *abbr* **o'er** *adj*
'o:ɹ,dəɪd
**sp** o're-dy'd[1]
> dye

**overearnest** *adj*
'o:vəɹ'ɐ:ɹnɪst
**sp** ouer-earnest[1]
> earnest

**overears,** *abbr* **o'er** *adj*
,o:ɹ'i:ɹz
**sp** o're eares[1]
> ear

**overeaten,** *abbr* **o'er** *adj*
,o:ɹ'i:tən
**sp** ore-eaten[1]
> eat

**overey·e,** *abbr* **o'er / ~ing** *v*
,o:ɹ'əɪ / 'o:vəɹ'əɪɪn, -ɪŋ
**sp** ore-eye[1] / ouer-eying[1]
**rh** sky *LLL 4.3.78*
> eye

**overfar** *adv*
'o:vəɹ'fɑ:ɹ
**sp** ouer-farre[1]
> far

**overflourish,** *abbr* **o'er / ~ed** *v*
,o:ɹ'flɤrɪʃt
**sp** ore-flourish'd[1]
> flourish

**overflow,** *abbr* **o'er / ~s / ~ed / ~n** *v*
'o:vəɹ'flo:, *abbr* ,o:ɹ- / ,o:ɹ'flo:s / 'o:vəɹ'flo:d / 'o:vəɹ'flo:n
**sp** ouerflow[2], *abbr* oreflow[2] / ore'flowes[1], ore-flowes[2] / ouerflow'd[1] / ouer-flowne[1]
**rh** knows *Luc 1119* / bestowed *Per 4.4.40*
> flow

**overflowing,** *abbr* **o'er** *adj*
ˌoːɹ'floːɪn, -ɪŋ
**sp** o're-flowing[1]
> flow

**overfly** *VA* *v*
'oːvəɹ'fləɪ
**sp** ouerfly[1]
**rh** overfly them hie them *VA 324*
> fly

**overfond** *adj*
'oːvəɹ'fɒnd
**sp** ouer-fond[1]
> fond

**overfraught,** *abbr* **o'er** *adj*
'oːɹˌfrɔːt
**sp** o're-fraught[1]
> fraught

**overfull** *adj*
'oːvəɹ'fʊl
**sp** ouer-full[1]
> full

**overgall,** *abbr* **o'er / ~ed** *v*
ˌoːɹ'gɑːlɪd
**sp** ore-galled[1]
> gall

**overglance,** *abbr* **o'er / ~d** *v*
'oːvəɹ'glans / ˌoːɹ'glanst
**sp** ouerglance[1] / o're-glanc't[1]
> glance

**over·go / ~gone,** *abbr* **o'er** *v*
'oːvəɹ'goː / 'oːvəɹ'goːn, *abbr* ˌoːɹ-, -'gɒn
**sp** ouer-go[1] / ouergone[1], *abbr* ore-gone[1] /
> go

**overgorge / ~d** *v*
'oːvəɹ'gɔːɹʤd
**sp** ouer-gorg'd[1]
> gorge

**overgreat,** *abbr* **o'er** *adj*
'oːɹˌgrɛːt
**sp** ore-great[1]
> great

**overgreedy** *adj*
'oːvəɹ'griːdəɪ
**sp** ouer-greedy[1]
> greedy

**overgrow,** *abbr* **o'er** *v*
ˌoːɹ'groː
**sp** o're-grow[1]
> grow

**overgrown,** *abbr* **o'er** *adj*
'oːvəɹ'groːn, *abbr m* ˌoːɹ'groːn, 'oːɹˌgroːn
**sp** ouer-growne[1], *abbr* ore-growne[3]
> grow

**overhang,** *abbr* **o'er** *v*
ˌoːɹ'aŋ, -'ha-
**sp** o're-hang[1]
> hang

**overhanging,** *abbr* **o'er** *adj*
ˌoːɹ'aŋgɪn, -ɪŋ, -'ha-
**sp** ore-hanging[1]
> hang

**overhappy** *adj*
'oːvəɹ'apəɪ, -'ha-
**sp** ouer-happy[1]
> happy

**overhasty,** *abbr* **o'er** *adj*
ˌoːɹ'astəɪ, -'ha-
**sp** o're-hasty[1]
> hasty

**overhead** *adv*
'oːvəɹ'ed, -'he-
**sp** ouer head[1]
**rh** tread *LLL 4.3.279*
> head

**overhear,** *abbr* **o'er / ~d / ~dest** *v*
'oːvəɹ'iːɹ, -ɛːɹ, -'h-, *abbr* ˌoːɹ- / 'oːvəɹ'ɛːɹd, -'ɐːɹd, -'h-, *abbr* ˌoːɹ- / -st
**sp** ouer-heare[2], *abbr* o're-heare[1], / ouerheard[2], ouer-heard[4], *abbr* ore-heard[3] / ouer-heardst[1], ouer heard'st[1]
**rh** here *LLL 5.2.95*

**overhold** *v*
'oːvəɹ'oːld, -'hoː-
**sp** ouerhold[1]
> hold

**overjoyed,** *abbr* **o'er** *adj*
'oːvəɹ'ʤəɪd, *abbr* ˌoːɹ-
**sp** ouer-ioyed[2], *abbr* ore-ioy'd[1]
> joy

**overkind** *adj*
'oːvəɹ'kəɪnd
**sp** ouer-kind[1]
> kind

**overkindness** *n*
'oːvəɹ'kəɪndnəs
**sp** ouerkindnesse[1]
> kind

**overlaboured,** *abbr* **o'er** *adj*
ˌoːɹ'lɛːbəɹd
**sp** ore-labor'd[1]
> labour

**overleap,** *abbr* **o'er / ~s** *v*
ˌoːɹ'liːp / -s
**sp** o're-leape[2] / ore-leapes[1]
> leap

**overleather** *n*
'oːvəɹˌleðəɹ
**sp** o-uer-leather[1]
> leather

**overlive** *v*
'oːvəɹ'lɪv
**sp** ouer-liue[1]
> live

**overlong** *adj*
'oːvəɹ'lɒŋ
**sp** ouer-long[1]
> long

**overlook,** *abbr* **o'er / ~s / ~ed** *v*
'oːvəɹ'lʊk, *abbr* ˌoːɹ- / -s / -t
**sp** ouer-looke[3], *abbr* orelooke[1], o're-looke[2] / ouer-lookes[2] / ouerlook'd[1], *abbr* ore-look'd[3], ore-lookt[1]
**rh** book *MND 2.2.127, S 82.2*; **over-look** them forsook them *VA 178*

**overlooking**, *abbr* **o'er** *n*
'o:vəɹˌlʊkɪn, -ɪŋ, *abbr* ˌo:ɹ-'l-
**sp** ouer looking[1], *abbr* ore-loo-king[1]
> look

**overlusty** *adj*
'o:vəɹ'lɤstəɪ
**sp** ouerlustie[1], ouer-lustie[1]
> lust

**overmaster**, *abbr* **o'er / ~est / ~ed** *v*
ˌo:ɹ'mastəɹ / *m* ˌo:ɹ'mastəˌrest / 'o:vəɹ'mastəɹd
**sp** o'remaster't [overmaster it][1] / ore-masterest[1] / ouer-mastred[1]
> master

**overmatched**, *abbr* **o'er** *adj*
'o:ɹˌmatʃt
**sp** ore-matcht[1]
> match

**overmatching** *adj*
'o:vəɹ'matʃɪn, -ɪŋ
**sp** ouer-matching[1]
> match

**overmeasure** *n*
'o:vəɹˌmezəɹ
**sp** ouer measure[1]
> measure

**overmerry** *adj*
'o:vəɹ'merəɪ
**sp** ouer-merrie[1]
> merry

**overmount**, *abbr* **o'er** *v*
ˌo:ɹ'məʊnt
**sp** o're-mount[1]

**overmounting** *adj*
'o:vəɹ'məʊntɪn, -ɪŋ
**sp** ouer-mounting[1]
> mount

**overmuch** *adv*
'o:vəɹ'mɤtʃ
**sp** ouer-much[2]
> much

**overname** *v*
'o:vəɹ'nɛ:m
**sp** ouer-name[1]
> name

**overnight**, *abbr* **o'er / ~'s** *n*
'o:vəɹ'nəɪt, *abbr* ˌo:ɹ- / -s
**sp** ouer-night[1], *abbr* ore-night[1] / o're-nights[1]
> night

**overoffice / ~s**, *abbr* **o'er** *v*
ˌo:ɹ'ɒfɪsɪz
**sp** o're of-fices[1]
> office

**overpaid**
> overpay

**overparted**, *abbr* **o'er** *adj*
ˌo:ɹ'pɑ:ɹtɪd
**sp** ore-parted[1]
> part

**overpass / ~ed** *v*
'o:vəɹ'past
**sp** ouer-past[1]

**overpassed**, *abbr* **o'er** *adj*
ˌo:ɹ'past
**sp** ore-past[1], *R3 4.4.396 emend of* repast[1]
**rh** hast *R3 4.4.396*

**over·pay**, *abbr* **o'er / ~pays / ~paid** *v*
'o:vəɹ'pɛ: / ˌo:ɹ'pɛ:z / ˌo:ɹ'pɛ:d
**sp** ouer-pay[1] / ore-payes[1] / ore-pai'd[1]
> pay

**overpeer**, *abbr* **o'er / ~ing / ~ed** *v*
'o:vəɹ'pi:ɹ, *abbr* ˌo:ɹ- / -ɪn, -ɪŋ / -d
**sp** ouer-peere[2], *abbr* o're-peere[1] / ouer-peering[1] / ouer-peer'd[1]
> peer

**overperch**, *abbr* **o'er** *v*
ˌo:ɹ'pɛ:ɹtʃ
**sp** ore-perch[1]
> perch

**overpictur·e / ~ing**, *abbr* **o'er** *v*
ˌo:ɹ'pɪktrɪn, -ɪŋ, -tər-
**sp** o're-picturing[1]
> picture

**overplus** *adj / n*
'o:vəɹ'plɤs
**sp** ouer-plus[1] / ouer-plus[1]
**rh** thus *S 135.2*

**overposting**, *abbr* **o'er** *n*
ˌo:ɹ'po:stɪn, -ɪŋ
**sp** o're-posting[1]
> post

**overpower / ~ed**, *abbr* **o'er** *v*
ˌo:ɹ'po:ɹd
**sp** o're-powr'd[2]
> power

**overpressed**, *abbr* **o'er** *adj*
'o:ɹˌprest
**sp** o're-prest[1]
> press

**overprize**, *abbr* **o'er / ~d** *v*
ˌo:ɹ'prəɪzd
**sp** ore-priz'd[1]
> prize

**overproud** *adj*
'o:vəɹ'prəʊd
**sp** ouer-proud[1], ouer proud[1]
> proud

**over-rate**, *abbr* **o'er** *v*
ˌo:ɹ'rɛ:t
**sp** o're-rate[1]
> rate

**over-reach**, *abbr* **o'er / -raught** *v*
'o:vəɹ'ri:tʃ, *abbr* ˌo:ɹ- / ˌo:ɹ'rɔ:t
**sp** ouer-reach[1], *abbr* ore-reach[1] / ore-wrought[2]
> reach

**over-reaching**, *abbr* **o'er** *n*
ˌo:ɹ'ri:tʃɪn, -ɪŋ
**sp** ore-reaching[1]
> reach

**over-read,** *abbr* **o'er** *present / past v*
'o:vəɹ'ri:d, *abbr* ˌo:ɹ- / ˌo:ɹ'red
**sp** ouer-reade[1], *abbr* ore-read[1], ore-reade[1] / ore-read[1]
**rh** dead *S 81.10*
> read

**over-red** *v*
'o:vəɹ'red
**sp** ouer-red[1]
> red

**over-rested,** *abbr* **o'er** *adj*
ˌo:ɹ'restɪd
**sp** ore-rested[1]
> rest

**over-ride / ~rode** *v*
'o:vəɹ'rɒd
**sp** ouer-rod[1]
> ride

**over-ripened** *adj*
'o:vəɹ'rəɪpənd
**sp** ouer-ripen'd[1]
> ripe

**over-roasted** *adj*
'o:vəɹ'ro:stɪd
**sp** ouer-roasted[1], ouer-rosted[1]
> roast

**over-rule,** *abbr* **o'er / ~s / ~d** *v*
ˌo:ɹ'ru:l / -z / 'o:vəɹ'ru:ld
**sp** ore-rule[1], o're-rule[1], o'rerule[1] / ore-rules[1] / ouer-rul'd[2]
> rule

**over-run,** *abbr* **o'er / ~s** *v*
'o:vəɹ'rɤn, *abbr* ˌo:ɹ- / -z
**sp** ouer-run[1], *abbr* ore-run[5] / ore-runs[1]

**over-running** *n*
'o:vəɹ'rɤnɪn, -ɪŋ
**sp** ouer-running[1]
> run

**overseas,** *abbr* **o'er** *adv*
ˌo:ɹ'si:z
**sp** ore-seas[1]
> sea

**overset,** *abbr* **o'er** *v*
'o:vəɹ'set, *abbr* ˌo:ɹ-
**sp** ouer set[1], *abbr* o're-set[1]
> set

**overshade,** *abbr* **o'er / ~s** *v*
ˌo:ɹ'ʃɛ:d / 'o:vəɹ'ʃɛ:dz, *abbr* ˌo:ɹ-
**sp** ore-shade[1] / ouer-shades[1], *abbr* ore-shades[2]
> shade

**overshine,** *abbr* **o'er / ~s** *v*
'o:vəɹ'ʃəɪn, *abbr* ˌo:ɹ- / 'o:vəɹ'ʃəɪnz
**sp** ouer-shine[2], *abbr* o're-shine[1] / ouershines[1]
> shine

**overshoes,** *abbr* **o'er** *adj / adv / n*
'o:vəɹˌʃu:z, *abbr* 'o:ɹ-
**sp** ouer-shooes[1], *abbr* oreshooes[1] / o-uer-shooes[1] / ouer shooes[1]
> shoe

**over·shoot,** *abbr* **o'er / ~shot** *v*
'o:vəɹ'ʃɒt, *abbr* ˌo:ɹ-
**sp** ouershot[1], ouer-shot[1], *abbr* ore'shot[1], o're-shot[1]
**rh** forgot *LLL 1.1.140*; not *LLL 4.3.158*
> shoot

**overshower,** *abbr* **o'er / ~ed** *Per v*
ˌo:ɹ'ʃo:ɹd
**sp** ore-showr'd[1]
**rh** devoured *Per 4.4.26*

**oversight / ~s** *n*
'o:vəɹˌsəɪt / -s
**sp** ouer-sights[1]
> sight

**oversize,** *abbr* **o'er / ~d** *v*
*m* ˌo:ɹ'səɪzɪd
**sp** o're-sized[1]
> size

**overskip,** *abbr* **o'er** *v*
ˌo:ɹ'skɪp
**sp** *Q* o're scip[1]
**rh** fellowship *KL 3.6.104*
> skip

**overslip,** *abbr* **o'er / ~s** *v*
ˌo:ɹ'slɪps
**sp** ore-slips[1]
> slip

**overspread,** *abbr* **o'er / ~s** *v*
'o:vəɹ'spred / ˌo:ɹ'spredz
**sp** ouer-spread[1] / ore-spreds[1]
> spread

**overstain / ~ed** *v*
'o:vəɹ'stɛ:nd
**sp** ouer-staind[1]
> stained

**overstare,** *abbr* **o'er** *v*
ˌo:ɹ'stɛ:ɹ
**sp** ore-stare[1]
> stare

**over·stink,** *abbr* **o'er / ~stunk** *v*
ˌo:ɹ'stɤŋk
**sp** ore-stunck[1]
> stink

**overstop,** *abbr* **o'er** *v*
ˌo:ɹ'stɒp
**sp** ore-stop[1]
> stop

**overstrawed,** *abbr* **o'er** *adj*
ˌo:ɹ'strɔ:d
**sp** ore-strawd[1]
**rh** fraud *VA 1143*
> straw

**oversway,** *abbr* **o'er / ~s / ~ed** *v*
ˌo:ɹ'swɛ: / -z / 'o:vəɹ'swɛ:d
**sp** ore-sway[1], o'resway[1] / o're-swaies[1] / ouerswayed[1]
**rh** obeyed *VA 109*
> sway

**overswear** *v*
'o:vəɹ'swɛ:ɹ

**sp** ouer sweare[1]
> swear

**overswell,** *abbr* **o'er** *v*
ˌoːɹ'swel
**sp** ore-swell[3]
> swell

**over·take,** *abbr* **o'er / ~taketh / ~took / ~tane** *v*
'oːvəɹ'tɛːk, *abbr* ˌoːɹ- / 'oːvəɹ'tɛːkəθ / 'oːvəɹ'tʊk, *abbr* ˌoːɹ- / 'oːvəɹ'tɛːn, *abbr* ˌoːɹ-
**sp** ouertake[5], ouer-take[2], *abbr* ore-take[3], o'retake[1], o're-take[3] / ouer-taketh[1] / ouer-tooke[1], *abbr* o'retooke[1], o're-tooke[1] / ouertane[1], ouerta'ne[1], *abbr* ore-tane[2]
> take

**overtedious** *adj*
'oːvəɹ'tɪdɪəs
**sp** ouer-tedious[1]
> tedious

**overteemed,** *abbr* **o'er** *adj*
*m* ˌoːɹ'tiːmɪd
**sp** ore-teamed[1]
> teem

**overthrow** *n*
'oːvəɹˌθroː
**sp** ouerthrow[12]

**overthrow,** *abbr* **o'er / ~s / ~n** *v*
'oːvəɹ'θroː, *abbr* *m* ˌoːɹ'θroː, 'oːɹˌθroː / ˌoːɹ'θroːz / 'oːvəɹ'θroːn, *abbr* ˌoːɹ'θroːn
**sp** ouerthrow[3], *abbr* orethrow[1], o'rethrow[1], o're-throw[1] / orethrowes[1] / ouerthrowne[11], *abbr* o'rethrown[1], orethrowne[1], ore-throwne[1], o'rethrowne[1], o're-throwne[2]
**rh** grow *TN 5.1.165*; woe *S 90.8* / foes *RJ Prol.7* / own *Ham 3.2.222, LLL 5.2.153, Tem Epil.1*
> throw

**overtook**
> overtake

**overtop,** *abbr* **o'er / ~ping / ~ped** *v*
*m* 'oːɹˌtɒp, -'tɒp, / 'oːɹ'tɒpɪn, -ɪŋ / 'oːvəɹ'tɒpt
**sp** ore-top[1], o're top[1] / ore-topping[1], / ouer-top'd[1]
> top

**overtopping** *n*
'oːvəɹ'tɒpɪn, -ɪŋ
**sp** ouer-topping[1]

**overtrip,** *abbr* **o'er** *v*
ˌoːɹ'trɪp
**sp** ore-trip[1]
> trip

**overture** *n*
*m* 'oːvəɹˌtuːɹ, -ɹtəɹ
**sp** ouerture[5], ouer-ture[1]

**overturn,** *abbr* **o'er / ~ed** *v*
ˌoːɹ'tɐːɹn / 'oːvəɹ'tɐːɹnd
**sp** o're-turne[2] / ouer-turn'd[1]
**rh** burn *S 55.5*
> turn

**overvalue,** *abbr* **o'er / ~s** *v*
ˌoːɹ'valjəz, -juːz
**sp** o're-values[1]
> value

**overveil / ~ed** *v*
'oːvəɹ'vɛːld
**sp** ouer-vayl'd[1]
> veil

**overview** *n*
'oːvəɹˌvjuː
**sp** ouer-view[1]
**rh** you *LLL 4.3.173*
> view

**overwalk,** *abbr* **o'er** *v*
ˌoːɹ'wɔːk
**sp** o're-walke[1]
> walk

**overwatched,** *abbr* **o'er** *adj*
'oːvəɹ'wɑʧt, *abbr* ˌoːɹ-
**sp** ouer-watcht[1], *abbr* ore-watch'd[1]
> watch

**overween,** *abbr* **o'er / ~s** *v*
'oːvəɹ'wiːn, *abbr* ˌoːɹ- / -z
**sp** ouer-weene[2], *abbr* oreweene[1] / o're-weenes[1]

**overweening,** *abbr* **o'er** *adj*
'oːvəɹ'wiːnɪn, -ɪŋ, *abbr* ˌoːɹ-
**sp** ouer-weening[5], *abbr* ore-weening[1]
> ween

**overweigh,** *abbr* **o'er / ~s** *v*
'oːvəɹ'wɛː, *abbr* ˌoːɹ- / ˌoːɹ'wɛːz
**sp** ouer-weigh[1], *abbr* o're-way[1] / ore-weighs[1]
> weigh

**overwhelm,** *abbr* **o'er / ~ed** *v*
'oːvəɹ'ʍelm, *abbr* ˌoːɹ- / *m* 'oːvəɹ'ʍelmd, -mɪd, *abbr* ˌoːɹ-
**sp** ouer-whelme[1], *abbr* orewhelm[1], ore-whelme[3], o'rewhelme[1], / ouerwhelm'd[1], ouer-whelmed[1], *abbr* o'rewhelm'd[1], o're-whelm'd[1], o're-whelmed[1]

**overwhelming** *adj*
'oːvəɹ'ʍelmɪn, -ɪŋ
**sp** ouerwhelming[1]
> whelm

**overwithered** *adj*
'oːvəɹ'wɪðəɹd
**sp** ouer-wither'd[1]
> wither

**overworn,** *abbr* **o'er** *adj*
'oːvəɹ'wɔːɹn, *abbr* ˌoːɹ-
**sp** ouer-worne[1], *abbr* ore-worne[1]
**rh** horn *VA 866*; morn *S 63.2*
> wear

**Ovid / ~'s** *n*
'ɒvɪd
**sp** Ouid[2] / Ouids[1]

**Ovidius** *n*
ə'vɪdɪəs
**sp** O-uiddius[1]

**owe / ~est / ~es / ~eth / ~ing / ~ed / ~edest / ought** *v*
oː / ˈoːst, ˈoːəst / oːz / oːəθ / ˈoːɪn, -ɪŋ / oːd / oːdst / ɔːt
**sp** owe[71] / owest[2], ow'st[5] / owes[25], ows[1] / oweth[1] / owing[1] / ow'd[7], owed[3] / owd'st[1] / ought[1]
**rh** Dromio *CE 3.1.42*; grow *MND 3.2.85*; grow, show *Luc 299*; know *CE 3.2.43, LLL 1.2.101, Mac 5.4.18, TN 2.4.104*; Mercutio *RJ 3.1.183*; show *S 70.14*; show, so *Luc 82*; so *TN 1.5.300*; throw *MND 2.2.85*; **owe it** know it *AW 4.3.225, VA 411*; **owe me** know me *VA 523*; **owe them** bestow them *LC 140* / goest, knowest, showest, throwest, trowest *KL 1.4.119*; growest *S 18.10* / shows *Tim 3.4.24* / bestowed, glowed *LC 327*
> honour-owing, unowed

**Owen** *n*
ˈoːɪn
**sp** Owen[9]

**owl / ~s** *n*
əʊl / -z
**sp** oule[1], owle[18] / owles[3]
**rh** *1* foul *LLL 4.1.140, 5.2.906*; **rh** *2* bowl *LLL 4.1.140, 5.2.915*
> night-, screech-owl

**own** *adj, pro*
oːn
**sp** own[16], owne[705], own's [own is][1]
**rh** *1* alone *TG 2.4.166*; blown *VA 776*; known *Luc 241*; known, shown *MND 3.2.459*; o'erthrown, overthrown *Ham 3.2.223, LLL 5.2.154, Tem Epil.2*; over-blown *R2 3.2.191*; shown *PP 20.18, RJ 1.1.189, 1.2.100, S 69.6, 121.10*; unknown *Luc 35*; **rh** *2* none *Per Prol.27*

**own / ~s / ~ing** *v*
oːn / -z / ˈoːnɪn, -ɪŋ
**sp** owne[1] / ownes[1] / owning[1]

**owner / ~s** *n*
ˈoːnəɹ / -z
**sp** owner[13], owners[4]

**ox / ~en** *n*
=
**sp** oxe[12] / oxen[7]
**rh** mocks *LLL 5.2.250*
> draught-oxen

**Oxford** *n*
ˈɒksfəɹd
**sp** Oxford[38], Ox-ford[1]

**Oxfordshire** *n*
*m* ˈɒksfəɹdˌʃəɪɹ
**sp** Oxfordshire[1]

**ox-head** *n*
ˈɒks-ˌed, -ˌhed
**sp** oxe-head[1]
> head

**oxlip / ~s** *n*
=
**sp** oxlips[1], oxslips[1]

**oyes** *n*
əɪz
**sp** oyes[2]
**rh** toys *MW 5.5.41*

**oyster** *n*
ˈəɪstəɹ
**sp** oyster[6], oy-ster[1]

**oyster-wench** *n*
ˈəɪstəɹ-ˌwentʃ
**sp** oyster-wench[1]

**ozier / ~s** *n*
ˈoːzɪəɹz
**sp** oziers[1]

# P

**P** [letter] / ~s *n*
=
**sp** P's[1]

**pace** / ~s *n*
pɛ:s / ˈpɛ:s·ɪz
**sp** pace[20] / paces[6]
**rh** case, grace *Luc 709*; race *S 51.9* / faces, interlaces *Luc 1391*

**pac·e** / ~ing / ~ed *v*
pɛ:s / ˈpɛ:s·ɪz / -ɪn, -ɪŋ / pɛ:st
**sp** pace[7] / pacing[1] / pac'd[2]
**rh** grace *WT 4.1.23*
> snail-paced

**Pace** [name] *n*
pɛ:s
**sp** Pace[1]

**pacif·y** / ~ied *v*
ˈpasɪfəɪ / -d
**sp** pacifie[1] / pacified[2]

**pack** / ~s *n*
=
**sp** pack[4], packe[8] / packs[1]

**pack** / ~ing / ~ed *v*
= / ˈpakɪn, -ɪŋ / =
**sp** pack[1], packe[8] / packing[8] / pack'd[2], packt[6]
> unpack

**packet** / ~s *n*
=
**sp** packet[8] / packets[2]

**pack-horse** *n*
ˈpak-ˌɔ:ɹs, -ˌhɔ:- / -ɪz
**sp** packe-horse[1] / pack-horses[1]
> horse

**packing** / ~s *n*
ˈpakɪnz, -ɪŋz
**sp** packings[1]

**pack-saddle** *n*
ˈpak-ˌsadl
**sp** packe-saddle[1]
> saddle

**pack-thread** *n*
=
**sp** packthred[2]
> thread

**Pacorus** *n*
pəˈkɔ:rəs
**sp** Pacorus[1], Paco-rus[1]

**paction** *n*
ˈpaksɪən
**sp** paction[1]

**paddl·e** / ~ing *v*
= / ˈpadlɪn, -ɪŋ
**sp** paddle[1] / padling[2]

**paddock** *n*
=
**sp** paddocke[1]

**Paddock** [name] *n*
=
**sp** Padock[1]

**Padua** *n*
*m* ˈpadju:ˌa, [2 *sylls*] ˈpadjʊə
**sp** Padua[29]

**pagan** *adj*
ˈpɛ:gən
**sp** pagan[3]

**pagan** / ~s *n*
ˈpɛ:gən / -z
**sp** pagan[3] / pagans[3]

**page** / ~'s / ~s *n*
pɛ:ʤ / ˈpɛ:ʤɪz
**sp** page[39] / pages[1] / pages[8]
**rh** age *MW 1.3.79, S 108.12*; embassage *LLL 5.2.97* / rages *Luc 910*

**page** *v*
pɛ:ʤ
**sp** page[1]

**Page** / ~'s [name] *n*
pɛ:ʤ / ˈpɛ:ʤɪz
**sp** Page[116] / Pages[4]

**pageant** / ~s *n*
ˈpaʤɪənt, -ʤənt / -s
**sp** pageant[9], page-ant[1] / pageants[5]

**pageant** / ~s *v*
ˈpaʤɪənts, -ʤənts
**sp** pageants[1]

**pah** *interj*
=
**sp** pah[2]

**paid**
> pay

**pail** / ~s *n*
pɛ:l / -z
**sp** paile[1] / pailes[1]
**rh** nail *LLL 5.2.904*

**pailful** / ~s *n*
ˈpɛ:lfʊlz
**sp** paile-fuls[1]

**pain / ~s** *n*
pɛ:n / -z
**sp** pain[1], paine[58] / paines[83], pains[5]
**rh** again *Cym 4.2.290, MND 1.1.250, VA 1034*; again, disdain *Luc 690*; again, distain *Luc 789*; complain *CE 2.1.36*; disdain *3H6 3.3.128, S 132.4, 140.4*; disdain, gain *PP 15.9*; Dumaine *LLL 4.3.170*; gain *Luc 861, S 141.14*; gain, remain *Luc 733*; maintain *2H4 4.5.222*; plain *LLL 4.3.120*; slain *S 139.14*; vain *LLL 1.1.73, PP 20.20, R2 2.1.8* / gains *Mac 4.1.39, R2 5.6.11*; retains *TNK Prol.8*
> hell-pains

**pain / ~s / ~ed** *v*
pɛ:n / -z / -d
**sp** paines[1] / pain'd[1]

**pained** *adj*
*m* 'pɛ:nɪd
**sp** pained[1]

**pained** *Luc* *n*
pɛ:nd
**sp** pained[1]
**rh** chained, obtained *Luc 901*

**painful** *adj*
'pɛ:nfʊl
**sp** painefull[3], painfull[3], pain-full[1]

**painfully** *adv*
*m* 'pɛ:nfʊˌləɪ
**sp** painefully[3], painfully[1]

**paint / ~s / ~ed** *v*
pɛ:nt / -s / 'pɛ:ntɪd
**sp** paint[16] / paints[1] / painted[23]
**rh** attaint *Luc 1074* / acquainted *S 20.1*; fainted *Luc 1541*

**painted** *adj*
'pɛ:ntɪd
**sp** painted[23]
> well-painted

**painter** *n*
'pɛ:ntəɹ
**sp** painter[9]

**painting** *adj*
'pɛ:ntɪn, -ɪŋ
**sp** painting[1]

**painting / ~s** *n*
'pɛ:ntɪn, -ɪŋ / -z
**sp** painting[14] / paintings[1]
> nose-painting

**pair / ~s** *n*
pɛ:ɹ / -z
**sp** paire[26], payre[12] / paires[1]

**pair / ~ed** *v*
pɛ:ɹ / -d
**sp** paire / payr'd[1]

**pair-taunt-like** *adj*
'pɛ:ɹ-tɔ:nt-ˌləɪk
**sp** pertaunt like[1]

**pajock** *n*
'pɛ:dʒək
**sp** paiocke[1]

**palabras** *Span* *n*
pa'labras, *Sly TS Induction 1.5*
pa'labri:s
**sp** palabras[1], *Sly* pallabris[1]

**palace** *adj*
=
**sp** pallace[4]

**palace / ~s** *n*
=
**sp** palace[4], pallace[22] / palaces[1], pallaces[6]

**Palamedes** *n*
ˌpala'mi:di:z
**sp** Palamedes[1]

**palate / ~s** *n*
=
**sp** pa-lat[1], pallat[3], pallate[3] / palats[1], pallats[2]

**palat·e / ~s / ~ing** *v*
= / 'palətɪn, -ɪŋ
**sp** pallates[2] / pallating[1]

**pale / ~r** *adj*
pɛ:l / 'pɛ:ləɹ
**sp** pale[113], pale-[primrose][1] / paler[3]
**rh** scale *Luc 441*; scale, tale *Luc 478*; tale *VA 76,1123*; tale, vale *LC 5*
> maid-pale

**pale / ~s** *n*
pɛ:l / -z
**sp** pale[8] / pales[1]
**rh** dale *MND 2.1.4, VA 230, WT 4.3.4*; stale *CE 2.1.100*; tale *VA 589*

**pale / ~s / ~ed** *v*
pɛ:l / -z / -d
**sp** pale[2] / pales[2] / pal'd[1]

**pale-dead** *adj*
'pɛ:l-ˌded
**sp** pale-dead[1]
> dead

**pale-faced** *adj*
'pɛ:l-ˌfɛ:st
**sp** pale-fac'd[3], pale-fac't[1]
> face

**pale-hearted** *adj*
*m* ˌpɛ:l-'ɑ:ɹtɪd, -'hɑ:-
**sp** pale-hearted[1]
> heart

**paleness** *n*
'pɛ:lnəs
**sp** palenesse[2]

**Palentine** *n*
'paləntəɪn
**sp** Palentine[2]

**Palestine** *n*
*m* 'paləstəɪn, -sˌt-
**sp** Palestine[2]

**pale-visaged** *adj*
*m* ˌpɛ:l-'vɪzɪdʒd
**sp** pale-visag'd[1]
> visage

**palfrey / ~s** *n*
'palfrəɪ / -z

**sp** palfray[1], palfrey[1] / palfrayes[1], palfries[1]

**palizado / ~es** *n*
ˌpalɪˈzɑːdoːz
**sp** palizadoes[1]

**pall** *v*
pɑːl, pɔːl
**sp** pall[1], paule[1]

**pallabris**
> palabras

**Pallas** *n*
ˈpaləs
**sp** Pallas[3]

**palled** *adj*
*m* ˈpɑːlɪd, ˈpɔː-
**sp** paul'd[1]

**pallet / ~s** *n*
ˈpalət / -s
**sp** pallads[1]

**palliament** *n*
*m* ˈpalɪəˌment
**sp** palliament[1]

**palm** [hand] **/ ~s** *n*
pɔːm / -z
**sp** palme[20] / palmes[1], palms[1]
**rh** balm *VA 25*

**palm** [tree] *n*
pɔːm
palme[5]

**palmer / ~'s / ~s** *n*
ˈpɔːməɹz
**sp** palmers[3] / palmers[2]

**palm-tree** *n*
ˈpɔːm-ˌtriː
**sp** palme tree[1]

**palpable** *adj*
=
**sp** palpable[6]

**palsied** *adj*
ˈpɔːlzəɪd, ˈpɑːl-
**sp** palsied[1], palsied-[eld][1]

**pals·y / ~ies** *n*
ˈpɔːlzəɪ, ˈpɑːl- / -z
**sp** palsie[3] / palsies[1]

**palter** *v*
ˈpɔːltəɹ
**sp** palter[5]

**paltering** *n*
ˈpɔːltrɪn, -ɪŋ
**sp** paltring[1]

**paltry** *adj*
ˈpɔːltrəɪ
**sp** paltrie[2], paltry[8], paultry[1]

**paly** *adj*
ˈpɛːləɪ
**sp** palie[1], paly[1]

**pamper** *v*
ˈpampəɹ
**sp** pamper[1]

**pampered** *adj*
ˈpampəɹd
**sp** pampred[1]

**pamphlet / ~s** *n*
=
**sp** pamphlets[11]

**pancake / ~s** *n*
ˈpankɛːk / -s
**sp** pancake[1] / pancakes[2], pan-cakes[1]

**Pandarus,** *abbr* **Pandar / ~'s** *n*
*m* ˈpandəˌrɤs, -dərəs, -drəs, *abbr* ˈpandəɹ / ˈpandəɹz
**sp** Pandarus[30], *abbr* Pandar[4], Pander[1], *abbr in s.d.* Pand[3] / Pandar's[2], Panders[1]

**pander / ~s** *n*
ˈpandəɹ / -z
**sp** pandar[3], pander[3] / pandars[1], panders[2]

**pander / ~s** *v*
ˈpandəɹz
**sp** panders[1]

**panderly** *adj*
ˈpandəɹləɪ
**sp** panderly[1]

**Pandulph** *n*
ˈpandəlf
**sp** Pandolph[1], Pandulph[3], *in s.d.* Pandulpho[2]

**pang / ~s** *n*
=
**sp** pang[4] / pangs[13]

**pang / ~ing / ~ed** *v*
ˈpaŋgɪn, -ɪŋ / =
**sp** panging[1] / pang'd[1]

**pannel** *n*
=
**sp** pannell[1]

**pannel / ~led** *v*
=
**sp** pannelled[1]

**pannier** *n*
ˈpanɪəɹ
**sp** pannier[1]

**Pannonian / ~s** *n*
pəˈnoːnɪənz
**sp** Pannonians[2]

**Pansa** *n*
ˈpansə
**sp** Pansa[1]

**pans·y / ~ies** *n*
ˈpanzəɪz
*sp Ham 4.5.177 emend of* paconcies[1]

**pant / ~s** *n*
=
**sp** pants[2]

**pant / ~s / ~eth** *Luc* **/ ~ing / ~ed** *v*
= / = / = / ˈpantɪn, -ɪŋ / =
**sp** pant[3] / pants[1] / pa[n]teth[1] / painting[1] / panted[1]
**rh** *1* granteth *Luc 555*; **rh** *2* wanteth *Luc 555*

**pantaloon** *n*
ˌpantəˈluːn
**sp** pantaloone[1], pantalowne[1], pantelowne[1]

**Pantheon** *n*
ˈpantɪən, -nθɪ-
**sp** Panthean[1], Pathan[1]

**panther** *n*
ˈpanθəɹ
**sp** panther[3]

**Panthino** *n*
panˈtiːnoː
**sp** Panthino[2], Panthion[2]

**panting** *adj / n*
ˈpantɪn, -ɪŋ
**sp** panting[2] / panting[1]

**pantler** *n*
ˈpantləɹ
**sp** pantler[4]

**pantry** *n*
ˈpantrəɪ
**sp** pan-tery[1]

**pap / ~s** *n*
=
**sp** pap[3] / pappes[1]
**rh** hop *MND 5.1.290*

**paper** *adj*
ˈpɛːpəɹ
**sp** paper[3]

**paper / ~s** *n*
ˈpɛːpəɹ / -z
**sp** paper[74], pa-per[1] / papers[11]

**paper / ~s** *v*
ˈpɛːpəɹz
**sp** papers[1]

**paper-faced** *adj*
ˈpɛːpəɹ-ˌfɛːst
**sp** paper-fac'd[1]
> face

**paper-mill** *n*
ˈpɛːpəɹ-ˌmɪl
**sp** paper-mill[1]
> mill

**Paphlagonia** *n*
ˌpafləˈgoːnɪə
**sp** Paphlagonia[1]

**Paphos** *n*
ˈpafɒs
**sp** Paphos[1]

**papist** *n*
ˈpapɪst
**sp** papist[1]

**par** *Fr prep*
paɹ
**sp** par[1]

**par** *nonsense word*
pɑːɹ
**sp** par[1]

**parable** *n*
=
**sp** parable[1]

**Paracelsus** *n*
ˌparəˈselsəs
**sp** Paracelsus[1]

**paradise** *n*
*m* ˈparəˌdəɪs, -ˌdəɪz, -əd-
**sp** paradise[11]
**rh** wise *LLL 4.3.71, PP 3.14, Tem 4.1.124*
> demi-paradise

**paradox / ~es** *n*
=
**sp** paradox[2], paradoxe[1] / paradoxes[2]

**paragon** *n*
*m* ˈparəˌgɒn, -əgən
**sp** paragon[5], pa-ragon[1], parragon[1]

**paragon / ~s / ~ed** *v*
*m* ˈparəˌgɒn / -z / -d
**sp** paragon[1] / paragons[1] / parragon'd[1]
> unparagoned

**parallel** *adj*
*m* ˈpɑːɹlel, -rəl-
**sp** paralell[1]

**parallel / ~s** *n*
=
**sp** paralell[3] / paralels[1]

**parallel / ~s / ~led** *v*
=
**sp** paralell[2] / paralels[1] / paralel'd[1]
**rh** well *TC 2.2.163*
> unparallelled

**paramour / ~s** *n*
ˈparəˌmɔːɹ / -z
**sp** paramour[5] / paramours[1]
> out-paramour

**parapet / ~s** *n*
ˈparəˌpɪts
**sp** parapets[1]

**paraquito** *n*
ˌparəˈkiːtoː
**sp** paraquito[1]

**parasite / ~'s / ~s** *n*
ˈparəˌsɪt / -s
**sp** parasite[2] / parasites[1] / parasites[1]
**rh** wits *VA 848*

**Parca / ~'s** *n*
ˈpɑːɹkəz
**sp** Parcas[1]

**parcel / ~s** *n*
ˈpɑːɹsəl / -z
**sp** parcel[1], parcell[10], par-cell[1] / parcells[1], parcels[6]

**parcel-bawd** *n*
ˈpɑːɹsəl-ˌbɔːd
**sp** parcell baud[1]

**parcel-gilt** *adj*
ˈpɑːɹsəl-ˌgɪlt
**sp** parcell gilt[1]

**parcell** *v*
ˈpɑːɹsəl
**sp** parcell[1]

**parcelled** *adj*
'pɑ:ɹsəld
**sp** parcell;d[1]

**parch / ~ed** *v*
pɑ:ɹʧ / -t
**sp** parch[1] / parcht[1]

**parched** *adj*
*m* 'pɑ:ɹʧɪd
**sp** parched[1]

**parching** *adj*
'pɑ:ɹʧɪn, -ɪŋ
**sp** parching[3]

**parchment** *adj / n*
'pɑ:ɹʧmənt
**sp** parchment[1] / parchment[7]

**pard** *n*
pɑ:ɹd
**sp** pard[4]

**pardon / ~s** *n*
'pɑ:ɹdən / -z
**sp** pardon[95], pardon's [pardon is][1] / pardons[5]

**pardon / ~s / ~ing / ~ed** *v*
'pɑ:ɹdən / -z / -ɪn, -ɪŋ, -dn- / -d
**sp** pardon[201], par-don[1], pardon't [pardon it][1] / pardons[2] / pardoning[2] / pardon'd[10], pardoned[1]
> unpardonable

**pardoner** *n*
*m* 'pɑ:ɹdəˌnɐ:ɹ
**sp** pardoner[1]

**pardon-me / ~s** *n*
'pɑ:ɹdən-'mi:z
**sp** par-don-mee's[1]
> me

**pardonner / pardonne / ~z** *Fr v*
paɹdɔ'ne / paɹ'dɔn / paɹdɔ'nez
**sp** pardonner[1], par-donner[1] / pardon'ne, perdonne[1] / pardonne

**pardy**
> perdy

**pare / ~d** *v*
pɛ:ɹ / -d
**sp** paire[3], payre[1] / pared[1], par'd[2]

**parent / ~s / ~s'** *n*
'parənt / -s
**sp** parent[2] / parents[11], pa-rents[1] / parents[3]

**parentage** *n*
'parəntɪʤ
**sp** parentage[9]

**paricide / ~s** *n*
*m* 'parɪˌsəɪd / -z
**sp** parricide[1] / paricides[1]

**paring / ~s** *n*
'pɛ:rɪn, -ɪŋ / -z
**sp** payring[1] / parings[3]

**paring-knife** *n*
'pɛ:ɹɪn-ˌnəɪf, -ɪŋ, ˌkn-
**sp** pairing-knife[1]
> knife

**Paris / ~'** *n*
= / 'parɪs
**sp** Paris[89], Paris-[balls][1], *abbr* Par[1] / Paris[3]

**parish** *adj / n*
=
**sp** parish[6] / parish[3]

**parishioner ~s** *n*
pə'rɪʃənəɹz
**sp** parishioners[2]

**Parisian / ~s** *n*
=
**sp** Parisians[1]

**Paris-ward** *adv*
'parɪs-ˌwɑ:ɹd
**sp** Paris-ward[1]

**paritor / ~s** *n*
'parɪtəɹz
**sp** parrators[1]

**park** *adj*
pɑ:ɹk
**sp** parke[1], parke-[corner][1]

**park / ~s** *n*
pɑ:ɹk / -s
**sp** park[1], parke[16] / parkes[2]
**rh** bark *VA 239*

**park / ~ed** *v*
pɑ:ɹkt
**sp** park'd[1]

**park-ward** *adv*
'pɑ:ɹk-ˌwɑ:ɹd
**sp** parke-ward[1]

**parle** *n*
pɑ:ɹl
parle[10], par'le[1]
**rh** wall *3H6 5.1.16*

**parler / parle / ~s / ~z** *Fr v*
paɹ'le / paɹl / paɹl / paɹ'lez
*sp H5 3.4.5 emend of* par-len / parle[2] / parlas[1] / parleis[1]

**parley** *n*
'pɑ:ɹləɪ
**sp** parley[18], parly[3]

**parley / ~ed** *v*
'pɑ:ɹləɪ / -d
**sp** parlee[2], parley[4], parlie[1] / parlied[1]

**parliament** *n*
*m* 'pɑ:ɹləˌment, -ləmənt, -lmənt
**sp** parliament[22], parlia-ment[1]

**parlour / ~s** *n*
'pɑ:ɹləɹ / -z
**sp** parlour[1] / parlours[1]

**parlous** *adj*
'pɑ:ɹləs
**sp** parlous[3]

**parmacety** *n*
ˌpɑ:ɹmə'seti:
**sp** parmacity[1]

**Parolles** *n*
pa'ro:lɪs
**sp** Parolles[13], Parrolles[15]

**parrot / ~s** *n*
=
**sp** parrat[3], parret[1], parrot[2] / parrats[2]

**parrot-teacher** *n*
'parət-ˌti:ʧəɹ
**sp** parrat teacher[1]
> teacher

**parsley** *n*
'pɑ:ɹsləɪ
**sp** parseley[1]

**parson / ~'s** *n*
'pɑ:ɹsən / -z
**sp** parson[16], parsons[2]

**Parson** [name] *n*
'pɛ:ɹsən
**sp** Person[3]
**pun** *Holofernes LLL 4.2.82* pierce

**part / ~'s / ~s / ~s'** *n*
pɑ:ɹt / -s
**sp** part[323] / parts[1] / parts[93] / parts[1]
**rh** *1* art *AW 2.1.132, Mac 3.5.8, S 48.12*; art, heart *LC 144*; heart *AY 3.2.143, CE 3.1.28, 3.2.61, JC 5.3.89, LLL 4.1.32, 5.2.150, 336, Luc 294, 1135, 1830, MND 3.2.165, PP 20.54, R2 5.1.95, 97, RJ 1.2.17, 2.3.21, S 23.2, 46.12, 46.13, 47.8, 53.13, 62.2, 113.7, 122.7, 132.12, VA 892*; mart *TS 2.1.319*; **rh** *2* desert *S 49.12* / **rh** *1* hearts *AW 5.3.336, AY 3.2.145, MND 3.2.153, S 31.3, TS 5.2.167*; **rh** *2* deserts *S 17.4*

**part / ~est / ~s / ~ing / ~ed** *v*
pɑ:ɹt / -s, -st / -s / 'pɑ:ɹt·ɪn, -ɪŋ / -ɪd
**sp** part[98] / par'tst[1] / parts[5] / parting[7] / parted[41]
**rh** *1* heart *AY 5.4.128, LLL 5.2.57, 806, MV 2.7.77, R2 5.1.81, VA 421*; **rh** *2* short *LLL 5.2.57, R2 2.1.222*
> a-, depart, im-part

**partake / ~n** *v*
pɑ:ɹ'tɛ:k / -ən
**sp** partake[7] / pertaken[1]
**rh** sake *S 149.2*

**partaker / ~s** *n*
pɑ:ɹ'tɛ:kəɹ / -z
**sp** partaker[3], partakers[1]

**part-created** *adj*
'pɑ:ɹt-kri:'ɛ:tɪd
**sp** part-created[1]
> create

**parted** *adj*
'pɑ:ɹtɪd
**sp** parted[1]
> long-, over-, peace-, timely-parted

**Parthia** *n*
'pɑ:ɹtɪə, -θɪ-
**sp** Parthia[6], Parthya[1]

**Parthian** *adj*
'pɑ:ɹtɪən, -θɪ-
**sp** Parthian[3]

**Parthian / ~s** *n*
'pɑ:ɹtɪən, -θɪ- / -z
**sp** Parthian[1], Parthians[1]

**partial** *adj*
'pɑ:ɹsɪɑl
**sp** partiall[6]
> im-, un-partial

**partialize** *v*
*m* 'pɑ:ɹsɪɑˌləɪz
**sp** partialize[1]

**partially** *adv*
'pɑ:ɹsɪɑləɪ
**sp** partially[1]

**participate** *v*
pɑ:ɹ'tɪsɪˌpɛ:t
**sp** participate[2]

**participation** *n*
pɑ:ɹˌtɪsɪ'pɛ:sɪən
**sp** participation[2]

**particle** *n*
'pɑ:ɹtɪkəl
**sp** particle[2]

**parti-coated** *adj*
'pɑ:ɹtəɪ-ˌko:tɪd
**sp** partie-coated[1]
> coat

**parti-coloured** *adj*
'pɑ:ɹtəɪ-ˌkɤləɹd
**sp** party-colour'd[1]
> colour

**particular** *adj*
pɑ:ɹ'tɪkləɹ, -kjəl-
**sp** particular[34], par-ticular[1], particuler[1], perticular[1]

**particular / ~s** *n*
pɑ:ɹ'tɪkləɹ, -kjəl- / -z
**sp** particular[14] / particulars[10]

**particularit·y / ~ies** *n*
*m* pɑ:ɹˌtɪkjə'larɪˌtəɪz, -ɪt-
**sp** particularities[1], particula-rities[1]

**particularize** *v*
pɑ:ɹ'tɪkjələɹəɪz
**sp** particularize[1]

**particularly** *adv*
*m* pɑ:ɹ'tɪkjəɹləɪ
**sp** particularly[2]

**parting** *adj / n*
'pɑ:ɹtɪn, -ɪŋ
**sp** parting[4] / parting[17]

**partisan / ~s** *n*
*m* 'pɑ:ɹtɪˌzan, -ɪzən / -z
**sp** partizan[2] / partisons[1], partizans[2]

**partition** *n*
*m* pɑ:ɹ'tɪsɪən, -ɪˌɒn
**sp** partition[4]

**Partlet** *n*
'pɑ:ɹtlət
**sp** Partlet[2]

**partly** *adv*
'pɑ:ɹtləɪ
**sp** partely[1], partlie[1], partly[32]

**partner / ~s** *n*
'pɑ:ɹtnəɹ / -z

**sp** partner[15], partner's [partner is][1] / partners[6]
> co-partner, fellow-partner

**partner / ~ed** *v*
'pɑːɹtnəɹ / -d
**sp** partner'd[1]

**partridge** *adj / n*
'pɑːɹtrɪdʒ
**sp** par-tridge[1] / partridge[1]

**part·y / ~ies** *n*
'pɑːɹtəɪ / -z
**sp** partie[21], par-tie[1], party[22] / parties[15]

**party-verdict** *n*
'pɑːɹtəɪ-ˌvɐːɹdɪkt
**sp** party-verdict[1]
> verdict

**pas** *Fr adv*
pa
**sp** pas[1], *emend of H5 3.4.38*

**pash** *n / v*
=
**sp** pash[1] / pash[1]

**pashed** *adj*
*m* 'paʃɪd
**sp** pashed[1]

**pass** *n*
pas / 'pas·ɪz
**sp** passe[11] / passes[3]
**rh** ass *CE 3.1.17*

**pass / ~es / ~eth / ~ing / ~ed** *v*
pas / 'pas·ɪz / -əθ / -ɪn, -ɪŋ / -*m* ɪd, past
**sp** passe[126] / passes[7] / passeth[2] / passing[9] / pass'd[6], passed[1], past[31]
**rh** *1* ass *AW 4.3.325, AY 2.5.47, MND 3.2.33, 4.1.77*; glass *AW 2.1.166, Per 2.3.35, R3 1.2.263, VA 982*; lass *AY 5.3.17*; **rh** *2* was *Ham 2.2.417, S 49.5, WT 4.1.9* / glassed *LLL 2.1.231*
> re-pass

**passable** *adj*
'pasəbəl
**sp** passable[2]

**passado** *n*
pa'sɑːdoː
**sp** passado[3]

**passage / ~s** *n*
=
**sp** passage[32], pas-sage[1] / passages[8]

**passant** *adv*
'pasənt
**sp** passant[1]

**passed** *adj*
*m* 'pasɪd
**sp** passed[2]

**passenger / ~s** *n*
'pasɪndʒəɹ / -z
**sp** passenger[2] / passengers[4]

**passing** *adj / adv*
'pasɪn, -ɪŋ
**sp** passing[3] / passing[23]

**passio** *Lat n*
'pasɪoː
**sp** passio[1]

**passion / ~'s / ~s** *n*
'pasɪən / -z
**sp** passion[98], pas-sion[2], passi-on[1] / passions[1] / passions[13], passi-ons[1]
**rh** affection *TS 3.1.72*; fashion *AY 2.4.55, LLL 4.3.138, Luc 1317, S 20.2*

**passion / ~s / ~ing** *v*
'pasɪən / -z / -ɪn, -ɪŋ
**sp** passion[1] / passions[1] / passioning[1]

**passionate** *adj*
*m* 'pasɪənət, -ˌnɛːt
**sp** passionate[9]

**passive** *adj*
=
**sp** passiue[1]

**passport** *n*
'paspɔːɹt
**sp** pasport[2]

**passy-measures** *adj*
'pasəɪ-ˌmezəɹz
**sp** passy measures[1]
> measure

**past** *adj / adv / n / prep*
past
**sp** past[16], past-[euills][1] / past[44] / past[3] / past[78]
**rh** *adj* waste *S 30.2* / **rh** *1 adv* fast *Luc 1671*; last *R2 2.1.14*; **rh** *2 adv* haste *Luc 1671* / *n* haste *S 123.10*
> fore-, overpass; pass

**past-cure** *adj*
'past-ˌkjuːɹ
**sp** past-cure[1]
> cure

**paste** *n*
past
**sp** paste[5]

**pastime / ~s** *n*
'pastəɪm / -z
**sp** pastime[13], pa-stime[1] / pastimes[2]

**pastor / ~'s** *n*
'pastəɹ / -z
**sp** pastors[1] / pastors[1]

**pastoral / ~s** *n*
'pastərɑl / -z
**sp** pastorall[1], [pastoricall-comicall-historicall]-pastorall[1], [tragicall-comicall-historicall]-pastorall[1] / [Whitson]-pastorals[1]

**pastorical** *n*
pas'tɒrɪkɑl
**sp** pastoricall-[comicall-historicall-pastorall][1]

**pastry** *n*
'pastrəɪ
**sp** pastrie[1]

**past-saving** *adj*
'past-ˌsɛ:vɪn, -ɪŋ
**sp** past-sauing[1]
> save

**pasture** *n*
'pastəɹ
**sp** pastour[1], pasture[11]
> repasture

**past·y / ~ies** *n*
'pastəɪ / -z
**sp** pasty[2] / pasties[1]

**pat** *adv*
=
**sp** pat[6]

**patch / ~es** *n*
=
**sp** patch[8] / patches[5]
**rh** hatch *CE 3.1.32*

**patch / ~ed** *v*
=
**sp** patch[4] / patch'd[3], patcht[4]

**patched** *adj*
=
**sp** patch'd[1]

**patchery** *n*
'paʧrəɪ, -ʧər-
**sp** patcherie[1], patchery[1]

**pate / ~s** *n*
pɛ:t / -s
**sp** pate[30] / pates[3]
**rh** gate *CE 3.1.74, TS 1.2.12*; gate, late *CE 2.2.228*
> bald-, curled-, smooth-pate; knot-, periwig-, russet-pated

**paten /~s** *n*
=
**sp** pattens[1]

**patent / ~s** *n*
'patənt / -s
**sp** patent[1], pattent[2] / patents[3]

**pat·er / ~rum** *Lat n*
'patrʊm
**sp** patrum[1]

**paternal** *adj*
pə'tɐ:ɹnɑl
**sp** paternall[1]

**path / ~s** *n*
paθ / -s
**sp** path[8] / pathes[3], paths[3]
> by-, foot-path; unpathed

**path** *v*
paθ
**sp** path[1]

**pathetical** *adj*
pə'θetɪkɑl
**sp** patheticall[3]

**pathway / ~s** *n*
'paθwɛ: / -z
**sp** pathway[2] / path-wayes[1]
> way

**patience** *n*
'pɛ:sɪəns
**sp** pacience[1], patience[178], patie[n]ce[1], pa-tience[1], pati-ence[2]
> impatience

**patient** *adj*
'pɛ:sɪənt
**sp** patient[84] pa-tient[1]

**patient / ~'s / ~s** *n*
'pɛ:sɪənts
**sp** patients[3] / patients[1]

**patiently** *adv*
*m* 'pɛ:sɪənt,ləɪ
**sp** patientlie[1], patiently[16]
**rh** *1* clemency, tragedy *Ham 3.2.160*;
**rh** *2* cry *Luc 1641*

**patrician / ~s** *n*
pə'trɪsɪən / -z
**sp** patritian[1] / patricians[15], patri-cians[1]

**Patrick / ~'s** *n*
=
**sp** Patricke[1] / Patrickes[1], Patricks[2]

**patrimony** *n*
'patrɪˌmʏnəɪ
**sp** patrimonie[2], patrimony[2]

**Patroclus** *n*
pə'trɒkləs
**sp** Patroclus[30], Pa-troclus[1], Patro-clus[1]

**patron / ~s** *n*
'patrən / -z
**sp** patron[8], patrone[1] / patrons[1]

**patronage** *v*
*m* 'patrəˌnɑ:ʤ
**sp** patronage[2]

**patroness** *n*
*m* 'patrəˌnes
**sp** patronesse[1], patronnesse[1]

**patrum** *Lat*
> pater

**pattern / ~s** *n*
'patəɹn / -z
**sp** patterne[10] / patternes[2]

**pattern / ~ed** *v*
'patəɹn / -d
**sp** patterne[2] / patern'd[1]

**pauca / ~s** *Lat adj, n*
'pɔ:ka / -s
**sp** pauca[6] / pau-cas[1]

**Paul / ~'s** *n*
=
**sp** Paul[5] / Paules[3], Poules[1], Powles[1]

**Paulina / ~'s** *n*
pɒ'ləɪnə / -z
**sp** Paulina[21] / Paulina's[1]

**paunch / ~es** *n*
=
**sp** paunch[2] / paunches[1]

**paunch** *v*
=
**sp** paunch[1]

**pause / ~s** *n*
=
**sp** pause[8], pawse[5] / pawses[1]
**rh** cause *VA 218*; claws, laws *Luc 541*

**pause** *v*
=
**sp** pause[20], pawse[5]
**rh** cause *CE 2.1.32*; laws *R2 2.3.167*

**pauser** *n*
'pɔ:zəɹ
**sp** pawser[1]

**pausingly** *adv*
*m* 'pɔ:zɪn,ləɪ, -ɪŋ-
**sp** pausingly[1]

**pauvre** *Fr adj*
'po:vrə
**sp** pouure[1]

**pave / ~d** *v*
*m* pɛ:vd, pɛ:vɪd
**sp** pau'd[1], paued[2]

**paved** *adj*
pɛ:vɪd
**sp** paued[2]
> unpaved

**pavement** *n*
'pɛ:vmənt
**sp** pauement[2]

**pavilion / ~s** *n*
*m* pə'vɪlɪən, -lɪ,ɒn / pə'vɪlɪənz
**sp** pauilion[1], pauillion[5] / pauillions[1]
**rh** anon *H5 4.1.27*, Ilion *LLL*

**pavilion / ~ed** *v*
pə'vɪlɪənd
**sp** pauillion'd[1]

**pavin** *n*
=
**sp** pauyn[1]

**paw / ~s** *n*
=
**sp** paw[3] / pawes[2]
**rh** jaws *S 19.1*

**pawn / ~s** *n*
=
**sp** paune[1], pawne[8] / pawnes[1]

**pawn / ~ed** *v*
=
**sp** pawne[17] / paund[1], pawn'd[8]

**pax** *n*
=
**sp** pax[2]

**pay** *n*
pɛ:
**sp** pay[14]
**rh** day *3H6 4.7.87*; way *VA 89*

**pay / ~est / ~s / ~ing / paid** *v*
pɛ: / -st / -z / 'pɛ:ɪn, -ɪŋ / pɛ:d
**sp** pay[119], pay't [pay it][1] / paiest[1] / paies[4], payes[20] / paying[6] / paid[34], paide[4], paied[2], payd[4], pay'd[8], payde[2], payed[8]
**rh** day *AW 5.3.334*; say *Mac 1.4.22, 4.1.131, S 79.14*; stay *MND 3.2.86* / weighing *MM 3.2.253* / maid *AW 2.1.146, Tem 4.1.96*
> over-, re-, un-pay; well-paid

**payment / ~s** *n*
'pɛ:mənt / -s
**sp** paiment[4], payment[9], pay-ment[1] / payments[1]

**paysan / ~s** *Fr n*
pei'zɑ̃
**sp** pesant[1] / peasauns[1]

**pea / ~s** *n*
=
**sp** pease[4]
**rh** leas *Tem 4.1.61*; please *LLL 5.2.315*

**peace / ~s** *n*
pi:s, pɛ:s / 'pi:sɪz, 'pɛ:s-
**sp** peace[528] / peaces[1]
**rh** *1* cease *Cym 5.5.486*; increase *R3 5.5.39*; release *MND 3.2.377*; **rh** *2* bless *MND 5.1.408*
**pun** *KJ 4.3.93* piece

**peace** *v*
pi:s, pɛ:s
**sp** *Caius* peace-[a-your][1]

**peaceable** *adj*
'pi:səbəl, 'pɛ:s-
**sp** peaceable[1]
> unpeaceable

**peaceably** *adv*
'pi:səbləɪ, 'pɛ:s-
**sp** peacea-blie[1], peaceably[1]

**peaceful** *adj*
'pi:sfʊl, 'pɛ:s-
**sp** peacefull[11]

**peace-maker / ~s** *n*
'pi:s-,mɛ:kəɹ, 'pɛ:s- / -z
**sp** peace-maker[1] / peace-makers[2]
> make

**peace-parted** *adj*
*m* ,pi:s-'pɑ:ɹtɪd, ,pɛ:s-
**sp** peace-parted[1]
> part

**peach / ~es** *v*
=
**sp** peach[1] / peaches[1]

**peach-coloured** *adj*
'pi:ʧ-,kɤləɹd
**sp** peach-colour'd[2]
> colour

**peacock / ~'s / ~s** *n*
=
**sp** peacock[2], pea-cocke[1] / peacocks[1] / peacocks[1]
> cock

**peak / ~ing** *v*
= / 'pi:kɪn, -ɪŋ
**sp** peake[2] / peaking[1]

**peal / ~s** *n*
=
**sp** peale[7] / peales[1]

**pear / ~s** *n*
pɛ:ɹ / -z
**sp** peare[3], [dride]-peare[1] / peares[1]
**rh** were *RJ 2.1.38*

**pearl / ~s** *n*
pɐːɹl / -z
**sp** pearle[23], [saphire]-pearle[1] / pearles[9], pearls[1]

**peasant** *adj*
=
**sp** peasant[1], peasant-[townes][1], pesant[3]

**peasant / ~s** *n*
=
**sp** peasant[1], peazant[1], pesant[6], pezant[9] / peazants[1], pesants[1], pezants[5]

**Peaseblossom** *n*
=
**sp** Peaseblossome[1], Pease-blossome[4], Pease Blossome[1],
> blossom

**peasecod** *n*
'peskəd, 'piːz-
**sp** peascod[1], pescod[2]

**Peasecod** [name] *n*
'peskəd, 'piːz-
**sp** Peascod[1]

**peasecod-time** *n*
'peskəd-ˌtəɪm, 'piːz-
**sp** pescod-time[1]
> time

**peat** *n*
pɛːt
**sp** peate[1]

**pebble** *adj*
=, 'pɪbəl
**sp** peeble[1], pibble[1]

**pebble / ~s** *n*
=, 'pɪbəl / -z
**sp** pebble[1], peeble[1] / peebles[1], pibbles[1]

**peck** *n*
=
**sp** pecke[2]

**peck / ~ed** *v*
=
**sp** peck[1], pecke[10] / peckt[1]

**Pecke** [name] *n*
=
**sp** Pecke[2]

**peculiar** *adj*
pɪ'kjulɪəɹ
**sp** peculiar[8]

**pecus** *Lat n*
'pekʊs
**sp** *emend of LLL 4.2.92* pecas[1]

**pedant** *n*
=
**sp** pedant[18]

**pedantical** *adj*
*m* pe'dantɪˌkɑl
**sp** pedanticall[1]

**pedascule** *n*
pe'daskjʊˌliː
**sp** pedascule[1]

**pedigree** *n*
=
**sp** pedigree[4]
**rh** he *1H6 2.5.77*

**pedlar / ~'s / ~s** *n*
'pedləɹ / -z
**sp** pedler[6] / pedlers[4] / pedlers[4]
**rh** meddler *WT 4.4.319*

**Pedro** *n*
'pedroː
**sp** Pedro[7]

**peel** *v*
=
**sp** pil'd[1]

**peeled** *adj*
=
**sp** piel'd[1]

**peep / ~s / ~ing / ~ed** *v*
piːp / -s / 'piːpɪn, -ɪŋ / piːpt
**sp** peepe[15] / peepes[3] / peeping[2] / peep'd[1], pee-ped[1]
**rh** creep, sleep *Luc 1251*; sleep *MND 4.1.83*; weep *VA 1088* / sleeping, weeping *Luc 1089*
> bo-, under-peep

**peer / ~s** *n*
piːɹ / -z
**sp** peere[11] / peeres[36], [hart-sorowing]-peeres[1]
**rh** *1* dear *Oth 2.3.84, R2 5.5.67*; **rh** *2* heir *Per Prol.21* / tears [cry] *H5 4.2.12*; years *R2 1.3.93*

**peer** *v*
piːɹ / -z / 'piːr·əθ / -ɪn, -ɪŋ / piːɹd
**sp** peere[3], peere-[out][2] / peers[1] / peereth[1] / peering[4] / peer'd[1]
**rh** year *WT 4.3.1*
> out-, over-peer; highest-, still-peering

**peerless** *adj*
'piːɹləs
**sp** peerelesse[5], peerlesse[1]

**peevish** *adj*
=
**sp** peeuish[28]

**peevishly** *adv*
'piːvɪʃləɪ
**sp** peeuishly[1]

**peg / ~s** *n*
=
**sp** peggs[1]

**peg** *v*
=
**sp** peg-[thee][1]
unpeg

**Peg-a-Ramsey** *n*
'peg-ə-'ramzəɪ
**sp** Peg-a-ramsie[1]

**Pegasus** *n*
*m* 'pegəˌsɤs, -əsəs
**sp** Pegasus[3]

**peize / ~d** *v*
pɛːz / *m* 'pɛːzɪd
**sp** peize[2] / peysed[1]

**pelf** *n*
=
**sp** pelfe[1]

**rh** himself *Per 2.Chorus.35*; myself *PP 14.12, Tim 1.2.61*

**pelican** *adj*
=
**sp** pelicane[1], pellican[1]

**Pelion** *n*
'pi:lɪən
**sp** Pelion[2]

**Pella** *n*
'pelə
**sp** Pella[1]

**pelleted** *adj*
=
**sp** pelleted[1]

**pell-mell** *adv*
=
**sp** pell-mell[3]; pell, mell[1]; pell mell[1]
**rh** hell *KJ 2.1.406, R3 5.3.313*

**Peloponnesus** *n*
ˌpeləpə'ni:səs
**sp** Peloponnesus[1]

**pelt** *v*
=
**sp** pelt[2]

**pelting** *adj / n*
'peltɪn, -ɪŋ
**sp** pelting[4] / pelting[1]

**Pembroke** *n*
'pembrʊk
**sp** Pembroke[9], Pem-broke[1], Pembrooke[5], Penbroke[2], Penbrooke[1], *abbr in s.d.* Pem[1]

**pen / ~s** *n*
=
**sp** pen[24], penne / pennes[1], pens[1]
**rh** again *S 79.6*; Amen *S 85.8*; men *H5 Epil.1, Luc 1289, S 16.10, 19.10, 32.6, 81.13*; then *MV 5.1.237*; when *Per 4.Chorus.28*
> goose-pen

**pen / ~s / ~ned** *v*
=
**sp** pen[3] / pennes[1] / pend[1]
> penned *adj*

**penalt·y / ~ies** *n*
*m* 'penəlˌtəɪ, -lt- / 'penəlˌtəɪz
**sp** penaltie[7], penalty[4] / penalties[3]
**rh** gentility *LLL 1.1.126*

**penance** *n*
=
**sp** penance[8], pennance[10]

**pence** *n*
=
**sp** pence[9], [three]pence[1], [three]-pence[1], [twelve]-pence[1], *abbr* d.[5]
> half-, six-, two-pence; penny

**pencil / ~s** *n*
=
**sp** pencill[1], pensill[1] / pensals[1]

**pencilled** *adj*
=
**sp** pensil'd[1]

**pendent** *adj*
=
**sp** pendant[4], [ribonds]-pendant[1]

**Pendragon** *n*
pen'dragən
**sp** Pendragon[1]

**pendulous** *adj*
'pendləs, -djəl-
**sp** pendulous[1]

**pene** *Lat adv*
'pene
**sp** pine[1]

**Penelope** *n*
=
**sp** Penelope[1]

**penetrable** *adj*
*m* 'penəˌtrabəl
**sp** penetrable[2]

**penetrate** *v*
'penəˌtrɛ:t
**sp** penetrate[4], pene-trate[1]

**penetrative** *adj*
'penəˌtratɪv
**sp** penetratiue[1]

**penitence** *n*
*m* 'penɪˌtens, -təns
**sp** penitence[6]

**penitent / ~s** *n*
*m* 'penɪˌtent, -tənt / 'penɪˌtents
**sp** penitent[14] / penitents[1]

**penitential** *adj*
ˌpenɪ'tensɪəl
**sp** penitentiall[1]

**penitently** *adv*
'penɪtəntləɪ
**sp** penitently[1]

**Penker** *n*
'peŋkəɹ
**sp** Penker[1]

**pen-knife** *n*
'penˌnəɪf, -ˌkn-
**sp** pen-knife[1]
> knife

**penned** *adj*
=
**sp** pen'd[3], penn'd[1]
**rh** end, friend *LLL 5.2.402*
> pen

**penner** *TNK* *n*
'penəɹ
**sp** penner[1]
**rh** tenor *TNK 3.5.123*

**penning** *n*
'penɪn, -ɪŋ
**sp** penning[1]

**pennon / ~s** *n*
=
**sp** penons[1]

**penny** *adj / n*
'penəɪ
**sp** penny[3] / penie[1], penny[8], penny-[cord][1], peny[7], *abbr* d[1]
**rh** many *TS 3.2.80*
> half-, eight-, six-penny; pence

**pennyworth / ~s** *n*
*m* 'penɪˌwɔːɹθ, 'penəɹθ / -s
**sp** peniworth[1], pennie-worth[1], penny-worth[3], penny worth[1], penyworth[1], peny-worth[1] / peniworths[1], penyworths[1]

**penser / pense** *Fr v*
pɑ̃s
**sp** [mal-y]-pence[1], pense[5]

**pension** *n*
'pensɪən
**sp** pension[2], pensi-on[1]

**pensioner / ~s** *n*
'pensɪənəɹ / -z
**sp** pensioners[1], pentioners[1]

**pensive** *adj*
=
**sp** pensiue[2]

**pensively** *adv*
'pensɪvləɪ
**sp** pensiuely[1]

**pent** *adj / v*
=
**sp** pent[2] / pent[4]

**Pentapolis** *Per* *n*
pen'tapəˌlɪs
**sp** Pantapoles[1], Penlapolis[1], Pentapolis[3]
**rh** this *Per 3.Chorus.34*

**Pentecost** *n*
=
**sp** Pentecost[2], Pentycost[1]

**Penthesilea** *n*
ˌpentɪsɪ'lɛːə
**sp** Penthisilea[1]

**penthouse** *adj / n*
'pentəʊs, -həʊs
**sp** pent-house[1] / penthouse[2]
> house

**penthouse-like** *adj*
'pentəʊs-ˌləɪk, -həʊs-
**sp** penthouse-like[1]

**pent-up** *adj*
'pent-ˌɤp
**sp** pent-vp[2]

**penurious** *adj*
pen'juːrɪəs
**sp** penurious[1]

**penury** *n*
*m* 'penjərəɪ, -ˌrəɪ
**sp** penurie[2], penury[3]

**people / ~'s** *n*
=
**sp** people[188], peo-ple[4] / peoples[19]

**people / ~s / ~d** *v*
=
**sp** people[1] / peoples[1] / peopel'd[1], peopled[2]
> unpeople

**peopled** *adj*
=
**sp** peopled[2]

**Pepin / ~'s** *n*
'pepɪn / -z
**sp** Pepin[2], Pippen[1], Pippin[1] / Pepins[1]

**pepper** *adj / n*
'pepəɹ
**sp** pepper[1] / pepper[1]

**pepper / ~ed** *v*
'pepəɹd
**sp** pepper'd[3]

**pepperbox** *n*
'pepəɹˌbɒks
**sp** pepper-boxe[1]

**peppercorn** *n*
'pepəɹˌkɔːɹn
**sp** pepper-corne[1]

**per** *Lat prep*
peɹ
**sp** per[2]
> per se

**peradventure / ~s** *adv*
ˌperəd'ventəɹ / -z
**sp** peraduenture[11], per-aduenture[4] / perad-uentures[1]

**perceive / ~s / ~th / ~d** *v*
pəɹ'siːv / -z / -əθ / -d
**sp** perceiue[87], perceiue's [perceive his][1], perceiue't [perceive it][1], perceiu't [perceive it][1], perceyue[1] / perceiues[3] / perceiueth[1] / perceiued[4], perceiu'd[9]
**rh** leave *TNK Prol.31* / deceived *S 104.10*

**perch / ~ed** *v*
pɐːɹʧ / -t
**sp** pearch[2] / pearch'd[1]
**rh** *n* search *Per 3.Chorus.15*
> overperch

**perchance** *adv*
pəɹ'ʧans
**sp** perchance[48], per-chance[1]
> chance

**percussion** *n*
pəɹ'kɤsɪən
**sp** percussion[1]

**Percy / ~'s / ~s** *n*
'pɛːɹsəɪ / -z
**sp** Percie[18], Percies [Percy is][1], Percy[37], Per-cy[1] / Percies[7], Percyes[1] / Percies[1]
**pun** *1H4 5.3.56* pierce

**Perdita** *n*
*m* 'pɐːɹdɪˌta, -ɪtə
**sp** Perdita[12]

**perdition** *n*
pəɹ'dɪsɪən
**sp** perdition[9]

**perdonato** *Ital v*
ˌpɑːɹdə'nɑːtoː
**sp** pardonato[1]

**perdre / perdu** *Fr v*
pɛɹ'dy
**sp** perdia[1], perdie[1]

**perdurable** *adj*
*m* 'pɐːɹdjəˌrabəl
**sp** perdurable[2]

**perdurably** *adv*
*m* 'pɐːɹdjəˌrabləɪ
**sp** perdurablie[1]

**perdy** *interj*
pəɹ'diː, -'dəɪ
**sp** perdie[4], perdy[1]
**rh** *1* comedy *Ham 3.2.302*; **rh** *2* fly *KL 2.4.81*

**père** *Fr n*
pɛːɹ
**sp** pere[1]

**Peregenia** *n*
ˌperɪ'dʒenɪə
**sp** Peregenia[1]

**peregrinate** *adj*
'perɪgrɪnət
**sp** pere-grinat[1]

**peremptorily** *adv*
pə'remtəɹləɪ, -mpt-
**sp** peremptorily[1]

**peremptory** *adj*
*m* 'perəmˌtɒrəɪ, -mtərəɪ, -mtrəɪ, pə'remtrəɪ, -təˌr-, -mpt-
**sp** peremptorie[7], peremptory[5]

**perfect / ~er / ~est** *adj*
'pɐːɹfɪt / -əɹ / -st
**sp** perfect[45], per-fect[3], perfit[2] / perfecter[1] / perfectest[1], perfect'st[1]
> imperfect

**perfect / ~ed** *v*
'pɐːɹfɪt / -ɪd
**sp** perfect[3] / perfected[3]

**perfection / ~s** *n*
*m* pəɹ'feksɪən, -sɪˌɒn / -z
**sp** perfection[22], per-fection[1] / perfections[7]

**perfectly** *adv*
*m* 'pɐːɹfɪtˌləɪ
**sp** perfectly[3], perfitly[1]

**perfectness** *n*
*m* 'pɐːɹfɪtˌnes
**sp** perfectnesse[2]
> unperfectness

**perfidious** *adj*
*m* pəɹ'fɪdɪəs, -ɪˌɤs
**sp** perfidious[4]

**perfidiously** *adv*
*m* pəɹ'fɪdɪəsˌləɪ
**sp** perfidiously[1]

**perforce** *adv*
pəɹ'fɔːɹs
**sp** perforce[44]

**perform / ~s / ~ed** *v*
pəɹ'fɔːɹm / -z / *m* -d, -ɪd
**sp** performe[38], perform't [perform it][2] / performes[2] / performd[1], perform'd[33], performed[3]
**rh** storm *Per 3.Chorus.54* / adjourned, turned *Cym 5.4.76*

**performance / -s** *n*
pəɹ'fɔːɹməns / -ɪz
**sp** performance[16] / performances[2]
> non-performance

**performer / ~s** *n*
pəɹ'fɔːɹməɹ / -z
**sp** perfor-mer[1] / performers[2]

**performing** *n*
pəɹ'fɔːɹmɪn, -ɪŋ
**sp** perfor-ming[1]
> love-performing

**perfume / ~s** *n*
*m* 'pɐːɹfjəm, pəɹ'fjuːm / -z
**sp** perfume[8] / perfumes[2], per-fumes[1]

**perfume / ~s / ~d** *v*
pəɹ'fjuːm / -z / *m* -d, -ɪd
**sp** perfume[2] / perfumes[2] / perfum'd[2], perfumed[2]

**perfumed** *adj*
'pɐːɹfjəmd
**sp** perfum'd[2]

**perfumer** *n*
'pɐːɹfjəməɹ
**sp** perfumer[1]

**perg·o / ~e** *Lat v*
'pɛɹge
**sp** perge[2]

**perhaps** *adv*
pəɹ'aps, -'haps
**sp** perhappes[2], perhaps[41]
**rh** statute-caps *LLL 5.2.279*

**periapt / ~s** *n*
'perɪˌapts
**sp** periapts[1]

**Pericles** *n*
'perɪkliːz
**sp** Pericles[60]
**rh** appease [*emend of* oppress] *Per 3.Chorus.30*; seas *Per 4.4.9*

**Perigort** *n*
'perɪˌgɔːɹt
**sp** Perigort[1]

**peril / ~s** *n*
=
**sp** perill[42], perrill[1] / perilles[1], perils[5]
> apperil

**perilous** *adj*
*m* 'pɛːɹləs, 'perɪləs, -ˌlɤs
**sp** perillous[11], perilous[2]

**period / ~s** *n*
'perɪəd / -z
**sp** period[13] / periods[1]

**period / ~s** *v*
'perɪədz
**sp** periods[1]

**perish / ~est / ~eth / ~ing / ~ed** *v*
= / 'perɪʃ·əst / -əθ / -ɪn, -ɪŋ / 'perɪʃt
**sp** perish[29] / perishest[1] / perisheth[1] / perishing[1] / perishd[1], perish'd[2]
**rh** cherish *Luc 1547, S 11.10*

**perished** *adj*
=
**sp** perished[1]

**perishing** *adj*
'perɪʃɪn, -ɪŋ
**sp** perishing[1]

**periwig** *n*
=
**sp** perewig[1], perrywig[1]

**periwig-pated** *adj*
'perɪwɪg-ˌpɛ:tɪd
**sp** pery-wig-pated[1]
> pate

**perjure** *n*
'pɐ:ɹʤəɹ
**sp** periure[1]

**perjure / ~d** *v*
'pɐ:ɹʤəɹ / -d
**sp** periure[1] / periur'd[4], periurde[1], periured[1]

**perjured** *adj*
'pɐ:ɹʤəɹd
**sp** periur'd[20]

**perjur·y / ~ies** *n*
*m* 'pɐ:ɹʤəˌrəɪ, -ʤər-, -ʤr- / 'pɐ:ɹʤəˌrəɪz
**sp** periurie[12], periury[8] / periuries[1]
**rh** *1* me, Muscovy *LLL 5.2.394*; **rh** *2* eye *LLL 4.3.60, PP 3.3*

**perk / ~ed** *v*
pɐ:ɹkt
**sp** perk'd[1]

**Perkes** [name] *n*
pɐ:ɹks
**sp** Perkes[1]

**permafoy** [*Pistol Fr*] *interj*
ˌpɐ:ɹma'fwɛ, -'fəɪ
**sp** permafoy[1]

**permanent** *adj*
'pɐ:ɹmənənt
**sp** permanent[1]

**permission** *n*
*m* pəɹ'mɪsɪən, -sɪˌɒn
**sp** permission[4]

**permissive** *adj*
pəɹ'mɪsɪv
**sp** permissiue[1]

**permit / ~ted** *v*
pəɹ'mɪt / -ɪd
**sp** permit[12] / permitted[2]

**pernicious** *adj*
*m* pəɹ'nɪsɪəs, -ɪˌɤs
**sp** pernicious[12], pernitious[10]

**perniciously** *adv*
*m* pəɹ'nɪsɪəsˌləɪ
**sp** perniciously[1]

**peroration** *n*
ˌperə'rɛ:sɪən
**sp** *2H6 1.1.103 emend of* preroration[1]

**perpend** *v*
pəɹ'pend
**sp** perpend[4], per-pend[1]

**perpendicular** *adj*
ˌpɐ:ɹpən'dɪkjələɹ
**sp** perpendicular[1]

**perpendicularly** *adv*
ˌpɐ:ɹpən'dɪkjəˌlɐ:ɹləɪ
**sp** perpendicularly[1]

**perpetual** *adv*
*m* pəɹ'petjal, -jʊal, -jʊˌɑ:l
**sp** perpetuall[19]
**rh** thrall, wall *Luc 726*; thrall *S 154.10*

**perpetually** *adv*
*m* pəɹ'petjaˌləɪ, -jʊa-
**sp** perpetually[1], perpe-tually[1]
**rh** purify *Luc 686*

**perpetuity** *n*
*m* ˌpɐ:ɹpɪ'tju:ɪˌtəɪ
**sp** perpetuitie[2], perpetuity[1]
**rh** tyranny *1H6 4.7.20*

**perplex** *v*
pəɹ'pleks
**sp** perplex[1]

**perplexed** *adj*
*m* pəɹ'plekst, -sɪd
**sp** perplexed[2], perplex'd[1], perplext[3]

**perplexity** *n*
*m* pəɹ'pleksɪtəɪ, -ˌtəɪ
**sp** perplexitie[3]

**per se** *Lat adj*
ˌpɐ:ɹ 'se
**sp** per se
> per

**persecute / ~d** *v*
'pɐ:ɹsɪkju:tɪd
**sp** persecuted[1]

**persecution / ~s** *n*
ˌpɐ:ɹsɪ'kju:sɪənz
**sp** persecutions[1]

**persecutor** *n*
'pɐ:ɹsɪkju:təɹ
**sp** persecutor[1]

**Perseus / ~'** *n*
'pɐ:ɹsɪəs
**sp** Perseus[2] / Perseus[1]

**persever / ~s** *v*
pəɹ'sevəɹ / -z
**sp** perseuer[8] / perseuers[1]
**rh** ever *AW 4.2.37*

**perseverance** *n*
*m* pəɹ'sevrəns, -vər-
**sp** perseuerance[2]

**Persia** *n*
'pɐ:ɹsɪə
**sp** Persia[1]

**Persian** *adj*
'pɐ:ɹsɪən
**sp** Persian[2]

**persist / ~s** *v*
pəɹ'sɪst / -s
**sp** persist[1] / persists[1]

**persisted** *adj*
pəɹ'sɪstɪd
**sp** persisted[1]

**persistency** *n*
pəɹ'sɪstənsəɪ
**sp** persistencie[1]

**persistive** *adj*
pəɹ'sɪstɪv
**sp** persistiue[1]

**person / ~'s / ~s** *n*
'pɐ:ɹsən / -z
**sp** person[142], per-son[1], person's [person is][1] / persons[3] / persons[18]

**personage /~s** *n*
*m* ˌpɐ:ɹsə'nɑ:ʤ, -s'n- / -ɪz
**sp** personage[3] / personages[2]

**personal** *adj*
'pɐ:ɹsnɑl, -sən-
**sp** personal[1], personall[9], perso-nall[1]

**personally** *adv*
*m* 'pɐ:ɹsnɑˌləɪ
**sp** personally[3]

**personate / ~s / ~d** *v*
*m* 'pɐ:ɹsnɛ:t, -sən- / pəɹ'sɒnɛ:ts / 'pɐ:ɹsnɛ:tɪd, -sən-
**sp** personate[1] / personates[1] / personated[1]

**personating** *n*
*m* ˌpɐ:ɹsə'nɛ:tɪn, -ɪŋ
**sp** personating[1]

**perspective / ~s** *adj*
*m* ˌpɐ:ɹspek'tɪv / -z
**sp** perspectiue[2] / perspectiues[1]

**perspectively** *adv*
*m* ˌpɐ:ɹspek'tɪvləɪ
**sp** perspec-tiuely[1]

**perspicuous** *adj*
pəɹ'spɪkjəs, -jʊəs
**sp** perspicuous[1]

**persuad·e / ~s / ~ing / ~ed** *v*
pəɹ'swɛ:d / -z / -ɪn, -ɪŋ / -ɪd
**sp** perswade[30] / perswades[6] / perswading[1], per-swading[1] / perswaded[19]
**rh** made *Luc 29*

**persuading** *adj*
pəɹ'swɛ:dɪn, -ɪŋ
**sp** perswading[1]

**persuasion** *n*
*m* pəɹ'swɛ:sɪən, -sɪˌɒn
**sp** perswasion[16], per-swasion[2], perswasions[2]
**rh** invasion *Luc 286*

**pert** *adj*
pɐ:ɹt
**sp** pert[2]

**pertain / ~s / ~ing** *v*
pəɹ'tɛ:n / -z / -ɪn, -ɪŋ
**sp** pertaine[2] / pertaines[4] / pertaining[1]

**pertinent** *adj*
*m* 'pɐ:ɹtɪˌnent
**sp** pertinent[2]
> appertinent

**pertly** *adv*
'pɐ:ɹtləɪ
**sp** pertly[2]

**perturbation / ~s** *n*
*m* ˌpɐ:ɹtəɹ'bɛ:sɪən, -sɪˌɒn / -sɪˌɒnz
**sp** perturbation[4] / perturbations[1]

**perturbed** *adj*
*m* pəɹ'tɐ:ɹbɪd, 'pɐ:ɹtɐ:ɹbd
**sp** perturb'd[1], perturbed[1]

**perusal** *n*
pə'ru:zɑl
**sp** perusall[1]

**perus·e / ~ing / ~ed** *v*
pə'ru:z / -ɪn, -ɪŋ / -d
**sp** peruse[13], pervse[1] / perusing[1] / perus'd[6], perused[1]
**rh** abused *Luc 1527*

**perverse** *adj*
pəɹ'vɐ:ɹs
**sp** peruerse[3]

**perversely** *adv*
pəɹ'vɐ:ɹsləɪ
**sp** peruersly[1]

**perverseness** *n*
pəɹ'vɐ:ɹsnəs
**sp** peruersenesse[1]

**pervert / ~ed** *v*
pəɹ'vɐ:ɹt / -ɪd
**sp** peruert[2] / peruerted[1]

**pester / ~ing / ~ed** *v*
'pestəɹ / 'pestrɪn, -ɪŋ / 'pestəɹd
**sp** pester[1] / pestring[1] / pestered[1], pestred[1]

**pestered** *adj*
'pestəɹd
**sp** pester'd[1]

**pestiferous** *adj*
pes'tɪfrəs, -fər-
**sp** pestiferous[1], pestifferous[1]

**pestilence** *n*
*m* 'pestɪˌlens, -ɪləns
**sp** pestilence[12]

**pestilent** *adj*
*m* 'pestɪˌlent, -ɪlənt
**sp** pestilent[7]

**Peter / ~'s** *n*
'pi:təɹ / -z
**sp** Peter[44], Pe-ter[1] / Peters[4]

**petit** *Fr adj*
pə'ti
**sp** petit[1]

**petition / ~s** *n*
pə'tɪsɪən / -z
**sp** petition[17] / petitions[6]

**petition / ~ed** *v*
pə'tɪsɪən / -d
**sp** petition[1] / petition'd[1]

**petitionary** *adj*
*m* pəˈtɪsɪəˌnarəɪ
**sp** petitionary[2]

**petitioner / ~s** *n*
pəˈtɪsɪənəɹ / -z
**sp** peticioner[1] petitioner[2] / petitioners[3]

**Peto** *n*
ˈpiːtoː
**sp** Peto[9]

**Petrarch** *n*
ˈpetrɑːɹk
**sp** Petrarch[1]

**Petruchio / ~'s** *n*
*m* pəˈtruːkɪoː, -ɪˌoː / -ɪoːz
**sp** Petruchio[46] / Petruchio's[3]
**rh** venuto *TS 1.2.26*

**petticoat / ~s** *n*
ˈpetɪˌkoːt / -s
**sp** petticoat[3], petticoate[2], petticote[1], petty-coate[1] / petticoats[1], petty-coates[1]
> coat

**pettiness** *n*
=
**sp** petti-nesse[1]

**pettish** *adj*
=
**sp** pettish[1]

**petty** *adj*
ˈpetəɪ
**sp** pettie[6], petty[22], petty-[brands][1], petty-[toes][1]

**peu** *Fr n*
pø
**sp** peu[2]

**pew** *n*
=
**sp** pue[1]

**pew-fellow** *n*
ˈpjuː-ˌfelə, -loː
**sp** pue-fellow[1]
> fellow

**pewter** *n*
ˈpjuːtəɹ
**sp** pewter[2]

**pewterer / ~'s** *n*
ˈpjuːtrəɹz, -tər-
**sp** pewterers[1]

**Phaeton** *n*
ˈfɛːəˌtɒn [3 *sylls*]
**sp** Phaeton[5]

**phantasim / ~s** *n*
ˈfantəsɪm / -z
**sp** phantasime[1] / phantasims[1]

**phantasma** *n*
fanˈtazmə
**sp** phantasma[1]

**Pharamond** *n*
ˈfarəˌmɒnd
**sp** Pharamond[3]

**Pharaoh / ~s** *n*
ˈfaroːz
**sp** Pharaoes[1], Pharaohs[1]

**Pharsalia** *n*
fəɹˈsalɪə
**sp** Pharsalia[1]

**pheasant** *n*
=
**sp** pheazant[2]

**pheazar** *n*
ˈfiːzəɹ
**sp** pheazar[1]

**Phebe / ~'s** *n*
ˈfiːbiː / -z
**sp** Phebe[21] / Phebes[1]
> Phoebe

**Phebe / ~s** *v*
ˈfiːbiːz
**sp** Phebes[1]

**pheeze, feeze** *v*
fiːz
**sp** pheeze[1], phese[1]

**Philadelphos** *n*
ˌfɪləˈdelfəs
**sp** Philadelphos[1]

**Philario / ~s** *n*
fɪˈlɑːrɪoː / -z
**sp** Philario[2] / Filorio's[1]

**Philarmonus** *n*
ˌfɪləɹˈmɒnəs
**sp** Philarmonus[1]

**Philemon / ~'s** *n*
fɪˈliːmənz
**sp** Philemons[1]

**Philip / ~'s** *n*
=
**sp** Philip[17], Phillip[6] / Philips[1]

**Philippi** *n*
fɪˈlɪpəɪ
**sp** Philippi[12], Phillippi[2]

**Phillida** *n*
ˈfɪlɪdə
**sp** Phillida[1]

**Phillippan** *adj*
fɪˈlɪpən
**sp** Phillippan[1]

**Philo** *n*
ˈfəɪloː
**sp** Philo[1]

**Philomel** *n*
*m* ˈfɪləˌmel
**sp** Philomel[4], Philomele[3]

**Philomela** *n*
ˌfɪləˈmiːlə
**sp** Philomela[2]

**philosopher / ~'s / ~s** *n*
fɪˈlɒsəfəɹ / -z
**sp** philosopher[8], philoso-pher[1], phylosopher[1] / philosophers[1] / philosophers[1]

**philosophical** *adj*
ˌfɪləˈsɒfɪkɑl
**sp** philosophicall[1]

**philosophy** *n*
*m* fɪˈlɒsəˌfəɪ, -əf-
**sp** philosophie[9], philosophy[5]
**rh** *1* harmony *TS 3.1.13*; **rh** *2* die *LLL 1.1.32*

**Philostrate** *n*
ˈfɪləˌstrɛːt
**sp** Philostrate[1]

**Philotus** *n*
fɪˈloːtəs
**sp** Philotus[2]

**phlegmatic** *adj*
=
**sp** flegmaticke[1]

**Phoebe** [goddess] *n*
ˈfiːbiː
**sp** Phoebe[1]
> Phebe

**Phoebus / ~'** *n*
ˈfiːbəs, *Bottom MND 1.2.31* ˈfɪbəs / ˈfiːbəs
**sp** Phebus[2], Phoebus[8], *Bottom* Phibbus[1] / Phoebus[8]

**Phoenecia** *n*
fəˈniːsɪə
**sp** Phoenetia[1]

**Phoenician / ~s** *n*
fəˈniːsɪənz
**sp** Phoenicians[1]

**phoenix** *n*
=
**sp** phenix[2] , phoenix[6]

**Phoenix** [name] *n*
=
**sp** Phoenix[4]

**Photinus** *n*
fəˈtiːnəs
**sp** Photinus[1]

**phrase / ~s** *n*
frɛːz / ˈfrɛːzɪz
**sp** phrase[26] / phrases[5]

**Phrygia** *n*
ˈfrɪʤɪə
**sp** Phrigia[1], Phrygia[2]

**Phrygian** *adj*
ˈfrɪʤɪən
**sp** Phrygian[4]

**Phrynia** *n*
ˈfrɪnɪə
**sp** Phrynia[1], *Tim 4.3.49 emend of* Phrinica[1]

**physic** *n*
=
**sp** phisicke[3], physick[3], physicke[20], phy-sicke[1]

**physic / ~s** *v*
=
**sp** physicke[3] / physicks[2]

**physical** *adj*
ˈfɪzɪˌkɑl
**sp** physicall[2]

**physician / ~'s / ~s** *n*
*m* fɪˈzɪsɪən, -ɪˌɒn / -z
**sp** physician[6], physitian[12], physition[3] / phisitians[1], physitians[2] / phisitions[2], physitians[4]
**rh** incision *R2 1.1.154*

**pia mater** *Lat* *n*
ˌpiːə ˈmɑːtəɹ
**sp** piamater[1], pia-mater[1], *LLL 4.2.70 emend of* primater[1]

**pibble-pabble**
> bibble-babble

**Picardy** *n*
*m* ˈpɪkəɹˌdəɪ
**sp** Picardy[1], Piccardie[1]

**pick / ~s / ~ing / ~ed** *v*
= / = / ˈpɪkɪn, -ɪŋ / =
**sp** pick[1], picke[14] / pickes[1] / picking[3] / pickd[1], pick'd[6], pickt[10]
> unpick

**pick-axe / ~s** *n*
*Gravedigger Hamlet 5.1.92* ˈpɪk-ˌhaks / =
**sp** *Hamlet* pickhaxe[1] / pickaxes[1]

**Pickbone** [name] *n*
ˈpɪkboːn
**sp** Pick-bone[1]

**picked** *adj*
=
**sp** picked[3], pickt[1]
> bare-, un-picked

**picker / ~s** *n*
ˈpɪkəɹz
**sp** pickers[1]

**picking** *adj / n*
ˈpɪkɪn, -ɪŋ
**sp** picking[1] / picking[2]

**pickle** *n*
=
**sp** pickle[4]

**picklock** *n*
=
**sp** pick-lock[1]

**pickpurse / ~s** *n*
ˈpɪkˌpɐːɹs / -ɪz
**sp** picke-purse[1], picke purse[1], pick-purse[1] / picke-purses[1]
> purse

**pickthank / ~s** *n*
=
**sp** pick-thankes[1]

**Pickt-hatch** [name] *n*
ˈpɪkt-ˌaʧ, -ˌha-
**sp** Pickt-hatch[1]

**picture / ~s** *n*
ˈpɪktəɹ / -z
**sp** picture[35], pic-ture[2] / pictures[8]

**picture / ~d** *v*
ˈpɪktəɹd
**sp** pictur'd[1]
> overpicturing

**picture-like** *adj*
ˈpɪktəɹ-ləɪk
**sp** picture-like[1]

**pie / ~s** *n*
pəɪ / -z
**sp** pie[4], pye[4] / pies[2], pyes[1]
**rh** *1* fly *TNK 1.1.21*; **rh** *2* presently *Tit 5.3.59*

**Pie** [name] *n*
pəɪ
**sp** Py-[Corner][1]

**piece / ~s** *n*
=
**sp** peece[67], [three pild]-peece[1], piece[2] / peeces[28], pieces[6]
**rh** Greece *Luc 1366*
**pun** *KJ 4.3.93* peace
> a-, birding-, chimmey-, cod-, head-, master-, mortar-piece

**piece / ~s / ~d** *v*
=
**sp** peece[6], piece[9] / pee-ces[1] / peec'd[2], piec'd[1]

**pied** *adj*
pəɪd
**sp** pied[2], py'de[1]

**pied** *Fr n*
pje
**sp** pied[1]

**piedness** *n*
ˈpəɪdnəs
**sp** pidenesse[1]

**pier / ~s** *n*
piːɹ / -z
**sp** peer[1] / peers[1]

**pierc·e / ~es / ~eth / ~ing / ~ed** *v*
pɛːɹs / ˈpɛːɹs·ɪz / -əθ / -ɪn, -ɪŋ / pɛːɹst
**sp** pearce[2], pierce[22] / pierces[1] / pierceth[1] / piercing[3], persing[1] / pearst[1], perst[1], pierc'd[2], pierst[1], pier'st[2]
**rh** rehearse *R2 5.3.126*
**pun** *Falstaff 1H4 5.3.56* Percy; *Holofernes LLL 4.2.82* pierce

**Pierce** [name] *n*
pɛːɹs
**sp** Pierce[1]

**piercing** *adj / n*
ˈpɛːɹsɪn, -ɪŋ
**sp** peircing[1], piercing[6] / piercing[1]
> ear-, side-piercing

**piety** *n*
*m* ˈpəɪəˌtəɪ, -ət-
**sp** pietie[1], piety[5]
**rh** eye *Luc 542*

**pig** *n*
=
**sp** pig[3], pigge[4]
> boar-, hedge-, tithe-pig

**pigeon / ~s** *n*
ˈpɪʤənz, -ʤɪə-
**sp** pidgions[1], pigeons[9], pigions[3]
> cock-pigeon

**pigeon-egg** *n*
ˈpɪʤən-ˌeg, -ʤɪə-
**sp** pidgeon-egge[1]
> egg

**pigeon-livered** *adj*
ˈpɪʤən-ˌlɪvəɹd, -ʤɪə-
**sp** pigeon-liuer'd[1]
> liver *adj*

**pight** *adj / v*
pəɪt
**sp** pight[1] / pight[1]
> straight-pight

**pigmy** *adj*
ˈpɪgməɪ
**sp** pigmy[1]

**pigm·y / ~y's / ~ies** *n*
ˈpɪgməɪz
**sp** pigmies[1] / pigmies[1]

**pignut / ~s** *n*
=
**sp** pig-nuts[1]
> nut

**Pigrogromitus** *n*
ˌpɪgrəˈgrɒmɪtəs
**sp** Pigrogromitus[1]

**pike / ~s** *n*
pəɪk / -s
**sp** pike[3], pyke[1] / pikes[7], pykes[1]

**Pilate / ~s** *n*
ˈpəɪlət / -s
**sp** Pilate[2] / Pilates[1]

**pilchard / ~s** *n*
ˈpɪlʧəɹz
**sp** pilchers[1]

**pilcher** *n*
ˈpɪlʧəɹ
**sp** pilcher[1]

**pile / ~s** *n*
pəɪl / -z
**sp** pile[4] / piles[2]

**pile / ~d** *v*
pəɪl / -d
**sp** pile[4] / pyl'd[2]

**piled** *adj*
pəɪld
**sp** pil'd[2]

**pilfering** *adj*
ˈpɪlfrɪn, -ɪŋ, -fər-
**sp** pilfering[1]

**pilgrim / ~s / ~s'** *n*
=
**sp** pilgrim[5], pilgrime[4] / pilgrimes[1], pilgrims[1] / pilgrims[1]

**pilgrimage** *n*
*m* ˈpɪlgrɪˌmɛːʤ, -ɪmɪʤ
**sp** pilgrimage[14]
**rh** age *AY 3.2.126, Luc 960, R2 1.3.230, S 7.8*; assuage *Luc 791*

**pill / ~s** *n*
=
**sp** pilles[1], pils[1]

**pill / ~ed** *v*
=
**sp** pill[1] / pil'd pill'd[1]

**pillage** *n*
=
**sp** pillage[5]

**pillar / ~s** *n*
'pɪləɹ / -z
**sp** pillar[3] / pillars[2], pillers[3]
**rh** well-willer *TNK 3.5.114*

**pilled** *adv*
=
**sp** pil'd[1]

**Pillicock** *n*
'pɪlɪkɒk
**sp** Pillicock[2]

**pillory** *n*
'pɪlrəɪ, -lər-
**sp** pillorie[2]

**pillow / ~s** *n*
'pɪlə, -lo: / -z
**sp** pillow[14], [trunke]-pillow[1] / pillowes[3]
> down-pillow

**pilot / ~'s / ~s** *n*
'pəɪlət / -s
**sp** pilot[3], pylot[3] / pilots[2], pylots[1] / pylots[1]

**Pimpernell** *n*
*m* 'pɪmpəɹ,nel
**sp** Pimpernell[1]

**pin** *adj*
=
**sp** pin[1]

**pin / ~'s / ~s / ~s'** *n*
=
**sp** pin[16], pinne[2] / pins[1] / pinnes[2], pins[4] / pinnes[1], pinnes-[heads][1]
**rh** in *LLL 4.1.137*
> push-pin

**pin / ~s / ~ned** *v*
=
**sp** pinnes[1] / pins[1] / pin'd[1]
> unpin

**pinch / ~es** *n*
=
**sp** pinch[5] / pinches[3]

**pinch / ~es / ~ed** *v*
=, *Evans MW 5.5.129* pɪns / =
**sp** pinch[15], *Evans* pinse[1] / pinches[2] / pinch'd[5], pincht[4]

**Pinch** [name] **/ ~'s** *n*
=
**sp** Pinch[3] / Pinches[1]

**pinched** *adj*
=
**sp** pinch'd[1]

**pinching** *adj*
'pɪnʧɪn, -ɪŋ
**sp** pinching[2]

**pinch-spotted** *adj*
=
**sp** pinch-spotted[1]

**Pindarus** *n*
*m* 'pɪndə,rʏs, -ərəs
**sp** Pindarus[12]

**pine** *n*
pəɪn / -z
**sp** pine[4], pyne[4] / pines[3]
**rh** Collatine, divine *Luc 1167*

**pine / ~s / ~d** *v*
pəɪn / -s / *m* -d, 'pəɪnɪd
**sp** pine[6], pyne[1] / pines[1] / pin'd[1], pinde[1], pined[2]
**rh** brine, mine *Luc 795*; design, mine *LC 275*; mine *Mac 1.3.23*

**pinfold** *n*
'pɪnfo:ld
**sp** pinfold[2]

**pining** *adj*
'pəɪnɪn, -ɪŋ
**sp** pining[2]

**pinion** *n*
=
**sp** pinnion[1]

**pinion / ~ed** *v*
=
**sp** pinnion[1] / pinnion'd[2]
> nimble-pinioned, opinion *v*

**pink** *adj / n*
=
**sp** pinke[2] / pinck[1]

**pinked** *adj*
=
**sp** pinck'd[1]
> unpinked

**pinnace** *n*
'pɪnɪs
**sp** pinnace[2], pinnasse[1]

**pint** *n*
pəɪnt
**sp** pint[2]
> half-pint

**pint-pot** *n*
'pəɪnt-,pɒt
**sp** pint-pot[1]
> pot

**pioned** *adj*
*m* 'pəɪə,nɪd
**sp** pioned[1]

**pioneer / ~s** *n*
,pəɪə'ni:ɹ / -z
**sp** pioner[1], *Luc* pyoner[1] / pioners[1], pyoners[1]
**rh** appear *Luc 1380*

**pious** *adj*
'pəɪəs
**sp** pious[9], *Ham 2.2.418 emend of* pons[1]
> impious

**Pious** [name] *n*
'pəɪəs
**sp** Pious[1]

**pip** *n*
=
**sp** peepe[1]

**pipe / ~s** *n*
pəɪp / -s
**sp** pipe[11] / pipes[6]
> bag-, cluster-, horn-, organ-, wind-pipe

**pip·e / ~ing** *v*
pəɪp / 'pəɪpɪn, -ɪŋ
**sp** pipe[2] / piping[1]

**piper / ~s** *n*
'pəɪpəɹz
**sp** pipers[1]

**pipe-wine** *n*
'pəɪp-ˌwəɪn
**sp** pipe-wine[1]
> wine

**piping** *adj*
'pəɪpɪn, -ɪŋ
**sp** piping[1]

**Pippen**
> Pepin

**pippin / ~s** *n*
=
**sp** pippin[1] / pip-pins[1]

**pirate / ~s** *n*
'pəɪrət / -s, *MV 1.3.23* 'pəɪˌrats
**sp** pirat[1], pirate[1], pyrate[5] / pirates[1], pirats[1], pyrates[2], pyrats[2]
**pun** *MV 1.3.23* rats

**Pisa** *n*
=
**sp** Pisa[14]

**Pisanio / ~'s** *n*
pɪ'sɑ:nɪo: / -z
**sp** Pasanio[1], Pisanio[37], *abbr in s.d.* Pisa[1] / Pisanio's[1]

**pish** *interj*
=
**sp** pish[4]

**pismire / ~s** *n*
'pɪsməɪɹz
**sp** pismires[1]

**piss** *v*
=
**sp** pisse[1]

**pissing** *adj*
'pɪsɪn, -ɪŋ
**sp** pissing[2]

**pistol / ~s** *n*
=
**sp** pistoll[4] / pistols[1]

**Pistol / ~'s** *n*
=, 'pɪsəl, *Hostess 2H4 2.4.156* 'pi:səl / -z
**sp** Pistol[10], Pistoll[39], Pi-stoll[2], *Hostess* Peesel[1] / Pi-stols[1]
> bulls-pizzle

**Pistol-proof** *adj*
=, 'pɪsəl-ˌprʊf, -ˌpru:f
**sp** Pistoll-proofe[1]
> proof

**pit / *VA* ~s** *n*
=
**sp** pit[22] / pits[1]
**rh** sit *R2 4.1.218* / wits *VA 247*
> cock-, saw-pit

**pitch** *adj / n*
=
**sp** pitch[1] / pitch[18], pytch[3]
**rh** *n* itch *Tem 2.2.51*

**pitch / ~ed** *v*
=
**sp** pitch[7] / pitched[1], pitcht[2]

**pitched** *adj*
=
**sp** pitched[1], pitcht[2]

**pitcher / ~s** *n*
'pɪʧəɹz
**sp** pitchers[2]

**pitchy** *adj*
'pɪʧəɪ
**sp** pitchy[3]

**piteous** *adj*
'pɪtɪəs [*2 sylls*]
**sp** piteous[2], pitious[1], pitteous[11], pittious[6]

**piteously** *adv*
*m* 'pɪtɪəsˌləɪ [*3 sylls*]
**sp** pitteously[1], pittiously[1]

**pitfall** *n*
'pɪtfɑ:l
**sp** pitfall[1]

**pith** *n*
=
**sp** pith[5], pyth[1]

**pithless** *adj*
=
**sp** pyth-lesse[1]

**pithy** *adj*
'pɪθəɪ
**sp** pithy[1]

**pitié** *Fr n*
pit'je
**sp** pitez[1]

**pitiful** *adj*
*m* 'pɪtɪˌfʊl, -ɪfəl
**sp** pitifull[1], pittiful[1], pittifull[26], pit-tifull[1], pitti-full[1]

**pitiful-hearted** *adj*
'pɪtɪfəl-ˌɑ:ɹtɪd, -ˌhɑ:-
**sp** pittifull hearted[1]
> heart

**pitifully** *adv*
*m* 'pɪtɪˌfʊləɪ, -ɪfələɪ, -ɪfləɪ
**sp** pittifully[3]
> unpitifully

**pitikins** *interj*
=
**sp** ['ods] pittikins[1]

**pitiless** *adj*
*m* 'pɪtɪˌles, -ɪləs
**sp** pittilesse[4]

**pittance** *n*
=
**sp** pittance[1]

**pittie-ward** *adv*
'pɪtəɪ-ˌwɑːɹd
**sp** pittie-ward[1]

**pit·y / ~ies** *n*
'pɪtəɪ / -z
**sp** pitie[5], pittie[35], pittie's [pity is][1], pitty[106], pity[3] / pitties[1]
**rh** city *LC 178, Luc 468, 1553*; ditty *PP 20.12*

**pit·y / ~ies / ~ing / ~ied / ~iedest** *v*
'pɪtəɪ / -z / -ɪn, -ɪŋ / -d / -dst
**sp** pitie[1], pittie[14], pitty[43], pity[1] / pitties[5] / pittying[4] / pittied[18] / pittied'st[1]
> unpitied

**place / ~'s / ~s** *n*
plɛːs / 'plɛːs·ɪz
**sp** place[365], [selfe]-place[1], [Yorke]-Place[1], [Yorke]-place[1] / place's[1] / places[36]
**rh** *1* case *1H6 2.1.73, RJ 1.1.102, S 108.11*; case, face *KJ 1.1.145, Luc 310*; case, grace *LC 117*; chase *Luc 1735, VA 885*; deface *S 6.3*; disgrace, face *Luc 803*; face *1H6 1.3.43, 46, LLL 3.1.66, Luc 1746, MND 1.1.203, 3.2.423, S 93.4, 131.12, 137.10*; face, grace *LC 82, Luc 565*; face, space *Luc 1773*; grace *3H6 4.6.31, KL 1.1.274, LC 318, LLL 2.1.179, 3.1.66, Mac 5.6.112, MND 5.1.390, Per 2.3.18, 4. Chorus.10, R2 3.4.104, S 79.4, Tem 4.1.73*; grace, space *LC 263*; race *Per 5.Chorus.11*; **rh** *2* ass *CE 3.1.46* / faces *Luc 1525*
> baiting-, birth-, burying-, dwelling-, judgement-, learning-, market-, meeting-, show-place; high-placed

**plac·e / ~es / ~eth / ~ing / ~ed** *v*
plɛːs / 'plɛːs·ɪz / -əθ / -ɪn, -ɪŋ / *m* -ɪd, plɛːst
**sp** place[18] / places[3] / placeth[2] / placing[2] / plac'd[14], placed[8], plac't[4]
**rh** place him embrace him *Luc 517*
> dis-, mis-place

**Placentio** *n*
plə'sensɪoː
**sp** Placentio[1]

**placing** *n*
'plɛːsɪn, -ɪŋ
**sp** placing[1]

**placket / ~s** *n*
=
**sp** placket[2] / placcats[1], plackets[2]

**plague / ~s** *n*
plɛːg / -z
**sp** plague[77], [red]-plague[1], plague-[tribunes][1] / plagues[11]

**plague / ~s / ~d** *v*
plɛːg / -z / *m* -gd, 'plɛːgɪd
**sp** plague[13] / plagues[2] / plagu'd[2], plagued[2]
> unplague

**plaguing** *adj*
'plɛːgɪn, -ɪŋ
**sp** plaguing[1]

**plaguy** *adj*
'plɛːgəɪ
**sp** plaguy[1]

**plain / ~er / ~est** *adj*
plɛːn / 'plɛːnəɹ / -əst
**sp** plain[4], plaine[87] / plainer[4] / plainest[2]
**rh** again *LLL 5.2.452, VA 407*; certain *MND 5.1.127*; pain *LLL 4.3.119*; rain *LLL 4.3.270, Luc 1786, VA 359*; sain [said] *LLL 3.1.80*

**plain / ~s** *n*
plɛːn / -z
**sp** plaine[7] / plaines[6]
**rh** rain *VA 236*; remain *Luc 1247* / swains *PP 17.30*

**plain-dealing** *adj / n*
'plɛːn-ˌdiːlɪn, -ɪŋ / 'plɛːn-'diːlɪn, -ɪŋ
**sp** plain dea-ling[1] plaine dealing[1] / plain-dealing[1], plaine dealing[1]
> deal

**plaining / ~s** *n*
'plɛːnɪn, -ɪŋ / -z
**sp** plaining[1] / playnings[1]
**rh** raining *Luc 559*

**plainly** *adv*
'plɛːnləɪ
**sp** plainely[7], plainlie[1], plainly[12]

**plainness** *n*
'plɛːnəs
**sp** plainenesse[1], plainnesse[10]

**plainsong** *adj / n*
'plɛːnsɒŋ
**sp** plainsong[1] / plaine-song[2]
> song

**plaint / ~s** *n*
plɛːnts
**sp** plaints[3]

**plaintiff / ~s** *n*
'plɛːntɪf / -s
**sp** plaintiffe[2] / plaintiffes[1]

**plait** *LC* *n*
plat
**sp** plat[1]
**rh** hat *LC 29*

**plait / ~s** *v*
plats
**sp** plats[1]

**planched** *adj*
'planʧɪd
**sp** planched[1]

**planet / ~s** *n*
=
**sp** planet[7], plannet[2] / planets[7]

**planetary** *adj*
*m* 'planɪˌtarəɪ, -ɪtərəɪ, -ɪtrəɪ
**sp** planatary[1], plannetary[1]

**plank / ~s** *n*
=
**sp** plankes[2]

**plant / ~s** *n*
plant, plɔ:nt / -s
**sp** plant[4] / plants[10]
**rh** predominant *RJ 2.3.26*

**plant / ~s / ~eth / ~ed** *v*
plant, plɔ:nt / -s / 'plant·əθ, 'plɔ:- / -ɪd
**sp** plant[19] / plants[1] / planteth[1] / planted[9]
**rh** *1* granted *LLL 1.1.162*; **rh** *2* haunted *LLL 1.1.162*
> displant; new-, sky-planted

**plantage** *n*
'plantɪʤ, 'plɔ:-
**sp** plantage[1]

**Plantagenet / ~s** *n*
*m* plan'taʤɪˌnet, -nət, plɔ:n- / -s
**sp** Plantagenet[40], Plantaginet[4] / Plantagenets[2]
**rh** *1* debt *R3 4.4.20*; **rh** *2* great *KJ 1.1.162*

**plantain** *adj / n*
'plantən, 'plɔ:n-
**sp** plantan[1] / plantan[4]

**plantation** *n*
plan'tɛ:sɪən, plɔ:n-
**sp** plantation[1]

**plash** *n*
=
**sp** plash[1]

**plaster** *n / v*
'plastəɹ
**sp** plaister[1], plaster[2] / plaister[1]
**rh** *n* master *VA 916*

**plasterer** *n*
'plastrəɹ, -tər-
**sp** playsterer[1]

**plastering** *adj*
'plastrɪn, -ɪŋ
**sp** plaist'ring[1]

**plate / ~s** *n*
plɛ:t / -s
**sp** plate[10] / plates[1]
> breastplate

**plated** *adj*
plɛ:tɪd
**sp** plated[1]

**platform / ~s** *n*
'platfɔ:ɹm / -z
**sp** platforme[3] / plat-formes[1]

**plausible** *adj*
=
**sp** plausible[1]

**plausive** *adj*
=
**sp** plausiue[2]
> unplausive

**Plautus** *n*
'plɔ:təs
**sp** Plautus[1]

**play / ~s** *n*
plɛ: / -z
**sp** play[81], play's [play is][1], [faire]-play[1], [faire]-play-[orders][1], [foule]-play[1], [fowle]-play[1] / playes[2]
**rh** away *TC Prol.29*; day *LLL 5.2.867, MND 3.2.11, TNK Prol.3*; Grey *R3 4.4.68*; may *H5 2.Chorus.40*; pray *H5 Prol.34*; say *AY 3.4.54, TNK Epil.1*; stay, way *LLL 4.3.76*; they *H8 Prol.14*; way *LLL 5.2.863*

**play / ~est / ~s / ~eth / ~ing / ~ed / ~edest** *v*
plɛ: / -st / -z / 'plɛ:·əθ / -ɪn, -ɪŋ / plɛ:d / -st
**sp** plaie[2], play[208] / play'st[1] / plaies[8], playes[23] / playeth[1] / playing[15], play-ing[1] / plaid[32], plaide[4], playd[1], play'd[10], played[4] / playd'st[1]
**rh** *1* away *AW 4.4.24, Ham 3.2.281, S 98.14*; away, hay *LLL 5.1.146*; prey *LLL 4.1.92*; well-a-day *Per 4.4.48*; **rh** *2* sea *H8 3.1.9* [song] / swayest *S 128.1* / delays *Luc 553* / afraid *PP 17.19*

**player / ~s** *n*
plɛ:əɹ / -z
**sp** plaier[1], player[5] / plaiers[1], players[28]

**playfellow / ~s** *n*
'plɛ:felə, -lo: / -z
**sp** play-fellow[6] / playfellowes[1], play-fellowes[1]
**rh** bedfellow *Per Prol.34*
> fellow

**playhouse** *n*
'plɛ:əʊs, -həʊs
**sp** playhouse[1], play-house[1]
> house

**playing** *adj / n*
'plɛ:ɪn, -ɪŋ
**sp** playing[2] / playing[1]

**plea** *n*
=
**sp** plea[6]
**rh** sea *S 65.3*

**pleached** *adj*
*m* 'pli:ʧɪd, pli:ʧt
**sp** pleach'd[1], pleached[1], pleacht[1]
> thick-pleached

**plead / ~s / ~eth** *Luc* **/ ~ing / ~ed** *v*
=, pled / -z / 'pli:d·əθ, 'pled- / -ɪn, -ɪŋ / -ɪd
**sp** plead[23], plea'd[1], pleade[21] / pleades[3] / pleadeth[1] / pleading[5] / pleaded[3]
**rh** *1* leadeth *Luc 268*; **rh** *2* dreadeth *Luc 268*

**pleader / ~s** *n*
'pli:dəɹ, 'pled- / -z
**sp** pleader[1] / pleaders[1]

**pleading** *n*
'pli:dɪn, -ɪŋ, 'pled-
**sp** pleading[1]

**pleasance** *n*
'plezəns, -esə-
**sp** pleasance[1]

**pleasant / ~est** *adj*
'plezənt, -esə- / -st, -nst
**sp** pleasant[33] / pleasant'st[1]
> unpleasant

**pleasantly** *adv*
'plezənt,ləɪ, -esə-
**sp** pleasantly[1]

**pleasantry** *n*
*m* 'plezən,trəɪ, -esə-
**sp** pleasantry[1]

**pleasant-spirited** *adj*
'plezənt-,spɪɹɪtɪd
**sp** pleasant spirited[1]
> spirit

**pleas·e / ~est / ~es / ~eth / ~ing / ~ed** *v*
= / = / = / = / 'pli:zɪn, -ɪŋ / *m* =, 'pli:zɪd
**sp** please[378], 'please[2], please'[1], pleas't [please it][1] / pleasest[2] / pleases[16], plea-ses[1] / pleaseth[17] / pleasing[1] / pleas'd[65], pleased[6]
**rh** disease *S 147.4*; ease *AY 2.5.50, H8 Epil.1, TS 5.2.177*; knees *Per 1.2.46*; peas *LLL 5.2.316*; these *LLL 1.1.50* / appeased *TG 5.4.80*
> unpleased

**pleased** *adj*
=
**sp** pleasd[1], pleas'd[6]

**please-man** *n*
=
**sp** please-man[1]

**pleasing** *adj / n*
'pli:zɪn, -ɪŋ
**sp** pleasing[18] / pleasing[1]

**pleasure / ~'s / ~s** *n*
'plezəɹ / -z
**sp** pleasure[164], plea-sure[2] / pleasures[1] / pleasures[33]
**rh** *1* leisure *S 58.2*; measure *S 91.5*; treasure *S 20.13, 52.4, 75.8, 126.9*; **rh** *2* seizure *PP 11.12* / measures *AY 5.4.189*
> displeasure

**Pleb / ~s** *n*
=
**sp** Plebs[1]

**Plebeian / ~s** *n*
*m* 'plebɪənz, -ɪ,anz, plə'bi:ənz
**sp** Plebeans[3], Plebeians[13]

**Plebeii** *n*
'plebəɪ,i:
**sp** Plebeij[1]

**pledge / ~s** *n*
=
**sp** pledge[13] / pledges[3]

**pledge / ~s** *v*
=
**sp** pledge[6] / pledges[1]

**plein / ~es** *Fr adj*
plɛ̃
**sp** plein[1]

**plenteous** *adj*
'plentɪəs [*2 sylls*]
**sp** plenteous[9], plen-teous[1], plentious[1]

**plenteously** *adv*
*m* 'plentɪəs,ləɪ [*3 sylls*]
**sp** plenteously[1]

**plentiful** *adj*
*m* 'plentɪ,fʊl, -ɪfəl
**sp** plentifull[3]

**plentifully** *adv*
*m* 'plentɪ,fʊləɪ, -fələɪ, -fləɪ
**sp** plentifully[3]

**plent·y / ~ies** *n*
'plentəɪ / -z
**sp** plentie[6], plen-tie[2], plenty[5] / plentyes[1]
**rh** *1* twenty *TN 2.3.48, VA 20*; **rh** *2* empty *Tem 4.1.110*

**Pleshey** *n*
'plaʃəɪ
**sp** Plashie[2], Plashy[1]

**pliant** *adj*
'pləɪənt
**sp** pliant[1]

**plied, plies**
> ply

**plight** *n*
pləɪt
**sp** plight[9]
**rh** fight *PP 17.22*; flight *3H6 3.3.37*; night *S 28.1*
> troth-plight

**plight ~ed** *v*
pləɪt / 'pləɪtɪd
**sp** plight[2] / plighted[2]
**rh** alight *KL 3.4.117*

**plighted** *adj*
'pləɪtɪd
**sp** plighted[1]

**plighter** *n*
'pləɪtəɹ
**sp** plighter[1]

**plod / ~ded** *v*
=
**sp** plod[3], plodde[1] / plodded[2]

**plodder / ~s** *n*
'plɒdəɹz
**sp** plodders[1]

**plodding** *n*
'plɒdɪn, -ɪŋ
**sp** plodding[1]

**plot** [ground] *n*
=
**sp** plot[6], [dazied]-plot[1], [grasse]-plot[1], plotte[1]
**rh** not *S 137.9*

**plot** [scheme] **/ ~s** *n*
=
**sp** plot[42] / plots[6]
**rh** blot *R2 4.1.323*

**plot / ~s / ~ted** *v*
=
**sp** plot[1], plots[8] / plotted[9]
**rh** got *Tem 4.1.88*

**plot-proof** *adj*
*m* ˌplɒt-ˈprʊf, -ˈpru:f
**sp** plot-proofe[1]

**plotted** *adj*
=
**sp** plotted[1]

**plotter** *n*
ˈplɒtəɹ
**sp** plotter[1]

**plough** *n*
pləʊ
**sp** plough[1]

**plough / ~est / ~ed** *v*
pləʊ / -st / -d
**sp** plough[4] / plow'st[1] / ploughed[1], plowed[1], plowgh'd[1]

**plough-irons** *n*
ˈpləʊ-ˌəɪrənz
**sp** plough-irons[1]

**ploughman** *adj*
ˈpləʊmən
**sp** ploughman[1]

**plough·man / ~men's** *n*
ˈpləʊmən / -z
**sp** ploughman[1], plough-man[1] / ploughmens[1]

**plough-torn** *adj*
ˈpləʊ-ˌtɔ:ɹn
**sp** plough-torne[1]
> tear *v*

**pluck / ~s / ~ing / ~ed** *v*
plɤk / -s / ˈplɤkɪn, -ɪŋ / plɤkt
**sp** pluck[23], pluck-[back][1], plucke[78] / pluckes[8], plucks[4] / plucking[5] / pluck'd[8], pluckt[24]
**rh** luck *S 14.1* / sucked *VA 574*

**plucker-down** *n*
ˈplɤkəɹ-ˈdəʊn
**sp** plucker downe[1]
> down

**plucking** *n*
ˈplɤkɪn, -ɪŋ
**sp** plucking[1]

**plum / ~s** *n*
plɤm / -z
**sp** plum[1] / plummes[1]

**plume / ~s** *n*
=
**sp** plume[4], plumbe[1] / plumes[5]
**rh** fume *VA 314* / assumes *TC 1.3.386*

**plume / ~d** *v*
=
**sp** plume[1] / plum'd[1]

**plumed** *adj*
*m* ˈplu:mɪd
**sp** plumed[2]

**plume-plucked** *adj*
ˈplu:m-ˌplɤkt
**sp** plume-pluckt[1]

**plummet** *n*
ˈplɤmɪt
**sp** plummet[3]

**plump** *adj*
plɤmp
**sp** plumpe[1]

**plumpy** *adj*
ˈplɤmpəɪ
**sp** plumpie[1]

**plum-tree** *adj / n*
ˈplɤm-ˌtri:
**sp** plum-tree[1] / plum-tree[1]
> tree

**plunge / ~d** *v*
plɤnʤ / *m* -d, ˈplɤnʤɪd
**sp** plundge[3], plunge[2] / plung'd[2], plunged[1]

**plural** *adj*
ˈplu:ral
**sp** plurall[2]

**plus** *Fr adv*
ply
**sp** plus[2]

**Pluto / ~'s** *n*
ˈplu:to: / -z
**sp** Pluto[4] / Plutoes[3], Pluto's[2]

**Plutus** *n*
ˈplu:təs
**sp** Plutus[1], Platus[1]

**pl·y / ~ies / ~ied** *v*
pləɪ / -z / -d
**sp** ply[4] , plye[1] / plies[2], plyes[2] / plied[1]

**Po** *n*
po:
**sp** Poe[1]
**rh** so *KJ 1.1.203*

**pocket / ~s** *n*
=
**sp** pocket[27], poc-ket[1] / pockets[7]

**pocket** *v*
=
**sp** pocket[5]

**pocketting-up** *n*
ˈpɒkɪtɪn-ˈɤp, -ɪŋ-
**sp** pocketting vp[1]

**pocky** *adj*
ˈpɒkəɪ
**sp** pocky[1]

**poem** *n*
ˈpo:ɪm
**sp** po-em[1]

**poesy** *n*
*m* ˈpo:ɪzəɪ, -ɪˌz-
**sp** poesie[4]

**poet / ~'s / ~s / ~s'** *n*
ˈpo:ɪt / -s
**sp** poet[18] / poets[3] / poets[7] / poets[1]

**poetical** *adj*
po:ˈetɪkal
**sp** poetical[1], poeticall[3]

**poetry** *n*
*m* 'po:ɪtrəɪ, -ɪˌt-
**sp** poetrie[6], poetry[3]

**Poins** *n*
pəɪnz
**sp** Poines[15], Points[1], Pointz[7], Poynes[4]

**point / ~s** *n*
pəɪnt / -s
**sp** point[110], poynt[6] / points[25]
> counterpoint

**point / ~est / ~s / ~ing / ~ed** *v*
pəɪnt / -st, pəɪnst / -s / 'pəɪnt·ɪn, -ɪŋ / -ɪd
**sp** point[18] / point'st[1] / points[3] / pointing[2] / poynted[1]

**point** *Fr adv*
pwɛ̃
**sp** point[2]

**point-blank** *adv*
ˌpəɪnt-'blaŋk
**sp** point-blanke[2]
> blank

**point-device** *adj / adv*
ˌpəɪnt-dɪ'vəɪs
**sp** point deuice[1], poynt deuise[1] / point deuise[1]
> device

**pointed** *adj*
'pəɪntɪd
**sp** pointed[4]
> sharp-pointed

**pointing** *adj*
'pəɪntɪn, -ɪŋ
**sp** pointing[1]

**poise** *n*
pəɪz
**sp** poise[1], poize[3], poyse[1]

**pois·e / ~ing / ~ed** *v*
pəɪz / 'pəɪzɪn, -ɪŋ / pəɪzd
**sp** poize[1] / poizing[1] / poiz'd[1], poys'd[1], poyz'd[1]
> counterpoise

**poison / ~s** *n*
'pəɪzən / -z
**sp** poison[5], poyson[70], poy-son[1] / poisons[1], poysons[4]

**poison / ~s / ~ed** *v*
'pəɪzən / -z / -d
**sp** poison[3] / poysons[4] / poison'd[3], poyson'd[11]

**poisoned** *adj*
'pəɪzənd
**sp** poysond[1], poyson'd[4], poysoned[1]

**poisoner** *n*
'pəɪznəɹ, -zən-
**sp** poysoner[3]

**poisoning** *n*
'pəɪznɪn, -ɪŋ, -zən-
**sp** poysoning[1]

**poisonous** *adj*
'pəɪznəs, -zən-
**sp** poysonous[10]

**poisonous-tongued** *adj*
'pəɪznəs-ˌtɒŋd, -zən-, -ˌtʊ-
**sp** poysonous tongu'd[1]
> tongue

**Poitiers** *n*
*m* pwɛ'ti:ɹ, 'pwɛti:ɹ
**sp** Poictiers[2], Poyctiers[3], Poytiers[1]

**poke** *n*
po:k
**sp** poake[1]

**poking-stick / ~s** *n*
'po:kɪn-ˌstɪks, -ɪŋ-
**sp** poaking-stickes[1]
> stick

**Polack** *n*
'po:lək
**sp** Polake[1], Poleak[2]

**Poland** *adj / n*
'po:lənd
**sp** Poland[1] / Poland[2]

**pole / ~s** *n*
po:l / -z
**sp** pole[7], [North]-pole[1] / poles[1]
> maypole

**Pole** [name] *n*
pu:l
**sp** Pole[4], Poole[9]

**pole-axe** *n*
'po:l-ˌaks
**sp** pollax[2]

**polecat / ~s** *n*
'po:lkat, pɤl- / -s
**sp** poulcat[1] / powlcats[2]
> cat

**pole-clipped** *adj*
'po:l-ˌklɪpt
**sp** pole-clipt[1]
clip

**Polemon** *n*
pə'li:mən
**sp** Polemen[1]

**polic·y / ~ies** *n*
*m* 'pɒlɪˌsəɪ, -ɪs- / 'pɒlɪˌsəɪz
**sp** policie[14], poli-cie[1], policy[11], pollicie[10], pollicy[7] / pollicies[1]
**rh** company *LLL 5.2.510*; me *R2 5.1.84*
> unpolicied

**Polidamus** *n*
pə'lɪdəməs
**sp** Polidamus[1]

**polished** *adj*
=
**sp** pollish'd[1]
> unpolished

**politic** *adj*
*m* 'pɒlɪˌtɪk, -lɪt-
**sp** politick[1], politicke[5], poli-ticke[1], politike[3], politique[3], pollitick[1]
**rh** heretic *S 124.11*

**politically** *adv*
*m* ˌpɒlɪ'tɪkləɪ, 'plɪtɪkˌləɪ
**sp** politickely[1], politikely[1]

**politician / ~s** *n*
ˌpɒlɪ'tɪsɪən / -z
**sp** politician[3], politi-cian[1], polititian[1] / politicians[1]

**Polixena** *n*
pə'lɪksəˌna
**sp** Polixena[1]

**Polixenes** *n*
*m* pə'lɪksəˌni:z, -sən-, -sn-
**sp** Polixenes[20]

**poll / ~ed** *n / adj*
po:l / po:ld
**sp** pole[4], poll[1] / poul'd[1]
**rh** soul *Ham 4.5.196*
> clodpoll

**pollax**
> pole-axe [*debated reading*]

**pollute** *Luc* **/ ~d** *v*
pə'lu:t / -ɪd
**sp** pollute[2] / polluted[1]
**rh** absolute *Luc 854*; fruit *Luc 1063*

**polluted** *adj*
pə'lu:tɪd
**sp** polluted[1]
> unpolluted

**pollution** *n*
pə'lu:sɪən
**sp** pollution[2], polusion[1]
**rh** confusion, conclusion *Luc 1157*

**Polonius / ~'** *n*
pə'lo:nɪəs
**sp** Pollonius[1], Polonius[19] / Polonius[1]

**poltroon / ~s** *n*
'po:ltru:nz
**sp** poultroones[1]

**pol·us / ~i** *Lat n*
pɒ'li:
**sp** poli[1]

**Polydore** *n*
'pɒlɪˌdɔ:ɹ
**sp** Paladour[1], Polidore[7]

**Polyxenes** *n*
pə'lɪksəˌni:z
**sp** Polixines[1]

**pomander** *n*
*m* 'pɒməndəɹ, pə'man-
**sp** pomander[1]

**pomegranate** *n*
*m* pɒm'granɪt
**sp** pomgranat[1]

**pomegranate-tree** *n*
*m* pɒm'granɪt-ˌtri:
**sp** pomgranet tree[1]
> tree

**Pomfret** *adj / n*
'pɤmfrɪt
**sp** Pomfret[1] / Pomfret[14], Pumfret[1]

**Pomgarnet** *n*
pɒm'gɑ:ɹnət
**sp** Pomgar-net[1]

**pommel** *n*
'pɤməl
**sp** pummell[1]

**pomp / ~s** *n*
=
**sp** pomp[1], pompe[31] / pompes[1]

**Pompeius** *n*
pəm'pɛ:əs
**sp** Pompeius[3]

**Pompey / ~'s** *n*
'pɒmpəɪ, *Costard LLL 5.2.501* 'pɒmpɪən / -z
**sp** Pompey[85], *Costard* Pompion[1] / Pompeyes[9], Pompey's[1]

**pompous** *adj*
=
**sp** pompous[2]

**pomwater** *n*
'po:mˌwɑtəɹ
**sp** pomwater[1]

**pond / ~s** *n*
=
**sp** pond[4] / ponds[1]
> fishpond

**ponder** *v*
'pɒndəɹ
**sp** ponder[1]

**ponderous** *adj*
*m* 'pɒndəˌrɤs, -ərəs, -drəs
**sp** ponderous[4]

**poniard / ~s** *n*
'pɒnjɑ:ɹd / -z
**sp** poyniard[1] / poniards[2], ponyards[1], poynyards[1]

**Pont** *n*
=
**sp** Pont[1]

**Pontic** *adj*
=
**sp** Ponticke[1]

**pontifical** *adj*
*m* pən'tɪfɪˌkɑl
**sp** pontificall[1]

**Ponton** *n*
'pɒntən
**sp** Ponton[1]

**pool** *n*
=
**sp** poole[4]

**poop** *n*
=
**sp** poope[2]

**poor** *adj*
po:ɹ / 'po:r·əɹ / -əst
**sp** poor[9], poore[585], poore-[old-man][1], poore-[old-woman][1], *Cym 3.4.85 emend of* pooru[1] / poorer[4] / poorest[7], poor'st[2]
**rh** store *LLL 5.2.378, RJ 1.1.215*

**poor** *n*
poːɹ
**sp** poor[2], poore[10]
**rh** whore *KL 2.4.51*

**poorest** *n*
'poːrəst
**sp** poorest[1]

**poor-John** *n*
'poːr-ˌʤɒn
**sp** poore-Iohn[1]

**poorly** *adv*
'poːɹləɪ
**sp** poorely[6]

**pop / ~s / ~ped** *v*
=
**sp** pops[1] / popt[1], pop't[1]

**pope** *n*
poːp
**sp** pope[19]
**rh** rope *1H6 1.3.52*

**popedom** *n*
'poːpdəm
**sp** popedome[1]

**Popilius** *n*
pə'pɪlɪəs
**sp** Popillius[3]

**popinjay** *n*
'pɒpɪnˌʤɛː
**sp** popingay[1]

**popish** *adj*
'poːpɪʃ
**sp** popish[1]

**poppering** *adj*
'pɒprɪn, -ɪŋ
**sp** poprin[1]

**poppy** *n*
'pɒpəɪ
**sp** poppy[1]

**popular** *adj*
*m* 'pɒpləɹ, -jələɹ
**sp** popular[6]

**popularity** *n*
*m* ˌpɒpjə'larɪˌtəɪ
**sp** popularitie[2]

**populous** *adj*
*m* 'pɒpjəˌlɤs, -ələs, 'pɒpləs
**sp** populous[4], populus[1]

**porch / ~es** *n*
pɔːɹʧ / 'pɔːɹʧɪz
**sp** porch[4] / porches[1]

**pore** *v*
pɔːɹ
**sp** poare[1], pore[1]

**poring** *adj*
'pɔːrɪn, -ɪŋ
**sp** poring[1]

**pork** *n*
pɔːɹk
**sp** porke[2]

**pork-eater / ~s** *n*
'pɔːɹk-ˌiːtəɹz
**sp** porke-eaters[1]

**porpentine** *n*
'pɔːɹpənˌtəɪn
**sp** porpentine[3]

**Porpentine** [name] *n*
'pɔːɹpənˌtəɪn
**sp** Porpentine[4], Porpen-tine[1]

**porridge** *n*
=
**sp** porrage[1], porredge[6], porridge[1]

**porringer** *n*
'pɒɹɪnʤəɹ
**sp** porrenger[2]

**port / ~s** *n*
pɔːɹt / -s
**sp** port[15] / ports[9]
> Cinque Ports

**portable** *adj*
'pɔːɹtəbəl
**sp** portable[2]

**portage** *n*
'pɔːɹtɪʤ
**sp** portage[1]

**portal** *n*
'pɔːɹtl
**sp** portall[2]

**portance** *n*
'pɔːɹtəns
**sp** portance[2]

**Port Blanc**
> Le Port Blanc

**portcullis / ~ed** *v*
pəɹ'kɤlɪst
**sp** percullist[1]

**portend / ~s** *v*
pɔːɹ'tend / -z
**sp** portend[3], por-tend[1] / portends[3]

**portendous** *adj*
pɔːɹ'tendəs
**sp** portendous[1]

**portent / ~s** *n*
pɔːɹ'tent / -s
**sp** portent[1] / portents[4]

**portentous** *adj*
pɔːɹ'tentəs
**sp** portentous[1]

**porter / ~s** *n*
'pɔːɹtəɹ / -z
**sp** porter[21] / porters[2]

**Portia / ~'s** *n*
*m* 'pɔːɹsɪə, -sɪˌa / 'pɔːɹsɪəz
**sp** Portia[36] / Portias[3]

**portion** *n*
'pɔːɹsɪən
**sp** portion[7]

**portly** *adj*
'pɔːɹtləɪ
**sp** portly[6]

**portotartarossa** *nonsense word*
'pɔ:ɹto:'tɑ:ɹtə'rɒsə
**sp** portotartarossa[1]

**portrait** *n*
'pɔ:ɹtrɛ:t
**sp** portrait[1]

**portraiture** *n*
'pɔ:ɹtretəɹ
**sp** portraiture[1]

**Portugal** *n*
'pɔ:ɹtɪgɑl
**sp** Portugall[1]

**pose** *v*
po:z
**sp** poze[1]

**position** *n*
*m* pə'zɪsɪən, -sɪ,ɒn
**sp** position[3], po-sition[1]

**positive** *adj*
*m* 'pɒsɪ,tɪv, -ɪt-
**sp** positiue[2], possitiue

**positively** *adv*
*m* 'pɒsɪ,tɪvləɪ
**sp** positiuely[1], possitiuely[1]

**possess / ~es / ~eth / *S* ~ing / ~ed** *v*
= / = / = / pə'zes·ɪn, -ɪŋ / *m* -t, -ɪd
**sp** possesse[29] / possesses[2] / possesseth[1] / possessing[2] / possess'd[2], possessed[3], possest[38]
**rh** excess, less *Luc 135*; less *LLL 5.2.383, RJ 1.3.94*; possess thee guide thee, tend thee, with me *R3 4.1.93* / releasing *S 87.1* / least *S 29.6*
> dis-, re-possess; unpossessed, unpossessing

**possession / ~s** *n*
*m* pə'zesɪən, -sɪ,ɒn / pə'zesɪənz
**sp** possession[28], possessio[n][1], pos-session[1] / possessions[5]
**rh** observation *3H6 2.6.110*; succession *CE 3.1.106*

**possession** *Fr n*
pɔsɛs'jɔ̃
**sp** possession[1], pos-session[1]

**possessor** *n*
pə'zesəɹ
**sp** possesser[1], possessor[1]

**posset / ~s** *n*
'pɒsɪt / -s
**sp** posset[1], pos-set[1] / possets[1]

**posset** *v*
'pɒsɪt
**sp** posset[1]

**possibility / ~ies** *n*
*m* ,pɒsɪ'bɪlɪ,təɪ, -ɪt- / -z
**sp** possibilitie[1], possibility[2] / possibilities[2]

**possible** *adj*
=
**sp** possible[57]
> impossible

**possibly** *adv*
'pɒsɪbləɪ
**sp** possibly[3]

**possitable** *adv*
*Evans MW 1.1.220* 'pɒsɪtəbəl
**sp** possitable[1]

**possum / posse** *Lat v*
'pɒse
**sp** *emend of 2H6 1.4.61* posso[1]

**post** *adv*
po:st
**sp** post[1], poste[1]

**post / ~s** *n*
po:st / -s
**sp** poast[2], post[21], poste[16] / postes[6], posts[4]
**rh** host *Luc 1*

**post / ~s / ~ing / ~ed** *v*
po:st / -s / 'po:st·ɪn, -ɪŋ / -ɪd
**sp** poast[1], post[11], poste[8] / postes[2] / poasting[1] / poasted[2], posted[4]

**poster / ~s** *n*
'po:stəɹz
**sp** posters[1]

**posterior / ~s** *n*
pɒ'sti:rɪəɹ / -z
**sp** posterior[2] / posteriors[1]

**posterity** *n*
*m* pɒ'sterɪ,təɪ
**sp** posteritie[4], posterity[5]
**rh** chastity, infirmity *PT 59*; enmity *S 55.11*; husbandry *S 3.8*; obscurity *VA 758*; severity *RJ 1.1.220*; thee *S 6.12*

**postern / ~s** *n*
'pɒstəɹn / -z
**sp** posterne[3] / posternes[3]

**post-haste** *adv*
,po:st-'ast, -'ha-
**sp** post-hast[1], post-haste[2], post haste[2]
> haste

**post-horse / ~s** *n*
*m* 'po:st-,ɔ:ɹs, -,hɔ:- / ,po:st-'ɔ:ɹsɪz, -'hɔ:-
**sp** post-horse[2] / post-horses[1]

**Posthumus** *n*
pɒ'stju:məs
**sp** Posthumus[45], Posthu-mus[1]

**posting** *adj*
'po:stɪn, -ɪŋ
**sp** posting[2]

**postmaster / ~'s** *n*
'po:s,mastəɹz, 'po:st-
**sp** post-masters[2]
> master

**postscript** *n*
'po:,skrɪpt, 'po:st-
**sp** postscript[1], post-script[1]

**posture / ~s** *n*
'pɒstəɹ / -z
**sp** posture[5] / postures[3]

**pos·y / ~ies** *n*
'po:zəɪ / -z
**sp** poesie[3] / posies[2]
**rh** roses *MW 3.1.19, PP 19.10*

**pot / ~s** *n*
=
**sp** pot[13] / pots[2]
**rh** *1* got *Mac 4.1.9*; **rh** *2* note *LLL 5.2.909, 918*
> chamber-, pint-, pottle-, water-pot

**potable** *adj*
'po:təbəl
**sp** potable[1]

**potation / ~s** *n*
pə'tɛ:sɪənz
**sp** potations[1], pota-tions[1]

**potato** *adj*
pə'tato:
**sp** potato[1]

**potato / ~oes** *n*
pə'tato:z
**sp** potatoes[1]

**potch** *v*
=
**sp** potche[1]

**potency** *n*
*m* 'po:tən,səɪ
**sp** potencie[4], potency[1]
> impotence

**potent** *adj*
'po:tənt
**sp** potent[19]

**potent / ~s** *n*
'po:tənts
**sp** potents[1]

**potentate / ~s** *n*
*m* 'po:tən,tɛ:ts
**sp** potentates[3]

**potential** *adj*
pə'tensɪɑl
**sp** potentiall[2]

**potently** *adv*
*m* 'po:tənt,ləɪ
**sp** potently[2]

**pothecary**
> apothecary

**pother** *n*
'pɤðəɹ, 'po:-
**sp** poother[1]

**potion / ~s** *n*
'po:sɪən / -z
**sp** potion[4] / potions[4]

**Potpan** [name] *n*
=
**sp** Potpan[2]

**potter / ~'s** *n*
'pɒtəɹz
**sp** potters[1]

**potting** *n*
'pɒtɪn, -ɪŋ
**sp** potting[1]

**pottle** *n*
=
**sp** pottle[4]

**pottle-deep** *adj*
=
**sp** pottle-deepe[1]
> deep

**pottle-pot / ~'s** *n*
=
**sp** pottle pot[1] / pottle-pots[1]
> pot

**pouch** *n*
pəʊʧ
**sp** pouch[3]

**poulter / ~'s** *n*
'po:ltəɹz
**sp** poulters[1]

**poultice** *n*
'po:ltɪs
**sp** poultis[1]

**Poultney** *n*
'po:ltnəɪ
**sp** Poultney[1]

**pouncet-box** *n*
'pəʊnsɪt-,bɒks
**sp** pouncet-box[1]

**pound / ~s** *n*
pəʊnd / -z
**sp** pound[52] / pounds[17]

**pound** *v*
pəʊnd
**sp** pound[1]

**pour** *Fr prep*
pu:ɹ
**sp** pour[8]

**pour / ~est / ~s / ~ing / ~ed** *v*
po:ɹ / -st / -z / 'po:rɪn, -ɪŋ / po:ɹd
**sp** poure[15], power[1], powr[1], powre[10] / powr'st[2] / pour's[1], powres[4] / pouring[1], powring[1] / pour'd[2], powr'd[4]

**pourquoi** *Fr adv*
puɹ'kwɛ
**sp** purquoy[1], pur-quoy[1]

**pout** *v*
pəʊt
**sp** powt[1]

**poverty** *n*
*m* 'pɒvəɹ,təɪ, -ɹt-
**sp** pouertie[11], pouerty[10]
**rh** *1* injury *S 40.10*; **rh** *2* eye *LLL 5.2.380*

**powder** *n / v*
'pəʊdəɹ, 'po:-
**sp** powder[7], pow-der[1] / powder[1]
> gunpowder

**powdered** *adj*
'pəʊdəɹd, 'po:-
**sp** pouder'd[1]

**powdering** *adj*
'pəʊdrɪn, -ɪŋ, 'po:-
**sp** poudring[1]

**power / ~s** *n*
po:ɹ / -z
**sp** power[287], pow'r[2], powre[36] / powers[46], powres[30], pow'rs[2]
**rh** bower *S 127.5*; deflower, hour *Luc 345*; flower *LC 146, MND 4.1.73, RJ 2.3.20, S 65.2, VA 944*; flower, hour *LC 74*; hour *3H6 4.1.148, S 126.1, Tim 3.1.62, WT 4.1.7*; sour *R2 3.2.192* / hours *Luc 295*
> overpowered

**powerful** *adj*
'po:ɹfʊl
**sp** powerfull[7], powrefull[10], powrfull[1], pow'rfull[1]

**powerfully** *adv*
'po:ɹfʊləɪ, -fl-
**sp** powerfully[1]

**powerless** *adj*
'po:ɹləs
**sp** powerlesse[1]

**pow waw** *interj*
'po:-'wɔ:
**sp** pow waw[1]

**pox** *n*
=
**sp** pox[16], 'pox[1], poxe[4]

**poyes**
> boy

**Poysam** *n*
'pəɪzəm
**sp** Poysam[1]

**prabble / ~s** *n*
=
**sp** prabbles[2], prables[2]

**practic** *adj*
=
**sp** practique[1]

**practice / ~s** *n*
=
**sp** practice[11], practise[33] / practises[13]

**practisant / ~s** *n*
*m* 'praktɪˌsants
**sp** practisants[1]

**practis·e / ~es / ~ing / ~ed** *v*
= / = / 'praktɪsɪn, -ɪŋ / =
**sp** practice[3], practise[13] / practises[1] / practising[3] / practic'd[1], practis'd[6], pra-ctis'd[1]
> death-, un-, well-practised

**practised** *adj*
=
**sp** practis'd[1], practiz'd[1]

**practiser / ~s** *n*
'praktɪsəɹ / -z
**sp** practiser[2] / practizers[1]

**praeclarissimus** *Lat adj*
ˌprekla'rɪsɪmʊs
**sp** praeclarissimus[1]

**praetor / ~'s / ~s** *n*
'pretəɹz
**sp** praetors[1], pretors[1]

**Prague** *n*
=
**sp** Prage[1]

**prains**
> brain

**praise / ~s** *n*
prɛ:z / 'prɛ:zɪz
**sp** praise[85], prayse[15] / praises[15], prayses[7]
**rh** days *3H6 4.6.44, LLL 4.1.23, 5.2.366, S 2.8, 38.14, 59.14, 70.11, 82.6, 95.7, Tit 1.1.171*; obeys, raise *LC 226*; ways *PP 18.15*

**prais·e / ~est / ~es / ~ing / ~ed** *v*
prɛ:z / 'prɛ:z·əst / -ɪz / -ɪn, -ɪŋ / *m* -ɪd, prɛ:zd
**sp** praise[51], prayse[5] / praisest[1] / praises[2] / praising[8], praysing[1] / praisd[1], prais'd[23], praised[7], prays'd[1], praysed[3]
**rh** days *S 62.13, 106.14*
> dis-, super-praise; all-praised

**praised** *n*
*m* 'prɛ:zɪd
**sp** praised[1]

**praiseworthy** *adj*
'prɛ:zˌwɔ:ɹðəɪ
**sp** praise worthie[1]
> worthy

**praising** *n*
'prɛ:zɪn, -ɪŋ
**sp** praising[1]

**pranc·e / ~ing** *v*
'prɔ:nsɪn, -ɪŋ
**sp** prauncing[1]

**prank / ~s** *n*
=
**sp** prancks[2], prankes[5], pranks[1]

**prank / ~s / ~ed** *v*
=
**sp** pranke[1] / prankes[1] / prank'd[1]

**prat** *v*
=
**sp** prat-[her][1]

**Prat** [name] *n*
=
**sp** Prat[1]

**prate** *n*
prɛ:t
**sp** prate[2]
> love-prate

**prat·e / ~est / ~es / ~ing** *v*
prɛ:t / -st / -s / 'prɛ:tɪn, -ɪŋ
**sp** prate[11] / pratest[2], prat'st[3] / prating[1] / prated[1]

**prater** *n*
'prɛ:təɹ
**sp** prater[1]

**prating** *adj / n*
'prɛ:tɪn, -ɪŋ
**sp** prating[7], pra-ting[1] / prating[3]

**prattle** *n / v*
=
**sp** pratle[1], prattle[1], prattle[6]

**prattler** *n*
'pratləɹ
**sp** pratler[1]

**prattling** *adj*
'pratlɪn, -ɪŋ
**sp** pratling[2]

**prattling / ~s** *n*
'pratlɪn, -ɪŋ / -z
**sp** pratling[2] / pratlings[1]

**prave**
> brave

**prawls**
> brawl

**prawn / ~s** *n*
=
**sp** prawnes[1]

**pray / ~est / ~s / ~ing / ~ed** *v*
prɛ: / -st / -z / 'prɛ:ɪn, -ɪŋ / prɛ:d
**sp** pra'[1], praie[21], pray[680], 'pray [I pray][14], pray'[I pray][1], praye[1], pray'thee[1], pray'[ye][1] / prai'st[1] / praies[6], prayes[11] / praying[6] / praid[3], prai'd[2], pray'd[9]
**rh** away *TS 1.2.224*; day *R2 1.1.150*; may *R2 5.3.82*; play *H5 Prol.33*; today *CE 1.2.51, RJ 2.3.59*; way *TG 1.2.40* / decays *Luc 714* / decayed *1H6 1.1.33*
**pun** *1H4 2.1.81* prey
> a-praying, outpray, prithee

**prayer / ~'s / ~s / ~s'** *n*
*m* 'prɛ:ɹ, -ɛ:əɹ / -z
**sp** praier[5], [morne]-praier[1], prayer[30], pray'r[1] / prayers[1] / praiers[8], prair's[1], prayers[66], prayres[10], prayrs[1], pray'rs[1] / prayers[1]
**rh** despair *RJ 1.5.102, Tem Epil.16*; fair *Luc 344*; fair, repair *PT 67*

**prayer-book / ~s** *n*
'prɛ:ɹ-ˌbʊk / -s
**sp** prayer-booke[1], prayer booke[1] / prayer bookes[1]
> book

**praying** *adj / n*
'prɛ:ɪn, -ɪŋ
**sp** praying[1] / praying[1]

**preach / ~es / ~ing / ~ed** *v*
= / = / 'pri:ʧɪn, -ɪŋ / =
**sp** preach[3] / preaches[1] / preaching[1] / preach'd[1]
**rh** teach *1H6 3.1.128*

**preacher / ~s** *n*
'pri:ʧəɹz
**sp** preachers[1]

**preachment** *n*
'pri:ʧmənt
**sp** preachment[1]

**pread**
> bread

**preambulate** *v*
pri:'ambjʊˌlɛ:t
**sp** preambulat[1]

**precedence** *n*
*m* prə'si:dəns, 'presɪˌdens
**sp** precedence[2]

**precedent** *adj*
prɪ'si:dənt
**sp** precedent[3], president[13]

**precedent** *n*
*m* 'presɪˌdent, -sɪdənt
**sp** precedent[2]
**rh** content *LC 155*

**preceding** *adj*
prɪ'si:dɪn, -ɪŋ
**sp** preceding[1]

**precept** *n*
pri:'sept / *m* pri:'seps, 'pri:seps, -pts
**sp** precept[1] / precepts[8]

**preceptiall** *adj*
pri:'sepsɪɑl
**sp** preceptiall[1]

**precinct** *n*
pri:'sɪŋkt
**sp** precinct[1]

**precious** *adj*
'presɪəs
**sp** precious[67], preci-ous[1], pretious[3], *MM 3.1.100 emend of* prenzie[1]

**precious-juiced** *adj*
*m* 'presɪəs-ˌʤəɪsɪd
**sp** precious iuced[1]
> juice

**preciously** *adv*
*m* 'presɪəsˌləɪ
**sp** preciously[1]

**precious-princely** *adj*
'presɪəs-ˌprɪnsləɪ
**sp** precious princely[1]
> prince

**precipice** *n*
=
**sp** *H8 5.1.139 emend of* precepit[1]

**precipitat·e / ~ing** *v*
prə'sɪpɪˌtɛ:tɪn, -ɪŋ
**sp** precipitating[1]

**precipitation** *n*
*m* prəˌsɪpɪ'tɛ:sɪən, -sɪˌɒn
**sp** precipitation[2]

**precise** *adj*
prɪ'səɪs
**sp** precise[6], *MM 3.1.97 emend of* prenzie[1]
**rh** flies *LLL 5.2.406*

**precisely** *adv*
prɪ'səɪsləɪ
**sp** precisely[5]

**preciseness** *n*
prɪ'səɪsnəs
**sp** precisenesse[1]

**precisian** *n*
prɪˈsɪzɪən
**sp** precisian[1]

**pre-contract** *n*
ˈpriː-kənˌtrakt
**sp** pre-contract[1]
> contract

**precor** *Lat v*
ˈprekɔːɹ
**sp** precor[1]

**precurser / ~s** *n*
prɪˈkɐːɹsəɹz
**sp** precursers[1]

**predeceased** *adj*
ˈpriːdɪˌsɛːst
**sp** predeceased[1]
> decease

**predecessor / ~s** *n*
ˈpriːdɪˌsesəɹ / -z
**sp** predecessor[1] / predecessors[4]

**predestinate** *adj*
prɪˈdestɪnət
**sp** predestinate[1]

**predicament** *n*
*m* prɪˈdɪkəˌment
**sp** predicament[3]

**prediction / ~s** *n*
prɪˈdɪksɪən / -z
**sp** prediction[3] / predictions[1]

**predominance** *n*
*m* prɪˈdɒmɪˌnans, -ɪnəns
**sp** predominance[3]

**predominant** *adj*
*m* prɪˈdɒmɪˌnant, -ɪnənt
**sp** predominant[5]
**rh** plant *RJ 2.3.25*

**predominate** *v*
*m* prɪˈdɒmɪˌnɛːt
**sp** predominate[2]

**preeches**
> breeches

**pre-eminence** *n*
priːˈhemɪˌnens
**sp** preheminence[2]
> eminence

**pre-employ / ~ed** *v*
ˈpriː-emˌpləɪd
**sp** pre-employ'd[1]
> employ

**preface** *n*
=
**sp** preface[1]

**prefer / ~est / ~s / ~eth / ~ring / ~red** *v*
prɪˈfɐːɹ / -st / -z / -əθ / -ɪn, -ɪŋ / -d
**sp** prefer[5], preferre[13] / preferr'st[1] / prefers[1] / preferreth[1] / preferring[1] / preferd[1], prefer'd[2], preferr'd[7], preferred[1]
**rh** interred *Cym 4.2.400*

**preferment / ~s** *n*
prɪˈfɐːɹmənt / -s
**sp** preferment[10], prefer-ment[1] / preferments[2]

**prefigur·e / ~ing** *S* *v*
priːˈfɪgəˌrɪŋ
**sp** prefiguring[1]
**rh** sing *S 106.10*

**prefix** *v*
priːˈfɪkst
**sp** prefix'd[1], prefixt[2]

**prefixed** *adj*
*m* priːˈfɪksɪd
**sp** prefixed[1]

**pre-formed** *adj*
*m* priː-ˈfɔːɹmɪd
**sp** pre-formed[1]
> form

**pregnancy** *n*
ˈpregnənsəɪ
**sp** pregnan-cie[1]

**pregnant** *adj*
=
**sp** pregnant[15]
> unpregnant

**pregnantly** *adv*
ˈpregnəntləɪ
**sp** pregnantly[1]

**prejudicate / ~s** *v*
*m* priːˈʤuːdɪˌkɛːts
**sp** preiudicates[1]

**prejudice** *n*
*m* ˈpreʤəˌdɪs, -əd-
**sp** preiudice[3]

**prejudicial** *adj*
ˌpreʤəˈdɪsɪɑl
**sp** preiudiciall[1]

**prelate** *n*
=
**sp** prelate[9]

**premeditate** *Luc* *v*
*m* priːˈmedɪˌtɛːt
**sp** premeditate[1]
**rh** debate *Luc 183*
> meditate

**premeditated** *adj*
priːˈmedɪˌtɛːtɪd
**sp** premeditated[3]
> unpremeditated

**premeditation** *n*
priːˌmedɪˈtɛːsɪən
**sp** premeditation[1]

**premise / ~s** *n*
=
**sp** premises[3]

**premised** *adj*
ˈpremɪst
**sp** premised[1]

**premunire** *n*
ˌpreməˈniːriː
**sp** premunire[1]

**prendre / prenez** *Fr v*
prɛˈnez
**sp** prennes[1]

**prenominate** *adj / v*
*m* priːˈnɒmɪnət / -ɪˌnɛːt
**sp** prenominate[1] / prenominate[1]
> nominate

**prentice / ~s** *n*
=
**sp** prentice[2], prentize[1] / prentices[2]

**pre-occupy** *v*
*m* priːˈɒkjəˌpəɪd
**sp** pre-occupy'd[1]
> occupy

**pre-ordinance** *n*
*m* priːˈɔːɹdɪˌnans
**sp** pre-ordinance[1]
> ordinance

**preparation / ~s** *n*
*m* ˌprepəˈrɛːsɪən, -sɪˌɒn / -z
**sp** preparation[25], prepara-tion[3] / preparations[3]

**prepar·e / ~es / ~ing / ~ed** *v*
prɪˈpɛːɹ / -z / -ɪn, -ɪŋ / -d
**sp** prepare[62], pre-pare[1] / prepares[1] / preparing[1], pre-paring[1] / prepar'd[31], prepared[4]
**rh** *1* care *LLL 5.2.506*; rare *Per 4. Chorus.38*; snare *Tim 5.2.16*; **prepare** it share it *TN 2.4.55*; **rh** *2* are *LLL 5.2.81, S 13.3* / stares *VA 303*

**prepared** *adj*
prɪˈpɛːɹd
**sp** prepar'd[2], prepared[3]
> unprepared

**preparedly** *adv*
*m* prɪˈpɛːrɪdˌləɪ
**sp** preparedly[1]

**preposterous** *adj*
prɪˈpɒstrəs, -tər-
**sp** preposterous[3], preposte-rous[1], prepostorous[1], prepostrous[2]

**preposterously** *adv*
*m* prɪˈpɒstrəsləɪ, -ˌləɪ, -tər-
**sp** preposterously[3] , prepostrously[1]
**rh** me *MND 3.2.121*

**prerogative / ~s** *n*
*m* prɪˈrɒgəˌtɪv, -ət- / *Fluellen H5 4.1.67* prɪˈrɒgəˌtɪfs
**sp** prerogatiue[8] / *Fluellen* prerogatifes[1]

**prerogative / ~ed** *v*
*m* prɪˈrɒgəˌtɪvd
**sp** prerogatiu'd[1]

**presage** *n*
*m* ˈpresɪʤ / -ɪz
**sp** presage[2] / presages[2]
**rh** age *S 107.6*

**presage / ~s / ~th** *v*
prɪˈsɛːʤ / -ɪz / -əθ
**sp** presage[4] / presages[3] / presageth[2]

**presaging** *adj*
prɪˈsɛːʤɪn, -ɪŋ
**sp** presaging[1]

**prescience** *n*
=
**sp** prescience[3]

**prescribe / ~d** *v*
prɪˈskrəɪb / -d
**sp** prescribe[4] / prescrib'd[1]

**prescript** *adj / n*
ˈpriːskrɪpt
**sp** prescript[1] / prescript[1]

**prescription / ~s** *n*
prɪˈskrɪpsɪən / -s
**sp** prescription[4] / prescriptions[2]

**presence / ~s** *n*
=
**sp** presence[99], pre-sence[1] / presences[1]

**present** *adj*
ˈprezənt
**sp** present[150]

**present / ~s** *n*
ˈprezənt / -s
**sp** present[32], pres-ent[1], pre-sent[2] / presents[4]

**present / ~s / ~eth / ~ing / ~ed** *v*
prɪˈzent / -s, *Costard LLL 5.2.488* pəɹˈzents / -əθ / -ɪn, -ɪŋ / -ɪd
**sp** present[50], pre-sent[3] / presents[7], *Costard* pursents[1] / presenteth[2] / presenting[1] / presented[15]
**rh** content *MND 5.1.130* / contents *LLL 5.2.516*

**présent** *Fr n*
preˈzɑ̃
**sp** present[1]

**presentation** *n*
ˌprezənˈtɛːsɪən
**sp** presentation[2]

**presented** *adj*
=
**sp** presented[1]

**presenter / ~s** *n*
prɪˈzentəɹz
**sp** presenters[1]

**presently** *adv*
*m* ˈprezəntˌləɪ, -tl-
**sp** presentlie[6], presently[131], pre-sently[2]
**rh** *1* suddenly *PP 13.4*; **rh** *2* die *Tit 5.1.146*; pie *Tit 5.3.58*

**presentment** *n*
prɪˈzentmənt
**sp** presentment[2]

**preservation** *n*
ˌprezəɹˈvɛːsɪən
**sp** preseruation[6]

**preservatiue** *n*
prɪˈzɐːɹvətɪv
**sp** preseruatiue[1]

**preserv·e / ~ing / ~ed** *v*
prɪˈzɐːɹv / -ɪn, -ɪŋ / -d
**sp** preserue[22], pre-serue[1] / preseruing[1] / preseru'd[9], preserued[1]

**preserved** *adj*
prɪ'zɐːɹvɪd
**sp** preserued[1]
> ever-, nice-preserved

**preserver / ~s** *n*
prɪ'zɐːɹvəɹ / -z
**sp** preseruer[3] / preseruers[1]

**preserving** *adj*
prɪ'zɐːɹvɪn, -ɪŋ
**sp** preseruing[1]
> life-preserving

**president** *n*
'presɪdənt
**sp** president[1]

**press / ~es** *n*
=
**sp** prease[1], preasse[1], presse[5] / presses[1]

**press / ~es / ~ed** *v*
=
**sp** prease[1], presse[22] / presses[3] / preast[1], prest[14]
**rh** express *S 140.1* / breast *RJ 1.1.187*; rest *MND 2.2.71*

**pressed** *adj*
*m* 'presɪd, prest
**sp** pressed[1], prest-[bed][1]
> over-, un-pressed

**pressing** *adj / n*
'presɪn, -ɪŋ
**sp** pressing[1] / pressing[1]

**press-money** *n*
'pres-ˌmɤnəɪ
**sp** presse-money[1]
> money

**pressure / ~s** *n*
'presəɹ / -z
**sp** pressure[1] / presures[1]
> impressure

**Prester** *n*
'prestəɹ
**sp** Prester[1]

**presum·e / ~es / ~ing** *v*
prɪ'zjuːm / -z / -ɪn, -ɪŋ
**sp** presume[20] pre-sume[1] / presumes[1] / presuming[2]

**presumption** *n*
*m* prɪ'zɤmpsɪən, -sɪˌɒn
**sp** presumption[6]

**presumptuous** *adj*
*m* prɪ'zɤmtjəs, -tjʊəs, -mpt-
**sp** presumptuous[5]
> sumptuous

**presuppose / ~d** *v*
ˌpriːsə'poːzd
**sp** presuppos'd[1]

**presurmize** *v*
ˌpriːsəɹ'məɪz
**sp** presurmize[1]

**prêt** *Fr adj*
prɛ
**sp** prest

**pretence / ~s** *n*
=
**sp** pretence[9] / pretences[1]

**pretend / ~ing / ~ed** *v*
= / prɪ'tendɪn, -ɪŋ / =
**sp** pretend[6] / pretending[1], preten-ding[1] / pretended[1]
**rh** amended, ended *Luc 576*

**pretended** *adj*
=
**sp** pretended[1]

**pretext** *n*
priː'tekst
**sp** pretext[1]

**pretia** *Ital v*
'pretsɪa
**sp** *LLL 4.2.97 emend of* perreche[1]
**rh** Venetia

**prettily** *adv*
*m* 'prɪtɪˌləɪ
**sp** prettily[5]
**rh** deny, lie *MND 2.2.59*

**prettiness** *n*
*m* 'prɪtɪˌnes
**sp** prettinesse[1]

**prett·y / ~ier / ~iest** *adj*
'prɪtəɪ / -əɹ / -əst
**sp** prettie[28], pretty[79], pret-ty[1], prety[2], pritty[1] / prettier[1] / prettiest[8], prettyest[1]
**rh** ditty *PP 14.21*

**prevail / ~s / ~eth / ~ing / ~ed** *v*
prɪ'vɛːl / -z / -əθ / -ɪn, -ɪŋ / -d
**sp** preuaile[12] preuayle[9] / preuailes[4] / preuayleth[1] / preuailing[1] / preuaild[2], preuail'd[11] preuayl'd[10]
**rh** prevail with me fail with me *H5 3.2.14* / scales *2H6 2.1.200* / assailed *S 41.8*

**prevailing** *adj / n*
prɪ'vɛːlɪn, -ɪŋ
**sp** preualing[1] / preuai-ling[1]

**prevailment** *n*
prɪ'vɛːlmənt
**sp** preuailment[1]

**prevent / ~s / ~ed** *v*
=
**sp** preuent[24] / preuents[3] / preuented[19]
**rh** intent *Luc 220, VA 471*
> unprevented

**prevention / ~s** *n*
*m* prɪ'vensɪən, -sɪˌɒn / -z
**sp** preuention[6] / preuentions[1]

**prey / ~s** *n*
prɛː / -z
**sp** pray[3], prey[26] / prey's[1]
**rh** away *MND 2.2.156*; day *VA 1097*; obey *VA 63, 547*; play *LLL 4.1.90*; stay *Luc 421*

**prey / ~s / ~ed** *v*
prɛː / -z / -d
**sp** pray[1], prey[5] / preyes[1] / praide[1], preied[1]
**pun** *1H4 2.1.81* pray

**preyful** *adj*
'prɛ:fʊl
**sp** prayfull[1]

**Priam / ~'s** *n*
'prəɪəm / -z
**sp** Priam[20] / Priams[11]

**Priam·us / ~i** *Lat n*
'pri:əm·əs, 'prəɪ- / -i
**sp** Priamus[2] / Priami[3]

**pribble / ~s** *n*
=
**sp** pribbles[1], pribles[1]

**price** *n*
prəɪs
**sp** price[29]
**rh** advice *KL 2.1.119*; nice *LLL 5.2.223*

**prick / ~s** *n*
=
**sp** prick[1], pricke[5] / prickes[1], [wodden]-prickes[1], pricks[2]
**rh** sick, thick *Luc 781*

**prick / ~est / ~s / ~ing / ~ed** *v*
= / prɪkst / = / 'prɪkɪn, -ɪŋ / =
**sp** prick[4], pricke[21], prick't [prick it][1] / prick'st[1] / prickes[3], pricks[4] / pricking[1] / prick'd[4], prickt[11]
**rh** sticks, tricks *Luc 319*

**prick-eared** *adj*
'prɪk-ˌi:ɹd
**sp** prickeard[1]

**pricket** *n*
=
**sp** pricket[5]
**rh** thicket *LLL 4.2.57*

**pricket-sore** *n*
'prɪkɪt-ˌsɔ:ɹ
**sp** pricket-sore[1]
> sore

**pricking** *adj / n*
'prɪkɪn, -ɪŋ
**sp** pricking[1] / pricking[2]

**pricksong** *n*
=
**sp** pricksong[1]
> song

**pride / ~s** *n*
prəɪd / -z
**sp** pride[95] / prides[1]
**rh** abide *R2 5.6.23, S 76.1*; beside *S 103.2*; beside, bide *LC 30*; bride *RJ 1.2.10*; chide *S 99.3*; died *1H6 4.7.16*; dignified, hide *Luc 662*; dyed *S 99.3*; eyed *S 104.4*; hide *RJ 1.3.90, S 52.12, TN 3.1.148*; lied *MND 2.2.60*; ride *S 80.12*; side 1H6 4.6.57, *Luc 1809, PP 2.8, R2 3.2.81, R3 5.3.177, S 144.8, 151.10*; tide *Luc 1669*; tried *VA 278*

**pridge**
> bridge

**prief**
> brief

**prier / prie** *Fr v*
pri
**sp** prie[1]

**priest / ~s** *n*
=
**sp** priest[57], [scuruy-iack-dog]-priest[1] / priests[15]
**rh** list *TS 3.2.163*
> hedge-, Jack-priest

**priesthood** *n*
'pri:stʊd, -hʊ-
**sp** priesthood[1], priest-hood[1]

**priestlike** *adj*
'pri:stləɪk
**sp** priest-like[2]

**prig** *n*
=
**sp** prig[2]

**primal** *adj*
'prəɪmɑl
**sp** primall[2]

**prime / ~r / ~st** *adj*
prəɪm / 'prəɪm·əɹ / -əst
**sp** prime[5] / primer[1] / primest[1]

**prime** *n*
prəɪm
**sp** prime[8]
**rh** time *AY 5.3.35, Luc 332, R2 5.2.51, S 3.10, 12.3, 70.8, 97.7, VA 131*

**primero** *n*
prɪ'mɛ:ro:
**sp** primero[2]

**primitive** *adj*
=
**sp** primatiue[1]

**primo** *Ital adv*
'pri:mo:
**sp** primo[1]

**primogenitive** *n*
ˌprəɪmə'ʤenɪtɪv
**sp** primogenitiue[1]

**primrose / ~s** *n*
'prɪmro:z / -ɪz
**sp** primrose[3], [pale]-primrose[1], prim-rose[1] / prime-roses[2]
> rose

**primy** *adj*
'prəɪməɪ
**sp** primy[1]

**prince / ~'s / ~s / ~s'** *n*
=
**sp** prince[378] / princes[27], prin-ces[1] / princes[93], [clowdy]-princes[1], prin-ces[1] / princes[3]
**rh** convince *Per 1.2.124*
> Black Prince

**prince** *v*
=
**sp** prince[1]

**prince-like** *adj*
'prɪns-ləɪk
**sp** prince-like[1]

**princely** *adj / adv*
'prɪnsləɪ
**sp** princely[76] / princely[1]
> precious-princely

**princess / ~'** *n*
'prɪnses
**sp** princes[1], princesse[60] / princesse[1]

**principal** *adj / n*
*m* 'prɪnsɪ,pɑl, -ɪp-
**sp** principal[1], principall[1] / principall[6]

**principalit·y / ~ies** *n*
*m* ,prɪnsɪ'palɪ,təɪ / -ɪtəɪz
**sp** principalitie[1] / principalities[1]

**principle / ~s** *n*
=
**sp** principle[2] / principles[1]

**princox** *n*
'prɪnkɒks
**sp** princox[1]

**prings**
> brings

**print / ~s** *n*
=
**sp** print[11] / prints[1]
**rh** dint *VA 353*

**print / ~ing / ~ed** *v*
= / 'prɪntɪn, -ɪŋ / =
**sp** print[3] / printing[1] / printed[2]

**printing** *n*
'prɪntɪn, -ɪŋ
**sp** printing[1]

**printless** *adj*
=
**sp** printlesse[1]

**prior·ess** *n*
'prəɪə,res
prioresse[1]

**priority** *n*
*m* prəɪ'ɒrɪtəɪ, -,təɪ
**sp** priority[2]

**prior·y / ~ies** *n*
'prəɪərəɪ / -z
**sp** priorie[2] / priories[1]

**Priscian** *n*
'prɪsɪən
**sp** Prescian[1]

**prison** *adj*
=
**sp** prison[2]

**prison / ~s** *n*
=
**sp** prison[78], prison-[house][1], pri-son[1] / prisons[4]
> imprison

**prisoned** *adj*
=
**sp** prison'd[1]

**prisoner** *adj*
*m* 'prɪznəɹ, -zən-
**sp** prisoner[1]

**prisoner / ~'s / ~s / ~s'** *n*
*m* 'prɪznəɹ, -zən- / -z
**sp** prisoner[74] / prisoners[1], pri-soners[1] / prisoners[37] / prisoners[1]

**prisonment** *n*
*m* 'prɪzən,ment
**sp** prisonment[1]

**prisonnier** *Fr n*
prizɔ̃'je
**sp** prisonner[1]

**pristine** *adj*
=
**sp** pristine[2]

**prithee** *interj*
'preði:, 'prɪ-
**sp** preethe[1], prethe[1], 'prethe[1], prethee[88], 'prethee[5], pre-thee[5], 'pre-thee[1], pre'thee[14], prethy[1], prithee[2], prythe[1], prythee[104], 'prythee[1], pry-thee[2], pry'thy[1]
> pray

**privacy** *n*
*m* 'prəɪvəsəɪ, -ə,s-
**sp** priuacie[2], priua-cy[1]

**private** *adj / adv*
'prəɪvət
**sp** priuat[1], priuate[48] / priuate[1]

**private / ~s** *n*
'prəɪvət / -s
**sp** priuate[15] / priuates[2]

**privately** *adv*
*m* 'prəɪvət,ləɪ, -tl-
**sp** priuately[5], priuatly[1]

**privilege / ~s** *n*
*m* 'prɪvleʤ, -vɪl-, -vɪ,l- / 'prɪvlə,ʤɪz
**sp** priuiledge[28], priui-ledge[1] / priuiledges[1]
**rh** edge *S 95.13*

**privilege / ~d** *v*
*m* 'prɪvleʤ, -vɪl-, -vɪ,l- / -d
**sp** priuiledge[2] / priuiledg'd[3]

**privileged** *adj*
*m* 'prɪvleʤd, -vɪl-, -vɪ,leʤɪd
**sp** priuiledg'd[1], priuiledged[1]

**privilegi·um / ~o** *Lat n*
,prɪvɪ'leʤɪo:
**sp** preuilegio[1], priuilegio[1]

**privily** *adv*
*m* 'prɪvɪ,ləɪ, -ɪl-
**sp** priuily[4]

**privity** *n*
*m* 'prɪvɪ,təɪ
**sp** priuity[1]

**privy** *adj*
'prɪvəɪ
**sp** priuie[7], priuy[8]

**privy-kitchen** *n*
'prɪvəɪ-,kɪʧɪn
**sp** priuy-kitchin[1]
> kitchen

**prize / ~s** *n*
prəɪz / 'prəɪzɪz
**sp** prize[33] / prizes[1]
**rh** eyes *MV 3.2.141*; lies *Luc 279*

**prize / ~st / ~s / ~d** *v*
prəɪz / 'prəɪz·əst / -ɪz / *m* -ɪd, prəɪzd
**sp** prise[1], prize[12] / prizest[1] / prizes[4] / pris'd[1], prisde[1], priz'd[6], prized[1]
**rh** devised *AY 3.2.148*
> dis-, out-, under-prize; over-, un-prized; unprizable

**prizer** *n*
'prəɪzəɹ
**sp** priser[1], prizer[1]

**probable** *adj*
=
**sp** probable[10]

**probal** *adj*
'pro:bɑl
**sp** proball[1]

**probation** *n*
*m* prə'bɛ:sɪən, -sɪ,ɒn
**sp** probation[7]

**proceed / ~s / ~ing / ~ed** *v*
= / = / prə'si:dɪn, -ɪŋ / =
**sp** proceed[51], proceede[19] / proceeds[3], proceedes[3] / proceeding[4] / proceeded[13]
**rh** deed *AW 2.1.209, 2.3.124, Luc 251*; need *LLL 4.3.285*; weed *S 76.8* / **rh** *1* bleeds *Luc 1552*; bleeds, deeds *Luc 1825*; deeds *AW 4.2.62, S 131.14*; **rh** *2* sheds *Luc 1552*

**proceeder / ~s** *n*
prə'si:dəɹz
**sp** proceeders[1]

**proceeding / ~s** *n*
prə'si:dɪn, -ɪŋ / -z
**sp** proceeding[21] / proceedings[16]
**rh** a-bleeding *RJ 3.1.188*; a-breeding *LLL 1.1.95*

**process** *n*
'pro:ses
**sp** processe[18]

**procession** *n*
*m* prə'sɛ:sɪən, -sɪ,ɒn
**sp** procession[3]

**process-server** *n*
'pro:ses-,sɐ:ɹvəɹ
**sp** processe-seruer[1]

**proclaim / ~s / ~eth / ~ed** *v*
prə'klɛ:m / -z / -əθ / *m* -d, -ɪd
**sp** proclaime[33], proclayme[5] / proclaimes[7], proclaymes[1] / proclaimeth[1] / proclaim'd[16], proclaimed[7], proclaym'd[4], proclaymed[1]
**rh** aim *AW 2.1.155*

**proclaimed** *adj*
*m* prə'klɛ:md, -mɪd
**sp** proclaim'd[71], proclaymed[1]

**proclamation / ~s** *n*
*m* prɒklə'mɛ:sɪən, -sɪ,ɒn / -z
**sp** proclamation[21], proclamatio[n][1] / proclamations[2]

**pro-consul** *n*
,pro:-'kɒnsəl
**sp** pro-consull[1]
> consul

**procrastinate** *v*
prə'krasti,nɛ:t
**sp** procrastinate[1]

**procreant** *adj*
'pro:krɪənt
**sp** procreant[1]

**procreant / ~s** *n*
*m* 'pro:krɪ,ants
**sp** procreants[1]

**procreation** *n*
,pro:krɪ'ɛ:sɪən
**sp** procreation[1]

**Procris** *n*
*Bottom mispronunciation MND 5.1.195f* 'prɒkrəs
**sp** Procrus[2]

**Proculeius** *n*
,prɒkjə'lɛ:əs, -jʊ-
**sp** Proculeius[9]

**procurator** *n*
'prɒkjə,rɛ:təɹ
**sp** procurator[1]

**procur·e / ~s / ~ed** *v*
prə'kju:ɹ / -z / -d
**sp** procure[19] / procures[1], pro-cures[1] / procur'd[2], procured[1]
**rh** enured *LC 252* [*emend of* procure]

**procuring** *n*
prə'kju:rɪn, -ɪŋ
**sp** procuring[1]

**prodigal** *adj / adv*
*m* 'prɒdɪ,gɑl, -ɪg-
**sp** prodigall[10] / prodigall[2]

**prodigal / ~'s / ~s** *n*
*m* 'prɒdɪ,gɑl, -ɪg- / 'prɒdɪgɑlz
**sp** prodigall[9] / prodigals[1] / prodigalls[1]
**rh** call *PP 20.37*

**prodigality** *n*
*m* ,prɒdɪ'gɑlɪ,təɪ
**sp** prodigallity[1]

**prodigally** *adv*
*m* 'prɒdɪ,gɑləɪ
**sp** prodigally[1]

**prodigious** *adj*
*m* prə'dɪʤəs, -ʤɪəs-, -ʤɪ,ɤs
**sp** prodigeous[1], prodigious[5], prodigi-ous[1]

**prodigiously** *adv*
*m* prə'dɪʤəs,ləɪ, -ɪəs-
**sp** prodigiously[1]

**prodig·y / ~ies** *n*
*m* 'prɒdɪ,ʤəɪ / -z
**sp** prodegie[1], prodigie[3] / prodigies[4]
**rh** prophecies *VA 926*

**proditor** *n*
*m* 'prɒdɪ,tɔ:ɹ
**sp** proditor[1]

**produc·e / ~es / ~ing / ~ed** *v*
prə'dju:s / -ɪz / -ɪn, -ɪŋ / -t
**sp** produce[16], pro-duce[1] / produces[1] / producing[2] / produc'd[1], produc't[1], *emend of Oth 1.1.147* producted[1]

**proface** *interj*
prə'fas
**sp** proface[1]

**profanation** *n*
*m* ˌprɒfə'nɛ:sɪən, -sɪˌɒn
**sp** prophanation[3]

**profane** *adj*
prə'fɛ:n
**sp** prophane[8]

**profan·e / ~ing / ~ed** *v*
prə'fɛ:n / -ɪn, -ɪŋ / *m* -d, -ɪd
**sp** prophane[9] / prophaning[1] / prophan'd[4], prophaned[1]

**profanely** *adv*
prə'fɛ:nləɪ
**sp** prophanely[1]

**profaneness** *n*
prə'fɛ:nəs
**sp** prophanenesse[1]

**profaner / ~s** *n*
prə'fɛ:nəɹz
**sp** prophaners[1]

**profess / ~es / ~ed** *v*
= / = / *m* prə'fest, -sɪd
**sp** professe[24], pro-fesse[2] / professes[7], pro-fesses[1] / profess'd[1], professed[2], profest[4]

**professed** *adj*
prə'fest
**sp** profest[2]

**profession / ~s** *n*
prə'fesɪən / -z
**sp** profession[16], profession's [profession is][1] / professions[4]

**professor / ~s** *n*
prə'fesəɹz
**sp** professors[3]

**proffer / ~s** *n*
'prɒfəɹ / -z
**sp** proffer[2] / proffers[1]
**rh** offer *PP 4.10*

**proffer / ~s / ~ed** *v*
'prɒfəɹ / -z / -d
**sp** proffer[2] / proffers[1] / proffer'd[1]

**proffered** *adj*
'prɒfəɹd
**sp** proffer'd[4]

**profferer** *n*
'prɒfrəɹ, -fər-
**sp** profferer[1]

**proficient** *adj*
prə'fɪsɪənt
**sp** proficient[1]

**profit / ~'s / ~s** *n*
=
**sp** profit[26], profite[1], profit's [profit is][1] / profits[1] / profits[5]

**profit / ~s / ~ing /~ed** *v*
= / = / 'prɒfɪtɪn, -ɪŋ / =
**sp** profit[26] / profits[2], pro-fits[1] / profiting[1] / profited[2]
> unprofited

**profitable** *adj*
*m* 'prɒfɪtˌabəl, -təb-
**sp** profitable[4]
> unprofitable

**profitably** *adv*
'prɒfɪtəbləɪ
**sp** profitably[2]

**profiting** *n*
'prɒfɪtɪn, -ɪŋ
**sp** profiting[1]

**profitless** *adj*
*m* 'prɒfɪtˌles
**sp** profitlesse[2]

**profound / ~est** *adj*
*m* prə'fəʊnd, 'pro:fəʊnd / prə'fəʊndəst
**sp** profound[14] / profoundest[1]
**rh** ground *LLL 5.2.116, Mac 3.5.24*

**profoundly** *adv*
prə'fəʊndləɪ
**sp** profoundly[1]

**progenitor / ~s** *n*
prə'ʤenɪˌtɔ:ɹz
**sp** progenitors[3]
**rh** none of ours *Luc 1756*

**progeny** *n*
*m* 'prɒʤɪˌnəɪ
**sp** progenie[2], progeny[3]

**Progne** *n*
'prɒgnɪ:
**sp** Progne[1]

**prognosticate** *S* *v*
*m* prɒg'nɒstɪˌkɛ:t
**sp** prognosticate[1]
**rh** date *S 14.13*

**prognostication** *n*
prɒgˌnɒstɪ'kɛ:sɪən
**sp** prog-nostication[1], progno-stication[1]

**progress** *n / v*
'pro:gres
**sp** progresse[10] / progresse[1]

**progression** *n*
prə'gresɪən
**sp** progression[1]

**prohibit** *v*
pro:'ɪbɪt, -'hɪ-
**sp** prohibite[1]

**prohibition** *n*
ˌpro:ɪ'bɪsɪən, -hɪ'-
**sp** prohibition[1]

**project / ~'s / ~s** *n*
'prɒʤɪkt / -s
**sp** proiect[10] / proiects[1] / proiects[1]

**project** *v*
'prɒʤɪkt
**sp** proiect[1]

**projection** *n*
prə'ʤeksɪən
**sp** proiection[1]

**prolixious** *adj*
prə'lɪksɪəs
**sp** prolixious[1]

**prolixity** *n*
*m* prə'lɪksɪtəɪ, -ˌtəɪ
**sp** prolixitie[1], prolixity[1]

**prologue / ~s** *n*
'pro:lɒg / -z
**sp** prologue[2] / prologues[2]

**prologue / ~s** *v*
'pro:lɒgz
**sp** prologues[1]

**prologue-like** *adj*
'pro:lɒg-ˌləɪk
**sp** prologue-like[1]

**prolong / ~s / ~ed** *v*
prə'lɒŋ / -z / -d
**sp** prolong[2] / prolongs[1] / prolong'd[4]
**rh** long *TNK Epil.16*

**Promethean** *adj*
prə'mi:tɪən, -i:θɪ-
**sp** Promethaean[1], Promethean[2]

**Prometheus** *n*
prə'mi:tɪəs, -i:θɪ-
**sp** Prometheus[1]

**promettre / promis** *Fr v*
prɔ'mi
**sp** pro-mets[1]

**promise / ~s** *n*
=
**sp** pro-mise[53], pro-mise[2] / promises[11]

**promis·e / ~es / ~eth / ~ing / ~ed / ~edest** *v*
= / = / = / 'prɒmɪs·ɪn, -ɪŋ / *m* -ɪd, 'prɒmɪst / -ɪdst
**sp** promise[46], pro-mise[2] / promises[12] / promiseth[3] / promising[3] / promisd[2], promis'd[40], promised[13], promist[6] / promised'st[1]

**promise-breach** *n*
'prɒmɪs-ˌbri:ʧ
**sp** promise-breach[1]
> breach

**promise-breaker** *n*
'prɒmɪs-ˌbrɛ:kəɹ
**sp** promise-breaker[2]
> break

**promise-crammed** *adv*
'prɒmɪs-ˌkramd
**sp** promise-cramm'd[1]
> cram

**promised** *adj*
*m* 'prɒmɪˌsɪd, 'prɒmɪst
**sp** promis'd[6], promised[1], promist[4]

**promise-keeping** *n*
'prɒmɪs-ˌki:pɪn, -ɪŋ
**sp** promise keeping[1]
> keep

**promising** *adj / n*
'prɒmɪsɪn, -ɪŋ
**sp** promising[2] / promising[1]

**promontory** *n*
*m* 'prɒməntrəɪ, -tər-, -ˌtɒrəɪ
**sp** promontary[1], promontorie[3], promontory[2]

**promotion / ~s** *n*
*m* prə'mo:sɪən, -sɪˌɒn / -z
**sp** promotion[4] / promotions[3]

**prompt** *adj*
prɒmt, -pt
**sp** prompt[4]

**prompt / ~s / ~ing / ~ed** *v*
prɒmt, -pt / -s / 'prɒmt·ɪn, -ɪŋ, -pt- / -ɪd
**sp** prompt[8] / promps[1], prompts[4] / prompting[1] / prompted[3]

**prompted** *adj*
'prɒmtɪd, -pt-
**sp** prompted[1]

**promptement** *Fr adv*
prɔ̃t'mɑ̃
**sp** promptement[1]

**prompter** *n*
'prɒmtəɹ, -pt-
**sp** prompter[1]

**prompting** *adj*
'prɒmtɪn, -ɪŋ, -pt-
**sp** prompting[1]

**prompture** *n*
'prɒmtəɹ, -pt-
**sp** prompture[1]

**promulgate** *v*
prə'mɤlgɛ:t
**sp** promulgate[1]

**prone** *adj*
pro:n
**sp** prone[4]
**rh** alone *S 141.6*

**prononc·er / ~ez** *Fr v*
prɔnɔ̃'se / -z
**sp** pronouncer[1] / pronoun-cies[1]

**pronoun / ~s** *n*
'pro:nəʊn / -z
**sp** pronoune[1] / pronounes[1]

**pronounc·e / ~ing / ~ed** *v*
prə'nəʊns / -ɪn, -ɪŋ / -t
**sp** pronounce[29], *RJ 2.1.10 emend of* prouant[1] / pronouncing[3] / pronounc'd[9], pronounced[2], pronounc'st[1], pronounc't[1]

**proof / ~s** *n*
=, prʊf / -s
**sp** proofe[73] / proofes[12], proofs[1]
**rh** aloof, behoof *LC 163*
> ague-, ap-, high-, Pistol-, plot-, shame-proof

**prop / ~s** *n*
=
**sp** prop[4] / props[2]

**prop / ~ped** *v*
=
**sp** prop[1] / propt[1]
> underprop

**propagate** *v*
'prɒpə,gɛ:t
**sp** propagate[3]
**rh** state *AW 2.1.197*

**propagation** *n*
,prɒpə'gɛ:sɪən
**sp** propogation[1]

**propend** *v*
prə'pend
**sp** propend[1]

**propension** *n*
prə'pensɪən
**sp** propension[1]

**proper / ~er / ~est** *adj*
'prɒp·əɹ / -rəɹ, -ərəɹ / -rəst
**sp** proper[61], pro-per[2] / properer[3] / proprest[1]
> unproper

**properly** *adv*
'prɒpəɹləɪ
**sp** properly[5]
> unproperly

**propert·y / ~ies** *n*
*m* prɒpəɹ,təɪ, -ɹt- / -z
**sp** propertie[7], property[8] / properties[2], pro-perties[1]
**rh** *1* immediately *Ham 3.2.268*; **rh** *2* die *AW 2.1.187*; eye *MND 3.2.367*

**propert·y / ~ies / ~ied** *v*
'prɒpəɹtəɪz / *m* 'prɒpəɹ,təɪd, -ɹt-
**sp** properties[1] / propertied[2], proportied[1]
> disproperty

**prophec·y / ~ies** *n*
*m* 'prɒfɪ,səɪ, -ɪs- / -z
**sp** prophecie[7], prophesie[9] / prophecies[3], prophesies[4]
**rh** *1* prodigies *VA 928*; **rh** *2* eyes *S 106.9*

**prophesier** *n*
'prɒfɪ,səɪəɹ
**sp** prophesier[1]

**prophes·y / ~ying / ~ied** *v*
*m* 'prɒfɪ,səɪ / -ɪn, -ɪŋ / -d
**sp** prophecie[6], prophesie[10] / prophecying[1] / prophecied[1], prophesi'd[1], prophesi'de[1], prophesied[2]
**rh** jealousy *VA 1135*

**prophesying** *adj*
'prɒfɪ,səɪɪn, -ɪŋ
**sp** prophesying[1]

**prophet / ~'s / ~s** *n*
=
**sp** prophet[13] / prophets[1] / prophets[3]

**prophetess** *n*
=
**sp** prophetesse[4]

**prophetic** *adj*
=
**sp** propheticke[3], prophetique[1], prophetticke[1]

**prophetically** *adv*
*m* prə'fetɪ,kaləɪ, -ɪkl-
**sp** prophetically[2]

**prophet-like** *adj*
'prɒfɪt-,ləɪk
**sp** prophet-like[1]

**propinquity** *n*
*m* prə'pɪnkwɪ,təɪ
**sp** propinquity[1]

**Propontic** *n*
prə'pɒntɪk
**sp** Proponticke[1]

**proportion / ~s** *n*
*m* prə'pɔ:ɹsɪən, -sɪ,ɒn / prə'pɔ:ɹsɪənz
**sp** proportion[22], pro-portion[1] / proportions[6]

**proportion / ~ed** *v*
prə'pɔ:ɹsɪən / -d
**sp** proportion[1] / proportion'd[2]
> disproportion; un-, well-proportioned

**proportionable** *adj*
prə'pɔ:ɹsɪənəbəl
**sp** proportionable[1]

**propos·e / ~es / ~ing / ~ed** *v*
prə'po:z / -ɪz / -ɪn, -ɪŋ / -d
propose[10] / proposes[1] / proposing[1] / propos'd[5]
**rh** lose *Ham 3.2.204* / supposed *Luc 132*

**proposed** *adj*
prə'po:zɪd
**sp** proposed[2]

**proposer** *n*
prə'po:zəɹ
**sp** proposer[1]

**proposition / ~s** *n*
,prɒpə'zɪsɪən / -z
**sp** proposition[1] / propositions[1]

**propound / ~ed** *v*
prə'pəʊndɪd
**sp** propounded[1]

**propre** *Fr adj*
'prɔprə
**sp** propre[1]

**propriety** *n*
*m* prə'prəɪə,təɪ
**sp** propriety[2]

**propugnation** *n*
,prɒpəg'nɛ:sɪən
**sp** propugnation[1]

**prorogue / ~d** *v*
pro:'ro:g / *m* pro:'ro:gɪd
**sp** prorogue[2] / proroged[1]

**proscription / ~s** *n*
*m* prəˈskrɪpsɪən, -sɪˌɒn / prəˈskrɪpsɪənz
**sp** proscription[3] / proscriptions[1]

**prose** *n*
proːz
**sp** prose[2]
**rh** hose *LLL 4.3.55*

**prosecute** *v*
=
**sp** prosecute[4]

**prosecution** *n*
ˌprɒsɪˈkjuːsɪən
**sp** prosecution[1]

**proselyte / ~s** *n*
*m* ˈprɒsɪˌləɪts
**sp** proselytes[1]

**Proserpina / ~'s** *n*
prəˈzɐːɹpɪnə / -z
**sp** Proserpina[1] / Proserpina's[1]

**prospect** *n*
ˈprɒspekt
**sp** prospect[6]

**prosper / ~s / ~ed** *v*
ˈprɒspəɹ / -z / -d
**sp** prosper[20] / prospers[1] / prosper'd[1]

**Prosper** [name] *n*
ˈprɒspəɹ
**sp** Prosper[4]
> Prospero

**prosperity** *n*
*m* prəˈsperɪˌtəɪ, -ɪt-
**sp** prosperitie[9], prosperitie's [prosperity is][1], prosperity[5]
**rh** amity, be, jollity, me, solemnly, triumphantly *MND 4.1.89*

**Prospero** *n*
*m* ˈprɒspəroː, -proː
**sp** Prospero[21]
> Prosper

**prosperous** *adj*
*m* ˈprɒsprəs, -pər-, -pəˌrɤs
**sp** prosperous[20], prosp'rous[3]

**prosperously** *adv*
ˈprɒsprəsˌləɪ, -pər-
**sp** prosperously[2]

**prostitute** *v*
ˈprɒstɪtjuːt
**sp** prostitute[1]

**prostrate** *adj*
ˈprɒstrɛːt
**sp** prostrate[6]

**protect / ~s / ~ed** *v*
=
**sp** protect[12] / protects[3] / protected[2]

**protection** *n*
*m* prəˈteksɪən, -sɪˌɒn
**sp** protection[13]

**protector / ~s** *n*
prəˈtektəɹ / -z *n*
**sp** protector[48], pro-tector[1] / protectors[9]

**protectorship** *n*
*m* prəˈtektəɹˌʃɪp
**sp** protectorship[3]

**protectress** *n*
=
**sp** protectresse[1]

**protest / ~s / ~ing / ~ed** *v*
= / = / prəˈtestɪn, -ɪŋ / =
**sp** protest[52], pro-test[1] / protests[4] / protesting[1] / protested[1]
**rh** breast *VA 581*; expressed *LLL 5.2.410*; guest *LLL 5.2.352*

**protestation / ~s** *n*
*m* ˌprɒtɪsˈtɛːsɪən, -sɪˌɒn / -z
**sp** protestation[6] / protestations[2]

**protester** *n*
prəˈtestəɹ
**sp** protester[1]

**protesting / ~s** *PP* *n*
prəˈtestɪnz, -ɪŋz
**sp** protestings[1]
**rh** jestings *PP 7.11*

**Proteus** *n*
*m* ˈproːtɪəs, -ɪˌɤs
**sp** Proteus[1], Protheus[66]
**rh** in us *TG 1.2.14*

**protract** *v*
=
**sp** protract[2]

**protractive** *adj*
=
**sp** protractiue[1]

**proud / ~er / ~est** *adj*
prəʊd / ˈprəʊd·əɹ / -əst, prəʊdst
**sp** proud[148], prowd[38] / prouder[5], prowder[2] / proudest[6], proud'st[1], prowdest[1]
**rh** aloud *VA 260, 884*; bowed *Luc 1371*; loud *Oth 2.1.145*
> mis-, over-, top-proud

**proud / ~s** *n*
prəʊd / -z
**sp** proud[1] / prouds[1]

**proud** *v*
prəʊd
**sp** proud[1]

**proudest** *n*
ˈprəʊdəst
**sp** proudest[4], prowdest[2]

**proud-hearted** *adj*
*m* ˌprəʊd-ˈɑːɹtɪd, -ˈhɑː-
**sp** prowd-hearted[1]
> heart

**proudl·y / ~ier** *adv*
ˈprəʊdləɪ / -əɹ
**sp** proudly[7], prowdly[3] / proudlier[1]

**proud-minded** *adj*
*m* ˌprəʊd-ˈməɪndɪd
**sp** proud minded[1]
> mind

**provand** *n*
'prɒvənd
**sp** prouand[1]

**prove / ~s / ~th / ~d** *v*
prɤv, pru:v / -z / 'prɤvəθ, 'pru:- / prɤvd, pru:vd
**sp** prooue[7], proue[230] / prooues[1], proues[14] / proueth[2] / prooued[2], prou'd[28], proued[6], pro-ued[1]
**rh** *1* love *AW 3.3.10, Ham 3.2.212, LLL 4.2.107, 4.3.62, 282, Luc 613, MND 2.1.265, PP 3.5, 5.3, 19.2, RJ 2.3.87, S 10.12, 32.13, 39.9, 72.4, 117.13, 136.7, 151.4, 153.7, 154.13, TC 1.3.287, TG 1.1.37, TN 2.4.116, 3.3.10, 3.4.374, TS 1.2.174, VA 40, 597*; prove me love thee *S 26.14*; **rh** *2* move *R2 1.1.46*; remove *Luc 613, RJ 1.1.141* / loved *S 116.13, VA 608*
> ap-, dis-prove

**proved** *adj*
prɤvd, pru:vd
**sp** prou'd[1]
> unimproved

**provender** *n*
'prɒvɪndəɹ
**sp** prouender[5]

**proverb / ~s** *n*
'prɒvəɹb, 'pro:- / -z
**sp** prouerb[3], prouerbe[9], pro-uerbe[1] / prouerbes[2], prouerbs[3]

**proverb / ~ed** *v*
'prɒvəɹbd, 'pro:-
**sp** prouerb'd[1]

**provide / ~s / ~d** *v*
prə'vəɪd / -z / -ɪd
**sp** prouide[29] / prouides[1] / prouided[20]
**rh** beside *Mac 3.5.18*; betide *3H6 4.6.87*; chide *S 111.3*; tide *Tim 3.4.118*

**provided** *adj / conj*
prə'vəɪdɪd
**sp** prouided[2] / prouided[8]
> sharp-, un-provided

**providence** *n*
*m* 'prɒvɪˌdens, -ɪdəns
**sp** prouidence[6]

**provident** *adj*
*m* 'prɒvɪˌdent
**sp** prouident[2]
> unprovident

**providently** *adv*
*m* 'prɒvɪˌdentləɪ
**sp** prouidently[1]

**provider** *n*
prə'vəɪdəɹ
**sp** prouider[1]

**province / ~s** *n*
=
**sp** prouince[3] / prouinces[6]

**provincial** *adj*
prə'vɪnsɪɑl
**sp** prouinciall[2]

**provision** *n*
prə'vɪzɪən
**sp** prouision[7]

**proviso** *n*
prə'vəɪzo:
**sp** prouiso[1]

**provocation** *n*
ˌprɒvə'kɛ:sɪən
**sp** prouocation[2]

**provoke / ~st / ~s / ~th / ~d** *v*
prə'vo:k / -st / -s / -əθ / -t
**sp** prouoake[1], prouoke[14] / prouoakst[1], prouok'st[1] / prouokes[10] / prouoketh[1] / prouoak'd[1], prouok'd[9], prouoked[4], prouok't[2]
**rh** *1* smoke *Per 1.1.138*; spoke *LLL 5.2.347*; **rh** *2* took *Per Prol.26*
> unprovokes

**provoker** *n*
prə'vo:kəɹ
**sp** prouoker[1]

**provoking** *adj*
prə'vo:kɪn, -ɪŋ
**sp** prouoking[2]

**provost** *n*
=
**sp** prouost[37]

**prowess** *n*
*m* 'pro:ɪs
**sp** prowesse[3]

**Prudence** [name] *n*
=
**sp** Prudence[2]

**prudent** *adj / n*
=
**sp** prudent[3] / prudent[1]

**prune / ~s** *n*
= / =, *Pompey MM 2.1.87ff*
'pru:ɪnz
**sp** prune[1] / [stew'd]-pruines[1], prunes[1], *Pompey* prewyns[4]

**prun·e / ~est / ~es / ~ing** *v*
= / pru:nst / = / 'pru:nɪn, -ɪŋ
**sp** prune[1] / prun'st[1] / prunes[1] / pruning[1]
> unpruned

**pruning** *n*
'pru:nɪn, -ɪŋ
**sp** pruning[1]

**pr·y / ~ies / ~ied** *v*
prəɪ / -z / -d
**sp** prie[5], pry[2] / pries[1] / pried[1]
**rh** jealousy *S 61.6*

**prying** *adj*
'prəɪɪn, -ɪŋ
**sp** prying[1]

**psalm / ~s** *n*
=, sɔ:mz
**sp** psalmes[1], psalms[1]

**psalter·y / ~ies** *n*
*m* 'sɔ:təˌrəɪz
**sp** psalteries[1]

**Ptolemy / ~s / ~s'** *n*
*m* 'tɒlə,məɪ / 'tɒləməɪz
**sp** Ptolomy[3] / Ptolomies[1] / Ptolomies[1]

**public** *adj / n*
'pɤblɪk
**sp** publicke[3], publike[17], publique[10] / pub-licke[1], publique[1]

**publican** *n*
'pɤblɪkən
**sp** publican[1]

**publication** *n*
,pɤblɪ'kɛ:sɪən
**sp** publication[1]

**publicly** *adv*
*m* 'pɤblɪk,ləɪ, -kl-
**sp** publikely[7], publiquely[3]

**Publicola** *n*
*m* pʊb'lɪkə,la
**sp** Publicola[2]

**publish / ~ing / ~ed** *v*
'pɤblɪʃ / -ɪn, -ɪŋ / *m* -ɪd, 'pɤblɪʃt
**sp** publish[8] / publishing[1] / publishd[1], publish'd[2], published[1]

**published** *adj*
'pɤblɪʃt
**sp** publish'd[1]
> **unpublished**

**publisher** *n*
'pɤblɪʃəɹ
**sp** publisher[1]
**rh** orator, singular *Luc 33*

**Publius** *n*
'pɤblɪəs
**sp** Publius[21], Pub-lius[1]

**Pucelle** *n*
*m* 'pu:sel, pu:'sel, -ze-
**sp** Pucel[1], Pucell[12], Pussel[1], Puzel[11], Puzell[1]

**Puck** *n*
pɤk
**sp** Puck[10], Pucke[12]
**rh** luck *MND 2.1.40, 5.1.421*

**pudder** *n*
'pɤdəɹ
**sp** pudder[1]

**pudding / ~s** *n*
'pʊdɪn, -ɪŋ / -z
**sp** pudding[5] / puddings[2]
> **hodge-pudding**

**puddle** *n*
'pɤdl
**sp** puddle[2]

**puddle / ~d** *v*
'pɤdld
**sp** pudled[1]

**puddled** *adj*
'pɤdld
**sp** puddled[1]

**pudency** *n*
*m* 'pju:dən,səɪ
**sp** pudencie[1]

**pueritia** *Lat n*
pu:ə'rɪtsɪə
**sp** puericia[1]

**puff / ~s / ~ing / ~ed** *v*
pɤf / -s / 'pɤfɪn, -ɪŋ / pɤft
**sp** puffe[2] / puffes[1] / puffing[2] / pufft[1], puff 't[1], puft[3]

**Puff** [name] *n*
pɤf
**sp** puffe[2]

**puffed** *adj*
pɤft
**sp** puft[3]

**puffing** *adj*
'pɤfɪn, -ɪŋ
**sp** puffing[1]

**pugging** *adj*
'pɤgɪn, -ɪŋ
**sp** pugging[1]

**puh** *interj*
=
**sp** puh[2]

**puis** *Fr adv*
pwi
**sp** puis[1]

**puisny** *adj*
'pju:nəɪ
**sp** puisny[1]

**puissance** *n*
*m* 'pu:ɪ,sɔ:ns, 'pwɪ-
**sp** puisance[2], puissance[7]

**puissant** *adj*
'pwɪsɔ:nt
**sp** puisant[1], puissant[7]
> **thrice-puissant**

**puissant** *Fr adj*
pwi'sɑ̃
**sp** [tres]-puissant[1]

**puk·e / ~ing** *v*
'pju:kɪn, -ɪŋ
**sp** puking[1]

**puke-stocking** *n*
'pju:k-,stɒkɪn, -ɪŋ
**sp** puke stocking[1]

**pulcher** *Lat adj*
'pʊlkeɹ
**sp** pulcher[1]

**puling** *adj / adv / n*
'pju:lɪn, -ɪŋ
**sp** puling[2] / puling[1] / [faint]-puling[1]

**pull / ~s** *n*
=
**sp** pulls[1]

**pull / ~s / ~ing / ~ed** *v*
= / -s / 'pʊlɪn, -ɪŋ / =
**sp** pull[12], pull't [pull it][1] / pulls[2] / pulling[1] / puld[3], pul'd[2], pull'd[4]
**rh** dull *AW 1.1.214*

**puller-down** *n*
'pʊləɹ-'dəʊn
**sp** puller downe[1]
> down

**pullet-sperm** *n*
'pʊlɪt-ˌspɐːɹm
**sp** pullet-spersme[1]

**pulpit / ~s** *n*
'pʊlpɪt / -s
**sp** pulpit[5] / pulpits[1]

**pulse** *n*
pɤls
**sp** pulse[9]

**pulsidge** *n*
'pɤlsɪʤ
**sp** pulsidge[1]

**pump / ~s** *n*
pɤmp / -s
**sp** pump[2] / pumpes[1], pumps[1]

**pumpion** *n*
'pɤmpɪən
**sp** pumpion[1]

**pun** *v*
pɤn
**sp** pun[1]

**punch / ~ed** *v*
*m* 'pɤnʧɪd
**sp** punched[1]

**punish / ~es / ~ed** *v*
'pɤnɪʃ / -ɪz / *m* 'pɤnɪʃt, -ʃed
**sp** punish[17], punnish[1] / punnishes[1] / punish'd[14], punished[2], punisht[3]
**rh** languish *Per 1.2.33* / head *RJ 5.3.308*

**punished** *adj*
'pɤnɪʃt
**sp** punisht[1]

**punishment / ~s** *n*
'pɤnɪʃˌment, -ʃmənt / -ʃmənts
**sp** punishment[20], punish-ment[1] / punishments[1]
**rh** argument *LLL 4.3.61, PP 3.4*

**punk** *n*
pɤŋk
**sp** puncke[2], punke[2]

**punto** *n*
'pʊnto:
**sp** puncto[1], punto[1]

**puny** *adj*
'pju:nəɪ
**sp** punie[3], punie-[sword][1], puny[2]

**pupil** *adj*
=
**sp** pupill[2]

**pupil / ~s** *n*
=
**sp** pupill[7] / pupils[1]

**pupil-like** *adj*
'pju:pɪl-ˌləɪk
**sp** pupill-like[1]

**puppet / ~'s** *n*
'pɤpɪt / -s
**sp** puppet[8] / puppets[2]
> demi-puppet

**pupp·y / ~ies** *n*
'pɤpəɪ / -z
**sp** puppie[2], puppy[2] / puppies[4]

**puppy-dog / ~s** *n*
'pɤpəɪ-ˌdɒg / -z
**sp** puppy-dog[1] / puppi-dogges[1]
> dog

**puppy-headed** *adj*
'pɤpəɪ-ˌedɪd, -ˌhe-
**sp** puppi-hea-ded[1]
> head

**purblind** *adj*
'po:ɹbləɪnd, 'pu:-
**sp** purblind[3], purblinde[1]
> blind

**purblinded** *adj*
'po:ɹbləɪndɪd, 'pu:-
**sp** purblinded[1]

**purchase / ~es** *n*
'pɐːɹʧɪs / -ɪz
**sp** purchase[6] / purchases[2]

**purchas·e / ~eth / ~ing / ~ed** *v*
'pɐːɹʧɪs / -əθ / -ɪn, -ɪŋ / -t
**sp** purchase[20] / purchaseth[1] / purchasing[2] / purchas'd[7], purchased[1], purcha-sed[1], purchast[3]

**purchased** *adj*
'pɐːɹʧɪst
**sp** purchast[1], purchaste[1]

**purchasing** *n*
'pɐːɹʧɪsɪn, -ɪŋ
**sp** purchasing[1]

**pure / ~r / ~st** *adj*
pju:ɹ / 'pju:ɹəɹ / -əst
**sp** pure[63] / purer[1] / purest[4]
**rh** endure *LLL 5.2.351, Luc 1658*; sure *TNK Prol.10*
> impure, thrice-repured

**purely** *adv*
'pju:ɹləɪ
**sp** purely[1]

**purer** *n*
'pju:rəɹ
**sp** purer[1]

**purest** *n*
'pju:rəst
**sp** purest[1]

**purgation** *n*
*m* pəɹ'gɛ:sɪən, -sɪˌɒn
**sp** purgation[6]

**purgative** *adj*
*m* pəɹ'gɛ:tɪv
**sp** purgatiue[1]

**purgatory** *n*
*m* 'pɐːɹgəˌtɒrəɪ, -ətər-, -ətr-
**sp** purgatorie[1], purgatory[1]

**purge** *n*
pɐːɹʤ
**sp** purge[1]

**purg·e / ~ing / ~ed** *v*
pɐːɹʤ / ˈpɐːɹʤ·ɪn, -ɪŋ / *m* -ɪd, pɐːɹʤd
**sp** purge[18] / purging[1] / purg'd[9], purged[1]
**rh** urge *S 118.4* / urged *RJ 1.5.107*

**purged** *adj*
*m* ˈpɐːɹʤɪd
**sp** purged[1]
> unpurged

**purger / ~s** *n*
ˈpɐːɹʤəɹz
**sp** purgers[1]

**purging** *n*
ˈpɐːɹʤɪn, -ɪŋ
**sp** purging[1]

**purif·y** *Luc* **/ ~ies /** *Luc* **~ied** *v*
*m* ˈpjuːrɪˌfəɪ / -z / -d
**sp** purifie[1] / purifies[1] / purified[1]
**rh** perpetually *Luc 685* / applied *Luc 532*

**purifying** *n*
ˈpjuːrɪˌfəɪɪn, -ɪŋ
**sp** pu-rifying[1]

**Puritan** *n*
ˈpjuːrɪtən
**sp** Puritan[3], Puri-tan[1], Puritane[2]

**purity** *n*
*m* ˈpjuːrɪˌtəɪ, -ɪt-
**sp** puritie[8], purity[1]

**purlieus** *n*
ˈpɐːɹljuːz
**sp** purlews[1]

**purple** *adj*
ˈpɐːɹpəl
**sp** purple[12]

**purple / ~s** *n*
ˈpɐːɹpəl / -z
**sp** purple[1] / purples[1]

**purpled** *adj*
ˈpɐːɹpəld
**sp** purpled[2]

**purple-hued** *adj*
ˈpɐːɹpəl-ˌjuːd, -ˌhj-
**sp** [mustachio]-purple-hu'd-[maltwormes][1]

**purple-in-grain** *adj*
ˈpɐːɹpəl-ɪn-ˈgrɛːn
**sp** purple in graine[1]
> grain

**purport** *n*
pəɹˈpɔːɹt
**sp** purport[1]

**purpose / ~s** *n*
ˈpɐːɹpəs / -ɪz
**sp** purpose[181], pur-pose[3] / purposes[36]

**purpose / ~es / ~eth / ~ing / ~ed** *v*
ˈpɐːɹpəs / -ɪz / -əθ / -ɪn, -ɪŋ / *m* -ɪd, ˈpɐːɹpəst
**sp** purpose[20] / purposes[2] / purposeth[2] / purposing[1] / purpos'd[10], purposed[3]

**purpose-changer** *n*
ˈpɐːɹpəs-ˌʧɛːnʤəɹ
**sp** purpose-changer[1]

**purposed** *adj*
ˈpɐːɹpəst
**sp** purpos'd[5]
> unpurposed

**purposely** *adv*
*m* ˈpɐːɹpəsˌləɪ, -sl-
**sp** purposely[4]

**purr** *n*
pɐːɹ
**sp** purre[1]

**purse / ~s** *n*
pɐːɹs / ˈpɐːɹsɪz
**sp** purse[76], pursse[1] / purses[10], pur-ses[1]
> cut-, pick-purse

**purse** *v*
pɐːɹs / -t
**sp** purse[2] / purst[1]

**purse-bearer** *n*
ˈpɐːɹs-ˌbɛːrəɹ
**sp** purse-bearer[1]
> bear

**purse-taking** *n*
ˈpɐːɹs-ˌtɛːkɪn, -ɪŋ
**sp** purse-taking[1]
> take

**pursue / ~st / ~s / ~th / ~ing / ~d** *v*
pəɹˈsjuː / -st / -z / -əθ / -ɪn, -ɪŋ / -d
**sp** persue[1], pursue[32], pur-sue[1] / pursuest[2] / pursues[7] / pursueth[1] / pursuing[5] / pursu'd[7], pursu'de[2], pursued[6]

**pursued** *adj*
pəɹˈsjuːd
**sp** pursu'de[1]

**pursuer / ~s** *n*
pəɹˈsjuːəɹz
**sp** pursuers[1]

**pursuit** *n*
pəɹˈsjuːt
**sp** pursuit[7], pursuite[8]

**pursuivant / ~s** *n*
ˈpɐːɹsɪˌvant, -swɪ- / -s
**sp** purse-uant[1], pursuiuant[4] / purseuants[1], pursuiuants[1]

**pursuivant-at-arms** *n*
ˈpɐːɹsɪˌvant-ət-ˈɑːɹmz, -swɪ-
**sp** pursuiuant at armes[1]
> arm

**pursy** *adj*
ˈpɐːɹsəɪ
**sp** pursie[2]

**purus** *Lat adj*
ˈpjuːrʊs
**sp** purus[1]

**purveyor** *n*
*m* 'pɐːɹvɪˌjɔːɹ
**sp** purueyor[1]

**push** *interj / n*
=
**sp** push[1] / push[8]

**push / ~es / ~ed** *v*
=
**sp** push[11], push-[on][2] / pushes[2] / pusht[1]

**push-pin** *n*
=
**sp** push-pin[1]
> pin

**pusillanimity** *n*
ˌpjuːsɪlə'nɪmɪtəɪ
**sp** pusillanimitie[1]

**put / ~test / ~s / ~ting** *v*
= / *m* pʊts, -t, 'pʊtəst / = / 'pʊtɪn, -ɪŋ
**sp** put[476], put-[off][1], put's [put his][2], put't [put it][1] / put'st[2], puttest[1] / puts[38], put's[3], puttes[1], putt's[1] / putting[12]

**putrified** *adj*
*m* 'pjuːtrɪˌfəɪd
**sp** putrified[1]
**rh** abide *Luc 1750*

**putrify** *v*
*m* 'pjuːtrɪˌfəɪ
**sp** putrifie[1]

**putter**
> butter

**putter-on** *n*
'pʊtəɹ-'ɒn
**sp** putter on[2]

**putter-out** *n*
'pʊtəɹ-'əʊt
**sp** putter out[1]

**putting-by** *n*
'pʊtɪn-'bəɪ, -ɪŋ-
**sp** putting by[1]

**putting-down** *n*
'pʊtɪn-'dəʊn, -ɪŋ-
**sp** putting down[1]

**putting-off** *n*
'pʊtɪn-'ɒf, -ɪŋ-
**sp** putting off[1]

**putting-on** *n*
'pʊtɪn-'ɒn, -ɪŋ-
**sp** putting on[4]

**puttock / ~'s** *n*
'pɤtək / -s
**sp** puttocke[2] / puttocks[1]

**puzzle / ~s / ~d** *v*
'pɤzəl / -z / -d
**sp** puzle[1] / puzels[1] / puzel'd[1]

**Pygmalion / ~'s** *n*
pɪg'mɛːlɪənz
**sp** Pigmalions[1]

**pyramid / ~s** *n*
=
**sp** pyramid[1] / pyramides[1], pyramids[1]

**pyramis / ~es** *n*
'pɪrəmɪs / -ɪz
**sp** pyramis[1] / pyra-misis[1]

**Pyramus** *n*
'pɪrəməs
**sp** Piramus[36], Pi-ramus[1], Pira-mus[1], Pyramus[10], Py-ramus[1], *abbr in s.d.* Pir[1]
**rh** thus *MND 5.1.289*

**Pyrenean** *n*
ˌpɪrə'niːən
**sp** Perennean[1]

**Pyrrhus** *n*
'pɪrəs
**sp** Pirhus[1], Pyrrhus[10]

**Pythagoras / ~s'** *n*
pɪ'tagərəs, -'θa-
**sp** Pythagoras[3] / Pythagoras[1]

**quadrangle** *n*
'kwɑdraŋgəl
**sp** quadrangle[1]

**quae** *Lat*
> qui

**quaff / ~ing / ~ed** *v*
kwɑf / 'kwɑfɪn, -ɪŋ / kwɑft
**sp** quaffe[1] / quaffing[1] / quafft[1], quaft[1]

**quagmire** *n*
'kwɑgməɪɹ
**sp** quagmire[1], quag-mire[1]

**quail / ~s** *n*
kwɛ:lz
**sp** quailes[2]

**quail** *v*
kwɛ:l
**sp** quaile[4]

**quailing** *adj / n*
'kwɛ:lɪn, -ɪŋ
**sp** quailing[1] / quailing[1]

**quaint** *adj*
kwɛ:nt
**sp** quaint[3], queint[7], quient[1]
**rh** faint *TNK 1.1.5*

**quaintly** *adv*
'kwɛ:ntləɪ
**sp** quaintly[3], queintly[2]

**quake / ~s / ~d** *v*
kwɛ:k / -s / -t
**sp** quake[13] / quakes[1] / quak'd[2]
**rh** take *1H6 1.1.156* / shakes *VA 1045*
> earthquake

**qualification** *n*
ˌkwɑlɪfɪ'kɛ:sɪən
**sp** qualification[1]

**qualified** *adj*
'kwɑlɪfəɪd
**sp** qualified[1]

**qualif·y / ~ies / ~ied** *v*
*m* 'kwɑlɪˌfəɪ, -ɪf-/ -ɪˌfəɪz / *m* -ɪˌfəɪd, -ɪf-
**sp** qualifie[7] / qualifies[1] / qualified[5], qual-lified[1]
**rh** lie *S 109.2* / satisfied, side *Luc 424*

**qualifying** *adj*
'kwɑlɪˌfəɪɪn, -ɪŋ
**sp** qualifying[1]

**qualité** *Fr n*
ˌkalɪ'te
**sp** qua-litee[1]

**qualit·y / ~ies** *n*
*m* 'kwɑlɪˌtəɪ, -ɪt- / -ɪˌtəɪz
**sp** qualitie[22], quality[28], qua-lity[1], quallitie[1] / qualities[23]
**rh** *1* astronomy *S 14.4*; destiny *MW 5.5.40*; discovery, uncertainly *Luc 1313*; opportunity *Luc 874*; **rh** *2* amplify *LC 210* / **rh** *1* maladies *VA 747*; **rh** *2* eyes *MND 1.1.231*; lies *RJ 2.3.12*
> unqualitied

**qualm** *n*
kwɔ:m
**sp** qualm[1], qualme[2]
> stomach-qualmed

**qualmish** *adj*
'kwɔ:mɪʃ
**sp** qualmish[1]

**qualtitie calmie custure me** [*Pistol H5 4.4.4*]
'kaltɪti: 'kɔ:mi: kʊ'stu:re: 'me:
**sp** [*as headwords*]

**quam** *Lat conj*
kwam, kam
**sp** quam[1]

**quand** *Fr adv*
kɑ̃
**sp** quand[2]

**quando** *Lat conj*
'kwando:, 'ka-
**sp** quando[1]

**quantit·y / ~ies** *n*
*m* 'kwɒntɪˌtəɪ, -ɪt- / -ɪtəɪz
**sp** quantitie[8], quantity[4] / quantities[2]
**rh** dignity *MND 1.1.232*; extremity *Ham 3.2.177*
> disquantity

**quare** *Lat adv*
'kwɑ:re, 'kɑ:-
**sp** quari[1]

**quarrel / ~s** *n*
'kwɑrəl / -z
**sp** quarell[1], quarrel[8], quarrell[73], quar-rell[1], quarrel's [quarrel is][1] / quarrells[1], quarrels[14], quar-rels[1]

**quarrel / ~s / led** *v*
'kwɑrəl / -z / -d
**sp** quarrel[2], quarrell[10] / quarrels[1] / quar-rel'd[1]

**quarreller** *n*
'kwɑrələɹ
**sp** quarreller[1]

**quarrelling** *n*
'kwarəlɪn, -ɪŋ
**sp** quarelling[1], quarreling[2], quarrelling[2], quar-relling[1], quarrel-ling[1]

**quarrellous** *adj*
'kwaɹləs, -rəl-
**sp** quarrellous[1]

**quarrelsome** *adj*
'kwarəlsəm
**sp** quarrelsome[2], quar-relsome[1]

**quarr·y / ~ies** *n*
'kwarəɪ / -z
**sp** quarrie[1], quarry[3] / quarries[1]

**quart** *adj*
kwaɹt
**sp** quart[1]

**quart / ~s** *n*
kwaɹt / -s
**sp** quart[3] / quarts[1]

**quarter / ~s** *n*
'kwaɹtəɹ / -z
**sp** quarter[17], quar-ter[1] / quarters[7]

**quarter / ~ed** *v*
'kwaɹtəɹ / -d
**sp** quarter[2] / quarter'd[5], quartered[2]

**quartered** *adj*
'kwaɹtəɹd
**sp** quarter'd[2]

**quartering** *adj*
'kwaɹtrɪn, -ɪŋ, -tər-
**sp** quartering[1]

**quasi** *adv*
'kwazi
**sp** quasi[1]

**quat** *n*
kwat
**sp** quat[1]

**quatch-buttock** *n*
'kwaʧ-ˌbɤtək
**sp** quatch-buttocke[1]

**que,** *abbr* **qu'** *Fr conj*
kə, *abbr* k
**sp** que[17], ques[1], *abbr* qu'[2]

**quean** *n*
kwi:n
**sp** queane[4]
> cotquean

**queas** *Lat*
> queo

**queasy** *adj*
'kwi:zəɪ
**sp** queasie[1], queazie[2]

**queasiness** *n*
=
**sp** queasinesse[1]

**queen / ~'s / ~s** *n*
=
**sp** queen[26] queene[453], queenes [queen is][1], queene's [queen is][1], queens [queen is][1], *abbr* Q[ueene][2], Qu[eene][1] / queenes[25], queens[3] / queenes[9], queens[2]
**rh** green *MND 2.1.8, PP 4.4, Tem 4.1.82*; seen *Luc 66; MND 1.1.173, 2.2.12, PT 31, R2 2.2.24, 3.4.107; S 96.5, TN 5.1.385, VA 503, 1193*; spleen *3H6 2.1.122*
> mother-queen

**queen** *v*
=
**sp** queene[1]
> unqueened

**quell** *n / v*
=
**sp** quell[1] / quell[5]
**rh** fell *MND 5.1.279*
> boy-, man-, woman-queller

**quench / ~ing / ~ed** *v*
= / 'kwenʧɪn, -ɪŋ / =
**sp** quench[24] / quenching[2] / quench'd[4], quenched[1], quencht[1]
> never-quenching

**quenchless** *n*
=
**sp** quenchlesse[1]

**que·o / ~as** *Lat v*
'kweas, 'ke-
**sp** queas[1]

**quern** *n*
kwɐ:ɹn
**sp** querne[1]
**rh** churn *MND 2.1.36*

**quest / ~s** *n*
=
**sp** quest[8] / quests[1]

**questant** *n*
'kwestənt
**sp** questant[1]

**question / ~s** *n*
*m* 'kwestɪən, -ɪˌɒn / -ɪənz
**sp** question[99], questio[n] [1], que-stion[3], questi-on[1], questions [question is][1], question's [question is][1] / questions[12]

**question** *Fr n*
kɛst'jɔ̃
**sp** question[1]

**question / ~ed / ~edest** *v*
'kwestɪən / *m* -d, -ˌned / -st, -dst
**sp** question[36] / question'd[7], *Luc* questioned[1] / questioned'st[1]
**rh** bed *Luc 122*
> unquestioned

**questionable** *adj*
*m* 'kwestɪəˌnabəl
**sp** questionable[1]
> unquestionable

**questioning** *n*
'kwestɪənɪn, -ɪŋ
**sp** questioning[1]
**rh** sing *AY 5.4.135*

**questionless** *n*
*m* 'kwestɪənˌles
**sp** questionlesse[1]

**questrist / ~s** *n*
=
**sp** questrists[1]

**Queubus** *n*
kwe'u:bəs
**sp** Queubus[1]

**qui** *Fr pro*
ki
**sp** che[2], qui[1]

**qui** *Lat pro / pluralized in English ~es*
kwi:, ki: / kwi:z, ki:z
**sp** qui[3], / quies[1]

*quae / pluralized in English ~s*
kwɛ:, kɛ: / -z
**sp** que[2] / ques[2]

*quo*
kwo:
**sp** quo[1]
**rh** so *1H6 5.3.109*

*quod / pluralized in English ~s*
kwɒd, kɒd / -z
**sp** quod[1] / quods[1]

**quick / ~er / ~est** *adj*
= / 'kwɪkəɹ / kwɪkst
**sp** quick[9], quicke[61] / quicker[1] / quick'st[1]
**rh** kick *AW 5.3.301*

**quick** *adv / n*
=
**sp** quick[5], quicke[15] / quick[2], quicke[5]

**quick-answered** *adj*
*m* ˌkwɪk-'ansəɹd
**sp** quicke-answer'd[1]
> answer

**quicken / ~s / ~ed** *v*
=
**sp** quicken[9] / quickens[2] / quicken'd[1], quickned[1]

**quickly** *adv*
'kwɪkləɪ / -əɹ
**sp** quickly[87], quickely[15] / quicklier[1]
**rh** unlikely *VA 990*

**Quickly** [name] *n*
'kwɪkləɪ
**sp** Quickely[1], Quickly[15], [nursh-a]-Quickly[1], Quick-ly[1]

**quickness** *n*
=
**sp** quicknesse[1]

**quickning** *adj / n*
'kwɪknɪn, -ɪŋ
**sp** quickning[1] / quickning[1]

**quick-raised** *adj*
*m* ˌkwɪk-'rɛ:zɪd
**sp** quick-raysed[1]

**quicksand / ~s** *n*
=
**sp** quick-sand[1] / quicke-sands[1]

**quicksilver** *n*
'kwɪk-ˌsɪlvəɹ
**sp** quick-siluer[2]
> silver

**quick-witted** *adj*
=
**sp** quicke witted[1]

**quid** *Lat pro*
=, kɪd
**sp** quid[2]

**quiddit / ~s** *n*
=
**sp** quiddits[1]

**quiddity / ~ies** *n*
'kwɪdɪtəɪz
**sp** quiddities[1]

**quiet** *adj / adv / n / v*
'kwəɪət
**sp** quiet[51], quyet[1] / quiet[5] / quiet[17] / quiet[2]
**rh** riot *VA 1149*
> dis-, un-quiet

**quieter** *n*
'kwəɪətəɹ
**sp** quieter[1]

**quietly** *adv*
'kwəɪətləɪ
**sp** quietly[8]
> unquietly

**quietness** *n*
'kwəɪətnəs
**sp** quietnes[1], quietnesse[6]
> unquietness

**quietus** *n*
kwɪ'ɛ:təs
**sp** quietus[1]

**qu'il / ~s** *Fr pro*
kil
**sp** qu'il[1] / qu'ils[1]

**quill / ~s** *n*
=
**sp** quill[2] / quilles[1]
**rh** bill *MND 3.1.121*; ill, will *Luc 1297*; still *S 85.3*
> goose-quill, sharp-quilled

**quillet / ~s** *n*
'kwɪləts
**sp** quillets[6]

**qu'ils**
> qu'il

**quilt** *n*
=
**sp** quilt[1]

**Quinapalus** *n*
kwɪ'napləs, -pəl-
**sp** Quinapalus[1]

**quince / ~s** *n*
=
**sp** quinces[1]

**Quince** [name] *n*
=
**sp** Quince[12]

**quintessence** *n*
'kwɪntəˌsens
**sp** quintessence[2]

**quintain** *n*
'kwɪntən
**sp** quintine[1]

**Quintus** *n*
'kwɪntəs
**sp** Quintus[1]

**quip / ~s** *n*
=
**sp** quip[1], quip-[modest][1] / quips[4]

**quire, quiring**
> choir, choiring

**quirk / ~s** *n*
kwɐ:ɹk / -s
**sp** quirke[1] / quirkes[3]

**quirister**
> chorister

**quis** *Lat pro*
kwɪs, kɪs
**sp** quis[3]

**quit / ~s / ~ting / ~ted** *v*
= / = / 'kwɪtɪn, -ɪŋ / =
**sp** quit[44] / quits[3] / quitting[1] / quitted[1]

**quite** *adv / v*
kwəɪt
**sp** quight[1], quite[80] / quite[1]
**rh** *adv* delight *LLL 1.1.70*; night *Oth 5.1.129*; recite *S 72.3*; sight *MND 3.2.88*; sprite *MND 2.1.32*; tonight *LLL 5.2.272*; write *S 103.7*

**quittance** *n / v*
=
**sp** quittance[5] / quittance[1]

**quiver** *adj / n*
'kwɪvəɹ
**sp** quiuer[1] / quiuer[1]

**quiver / ~s** *v*
'kwɪvəɹ / -z
**sp** quiuer[2] / quiuers[1]

**quivering** *adj*
'kwɪvrɪn, -ɪŋ, -vər-
**sp** quiuering[1]

**quo, quod** *Lat*
> qui

**Quoint** [name] *n*
kəɪnt, kw-
**sp** Quoint[1]

**quoit / ~s** *n*
kəɪts
**sp** quoits[1]

**quoit** *v*
kəɪt
**sp** quoit[1]

**quondam** *adj*
'kwɒndam, 'kɒ-
**sp** quondam[6]

**quoniam** *Lat adv*
'kwo:nɪam, 'ko:-
**sp** quoniam[1]

**quote / ~s / ~d** *v*
ko:t, kw- / -s / 'ko:tɪd, 'kw-
**sp** coat[1], coate[1], quoat[2], quote[1] / quotes[1] / quoted[4]
**rh** noted *LLL 4.3.85*
> misquote

**quoth** *v*
kɒθ, kw-, -o:θ
**sp** quoth[62], quoth-[a][3], qua-th[a][1]

**quotidian** *n*
ko:'tɪdɪən, kw-
**sp** quotidian[2]

# R

**rabbit** *n*
=
**sp** rabbet[2], rabit[1]

**rabbit-sucker** *n*
'rabɪt-ˌsɤkəɹ
**sp** rabbet-sucker[1]

**rabble / ~'s** *n*
=
**sp** rabble[11], rable[2] / rabbles[1]
**rh** fable *TNK 3.5.105*

**rabblement** *n*
=
**sp** rabblement[2]

**race** *n*
rɛ:s
**sp** race[14]
**rh** pace *S 51.11*; place *Per 5.Chorus.9*

**rac·e / ~ing / ~ed** *v*
rɛ:s / 'rɛ:sɪn, -ɪŋ / rɛ:st
**sp** race[2] / racing[1] / rac'd[1]

**raced** *adj*
rɛ:st
**sp** rac'd[1]

**rack / ~s** *n*
=
**sp** racke[9] / racks[2]

**rack / ~ed** *v*
=
**sp** racke[4] / rack'd[2], rackt[3]

**racker / ~s** *n*
'rakəɹz
**sp** rackers[1]

**racket / ~s** *n*
=
**sp** racket[1], rackets[1]

**racking** *adj*
'rakɪn, -ɪŋ
**sp** racking[1]

**radiance** *n*
'rɛ:dɪəns
**sp** radience[2]

**radiant** *adj*
'rɛ:dɪənt
**sp** radiant[7], radient[1]

**radish** *n*
=
**sp** radish[2]

**raft** *n*
raft
**sp** rafte[1]

**rag / ~s** *n*
=
**sp** ragge[5] / ragges[11], raggs[1], rags[3]
**rh** bags *KL 2.4.46*
> tag-rag

**ragamuffin** *n*
'ragəˌmɤfɪn
**sp** rag of muffins[1]

**rage / ~s** *n*
rɛ:ʤ / 'rɛ:ʤ·ɪz
**sp** rage[96], [tiger-footed]-rage[1] / rages[4]
**rh** *1* age *1H6 4.6.13, 34, LC 13, S 17.11, 64.4*; age, gage *Luc 145*; assuage *VA 332*; sage *Luc 219*; stage *RJ Prol.10, S 23.3*; **rh** *2* marriage *[3 sylls] Luc 219* / pages *Luc 909*; wages *Cym 4.2.259*

**rag·e / ~s / ~eth / ~ing / ~ed** *v*
rɛ:ʤ / 'rɛ:ʤ·ɪz / -əθ / -ɪn, -ɪŋ / *m* -ɪd, rɛ:ʤd
**sp** rage[15] / rages[7], ra-ges[1] / rageth[1] / raging[2] / rag'd[2], raged[1]

**ragged / ~est** *adj*
'ragɪd / -st
**sp** rag'd-[hornes][1], ragged[21] / ragged'st[1]

**raggedness** *n*
=
**sp** raggednesse[1]

**raging** *adj / n*
'rɛ:ʤɪn, -ɪŋ
**sp** raging[15] / raging[1]

**Ragozine** *n*
'ragəˌzəɪn
**sp** Ragozine[3]

**rah-tah-tah** *interj*
=
**sp** rah, tah, tah[1]

**rail** *n*
rɛ:l
**sp** raile[1]

**rail / ~est / ~s / ~eth / ~ed** *v*
rɛ:l / -st / -z / 'rɛ:ləθ / rɛ:ld
**sp** raile[21], rayle[7] / railest[1], rayl'st[1] / railes[5], rayles[1] / raileth[1] / raild[2], rail'd[6], rayl'd[1]

**railer** *n*
'rɛ:ləɹ
**sp** rayler[1]

**railing** *adj / n*
'rɛ:lɪn, -ɪŋ
**sp** railing[1], rayling[2] / railing[3], rayling[2]

**raiment** *n*
'rɛ:mənt
**sp** raiment[4], rayment[3]

**rain** *n*
rɛ:n
**sp** raine[35], rayne[1]
**rh** again *Mac 1.1.2, VA 959, 965*; a-twain *LC 7*; plain *LLL 4.3.268, Luc 1788, VA 238*

**rain / ~s / ~eth / ~ing / ~ed** *v*
rɛ:n / -z / 'rɛ:n·əθ / -ɪn, -ɪŋ / rɛ:nd
**sp** raigne[1], raine[13] / raines[2] / raineth[2] / raining[1] / rain'd[4], rayn'd[1]
**rh** gain *KL 2.4.76*; plain *VA 360*; remain *VA 799* / staineth *VA 458* / complaining, sustaining *Luc 1271*; plaining *Luc 560*

**rainbow** *n*
'rɛ:nbo:
**sp** raine-bow[3]

**Rainold** *n*
'rɛ:nəld
**sp** Rainald[1]

**rainwater** *n*
'rɛ:nˌwɑtəɹ
**sp** rain-water[1]

**rainy** *adj*
'rɛ:nəɪ
**sp** rainie[1], raynie[2]

**rais·e / ~es / ~ing / ~ed** *v*
rɛ:z / 'rɛ:z·ɪz / -ɪn, -ɪŋ / rɛ:zd
**sp** raise[32], rayse[13] / raises[1] / raising[3], raysing[2] / raisd[1], rais'd[24], rays'd[1]
**rh** days *1H6 1.2.130*; obeys, praise *LC 228*

**raised** *adj*
'rɛ:zɪd
**sp** raised[2]
> unraised

**raisin / ~s** *n*
'rɛ:zənz
**sp** reysons[1]
**pun** *1H4 2.4.235*, reasons

**raising** *n*
'rɛ:zɪn, -ɪŋ
**sp** raising[1]

**rake / ~s** *n*
rɛ:ks
**sp** rakes[1]

**rake / ~d** *v*
rɛ:k / -t
**sp** rake[4] / rakt[1]
> unraked

**Ralph** *n*
rɑ:f
**sp** Rafe[1], Ralfe[1], Raphe[1]

**ram / ~'s / ~s** *n*
=
**sp** ram[2], ramme[3] / rams[1] / rammes[4], rams[1]

**ram / ~med** *v*
=
**sp** ramme[1] / ram'd[1], ramm'd[1]

**Rambures** *n*
*Eng* 'rɒmbu:ɹ, *Fr* rɔ̃'by:ɹ
**sp** Rambures[3], Ramburs[2]

**ramp / ~s** *n*
=
**sp** rampes[1]

**rampallian** *n*
ram'palɪən
**sp** rampallian[1]

**rampant** *adj*
=
**sp** rampant[1]

**ramping** *adj*
'rampɪn, -ɪŋ
**sp** ramping[3]

**rampired** *adj*
'rampəɪɹd
**sp** rampyr'd[1]

**Ramston** *n*
'ramstən
**sp** *emend of R2 2.1.283* Rainston[1]

**ram-tender** *n*
'ram-ˌtendəɹ
**sp** ram-ten-der[1]

**ran**
> run

**rancorous** *adj*
'raŋkrəs, -kər-
**sp** rancorous[5]

**rancour / ~'s / ~s** *n*
'raŋkəɹ / -z
**sp** rancor[1], rancour[5] / rancours[2] / rancours[2]

**random** *n*
'randən, -əm
**sp** randome[1], randon[1], randone[1]

**rang**
> ring

**range / ~s** *n*
'rɛ:nʤ·ɪz, 'rɔ:-
**sp** ranges[1]

**rang·e / ~es / ~ing / ~ed** *v*
rɛ:nʤ, rɔ:- / 'rɛ:nʤ·ɪz, 'rɔ:- / -ɪn, -ɪŋ / rɛ:nʤd, rɔ:-
**sp** range[6], raunge[2] / ranges[1], raunges[1] / ranging[2] / rang'd[2]
**rh** changing *TS 3.1.89* / exchanged *S 109.5*

**ranged** *adj*
rɛ:nʤd, rɔ:-
**sp** raing'd[1]

**ranger / ~s** *n*
'rɛ:nʤəɹz, 'rɔ:-
**sp** rangers[1]

**rank / ~er / ~est** *adj*
= / 'raŋkəɹ / =
**sp** ranck[1], rancke[2], rank[3], ranke[24] / ranker[1] / rankest[2]
**rh** bank *VA 71*

**rank / ~s** *n*
=
**sp** ranck[1], ranke[9] / rankes[14], ranks[1]
**rh** banks *Luc 1441*
> fore-rank

**rank / ~ing / ~ed** *v*
= / 'raŋkɪn, -ɪŋ / =
**sp** ranke[5] / ranking[1] / ranck'd[1], rank'd[2], rankt[1]

**rankness** *n*
=
**sp** ranckenesse[1], ranknesse[2]

**rankle** *v*
=
**sp** ranckle[1], rankle[1]

**rankly** *adv*
'raŋkləɪ
**sp** rankly[1]

**rank-scented** *adj*
=
**sp** ranke-sented[1]

**Rannius** *n*
'ranɪəs
**sp** Rannius[1]

**ransack / ~ing / ~ed** *v*
= / 'ransakɪn, -ɪŋ / =
**sp** ransacke[1] / ransacking[1] / ransack'd[1], ransackt[1]

**ransacked** *adj*
=
**sp** ransack'd[1]

**ransom / ~s** *n*
=
**sp** ransom[3], ransome[40], ransome's [ransome is][1] / ransomes[1]

**ransom / ~ing / ~ed** *v*
= / 'ransəmɪn, -ɪŋ / =
**sp** ransome[9] / ransoming[1] / ransom'd[5], ransomed[1]

**ransomless** *n*
=
**sp** ransomlesse[2]

**rant** *v*
=
**sp** rant[1]

**ranting** *adj*
'rantɪn, -ɪŋ
**sp** ranting-[host][1]

**rap / ~s** *n*
=
**sp** rap[2], rappe[1] / rap's[1]

**rape / ~s** *n*
rɛ:p / -s
**sp** rape[15] / rapes[3]

**rapier / ~'s / ~s** *n*
'rapɪəɹ / -z
**sp** rapier[22], ra-pier[1] / rapiers[5] / rapiers[3]

**rapine** *n*
'rapəɪn
**sp** rapine[3]

**rapt** *adj*
=
**sp** rapt[7]

**rapture / ~s** *n*
'raptəɹ / -z
**sp** rapture[2], raptures[1]

**rare / ~r / ~st** *adj*
rɛ:ɹ / 'rɛ:r·əɹ / -əst, rɛ:ɹst
**sp** rare[54] / rarer[4] / rarest[4], rar'st[1]
**rh** *1* care *S 56.14*; compare *S 21.7, 130.13*; prepare *Per 4.Chorus.37*; **rh** *2* are *S 52.5*

**rarely** *adv*
'rɛ:ɹləɪ
**sp** rarely[9]

**rareness** *n*
'rɛ:ɹnəs
**sp** rarenesse[2]

**rarest** *n*
'rɛ:rəst, rɛ:ɹst
**sp** rarest[3], rar'st[1]

**rariet·y / ~ies** *n*
rə'rəɪətəɪ / -z
**sp** rariety[1] / rarieties[1]

**rarity** *n*
*m* 'rɛ:rɪtəɪ, -ˌtəɪ
**sp** raritie[1], rarity[1]
**rh** *1* simplicity *PT 53*; **rh** *2* lie *PT 53*

**rascal / ~lest** *adj*
'raskɑl / -əst, -kləst
**sp** rascal[1], rascall[8] / rascallest[1]

**rascal / ~s** *n*
'raskɑl / -z
**sp** rascall[46], [epicurian]-rascall[1], [wide-chopt]-rascall[1], ras-call[1], rascall's [rascal is][1] / rascalls[4], rascals[12], [traitorly]-rascals[1], raskalls[1]

**rascal-like** *adj*
'raskɑl-ˌləɪk
**sp** rascall-like[1]

**rascally** *adv*
'raskləɪ, -kɑl-
**sp** rascally[9], [iealious]-rascally-[knaue][1], rascally-[yea-forsooth-knaue][1]

**rash** *adj*
=
**sp** rash[32]
**rh** flash *Cym 4.2.272*
> heady-rash

**Rash** [name] *n*
=
**sp** Rash[1]

**rasher** *n*
'raʃəɹ
**sp** rasher[1]

**rash-levied** *adj*
*m* ˌraʃ-'levəɪd
**sp** rash leuied[1]

**rashly** *adv*
ˈraʃləɪ
**sp** rashly[4]

**rashness** *n*
=
**sp** rashnes[1], rashnesse[9]

**rat / ~s** *n*
=
**sp** rat[10] / rats[9], rattes[1]

**rat-catcher** *n*
ˈrat-ˌkatʃəɹ
**sp** rat-catcher[1]

**Ratcliffe** *n*
=
**sp** Ratclif[1], Ratcliff[1], Ratcliffe[23], Ratliffe[1]

**rate / ~s** *n*
rɛ:t / -s
**sp** rate[20] / rates[2]
**rh** mate, state *Luc 19*; state *MND 3.1.145*

**rat·e / ~es / ~ing / ~ed** *v*
rɛ:t / -s / ˈrɛ:t·ɪn, -ɪŋ / -ɪd
**sp** rate[8] / rates[3] / rating[1] / rated[15]
**rh** estimate *AW 2.1.179*
> over-rate

**rated** *adj*
ˈrɛ:tɪd
**sp** rated[1]
> low-rated

**rather / ~est** *adj*
ˈraðəɹ / -st
**sp** rather[313], ra-ther[6] / rathe-rest[1]
**rh** father *R2 1.3.237*

**ratifier / ~s** *n*
ˈratɪˌfəɪɹz
**sp** ratifiers[1]

**ratif·y / ~ied** *v*
*m* ˈratɪˌfəɪ, -ɪf- / -d
**sp** ratifie[4] / ratified[4]

**rational** *adj*
ˈrasɪənɑl
**sp** rationall[2]

**Ratolorum** [*malap for* rotulorum] *Lat n*
ˈratəˌlɔ:rʊm
**sp** Ratolorum[1]

**ratsbane** *n*
ˈratsbɛ:n
**sp** rats-bane[3]

**rattle / ~s** *v*
=
**sp** rattle[1] / rattles[1]

**rattling** *adj*
ˈratlɪn, -ɪŋ
**sp** ratling[5]

**raught**
> reach

**rave / ~s / ~d** *v*
rɛ:v / -z / -d
**sp** raue[3] / raues[2] / rau'd[1]
**rh** crave, slave *Luc 982*

**ravel** *v*
ˈravəl
**sp** rauell[3]

**ravelled** *adj*
ˈravəld
**sp** rauel'd[1]

**raven / ~'s / ~s** *n*
ˈrɛ:vən / -z
**sp** rauen[16] / rauens[5] / rauens[5]
> night-raven

**raven** *v*
ˈravɪn / -ɪn, -ɪŋ, -vn-
**sp** rauen[1], rauyn[1] / rauening[1]
> wolvish-ravening

**raven-coloured** *adj*
ˈrɛ:vən-ˌkɤləɹd
**sp** rauen coloured[1]
> colour

**ravenous** *adj*
*m* ˈravnəs, -vɪn-, -vɪˌnɤs
**sp** rauenous[6], rau'nous[2]

**Ravenspurgh** *n*
ˈravɪnzˌpɐ:ɹ
**sp** Rauenspurg[1], Rauenspurgh[7], Rauenspurre[1]

**ravine** *adj*
ˈravɪn
**sp** rauine[1]

**ravined** *adj*
ˈravɪnd
**sp** rauin'd[1]

**ravish / ~ed** *v*
= / *m* ˈravɪʃt, -ˌʃɪd
**sp** rauish[10], ra-uish[1] / rauished[3], rauisht[7]

**ravished** *adj*
ˈravɪʃt
**sp** rauish'd[2]

**ravisher** *n*
ˈravɪʃəɹ
**sp** rauisher[2]
**rh** conspirator *Luc 770*

**ravishing** *adj*
ˈravɪʃɪn, -ɪŋ
**sp** rauishing[2]

**ravishment** *Luc* **/ ~s** *n*
=
**sp** rauishment[2] / rauishments[1]
**rh** languishment *Luc 1128*

**raw** *adj*
=
**sp** raw[8], raw-[rumaticke][1], rawe[2]
**rh** saw *LLL 5.2.913, Luc 1592*

**raw-boned** *adj*
ˈrɔ:-ˌbo:nd
**sp** raw-bon'd[1]
> bone

**rawly** *adv*
ˈrɔ:ləɪ
**sp** rawly[1]

**rawness** *n*
=
**sp** rawnesse[1]

**ray / ~s** *n*
rɛ: / -z
**sp** ray[1] / rayes[4], rayse[1]

**ray / ~ed** *v*
rɛ:d
**sp** raide[1], raied[1]

**raze ~s** *n*
'rɛ:zɪz
**sp** razes[1]

**raze / ~th / ~d** *v*
rɛ:z / 'rɛ:zəθ / rɛ:zd
**sp** raze[3] /razeth[1] / raiz'd[1], rased[1], raz'd[2]
> down-razed

**razor / ~s** *n*
'rɛ:zəɹz
**sp** razors[2]

**razorable** *adj*
*m* 'rɛ:zəˌrabəl
**sp** razor-able[1]

**razure** *n*
'rɛ:zəɹ
**sp** razure[1]

**reach** *n*
=
**sp** reach[10]

**reach / ~es / ~eth / ~ed / raught** *v*
=
**sp** reach[15] / reaches[3] / reacheth[1] / reach'd[1] / raught[4]
> over-reach

**reaching** *adj*
'ri:ʧɪn, -ɪŋ
**sp** reaching[1]
> high-reaching

**read** *adj*
red
**sp** read[4]

**read** *present* **/ ~est / ~s / ~ing / read** *past* *v*
= / 'ri:dst / = / 'ri:dɪn, -ɪŋ / =
**sp** read[74], reade[80] / read'st[1] / reades[14], reads[10] / reading[19], rea-ding[2] / read[37]
**rh** *present* indeed *S 62.11* / *past* said *LLL 4.3.191*
> over-, un-read

**reader** *n*
'ri:dəɹ
**sp** reader[1]

**readily** *adv*
'redɪləɪ
**sp** readily[1]
**rh** *1* mutiny *Luc 1152*; **rh** *2* fly *Luc 1152*

**readiness** *n*
=
**sp** readinesse[14], readines[1]
**rh** forwardness *3H6 5.4.64*

**reading** *n*
'ri:dɪn, -ɪŋ
**sp** reading[7]
**rh** weeding *LLL 1.1.94*

**Reading** [name] *n*
'redɪn, -ɪŋ
**sp** Reading[1]

**read·y / ~iest** *adj*
'redəɪ / -əst
**sp** readie[40], rea-die[1], ready[99], rea-dy[1] / readiest[4]
> unready

**real** *adj*
'ri:ɑl
**sp** reall[2]
> unreal

**realm / ~s** *n*
rɛ:m / -z
**sp** realme[53] / realmes[6], realms[1]

**re-answer** *v*
ri:'ansəɹ, -'ɔ:n-
**sp** re-answer[1]
> answer

**reap / ~s / ~ed** *v*
=
**sp** reap[1], reape[12] / reapes[1] / reap'd[2], reapt[1]
**rh** leap *S 128.7*

**reaper / ~s** *n*
'ri:pəɹz
**sp** reapers[2]

**reaping** *n*
'ri:pɪn, -ɪŋ
**sp** reaping[1]

**rear** *n*
ri:ɹ
**sp** reare[1], reare'[1]

**rear** *v*
ri:ɹ / -z / -d
**sp** reare[8], rere[1] / reares[1] / reard[1], rear'd[4]
**rh** here *R2 5.3.89* / afeared *1H6 4.7.92*
> uprear

**reared** *adj*
ri:ɹd
**sp** rear'd[1]
> high-reared

**rearmouse / ~mice** *n*
'ri:ɹməɪs
**sp** reremise[1]

**rearward** *adv*
'ri:ɹwɑɹd
**sp** rereward[1], rere-ward[2]

**reason / ~'s / ~s** *n*
'rɛ:zən / -z
**sp** reason[240], rea-son[4] / reasons[2] / reason's[1], reasons[64]
**rh** season *CE 2.2.49*; season, treason *Luc 880*; treason *S 151.8, VA 727*
**pun** *1H4 2.4.235*, raisins

**reason / ~s / ~ing / ~ed** *v*
'rɛ:zən / -z / -ɪn, -ɪŋ, -zn- / -d
**sp** reason[24], rea-son[1] / reasons[1] / reasoning[1] / reasond[1], reason'd[1], reasoned[1]
**rh** season *CE 4.2.56, MND 2.2.124*

**reasonable** *adj*
*m* 'rɛ:zəˌnabəl, -znəbəl
**sp** reasonable[16], rea-sonable[1], reaso-nable[1], reasonnable[1]
> unreasonable

**reasonably** *adv*
*m* 'rɛ:zəˌnabləɪ
**sp** reasonably[1]
> unreasonably

**reasonless** *adj*
*m* 'rɛ:zənˌles
**sp** reasonlesse[2]

**reave / reft / ~est** *v*
= / = / refts, -t
**sp** reaue[2] / reft[4] / refts[1]

**rebate** *v*
rɪ'bɛ:t
**sp** rebate[1]

**rebato** *n*
rɪ'bɑ:to:
**sp** rebato[1]

**Rebeck** [name] *n*
'rebɪk
**sp** Rebicke[1]

**rebel** *adj*
=
**sp** rebell[1]

**rebel / ~'s / ~s / ~s'** *n*
= ['rebəl]
**sp** rebel[1], rebell[9] / rebells[1], rebels[2] / rebells[1], rebels[22] / rebells[1] , rebels[2]

**rebel / ~s / ~led** *v*
= [rɪ'bel]
**sp** rebell[5], / rebells[1], rebels[4] / rebell'd[2]
**rh** tell *R2 3.2.119*

**rebelling** *adj*
rɪ'belɪn, -ɪŋ
**sp** rebelling[1]

**rebellion** *n*
*m* rɪ'belɪən, -ɪˌɒn
**sp** rebellion[29], re-bellion[1]

**rebellious** *adj*
=
**sp** rebellious[11]

**rebound** *n*
rɪ'bəʊnd
**sp** rebound[1]

**rebukable** *adj*
=
**sp** rebukeable[1]

**rebuke / ~s** *n*
=
**sp** rebuke[13] / rebukes[4]

**rebuke / ~d** *v*
=
**sp** rebuke[5] / rebuk'd[2]

**rebused**
> abuse *v*

**recall / ~ed** *v*
rɪ'kɑ:l / -d
**sp** recall[2] / recal'd[1], recall'd[2]
> call

**recant** *v*
=
**sp** recant[1]

**recantation** *n*
ˌri:kən'tɛ:sɪən
**sp** recantation[1], re-cantation[1]

**recanter** *n*
rɪ'kantəɹ
**sp** re-canter[1]

**recanting** *adj*
rɪ'kantɪn, -ɪŋ
**sp** recanting[2]

**receipt / ~s** *n*
rɪ'si:t, -'sɛ:- / -s
**sp** receipt[3], receit[5], receite[2], receyt[1] / receits[1]
**rh** conceit *Luc 703*

**receiv·e / ~est / ~es / ~eth / ~ing / ~ed** *v*
rɪ'si:v, -'sɛ:- / -st / -z / -əθ / -ɪn, -ɪŋ / -d
**sp** receiue[81], receiue't [receive it][1], receyue[8], recieue[2], reciue't [receive it][1] / receiuest[1] / receiues[9], receyues[1] / receiueth[1] / receiuing[2], receyuing[1] / receiud[1], receiu'd[54], receiude[1], receiued[15], receyu'd[5], receyued[2]
**rh** leave *AW 2.3.83, LC 241, MV 3.2.140, TC 4.5.36*; **receive** it leave it *2H6 2.3.36* / deceivest *S 40.5* / deceives, leaves *LC 303*

**received** *adj*
rɪ'si:vd, -'sɛ:-
**sp** receiu'd[3]

**receiver** *n*
rɪ'si:vəɹ, -'sɛ:-
**sp** receiuer[1]

**receiving** *adj / n*
rɪ'si:vɪn, -ɪŋ, -'sɛ:-
**sp** receiuing[1] / receiuing[2]

**receptacle** *n*
*m* 'resɪpˌtakəl
**sp** receptacle[3]

**recheat** *n*
rɪ'ʧɛ:t
**sp** rechate[1]

**reciprocal** *adj*
rɪ'sɪprəkɑl
**sp** reciprocall[1]

**reciprocally** *adv*
*m* rɪ'sɪprəˌkləɪ
**sp** reciprocally[1]

**recite** *S* *v*
rɪ'səɪt
**sp** recite[1]
**rh** quite *S 72.1*

**réciter / ~ai** *Fr v*
resitə'rɛ
**sp** recitera[2]

**reck / ~s** *v*
=
**sp** reake[1], reaks[1]

**reckless** *adj*
=
**sp** recklesse[2], reck-lesse[1]

**reckon / ~ing / ~ed** *v*
= / 'reknɪn, -ɪŋ / =
**sp** reckon[6], rec-kon[1] / reckning[1] / reckon'd[5]

**reckoning / ~s** *n*
*m* 'reknɪn, -ɪŋ, -kən-, -kəˌn- / 'reknɪnz, -ɪŋz, -kən-
**sp** reckning[6], reck'ning[3], reckoning[9], rec-koning[1], recko-ning[1] / recknings[3], reckonings[2]
**rh** beckoning [*2 sylls*] *TNK 3.5.129*

**reclaim / ~s / ~ed** *v*
rɪ'klɛːm·z / -d
**sp** reclaimes[1] / reclaim'd[1], reclaym'd[1]
> claim, unreclaimed

**reclusive** *adj*
=
**sp** reclusiue[1]

**recognizance / ~s** *n*
*m* rɪ'kɒgnɪˌzans / -ɪz
**sp** recognizance[1] / recog-nizances[1]

**recoil / ~ing** *v*
rɪ'kəɪl / -ɪn, -ɪŋ
**sp** recoile[1], recoyle[4], requoyle[1] / recoyling[1]

**recollect** *Per* *v*
=
**sp** recollect[1]
**rh** detect *Per 2.1.50*

**recollected** *adj*
=
**sp** recollected[1]

**recomforted** *n*
rɪ'kɤmfəɹtɪd
**sp** recomforted[1]
> comfort

**recomforture** *n*
rɪ'kɤmfəɹtəɹ
**sp** recomforture[1]
> comfort

**recommend / ~s / ~ed** *v*
=
**sp** recommend[1] / recommends[2] / recommended[1]
> commend

**recompense** *n*
=
**sp** recompence[20], recom-pence[1]
**rh** eloquence *S 23.11*; hence *1H6 1.2.116*; sense *LLL 1.1.58, MND 3.2.180*

**recompense / ~d** *v*
=
**sp** recompence[4], re-compence[1] / recompenc'd[2], recompenc't[1]

**recompt** *n*
rɪ'kɒmt, -mpt
**sp** recompt[1]
> recount

**reconcile / ~s / ~ed** *v*
'rekənˌsəɪl / -z / -d
**sp** reconcile[8] / reconciles[1] / reconcil'd[6], reconciled[1], re-conciled[1]
**rh** awhile *Per 4.4.22*; reconciles thee defile thee *KL 3.6.111* [*Q*]
> irreconciled, un-reconciled

**reconcilement** *n*
*m* ˌrekən'səɪlmənt
**sp** reconcilement[1]

**reconciler** *n*
'rekənsəɪləɹ
**sp** reconciler[1]

**reconciliation** *n*
ˌrekənsɪlɪ'ɛːsɪən
**sp** reconciliation[1]

**record / ~s** *n*
*m* rɪ'kɔːɹd, 'rekəɹd / -z
**sp** record[16], records[2]
**rh** 1 sword *Luc 1643*; **rh** 2 word *Luc 1643*

**record / ~s / ~ed** *v*
rɪ'kɔːɹd / -z / -ɪd
**sp** record[4] / records[1] / recorded[5]

**recordation** *n*
ˌrekəɹ'dɛːsɪən
**sp** recordation[2]

**recorded** *adj*
rɪ'kɔːɹdɪd
**sp** recorded[2]

**recorder / ~s** *n*
rɪ'kɔːɹdəɹ / -z
**sp** recorder[4] / recorders[1]

**recount / ~s / ~ed** *v*
rɪ'kəʊnt / -s / -ɪd
**sp** recount[9], re-count[1] / recounts[1] / recounted[1]
> recompt, unrecounted

**recountment / ~s** *n*
rɪ'kəʊntmənt / -s
**sp** recountments[1]

**recourse** *n*
rɪ'kɔːɹs
**sp** recourse[4]

**recover / ~s / ~ed** *v*
rɪ'kɤvəɹ / -z / *m* rɪ'kɤvəɹd, -əˌrɪd
**sp** recouer[25], re-couer[1], reco-uer[1] / recouers[2], reco-uers[1] / recouer'd[7], recouered[9]

**recoverable** *adj*
rɪ'kɤvrəbəl
**sp** recouerable[1]
> irrecoverable

**recover·y / ~ies** *n*
*m* rɪ'kɤvrəɪ, -vəˌrəɪ / -vərəɪz, -vrəɪz
**sp** recouerie[5], recouery[3], recou'ry[1] / recoueries[1], reco-ueries[1]

**recreant** *adj*
*m* 'rekrɪənt, -ɪˌant
**sp** recreant[7]

**recreant** *n*
*m* 'rekrɪənt, -ɪˌant / -s
**sp** recreant[6] / recreants[2]

**recreate** *v*
'rekrɪɛ:t
**sp** recreate[1]

**recreation / 's** *n*
*m* ˌrekrɪɛ':sɪən, -sɪˌɒn / -z
**sp** recreation[7] / recreation [sake][1]

**rectify** *v*
*m* 'rektɪˌfəɪ
**sp** rectifie[3]

**rector** *n*
'rektəɹ
**sp** rector[1]

**rectorship** *n*
*m* 'rektəɹˌʃɪp
**sp** rectorship[1]

**recure / *S* ~d** *v*
rɪ'kju:ɹ / -d
**sp** recure[1] / recured[1]
**rh** assured *S 45.9*
> unrecuring

**red / ~der / ~dest** *adj*
= / 'redəɹ / =
**sp** red[55], red-[plague][1], red-[rose][1], redde[3] / redder[1] / reddest[1]
**rh** bed *VA 107*; bred *LLL 1.2.94*; dead *VA 468*; entituled *Luc 59*; head *Luc 1417, S 130.2, VA 116*; spread *VA 901*; tread *MND 3.2.391*
> over-red

**red-breast** *n*
=
**sp** [robin]-red-breast[1], red-brest[1]
> breast

**rede** *n*
ri:d
**sp** reade[1]

**redeem / ~est / ~s / ~ing / ~ed** *v*
= / rɪ'di:mst / = / rɪ'di:mɪn, -ɪŋ / =
**sp** redeem[1], redeeme[20], re-deeme[1] / redeem'st[1] / redeemes[3] / redeeming[3] / re-deem'd[1], redeem'd[6]

**redeemed** *adj*
*m* rɪ'di:mɪd
**sp** redeemed[1]

**redeemer** *n*
rɪ'di:məɹ
**sp** redeemer[2]

**redeliver** *v*
ˌri:dɪ'lɪvəɹ
**sp** redeliuer[1], re-deliuer[1]

**redemption** *n*
*m* rɪ'dempsɪən, -sɪˌɒn
**sp** redemption[8]

**red-faced** *adj*
'red-ˌfɛ:st
**sp** red-fac'd[1]
> face

**red-hipped** *adj*
'red-ˌɪpt, -ˌhɪ-
**sp** red hipt[1]
> hip

**red-hot** *adj*
*m* 'red-ˌɒt, ˌred-'ɒt, -hɒ-
**sp** red-hot[1], red hot[2]
> hot

**redim·o / ~e** *Lat v*
re'di:me
**sp** redime[1]

**red-lattice** *adj*
=
**sp** red-lattice[1]

**red-looked** *adj*
=
**sp** red-look'd[1]

**redness** *n*
=
**sp** rednesse[1]

**red-nose** *adj*
'red-ˌno:z
**sp** red-nose[1]
> nose

**redouble / ~d** *v*
ri:'dɤbəld
**sp** redoubled[3]
**rh** troubled *VA 832*
> double

**redoubted** *adj*
rɪ'dəʊtɪd
**sp** redoubted[5]
> doubt

**redound** *v*
rɪ'dəʊnd
**sp** redound[1]

**redress / ~es** *n*
=
**sp** redresse[8] / redresses[2]
**rh** heaviness *Luc 1603*

**redress / ~ed** *v*
=
**sp** redresse[18] / redress'd[1], redressed[1], redrest[1]
**rh** refresh *PP 13.10*

**red-tailed** *adj*
'red-ˌtɛ:ld
**sp** red-tail'd[1]
> tail

**reduce** *v*
=
**sp** reduce[3]

**reechy** *adj*
'ri:ʧəɪ
**sp** rechie[1], reechie[2]

**reed** *adj*
=
**sp** reede[1]

**reed / ~s** *n*
=
**sp** reede[2] / reeds[3]

**re-edif·y / ~ied** *v*
ri:'edɪˌfəɪd
**sp** re-edified[1], re-edify'd[1]

**reek** *n*
=
**sp** reeke[1]

**reek / *S* ~s / ~ing** *v*
= / = / 'ri:kɪn, -ɪŋ
**sp** reek[1], reeke[4] / reekes[1] / reeking[1]
**rh** cheeks *S 130.8*

**reeking** *adj / adv*
'ri:kɪn, -ɪŋ
**sp** reeking[3] / reeking[1]

**reeky** *adj*
'ri:kəɪ
**sp** reckie[1]

**reel / ~s** *n*
=
**sp** reeles[3]

**reel / ~s / ~ing** *v*
= / = / 'ri:lɪn, -ɪŋ
**sp** reele[3] / reeles[1] / reeling[2]
**rh** wheels *RJ 2.2.190*

**reeling** *adj*
'ri:lɪn, -ɪŋ
**sp** reeling[1]

**refell / ~ed** *v*
rɪ'feld
**sp** refeld[1]

**refer / ~red** *v*
rɪ'fɐ:ɹ / -d
**sp** referre[3] / referr'd[2]

**reference** *n*
*m* 'refrəns, -fəˌrens
**sp** reference[5]

**refine / ~d** *v*
rɪ'fəɪnd
**sp** refin'de[1]

**refined** *adj*
*m* rɪ'fəɪnɪd
**sp** refined[2]

**reflect** *v*
=
**sp** reflect[3]
**rh** effect *VA 1130*

**reflecting** *adj*
rɪ'flektɪn, -ɪŋ
**sp** reflecting[1]

**reflection** *n*
rɪ'fleksɪən
**sp** reflection[6]

**reflex** *n / v*
*m* rɪ'fleks
**sp** reflexe[1] / reflex[1]

**reform / ~ed** *v*
rɪ'fɔ:ɹm / -d
**sp** reforme[3] / reform'd[3], reformed[1]

**reformation** *n*
*m* ˌrefəɹ'mɛ:sɪən, -sɪˌɒn
**sp** reformation[6]

**reformed** *adj*
*m* rɪ'fɔ:ɹmd, -mɪd
**sp** reform'd[1], reformed[1]

**refractory** *adj*
*m* rɪ'fraktəˌrəɪ
**sp** refracturie[1]

**refrain** *v*
rɪ'frɛ:n
**sp** refraine[4]
**rh** complain *PP 20.16*

**refresh** *v*
=
**sp** refresh[4]
**rh** redress *PP 13.8*
> fresh

**refreshed** *adj*
=
**sp** refresht[1]

**refreshing** *adj*
rɪ'freʃɪn, -ɪŋ
**sp** refreshing[1]

**reft**
> reave

**refuge** *n*
'refju:ʤ
**sp** refuge[1]

**refuge** *v*
rɪ'fju:ʤ
**sp** refuge[1]

**refusal** *n*
rɪ'fju:zɑl
**sp** refusall[1]

**refus·e / *S* ~est / ~ing / ~ed** *v*
= / rɪ'fju:z·əst / -ɪn, -ɪŋ / =
**sp** refuse[28], re-fuse[1] / refusest[1] / refusing[3] / refus'd[10], refused[1]
**rh** usest *S 40.8* / abused *MND 2.2.139*

**regal** *adj*
'ri:gɑl
**sp** regall[12]

**Regan / ~'s** *n*
=
**sp** Regan[25], Re-gan[1] / Regans[1]

**regard / ~s** *n*
rɪ'gɑ:ɹd / -z
**sp** regard[31], re-gard[1] / regards[1]
**rh** 1 hard *LC 213*; **rh** 2 heard *Luc 305, R2 2.1.28*; **rh** 3 ward *Luc 305*
> non-regardance

**regard / ~s / ~ed** *v*
rɪ'gɑ:ɹd / -z / -ɪd
**sp** regard[9] / regards[6] / regarded[7]
**rh** hard *VA 377*
> best-, un-regarded

**regardfully** *adv*
*m* rɪ'gɑ:ɹdfəˌləɪ
**sp** regardfully[1]

**regarding** *conj*
rɪ'gɑ:ɹdɪn, -ɪŋ
**sp** regarding[1]

**regenerate** *v*
*m* rɪ'ʤenəˌrɛ:t
**sp** regenerate[1]

**regent** *n*
=
**sp** regent[17]

**regentship** *n*
*m* 'ri:ʤənt,ʃɪp
**sp** regent-ship[1]

**regia** *Lat n*
'reʤɪa
**sp** regia[3]

**regiment / ~s** *n*
*m* 'reʤɪmənt, -,ment / -,ments
**sp** regiment[7] / regiments[1]

**regina** *Lat n*
re'ʤi:na
**sp** regina[1]

**region** *adj*
'ri:ʤɪən
**sp** region[1]

**region / ~s** *n*
*m* 'ri:ʤɪən, -ɪ,ɒn / -z
**sp** region[13] / regions[8]
**rh** imagination *Per 4.4.4*

**register** *n*
'reʤɪstəɹ
**sp** register[2]

**register** *S* **/ ~ed** *v*
'reʤɪstəɹ / -d
**sp** register[1] / registred[4]
**rh** character *S 108.3*
> unregistered

**regreet / ~s** *n*
*m* rɪ'gri:t
**sp** regreete[1] / regreets[1]

**regreet** *v*
*m* rɪ'gri:t
**sp** regreet[1], regreete[2]
**rh** sweet *R2 1.3.67*
> greet

**regress** *n*
'ri:gres
**sp** regresse[1]
> egress

**reguerdon** *n*
rɪ'gɐ:ɹdən
**sp** reguerdon[1]
> guerdon

**reguerdon / ~ed** *v*
rɪ'gɐ:ɹdənd
**sp** reguerdon'd[1]

**regular** *adj*
'regləɹ, -gəl-
**sp** regular[1]
> irregular

**rehearsal** *n*
rɪ'ɐ:ɹsɑl, -'hɐ:-
**sp** rehearsall[2]

**rehearse / ~d** *v*
rɪ'ɐ:ɹs, -'hɐ:- / -t
**sp** rehearse[10] / rehearst[3]
**rh** *1* verse *S 21.4, 38.4, 71.11, 81.11*;
**rh** *2* pierce *R2 5.3.127*

**reign / ~s** *n*
rɛ:n / -z
**sp** raigne[4], reign[1] / reigne[8], reignes[7]
**rh** complain *S 28.5*; gain *Per 2. Chorus.7, Tim 5.1.221*; remain, vein *Luc 1451*

**reign / ~s / ~ing / ~ed** *v*
rɛ:n / -z / 'rɛ:nɪn, -ɪŋ / rɛ:nd
**sp** raigne[6], reigne[20] / raignes[4], raigns[1], reignes[1] / reigning[2] / raign'd[1], rain'd[1], reign'd[4]
**rh** brain *RJ 2.3.34*; maintain *S 121.14*; remain *LC 127*; sovereign *Per 2.4.38* / gains *R3 1.1.161* / stained *S 109.9*

**Reignier** *n*
'renje
**sp** Reignard[1], Reigneir[4], Reignier[15]

**rein / ~s** *n*
rɛ:n / -z
**sp** raine[1], reine[4], reyne[2] / raines[1], reines[3]
**rh** disdain *VA 31, 392*

**rein / ~ed** *v*
rɛ:n / -d
**sp** reine[2] / rein'd[1]

**reinforce / ~d** *v*
,ri:ɪn'fɔ:ɹs / -t
**sp** re-inforce[1] / re-enforc'd[1]

**reinforcement** *n*
,ri:ɪn'fɔ:ɹsmənt
**sp** re-enforcement[1], re-inforcement[1]

**reiterate** *v*
*m* ri:'ɪtə,rɛ:t
**sp** reiterate[1]

**reject /** *VA* **~ed** *v*
=
**sp** reiect[1] / reiected[1]
**rh** **reject her** respect her *LLL 5.2.438* / affected *VA 159*

**rejoic·e / ~es / ~eth / ~ing / ~ed** *v*
rɪ'ʤəɪs / -ɪz / -əθ / -ɪn, -ɪŋ / -t
**sp** reioice[1], reioyce[24] / reioyces[2] / reioyceth[1] / reioycing[1] / reioyc'd[1]
**rh** voice *VA 977*

**rejoicing** *n*
rɪ'ʤəɪsɪn, -ɪŋ
**sp** reioycing[3], re-ioycing[1]

**rejoicing-fire / ~s** *n*
rɪ'ʤəɪsɪn-'fəɪɹz, -ɪŋ-
**sp** reioycing-fires[1]
> fire

**rejoicingly** *adv*
rɪ'ʤəɪsɪnləɪ, -ɪŋ-
**sp** reioycingly[1]

**rejoindure** *n*
rɪ'ʤəɪndəɹ
**sp** reioyndure[1]

**rejourn** *v*
rɪ'ʤɐ:ɹn
**sp** reiourne[1]

**relapse** *n*
'ri:laps
**sp** relapse[1]

**relate / ~s** *v*
rɪ'lɛ:t / -s

**sp** relate[9] / relates[1]
**rh** arbitrate *Mac 5.4.19*; debate *LLL 1.1.169*; extenuate *Oth 5.2.337*; state *Oth 5.2.367*

**relation / ~s** *n*
rɪ'lɛ:sɪən / -z
**sp** relation[7], re-lation[1] / relations[1]

**relative** *adj*
=
**sp** relatiue[1]

**release** *n*
rɪ'li:s, -'lɛ:s
**sp** release[1]

**releas·e / *VA, S* ~ing / ~ed** *v*
rɪ'li:s, -'lɛ:s / -ɪn, -ɪŋ / -t
**sp** release[6] / releasing[2] / releasd[1], releas'd[2], released[2]
**rh** peace *MND 3.2.376* / **rh** *1* increasing *VA 256*; **rh** *2* possessing *S 87.3*
> lease

**relent / ~s / *VA* ~eth / ~ing** *v*
= / = / = / rɪ'lentɪn, -ɪŋ
**sp** relent[16] / relents[1] / relenteth[1] / relenting[2]
**rh** tormenteth *VA 200*
> unrelenting

**reliance / ~s** *n*
rɪ'ləɪənsɪz
**sp** reliances[1]

**relic / ~s** *n*
=
**sp** reliques[5]

**relief** *n*
=
**sp** releefe[7], reliefe[4], re-liefe[1]
**rh** grief *3H6 3.3.20, S 34.11*

**relier *Luc*** *n*
rɪ'ləɪəɹ
**sp** relier[1]
**rh** desire, retire *Luc 639*

**reliev·e / ~es / *VA* ~eth / ~ing / ~ed** *v*
=, rɪ'lɪv / -z / -əθ / -ɪn, -ɪŋ / -d
**sp** releeue[9], relieue[3] / releeues[1] / releeueth[1] / relieuing[1] / releeu'd[5], releeued[2], relieu'd[2], relieued[1]
**rh** *1* **relieve them** grieve for them *Per 1.2.99*; **rh** *2* **relieve me** give me *Per 5.2.4* [*Chorus*] / upheaveth *VA 484*

**religion / ~s** *n*
*m* rɪ'lidʒɪən, -ɪˌɒn / -ɪənz
**sp** religion[16] / religions[1]

**religious** *adj*
*m* rɪ'lidʒɪəs, -ɪˌɤs
**sp** religious[18], religous[1]
> irreligious

**religiously** *adv*
*m* rɪ'lidʒɪəsləɪ, -ˌləɪ
**sp** religiouslie[1], religiously[6]

**relinquish / ~ed** *v*
=
**sp** relinquisht[1]

**reli·nquo / ~quit** *Lat v*
'relɪkwɪt
**sp** reliquit[1]

**relish** *n*
=
**sp** rallish[1], relish[1], rellish[4], rel-lish[1]

**relish / ~ed** *v*
=
**sp** rallish[1], rellish[10] / rellish'd[1]
> disrrelish

**relume** *v*
rɪ'lju:m
**sp** re-lume[1]

**rely / ~ing** *v*
rɪ'ləɪ / -ɪn, -ɪŋ
**sp** rely[2], relye[3] / relying[1]
**rh** I *AW 2.1.204*

**remain / ~s** *n*
rɪ'mɛ:n / -z
**sp** remaine[2] / remaines[2]

**remain / ~s / ~eth / ~ing / ~ed** *v*
rɪ'mɛ:n / -z / -əθ / -ɪn, -ɪŋ / -d
**sp** remain[2], remaine[55] / remaines[34], remains[1] / remaineth[1], remayneth[1] / remaining[5] / remain'd[2]
**rh** brain *S 122.3*; dame *PP 17.12*; disdain *Luc 519*; feign *PP 8.14*; gain *H8 5.3.180*; gain, pain *Luc 732*; plain *Luc 1249*; rain *VA 801*; reign *LC 129*; reign, vein *Luc 1453*; slain *Per 4.1.102*; twain *MND 5.1.150, PT 48, S 36.3, 39.14*; vein *MND 3.2.83* / contains *LC 188, S 74.14* / complaining, sustaining *Luc 1572* / stained *Luc 1742*

**remainder** *adj*
rɪ'mɛ:ndəɹ
**sp** remainder[2]

**remainder** *n*
rɪ'mɛ:ndəɹ / -z
**sp** remainder[8] / remainders[3]

**remarkable** *adj*
rɪ'mɑ:ɹkəbəl
**sp** remarkeable[1], re-markeable[1]

**remarked** *n*
rɪ'mɑ:ɹkt
**sp** remark'd[1]

**remediate** *adj*
rɪ'mi:dɪət
**sp** remediate[1]

**remed·y / ~ies** *n*
*m* 'remɪˌdəɪ, -ɪd- / -z
**sp** remedie[32], remedy[22] / remedies[8]
**rh** *1* archery, gloriously MND 3.2.109; courtesy 1H6 2.2.57; **rh** *2* apply, eye *MND 3.2.452*; by *S 154.11*; by, dye, espy, sky *MND 3.2.109*; die *RJ 3.5.242, 4.1.67*; eye *S 62.3*; try *AW 2.1.135* / eyes *R2 3.3.203*; lies *RJ 2.3.47*

**remed·y / ~ied** *v*
*m* 'remɪˌdəɪ, -ɪd- / -d
**sp** remedie[3] / remedied[1], remedy'd[1]

**remember / ~est / ~s / ~ing / ~ed** *v*
rɪˈmembəɹ / -st / -z / rɪˈmemb·rɪn, -ɪŋ / *m* -əɹd, -əˌred
**sp** remember[183], reme[m]ber[1], re-member[2], remem-ber[1], remember't [remember it][1] / remember'st[1], remembrest[4] / remembers[3] / remembring[5] / remembred[22], reme[m]bred[1], remem-bred[2], re-membred[1]
**rh** dead *S 74.12*; tendered *S 120.9*
> well-remembered

**remembrance / ~s** *n*
*m* rɪˈmembrəns, -bəˌrans, -ˌrɔ:ns / -brənsɪz, -ˌsɪz
**sp** remembrance[59], remem-brance[1], remembraunce[1] / remembrances[5]

**remembrancer** *n*
rɪˈmembrənsəɹ
**sp** remembrancer[2]

**remercîment / ~s** *Fr n*
rəmɛɹsiˈmɑ̃
**sp** remercious[1]

**remiss** *adj*
=
**sp** remisse[5]

**remission** *n*
*m* rɪˈmɪsɪən, -sɪˌɒn
**sp** remission[4]

**remissness** *n*
=
**sp** remissenesse[1]

**remit** *v*
=
**sp** remit[4]

**remnant / ~s** *n*
=
**sp** remnant[5] / remnants[3]

**remonstrance** *n*
*m* rɪˈmɒnstrəns
**sp** remonstrance[1]

**remorse** *n*
rɪˈmɔ:ɹs
**sp** remorse[28]
**rh** horse *VA 257*

**remorseful** *adj*
rɪˈmɔ:ɹsfʊl
**sp** remorsefull[3], remorse-full[1]

**remorseless** *adj*
rɪˈmɔ:ɹsləs
**sp** remorselesse[3]

**remote** *adj*
rɪˈmo:t
**sp** remote[6]

**remotion** *n*
rɪˈmo:sɪən
**sp** remotion[2]

**remove / ~s** *n*
rɪˈmɤv, -ˈmu:v / -z
**sp** remoue[5] / remoues[2]

**remov·e / ~es / ~ing / ~ed** *v*
rɪˈmɤv, -ˈmu:v / -z / -ɪn, -ɪŋ / -d
**sp** remoue[22] / remoues[1] / remouing[2] / remoou'd[2], remooued[1], remou'd[12], remoued[9]
**rh** *1* love *AY 3.4.51, LC 237, Luc 614, PP 17.8, RJ Prol.11, S 116.4, VA 81, 186;* **rh** *2* prove *Luc 614, RJ 1.1.142* / loves *LLL 5.2.135* / beloved *S 25.14*
> move; irremovable, un-removable

**removed** *adj*
*m* rɪˈmɤvɪd, -vd, -ˈmu:v-
**sp** remoued[6]

**removedness** *n*
rɪˈmɤvɪdnəs, -ˈmu:v-
**sp** remouednesse[1]

**removing** *n*
rɪˈmɤvɪn, -ɪŋ, -ˈmu:v-
**sp** remouing[1]
**rh** *1* loving; **rh** *2* reproving *Luc 243*

**remunerate** *v*
*m* rɪˈmju:nəˌrɛ:t
**sp** remunerate[1]

**remuneration** *n*
rɪˌmju:nəˈrɛ:sɪən
**sp** remuneration[11], remune-ration[1]

**rend** *v*
=
**sp** rend[12]

**render** *n*
ˈrendəɹ
**sp** render[3]

**render / ~est / ~s / ~ing / ~ed** *v*
ˈrendəɹ / -st / -z / ˈrendrɪn, -ɪŋ / ˈrendəɹd
**sp** render[36] / render'st[1] / renders[4] / rendring[1], rend'ring[1] / render'd[4], rendred[9]
**rh** ender, tender *LC 221*
> life-rendering

**rendezvous** *n*
*m* ˈrendəˌvu:, -əvu:
**sp** randeuous[1], rendeuous[3]

**renegado** *n*
renɪˈgaðo:
**sp** renegatho[1]

**renege / ~s** *v*
rɪˈnegz
**sp** reneages[1]

**renew / *S* ~est / ~s / ~ed** *v*
= / rɪˈnju:st / =
**sp** renew[12] / renewest[1] / renewes[1] / renew'd[1], renewed[1]
**rh** viewest *S 3.3* / ensues, views *Luc 1103* / subdued *S 111.8*

**renewed** *adj*
=
**sp** renew'd[1]

**renounc·e / ~ing** *v*
rɪˈnəʊns / -ɪn, -ɪŋ
**sp** renounce[4], renownce[1] / renouncing[1]

**renouncement** *n*
rɪˈnəʊnsmənt
**sp** renouncement[1]

**renown** *n*
rɪ'nəʊn
**sp** renown[1], renowne[19]
**rh** crown *AW 4.4.36*; down *Oth 2.3.88*; frown *PP 20.46*; town *AY 5.4.142*

**renown / ~ed** *v*
rɪ'nəʊn / -d
**sp** renowne[1] / renowned[1]

**renowned** *adj*
*m* rɪ'nəʊnɪd, -nd
**sp** renown'd[5], renowned[32]
> thrice-renowned

**rent** *n*
=
**sp** rent[2] / rents[2]
**rh** spent *S 125.6* / ornaments *S 142.8*

**rent / ~s** *v*
=
**sp** rent[9] / rents[1]
**rh** contents *LC 55*

**repair** *n*
rɪ'pɛ:ɹ
**sp** repaire[4], repayre[1]
**rh** fair *LLL 2.1.226*

**repair / ~s / ~ed** *v*
rɪ'pɛ:ɹ / -z / -d
**sp** repair[1], repaire[23], repayre[13] / repaires[3] / repaired[1], repayr'd[1]
**rh** air *LLL 5.2.292*; fair *CE 2.1.99, S 16.9*; fair, prayer *PT 65*; fair, there *TG 4.2.45*
> a-repairing

**repairing** *adj*
rɪ'pɛ:rɪn, -ɪŋ
**sp** repayring[1]

**re-pass / ~ed** *v*
'ri:-ˌpast
**sp** re-pass'd[1]
> pass

**repast** *n / v*
rɪ'past
**sp** repast[3] / repast[1]
**rh** hast *R3 4.4.396* [*F*]

**repasture** *n*
rɪ'pastəɹ
**sp** repasture[1]
> pasture

**repay / ~s / ~ing / repaid** *v*
rɪ'pɛ: / -z / -ɪn, -ɪŋ / -d
**sp** repaie[1], repay[3] / repayes[3] / repaying[1] / repaid[2], repaide[1], repaie[1], repayed[1]
**rh** day *S 117.2*
> pay

**repeal** *n*
=
**sp** repeale[4]
**rh** appeal *Luc 640*

**repeal / ~s / ~ed** *v*
=
**sp** repeale[4] / repeales[2] / repeal'd[6]

**repealing** *n*
rɪ'pi:lɪn, -ɪŋ
**sp** repealing[1]

**repeat / ~est / ~s / ~ed** *v*
rɪ'pi:t / -s, -st / -s / -ɪd
**sp** repeat[8], repeate[4] / repeat'st[1] / repeats[1] / repeated[2]
**rh** *1* deceit *Per 1.4.74*; **rh** *2* great *Per 1.4.31*

**repeating** *n*
rɪ'pi:tɪn, -ɪŋ
**sp** repeating[1]

**repel** *v*
=
**sp** repell[1]

**repent / ~s / ~ed** *v*
=
**sp** repent[56], re-pent[2] / repents[2], re-pents[1] / repented[4]
**rh** bent *PP 18.27*; content, spent *MND 2.2.117*; repent you content you *MND 5.1.115*
> high-repented

**repentance** *n*
=
**sp** repentance[8]

**repentant** *adj*
=
**sp** repentant[2]

**repenting** *n*
rɪ'pentɪn, -ɪŋ
**sp** repenting[1]

**repetition / ~s** *n*
*m* ˌrepɪ'tɪsɪən, -sɪˌɒn / -sɪˌɒnz
**sp** repetition[6] / repetitions[1]

**répétition** *Fr n*
repeti'sjɔ̃
**sp** repiticio[1]

**repine** *VA* **/ ~d** *v*
rɪ'pəɪn / -d
**sp** repine[1] / repin'd[1]
**rh** shine *VA 490*; thine *1H6 5.2.20*

**repining** *adj*
rɪ'pəɪnɪn, -ɪŋ
**sp** repining[1]

**replant** *v*
*m* 'ri:plant
**sp** replant[1]

**replenish** *Luc* *v*
=
**sp** replenish[1]
**rh** blemish *Luc 1357*

**replenished** *adj*
*m* rɪ'plenɪʃt, -ˌʃɪd
**sp** replenish'd[1], replenished[2]

**replete** *adj*
=
**sp** repleat[3], repleate[3], replete[1]

**replication** *n*
ˌreplɪ'kɛ:sɪən
**sp** replication[2], re-plication[1]

**repl·y / ~ies** *n*
rɪ'pləɪz
**sp** replies[1], replyes[1]

**repl·y / ~iest / ~ies / ~ying / ~ied** *v*
rɪˈpləɪ / -st / -z / -ɪn, -ɪŋ / -d
**sp** replie[2], reply[22] / repli'st[1] / replies[2], replyes[1] / replying[2] / replide[2], replied[2], reply'd[1], replyed[3]
**rh** advisedly *1H4 5.1.113*; modesty *TG 2.1.157* / eyes *AW 2.3.80*; skies *VA 695*

**report / ~s** *n*
rɪˈpɔːɹt / -s
**sp** report[87], re-port[4] / reports[11], re-ports[1]
**rh** court *Cym 4.2.34*; short *S 83.5*; sort *MND 3.2.22, S 36.14, 96.14, 95.8*

**report ~est / ~s / ~ed** *v*
rɪˈpɔːɹt / -st / -s / -ɪd
**sp** report[50] / reportest[1], reportst[1], report'st[1] / reports[6] / reported[15]
> misreport

**reporter** *n*
rɪˈpɔːɹtəɹ
**sp** reporter[1]

**reporting** *n*
rɪˈpɔːɹtɪn, -ɪŋ
**sp** reporting[1]

**reportingly** *adv*
*m* rɪˈpɔːɹtɪnˌləɪ, -ɪŋ-
**sp** reportingly[1]
**rh** I *MA 3.1.116*

**reposal** *n*
rɪˈpoːzɑl
**sp** reposall[1]

**repose** *n*
rɪˈpoːz
**sp** repose[12]

**repos·e / ~eth / ~ing** *v*
rɪˈpoːz / -əθ / -ɪn, -ɪŋ
**sp** repose[12] / reposeth[1] / reposing[3]
**rh** foes, woes Luc 933

**repossess** *v*
=
**sp** repossesse[2], re-possesse[2]
> possess

**reprehend / ~ing / ~ed** *v*
ˌreprɪˈend, -ˈhe- / -ɪn, -ɪŋ / -ɪd
**sp** reprehend[3] / reprehending[1] / reprehended[3]
**rh** mend *MND 5.1.419*; reprehend her defend her *VA 470*

**represent** *v*
=
**sp** represent[3]

**reprieve / ~s** *n*
=
**sp** repreeue[3], reprieue[1] / repreeues[2]

**reprieve** *v*
=
**sp** repreeue[2]
> unreprievable

**reprisal** *n*
rɪˈprəɪzɑl
**sp** reprizall[1]

**reproach / ~es** *n*
rɪˈproːʧ / -ɪz
**sp** reproach[1] / reproaches[1], reproches[1]

**reproach** *v*
rɪˈproːʧ
**sp** reproach[17]

**reproachful** *adj*
rɪˈproːʧfʊl
**sp** reproachfull[1], reprochfull[1]

**reproachfully** *adv*
*m* rɪˈproːʧfʊˌləɪ
**sp** reproachfully[1]

**reprobance** *n*
*m* ˈreprəˌbans
**sp** reprobance[1]

**reprobate** *adj / n*
*m* ˈreprəbət / ˈreprəˌbɛːt
**sp** reprobate[1] / reprobate[1]

**reproof** *n*
rɪˈprɤf, -ruːf
**sp** reproofe[16]

**reprovable** *adj*
rɪˈprɤvəbəl, -ruːv-
**sp** reprouable[1]

**reprove / ~s / *S* ~ing / ~d** *v*
rɪˈprɤv, -ruːv / -z / -ɪn, -ɪŋ / -d
**sp** re-prooue[1], reproue[5] / reproues[1] / reproouing[1] / reprou'd[1]
**rh** love *LLL 4.3.151, VA 787* / loving *S 142.4*

**reproving *Luc*** *n*
rɪˈprɤvɪn, -ɪŋ, -ruːv-
**sp** reproouing[1]
**rh** *1* loving *Luc 242*; **rh** *2* removing *Luc 242*
> self-reproving

**repugn** *v*
rɪˈpjuːn
**sp** repugne[1]

**repugnancy** *n*
*m* rɪˈpɤgnənˌsəɪ
**sp** repugnancy[1]

**repugnant** *adj*
rɪˈpɤgnənt
**sp** repugnant[1]

**repulse** *n*
rɪˈpɤls
**sp** repulse[5]

**repulse** *v*
rɪˈpɤlst
**sp** repulsed[1]

**repurchase / ~d** *v*
rɪˈpɐːɹʧɪst
**sp** re-purchac'd[1]

**repure**
> thrice-repured

**reputation** *n*
*m* ˌrepjəˈtɛːsɪən, -sɪˌɒn
**sp** reputation[44], repu-tation[1], reputati-on[1]
**rh** disputation *Luc 820*

**repute** *n*
=
**sp** repute[3]

**repute / ~es / ~ing / ~ed** *v*
= / = / rɪ'pju:tɪn, -ɪŋ / =
**sp** repute[7] / reputes[2] / reputing[1] / reputed[7]

**reputed** *adj*
=
**sp** reputed[2]
> well-reputed

**reputeless** *adj*
=
**sp** reputelesse[1]

**request / ~'s / ~s** *n*
=
**sp** request[52], request's [request is][1] / requests[1] / requests[8]
**rh** rest *MM 2.4.186*

**request / ~s / ~ing / ~ed** *v*
= / = / rɪ'kwestɪn, -ɪŋ / =
**sp** request[12] / requests[6] / requesting[1] / requested[3]

**requicken / ~ed** *v*
=
**sp** requickned[1]

**requiem** *n*
=
**sp** requiem[1]

**require / ~s / ~th / ~d** *v*
rɪ'kwəɪɹ / -z / -əθ / -d
**sp** require[21] / requires[14] / requireth[1] / requir'd[7]
**rh** desire *S 57.4*

**required** *adj*
*m* rɪ'kwəɪɹd, -rɪd
**sp** requir'd[2], required[2]

**requiring** *n*
rɪ'kwəɪrɪn, -ɪŋ
**sp** requiring[2], requi-ring[1]
**rh** firing *Tem 2.2.178*

**requisite / ~s** *n*
=
**sp** requisite[1] / requisites[1]

**requit / ~s / ~ted** *v*
rɪ'kwɪt / -s / -ɪd
**sp** requit[5] / requits[1] / requitted[1]

**requital** *n*
rɪ'kwɪtɑl
**sp** requital[1], requitall[6]

**requite / ~s / ~d** *v*
rɪ'kwəɪt / -s / -ɪd
**sp** requite[20] / requites[1] / requited[4]
**rh** requite thee incite thee *MA 3.1.111*

**resalute** *v*
ˌri:sə'lu:t
**sp** resalute[2]
> salute

**rescue** *n*
=
**sp** rescu[3], rescue[16], res-cue[1]

**rescu·e / ~es / ~ing / ~ed** *v*
= / = / 'reskju:ɪn, -ɪŋ / =
**sp** rescue[8], reskew[1], reskue[1] / rescues[2] / rescuing[1] / rescu'd[5], rescued[5]

**resemblance** *n*
rɪ'semblɔ:ns, -ləns, -'z-
**sp** resemblance[2], re-semblance[1]

**resembl·e / ~es / ~eth / ~ing / ~ed** *v*
rɪ'sembl, -'z- / -z / -əθ / -ɪn, -ɪŋ / -d
**sp** resemble[7] / resembles[4] / resembleth[1] / resembling[2] / resembled[2], resem-bled[1]
**rh** assemble *S 114.6*; tremble *Luc 1392*

**resend** *v*
=
**sp** resend[1]
> send

**reservation** *n*
ˌresəɹ'vɛ:sɪən, ˌrez-
**sp** reseruation[5]

**reserve / ~s / ~ed** *v*
rɪ'sɐ:ɹv, -'z- / -z / -d
**sp** reserue[7], re-serue[1] / reserues[1] / reseru'd[12], reserued[1]

**resid·e / ~s / ~ing** *v*
rɪ'səɪd, -'z- / -z / -ɪn, -ɪŋ
**sp** recide[3] / recides[4], resides[2] / reciding[2], residing[1]

**residence** *n*
*m* 'resɪˌdens, -dəns, -'rez-
**sp** residence[8], resi-dence[1]

**resident** *adj*
*m* 'resɪˌdent, -'rez-
**sp** resident[2]

**residue** *n*
'resdju:, 'rez-, -sɪd-, -zɪd-
**sp** residue[1]

**resign / ~ed** *v*
rɪ'səɪn, -'z- / -d
**sp** resigne[21] / resign'd[3]
**rh** mine *2H6 2.3.33, R2 4.1.189*

**resignation** *n*
ˌresɪg'nɛ:sɪən, ˌrez-
**sp** resignation[1]

**resist / ~s / *VA* ~eth / ~ing** *v*
rɪ'sɪst, -'z- / -s / -əθ / -ɪn, -ɪŋ
**sp** resist[8] / resists[2] / resisteth[1] / resisted[5]
**rh** consist *Per 1.4.84*; desist *Per 1.1.41* / listeth *VA 563*

**resistance** *n*
rɪ'sɪstɔ:ns, -təns, -'z-
**sp** resistance[3]

**resisting** *adj*
rɪ'sɪstɪn, -ɪŋ, -'z-
**sp** resisting[1]

**resolute** *adj*
*m* 'resəˌlju:t, -sl-, 'rez-
**sp** resolute[12]

**resolute / ~s** *n*
*m* 'resəˌlju:ts, 'rez-
**sp** resolutes[1]

**resolutely** *adv*
*m* 'resə,lju:tləɪ, 'rez-
**sp** resolutely[2], reso-lutely[1]

**resolution** *n*
*m* ,resə'lu:sɪən, -sɪ,ɒn, ,rez-
**sp** resolution[27], re-solution[1], resolution's [resolution is][1]
**rh** absolution, dissolution *Luc 352*

**resolve** *n*
rɪ'sɒlv, -'z-
**sp** resolue[5]

**resolve / ~s / ~th /** *Luc* **~ing / ~d** *v*
rɪ'sɒlv, -'z- / -z / -əθ / -ɪn, -ɪŋ / -d
**sp** resolue[23], re-solue[1] / resolues[2] / resolueth[1] / resoluing[1] / resolud[1], resolu'd[35], resolued[1]
**rh** revolving *Luc 129*

**resolved** *adj*
*m* rɪ'sɒlvd, -vɪd, -'z-
**sp** resolu'd[2], resolued[3], resolv'd[1]
> high-, un-resolved

**resolvedly** *adv*
*m* rɪ'sɒlvɪd,ləɪ, -'z-
**sp** resoluedly[1]

**resort** *n*
rɪ'sɔ:ɹt, -'z-
**sp** resort[7]

**resort / ~ed** *v*
rɪ'sɔ:ɹt, -'z- / -ɪd
**sp** resort[5] / resorted[1]
**rh** short, sport *Luc 989*; sport *S 96.4*

**resound / ~s** *v*
rɪ'səʊndz, -'z-
**sp** resounds[1]

**resounding** *adj*
rɪ'səʊndɪn, -ɪŋ, -'z-
**sp** resounding[1]

**respeak / ~ing** *v*
ri:'spi:kɪn, -ɪŋ, -'spɛ:k-
**sp** respeaking[1]
> speak

**respect / ~s** *n*
= / rɪ'speks, -kts
**sp** respect[78], re-spect[3] / respects[9], re-spects[1]
**rh** aspect *S 26.12*; defect *Luc 1347*; deject *TC 2.2.49*; effect *S 36.5*; neglect *KL 1.1.255* / defects *S 49.4*

**respect / ~est / ~s / ~ing / ~ed** *v*
= / rɪ'spek·st, -tst / -s, -ts / -tɪn, -tɪŋ / =
**sp** respect[15] / respect'st[1] / respects[7] / respecting[4] / respected[7]
**rh** defect *S 149.9*; effect *S 85.13*; **respect her** reject her *LLL 5.2.437* / neglected *Per 2.2.13* / effecting *VA 911*

**respected** *adj*
=
**sp** respected[4]
> well-respected

**respective** *adj*
=
**sp** respectiue[4]
> unrespective

**respectively** *adv*
rɪ'spektɪvləɪ
**sp** re-spectiuely[1]

**respic·io / ~e** *Lat v*
re'spi:se
**sp** respice[1]

**respite / ~s** *n*
'respɪt / -s
**sp** respit[3], respite[2] / respits[1]

**responsive** *adj*
=
**sp** responsiue[1]

**rest** *n*
=
**sp** rest[243]
**rh** *1* addressed *LLL 5.2.91*; best *Per 2.Chorus.26, PP 1.8, S 91.6, 115.12, TG 1.2.20*; breast *Ham 3.2.187, 3H6 2.6.29, LLL 5.2.809, Luc 757, 1844, MND 5.1.148, RJ 2.2.123, VA 647, 784, 853, 1185*; jest *LLL 1.1.53*; oppressed *S 28.2*; pressed *MND 2.2.70*; request *MM 2.4.187*; suppressed *3H6 4.3.5*; west *S 73.8*; **rh** *2* beast *CE 5.1.83*; east *PP 14.15*; feast *TS 5.1.128*
> night-, un-rest

**rest / ~s / ~eth / ~ing / ~ed** *v*
= / = / = / 'restɪn, -ɪŋ / =
**sp** rest[89], rest-[them][1] / rests[16], rest's[1] / resteth[3] / resting[2] / rested[6]
**rh** best *Per 2.3.114*; blest/blessed *AW 2.1.207; MND 5.1.410*; breast *RJ 2.2.187*; breast, nest, rest *PT 58*; oppressed *Cym 5.4.97*; **rest them** blessed them *TG 3.1.144* / breasts, guests *Luc 1124*
> over-rested

**re-stem** *v*
=
**sp** re-stem[1]
> stem

**restful** *adj*
=
**sp** restfull[1]

**resting** *adj / n*
'restɪn, -ɪŋ
**sp** resting[1] / resting[1]

**restitution** *n*
*m* ,restɪ'tu:sɪən, -sɪ,ɒn
**sp** restitution[4]

**restless** *adj*
=
**sp** restlesse[4]

**restoration** *n*
,restə'rɛ:sɪən
**sp** restauratian[1]

**restorative / ~s** *Per* *n*
*m* rɪ'stɔ:rə,təɪvz
**sp** restoratiues[1]
**rh** lives [*n*] *Per Prol.8*

**restore / ~s / ~d** *v*
rɪ'stɔ:ɹ / -z / -d
**sp** restore[18] / restores[1] / restor'd[12]
**rh** bore *LC 301*

**restored** *adj*
rɪ'stɔ:rɪd
**sp** restored[4]
> unrestored

**restoring** *n*
rɪ'stɔ:rɪn, -ɪŋ
**sp** restoring[1]

**restrain / ~est / ~s / ~ing / ~ed** *v*
rɪ'strɛ:n / -st / -z / -ɪn, -ɪŋ / -d
**sp** restraine[6] / restrain'st[1] / restraines[1] / restraining[1], restrayning[1] / restrain'd[5], restrained[3]
**rh restrain him** detain him *VA 579* / veins *Luc 426*

**restrained** *adj*
rɪ'strɛ:nɪd
**sp** restrained[1]
> unrestrained

**restraint** *n*
rɪ'strɛ:nt
**sp** restraint[12], re-straint[1]

**resty** *adj*
'restəɪ
**sp** restie[1]

**result / ~ing** *v*
rɪ'sɤltɪn, -ɪŋ, -z-
**sp** resulting[1]

**resume / ~d** *v*
rɪ'sju:m, -'z- / -d
**sp** resume[4] / resum'd[1]

**resurrection / ~s** *n*
*Evans MW 1.1.49*
ˌresə'reksɪəns
**sp** resurrections[1]

**re-survey** *v*
'ri:-səɹ'vɛ:
**sp** re-suruey[1]
**rh** day *S 32.3*

**retail / ~s / ~ed** *v*
rɪ'tɛ:l / -z / -d
**sp** retaile[2] / retailes[1] / retayl'd[1]

**retain / ~s / ~ing / ~ed** *v*
rɪ'tɛ:n / -z / -ɪn, -ɪŋ / -d
**sp** retaine[7] / retaines[1] / retaining[1] / retain'd[1], retein'd[1]
**rh** pains *TNK Prol.7*

**retainer / ~s** *n*
rɪ'tɛ:nəɹz
**sp** retainers[1]

**retell / retold** *v*
ri:'tel / ri:'to:ld
**sp** re-tell[1] / retold[1], re-told[1]
> tell

**retention** *n*
rɪ'tensɪən
**sp** retention[3]

**retentive** *adj*
=
**sp** retentiue[2]

**retinue** *n*
=
**sp** retinue[2]

**retire / ~es** *n*
rɪ'təɪɹ / -z
**sp** retire[6], retyre[5] / retires[1]
**rh** desire *LLL 2.1.220, Luc 573*

**retir·e / ~es / ~ing / ~ed** *v*
rɪ'təɪɹ / -z / -ɪn, -ɪŋ / -d
**sp** retire[12], retyre[11] / retires[2], retyres[2] / retyring[2] / retir'd[1], retyr'd[6], retyred[3]
**rh** desire, relier *Luc 641*; desire *Luc 174*

**retired** *adj*
*m* rɪ'təɪɹd, -rɪd
**sp** retir'd[1], retired[1]

**retirement** *n*
rɪ'təɪɹmənt
**sp** retirement[1], retirment[1], retyrement[3]

**retiring** *adj*
rɪ'təɪrɪn, -ɪŋ
**sp** retyring[1]

**retold**
> retell

**retort** *n*
rɪ'tɔ:ɹt
**sp** retort[2]

**retort / ~s** *v*
rɪ'tɔ:ɹt / -s
**sp** retort[3] / retorts[1]

**retourn·er / é** *Fr v*
rətuɹ'ne
**sp** retourne[1]

**retract** *v*
=
**sp** retract[1]

**retreat** *n*
rɪ'trɛ:t, -et
**sp** retrait[1], retreat[24], retreate[2], re-treit[1]

**retrograde** *adj*
*m* 'retrəˌgrɛ:d
**sp** retrograde[2]

**return / ~s** *n*
rɪ'tɐ:ɹn / -z
**sp** returne[44], re-turne[1] / returnes[1]

**return / ~est / ~s / ~eth / ~ing / ~ed** *v*
rɪ'tɐ:ɹn / -st / -z / -əθ / -ɪn, -ɪŋ / *m* -d, -ɪd
**sp** return[2], returne[139], re-turne[3] / returnst[1] / returnes[16] / returneth[1], re-turneth[1] / returning[4] / returnd[1], return'd[47], re-turn'd[2], returned[4]
**rh** sojourned *MND 3.2.172*

**returned** *adj*
*m* rɪ'tɐ:ɹnɪd
**sp** returned[1]

**re-unite / ~d** *v*
ˌr:i-jə'nəɪtɪd
**sp** re-vnited[1]

**revania** *nonsense word*
re'vanɪə
**sp** reuania[1]

**reveal / ~s / ~ed** *v*
=
**sp** reueale[5] / reueales[1] / reueal'd[3]

**revel / ~s** *n*
=
**sp** reuell[4] / reuels[12], re-uels[1]

**revel / ~s / ~ling / ~led** *v*
= / = / 'revəlɪn, -ɪŋ / =
**sp** reuell[11] / reuels[2] / reuelling[1] / reuel'd[1], reuell'd[2]

**reveller / ~s** *n*
'revləɹ, -vəl- / -z
**sp** reueller[2] / reuellers[2]

**revelling** *n*
'revlɪn, -ɪŋ, -vəl-
**sp** reuelling[2]

**revelry** *n*
'revəlrəɪ
**sp** reuelrie[1]
**rh** dignity *AY 5.4.174*

**revenge / ~'s / ~s** *n*
=
**sp** reuenge[104], re-uenge[4] / reuenges[1] / reuenges[15]

**revenge / ~d** *v*
=
**sp** reuenge[44], re-uenge[1], reueng'd[37], reuenged[5]
> unrevenged

**revengeful** *adj*
=
**sp** reuengefull[7], re-uengefull[1]

**revengement** *n*
=
**sp** reuengement[1]

**revenger / ~s** *n*
rɪ'venʤəɹ / -z
**sp** reuenger[1] / reuengers[1]

**revenging** *adj*
rɪ'venʤɪn, -ɪŋ
**sp** reuenging[2]

**revengingly** *adv*
rɪ'venʤɪnləɪ, -ɪŋ-
**sp** reuengingly[1]

**revenue / ~s** *n*
*m* rə'venju:, = / -z
**sp** reuenew[4], reuennew[12], reuennue[1], reuenue[2] / reuenewes[1], reuennewes[1], reuenues[3]

**reverb** *v*
rɪ'vɐ:ɹb
**sp** reuerbe[1]

**reverberate** *adj / v*
rɪ'vɐ:ɹbrət, -bər-
**sp** reuerberate[1] / reuerberate[1], reuerb'rate[1]

**reverence** *n*
*m* 'revrəns, -vər-, -əˌrens
**sp** reuerence[41], reue-rence[1]

**reverence / ~d** *v*
'revrəns, -vər- / -t
**sp** reuerence[1] / reuerenc'd[1], reuerenc't[1]

**reverend / ~est** *adj*
'revrənd, -vər- / -z, -nz
**sp** reuerend[42], reueren'd[3], re-uerend[1] / reuerends [throat][1]
> unreverend, unreverent

**reverent** *adj*
*m* 'revrənt, -vər-, -əˌrent
**sp** reuerent[15]

**reverently** *adv*
*m* 'revrəntləɪ, -vər-, -ˌləɪ
**sp** reuerently[3]

**reverse** *n*
rɪ'vɐ:ɹs
**sp** reuerse[1]

**reverse / ~d** *v*
rɪ'vɐ:ɹs / -t
**sp** reuerse[2] / reuerst[1]
> unreversed

**reversion** *n*
*m* rɪ'vɐ:ɹsɪən, -sɪˌɒn
**sp** reuersion[4]

**reverso** *Ital adj*
re'vɛ:ɹso:
**sp** reuerso[1]

**revert / ~ed** *v*
rɪ'vɐ:ɹtɪd
**sp** reuerted[2]

**re-view** *v*
ˌr:i-'vju:
**sp** re-view[1]
**rh** due *S 74.5*

**revile / ~d** *v*
rɪ'vəɪl / -d
**sp** reuile[1] / reuil'd[2]

**revisit / ~s** *v*
ri:'vɪzɪts
**sp** reuisits[1]

**reviv·e / ~es / *VA* ~eth / ~ing** *v*
rɪ'vəɪv / -z / -əθ / -ɪn, -ɪŋ
**sp** reuiue[10] / reuiues[3] / reuiueth[1] / reuiu'd[6]
**rh** thriveth *VA 464*

**reviving** *adj*
rɪ'vəɪvɪn, -ɪŋ
**sp** reuiuing[2]

**revoke / ~d** *v*
rɪ'vo:k / -t
**sp** reuoke / reuok'd[1]

**revokement** *n*
rɪ'vo:kmənt
**sp** reuokement[1]

**revolt / ~s** *n*
rɪ'vɒlt, -'vo:- / -s
**sp** reuolt[22] / reuolts[5]

**revolt / ~s / ~ed** *v*
rɪ'vɒlt, -'vo:- / -s / -ɪd
**sp** reuolt[19] / reuolts[1] / reuolted[4]

**revolted** *adj*
rɪ'vɒltɪd, -'vo:-
**sp** reuolted[8]

**revolting** *adj*
rɪ'vɒltɪn, -ɪŋ, -'voː-
**sp** reuolting[4]

**revolution / ~s** *n*
ˌrevə'luːsɪən / -z
**sp** reuolution[3] / reuolutions[1]

**revolv·e / ~ing** *v*
rɪ'vɒlv / -ɪn, -ɪŋ
**sp** reuolue[4], reuoluing[2]
**rh** resolving *Luc 127*
> deep-revolving

**reward / ~s** *n*
rɪ'wɑːɹd / -z
**sp** reward[24] / rewards[6]
**rh** *1* barred *AW 2.1.147*; guard *Per 2.4.15*; **rh** *2* heard *Per Epil.2*

**reward,** *abbr* **ward / ~s / ~ing / ~ed** *v*
rɪ'wɑːɹd, *abbr* wɑːɹd / -z / -ɪn, -ɪŋ / -ɪd
**sp** reward[12], *abbr* ward[1] / rewards[3], re-wards[1] / rewarding[1] / rewarded[2]
> unrewarded

**rewarder** *n*
rɪ'wɑːɹdəɹ
**sp** rewarder[1]

**re-word /** *LC* **~ed** *v*
ˌriː-'wɔːɹd / ˌriː-'wɔːɹdɪd
**sp** re-word[1] / reworded[1]
**rh** accorded *LC 1*

**rex** *Lat n*
reks
**sp** rex[2]

**Reynard** *n*
re'nɑːɹd
**sp** Reynard[1]

**Reynoldo** *n*
rɪ'nɒldoː
**sp** Reynoldo[4]

**rhapsody** *n*
*m* 'rapsəˌdəɪ
**sp** rapsidie[1]

**Rheims** *n*
riːmz
**sp** Rheimes[2], Rhemes[1]

**Rhenish** *n*
'renɪʃ
**sp** Reinish-[wine][1], Renish[2], rennish[1]

**Rhesus / ~'** *n*
'riːsəs
**sp** Rhesus[1]

**rhetoric** *n*
'retrɪk, -tər-
**sp** rethoricke[1], rhetoricke[4], rhetorike[1]

**rheum / ~s** *n*
ruːm / -z
**sp** rheume[7], rhewme[6], rume[1] / rheumes[1]

**rheumatic** *adj*
'ruːmətɪk
**sp** rheumaticke[1], rheumatike[1], [raw]-rumaticke[1], rumatique[1]

**rheumy** *adj*
'ruːməɪ
**sp** rhewmy[1]

**rhinoceros** *n*
*m* rɪ'nɒsəˌrɒs, rəɪ-
**sp** rhinoceros[1]

**Rhodes** *n*
roːdz
**sp** Rhodes[6]

**Rhodope / ~'s** *n*
*m* 'rɒdəˌpiːz
**sp** Rhodophe's[1]

**rhubarb** *n*
'ruːbɑːɹb
**sp** rubarb[1]

**rhyme / ~s** *n*
rəɪm / -z
**sp** rime[21], ryme[1], rymme[1] / rimes[7]
**rh** time *LLL 1.1.99, 4.3.179, MW 5.5.91, Per 4.Chorus.48, S 16.4, 17.14, 32.7, 55.2, 106.3, 107.11* / times *LLL 5.2.64, Luc 524, Per Prol.12*
> love-rhyme

**rhym·e / ~ing ~ed** *v*
rəɪm / 'rəɪmɪn, -ɪŋ / rəɪmd
**sp** rime[4], ryme[1] / riming[1] / rim'd[1]

**rhymer / ~s** *n*
'rəɪməɹz
**sp** rimers[1]

**rhyming** *adj*
'rəɪmɪn, -ɪŋ
**sp** ri-ming[1]

**Rhys ap Thomas** *n*
'riːs ap 'tɒməs
**sp** Rice ap Thomas[1]

**Rialto** *n*
rɪ'altoː
**sp** Ryalta[2], Ryalto[3]

**rib / ~s** *n*
=
**sp** ribbe[1] / ribbes[8], ribs[9]

**rib / ~bed** *v*
=
**sp** rib[1] / ribb'd[1]
> bare-, strong-, thick-ribbed

**ribald** *adj*
'rɪbɔːld
**sp** ribauld[1]

**riband / ~s** *n*
=
**sp** riband[1] / ribbands[1], ribonds-[pendant][1]

**ribaudred** *adj*
'rɪbədrɪd
**sp** ribaudred[1]

**ribbon / ~s** *n*
=
**sp** ribbon[2] / ribbons[2]

**rib-breaking** *adj*
'rɪb-ˌbrɛ:kɪn, -ɪŋ
**sp** rib-breaking[1]
> break

**rice** *n*
rəɪs
**sp** rice[2]

**rich / ~er / ~est** *adj*
= / 'rɪʧəɹ / =
**sp** rich[139], rich[men][2], rich-[ones][1] / richer[17], ri-cher[1] / richest[6]

**rich / ~es** *n*
=
**sp** rich[6] / riches[19]

**rich / ~ed** *v*
=
**sp** rich'd[1]
> enrich

**Richard / ~'s** *n*
'rɪʧəɹd / -z
**sp** Richard[209], Ri-chard[1], *abbr in line and in s.d.* Rich[3] / Richards[18]

**rich-jewelled** *adj*
=
**sp** rich-iewel'd[1]
> jewel

**rich-left** *adj*
=
**sp** rich-left-[heyres][1]

**richly** *adv*
'rɪʧləɪ
**sp** richly[14]

**Richmond / ~'s / ~s** *n*
=
**sp** Richmond[40], Rich-mond[1] / Richmonds[2] / Richmonds[1]

**rid / ~s** *v*
=
**sp** rid[25], ridde[4] / rids[2]

**riddance** *n*
=
**sp** riddance[2]

**riddle / ~s** *n*
=
**sp** riddle[7] / riddles[4]

**riddle / ~s** *v*
=
**sp** riddles[1]

**riddle-like** *adj*
'rɪdl-'ləɪk
**sp** riddle like[1]
> like

**riddling** *adj*
'rɪdlɪn, -ɪŋ
**sp** riddling[1], ridling[2]

**ride** *n*
rəɪd
**sp** ride[1]

**rid·e / ~est / ~es / ~eth / ~ing / rid / rode / ridden** *v*
rəɪd / -st / -z / 'rəɪd·əθ / -ɪn, -ɪŋ / = / ro:d / =
**sp** ride[51], ride's [ride us][1] / ridest[1] / rides[8] / rideth[1] / riding[4], ri-ding[1] / rid[1] / rod[1], rode[12], rode-[on][1] / ridden[2]
**rh** hide *S 33.5*; pride *S 80.10*; side *R2 1.3.251*; tied *LC 22, S 137.6*; wide *TNK 3.4.22*
> out-, over-rod

**rider / ~s** *n*
'rəɪdəɹ / -z
**sp** rider[6] / riders[1]

**ridge / ~s** *n*
=
**sp** ridge[1] / ridges[2]

**ridiculous** *adj*
=
**sp** rediculous[2], ridiculous[13]
**rh** *1* credulous *VA 988*; **rh** *2* to us *LLL 5.2.306*

**riding** *adj*
'rəɪdɪn, -ɪŋ
**sp** riding[4]
> ride

**rien** *Fr pro*
rjɛ̃
**sp** rien[1]

**rife** *adj*
rəɪf
**sp** rife[1]

**rifle** *v*
'rəɪfəl
**sp** rifle[1]

**rift** *n*
=
**sp** rift[2]

**rift / ~ed** *v*
=
**sp** rift[1] / rifted[1]

**rig / ~gest / ~ged** *v*
= / rɪgst / =
**sp** rigge[1] / rigg'st[1] / rig'd[2], rigg'd[1]

**riggish** *adj*
=
**sp** riggish[1]

**right** *adj / adv / v*
rəɪt
**sp** right[93] / right[78] / right[10], rite[1]
**rh** *adj* fight *R2 1.3.55, TC 3.2.170*; knight *KL 3.2.87*; *adv* knight, might *LLL 5.2.562*; night *WT 4.3.18*; spite *Ham 1.5.189*; tonight *RJ 2.3.37*
> down-, forth-, out-right

**right / ~s** *n*
rəɪt / -s
**sp** right[156] / rights[17], rites[1]
**rh** appetite *Luc 545*; despite, night *Luc 1027*; fight *1H6 4.2.55, 3H6 4.7.73, Luc 67, R2 3.2.62*; flight *KJ 5.4.61*; incite *KL 4.4.28*; knight *2H4 5.3.73, 3H6 2.2.62*; light, night *Luc 943*; night *KJ 1.1.170, R3 4.4.15, VA 1184*; sight *PT 34, S 46.4, 117.6*; spite *CE 4.2.7*; white *Luc 67, PT 16*
> bed-, birth-right

**right-drawn** *adj*
'rəɪt-ˌdrɔ:n
**sp** right drawn[1]

**righteous** *adj*
'rəɪtɪəs
**sp** righteous[6]
> unrighteous

**righteously** *adv*
'rəɪtɪəsləɪ
**sp** righteously[1]
> uprighteously

**rightful** *adj*
'rəɪtfʊl
**sp** rightful[1], rightfull[12]
> unrightful

**rightfully** *adv*
*m* 'rəɪtfʊˌləɪ
**sp** rightfully[1]

**right-hand** *adj*
'rəɪt-ˌand, -ˌha-
**sp** right hand[1]

**rightly** *adv*
'rəɪtləɪ
**sp** rightlie[2], rightly[20], right-ly[1]

**rigol** *n*
'rɪgɒl
**sp** rigoll[1]

**rigorous** *adj*
'rɪgrəs, -gər-
**sp** rigorous[3]

**rigorously** *adv*
*m* 'rɪgrəsˌləɪ, -gər-
**sp** rigorously[1]

**rigour** *n*
'rɪgəɹ
**sp** rigor[4], rigour[4]
**rh** vigour *VA 954*

**rind** *n*
rəɪnd
**sp** rind[1], rinde[1]
**rh** Rosalind *AY 3.2.105*

**ring** *adj*
=
**sp** *AY 5.4.18 emend of* rang[1]

**ring / ~s** *n*
=
**sp** ring[137], ring's [ring is][1] / rings[11]
**rh** bring *AW 2.1.162*; sing *Mac 4.1.42, MW 5.5.66*; thing *MV 5.1.3075*; ring time spring-time *AY 5.3.18, 24, 30, 36* / things *TS 4.3.55*
> horn-, seal-, thumb-ring

**ring / ~s / ~ing / ~ed / rung** *v*
= / = / 'rɪŋɪn, -ɪŋ / = / rɤŋ
**sp** ring[18] / rings[3] / ringing[2] / ring'd[1] / rung[6]
**rh** thing *CE 4.2.51*; ring it sing it *TS 1.2.16*

**ring-carrier** *n*
'rɪŋ-ˌkarɪəɹ
**sp** ring-carrier[1]

**ring-leader** *n*
'rɪŋ-ˌli:dəɹ, -ˌlɛ:-
**sp** ring-leader[1]
> lead

**ringlet / ~s** *n*
=
**sp** ringlets[2]

**Ringwood** *n*
=
**sp** Ring-wood[1]

**riot / ~s** *n*
'rəɪət / -s
**sp** riot[9], riots[4], ryot[4] / ryots[2]
**rh** quiet *VA 1147*

**riot / ~ing** *v*
'rəɪətɪn, -ɪŋ
**sp** rioting[1]

**rioter** *n*
'rəɪətəɹ
**sp** riotor[1]

**riotous** *adj*
'rəɪətəs
**sp** riotous[10]

**rip / ~ping / ~ped** *v*
= / 'rɪpɪn, -ɪŋ / =
**sp** rip[2] / ripping[1] / ript[3]

**ripe / ~er / ~st** *adj*
rəɪp / 'rəɪp·əɹ / -əst
**sp** ripe[29] / riper[1] / ripest[2]
> unripe

**ripe** *adv / v*
rəɪp
**sp** ripe[5] / ripe[6]

**ripely** *adv*
'rəɪpləɪ
**sp** ripely[1]

**ripen / ~s / ~ed** *v*
'rəɪpən / -z / -d
**sp** ripen[3] / ripens[2], ripen's[1] / ripened[2]
> a-ripening

**ripened** *adj*
'rəɪpənd
**sp** ripened[2]
> over-ripened

**ripeness** *n*
'rəɪpnəs
**sp** ripenesse[2]

**ripening** *adj / n*
'rəɪpnɪn, -ɪŋ, -pən-
**sp** ripening[1] / ripening[1]

**riping** *n*
'rəɪpɪn, -ɪŋ
**sp** riping[1]

**rise** *n*
rəɪz
**sp** rise[1]
> uprise

**ris·e / ~es / ~eth / ~ing / rose / risen** *v*
rəɪz / 'rəɪz·ɪz / -əθ / -ɪn, -ɪŋ / ro:z / 'rɪzən
**sp** rise[75] / rises[9] / riseth[5] / rising[8] / rose[11] / risen[4]
**rh** eyes, lies *Luc 257*; eyes *Ham 1.2.257, Per 1.4.9, PP 14.14, Tim 1.2.124*; moralise *VA 710*
> new-risen

**rising** *adj / n*
'rəɪzɪn, -ɪŋ
**sp** rising[3] / rising[5]
> sun-, up-rising

**rite / ~s** *n*
rəɪt / -s
**sp** right[2] / rightes[1], rights[6], rite[5], rites[16]
**rh** might *S 23.6*; night *MA 5.3.23*; tonight *RJ 5.3.20* / delights *AY 5.4.194*

**rivage** *n*
'rɪvɪʤ
**sp** riuage[1]

**rival** *adj*
'rəɪvəl
**sp** riuall[2]

**rival / ~s** *n*
'rəɪvəl / -z
**sp** riuall[4] / riuals[8]

**rival / ~led** *v*
'rəɪvəld
**sp** riuald[1]
> unrivalled

**rivality** *n*
rəɪ'valɪtəɪ
**sp** riuality[1]

**rive / ~d** *v*
rəɪv / -d
**sp** riue[5], ryue[1] / riu'd[2]

**river / ~s** *n*
'rɪvəɹ / -z
**sp** riuer[21] / riuers[11]

**Rivers** [name] *n*
'rɪvəɹz
**sp** Rivers[20]

**rivet / ~s** *n*
=
**sp** riuet[1] / riuets[2]

**rivet / ~ed** *v*
=
**sp** riuet[1] / riueted[2]

**riveted** *adj*
=
**sp** riueted[1]

**rivo** *interj*
'rəɪvo:
**sp** riuo[1]

**road / ~s** *n*
'ro:d / -z
**sp** road[2], roade[3], rode[8] / rodes[2]

**roadway** *n*
'ro:dwɛ:
**sp** rode-way[1]
> way

**roam / ~ing** *v*
ro:m / 'ro:mɪn, -ɪŋ
**sp** roame[1], rome[2] / roming[3]
**rh** coming *TN 2.3.37*

**roan** *adj / n*
ro:n
**sp** roane[2] / *sp* roane[2]

**roar** *n*
rɔ:ɹ
**sp** roare[1], rore[2]
> uproar

**roar / ~s / ~ing / ~ed** *v*
rɔ:ɹ / -z / 'rɔ:rɪn, -ɪŋ / rɔ:ɹd
**sp** roare[17], rore[7] / roares[4], rores[3] / roaring[4] / roard[1], roar'd[10], roared[2], roa-red[1]
**rh** before *LLL 4.1.89*; floor *MND 5.1.218*; more *KJ 2.1.294*; snores *MND 5.1.361*
> out-, up-roar

**roarer / ~z** *n*
'rɔ:rəɹz
**sp** roa-rers[1]

**roaring** *adj / n*
'rɔ:rɪn, -ɪŋ
**sp** roaring[14], roring[2] / roaring[5]

**roast** *n*
ro:st
**sp** rost[1]

**roast** *v*
ro:st / 'ro:stɪd
**sp** roast[1], rost[2] / roasted[1]

**roasted** *adj*
'ro:stɪd
**sp** roasted[2], rosted[2]
> ill-, over-roasted

**rob / ~best / ~s / ~bing / ~bed** *v*
= / rɒbst / = / 'rɒbɪn, -ɪŋ / =
**sp** rob[34], robbe[1] / robst[1] / robbes[1], robs[5] / robbing[1] / robb'd[10], robd[1], rob'd[10]

**robbed** *n*
=
**sp** rob'd[1]

**robber / ~'s / ~s / ~s'** *n*
'rɒbəɹ / -z
**sp** robber[1] / robbers[1] / robbers[6] / robbers[1]

**robbery** *n*
'rɒbrəɪ, -bər-
**sp** robberie[1], robbe-rie[1], robbery[5]

**robbing** *n*
'rɒbɪn, -ɪŋ
**sp** robbing[4]

**robe / ~s** *n*
ro:b / -z
**sp** robe[17] / roabes[1], robes[19]
> disrobe, fire-robed

**robe** *Fr n*
rɔb
**sp** *H5 3.4.46 emend of* roba[1]

**Robert / ~'s** *n*
'rɒbəɹt / -s
**sp** Robert[26] / Roberts[9]

**robin / Robin** [name] *n*
=
**sp** robin-[red-breast][1] / Robin[24]

**Robin Hood / 's** *n*
'rɒbɪn 'ʊd, -'hʊd / -z

**sp** Robin-hood[1], Robin Hood[1] / Robin Hoods[1]
> hood

**robustious** *adj*
rə'bɤstɪəs
**sp** robustious[2]

**Rochester** *n*
'rɒʧɪstəɹ
**sp** Rochester[2]

**Rochford** *n*
'rɒʧfəɹd
**sp** Rochford[1]

**rock / ~s** *n*
=
**sp** rock[7], rocke[26] / rockes[7], [gutter'd]-rockes[1], rocks[9]
**rh** flocks *PP 19.5*; locks, shocks *MND 1.2.27*

**rock / *Luc* ~ed** *v*
=
**sp** rock[1], rocke[4] / rockt[1]
**rh** locked *Luc 262*

**rocky** *adj*
'rɒkəɪ
**sp** rockie[1], rocky[2]

**rocky-hard** *adj*
'rɒkəɪ-'ɑ:ɹd, -'hɑ:-
**sp** rockey-hard[1]
**rh** vineyard *Tem 4.1.69*

**rod / ~s** *n*
=
**sp** rod[14], rodde[1] / rods[4]

**Roderigo / ~'s** *n*
*m* ˌrɒdə'ri:go:, rə'dri:- / ˌrɒdə'ri:go:z
**sp** Roderigo[1], Rodorigo[36], Rodo-rigo[1] / Rodorigo's[1]

**roe / ~s** *n*
ro: / -z
**sp** roe[3] / roes[1]

**Roger** *n*
'rɒʤəɹ
**sp** Roger[5]

**Rogero** *n*
rə'ʤɛ:ro:
**sp** Rogero[1]

**rogue / ~'s / ~s** *n*
ro:g / -z
**sp** roague[4], rogue[73] / rogues[1], [cuckoldly]-rogues[1] / rogues[22]

**roguery** *n*
'ro:grəɪ, -gər-
**sp** roguery[2]

**roi** *Fr n*
rwɛ
**sp** Roy[5]

**roisting** *adj*
'rəɪstɪn, -ɪŋ
**sp** roisting[1]

**Roland / ~'s / ~s** *n*
'ro:lənd / -z
**sp** Roland[1], Ro-land[1], Rowland[5] / Rolands[1], Roulands[1], Rowlands[2] / Rowlands[1]

**roll / ~s** *n*
ro:l / -z
**sp** role[1], roll[5] / rolles[1]

**roll / ~s / ~ing / ~ed** *v*
ro:l / -z / 'ro:lɪn, -ɪŋ / ro:ld
**sp** roule[1], rowle[1] / rowles[3] / rolling[1] / roll'd[1], rolled[1]
**rh** controlling *S 20.5*; behold, told *Luc 1398*
> a-rolling, unrolled

**rolling** *adj*
'ro:lɪn, -ɪŋ
**sp** rolling[2]

**romage** *n*
'rɤmɪʤ
**sp** romage[1]

**Roman** *adj*
'ro:mən
**sp** Romaine[13], Roman[21], Romane[16], Ro-mane[1]

**Roman / ~'s / ~s** *n*
'ro:mən / -z
**sp** Romaine[2], Roman[33], Romane[7] / Romanes, Romans[2] / Romaines[12], Romanes[15], Romans[25]

**Romano** [name] *n*
rə'mɑ:no:
**sp** Romano[1]

**Romanos** *Lat n*
ro:'mɑ:nɒs
**sp** Romanos[1]

**Rome / ~'s** *n*
ru:m, ro:m / -z
**sp** Rome[279] / Romes[23]
**rh** *1* home *JC 1.1.33*; **rh** *2* doom *Luc 715, 1851*; groom *Luc 1644*
**pun** *JC 1.2.155* room

**Romeo / ~'s** *n*
*m* 'ro:mɪo:, -ˌo: / 'ro:mɪo:z
**sp** Romeo[133], Romeos [Romeo is][1] / Romeo's[8], Romeos[4]
**rh** Mercutio *RJ 3.1.144*; woe *RJ 5.3.310*

**Romish** *adj*
'ru:mɪʃ, 'ro:-
**sp** Romish[1]

**ronyon**
> runnion

**rood** *n*
=, rʊd
**sp** rood[4], roode[1]

**roof / ~s** *n*
=, rʊf / -s
**sp** roofe[14], rough[1], roofe's [roof is][1] / roofes[4]

**roof / ~ed** *v*
=, rʊft
**sp** roof 'd[1]
> unroofed

**rook / ~s** *n*
=
**sp** rooke[1], [bully]-rooke[3] / rookes[2]

**rook / ~ed** *v*
=
**sp** rook'd[1]

**rooky** *adj*
'rʊkəɪ
**sp** rookie[1]

**room** *n*
=, rʊm / -z
**sp** room[1], roome[44] / roomes[3]
**rh** doom *3H6 5.6.92, MW 5.5.57, R2 5.6.25, S 55.10*
**pun** *JC 1.2.155* Rome
> bed-, by-room

**root / ~s** *n*
=, rʊt / -s
**sp** root[12], roote[20] / rootes[5], roots[5]
**rh** *1* to't *Tim 1.2.70*; **rh** *2* foot *Luc 665*

**root / ~eth / ~ed** *v*
=, rʊt / =, 'rʊtəθ / =, 'rʊtɪd
**sp** root[6], roote[3] / rooteth[1] / rooted[5]
> en-, un-root

**rooted** *adj*
=, 'rʊtɪd
**sp** rooted[2]
> ill-, shallow-rooted

**rootedly** *adv*
*m* 'ru:tɪdˌləɪ, 'rʊt-
**sp** rootedly[1]

**rooting** *adj*
'ru:tɪn, -ɪŋ, 'rʊt-
**sp** rooting[1]

**rope / ~'s / ~s** *n*
ro:p / -s
**sp** rope[10] / ropes[5] / ropes[1], rope's[1]
**rh** pope *1H6 1.3.53*
> wainrope

**rope-maker** *n*
'ro:p-ˌmɛ:kəɹ
**sp** rope-maker[1]
> make

**ropery** *n*
'ro:prəɪ, -pər-
**sp** roperie[1]

**rope-trick / ~s** *n*
'ro:p-ˌtrɪks
**sp** rope trickes[1]
> trick

**roping** *adj*
'ro:pɪn, -ɪŋ
**sp** roping[1]
> down-roping

**Rosalind** *n*
'rɒzələɪnd
**sp** Rosalind[39], Ro-salind[1], Rosa-lind[2], Rosalinde[21], *abbr in s.d* Ros[1]
**rh** *1* bind *AY 3.2.104*; find *AY 3.2.108*; hind *AY 3.2.98*; Ind *AY 3.2.85*; kind *AY 3.2.100*; lined *AY 3.2.89, 102*; mind *AY 3.2.91*; rind *AY 3.2.106*; **rh** *2* wind *AY 3.2.87*

**Rosalinda** *n*
ˌrɒzə'lɪndə
**sp** Rosalinda[1]

**Rosaline / ~'s** *n*
'rɒzələɪn / -z
**sp** Rosalin[1], Rosaline[23], Ro-saline[1] / Rosalines[1]
**rh** brine *RJ 2.3.66*; mine *LLL 4.1.56, 106, 5.2.442, RJ 2.3.40, 77*; thine *LLL 4.3.219, 5.2.133, RJ 2.3.74*

**Roscius** *n*
'rɒsɪəs
**sp** Rossius[2]

**rose / ~s** *n*
ro:z / 'ro:zɪz
**sp** rose[40], [milke-white]-rose[1], [red]-rose[1] / roses[19]
**rh** clothes *Ham 4.5.52*; enclose *S 95.2*; flows *LLL 4.3.25, TNK 5.1.165*; goes *KJ 1.1.142*; grows, shows *LLL 1.1.105*; those *S 98.10*; throws *VA 590* / **rh** *1* composes *Per 5.Chorus.7*; discloses *S 54.6*; encloses *LC 286, Luc 71*; noses *WT 4.4.222*; **rh** *2* posies *MW 3.1.18, PP 19.9*
> cheek-, musk-, prim-rose

**Rose** [name] *n*
ro:z
**sp** Rose[1]

**rose / ~d** *v*
ro:zd
**sp** ros'd[1]

**rose-cheeked** *adj*
'ro:z-ˌʧi:kt
**sp** rose-cheekt[1]

**rosed** *adj*
*m* 'ro:zɪd
**sp** rosed[1]

**rose-lipped** *adj*
'ro:z-ˌlɪpt
**sp** rose-lip'd[1]

**rosemary** *n*
*m* 'ro:zmərəɪ, -ˌrəɪ
**sp** rosemarie[2], rosemary[2]

**Rosemary** [name] *n*
'ro:zmərəɪ
**sp** Rosemarie[1], Rosemary[1]

**Rosencrantz** *n*
'ro:zənˌkrants
**sp** Rosincran[1], Rosincrance[10], Ro-sincrance[1], Rosincrane[3], *abbr in s.d.* Ros.[2]

**rose-water** *n*
'ro:z-ˌwɑtəɹ
**sp** rose-water[1]

**Ross, Rosse** *n*
=
**sp** Ross[1], Rosse[19]

**Rossillion** *n*
rɒ'sɪlɪən
**sp** Rosillion[2], Rossillion[15], Ros-sillion[1], *AW 1.2.18 emend of* Rosignoll[1]

**rosy** *adj*
'ro:zəɪ
**sp** rosie[2]

**rot** *n*
=
**sp** rot[1]

**rot / ~s / ~ting / ~ted** *v*
= / = / 'rɒtɪn, -ɪŋ / =
**sp** rot[18] / rots[1] / rotting[1] / rotted[2]
**rh** forgot *CE 3.2.3* / allotted, unspotted *Luc 823*

**rote** *n*
ro:t
**sp** roate[2], rote[2]
**rh** note *MND 5.1.387*

**rote / ~d** *v*
'ro:tɪd
**sp** roated[1]

**rotten** *adj*
=
**sp** rotten[35]
**rh** forgotten *S 81.2*

**rottenness** *n*
*m* 'rɒtə,nes, -ənəs
**sp** rottennesse[2]

**rotundity** *n*
rə'tʏndɪtəɪ
**sp** rotundity[1]

**Rouen** *n*
*m* ru:n, 'ru:ən
**sp** Roan[12]

**rough / ~er / ~est** *adj*
rʏf / 'rʏf·əɹ / -əst
**sp** rough[64], ruffe[2] / rougher[2] / roughest[2]
**rh** buff *CE 4.2.35*; enough *VA 237*
> unrough

**roughcast** *n*
'rʏf,kast
**sp** rough-cast[2], rough cast[1]
> cast

**rough-hew** *v*
*m* ,rʏf'ju:, -'hju:
**sp** rough-hew[1]

**roughly** *adv*
'rʏfləɪ
**sp** roughly[6]

**roughness** *n*
'rʏfnəs
**sp** roughnes[1]

**round / ~er / ~est** *adj*
rəʊnd / 'rəʊnd·əɹ / -əst
**sp** round[25] / rounder[1] / roundest[1]

**round** *adv / prep*
rəʊnd
**sp** round[38] / round[3]
**rh** *adv* bound *Luc 1499*; crowned, drowned *AC 2.7.115*; ground *Ham 3.2.164*; sound *Per 3.Chorus.35*

**round / ~s** *n*
rəʊnd / -z
**sp** round[6] / rounds[1]
**rh** *1* hound *MND 3.1.100*; sound *Mac 4.1.129*; **rh** *2* wound *VA 368*

**round / ~s / ~ing / ~ed** *v*
rəʊnd / -z / 'rəʊnd·ɪn, -ɪŋ / -ɪd
**sp** round[1] / rounds[3] / rounding[1] / rounded[4]

**roundel** *n*
'rəʊndl
**sp** roundell[1]

**rounder** *n*
'rəʊndəɹ
**sp** rounder[1]

**roundly** *adv*
'rəʊndləɪ
**sp** roundlie[1], roundly[9]

**round-wombed** *adj*
*m* ,rəʊnd-'wu:md
**sp** round womb'd[1]
> womb

**rouse** *n*
rəʊs
**sp** rouce[1], rouse[2], rowse[1]
**rh** house *Per 3.Chorus.1* [*emend of* rout]

**rouse / ~d** *v*
rəʊz / *m* -d, 'rəʊzɪd
**sp** rouse[3], rouze[3], rowse[11], rowze[9] / rouz'd[4], rows'd[2], rowsed[1], rowz'd[1]
**rh** drowse *Mac 3.2.53*

**roused** *adj*
*m* 'rəʊzɪd
**sp** rowsed[1]
> uproused

**Roussi** *n*
*m* ru:'si:, 'ru:si:
**sp** Roussi[1], Roussie[1]

**rout / ~s** *n*
rəʊt / -s
**sp** rout[7], rowt[3] / routs[1]
**rh** out *TNK 3.5.146*

**rout** *v*
rəʊt
**sp** rowts[1]

**routed** *n*
'rəʊtɪd
**sp** routed[1]

**rove** *v*
ro:v
**sp** roue[1]

**rover** *n*
'ro:vəɹ
**sp** rouer[1]

**row** [line] *n*
ro:
**sp** rowe[2]
> a-row

**rowel** *n*
'ro:əl
**sp** rowell[1]

**rowel-head** *n*
'ro:əl-'ed, -'he-
**sp** rowell head[1]

**royal** *adj*
'rəɪəɑl
**sp** roiall[1], royal[4], royall[203], [blood]-royall[1]
**rh** loyal *R3 1.4.168*
> face-, tent-royal

**royalize** *n*
*m* 'rəɪɑˌləɪz
**sp** royalize[1]

**royally** *adv*
*m* 'rəɪɑˌləɪ, 'rəɪləɪ
**sp** royally[9]
**rh** victory *1H6 1.6.30*

**royalt·y / ~y's / ~ies** *n*
*m* 'rəɪɑlˌtəɪ, 'rəɪlt- / -z / -z, 'rəɪlt-
**sp** roialtie[1], royaltie[11], royalty[11] / royalties[1] / roalties[1], royalties[6]

**roynish** *adj*
'rəɪnɪʃ
**sp** roynish[1]

**rub / ~s** *n*
rɤb / -z
**sp** rub[5], rubbe[1] / rubs[2]

**rub / ~s / ~bing / ~bed** *v*
rɤb / -z / 'rɤbɪn, -ɪŋ / rɤbd
**sp** rub[6] / rubbes[1], rubs[2] / rubbing[1] / rub'd[3]

**rubbing** *n*
'rɤbɪn, -ɪŋ
**sp** rubbing[1]

**rubbish** *n*
'rɤbɪʃ
**sp** rubbish[2]

**rubious** *adj*
'ru:bɪəs
**sp** rubious[1]

**ruby** *adj*
'ru:bəɪ
**sp** ruby[1]

**rub·y / ~ies** *n*
'ru:bəɪ / -z
**sp** rubie[1] / rubies[4]

**rudder** *n*
'rɤdəɹ
**sp** rudder[2]

**ruddiness** *n*
*m* 'rɤdɪˌnes
**sp** ruddinesse[1]

**ruddock** *n*
'rɤdək
**sp** raddocke[1]

**ruddy** *adj*
'rɤdəɪ
**sp** ruddy[1]

**rude / ~r / ~st** *adj*
= / 'ru:d·əɹ / *m* -əst, ru:dst
**sp** rude[68] / ruder[2] / rudest[1], rud'st[1]
**rh** ingratitude *AY 2.7.180*

**rude-growing** *adj*
*m* ˌru:d-'gro:ɪn, -ɪŋ
**sp** rude growing[1]

**rudely** *adv*
'ru:dləɪ
**sp** rudely[5]

**rudeness** *n*
=
**sp** rudenes[1], rudenesse[4]

**rudesby** *n*
'ru:dzbəɪ
**sp** rudesbey[1], rudesby[1]

**rudiments** *n*
*m* 'ru:dɪˌments
**sp** rudiments[2]

**rue** *n*
=
**sp** rew[3], rue[2]

**rue / ~d** *v*
=
**sp** rue[13] / rew'd[1]
**rh** adieu *KJ 3.1.325*; true *KJ 5.7.117*

**ruff / ~s** *n*
rɤf / -s
**sp** ruffe[3] / ruffes[1]

**ruffian** *adj / v*
'rɤfɪən
**sp** ruffian[4] / ruffiand[1]

**ruffian / ~s** *n*
'rɤfɪən / -z
**sp** ruffian[11] / ruffians[3]

**ruffle** *v*
'rɤfəl
**sp** ruffle[4]

**ruffling** *adj*
'rɤflɪn, -ɪŋ
**sp** ruffling[1]

**Rugby** *n*
'rɤgbəɪ
**sp** Rugby[18]

**rugged** *adj*
'rɤgɪd
**sp** rugged[5]

**rug-headed** *adj*
*m* ˌrɤg-'edɪd, -'he-
**sp** rug-headed[1]
> head

**ruin / ~'s / ~s** *n*
=
**sp** ruin[1], ruine[34] / ruines[1] / ruines[5]

**ruin / ~ed** *v*
=
**sp** ruine[1] / ruin'd[4]

**ruinate** *adj / v*
*m* 'ru:ɪˌnɛ:t
**sp** ruinate[1] / *sp* ruinate[2]
**rh** *v* hate *S 10.7*; state [*F, at Tit 5.3.199*]

**ruined** *adj*
=
**sp** ruin'd[6]

**ruining** *S* *n*
'ru:ɪnɪn, -ɪŋ
**sp** ruining[1]
**rh** honouring *S 125.4*

**ruinous** *adj*
*m* 'ru:ɪˌnɤs
**sp** ruinous[5]
**rh** Antipholus *CE 3.2.4*

**rule / ~s** *n*
=
**sp** rule[19] / rules[5]
> night-rule

**rul·e / ~es / ~ing / ~ed** *v*
= / = / ˈruːlɪn, -ɪŋ / =
**sp** rule[29] / rules[3] / ruling[1] / rul'd[29], ruled[3]
> hard-ruled, over-rule

**ruler / ~s** *n*
ˈruːləɹ / -z
**sp** ruler[6] / rulers[1]

**rumble** *v*
ˈrɤmbəl
**sp** rumble[1]

**ruminate / ~s / ~d** *v*
*m* ˈruːmɪˌnɛːt / -s / -ɪd
**sp** ruminate[7] / ruminates[1], rumi-nates[1] / ruminated[2]
**rh** hate *TG 1.2.49*; state *S 64.11*

**rumination** *n*
ˌruːmɪˈnɛːsɪən
**sp** rumination[1]

**rumin·o / ~at** *Lat v*
ˈruːmɪnat
**sp** ruminat[1]

**rumour / ~'s / ~s** *n*
ˈruːməɹ / -z
**sp** rumor[8], rumour[9] / rumors[1], rumours[1] / rumors[2], rumours[1]

**rumour / ~ed** *v*
ˈruːməɹ / -d
**sp** rumor[1] / rumour'd[2]

**rumourer** *n*
ˈruːmərəɹ
**sp** rumorer[1]

**rump** *n*
rɤmp
**sp** rumpe[1]

**rump-fed** *adj*
ˈrɤmp-ˌfed
**sp** rumpe-fed[1]
> feed

**run** *n*
rɤn
**sp** run[1]

**run / ~st / ~s / ~ning / ran / ~st** *v*
rɤn / -st / -z / ˈrɤnɪn, -ɪŋ / = / ranst
**sp** run[122], run-[by][1], runne[64] / runst[3], run'st[1] / runnes[18], runs[22] / running[24], running *Ham 1.3.109 emend of* roaming[1] / ran[22], ranne[11] / ranst[1], ran'st[2]
**rh** *1* begun *Ham 3.2.221*; done *LLL 5.2.482*; sun *MND 5.1.373*; undone *VA 781*; won *TS 4.5.24*; **rh** *2* dumb *Per 5.2.1* [*Chorus*] / began, than [then] *Luc 1437*
> fore-, out-, over-run; ever-running

**runagate / ~s** *n*
*m* ˈrɤnəˌgɛːt, -əg- / -əgɛːts
**sp** run-agate[1], runnagate[2] / runnagates[2]

**runaway / ~s** *n*
*m* ˈrɤnəˌwɛː / -z
**sp** runaway[1], run-away[1] / runawaies[1], run-awayes[3]
> away

**rung**
> ring

**runner ~s** *n*
ˈrɤnəɹ / -z
**sp** runner[1] / runners[1]

**running** *adj / n*
ˈrɤnɪn, -ɪŋ
**sp** running[4] / runing[1], running[5]

**runnion** *n*
ˈrɤnɪən
**sp** ronyon[1], runnion[1]

**rupture / ~s** *n*
ˈrɤptəɹ / -z
**sp** rupture[1] / ruptures[1]

**rural** *adj*
ˈruːrɑl
**sp** rurall[3]

**rush** *adj*
rɤʃ
**sp** rush[1]

**rush / ~es** *n*
rɤʃ / ˈrɤʃɪz
**sp** rush[5] / rushes[9]

**rush / ~es / ~ing / ~ed** *v*
rɤʃ / ˈrɤʃ·ɪz / -ɪn, -ɪŋ / rɤʃt
**sp** rush[15] / rushes[1] / rushing[5] / rush'd[2], rusht[3]
**rh** bushes *VA 630*

**rushling** *adj*
ˈrɤʃlɪn, -ɪŋ
**sp** rushling[1]

**rushy** *adj*
ˈrɤʃəɪ
**sp** rushie[1]

**russet** *adj*
ˈrɤsɪt
**sp** russet[2]

**russet-pated** *adj*
ˈrɤsɪt-ˌpɛːtɪd
**sp** russed-pated[1]
> pate

**Russia** *n*
ˈrɤsɪə, -ʃɪ-
**sp** Russia[4]

**Russian** *adj*
ˈrɤsɪən, -ʃɪ-
**sp** Russian[3]

**Russian / ~s** *n*
ˈrɤsɪən, -ʃɪ- / -z
**sp** Russian[1], *LLL 6.2.368 emend of* Russia[1] / Russians[3]

**rust** *n*
rɤst
**sp** rust[2]

**rust / ~s / ~ed** *v*
rɤst / -s / ˈrɤstɪd
**sp** rust[7] / rusts[1] / rusted[1]
**rh** dust *Per 2.2.53*

**rustic** *adj*
ˈrɤstɪk
**sp** rusticke[3]

**rustic / ~s** *n*
ˈrɤstɪks
**sp** rustiques[1]

**rustically** *adv*
ˈrɤstɪkləɪ
**sp** rustically[1]

**rustl·e / ~ing** *v*
ˈrɤsəl / ˈrɤslɪn, -ɪŋ
**sp** russle[1] / rustling[2]

**rustling** *n*
ˈrɤslɪn, -ɪŋ
**sp** rustling[1]

**rusty** *adj*
ˈrɤstəɪ
**sp** rustie[3], ru-stie[1], rusty[3]
**rh** trusty *PP 7.4*

**ruth** *n*
=
**sp** ruth[3]
**rh** youth *PP 9.11*

**ruthful** *adj*
=
**sp** ruthfull[4]

**ruthless** *adj*
=
**sp** ruthlesse[10]

**Rutland / ~'s** *n*
ˈrɤtlənd / -z
**sp** Rutland[15] / Rutlands[3]

**rut-time** *n*
ˈrɤt-ˌtəɪm
**sp** rut-time[1]
> time

**ruttish** *adj*
ˈrɤtɪʃ
**sp** ruttish[1]

**rye** *n*
rəɪ
**sp** rie[1], rye[1]
**rh** lie *AY 5.3.21*

**rye-straw** *n*
ˈrəɪ-ˌstrɔ:
**sp** rye-straw[1]
> straw

**Rynaldo** *n*
rɪˈnaldo:
**sp** Rynaldo[2]

# S

**Saba** *n*
ˈsɑːbə
**sp** Saba[1]

**Sabbath** *n*
ˈsabət, -əθ
**sp** Sabbath[1], Sabboth[1]

**sable** *adj*
ˈsɛːbəl
**sp** sable[1]

**sable / ~s** *n*
ˈsɛːbəl / -z
**sp** sable[1] / sables[1]

**sable-coloured** *adj*
ˈsɛːbəl-ˌkɤləɹd
**sp** sable coloured[1]
> colour

**sack / ~s** *n*
=
**sp** sack[14], sacke[36] / sacks[3]
> sherris-sack

**sack / ~ed** *v*
=
**sp** sack[1], sacke[5], sacked[1]

**sackbut / ~s** *n*
=
**sp** sack-buts[1]

**sack-cloth** *n*
=
**sp** sacke-cloath[1]
> cloth

**Sackerson** *n*
ˈsakəɹsən
**sp** *MW 1.1.275 emend of* Saskerson[1]

**sacrament** *n*
*m* ˈsakrəˌment, -əmənt
**sp** sacrament[8]

**sacred** *adj*
ˈsɛːkrɪd
**sp** sacred[44]

**sacrifice / ~s** *n*
*m* ˈsakrɪˌfəɪs, -ɪf- / -ɪˌfəɪsɪz
**sp** sacrifice[15] / sacrifices[6]
**rh** enterprise *TC 1.2.282*; wise *Per 5.2.12* [*Chorus*]
> blood-sacrifice

**sacrifice / ~d** *v*
*m* ˈsakrɪˌfəɪs / -t
**sp** sacrifice[4] / sacrific'd[2]

**sacrificer / ~s** *n*
*m* ˈsakrɪˌfəɪsəɹz
**sp** sacrificers[1]

**sacrificial** *adj*
ˌsakrɪˈfɪsɪɑl
**sp** sacrificiall[1]

**sacrificing** *adj*
*m* ˈsakrɪˌfəɪsɪn, -ɪŋ
**sp** sacrificing[1], sacrifising[1]

**sacrilegious** *adj*
ˈsakrɪˌleʤɪəs
**sp** sacrilegious[2]

**sacring** *adj*
ˈsakrɪn, -ɪŋ
**sp** sacring[1]

**sad / ~der / ~dest** *adj*
= / ˈsadəɹ / =
**sp** sad[150], sadde[3] / sadder[3] / saddest[2]
**rh** *1* glad *S 45.14*; had *3H6 3.2.110, Luc 1386*; lad, mad *MND 3.2.439*;
**rh** *2* shade *MND 4.1.94*

**saddle / ~s** *n*
=
**sp** saddle[3], sad-dle[1] / saddles[1]
> pack-saddle

**saddle** *v*
=
**sp** saddle[4], sadle[1]

**saddle-bow** *VA* *n*
ˈsadl-ˌboː
**sp** saddle bow[1]
**rh** know *VA 14*

**saddler** *n*
ˈsadləɹ
**sp** sadler[2]

**sad-eyed** *adj*
ˈsad-ˌəɪd
**sp** sad-ey'd[1]
> eye

**sad-faced** *adj*
ˈsad-ˌfɛːst
**sp** sad fac'd[1]
> face

**sad-hearted** *adj*
*m* ˌsad-ˈɑːɹtɪd, -ˈhɑː-
**sp** sad-hearted-[men][1]
> heart

**sadly** *adv*
ˈsadləɪ
**sp** sadly[16]
**rh** gladly *S 8.1*

**sadness** *n*
=
**sp** sadnes[1], sadnesse[22]
**rh** gladness *TC 1.1.42*

**safe / ~r / ~st** *adj*
sɛ:f / 'sɛ:f·əɹ / -əst
**sp** safe[46] / safer[16] / safest[5]
> unsafe

**safe / ~r / ~st** *adv*
sɛ:f / 'sɛ:f·əɹ / -əst
**sp** safe[35] / safer[1] / safest[1]

**safe / ~d** *v*
sɛ:f / -t
**sp** safe[1] / saf't[1]

**safe-conduct / ~ing** *v*
*m* ˌsɛ:f-'kɒndəktɪn, -ɪŋ
**sp** safe-conducting[1]
> conduct

**safeguard** *n / v*
'sɛ:fgɑ:ɹd
**sp** safegard[4], safe-guard[1] / safegard[2]
> guard

**safely** *adv*
'sɛ:fləɪ
**sp** safelie[2], safely[24]

**safer** *n*
'sɛ:fəɹ
**sp** safer[1]

**safet·y / ~ies** *n*
'sɛ:ftəɪ, -fət- / -z
**sp** safetie[24], safe-tie[1], safety[48] / safeties[1]

**saffron** *adj / n*
=
**sp** saffron[2] / saffron[2]

**sag** *v*
=
**sp** sagge[1]

**sage** *adj / n*
sɛ:ʤ, sɑ:ʤ
**sp** sage[4] / sage[2]
**rh** *n* age, stage *Luc 277*; marriage [*3 sylls*] *Luc 222*; rage *Luc 222*

**sage** *Fr adj*
sa:ʒ
**sp** sage[1]

**Sagittary** *n*
*m* 'saʤɪˌtarəɪ, -ɪtərəɪ, -ɪtrəɪ
**sp** Sagitary[2], Sagittary[1]

**said, saidst**
> say

**sail / ~s** *n*
sɛ:l / -z
**sp** saile[27], [vnder]saile[1], sayle[10] / sailes[13], sayles[2]
**rh** fails *Tem Epil.11*

**sail / ~s / ~ing / ~ed** *v*
sɛ:l / -z / 'sɛ:lɪn, -ɪŋ / sɛ:ld
**sp** saile[4], sayle[2] / sailes[2] / sayling[1] / saild[1], sayld[1], sayl'd[1]
**rh** tail *Mac 1.3.8*

**sailing** *adj / n*
'sɛ:lɪn, -ɪŋ
**sp** sayling[1] / sayling[1]

**sail-maker** *n*
'sɛ:l-ˌmɛ:kəɹ
**sp** saile-maker[1]
> make

**sailor / ~'s / ~s** *n*
'sɛ:ləɹ / -z
**sp** sailor[2], sayler[1], saylor[4] / saylors[2] / sailors[1], saylers[3], saylors[8]

**sain**
> say

**saint / ~s** *n*
sɛ:nt / -s
**sp** saint[115], *abbr as* S.[50] / saints[14]
**rh** attaint *CE 3.2.14, PP 18.44*

**sainted** *adj*
'sɛ:ntɪd
**sp** sainted[4], sainted-[king][1]
> outward-sainted

**saint-like** *adj*
'sɛ:nt-ləɪk
**sp** saint-like[3]

**saint-seducing** *adj*
'sɛ:nt-səˌdju:sɪn, -ɪŋ
**sp** sainct-seducing[1]

**saist, saith**
> say

**sake / ~s** *n*
sɛ:k / -s
**sp** sake[159], [mercy]-sake[1], [truths]-sake[1], [wealths]-sake[1] / sakes[3]
**rh** ache *CE 3.1.57*; awake *MND 2.2.109, 3.2.68, R3 5.3.151, S 61.12*; make *LC 322, MV 1.1.185, S 145.3*; partake *S 149.4*; take *AW 2.3.89, H5 Epil.13, Luc 533, RJ 1.5.105, S 134.11*; take, wake *MND 2.2.35*

**sal**
> shall

**Sala** *n*
'sɑ:lə
**sp** Sala[3]

**salad** *n*
=
**sp** sallad[1]
**pun** *2H6 4.10.8* sallet

**salamander** *n*
'saləmandəɹ
**sp** salamander[1]

**Salanio**
> Solanio

**Salarino** *n*
salə'ri:no:
**sp** Salarino[5]

**salary** *n*
'salrəɪ, -lər-
**sp** sallery[1]

**sale** *n*
sɛ:l
**sp** saile[1], sale[7]

**Salerio** *n*
sə'li:rɪo:
**sp** Salerio[6], *MV 2.5.55 s.d. emend of* Salino[1]

**sale-work** *n*
'sɛ:l-ˌwɔ:ɹk
**sp** sale-worke[1]
> work

**Salic** *adj*
'salɪk
**sp** Salike[8], Salique[1]

**Salic·a / ~m** *Lat n*
'salɪkam
**sp** Salicam[1]

**Salisbury / ~'s** *n*
*m* 'sɑ:lzbrəɪ, -bərəɪ, -bəˌrəɪ / -brəɪz
**sp** Salisburie[4], Salisbury[55], Salis-bury[1], Salsburie[1], Salsbury[10] / Salisburies[1]

**sall**
> shall

**sallet / ~s** *n*
=
**sp** sallet[5] / sallets[3]
**pun** *2H6 4.10.10* salad

**sallow** *adj*
'salə, -lo:
**sp** sallow[1]

**sally** *n*
'saləɪ
**sp** sallie[1]

**sall·y / ~ies** *v*
'saləɪ / -z
**sp** sallie[1], sally[1] / sallies[1]

**salmon / ~'s / ~s** *n*
=
**sp** salmons[1] / salmons[1]

**salt / ~er** *adj*
= / 'sɒltəɹ
**sp** salt[26], salt-[fish][1], salt-[water][1], salte[1] / salter[1]

**salt** *n*
=
**sp** salt[16], sault[1]

**salt-butter** *adj*
'sɒlt-ˌbɤtəɹ
**sp** [mechanicall]-salt-butter[1]

**saltness** *n*
=
**sp** saltnesse[1]

**saltpetre** *n*
ˌsɒlt-'pi:təɹ
**sp** salt-peter[1]

**salt-water** *adj*
'sɒlt-ˌwɑtəɹ
**sp** salt-water[1], salt-water-[girdle][1]

**salutation / ~s** *n*
ˌsɑljə'tɛ:sɪən / -z
**sp** salutation[6] / salutations[3]

**salute / ~s / ~th / ~d** *v*
sə'lu:t / -s / -əθ / -ɪd
**sp** salute[16], sa-lute[1] / salutes[4] / saluteth[2] / saluted[1]
> resalute, unsaluted

**salvation** *n*
sal'vɛ:sɪən
**sp** saluation[5]

**salve** *n*
sɔ:v, sɑlv
**sp** salue[2]

**salve / ~d** *v*
sɔ:v, sɑlv / -d
**sp** salue[7] / salu'd[1]

**same** *adj / n*
sɛ:m
**sp** same[144] / same[68]
**rh** blame *LLL 1.2.100*; frame *S 5.3, 59.12*; name *Cym 4.2.380, LLL 2.1.180, PT 38, S 76.5, 108.6*; name, shame *LLL 1.1.116, Luc 600*
> self-same

**samingo** *interj*
sə'mɪŋgo:
**sp** samingo[1]

**sampire** *n*
'sampəɪɹ
**sp** sampire[1]

**sample** *n*
=
**sp** sample[1]

**sampler** *n*
'sampləɹ
**sp** sampler[2]

**Sampson / ~'s / ~s** *n*
'samsən, -mps- / -z
**sp** Sampson[8] / Sampsons[1] / Samsons[1]

**sanctified** *adj*
*m* 'saŋtɪˌfəɪd, -ɪf-, -ŋkt-
**sp** sanctified[4]

**sanctif·y / ~ies / ~ied** *v*
'saŋtɪˌfəɪ, -ŋkt- / -ɪfəɪz / -ɪˌfəɪd
**sp** sanctifie[4] / sanctifies[1] / sanctified[1], sanctify'd[1]
**rh** hie *AW 3.4.11*
> unsanctified

**sanctimonious** *adj*
ˌsaŋtɪ'mo:nɪəs, -ŋkt-
**sp** sanctimonious[2]

**sanctimony** *n*
'saŋtɪmənəɪ, -ŋkt-
**sp** sanctimonie[4]

**sanctit·y / ~ies** *n*
*m* 'saŋtɪˌtəɪ, -ɪt-, -ŋkt- / -ɪˌtəɪz
**sp** sanctitie[2], sanctity[4] / sanctities[1]

**sanctuarize** *v*
*m* 'saŋtjəˌrəɪz, -ŋkt-
**sp** sancturize[1]

**sanctuary** *n*
*m* 'saŋtjəˌrəɪ, -tjʊˌarəɪ, -ŋkt-
**sp** sanctuarie[6], sanctuary[7]

**sanct·us / ~a** *Lat adj*
'saŋkta
**sp** sancta[1]

**sand / ~s** *n*
=
**sp** sand[7] / sands[17]
**rh** hands *Tem 1.2.375*; lands *Luc 335*

**sandal / Sandal** [name] *n*
'sandɑl
**sp** sandal[1] / Sandall[1]

**sandbag** *n*
=
**sp** sand-bagge[2]
> bag

**sand-blind** *adj*
'sam-ˌbləɪnd, 'sand-
**sp** sand-blinde[1], sand blinde[1]
> blind

**sanded** *adj*
=
**sp** sanded[1]

**Sands** [name], **Sandys** *n*
sandz
**sp** Sands[6], Sandys[1]

**sandy** *adj*
'sandəɪ
**sp** sandie[5], sandy[1]

**sandy-bottomed** *adj*
'sandəɪ-ˌbɒtəmd
**sp** sandy-bottom'd[1]
> bottom

**Sandys**
> Sands

**sang**
> sing

**sanguine** *adj*
=
**sp** sanguine[3], san-guine[1]

**sanguis** *Lat n*
'sangwɪs
**sp** sanguis[1]

**sanity** *n*
'sanɪtəɪ
**sp** sanitie[1]

**sans** *prep*
sanz, sɔ:nz
**sp** sans[15]

**Santrailles** *n*
sɒn'trel
**sp** Santrayle[1]

**sap** *n*
=
**sp** sap[7], sappe[2]

**sap-consuming** *adj*
'sap-kənˌsju:mɪn, -ɪŋ
**sp** sap-consuming[1]
> consume

**sap·io / ~it** *Lat v*
'sapɪt
**sp** *emend of LLL 4.2.79* sapis[1]

**sapless** *adj*
=
**sp** saplesse[1], sappe-lesse[1]

**sapling** *n*
'saplɪn, -ɪŋ
**sp** sapling[2]

**sapphire / ~s** *n*
'safəɪɹ / -z
**sp** saphire-[pearle][1] / saphires[1]

**Saracen / ~s** *n*
*m* 'sarəˌsenz
**sp** Saracens[1]

**sarcenet** *adj*
'sɑ:ɹsnət, -sən-
**sp** sarcenet[2]

**Sardian ~s** *n*
*m* 'sɑ:ɹdɪˌanz
**sp** Sardians[1]

**Sardinia** *n*
sɑ:ɹ'dɪnɪə
**sp** Sardinia[1]

**Sardis** *n*
'sɑ:ɹdɪs
**sp** Sardis[3]

**Sarum** *n*
'sɑ:ɹəm
**sp** Sarum[1]

**sat**
> sit

**Satan** *n*
'satən
**sp** Sathan[6], sathan[2]

**satchel** *n*
=
**sp** satchell[1]

**sate / ~d** *v*
sɛ:t / 'sɛ:tɪd
**sp** sate[1] / sated[1]

**satiate** *v*
'sasɪət
**sp** satiate[1]
> unsatiate

**satiety** *n*
sə'səɪətəɪ
**sp** sacietie[1], saciety[1], satiety[1]
**rh** variety *VA 19*

**satin** *n*
=
**sp** satten[3]

**satire** *n*
'satəɪɹ
**sp** satire[1]

**satirical** *adj*
sə'tɪrɪkɑl
**sp** satyricall[1]

**satis** *Lat adv*
'satɪs
**sp** satis[1]

**satisfaction** *n*
*m* ˌsatɪs'faksɪən, -sɪˌɒn
**sp** satisfaction[31], satisfa-ction[1]

**satisfy / ~ies / ~ying / ~ied** *v*
'satɪsfəɪ / -z / -ɪn, -ɪŋ / -d
**sp** satisfie[27] / satisfies[1] / satisfying[3] / satisfi'd[6], satisfide[3], satisfied[36], satisfy'd[3]
**rh** *1* eye *Luc 96*; **rh** *2* majesty *Luc 96* / qualified, side *Luc 422*
> unsatisfied

**Saturday / ~s** *n*
'satəɹˌdɛ: / -z
**sp** Saterday[1] / Saterdaies[1]

**Saturn** *n*
'satəɹn
**sp** Saturne[4]

**Saturnin·e / ~us / ~us'** *n*
*m* 'satəɹˌnəɪn / -əs
**sp** Saturnine[18] / Saturninus[6] / Saturninus[1]

**satyr / ~s** *n*
'satəɹ / -z
**sp** satyre[3] / satyres[1], *malap WT 4.4.325* saltiers[1]

**sauce** *n*
=
**sp** sauce[1], sawce[10]
> Jack-sauce

**sauce / ~d** *v*
=
**sp** sauce[2], sawce[3] / sauced[1], sawc'd[1], sawc'st[2]

**saucer / ~s** *n*
'sɔ:səɹz
**sp** sawcers[1]

**saucily** *adv*
'sɔ:sɪləɪ
**sp** sawcily[2]
**rh** audacity, leisurely *Luc 1348*

**sauciness** *n*
*m* 'sɔ:sɪnəs, -ˌnes
**sp** saucinesse[1], sawcines[1], sawcinesse[4]

**saucy** *adj*
'sɔ:səɪ
**sp** saucie[2], saucy[2], sawcie[14], sawcy[15]

**sauf** *Fr prep*
sof
**sp** sauf[4], sans[1]

**Saunder** *n*
'sɔ:ndəɹ
**sp** Saunder[2]

**savage** *adj*
=
**sp** sauage[30]

**savage / ~s** *n*
=
**sp** sauage[2] / saluages[1], sauages[3]

**savagely** *adv*
'savɪʤləɪ
**sp** sauagely[1]

**savageness** *n*
=
**sp** sauagenes[1], sauagenesse[2]

**savagery** *n*
*m* 'savɪʤˌrəɪ, -ʤr-
**sp** sauagery[2]
**rh** fumitory *H5 5.2.47*

**save** *prep*
*str* sɛ:v, *unstr* sev
**sp** saue[47]

**sav·e / ~es / ~ing / ~ed** *v*
sɛ:v / -z / 'sɛ:vɪn, -ɪŋ / sɛ:vd
**sp** saue[147], 'saue[10], [God save], *Macmorris H5 3.2.107f* sa'me [save me][2] / saues[6] / sauing[2] / sau'd[19], saued[19], *Caius MW 2.3.6* saue[1]
**rh** grave *TN 2.4.62*

**savez** *Fr*
> savoir

**saving** *adj / prep*
'sɛ:vɪn, -ɪŋ
**sp** sauing[1] / sauing[12]
> past-saving

**Saviour / ~'s** *n*
'sɛ:vɪəɹ
**sp** Sauiours[1]

**savoir / savez** *Fr v*
sa'vez
**sp** saaue[1]

**savour / ~s** *n*
'sɛ:vəɹ / -z
**sp** sauour[3] / sauors[3], sauours[3]
**rh** favour *S 125.7* / favours *MND 2.1.13*

**savour / ~s / ~ing** *v*
'sɛ:vəɹ / -z / -ɪn, -ɪŋ, 'sɛ:vr-
**sp** sauour[3] / sauors[1], sauours[2] / sauouring[1]
> sweet-savoured

**savoury** *adj / n*
'sɛ:vrəɪ, -vər-
**sp** sa-uory[1], sauoury[1] / sauory[1]
> unsavoury

**Savoy** *n*
sə'vəɪ
**sp** Sauoy[1]

**saw / ~s** *n*
=
**sp** saw[2] / sawes[4]
**rh** awe *Luc 244*; draw *Luc 1672*; raw *LLL 5.2.911*
> handsaw

**saw / ~ed** *v*
=
**sp** saw[1] / saw'de[1]

**saw** *v*
> see

**sawpit** *n*
=
**sp** saw-pit[1]
> pit

**sawyer** *n*
'sɔ:jəɹ
**sp** sawyer[1]

**Saxon / ~s** *n*
=
**sp** Saxons[2]

**Saxony / ~'s** *n*
'saksənəɪz
**sp** Saxonies[1]

**say / ~est / ~s / saith / saying / said / saidest / sain** *v*
sɛ: / -st / -z, sez / sɛ:θ, seθ / 'sɛ:ɪn, -ɪŋ / sɛ:d, sed / -st / sɛ:n
**sp** saie[3], say[1615], say't [say it][5] / saiest[3], saist[34], sai'st[2], sayest[8], sayst[6], say'st[29] / saies[103], sayes[131] / saith[4], sayth[2] / saying[26] / said[327], saide[28], sayd[10], sayde[3], sed[2], [well]-sed[1] / saidst[1], said'st[1], sayd'st[1] / *emend of LLL 3.1.81* faine[1]
**rh** *1* away *AY 3.3.94, CE 4.2.25, Luc 1709, R2 1.3.243, RJ 2.4.192, 5.3.66, TG 3.1.100, VA 253, 805*; away, fray *MND 3.2.344*; away, lay *Luc 1797*; away, stay *R2 5.5.97*; day *CE 4.2.58, Ham 2.1.57, 2H4 5.2.144, 1H6 2.4.133, H8 Prol.31, LLL 1.1.113, 4.3.87, 5.2.817, R2 3.2.197, TS 4.4.92*; decay *S 23.5*; delay *R2 5.1.102*; denay *TN 2.4.122*; fray *TS 1.2.24*; gay *VA 284*; lay *Luc 1618*; *Mac 2.3.52, S 101.5*; may *WT 4.1.31*; nay *PP 18.34*; obey *KL 5.3.322, LC 132*; pay *Mac 1.4.21, 4.1.130, S 79.13*; play *AY 3.4.53, TNK Epil.2*; stay *RJ 1.2.36*; sway *LC 106*; they *LLL 5.2.88, S 59.9*; today *1H6 4.7.27, TC 5.6.25*; way *Cym 3.2.82, Luc 629, S 50.3*; **say ye** stay ye *TNK Epil.10*; **rh** *2* Syria *Per Prol.20* / assays, delays *Luc 1717*; days *R2 4.1.219*; lays *Per 5.Chorus.2* / **rh** *1* afraid, maid *LC 180*; aid *Luc 1785*; aid, appaid *Luc 915*; aid, bewrayed *Luc 1699*; allayed *S 56.1*; bewrayed *PP 18.53*; maid *AW 2.3.140, 1H6 4.7.37, KL 1.1.183, MND 2.2.64, 78, MW 5.5.50, Per 4.Chorus.18*; stayed *VA 333*; **rh** *2* read [red] *LLL 4.3.192* / plain *LLL 3.1.81*
> for-, sooth-, un-say

**Say** [name] *n*
sɛ:
**sp** Say[7]

**saying / ~s** *n*
'sɛ:ɪn, -ɪŋ / -z
**sp** saying[28], say-ing[1] / sayings[5]

**'sblood**
> blood

**scab / ~s** *n*
=
**sp** scab[3], scabbe[1] / scabs[1]

**scabbard** *n*
'skabəɹd
**sp** scabbard[2], scabberd[2]

**scaffolage** *n*
'skafəlɪʤ
**sp** scaffolage[1]

**scaffold** *n*
'skafo:ld
**sp** scaffold[2]

**scald** *adj*
skɔ:ld
**sp** scald[2], scall[1], scauld[3]

**scald / ~est / ~ed** *v*
skɔ:ld / -st, skɔ:lst / 'skɔ:ldɪd
**sp** scald[1], scal'd[2] / scald'st[1] / scalded[1]

**scalding** *adj / n*
'skɔ:ldɪn, -ɪŋ
**sp** scalding[1] / scalding[1]

**scale / ~s** *n*
skɛ:l / -z
**sp** scale[10] / scales[6]
**rh** prevails *2H6 2.1.199*; tales *MND 3.2.132*

**scal·e / ~ing / ~ed** *v*
skɛ:l / 'skɛ:lɪn, -ɪŋ / skɛ:ld
**sp** scale[2], scale't [scale it][1] / skaling[1] / scaled[1]
**rh** pale *Luc 440*; pale, tale *Luc 481*
> unscalable

**scaled** *adj*
*m* skɛ:ld, 'skɛ:lɪd
**sp** scal'd[1], scaled[1]

**Scales** [name] *n*
skɛ:lz
**sp** Scales[4]

**scaling** *adj*
'skɛ:lɪn, -ɪŋ
**sp** scaling[2]

**scalp / ~s** *n*
=
**sp** scalpe[2] / scalps[1]

**scaly** *adj*
'skɛ:ləɪ
**sp** scalie[1]

**scamble** *v*
=
**sp** scamble[1]

**scambling** *adj / n*
'skamblɪn, -ɪŋ
**sp** scambling[2] / skambling[1]

**scamels** *n*
'skaməlz
**sp** scamels[1]

**scan / ~ned** *v*
=
**sp** scan[1] / scand[1], scan'd[1], scann'd[1]
**rh** man *Per 2.2.55* / hand *Mac 3.4.139*; understand *CE 2.2.159*
> unscanned

**scandal** *n*
'skandɑl
**sp** scandall[2]

**scandal / ~led** *v*
'skandɑl / -d
**sp** scandall[2] / scandal'd[1]

**scandalized** *adj*
'skandɑˌləɪzd
**sp** scandaliz'd[2]

**scandalled** *adj*
'skandɑld
**sp** scandald[1]

**scandalous** *adj*
'skandləs, -dɑl-
**sp** scandalous[2]

**scant / ~er** *adj*
= / 'skantəɹ
**sp** scant[1] / scanter[1]

**scant** *adv*
=
**sp** scant[1]

**scant / ~s / ~ing / ~ed** *v*
= / = / 'skantɪn, -ɪŋ / =
**sp** scant[7] / scants[1] / scanting[1] / scanted[3]
**rh** want *PP 20.35* / wanted *KL 1.1.278*

**scanted** *adj*
=
**sp** scanted[1]

**scantling** *n*
'skantlɪn, -ɪŋ
**sp** scantling[1]

**scantly** *adv*
'skantləɪ
**sp** scantly[1]

**scape**
> escape

**scar / ~s** *n*
skɑ:ɹ / -z
**sp** scar[2], scarre[7], scarre's [scar is][1], skarre[1] / scarres[8], scars[3], skarres[3]
**rh** *1* afar *Luc 828*; are *MND 5.1.401*; **rh** *2* war *Luc 828* / wars *H5 5.1.84*

**scar / ~red** *v*
skɑ:ɹ / -d
**sp** scarre[1] / scar'd[1], scarr'd[2]
> unscarred

**scarce** *adj / adv*
skɑ:ɹs
**sp** scarce[3], scarse[3] / scarce[32], scarse[33]

**scarce-bearded** *adj*
*m* ˌskɑ:ɹs-'bɛ:ɹdɪd, -'bɐ:ɹ-
**sp** scarse-bearded[1]
> bearded

**scarce-cold** *adj*
'skɑ:ɹs-ˌko:ld
**sp** scarse-cold[1], scarse-cold-[battaile][1]
> cold

**scarcely** *adv*
'skɑ:ɹsləɪ
**sp** scarcely[4], scarce-ly[1], scarsely[9]

**scarcity** *n*
*m* 'skɑ:ɹsɪˌtəɪ
**sp** scarcity[1], scarsitie[2]
**rh** chastity *VA 753*

**scar·e / ~ing / ~ed** *v*
skɑ:ɹ / 'skɑ:rɪn, -ɪŋ / skɑ:ɹd
**sp** scarre[4] / skaring[1] / scar'd[4], scarr'd[2]

**scarecrow / ~s** *n*
'skɑ:ɹkro: / -z
**sp** scar-crow[2] / skar-crowes[1]
> crow

**scarf / ~s** *n*
skɑ:ɹf / -s
**sp** scarfe[6], scarph[1], skarfe[1] / scarfes[2], scarffes[3]

**scarf / ~ed** *v*
skɑ:ɹf / -t
**sp** skarfe[1] / scarft[1]

**scarfed** *adj*
'skɑ:ɹfɪd
**sp** skarfed[1]

**scarlet** *adj / n*
'skɑ:ɹlɪt
**sp** scarlet[7] / scarlet[3]

**Scarlet** [name] *n*
'skɑ:ɹlɪt
**sp** Scarlet[2]

**Scarus** *n*
'skarəs
**sp** Scarrus[5], Scarus[1]

**scathe** *n / v*
skað
**sp** scath[1], scathe[3] / scath[1]

**scatheful** *adj*
'skaðfʊl
**sp** scathfull[1]

**scatter / ~s / ~ed** *v*
'skatəɹ / -z / -d
**sp** scatter[4] / scatters[3] / scattered[4], scattred[4]

**scattered** *adj*
'skatəɹd
**sp** scatter'd[2], scattred[3]

**scattering** *adj*
'skatrɪn, -ɪŋ, -tər-
**sp** scattering[1]

**scel·us / ~era / ~erisque** *Lat n + conj*
'skelə·ra / -'ri:skwe, -ke
**sp** scelera[1] / scelerisque[1]

**scene / ~s** *n*
=, sen / -z
**sp** sceane[2], scene[29], scoene[2] / scenes[1], scoenes[2]
**rh** *1* Threne *PT 52*; unclean *RJ Prol.2*;
**rh** *2* then *H5 2.Chorus.42*

**scent** *n / v*
=
**sp** sent[2] / sent[1]

**sceptre / ~'s / ~s** *n*
'septəɹ / -z
**sp** scepter[29] / scepters[3] / scepters[5]

**sceptred** *adj*
'septəɹd
**sp** sceptred[4]

**schedule / ~s** *n*
'sedju:l / -z
**sp** scedule[4], schedule[1] / scedules[1]
> enschedule

**scholar / ~'s / ~s** *n*
'skɒləɹ / -z
**sp** scholler[17] / schollers[1] / schollers[5]
> fellow-scholar

**scholarly** *adv*
'skɒləɹləɪ
**sp** schollerly[1]

**school** *n*
=
**sp** schoole[22] / schooles[3], schools[1], sculs[1]
**rh** fool *LLL 4.2.31, 5.2.71, Luc 1820* / fools *Luc 1018*
> dancing-, taming-school

**school** *v*
=
**sp** schoole[1], school'd[3]
> ill-, un-schooled

**schoolboy / ~'s / ~s'** *n*
'sku:lbəɪ / -z
**sp** school-boy[1], schoole-boy[4] / school-boies[1], school-boyes[1] / school-boyes[1]
> boy

**schooldays / ~s'** *n*
'sku:ldɛ:z
**sp** school-daies[1], schoole dayes[1] / schooledaies[1]
> day

**schooling** *n*
'sku:lɪn, -ɪŋ
**sp** schooling[1]

**schoolmaid / ~s** *n*
'sku:lˌmɛ:dz
**sp** schoole-maids[1]
> maid

**schoolmaster / ~s** *n*
'sku:lˌmastəɹ / -z
**sp** schoolemaster[7], schoole-master[3], schoolmaster[2] / schoolemasters[2], schoole-masters[1]
> fellow-schoolmaster, master

**sciatica** *n*
səɪ'atɪkə
**sp** ciatica[1], sciatica[1]

**science / ~s** *n*
'səɪəns / -ɪz
**sp** science[2] / sciences[2]

**Scilla** *n*
'sɪlə
**sp** Scilla[1], Sylla[1]

**scimitar / ~'s** *n*
'sɪmɪˌtɑ:ɹ / -z
**sp** cemitar[1], symitare[1] / semitars[1]

**scion / ~s** *n*
'səɪən / -z
**sp** seyen[1], sien[1] / syens[1]

**scissors** *n*
'sɪzəɹz
**sp** cizers[1]

**scoff / ~s** *n*
=
**sp** scoffe[1] / scoffes[3]
**rh** off *LLL 5.2.263*

**scoff / ~ing** *v*
= / 'skɒfɪn, -ɪŋ
**sp** scoffe[1] / scoffing[1]

**scoffer** *n*
'skɒfəɹ
**sp** scoffer[1]
**rh** offer *AY 3.5.62*

**Scoggin / ~'s** *n*
'skɒgɪnz
**sp** Scoggan's[1]

**scold** *n*
sko:ld
**sp** scold[2]

**scold / ~est / ~s** *v*
sko:ld / -st, -əst / -z
**sp** scold[5], scoul'd[1] / scold'st[1] / scolds[1]
> outscold

**scolding** *adj / n*
'sko:ldɪn, -ɪŋ
**sp** scolding[5] / scolding[1]

**sconce** *n*
=
**sp** sconce[7]
> ensconce

**Scone** [name] *n*
sko:n
**sp** Scone[3]
**rh** one *Mac 5.6.114*

**scope** *n*
sko:p
**sp** scope[23]
**rh** hope *Ham 3.2.229* [Q2], *S 29.7, 52.13*

**scorch / ~ed** *v*
skɔ:ɹʧ / *m* -t, 'skɔ:ɹʧɪd
**sp** scorch[2] / scorch'd[2], scorched[1]
**rh** torch *Luc 314*
> unscorch

**score / ~s** *n*
skɔ:ɹ / -z
**sp** score[22], [sixe]-score[1], [twelve]-score[2] / scores[1]
**rh** before *AW 4.3.219*; door, more, whore *KL 1.4.126*; hoar *RJ 2.4.135*; more *Mac 5.6.91*
> five-, four-score

**score / ~s / ~ed** *v*
skɔ:ɹ / -z / -d
**sp** score[3] / scores[1] / scoar'd[1]
**rh** more *S 122.10*

**scoring** *n*
'skɔ:rɪn, -ɪŋ
**sp** scoring[1]

**scorn / ~s** *n*
skɔ:ɹn / -z
**sp** scorn[3], scorne[54] / scornes[9], skornes[1]
**rh** born *AW 2.3.132, Cym 4.4.53, 5.4.125, 1H6 4.7.39, Luc 1189, Mac 4.1.78, 5.6.22, MND 2.2.130, 3.2.122*; borne *Cym 5.2.7, 1H6 4.7.18*; forlorn *VA 252*; forsworn *S 88.2*; horn *AY 4.2.19*; morn *VA 4*; sworn *LLL 1.1.296*; thorn *MND 5.1.136* / horns *TC 4.5.30*

**scorn / ~est / ~s / ~ing / ~d / ~dest** *v*
skɔ:ɹn / -st / -z / 'skɔ:ɹnɪn, -ɪŋ / skɔ:ɹn·d / -st, -dst

**sp** scorne[36] / scorn'st[1] / scornes[10], scorns[1] / scorning[4] / scornd[1], scorn'd[10], scorned[2] / scornd'st[1]
**rh** horn *TC 1.1.113*

**scornful** *adj*
'skɔ:rnfʊl
**sp** scornefull[1], scornfull[6]

**scornfully** *adv*
*m* 'skɔ:rnfʊ,ləɪ
**sp** scornefully[2], scornfully[1]

**scorpion / ~'s / ~s** *n*
'skɔ:rpɪən / -z
**sp** scorpion[1] / scorpions[1] / scorpions[1]

**scot** *n*
=
**sp** scot[1]

**Scot / ~s** *n*
=
**sp** Scot[16] / Scots[7], Scottes[1]

**scotch / ~es** *n*
=
**sp** scotches[1]

**scotch / ~ed** *v*
=
**sp** scotcht[1]

**Scotch** *adj*
=
**sp** Scotch[2]

**Scotland** *n*
=
**sp** Scotland[28]

**Scottish** *adj*
=
**sp** Scottish[2]

**scoundrel / ~s** *n*
'skəʊndrəlz
**sp** scoundrels[1]

**scour / ~ing / ~ed** *v*
sko:ɹ / 'sko:ɹ·ɪn, -ɪŋ / *m* -ɪd, sko:ɹd
**sp** scoure[3], scowre[5] / scowring[1], scow-ring[1] / scowr'd[1], scowred[1]
**rh** flower *MW 5.5.61*
> unscoured

**scourge** *n*
skɐ:ɹʤ
**sp** scourge[12]

**scourge / ~d** *v*
skɐ:ɹʤ / -d
**sp** scourge[4] / scourg'd[2]

**scouring** *n*
'sko:ɹɪn, -ɪŋ
**sp** scouring[1]

**scout / ~s** *n*
skəʊt / -s
**sp** scout[3] / scouts[5]

**scout** *v*
skəʊt
**sp** scout[1], skowt[1]
**rh** scout 'em flout 'em, *emend of* cout 'em *Tem 3.2.123*

**scowl /** *VA* **~ing** *v*
skəʊl / 'skəʊlɪn, -ɪŋ
**sp** scowle[3] / skowling[1]
**rh** howling *VA 917*

**scrap / ~s** *n*
=
**sp** scraps[4]

**scrape / ~ed** *v*
skrɛ:p / -t
**sp** scrape[3] / scrap'd[3]

**scraping** *adj*
'skrɛ:pɪn, -ɪŋ
**sp** scraping[1]

**scratch / ~es** *n*
=
**sp** scratch[3] / scratches[1]

**scratch / ~ed** *v*
=
**sp** scratch[13] / scratch'd[3], scratcht[2]
**rh** wretch *VA 705*

**scratched** *adj*
=
**sp** scratcht[2]
> unscratched

**scratching** *n*
'skraʧɪn, -ɪŋ
**sp** scratching[3]

**scream / ~s** *n*
=
**sp** schreemes[1]

**scream** *v*
=
**sp** schreame[1]

**screech / ~ing** *v*
'skri:ʧɪn, -ɪŋ
**sp** scritching[1]

**screech-owl / ~s** *n*
'skri:ʧ-,əʊl / -z
**sp** schreechowle[1], screechoule[1], scritch-owle[1] / screech-owles[2]
> owl

**screen / ~s** *n*
=
**sp** schreene[1] / skreenes[1]

**screen / ~ed** *v*
=
**sp** screen'd[1]
> bescreen

**screw / ~s / ~ed** *v*
=
**sp** screw[1] / screwes[1] / screw'd[1]

**scribble / ~d** *v*
=
**sp** scribeld[1]

**scribbled** *adj*
=
**sp** scribled[1]

**scribe / ~s** *n*
skrəɪb / -z
**sp** scribe[2] / scribes[3]

**scrip** *n*
=
**sp** scrip[2]

**scrippage** *n*
=
**sp** scrippage[1]

**scripture / ~s** *n*
'skrɪptəɹ / -z
**sp** scripture[4] / scriptures[1]

**scrivener** *n*
'skrɪvnəɹ, -vən-
**sp** scriuener[2]

**scroll / ~s** *n*
skro:l / -z
**sp** scrole[1], scroule[5], scrowle[5] / scrowles[1]

**Scroop** *n*
=
**sp** Scroop[1], Scroope[13]

**scroyle / ~s** *n*
skrəɪlz
**sp** scroyles[1]

**scrubbed** *adj*
*m* 'skrɤbɪd
**sp** scrubbed[2]

**scruple / ~s** *n*
=
**sp** scruple[21], scru-ple[1] / scruples[4]

**scrupulous** *adj*
*m* 'skru:pləs, -pəl-
**sp** scrupulous[2]

**scuffle / ~s** *n*
'skɤfəlz
**sp** scuffles[1]

**scuffling** *n*
'skɤflɪn, -ɪŋ
**sp** scuffling[1]

**scull / ~s** *n*
skɤl / -z
**sp** scul[1], scull[10] / sculles[2], sculls[2]

**scullion** *n*
'skɤlɪən
**sp** scullion[2]

**scum** *n*
skɤm
**sp** scum[4]

**scurril** *adj*
'skɤrɪl
**sp** scurrill[1]

**scurrility** *n*
skə'rɪlɪtəɪ
**sp** scurilitie[1], scur-rillity[1]
**rh** facility *LLL 4.2.54*

**scurrilous** *adj*
'skɤrɪləs
**sp** scurrilous[1]

**scurvy** *adj*
'skɐ:ɹvəɪ
**sp** scuruie[8], scuruy[16], scuruy-[iack-dog-priest][1], scur-uy-[cogging-companion][1], skuruy[1]

**scuse**
> excuse

**scut** *n*
skɤt
**sp** scut[1]

**scutcheon / ~s** *n*
'skɤʧɪən / -z
**sp** scutcheon[2] / scutcheons[1]

**scythe / ~s** *n*
səɪð / -z
**sp** sythe[2] / sythes[1]

**Scythia** *n*
'sɪðɪə
**sp** Scythia[2]

**Scythian** *adj / n*
'sɪðɪən
**sp** Scythian[1] / Scythian[1]

**'sdeath**
> death

**se** *Lat pro*
se
**sp** se[2]

**sea / ~'s / ~s** *n*
=
**sp** sea[193], sea-[fight][2], sea-[wing][1], [south]-sea[1], seas [sea is][1] / seas[1] / seas[43]
**rh** *1* plea *S 65.1*; thee *RJ 2.2.133*;
**rh** *2* play *H8 3.1.10 /* ease *Per 2. Chorus.27, 2.4.43*; Pericles *Per 4.4.10*; these *CE 2.1.21*
> overseas

**sea-bank / ~s** *n*
=
**sp** sea-banke[1] / sea bankes[1]
> bank

**sea-boy** *n*
'si:-'bəɪ
**sp** *2H4 3.1.27 emend as* sea-son
> boy

**sea-cap** *n*
=
**sp** sea-cap[1]
> cap

**sea-change** *n*
'si:-'ʧɛ:nʤ
sea-change[1]
**rh** strange *Tem 1.2.401*
> change

**sea-coal** *adj*
'si:-ˌko:l
**sp** sea-cole[1], sea-cole-[fire][1]
> coal

**Seacoal** [name] *n*
'si:ko:l
**sp** Sea-coale[3]

**seafaring** *adj*
'si:ˌfɛ:rɪn, -ɪŋ
**sp** sea-faring[1]
> fare

**sea-gown** *n*
'si:-ˌgəʊn
**sp** sea-gowne[1]
> gown

**seal / ~s** *n*
=
**sp** seale[31] / seales[6]

**seal / ~s / ~ing / ~ed** *v*
= / = / 'si:lɪn, -ɪŋ / =
**sp** seal[1], seale[32] / seales[6] / sealing[2] / seal'd[20], seald[2], sealed[1]
**rh** dealing *VA 512*
> counter-, un-seal

**sealed** *adj*
=
**sp** seal'd[2], sealed[4]

**sealed-up** *adj*
'si:ld-ɤp
**sp** seal'd-vp[2]

**sea-like** *adj*
'si:-ˌləɪk
**sp** sea-like[1]
> like

**sealing** *adj*
'si:lɪn, -ɪŋ
**sp** sealing[1]

**seal-ring** *n*
=
**sp** seale-ring[2]
> ring

**seam** *n*
=
**sp** seame[1]

**sea-maid / ~'s** *n*
'si:-ˌmɛ:d / -z
**sp** sea-maid[1] / sea-maids[1]
> maid

**sea·man / ~men** *n*
=
**sp** sea-men[1]
> man

**sea-marge** *n*
'si:-ˌmɑ:ɹʤ
**sp** sea-marge[1]

**sea-mark** *n*
'si:-ˌmɑ:ɹk
**sp** sea-marke[2]
> mark

**sea-monster** *n*
'si:-ˌmɒnstəɹ
**sp** sea-monster[2]
> monster

**seamy** *adj*
'si:məɪ
**sp** seamy-[side][1]

**sea-nymph / ~s** *n*
=
**sp** sea-nimphs[1]
> nymph

**sear / ~ed** *v*
si:ɹ / -d
**sp** seare[4] / sear'd[1]
> ensear

**search** *n*
sɐ:ɹʧ
**sp** search[15]
**rh** perch *Per 3.Chorus.16*

**search / ~es / ~eth / ~ing / ~ed** *v*
sɐ:ɹʧ / 'sɐ:ɹʧ·ɪz / -əθ / -ɪn, -ɪŋ / sɐ:ɹʧt
**sp** search[25], serch[3] / searches[1] / searcheth[1] / searching[2] / search'd[6], searcht[1]
> unsearched

**searcher / ~s** *n*
'sɐ:ɹʧəɹz
**sp** searchers[1]

**searching** *adj*
'sɐ:ɹʧɪn, -ɪŋ
**sp** searching[2], sear-ching[1], serching[1]

**seared** *adj*
si:ɹd
**sp** seard[1]

**seasick** *n*
=
**sp** sea-sick[1], sea-sicke[2]
> sick

**seaside** *n*
'si:səɪd
**sp** sea-side[6], sea side[1]
> side

**season / ~'s / ~s** *n*
'sɛ:zən / -z
**sp** season[32] / seasons[2] / seasons[5]
**rh** reason *CE 2.2.48, 4.2.57, MND 2.2.123*; reason, treason *Luc 879*

**season / ~s / ~ed** *v*
'sɛ:zən / -z / -d
**sp** season[8] / seasons[4] / season'd[4]
> unseason

**sea-son** *n*
'si:-'sɤn
**sp** *emend of 2H4 3.1.27* sea-boy
> son

**seasoned** *adj*
'sɛ:zənd
**sp** season'd[2]

**sea-sorrow** *n*
'si:-'sɒrə, -ro:
**sp** sea-sorrow[1]
> sorrow

**sea-storm** *n*
'si:-'stɔ:ɹm
**sp** sea-storme[1]
> storm

**sea-swallowed** *adj*
'si:-ˌswɒləd, -lo:d
**sp** sea-swallow'd[1]
> swallow

**seat / ~'s / ~s** *n*
=
**sp** seat[24], seate[28] / seates[1] / seates[2], seats[3]
**rh** great *Luc 70, Per Prol.18*

**seat / ~s / ~ed** *v*
=
**sp** seat[3] / seats[1] / seated[9], [darke] seated[1]
> dis-seat

**seated** *adj*
=
**sp** seated[1]

**sea-walled** *adj*
'siː-ˌwɑːld
**sp** sea-walled[1]
> wall

**sea-water** *n*
'siː-ˌwɑtəɹ
**sp** sea-water[1], sea water[1]
> water

**Sebastian** *n*
sə'bastɪən
**sp** Sebastian[27]

**second** *adj*
=
**sp** second[68], se-cond[1]

**second / ~s** *n*
=
**sp** second[15] / seconds[4]

**second / ~s / ~ed** *v*
'sekənd / -z / -ɪd
**sp** second[11], se-cond[1] / seconds[1] / seconded[3]
> unseconded

**secondarily** *adv*
*m* 'sekənˌdarɪləɪ
**sp** secondarily[1]

**secondary** *adj*
*m* 'sekənˌdarəɪ, -dərəɪ, -drəɪ
**sp** secondary[2]

**secrec·y / *Luc* ~ies** *n*
*m* 'siːkrəsəɪ, -ˌsəɪ / 'siːkrəˌsəɪz
**sp** secrecie[10], secrecy[2], secricie[1] / secrecies
**rh** affectedly *LC 49* / eyes *Luc 101*

**secret / ~est** *adj*
= / 'siːkrəts
**sp** secret[44] / secret'st[1]
> unsecret

**secret / ~s** *n*
=
**sp** secret[17] / secrets[23], se-crets[1]

**secretar·y / ~ies** *n*
*m* 'sekrəˌtrəɪ, -ət- -ˌtarəɪ / -ətrəɪz
**sp** secretary[7], *abbr in s.d.* secret[1] / secretaries[1]

**secret-false** *adj*
'siːkrət-'fɑls
**sp** secret false[1]

**secretly** *adv*
*m* 'siːkrətləɪ, -ˌləɪ
**sp** secretly[12]
**rh** Thisbe *MND 5.1.158*

**sect / ~s** *n*
=
**sp** sect[5] / sects[3]

**sectary** *n*
*m* 'sektəˌrəɪ
**sp** sectary[1]

**secundo** *Ital n*
se'kʊndoː
**sp** secundo[1]

**secure** *adj / adv*
sɪ'kjuːɹ
**sp** secure[21] / secure[5]

**secur·e / ~ing** *v*
sɪ'kjuːɹ / -ɪn, -ɪŋ
**sp** secure[5] / securing[1]

**securely** *adv*
sɪ'kjuːɹləɪ
**sp** securely[6]

**security** *n*
*m* sɪ'kjuːɹtəɪ, -ɹɪtəɪ, -ɹɪˌtəɪ
**sp** securitie[5], security[11]
**rh** enemy *Mac 3.5.32*

**sedge / ~s** *n*
=
**sp** sedge[1], sedges[3]

**sedged** *adj*
=
**sp** sedg'd[1]

**sedgy** *adj*
'sedʒəɪ
**sp** siedgie[1]

**sedition** *n*
sɪ'dɪsɪən
**sp** sedition[3]

**seditious** *adj*
sɪ'dɪsɪəs
**sp** seditious[2]

**seduc·e / ~ing / ~ed** *v*
sɪ'djuːs / -ɪn, -ɪŋ / *m* -ɪd, -t
**sp** seduce[3] / seducing[1] / seduc'd[5], seduced[3]
> unseduced

**seducer** *n*
sɪ'djuːsəɹ
**sp** seducer[1]

**see** *n*
=
**sp** sea[2]

**see / ~st / ~s / ~ing / saw / ~est / *LC* sawn / seen** *v*
= / siːst / = / 'siːɪn, -ɪŋ / = / sɔːst / sɔːn / =
**sp** see[1398], see's [see us][1], see't [see it][21] / seest[48], see'st[2] / sees[40], see's[3] / seeing[19] / saw[243], sawe[1], saw't [saw it][6] / saw'st[12] / sawne[1] / seen[13], seene[234], seene't [seen it][1], seen't [seen it][2]
**rh** agree *H8 Prol.9*; audaciously *LLL 5.2.103*; be *AC 1.3.64, AY 2.4.83, Cor 5.3.130, H5 4.Chorus.52, Ham 5.1.294, LC 183, LLL 2.1.224, Luc 750, 1084, Mac 1.4.54, MM 1.3.53, MND 2.1.11, 3.2.114, 4.1.71, 5.1.271, MV 2.9.99, MW 5.5.68, RJ 1.2.30, S 56.11, 137.2, TC 1.2.284, TN 1.2.64, VA 939*; be, free *LC 102*; be, three *PP 15.3*; chivalry *R2 1.1.202*; company *Per 5.2.17 [Chorus]*; constancy *S 152.12*; enemy *AY 2.5.6, 40*; free *LLL 5.2.423*; he *AY 2.5.52, 3.5.78*; mannerly *MV 2.9.99*; me *AW 2.3.71, 2.5.52, Ham 3.1.162, 1H6 1.2.86, LLL 2.1.243, 4.3.147, Mac 3.5.34, MND 1.1.204, 3.2.427, 5.1.176, R2 1.2.67, 3.3.170, TS 1.2.190*; me, thee *Luc 1306*; misery

*H8 Prol.29*; she *LLL 4.3.275*; sobriety *TS 1.1.70*; solemnity *AC 5.2.363*; story *H8 Prol.25*; thee *KJ 3.1.144, Luc 1770, Oth 1.3.289, S 3.11, 18.13, 27.8, 43.1, 95.12, 99.14, TC 5.2.110, VA 437, 952*; three *LLL 4.3.159, 5.2.418*; we *KL 1.1.263*; see it be it, free it *Luc 1206*; see't feet *KL 3.2.93* / agrees *Luc 1093, VA 287*; knees *R2 5.3.93* / agreeing , 'greeing *Ham 3.2.265, S 114.9*; being *S 121.4* / law *Cym 5.4.36*; maw *VA 604*; raw *Luc 1590*; straw *LC 10* / drawn *LC 91* / been *R2 5.6.29, S 97.3*; green *S 33.1, 63.13, 68.9, 104.6, VA 148*; keen *AY 2.7.179, LC 160, LLL 5.2.258, Per Epil.3*; queen *Luc 64, MND 1.1.174, 2.2.10, PT 30, R2 2.2.25, 3.4.106, S 96.7, TN 5.1.384, VA 504, 1194*; teen *LC 190, LLL 4.3.161, R3 4.1.95*; seen them between them *VA 357*
> foresee, unseen

**seed / ~s** *n*
=
**sp** seed[4], seede[2] / seedes[5], seeds[1]
**rh** breeds *AW 1.3.141*
> fern-, hag-, honey-, Mustard-, nettle-seed

**seeded** *adj*
=
**sp** seeded[1]

**seedness** *n*
=
**sp** seednes[1]

**seedsman** *n*
=
**sp** seedsman[1]

**seeing** *adj / conj / n*
'si:ɪn, -ɪŋ
**sp** seeing[2] / seeing[15] / seeing[6]
> all-, un-seeing

**seek / ~est / ~s / ~ing / sought / ~est** *v*
= / si:kst / = / 'si:kɪn, -ɪŋ / = / sɔ:tst
**sp** seek[12], seek't[1], seeke[211] / seek'st[6] / seekes[23], seeks[1] / seeking[21] / sought[31] / sought'st[1]
**rh** cheek *LLL 4.3.235, S 67.7*; Greek *TC 4.5.85, 5.8.10*; week *AY 2.3.73, LLL 5.2.62, Luc 211* / cheeks *VA 52, 477* / fought *Luc 1438*; thought *S 30.3*; thought, wrought *Luc 340*
> unsought

**seeking** *n*
'si:kɪn, -ɪŋ
**sp** seeking[2]

**seel** *v*
=
**sp** seele[4]

**seeling** *adj*
'si:lɪn, -ɪŋ
**sp** seeling[1]

**seely** *adj*
'si:ləɪ
**sp** seely[1]

**Seely** [name] *n*
'si:ləɪ
**sp** Seely[1]

**seem / ~est / ~s / ~eth / ~ing / ~ed** *v*
= / si:mst / = / = / 'si:mɪn, -ɪŋ / =
**sp** seem[4], seeme[158] / seem'st[6] / seemes[108], seeme's [seems][1], seems[4], / seemeth[9] / seeming[20] / seem'd[31], seemed[1]
**rh** deem *S 54.1*; esteem *S 127.10* / extremes *VA 985*

**seemer / ~s** *n*
'si:məɹz
**sp** seemers[1]

**seeming** *adj / n*
'si:mɪn, -ɪŋ
**sp** seeming[14], see-ming[1] / seeming[19]
**rh** esteeming *S 102.1*
> ill-, summer-, un-, well-seeming

**seemingly** *adv*
*m* 'si:mɪn,ləɪ, -ɪŋ-
**sp** seemingly[1]

**seemly** *adv*
'si:mləɪ
**sp** seemely[1]

**seer**
> all-seer

**seethe** *v*
=
**sp** seeth[1] / seethes[1]

**seething** *adj*
'si:ðɪn, -ɪŋ
**sp** seething[1]

**segregation** *n*
ˌsegrɪ'gɛ:sɪən
**sp** segregation[1]

**seigneur / ~s** *Fr n*
*Fr* se'ɲœ:ɹ, *Eng* sen'jɔ:ɹ / -z
**sp** seigneur[5], seignieur[1], seignior[2], signeur[2], signieur[5] / seigneurs[1]
> signor

**seiz·e / ~s / ~eth / ~ing / ~ed** *v*
= / = / = / 'si:zɪn, -ɪŋ / =
**sp** ceaze[2], seaze[2], seise[1], seize[23] / ceizes[1], seizes[1] / ceazeth[1] / seizing[1] / ceazed[1], ceiz'd[1], seaz'd[1], seiz'd[13]

**seizure** *n*
'si:zəɹ, -jəɹ
**sp** seizure[2], seysure[1]
**rh** pleasure *PP 11.10*

**seld** *adv*
=
**sp** seld[1]

**seldom** *adv*
=
**sp** seldome[18], sel-dome[1], sildome[8]

**seld-shown** *adj*
'seld-ˌʃo:n
**sp** seld-showne[1]
> show

**select** *adj / v*
=
**sp** select[1] / select[1]

**Seleucus** *n*
sel'ju:kəs
**sp** Seleucus[4]

**self** *adj*
=
**sp** selfe[55], selfe-[hand][1], selfe-[mettle][1], selfe-[place][1]

**self / ~'s / selves** *n*
=
**sp** self[1] / selfes[2] / selues[12], [grosse]-selues[1]

**self** *pro*

***herself***
*m* əɹ'self, hə-, 'ɐ:ɹself, 'hɐ:-
**sp** her self[3], her selfe[79], her selfe's [herself is][1]

***himself***
*m* ɪm'self, hɪ-, 'ɪmself, 'hɪ-
**sp** him selfe[1], him-selfe[7]

***itself***
*m* ɪt'self, 'ɪtself
**sp** it selfe[234]

***myself***
*m* mɪ'self, 'məɪself
**sp** my self[1], my selfe[547]
**rh** itself *R3 1.3.67*; pelf *PP 14.11*, *Tim 1.2.62*; thyself *R3 1.2.85*, *Tim 4.3.220*; yourself *R3 4.4.420*

***our·self / ~selves***
*m* o:ɹ'self / o:ɹ'selvz
**sp** our selfe[27] / our selues[110]

***themselves***
*m* ðəm'selvz, 'ðemselvz
**sp** themselues[142], them-selues[6]

***thyself***
*m* ðɪ'self, 'ðəɪself
**sp** thy self[2], thy selfe[194]

***your·self / ~self 's / -selves***
*m* jəɹ'self, 'ju:ɹself / jəɹ'selfs / jəɹ'selvz, 'ju:ɹselvz
**sp** your self[6], your selfe[259] / your selfes[1] / your selues[69]

**self-abuse** *n*
=
**sp** self-abuse[1]
**rh** use *Mac 3.4.141*
> abuse

**self-admission** *n*
'self-əd'mɪsɪən
**sp** selfe admission[1]
> admit

**self-affected** *adj*
=
**sp** selfe affected[1]
> affect

**self-affrighted** *adj*
'self-ə'frəɪtɪd
**sp** selfe-affrighted[1]
> affright, fright

**self-appl·y / ~ied** *LC* *v*
'self-ə'pləɪd
**sp** selfe applyed[1]
**rh** beside *LC 76*
> apply

**self-assumption** *n*
'self-ə'sɤmpsɪən
**sp** selfe-assumption[1]
> assume

**self-born / ~e** *adj*
'self-ˌbɔ:ɹn
**sp** selfe-borne[1] / selfe-borne[1]
> bear, born

**self-bounty** *n*
ˌself-'bəʊntəɪ
selfe-bounty[1]
> bounty

**self-breath** *n*
=
**sp** selfe-breath[1]
> breath

**self-charity** *n*
ˌself-'ʧɑ:ɹtəɪ, -ɹɪt-
**sp** selfe-charitie[1]
> charity

**self-comparison / ~s** *n*
*m* 'self-kəm'parɪˌsɒnz
**sp** selfe-comparisons[1]
> comparison

**self-danger** *n*
ˌself-'dɛ:nʤəɹ
**sp** selfe-danger[1]
> danger

**self-drawing** *adj*
ˌself-'drɔ:ɪn, -ɪŋ
**sp** selfe-drawing[1]
> draw

**self-endeared** *adj*
'self-en'di:ɹd -'dɛ:-
**sp** selfe indeared[1]
> endear

**self-explication** *n*
'self-ˌekspl ɪ'kɛ:sɪən
**sp** selfe-explication[1]
> explication

**self-figured** *adj*
ˌself-'fɪgəɹd
**sp** selfe-figur'd[1]
> figure

**self-glorious** *adj*
=
**sp** selfe-glorious[1]
> glorious

**self-harming** *adj*
ˌself-'ɑ:ɹmɪn, -ɪŋ, -'hɑ:-
**sp** selfe-harming[2]
> harm

**self-killed** *S* *adj*
=
**sp** selfe kil'd[1]
**rh** distilled *S 6.4*
> kill

**self-love** *n*
'self-'lɤv
**sp** selfe-loue[4]
> love

**self-loving** *adj*
'self-'lɤvɪn, -ɪŋ
selfe-louing[1]

**self-mettle** *n*
=
**sp** selfe-mettle[1]
> mettle

**self-misused** *adj*
=
**sp** selfe-misvs'd[1]
> misuse

**self-mould** *n*
ˌself-'mo:ld
**sp** selfe-mould[1]
> mould

**self-neglecting** *n*
'self-nɪ'glektɪn, -ɪŋ
**sp** selfe-neglecting[1]
> neglect

**self-offence / ~s** *n*
=
**sp** selfe-offences[1]
> offence

**self-reproving** *adj*
'self-rɪ'prɤvɪn, -ɪŋ, -ru:v-
**sp** selfereprouing[1]
> reprove

**selfsame** *adj*
'selfsɛ:m
**sp** selfesame[7], selfe-same[13], selfe same[2]
> same

**self-slaughter** *n*
ˌself-'slɔ:təɹ
**sp** selfe-slaughter[2]
> slaughter

**self-sovereignty** *n*
*m* ˌself-'sɒvrənˌtəɪ
**sp** selfe-soueraigntie[1]
**rh** be *LLL 4.1.36*
> sovereign

**self-subdued** *adj*
'self-səb'dju:d
**sp** selfe-subdued[1]
> subdue

**self-trust** *Luc* *n*
ˌself-'trɤst
**sp** selfe-trust[1]
**rh** just, lust *Luc 158*

**self-unable** *adj*
'self-ən'ɛ:bəl
**sp** selfe vnable[1]
> unable

**self-willed** *adj*
*m* 'selfˌwɪld, ˌself'wɪld
**sp** selfe-wild[1], selfe-will'd[2]
> will

**self-wrong** *n*
=
**sp** selfe wrong[1]
**rh** song *CE 3.2.171*
> wrong

**sell / ~s / ~ing / sold / ~est** *v*
= / = / 'selɪn, -ɪŋ / so:ld / so:lst, -dst
**sp** sel[3], sell[35] / sels[1] / selling[2] / sold[32], solde[2] / soldest[1]
**rh** well *S 21.14, TC 4.1.79*; *emend* of sale *PP 18.12* / behold, bold, cold, enfold, gold, inscrolled, old, told *MV 2.7.67*; bold *R3 5.3.306*; cold *CE 3.1.72*
> outsell

**seller / ~'s** *n*
'seləɹz
**sp** sellers[1]

**semblable** *adj / n*
*m* 'sembləˌbɤl, -əbəl / -əˌbɤl
**sp** semblable[2] / semblable[1]

**semblable** *Fr adj*
sɑ̃'blablə
**sp** semblable[1]

**semblably** *adv*
*m* sem'blabləɪ
**sp** semblably[1]

**semblance / ~s** *n*
=
**sp** semblance[18] / semblances[2]

**semblative** *adj*
*m* 'sembləˌtɪv
**sp** semblatiue[1]

**semicircle** *n*
'semɪ-ˌsɐ:ɹkəl
**sp** cemicircle[1]
> circle

**semi-circled** *adj*
'semɪ-ˌsɐ:ɹkəld
**sp** semi-circled[1]

**Semiramis** *n*
sə'mɪrəˌmɪs
**sp** Semeramis[1], Semiramis[1], Semirimis[1]

**semper** *Lat adv*
'sempeɹ
**sp** semper[1]

**Sempronius** *n*
sem'pro:nɪəs
**sp** Sempronius[4]

**senate** *adj*
=
**sp** senat[1], senate[2], senate-[house][4]

**senate / ~'s** *n*
=
**sp** senat[2], senate[26] / senates[2]

**senator / ~s** *n*
'senətəɹ / -z
**sp** senator[2], senatour[1] / senators[46], senatours[4]

**send / ~s / ~eth / ~ing / sent / ~est** *v*
= / = / = / 'sendɪn, -ɪŋ / = /senst, -tst
**sp** send[254], *Caius MV 1.4.86* send-a[1] / sends[39] / sendeth[1] / sending[7] / sent[265] / sentst[1]
**rh** end *VA 274*; mend *Oth 4.3.103* / Kent *R2 5.6.7*; tent *TC 5.9.7*; sent her contents her *TG 3.1.92*; sent me lent me *LC 197*

**sender** *n*
'sendəɹ
**sp** sender[4]

**sending** *n*
'sendɪn, -ɪŋ
**sp** sending[4]

**Seneca** *n*
'senəkə
**sp** Seneca[1]

**sen·ex / ~is** *Lat n*
'senɪs
**sp** senis[3]

**Senior** *n*
'si:nɪəɹ
**sp** Senior[2], *abbr in s.d.* Sen[1]

**seniory** *n*
*m* 'si:nɪə,rəɪ
**sp** signeurie[1]

**senis** *Lat*
> senex

**sennet** *n*
=
**sp** senet[7], senit[1], sennet[9], sennit[1]

**sennight / ~'s / ~s** *n*
'senəɪt / -s
**sp** sennight[1], seue' night[1], seuen night[1] / senights[1] / seu'nights[1]
> night

**Senoys** *n*
'senəɪz
**sp** Senoys[1]

**sense / ~s** *n*
=
**sp** sence[59], sense[52] / sences[23], senses[11]
**rh** commence *S 35.9*; defence *PP 8.6*; dispense *S 112.10*; hence *TNK 1.1.15*; recompense *LLL 1.1.57, MND 3.2.179*
> common sense

**senseless** *adj*
=
**sp** senceles[1], sencelesse[8], sence-lesse[2], senselesse[13], senslesse[3]

**sensible** *adj*
=
**sp** sencible[2], sensible[18], sen-sible[2], sensi-ble[1]
**rh** invisible *LLL 5.2.259, VA 436*
> insensible

**sensibly** *adv*
*m* 'sensɪ,bləɪ
**sp** sencibly[1], sensibly[2]

**sensual** *adj*
'sensjʊal
**sp** sensuall[2]

**sensuality** *n*
*m* ,sensjʊ'alɪ,təɪ
**sp** sensualitie[1], sensu-alitie[1]

**sent**
> send

**sentence / ~s** *n*
=
**sp** sentence[35] / sentences[7]

**sentence / ~d** *v*
=
**sp** sentence[2] / sentenc'd[6]

**sententious** *adj*
sen'tensɪəs
**sp** sententious[3]

**sentinel / ~s** *n*
*m* 'sentɪ,nel / *m* -z, -ɪnəlz
**sp** centinell[2] / centinels[5], sentinels[1]
**rh** *1* kill *VA 650*; **rh** *2* well *MND 2.2.32*

**sentr·y / ~ies** *n*
*m* 'sentrəɪ, -ə,rəɪ / -trəɪz
**sp** centerie[1], centery[1] / centuries[1]

**separate** *v*
*m* 'sepə,rɛ:t / -s / -ɪd
**sp** separate[3] / seperates[1] / seperated[2]
> in-, un-separable

**separated** *adj*
*m* 'sepə,rɛ:tɪd
**sp** seperated[2]

**separation** *n*
*m* ,sepə'rɛ:sɪən, -sɪ,ɒn
**sp** separation[3], seperati-on[1]

**Septentrion** *n*
*m* sep'tentrɪ,ɒn
**sp** Septentrion[1]

**sepulchre / ~s** *n*
*m* 'sepəl,kɐ:ɹ, -lkəɹ, se'pɤl- / *m* 'sepəl,kɐ:ɹz
**sp** sepulcher[9], sepulchre[2] / sepulchers[1]

**sepulchr·e / ~ing** *v*
se'pɤlk·əɹ / -rɪn, -rɪŋ
**sp** sepulcher[1] / sepulchring[1]

**sequel** *n*
=
**sp** sequele[2], sequell[8]

**sequence** *n*
=
**sp** sequence[4]

**sequent** *adj / n*
=
**sp** sequent[6], *Ham 5.2.54 emend of* sement[1] / se-quent[1]

**sequester / ~ing / ~ed** *v*
sɪ'kwest·əɹ / -rɪn, -ɪŋ / -əɹd
**sp** sequester[1] / sequestring[1] / sequestred[1]

**sequestered** *adj*
sɪ'kwestəɹd
**sp** sequestred[1]

**sequestration** *n*
,sɪkwes'trɛ:sɪən
**sp** sequestration[2], seque-stration[1]

**sere** *n*
si:ɹ, sɛ:ɹ
**sp** seare[1], sere[2]
**rh** everywhere *CE 4.2.19*

**seren·us / ~issima** *Lat adj*
,sere'nɪsɪma
**sp** serenissima[1]

**serge** *n*
sɐːɹʤ
**sp** serge[1]

**sergeant** *n*
ˈsɐːɹʤɪənt, -ʤənt
**sp** sergeant[4], serieant[5]

**sergeant-at-arms** *n*
ˈsɐːɹʤɪənt-ət-ˈɑːɹmz, -ʤənt-
**sp** sergeant at armes[2]

**serious** *adj*
=, ˈserɪəs
**sp** serious[22], serrious[1]

**seriously** *adv*
*m* ˈsiːrɪəsˌləɪ, ˈse-
**sp** seriouslie[1], seriously[4]

**sermon / ~s** *n*
ˈsɐːɹmən / -z
**sp** sermon[1] / sermons[1]

**sermon** *v*
ˈsɐːɹmən
**sp** sermon[1]

**serpent / ~'s / ~s** *n*
ˈsɐːɹpənt / -s
**sp** serpent[23] / serpents[8] / serpents[6]

**serpentine** *adj*
*m* ˈsɐːɹpənˌtəɪn
**sp** serpentine[1]

**serpent-like** *adj*
ˈsɐːɹpənt-ˌləɪk
**sp** serpent-like[1]

**serpigo** *n*
ˈsɤpɪgoː, ˈsɐːɹ-, səˈpəɪgoː
**sp** sapego[1], suppeago[1]

**servant** *adj*
ˈsɐːɹvənt
**sp** seruant[4]

**servant / ~'s / ~s** *n*
ˈsɐːɹvənt / -s
**sp** seruant[139], ser[u]ant[1], ser-uant[2], *abbr in s.d.* Ser [servants][1] / seruants[6] / seruants[68]
> fellow-, joint-servant

**servant / ~ed** *v*
ˈsɐːɹvəntɪd
**sp** seruanted[1]

**serv·e / ~est / ~s / ~eth / ~ing / ~ed** *v*
sɐːɹv / -st / -z / ˈsɐːɹv·əθ / -ɪn, -ɪŋ / sɐːɹvd
**sp** serue[180] / seru'st[3] / serues[37] / serueth[1] / seruing[2] / seru'd[49], serued[4], serv'd[1]
**rh** carve *LLL 4.1.59* / observed *AW 2.1.202*

**service / ~s** *n*
ˈsɐːɹvɪs / -ɪz
**sp** seriuce[1], seruice[212], ser-uice[3] / seruices[34]
> land-service

**serviceable** *adj*
*m* ˈsɐːɹvɪsəbəl, -ˌabəl
**sp** seruiceable[5]
> super-, un-serviceable

**servile** *adj*
ˈsɐːɹvəɪl
**sp** seruile[7]

**servility** *n*
səɹˈvɪlɪtəɪ
**sp** seruility[1]

**Servilius** *n*
səɹˈvɪlɪəs
**sp** Seruilius[9], Seruili-us[1], *abbr in s.d.* Seruil[1]

**serving** *adj / n*
ˈsɐːɹvɪn, -ɪŋ
**sp** seruing[2] / seruing[2]

**serving·man / ~men** *n*
ˈsɐːɹvɪnmən, -ɪŋ-
**sp** seruingman[14], seruing-man[4], seruing man[1] / seruingmen[8], seruing-men[1], seruing men[1]

**serviteur** *Fr n*
sɛɹviˈtœːɹ
**sp** seruiteur[1], seruiture[1]

**servitor / ~s** *n*
*m* ˈsɐːɹvɪˌtɔːɹ, -ɪtəɹ / -z
**sp** seruitor[1], seruitour[2], seruiture[1] / seruitors[3]

**servitude** *n*
*m* ˈsɐːɹvɪˌtjuːd, -ɪt-
**sp** seruitude[3]

**sese, sesey, sessa** *interj*
ˈsesə
**sp** sese[1], sesey[1], sessa[1]

**session / ~s** *n*
ˈsesɪən / -z
**sp** session[6] / sessions[3]

**set** *adj / n*
=
**sp** set[3] / set[8], sett[1]
> firm-, on-, sun-, un-set

**set / ~test / ~s / ~ting** *v*
= / -s, -st / -s / ˈsetɪn, -ɪŋ
set[436], sette[1] / setst[1], set'st[1], sett'st[1] / sets[20], set's[1], setts[1] / setting[815], set-ting[1]
**rh** Capulet *RJ 2.3.53*; carcanet *S 52.6*; counterfeit *S 53.7*; debt *S 83.2*; forget *MW 5.5.77*; fret *VA 619*; get *LC 136*; jet, wet *LC 39*; Juliet *RJ 5.3.301*; let *Luc 8*; violet *VA 935*; wet *Luc 1226*
> overset

**Setebos** *n*
ˈsetɪˌbɒs
**sp** Setebos[2]

**setter** *n*
ˈsetəɹ
**sp** setter[1]

**setter-up** *n*
ˈsetəɹ-ˈɤp
**sp** setter vp[2]

**setting** *adj / n*
ˈsetɪn, -ɪŋ
**sp** setting[3] / setting[4]

**setting-down** *n*
'setɪn-'dəʊn, -ɪŋ-
**sp** setting downe[1]

**setting-on** *n*
'setɪn-'ɒn, -ɪŋ-
**sp** setting on[1]

**settle / ~st / ~d** *v*
= / 'setlst / =
**sp** settle[3] / setlest[1] / setled[3], settled[2]
> unsettle

**settled** *adj*
=
**sp** setled[10]

**settling** *n*
'setlɪn, -ɪŋ
**sp** setling[1]

**seven** *adj / n*
*m* 'sɛ:n, 'sevn, -vən-
**sp** seauen[7], seuen[50], se-uen[1] / seauen[3], seuen[11], *abbr* vii.[1]
**rh** uneven *R2 2.2.121*
> twenty-seven

**sevenfold** *adj / adv*
'sɛ:nfo:ld, 'sevn-, -vən
**sp** seuen-fold[1] / seuen-fold[1]
> fold

**seventeen** *adj*
'sɛ:nti:n, 'sevn-, -vən-
**sp** seauenteene[1], seuenteene[4]

**seventh** *adj / n*
sɛ:nθ, 'sevnθ, -vən-
**sp** sea-uenth[1], seuenth[5] / seauenth[2], seuenth[1]

**seventy** *adj / n*
'sɛ:ntəɪ, 'sevn-, -vən-
**sp** seauentie[1], seuenty[1] / seuentie[1], seuenty[1]

**seventy-five** *adj*
'sɛ:ntəɪ-'fəɪv, 'sevn-, -vən-
**sp** seuenty fiue[1]

**sever / ~ed / ~ing** *v*
'sɛ:vəɹ / -z / -d
**sp** seuer[2] / seuers[1] / seuer'd[8], seuered[1]
> unsevered

**several** *adj*
'sɛ:vrɑl, -vər-
**sp** seueral[1], seuerall[75], seu'rall[1]

**several / ~s** *n*
'sɛ:vrɑlz, -vər-
**sp** seueralls[2], seuerals[1]

**severally** *adv*
*m* 'sɛ:vrɑləɪ, -ˌləɪ
**sp** seuerally[9]

**severe / ~st** *adj*
sɪ'vi:ɹ, -vɛ:ɹ / -əst
**sp** seueare[1], seuere[6] / seuerest[1]
**rh** *1* fear *VA 1000, 1155*; **rh** *2* bear *MM 3.2.250*

**severed** *adj*
'sɛ:vəɹd
**sp** seuer'd[2]

**severely** *adv*
sɪ'vi:ɹləɪ, -vɛ:-
**sp** seuerely[2]

**severing** *adj / n*
'sevərɪn, -ɪŋ
**sp** seuering[1] / seuering[1]

**severity** *n*
*m* sɪ'verɪˌtəɪ
**sp** seueritie[2], seuerity[2]
**rh** posterity *RJ 1.1.219*

**Severn / ~'s** *n*
'sevəɹn / -z
**sp** Seuern[1], Seuerne[3] / Seuernes[2]

**sew / ~ing / ~ed** *v*
so: / 'so:ɪn, -ɪŋ / so:d
**sp** sow[1], sowe[3], / sowing[2] / sow'd[2], sowed[2]
**pun** *TG 3.1.298* so

**sewer** *n*
'sju:əɹ, 'ʃu:-
**sp** sewer[1], sure[1]

**sex** *n*
=
**sp** sex[10], sexe[8]
> unsex

**sexton / ~'s** *n*
=
**sp** sexton[5], *Ham 5.1.160 emend of* sixeteene[1] / sextons[2]

**Sextus** *n*
'sekstəs
**sp** Sextus[3]

**Seymour** *n*
'sɛ:mu:ɹ, 'si:-
**sp** Seymor[1]

**Seyton** *n*
'sɛ:tən, 'si:-
**sp** Seyton[6]

**Seyward / ~'s** *n*
'sɛ:wəɹd, 'si:- / -z
**sp** Seyward[10] / Seywards[2]

**'sfoot**
> foot

**shackle / ~s** *n*
=
**sp** shackles[1]

**shackle / ~s** *v*
=
**sp** shackle[1] / shackles[1]

**shade / ~s** *n*
ʃɛ:d / -z
**sp** shade[21] / shades[2]
**rh** *1* blade *Luc 507, MND 5.1.147*; fade *S 18.11*; made *Luc 805, PP 6.2, 20.3, S 43.11, 53.3*; **rh** *2* sad *MND 4.1.95*

**shade / *PP* ~d** *v*
ʃɛ:d / 'ʃɛ:dɪd
**sp** shade[3] / shaded[1]
**rh** vaded *PP 10.3*
> overshade

**shadow / ~'s / ~s** *n*
'ʃadə, -do: / -z

**sp** shadow[60] / shadowes[2] / shadowes[23], shadows[2]

**shadow / ~ing / ~ed** *v*
'ʃadə, -doː / -wɪn, -wɪŋ / -d
**sp** shadow[1] / shadowing[1] / shadow'd[1]

**Shadow** [name] *n*
'ʃadə, -doː
**sp** shadow[7]

**shadowed** *adj*
'ʃadəd, -doːd
**sp** shadowed[1]

**shadowing** *adj*
'ʃadəwɪn, -ɪŋ, -doː-
**sp** shadowing[2]

**shadowy** *adj*
'ʃadəwəɪ, -doː-
**sp** shadowie[1], shadowy[1]

**shady** *adj*
'ʃɛːdəɪ
**sp** shadie[1], shady[1]

**Shafalus** *n*
'ʃafələs
**sp** Shafalus[2]

**shaft / ~s** *n*
ʃaft / -s
**sp** shaft[9] / shafts[1]

**shag-eared** *adj*
'ʃag-ˌiːɹd
**sp** shagge-ear'd[1]
> ear

**shag-haired** *adj*
'ʃag-ˌɛːɹd, -ˌhɛː-
**sp** shag-hayr'd[1]
> hair

**shak·e / ~est / ~es / ~ing / ~ed / ~en / shook** *v*
ʃɛːk / -st / -s / 'ʃɛːkɪn, -ɪŋ / ʃɛːkt / 'ʃɛːkən / =
**sp** shake[98] / shak'st[2] / shakes[17] / shaking[3] / shak'd[5] / shaken[3] / shook[1], shooke[26]
**rh** make *Luc 227* / quakes *VA 1047*; takes *Per 3.Chorus.44* / taken *S 116.6, 120.5*
> unshake; a-shaking; love-, wind-shaked

**shaking** *adj / n*
'ʃɛːkɪn, -ɪŋ
**sp** shaking[1] / shaking[6]
> all-shaking

**shale / ~s** *n*
ʃɛːlz
**sp** shales[1]

**shall / shalt** *v*
*str* ʃɒl, ʃɑl, *unstr* ʃəl, *Jamy H5 3.2.99ff, Fluellen H5 4.7.23, Katherine H5 5.2.247* sɑl / *str* ʃɒlt, ʃɑlt, *unstr* ʃəlt, ʃlt
**sp** shal[227], shal[be][16], shall[3397], shall [be][3], shall's [shall us][4], shal's [shall us][1], shal't [shall it][2], *Jamy* sal[1], sall[4], *Fluellen* sall[1], *Katherine* sall[1], *RJ 1.2.98 emend of* shell[1] / shall't[2], shalt[278]
**rh** *1* fall *Ham 4.5.217, Tit 5.3.134*; gall *RJ 1.5.91*; withal *LLL 5.2.141*;
**rh** *2* funeral *AC 5.2.361*
> should

**shallow / ~est** *adj*
'ʃalə, -loː / -st
**sp** shal-low[4], shallow[39], shallowe[1] / shallowest[1]

**Shallow** [name] *n*
'ʃalə, -loː
**sp** Shallow[58]

**shallow-changing** *adj*
'ʃalə-'ʧɛːnʤɪn, -ɪŋ, -loː-
**sp** shallow-changing[1]
> change

**shallow-hearted** *adj*
'ʃalə-'ɑːɹtɪd, 'hɑː- , -loː-
**sp** shallow harted[1]
> heart

**shallowly** *adv*
*m* 'ʃaləˌləɪ, -loː-
**sp** shallowly[1]

**shallow-rooted** *adj*
'ʃalə-'ruːtɪd, -loː-
**sp** shallow-rooted[1]
> root

**shallows** *n*
'ʃaləz, -loːz
**sp** shallowes[1], shallows[1]

**shambles** *n*
=
**sp** shambles[2]

**shame / ~'s / ~s** *n*
ʃɛːm / -z
**sp** shame[251], shames [shame is][1] / shames[2] / shames[14]
**rh** blame *Ham 4.5.60, 1H6 4.5.46, Luc 223, 1260, 1344, R3 5.1.28, S 129.1*; blame, defame *Luc 765*; blame, name *Luc 618*; came, dame *Luc 1629*; dame, defame *Luc 54, 1031*; fame, inflame *LC 271*; defame, name *Luc 816*; fame *1H6 4.6.44, MA 5.3.7*; game *LLL 5.2.156, 358*; name *AW 2.1.171, CE 2.1.113, 1H6 4.4.8, 2H6 2.1.193, LLL 1.1.118, 155, 2.1.186, 4.3.47, 202, Luc 890, R2 1.1.166, S 36.10, 95.1, 127.4, TC 5.3.123* [Q], *5.10.33, TG 1.2.17*; name, same *Luc 597*; same *LLL 1.1.118*; tame *R2 1.1.175*

**sham·e / ~est / ~es / ~ing / ~ed** *v*
ʃɛːm / -st / -z / 'ʃɛːmɪn, -ɪŋ / ʃɛːmd
**sp** shame[33] / sham'st[5] / shames[1] / shaming[1] / sham'd[13]

**shamed** *adj*
*m* ʃɛːmd, 'ʃɛːmɪd
**sp** sham'd[1], shamed[1]

**shamefaced** *adj*
'ʃɛːmˌfɛːst
**sp** shamefac'd[2]
> face

**shameful** *adj*
'ʃɛːmfʊl
**sp** shamefull[15]

**shamefully** *adv*
*m* 'ʃɛ:mfʊˌləɪ
**sp** shamefully$^{4}$

**shameless** *adj*
'ʃɛ:mləs
**sp** shamelesse$^{7}$

**shame-proof** *adj*
'ʃɛ:m-ˌprɤf, -ˌpru:f
**sp** shame-proofe$^{1}$
> proof

**shank / ~s** *n*
=
**sp** shanke$^{1}$ / shankes$^{1}$, shanks$^{2}$

**shape / ~s** *n*
ʃɛ:p / -s
**sp** shape$^{69}$ / shapes$^{24}$
**rh** ape *CE 2.2.206*

**shape / ~s / ~d** *v*
ʃɛ:p / -s / -t
**sp** shape$^{11}$ / shapes$^{5}$ / shap'd$^{6}$
> ill-shaped, mis-, trans-, un-shape

**shapeless** *adj*
'ʃɛ:pləs
**sp** shapelesse$^{4}$

**shaping** *adj*
'ʃɛ:pɪn, -ɪŋ
**sp** shaping$^{1}$

**shard / ~s** *n*
ʃɑ:ɹdz
**sp** shardes$^{1}$, shards$^{1}$

**shard-borne** *adj*
'ʃɑ:ɹd-ˌbɔ:ɹn
**sp** shard-borne$^{1}$
> bear

**sharded** *adj*
'ʃɑ:ɹdɪd
**sp** sharded-[beetle]$^{1}$

**share / ~s** *n*
ʃɛ:ɹ / -z
**sp** share$^{7}$ / shares$^{3}$
**rh** care *PP 14.1*

**shar·e / ~es / ~ing / ~ed** *v*
ʃɛ:ɹ / -z / 'ʃɛ:rɪn, -ɪŋ / ʃɛ:ɹd
**sp** share$^{21}$ / shares$^{1}$ / sharing$^{3}$ / shar'd$^{3}$
**rh** share it prepare it *TN 2.4.57*

**shark** *n*
ʃɑ:ɹk
**sp** sharke$^{1}$
**rh** dark *Mac 4.1.24*

**shark up / ~ed ~** *v*
'ʃɑ:ɹkt 'ɤp
**sp** shark'd vp$^{1}$

**sharp / ~er / ~est** *adj*
ʃɑ:ɹp / 'ʃɑ:ɹp·əɹ / *m* -əst, ʃɑ:ɹpst
**sp** sharp$^{4}$, sharpe$^{59}$ / sharper$^{5}$ / sharpest$^{1}$, sharp'st$^{1}$
**rh** warp *AY 2.7.189*

**sharp** *adv*
ʃɑ:ɹp
**sp** sharp$^{1}$

**sharp / ~s** *n*
ʃɑ:ɹps
**sp** sharpes$^{1}$

**sharpen / ~s** *v*
'ʃɑ:ɹpən / -z
**sp** sharpen$^{1}$ / sharpens$^{1}$

**sharper** *n*
'ʃɑ:ɹpəɹ
**sp** sharper$^{1}$

**sharpest** *n*
'ʃɑ:ɹpəst
**sp** sharpest$^{1}$

**sharp-ground** *adj*
'ʃɑ:ɹp-ˌgrəʊnd
**sp** sharpe ground$^{1}$
> ground

**sharp-looking** *adj*
'ʃɑ:ɹp-ˌlʊkɪn, -ɪŋ
**sp** [hollow-ey'd]-sharpe-looking-[wretch]$^{1}$
> look

**sharply** *adv*
'ʃɑ:ɹpləɪ
**sp** sharpely$^{4}$

**sharpness** *n*
'ʃɑ:ɹpnəs
**sp** sharpenesse$^{1}$, sharpnesse$^{1}$

**sharp-pointed** *adj*
*m* ˌʃɑ:ɹp-'pəɪntɪd
**sp** sharpe-pointed$^{1}$
> point

**sharp-provided** *adj*
'ʃɑ:ɹp-prəˌvəɪdɪd
**sp** sharp prouided$^{1}$
> provide

**sharp-quilled** *adj*
'ʃɑ:ɹp-ˌkwɪld
**sp** sharpe-quill'd$^{1}$
> quill

**sharp-toothed** *adj*
*m* ˌʃɑ:ɹp-'tʊθt, -'tu:-
**sp** sharpe-tooth'd$^{1}$
> tooth

**shatter** *v*
'ʃatəɹ
**sp** shatter$^{1}$

**shave / ~d** *v*
ʃɛ:v / -d
**sp** shaue$^{2}$, shaue't [shave it]$^{1}$ / shau'd$^{1}$

**shaven** *adj*
'ʃɛ:vən
**sp** shauen$^{1}$

**Shaw** *n*
=
**sp** Shaw$^{1}$

**she / ~s** *n*
=
**sp** shees$^{1}$

**she** *pro*
*str* ʃi:, *unstr* ʃɪ, ʃ
**sp** sh'$^{1}$, she$^{1866}$, shee$^{266}$, shee-[knight-arrant]$^{1}$, shees [she is]$^{1}$,

shee's [she is][63], shes [she is][1], she's [she is][89]
**rh** be *LLL 4.3.93, MND 1.1.227, Per 4. Chorus.19, PT 63, TG 4.2.40*; extremity *R3 1.1.64*; free *TS 1.2.231*; he *AY 5.4.121, VA 717*; me *AW 2.3.142, Ham 4.5.63, 1H6 5.5.78, Luc 1688, 1700, MND 2.1.53*; see *LLL 4.3.273*; tree *AY 3.2.10*; we *LLL 5.2.469*; what is she wise is she *TG 4.2.38*
> her

***she will*** *abbr*
*str* ʃiːl, *unstr* ʃɪl, ʃl
**sp** sheel[1], shee'l[13], sheele[4], shee'le[6], shee'll[5], she'l[5], she'le[3], she'll[4]

***she would*** *abbr*
*str* ʃiːd, ʃiːld, *unstr* ʃɪd, ʃɪld
**sp** she'ld[1], she'l'd[1]

**sheaf / *S* sheaves** *n*
=
**sp** sheafe[1]
**rh** leaves *S 12.7*

**sheaf** *v*
=
**sp** sheafe[1]

**she-angel** *n*
ˈʃiː-ˌɛːnʤəl
**sp** shee-angell[1]
> angel

**shear / shore / shorn** *v*
ˈʃiːɹ / ʃɔːɹ / ʃɔːɹn
**sp** sheere[2] / shore[2] / shorne[1]
> sheep-shearing

**shearer / ~s** *n*
ˈʃiːɹəɹz
**sp** shea-rers[1], sheerers[1]

**shearing** *n*
ˈʃiːɹɪn, -ɪŋ
**sp** shearing[1]

**shearman** *n*
ˈʃiːɹmən
**sp** sheareman[1]

**shears** *n*
ˈʃiːɹz
**sp** sheeres[4]

**sheath** *n*
=
**sp** sheath[4]

**sheath / ~ing / ~ed** *v*
= / ˈʃiːðɪn, -ɪŋ / =
**sp** sheath[9] / sheathing[1] / sheath'd[2]
> unsheath; ill-, mis-, un-sheathed

**sheathing** *n*
ˈʃiːðɪn, -ɪŋ
**sp** sheathing[1]

**sheaves**
> sheaf

**she-bear** *n*
*m* ˌʃiː-ˈbɛːɹ
**sp** she bear[1]
> bear *n*

**she-beggar** *n*
*m* ˌʃiː-ˈbegər
**sp** shee-begger[1]
> beg

**shed / ~s / ~ding** *v*
= / = / ˈʃedɪn, -ɪŋ
**sp** shead[1], shed[47], shedde[2] / sheds[2] / shedding[3]
**rh** bed, head *Luc 683*; dead *R2 1.3.57*; encountered [*4 sylls*] *1H6 4.6.19*; head *VA 665*
> blood-, new-shed; sheed, silver-shedding

**sheed / *Luc, S* ~s** *v*
=
**sp** sheeds[2]
**rh** bleeds, proceeds *Luc 1549*; deeds *S 34.13*
> shed

**sheen** *n*
=
**sp** sheene[2]
**rh** been *Ham 3.2.166*; green *MND 2.1.29*

**sheep / ~'s / ~s** *n*
=
**sp** sheep[1], sheepe[39] / sheepes[5] / sheepes[5]
**rh** keep *Tem 4.1.62, VA 685*

**sheep-biter** *n*
ˈʃiːp-ˌbəɪtəɹ
**sp** sheepe-biter[1]
> bite

**sheep-biting** *adj*
ˈʃiːp-ˌbəɪtɪn, -ɪŋ
**sp** sheepe-biting[1]

**sheepcote / ~s** *n*
ˈʃiːpkoːt / -s
**sp** sheep-coat[3] / sheeps-coates[1]

**sheep-hook** *n*
ˈʃiːp-ˌʊk, -ˌhʊk
**sp** sheepe-hooke[1]
> hook

**sheep-shearing** *adj*
ˈʃiːp-ˈʃiːrɪn, -ɪŋ
**sp** sheepe-shearing[4], sheepe-shearing-[feast][1]
> shear

**sheepskin / ~s** *n*
=
**sp** sheep-skinnes[1]
> skin

**sheep-whistling** *adj*
ˈʃiːp-ˌʍɪslɪn, -ɪŋ
**sp** sheepe-whistling[1]

**sheer** *adj*
ʃiːɹ
**sp** sheere[2]

**sheet / ~s** *n*
=
**sp** sheet[8], sheete[4], [shrowding]-sheete[1] / sheetes[8], sheets[11]
**rh** meet *Ham 5.1.93*
> winding-sheet

**Sheffield** *n*
=
**sp** Sheffeild[1]

**she-lamb** *n*
=
**sp** shee-lambe[1]
> lamb

**shelf / shelves** *n*
=
**sp** shelfe[1] / shelues[2]

**shell** *n*
=
**sp** shell[4]
> in-, mussel-, nut-, walnut-shell

**shelled** *adj*
=
**sp** sheal'd[1]

**shelter / ~s** *n*
'ʃeltəɹ / -z
**sp** shelter[9] / shelters[1]

**shelter** *v*
'ʃeltəɹ
**sp** shelter[4]
> enshelter

**sheltered** *adj*
'ʃeltəɹd
**sp** sheltred[1]

**shelving** *adj*
'ʃelvɪn, -ɪŋ
**sp** sheluing[1]

**shelvy** *adj*
'ʃelvəɪ
**sp** sheluy[1]

**she-Mercury** *n*
*m* ˌʃiː-'mɐːɹkjərəɪ
**sp** shee- Mercurie[1]

**shent** *v*
=
**sp** shent[4]
**rh** consent *Ham 3.2.405*

**shepherd** *adj*
'ʃepəɹd
**sp** shepheard[3]

**shepherd / ~'s / ~s** *n*
'ʃepəɹd / -z
**sp** sheepe-heard[1], shepheard[45], shep-heard[3], shepherd[6] / shepheards[9], shepherds[4] / shepheards[7], shepherds[1], shep-herds[1]
> herd, neighbour-shepherd

**shepherdess / ~es** *n*
*m* 'ʃepəɹˌdes, -ɹd- / -ɹdesɪz
**sp** shepheardesse[2], shepherdesse[3] / shepheard desses[1]

**sheriff / ~'s** *n*
=
**sp** sherife[12], sheriffe[2] / sheriffes[1]

**sherris** *n*
'ʃerɪs
**sp** sherris[4]

**sherris-sack** *n*
'ʃerɪs-ˌsak
**sp** sherris-sack[1]
> sack

**shew**
> show

**she-wolf** *n*
=
**sp** shee-wolfe[1]
> wolf

**shield / ~s** *n*
=
**sp** sheeld[1], shield[8] / shields[2]
**rh** *1* field *H5 3.2.8, LLL 5.2.549* [*F end line*], *Luc 61, R3 4.3.56*; **rh** *2* gild *Luc 61*

**shield / ~ed** *v*
=
**sp** sheeld[1], sheild[1], [God]sheild[1], shield[8] / sheelded[1]
**rh** *1* yielded *LC 151*; **rh** *2* builded *LC 151*

**shift / ~s** *n*
=
**sp** shift[14] / shifts[4]
**rh** *1* shrift *3H6 3.2.108*; **rh** *2* theft *Luc 920* / gifts *CE 3.2.190*; hits *AW 2.1.144* [*F*]

**shift / ~s / ~ing / ~ed** *v*
= / = / 'ʃɪftɪn, -ɪŋ / =
**sp** shift[14] / shifts[3] / shifting[2] / shifted[3]

**shifted** *adj*
=
**sp** shifted[1]

**shilling / ~s** *n*
'ʃɪlɪŋ, -ɪn, *Fluellen H5 4.8.71* 'sɪlɪŋ, -ɪn / -z
**sp** shilling[5], *abbr* s.[2], *Fluellen* silling[1] / shillings[8]
**rh** willing *H8 Prol.12*

**shin / ~s** *n*
=
**sp** shin[7], shinne[1] / shinnes[1], shins[3]
**rh** begin, in *LLL 3.1.68, 104*; within *LLL 3.1.115* / sins *MW 5.5.54*

**shine / ~est / ~s / ~eth / ~ing / shone** *v*
ʃəɪn / -st / -z / 'ʃəɪn·əθ / -ɪn, -ɪŋ / =
**sp** shine[40] / shin'st[1] / shines[27] / shineth[1] / shining[3] / shone[5]
**rh** divine *LLL 4.3.244, VA.728*; eyne *LLL 5.2.205*; mine *LLL 4.3.67, 89, PP 3.10, PT 33, S 33.9, TN 4.3.34*; repine *VA 488*; thine *S 135.8* / declines *S 18.5*
> moon-, over-, sun-shine

**shining** *adj*
'ʃəɪnɪn, -ɪŋ
**sp** shining[7]
> bright-, clear-, out-shining

**shiny** *adj*
'ʃəɪnəɪ
**sp** shiny[1]

**ship / ~s** *n*
=
**sp** ship[40], shippe[4] / shippes[7], ships[16]
**rh** split *Per 2.Chorus.31* / lips *LLL 2.1.205*

**ship / ~ped** *v*
=

**sp** ship[1], shippe[1] / ship'd[5], shipped[1], shipt[5]

**shipboard** *n*
'ʃɪpˌbɔ:ɹd
**sp** ship-boord[1], shipbord[1]

**ship-boy / ~'s / -s** *n*
'ʃɪp-ˌbəɪ / -z
**sp** ship-boyes[2] / ship-boyes[1]
> boy

**ship·man / ~man's / ~men** *n*
=
**sp** ship-mans[1] / shipmen[1]

**shipmaster** *n*
'ʃɪpˌmastəɹ
**sp** ship-master[1]
> master

**shipping** *n*
'ʃɪpɪn, -ɪŋ
**sp** shipping[5]

**ship-tire** *n*
'ʃɪp-ˌtəɪɹ
**sp** ship-tyre[1]
> tire

**shipwreck** *n*
'ʃɪprak
**sp** shipwracke[2]
> wrack

**shipwreck / ~ed** *v*
'ʃɪprakt
**sp** shipwrack'd[1]

**shipwrecked** *adj*
'ʃɪprakt
**sp** ship-wrackt[1]

**shipwrecking** *adj*
'ʃɪprakɪn, -ɪŋ
**sp** shipwracking[1]

**shipwright / ~s** *n*
'ʃɪprəɪt / -s
**sp** shipwright[1], ship-wright[1] / ship-wrights[1]

**shire** *n*
ʃəɪɹ
**sp** shire[1]

**Shirley** *n*
'ʃɐ:ɹləɪ
**sp** Sherly[1]

**shirt / ~s** *n*
ʃɐ:ɹt / -s
**sp** shirt[15] / shirts[6]

**shive** *n*
ʃəɪv
**sp** shiue[1]

**shiver / ~s** *n*
'ʃɪvəɹ / -z
**sp** shiuers[2]

**shiver / ~ed** *v*
'ʃɪvəɹ / -d
**sp** shiuer[1] / shiuer'd[1]

**shivering** *adj*
'ʃɪvrɪn, -ɪŋ, -vər-
**sp** shiuering[2]

**shoal / ~s** *n*
ʃo:l / -z
**sp** *Mac 1.7.6 emend of* schoole[1] / shoales[1]

**shock / ~s** *n*
=
**sp** shock[1], shocke[3] / shockes[1], shocks[1]
**rh** locks, rocks *MND 1.2.28*

**shock** *v*
=
**sp** shocke[1]

**shoe / ~s / shoon** *n*
= / ʃo:n, ʃu:n
**sp** shoo[4], shooe[8] / shoes[1], shooes[14] / shooen[1], shoone[1]
**rh** one *Ham 4.5.26*
> dancing-shoe, overshoes

**shoe** *v*
=
**sp** shoo[2]

**shoeing** *n*
'ʃu:ɪn, -ɪŋ
**sp** shooing[1]

**shoeing-horn** *n*
'ʃu:ɪn-ˌɔ:ɹn, -ɪŋ, -ˌh-
**sp** shooing-horne[1]
> horn

**shoemaker** *n*
'ʃu:ˌmɛ:kəɹ
**sp** shoo-maker[1]
> make

**shoe-tie / Shoe-tie** [name] *n*
'ʃu:-ˌtəɪ
**sp** shooe-tye[1] / Shootie[1]
> tie

**shog** *v*
=
**sp** shogg[1], shogge[1]

**shone**
> shine

**shook**
> shake

**shoon**
> shoe

**shoot / ~s** *n*
=
**sp** shoot[1], shoote[6] / shoots[1]
**rh** do't *LLL 4.1.26*

**shoot / ~s / ~ing / shot** *v*
= / = / 'ʃu:tɪn, -ɪŋ / =
**sp** shoot[11], shoote[11] / shootes[2], shoots[3] / shooting[1] / shot[24]
> upshoot; grief-, over-shot

**shooter** *n*
'ʃu:təɹ
**sp** shooter[3]
**pun** *LLL 4.1.109* suitor

**shooting** *adj / n*
'ʃu:tɪn, -ɪŋ
**sp** shooting[2] / shooting[1]
**rh** *n* a-hooting *LLL 4.2.58*

**shop / ~s** *n*
=
**sp** shop[12], shoppe[1] / shoppes[1], shops[2]

**shore** *n*
ʃɔːɹ / -z
**sp** shore[47], [vast]-shore-[washet][1] / shoares[1], shores[16]
**rh** before *S 60.1*; gore *MND 5.1.332*; more *Luc 1114, MA 2.3.62, VA 817*; store *S 64.6*

**shore** *v*
ʃɔːɹ
**sp** shoare[1]

**shore, shorn** *v*
> shear

**Shore / ~'s** [name] *n*
ʃɔːɹ / -z
**sp** Shore[5] / Shores[2]

**short / ~er** *adj*
ʃɔːɹt / ˈʃɔːɹtəɹ
**sp** short[65] / shorter[4]
**rh** *1* for't *Per 4.4.1*; sport *1H4 1.3.295, LLL 1.1.178, VA 23, 842*; **rh** *2* heart *AY 3.5.138, LLL 5.2.56, R2 5.1.91*; part *LLL 5.2.56, R2 2.1.223*; **rh** *3* cold *PP 12.5*

**short / ~er** *adv*
ʃɔːɹt / ˈʃɔːɹtəɹ
**sp** short[19] / shorter[2]
**rh** report *S 83.7*; resort, sport *Luc 991* / departure *KL 1.5.49*

**short** *n / v*
ʃɔːɹt
**sp** short[3] / short[1]

**short-armed** *adj*
ˈʃɔːɹt-ˌɑːɹmd
**sp** short-arm'd[1]
> arm

**Shortcake** [name] *n*
ˈʃɔːɹtkɛːk
**sp** Short-cake[1]

**shorten / ~s / ~ed** *v*
ˈʃɔːɹtən / -z / -d
**sp** shorten[5] / shortens[3] / shortned[3]

**shortening** *n*
ˈʃɔːɹtnɪn, -ɪŋ
**sp** shortning[1]

**shortest** *n*
ʃɔːɹtst
**sp** short'st[1]

**short-grassed** *adj*
ˈʃɔːɹt-ˌgrast
**sp** short gras'd[1]
> grass

**short-legged** *adj*
ˈʃɔːɹt-ˌlegd
**sp** short-legg'd[1]
> leg

**short-lived** *adj*
ˈʃɔːɹt-ˌlɪvd
**sp** short liu'd[2]
> live

**shortly** *adv*
ˈʃɔːɹtləɪ
**sp** shortlie[2], shortly[43], short-ly[1]

**shortness** *n*
ˈʃɔːɹtnəs
**sp** shortnesse[4]

**short-winded** *adj*
*m* ˌʃɔːɹt-ˈwəɪndɪd
**sp** short-winded[1], shortwinded[1]
> wind

**shot** *n*
=
**sp** shot[20]
**rh** begot *KJ 1.1.174*
> cannon-shot

**shot-free** *adj*
=
**sp** shot-free[1]
> free

**shotten** *adj*
=
**sp** shotten[1]
> nook-, shoulder-shotten

**shough / ~s** *n*
ʃɒks
**sp** showghes[1]

**should / ~est** *v*
*str* =, ʃʊld, *unstr* ʃd, *Edgar's assumed dialect KL 4.6.238* ʧʊd [I should] / -st
**sp** shold[22], should[1495], *Edgar* 'chud[1] / shouldest[1], shold'st[1], shouldst[20], should'st[48]
**rh** *1* could *Tim 1.2.158*; would *LLL 1.1.142*; **rh** *2* cool'd *VA 385*
> shall

**shoulder / ~s** *n*
ˈʃoːldəɹ / -z
**sp** shoulder[22], shoul-der[2] / shoulders[33]
**rh** bolder *LLL 5.2.107*

**shoulder / ~ed** *v*
ˈʃoːldəɹ / -d
**sp** shouldred[1]

**shoulder-blade** *n*
ˈʃoːldəɹ-ˌblɛːd
**sp** shoulder-blade[1]

**shoulder-bone** *n*
ˈʃoːldəɹ-ˌboːn
**sp** shoulder-bone[1]

**shoulder-clapper** *n*
ˈʃoːldəɹ-ˌklapəɹ
**sp** shoulder-clapper[1]

**shouldering** *n*
ˈʃoːldrɪn, -ɪŋ, -dər-
**sp** shouldering[1]

**shoulder-shotten** *adj*
ˈʃoːldəɹ-ˌʃɒtən
**sp** shoulder-shotten[1]
> shot

**shout / ~s** *n*
ʃəʊt / -s
**sp** shout[14], showt[4] / shouts[3], showts[7]
**rh** doubt *MV 3.2.143*

**shout / ~ing / ~ed** *v*
ʃəʊt / ˈʃəʊt·ɪn, -ɪŋ / -ɪd
**sp** shout[4], showt[1] / shooting[1] / shouted[1], showted[1]
> a-shouting, unshout

**shouting** *adj / n*
ˈʃəʊtɪn, -ɪŋ
**sp** shouting[1], showting[2] / showting[1]

**shove / ~d** *v*
ʃɤv / -d
**sp** shoue[1] / shou'd[2]

**shove-groat** *n*
ˈʃɤv-ˌgroːt
**sp** shoue-groat[1]
> groat

**shovel** *n*
ˈʃɤvəl
**sp** shouell[1]
> fire-shovel

**shovel / ~s** *v*
ˈʃɤvəlz
**sp** shouels-[in]

**shovel-board / ~s** *n*
ˈʃɤvəl-ˌbɔːɹdz
**sp** sho-uelboords[1]

**show / ~s** *n*
ʃoː / -z
**sp** shew[45], shewe[1], show[18] / shewes[11], showes[6]
**rh** grow *MND 3.2.139, S 69.13, 93.14*; grow, owe *Luc 296*; know *AY 3.2.136, H8 Prol.18, LLL 5.2.320, Mac 1.7.81, MND 5.1.116, 126, PP 18.38*; owe *S 70.13*; owe, so *Luc 81*; so *LLL 5.2.536, MND 3.2.151, S 43.6, 54.9*; so, woe *Luc 1507, 1810*; woe *Ham 1.2.85, Per 4.4.23, R2 3.3.71* / foes, woes *TNK 1.5.7*; grows *S 15.3*; grows, rose *LLL 1.1.106*; knows *AW 2.1.150*; suppose *Per 5.2.6* [*Chorus*]; woes *LC 308*
> dumb-, fore-, urchin-show

**show / ~est / ~s / ~ing / ~ed / ~edest / ~n** *v*
ʃoː / -st / -z / ˈʃoːɪn, -ɪŋ / *m* ʃoːd, ˈʃoːɪd / ˈʃoːdst / ʃoːn
**sp** shew[281], shew's [show us][1], shew't [show it][1], shoe[1], show[45], showe[1] / shew'st[3], showest[1] / shewes[68], shewes-[off][1], shooes[1], showes[5] / shewing[7], showing[1] / shewd[1], shew'd[47], shewed[7], show'd[2] / shew'dst[1] / shewn[1], shewne[15], showne[11]
**rh** *1* crow *RJ 1.2.85*; foe, know *Luc 474*; grow *S 83.6*; know *CE 3.1.12, Cym 5.1.30, MM 5.1.535, R2 1.3.250, 5.3.49, S 53.10, 77.5*; low, throw *Mac 4.1.67*; no *AY 3.2.124*; owe, so *Luc 81*; slow *S 94.2*; so *MND 5.1.159, S 105.2*; woe *LLL 4.3.35*; **show it** bestow it *S 26.6*; **show not** know not *CE 3.2.31*; **show their love** know their love *TG 1.2.31*; **rh** *2* shrew *TS 4.1.197* / goest, knowest, owest, throwest, trowest *KL 1.4.117*; grow'st *S 126.3* / crows *RJ 1.5.49*; foes *S 40.13*; goes, woes *Luc 1748*; owes *Tim 3.4.23* / blown *LLL 5.2.296*; flown *AW 2.1.138*; known *LLL 1.2.97, PP 20.17, RJ 1.1.188, 1.2.99, S 69.8, 121.12*; known, own *MND 3.2.460*
> seld-, un-shown

**shower / ~s** *n*
ʃoːɹ / -z
**sp** shower[3], showre[6] / showers[4], showres[9]
**rh** flowers *Ham 4.5.40, H8 3.1.7, Tem 4.1.79, VA 66*; hours *S 124.12*

**shower / ~ing / ~ed** *v*
ʃoːɹ / ˈʃoːrɪn, -ɪŋ / ʃoːɹd
**sp** showre[1] / showring[2] / showr'd[1]

**showing** *n*
ˈʃoːɪn, -ɪŋ
**sp** shewing[2]

**showplace** *n*
ˈʃoː-ˌplɛːs
**sp** shew place[1]
> place

**shred / ~s** *n*
=
**sp** shreds[2]

**shrew / ~s** *n*
ʃroː / -z
**sp** shrew[11], shrow[2] / shrewes[1], shrowes[1]
**rh** show *TS 4.1.196*; so *TS 5.2.187*; woe *TS 5.2.28* / O's *LLL 5.2.46*
> beshrew

**shrewd** *adj*
ʃroːd
**sp** shrew'd[9], shrewd[14], shrow'd[3]

**shrewdly** *adv*
ˈʃroːdləɪ
**sp** shrewdly[8], shrowdly[2]

**shrewdness** *n*
ˈʃroːdnəs
**sp** shrodenesse[1]

**shrewish** *adj*
ˈʃroːɪʃ
**sp** shrewish[1]

**shrewishly** *adv*
ˈʃroːɪʃləɪ
**sp** shrewishly[1]

**shrewishness** *n*
*m* ˈʃroːɪʃˌnes
**sp** shrewishnesse[1]

**Shrewsbury** *n*
*m* ˈʃroːzbəˌrəɪ, -bərəɪ, -brəɪ
**sp** Shrewsburie[4], Shrewsbury[14]

**shriek** *n*
=
**sp** shreeke[1] / shriekes[1], shrieks[1], shrikes[1]
> night-shriek

**shriek / ~ing / ~ed** *v*
= / ˈʃriːkɪn, -ɪŋ / =
**sp** shrieke[2], shrike[3] / shreeking[1] / shriek'd[3], shrekt[1]

**shrieking** *adj*
ˈʃriːkɪn, -ɪŋ
**sp** shreeking[1]
> shrill-shrieking

**shrieve / ~'s** *n*
=
**sp** shrieues[1]

**shrift** *n*
=
**sp** shrift[8]
**rh** drift *RJ 2.3.52*; shift *3H6 3.2.107*

**shrill / ~er** *adj*
= / 'ʃrɪləɹ
**sp** shril[1], shrill[4] / shriller[1]

**shrill / ~s** *v*
=
**sp** shrils[1]

**shrill-gorged** *adj*
'ʃrɪl-ˌgɔːɹʤd
**sp** shrill-gorg'd[1]
> gorge

**shrill-shrieking** *adj*
*m* ˌʃrɪl-'ʃriːkɪn, -ɪŋ
**sp** shrill-shriking[1]
> shriek

**shrill-sounding** *adj*
*m* ˌʃrɪl-'səʊndɪn, -ɪŋ
**sp** shrill-sounding[1]
> sound

**shrill-tongued** *adj*
*m* 'ʃrɪl-ˌtɒŋd, ˌʃrɪl-'tɒŋd, -ˌtʊ-
**sp** shrill-tongu'd[1], shrill tongu'd[1]
> tongue

**shrill-voiced** *adj*
'ʃrɪl-ˌvəɪst
**sp** shrill-voic'd[1]
> voice

**shrilly** *adv*
'ʃrɪləɪ
shrilly[2]

**shrimp** *n*
=
**sp** shrimpe[2]
**rh** imp *LLL 5.2.586*

**shrine** *n*
ʃrəɪn
**sp** shrine[6]
**rh** divine, thine *Luc 194*
> enshrine

**shrink / ~s / ~ing / shrunk** *v*
= / = / 'ʃrɪŋkɪn, -ɪŋ / ʃrɤŋk
**sp** shrinke[11] / shrinkes[3] / shrinking[2] / shrunke[3]
**rh** think *R2 2.2.32*
> custom-shrunk

**shrinking** *adj*
'ʃrɪŋkɪn, -ɪŋ
**sp** shrinking[1]
> unshrinking

**shrive / ~s / ~d** *v*
ʃrəɪv / -z / -d
**sp** shriue[2] / shriues[1] / shriu'd[1]

**shriver** *n*
'ʃrəɪvəɹ
**sp** shriuer[1]

**shriving** *adj*
'ʃrəɪvɪn, -ɪŋ
**sp** shriuing[2]

**shroud / ~s** *n*
ʃrəʊd / -z
**sp** shrowd[5], shrow'd[3] / shrowdes[1], shrowds[2]
**rh** allowed *LLL 5.2.479*; loud *MND 5.1.368*

**shroud / ~ed** *v*
ʃrəʊd / 'ʃrəʊdɪd
**sp** shrowd[3], shrow'd[1] / shrowded[3]

**shrouding** *adj*
'ʃrəʊdɪn, -ɪŋ
**sp** showding-[sheete][1]

**Shrovetide** *n*
'ʃroːvˌtəɪd
**sp** Shrouetide[1]

**Shrove Tuesday** *n phrase*
'ʃroːv 'tjuːzdɛː
**sp** Shroue-Tuesday[1]
> Tuesday

**shrub / ~s** *n*
ʃrɤb / -z
**sp** shrub[2] / shrubs[2]
> unshrubbed

**shrug / ~s** *n*
ʃrɤg / -z
**sp** shrug[2] / shrugs[1]

**shrug / ~gest** *v*
ʃrɤg / -st
**sp** shrug[1] / shrug'st[1]

**shrunk** *adj*
ʃrɤŋk
**sp** shrunke[4]

**shrunk** *v*
> shrink

**shudder** *VA* **/ ~s** *n*
'ʃɤdəɹ / -z
**sp** shudder[1] / shudders[1]
**rh** adder *VA 880*

**shuddering** *adj*
'ʃɤdrɪn, -ɪŋ
**sp** shuddring[1]

**shuffle / ~d** *v*
'ʃɤfəl / -d
**sp** shuffle[2], shufflle[1] / shuffel'd[2]

**shuffling** *adj / n*
'ʃɤflɪn, -ɪŋ
**sp** shuffling[1] / *sp* shuffling[2]

**shun / ~s / ~ning / ~ned** *v*
ʃɤn / -z / 'ʃɤnɪn, -ɪŋ / ʃɤnd
**sp** shun[14], shunne[3] / shunnes[1], shuns[3] / shunning[1] / shund[1], shun'd[4], shunn'd[3]
**rh** nun *LC 234*; sun *AY 2.5.35*; shun you on you *Tem 4.1.116*
> unshunnable, unshunned

**shunless** *adj*
'ʃɤnləs
**sp** shunlesse[1]

**shunning** *n*
'ʃɤnɪn, -ɪŋ
**sp** shunning[1]

**shut / ~s** *v*
ʃɤt / -s
**sp** shut[56] / shuts[4]

**shuttle** *n*
'ʃɤtl
**sp** shuttle[1]

**shy** *adj*
ʃəɪ
**sp** shie[2]

**Shylock / ~'s** *n*
'ʃəɪlɒk/ -s
**sp** Shylock[2], Shylocke[17], Shylok[1] / Shylockes[1]

**si** *Fr conj / Ital conj*
si
**sp** si[1] / si[2]

**sibyl / ~s** *n*
=
**sp** sybill[1]/ sibyls[1]

**Sibyl / ~'s** *n*
=
**sp** Sibell[1] / Sibels[1]

**Sibylla** *n*
sɪ'bɪlə
**sp** Sibilla[1]

**Sicil / ~s** *n*
'sɪsɪl / -z
**sp** Sicill[1] / Sicils[2]

**Sicilia** *n*
sɪ'sɪlɪə
**sp** Sicilia[9], Sicillia[5]

**Sicilian** *adj*
sɪ'sɪlɪən
**sp** Sicilian[1]

**Sicilius / ~'** *n*
sɪ'sɪlɪəs
**sp** Sicillius[2] / Sicilius[1]

**Sicily** *n*
*m* 'sɪsləɪ, 'sɪsɪ,ləɪ
**sp** Cicelie[3], Cicilie[1], Sicily[1]

**Sicinius** *n*
sɪ'sɪnɪəs
**sp** Scicinius[4], Sicinius[12], *abbr in s.d.* Scic.[1]

**sick** *adj / n*
=
**sp** sick[12], sick[mans][1], sicke[141] / sick[1], sicke[1]
**rh** *adj* prick, thick *Luc 779*; trick *LLL 5.2.417*
> brain-, fancy-, heart-, love-, sea-, thought-sick

**sick / ~ed** *v*
=
**sp** sick'd[1]

**sicken / ~s / ~ed** *v*
=
**sp** sicken[6] / sickens[2] / sicken'd[1]

**sicker** *n*
'sɪkəɹ
**sp** sicker[1]

**sick-fallen** *adj*
'sɪk-,fɑ:ln
**sp** sicke-falne[1]
> fall

**sickle / ~s** *n*
'sɪkəlz
**sp** sickles[1]

**sickle·man / ~men** *n*
=
**sp** sicklemen[1]

**sickliness** *n*
*m* 'sɪkləɪ,nes
**sp** sicklinesse[1]

**sickly** *adj / adv*
'sɪkləɪ
**sp** sickely[3], sick-ly[1], sickly[10] / sickly[3]

**sickl·y over / ~ied ~** *v*
'sɪkləɪd 'o:ɹ
**sp** sicklied o're[1]

**sickness** *n*
=
**sp** sickenesse[4] , sicknes[1], sicknesse[46], [greene]-sicknesse[2]

**Sicyon** *n*
'sɪsɪən
**sp** Scicion[3]

**side / ~s** *n*
səɪd / -z
**sp** side[157], [north]-side[1], [seamy]-side[1] / sides[43]
**rh** applied, divide *LC 65*; bide *MND 3.2.185*; died *Luc 381*; divide *1H6 4.5.48, Luc 1739*; eyed *MND 3.2.39*; guide *VA 180*; hide *MM 3.2.260, S 50.12*; pride *1H6 4.6.56, Luc 1807, PP 2.6, R2 3.2.80, R3 5.3.176, S 144.6, 151.12*; qualified, satisfied *Luc 425*; ride *R2 1.3.252*
> a-, back-, be-, broad-, in-, out-, sea-, water-side; both-sides

**side / ~d** *v*
'səɪdɪd
**sp** sided[1]

**side-piercing** *adj*
'səɪd-,pɛ:ɹsɪn, -ɪŋ
**sp** side-piercing[1]
> piercing

**side-stitch / ~es** *n*
'səɪd-,stɪʧɪz
**sp** side-stitches[1]

**siege / ~s** *n*
=
**sp** seige[2], siedge[4], siege[23] / sieges[1]
> besiege

**Siena / ~'s** *n*
si:'enəz
**sp** Syenna's[1]

**sieve** *n*
=
**sp** siue[2], syue[1]

**sift / ~ed** *v*
=
**sp** sift[3] / sifted[1]
> unsifted

**Sigeia** *adj*
sɪ'ʤɛ:ə
**sp** sigeria[3]

**sigh / ~s** *n*
səɪ / -z
**sp** sigh[13], sighe[3] / sighes[43], sighs[1]
**rh** eyes *RJ 1.1.190, TG 2.4.130*

**sigh / ~est / ~s / ~ing / ~ed** *v*
səɪ / -st / -z / ˈsəɪɪn, -ɪŋ / səɪd
**sp** sigh[30], sighe[4] / sighest[1] / sighes[3] / sighing[6] / sigh'd[8], sighed[1]

**sighing** *adj / n*
ˈsəɪɪn, -ɪŋ
**sp** sighing[1] / sighing[2]

**sight / ~s** *n*
səɪt / -s
**sp** sight[185], [earnest-gaping]-sight[1] / sights[19]
**rh** aright *S 148.2*; bright, light *Luc 373, MND 5.1.267*; delight *Luc 384, MND 3.2.456, Per 1.4.28, S 47.13, 75.9*; fight, white *Luc 1404*; goodnight *Mac 5.1.74*; height *R2 1.1.188*; light *Luc 104, S 7.3, 38.6*; midnight *MND 1.1.222*; might *AY 3.5.82, MND 3.2.369, Per 5.Chorus.21, S 123.4, 139.5, 150.3*; night *CE 3.2.57, PP 14.22, RJ 1.5.52, S 15.10, 27.9, 30.8, 61.4, 63.7, 113.9, VA 124, 822*; quite *MND 3.2.89*; right *PT 35, S 46.2, 117.8*; sprite *VA 183*; tonight *MND 2.1.19*; white *VA 1166* / lights *Luc 462*
> eye-, over-sight

**sighted** *adj*
ˈsəɪtɪd
**sp** sighted[1]
> eagle-, high-sighted

**sight-hole / ~s** *n*
ˈsəɪt-ˌoːlz, -ˌh-
**sp** sight-holes[1]

**sightless** *adj*
ˈsəɪtləs
**sp** sightlesse[3]

**sightly** *adv*
ˈsəɪtləɪ
**sp** sightly[1]
> unsightly

**sign / ~s** *n*
səɪn / -z
**sp** signe[46] / signes[31]

**sign / ~s / ~ed** *v*
səɪn / -z / -d
**sp** signe[4] / signes[1] / sign'd[3]

**signal** *n*
ˈsɪgnɑl
**sp** signall[10]

**signet** *n*
=
**sp** signet[3]

**significant / ~s** *n*
=
**sp** significant[1] / significants[1]

**signif·y / ~ies / ~ying / ~ied** *v*
*m* ˈsɪgnɪfəɪ, -ˌfəɪ / -z / -ɪn, -ɪŋ / -d
**sp** signifie[24], sig-nifie[1] / signifies[4] / signifying[1] / signified[2], signify'd[1]

**signor / ~s** *Sp, Ital n*
siːnˈjɔːɹ / -z
**sp** seigneur[3], signeor[1], signeur[5], signior[114], sig-nior[6], signi-or[2], signiour[3], signor[2] / signiors[3]
> seigneur

**signor·y / ~ies** *n*
*m* ˈsɪnjəˌrəɪ / ˈsɪnjərəɪz, -ˌrəɪz
**sp** signorie[1] / seignories[3], signories[1]

**signum** *Lat n*
ˈsɪgnʊm
**sp** signum[1]

**silence / Silence** [name] *n*
ˈsəɪləns
**sp** silence[49], si-lence[2] / Silence[14]

**silenc·e / ~ing / ~d** *v*
ˈsəɪləns / -ɪn, -ɪŋ / -t
**sp** silence[21] / silencing[1] / silenc'd[4], silenced[1]

**silent** *adj*
ˈsəɪlənt
**sp** silent[34]

**silently** *adv*
ˈsəɪləntləɪ
**sp** silently[1]
**rh** *1* chastity *MND 3.1.196*; **rh** *2* eye *MND 3.1.196*

**Silicia** *n*
sɪˈlɪsɪə
**sp** Silicia[1]

**Silius** *n*
ˈsɪlɪəs
**sp** Sillius[3]

**silk** *adj*
=
**sp** silk[2], silke[1]

**silk / ~s** *n*
=
**sp** silke[13] / silkes[4]
**rh** milk *MND 5.1.333, Per 4.Chorus.21*
> sleave-silk

**silken** *adj*
=
**sp** silken[14], [cockred]-silken[1]

**silken-coated** *adj*
ˈsɪlkən-ˌkoːtɪd
**sp** silken-coated[1]

**silkman** *n*
=
**sp** silkman[1]

**silly** *adj*
ˈsɪləɪ / -əst
**sp** sillie[2], silly[14] / silliest[1]

**silly-ducking** *adj*
ˈsɪləɪ-ˈdɤkɪn, -ɪŋ
**sp** silly-ducking[1]
> duck

**sillyness** *n*
ˈsɪləɪnəs
**sp** sillynesse[1]

**silver** *adj / n*
'sɪlvəɹ
**sp** siluer[36] / siluer[25]
> quicksilver

**silver / ~ed** *v*
'sɪlvəɹd
**sp** siluer'd[1]

**silvered** *adj*
'sɪlvəɹd
**sp** siluer'd[2]

**silverly** *adv*
*m* 'sɪlvəɹ,ləɪ
**sp** siluerly[1]

**silver-shedding** *adj*
'sɪlvəɹ-'ʃedɪn, -ɪŋ
**sp** siluer-shedding[1]
> shed

**silver-sweet** *adj*
'sɪlvəɹ-'swi:t
**sp** siluer sweet[1]
> sweet

**silver-white** *adj*
'sɪlvəɹ-'ʍəɪt
**sp** siluer white[1]
**rh** delight *LLL 5.2.884*
> white

**Silvia / ~'s** *n*
=
**sp** Siluia[61], Siluia's [Silvia is][1], *abbr in s.d.* Sil.[1] / Siluias[1], Siluia's[2]

**Silvius** *n*
'sɪlvɪəs
**sp** Siluius[13], *abbr in s.d.* Sil.[1]

**simile / ~s** *n*
*m* 'sɪmɪləɪ / -ɪ,ləɪz
**sp** simile[1] / similes[1], similies[1]

**Simois** *Lat n*
'sɪmo:i:s
**sp** Simois[2], Si-mois[1]

**Simon** *n*
'səɪmən
**sp** Simon[2], Symon[1]

**Simonides** *Per* *n*
sɪ'mɒnɪ,di:z
**sp** Simonides[3], Symonides[7], Simonydes[1]
**rh** these *Per 3.Chorus.23*

**simony** *n*
'sɪmənəɪ
**sp** symonie[1]

**Simpcox** [name] *n*
'sɪmkɒks, -mpk-
**sp** Simpcoxe[1]

**simpering** *adj / n*
'sɪmprɪn, -ɪŋ
**sp** simpring[1] / simpring[1]

**simple / ~r** *adj*
= / 'sɪmpləɹ
**sp** simple[60], sim-ple[2] / simpler[2]
**rh** dimple *VA 244*

**simple / ~s** *n*
=
**sp** simples[5]

**Simple** [name] *n*
=
**sp** Simple[9]

**simple-answered** *adj*
'sɪmpəl-'ansəɹd
**sp** simple answer'd[1]

**simpleness** *n*
=
**sp** simplenesse[5]

**simplicity** *adj / n*
*m* sɪm'plɪsɪtəɪ, -,təɪ
**sp** simplicity[1] / simplicitie[9], simplicity[3]
**rh** *1* authority *S 66.11*; capacity *MND 5.1.104*; hypocrisy *LLL 5.2.52*; rarity *PT 54*; society *LLL 4.3.52*; **rh** *2* apply *LLL 5.2.78*; lie *PT 54*

**simply** *adv*
'sɪmpləɪ
**sp** simply[11]

**simular** *adj*
*m* 'sɪmləɹ, -mjəl-
**sp** simular[1]

**simular** *n*
'sɪmjə,lɐ:ɹ
**sp** simular[1]

**simulation** *n*
,sɪmjə'lɛ:sɪən
**sp** simulation[1]

**sin / ~'s / ~s** *n*
=
**sp** sin[37], sinne[92] sinn's [sin is][1] / sinnes[3] / sinnes[24], sins[7]
**rh** *1* begin *Luc 343, Per Prol.30, R2 1.1.187, S 114.13*; in *LLL 4.3.175, MM 4.2.105, R2 5.3.81, R3 4.2.63*; kin *KJ 1.1.275, RJ 1.5.59*; win *AW 4.2.75*; **rh** *2* been *Luc 209*; **rh** *3* him *Per 2. Chorus.23* / shins *MW 5.5.53*; wins *TNK 4.2.156*

**sin / ~s / ~ning / ~ned** *v*
= / = / 'sɪnɪn, -ɪŋ / =
**sp** sin[3], sinne[10] / sins[1] / sinning[1] / sin'd[1], sinn'd[4]

**sin-absolver** *n*
'sɪn-əb'zɒlvəɹ
**sp** sin-absoluer[1]
> absolve

**since** *adv / conj*
=
**sp** since[65] / since[347]

**sincere** *adj*
sɪn'si:ɹ
**sp** sincere[4]

**sincerely** *adv*
sɪn'si:ɹləɪ
**sp** sincerely[3]

**sincerity** *n*
*m* sɪn'serɪtəɪ, -,təɪ
**sp** sinceritie[3], sincerity[3]

**sin-conceiving** *adj*
'sɪn-kən'si:vɪn, -ɪŋ
**sp** sinne-conceiuing[1]

**sine** *Lat prep*
'si:ne
**sp** fine[1]

**Sinell / ~'s** *n*
'sɪnəlz
**sp** Sinells[1]

**sinew / ~s** *n*
=
**sp** sinew[2] / sinewes[19], sinews[1], sinnewes[2]

**sinew / ~ed** *v*
=
**sp** sinow[1] / sinew'd[1]
> in-, treble-, un-, well-sinewed

**sinewy** *adj*
'sɪnju:əɪ
**sp** si-newie[1], sinnowie[1], sinnowy[1], synowie[1]

**sinful** *adj*
=
**sp** sinfull[7], sinnefull[1]

**sinfully** *adv*
'sɪnfləɪ, -fʊl-
**sp** sinfully[2]

**sing / ~est / ~s / ~eth / ~ing / *S* sang / sung** *v*
= / 'sɪŋst / = / = / 'sɪŋgɪn, -ɪŋ / = / sɤŋ
**sp** sing[132] / singst[1], sing'st[1] / singes[1], sings[39] / singeth[1] / singing[11], sin-ging[1] / sang[1] / sung[16]
**rh** bring *Per Prol.13, S 39.1, TNK 1.1.22*; bring, thing *TG 4.2.48*; ding, spring *AY 5.3.19, 25, 31, 37*; dwelling, excelling *TG 4.2.48*; king *2H4 5.5.110, R2 2.1.263, 3.3.183, WT 4.3.6*; ordering *S 8.12*; prefiguring *S 106.12*; questioning *AY 5.4.134*; ring *Mac 4.1.41, MW 5.5.65*; sorrowing *PP 20.25*; spring *H8 3.1.5, LLL 1.1.103, Luc 871, PP 20.5, S 102.7*; spring, thing *Luc 333*; sting *TC 5.10.42*; ushering *LLL 5.2.327*; wing *S 78.5*; sing it ring it *TS 1.2.17* / springs *Cym 2.3.19*; wings *VA 305* / hang *S 73.4* / **rh** *1* along *VA 1095*; **rh** *2* among *KL 1.4.172*; **rh** *3* come *Per Prol.1*

**sing·e / ~ing / ~ed** *v*
= / 'sɪnʤɪn, -ɪŋ / =
**sp** sindge[2] / sindging[1] / sindg'd[1], sing'd[1]

**singer** *n*
'sɪŋgəɹ
**sp** singer[4]

**singing** *adj / n*
'sɪŋgɪn, -ɪŋ
**sp** singing[1], sin-ging[1] / singing[5]

**single** *adj*
=
**sp** single[50]

**single / ~d** *v*
=
**sp** single[4] / singled[4]
**rh** mingled *VA 693*

**singleness** *n*
=
**sp** singlenesse[1]

**single-soled** *adj*
'sɪŋgəl-ˌso:ld
**sp** single sol'd[1]

**singly** *adv*
'sɪŋgləɪ
**sp** singly[5]

**singular** *adj*
*m* 'sɪŋgjələɹ, -ˌlɐ:ɹ
**sp** singular[6]
**rh** orator, publisher *Luc 32*
> sole-singular

**singulariter** *Lat adv*
ˌsɪŋgjʊ'larɪˌteɹ
**sp** singulariter[1]

**singularity / ~ies** *n*
*m* ˌsɪŋgjə'larɪˌtəɪ, -ɪt- / -z
**sp** singularitie[1], singularity[2] / singularities[1]

**sinister** *adj*
sɪ'nɪstəɹ
**sp** sinister[6]
**rh** whisper *MND 5.1.161*

**sink** *n*
=
**sp** sinck[1], sinke[3]

**sink / ~s / ~ing / sunk** *v*
= / = / 'sɪŋkɪn, -ɪŋ / sɤŋk
**sp** sincke[1], sink[1], sinke[27] / sinkes[6] / sinking[2] / suncke[1], sunke[2]
**rh** think *CE 3.2.52, Tim 2.2.236*

**sinking** *adj / n*
'sɪŋkɪn, -ɪŋ
**sp** sinking[1] / sinking[1], sink-ing[1]

**Sinklo** [name] *n*
'sɪŋklo:
**sp** Sinklo[1]

**sinner / ~s** *n*
'sɪnəɹ / -z
**sp** sinner[3], synner[1] / sinners[4]
**rh** dinner *CE 2.2.197*

**Sinon / ~'s** *n*
'səɪnən / -z
**sp** Sinon[1], Synon[1] / Synons[1]

**sip** *n*
=
**sp** sip[1]

**sip / ~ping** *v*
= / 'sɪpɪn, -ɪŋ
**sp** sip[1], sippe[1] / sipping[1]

**sir, Sir / ~'s / ~s** *n*
sɐ:ɹ, *Edgar's assumed dialect KL 4.6.235* zɐ:ɹ / -z
**sp** sir[2475], *Edgar* zir[2] / sirs[1] / sirs[42]

**Siracusa, Siracuse, Siracusian**
> Syracusa, Syracuse, Syracusian

**sire** *n / v*
səɪɹ
**sp** sire[11], syre[3] / syre[1]
**rh** *n* desire *Luc 232, VA 1178*; fire *VA 1160*

**siren** *n*
'səɪɹən
**sp** siren[1], syren[1]

**sirrah** *n*
'sɪrə
**sp** sirha[16], sirra[60], sirrah[53], sir-rah[2], sirrha[16]

**sister / ~'s / ~s / ~s'** *n*
'sɪstəɹ / -z
**sp** sister[181], si-ster[1], sisters [sister is][1], sister's [sister is][1] / sisters[12] / sisters[23] / sisters[2]

**sisterhood** *n*
'sɪstəɹ,ʊd, -,hʊd
**sp** sisterhood[4], sister-hood[1]

**sisterly** *adv*
'sɪstəɹləɪ
**sp** sisterly[1]

**sit / ~test / ~s / ~ting / sat** *v*
= / sɪts, -st / = / 'sɪtɪn, -ɪŋ / =
**sp** sit[199] sitte[2] / sitt'st[1] / sit's[1], sits[52] / sitting[20] / sat[15], sate[14]
**rh** *1* hit *VA 1035*; it *KJ 3.1.73, S 103.13*; pit *R2 4.1.217*; wit *S 37.7*;
**rh** *2* yet *RJ 2.3.71* / commits *S 9.13*; fits *VA 325*; fits, wits *Luc 858*; wits *Luc 288, RJ 1.4.46* / bat *LC 66*; gnat *LLL 4.3.163*; hat *VA 349*

**sit** *Lat*
> esse

**sith** *conj*
sɪθ
**sp** sith[18]

**sithence** *adv / conj*
'sɪθəns
**sp** sithence[1] / sithence[1]

**sitting** *n*
'sɪtɪn, -ɪŋ
**sp** sitting[2]

**situate** *v*
'sɪtjʊɛ:t
**sp** situate[2]

**situation / ~s** *n*
,sɪtjʊ'ɛ:sɪən / -s
**sp** situation[1] / situations[1]

**six** *adj / n*
=
**sp** six[20], sixe[33], sixe-[score][1], *abbr* vi.[1] / six[8], sixe[4]

**six-gated** *adj*
'sɪks-'gɛ:tɪd
**sp** six-gated[1]
> gate

**sixpence** *n*
'sɪkspəns
**sp** sixepence[1], sixe-pence[1], sixe pence[3], sixpence[2], six-pence[1], six pence[5]
> mill-sixpence

**sixpenny** *adj*
'sɪkspnəɪ, -pən-
**sp** six-penny[1]
> penny

**sixteen** *adj / n*
=
**sp** sixteene[10] / sixteen[1], sixteene[1]

**sixth** *adj / adv / n*
sɪkst
**sp** sixt[6] / sixt[2] / sixt[17]

**sixty** *adj / n*
'sɪkstəɪ
**sp** sixty[1] / sixty[3]

**size / ~s** *n*
səɪz / 'səɪzɪz
**sp** size[11] / sizes[2]

**sized** *adj*
səɪzd
**sp** siz'd[1]
> great-, over-sized

**skaines-mate / ~s** *n*
'skɛ:nz-'mɛ:ts
**sp** skaines-mates[1]
> mate

**skein** *n*
skɛ:n
**sp** skeine[1], skiene[1]

**skilful** *adj*
=
**sp** skilful[1], skilfull[5], skil-full[1]
> unskilful

**skilfully** *adv*
*m* 'skɪlfʊ,ləɪ
**sp** skilfully[1]
**rh** eye, lie *LLL 2.1.240*

**skill** *n*
=
**sp** skil[1], skill[39]
**rh** ill *S 66.10, 91.1, 150.7*; ill, still *Luc 1528*; ill, will *Luc 1243*; kill *LLL 4.1.28, S 126.7*; still *Luc 1099, 1134, 1506, MND 1.1.195, Per 4.Chorus.30, S 16.14, 24.5*; will *Cym 2.4.184, 1H4 1.2.214, LC 125, MND 2.2.125, 5.1.110, TG 2.4.212*

**skill / ~s / ~ed** *v*
=
**sp** skilles[1], skills[2] / skild[1], skil'd[1], skill'd[1]

**skilless** *adj*
=
**sp** skillesse[4]

**skillet** *n*
=
**sp** skillet[1]

**skim** *v*
=
**sp** skim[1]

**skimble-skamble** *adj*
=
**sp** skimble-skamble[1]

**skimmed** *adj*
=
**sp** skim'd[1]

**skin / ~s** *n*
=
**sp** skin[15], skin's [skin is][1], skinne[6] / skinnes[3], skins[3]
**rh** chin *LC 94, Luc 419*; in *MND 2.1.255*; win *2H6 3.1.300*
> calf's-, eel-, elf-, lamb-, sheep-, sow-, thick-skin

**skin / ~s** *v*
=
**sp** skin[1] / skins[1]

**skin-coat** *n*
'skɪn-ˌkoːt
**sp** skin-coat[1]
> coat

**skinny** *adj*
'skɪnəɪ
**sp** skinnie[1]

**skip / *PP* ~s / ~ped** *v*
=
**sp** skip[5], skippe[1] / skips[1] / skipt[1]
**rh** lips *PP 11.11*
> overskip

**skipper** *n*
'skɪpəɹ
**sp** skipper[1]

**skipping** *adj*
'skɪpɪn, -ɪŋ
**sp** skipping[5]

**skirmish / ~es** *n*
'skɐːɹmɪʃ / -ɪz
**sp** skirmish[5] / skirmishes[1]

**skirmish** *v*
'skɐːɹmɪʃ
**sp** skirmish[2]

**skirr** *v*
skɐːɹ
**sp** sker[1], skirre[1]

**skirt / ~s** *n*
skɐːɹts
**sp** skirts[6]
> fore-skirt

**skirted** *adj*
'skɐːɹtɪd
**sp** skirted[1]
> wide-skirted

**skittish** *adj*
=
**sp** skittish[3]

**skulk / ~ing** *v*
'skɤlkɪn, -ɪŋ
**sp** skulking[1]

**skull** *n*
skɤl
**sp** skull[2]

**sky / skies** *n*
skəɪ / -z
**sp** skie[24], sky[10], skye[4] / skies[7]
**rh** *1* by *VA 348*; by, dye, espy, eye, gloriously, remedy *MND 3.2.107*; die *MND 5.1.295*; eye *CE 2.1.17, Luc 1230, 1587, R2 3.2.194, VA 184, 485, 815*; fly *Luc 1407, MND 3.2.23, R2 1.1.41*; I *Tem 4.1.70*; lie *AW 1.1.213, VA 153*; nigh *AY 2.7.185*; o'er-eye *LLL 4.3.77*; **rh** *2* archery, gloriously *MND 3.2.107*; company *Luc 1587*; memory *S 15.6*; mortality *1H6 4.7.21*; sympathy *Luc 1230* / dies, lies *Luc 506*; hies *VA 1191*; replies *VA 696*
> ensky

**skyey** *adj*
'skəɪəɪ
**sp** skyie-[influences][1]

**skyish** *adj*
'skəɪɪʃ
**sp** skyish[1]

**sky-planted** *adj*
'skəɪ-'plɔːntɪd, -'pla-
**sp** sky-planted[1]
> plant

**slab** *adj*
=
**sp** slab[1]
**rh** *1* drab *Mac 4.1.32*; **rh** *2* babe *Mac 4.1.32*

**slack** *adj / v*
=
**sp** slacke[5] / slack[1], slacke[4]
**rh** *adj* back *PP 18.23*

**slackly** *adv*
'slakləɪ
**sp** slackely[1]

**slackness** *n*
=
**sp** slacknesse[2]

**slain** *adj*
slɛːn
**sp** slaine[3]
> slay

**slake / *Luc* ~th** *v*
slɛːk / 'slɛːkəθ
**sp** slake[1] / slaketh[1]
**rh** awaketh, maketh *Luc 1677*

**slander / ~'s / ~s** *n*
'slɔːndəɹ, 'slan- / -z
**sp** slander[25], slan-der[1], slaunder[2] / slanders[2] / slanders[11]
**rh** commander *VA 1006*

**slander / ~s / ~ing / ~ed** *v*
'slɔːndəɹ, 'slan- / -z / 'slɔːndrɪn, -ɪŋ, 'slan-, -dər- / 'slɔːndəɹd, 'slan-
**sp** slander[13], slan-der[1] / slanders[5] / slandering[1] / slanderd[1], slander'd[3], slandered[2], sland'red[1], slaundred[1]

**slanderer / ~s** *n*
*m* 'slɔːndrəɹ, -dər-, -dəˌrɐːɹ, 'slan- / -dəˌrɐːɹz
**sp** slanderer[4] / slanderers[1]

**slanderous** *adj*
*m* 'slɔːndrəs, -dəˌrɤs, 'slan-
**sp** slanderous[4], slandrous[1], sland'rous[5]

**slash** *v*
=
**sp** slash[2]

**slaughter / ~'s / ~s** *n*
'slɔːtəɹ / -z
**sp** slaughter[23] / slaughters[1] / slaughters[3]
**rh** *1* caught her, daughter *KL 1.4.316*; daughter *Luc 955, Per 4.4.37, R3 4.4.210*;
**rh** *2* after, halter *KL 1.4.316*
> self-slaughter

**slaughter / ~s / ~ed** *v*
'slɔ:təɹ / -z / -d
**sp** slaughter[4] / slaughters[2] / slaughter'd[7], slaughtered[1], slaughtred[3], slaught'red[3]
**rh** butchered *R3 4.4.391*

**slaughtered** *adj / n*
'slɔ:təɹd
**sp** slaughter'd[2], slaughtered[1], slaughtred[3], slaught'red[1] / slaught'red[1]

**slaughterer** *n*
'slɔ:trəɹ, -tər-
**sp** slaughterer[1]

**slaughter-house** *n*
'slɔ:təɹ-ˌəʊs, -ˌhəʊs
**sp** slaughter-house[6]
> house

**slaughtering** *adj / n*
'slɔ:trɪn, -ɪŋ, -tər-
**sp** slaughtering[1], slaughtring[1] / slaught'ring[1]

**slaughter·man / ~-men** *n*
'slɔ:təɹ-ˌman / -ˌmen
**sp** slaughter-man[2], slaughter man[1], slaughter-men[2]
**rh** countrymen *1H6 3.3.75*
> man

**slaughterous** *adj*
'slɔ:trəs, -tər-
**sp** slaughterous[1]

**slave** *adj / v*
slɛ:v
**sp** slaue-[man][1] / slaue[1]

**slave / ~'s / ~s** *n*
slɛ:v / -z
**sp** slaue[117], [villaine]-slaue[1], [thick-lipt]-slaue[1] / slaues[2] / slaues[36], [knee]-slaues[1]
**rh** *1* crave *S 58.1*; crave, rave *Luc 984*; grave *AW 2.3.136, Luc 200, 659*; *rh 2* have *AY 3.2.150, Luc 200, 1001, VA 101*
> bond-, Jack-slave

**slave-like** *adj*
'slɛ:v-ləɪk
**sp** slaue-like[1]

**slaver** *v*
'slavəɹ
**sp** slauuer[1]

**slavery** *n*
*m* 'slɛ:vrəɪ, -vər-, -vəˌrəɪ
**sp** slauerie[2], slauery[2]

**slavish** *adj*
'slɛ:vɪʃ
**sp** slauish[5]

**slay / ~s / slew / ~est / slain** *v*
slɛ: / -z / = / slu:st / slɛ:n
**sp** slay[25] / slayes[1] / slew[36], slewe[1] / slew'st[2] / slain[2], slaine[119]
**rh** away *VA 765*; decay, way *Luc 515*; fray *RJ 3.1.152*, way *AW 2.1.177, VA 624*; drew *Luc 1522* / again *1H6 4.5.18, RJ 3.1.122, S 22.13, VA 473, 1019, 1111*; amain *TC 5.8.14*; disdain *VA 243, 762*; Maine *2H6 1.1.211*; maintain, twain *Cym 5.4.72*; pain *S 139.13*; remain *Per 4.1.103*; stain *1H6 4.5.43, MND 5.1.144*; twain *PT 28*; vain *Luc 1046*; vein *1H6 4.7.96*
> blood-slain

**slaying** *n*
'slɛ:ɪn, -ɪŋ
**sp** slaying[1]

**sleave-silk** *n*
'sli:v-ˌsɪlk
**sp** *TC 5.1.28 emend of* sleyd silke[1]

**sledded** *adj*
=
**sp** sledded[1]

**sleek** *adj / v*
=
**sp** sleeke[2] / sleeke[1]

**sleek-headed** *adj*
ˌsli:k-'edɪd, -'he-
**sp** sleeke-headed[1]
> head

**sleep / ~s** *n*
=
**sp** sleep[5], sleepe[97] / sleepes[5]
**rh** creep *MND 3.2.364*; deep *MND 3.2.47*; keep *TNK Prol.29*; peep *MND 4.1.82*

**sleep / ~est / ~s / ~ing / slept** *v*
= / sli:ps, -st / = / 'sli:pɪn, -ɪŋ / =
**sp** sleep[6], sleepe[244] / sleepest[1], sleep'st[4] / sleepes[28], sleeps[2] / sleeping[25] / slept[36]
**rh** creep, peep *Luc 1250*; deep *MND 3.1.150, TC 2.3.262*; deep, weep *LC 123*; keep *LLL 1.1.48*; steep *TN 4.1.62*; weep *Ham 3.2.282, 1H6 4.3.29, PP 20.52* / creeps *Luc 1574*; weeps *Luc 904* / peeping, weeping *Luc 1090*; weeping *Tim 4.3.488* / crept *TC 2.2.212*
> a-sleeping, outsleep

**sleeper / ~s** *n*
'sli:pəɹ / -z
**sp** sleeper[1] / sleepers[5]

**sleeping** *adj / n*
'sli:pɪn, -ɪŋ
**sp** sleeping[18] / sleeping[4]
**rh** weeping *VA 951*

**sleepy** *adj*
'sli:pəɪ
**sp** sleepie[6], sleepy[5]

**sleeve / ~s** *n*
=
**sp** sleeue[21] / sleeues[8]
**rh** *1* believe *CE 3.2.23, TC 5.3.96*; Eve *LLL 5.2.321*; **rh** *2* give *LLL 5.2.455*

**sleeve-hand** *n*
'sli:v-ˌand, -ˌhand
**sp** sleeue-hand[1]
> hand

**sleeveless** *adj*
=
**sp** sleeuelesse[1]

**sleight / ~s** *n*
sləɪt / -s
**sp** sleight[1] / slights[1]
**rh** sprites *Mac 3.5.26*

**slender / ~er** *adj*
'slendəɹ / -əɹ, -drəɹ
**sp** slender[10] / slenderer[1]

**Slender** [name] **/ ~'s** *n*
'slendəɹ / -z
**sp** Slender[32], Slen-der[2], Slender's [Slender is][1] / Slenders[2]

**slenderly** *adv*
'slendəɹləɪ
**sp** slenderly[1]

**slept**
> sleep

**slew**
> slay

**slice** *v*
sləɪs
**sp** slice[2]

**slickly** *adv*
'slɪkləɪ
**sp** slickely[1]

**'slid**
> lid

**slide / ~s** *v*
sləɪd / -z
**sp** slide[4] / slides[1]
**rh** abide *S 45.4*; untried *WT 4.1.5*

**sliding** *n*
'sləɪdɪn, -ɪŋ
**sp** sliding[1]

**slight / ~est** *adj*
sləɪt / 'sləɪtəst
**sp** slight[26], sleight[1] / sleightest[1], slightest[2]

**slight** *adv*
sləɪt
**sp** slight[1]

**slight / ~s / ~ed** *v*
sləɪts / 'sləɪtɪd
**sp** slights[1] / slighted[3]

**'slight**
> light

**slightly** *adv*
'sləɪtləɪ
**sp** sleightly[1], slightly[8]

**slightness** *n*
'sləɪtnəs
**sp** slightnesse[1]

**slily**
> sly

**slime** *n*
sləɪm
**sp** slime[5]

**slimy** *adj*
'sləɪməɪ
**sp** slimy[2]

**sling / ~s** *n*
=
**sp** slings[2]

**slink / slunk** *v*
= / slɤŋk
**sp** slinke[3] / slunke[1]

**slip / ~s** *n*
=
**sp** slip[8], slippe[1] / slippes[2], slips[5]
**rh** slips *VA 515*

**slip / ~s / ~ped** *v*
=
**sp** slip[13] / slippes[1] / slipt[8]
**rh** lip *VA 129*
> overslip, unslipping

**slipper** *adj*
'slɪpəɹ
**sp** slipper[1]

**slipper / ~s** *n*
'slɪpəɹ / -z
**sp** slipper[2] / slippers[2]

**slippered** *adj*
'slɪpəɹd
**sp** slipper'd[1]

**slippery** *adj*
'slɪprəɪ, -pər-
**sp** slipp'ry[4], slipperie[1], slippery[6]

**slip-shod** *adj*
=
**sp** slip-shod[1]

**slish** *v*
=
**sp** slish[1]

**slit** *v*
=
**sp** slit[1]

**sliver** *n*
'slɪvəɹ
**sp** sliuer[1]

**sliver / ~ed** *v*
'slɪvəɹd
**sp** sliuer'd[1]

**slobbery** *n*
'slɒbrəɪ
**sp** slobbry[1]

**slop / ~s** *n*
=
**sp** slop[1] / slops[1]

**slope** *v*
slo:p
**sp** slope[1]

**sloth** *n*
slo:θ
**sp** sloth[5], slouth[1]

**slothful** *adj*
'slo:θfʊl
**sp** slouthfull[1]

**slough** *n*
sləʊ
**sp** slough[5]

**slovenly** *adj*
*m* 'slɤvən,ləɪ
**sp** slouenly[1]

**slovenry** *n*
*m* 'slɤvən,rəɪ
**sp** slouenrie[1]

**slow** *adj*
slo: / 'slo:əɹ
**sp** slow[38] / slower[2]
**rh** go *1H4 3.1.256*; know *S 51.6*; no, so *LLL 3.1.57*; show *S 94.4*; so *RJ 2.6.15*; woe *S 44.13*
> snail-slow

**slow / ~er** *adv*
slo: / 'slo:əɹ
**sp** slow[6] / slower[1]
**rh** go *S 51.13*
> wilful-slow

**slow** *n*
slo:
**sp** slow[1]

**slow / ~ed** *v*
slo:d
**sp** slow'd[1]
> foreslow

**slow-gaited** *adj*
'slo:-'gɛ:tɪd
**sp** slow gated[1]
> gait

**slowly** *adv*
'slo:ləɪ
**sp** slowly[5]

**slowness** *n*
'slo:nəs
**sp** slownesse[2]

**slow-winged** *adj*
'slo:-,wɪŋd
**sp** slow-wing'd[1]
> winged

**slubber** *v*
'slɤbəɹ
**sp** slubber[2]
> beslubber

**slug** *n*
slɤg
**sp** slug[2]

**slug-a-bed** *n*
'slɤgəbed
**sp** sluggabed[1]

**sluggard** *n*
'slɤgəɹd
**sp** sluggard[2]

**sluggardized** *adj*
*m* 'slɤgəɹ,dəɪzd
**sp** sluggardiz'd[1]

**sluggish** *adj*
'slɤgɪʃ
**sp** sluggish[1]

**sluice / ~s** *Luc* *n*
=
**sp** sluces[2]
**rh** abuses, excuses *Luc 1076*

**sluice / ~d** *v*
=
**sp** sluc'd[1], sluyc'd[1]

**slumber / ~s** *n*
'slɤmbəɹ / -z
**sp** slumber[14], *Macmorris H5 3.2.111* slomber[1] / slumbers[3], [faint]-slumbers[1]

**slumber / ~ed** *v*
'slɤmbəɹ / -d
**sp** slumber[3] / slumbred[1]

**slumbery** *adj*
'slɤmbrəɪ
**sp** slumbry[1]

**slunk**
> slink

**slut / ~s** *n*
slɤt / -s
**sp** slut[2] / sluts[2]

**sluttery** *n*
'slɤtrəɪ, -tər-
**sp** sluttery[2]
**rh** bilberry *MW 5.5.46*

**sluttish** *adj*
'slɤtɪʃ
**sp** sluttish[3]

**sluttishness** *n*
'slɤtɪʃnəs
**sp** slut-tishnesse[1]

**sly** *adj*
sləɪ
**sp** slie[1], sly[1], slye[7]

**Sly** [name] **/ ~'s / ~s** *n*
sləɪ / -z
**sp** Slie[3], Sly[2] / Slies[1] / Slies[1]

**slyly** *adv*
'sləɪləɪ
**sp** slily[1], slyly[5]

**smack** *n*
=
**sp** smack[1], smacke[3]

**smack / ~s / ~ing** *v*
= / = / 'smakɪn, -ɪŋ
**sp** smack[3], smacke[1] / smackes[2] / smacking[1]

**small** *adj*
smɑ:l / 'smɑ:l·əɹ / *m* -əst, -st
**sp** smal[2], small[75] / smaller[3] / smallest[14], small'st[1]
**rh** all *Per 3.4.18, TG 1.2.29*; small ones tall ones *TNK 3.5.110*

**small** *adv / n*
smɑ:l
**sp** small[3]/ small[7]

**smallest** *n*
'smɑ:ləst
**sp** smallest[2]

**small-knowing** *adj*
'smɑ:l-,no:ɪn, -ɪŋ
**sp** small knowing[1]
> know

**smallness** *n*
'smɑ:lnəs
**sp** smalnesse[1]

**Smalus** *n*
'smaləs
**sp** Smalus[1]

**smart** *adj*
smɑ:ɹt
**sp** smart[3]

**smart / *Luc* ~s** *n*
smɑ:ɹt / -s
smart[2] / smarts[1]
**rh** art *Cym 5.4.42; TC 4.4.18* / hearts *Luc 1238*

**smart / ~ing** *v*
smɑ:ɹt / -ɪn, -ɪŋ
**sp** smart[4] / smarting[1]
**rh** heart *1H6 4.6.42*
> all-smarting

**smartly** *adv*
'smɑ:ɹtləɪ
**sp** smartly[1]

**smatch** *n*
=
**sp** smatch[1]

**smatter** *v*
'smatəɹ
**sp** smatter[1]

**smear / ~ed** *v*
smi:ɹ / -d
**sp** smeare[1] / smear'd[4], smeered[1]
> besmear

**smell / ~s** *n*
=
**sp** smell[10] / smels[1]
**rh** tell *S 98.5*; yell *VA 686*

**smell / ~est / ~s / ~ing / ~ed / smelt** *v*
= / smelst / = / 'smelɪn, -ɪŋ / smeld / smelt
**sp** smel[2], smel't [smell it][1], smell[30] / smell'st[1] / smelles[1], smells[3], smels[6] / smelling[4] / smell'd[1] / smelt[7]
**rh** dwell *VA 1171*; tell *PP 18.9* / dwells *S 99.2* / excelling *VA 444*
> tender-smelling

**smile / ~s** *n*
sməɪl / -z
**sp** smile[12], smyle[1] / smiles[18]

**smil·e / ~est / ~es / ~ing / ~ed / ~edest** *v*
sməɪl / -st / -z / 'sməɪlɪn, -ɪŋ / sməɪld / -st
**sp** smile[62], smoile[1] / smilest[1], smil'st[2] / smiles[27] / smiling[13], smyling[1] / smild[1], smil'd[9] / smil'dst[1]
**rh** awhile *Per 1.4.108, TNK Epil.4*; beguile *MND 2.1.44, Oth 1.3.209*; exile *PP 14.7*; while *H8 Epil.11* / beguiled *PP 20.27*

**Smile** [name] *n*
sməɪl
**sp** Smile[2]

**smiling** *adj / n*
'sməɪlɪn, -ɪŋ
**sp** smiling[11] / smiling[3], smyling[2]
**rh** beguiling, defiling *LC 172*

**smilingly** *adv*
'sməɪlɪn,ləɪ, -ɪŋ-
**sp** smilingly[2]

**smirch** *v*
smɐ:ɹʧ
**sp** smirch[1]

**smirched** *adj*
smɐ:ɹʧt
**sp** smircht[1], smyrcht[1]
> unsmirched

**smite / ~s / *Luc* ~th / smit / smote** *v*
sməɪt / -s / 'sməɪtəθ / = / smo:t, smɒt
**sp** smite[1] / smites[1] / smiteth[1] / smit[1] / smoate[1], smot[3], smote[1]
**rh** lighteth *Luc 176* / not *LLL 4.3.26*

**smith / ~'s** *n*
=
**sp** smith[1], smyth[1] / smithes[1]

**Smith** [name] *n*
=
**sp** Smith[2]

**Smithfield** *n*
=
**sp** Smithfield[5]

**smock / ~s** *n*
=
**sp** smock[1], smocke[7] / smockes[2]
**rh** clocks *LLL 5.2.895*
> lady-smock

**smoke / ~s** *n*
smo:k / -s
**sp** smoke[4], smoake[11] / smoakes[1]
**rh** cloak *Luc 799, S 34.4*; provoke *Per 1.1.139*

**smok·e / ~es / ~ing / ~ed** *v*
smo:k / -s / 'smo:kɪn, -ɪŋ / smo:kt
**sp** smoake[6] / smoakes[2] / smoaking[1], smoa-king[1] / smoak'd[2]

**smoking** *adj*
'smo:kɪn, -ɪŋ
**sp** smoaking[2]

**smoky** *adj*
'smo:kəɪ
**sp** smoakie[5]

**smooth** *adj / adv*
=
**sp** smooth[20], smooth-[comforts-false][1], smoothe[1] / smooth[5]

**smooth / ~est / ~s / ~ed** *v*
= / smu:ðst / = / *m* smu:ðd, 'smu:ðɪd
**sp** smooth[9] / smooth'st[1] / smooths[1] / smooth'd[2], smoothed[1]

**Smooth** [name] *n*
=
**sp** Smoothes [Smooth is][1]

**smoothed** *adj*
*m* 'smu:ðɪd
**sp** smoothed[1]

**smooth-faced** *adj*
'smu:ð-ˌfɛ:st
**sp** smoothfac'd[1], smooth-fac'd[2]
> face

**smoothing** *adj*
'smu:ðɪn, -ɪŋ
**sp** smoothing[2]

**smoothly** *adv*
'smu:ðləɪ
**sp** smoothly[2]

**smoothness** *n*
'smu:ðnəs
**sp** smoothnes[1], smoothnesse[1]

**smooth-pate / ~s** *n*
'smu:ð-ˌpɛ:ts
**sp** smooth-pates[1]
> pate

**smother** *n*
'smɤðəɹ
**sp** smother[1]
**rh** brother *AY 1.2.276*

**smother / ~s / ~ed** *v*
'smɤðəɹ / -z / -d
**sp** smother[5] / smothers[1] / smother'd[6], smothered[2], smothred[1]
**rh** another, brother *Luc 634*; other *S 47.4*

**smothering** *n*
'smɤðrɪn, -ɪŋ, -ðər-
**sp** smothering[1]

**smug** *adj*
smɤg
**sp** smug[2], smugge[1]

**Smulkin** *n*
'smɤlkɪn
**sp** Smulkin[1]

**smutch / ~ed** *v*
smɤʧt
**sp** smutch'd[1]

**snaffle** *n*
=
**sp** snaffle[1]

**snail / ~s** *n*
snɛ:l / -z
**sp** snaile[6], snayle[1] / snayles[1]

**snail-paced** *adj*
'snɛ:l-ˌpɛ:st
**sp** snaile-pac'd[2]
> pace

**snail-slow** *adj*
'snɛ:l-'slo:
**sp** snaile-slow[1]
> slow

**snake / ~s** *n*
'snɛ:k / -s
**sp** snake[12] / snakes[5]
**rh** bake *Mac 4.1.12*

**snaky** *adj*
'snɛ:kəɪ
**sp** snakie[1]

**snap / ~ped** *v*
=
**sp** snap[3] / snapt[1]

**snapper-up** *n*
'snapəɹ-'ɤp
**sp** snapper-vp[1]

**snare / ~s** *n*
snɛ:ɹ / -z
**sp** snare[2] / snares[4]
**rh** are, care *Luc 928*; prepare *Tim 5.2.17*

**snare / ~s / ~d** *v*
snɛ:ɹ / -z / -d
**sp** snare[1] / snares[1] / snar'd[2]
> ensnare

**Snare** [name] *n*
snɛ:ɹ
**sp** Snare[7]

**snarl / ~eth / ~ing** *v*
snɑ:ɹl / 'snɑ:ɹl·əθ / -ɪn, -ɪŋ
**sp** snarle[1] / snarleth[1] / snarling[1]

**snatch / ~es** *n*
=
**sp** snatch[1] / snatches[3]

**snatch / ~es / ~ed** *v*
=
**sp** snatch[8] / snatches[3] / snacht[1], snatch'd[5], snatcht[1]
**rh** catch *MND 3.2.29*

**snatcher / ~s** *n*
'snaʧəɹz
**sp** snatchers[1]

**sneak / ~ing** *v*
= / 'sni:kɪn, -ɪŋ
**sp** sneake[1] / sneaking[2]

**Sneak** [name] **/ ~'s** *n*
=
**sp** Sneake[1] / Sneakes[1]

**sneak-cup** *n*
'sni:k-ˌkɤp
**sp** sneake-cuppe[1]
> cup

**sneaking** *adj*
'sni:kɪn, -ɪŋ
**sp** sneaking[1]

**sneap** *n*
=
**sp** sneape[1]

**sneaping** *adj*
'sni:pɪn, -ɪŋ
**sp** sneaping[2]

**sneck** *n*
=
**sp** snecke[1]

**snip** *n*
=
**sp** snip[3]

**snipe** *n*
snəɪp
**sp** snipe[1]

**snipped** *adj*
=
**sp** snipt[1]

**snore / ~s** *n*
snɔːɹz
**sp** snores[2]

**snor·e / ~es / ~ing** *v*
snɔːɹ / -z / ˈsnɔːrɪn, -ɪŋ
**sp** snore[3] / snores[2] / snoaring[1]
**rh** roars *MND 5.1.363*

**snort / ~ing** *v*
ˈsnɔːrtɪn, -ɪŋ
**sp** snorting[1]

**snorting** *adj*
ˈsnɔːrtɪn, -ɪŋ
**sp** snorting[1]

**Snout** [name] *n*
snəʊt
**sp** Snout[3], Snowt[4]

**snow** *adj / n*
snoː
**sp** snow[1] / snow[33]
**rh** blow *LLL 5.2.912*; crow *MND 3.2.141, WT 4.4.220*; foe *VA 362*; go *Ham 4.5.36*; so *Luc 1218*

**snowball / ~s** *n*
ˈsnoːbɑːlz
**sp** snow-bals[1]
> ball

**snow-broth** *n*
ˈsnoː-ˌbrɒθ
**sp** snow-broth[1]
> broth

**snow-white** *adj*
ˈsnoː-ˌʍəɪt
**sp** snow-white[3]
> white

**snowy** *adj*
ˈsnoːəɪ
**sp** snowy[1]

**snuff / ~s** *n*
snɤf / -s
**sp** snuffe[6] / snuffes[1]

**snuff / ~ed** *v*
snɤf / -t
**sp** snuffe[1] / snuft[1]

**Snug** [name] *n*
snɤg
**sp** Snug[4], Snugge[1]

**so** *adv*
soː
**sp** so[4869], ’so[1], soe[1], so’s [so is][1] / *abbr* s’[1]
**rh** Bassanio *MV 2.8.38*; blow *LLL 4.3.108, PP 16.10*; blow, woe *Luc 1664*; crow *CE 3.1.81, 85, MND 2.1.268, Per 4.Chorus.31*; foe *Luc 1036, 1197, 1681, 1826, MND 3.2.43, RJ 1.5.60, Tim 2.2.239*; go *AW 2.3.128, 298, CE 2.2.225, Cor 2.3.120, Ham 3.1.188, LLL 2.1.36, 4.3.185, 5.2.59, 5.2.621, MND 1.1.186, 2.2.92, 3.1.151, 3.2.183, 5.1.201, MV 2.7.79, R2 1.2.63, 1.3.247, 2.1.297, RJ 3.5.24, Tem 4.1.45, TN 2.1.42, VA 381, 612*; go, know *CE 4.3.78*; go, moe, woe *MA 2.3.70*; grow *LLL 2.1.52, 5.2.252, R3 2.4.8, S 115.13, TN 2.4.40*; know *CE 3.2.53, Ham 3.2.180, LLL 1.1.59, 2.1.52, 4.3.49, 128, 5.2.489, Luc 1060, MND 1.1.228, 3.2.162, 173, 190, Oth 4.3.102, R2 3.4.90, S 13.14, 140.6, Tit 5.3.139, TN 3.4.371, VA 1110*; know, no *LLL 1.1.67*; minimo [*Lat*] *TS 1.1.158*; moe, woe *Luc 1481*; no *CE 3.2.59, 4.2.1, LLL 2.1.198, 4.1.13, MND 3.2.80, MV 3.2.146, R2 3.3.208, S 148.6, TC 4.4.133, VA 851*; owe *TN 1.5.301*; owe, show *Luc 79*; Po *KJ 1.1.204*; quo *1H6 5.3.108*; show *LLL 5.2.537, MND 3.2.152, 5.1.160, S 43.8, 54.11, 105.4*; show, woe *Luc 1510, 1811*; shrew *TS 5.2.188*; slow *LLL 3.1.59, RJ 2.6.14*; snow *Luc 1217*; though *KJ 1.1.168, MND 2.2.114*; venuto *TS 1.2.278*; woe *CE 2.1.14, 3H6 2.3.47, 2.5.19, LLL 4.1.13, Luc 1224, MM 2.1.270, 4.1.12, R2 2.1.151, 3.4.27, 4.1.148, S 71.6, 90.14, 127.14, 129.9, Tit 5.3.146, VA 713, 834, 840, 969*
**pun** *TG 3.1.299* sew
> so-so, well

**soak / ~s / ~ing / ~ed** *v*
soːks / ˈsoːkɪn, -ɪŋ / soːkt
**sp** sokes[1] / soaking[2] / soak’d[1]

**soar / ~s / ~ing** *v*
soːɹ / -z / ˈsoːrɪn, -ɪŋ
**sp** soare[6], sore[1] / soares[1] / soaring[1]
**pun** *RJ 1.4.20* sore

**soaring** *adj*
ˈsoːrɪn, -ɪŋ
**sp** soaring[1]
> high-soaring

**sob / ~s** *n*
=
**sp** sob[1] / sobs[2]

**sob / ~s** *v*
=
**sp** sob[1] / sobs[2]

**sobbing** *adj*
ˈsɒbɪn, -ɪŋ
**sp** sobbing[1]

**sober** *adj*
ˈsoːbəɹ
**sp** sober[16]

**sober-blooded** *adj*
ˈsoːbəɹ-ˌblɤdɪd
**sp** so-ber-blooded[1]

**soberly** *adv*
*m* ˈsoːbəɹˌləɪ
**sp** soberly[1]

**sober-suited** *adj*
ˈsoːbəɹ-ˌʃuːtɪd, -ˌsju-
**sp** sober suted[1]

**sobriety** *n*
*m* səˈbrəɪətəɪ, -ˌtəɪ
**sp** sobrietie[2]
**rh** see *TS 1.1.71*

**sociable** *adj*
*m* ˈsoːsɪˌabəl, -sɪəbəl
**sp** sociable[6]
> insociable

**societ·y / ~ies** *n*
*m* sə'səɪəˌtəɪ, -təɪ / -z
**sp** societie[12], so-cietie[1], society[9], so-ciety[1] / societies[4]
**rh** charity *LLL 4.3.126*; company, deity *Tem 4.1.91*; company, melody *Luc 1111*; impiety *S 67.4*; simplicity *LLL 4.3.51*

**sock / ~s** *n*
=
**sp** socks[1]

**Socrates / ~'** *n*
'sɒkrəˌti:z
**sp** Socrates[1]

**sodden** *adj*
=
**sp** sodden[2]

**sodden-witted** *adj*
=
**sp** sodden-witted[1]
> wit

**soever,** *abbr* **soe'er** *adv*
so:'evəɹ, *abbr* so:'ɛ:ɹ
**sp** soeuer[6], *abbr* soere[1], so ere[5]
**rh** there *TN 1.1.12*
> ever

**so-forth** *n*
'so:-ˌfɔ:ɹθ
**sp** so-forth[1]
> forth

**soft / ~er / ~est** *adj*
= / 'sɒftəɹ / =
**sp** soft[51] / softer[3] / softest[3]
> flower-soft

**soft** *adv / interj / n*
=
**sp** soft[5] / soft[58] / soft[1]

**soft-conscienced** *adj*
'sɒft-ˌkɒnsɪənst
**sp** soft conscienc'd[1]

**soften / ~s / ~ed** *v*
=
**sp** soften[5] / softens[1] / softned[2]

**soft-hearted** *adj*
*m* ˌsɒft-'ɑ:ɹtɪd, -'h-
**sp** soft harted[1], soft-hearted[1]

**softly** *adv / interj*
'sɒftləɪ
**sp** softly[13], soft-ly[1] / softly[7]

**softly-sprighted** *adj*
'sɒftləɪ-'sprəɪtɪd
**sp** softly-sprighted[1]

**softness** *n*
=
**sp** softnesse[1]

**so-ho** *interj*
ˌso:-'ho:
**sp** soa hough[1], so-hough[1]

**soil / ~'s** *n*
səɪl / -z
**sp** soil[1], soile[6], soyle[15] / soyles[1]

**soil / ~ed** *v*
səɪl / -d
**sp** soyle[2] / soil'd[1], soyld[1], soyl'd[1]

**soiled** *adj*
səɪld
**sp** soyled[1]
> unsoiled

**soilure** *n*
'səɪljəɹ
**sp** soylure[1]

**soit** *Fr*
> être

**sojourn** *n*
'sɒʤəɹn
**sp** soiourne[1]

**sojourn / ~ed** *v*
'sɒʤəɹn / -d
**sp** soiourne[5] / soiourn'd[3]
**rh** returned *MND 3.2.171*

**sol** [music] *n*
=
**sp** sol[4]

**Sol** [name] *n*
=
**sp** Sol[1]

**sola** *interj*
sə'la:, so:-
**sp** sola[3], sowla[2]

**solace** *n / v*
=
**sp** solace[2] / solace[4], sollace[1]

**Solanio** *n*
sə'lanɪo:
**sp** Salanio[2], Solanio[4]

**sold**
> sell

**soldat** *Fr n*
sɔl'da
**sp** soldat[1]

**solder / ~est** *v*
'sɔ:dəɹ, 'so:- / -st
**sp** soalder[1] / souldrest[1]

**soldier / ~'s / ~s / ~s'** *n*
'so:dɪəɹ / -z
**sp** soldier[19], sol-dier[1], soldiour[8], souldier[106], souldiers [soldier is][1], souldior[2], souldiour[4] / soldiers[4], souldiers[9], soul-diers[2], souldiors[13], souldiours[1] / soldiers[37], soldiours[4], souldiers[107], souldiours[5] / soldiers[1], souldiers[5], souldiors[1]
> fellow-soldier

**soldier-breeder** *n*
'so:dɪəɹ-ˌbri:dəɹ
**sp** souldier-breeder[1]
> breeder

**soldier-like** *adj*
'so:dɪəɹ-ləɪk
**sp** souldier-like[2]

**soldiership** *n*
*m* 'so:dɪəɹˌʃɪp, -ɹʃ-
**sp** soldiership[1], souldiership[7], souldier-ship[1]

**sole** *adj*
so:l
**sp** soale[1], sole[20]

**sole / ~s** *n*
so:l / -z
**sp** sole[3] / soales[1], soles[1]
**pun** *MV 4.1.123* soul

**solely** *adv*
'so:ləɪ
**sp** solely[3], solie[3], soly[2]

**solemn** *adj*
=
**sp** solemn[3], solemne[37], sollemne[1]

**solemnly** *adv*
*m* 'sɒləm,ləɪ, -ml-
**sp** solemnely[1], solemnly[5], sollemnly[1]

**solemness** *n*
=
**sp** solemnesse[1]

**solemnit·y / ~ies** *n*
*m* sə'lemnɪ,təɪ, -ɪt- / -ɪ,təɪz
**sp** solemnitie[6], solemnity[5] / solemnities[1]
**rh** amity, be, jollity, me, prosperity, triumphantly *MND 4.1.87*; jollity *MND 5.1.359*; see *AC 5.2.364*; three *MND 4.1.184*

**solemnize / ~d** *v*
'sɒləm,nəɪz / *m* -d, -mnəɪzd, sɒ'lemnɪ,zɪd
**sp** solemnize[2] / solemnizd[1], solemniz'd[3], solemnized[2]

**sole-singular** *adj*
'so:l-'sɪŋgjələɹ
**sp** sole-singular[1]
> singular

**solicit / ~s / ~ing / ~ed** *v*
= / = / sə'lɪsɪtɪn, -ɪŋ / =
**sp** solicit[2], solicite[5], soli-cite[1], sollicit[1], sollicite[2] / solicites[3] / soliciting[1], sollicting[1] / solicited[3]
> still-soliciting, unsolicited

**solicitation** *n*
sə,lɪsɪ'tɛ:sɪən
**sp** solicitation[1]

**soliciter** *n*
sə'lɪsɪtəɹ
**sp** soliciter[1], solicitor[1]

**soliciting** *n*
sə'lɪsɪtɪn, -ɪŋ
**sp** soliciting[1], sollicting[1]

**solicity** *n*
sə'lɪsɪtəɪ
**sp** solicity[1]

**solid** *adj*
=
**sp** solid[3], solide[1]

**solidare / ~s** *n*
'sɒlɪdɛ:ɹz
**sp** solidares[1]

**solidity** *n*
*m* sə'lɪdɪ,təɪ
**sp** solidity[1]

**Solinus** *n*
sə'ləɪnəs
**sp** Solinus[1]

**solitary** *adj*
*m* 'sɒlɪ,trəɪ, -ɪt-
**sp** solitarie[1], solitary[1]

**Solomon** *n*
=
**sp** Salomon[2]

**Solon / ~'s** *n*
'so:lənz
**sp** Solons[1]

**sol·us / ~um** *Lat adj*
'so:lʊm
**sp** *emend of TS 4.4.90* solem[1]

**solus** *Lat adv / n*
'so:lʊs
**sp** solus[8] / solus[3]

**Solyman** *n*
'sɒlɪmən
**sp** Solyman[1]

**some** *det / n*
*str* sɤm, *unstr* sm / sɤm
**sp** som[2], some[1229] / some[226], [other] some[1], [other]-some[1]
**rh** come *LLL 5.2.819, Luc 1445*; crumb, mum *KL 1.4.194*
**pun** *2H4 2.1.71* sum

**somebody** *pro*
*m* 'sɤmbədəɪ, sɤm'bɒdəɪ
**sp** some bodie[2], somebody[2], some-body[1], some body[3]
> body

**someone** *pro*
*m* 'sɤmo:n, -ən, sɤm'o:n, -'wɒn
**sp** some one[7]
> one

**Somerset / ~'s** *n*
*m* 'sɤməɹ,set, -ɹs- / -ɹ,sets
**sp** Somerset[87], Somer-set[1] / Somersets[2]
**rh** get *1H6 4.3.33*

**Somervile** *n*
*m* 'sɤməɹ,vɪl
**sp** Someruile[2]

**something** *pro*
*m* 'sɤmθɪŋ, sɤm'θɪŋ
**sp** something[156], some-thing[5], some thing[1], something's [something is][1], somthing[12], som-thing[1], som thing[1]
> thing

**sometime** *adj / adv*
'sɤmtəɪm / *m* 'sɤmtəɪm, sɤm'təɪm
**sp** sometime[3] / sometime[63], somtime[5], som-time[1]
> time

**sometimes** *adv*
*m* 'sɤmtəɪmz, sɤm'təɪmz
**sp** sometimes[48], some-times[3], somtimes[2]
**rh** crimes *LLL 4.1.30*

**somever** *adv*
sʏm'evəɹ
**sp** someuer[1]
> howsomever

**somewhat** *adv*
'sʏmʌɑt
**sp** somewhat[16], somwhat[1]

**somewhere** *adv*
'sʏmʌɛːɹ
**sp** somewhere[1], some-where[1], some where[1]

**somewhither** *adv*
sʏm'ʌɪðəɹ
**sp** some whether[1]
> whither

**Somme** *n*
sɒm
**sp** Some[1]

**son / ~'s / ~s / ~s'** *n*
sʏn / -z
**sp** son[67], son's [son is][1], sonne[548], [bitch-wolfes] sonne[1], [Hydra]-sonne[1], sonne's [son is][2] / sonnes[13] / sonnes[175], sons[7] / sonnes[4], sons[1]
**rh** *1* begun *KJ 1.1.159, R2 1.1.159*; done *1H6 4.3.37, 4.6.6, Mac 3.5.11, R2 1.3.224, 5.2.101, R3 4.4.25, Tem 2.1.332, 4.1.93, Tit 1.1.345*; undone *Per 1.1.119*; won *1H6 4.6.51, S 41.7*; **rh** *2* afternoon *1H6 4.5.52*; noon *S 7.14*; **rh** *3* gone *R3 1.3.9* / nuns *VA 754*
**pun** *R3 1.1.2* sun

**son** *Fr det*
> il

**son** *Fr n*
sɔ̃
**sp** son[1]

**sonance** *n*
'soːnəns
**sp** sonuance[1]

**song / ~s** *n*
=
**sp** song[81], songue[1] / songs[12]
**rh** *1* long *PP 18.50, S 100.3*; self-wrong *CE 3.2.172*; **rh** *2* tongue *LLL 5.2.405, S 17.12, 102.14* / tongues *VA 777*
> love-, plain-, prick-song

**song·man / ~men** *n*
=
**sp** song-men[1]

**son-in-law / ~'s** *n*
'sʏn-ɪn-ˌlɔː / -z
**sp** son-in-law[2], son in lawes[1], sonne-in-law[2], sonne in-law[1], sonne in law[6] / sonne in lawes[1]
> law

**sonnet / ~s** *n*
=
**sp** sonnet[12] / sonnets[3]

**sonneting** *n*
'sɒnɪtɪn, -ɪŋ
**sp** sonnetting[1]
**rh** thing *LLL 4.3.156*

**sont** *Fr*
> être

**sonties** *n*
'sɒntəɪz
**sp** sonties[1]

**soon / ~er / ~est** *adv*
= / 'suːnəɹ / =
**sp** soon[2], soone[134], [as]soone[4], [as]-soone[1] / sooner[46], soo-ner[1] / soonest[4]
**rh** *1* moon *LLL 5.2.211, Luc 370, MND 3.2.52, 4.1.96, PP 14.25*; noon *TN 3.1.144*; **rh** *2* doom *Per 5.2.19 [Chorus]*

**sooner** *n*
'suːnəɹ
**sp** sooner[12]

**soonest** *adj*
=
**sp** soonest[2]

**sooth** *n*
=, sʊθ
**sp** sooth[31], [good]sooth[1], [good]-sooth[2], [in]sooth[10], sooth-[law][1]
> forsooth

**soothe / ~est / ~ing / ~ed** *v*
= / -st / 'suːðɪn, -ɪŋ / =
**sp** sooth[4] / sooth'st[1] / soothing[1] / sooth'd[1]

**soother / ~s** *n*
'suːðəɹz
**sp** soothers[1]

**soothing** *n*
'suːðɪn, -ɪŋ
**sp** soothing[1]

**soothsay** *v*
'suːθˌsɛː, 'sʊθ-
**sp** soothsay[1]
> say

**soothsayer** *n*
'suːθˌsɛːəɹ, 'sʊθ-
**sp** soothsaier[1], soothsayer[6], sooth-sayer[2], southsayer[1]

**sooty** *adj*
'sʊtəɪ
**sp** sootie[1]

**sop / ~s** *n*
=
**sp** sop[2], soppe[1] / sops[2]
> milksop

**sophister** *n*
'sɒfɪstəɹ
**sp** sophister[1]

**sophisticated** *adj*
sə'fɪstɪˌkɛːtɪd
**sp** sophisticated[1]

**Sophy** *n*
'soːfəɪ
**sp** Sophie[1], Sophy[2]

**sorcerer / ~s** *n*
'sɔːɹsərəɹ / *m* -z, -əˌrɐːɹz
**sp** sorcerer[1] / sorcerers[3]

**sorceress** *n*
ˈsɔːɹsəˌres
**sp** sorceresse[3]

**sorcer·y / ~ies** *n*
ˈsɔːɹsəˌrəɪ / ˈsɔːɹsrəɪz, -sər-
**sp** sorcerie[1], sorcery[1] / sorceries[1]

**sore / ~r** *adj*
sɔːɹ / ˈsɔːɹəɹ
**sp** sore[17] / sorer[1]
**rh** o'er *Luc 1568*

**sore** *adv*
sɔːɹ
**sp** sore[9]
**rh** before, door *CE 3.1.65*
**pun** *RJ 1.4.20* soar

**sore / ~s** *n*
sɔːɹ / -z
sore[14] / sores[7]
**rh** boar *PP 9.12*; more *R2 1.3.303, TC 3.1.117*
> eye-, heart-, pricket-sore

**sore-betrayed** *LC* *adj*
ˈsɔːɹ-bɪˈtrɛːd
**sp** sore-betrayed[1]
**rh** maid *LC 328*
> betray

**sorely** *adv*
**sp** sorely[5], sore-ly[1]
ˈsɔːɹləl

**sorrel** *n*
ˈsɒrəl
**sp** sorell[2], sorrell[1]
**rh** more 'L' *LLL 4.2.61*

**sorrier** *n*
ˈsɒrəɪəɹ
sorrier[1]
sorry

**sorrow / ~'s / ~s** *n*
ˈsɒrə, -roː / -z
**sp** sorow[3], sorrow[160], [hearts]-sorrow[1], sorrow's [sorrow is][1] / sorrowes[108] / sorowes[1], sorrowes[2]
**rh** borrow *Luc 1497, Oth 1.3.212, VA 963*; borrow, morrow *Luc 1080*; good-morrow *Luc 1221*; morrow *Luc 1569, R2 1.3.227, RJ 2.2.184, S 90.5*; tomorrow *AW 2.3.294, 2H4 4.2.83, PP 14.6, 14.23, VA 583, 671*
> canker-, sea-sorrow; heart-sorrowing

**sorrow / ~est / ~s / ~ed** *v*
ˈsɒrə, -roː / -əwəst, -oːəst / -əz, -oːz / -əd, -oːd
**sp** sorrow[5] / sorrowest[1] / sorrowes[1] / sorrowed[1]

**sorrowed** *adj*
ˈsɒrəd, -roːd
**sp** sorrowed[1]

**sorrowful** *adj*
ˈsɒrəfʊl, -roː-
**sp** sorrowfull[5]

**sorrowing** *PP* *n*
ˈsɒrəwɪn, -ɪŋ, -roː-
**sp** sorrowing[1]
**rh** sing *PP 20.26*

**sorrow-wreathen** *adj*
ˈsɒrə-ˌriːðən, -roː-
**sp** sorrow-wreathen[1]

**sorr·y / ~iest** *adj*
ˈsɒrəɪ / -əst
**sp** sorrie[15], sorry[75] / sorryest[1]
**rh** glory, story *Luc 1524*
> sorrier *n*

**sort / ~s** *n*
sɔːɹt / -s
**sp** sort[52] / sorts[8]
**rh** extort, sport *MND 3.2.159*; report *MND 3.2.21, S 36.13, 96.13*; sport *MND 3.2.13, 388*

**sort / ~s / ~ing / ~ed** *v*
sɔːɹt / -s / ˈsɔːɹt·ɪn, -ɪŋ / -ɪd
**sp** sort[14] / sorts[5] / sorting[1] / sorted[4]
**rh** sport *MND 3.2.352*
> unsorted

**sortance** *n*
ˈsɔːɹtəns
**sp** sortance[1]

**so-seeming** *adj*
ˈsoː-ˈsiːmɪn, -ɪŋ
**sp** so-see-ming[1]
> seem

**so-so** *adv*
ˌsoː-ˈsoː
**sp** so, so[4]; so so[1]
**rh** Mercatio *TG 1.2.13*
> so

**Sossius** *n*
ˈsɒsɪəs
**sp** Sossius[1]

**sot / ~s** *n*
=
**sp** sot[6], [make-a-de]-sot[1] / sottes[1]
**rh** not *CE 2.2.203*

**Soto** *n*
ˈsoːtoː
**sp** Soto[1]

**sottish** *adj*
=
**sp** *emend of* sortish[1]

**sought**
> seek

**soul / ~'s / ~s** *n*
ˈsoːl / -z
**sp** soale[1], soule[419], [Christians]-soule[1], [sad]-soule[1], [stranger]-soule[1] / soules[19] / soules[108]
**rh** control *Luc 498, 1779, S 107.1, 125.13*; hole *Luc 1176*; poll *Ham 4.5.199* / fowls *CE 2.1.22*
**pun** *MV 4.1.123* sole

**soul-confirming** *adj*
ˈsoːl-kənˈfɐːɹmɪn, -ɪŋ
**sp** soule-confirming[1]
> confirm

**soul-curer** *n*
ˈsoːl-ˌkjuːrəɹ
**sp** soule-curer[1]
> curer

**soul-fearing** *adj*
*m* ˌsoːl-ˈfiːrɪn, -ɪŋ
**sp** soule-fearing[1]
> fear

**soul-killing** *adj*
*m* ˌso:l-ˈkɪlɪn, -ɪŋ
**sp** soule-killing[1]
> kill

**soulless** *adj*
ˈso:ləs
**sp** soule-lesse[1]

**soul-vexed** *adj*
*m* ˌso:l-ˈvekst
**sp** soule-vext[1]
> vex

**sound** *adj*
səʊnd / ˈsəʊndəɹ / -əst
**sp** sound[34] / sounder[2] / soun-dest[1]
**rh** wound *Per 4.Chorus.24*
> unsound

**sound** *adv*
səʊnd
**sp** sound[8]
**rh** confound *R2 5.3.84*; ground *MND 2.2.80, 3.2.449*

**sound** *n*
səʊnd / -z
**sp** sound[46] / sounds[17]
**rh** *1* drowned *PP 8.9*; found MND *3.2.182, R2 2.1.19* [*also emend as* fond]; ground *S 130.10*; round *Mac 4.1.128*; sound-a bound-a *TNK 3.5.67*; **rh** *2* wound *Luc 1464, RJ 4.5.127* / confounds *S 8.5*

**sound** [noise] / ~s / ~ing / ~ed *v*
səʊnd / -z / ˈsəʊnd·ɪn, -ɪŋ / -ɪd
**sp** sound[118] / sounds[28] / sounding[4] / sounded[21]
**rh** bound *RJ 3.2.126*; round *Per 3. Chorus.36* / confounds *S 128.2* / wounding *VA 431*
> unsounded

**sound** [swoon] / ~ed *v*
səʊnd / ˈsəʊndɪd
**sp** sound[1] / sounded[2]
> swoon, swound

**sounder** *n*
ˈsəʊndəɹ
**sp** sounder[1]

**soundest** *n*
ˈsəʊndəst
**sp** soundest[1]

**sounding** *adj*
ˈsəʊndɪn, -ɪŋ
**sp** sounding[1]
> re-, shrill-sounding

**sounding** *n*
ˈsəʊndɪn, -ɪŋ
**sp** sounding[2]

**soundless** *adj*
ˈsəʊndləs
**sp** soundlesse[1]

**soundly** *adv*
ˈsəʊndləɪ
**sp** soundly[22], sound-ly[1]

**soundness** *n*
ˈsəʊndnəs
**sp** soundnesse[1]

**Soundpost** [name] *n*
ˈsɔʊnpo:st, -ndp-
**sp** Sound-Post[1]

**sour** / ~est *adj*
so:ɹ / -əst
**sp** soure[1], sower[5], sowre[21] / sowrest[3]
**rh** hour *S 57.7*; lour *R2 1.3.236*; power *R2 3.2.193*

**sour** *adv*
so:ɹ
**sp** sowre[2]

**sour** / *Luc* ~s / *Luc* ~ing / ~ed *v*
so:ɹ / -z / ˈso:rɪn, -ɪŋ / so:ɹd
**sp** sowre[2] / sowres[1] / sowring[1] / sowr'd[1]
**rh** ours *Luc 867* / devouring *Luc 699*

**source** / ~s *n*
sɔ:ɹs / ˈsɔ:ɹsɪz
**sp** source[2], sourse[4] / sources[1]

**sourest-natured** *adj*
ˈso:rəst-ˌnɛ:təɹd
**sp** sowrest natured[1]

**sour-eyed** *adj*
*m* ˌso:ɹ-ˈəɪd
**sp** sower-ey'd[1]
> eye

**sourly** *adv*
ˈso:ɹləɪ
**sp** sowrely[1]

**souse** *v*
səʊs
**sp** sowsse[1]

**soused** *adj*
səʊst
**sp** sowc't-[gurnet][1]

**south** *adj* / *adv* / *n*
səʊθ
**sp** south[2], south-[fog], south-[sea], south-[wind][1] / south[2] / south[18]
**rh** *n* mouth *KJ 2.1.413*

**Southam** *n*
ˈsɤðəm
**sp** Southam[2]

**Southampton,** *abbr* **Hampton** *n*
səʊθˈamtən, *abbr* ˈhamtən, ˈam-, -mpt-
**sp** Southampton[4], *abbr* Hampton[1]

**southerly** *adv*
ˈsɤðəɹləɪ
**sp** southerly[1]

**southern** *adj*
ˈsɤðəɹn
**sp** southerne[4]

**southward** *adv*
ˈsəʊθwaɹd
**sp** southward[1], south-ward[1]

**Southwark** *n*
ˈsɤðəɹk
**sp** Southwarke[2]

**Southwell** *n*
'sɤðəl
**sp** Southwell[2]

**south-west** *n*
'səʊθˌwest
**sp** southwest[1]

**souviendrai** *Fr v*
suvjɛ̃'drɛ
**sp** *emend of H5 3.4.9* souemeray[1]

**sovereign / ~est** *adj*
'sɒvrən, -vər- / -st
**sp** soueraign[1], soueraigne[44], soue-raigne[1] / soueraign'st[1]

**sovereign / ~'s** *n*
*m* 'sɒvrən, -vər-, -vəˌren / 'sɒvrənz, -vər-
**sp** soueraign[3], soueraigne[89], so-ueraigne[1] / soueraignes[10], soueraigns[1], sou'raignes[1], sou'rains[1]
**rh** reign *Per 2.4.39*

**sovereignly** *adv*
*m* 'ɜɒvrənˌləɪ
**sp** soueraignely[1]

**sovereignty** *n*
*m* 'sɒvrənˌtəɪ
**sp** soueraigntie[10], soueraignty[13]
**rh** be *Luc 36*; dignity *LLL 4.3.232*
> self-sovereignty

**sow** [animal] **/ ~'s** *n*
səʊ / -z
**sp** sow[2] / sowes[1]

**sow** [grow] **/ ~ing / ~ed** *v*
so: / 'so:ɪn, -ɪŋ / -d
**sp** sow[1], sowe[4], sow't [sow it][1] / sowing[1] / sow'd[4], sowed[1]
**rh** go *MM 4.1.75*

**sowl** *v*
so:l
**sp** sole[1]

**sow-skin** *adj*
'səʊ-ˌskɪn
**sp** sow-skin[1]

**Sowter** *n*
'so:təɹ
**sp** Sowter[1]

**space / ~s** *n*
spɛ:s / 'spɛ:sɪz
**sp** space[26], [blancke]-space[1] / spaces[1]
**rh** face, place *Luc 1776*; grace *AW 2.1.159, LLL 1.1.52, 148*; grace, place *LC 264*

**spacious** *adj*
'spɛ:sɪəs
**sp** spacious[11]
**rh** gracious *S 135.5*

**spade** *n*
spɛ:d
**sp** spade[8]
**rh** made *Ham 5.1.92*

**Spain** *n*
spɛ:n
**sp** Spaine[12]
**rh** brain *LLL 1.1.161*

**spake**
> speak

**span / ~s** *n*
=
**sp** span[4] / spannes[1]
**rh** man *AY 3.2.127, Oth 2.3.67, Tim 5.3.3*

**span / ~ned** *v*
=
**sp** spand[1]

**span-counter** *n*
'span-ˌkəʊntəɹ
**sp** span-counter[1]

**spangle / ~d** *v*
=
**sp** spangle[1] / spangled[1]

**spangled** *adj*
=
**sp** spangled[1]

**Spaniard / ~'s** *n*
'spanɪəɹd / -z
**sp** Spaniard[4] / Spa-niards[1]

**spaniel** *adj*
=
**sp** spaniell[1]

**spaniel / ~s** *n*
=
**sp** spaniel[1], spaniell[3] / spaniels[1]
> water-spaniel

**spaniel-like** *adv*
'spanɪəl-ˌləɪk
**sp** spaniel-like[1]

**Spanish** *adj*
=
**sp** Spanish[3]

**spare** *adj / n*
spɛ:ɹ
**sp** spare[4] / spare[1]

**spar·e / ~es / ~ing / ~ed** *v*
spɛ:ɹ / -z / 'spɛ:rɪn, -ɪŋ / spɛ:ɹd
**sp** spare[55] / spares[2] / sparing[1] / spar'd[6]
**rh** spare me ensnare me *Luc 582*; spare not dare not *TN 2.3.108*

**sparing** *adj / n*
'spɛ:rɪn, -ɪŋ
**sp** sparing[2] / sparing[1]
> none-sparing

**sparingly** *adv*
*m* 'spɛ:rɪnˌləɪ, -ɪŋ-
**sp** sparingly[2]

**spark / ~s** *n*
spɑ:ɹk / -s
**sp** spark[3], sparke[6] / sparkes[9]

**sparkl·e / ~es / ~ing** *v*
'spɑ:ɹkəl / -z / -klɪn, -klɪŋ
**sp** sparcle[1], sparkle[3] / sparkles[1] / sparkling[5]

**sparkling** *adj*
'spɑ:ɹklɪn, -ɪŋ
**sp** sparkling[2]

**sparrow / ~s** *n*
'sparə, -roː / -z
**sp** sparrow[10] / sparrowes[2], spar-rowes[1], sparrows[1]
**rh** arrows *Tem 4.1.100*
> hedge-sparrow

**Sparta / ~'s** *n*
'spɑːɹtə / -z
**sp** Sparta[2] / Sparta's[1]

**Spartan** *adj*
'spɑːɹtən
**sp** Spartan[1], Sparton[1]

**spavin / ~s** *n*
'spavɪn / -z
**sp** spauen[1] / spauins[1]

**spawn** *n*
=
**sp** spawne[1]

**spawn / ~ed** *v*
=
**sp** spawn'd[1]

**speak / ~est / ~s / ~eth / ~ing / spake / ~st / spoke / ~st / ~n** *v*
spiːk, spɛːk, spek / -st / -s / 'spiːk·əθ, 'spɛː-, 'spe- / -ɪn, -ɪŋ / spak / -st / spoːk / -st / -ən
**sp** speak[70], speake[1082], speake-[a-your][1], speak't [speak it][2] / speakest[5], speakst[1], speak'st[35] / speakes[113], speaks[17], speak's[1] / speaketh[1] / speaking[41] / spake[48] / spak'st[2] / spoake[1], spoke[142] / spoak'st[1], spok'st[2] / spoken[58]
**rh** *1* cheek *Per 5.1.95*; leak *KL 3.6.27* [*Q*]; weak *AW 2.1.175, 3.4.42, CE 3.2.33, Luc 1648, VA 1146*; **rh** *2* break *Ham 3.2.196, LLL 1.1.133, Luc 1268, 1718, Mac 4.3.209, S 34.7, TC 3.3.214, VA 221*; **rh** *3* deck *Per 3.Chorus.60* / breaks *Luc 567* / breaking *TC 4.4.19* / broke *MND 1.1.176*; provoke *LLL 5.2.349*; stroke *VA 943*
> be-, fore-, mis-, out-speak; re-, un-speaking; un-, well-spoken

**speaker / ~s** *n*
ˌspiːkəɹ, spɛː- / -z
**sp** speaker[8] / speakers[1]

**spear / ~s** *n*
spiːɹ / -z
**sp** speare[7] / speares[1]
**rh** *1* career *R2 1.2.47*; here *R2 1.1.171*; tear [cry] *R2 1.3.60*; **rh** *2* there *Luc 1424, VA 1112*
> boar-spear

**spear-grass** *n*
'spiːɹ-ˌgras
**sp** spear-grasse[1]

**special** *adj*
'spesɪɑl
**sp** special[2], speciall[33], spe-ciall[1]
> especial

**special-blest** *S* *adj*
'spesɪɑl-'blest
**sp** speciall blest[1]
**rh** chest *S 52.11*

**specially** *adv*
*m* 'spesɪɑˌləɪ
**sp** specially[2]

**specialt·y / ~ies** *n*
*m* 'spesɪɑlˌtəɪ / -z
**sp** specialty[1] / specialties[2]

**specify** *v*
*m* 'spesɪˌfəɪ, -ɪf-
**sp** specifie[4]

**speciously** *adv*
*m* 'spiːsɪəsˌləɪ
**sp** speciously[1], spe-ciously[1]

**spectacle / ~s** *n*
=
spectacle[9] / spectacles[8]

**spectacle / ~d** *v*
=
**sp** spectacled[1]

**spectator / ~s** *n*
spek'tɛːtəɹz
**sp** spectators[4]

**spectatorship** *n*
spek'tɛːtəɹˌʃɪp
**sp** spectatorship[1]

**speculation / ~s** *n*
*m* ˌspekjə'lɛːsɪən, -sɪˌɒn / -sɪənz
**sp** speculation[3] / speculations[1]

**speculative** *adj*
*m* 'spekjəlˌtɪv, -ələ-
**sp** speculatiue[2]

**sped**
> speed

**speech / ~es** *n*
=
**sp** speach[1], spech[1], speech[127] / speeches[21]
**rh** beseech *CE 4.2.15*; eche [eke] *Per 3.Chorus.14*; teach *R2 5.3.113*

**speechless** *adj*
=
**sp** speechlesse[11]

**speed** *n*
=
**sp** speed[54], speede[23]
**rh** breed, deed *Luc 501*; meed *Cym 3.5.162*; need *2H4 1.1.214*

**speed / ~s / ~ed / sped** *v*
=
**sp** speed[27], speed[131], speede[29] / speedes[1], speeds[4] / speeded[2] / sped[10]
**rh** deed *AW 3.7.44*; indeed *Tim 3.2.63*; need *KJ 1.1.178, S 51.2* / weeds *MA 5.3.32* / bed *TS 5.2.184*; bed, head *MV 2.9.72*

**Speed** [name] *n*
=
**sp** Speed[6]

**speedier** *n*
'spiːdəɪəɹ
**sp** speedier[1]

**speediest** *n*
'spiːdəɪəst
**sp** speediest[1]

**speedily** *adv*
*m* ˈspiːdɪləɪ, -ˌləɪ
**sp** speedily[11], spee-dily[1]
**rh** Brittany *3H6 4.6.102*; merrily *1H4 4.1.133*

**speediness** *n*
=
**sp** speedinesse[1]

**speeding** *adj / n*
ˈspiːdɪn, -ɪŋ
**sp** speeding[1] / speeding[2]

**speed·y / ~ier / ~iest** *adj*
ˈspiːdəɪ / -əɹ / -əst
**sp** speedie[5], speedy[14] / speedier[1] / speediest[2]

**spell / ~s** *n*
=
**sp** spell[8] / spelles[1], spels[4]
**rh** dwell *Tem Epil.8*

**spell / ~ed** *v*
=
**sp** spell[2] / speld[1]
**rh** well *RJ 2.3.84*

**spelling** *adj*
ˈspelɪn, -ɪŋ
**sp** spelling[1]

**spell-stopped** *adj*
=
**sp** spell-stopt[1]

**Spencer** *n*
ˈspensəɹ
**sp** Spencer[1]

**spend / ~est / ~s / ~ing / spent** *v*
= / spenst, -ndst / = / ˈspendɪn, -ɪŋ / =
**sp** spend[59] / spendest[1], spend'st[1] / spends[3] / spending[2] / spent[60]
**rh** end *Mac 3.5.20, S 9.9, 146.6, Tim 3.4.57*; friend *PP 20.34, S 149.7*; lend *S 4.1*; tend *S 57.3* / argument *S 76.12, 100.6, 105.11, Tim 3.5.22*; attent *Per 3. Chorus.12*; banishment *R2 1.3.211, RJ 3.2.130*; content *AY 2.3.67, Cym 5.4.104, Mac 3.2.4, S 119.14*; content, repent *MND 2.2.118*; descent *R2 1.1.108*; detriment, discontent *Luc 1577*; discontent, event *Luc 1600*; element *Luc 1589*; event *2H6 3.1.325*; exigent *1H6 2.5.8*; instrument *R2 2.1.150*; Lent *RJ 2.4.136*; monument *S 107.14*; rent *S 125.8*; tent *TC 5.1.43*; testament *Luc 1182*
> forespend

**spendthrift** *n*
=
**sp** spend-thrift[1]

**spent** *adj*
=
**sp** spent[1]

**spera / ~to** *Ital v*
ˈspera / speˈrɑːto:
**sp** spera[1] / *Pistol 2H4 2.4.176* sperato[1]

**sphere / ~s** *n*
sfiːɹ / -z
**sp** spheare[3], sphere[7] / sphceres[3], spheres[4]
**rh** *1* clear *MND 3.2.61*; **rh** *2* every-where *MND 2.1.7*

**sphere / ~d** *v*
sfiːɹd
**sp** sphear'd[1]
> unsphere

**sphered** *adj*
*m* ˈsfiːrɪd
**sp** sphered[1]

**spherical** *adj*
ˈsferɪkɑl
**sp** sphericall[3]

**sphery** *adj*
ˈsfiːrəɪ
**sp** sphery[1]

**sphinx** *n*
=
**sp** sphinx[1]

**spice / ~s** *n*
spəɪs / ˈspəɪsɪz
**sp** spice[3] / spices[5]

**spice / ~s** *v*
ˈspəɪsɪz
**sp** spices[1]

**spiced** *adj*
*m* ˈspəɪsɪd
**sp** spiced[1]

**spicery** *n*
ˈspəɪsrəɪ, -sər-
**sp** spicery[1]

**spider / ~'s / ~s** *n*
ˈspəɪdəɹ / -z
**sp** spider[9] / spiders[2] / spiders[3]

**spider-like** *adv*
ˈspəɪdəɹ-ˌləɪk
**sp** spider-like[1]

**spigot** *n*
=
**sp** spigot[1]

**spill / ~s / ~ing / ~ed / ~t** *v*
= / = / ˈspɪlɪn, -ɪŋ / =
**sp** spill[5] / spilles[1], spill's[1] / spilling[1] / spild[1] / spilt[5]
**rh** ill *LLL 4.1.34*; ill, kill *Luc 999* / filling, willing *Luc 1236* / **rh** *1* filled, killed *Luc 1801*; killed *VA 1167*; **rh** *2* child *RJ 3.1.147* / guilt *Ham 4.5.20*

**spilth** *n*
=
**sp** spilth[1]

**spin / spun** *v*
= / spɤn
**sp** spin[4] / spun[2]

**Spinii** *n*
ˈspɪniː
**sp** Spinij[1]

**spinner / ~s'** *n*
ˈspɪnəɹz
**sp** spinners[1] / spin-ners[1]

**spinster / ~s** *n*
'spɪnstəɹ / -z
**sp** spinster[1] / spinsters[2]

**spire** *n*
'spəɪɹ
**sp** spire[1]

**spirit / ~s** *n*
*m* =, spɪɹt / -s, sprəɪts
**sp** spirit[238], [ill]-spirit[1], spi-rit[2], spirite[2], spirit's [spirit is][1] / spirites[3], spirits[118], sprights[1]
**rh** merit *S 108.2*

**spirit / ~ed** *v*
=
**sp** spirited[1]
> barren-, ill-, low-, pleasant-spirited

**spiritless** *adj*
*m* 'spɪrɪt,les
**sp** spiritlesse[1]

**spirit-stirring** *adj*
'spɪrɪt-,stɐ:rɪn, -ɪŋ
**sp** spirit-stirring[1]

**spiritual** *adj*
*m* 'spɪrɪt,ju:ɑl, -tjɑl
**sp** spirituall[6]

**spiritualty** *n*
*m* ,spɪrɪ'tju:ɑltəɪ
**sp** spiritualtie[1]

**spirt** *v*
spɐ:ɹt
spirt[1]

**spit / ~s** *n*
=
**sp** spit[4], spits[3]

**spit / ~s / ted** *v*
=
**sp** spet[3], spit[21] / spets[1], spits[2] / spitted[1]

**spital**
> spittle

**spite / ~s** *n*
spəɪt / -s
**sp** spight[30], spite[1] / spights[1]
**rh** delight *S 36.6, 37.3*; fight, knight *PP 15.7*; knight *MND 5.1.268*; light *MND 3.2.420, VA 1133*; might *S 90.10*; night *Luc 762, RJ 1.5.62*; right *CE 4.2.8, Ham 1.5.188*; tonight *2H6 5.1.213* / sprites *CE 2.2.198*
> despite

**spite / ~s / ~d** *v*
spəɪt / -s / 'spəɪtɪd
**sp** spight[5] / spights[1] / spighted[1]

**spite of, (in)** *prep*
(ɪn)'spəɪtəv
**sp** in spight of[12], [in]spight of[2], spight of[3]
> despite of

**spiteful** *adj*
'spəɪtfʊl
**sp** spightfull[2], spitefull[1]

**spitting** *adj / n*
'spɪtɪn, -ɪŋ
**sp** spitting[1] / spitting[1]

**spittle, spital** *n*
=
**sp** spittle[2]

**spittle-house** *n*
'spɪtl-,əʊs, -,həʊs
**sp** spittle-house[1]
> house

**splay** *v*
splɛ:
**sp** splay[1]

**spleen / ~s** *n*
=
**sp** spleene[28] / spleenes[3]
**rh** been *PP 6.6*; queen *3H6 2.1.123*

**spleenful** *adj*
=
**sp** spleenefull[1], spleenfull[1]

**spleeny** *adj*
'spli:nəɪ
**sp** spleeny[1]

**spleet / ~s** *v*
=
**sp** spleet's[1]

**splenative** *adj*
*m* 'spli:nə,tɪv
**sp** spleenatiue[1]

**splendour** *n*
'splendəɹ
**sp** splendor[2]

**splinter / ~s** *n*
'splɪntəɹ / -z
**sp** splinter[1] / splinters[1]

**splinter / ~ed** *v*
'splɪntəɹ / -d
**sp** splinter[1] / splinter'd[1]

**split / ~est / ~s / ~ting / ~ted** *v*
= / splɪts, -tst / = / 'splɪtɪn, -ɪŋ / =
**sp** split[16] / splitt'st[1] / splits[2] / splitting[1] / splitted[3]
**rh** ship *Per 2.Chorus.32*

**splitted** *adj*
=
**sp** splitted[1]

**splitting** *adj*
'splɪtɪn, -ɪŋ
**sp** splitting[2]

**spoil / ~s** *n*
spəɪl / -z
**sp** spoile[4], spoyle[10] / spoiles[3], spoyles[2]
**rh** boil *VA 553*; foil *LC 154*

**spoil / ~s / ~ed** *v*
spəɪl / -z / -d
**sp** spoile[1], spoyle[8] / spoyles[5] / spoil'd[2], spoyl'd[7]

**spoke / ~s** *n*
spo:ks
**sp** spoakes[1], spokes[2]

**spokesman** *n*
'spo:ksmən
**sp** spokes-man[1]

**sponge** *n*
spɤndʒ
**sp** spundge[3], spunge[1]

**spongy** *adj*
'spɤndʒəɪ
**sp** spungie[3], spungy[1]

**spoon / ~s** *n*
=
**sp** spoone[4] / spoones[3]

**spoon-meat** *n*
=
**sp** spoon-meate[1]

**sport / ~s** *n*
spɔ:ɹt / -s
**sp** sport[114], [table]-sport[1] / sports[9]
**rh** court *LLL 4.1.100*; extort, sort *MND 3.2.161*; report *S 95.6*; resort *S 96.2*; resort, short *Luc 992*; short *1H4 1.3.296, LLL 1.1.177, VA 24, 844*; sort *MND 3.2.14, 353, 389*

**sport** *v*
spɔ:ɹt
**sp** sport[6]
**rh** sport me support me *VA 154*
> dis-, out-sport

**sportful** *adj*
'spɔ:ɹtfʊl
**sp** sportfull[4]

**sporting** *adj*
'spɔ:ɹtɪn, -ɪŋ
**sp** sporting[1]

**sportive** *adj*
'spɔ:ɹtɪv
**sp** sportiue[3]

**spot / ~s** *n*
=
**sp** spot[9], spotte[1] / spottes[1], spots[8]

**spot / ~ted** *v*
=
**sp** spotted[4]
**rh** blotted *Oth 5.1.36*

**spotless** *adj*
=
**sp** spotlesse[7]

**spotted** *adj / n*
=
**sp** spotted[6] / spotted[1]
> blood-be-, cinque-, pinch-, toad-, un-spotted

**spousal** *adj / n*
'spəʊzɑl
**sp** spousall[1] / spousall[1]

**spouse** *n*
spəʊz
**sp** spouse[4]

**spout / ~s** *n*
spəʊt / -s
**sp** spout[1] / spouts[3]

**spout / ~ing** *v*
spəʊt / 'spəʊtɪn, -ɪŋ
**sp** spout[3], spowt[1] / spouting[1]

**sprack** *n*
*Evans MW 4.1.77* sprag
**sp** sprag-[memory][1]

**sprang**
> spring

**sprat** *n*
=
**sp** sprat[1]

**sprawl / ~est** *v*
sprɔ:l, -rɑ:l / 'sprɔ:lst, -rɑ:l-
**sp** sprall[1] / sprawl'st[1]
**rh** withal *Tit 5.1.51*

**spray / ~s** *n*
sprɛ: / -z
**sp** spray[1] / sprayes[3]
**rh** days *2H6 2.3.45*

**spread / ~ing** *v*
= / 'spredɪn, -ɪŋ
**sp** spread[14], spred[11] / spreading[1]
**rh** buried *S 25.5*; dead *Luc 1266*; red *VA 903*
> overspread

**spreading** *adj*
'spredɪn, -ɪŋ
**sp** spreading[1]

**sprig / ~s** *n*
=
**sp** sprigs[1]

**spright**
> sprite

**spring / ~s** *n*
=
**sp** spring[37] / springs[7]
**rh** bring *VA 656*; ding, sing *AY 5.3.20, 26, 32, 38*; everything *TN 3.1.146*; king *Per 1.1.13, R2 5.2.47, S 63.8*; king, thing *Luc 604*; niggarding *S 1.10*; sing *H8 3.1.8, LLL 1.1.101, Luc 869, S 102.5*; sing, thing *Luc 331*; sting *PP 10.2*; thing *S 98.1* / kings *R2 1.3.214*; sings *Cym 2.3.21*; things, wings *Luc 950*
> love spring

**spring / ~s / ~eth / ~ing / sprung / sprang / ~est** *v*
= / = / = / 'sprɪŋgɪn, -ɪŋ / sprɤŋ / = / spraŋst
**sp** spring[12] / springs[5] / springeth[1] / springing[2] / sprung[10] / sprang[1] / sprang'st[1]
**rh** sing *PP 20.6*

**springe / ~s** *n*
'sprɪndʒ / -ɪz
**sp** sprindge[2] / springes[1]

**springhalt** *n*
'sprɪŋˌɔ:t, -ˌhɔ:t
**sp** spring-halt[1]

**springtime** *n*
'sprɪŋtəɪm
**sp** spring-time[3], spring time[5]
**rh** ring-time *AY 5.3.18, 24, 30, 36*

**sprinkle / ~s** *v*
=
**sp** sprinkle[3] / sprinkles[1]

**sprite, spright / ~s** *n*
sprəɪt / -s
**sp** spright[2], sprights[7], sprite[2]
**rh** fight, night *Luc 121*; light *MND 5.1.383*; night *Luc 451, MND 5.1.371*; quite *MND 2.1.33*; sight *VA 181*; write *AY 3.2.135* / delights *Mac 4.1.126*; sleights *Mac 3.5.27*; spites *CE 2.2.199*

**sprite, spright / ~ed** *v*
sprəɪtɪd
**sp** sprighted[1]

**spriteful, sprightful** *adj*
'sprəɪtfʊl
**sp** sprightfull[1]

**spritefully, sprightfully** *adv*
*m* 'sprəɪtfʊˌləɪ
**sp** sprightfully[1]

**spritely, sprightly** *adj*
'sprəɪtləɪ
**sp** sprightly[8], spritely[1]

**spriting, sprighting** *n*
'sprəɪtɪn, -ɪŋ
**sp** spryting[1]

**sprout** *v*
sprəʊt
**sp** sprowt[1]

**spruce** *adj*
=
**sp** spruce[3]

**spur / ~s** *n*
spɐ:ɹ / -z
**sp** spur[2], spurre[13], [cold]-spurre[1], [hot]-spurre[1] / spurres[7], spurs[3]
**rh** stir *VA 285*

**spur / ~s / ~ring / ~red** *v*
spɐ:ɹ / -z / 'spɐ:ɹɪn, -ɪŋ / spɐ:ɹd
**sp** spur[4], spurre[10] / spurres[3], spurs[2] / spurring[1] / spurd[2], spurr'd[1]
> fore-spurrer

**spur-gall / ~ed** *v*
*m* ˌspɐ:ɹ-'gɑ:ld
**sp** spur-gall'd[1]
> gall

**Spurio** *n*
'spɤrɪo:
**sp** Spurio[2]

**spurn / ~s** *n*
spɐ:ɹn / -z
**sp** spurne[2], spurnes[1]

**spurn / ~s / ~ed** *v*
spɐ:ɹn / -z / -d
**sp** spurne[24] / spurnes[5] / spurn'd[1]

**spurring** *n*
'spɐ:rɪn, -ɪŋ
**sp** spurring[2]

**sp·y / ~ies** *n*
spəɪ / -z
**sp** spy[2] / spies[8], spyes[1]
**rh** jealousy *VA 655* / eyes *S 121.7*

**spy / ~est / spies / ~ing / spied** *v*
spəɪ / spəɪst / spəɪz / 'spəɪɪn, -ɪŋ / spəɪd
**sp** spie[14], spy[8], spye[1] / spy'st[1] / spies[1], spyes[1] / spying[2] / spied[4], spy'd[1], spyed[2]
**rh** eye *MND 3.2.19, TG 5.4.115*; spy him by him *Luc 881* / eyes *Luc 1086*; flies *VA 1029*; lies *Luc 316* / belied *Luc 1532*
> espy

**squabble** *v*
'skwɑbəl, -wɒ-
**sp** squabble[1]

**squadron / ~s** *n*
'skwɑdrən, -wɒ- / -z
**sp** squadron[1] / squadrons[3]

**squander / ~ed** *v*
'skwɑndəɹd, -wɒ-
**sp** squandred[1]

**squandring** *adj*
'skwɑndrɪn, -ɪŋ, -wɒ-
**sp** squandring[1]

**square** *adj*
skwɛ:ɹ
**sp** square[2]

**square / ~s** *n*
skwɛ:ɹ / -z
**sp** square[3] / squares[2]
> squier

**square / ~st / ~d** *v*
skwɛ:ɹ / -st / -d
**sp** square[8] / squar'st[1] / squar'd[2]
> unsquared

**squarer** *n*
'skwɛ:rəɹ
**sp** squarer[1]

**squash** *n*
skwɑʃ
**sp** squash[3]

**squeak** *v*
=
**sp** squeak[1]

**squeaking** *adj*
'skwi:kɪn, -ɪŋ
**sp** squeaking[1]

**squeal** *v*
=
**sp** squeale[1]

**squealing** *n*
'skwi:lɪn, -ɪŋ
**sp** squealing[1]

**squeez·e / ~ing** *v*
'skwi:zɪn, -ɪŋ
**sp** squee-zing[1]

**Squele** [name] *n*
skwi:l
**sp** Squele[1]

**squier** [square] *n*
skwəɪɹ
**sp** squier[1]
**rh** fire *LLL 5.2.474*
> square

**squinny** *v*
'skwɪnəɪ
**sp** squiny[1]

**squint / ~s** *v*
=
**sp** squints[1]
> asquint

**squire / ~'s / ~s** *n*
skwəɪɹ / -z
**sp** squier[1], squire[10] / squires[2] / squires[4]
**rh** desire *KJ 1.1.177*
> esquire, mountain-squire

**squirelike** *adv*
'skwəɪɹləɪk
**sp** squire-like[1]

**squirrel / ~'s** *n*
=
**sp** squirrel[1], squirrill[1] / squirrels[1]

**stab / ~s** *n*
=
**sp** stab[1] / stabs[2]

**stab / ~best / ~s / ~bed** *v*
= / stabst / =
**sp** stab[16] / stab'st[1] / stabbes[2], stabs[6] / stabb'd[7], stabd[1], stab'd[12]

**stabbing** *adj / n*
'stabɪn, -ɪŋ
**sp** stabbing[2] / stabbing[2]

**stable** *adj*
'stɛ:bəl
**sp** stable[2]

**stable / ~s** *n*
'stɛ:bəl / -z
**sp** stable[4], stables[3]

**stableness** *n*
*m* 'stɛ:bəlˌnes
**sp** stablenesse[1]

**stablishment** *n*
=
**sp** stablishment[1]
> establish

**staff** *n*
staf
**sp** staff[1], staffe[40]
**rh** laugh *CE 3.1.51*
> cowl-, long-, torch-staff; stave

**Stafford / ~'s / ~s** *n*
'stafəɹd / -z
**sp** Stafford[11], Staf-ford[1] / Staffords[3] / Staffords[3]

**Staffordshire** *n*
*m* 'stafəɹdʃəɹ, -ˌʃəɪɹ
**sp** Staffordshire[1]

**stag / ~s** *n*
=
**sp** stag[2], stagge[2] / stagges[1], stags[1]

**stage / ~s** *n*
stɛ:ʤ / 'stɛ:ʤɪz
**sp** stage[31] / stages[1]
**rh** age, sage *Luc 278*; rage *RJ Prol.12, S 23.1*

**stage / ~d** *v*
stɛ:ʤ / -d
**sp** stage[2] / stag'd[1]

**stagger / ~s** *n*
'stagəɹz
**sp** staggers[3]

**stagger / ~s** *v*
'stagəɹ / -z
**sp** stagger[3] / staggers[1]

**staggering** *n*
'stagrɪn, -ɪŋ, -gər-
**sp** staggering[1]

**staid / ~er** *adj*
'stɛ:dəɹ
**sp** stayder[1]
> unstaid

**stain / ~s** *n*
stɛ:n / -z
**sp** staine[12], stayne[2] / staines[3], staynes[1]
**rh** again *Luc 1708, S 109.8*; slain *1H6 4.5.42*

**stain / ~s / *S, VA* ~eth / ~ed** *v*
stɛ:n / -z / 'stɛ:n·əθ / *m* -ɪd, stɛ:nd
**sp** staine[20], stayne[2] / staines[2] / staineth[1], *emend of S* stainteh[1] / stain'd[12], staind[3], stained[2], stayn'd[5]
**rh** slain *MND 5.1.142* / disdaineth *S 33.14*; raineth *VA 460* / complained, maintained *Luc 1836*; reigned *S 109.11*; remained *Luc 1743*
> overstain

**stained** *adj*
*m* 'stɛ:nɪd, stɛ:nd
**sp** stain'd[2], stained[2], stayned[1]
> blood-, lust-, neighbour-, tear-, un-stained

**Staines** *n*
stɛ:nz
**sp** Staines[1]

**staining** *adj*
'stɛ:nɪn, -ɪŋ
**sp** staining[1]

**stainless** *adj*
'stɛ:nləs
**sp** stainlesse[2]

**stair / ~s** *n*
stɛ:ɹ / -z
**sp** staire[1] / staires[4], stayres[1]
> down-, up-stairs

**stair-work** *n*
'stɛ:ɹ-ˌwɔ:ɹk
**sp** staire-worke[1]
> work

**stake / ~s** *n*
stɛ:k / -s
**sp** stake[17] / stakes[1]

**stake / ~s** *v*
stɛ:ks
**sp** stakes[2]

**stale** *adj / n / v*
stɛ:l
**sp** stale[11] / stale[9], [bully]-stale[1] / stale[2] , staule[1]

**rh** *adj* tale *WT 4.1.13* / *n* pale *CE 2.1.101*

**stalk** *n*
stɔ:k
**sp** stalke[2]

**stalk / ~s** *v*
stɔ:k / -s
**sp** stalke[6] / stalkes[2]
**rh** walks *Luc 365*

**stalking-horse** *n*
'stɔ:kɪn-ˌɔ:ɹs, -ɪŋ-, -ˌhɔ:-
**sp** stalking-horse[1]
> horse

**stall / ~s** *n*
stɑ:l / -z
**sp** stall[1] / stalls[3], stals[1]
**rh** mechanicals *MND 3.2.10*

**stall / ~ed** *v*
stɑ:l / -d
**sp** stall[2] / stal'de[1], stall'd[1]

**stalling** *n*
'stɑ:lɪn, -ɪŋ
**sp** stalling[1]

**stallion** *n*
=
**sp** stallion[1]

**Stamford** *n*
'stamfəɹd
**sp** Stamford[1]

**stammer** *v*
'staməɹ
**sp** stammer[1]

**stamp / ~s** *n*
=
**sp** stampe[12] / stampes[1], stamps[1]

**stamp / ~s / ~ed** *v*
= / = / *m* 'stampɪd, stampt
**sp** stamp[1], stampe[7] / stampes[3], stamps[1] / stamp'd[1], stamped[1], stampt[6], stamp't[1]

**stamped** *adj*
=
**sp** stamped[1]

**stanch** *v*
stanʧ, stɔ:nʧ
**sp** stanch[1], staunch[1]
> unstanched

**stanchless** *adj*
'stanʧləs, 'stɔ:-
**sp** stanchlesse[1]

**stand / ~s** *n*
=
**sp** stand[15], [still]-stand[1] / stands[1]
**rh** hand, land *Luc 438*; hand *RJ 1.5.50*,

**stand / ~est / ~s / ~eth / ~ing / stood** *v*
= / *m* stans, -st, 'standəst / = / = / 'standɪn, -ɪŋ / =
**sp** stand[527], stand-[by][1], stand-[vnder][1] / standest[2], standst[2], stand'st[14] / stands[146] / standeth[3] / standing[21] / stood[88], stoode[2]
**rh** dial-hand *S 104.11*; hand *2H6 2.3.43, LC 143, Luc 1233, 1401, 1599, MND 5.1.400, R2 5.3.128, RJ 1.5.95, S 60.13, 99.8, 128.8*; land *Cym 2.1.63, KL 1.4.141* [Q], *S 44.5* / hands *AC 2.1.50, Per 2.4.58* / **rh** *1* blood, flood *Luc 1740*; blood *1H6 4.5.17, VA 1121, 1170*; flood *Luc 265, PP 6.13*; **rh** *2* good *AW 1.3.72, 73*
> out-, still-stand

**standard / ~s** *n*
'standəɹd / -z
**sp** standard[9] / standards[3]

**stander / ~s** *n*
'standəɹz
**sp** standers[1]

**stander-by / ~s-by** *n*
'standəɹ-'bəɪ / -ɹz-
**sp** stander-by[1] / standers by[4]
> by

**standing** *adj* / *n*
'standɪn, -ɪŋ
**sp** standing[7], sta[n]ding[1] / standing[5]
> water-standing

**standing-bed** *n*
'standɪn-ˌbed, -ɪŋ-
**sp** standing-bed[1]
> bed

**Stanley / ~'s** *n*
'stanləɪ / -z
**sp** Stanley[28], Stanly[2] / Stanleys[1]

**stanza / ~s** *n*
=
**sp** stanze[1], stanzo[1] / stanzo's[1]

**staple / ~s** *n*
'stɛ:pəl / -z
**sp** staple[1] / staples[1]

**star / ~s** *n*
stɑ:ɹ / -z
**sp** star[1], starre[35], [watry]-starre[1] / starres[50], stars[12]
**rh** are *LLL 1.1.89* / **rh** *1* bars *S 25.1*; **rh** *2* wars *MND 3.2.407, Per 1.1.38*
> ill-starred, lodestar

**star / ~red** *v*
stɑ:ɹd
**sp** star'd[1]

**star-blasting** *n*
'stɑ:ɹ-ˌblastɪn, -ɪŋ
**sp** starre-blasting[1]
> blast

**star-chamber** *adj*
'stɑ:ɹ-ˌʧambəɹ
**sp** star-chamber[1]
> chamber

**stare** *n*
stɛ:ɹ
**sp** stare[1]

**star·e / ~es / ~ing / ~ed** *v*
stɛ:ɹ / -z / 'stɛ:rɪn, -ɪŋ / stɛ:ɹd
**sp** stare[11] / stares[2] / staring[1], sta-ring[1] / star'd[3]
**rh** cares, fares *Luc 1591*; prepares *VA 301*
> out-, over-stare; upstaring

**staring** *adj*
'stɛ:rɪn, -ɪŋ
**sp** staring[3]

**staring / ~s** *n*
'stɛ:rɪnz, -ɪŋz
**sp** starings[1]

**stark** *adv*
stɑ:ɹk
**sp** starke[8], starke-[mad][1], starke-[nak'd][1]

**starkly** *adv*
'stɑ:ɹkləɪ
**sp** starkely[1]

**starlight** *adj / n*
'stɑ:ɹləɪt
**sp** star-light[1] / star-light[1], starre-light[1]

**starlike** *adj / adv*
'stɑ:ɹləɪk
**sp** starre-like[1] / star-like[1]

**starling** *n*
'stɑ:ɹlɪn, -ɪŋ
**sp** starling[1]

**starry** *adj*
'stɑ:rəɪ
**sp** starrie[1]

**start / ~s** *n*
stɑ:ɹt / -s
**sp** start[9], starts[5]

**start / ~est / ~s / ~eth / ~ing / ~ed** *v*
stɑ:ɹt / -s / -s / 'stɑ:ɹt·əθ / -ɪn, -ɪŋ / -ɪd
**sp** start[24] / starts [thou][1] / startes[1], starts[7] / starteth[1] / starting[2], star-ting[1] / started[3]
**rh** heart *1H6 4.7.12, MW 5.5.86* / imparteth *Luc 1037*

**starting** *adj / n*
'stɑ:ɹtɪn, -ɪŋ
**sp** *TC 4.5.2 emend* starring[1] / starting[1], star-ting[1]

**starting-hole** *n*
'stɑ:ɹtɪn-ˌo:l, -ɪŋ-, -ˌho:l
**sp** starting hole[1]

**startingly** *adv*
*m* 'stɑ:ɹtɪnˌləɪ, -ɪŋ-
**sp** startingly[1]

**startle / ~s** *v*
'stɑ:ɹtl / -z
**sp** startle[2] / startles[3]

**start-up** *n*
'stɑ:ɹt-ˌɤp
**sp** start-vp[1]

**starv·e / ~eth / ~ing / ~ed** *v*
stɑ:ɹv / -əθ / 'stɑ:ɹvɪn, -ɪŋ / stɑ:ɹvd
**sp** starue[9], sterue[6] / starueth[1] / staruing[1] / staru'd[4], steru'd[2]
**rh** deserve *Cor 2.3.112*
> hunger-, hungry-starved

**starved** *adj*
*m* 'stɑ:ɹvɪd, stɑ:ɹvd
staru'd[3], starued[5], steru'd[1]

**Starve-lackey** [name] *n*
'stɑ:ɹv-ˌlakəɪ
**sp** Starue-lackey[1]
> lackey

**starveling / Starveling** [name] *n*
'stɑ:ɹvlɪn, -ɪŋ
**sp** starueling[2] / Starueling[4], Starue-ling[1]

**state** *adj*
stɛ:t
**sp** state[3]

**state / ~'s / ~s** *n*
stɛ:t / -s
**sp** state[284], states [state is][1] / states[3] / states[13]
**rh** anticipate *S 118.11*; bait *CE 2.1.95*; communicate *CE 2.2.184*; debate *KL 5.1.68*; degenerate, hate *Luc 1006*; fate *LLL 5.2.67, MW 5.5.224, S 29.2*; fate, gate *Luc 1066*; gait *S 128.9, Tem 4.1.101*; gate *2H6 4.10.21, S 29.10*; hate *Luc 666, S 124.1, 142.3, 145.4, 150.12*; instigate *Luc 45*; late *Ham 3.2.173, LLL 5.2.363, R2 3.2.72*; mate, rate *Luc 16*; propagate *AW 2.1.198*; rate *MND 3.1.146*; relate *Oth 5.2.366*; ruinate [*F, at Tit 5.3.199*]; ruminate *S 64.9*; translate *S 96.12*
> en-, un-state

**statel·y / ~ier** *adj*
'stɛ:tləɪ / -əɹ
**sp** stately[9] / statelyer[1]

**stately** *adv*
'stɛ:tləɪ
**sp** stately[1]

**statesman / ~men** *n*
'stɛ:tsmən
**sp** statesman[1], states-man[1] / statesmen[1]

**state-statue / ~s** *n*
'stɛ:t-'statju:z
**sp** state-statues[1]
> statue

**Statilius** *n*
stə'tɪlɪəs
**sp** Statillius[1]

**station** *n*
'stɛ:sɪən
**sp** station[6], sta-tion[1]

**statist / ~s** *n*
'stɛ:tɪst / -s
**sp** statist[1] / statists[1]

**statue / ~s** *n*
'statju: / -z
**sp** statue[18] / statues[2]
> state-statue

**stature / ~s** *n*
'statjəɹ / -z
**sp** stature[4] / statures[1]

**statute / ~s** *n*
'statju:t / -s
**sp** statute[4] / statutes[11]

**statute-cap / ~s** *n*
'statju:t-ˌkaps
**sp** statute caps[1]
**rh** perhaps *LLL 5.2.281*
> cap

**stave / ~'s / ~s** *n*
'stɛ:vz
**sp** staues[9] / staues[9]
> staff; tip-, torch-staff

**stay / ~s** *n*
'stɛ: / -z
**sp** stay[24] / stayes[1]
**rh** away *1H6 4.6.40, MV 3.2.325, R2 5.5.95, RJ 1.1.158*; clay *KJ 5.7.68*; day *MND 5.1.411*; decay *S 15.9*; pay *MND 3.2.87*; say *R2 5.5.95*

**stay / ~est / ~s / ~eth / ~ing / ~ed** *v*
stɛ: / -st / -z / 'stɛ:·əθ / -ɪn, -ɪŋ / stɛ:d
**sp** staie[5], stay[386] / stayest[1], stay'st[1] / staies[16], stayes[21] / stayeth[1] / staying[8] / staid[21], staide[1], stayd[2], stay'd[11], stayed[2]
**rh** array *1H6 1.3.54*; assay, way *LC 159*; away, day *Luc 1012*; away, may *LLL 2.1.113*; away *CE 3.2.192, 5.1.337, 1H6 4.5.30, 2H6 5.2.73, KJ 2.1.416, 4.3.8, KL 2.4.78, LLL 4.3.211, 5.2.623, MND 2.1.145, MV 2.6.59, R2 4.1.198, R3 1.4.286, RJ 3.1.136, 5.3.159, S 74.4, 92.3, 143.4, TN 5.1.141, TS 5.1.139*; day *AW 5.3.69, 1H6 4.6.36, 3H6 2.1.187, 2.2.176, MND 2.1.138, MV 5.1.302, S 43.12*; holiday *H8 5.5.75*; may *2H6 4.4.47*; play *LLL 4.3.75*; prey *Luc 423*; say *RJ 1.2.37*; way *LLL 4.3.75, Luc 311, 1364, Per 5.3.83, R2 1.3.305, S 44.4, 48.3, VA 706, 873*; **stay him** delay him *Luc 323*; **stay ye** say ye *TNK Epil.9* / days *Ham 3.3.95, RJ 1.3.105* / **rh** *1* maid *Luc 1275*; **rh** *2* said *VA 331*
> outstay

**stayer / ~s** *n*
'stɛ:əɹz
**sp** stayers[1]

**staying** *n*
'stɛ:ɪn, -ɪŋ
**sp** staying[3]

**stead** *n*
=
**sp** stead[3], steed[2], sted[2]
**rh** dead *1H6 4.6.31*
> instead

**stead / ~s** *v*
=
**sp** stead[1], sted[1] / steads[1]
**rh** dead *Per 4.Chorus.41*

**steadfast** *adj*
'stedfast
**sp** stedfast[1]
> unsteadfast

**steadfastly** *VA* *adv*
*m* 'stedfastˌləɪ
**sp** stedfastly[1]
**rh** three *VA 1063*

**steady** *adj*
'stedəɪ
**sp** steddier[1]

**steal / ~s / *Luc* ~eth / ~ing / stole / ~st / ~n** *v*
= / = / = / 'sti:lɪn, -ɪŋ / sto:l / -st / -n, 'sto:lən
**sp** steale[76], steale't [steal it][1] / steales[11], steals[1] / stealeth[1] / stealing[10] / stole[21] / stolest[1], stol'st[1] / stolen[1], stollen[1], stoln[1], stolne[51]
**rh** conceal *MND 1.1.213*; weal *1H6 1.1.176* / healeth *Luc 729*

**stealer / ~s** *n*
'sti:ləɹ / -z
stealer[2] / stealers[1]
> horse-stealer, thief-stolen

**stealing** *adj / n*
'sti:lɪn, -ɪŋ
**sp** stealing[2] / stealing[1]

**stealth** *n*
=
**sp** stealth[9]
**rh** wealth *CE 3.2.7, Tim 3.4.29*

**stealthy** *adj*
'stelθəɪ
**sp** stealthy[1]

**steed / ~'s / ~s** *n*
=
**sp** steed[13], steede[2] / steeds[1] / steedes[3], steeds[11]
**rh** deed *LC 112*; exceed *VA 290*; meed *VA 13*

**steed / ~s / ~ed** *v*
=
**sp** steed[5] / steeds[1] / steeded[1]

**steel** *adj / n*
=
**sp** steele[2] / steele[65]
**rh** feel *Luc 755, S 120.4, VA 199*; heel *WT 4.4.228*; wheel *CE 3.2.153, Luc 951*

**steel / ~ed** *v*
=
**sp** steele[6] / steel'd[3]
**rh** **steel it** feel it *VA 375* / held *S 24.1*

**steeled** *adj*
*m* 'sti:lɪd
**sp** steeled[3]

**steely** *adv*
'sti:ləɪ
**sp** steely[2]

**steep** *adj*
=
**sp** steepe[5]

**steep / ~s / ~ed** *v*
= / = / *m* =, 'sti:pɪd
**sp** steep[1], steepe[3] / steepes[1] / steep'd[7], steeped[1], steept[2], steep't[1]
**rh** asleep *S 153.3*; sleep *TN 4.1.61*

**steep-down** *adj*
'sti:p-ˌdəʊn
**sp** steepe-downe[1]

**steeple / ~s** *n*
=
**sp** steeple[1], steeples[2]
**rh** invisible *TG 2.1.129*

**steer / ~s** *n*
'sti:ɹ / -z
**sp** steere[1] / steeres[1]

**steer / ~s / ~ing / ~ed** *v*
sti:ɹ / -z / 'sti:ɹɪn, -ɪŋ / sti:ɹd
**sp** steere[3] / steeres[1] / steering[1] / steer'd[1]
**rh** cleared *Cym 4.3.46*

**steerage** *n*
'sti:rɪʤ
**sp** stirrage[1]

**stell / ~ed** *v*
steld
**sp** steld
**rh** beheld, dwelled *Luc 1444*

**stelled** *adj*
*m* 'stelɪd
**sp** stelled[1]

**stem** *n*
=
**sp** stem[4]

**stem / ~ming** *v*
= / 'stemɪn, -ɪŋ
**sp** stemme[1] / stemming[1]
> re-stem

**stench** *n*
=
**sp** stench[3]

**step / ~s** *n*
=
**sp** steepe[1], step[11], steppe[2] / steppes[4], steps[17]
**rh** leaps *VA 277*

**step / ~s / ~ping / ~ped** *v*
= / = / 'stepɪn, -ɪŋ / =
**sp** step[15] / steppes[2], steps[2] / stepping[1] / stepp'd[1], stept[6]

**stepdame** *n*
'stepdɛ:m
stepdame[2], step-dame[2]
> dame

**Stephano** *n*
ste'fɑ:no:
**sp** Stephano[19], Ste-phano[1]

**Stephen** *n*
=
**sp** Stephen[6]

**stepmother / ~s** *n*
'stepmɤðəɹz
**sp** step-mothers[1]
> mother

**sterile** *adj*
'sterɪl
**sp** sterrile[1], sterrill[1], ster-rill[1], stirrile[1], stirrill[1]

**sterility** *n*
stə'rɪlɪtəɪ
**sp** stirrility[1]

**sterling** *adj*
'stɐ:ɹlɪn, -ɪŋ
**sp** starling[1], sterling[2]

**stern / ~er / ~est** *adj*
stɐ:ɹn / 'stɐ:ɹn·əɹ / *m* -əst, stɐ:ɹnst
**sp** stearne[1], stern[1], sterne[27] / sterner[2] / sternest[1], stern'st[1]

**stern** *adv / n*
stɐ:ɹn
**sp** sterne[1] / sterne[3]

**sternage** *n*
'stɐ:ɹnɪʤ
**sp** sternage[1]

**sternness** *n*
'stɐ:ɹnəs
**sp** sternnesse[1]

**steterat** *Lat*
> sto

**stew / ~s** *n*
=
**sp** stew[2] / stewes[2]

**stew / ~ed** *v*
=
**sp** stewd[1], stew'd[4]

**steward** *n*
'stju:əɹd
**sp** steward[40], ste-ward[1], stew-ard[1]

**stewardship** *n*
*m* 'stju:əɹdˌʃɪp
**sp** stewardship[2]

**stewed** *adj*
'stju:d
**sp** stew'd[1], stew'd-[pruines][1], stewed[1], stu'de[1]

**stick / ~s** *n*
=
**sp** sticke[4] / stickes[1]
> poking-stick

**stick / ~est / ~s / ~ing / stuck** *v*
= / stɪkst / = / 'stɪkɪn, -ɪŋ / stɤk
**sp** stick[1], sticke[24] / stickest[1], stick'st[1] / stickes[6], sticks[3] / sticking[3] / stuck[3], stucke[14]
**rh** pricks, tricks *Luc 317*

**sticking** *adj*
'stɪkɪn, -ɪŋ
**sp** sticking[1]

**stickler-like** *adv*
'stɪkləɹ-ləɪk
**sp** stickler-like[1]

**stiff** *adj*
=
**sp** stiffe[11], stiffe-[newes][1]

**stiff-borne** *adj*
'stɪf-ˌbɔ:ɹn
**sp** stiffe-borne[1]
> bear

**stiffen** *v*
=
**sp** stiffen[1]

**stiffly** *adv*
'stɪfləɪ
stiffely[1]

**stifle / ~d** *v*
'stəɪfəl / -d
**sp** stifle[3] / stifled[3]

**stigmatic** *n*
*m* 'stɪgmaˌtɪk
**sp** stygmaticke[2]

**stigmatical** *adj*
*m* stɪg'matɪˌkɑl
**sp** stigmaticall[1]

**stile** *n*
stəɪl
**sp** stile[1], [*song*] stile-a[1]
**rh** mile-a *WT 4.3.122*
**pun** *MA 5.2.6* style

**still / ~er / ~est** *adj*
= / 'stɪləɹ / =
**sp** still[42] / stiller[1] / stillest[1]
**rh** kill *Luc 167*; will *2H6 5.2.29, JC 5.5.50*
> stone-still

**still** *adv*
=
**sp** stil[11] , still[445]
**rh** hill *S 7.7, VA 699*; ill *Luc 475, Mac 3.2.54, Per 1.1.77, PP 2.2, S 144.2, 147.1*; ill, kill *Luc 382*; ill, skill *Luc 1531*; kill *2H6 5.2.70, Luc 249, MND 5.1.193, TC 3.1.121, VA 617*; quill *S 85.1*; skill *Luc 1098, 1133, 1508, MND 1.1.194, Per 4.Chorus.29, S 16.13, 24.7*; Will *S 135.3, 135.9, 136.13, 143.14*; will *CE 2.1.110, 3.2.69, 4.2.17, Luc 249, 727, PP 10.10, RJ 1.1.171, 2.3.23, S 134.4, Tim 4.2.51, VA 480, 637*

**still / ~ed** *v*
=
**sp** still[4] / still'd[1]

**still-born** *adj*
*m* ˌstɪl-'bɔːɹn
**sp** still-borne[1]
> born

**still-breeding** *adj*
*m* ˌstɪl-'briːdɪn, -ɪŋ
**sp** still breeding[1]
> breed

**still-closing** *adj*
*m* ˌstɪl-'kloːzɪn, -ɪŋ
**sp** still closing[1]
> close

**still-discordant** *adj*
'stɪl-dɪs'kɔːɹdənt
**sp** still discordant[1]
> discord

**still-lasting** *adj*
*m* ˌstɪl-'lastɪn, -ɪŋ
**sp** stil lasting[1]
> last

**stillness** *n*
=
**sp** stillnesse[3], stilnes[1], stilnesse[1]

**still-peering** *adj*
*m* ˌstɪl-'piːrɪn, -ɪŋ
**sp** still peering[1]
> peer

**still-soliciting** *adj*
'stɪl-sə'lɪsɪtɪn, -ɪŋ
**sp** still soliciting[1]
> solicit

**still-stand** *n*
*m* 'stɪl-ˌstand
**sp** still-stand
> stand

**still-vexed** *adj*
*m* ˌstɪl-'vekst
**sp** still-vext[1]
> vexed

**still-waking** *adj*
*m* ˌstɪl-'wɛːkɪn, -ɪŋ
**sp** still waking[1]
> waking

**stilly** *adv*
'stɪləɪ
**sp** stilly[1]

**sting / ~s** *n*
=
**sp** sting[1] / stings[8]
**rh** bring *Luc 493*; sing *TC 5.10.43*; spring *PP 10.4*; thing *Luc 364*; wing *Mac 4.1.16*

**sting / ~s / stung** *v*
= / = / stɤŋ
**sp** sting[12] / stings[2] / stung[5]
**rh** king, thing *Luc 40* / tongue *MND 3.2.73*

**stinging** *adj*
'stɪŋɪn, -ɪŋ
**sp** stinging[3]

**stingless** *adj*
=
**sp** stinglesse[1]

**stink / ~s** *v*
=
**sp** stinke[4] / stinkes[1]
> overstunk

**stinking** *adj*
'stɪŋkɪn, -ɪŋ
**sp** stinking[8], stinking-[elder][1], stink-ing[2]

**stinkingly** *adv*
*m* 'stɪŋkɪnˌləɪ, -ɪŋ-
**sp** stinkingly[1]

**stint / ~s / ~ed** *v*
=
**sp** stint[4] / stints[1] / stinted[2]
**rh** flint *Per 4.4.42*

**stir / ~s** *n*
stɐːɹ / -z
**sp** stir[1], stirre[4] / stirres[2]
**rh** *1* her *TNK Prol.6*; incur *Luc 1471*; spur *VA 283*; **rh** *2* war *R2 2.3.51*

**stir / ~s / ~eth / ~ring / ~red** *v*
stɐːɹ / -z / 'stɐːr·əθ / -ɪn, -ɪŋ / stɐːɹd
**sp** stir[11], stirre[65] / stirres[8], stirs[6] / stirreth[1] / stirring[14] / stir'd[5], stirr'd[8]
> bestir

**stirrer / ~s** *n*
'stɐ:rəɹ / -z
**sp** stirrer[1] / stirrers[1]

**stirring** *adj / n*
'stɐ:rɪn, -ɪŋ
**sp** stirring[5] / stirring[1]

**stirrup / ~s** *n*
=
**sp** stirrop[3], styrrop[1] / stirrops[1]

**stitch / ~es** *n*
=
**sp** stitches[1]

**stitchery** *n*
'stɪʧrəɪ, -ʧər-
**sp** stitchery[1]

**stithy** *n*
'stɪðəɪ
**sp** stythe[1]

**stith·y / ~ied** *v*
'stɪðəɪd
**sp** stythied[1]

**sto / steterat** *Lat v*
'stetərat
**sp** staterat[1], steterat[2]

**stoccado / ~es** *n*
stə'kɑ:do: / -z
**sp** stucatho[1] / stoccado's[1]

**stock / ~s** *n*
=
stock[13], stocke[12] / stockes[13], stocks[9]
> laughing-, vlouting-, whip-stock; nether-stocks

**stock / ~ing / ~ed** *v*
'stɒkɪn, -ɪŋ / =
**sp** stocking[1] / stockt[2]

**stockfish / ~es** *n*
=
**sp** stocke-fish[1], stockfish[1], stock-fish[1] / stock-fishes[1]
> fish

**stockings** *n*
'stɒkɪnz, -ɪŋz
**sp** stockings[13], stock-ings[1]
> puke-, worsted-stocking

**stockish** *adj*
=
**sp** stockish[1]

**Stoic / ~s** *n*
'sto:ɪks
**sp** Stoickes[1]

**Stokesley** *n*
'sto:ksləɪ
**sp** *emend of H8 4.1.101* Stokeley[1]

**stole, stolen** *v*
> steal

**stolen** *adj*
*m* sto:ln, 'sto:lən
**sp** stolne[4]

**stomach / ~s** *n*
'stɒmək / -s
**sp** stomack[4], stomacke[38] / stomackes[7], stomacks[7], stomakes[1]
> high-stomached

**stomacher / ~s** *n*
'stɒmə,ʧɛ:ɹz
**sp** stomachers[2]
**rh** dears *WT 4.4.226*

**stomaching** *n*
'stɒməkɪn, -ɪŋ
**sp** stomacking[1]

**stomach-qualmed** *adj*
'stɒmək-,kwɔ:md
**sp** stomacke-qualm'd[1]
> qualm

**stone** *adj*
sto:n
**sp** stone[1], stone-[iugs][1]

**stone / ~s** *n*
sto:n / -z
**sp** stone[52], stones [stone is][1] / stones[59], [bruzing]-stones[1]
**rh** *1* alone *VA 211*; moan *LC 216*; **rh** *2* none *S 94.3*; **rh** *3* gone *Ham 4.5.32*; thirty-one *Mac 4.1.6* / bones *KJ 4.3.9, Tim 3.6.118*; groans *R2 1.2.69*; groans, moans *Luc 978*; moans *MND 5.1.187, Oth 4.3.44, RJ 5.3.13*
> agate-, brim-, corner-, grave-, grind-, gun-, hail-, mill-, thunder-, whet-stone

**stone / ~d** *v*
sto:nd
**sp** ston'd[2]

**stone-bow** *n*
'sto:n-,bo:
**sp** stone-bow[1]
> bow

**stone-cutter** *n*
'sto:n-,kɤtəɹ
**sp** stone-cutter[1]
> cut

**stone-hard** *adj*
'sto:n-,ɑ:ɹd, -,hɑ:-
**sp** stone-hard[1]

**stone-still** *adv*
,sto:n-'stɪl
**sp** stone still[1]
> still

**stony** *adj*
'sto:nəɪ
**sp** stonie[3], stony[4]

**stony-hearted** *adj*
'sto:nəɪ-,ɑ:ɹtɪd, -,hɑ:-
**sp** stony-hearted[1]

**Stony Stratford** *n*
,sto:nəɪ-'stratfəɹd
**sp** Stony Stratford[1]

**stood**
> stand

**stool / ~s** *n*
stʊl, stu:l / -z
**sp** stoole[13] / stooles[3]
**rh** fool *TS 1.1.64*
> close-, foot-, joint-stool

**stoop / ~s / ~ing / ~ed** *v*
= / = / 'stu:pɪn, -ɪŋ / stu:pt

**sp** stoop[2], stoope[24] / stoopes[3] / stooping[2], stoo-ping[1] / stoop'd[4], stoopt[1]

**stooping** *adj / n*
'stu:pɪn, -ɪŋ
**sp** stooping[1] / stooping[2]
> unstooping

**stop / ~s** *n*
=
**sp** stop[10], stoppe[2] / stoppes[2], stops[4]

**stop / ~s / ~ping / ~ped** *v*
= / = / 'stɒpɪn, -ɪŋ / =
**sp** stop[74], stopp[1], stoppe[3] / stoppes[4], stops[7] / stopping[3] / stop'd[4], stopp'd[4], stopt[18]
**rh** dropped *VA 956*
> overstop

**store** *n*
stɔ:ɹ
**sp** stoore[1], store[28]
**rh** *1* adore *Luc 1837*; before *Luc 692*; door *CE 3.1.34*; more *Luc 97, RJ 1.2.22, S 11.9, 37.8, 84.3, 135.10, 146.10, Tit 1.1.97*; shore *S 64.8*; **rh** *2* poor *LLL 5.2.377, RJ 1.1.216*
> new-store

**store / ~d** *v*
stɔ:ɹ / -d
**sp** store[3], stor'd[3]
**rh** yore *S 68.13*

**stored** *adj*
stɔ:ɹd
**sp** stor'd[1]

**storehouse / ~s** *n*
'stɔ:ɹ-ˌəʊs, -ˌhəʊ- / -ˌəʊzɪz, -ˌhəʊ-
**sp** store-house[3] / store-houses[1]
> house

**storm / ~s** *n*
stɔ:ɹm / -z
**sp** storm[1], storme[50], *emend of TC 1.1.39* [a]-scorne[1] / stormes[15]
**rh** form *KL 2.4.77, LC 101*; perform *Per 3.Chorus.53* / forms *Luc 1518*
> sea-storm

**storm / ~s / ~ed** *v*
stɔ:ɹm / -z / -d
**sp** storme[3] / stormes[1] / stormed[1]

**stormy** *adj*
'stɔ:ɹməɪ
**sp** stormie[2], stormy[1]

**stor·y / ~ies** *n*
'stɔ:rəɪ / -z
**sp** storie[20], story[41] / stories[5]
**rh** glory *H5 Epil.2, RJ 1.3.93, S 84.8, 88.6*; glory, sorry *Luc 1521*; oratory *Luc 813*; see *H8 Prol.26* / glories *VA 1013*

**stoup / ~s** *n*
stu:p / -s
**sp** stoope[1], stope[2], stoupe[7] / stopes[1]

**stout / ~er** *adj*
stəʊt / 'stəʊtəɹ
**sp** stout[17], stowt[1] / stouter[1]
**rh** out *S 65.7*

**stoutly** *adv*
'stəʊtləɪ
**sp** stoutly[3]

**stoutness** *n*
'stəʊtnəs
**sp** stoutnesse[2]

**stover** *n*
'sto:vəɹ
**sp** stouer[1]

**stow / ~ed** *v*
sto:d
**sp** stow'd[1], stowed[2]

**stowage** *n*
'sto:ɪʤ
**sp** stowage[1]

**Strachy** *n*
'strɛ:ʧəɪ
**sp** Stra-chy[1]

**straggler / ~s** *n*
'stragləɹz
**sp** straglers[1]

**straggling** *adj*
'straglɪn, -ɪŋ
**sp** stragling[1]

**straight / ~est** *adj*
strɛ:t / 'strɛ:təst
**sp** straight[4], strait[7], straite[2] / straightest[1]

**straight / ~er** *adv*
strɛ:t / 'strɛ:təɹ
straight[114], strait[18], straite[4], streight[1] / straiter[1]
**rh** *1* bait *S 129.5*; gate *Tim 2.1.9*; weight *TNK 3.5.116*; **rh** *2* conceit *CE 4.2.62*

**straight / ~s** *n*
strɛ:t / -s
straight[1] / straights[1]

**straightly** *adv*
'strɛ:tləɪ
**sp** straightly[1]

**straightness** *n*
'strɛ:tnəs
**sp** straitnesse[1]

**straight-pight** *adj*
*m* ˌstrɛ:t-'pəɪt
straight-pight[1]
> pight

**straightway** *adv*
'strɛ:twɛ:
**sp** straightway[3], straight way[4]
> way

**strain / ~s** *n*
strɛ:n / -z
**sp** straine[8] / straines[3], strains[1]

**strain / ~s / ~ing / ~ed** *v*
strɛ:n / -z / 'strɛ:nɪn, -ɪŋ / strɛ:nd
**sp** straine[19], strayne[1] / straines[2] / straining[2] / strain'd[3], strayn'd[1]

**strained** *adj*
strɛ:nd
**sp** strain'd[2]

**straining** *n*
'strɛ:nɪn, -ɪŋ
**sp** straining[1]

**strait / ~ed** *v*
'strɛ:tɪd
**sp** straited[1]

**strand**
> strond

**strange / ~r / ~st** *adj*
strɛ:nʤ / 'strɛ:nʤ·əɹ / -əst
**sp** strange[237], straunge[4] / stranger[8] / strangest[5]
**rh** change *Ham 3.2.210, LLL 5.2.210, S 76.4, 89.8, 93.8, 123.3*; sea-change *Tem 1.2.402*

**strange** *adv*
strɛ:nʤ
strange[3], stra[n]ge[1]

**Strange** [name] *n*
strɛ:nʤ
Strange[1]

**strange-achieved** *adj*
*m* 'strɛ:nʤ-ə,ʧi:vɪd, -ʧɪv-
**sp** strange-atchieued[1]
> achieve

**strangely** *adv*
'strɛ:nʤləɪ
**sp** strangelie[1], strangely[24]

**strangeness** *n*
'strɛ:nʤnəs
**sp** strangenes[2], strangenesse[9]

**stranger / ~s** *n*
'strɛ:nʤəɹ / -z
**sp** stranger[29], stranger-[bloud][1], stranger-[soule][1] / strangers[18], stran-gers[1]
**rh** danger *VA 790*

**stranger / ~ed** *v*
'strɛ:nʤəɹd
**sp** stranger'd[1]

**strangl·e / ~es / ~ing / ~ed** *v*
'straŋg·əl / -əlz / -lɪn, -lɪŋ / -əld
**sp** strangle[6] / strangles[2] / strangling[2] / strangled[54]
> birth-strangled

**strangled** *adj*
'straŋgəld
**sp** strangled[1]

**strangler** *n*
'straŋgləɹ
**sp** strangler[1]

**strap / ~s** *n*
=
**sp** straps[1]

**strappado** *n*
strə'pɑ:do:
**sp** strappado[1]

**stratagem / ~s** *n*
*m* 'stratə,ʤem, -ʤəm / -z
**sp** stratagem[7], stratageme[3] / stratagemes[1], stratagems[4]

**Strato** *n*
'strato:
**sp** Strato[9]

**straw / ~s** *n*
=
**sp** straw[13] / strawes[5]
**rh** law *Luc 1021*; saw *LC 8* / daws *LLL 5.2.892*
> overstrawed, rye-straw

**strawberr·y / ~ies** *n*
*m* 'strɔ:bə,rəɪ / -bə,rəɪz, -bərəɪz, -brəɪz
**sp** strawberry[1] / strawberries[3]

**straw-colour** *adj*
'strɔ:-,kɤləɹ
**sp** straw-colour[1]

**stray** *n*
strɛ:
**sp** stray[4]
**rh** today *2H4 4.2.120*

**stray / ~s / ~ing / ~ed** *v*
strɛ: / -z / 'strɛ:ɪn, -ɪŋ / strɛ:d
**sp** stray[6] / straies[1], strayes[2] / straying[3] / straid[1], strai'd[1], stray'd[1]
**rh** away *TG 1.1.74*; day *MND 5.1.392*; way *R2 1.3.206*

**straying** *adj*
'strɛ:ɪn, -ɪŋ
**sp** straying[3]

**streak / ~s** *n*
=
**sp** streakes[3], streaks[1]

**streak** *v*
=
**sp** streake[1]

**streaked** *adj*
=
**sp** streak'd[1], streakt[1]

**stream / ~s** *n*
=
**sp** stream[1], streame[26] / streames[11]
**rh** dream *Luc 1774, Oth 2.3.59, TN 4.1.59*; theme *VA 772* / beams *MND 3.2.393*

**stream / ~s / ~ing** *v*
= / = / 'stri:mɪn, -ɪŋ
**sp** streame[2] / streames[1] / streaming[1]

**streamer / ~s** *n*
'stri:məɹz
**sp** streamers[1]

**street / ~s** *n*
=
**sp** street[14], streete[7], [Fish]-streete[1], [Turnball]-street[1] / streetes[9], streets[40]
**rh** feet *CE 3.1.36* / meets *TNK 1.5.15*

**strength / ~s** *n*
=
**sp** strength[114] / strengths[6]
**rh** length *PP 18.31, TC 1.3.137*

**strengthen / ~ing / ~ed** *v*
= / 'streŋθnɪn, -ɪŋ / =

**sp** strengthen[8] / strength'ning[1] / strengthned[2], strength'ned[1]

**strengthless** *adj*
=
**sp** strengthlesse[1], strength-lesse[1]

**stretch / ~es / ~ing / ~ed** *v*
= / = / 'stretʃɪn, -ɪŋ / =
**sp** stretch[18] / stretches[3] / stretching[1] / stretch'd[4], stretched[1], stretcht[7]
> out-, wide-stretched

**stretched-out** *adj*
'stretʃt-ˌəʊt
**sp** stretcht-out[1]
> out

**stretching** *n*
'stretʃɪn, -ɪŋ
**sp** stretching[1]

**stretch-mouthed** *adj*
'stretʃ-ˌməʊðd
**sp** stretch-mouth'd[1]
> mouth

**strew / ~est / ~ing / ~ed / ~n** *v*
stro:, stru: / -st / 'stro:ɪn, -ɪŋ, -ru:- / stro:d, -ru:- / stro:n, -ru:-
**sp** strew[13] / strew'st[1] / strewing[1] / strewd[1], strew'd[8] / strewne[1]
**rh** dew *RJ 5.3.12* / thrown *TN 2.4.59*
> bestrew

**strewing / ~s** *n*
'stro:ɪnz, -ɪŋz
**sp** strewings[1]

**strewment / ~s** *n*
'stro:mənts
**sp** strewments[1]

**strict / ~er / ~est** *adj*
= / 'strɪktəɹ / =
**sp** strick'd[1], strict[15] / stricter[1] / strictest[1]
**rh** interdict *PT 12*

**strictly** *adv*
'strɪkləɪ, -ktl-
**sp** strictly[1]

**stricture** *n*
'strɪktəɹ
**sp** stricture[1]

**stride / ~s** *n*
strəɪd / -z
**sp** stride[3] / strides[2]

**strid·e / ~ing** *v*
strəɪd / 'strəɪdɪn, -ɪŋ
**sp** stride[2] / striding[1]
> bestride

**strife / ~s** *n*
strəɪf / -s
**sp** strife[31] / strifes[2]
**rh** life *1H6 4.4.39, Luc 143, 405, 689, MND 5.1.221, Oth 2.3.251, R2 5.6.27, RJ Prol.8, 3.1.178, S 75.3, Tim 1.1.38, VA 11, 291, 764*; life, wife *Luc 236, 1377*; wife *AW 2.3.289, CE 3.2.28, Ham 3.2.232, Luc 1791, MV 2.3.20, TN 1.4.41*

**strik·e / ~est / ~es / ~eth / ~ing / stroke / ~n / struck / ~est / ~en / stricken** *v*
strəɪk / -s, -st / -s / 'strəɪk·əθ / -ɪn, -ɪŋ / stro:k / 'stro:kən / strɤk / -st / 'strɤkən / 'strɪkən
**sp** strike[151] / strik'st[3] / strikes[34] / striketh[1] / striking[4] / stroke[9], strook[4], strooke[36] / stroken[2], strooken[2] / struck[9], strucke[16] / struck'st[1] / strucken[3] / stricken[2]
**rh** [strikes] might *PP 18.2* / liking *Luc 433*
> outstrike, heart-struck

**striker / ~s** *n*
'strəɪkəɹz
**sp** strikers[1]

**striking** *n*
'strəɪkɪn, -ɪŋ
**sp** striking[2]
**rh** liking *MM 3.2.255, VA 250*

**string / ~s** *n*
=
**sp** string[6] / strings[10]
**rh** things *MM 3.2.263*
> bow-, eye-, ham-, heart-, lute-string

**string / strung** *v*
strɤŋ
**sp** strung[2]
> unstringed

**stringless** *adj*
=
**sp** stringlesse[1]

**strip / ~ping / ~ped** *v*
= / 'strɪpɪn, -ɪŋ / =
**sp** strip[5], strippe[1] / stripping[1] / stript[3]
> outstrip

**stripe / ~s** *n*
strəɪps
**sp** stripes[4]

**stripling / ~s** *n*
'strɪplɪn, -ɪŋ / -z
**sp** stripling[2] / striplings[1]

**striv·e / ~est / ~es / ~ing / strove** *v*
strəɪv / -s, -st / -z / 'strəɪvɪn, -ɪŋ / stro:v, strɤv
**sp** striue[30] / striu'st[1] / striues[8] / striuing[7] / stroue[2]
**rh** alive *Per 2.Chorus.19, S 112.5* / contrives, gyves *LC 240* / arrived *Luc 52, Per 5.Chorus.16* / love *AW 1.1.222*

**stroke / ~s** *n*
stro:k / -s
**sp** stroake[9], stroke[23] / stroakes[7], strokes[14], *Cym 3.5.40 emend of* stroke[1]
**rh** oak *Cym 4.2.265*; spoke *VA 945*
> thunderstroke

**stroke / ~est / ~s** *v*
stro:k / -s, -st / -s
**sp** stroake[1], stroke[3] / stroakst[1] / stroakes[1]

**stroke** [strike]
> strike

**strond / ~s** *n*
strɒnd / -z
**sp** strond[4] / stronds[1]
**rh** hand *TS 1.1.167*

**strong / ~er / ~est** *adj*
= / ˈstrɒŋg·əɹ / -əst
**sp** strong[178] / stronger[31] / strongest[6], strongst[1], strong'st[1]
**rh** *1* belong *LC 257, S 58.9*; belong, wrong *Luc 1262*; long *Luc 865, S 73.13, TNK 3.5.154, VA 297*; wrong *MND 3.2.27, Tim 5.4.9*; **rh** *2* among *LC 257*; tongue *LC 122, MM 3.2.177*; young *Luc 865* / longer *S 28.14*
> headstrong

**strong / ~er** *adv*
= / ˈstrɒŋgəɹ
**sp** strong[4] / stronger[3]
**rh** young *VA 420*

**strong** *n*
=
**sp** strong[1]

**strong-barred** *adj*
ˈstrɒŋ-ˌbɑːɹd
**sp** strong barr'd[1]
> bar

**strong-based** *adj*
ˈstrɒŋ-ˌbast
**sp** strong bass'd[1]
> base

**stronger** *n*
ˈstrɒŋgəɹ
**sp** stronger[1]
**rh** longer *Luc 1767*

**strong-framed** *adj*
*m* ˌstrɒŋ-ˈfrɛːmd
**sp** strong fram'd[1]
> frame

**strong-jointed** *adj*
*m* ˌstrɒŋ-ˈʤɔɪntɪd
**sp** strong ioynted[2]
> joint

**strong-knit** *adj*
ˈstrɒŋ-ˌnɪt, -kn-
**sp** strong knit[2]
> knit

**strongly** *adv*
ˈstrɒŋləɪ
**sp** strongly[25], strong-ly[1]

**strong-ribbed** *adj*
ˈstrɒŋ-ˌrɪbd
**sp** strong ribb'd[1]
> rib

**strong-winged** *adj*
ˈstrɒŋ-ˌwɪŋd
**sp** strong wing'd[1]
> wing

**strossers** *n*
ˈstrɒsəɹz
**sp** strossers[1]

**strove**
> strive

**struck** *adj*
strɤk
**sp** struck-[foole][1]

**struck** *v*
> strike

**strucken** *adj*
ˈstrɤkən
**sp** strucken[1]

**struggl·e / ~ing** *v*
ˈstrɤg·əl / -lɪn, -lɪŋ
**sp** struggle[2] / strugling[2]

**strumpet / ~'s / ~s** *n*
ˈstrɤmpɪt / -s
**sp** strumpet[23], strumpet-[fortune][1] / strumpets[3] / strumpets[1]

**strumpet / ~ed** *v*
ˈstrɤmpɪtɪd
**sp** strumpeted[1]
**rh** disabled *S 66.6*

**strung**
> string

**strut / ~s / ~ted** *v*
strɤt / -s / ˈstrɤtɪd
**sp** strut[4] / struts[1] / strutted[1]

**strutting** *adj*
ˈstrɤtɪn, -ɪŋ
**sp** strutting[2]

**stubble** *adj / n*
ˈstɤbəl
**sp** stubble[1] / stubble[1]

**stubborn / ~est** *adj*
ˈstɤbəɹn / -st
**sp** stubborn[2], stubborne[21], stub-borne[3] / stubbor-nest[1]

**stubborness** *n*
*m* ˈstɤbəɹˌnes
**sp** stubbornesse[1], stubbornnesse[2]

**stubbornly** *adv*
*m* ˈstɤbəɹnˌləɪ
**sp** stubbornly[1]

**stuck** *n*
stɤk
**sp** stucke[1]

**stuck-in** *n*
ˈstɤk-ɪn
**sp** stucke in[1]

**stud / ~s** *n*
stɤdz
**sp** studs[1]
**rh** buds *PP 19.14*

**stud / ~ded** *v*
ˈstɤdɪd
**sp** studded[1]

**student / ~s** *n*
ˈstjuːdənt, -dɪənt / -s
**sp** student[1], studient[2] / students[1]
> fellow-student

**studied** *adj*
ˈstɤdəɪd
**sp** studied[4]

**studious** *adj*
'stju:dɪəs
**sp** studious[2]

**studiously** *adv*
*m* 'stju:dɪəs,ləɪ
**sp** studiously[1]

**study** *adj*
'stɤdəɪ
**sp** study[1]

**stud·y / ~y's / ~ies** *n*
'stɤdəɪ / -z
**sp** studie[14], stu-die[1], study[14] / studies[3] / studies[10]
**rh** muddy *TNK 3.5.120*

**stud·y / ~ies / ~ying / ~ied** *v*
'stɤdəɪ / -z / -ɪn, -ɪŋ / -d
**sp** studie[15], study[17] / studies[3] / studying[3] / studied[11]

**stuff / ~s** *n*
stɤf / -s
**sp** stuffe[39] / stuffes[1], stuffs[1]

**stuff / ~s / ~ing / ~ed** *v*
stɤf / -s / 'stɤfɪn, -ɪŋ / stɤft
**sp** stuffe[7], [Burdeux]-stuffe[1], [houshold]-stuffe[1] / stuffes[1] / stuffing[1] / stufft[3], stuft[9]

**stuffed** *adj*
stɤft
**sp** stuff'd-[sufficiency][1], stuft[2], stufft[1]
> unstuffed

**stuffing** *n*
'stɤfɪn, -ɪŋ
**sp** stuffing[1]

**stumbl·e / ~est / ~ing / ~ed** *v*
'stɤmb·əl / -ləst / -lɪn, -lɪŋ / -əld
**sp** stumble[9] / stumblest[1] / stumbling[3] / stumbled[3], stum-bled[1]
**rh** humble *LLL 5.2.627*

**stumbling** *adj / n*
'stɤmblɪn, -ɪŋ
**sp** stumbling[2] / stumbling[1]

**stump / ~s** *n*
stɤmp / -s
**sp** stump[1], stumpe[1] / stumpes[1], stumps[3]

**stung** *n*
stɤŋ
stung[1]

**stung** *v*
> sting

**stupef·y / ~ied** *v*
*m* 'stju:pɪ,fəɪ / -d
**sp** stupifie[1] / stupified[1]

**stupid** *adj*
'stju:pɪd
**sp** stupid[1]

**stuprum** *Lat n*
'stʊprʊm
**sp** stuprum[1]

**sturdy** *adj*
'stɐ:ɹdəɪ
**sp** sturdie[1]

**sty** *n / v*
stəɪ
**sp** stye[3] / sty-[me][1]

**Stygia** *n*
'stɪʤɪə
**sp** Stigia[1]

**Stygian** *adj*
'stɪʤɪən
**sp** Stigian[1]

**style** *n*
stəɪl
**sp** stile[14], style[3]
**rh** compile *S 78.11*; erewhile *LLL 4.1.97*
**pun** *MA 5.2.6* stile

**style / ~d** *v*
stəɪld
**sp** stil'd[1]

**Styx** *n*
stɪks
**sp** Stix[2]

**sub** *Lat prep*
sʊb
**sp** sub[1]

**subcontract / ~ed** *v*
,sɤbkən'traktɪd
**sp** sub-contracted[1]

**subdue / ~s / ~d** *v*
=
**sp** subdue[9] / subdewes[1], subdues[4] / subdu'd[9], subdude[2], subdu'de[3], subdued[1]
**rh** true *LC 248* / renewed *S 111.6*
> self-subdued

**subdued** *adj*
*m* 'sɤbdju:d
**sp** subdu'd[10]

**subduement / ~s** *n*
=
**sp** subduments[1]

**subject** *adj*
'sɤbʤɪkt
**sp** subject[16]

**subject / ~'s / ~s' / ~s** *n*
'sɤbʤɪkt / -s
**sp** subiect[74], sub-iect[4] / subiects[4] / subiects[4] / subiects[52], sub-iects[1]

**subject / ~ed** *v*
səb'ʤekt / -ɪd
**sp** subject[2] / subiected[1]

**subjected** *adj*
səb'ʤektɪd
**sp** subiected[1]

**subjection** *n*
səb'ʤeksɪən
**sp** subiection[4]
**rh** insurrection *Luc 724*

**submerge / ~d** *v*
səb'mɐːɹʤd
**sp** submerg'd[1]

**submission** *n*
*m* səb'mɪsɪən, -sɪˌɒn
**sp** submission[11]

**submissive** *adj / adv*
səb'mɪsɪv
**sp** submissiue[3] / submissiue[1]

**submit / ~s / ~ting** *v*
səb'mɪt / -s / -ɪn, -ɪŋ
**sp** submit[11] / submits[1] / submitting[1]

**suborn / ~ed** *v*
sə'bɔːɹn / *m* -d, -nɪd
**sp** suborne[1] / subborn'd[1], subborned[1], suborn'd[5], suborned[1]

**subornation** *n*
*m* ˌsɤbəɹ'nɛːsɪən, -sɪˌɒn
**sp** subornation[3]
**rh** abomination, inclination *Luc 919*

**subscribe / ~s / ~d** *v*
səb'skrəɪb / -z / -d
**sp** subscribe[15] / subscribes[1] / subscrib'd[4], subscribed[1]
**rh** tribes *S 107.10*

**subscription** *n*
səb'skrɪpsɪən
**sp** subscription[1]

**subsequent** *adj*
*m* səb'siːkwənt
**sp** subsequent[1]

**subsid·y / ~ies** *n*
*m* 'sɤbsɪdəɪ / -ˌdəɪz
**sp** subsidie[1] / subsidies[1]

**subsist** *S* **/ ~ing** *v*
= / səb'sɪstɪn, -ɪŋ
**sp** subsist[1] / subsisting[1]
**rh** missed *S 122.6*

**substance / ~s** *n*
*m* 'sɤbstəns / -ˌsɪz
**sp** substance[36] / substances[2]

**substantial** *adj*
*m* səb'stansɪɑl, -ɪˌɑl
**sp** substantiall[4]
> unsubstantial

**substitute / ~s** *n*
'sɤbstɪˌtjuːt, -ɪt- / -ˌtjuːts
**sp** substitute[9], substi-tute[1] / substitutes[4]

**substitute / ~d** *v*
'sɤbstɪˌtjuːtɪd
**sp** substituted[2]

**substitution** *n*
ˌsɤbstɪ'tjuːsɪən
**sp** substitution[1]

**substractor / ~s** *n*
səb'straktəɹz
**sp** substra-ctors[1]

**subtle** *adj*
'sɤtl
**sp** subtil[1], subtile[8], subtill[5], subtle[17]
> super-subtle

**subtlet·y / ~ies** *n*
*m* 'sɤtlˌtəɪ / -z
**sp** subtletie[1] / subtleties[1]
**rh** me *VA 675* / lies *S 138.4*

**subtle-witted** *adj*
'sɤtl-ˌwɪtɪd
**sp** subtile-witted[1]
> wit

**subtly** *adv*
'sɤtləɪ
**sp** subtilly[2], subtly[1]

**suburb / ~s** *n*
'sɤbəɹbz
**sp** suborbs[1], suburbes[1], suburbs[5], sub-urbs[1]

**subversion** *n*
səb'vɐːɹsɪən
**sp** subuersion[1]

**subvert / ~s** *v*
səb'vɐːɹts
**sp** subuerts[1]

**succed·o / ~ant** *Lat v*
sʊk'seːdant
sp succedant[1]

**succeed / ~s / ~ing / ~ed** *v*
= / = / sək'siːdɪn, -ɪŋ / =
**sp** succeed[7], succeede[6] / succeedes[2], succeeds[1] / succeeding[3] / succeeded[1]
**rh** bleed *H5 Epil.10*

**succeeder / ~s** *n*
sək'siːdəɹz
**sp** succeeders[2]

**succeeding** *adj / n*
sək'siːdɪn, -ɪŋ
**sp** succeeding[3] / succeeding[1]

**success** *n*
=
**sp** successe[47], suc-cesse[1] / successes[2]
**rh** express *Luc 112*

**successantly** *adv*
sək'sesəntləɪ
**sp** successantly[1]

**successful** *adj*
=
**sp** succesfull[1], successefull[5]

**successfully** *adv*
*m* sək'sesfəˌləɪ
**sp** successefully[3]

**succession** *n*
*m* sək'sesɪən, -sɪˌɒn
**sp** succession[16]
**rh** possession *CE 3.1.105*

**successive** *adj*
=
**sp** successiue[4]

**successively** *adv*
*m* sək'sesɪvˌləɪ
**sp** successiuely[3]

**successor / ~s** *n*
sək'sesəɹ / -z
**sp** successor[1] / successors[2]

**succour / ~s** *n*
'sɤkəɹ / -z
**sp** succor[1], succour[8] / succours[3]

**succour** *v*
'sɤkəɹ
**sp** succor[1], succour[3]

**such** *det*
sɤʧ
**sp** such[1349]
**rh** clutch *Ham 5.1.74*; much *LLL 4.3.129, MA 3.1.110*; touch *PP 8.7*

**suchlike** *adj*
'sɤʧləɪk
**sp** such[3]
> like

**suck** *n*
sɤk
**sp** sucke[2]

**suck / ~est / ~s / ~ing / ~ed** *v*
sɤk / -st / -s / 'sɤkɪn, -ɪŋ / sɤkt
**sp** suck[5], sucke[17] / suck'st[3] / suckes[3], sucks[2] / sucking[1] / suck'd[2], suckt[4], suck't[1]
**rh** plucked *VA 572*
> blood-, rabbit-sucker; fen-sucked

**sucked** *adj*
sɤkt
**sp** suck'd[1]

**sucking** *adj / n*
'sɤkɪn, -ɪŋ
**sp** sucking[4] / sucking[1]

**suckle** *v*
'sɤkəl
**sp** suckle[2]
> honeysuckle

**sudden** *adj / adv / n*
'sɤdən
**sp** sodain[2], sodaine[43], suddaine[3], sudden[18] / sodaine[1] / sodaine[9], so-daine[1], suddaine[1], sudden[2]

**sudden-bold** *adj*
'sɤdən-'bo:ld
**sp** sodaine bold[1]
> bold

**suddenly** *adv*
*m* 'sɤdən,ləɪ, -ləɪ
**sp** sodainely[4], so-dainely[2], sodainlie[1], sodainly[21], so-dainly[1], suddainely[3], suddenly[17]
**rh** be *AY 2.4.97*; presently *PP 13.2*

**sue / ~s / ~eth / ~ing / ~d** *v*
=, ʃu: / -z / 'sju:·əθ, ʃu:- / -ɪn, -ɪŋ / =, ʃu:d
**sp** sue[25], shue[1] / sues[5] / sueth[1] / suing[1] / sued[6]
**rh** knew *TC 1.2.291*; true, you *LLL 5.2.427* / wooing *VA 356*

**sued-for** *adj*
'sju:d-,fɔ:ɹ, 'ʃu:d-
**sp** su'd-for[1]

**suffer / ~est / ~s / ~ing / ~ed** *v*
'sɤfəɹ / -st / -z / -ɪn, -ɪŋ, 'sɤfr- / -d
**sp** suffer[78], suffer't [suffer it][1] / suffer'st[2] / suffers[8] / suffering[4], suffring[1], suff 'ring[1] / sufferd[3], suffer'd[20], suf-fer'd[1], suffered[6], suffred[3]

**sufferance / ~s** *n*
*m* 'sɤfrəns, -fər-, -fə,rans / -frən,sɪz
**sp** sufferance[21], suf-ferance[1], suffe-rance[1] / sufferances[1]

**suffered** *adj*
'sɤfəɹd
**sp** suffred[1]

**suffering** *adj / n*
'sɤfrɪn, -ɪŋ, -fər-
**sp** suffering[2] / suffering[4], suffring[1]

**suffice / ~s / ~th / ~d** *v*
sə'fəɪs / -ɪz / -əθ / -t
**sp** suffice[14] / suffises[1] / sufficeth[7] / suffic'd[1], suffis'd[1]
**rh** eyes *LLL 4.2.111, Luc 1679, PP 5.7* / despised *S 37.11*; sympathised *Luc 1112*

**sufficiency** *n*
*m* sə'fɪsɪən,səɪ, -ns-
**sp** sufficiencie[2], sufficiency[1], [stuff 'd]-sufficiency[1]

**sufficient** *adj*
*m* sə'fɪsɪənt, -ɪ,ent
**sp** sufficient[14], suffi-cient[2], suffici-ent[1]

**sufficient** *n*
sə'fɪsɪənt
**sp** sufficient[1]

**sufficiently** *adv*
*m* sə'fɪsɪənt,ləɪ, -tl-
**sp** sufficiently[1], suffici-ently[1]

**sufficing** *adj*
sə'fəɪsɪn, -ɪŋ
**sp** suffising[1]

**suffic·io / ~it** *Lat v*
sʊ'fɪsɪt
**sp** sufficit[1]

**suffigance** [*malap* sufficient] *adj*
sə'fɪʤɪəns
**sp** suffigance[1]

**suffocate** *v*
'sɤfə,kɛ:t
**sp** suffocate[3]

**suffocating** *adj*
'sɤfə,kɛ:tɪn, -ɪŋ
**sp** suffocating[1]

**suffocation** *n*
,sɤfə'kɛ:sɪən
**sp** suffocation[1]

**Suffolk / ~'s** *n*
'sɤfək / -s
**sp** Suffolk[3], Suffolke[94] / Suffolkes[9], Suf-folkes[1], Suffolks[1]

**suffrage / ~s** *n*
'sɤfrɪʤ / -ɪz
**sp** sufferage[1] / suffrages[2]

**suffrance** *n*
'sɤfrəns
**sp** suffrance[2]

**sugar** *adj / n*
'ʃʊgəɹ, 'ʃuː-
**sp** sugar[1], suger[1] / sugar[9], su-gar[1], suger[2]

**sugar-candy** *n*
'ʃʊgəɹ-ˌkandəɪ, 'ʃuː-
**sp** sugar-candie[1]

**sugared** *adj*
'ʃʊgəɹd, 'ʃuː-
**sp** sugred[4]

**Sugarsop** *n*
'ʃʊgəɹ-ˌsɒp, 'ʃuː-
**sp** Su-gersop[1]

**suggest / ~s / ~ed** *v*
=
**sp** suggest[6] / suggests[2] / suggested[4]

**suggestion / ~s** *n*
*m* sə'ʤɛːstɪən, -ɪˌɒn / -z
**sp** suggestion[9] / suggestions[3]

**suis** *Fr*
> être

**suit / ~s** *n*
ʃuːt, sjuːt / -s
**sp** suit[41], suite[79], suite's [suit is][1], sute[11], *emend of Tit 1.1.226* sure[1] / suites[19], sutes[4]
**rh** mute *AW 2.3.75, LLL 5.2.275, VA 206, 336*
> love-, non-suit

**suit / ~s / ~ing / ~ed** *v*
ʃuːt, sjuːt / -s / 'ʃuːtɪn, -ɪŋ, 'sjuː- / 'ʃuːtɪd, 'sjuː-
**sp** suite[3], sute[3] / suites[7], sutes[2] / suiting[1] / suited[2]

**suitable** *adj*
'ʃuːtəbəl, 'sjuː-
**sp** suteable[1]
> unsuitable

**suited** *adj*
'ʃuːtɪd, 'sjuː-
**sp** suited[2], suted[3]
> three-suited

**suitor / ~s** *n*
'ʃuːtəɹ, 'sjuː- / -z
**sp** suitor[6], suter[2], sutor[12] / suitors[1], suters[7], sutors[10]
**rh** tutor *TG 2.1.130* / tutors *KL 3.2.84*
**pun** *LLL 4.1.109* shooter

**suivre / suivez** *Fr v*
swi'vez
**sp** saaue[1]

**sullen** *adj*
'sɤlən
**sp** sullen[15]

**sullen / ~s** *n*
'sɤlənz
**sp** sullens[1]

**sull·y / ~ies** *n*
'sɤləɪz
**sp** sulleyes[1]

**sull·y / ~ied** *v*
'sɤləɪ / -d
**sp** sulley[1], sully[2] / sullied[1]
> unsullied

**sulphur** *n*
'sɤlfəɹ
**sp** sulpher[1], sulphure[3]

**sulphurous** *adj*
'sɤlfrəs, -fər-
**sp** sulpherous[1], sulph'rous[1], sulphurous[4]

**sultan** *n*
'sɤltən
**sp** sultan[1]

**sultry** *adj*
'sɤltrəɪ
**sp** soultry[2]

**sum / ~s** *n*
sɤm / -z
**sp** sum[12], summe[38] / summes[13], sums[1]
**rh** come *S 49.3* / bums *Tim 1.2.237*; comes *LC 231*
**pun** *2H4 2.1.70* some

**sum / ~s / ~med** *v*
sɤm / -z / -d
**sp** sum[1], summe[2] / summes[1] / summ'd[1]

**sum** *Lat*
> adsum

**sumless** *adj*
'sɤmləs
**sp** sum-lesse[1]

**summa** *Lat*
> summus

**summary** *n*
*m* 'sɤmrəɪ, -mər-, -məˌr-
**sp** summarie[2]

**summer** *adj*
'sɤməɹ
**sp** sommer[2], summer[14], sum-mer[1]

**summer / ~'s / ~s** *n*
'sɤməɹ / -z
**sp** sommer[10], summer[19], / sommers[1] / sommers[1], summers[23]
> midsummer

**summer / ~ed** *v*
'sɤməɹd
**sp** summer'd[1]

**summer-house** *n*
'sɤməɹ-ˌəʊs, -ˌhəʊs
**sp** summer-house[1]
> house

**summer-seeming** *adj*
'sɤməɹ-ˌsiːmɪn, -ɪŋ
**sp** summer-seeming[1]
> seem

**summer-swelling** *adj*
'sɤməɹ-ˌswelɪn, -ɪŋ

**sp** sommer-swelling[1]
> swell

**summit** *n*
'sɤmɪt
**sp** *Ham 3.3.18 emend of* somnet[2]

**summon / ~s / ~ed** *v*
'sɤmən / -z / -d
**sp** summon[12] / summons[1] / summon'd[2], summond[1]

**summoner / ~s** *n*
'sɤmnəɹz, -mən-
**sp** summoners[1]

**summons** *n*
'sɤmənz
**sp** summons[8]

**summ·us / ~a** *Lat adj*
'sʊma
**sp** summa[1]

**sumpter** *n*
'sɤmtəɹ, -mpt-
**sp** sumpter[1]

**sumptuous** *adj*
'sɤmtju:əs, -tɪəs, -mpt-
**sp** sumptuous[4]
> presumptuous

**sumptuously** *adv*
*m* 'sɤmtju:əsˌləɪ, -tɪəs-, -mpt-
**sp** sumptuously[1]

**sun / ~'s / ~s** *n*
sɤn / -z
**sp** sonne[2], sun[68], sunne[137], sunnes [sun is][1], sun's [sun is][1] / sunnes[8] / sunnes[6], suns[1]
**rh** *1* begun *LC 260, Luc 372, RJ 1.2.91*; begun, done *LC 9, Luc 25*; done *CE 1.1.28, Cym 4.2.258, Ham 4.5.66, Mac 1.1.5, S 24.11, 35.3, 59.6, TC 5.8.7, Tim 1.2.142, VA 198, 750, 800*; dun *S 130.1*; run *MND 5.1.375*; shun *AY 2.5.36*; undone *Mac 5.5.49*; won *Mac 1.1.5, LLL 1.1.84*; **rh** *2* gone *VA 190*
**pun** *R3 1.1.2* son
> unsunned

**sunbeam / ~s** *n*
'sɤnbi:mz
**sp** sun-beames[1]

**sunbeamed** *adj*
*m* ˌsɤn'bi:mɪd
**sp** sunne beamed[2]
> beam

**sun-bright** *adj*
'sɤn-ˌbrəɪt
**sp** sun-bright[1]

**sunburn / ~ing** *v*
'sɤnˌbɐ:ɹnɪn, -ɪŋ
**sp** sunne-bur-ning[1]

**sunburned** *adj*
'sɤnˌbɐ:ɹnt
**sp** sun-burn'd[2], sun-burnt[1]

**Sunday / ~s** *n*
'sɤndɛ: / -z
**sp** Sonday[6], Sunday[2], Sunday-[citizens][1] / Sundaies[2]
**rh** array *TS 2.1.317*
> citizen

**sunder** *n*
'sɤndəɹ
**sp** sunder[1]
**rh** under *Luc 388*

**sunder / ~s / ~ed** *v*
'sɤndəɹ / -z / -d
**sp** sunder[7] / sunders[1] / sundred[1]
**rh** wonder *MND 5.1.131*
> asunder

**sundered** *adj*
'sɤndəɹd
**sp** sundred[2]

**sundry** *adj*
'sɤndrəɪ
**sp** sundrie[1], sundry[3]

**sun-expelling** *adj*
'sɤn-ɪkˌspelɪn, -ɪŋ
**sp** sun-expelling[1]

**sung**
> sing

**sunk**
> sink

**sunken** *adj*
'sɤŋkən
**sp** sunken[2]

**sunlike** *adj*
'sɤnləɪk
**sp** sunne-like[1]

**sunny** *adj*
'sɤnəɪ
**sp** sunnie[1], sunny[2]

**sunrise** *n*
'sɤnrəɪz
**sp** sunne rise[1]

**sunrising** *n*
*m* ˌsɤn'rəɪzɪn, -ɪŋ
**sp** sun-rising[1]
> rise

**sunset** *n*
'sɤnset
**sp** sunset[2], sun-set[1]
> set

**sunshine** *adj / n*
'sɤnʃəɪn
sunne-shine[1], sun-shine[1] / sunne-shine[1], sunshine[2], sun-shine[2]
> shine

**sup / ~s / ~ped** *v*
sɤp / -s / -t
**sp** sup[16], suppe[4] / suppes[1], sups[4] / supp'd[1], supt[4]
> half-supped

**super-dainty** *adj*
'su:pəɹ-ˌdɛ:ntəɪ
**sp** super-daintie[1]
> dainty

**superficial** *adj*
ˌsu:pəɹ'fɪsɪɑl
**sp** superficiall[2]

**superficially** *adv*
*m* ˌsu:pəɹ'fɪsɪɑˌləɪ
**sp** superficially[2]

**superfluity** *n*
ˌsu:pəɹ'flu:ɪtəɪ
**sp** superfluitie[1], super-fluitie[1], superfluity[2]

**superfluous** *adj*
sʊ'pɐ:ɹflu:əs
**sp** superfluous[15]

**superfluously** *adv*
sʊ'pɐ:ɹflu:asləɪ
**sp** superflu-ously[1]

**superflux** *n*
'su:pəɹˌflɤks
**sp** superflux[1]

**superior** *n*
sʊ'perɪəɹ
**sp** superiour[1]

**supernal** *adj*
sʊ'pɐ:ɹnɑl
**sp** supernal[1]

**supernatural** *adj*
*m* ˌsu:pəɹ'natəˌrɑl
**sp** supernaturall[2]
> nature

**superpraise** *v*
'su:pəɹˌprɛ:z
**sp** superpraise[1]
> praise

**superscript** *n*
'su:pəɹˌskrɪpt
**sp** superscript[1]

**superscription** *n*
*m* ˌsu:pəɹ'skrɪpsɪən, -sɪˌɒn
**sp** superscription[1], superscripti-on[1]

**super-serviceable** *adj*
ˌsu:pəɹ'sɐ:ɹvɪsəbəl
**sp** super-seruiceable[1]

**superstition** *n*
ˌsu:pəɹ'stɪsɪən
**sp** superstition[1]

**superstitious** *adj*
ˌsu:pəɹ'stɪsɪəs
**sp** superstitious[4]

**superstitiously** *adv*
*m* ˌsu:pəɹ'stɪsɪəsˌləɪ
**sp** superstitiously[1]

**super-subtle** *adj*
'su:pəɹ-ˌsɤtl
**sp** super-subtle[1]

**supervise** *n / v*
'su:pəɹvəɪz
**sp** superuize[1] / superuise[1]

**supervision** *n*
ˌsu:pəɹ'vɪzɪən
**sp** super-vision[1]

**supper / ~s** *n*
'sɤpəɹ / -z
**sp** supper[62], sup-per[1] / suppers[1]

**supper-time** *n*
'sɤpəɹ-ˌtəɪm
**sp** supper time[10]
> time

**supping** *n*
'sɤpɪn, -ɪŋ
**sp** supping[1]

**supplant** *v*
sə'plant
**sp** supplant[6]

**supple / ~r** *adj*
'sɤp·əl / -ləɹ
**sp** supple[6] / suppler[2]

**suppliance** *n*
sə'pləɪəns
**sp** suppliance[1]

**suppliant** *adj*
*m* 'sɤplɪənt, -ɪˌant
**sp** suppliant[2]

**suppliant / ~s** *n*
*m* 'sɤplɪənt, -ɪˌant / -s
**sp** suppliant[4] / suppliants[1]

**supplication / ~s** *n*
ˌsɤplɪ'kɛ:sɪən / -z
**sp** supplication[6] / supplications[1], supplica-tions[1]

**supplier / supplie** *Fr v*
sy'pli
**sp** supplie[2]

**suppl·y / ~ies** *n*
sə'pləɪ / -z
**sp** supplie[1], supply[11] / supplies[2], supplyes[2]

**suppl·y / ~iest / ~ying / ~ied** *v*
sə'pləɪ / -əst / -ɪn, -ɪŋ /-d
**sp** supplie[2], supply[12], sup-ply[2] / suppliest[1] / supplying[1] / supplied[2], supply'd[6], supply'de[1]
**rh** mutiny *1H6 1.1.159* / beside *H5 1.1.17*

**supplyment** *n*
sə'pləɪmənt
**sp** supplyment[1]

**support** *n*
sə'pɔ:ɹt
**sp** support[1]

**support / ~ing / ~ed** *v*
sə'pɔ:ɹt / -ɪn, -ɪŋ / -ɪd
**sp** support[12] / supporting[1] / supported[1]
**rh** support me sport me *VA 152*

**supportable** *adj*
sə'pɔ:ɹtəbəl
**sp** supportable[1]
> insupportable

**supportance** *n*
sə'pɔ:ɹtəns
**sp** supportance[2]

**supporter / ~s** *n*
sə'pɔ:ɹtəɹ / -z
**sp** supporter[2] / supporters[1]

**supposal** *n*
sə'po:zɑl
**sp** supposall[1]

**suppose / ~s** *n*
sə'po:z / -ɪz
**sp** suppose[2] / supposes[1]

**suppos·e / ~est / ~es / ~ing / ~ed** *v*
sə'po:z / -əst / -ɪz / -ɪn, -ɪŋ / *m* -d, -ɪd
**sp** suppose[26] / supposest[1] / supposes[2] / supposing[3] / supposd[1], suppos'd[10], supposed[5]
**rh** shows *Per 5.2.5* [*Chorus*]; those *AW 1.1.221, S 57.10* / proposed *Luc 133*

**supposed** *adj*
*m* sə'po:zd, -ɪd
**sp** suppos'd[4], supposed[8]
**rh** enclosed *Luc 377*

**supposition** *n*
ˌsɤpə'zɪsɪən
**sp** supposition[4], suppo-sition[1]

**suppress / ~eth / ~ed** *v*
=
**sp** suppresse[5] / suppresseth[1] / supprest[3]
**rh** best *S 138.8*; rest *3H6 4.3.6*

**supremacy** *n*
*m* sə'premәˌsəɪ
**sp** supremacie[2], supremacy[1], supremicie[1]

**supreme** *adj*
*m* 'su:pri:m, sʊ'pri:m
**sp** supreame[4], supreme[3]

**sur** *Fr prep*
syɹ
**sp** sur[2]

**sur-addition** *n*
ˌsɐ:ɹ-ə'dɪsɪən
**sp** sur-addition[1]

**surance** *n*
'ʃu:rəns, 'sju:-
**sp** surance[1]
> assurance

**surcease** *n / v*
səɹ'si:s
**sp** surcease[1] / surcease[2]

**sure / ~r / ~st** *adj*
ʃu:ɹ / 'ʃu:ɹ·əɹ / -əst
**sp** sure[176], surer[2], surest[1], *Mac* 2.1.56 *emend* sowre[1]
**rh** pure *TNK Prol.9*
> unsured

**sure** *adv*
ʃu:ɹ
**sp** sure[112], *Q H5 1.2.8* shure
**rh** cure *AW 2.1.157*; endure *JC 1.2.318*

**Surecard** *n*
'ʃu:ɹkɑ:ɹd
**sp** Sure-card[1]
> card

**surely** *adv*
'ʃu:rləɪ
**sp** suerly[1], surelie[2], sure-lie[1], surely[35]

**surer** *adv*
'ʃu:rəɹ
**sp** surer[1]

**surest** *adv*
'ʃu:rəst
**sp** surest[1]

**suret·y / ~ies** *n*
'ʃu:ɹtəɪ, -ɹət- / -z
**sp** suretie[8], surety[12] / sureties[1]

**surety** *v*
'ʃu:ɹtəɪ, -ɹət-
**sp** surety[1]

**surfeit / ~s** *n*
'sɐ:ɹfɪt / -s
**sp** surfeit[2], surfet[5] / surfets[3]

**surfeit / ~s / ~ing / ~ed** *v*
'sɐ:ɹfɪt / -s / -ɪn, -ɪŋ / -ɪd
**sp** surfeit[1], surfet[5] / surfets[2] / surfetting[3] / surfeted[1], surfetted[2]

**surfeited** *adj*
'sɐ:ɹfɪtɪd
**sp** surfeted[1]

**surfeiter** *n*
'sɐ:ɹfɪtəɹ
**sp** surfetter[1]

**surfeiting** *adj*
'sɐ:ɹfɪtɪn, -ɪŋ
**sp** surfetting[1]

**surfeit-swelled** *adj*
'sɐ:ɹfɪt-ˌsweld
**sp** surfeit-swell'd[1]

**surge / ~'s / ~s** *n*
sɐ:ɹʤ / 'sɐ:ɹʤɪz
**sp** surge[7], [winde-shak'd]-surge[1] / surges[1] / surges[3]

**surge** *v*
sɐ:ɹʤ
**sp** surge[1]

**surgeon / ~'s / ~s** *n*
'sɐ:ɹʤɪən / -z
**sp** sur-gean[1], surgeon[10] / surgeons[1] / surgeons[3]

**surgery** *n*
*m* 'sɐ:ɹʤrəɪ, -ʤər-, -əˌrəɪ
**sp** surgerie[1], surge-rie[1], surgery[3]

**surg·o / ~ere** *Lat v*
'su:rʤere
**sp** surgere[1]

**surly** *adj / adv*
'sɐ:ɹləɪ
**sp** surley[1], surly[9] / surly[2]

**surmise / ~s** *n*
səɹ'məɪz / -ɪz
**sp** surmise[3], surmize[1] / surmises[3], surmizes[1]
**rh** eyes *Luc 83*

**surmise / ~d** *v*
səɹ'məɪz / -d
**sp** surmise[1] / surmiz'd[1]

**surmised** *adj*
*m* səɹ'məɪzɪd
**sp** surmised[1]

**surmount / ~s / ~ed** *v*
səɹ'məʊnt / -s / -ɪd
**sp** surmount[1] / surmounts[1] / surmounted[1]
**rh** account *S 62.8*
> mount

**surname** *n*
'sɐːɹnɛːm
**sp** surname[2], sur-name[1]
> name

**surname / ~d** *v*
'sɐːɹnɛːmd
**sp** surnam'd[2], sur-named[1]

**surpass / ~eth / ~ing** *v*
səɹ'pas·əθ / -ɪn, -ɪŋ
**sp** surpasseth[1] / surpassing[1]

**surplice** *n*
'sɐːɹplɪs
**sp** surplis[1]

**surplus** *n*
'sɐːɹpləs
**sp** surplus[2]

**surprise** *n*
səɹ'prəɪz
**sp** surprize[1]

**surprise / ~d** *v*
səɹ'prəɪz / *m* -d, -ɪd
**sp** surprize[6], sur-prize[1] / surpris'd[5], surprised[1], surpriz'd[15]
**rh** cries, eyes *Luc 166*; eyes *VA 1049* / disguised *LLL 5.2.84*
> fear-surprised

**sur-reined** *adj*
'sɐːɹ-ˌrɛːnd
**sp** sur-reyn'd[1]

**surrender** *n / v*
sə'rendəɹ
**sp** surrender[3] / surrender[2]

**Surrey** *n*
'sɤrəɪ
**sp** Surrey[18], Surrie[1]

**survey** *n*
səɹ'vɛː
**sp** suruey[4]

**survey / ~est / ~s / ~ing / ~ed** *v*
səɹ'vɛː / -st / -z / -ɪn, -ɪŋ / -d
**sp** suruay[1], suruey[7] / suruayest[1] / surueyes[1] / surueying[1] / suruey'd[1]
**rh** *1* decay *S 100.9*; sway *AY 3.2.2*;
**rh** *2* key *S 52.3*
> re-survey

**surveyor / ~s** *n*
səɹ'vɛːəɹ / -z
surueyor[6] / surueyors[1]

**survive / ~s** *v*
səɹ'vəɪv / -z
**sp** suruiue[8] / suruiues[2]
**rh** alive *VA 173*; alive, hive *Luc 1766*; contrive *Luc 204*

**survivor** *n*
səɹ'vəɪvəɹ
**sp** suruiuer[1], suruiuor[1]

**Susan** *n*
=
**sp** Susan[3]

**suspect / ~s** *n*
sə'spekt / -s
**sp** suspect[6] / suspects[2]
**rh** defect *S 70.3*

**suspect / ~s / ~ing / ~ed** *v*
sə'spekt / -s / -ɪn, -ɪŋ / -ɪd
**sp** suspect[29] / suspects[3] / suspecting[1] / suspected[7]
> unsuspected

**suspend** *v*
=
**sp** suspend[2]

**suspense** *n*
=
**sp** suspence[1]

**suspicion / ~s** *n*
*m* sə'spɪsɪən, -sɪˌɒn / -sɪənz
**sp** suspition[31] / suspitions[1]

**suspicious** *adj*
sə'spɪsɪəs
**sp** suspicious[2], suspitious[3]

**suspiration** *n*
ˌsɤspɪ'rɛːsɪən
**sp** suspiration[1]

**suspire** *v*
sə'spəɪɹ
**sp** suspire[2]

**sustain / ~d** *v*
sə'stɛːn / -d
**sp** sustaine[13], su-staine[1], sustayne[1] / sustain'd[2]
**rh** again *TN 4.2.125*; gain *Luc 139*; twain *KL 5.3.318*

**sustaining** *adj*
sə'stɛːnɪn, -ɪŋ
**sp** sustaining[2]
**rh** complaining, raining *Luc 1272*; complaining, remaining *Luc 1573*

**sustenance** *n*
'sɤstnəns, -tən-
**sp** sustenance[1]

**sutler** *n*
'sɤtləɹ
**sp** sut-ler[1]

**Sutton Coldfield** *n*
ˌsɤtən 'koːlfɪl, 'koːf-
**sp** Sutton-cop-hill[1]

**suum** *interj*
'suːəm
**sp** suum[1]

**suus / suum** *Lat det*
'suːəm
**sp** suum[1]

**swabber** *n*
'swɒbəɹ
**sp** swabber[2]

**swag-bellied** *adj*
'swag-ˌbelɘɪd
**sp** swag-belly'd[1]

**swagger / ~ing / ~ed** *v*
'swagɘɹ / -ɪn, -ɪŋ, -gr- / -d, *Edgar's assumed dialect KL 4.6.238* zwagɘɹd
**sp** swagger[5] / swagge-ring[1] / swag-ger'd[1], *Edgar* zwaggerd[1]

**swaggerer / ~s** *n*
'swagrɘɹ, -gɘr- / -z
**sp** swaggerer[3] / swaggerers[5]

**swaggering** *adj / n*
'swagrɪn, -ɪŋ, -gɘr-
**sp** swaggering[3], swagge-ring[1] / swaggering[2], swag-gering[1]

**swain / ~'s / ~s** *n*
swɛ:n / -z
**sp** swain[2], swaine[21] / swaines[1] / swaines[2]
**rh** plains *PP 17.29*

**swallow / ~'s / ~s** *n*
'swɒlɘ, -lo: / -z
**sp** swallow[4] / swallowes[1] / swallowes[2]

**swallow / ~s / ~ing / ~ed** *v*
'swɒlɘ, -lo: / -z / *m* -wɪn, -wɪŋ / -d
**sp** swallow[10] / swallowes[2] / swallowing[3] / swallow'd[8], swallowed[10]
> sea-swallowed

**swallowing** *adj / n*
'swɒlwɪn, -ɪŋ, -lɘw-
**sp** swallowing[2] / swallowing[1]

**swam**
> swim

**swan / ~'s / ~s** *n*
swɒn / -z
**sp** swan[6] / swannes[1], swannes-[nest][1], swans[1] / swans[1]
**rh** can *PT 15*

**swan-like** *adj*
'swɒnlɘɪk
**sp** swan-like

**sware**
> swear

**swarm** *n*
swɑ:ɹm
**sp** swarme[1]

**swarm / ~ing** *v*
swɑ:ɹm / 'swɑ:ɹmɪn, -ɪŋ
**sp** swarme[3] / swarming[2]
upswarm

**swart** *adj*
swɑ:ɹt
**sp** swart[3], swarth[1]

**swarthy** *adj*
'swɑ:ɹðɘɪ
swarthy[1]

**swasher / ~s** *n*
'swɑʃɘɹz
**sp** swashers[1]

**swashing** *adj*
'swɑʃɪn, -ɪŋ
**sp** swashing[1]

**swath** *n*
swɑθ
**sp** swath[2]

**swathe / ~s** *n*
swɑ:ðz
**sp** swarths[1]

**swathing** *adj*
'swɑ:ðɪn, -ɪŋ
**sp** swathing[3]

**sway** *n*
swɛ:
**sp** sway[18]
**rh** day *1H4 5.5.42* [*emend of* way]

**sway / *S* ~est / ~s / ~ing / ~ed** *v*
swɛ: / -st / -z / 'swɛ:ɪn, -ɪŋ / swɛ:d
**sp** sway[13], sway-[on][1] / swayst[1] / swaies[2], swayes[6] / swaying[1] / swai'd[1], sway'd[6], *TS 3.2.54 emend of* waid[1]
**rh** day *S 150.2*; obey *CE 2.1.28, TS 5.2.162*; say *LC 108*; survey *AY 3.2.4* / play'st *S 128.3* / maid *MND 2.2.121*
> over-, un-sway; unswayable

**swear / ~est / ~s / ~ing / swor·e / ~est / ~n** *v*
swɛ:ɹ / -st / -z / 'swɛ:rɪn, -ɪŋ / swɔ:ɹ / -st / -n
**sp** swear[5], sweare[243], swear't [swear it][3] / swearest[1], swear'st[6] / sweares[24], swears[1] / swearing[10] / sware[2], swore[48] / sworst[2], swor'st[1] / sworn[3], sworne[106], sworn't [sworn it][1], [be]sworne[1]
**rh** *1* anywhere *RJ 2.Chorus.10*; bear *Luc 1418, S 131.9*; there *Luc 1650, MND 2.1.56*; where *R2 5.3.141*; **rh** *2* ear *LLL 4.1.61, Luc 1418*; fear *1H6 4.5.28, Luc 1650, TN 5.1.168*; hear *LLL 4.3.144*; here *LLL 5.2.359*; **rh** *3* were *LLL 4.3.115, PP 16.15* / **rh** *1* hairs *Per 4.4.27*; **rh** *2* tears *VA 80* / **rh** *1* bearing *S 152.2*; **rh** *2* fearing *PP 7.8* / before *LLL 5.2.109, Luc 1848*; o'er *MND 3.2.134* / **rh** *1* horn *TC 4.5.45*; scorn *LLL 1.1.294*; thorn *LLL 4.3.109, PP 16.11*; **rh** *2* more *LLL 1.1.114*
> for-, out-, over-, un-swear

**swearer / ~s** *n*
'swɛ:rɘɹ / -z
**sp** swearer[1] / swearers[2]

**swearing** *adj*
'swɛ:rɪn, -ɪŋ
**sp** swearing[2]

**swearing / ~s** *n*
'swɛ:rɪn, -ɪŋ / -z
**sp** swearing[9], swea-ring[1] / swearings[2]

**sweat** *n*
=
**sp** sweat[10], sweate[2], swet[2]

**sweat** *v*
= / -s, -st / = / 'swet·ɪn, -ɪŋ / -ən
**sp** sweat[11], sweate[7], swet[4] / sweat'st[1] / sweates[3], sweats[2] / sweating[3] / sweaten[1]
**rh** *1* great *H8 Prol.28, LLL 5.2.549*; **rh** *2* heat *VA 175* / eaten *Mac 4.1.64*

**sweating** *adj*
'swetɪn, -ɪŋ
**sp** sweating[3]

**sweaty** *adj*
'swetəɪ
**sp** sweatie[1], sweaty[1]

**sweep** *n*
=
**sp** sweepe[1]

**sweep / ~s / swept** *v*
=
**sp** sweep[1], sweepe[10] / sweepes[3] / swept[2]
> unswept

**sweet / ~er / ~est** *adj*
= / 'swi:t·əɹ / -əst, -st
**sp** sweet[568], sweet-[goose][1], sweet-[heart][5], sweet-[heart's][1], sweet-[ladie][1], sweete[140] / sweeter[14], swee-ter[1] / sweetest[19], sweet'st[3], swetest[1]
**rh** Crete *1H6 4.6.55*; feet *LLL 5.2.329, TNK 1.1.13*; greet *S 145.6, TN 2.4.58*; meet *Ham 3.4.210* [*Q2*], *5.1.62, LLL 5.2.236, MND 1.1.216, R2 5.3.116, S 94.9*; regreet *R2 1.3.68*
> flattering-, honey-sweet; outsweetened

**sweet** *adv*
=
**sp** sweet[9], sweete[4]
**rh** meet *S 5.14*

**sweet / ~s** *n*
=
**sp** sweet[25], sweete[12] / sweetes[3], sweets[6]
**rh** discreet *RJ 1.1.194*; greet *LLL 5.2.373*; meet *AW 5.3.331, RJ 2. Chorus.14*; unmeet *LLL 4.3.112, PP 16.14* / fleet'st *S 19.7*

**sweeten / ~ed** *v*
=
**sp** sweeten[7], swee-ten[1] / sweetned[1]

**sweeter** *n*
'swi:təɹ
**sp** sweeter[1]

**sweet-faced** *adj*
'swi:t-ˌfɛ:st
**sp** sweet-fac'd[1]
> face

**Sweetheart** [name] *n*
'swi:tˌɑ:ɹt, -ˌhɑ:-
**sp** Sweet-heart[1]

**sweeting** *n*
'swi:tɪn, -ɪŋ
**sp** sweeting[4], [bitter]-sweeting[1]
**rh** meeting *TN 2.3.40*

**sweetly** *adv*
'swi:tləɪ
**sp** sweetely[1], sweetly[22], sweet-ly[1]

**sweetmeat / ~s** *n*
=
**sp** sweet meats[2]

**sweetness** *n*
=
**sp** sweetnes[1], sweetnesse[4]
**rh** meetness *S 118.5*

**sweet-savoured** *adj*
*m* ˌswi:t-'sɛ:vəɹd
**sp** sweet-sauour'd[1]
> savour

**sweet-suggesting** *adj*
'swi:t-səˌʤestɪn, -ɪŋ
**sp** sweet-suggesting[1]

**swell** *n*
=
**sp** swell[1]

**swell / ~est / ~s / ~ing / ~ed / swollen** *v*
= / -st / -z / 'swelɪn, -ɪŋ / sweld / swo:ln
**sp** swell[17], swell's [swell us][1] / swell'st[1] / swelles[1], swells[4], swels[4] / swelling[2] / sweld[1], swel'd[1], swell'd[3] / swolne[1]
> out-, over-swell; big-, high-swollen

**swelled** *adj*
=
**sp** swell'd[1]

**swelling** *adj*
'swelɪn, -ɪŋ
**sp** swelling[15]
> summer-swelling

**swelling / ~s** *n*
'swelɪn, -ɪŋ / -z
**sp** swelling[1] / swellings[1]

**sweltered** *adj*
'sweltəɹd
**sp** sweltred[1]

**Sweno** *n*
'swi:no:
**sp** Sweno[1]

**swerv·e / ~ing** *v*
swɐ:ɹv / 'swɐ:ɹvɪn, -ɪŋ
**sp** swerue[4] / sweruing[1]
**rh** deserve *Cym 5.4.129* / deserving *S 87.8*

**swerving** *n*
'swɐ:ɹvɪn, -ɪŋ
**sp** sweruing[1]

**swift / ~er / ~est** *adj*
= / 'swɪftəɹ / =
**sp** swift[43] / swifter[5] / swiftest[5]
**rh** drift *TG 2.6.42*
> night-, wind-swift

**swift / ~er** *adv*
= / 'swɪftəɹ
**sp** swift[15] / swifter[8]

**swift** *n*
=
**sp** swift[1]

**swiftly** *adv*
'swɪftləɪ
**sp** swiftly[7]

**swiftness** *n*
=
**sp** swiftnesse[4]

**swift-winged** *adj*
*m* ˌswɪft-'wɪŋɪd
**sp** swift-winged[2]
> winged

**swill / ~s / ~ed** *v*
=
**sp** swilles[1] / swill'd[1]

**swim / ~s / swam** *v*
= / = / swɑm
**sp** swim[8], swimme[4] / swimmes[2], swims[1] / swam[2], swom[2]
**rh** him *TNK Prol.24*

**swimmer / ~s** *n*
'swɪməɹ / -z
**sp** swimmer[1] / swimmers[1]

**swimming** *adj*
'swɪmɪn, -ɪŋ
**sp** swimming[2]

**swine** *n*
swəɪn
**sp** swine[8]
**rh** groin *VA 1115*

**swine-drunk** *adj*
'swəɪn-ˌdrɤŋk
**sp** swine-drunke[1]
> drunk

**swineherd / ~s** *n*
'swəɪn-ˌɐ:ɹdz, -ˌhɐ:-
**sp** swine-herds[1]
> herd

**swine-keeping** *n*
'swəɪn-ˌki:pɪn, -ɪŋ
**sp** swine-keeping[1]
> keep

**swing** *n*
=
**sp** swing[1]

**swing / swung** *v*
swɤŋ
**sp** swong[1]

**swinge / ~d** *v*
=
**sp** swinge[1] / swindg'd[2], swing'd[6]

**swinge-buckler / ~s** *n*
'swɪnʤ-ˌbɤkləɹz
**sp** swindge-bucklers[1]

**swinish** *adj*
'swəɪnɪʃ
**sp** swinish[1]

**Swinsted** *n*
'swɪnsted
**sp** Swinsted[2]

**switch / ~es** *n*
swɪts / =
**sp** swits[2] / switches[1]

**Swithold** *n*
'swɪto:ld
**sp** Swithold[1]

**Switzer / ~s** *n*
'swɪtzəɹz
**sp** Switzers[1]

**swollen** *adj*
swo:ln
**sp** swolne[4]

**swollen** *v*
> swell *v*

**swoon / ~s / ~ed / ~ded** *v*
= / = / = / 'swu:ndɪd
**sp** swoon[1], swoone[1] / swoonds[1] / swoond[3], swoon'd[1] / swoonded[1]
> sound [swoon], swound

**swoop** *n*
=
**sp** swoope[1]

**swoopstake** *adv*
'su:pstɛ:k, 'swu:-
**sp** soop-stake[1]

**sword / ~'s / ~s** *n*
sɔ:ɹd / -z
**sp** sword[329], [punie]-sword[1], [victor]-sword[1], sword's [sword is][1] / swords[1] / swords[68]
**rh** *1* lord *H5 Epil.6, TNK 3.1.42*; record *Luc 1640*; **rh** *2* word *1H6 4.6.3, LLL 5.2.276, Luc 1640, MND 2.2.113, 5.1.335* / words *Luc 1421, R2 3.3.132*
> half-, long-sword

**sworder** *n*
'sɔ:ɹdəɹ
**sp** sworder[2]

**sword-hilt / ~s** *n*
'sɔ:ɹd-ˌɪlts, -ˌhɪ-
**sp** sword hilts[1]
> hilt

**sword-man / ~-men** *n*
'sɔ:ɹdmən
**sp** sword-men[1]

**swore, sworn** *v*
> swear

**sworn** *adj*
swɔ:ɹn
**sp** sworn[3], sworne[15], sworne-[twelue][1]
**rh** born *LLL 5.2.282*
> deep-, un-sworn

**swound / ~s / ~ed** *v*
swəʊnd / -z, -nz / 'swəʊndɪd
**sp** swound[3], swowne[1] / swounds[1] / swownded[1]
**rh** *1* confounds *Luc 1486*; **rh** *2* wounds *Luc 1486*
> sound [swoon], swoon
> sibyl

**sycamore** *n*
'sɪkəˌmɔ:ɹ
**sp** siccamore[1], sycamour[1]
**rh** hour *LLL 5.2.89*

**sycamore-tree** *n*
ˈsɪkəmɔːɹ-ˈtriː
**sp** sicamour tree[1]
> tree

**Sycorax** *n*
ˈsɪkəˌraks
**sp** Sycorax[7]

**syllable / ~s** *n*
=
**sp** sillable[3], syllable[7] / syllables[1], sylla-bles[1]

**syllogism** *n*
=
**sp** sillogisme[1]

**symbol / ~s** *n*
=
**sp** simbols[1]

**sympathise / ~d** *v*
ˈsɪmpəˌθəɪz / -d
**sp** simpathize[1], sympathize[5]
**rh** *1* devised *S 82.11*; **rh** *2* sufficed *Luc 1113*

**sympathized** *adj*
*m* ˈsɪmpəˌθəɪzd, -zɪd
**sp** simpathis'd[1], simpathized[1]

**sympathy** *n*
ˈsɪmpəˌθəɪ
**sp** simpathie[4], simpathy[5]
**rh** eye, sky *Luc 1229*

**synagogue** *n*
=
**sp** sinagogue[2]

**synod / ~s** *n*
=
synod[4], synode[1] / synodes[1]

**Syracusa / Syracuse** *n*
ˈsɪrəˌkjuːzə
**sp** Siracusa[6], Siracusia[5], Syracusa[1] / Siracuse[2], *abbr in s.d.* S[1], Sir[2], Sira[1], Sirac[1]

**Syracusian** *adj*
ˈsɪrəˌkjuːzɪən
**sp** Siracusian[2], Syracusian[1]

**Syracusian / ~s** *n*
ˈsɪrəˌkjuːzɪən / -z
**sp** Siracusian[4] / Siracusians[1]

**Syria** *n*
=
**sp** Syria[5]
**rh** say *Per Prol.19*

**syrup / ~s** *n*
=
**sp** sirrups[1], syrrups[1]

# T

**T / ~s** *n*
=
**sp** T's[2]

**table** *adj*
'tɛ:bəl
**sp** table-[sport][1]

**table / ~s** *n*
'tɛ:bəl / -z
**sp** table[54], table-[sport][1], table's [table is][1] / tables[11]

**table / ~d** *v*
'tɛ:bəld
**sp** tabled[1]

**table-book** *n*
'tɛ:bəl-ˌbʊk
**sp** table-booke[3]
> book

**tablet** *n*
=
**sp** tablet[1]

**table-talk** *n*
'tɛ:bəl-ˌtɔ:k
**sp** table talke[1]

**tabor / ~s** *n*
'tabəɹ / -z
**sp** taber[4], tabor[5], ta-bor[1] / tabors[1]

**taborer** *n*
'tabrəɹ, -bər-
**sp** taborer[1]

**taborin / ~s** *n*
*m* 'tabrɪnz, -bər-, -bəˌr-
**sp** taborins[1], tabourines[1]

**taciturnity** *n*
*m* ˌtasɪ'tɐ:ɹnɪˌtəɪ
**sp** taciturnitie[1]

**tack / ~ed** *v*
=
**sp** tackt[1]

**tackle / ~s** *n*
=
**sp** tackle[4] / tackles[2]

**tackled** *adj*
=
**sp** tackled[1]

**tackling / ~s** *n*
'taklɪn, -ɪŋ / -z
**sp** tackling[1] / tacklings[1]

**tadpole** *n*
'tadpo:l, 'tɒ-
**sp** tadpole[1], tod-pole[1]

**taffeta** *adj / n*
=
**sp** taffata[2], taffety[1], taffata[3]

**tag** *n*
=
**sp** tagge[1]

**tag-rag** *adj*
=
**sp** tag-ragge[1]
> rag

**tail / ~s** *n*
tɛ:l / -z
**sp** taile[15], tayle[3] / tayles[1]
**rh** fail *TNK 3.5.50, TC 5.10.44*; frail *Oth 2.1.152*; sail *Mac 1.3.9*; trail *TC 5.8.21*
**pun** *Oth 3.1.8* tale
> horse-, long-, trundle-tail; red-tailed

**tailor / ~'s / ~s / ~s'** *n*
'tɛ:ləɹ / -z
**sp** tailor[17], tailour[2], tayler[1], taylor[14], taylour[1], *abbr in s.d.* Tail[1] / tailors[1], taylors / tailors[2], taylors[4] / taylors[1]

**taint / ~s** *n*
tɛ:nt / -s
**sp** taint[4] / taints[3]

**taint / ~s / ~ing / ~ed** *v*
tɛ:nt / -s / 'tɛ:nt·ɪn, -ɪŋ / -ɪd
**sp** taint[10], taynt[1] / taints[2] / tainting[1] / tainted[11]

**tainted** *adj*
'tɛ:ntɪd
**sp** tainted[4]
**rh** acquainted *CE 3.2.13*
> travel-, un-tainted

**tainting** *n*
'tɛ:nt·ɪn, -ɪŋ
**sp** tainting[2]

**taintingly** *adv*
*m* 'tɛ:ntɪnˌləɪ, -ɪŋ-
**sp** taintingly[1]

**tak·e / ~est / ~es / ~eth / ~ing / took / ~est / taken / tane** *v*
tɛ:k / -s, -st / -s / 'tɛ:k·əθ / -ɪn, -ɪŋ / = / -st / 'tɛ:kən / tɛ:n
**sp** take[1165], take-[a-your][1], take-[in][1], take-[off][1], take't [take it][8], tak't [take it][7] / tak'st[12] / takes[88] / taketh[2] / taking[21], ta-king[1] / took[6], tooke[145], took't [took it][4] / tookst[1], took'st[1] / taken[87], ta-ken[2], tak'n[1] / tane[70], 'tane[7], t'ane[4], ta'ne[13]
**rh** awake *Tem 2.1.307*; brake *MND 3.2.16*; make *AY 4.3.61, Luc 1200, S 81.3, 91.13*; quake *1H6 1.1.155*; sake *AW 2.3.88, H5 Epil.14, Luc 535, RJ 1.5.106, S 134.9*; sake, wake *MND 2.2.34*; take him forsake him *VA 319*; take it make it *AW 4.3.218* / mak'st *PT 19*; wak'st *MND 3.2.454* / makes *MND 3.2.177, Oth 1.3.204*; makes, takes *LC 107, 110*; shakes *Per 3. Chorus.43* / forsaken *S 133.5*; shaken *S 116.8, 120.7* / **rh** *1* book *RJ 1.5.108*; brook *VA 1101*; forsook, look *Luc 1537*; look *CE 2.1.89, S 47.1, 75.12*; **rh** *2* provoke *Per Prol.25*
> over-, under-take; action-taking, well-took, new-taken, ill-ta'en

**taker** *n*
'tɛ:kəɹ
**sp** taker[1], [life-wearie]-taker[1]

**taking** *n*
'tɛ:kɪn, -ɪŋ
**sp** taking[7], ta-king[1]
**rh** a-shaking, waking *Luc 453*
> leave-, purse-taking

**taking-up** *n*
'tɛ:kɪn-'ɤp, -ɪŋ-
**sp** taking-vp[1]

**taking-off** *n*
'tɛ:kɪn-'ɒf, -ɪŋ-
**sp** taking off[1]

**Talbonite / ~s** *n*
'tɑlbə,nəɪts
**sp** Talbonites[1]

**Talbot / ~'s / ~s** *n*
'tɑlbət / -s
**sp** Talbot[94], Talbot's [Talbot is][1], Talbots [Talbot is][1] / Talbots[13] / Talbots[2]

**tale / ~s** *n*
tɛ:l / -z
**sp** tale[106], tale's [tale is][1] / tales[20]
**rh** ale *MND 2.1.51*; ashy-pale *VA 74*; dale *Luc 1078*; pale *VA 591, 1125*; pale, scale *Luc 480*; pale, vale *LC 4*; stale *WT 4.1.14* / scales *MND 3.2.133*
**pun** *Oth 3.1.9* tail
> carry-, half-, tell-tale

**talent / ~s** *n*
=
**sp** talent[3] / talents[15]
**pun** talon *LLL 4.2.64*

**Taleporter** *n*
'tɛ:l,pɔ:ɹtəɹ
**sp** Tale-Porter[1]

**talk** *n*
=
**sp** talke[39]
**rh** *1* walk *TC 4.4.138*; **rh** *2* halt *PP 18.8*

**talk / ~est / ~s / ~ing / ~ed** *v*
= / -s, -st / -s / 'tɔ:kɪn, -ɪŋ / =
**sp** talk[2], talke[157] / talkest[3], talk'st[7] / talkes[13], talks[2] / talking[16], tal-king[1] / talk'd[17], talk'd-[of][1], talkt[8]
> out-talk; a-talking, untalked

**talker / ~s** *n*
'tɔ:kəɹ / -z
**sp** talker[2] / talkers[1]

**talking** *adj / n*
'tɔ:kɪn, -ɪŋ
**sp** talking[1] / talking[6], tal-king[2]

**tall / ~er** *adj*
tɑ:l / 'tɑ:ləɹ
**sp** tall[33], tall-[fellowes][1], taller[1]
**rh** all *2H4 5.3.33*; fall *MND 5.1.143*; tall ones small ones *TNK 3.5.111*

**taller** *n*
'tɑ:ləɹ
**sp** taller[2]

**tallest** *n*
'tɑ:ləst
**sp** tallest[2]

**tallow** *n*
'talə, -lo:
**sp** tallow[5]

**tallow-catch** *n*
'talə-,katʃ, -lo:-
**sp** tallow catch[1]

**tallow-face** *n*
'talə-,fɛ:s, -lo:-
**sp** tallow face[1]

**tally** *n*
'taləɪ
**sp** tally[1]

**talon / ~s** *n*
'talən, -t / 'talənz
**sp** talent[1] / tallons[2]
**pun** talent *LLL 4.2.64*

**tam** *Lat adv*
tam
**sp** tam[2]

**tame** *adj*
tɛ:m
**sp** tame[25]
**rh** came *LC 311*; lame *PP 12.8*; shame *R2 1.1.174*

**tam·e / ~es / ~ing / ~ed** *v*
tɛ:m / -z / 'tɛ:mɪn, -ɪŋ / tɛ:md
**sp** tame[10] / tames[1] / taming[1] / tam'd[4]

**tamed** *adj*
*m* 'tɛ:mɪd
**sp** tamed[1]

**tamely** *adv*
'tɛ:mləɪ
**sp** tamely[3]

**tameness** *n*
'tɛ:mnəs
**sp** tame-nesse[1]

**tamer** *n*
'tɛːməɹ
**sp** tamer[1]

**taming-school** *n*
'tɛːmɪn-ˌskuːl, -ɪŋ-
**sp** taming schoole[2]
> school

**Tamora / ~'s** *n*
*m* 'taməˌra, -mər-, -mrə / -məˌraz
**sp** Tamora[32] / Tamora's[1]

**Tamworth** *n*
'tamwəɹθ
**sp** Tamworth[1]

**tang** *n / v*
=
**sp** tang[1] / tang[1], *TN 3.4.71 emend of* langer[1]
**rh** hang *Tem 2.2.49*

**tangle / ~d** *v*
=
**sp** tangle[4] / tangled[1]
> untangle

**tangled** *adj*
=
**sp** tangled[1]

**tanling / ~s** *n*
'tanlɪnz, -ɪŋz
**sp** tanlings[1]

**tanned** *adj*
=
**sp** tan'd[1]

**tanner** *n*
'tanəɹ
**sp** tanner[2]

**tanquam** *Lat adv*
'tankwam, -ka-
**sp** tanquam[1]

**tant·us / ~a / ~aene** *Lat adj + particle*
'tant·a / -ene
**sp** tanta[1] / tantaene[1]

**tap** *n*
=
**sp** tap[2]

**tap / ~ped** *v*
=
**sp** tap[1], tapt[1]

**tape** *n*
tɛːp
**sp** tape[2]
**rh** cape *WT 4.4.313*

**taper / ~s** *n*
'tɛːpəɹ / -z
**sp** taper[10], tapor[1] / tapers[9]
night-taper

**taper-light** *n*
'tɛːpəɹ-ˌləɪt
**sp** taper-light[1]
**rh** might *Per Prol.15*
> light

**tapestr·y / ~ies** *n*
'tapɪsˌtrəɪ / -z
**sp** tapestrie[1], tapestry[1], tapistrie[1], tapistry[2] / tapistries[1]

**tap-house** *n*
'tap-ˌəʊs, -ˌhəʊs
**sp** tap-house[1]
> house

**tapster / ~'s / ~s** *n*
'tapstəɹ / -z
**sp** tapster[13] / tapsters[1] / tapsters[3]

**tar** *n*
tɑːɹ
**sp** tar[1], tarre[2]

**tar / ~red** *v*
tɑːɹ / -d
**sp** tarre[3] / tarr'd[1]

**tardily** *adv*
*m* 'tɑːɹdɪˌləɪ
**sp** tardily[1]

**tardiness** *n*
*m* 'tɑːɹdɪˌnes
**sp** tardinesse[1]

**tardy** *adj / adv*
'tɑːɹdəɪ
**sp** tardie[7], tardy[3] / tardie[3]

**tard·y / ~ied** *v*
'tɑːɹdəɪd
**sp** tardied[1]

**tardy-gaited** *adj*
'tɑːɹdəɪ-ˌgɛːtɪd
**sp** [creeple]-tardy-gated[1]

**targe / ~s** *n*
tɑːɹʤ / 'tɑːɹʤɪz
**sp** targe[1] / targes[2]

**target / ~s** *n*
'tɑːɹgɪt / -s
**sp** target[3], targuet[2] / targets[2]

**Tarientum** *n*
tarɪ'entəm
**sp** Tarientum[1]

**Tarpeian** *adj*
tɑːɹ'piːən
**sp** Tarpeian[5]

**Tarquin / ~'s / ~s** *n*
'tɑːɹkwɪn / -z
**sp** Tarquin[5], Tarquine[1] / Tarquins[2] / Tarquins[1]

**tarriance** *n*
=
**sp** tarriance[1]

**tarr·y / ~ies / ~ying / ~ied** *v*
'tarəɪ / -z / -ɪn, -ɪŋ / -d
**sp** tarrie[10], tarry[35] / taries[1], tarries[1] / tarrying[1] / tarried[4]

**tarrying** *n*
'tarəɪɪn, -ɪŋ
**sp** tarrying[3]

**tart** *adj / n*
tɑːɹt
**sp** tart[3] / tart[3]

**Tartar** *adj*
'tɑːɹtəɹ
**sp** Tartar[1]

**Tartar / ~'s / ~s** *n*
'tɑ:ɹtəɹ / -z
**sp** Tartar[3], [Bohemian]-Tartar[1] / Tartars[4] / Tarters[1]

**tartly** *adv*
'tɑ:ɹtləɪ
**sp** tartly[1]

**tartness** *n*
'tɑ:ɹtnəs
**sp** tartnesse[1], tart-nesse[1]

**task / ~s** *n*
task / -s
**sp** task[2], taske[19] / taskes[3]

**task / ~ing / ~ed** *v*
task / 'taskɪn, -ɪŋ / taskt
**sp** taske[6] / tasking[1] / task'd[1], taskt[1], task't[1]
**rh** masked *LLL 5.2.126*

**tasker** *n*
'taskəɹ
**sp** tasker[1]

**tassel** *n*
'tasəl
**sp** tassell[1]

**tassel-gentle** *n*
'tasəl-'ʤentl
**sp** tassell gentle[1]
> tercel

**taste** *n*
tast
**sp** tast[1], taste[31]
**rh** *1* last *VA 445*; **rh** *2* haste *Luc 651*

**tast·e / ~es / ~ing / ~ed** *v*
tast / -s / 'tast·ɪn, -ɪŋ / -ɪd
**sp** tast[5], taste[39] / tastes[2], tasts[1] / tasting[2] / tasted[7]
**rh** *1* fast *VA 528*; fast, last *Luc 893*; last *LC 167, S 90.11*; **rh** *2* haste *MND 1.1.236*; waste *RJ 2.3.68, S 77.4* / wasted *VA 128*
> untasted

**tattered** *adj*
'tatəɹd
**sp** tatter'd[2], tattred[1], totter'd[1]

**tatters** *n*
'tatəɹz
**sp** tatters[1]

**tattl·e / ~ing** *v*
= / 'tatlɪn, -ɪŋ
**sp** tattle[1] / tatling[1]
> tittle-tattling

**tattling** *adj*
'tatlɪn, -ɪŋ
**sp** tatling[1]

**tattling / ~s** *n*
'tatlɪnz, -ɪŋz
**sp** tatlings[1]

**taught**
> teach

**taunt / ~s** *n*
=, tɑ:nt / -s
**sp** taunt[1] / taunts[6]

**taunt / ~s / ~ed** *v*
=, tɑ:nt / -s / =, 'tɑ:ntɪd
**sp** taunt[6] / taunts[1] / taunted[1]

**taunting** *adj*
'tɔ:ntɪn, -ɪŋ, 'tɑ:-
**sp** tanting[1]

**Taurus / ~'s** *n*
'tɔ:rəs, 'to:-
**sp** Taurus[2], Towrus / Taurus[2]

**tavern** *adj*
'tavəɹn
**sp** tauerne[2]

**tavern / ~s** *n*
'tavəɹn / -z
**sp** tauern[1], tauerne[8] / tauernes[3]

**tawdry-lace** *n*
'tɔ:drəɪ-ˌlɛ:s
**sp** tawdry-lace[1]
> lace

**tawny** *adj*
'tɔ:nəɪ
**sp** tawney[1], tawnie[3], tawny[6]
> orange-tawny

**tawny-coat / ~s** *n*
'tɔ:nəɪ-ˌko:ts
**sp** tawney-coates[1], tawny-coats[1], tawny coats[1]

**tawny-finned** *adj*
'tɔ:nəɪ-ˌfɪnd
**sp** *emend of AC 2.5.12* tawny fine

**Tawyer** [name] *n*
'tɔ:əɹ
**sp** Tawyer[1]

**tax** *n*
=
**sp** taxe[1], taxes[1]

**tax / ~ing / ~ed** *v*
= / 'taksɪn, -ɪŋ / =
**sp** tax[1], taxe[8], *emend of AW 5.3.122* taze[1] / taxing[1] / tax'd[2], taxt[1]

**taxation / ~s** *n*
tak'sɛ:sɪən / -z
**sp** taxation[5] / taxations[2]

**taxing** *n*
'taksɪn, -ɪŋ
**sp** taxing[1]

**te** *Fr*
> tu

**teach / ~est / ~es / ~eth / ~ing / taught** *v*
= / 'ti:ʧ·əst / -ɪz / -əθ / -ɪn, -ɪŋ / =
**sp** teach[102] / teachest[4] / teaches[7] / teacheth[3] / teaching[5] / taught[44]
**rh** beseech *TC 1.2.292*; preach *1H6 3.1.130*; speech *R2 5.3.112*; teach thee beseech thee *VA 406*; teach you beseech you *Per 4.4.8*
> untaught

**teacher / ~s** *n*
'ti:ʧəɹ / -z
**sp** teacher[3] / teachers[2]
> parrot-teacher

**teaching** *n*
'ti:ʧɪn, -ɪŋ
**sp** teaching[7]

**team** *n*
=
**sp** teame[2], teeme[3]
**rh** dream *MND 5.1.374*

**tear** [cry] **/ ~s** *n*
ti:ɹ, tɛ:ɹ / -z
**sp** teare[27] / teares[265], tears[3]
**rh** *1* appear *S 31.5*; bier *Ham 4.5.168*; here *H8 Prol.6, LC 51, 289*; spear *R2 1.3.59*; **rh** *2* bear *LC 51*; bear, hair *Luc 1131*; there *Luc 1375*; wear *LC 289* / **rh** *1* appears *LC 296, LLL 4.3.153, 5.2.118, MND 3.2.123, VA 1176*; cheers *TNK 1.5.5*; clears *Luc 1713, S 148.10*; ears *Luc 1127*; fears *LC 296, S 119.1*; peers *H5 4.2.11*; years *Per 1.4.19, VA 1092*; **rh** *2* bears *LC 18, Luc 1713*; cares *3H6 3.3.13*; hairs *CE 3.2.46, VA 49, 192*; swears *VA 82*; theirs *Per 1.4.54*; wears *Luc 682*; **rh** *3* characters *LC 18*; hers *MND 2.2.98*

**tear** [rip] **/ ~s / ~ing / tore / torn** *v*
tɛ:ɹ, ti:ɹ / -z / 'tɛ:rɪn, -ɪŋ, ti:- / tɔ:ɹ / -n
**sp** tear[2], teare[46] / teares[3] / tearing[3] / tore[4] / torne[13]
**rh** *1* fear *Luc 739, R2 1.1.192*; here *Luc 1472*; **rh** *2* bear *Luc 1472*; there *Luc 739*; **tear it** fear it, hear it *LLL 4.3.198*; **tear thee rh** *1* bear thee *Luc 669*; **rh** *2* hear thee *Luc 669* / bears *Per 4.4.30* / more, o'er *Luc 1787* / forsworn *LLL 4.3.283, S 152.3*; born, outworn *Luc 1762*
> plough-torn

**tear-falling** *adj*
ˌti:ɹ-'fɔ:lɪn, -ɪŋ, ˌtɛ:-
**sp** teare-falling[1]

**tearful** *adj*
'ti:ɹfʊl, ˌtɛ:-
**sp** tearefull[1]

**tearing** *adj / n*
'tɛ:rɪn, -ɪŋ, ti:-
**sp** tearing[1] / tearing[1]

**Tearsheet** *n*
'tɛ:ɹʃi:t, 'ti:-
**sp** Teare-sheet[6], Teare-sheete[2]

**tear-stained** *adj*
'ti:ɹ-ˌstɛ:nd, 'tɛ:-
**sp** teare-stayn'd[1]
> stain

**teat** *n*
=
**sp** teat[2]

**Te Deum** *Lat n*
'tɛ: 'dɛ:ʊm
**sp** Te Deum[2]
> te

**tedious** *adj / n*
'tɪdɪəs
**sp** tedious[42] / tedious[1]
> overtedious

**tediously** *adv*
'tɪdɪəsləɪ
**sp** tediously[1]

**tediousness** *n*
*m* 'tɪdɪəsˌnes, -nəs
**sp** tediousnesse[4]

**teem / ~s** *v*
=
**sp** teeme[3] / teemes[3]
> overteemed

**teeming** *adj*
'ti:mɪn, -ɪŋ
**sp** teeming[4]

**teen** *n*
=
**sp** teene[4]
**rh** green *VA 808*; seen *LC 192, LLL 4.3.162, R3 4.1.96*

**teeth**
> tooth

**teipsum** *Lat*
> te

**Telamon** *n*
'teləmən
**sp** Telamon[1]

**Telamonius** *n*
*m* ˌtelə'mo:nɪˌʊs
**sp** Telamonius[1]

**tell / ~est / ~s / ~ing / told / ~est** *v*
= / tels, -st / = / 'telɪn, -ɪŋ / to:ld / to:ls, -lds, -st
**sp** tel[30], tell[1009], tell-[a-me][2], tell's [tell us][1], tel's [tell us][1] / tellst[1], tell'st[7], telst[1], tel'st[3] / telles[2], tells[13], tels[25] / telling[20] / told[220] / told'st[3], toldst[2]
**rh** bell, knell *Luc 1496*; cell *RJ 2.2.193*; dwell *S 84.7, 89.12, 93.12*; excel *LLL 4.3.39*; farewell *R2 2.1.212*; hell *2H6 5.1.215, Luc 1288, PP 2.10, S 144.10*; rebel *R2 3.2.120*; smell *PP 18.7, S 98.7*; well *CE 3.1.52, 3.2.187, 4.2.45, KL 1.4.342, 4.6.277, LC 253, MND 3.2.76, S 14.5, 103.12, WT 4.4.299* / bells *Luc 510* / behold *Luc 1324*; behold, bold, cold, enfold, gold, inscrolled, old, sold *MV 2.7.66*; behold, rolled *Luc 1397*; bold *Luc 1284, TNK Epil.12*; cold *VA 1126*; hold *Per 3.Chorus.57*; old *PP 1.12, S 76.14, 123.8, 138.12*
> all-telling, foretell; re-, un-told

**teller** *n*
'teləɹ
**sp** teller[1]

**telling** *n*
'telɪn, -ɪŋ
**sp** telling[6]
> fortune-telling

**tell-tale** *adj*
'tel-ˌtɛ:l
**sp** tell-tale[1]

**tell-tale / ~s** *n*
'tel-ˌtɛ:l / -z
**sp** tell-tale[2], tel-tale[1] / tell-tales[1], tel-tales[1]
> tale

**tellus** *Lat n*
'telʊs
**sp** tellus[2], tel-lus[1]

**Tellus / ~'s** *n*
'teləs
**sp** Tellus[1]

**temper** *n*
'tempəɹ / -z
**sp** temper[25] / tempers[1]

**temper / ~ing / ~ed** *v*
'tempəɹ / -ɪn, -ɪŋ, -pr- / -d
**sp** temper[9] / tempering[1], temp'ring[1] / temper'd[3], tempred[1], temp'red[1]
**rh** ventring *VA 565*
> best-, dis-, ill-, mis-tempered; untempering

**temperance** *n*
*m* 'tempəˌrans, -pər-, -prəns
**sp** temperance[8], temp'rance[2]

**temperate** *adj*
*m* 'tempəˌrɛ:t, -pər-, -prət
**sp** temperate[7], temp'rate[1]
**rh** date *S 18.2*

**temperately** *adv*
*m* 'temprətˌləɪ, -pər-
**sp** temperately[2], temp'rately[2]

**tempered** *adj*
'tempəɹd
**sp** temper'd[5]

**tempest / ~s** *n*
=
**sp** tempest[39] / tempests[4]

**tempest-dropping** *adj*
'tempəst-ˌdrɒpɪn, -ɪŋ
**sp** tempest-dropping-[fire][1]

**tempest-tossed** *adj*
'tempəs-ˌtɒst
**sp** tempest tossed[1], tempest-tost[1]
**rh** lost Mac *1.3.25*
> toss

**tempestuous** *adj*
tem'pestɪəs
**sp** tempestuous[3]

**temple** *adj*
=
**sp** temple[3]

**temple / ~s** *n*
=
**sp** temple[22], tem-ple[2] / temples[13]

**temple-haunting** *adj*
'templ-ˌɔ:ntɪn, -ɪŋ, -hɔ:-
**sp** temple-haunting[1]
> haunt

**temporal** *adj*
*m* 'tempəˌrɑl, -pər-, -prɑl
**sp** temporall[7]

**temporality** *n*
ˌtempə'ralɪtəɪ
**sp** temperalitie[1]

**temporary** *adj*
*m* 'tempəˌrarəɪ
**sp** temporary[1]

**temporise / ~d** *v*
*m* 'tempəˌrəɪz / -d
**sp** temporise[1], temporize[2] / temporiz'd[1]

**temporiser** *n*
*m* 'tempəˌrəɪzəɹ
**sp** temporizer[1]

**temps** *Fr n*
tɑ̃
**sp** temps[1]

**tempt / ~s / ~ed** *v*
temt, -mpt / -s / 'temtɪd, -mpt-
**sp** tempt[30] / tempts[6] / tempted[13]

**temptation / ~s** *n*
tem'tɛ:sɪən / -z, -mp-
**sp** temptation[3] / temptations[1]

**tempted** *adj / n*
'temtɪd, -mpt-
**sp** tempted[1] / tempted[1]

**tempter / ~s** *n*
'temtəɹ, -mpt- / -z
**sp** tempter[1] / tempters[2]

**tempting** *adj / adv / n*
'temtɪn, -ɪŋ, -mpt-
**sp** tempting[1] / tempting[1] / tempting[1]

**ten** *adj*
=
**sp** ten[92], tenne[11]

**ten / ~s** *n*
=
**sp** ten[33], tenne[8] / tens[1]
**rh** Englishmen *H5 3.7.152*; then *AW 1.3.77*

**tenant / ~s** *n*
=
**sp** tenant[2] / tenants[4]

**Tenantius** *n*
te'nansɪəs
**sp** Tenantius[2]

**tenantless** *adj*
*m* 'tenəntˌles
**sp** tenant-lesse[1]

**tench** *n*
=
**sp** tench[2]

**tend / ~s / ~ing / ~ed** *v*
= / = / 'tendɪn, -ɪŋ / =
**sp** tend[20] / tends[10] / tending[5] / tended[5]
**rh** amend, blend *LC 212*; friend *Ham 3.2.216*; lend *S 53.2*; mend *S 103.11*; spend *S 57.1*; tend thee guide thee, possess thee, with me *R3 4.1.92*

**tendance** *n*
=
**sp** tendance[4]

**tender** *adj*
'tendəɹ
**sp** tender[83]
> untender

**tender / ~s** *n*
'tendəɹ / -z
tender[10], ten-der[1] / tenders[3]
**rh** ender, render *LC 219*

**tender / ~s / ~ing / ~ed** *v*
'tendəɹ / -z / 'tendrɪn, -ɪŋ / 'tendəɹd
**sp** tender[34], tender't [tender it][1] / tenders[1] / tendering[1], tendring[4] / tenderd[1], tender'd[2], tendred[1]
**rh** remembered *S 120.11*

**tender-bodied** *adj*
'tendəɹ-ˌbɒdəɪd
**sp** tender-bodied[1]
> body

**tender-dying** *adj*
'tendəɹ-ˌdəɪɪn, -ɪŋ
**sp** tender-dying[1]
> die

**tender-feeling** *adj*
'tendəɹ-ˌfiːlɪn, -ɪŋ
**sp** tender-feeling[1]
> feel

**tender-hearted** *adj*
'tendəɹ-ˌɑːɹtɪd, -ˌhɑː-
**sp** tender-hearted[1]
> heart

**tender-hefted** *adj*
'tendəɹ-ˌeftɪd, -ˌhe-
**sp** tender-hefted[1]
> heft

**tenderly** *adv*
*m* 'tendəɹˌləɪ, -ɹl-
**sp** tenderly[5]

**tender-minded** *adj*
'tendəɹ-ˌməɪndɪd
**sp** tender minded[1]
> mind

**tenderness** *n*
*m* 'tendəɹˌnes, -ɹnəs
**sp** tendernes[1], tendernesse[12]

**tender-smelling** *adj*
'tendəɹ-ˌsmelɪn, -ɪŋ
**sp** tender smel-ling[1]
> smell

**tending** *n*
'tendɪn, -ɪŋ
**sp** tending[1]

**Tenedos** *n*
'tenəˌdɒs
**sp** Tenedos[1]

**tenement / ~s** *n*
*m* 'tenəˌment / -s
**sp** tenement[1] / tenements[1]

**tenfold** *adj / adv*
'tenfoːld
**sp** tenfold[1] / ten-fold[1]
> fold

**tennis** *n*
=
**sp** tennis[2]

**tennis-court** *adj*
'tenɪs-ˌkɔːɹt
**sp** tennis-court-[keeper][1]

**tenor** *n*
'tenəɹ
**sp** tenor[6]
**rh** penner *TNK 3.5.122*

**tent / ~s** *n*
=
**sp** tent[77] / tents[20]
**rh** intent *TC 1.3.307*; lent *Luc 15*; sent *TC 5.9.8*; spent *TC 5.1.42*

**tent** *v*
=
**sp** tent[3]
> untent

**tented** *adj*
=
**sp** tented[1]
> untented

**tenth** *adj*
tent
**sp** tenth[2]

**tenth / ~s** *n*
tent / -s
**sp** tenth[7] / tenths[1]

**ten-times** *adj*
'ten-ˌtəɪmz
**sp** ten times[1]

**tent-royal** *n*
*m* ˌtent-'rəɪəl
**sp** tent-royal[1]

**tenure / ~s** *n*
'tenjəɹ / -z
**sp** tenure[9] / tenures[2]

**tercel** *n*
'tɐːɹsəl
**sp** tercell[1]

**Tereus / ~s'** *n*
'terɪəs
**sp** Tereus[3] / Tereus[1]

**term / ~s** *n*
tɐːɹm, tɛːɹm / -z
**sp** tearme[3], terme[12], *1H4 1.3.45 emend of* tearme / tearmes[33], termes[36]

**term / ~s / ~ed** *v*
tɐːɹm, tɛːɹm / -z / *m* tɐːɹmd, 'tɐːɹmɪd, tɛː-
**sp** tearme[3], terme[6] / tearmes[2], termes[1] / tearm'd[3], tearmed[1], term'd[2]
> misterm

**termagant** *adj*
'tɐːɹməgənt
**sp** termagant[1]

**Termagant** *n*
'tɐːɹməgənt
**sp** Termagant[1]

**termination / ~s** *n*
ˌtɐːɹmɪ'nɛːsɪənz
**sp** terminations[1]

**terra / ~m / ~s** *Lat n*
'tera / -m / -s
**sp** terra[2] / terram[1] / terras[1]

**terrace** *n*
=
**sp** tarras[1]

**terre** *Fr n*
tɛːɹ
**sp** terre[1]

**terrene** *adj*
'teri:n
**sp** terrene[1]

**terrestrial** *adj*
tə'restrɪɑl
**sp** terrestriall[1]

**terrible** *adj*
=
**sp** terrible[26]

**terribly** *adv*
'terɪbləɪ
**sp** terribly[4]

**territor·y / ~ies** *n*
*m* 'terɪtrəɪ, -tər-, -ˌtɒrəɪ / 'terɪtrəɪz, -tər-
**sp** territorie[1], territory[1] / territories[11]

**terror / ~s** *n*
'terəɹ / -z
**sp** terror[28], terrour[1] / terrors[5], terrours[1]
**rh** error *LLL 5.2.470, WT 4.1.1*

**tertian** *n*
'tɐ:ɹsɪən
**sp** tertian[1]

**tertio** *Lat adv*
'teɹsɪo:
**sp** tertio[1]

**test** *n*
=
**sp** test[5]

**testament** *n*
=
**sp** testament[10]
**rh** spent *Luc 1183*

**tested** *adj*
=
**sp** tested-[gold][1]

**tester** *n*
'testəɹ
**sp** tester[2]

**testify** *v*
*m* 'testɪˌfəɪ, -ɪf-
**sp** testifie[5], testify[1]
**rh** die *Per Prol.40*

**testimon·y / ~ies** *n*
*m* 'testɪˌmɒnəɪ, -ɪmən- / -z
**sp** testimonie[5], testi-monie[1], testimony[5], te-stimony[1], testi-mony[1] / testimonies[2]

**testimon·y / ~ied** *v*
*m* 'testɪˌmɒnəɪd
**sp** testimonied[1]

**testiness** *n*
=
**sp** testinesse[1]

**testril** *n*
=
**sp** testrill[1]

**testy** *adj*
'testəɪ
**sp** testie[5]

**tetchy** *adj*
'tetʃəɪ
**sp** teachie[1], teachy[1], tetchy[1]

**tether** *n*
'teðəɹ
**sp** tether[1]

**tetter** *n / v*
'tetəɹ
**sp** tetter[1] / tetter[1]

**Tewksbury** *n*
*m* 'tju:ksbəˌrəɪ, -bərəɪ, -brəɪ
**sp** Teukesbury[1], Tewkesburie[1], Tewkesbury[3], Tewksburie[1], Tewksbury[1]

**text** *n*
=
**sp** text[10]
**rh** next *Per 2.Chorus.40, RJ 4.1.21*

**Thames** *adj / n*
=
**sp** Thames[1] / Thames[6]

**than** *conj*
=
**sp** than[24], then[1729], the[n][3], then's [than his][1]

**thane / ~s** *n*
θɛ:n / -z
**sp** thane[25] / thanes[6]

**thank / ~s / ~ed** *v*
=, *Caius MW 2.3.65, 82* taŋk / = / *m* =, 'θaŋkɪd
**sp** thank[24], thanke[261], *Caius MW 2.3.65* tanck[1], *MW 2.3.82* dancke[1], *emend Cym 5.3.233* thanks[1] / thankes[4], thanks[41] / thank'd[3], thanked[5], thank-ed[1], thankt[2]

**thankful** *adj*
=
**sp** thankefull[8], thankful[1], thankfull[10]
> unthankful

**thankfully** *adv*
*m* 'θaŋkfʊˌləɪ, -fləɪ
**sp** thankefully[2], thankfully[4], thank-fully[1]

**thankfulness** *n*
=
**sp** thankefulnesse[1], thanke-fulnesse[1], thankfulnes[2], thankfulnesse[1]
> unthankfulness

**thanking / ~s** *n*
'θaŋkɪn, -ɪŋ / -z
**sp** thanking[1] / thankings[3]

**thankless** *adj*
=
**sp** thankelesse[1], thanklesse[2]

**thanks** *n*
=
**sp** thankes[124], thanks[40]

**thanksgiving** *n*
ˌθaŋks'gɪvɪn, -ɪŋ
**sp** thanks-giuing[2]
**rh** living *LLL 2.1.128*
> giving

**Thasos** *n*
'θasɒs
**sp** Tharsus[1]

**that / those** *det, pro*
=, *Caius MW 1.4.53ff, Alice/ Katherine H5 5.2.119ff* dat
**sp** that[10433], [a']that[1], [o']that[10], thats [that is][3], that's [that is][393], *abbr* y[27], *Caius, Alice, Katherine* dat[24]
**rh** chat *LLL 5.2.229*; hat *LLL 1.1.293*

**those** *det, pro*
ðo:z
**sp** those[503]
**rh** depose *R2 4.1.192*; foes *Mac 2.4.40*; foes, woes *Luc 1461*; goes, glows *Luc 44*; grows *S 142.9*; rose *S 98.12*; suppose *AW 1.1.220, S 57.12*

**thatch** *n*
=
**sp** thatch[1]

**thatch / ~ed** *v*
=
**sp** thatch[1] / thatcht[1], thetchd[1]

**thatched** *adj*
=
**sp** thatch'd[1]

**thaw** *n*
=
**sp** thaw[2]

**thaw / ~s / ~ing / ~ed** *v*
= / = / 'θɔ:ɪn, -ɪŋ / =
**sp** thaw[2], thawe[1] / thawes[1] / thawing[1] / thaw'd[2]
**rh** bawd, laud *Luc 884*

**the, *abbr* th, t, y** *det*
=, *abbr* θ, ð / *Fr* də, *abbr* d
**sp** the[25481], [make-a]-the[1], *emend of Tit 5.1.126* few[1], *abbr* th'[541], 'th'[1], th'[aduantage][1], th[antoniad][1], th '[center][1], t'[1], y[50] / *Fr pron* de[63], [clapper]-de-[claw][2], [make-a]-de-[sot][1], *abbr* d'[4]

***by the*** *abbr*
bɪθ, bəɪθ, -ð
**sp** bi'th'[1], byth'[3], by'th[5], by'th'[26]

***in the*** *abbr*
ɪθ, -ð
**sp** ith[3], i'th[85], ith'[19], i'th'[184], i'the[3]

***of the*** *abbr*
əθ, ɒθ, -ð
**sp** ath'[2], a'th[19], a'th'[24], oth'[8], o't[201], o'th'[173]

***to the*** *abbr*
təθ, tʊθ, -ð
**sp** toth'[17], to'th[10], to'th'[69]

***the one*** *abbr*
tɒn
**sp** 'ton[1]

**theatre** *n*
*m* 'θi:ətəɹ, -ˌtɐ:ɹ
**sp** theater[5], thea-tre[1]

**Theban** *n*
'θi:bən
**sp** Theban[1]

**Thebe** *n*
'θi:bi:
**sp** Thebe[1]

**Thebes** *n*
'θi:bz
**sp** Thebes[1]

**thee**
> thou

**theft / ~s** *n*
=
**sp** theft[13] / thefts[2]
**rh** *1* bereft, left *Luc 838*; left *Mac 2.3.142, VA 160*; **rh** *2* shift *Luc 918*

**their, theirs, them**
> they

**theme / ~s** *n*
=
**sp** theame[27], theme[1] / theames[1]
**rh** dream *CE 2.2.190, MND 5.1.417*; stream *VA 770*

**themselves**
> they

**then** *adv*
= / *Katherine H5 5.2.247* den
**sp** than[12], then[2180], the[n][3], then's[1] [than his] / *Katherine* den[1]
**rh** *1* again *LLL 5.2.820, RJ 2.3.43*; den *LLL 4.1.93*; men *H5 4.8.124, LLL 5.2.344, MND 3.2.66, MV 2.1.45, Oth 4.3.52, PP 18.36, 18.45, RJ 2.3.75, S 146.14*; Mytilene *Per 4.4.50*; pen *MV 5.1.236*; ten *AW 1.3.74*; **rh** *2* scene *H5 2.Chorus.41*; **rh** *3* began, ran, then *Luc 1440*

**then** *conj*
> than

**thence** *adv*
=
**sp** thence[78]
**rh** diligence, offence *Luc 1850*; intelligence *S 86.12*; negligence *LC 34*; offence *Luc 736, S 51.3*

**theoric** *n*
=
**sp** theoricke[2], theorique[1]

**there** *adv*
ðɛ:ɹ / *Caius MW 1.4.61ff* dɛ:ɹ
**sp** ther[3], there[1784], there't [there it][1], theres [there is][7], there's [there is][341], ther's [there is][38] / *Caius* der[1], dere[2]
**rh** *1* bear *LLL 5.2.99, Tem 1.2.379*; everywhere *R2 1.2.71, S 5.6, 100.10*; fair, repair *TG 4.2.47*; forbear *S 41.11*; soe'er *TN 1.1.11*; swear *Luc 1649, MND 2.1.57*; tear [rip] *Luc 737*; where *TN 2.4.65*; **rh** *2* appear, fear *Luc 114*; appear, here *KL 1.4.145 [Q]*; cheer, dear *2H4 5.3.20*; dear *S 110.1, WT 4.3.17*; ear *PP 4.7, 18.14, R2 5.3.124, VA 780*; fear *Ham 3.2.182 [Q2], 1H6 5.2.16, Luc 307, 737, 1649, MND 2.1.31, 3.2.32, R2 2.1.300, VA 322*; here *LLL 4.3.187, MND 3.2.411, MV 2.9.53, Per 1.4.78*; near *MND 2.2.141, S 136.3*; spear *Luc 1422, VA 1114*; tear [cry] *Luc 1373*; year *2H4 5.3.20*; **rh** *3* harbinger *MND 3.2.381*

**thereabout / ~s** *adv*
'ðɛ:rə,bəʊt / -s
**sp** thereabout[2] / thereabouts[3]

**thereafter** *adv*
ðɛ:ɹ'aftəɹ, -'ɑ:təɹ
**sp** thereafter[1]

**thereat** *adv*
*m* ðɛ:ɹ'at, 'ðɛ:ɹat
thereat[2]

**thereby** *adv*
*m* ðɛ:ɹ'bəɪ, 'ðɛ:ɹbəɪ
**sp** thereby[23], there-by[1]
**rh** die *S 11.13*
> by

**therefore** *adv*
*m* ðɛ:ɹ'fɔ:ɹ, 'ðɛ:ɹfɔ:ɹ
**sp** therefore[580], there-fore[5], therfore[19], ther-fore[4]
**rh** more *MND 3.2.78*

**therein** *adv*
*m* ðɛ:ɹ'ɪn, 'ðɛ:ɹɪn
**sp** therein[53]
**rh** begin *TG 1.1.9*

**thereof** *adv*
*m* ðɛ:ɹ'ɒv, 'ðɛ:ɹɒv
**sp** thereof[36]

**thereon** *adv*
*m* ðɛ:ɹ'ɒn, 'ðɛ:ɹɒn
**sp** thereon[7]

**thereto** *adv*
*m* ðɛ:ɹ'tu:, 'ðɛ:ɹtu:
**sp** thereto[17]
**rh** you *TG 1.3.90*

**thereunto** *adv*
'ðɛ:ɹən'tu:
**sp** thereunto[3]
**rh** do *Oth 2.1.139*

**thereupon** *adv*
'ðɛ:ɹə'pɒn
**sp** thereupon[8]

**therewith** *adv*
'ðɛ:ɹwɪð, -ɪθ
**sp** therewith[2]

**therewithal** *adv*
'ðɛ:ɹwɪð'ɑ:l, -ɪθ-
**sp** therewithall[9]

**Thersites** *n*
θəɹ'səɪti:z
**sp** Thersites[29], Ther-sites[1]

**these**
> this

**Theseus / ~'s** *n*
*m* 'θi:sɪəs, -ɪ,ɤs / 'θi:sɪəs
**sp** Theseus[9] / Theseus[3], Thesus[1]

**Thessalian** *adj*
θə'sɛ:lɪən
**sp** Thessalian[1]

**Thessaly** *n*
*m* 'θesə,ləɪ, -əl-
**sp** Thessaly[2]

**Thetis / ~s'** *n*
'θetɪs
**sp** Thetis[2] / Thetis[2]

**thews** *n*
θju:z
**sp** thewes[3]

**they / their / ~s / them / ~selves** *pro*
ðɛ:, *unstr* ðɛ
**sp** they[2320]
**rh** play *H8 Prol.13*; say *LLL 5.2.87, S 59.11*; they do may do *MA 4.1.18*

***their / ~s***
ðɛ:ɹ / -z
**sp** their[1941], [o']their[1], theyr[1] / theirs[27], theyrs[1]
**rh** tears *Per 1.4.55*

***them***
=, *unstr* əm
**sp** them[1913], the[m][7], em[14], 'em[152], em'[1]

***themselves***
=
**sp** themselues[143], the[m]selues[1], them-selues[6]

***they are*** *abbr*
ðɛ:ɹ, *unstr* ðɛɹ
**sp** th'are[2], they'r[1], they're[6]

***they have*** *abbr*
ðɛ:v
they'aue[1], th'haue[2]

***they will*** *abbr*
ðɛ:l
**sp** thei'le[1], they'l[21], theyle[2], they'le[14], they'll[10]

***they would*** *abbr*
ðɛ:d, ðɛ:ld
**sp** they'ld[2]

**thick / ~er / ~est** *adj*
= / 'θɪkəɹ / =
**sp** thick[7], thicke[27] / thicker[2] / thickest[1]

**thick / ~er** *adv*
= / 'θɪkəɹ
**sp** thick[10] / thicker[1]
**rh** prick, sick *Luc 782*

**thick-coming** *adj*
*m* ,θɪk-'kɤmɪn, -ɪŋ
**sp** thicke-comming[1]
> come

**thicken / ~s** *v*
=
**sp** thicken[1] / thickens[2]

**thickest** *n*
=
**sp** thickest[3]

**thicket** *n*
=
**sp** thicket[5]
**rh** pricket *LLL 4.2.59*

**thick-eyed** *adj*
'θɪk-,əɪd
**sp** thicke-ey'd[1]
> eye

**thick-grown** *adj*
'θɪk-,gro:n
**sp** thicke growne[1]
> grow

**thick-lipped** *adj*
'θɪk-ˌlɪpt
**sp** thick-lipt-[slaue[1]]
> lip

**thick-lips** *n*
=
**sp** thicks-lips[1]
> lip

**thick-pleached** *adj*
'θɪk-ˌpliːʧt
**sp** thick pleached[1]
> pleached

**thick-ribbed** *adj*
*m* ˌθɪk-'rɪbɪd
**sp** thicke-ribbed[1]
> rib

**thick-skin** *n*
=
**sp** thick-skin[1]
> skin

**Thidias** *n*
'θɪdɪɔs
**sp** Thidias[4], Thidius[1], *abbr in s.d.* Thid[1]

**thief / thieves** *n*
=
**sp** theefe[56], thiefe[7] / theeues[45]
**rh** grief *Luc 888, Oth 1.3.206, S 40.9, 48.8* / grieves *VA 1022*

**thief-stolen** *adj*
'θiːf-ˌstoːln
**sp** theefe-stolne[1]
> steal

**thievery** *n*
'θiːvrəɪ, -vər-
**sp** theeuerie[1], theeuery[2]

**thievish** *adj*
=
**sp** theeuish[3]

**thigh / ~s** *n*
θəɪ / -z
**sp** thigh[9] / thighes[5]
**rh** lie *RJ 2.1.19* / **rh** *1* arise, butter-flies, eyes *MND 3.1.164*; **rh** *2* bees, courtesies, dewberries, mulberries *MND 3.1.164*

**thimble / ~s** *n*
=
**sp** thimble[2] / thimbles[1]

**thin** *adj / adv*
=
**sp** thin[14], thinne[5] / thinne[1]
**rh** in *CE 3.1.70*

**thin-belly** *adj*
'θɪnˌbeləɪ
**sp** thinbellie[1]
> belly

**thin-bestained** *adj*
*m* ˌθɪn-bɪ'stɛːnɪd
**sp** thin-bestained[1]

**thine**
> thou

**thin-faced** *adj*
'θɪn-ˌfɛːst
**sp** thin fac'd[1]
> face

**thing / ~s** *n*
=
**sp** thing[321], thing's [thing is][1] / things[321]
**rh** bring *TNK Prol.22*; bring, dwelling, excelling, sing *TG 4.2.50*; king *Ham 2.2.602, Luc 602, 1004, Per 3.Chorus.38, R2 5.3.78*; king, spring *Luc 607*; king, sting *Luc 39*; ring *CE 4.2.50, MV 5.1.306*; sing, spring *Luc 334*; sonneting *LLL 4.3.155*; spring *S 98.3*; sting *Luc 363* / brings *AW 1.1.219, MND 2.2.143, RJ 5.3.307*; kings *Luc 941, 1813, S 115.8, VA 996*; rings *TS 4.3.56*; springs, wings *Luc 947*; strings *MM 3.2.264*; wings *LLL 5.2.261*
> all-, any-, every-, no-, some-thing

**think / ~est / ~s / ~ing / thought / ~est** *v*
= / *m* θɪŋks, -st, 'θɪŋkəst / = / 'θɪŋkɪn, -ɪŋ / = / 'θɔːts
**sp** think[42], thinke[967], thinke't [think it][1], think't [think it][2] / thinkest[3], thinkst[9], think'st[40] / thinkes[48], thinks[9] / thinking[25], think-ing[2] / thoght[3], thought[243] / thoughtst [to][1]
**rh** chink *MND 5.1.155, 191*; drink *LLL 5.2.371, S 111.11*; ink *CE 3.1.14*; shrink *R2 2.2.31*; sink *CE 3.2.50, Tim 2.2.235* / bought *Luc 1065*; brought *H5 1.2.310, Luc 1576, Per 4.4.18, S 32.9, 44.1*; naught *Mac 4.1.68, R3 3.6.14, S 57.9, TG 1.1.69*; sought *S 30.1*; sought, wrought *Luc 338*; wrought *S 44.9*
> fore-, mis-, un-think; ill-thinking, methinks

**thinking / ~s** *n*
'θɪŋkɪn, -ɪŋ / -z
**sp** thinking[13], thin-king[2] / thinkings[3]

**thinly** *adv*
'θɪnləɪ
**sp** thinly[2]

**third** *adj*
θɐːɹd
third[41]

**third / ~'s / ~s** *n*
θɐːɹd, *Caius MW 3.3.222* tɐːɹd / -z
**sp** third[29], *Caius* turd[1] / thirds[1], third's[2] / thirds[1]
**pun** *Caius* turd

**thirdborough** *n*
'θɐːɹbrə
**sp** tharborough[1]

**thirdly** *adv*
'θɐːɹdləɪ
**sp** thirdlie[1], thirdly[1]

**thirst** *n*
θɐːɹst
**sp** thirst[3]

**thirst / ~s / ~ing** *v*
θɐːɹst / -s / 'θɐːɹstɪn, -ɪŋ
**sp** thirst[4] / thirsts[1] / thirsting[1]

**thirsty** *adj*
'θɐ:ɹstəɪ
**sp** thirstie[2], thirsty[4]

**thirteen** *adj / n*
'θɐ:ɹti:n
**sp** thirteene[1] / thirteen[1], thirteene[3]

**thirtieth** *n*
'θɐ:ɹtiət
**sp** thirtieth[1]

**thirty** *adj*
'θɐ:ɹtəɪ
**sp** thirtie[12], thirty[8]

**thirt·y / ~ies** *n*
'θɐ:ɹtəɪ / -z
**sp** thirtie[2], thirty[6] / thirties[1]

**thirty-one** *n*
ˌθɐ:ɹtəɪ-'o:n
**sp** thirty one[1]
**rh** stone *Mac 4.1.7*

**thirty-three** *adj*
ˌθɐ:ɹtəɪ-'θri:
**sp** thirtie three[1]

**this / these** *det, pro*
=
**sp** this[6436], 'this[1], this'[1], [o']this[1]
**rh** *1* amiss *CE 2.2.192, Ham 5.2.395, PP 17.4, S 35.5;* amiss, bliss, iwis, kiss *MV 2.9.63, 69*; bliss *MND 5.1.175, MV 3.2.135, Tit 3.1.148*; hiss *TC 5.10.54, TNK Prol.15*; kiss *AW 4.3.222, Oth 5.2.354, Per 1.2.78, RJ 1.5.94, 98, S 128.13, VA 205, 721*; miss *AW 1.3.250*; Pentapolis *Per 3.Chorus.33*; **rh** *2* is *MV 2.9.63, 69, R3 2.1.84, RJ 1.1.182, S 72.9, TC 1.2.288, Tim 1.2.193, 5.3.9, VA 613*

***these*** *det, pro*
= / *Caius MW 1.4.43* di:z / *Macmorris H5 3.2.110* ðe:z
**sp** these[1283], [o']these[1], [o']th's[1] / des-[toyes][1] / theise[1]
**rh** please *LLL 1.1.49*; seas *CE 2.1.20*; Simonides *Per 3.Chorus.24*

**Thisbe / ~'s** *n*
'θɪzbi:, *MND 1.2.48*
'θɪzni: / -z
**sp** Thisbie[15], Thisby[22], *MND 1.2.48* Thisne[2] / Thisbies[8]
**rh** secretly *MND 5.1.157*

**thistle / ~s** *n*
=
**sp** thissell[2], thistle[1] / thistles[1]

**thither** *adv*
'θɪðəɹ
**sp** thether[9], thither[80], thi-ther[2]
**rh** *1* whither *WT 4.4.300*; **rh** *2* together *Per 5.1.239, TC 1.1.117*; weather *Luc 113*; whether *PP 14.10*

**thitherward** *adv*
'θɪðəɹˌwɑ:ɹd
**sp** thitherward[1]

**Thoas** *n*
'θo:əs
**sp** Thous[1]

**Thomas** *n*
=
**sp** Thomas[55], Tho-mas[1], *abbr* Tho.[2]

**thorn** *adj*
θɔ:ɹn
**sp** thorne[2]

**thorn** *n*
θɔ:ɹn / -z
**sp** thorne[9] / thornes[10], thorns[2]
**rh** born *AW 1.3.124*; forlorn *PP 20.10*; scorn *MND 5.1.134*; sworn *LLL 4.3.110, PP 16.12*; unborn *R2 4.1.322*

**thorny** *adj*
'θɔ:ɹnəɪ
**sp** thornie[3], thorny[4]

**thorough** *prep*
'θɤrə, -ro:
**sp** thorough[5], tho-rough[1], thorow[2], tho-row[1]

**thoroughly** *adv*
*m* 'θɤrəˌləɪ, -əl-
**sp** thoroughly[1], tho-roughly[1], thorowly[2]

**those**
> that

**thou / thee / thine / thy / ~self** *pro*
ðəʊ
**sp** thou[5165], *abbr* y[58]
**rh** allow *R2 1.1.122*; now *LLL 5.2.337, MND 3.2.402*

***thou art*** *abbr*
ðɑ:ɹt, ðəʊɹt
**sp** th'art[23], thou'rt[19], th'ourt[1]

***thou hadst*** *abbr*
ðads, -t
**sp** th'hadst[2]

***thou hast*** *abbr*
ðast, ðəʊst
**sp** th'hast[4], thou'st[1]

***thou shalt*** *abbr*
ðəʊz
**sp** thou'se[1]

***thou wilt*** *abbr*
ðəʊl, -t
**sp** thou'lt[17], thou't[5]

***thou wouldest*** *abbr*
ðəʊds, -st, ðəʊlst
**sp** thou'dst[8], thoud'st[3], thou'd'st[1], thould'st[1]

***thee***
=, *unstr* ðɪ
**sp** thee[3002], [fare]thee[1], [far] thee[2], [fare]thee-[well][1], [far] thee[well][2], [far]-thee-[well][1], [far]the[well][1], [peg]-thee[1]
**rh** agony *R3 4.4.163*; authority *1H6 5.1.60*; be *CE 3.2.66, Cym 3.5.158, 2H6 4.10.30, Luc 1210, R2 2.1.135, 4.1.201, 5.3.34, S 1.14, 3.14, 4.13, 44.6, 78.10, 101.10, 123.14, 126.12, 136.12, 140.10, 141.10, 142.10, 151.9, VA 156*; be, me *Luc 1192*; Burgundy *1H6 4.6.15*; captivity *1H6 4.7.4*; commodity *KJ 2.1.598*; company

*3H6 5.2.3*; decree *Luc 1032*; degree *Oth 2.3.91*; fee *2H6 3.2.216, Luc 911, Tit 2.3.180*; free *3H6 4.6.17, S 125.12, TG 5.4.83, Tim 4.3.540*; he *Luc 1634*; he, knee *LLL 5.2.545*; honesty *KJ 1.1.180*; hospitality *Luc 577*; infancy [*F, at Tit 5.3.163*]; iniquity *Luc 624*; knee *KJ 1.1.83, R3 1.2.176*; lawlessly *TG 5.3.15*; loyalty *AY 2.3.69*; me *AC 1.3.104, AW 4.2.66, AY 4.3.57, CE 1.2.70, 2.1.38, H5 4.1.300, 1H6 4.5.38, 2H4 4.5.47, 2H6 3.2.299, 4.4.25, 3H6 4.7.38, 5.1.98, KJ 4.1.133, KL 1.4.138, LLL 4.3.32, 63, 114, Luc 917, Mac 2.1.34, MND 1.1.178, 3.1.148, 5.1.188, PP 3.6, 10.11, R2 2.1.87, 4.1.214, RJ 3.3.174, 5.1.86, S 10.14, 22.5, 24.12, 28.8, 31.13, 36.9, 37.13, 38.7, 39.4, 41.13, 43.13, 45.10, 47.12, 50.8, 61.5, 74.6, 88.10, 97.11, 122.13, 133.13, 143.9, 150.14, Tit 1.1.64, 110, 3.2.82, 5.2.44, TN 4.1.58, VA 137, 194, 519*; me, see *Luc 1304*; melancholy *S 45.6*; misery *PP 20.29, Tit 2.4.56*; opportunity *Luc 896, 902*; posterity *S 6.10*; sea *RJ 2.2.134*; see *KJ 3.1.146, Luc 1771, Oth 1.3.290, S 3.9, 18.14, 27.6, 43.3, 95.10, 99.15, TC 5.2.109, VA 438, 950*; three *LLL 5.2.230*; usury *S 6.7*; vanity *1H4 5.4.104*; victory *R3 5.3.167*; thee it is vapour is *PP 3.11*

***thine***
ðəɪn, *unstr* ðɪn
**sp** thine[405], thine's [thine is][2]
**rh** confine *LC 266*; divine *S 108.7*; divine, shrine *Luc 191*; eyne *VA 631*; mine *Cor 4.7.56, 1H6 4.6.22, Luc 482, R3 4.4.124, S 2.12, 26.7, 92.4, 134.1, 142.5, VA 115, 500*; repine *1H6 5.2.19*; Rosaline *LLL 4.3.218, 5.2.132, RJ 2.3.73*; shine *S 135.6*; vine *CE 2.2.182*

***thy***
ðəɪ, *unstr* ðɪ
**sp** thy[3727], [i']thy[1], [o']thy[1]

***thyself***
ðɪ'self, ðəɪ'self
**sp** thy self[2], thy selfe[194]
**rh** myself *R3 1.2.84, Tim 4.3.221*

**thou / ~est** *v*
ðəʊst
**sp** thou'st[1]

**though** *adv / conj*
ðo:
**sp** tho[1], though[6] / tho[2], thogh[7], though[572], though't [though it][4]
**rh** *adv* so *KJ 1.1.169, MND 2.2.115*
> although

**thought / ~'s / ~s' / ~s** *n*
=
**sp** thoght[5], thought[133], thought's [thought is][1] / thoghts[6], thoughts[1] / thoughts[1] / thoughts[218], [lay]-thoughts[1]
> love-thought

**thought-executing** *adj*
*m* ˌθɔ:t-'eksɪˌkju:tɪn, -ɪŋ
**sp** thought-executing[1]
> execute

**thoughtful** *adj*
=
**sp** thoughtfull[1]

**thought-sick** *adj*
=
**sp** thought-sicke[1]
> sick

**thousand** *adj*
'θəʊzənd
**sp** thousand[258], thou-sand[1]

**thousand / ~s** *n*
'θəʊzənd / -z
**sp** thousand[52], thou-sand[2], / thousands[16], thousand's[1], thou-sands[1]

**thousandfold** *n*
'θəʊzənˌfo:ld, -nd-
**sp** thousand fold[4]
> fold

**Thracian** *adj*
'θrɛ:sɪən
**sp** Thracian[5]

**thraldom** *n*
'θrɑ:ldəm
**sp** thraldome[1]

**thrall / ~s** *n*
θrɑ:l / -z
**sp** thrall[3] / thralles[1]
**rh** *1* gall *PP 17.14*; wall *Luc 725*;
**rh** *2* perpetual *Luc 725, S 154.12*

**thrall / ~ed** *v*
θrɑ:ld
**sp** thral'd[1]

**thrash** *v*
=
**sp** thrash[1], thresh[1]

**thrasonical** *adj*
θrə'sɒnɪkɑl
**sp** thrasonicall[2]

**thread** *n*
=
**sp** thred[19]
**rh** head *WT 4.4.316*
> pack-thread

**thread / ~ing** *v*
= / 'θredɪn, -ɪŋ
**sp** thred[2] / thredding[1]
> unthread

**threadbare** *adj*
'θredbɛ:ɹ
**sp** thred-bare[2]
> bare

**threaden** *adj*
'θredən
**sp** threaden[1]

**threat / ~s** *n*
=
**sp** threats[11]

**threat / ~est / ~s** *v*
= / θrets, -st / =
**sp** threat[9] / threatest[1] / threats[3]
**rh** get *Luc 547*

**threaten / ~est / ~s / ~ing / ~ed** *v*
= / 'θretnəst / = / 'θretnɪn, -ɪŋ / =
**sp** threaten[9] / threatnest[1] / threatens[7] / threatning[6] / threatend[1], threaten'd[2], threatned[6]

**threatened** *adj*
=
**sp** threatned[2]

**threatener** *n*
'θretnəɹ
**sp** threatner[1]

**threatening** *adj / n*
'θretnɪn, -ɪŋ
**sp** threatning[12] / threatning[1]

**threateningly** *adv*
*m* 'θretnɪn,ləɪ, -ɪŋ-
**sp** threatningly[1]

**threat-enraged** *adj*
'θret-en,rɛ:ʤd
**sp** threat-enrag'd[1]
> enrage

**three** *adj*
=
**sp** three[265], three[farthings][1], three-[farthings][1], three-[far-things][1], three[pence][1], three-[pence][1], *abbr* iij[1]
**rh** be *MND 5.1.397*; me *MND 5.1.328*

**three / ~s** *n*
=, *Caius MW 2.3.20, 33* tri: / =
**sp** three[109], *Caius* tree[2] / threes[3], [foure]-threes[1]
**rh** be, see *PP 15.1*; honesty, me *LLL 5.2.814*; humble-bee *LLL 3.1.84, 88, 94*; me *MND 3.2.193*; see *LLL 4.3.160, 5.2.419*; solemnity *MND 4.1.183*; steadfastly *VA 1064*; thee *LLL 5.2.231*; three-a Barbary-a [*song*] *TNK 3.5.63*
> thirty-three

**threefold** *adj*
'θri:fo:ld
**sp** threefold[3], three-fold[6]
> fold

**three-foot** *adj*
=
**sp** three-foot[2]
> foot

**three-headed** *adj*
*m* ,θri:-'edɪd, -'he-
**sp** three-headed[1]
> head

**three-hooped** *adj*
'θri:-,u:pt, -,hu:-
**sp** three hoop'd[1]
> hoop

**three-inch** *adj*
=
**sp** three inch[1]
> inch

**three-legged** *adj*
'θri:-,legd
**sp** three-legg'd[1]
> leg

**three-man** *adj*
=
**sp** three-man[1], three-man-[beetle][1]
> man

**three-nooked** *adj*
=
**sp** three nook'd[1]

**Three-pile** [name] *n*
'θri:-,pəɪl
**sp** Three-pile[1]

**three-piled** *adj*
'θri:-,pəɪld
**sp** three pil'd-[peece][1]

**threescore** *adj / n*
*m* 'θri:skɔ:ɹ, θri:'skɔ:ɹ
**sp** threescore[1] / threescore[4]

**three-suited** *adj*
'θri:-,ʃu:tɪd, ,sju:-
**sp** three-suited-[hundred][1]

**Threne** *n*
θri:n
**sp** Threne[1]
**rh** scene *PT 49*

**thresher** *n*
'θreʃəɹ
**sp** thresher[1]

**threshold** *n*
'θreʃo:ld
**sp** threshold[5]

**threw**
> throw

**thrice** *adv*
θrəɪs
**sp** thrice[64]

**thrice-crowned** *adj*
*m* ,θrəɪs-'krəʊnɪd
**sp** thrice crowned[1]
> crowned

**thrice-driven** *adj*
'θrəɪsdrɪvən
**sp** thrice-driuen[1]

**thrice-fair** *adj*
'θrəɪs-,fɛ:ɹ
**sp** thrice faire[1]

**thrice-famed** *adj*
*m* ,θrəɪs-'fɛ:md, -mɪd
**sp** thrice fam'd[1], thrice-famed[1]
> famed

**thrice-gentle** *adj*
*m* ,θrəɪs-'ʤentl
**sp** thrice-gentle[1]
> gentle

**thrice-gorgeous** *adj*
*m* ,θrəɪs-'gɔ:ɹʤɪəs
**sp** thrice-gorgeous[1]
> gorgeous

**thrice-gracious** *adj*
*m* ,θrəɪs-'grɛ:sɪəs
**sp** thrice-gracious[1], thrice gracious[1]
> gracious

**thrice-noble / ~r** *adj*
*m* ,θrəɪs-'no:bl, 'θrəɪs-,no:bl / ,θrəɪs-'no:bləɹ
**sp** thrice-noble[1], thrice noble[1] / thrice-nobler[1]
> noble

**thrice-puissant** *adj*
*m* ˌθrəɪs-ˈpwɪsɔ:nt
**sp** thrice-puissant[1]
> puissance

**thrice-renowned** *adj*
*m* ˈθrəɪs-rɪˌnəʊnɪd
**sp** thrice-renowned[1]
> renown

**thrice-repured** *adj*
*m* ˈθrəɪs-rɪˌpju:rɪd
**sp** *TC 3.2.20 emend of* thrice reputed[1]
> pure

**thrice-valiant** *adj*
*m* ˌθrəɪs-ˈvalɪənt
**sp** thrice-valiant[1], thrice valiant[1]
> valiant

**thrice-worthy** *adj*
*m* ˌθrəɪs-ˈwɔ:ɹðəɪ
**sp** thrice-worthy[1], thrice worthy[2]
> worthy

**thrift / ~s** *n*
=
**sp** thrift[11], [French]-thrift[1] / thrifts[1]
> unthrift

**thriftless** *adj*
=
**sp** thriftlesse[3]

**thrifty** *adj*
ˈθrɪftəɪ
**sp** thriftie[2], thrifty[3]
> unthrifty

**thrill / ~s / ~ed** *v*
=
**sp** thrill[2] / thrills[1] / thrill'd[1]

**thrilling** *adj*
ˈθrɪlɪn, -ɪŋ
**sp** thrilling[1]

**thrive / ~s / ~d** *v*
θrəɪv / -z / -d
**sp** thriue[54] / thriues[4] / thriued[1]
**rh** *1* alive *AW 4.3.328, VA 1011*; derive *AW 2.3.134, S 14.11*; five *LLL 5.2.534*; wive *TN 5.1.396*; **rh** *2* live *v R2 1.3.84* / reviveth *VA 466* / wived *Per 5.2.9* [*Chorus*]

**thriving** *adj*
ˈθrəɪvɪn, -ɪŋ
**sp** thriuing[2]

**throat / ~s** *n*
θro:t, *Caius MW 1.4.106* tro:t / -s
**sp** throat[33], throate[15], throte[2], *Caius* troat[1] / throates[6], throats[20]
**rh** note *AY 2.5.4, R2 1.1.44* / notes *Tim 1.2.51*
> cut-throat

**throb** *v*
=
**sp** throb[1], throbs[1]

**throbbing** *adj*
ˈθrɒbɪn, -ɪŋ
**sp** throbbing[1]

**throca** *nonsense word*
ˈθrɒka
**sp** throca[1]

**throe / ~s** *v*
θro:z
**sp** throwes[2]

**throes** *n*
θro:z
**sp** throwes[2]
**rh** foes *Cym 5.4.44*

**thromuldo** *nonsense word*
θrɒˈmʊldo:
**sp** thromuldo[1]

**throne / ~s** *n*
θro:n / -z
**sp** throane[1], throne[62] / throanes[1], thrones[1]
**rh** *1* groan *VA 1043*; **rh** *2* gone *2H6 2.3.38*

**throne / ~d** *v*
θro:n / *m* θro:nd, ˈθro:nɪd
**sp** throne[1] / thron'd[3], throned[2]
enthrone

**throned** *adj*
*m* θro:nd, ˈθro:nɪd
**sp** throaned[1], thron'd[1]

**throng / ~s** *n*
=
**sp** throng[7] / throngs[6]
**rh** long *H5 4.5.22* / tongues *KL 3.2.90*

**throng / ~ing / ~ed** *v*
= / ˈθrɒŋgɪn, -ɪŋ / =
**sp** throng[7] / thronging[2] / throng'd[2]
**rh** long *Luc 1783*; tongue *Luc 1783*

**thronging** *adj*
ˈθrɒŋgɪn, -ɪŋ
**sp** thronging[2]

**throstle** *n*
=
**sp** throstle[1], trassell[1]

**throttle** *v*
=
**sp** throttle[1]

**through** *adv / prep / v*
=
**sp** through[28] / throgh[1], through[226], through't [through it][1] / through[2]
**rh** *adv* do *Cor 2.3.122*

**throughfare / ~s** *n*
ˈθru:fɛ:ɹ / -z
**sp** through-fare[1] / throughfares[1]

**throughly** *adv*
ˈθru:ləɪ
**sp** throughlie[1], throughly[10], through-ly[1]

**throughout** *adv / prep*
θru:ˈəʊt
**sp** throughout[7] / throughout[7]

**throw / ~s** *n*
θro: / -z
**sp** throw[5] / throwes[2]

**throw / ~est / ~s / ~ing / threw / ~-est / thrown** *v*
θro: / 'θro:əst / θro:z / 'θro:ɪn, -ɪŋ / = / θru:st / θro:n
**sp** throw[95], throw-[out][1], throw't [throw it][2], throwe[1] / throwest[1] / throwes[11] / throwing[9] / threw[21], threw-[off][1] / threw'st[1] / thrown[3], throwne[26]
**rh** go *Mac 4.1.5*; low, show *Mac 4.1.65*; owe *MND 2.2.84* / goest, knowest, owest, showest, trowest *KL 1.4.122* / rose *VA 592* / crew, drew *Luc 1733*; drew *LC 38*; you *S 145.13* / **rh** *1* one *Cym 5.4.59*; **rh** *2* strewn *TN 2.4.61*
> overthrow

**thrower-out** *n*
'θro:əɹ-'əʊt
**sp** thrower-out[1]
> out

**throwing** *n*
'θro:ɪn, -ɪŋ
**sp** throwing[1]

**thrum** *n*
θrɤm
**sp** thrum[1]
**rh** come *MND 5.1.278*

**thrummed** *adj*
θrɤmd
**sp** thrum'd[1]

**thrush** *n*
θrɤʃ
**sp** thrush[1]

**thrust / ~s** *n*
θrɤst / -s
**sp** thrust[6] / thrusts[1]

**thrust / ~s / ~eth / ~ing** *v*
θrɤst / -s / 'θrɤst·əθ / -ɪn, -ɪŋ
**sp** thrust[46] / thrusts[3] / thrusteth[1] / thrusting[4]
**rh** dust, lust *Luc 1383*; just, mistrust *Luc 1517*; lust *VA 41*; trust *S 48.2*

**thrusting-on** *n*
'θrɤstɪn-'ɒn, -ɪŋ-
**sp** thru-sting on[1]

**thumb / ~s** *n*
θɤm / -z
**sp** thombe[1], thumb[4], thumbe[8] / thumbes[1]
**rh** come *LLL 5.2.111, Mac 1.3.27* /
**rh** comes *Mac 4.1.44*

**thumb-ring** *n*
'θɤm-ˌrɪŋ
**sp** thumbe-ring[1]
> ring

**thump / ~ed** *v*
θɤmp / -t
**sp** thump[1], thump-[her][1], thumpe[4] / thump'd[1], thumpt[1]
> bethump

**Thump** [name] *n*
θɤmp
**sp** Thumpe[2]

**thunder / ~'s / s** *n*
'θɤndəɹ / -z
**sp** thunder[52] / thunders[2] / thunders[1]
**rh** asunder *VA 268*; wonder *LLL 4.2.115, PP 5.11*

**thunder / ~est / ~s** *v*
'θɤnd·əɹ / -rəst / -əɹz
**sp** thunder[8] / thundrest[1] / thunders[6], thun-ders[1]

**thunder-bearer** *n*
'θɤndəɹ-ˌbɛ:rəɹ
**sp** thunder-bearer[1]
> bearer

**thunderbolt / ~s** *n*
'θɤndəɹˌbo:lt / -s
**sp** thunder-bolt[2], thunderbolt[3] / thunder-bolts[2]
> bolt

**thunderclap / ~s** *n*
'θɤndəɹˌklaps
**sp** thunder-claps[1]
> clap

**thunder-darter** *n*
'θɤndəɹ-ˌdɑ:ɹtəɹ
**sp** thunder-darter[1]

**thunderer** *n*
'θɤndrəɹ, -dər-
**sp** thunderer[1]

**thundering** *adj*
'θɤndrɪn, -ɪŋ
**sp** thundring[1]

**thunder-like** *adj*
'θɤndəɹ-ˌləɪk
**sp** thunder-like[1]

**thunder-master** *n*
'θɤndəɹ-ˌmastəɹ
**sp** thunder-master[1]
> master

**thunder-stone** *n*
'θɤndəɹ-ˌsto:n
**sp** thunderstone[1], thunder-stone[1]
**rh** moan *Cym 4.2.271*
> stone

**thunderstroke** *n*
'θɤndəɹˌstro:k
**sp** thunder-strok[1], thunder-stroke[1]
> stroke

**Thurio / ~'s** *n*
'θʊrɪo: / -z
**sp** Thurio[29] / Thurio's[1]

**Thursday** *n*
'θɐ:ɹzdɛ:
**sp** Thursday[17]

**thus** *adv*
ðɤs
**sp** thus[752]
**rh** *1* Demetrius *MND 2.2.91, 103, 3.2.363*; over-plus *S 135.4*; Pyramus *MND 5.1.292*; us *LLL 5.2.120*; **rh** *2* guess *LLL 5.2.120*

**thwack** *v*
=
**sp** thwack[1], thwacke[3]

**thwart** *adj / n*
θwɑːɹt
**sp** thwart[1] / thwart[1]

**thwart / ~ed** *v*
θwɑːɹt / ˈθwɑːɹtɪd
**sp** thwart[3] / thwarted[4]

**thwarting** *adj*
ˈθwɑːɹtɪn, -ɪŋ
thwarting[2]

**thy, thyself**
> thou

**ti** *Ital*
> tu

**Tib / ~'s** *n*
=
**sp** Tibs[1]

**Tiber** *n*
ˈtəɪbəɹ
**sp** Tiber[1], Tyber[7]

**Tiberio** *n*
*m* təɪˈbiːrɪˌoː
**sp** Tyberio[1]

**tick** *n*
=
**sp** ticke[1]

**tickle** *adj*
=
**sp** tickle[2]

**tickl·e / ~es / ~ing / ~ed** *v*
= / = / ˈtɪklɪn, -ɪŋ / =
tickle[7] / tickles[2] / tickling[2], tick-ling[1] / tickel'd[1], tickled[4], tick-led[1]

**tickle-brain** *n*
ˈtɪkəl-ˌbrɛːn
**sp** tickle-braine[1]
> brain

**tickling** *adj / n*
ˈtɪklɪn, -ɪŋ
**sp** tickling[2] / tickling[2]

**tick-tack** *n*
=
**sp** ticke-tacke[1]

**tiddle-taddle** *n*
=
**sp** tiddle tadle[1]

**tide / ~s** *n*
təɪd / -z
**sp** tide[28], tyde[13] / tides[5]
**rh** abide *Luc 645, 3H6 4.3.60*; beside *VA 979*; pride *Luc 1667*; provide *Tim 3.4.117*
**pun** *TG 2.3.34ff* tied
> Bartholomew-, Lammas-tide

**tidings** *n*
ˈtəɪdɪnz, -ɪŋz
**sp** tidings[19], tydings[30]

**tidy** *adj*
ˈtəɪdəɪ
**sp** tydie[1]

**tie** *n*
təɪ
**sp** tye[1]

**tie / ~s / tying / tied** *v*
təɪ / -z / ˈtəɪɪn, -ɪŋ / təɪd
**sp** tie[2], tye[14] / ties[1], tyes[2] / tying[4] / tide[6], ti'de[2], tied[7], ty'd[3], ty'de[1], tyed[4]
**rh** ride *LC 24, S 137.8*
**pun** *TG 2.3.34ff* tide
> shoe-, un-tie

**tied-up** *adj*
ˈtəɪd-ˌɤp
**sp** tyde-vp[1]

**tiger / ~'s / ~s** *n*
ˈtəɪgəɹ / -z
**sp** tiger[2], tyger[8], [male]-tyger[1] / tigers[2], tygres[1] / tigers[2], tygers[5]

**Tiger** [name] *n*
ˈtəɪgəɹ
**sp** Tiger[2]

**tiger-footed** *adj*
ˈtəɪgəɹ-ˌfʊtɪd
**sp** tiger-footed-[rage][1]
> foot

**tight** *adj*
təɪt
**sp** tight[2], tite[1], tyte[1]

**tightly** *adv*
ˈtəɪtləɪ
**sp** tightly[2]

**tile** *n*
təɪl
**sp** tile[1]

**till** *prep*
=
**sp** til[17], till[580], 'till[2], til't [till it][1]
> until

**till / ~ed** *v*
=
**sp** tyll'd[1]

**tilly-vally** *interj*
ˈtɪlɪ-ˈvaləɪ
**sp** tilly-fally[1], tilly vally[1]

**tilt / ~s** *n*
=
**sp** tilts[1]

**tilt / ~ing / ~s** *v*
= / ˈtɪltɪn, -ɪŋ / =
**sp** tilt[1] / tilting[3] / tilts[1]
> atilt

**tilter** *n*
ˈtɪltəɹ
tilter[2]

**tilth** *n*
=, tɪlt
**sp** tilth[2], *MM 4.1.75 emend of* tithes [tilth is][1]

**tiltyard** *n*
ˈtɪlt-ˌjɑːɹd
**sp** tilt-yard[2]
> yard

**Timandra** *n*
tɪˈmandrə
**sp** Timandra[3], *Tim 4.3.49 emend of* Timandylo[1]

**timber** *n*
ˈtɪmbəɹ
**sp** timber[3]

**timbered** *adj*
ˈtɪmbəɹd
**sp** timber'd[2], timbred[1]
> hardest-, un-timbered

**Timbria** *n*
ˈtɪmbrɪə
**sp** Timbria[1]

**time / ~'s / ~s** *n*
təɪm / -z
**sp** time[974], [holly-day]-time[1], time's [time is][1] / times 's[14] / times[200]
**rh** chime *Per 1.1.85*; climb, crime *Luc 774*; crime *Luc 930, 994, S 19.6, 58.10, 120.6, 124.13, WT 4.1.3*; prime *AY 5.3.33, Luc 330, R2 5.2.50, S 3.12, 12.1, 70.6, 97.5, VA 132*; rhyme *LLL 1.1.98, 4.3.180, MW 5.5.92, Per 4.Chorus.47, S 16.2, 17.13, 32.5, 55.4, 106.1, 107.9* / crimes *MM 3.2.262*; rhymes *LLL 5.2.63, Luc 525, Per Prol.11*
> bed-, dinner-, life-, milking-, peascod-, rut-, supper-time; after-, often-, some-times

**time / ~d** *v*
təɪmd
**sp** tim'd[1]

**time-bewasted** *adj*
ˈtəɪm-bɪˌwastɪd
**sp** time-bewasted[1]
> wasted

**time-honoured** *adj*
*m* ˌtəɪm-ˈɒnəɹd
**sp** time-honoured[1]

**timeless** *adj*
ˈtəɪmləs
**sp** timeles[1], timelesse[7]

**timely** *adj*
ˈtəɪmləɪ
**sp** timelie[1], timely[1]
> untimely

**time·ly / ~lier** *adv*
ˈtəɪmləɪ / -əɹ
**sp** timely[2] / timelier[1]

**timely-parted** *adj*
ˈtəɪmləɪ-ˌpɑːɹtɪd
**sp** timely-parted[1]
part

**time-pleaser / ~s** *n*
ˈtəɪm-ˌpliːzəɹ / -z
**sp** time-pleaser[1] / time-pleasers[1]

**Timon / ~'s** *n*
ˈtəɪmən / -z
**sp** Timon[90], Tymon[2] / Timons[27]
**rh** gone *Tim 4.3.98*

**timor** *Lat n*
ˈtɪmɔːɹ
timor[1]

**timorous** *adj*
ˈtɪmrəs, -mər-
**sp** timerous[1], timorous[5]

**timorously** *adv*
ˈtɪmrəsˌləɪ, -mər-
**sp** timorously[1]

**tinct** *n*
=
**sp** tinct[4]

**tincture / ~s** *n*
ˈtɪŋktəɹ / -z
**sp** taincture[1], tincture[1] / tinctures[1]
> lily-tincture

**tinder** *n*
ˈtɪndəɹ
**sp** tinder[1]

**tinderbox** *n*
ˈtɪndəɹˌbɒks
**sp** tinderbox[1]

**tinder-like** *adj*
ˈtɪndəɹ-ˌləɪk
**sp** tinder-like[1]

**tingling** *n*
ˈtɪŋglɪn, -ɪŋ
**sp** tingling[1]

**tinker / ~'s / ~s** *n*
ˈtɪŋkəɹ / -z
**sp** tinker[6] / tinkers[1] / tinkers[3]

**tinsel** *n*
=
**sp** tinsel[1]

**tiny** *adj*
ˈtəɪnəɪ
**sp** tine[2], tyne[1], [little]-tyne[1]

**tip** *n*
=
**sp** tip[1]

**tip / ~s / ~ped** *v*
=
**sp** tip[1] / tips[1] / tipt[1]

**tippl·e / ~ing** *v*
ˈtɪplɪn, -ɪŋ
**sp** tipling[1]

**tipsy** *adj*
ˈtɪpsəɪ
**sp** tipsie[1]

**tip·staff / -staves** *n*
ˈtɪpstɛːvz
**sp** tipstaues[1]
> staff

**tiptoe** *adv*
ˈtɪptoː
**sp** tipto[1]
> a-tiptoe

**tire / ~s** *n*
təɪɹ / -z
**sp** tire[2], tyre[1] / tires[1]
> ship-tire

**tir·e / ~est / ~es / ~ing / ~ed** *v*
təɪɹ / ˈtəɪrəst / təɪɹz / ˈtəɪrɪn, -ɪŋ / təɪɹd
**sp** tire[3], tyre[8] / tyrest[1] / tyres[4] / tyring[2] / tir'd[2], tyrd[1], tyr'd[4], tyred[1]

**rh** briar *MND 3.1.89*; desire *Luc 707*; mire [*F, at* LLL 2.1.113-129] / admired, desired *Luc 417*; expired *S 27.2*
> untireable

**tired** *adj*
təɹɪd
**sp** tired[3], tyred[6]
> untired

**tire-valiant** *n*
'təɹɪ-'valɪənt
**sp** tyre-valiant[1]
> valiant

**tiring** *adj*
'təɪrɪn, -ɪŋ
**sp** tyring[1]

**tiring-house** *n*
'təɪrɪn-ˌəʊs, -ɪŋ-, ˌhəʊs
**sp** tyring house[1]
> house

**tirra-lirra** *interj*
=
**sp** tirra lyra[1]

**tirrits** *n*
=
**sp** tirrits[1]

**'tis**
> it

**tisick** *n*
'tɪsɪk
**sp** tisicke[2]

**Tisick** [name] *n*
'tɪsɪk
**sp** Tisick[1]

**tissue** *n*
'tɪsju:, -ɪʃu:
**sp** tissue[1]
> intertissued

**Titan / ~'s** *n*
'təɪtən / -z
**sp** Titan[4] / Titans[3], Tytans[1]

**Titania** *n*
tɪ'tanɪə
**sp** Titania[5], Tytania[4]

**tithe** *adj / n / v*
təɪð
tythe[1] / tythe[1], *1H4 3.3.56 emend of* tight / tythe[1]

**tithed** *adj*
*m* 'təɪðɪd
**sp** tythed[1]

**tithe-pig / ~'s** *n*
'təɪð-ˌpɪgz
**sp** tithe pigs[1]

**tithe-woman** *n*
'təɪð-ˌwʊmən
**sp** tithe woman[1]

**tithing** *n*
'təɪðɪn, -ɪŋ
**sp** tything[2]

**Titinius** *n*
tɪ'tɪnɪəs
**sp** Titinius[23]

**title / ~'s / ~s** *n*
'təɪtl / -z
**sp** title[96], titles [title is][2], title's [title is][1] / titles[21]
> entitle

**titled** *adj*
'təɪtld
**sp** titled[2]

**title-leaf** *n*
'təɪtl-ˌli:f
**sp** title-leafe[1]
> leaf

**titleless** *adj*
*m* 'təɪtlˌles
**sp** titlelesse[1]

**tittle / ~s** *n*
=
**sp** tittles[1]

**tittle-tattl·e / ~ing** *v*
'tɪtl-ˌtatlɪn, -ɪŋ
**sp** tittle-tatling[1]
> tattle

**Titus / s'** *n*
'təɪtəs
**sp** Titus[64] / Titus[13]

**to** *adv, particle, prep / particle also abbr* **t**
*str* tu:, *unstr* tə, tʊ, *abbr* t
**sp** to[18419], to [and fro][1], too[137], too [and fro][1], [contrary] to[5], [go]-too[6], *abbr* t'[62]
**rh** do *R2 5.5.98, WT 4.1.11*; **to him** woo him *PP 11.4*; **to it** do it *LLL 5.2.216*; **to't rh** *1* do't *Cor 2.3.116, Ham 4.5.61*; root *Tim 1.2.69*; **rh** *2* foot *LLL 5.2.145*; **to me** woo me *AY 4.3.49*; **to us** ridiculous *LLL 5.2.307*; **to woo him** unto him *VA 6*; undo us *LLL 5.2.424*
> up to

***to have*** *abbr*
təv, tav
**sp** t'haue[6]

***to his*** *abbr*
tʊz
**sp** to's[4], too's[2]

***to it*** *abbr*
tʊt
**sp** toot[1], too't[90], to't[21]

***to the*** *abbr*
təθ, tʊθ, -ð
**sp** too'th[4], toth'[17], to'th[10], to'th'[69]

***to us*** *abbr*
tʊz
**sp** to's[3] too's[1]

**toad / ~s** *n*
to:d / -z
**sp** toad[11], toade[6] / toades[7], toads[1]

**toad-spotted** *adj*
*m* ˌto:d-'spɒtɪd
**sp** toad-spotted[1]

**toadstool** *n*
'to:dstʊl, -stu:l
**sp** toads stoole[1]

**to and fro** *adv*
'tu:ən'fro:
**sp** to and fro[1], too and fro[1]

**toast / ~s** *n*
to:st / -s
**sp** tost[1], toste[1] / tostes[2]

**toast** *v*
to:st
**sp** toste[1]

**toasted** *adj*
'to:stɪd
**sp** toasted[3]

**toasting-iron** *n*
'to:stɪn-ˌəɪrən, -ɪŋ-
**sp** tosting-iron[1]
> iron

**toaze** *v*
to:z
**sp** toaze[1]

**Toby / ~'s** *n*
'to:bəɪ / -z
**sp** Toby[48] / Tobyes[1]

**tod / ~s** *n*
=
**sp** tod[1] / toddes[1]

**today** *adv*
tə'dɛ:, tʊ-
**sp** to day[162]
**rh** away *2H6 2.1.156, LLL 4.3.271, MV 3.4.84*; fray *1H4 5.4.106, RJ 1.1.116*; may *CE 3.1.40, TC 1.1.115*; pray *CE 1.2.52, RJ 2.3.60*; say *1H6 4.7.28, TC 5.6.26*; stray *2H4 4.2.121*

**toe / ~s** *n*
to: / -z
**sp** toe[15] / toes[3]
**rh** mow *n Tem 4.1.46*; no *Tem 4.1.46*; woe *KL 3.2.31*

**tofore** *adv*
tə'fɔ:ɹ, tʊ-
**sp** tofore[1], to fore[1]
> before

**toged** *adj*
'to:gəd
*sp Oth 1.1.25 emend of* tongued[1]

**together** *adv*
tə'geðəɹ, tʊ-, -'geəɹ
**sp** together[232], to-gether[3], toge-ther[3], to gether[1], togither[4]
**rh** *1* feather *CE 3.1.83*; weather *AY 5.4.132, PP 12.1, VA 971*; **rh** *2* hither *AY 5.4.107, TNK 3.5.118*; thither *Per 5.1.241, TC 1.1.118*; whither *VA 902*; **rh** *3* neither *LLL 4.3.190, PT 42*

**toil / ~s** *n*
təɪl / -z
**sp** toile[3], toyle[19] / toyles[1]

**toil / ~s / ~ing / ~ed** *v*
təɪl / -z / 'təɪlɪn, -ɪŋ / təɪld
**sp** toile[2], toyle[2] / toyles[1] / toyling[2] / toyl'd[2], toyled[1]
**rh** foiled *S 25.12*

**token / ~s** *n*
'to:kən /-z
**sp** token[27] / tokens[12], to-kens[1]
> death-, love-token

**token** *v*
'to:kən
**sp** token[1]

**tokened** *adj*
'to:kənd
**sp** token'd[1]

**told, toldest**
> tell

**Toledo** *n*
tə'li:do:
**sp** Toledo[1]

**tolerable** *adj*
'tɒlrəbəl, -lər-
**sp** tollerable[2]
> intolerable

**toll** *v*
to:l
**sp** toll[1], toule[1], towle[1]

**Tom** *n*
=
**sp** Tom[19], Toms [Tom is][1], Tom's [Tom is][4] / Toms[2]

**tomb / ~s** *n*
tu:m, tʊm / -z
**sp** tomb[1], tombe[39], toomb[1], toombe[3] / tombes[2]
**rh** *1* come *RJ 5.2.29, S 17.3*; dumb *AW 2.3.139, MA 5.3.9, MND 5.1.320, S 83.12, 101.11*; **rh** *2* womb *1H6 4.5.34, RJ 2.3.5, S 3.7*

**tomber / tombé** *Fr v*
tɔ̃'be
**sp** [in]tombe[1]

**tombless** *adj*
'tu:mləs, 'tʊ-
**sp** tomblesse[1]

**tomboy** *n*
'tɒmbəɪz
**sp** tomboyes[1]
> boy

**tomorrow / ~'s** *adv*
tə'mɒrə, -ro:, tʊ-
**sp** tomorrow[1], to morow[2], to morrow[217], to mor-row[8], to morrow't [tomorrow it][1], too morrow[1] / to morrowes[3]
**rh** borrow *PP 14.30*; sorrow *AW 2.3.293, 2H4 4.2.84, PP 14.5, 14.24, VA 585, 672*

**Tomyris** *n*
*m* 'to:məˌrɪs
**sp** Tomyris[1]

**ton** *n*
tɤn
**sp** tonne[1]

**ton** *Fr*
> tu

**tongs** *n*
tɒŋz
**sp** tongs[2]
**pun** *TN 1.3.89-92* tongues

**tongue / ~'s / ~s** *n*
tɒŋ, tʊŋ / -z
**sp** tong[5], tongue[380], toong[4] / tongues[6], toungs[1] / tonges[1], tongues[66], ton-gues[1]
**rh** *1* belong *LLL 5.2.382*; long *LLL 5.2.242, Luc 1617, MND 5.1.423, TS 4.2.58*; long, throng *Luc 1780*; long, wrong *Luc 1465*; song *LLL 5.2.403, S 17.10, 102.13*; strong *LC 120, MM 3.2.178*; wrong *LLL 1.1.164, 4.2.118, Luc 78, 1463, MND 2.2.9, 3.2.360, PP 5.14, R2 1.1.190, 1.3.245, 3.2.216, S 89.9, 112.6, 139.3, Tit 5.3.56, VA 217, 330, 427, 1003*; **rh** *2* stung *MND 3.2.72*; young *PP 1.7, 1.11, 19.18, S 138.7* / belongs *LLL 4.3.236*; songs *VA 775*; throngs *KL 3.2.89*; wrongs *2H4 Induction.39, MA 5.3.3*
**pun** *TN 1.3.89-92* tongs
> honey-, lewd-, long-, poisonous-, shrill-, wasp-tongued

**tongue** *v*
tɒŋ, tʊŋ
**sp** tongue[1]
> out-tongue

**tongueless** *adj*
'tɒŋləs, tʊ-
**sp** tonguelesse[2], tongue-lesse[1], toonglesse[1]

**tongue-tied** *adj*
'tɒŋ-ˌtəɪd, tʊ-
**sp** tong-tide[1], tongue-tide[1], tongue-ty'd[5], tongue-tyed[1]

**tonight** *adv*
tə'nəɪt, tʊ-
**sp** to night[180]
**rh** delight *MV 2.6.68*; fight *Mac 5.6.7*; flight *Mac 3.1.141*; height *TC 5.1.1*; quite *LLL 5.2.270*; right *RJ 2.3.38*; rite *RJ 5.3.19*; sight *MND 2.1.18*; spite *2H6 5.1.214*
> night

**too** *adv*
=
**sp** too[1162], too-too[2], [go]-too[6], too-[farre][1], too-[long][1], too-[much][1], too[1]
**rh** ado *Tit 2.1.97*; do *Cym 5.3.62, Ham 3.2.183, LLL 1.1.23, 5.2.203, MND 3.2.38, 255, 150, R2 3.3.206, RJ 1.5.101, S 88.9, TNK 3.5.141, TS 1.2.222*; you *1H4 2.3.118*

**took**
> take

**tool / ~s** *n*
= / z
**sp** toole[2] / tooles[3]
**rh** fool *TNK 3.5.131*

**tooth / teeth** *n*
tʊθ, tu:θ / =
**sp** tooth[24] / teeth[54], teethes[1]
**rh** doth *TC 4.5.293* / with *VA 269*

**toothache** *n*
'tʊθɛ:ʧ, 'tu:-
**sp** tooth-ach[2], tooth-ache[1], tooth-ake[2]
> ache

**tooth-drawer** *n*
'tʊθ-ˌdrɔ:əɹ, 'tu:-
**sp** tooth-drawer[1]
> drawer

**toothed** *adj*
tʊθt, tu:θt
**sp** tooth'd[1]
> sharp-toothed

**tooth-pick** *n*
'tʊθ-ˌpɪk, 'tu:-
**sp** tooth-pick[1], tooth-picke[1]

**tooth-picker** *n*
'tʊθ-ˌpɪkəɹ, 'tu:-
**sp** tooth-picker[1]

**top / ~s** *n*
=
**sp** top[49], top-[branch] [1], toppe[1] / tops[9]

**top / ~ping / ~ped** *v*
= / 'tɒpɪn, -ɪŋ / =
top[2] / topping[1] / top'd[1]
> overtop

**Topas** *n*
'to:pəs
**sp** Topas[16]

**top-full** *adj*
=
**sp** topfull[1], top-full[1]

**topgallant** *n*
tɒp'galənt
**sp** top gallant[1]
> gallant

**topless** *adj*
=
**sp** toplesse[1]

**topmast** *n*
'tɒpmast
**sp** top-mast[4]
> mast

**topple / ~s** *v*
=
**sp** topple[2] / topples[1]

**top-proud** *adj*
'tɒp-ˌprəʊd
**sp** top-proud[1]
> proud

**topsail** *n*
'tɒpsɛ:l
**sp** toppe-sale[1]

**topsie-turvy** *adv*
'tɒpsəɪ-'tɐ:ɹvəɪ
**sp** topsie-turuy[1]

**torch / ~es** *n*
tɔ:ɹʧ / 'tɔ:ɹʧɪz
**sp** torch[21] / torches[18]

**torch-bearer / ~s** *n*
'tɔ:ɹʧ-ˌbɛ:rəɹ / -z
**sp** torch-bearer[4] / torch-bearers[2]
**rh** scorch *Luc 315*
> bearer

**torcher** *n*
'tɔːɹʧəɹ
**sp** torcher[1]

**torchlight** *n*
'tɔːɹʧləɪt
**sp** torch-light[1]

**torch-staff / ~staves** *n*
'tɔːɹʧ-ˌstɛːvz
**sp** torch-staues[1]
> staff

**torment / ~s** *n*
'tɔːɹment / -s
**sp** torment[15] / torments[6]

**torment / ~est / ~s / ~eth / ~ed** *v*
tɔːɹ'ment / -s, -st / -s / -əθ / -ɪd
**sp** torment[13] / torments[1], torment'st[1] / torments[5] / tormenteth[1] / tormented[1]
**rh** relenteth *VA 202*

**tormente** [*Pistol H4 2.4.176*] *v*
tɔːɹ'mɛntɛ
**sp** *Pistol 2H4 2.4.176* tormente[1]

**tormenting** *adj*
tɔːɹ'mentɪn, -ɪŋ
**sp** tormenting[2]

**tormento** *Ital or Span v*
tɔːɹ'mɛntoː
**sp** *Pistol 2H4 5.5.99* tormento[1]

**tormentor / ~s** *n*
tɔːɹ'mentəɹz
**sp** tormentors[1]

**torn**
> tear

**torrent** *n*
=
**sp** torrent[2], tor-rent[1]

**tortive** *adj*
'tɔːɹtɪv
**sp** tortiue[1]

**tortoise** *n*
'tɔːɹtəɪz
**sp** tortoyrs[1], tortoys[1]

**torture / ~s** *n*
'tɔːɹtəɹ / -z
**sp** torture[15] / tortures[5]

**torture / ~st / ~d** *v*
'tɔːɹtəɹ / -st, -trəst / -d
**sp** torture[14] / torturest[1] / tortured[1]

**tortured** *adj*
'tɔːɹtəɹd
**sp** tortur'd[4]

**torturer / ~s** *n*
'tɔːɹtəɹəɹ, -trəɹ / -z
**sp** torturer[2] / torturors[1]

**torturing** *adj*
'tɔːɹtrɪn, -ɪŋ
**sp** tortering[1], torturing[1]

**Toryne** *n*
'tɒrɪn
**sp** Toryne[1], Troine[1]

**toss / ~eth / ~ing / ~ed** *v*
= / = / 'tɒsɪn, -ɪŋ / =
**sp** tosse[4] / tosseth[1] / tossing[1] / toss'd[1], tost[3]
**rh** lost *Per 2.Chorus.34*
> be-, tempest-tossed

**tossing** *n*
'tɒsɪn, -ɪŋ
**sp** tossing[1]

**toss-pot / ~s** *n*
=
**sp** tospottes[1]

**total** *n*
'toːtɑl
**sp** totall[1]

**totally** *adv*
'toːtɑləɪ
**sp** totally[1]

**totter / ~s / ~ing** *v*
'tɒtəɹz / 'tɒtrɪn, -ɪŋ
**sp** totters[1] / tottring[1]

**tottering** *adj*
'tɒtrɪn, -ɪŋ
**sp** tott'ring[2]

**touch / ~es** *n*
tɤʧ / 'tɤʧɪz
**sp** touch[39], tutch[2] / touches[7], toutches[1], tutches[2]
**rh** much *MND 3.2.70*; such *PP 8.5*

**touch / ~es / ~eth / ~ing / ~ed** *v*
tɤʧ / 'tɤʧ·ɪz / -əθ / -ɪn, -ɪŋ / *m* -ɪd, tɤʧt
**sp** touch[69], tuch[1] / touches[13] / toucheth[3] / touching[23] / touch'd[32], touched[1], toucht[17], touch't[1]
**rh** much *RJ 1.5.99, VA 440*
> untouched

**touching** *adj / n*
'tɤʧɪn, -ɪŋ
**sp** touching[1] / touching[1]

**Touchstone** *n*
'tɤʧstoːn
**sp** Touchstone[4]

**tough** *adj*
tɤf / 'tɤfəɹ
**sp** tough[8] / tougher[1]

**toughness** *n*
'tɤfnəs
**sp** toughnesse[1]

**Touraine** *n*
tʊ'ren
**sp** Toraine[3], Torayne[1], Touraine[1]

**tournament / ~s** *n*
*m* 'tuːɹnəˌments
**sp** turnaments[1]

**Tours** *n*
tuːɹ
**sp** Toures[2], Tours[1]

**touse** *v*
təʊz
**sp** towze[1]

**tout / tous** *Fr adj*
tu, *before a vowel* tut
**sp** tout[1], toute[2] / touts[1]

**tow** *v*
to:
**sp** towe[1]

**toward** *adj / adv*
to:ɹd, to:əɹd
toward[2] / toward[10]
**rh** *adv 1* froward *PP 4.13, TS 1.1.68, 5.2.181*; **rh** *2* coward *VA 1157*
> untoward

**toward / ~s** *prep*
to:ɹd, to:əɹd / -z
**sp** toward[88] / towardes[1], towards[66], to-wards[1]

**towardly** *adj*
'to:ɹdləɪ, to:əɹ-
**sp** towardlie[1]
> untowardly

**towards** *adv*
to:ɹdz, to:əɹ-
**sp** towards[2]

**tower / ~s** *n*
to:ɹ / -z
**sp** tower[8], towre[4] / towers[3], towres[5]
**rh** hours *Luc 945*

**tower / ~s / ~ing** *v*
to:ɹ / -z / 'to:rɪn, -ɪŋ
**sp** towre[1] / towres[1] / towring[1]

**Tower** [name] *adj / n*
to:ɹ
**sp** Tower[3] / Tower[53], Towre[1]

**towered** *adj*
to:ɹd
**sp** toward[1]

**towering** *adj*
'to:rɪn, -ɪŋ
**sp** towring[1]

**town / ~'s / ~s** *n*
təʊn / -z
**sp** town[4], towne[109], towne-[bull][1], towne-[gates][1], towne-[way][1] / townes[30] / townes[30], [peasant]-townes[1]
**rh** *1* crown *AY 5.4.140*; down *CE 3.1.60, MND 3.2.398, PP 18.17*; renown *AY 5.4.143*; **rh** *2* known *H8 Prol.24*

**town crier** *n*
'təʊn 'krəɪəɹ
**sp** town-cryer[1]
> crier

**township** *n*
'təʊnʃɪp
**sp** towneship[1]

**towns·man / ~men** *n*
'təʊnzmən
**sp** townesmen[1], townes-men[1]

**toy / ~s** *n*
təɪ / -z
**sp** toy[13] / toyes[13]
**rh** boy *TN 5.1.388, TS 2.1.395, VA 34*; destroy, joy *Luc 214*; oyez *MW 5.5.42* / boys *Cym 4.2.193, LLL 4.3.168*

**trace / ~s** *n*
trɛ:s / 'trɛ:sɪz
**sp** trace[1] / 'traces[1]

**trace** *v*
trɛ:s
**sp** trace[8]

**track** *n*
=
**sp** *R2 3.3.66, R3 5.3.20 emend of* tract[2]

**tract** *n*
=
**sp** tract[2]

**tractable** *adj*
=
**sp** tractable[5]

**trade / ~s** *n*
trɛ:d / -z
**sp** trade[34] / trades[3]
**rh** made *TC 5.10.52*

**trade / ~s / ~d** *v*
trɛ:d / -z / 'trɛ:dɪd
**sp** trade[3] / trades[1] / traded[1]

**traded** *adj*
'trɛ:dɪd
**sp** traded[1]

**trade-fallen** *adj*
'trɛ:d-ˌfɑ:ln
**sp** trade-falne[1]
> fallen

**trader / ~s** *n*
'trɛ:dəɹz
**sp** traders[4]

**trades·man / ~man's / ~men** *n*
'trɛ:dz·mənz / -mən
**sp** tradesmans[1] / tradesmen[1], trades-men[1]

**trading** *n*
'trɛ:dɪn, -ɪŋ
**sp** trading[1]

**tradition** *n*
trə'dɪsɪən
**sp** tradition[3]

**traditional** *adj*
*m* trə'dɪsɪəˌnɑl
**sp** traditionall[1]

**traduce / ~d** *v*
trə'dju:s
**sp** traduc'd[4]

**traducement** *n*
trə'dju:smənt
**sp** traducement[1]

**traffic / ~'s** *n*
=
**sp** traffick[1], trafficke[6] / traffiques[1]

**traffic / ~sv**
=
**sp** trafficke[1] / traffickes[2]

**trafficker / ~s** *n*
'trafɪkəɹz
**sp** traffiquers[1]

**tragedian / ~s** *n*
trə'ʤi:dɪən / -z
**sp** tragedian[1] / tragedians[2]
**rh** clemency, patiently *Ham 3.2.158*

**tragedy** *n*
'traʤɪdəɪ / -z
**sp** tragedie[8], trage-die[1], tragedy[1] / tragedies[1]

**tragic** *adj*
=
**sp** tragicke[7]

**tragical** *adj*
*m* 'traʤɪkɑl, -ˌkɑl
**sp** tragicall[5], tragicall-[comicall][1], tragicall-[historicall][1]

**trail** *n*
trɛ:l
**sp** traile[4]

**trail / ~est** *v*
trɛ:l / -s, -st
**sp** traile[2] / trayl'st[1]
**rh** tail *TC 5.8.22*

**train / ~s** *n*
trɛ:n / -z
**sp** traine[53], trayne[5] / traines[3]

**train / ~ed** *v*
trɛ:n / -d, 'trɛ:nɪd
**sp** traine[5] / traind[1], train'd[5], trained[1], trayn'd[5]
**rh** gained *Per 4.Chorus.7*
> untrained

**training** *n*
'trɛ:nɪn, -ɪŋ
**sp** trayning[1]

**traitor / ~'s / ~s' / ~s** *n*
'trɛ:təɹ / -z
**sp** traitor[80], traitour[2], traytor[41] / traitors[8], traytors[3] / traitors[2], traytors[1] / traitors[39], trai-tors[1], traitours[1], trai-tours[1], traytors[13]

**traitoress** *n*
'trɛ:trəs, -tər-
**sp** traitoresse[1]

**traitorly** *adj*
'trɛ:təɹləɪ
**sp** traitorly-[rascals][1]

**traitorous** *adj*
'trɛ:trəs, -tər-
**sp** traiterous[1], traitorous[3], trayterous[1], traytorous[1], traytrous[1], trayt'rous[2]

**traitorously** *adv*
*m* 'trɛ:trəsˌləɪ, -sl-, -tər-
**sp** traiterously[3], traitorously[1]

**traject** *n*
'traʤekt
**sp** *MV 3.4.53 emend of* tranect[1]

**trammel** *v*
=
**sp** trammell[1]

**trampl·e / ~ing / ~ed** *v*
= / 'trampl·ɪn, -ɪŋ / =
**sp** trample[2] / trampling[1] / trampled[1]

**trance / ~s** *n*
trɔ:ns / *Luc* 'trɔ:nsɪz
**sp** trance[1], traunce[1] / trances[1]
**rh** chance *Luc 1595*; mischances *Luc 974*

**Tranio** *n*
*m* 'tranɪo:, -ɪˌo:
**sp** Tranio[43], Tra-nio[1], Trayno[1], Triano[1], Tronio[1]
**rh** Lucentio *TS 1.1.240*

**tranquil** *adj*
=
**sp** tranquill[1]

**tranquility** *n*
traŋ'kwɪlɪtəɪ
**sp** tranquilitie[1]

**transcend / ~s** *v*
=
**sp** transce[n]ds[1]
**rh** commends *TC 1.3.244*

**transcendence** *n*
=
**sp** tran-cendence[1]

**transfer / ~red** *S* *v*
trans'fɐ:ɹd
**sp** transferred[1]
**rh** erred *S 137.14*

**transfigure / ~d** *v*
trans'fɪgəɹd
**sp** transfigur'd[1]

**transform / ~ed** *v*
trans'fɔ:ɹm / *m* -d, -ɪd
**sp** transforme[6] / transform'd[6], trans-form'd[1], transformed[6]

**transformation / ~s** *n*
*m* ˌtransfəɹ'mɛ:sɪən, -sɪˌɒn / -sɪˌɒnz
**sp** transformation[5], trans-formation[1] / transformations[1]

**transformed** *adj*
*m* trans'fɔ:ɹmd, -ɪd
**sp** transformed[2]
> new-transformed

**transgress / ~es / ~ed** *v*
trans'gres, -nz-
**sp** transgresses[1] / transgrest[2]

**transgressing** *adj*
trans'gres-ɪn, -ɪŋ, -nz-
**sp** transgressing[2]

**transgression** *n*
trans'grɛ:sɪən, -nz-
**sp** transgression[7], trans-gression[1]
**rh** confession *LLL 5.2.431*; oppression *RJ 1.1.185*

**translate / ~s / ~d** *v*
trans'lɛ:t / -s / -ɪd, -nz-
**sp** translate[8] / translates[1] / translated[3], transla-ted[1]

**rh** state *S 96.10* / bated *MND 1.1.191*

**translation** *n*
trans'lɛ:sɪən, -nz-
**sp** translation[1]

**transmigrate / ~s** *v*
ˌtransmәɪ'grɛ:ts, -nz-
**sp** transmigrates[1]

**transmutation** *n*
ˌtransmjʊ'tɛ:sɪən, -nz-
**sp** transmutation[1]

**transparent** *adj*
trans'parәnt
**sp** transparant[2], transparent[3]

**transport / ~ing / ~ed** *v*
tran'spɔ:ɹt / -ɪn, -ɪŋ / -ɪd
**sp** transport[6] / transporting[2] / transported[10]

**transportance** *n*
tran'spɔ:ɹtәns
**sp** transportance[1]

**transpose** *v*
trans'po:z
**sp** transpose[2]

**trans-shape** *v*
tran'ʃɛ:p, -ns-
**sp** trans-shape[1]
> shape

**trap** *n*
=
**sp** trap[3]

**trap / ~s / ~ped** *v*
=
**sp** trap[1] / traps[2] / trap'd[1], trapt[1]
**rh** haps *MA 3.1.106*
> mousetrap

**trapping** *n*
'trapɪnz, -ɪŋz
**sp** trappings[2]

**trash** *n / v*
=
**sp** trash[1] / trash[9]

**travail** *n*
'travәl
**sp** trauaile[5], trauell[1]

**travail / ~s** *v*
'travәl / -z
**sp** trauaile[2] / trauailes[1]

**travel / ~s** *n*
=
**sp** trauaile[12], trauell[9] / trauells[2]

**travel / ~est / ~s / ~ling / ~led** *v*
= / 'travәlst / = / *m* 'travlɪn, -ɪŋ, -vәl- / =
**sp** trauaile[3], trauell[4] / trauellest[1] / trauels[2] / trauailing[2], trauelling[2] / trauaild[1], trauail'd[6], trauel'd[1]

**traveller / ~s** *n*
*m* 'travlәɹ, -vәl- / -z
**sp** trauailer[3], traueiler[1], traueller[6], trauel-ler[1], trauellor[1] / trauellers[1], trauellours[1] / trauailers[1], trauailors[1], trauellers[4]

**travelling** *adj*
'travlɪn, -ɪŋ, -vәl-
**sp** trauailing[1]

**travel-tainted** *adj*
'travәl-ˌtɛ:ntɪd
**sp** trauell-tainted[1]

**Travers** *n*
'travәɹz
**sp** Trauers[4]

**traverse** *adv / v*
'travәɹs
**sp** trauers[1] / trauers[1], trauerse[3]

**traversed** *adj*
'travәɹst
**sp** trauerst[1]

**tray-trip** *n*
'trɛ:-ˌtrɪp
**sp** tray-trip[1]

**treacher / ~s** *n*
'treʧәɹz
**sp** treachers[1]

**treacherous** *adj*
*m* 'treʧә,rɤs, -әrәs, -ʧrәs
**sp** treacherous[19], trecherous[6]

**treacherously** *adv*
*m* 'treʧә,rɤslәɪ
**sp** trecherously[1]

**treachery** *n*
*m* 'treʧә,rәɪ, әrәɪ, -ʧrәɪ
**sp** treacherie[7], treache-rie[1], treachery[11], trecherie[5]
**rh** lechery *MW 5.3.22*

**tread** *n*
=
**sp** tread[4]
**rh** overhead *LLL 4.3.277*

**tread / ~s / ~ing / trod / ~den** *v*
= / = / 'tredɪn, -ɪŋ / =
**sp** tread[28], treade[10] / treades[1], treads[6] / treading[1] / trod[11], trodd[1] / trodden[3], troden[3]
**rh** red *MND 3.2.390*
> untread; earth-, mis-treading; untrod, downtrodden

**treading** *n*
'tredɪn, -ɪŋ
**sp** trea-ding[1]

**treason / ~'s / ~s** *n*
'trɛ:zәn / -z
**sp** treason[85], trea-son[3] / treasons[3] / treasons[19]
**rh** reason, season *Luc 877*; reason *S 151.6, VA 729*

**treasonable** *adj*
'trɛ:znәbәl, -zәn-
**sp** treasonable[1]

**treasonous** *adj*
'trɛ:znәs, -zәn-
**sp** treasonous[3]

**treasure / ~s** *n*
'trezəɹ / -z
**sp** treasure[43], treasure's [treasure is][1] / treasures[3]
**rh** leisure *TS 4.3.60*; measure *LLL 4.3.362*; pleasure *S 20.14. 52.2. 75.6. 126.10* / measures *VA 1150*
> en-, un-treasured

**treasurer** *n*
'trezrəɹ, -zər-
**sp** treasurer[1]

**treasur·y / ~ies** *n*
*m* 'trezəˌrəɪ, -zər-, -zr- / 'trezəˌrəɪz
**sp** treasurie[4], treasury[2] / treasuries[1]

**treat / ~s** *v*
=
**sp** treat[1] / treates[1], treats[2]

**treatise** *n*
'tri:tɪs
**sp** treatise[2]

**treat·y / ~ies** *n*
'tri:təɪ / -z
**sp** treatie[4], treaty[2] / treaties[1]

**treble** *adj / n*
=
**sp** trebble[6], treble[1] / treble[1]

**treble / ~s / ~d** *v*
=
**sp** treble[1] / trebbles[2] / trebled[1]

**treble-sinewed** *adj*
=
**sp** trebble-sinewed[1]
> sinew

**Trebonius** *n*
tre'bo:nɪəs
**sp** Trebonius[9], Tre-bonius[1], Trebo-nius[1]

**tree / ~'s / ~s** *n*
=
**sp** tree[42] / trees[1] / trees[25]
**rh** bastardy *Tit 5.1.47*; be *AY 3.2.123, Ham 3.2.200, Mac 4.1.94, MW 5.5.79, PP 10.5, PT 2*; fee *VA 391*; he *LLL 5.2.887, 896, VA 263*; knee *Oth 4.3.38*; me *AY 2.5.1, LLL 5.2.285*; she *AY 3.2.9* / freeze *H8 3.1.3*
> axle-, bay-, box-, crab-, cypress-, elder-, fruit-, medlar-, olive-, palm-, plum-, pomegranet-, sycamore-, willow-tree

**trembl·e / ~est / ~es / ~ing / ~ed** *v*
= / 'trembləs, -st, -bəls, -st / = / 'tremblɪn, -ɪŋ / =
**sp** tremble[33], trem-ble[1] / tremblest[2], trembl'st[1] / trembles[8] / trembling[5] / trembled[4]
**rh** dissemble *VA 642*; resemble *Luc 1393*

**trembling** *adj / n*
'tremblɪn, -ɪŋ, *Evans MW 3.1.12* 'tremplɪn, -ɪŋ
trembling[8] / trembling[4], *Evans* trempling[1]

**tremblingly** *adv*
*m* 'tremblɪnˌləɪ, -ɪŋ-
**sp** tremblingly[1]

**tremor cordis** *n*
'tremɔ:ɹ 'kɔ:ɹdɪs
**sp** tremor cordis[1]

**trench / ~es** *n*
=
**sp** trenches[7]

**trench / ~ed** *v*
=
**sp** trench[1] / trenched[1]
**rh** drenched *VA 1052*

**trenchant** *adj*
'trenʧənt
**sp** trenchant[1]

**trenched** *adj*
'trenʧɪd
**sp** trenched[1]

**trencher / ~s** *n*
'trenʧəɹ / -z
**sp** trencher[7], tren-cher[1] / trenchers[1]

**trencher-friend / ~s** *n*
'trenʧəɹ-ˌfrendz
**sp** trencher-friends[1]
> friend

**trenchering** *n*
'trenʧrɪn, -ɪŋ, -ʧər-
**sp** trenchering[1]

**trencher-knight** *n*
'trenʧəɹ-ˌnəɪt
**sp** trencher-knight[1]

**trencherman** *n*
'trenʧəɹmən
**sp** trencher-man[1]

**trenching** *adj*
'trenʧɪn, -ɪŋ
**sp** trenching[1]

**Trent** *n*
=
**sp** Trent[4]
**rh** went *TNK Prol.12*

**très** *Fr adv*
trɛ
**sp** tres[1], tres[cher][2], tres-[puissant[1]]

**trespass / ~es** *n*
=
**sp** trespas[6], trespasse[9] / trespasses[2]

**trespass** *v*
=
**sp** trespasse[1]

**tress / ~es** *n*
=
**sp** tresses[2]

**Tressel** *n*
=
**sp** Tressel[1]

**trey / ~s** *n*
trɛ:z
**sp** treyes[1]

**Trey** [name] *n*
trɛ:
**sp** Trey[1]

**trial** *adj*
'trəɪɑl
**sp** triall[1], tryall[1]

**trial / ~s** *n*
'trəɪɑl / -z
**sp** trial[1], triall[35], tryall[16] / trials[3], tryalls[1]
**rh** denial, dial *Luc 326*

**trial-fire** *n*
'trəɪɑl-'fəɪɹ
**sp** triall-fire[1]

**tribe / ~s** *n*
trəɪb / -z
**sp** tribe[9] / tribes[2]
**rh** subscribes *S 107.12*

**tribulation** *n*
ˌtrɪbjə'lɛːsɪən
**sp** tribulation[1]

**tribunal** *adj / n*
trɪ'bjuːnɑl
**sp** tribunall[1] / tribunall[1]

**tribune / ~s** *n*
=
**sp** tribune[12] / tribunes[52], [plague]-tribunes[1]
> fellow-tribune

**tributary** *adj*
*m* 'trɪbjəˌtarəɪ
**sp** tributarie[3], tributary[1]

**tributary** *n*
*m* 'trɪbjəˌtrəɪ / *m* 'trɪbjəˌtrəɪz, -ˌtar-
**sp** tributary[1] / tributaries[2]

**tribute** *n*
=
**sp** tribute[25]

**trice** *n*
trəɪs
**sp** trice[4]
**rh** Vice *TN 4.2.124*

**trick / ~s** *n*
=
**sp** trick[7], tricke[41] / trickes[18], tricks[13]
**rh** Dick *LLL 5.2.465*; sick *LLL 5.2.416* / pricks, sticks *Luc 320*
> back-, rope-trick

**trick / ~ed** *v*
=
**sp** tricke[1] / trick'd[1]

**tricking** *n*
'trɪkɪn, -ɪŋ
**sp** tricking[1]

**trickling** *adj*
'trɪklɪn, -ɪŋ
**sp** trickling[1]

**tricksy** *adj*
'trɪksəɪ
**sp** tricksey[1], tricksie[1]

**trident** *n*
'trəɪdənt
**sp** trident[2]

**tried** *adj*
trəɪd
**sp** tried[1]

**trier** *n*
'trəɪəɹ
**sp** trier[1]

**trifle / ~s** *n*
'trəɪfəl / -z
**sp** trifle[15], trifle[2] / trifles[14]

**trifle / ~d** *v*
'trəɪfəl / -d
**sp** trifle[7] / trifled[1]

**trifler** *n*
'trəɪfləɹ
**sp** trifler[1]

**trifling** *adj / n*
'trəɪflɪn, -ɪŋ
**sp** trifling[4] / trifling[1]

**trigon** *n*
'trəɪgɒn
**sp** trigon[1]

**trim** *adj*
=
**sp** trim[9]
**rh** dim *TNK 1.1.12*; him *TC 4.5.33, VA 1079*

**trim / ~s** *n*
=
**sp** trim[4], trimme[1] / trimmes[1]
**rh** him *LC 118, S 98.2*

**trim / ~ming / ~med** *v*
= / 'trɪmɪn, -ɪŋ / =
**sp** trim[3] / trimming[1] / trim'd[7], trimm'd[3], trym'd[1]
> new-, un-trimmed

**trimly** *adv*
'trɪmləɪ
**sp** trimly[1]

**trimming** *n*
'trɪmɪn, -ɪŋ
**sp** trimming[1]

**Trinculo / ~'s / ~s** *n*
'trɪŋkjʊloː / -z
**sp** Trinculo[17], Trin-culo[1] / Trinculo's[1] / Trinculo's[1]

**trinket / ~s** *n*
=
**sp** trinkets[2]

**trip** *n*
=
**sp** trip[1]
> tray-trip

**trip / *VA* ~s / ~ping / ~ped** *v*
= *Evans MW 5.4.1, 4* trɪb / = / 'trɪpɪn, -ɪŋ / =
**sp** trip[10], *Evans* trib[4] / trips[1] / tripping[3] / tript[5]
**rh** lips *VA 722*
> overtrip

**tripartite** *adj*
*m* 'trɪpəɹ,təɪt
**sp** tripartite[1]

**tripe** *n*
trəɪp
**sp** tripe[1]

**tripe-visaged** *adj*
'trəɪp-,vɪzɪdʒd
**sp** tripe-visag'd[1]
> visage

**triple** *adj*
=
**sp** triple[4]

**triple-turned** *adj*
'trɪpəl-,tɐ:ɹnd
**sp** triple-turn'd[1]

**triplex** *n*
=
**sp** triplex[1]

**Tripoli / ~s** *n*
'trɪpə·li: / -lɪs
**sp** Tripolie[1] / Tripolis[2], Tri-polis[1]

**tripping** *adj / adv*
'trɪpɪn, -ɪŋ
**sp** tripping[1] / tripping[1]
> night-tripping

**trippingly** *adv*
'trɪpɪnləɪ, -ɪŋ-
**sp** trippinglie[1], trippingly[1]
**rh** me *MND 5.1.386*

**tristful** *adj*
=
**sp** tristfull[1], *emend of 2H4 2.4.386* trustfull[1]

**Triton** *n*
'trəɪtən
**sp** Triton[1]

**triumph / ~s** *n*
'trəɪəmf / -s
**sp** triumph[28] / triumphes[5], triumphs[2]

**triumph / ~s / ~ing / ~ed** *v*
'trəɪəmf / -s / trəɪ'ɤmf·ɪn, -ɪŋ / *m* -ɪd, 'trəɪəmft
**sp** triumph[15] / triumphs[2] / triumphing[3] / triumphed[1], triumpht[1]

**triumphant** *adj*
trəɪ'ɤmfənt
**sp** triumphant[12]

**triumphantly** *adv*
*m* trəɪ'ɤmfənt,ləɪ
**sp** triumphantly[3]
**rh** amity, be, jollity, me, solemnly, prosperity *MND 4.1.88*

**triumpher / ~s** *n*
trəɪ'ɤmfəɹ / -z
**sp** triumpher[1] / triumphers[1]

**triumvirate** *n*
trəɪ'ɤmfrət, -fər-
**sp** triumpherate[1]

**triumviry** *n*
trəɪ'ɤmfrəɪ, -fər-
**sp** triumphery[1]

**trivial** *adj*
'trɪvɪɑl
**sp** triuiall[7]

**Troien** *n*
'trəɪən
**sp** Troien[1]

**Troilus / ~s' / ~es** *n*
'trəɪləs / 'trəɪləs / -ɪz
**sp** Troilous[2], Troilus[1], Troylus[99], Troy-lus[3] / Troylus[3] / Troylusses[1]

**Trojan** *adj*
'tro:dʒən
**sp** Troian[10], Troyan[1]

**Trojan / ~'s / ~s** *n*
'tro:dʒən / -z
**sp** Troian[16], Troyan[9] / Troians[3] / Troyans[8]

**troll** *v*
tro:l
**sp** troule[1]

**troll-my-dame / ~s** *n*
'tro:l-mɪ-,dɛmz
**sp** troll-my-dames[1]
> dame

**tromperies** *Fr n*
trɔ̃pə'ri
**sp** tromperies[1]

**troop / ~s** *n*
=
**sp** troop[2], troope[17], troupe[5] / troopes[21], troops[1], troupes[6], troups[2]

**troop** *v*
= / 'tru:pɪn, -ɪŋ
**sp** troope[5] / trooping[1]

**trop** *Fr adv*
tro
**sp** trop[1]

**troph·y / ~ies** *n*
'tro:fəɪ / -z
**sp** trophe[1], trophee[4] / trophees[3], trophies[1]

**tropically** *adv*
'trɒpɪkləɪ, -kɑl-
**sp** tropically[1]

**trot** *n*
=
**sp** trot[2]

**trot / ~s** *v*
=
**sp** trot[7], trots[3]

**troth / ~s** *n*
tro:θ, *Caius MW 1.4.60, 4.5.81* tro:t / -s
**sp** troth[88], [in]troth[3], troth's [troth it's][2], *Caius* trot[2] / troths[1]
**rh** both *Luc 571, MND 2.2.48*; growth, oath *Luc 1059*; oath *LC 280, LLL 1.1.66, 4.3.141, 5.2.350, 450, Luc 571, 885, MND 2.2.56, 3.2.92*
> new-trothed

**troth-plight** *n*
'tro:θ-,pləɪt
**sp** troth-plight[4]
> plight

**trotting** *adj*
'trɒtɪn, -ɪŋ
**sp** trotting[2]

**trouble / ~s** *n*
'trɤbəl / -z
**sp** trouble[25] / troubles[7]
**rh** bubble *Mac 4.1.10, 18, 20, 35*; double *VA 522* / doubles *VA 680*

**trouble / ~st / ~s / ~d** *v*
'trɤb·əl / -ləs, -t, -əls, -t / -əlz / -əld
**sp** troble[1], trouble[49] / troublest [me][1] / troubles[6], trou-bles[1] / trobled[1], troubled[23], trou-bled[1]
**rh** doubled *VA 1068*

**troubled** *adj*
'trɤbəld
**sp** troubled[6]
**rh** redoubled *VA 830*
> untroubled

**troubler** *n*
'trɤbləɹ
**sp** troubler[1]

**troublesome** *adj*
*m* 'trɤbəlsəm, -ˌsɤm
**sp** troublesome[8]

**troublous** *adj*
'trɤbləs
**sp** troublous[4]

**trough** *n*
=
**sp** trough[1]

**trout / ~s** *n*
trəʊt / -s
trowt[1] / trowts[1]

**trovato** *Ital*
trɒ'vɑ:to:
**sp** trobatto[1]

**trow / ~est** *v*
tro: / *m* -s, -st, 'tro:əst
**sp** tro[1], troa[3], trow[10] / trowest[3]
**rh** blow, no *CE 3.1.54* / goest, knowest, owest, showest, throwest *KL 1.4.121*

**trowel** *n*
'tro:əl
**sp** trowell[1]

**Troy** *adj*
trəɪ
**sp** Troy[1]

**Troy / ~'s** *n*
trəɪ / -z
**sp** Troy[79] / Troyes[1]
**rh** annoy, destroy *Luc 1367*; boy *TC 5.3.36*; joy *AW 1.3.69, Luc 1429*

**truant** *adj / n / v*
=
**sp** trewant[1], truant[2] / treuant[1], trewant[2], truant[6] / truant[1]

**truce** *n*
=
**sp** truce[14]

**truckle-bed** *n*
'trɤkəl-ˌbed
**sp** truckle-bed[1], truckle bed[1]
> bed

**trudge** *v*
trɤʤ
**sp** trudge[6]

**true / ~r / ~st** *adj*
= / 'tru:əɹ / =
**sp** true[682], true-[love][1], true-[man][3], true-[men][1], true-[wrongs][1] / truer[11] / truest[8]
**rh** adieu *AY 5.4.117, MA 3.1.107, RJ 2.2.137*; adieu, new *R2 5.3.144*; anew *S 119.9*; ensue *MND 3.2.91*; hue *MND 3.1.120, S 67.8, TNK 1.1.6*; Montague *RJ 3.1.148*; new *PP 18.20, S 68.10, 93.1*; subdue *LC 246*; sue *LLL 5.2.426*; view *Luc 455, MV 3.2.132, S 148.9*; yew *TN 2.4.56*; you *LLL 5.2.426, 769, MND 3.2.127, 5.1.195, MV 3.2.147, RJ 1.4.52, S 85.9, 118.13, TC 4.5.43, Tem Epil.3, TN 3.4.366, 4.3.33*

**true / ~r / ~st** *adv*
= / 'tru:əɹ / =
**sp** true[60] / truer[3] / truest[1]
**rh** due *LLL 4.1.18*; Montague *RJ 3.1.177*; rue *KJ 5.7.118*; you *S 114.3*

**true / ~r / ~st** *n*
= / 'tru:·əɹ / =
**sp** true[3] / truer[1] / truest[1]
**rh** you *MM 2.4.170*

**true-begotten** *adj*
=
**sp** true begotten[1]
> beget

**true-betrothed** *adj*
*m* 'tru:-bɪˌtro:ðɪd
**sp** true betrothed[1]
> betrothed

**true-born** *adj*
'tru:-ˌbɔ:ɹn
**sp** true-borne[2]
> born

**true-bred** *adj*
=
**sp** true-bred[1], true bred[3]

**true-derived** *adj*
*m* 'tru:-dɪˌrəɪvɪd
**sp** true deriued[1]
> derive

**true-devoted** *adj*
'tru:-dɪˌvo:tɪd
**sp** true-deuoted[1]
> devoted

**true-disposing** *adj*
'tru:-dɪˌspo:zɪn, -ɪŋ
**sp** true-disposing[1]
> dispose

**true-divining** *adj*
'tru:-dɪˌvəɪnɪn, -ɪŋ
**sp** true diuining[1]
> divining

**true-hearted / truer-~** *adj*
'tru:-ˌɐ:ɹtɪd, -ˌhɐ:- / 'tru:əɹ-
**sp** true-har-ted[1], true-hearted[2] / truer-hearted[1]
> heart

**true-love** *adj*
'tru:-ˌlɤv
**sp** true-loue[3]

**true-meant** *adj*
=
**sp** true meant[1]

**truepenny** *n*
'tru:ˌpenəɪ
**sp** true-penny[1]

**truie** *Fr n*
trwi
**sp** *emend of H5 3.7.63* leuye

**trull / ~s** *n*
trɤl / -z
**sp** trull[4] / [kitchin]-trulles[1]

**truly** *adv*
'tru:ləɪ
**sp** truelie[1], truely[63], true-ly[2], trulie[2], truly[98], tru-ly[1]
**rh** duly *H5 3.2.18*

**trump** *n*
trɤmp
**sp** trumpe[6]

**trumpery** *n*
'trɤmprəɪ, -pər-
**sp** tromperie[1], trumpery[1]

**trumpet** *adj / v*
'trɤmpɪt
**sp** trumpet[3] / trumpet[2]

**trumpet / ~'s / ~s / ~s'** *n*
'trɤmpɪt / -s
**sp** trompet[2], trumpet[65], trum-pet[1], trumpets [trumpet is][1], trumpet's [trumpet is][1] / trumpets[2], *abbr in s.d.* trum[1] / trumpets[69], tru[m]pets[1], trumpettes[1] / trumpets[2]

**trumpeter / ~s** *n*
'trɤmpɪtəɹ / -z
**sp** trumpeter[2] / trum-peters[1], trumpetters[1]

**trumpet-tongued** *adj*
'trɤmpɪt-ˌtɒŋd, -ˌtʊ-
**sp** trumpet-tongu'd[1]

**trunchion / ~'s** *n*
'trɤnʃɪən / -z
**sp** truncheon[2], trunchion[2] / truncheons[1]

**trunchion** *v*
'trɤnʃɪən
**sp** trunchion[1]

**trunchioner / ~s** *n*
'trɤnʃɪənəɹz
**sp** truncheoners[1]

**trundle-tail** *n*
'trɤndl-ˌtɛ:l
**sp** troudle taile[1]
**rh** wail *KL 3.6.69*
> tail

**trunk** *adj*
trɤŋk
**sp** trunke[1]

**trunk / ~s** *n*
trɤŋk / -s
**sp** trunck[1], truncke[2], trunke[16], trunke-[pillow][1] / trunkes[3], truncks[1]

**trunk-inheriting** *adj*
'trɤŋk-ɪnˌerɪtɪn, -ɪŋ, -ˌhe-
**sp** trunke-inheriting[1]

**trunk-work** *n*
'trɤŋk-ˌwɔ:ɹk
**sp** trunke-worke[1]
> work

**truss / ~ed** *v*
trɤst
**sp** truss'd[1]
> untrussing

**trust** *n*
trɤst
**sp** trust[38]
**rh** lust *S 129.4*; must *AW 2.1.206*; thrust *S 48.4*; unjust *PP 18.19, S 138.11*

**trust / ~s / ~ing / ~ed** *v*
trɤst / -s / 'trɤst·ɪn, -ɪŋ / -ɪd
**sp** trust[136] / trusts[3] / trusting[3] / trusted[11]
> dis-, mis-trust

**truster / ~s'** *n*
'trɤstəɹ / -z
**sp** truster[1] / trusters[1]

**trusting** *n*
'trɤstɪn, -ɪŋ
**sp** trusting[3]

**trusty** *adj*
'trɤstəɪ
**sp** trustie[11], trusty[6]
**rh** rusty *PP 7.2*

**truth / ~'s / ~s** *n*
=
**sp** trueth[1], truth[300], truth's [truth is][2], / truths[2], truths-[sake][1] / truthes[2], truths[5], truth's[2]
**rh** youth *AW 1.3.127, LC 105, PP 1.1, S 37.4, 41.12, 54.14, 60.11, 110.5, 138.1, TN 3.1.155*
> untruth

**try** *n*
trəɪ
**sp** try[1]

**tr·y / ~ied** *v*
trəɪ / -d
**sp** trie[22], try[62], trye[5] / tride[7], tri'de[1], tried[6], try'd[2], try'de[1], tryed[1]
**rh** *1* die *AW 2.1.185, R2 1.1.184*; nigh *CE 2.1.42*; try her by her *PP 11.3*;
**rh** *2* enemy *Ham 3.2.218*; remedy *AW 2.1.134*; guide *Luc 353*; pride *VA 280*
> untried

**trying** *n*
'trəɪɪn, -ɪŋ
**sp** trying[1]

**tu** *Fr pro*
ty
**sp** tu[2]

*te* *pro*
tə
**sp** te[1]

*ton* *det*
tɔ̃
**sp** ton[1]

**tu** *Ital pr*

**ti**
ti:
**sp** te[2]

**tu** *Lat pro*
tu:
**sp** tu[1]
> Te Deum

*teipsum*
te'ɪpsʊm
**sp** teipsum[1]

*tuae*
'tu:e
**sp** tuae[1]

**tub / ~s** *n*
tɤb / -z
**sp** tub[3] / tubbes[1]

**Tubal** *n*
'tju:bɑl
**sp** Tuball[10]

**tuck** *n / v*
tɤk
**sp** tucke[2] / tucke[1]

**tucket** *n*
'tɤkɪt
**sp** tucket[10]

**Tuesday** *adj / n*
'tju:zdɛ:, 'tu:-
**sp** Tuesday[5] / Tuesday[2]
> Shrove Tuesday

**tuft / ~s** *n*
tɤft / -s
**sp** tufft[1], tuft[2] / [emrald]-tuffes[1]

**tug / ~ging / ~ged** *v*
tɤg / 'tɤgɪn, -ɪŋ / tɤgd
**sp** tug[2], tugge[2] / tugging[2] / tugg'd[2]

**tuition** *n*
tju:'ɪsɪən
**sp** tuition[1]

**Tullus / ~s'** *n*
'tɤləs
**sp** Tullus[11] / Tullus[1]

**Tully / ~'s** *n*
'tɤləɪ / -z
**sp** Tully[1] / Tullies[1]

**tumbl·e / ~est / ~es / ~ing / ~ed** *v*
'tɤmbəl / -st, -bləst / -z / -blɪn, -ɪŋ / -d
**sp** tumble[7] / tumblest[1] / tombles[1] / tumbling[2] / tumbled[4]

**tumbler / ~'s** *n*
'tɤmbləɹz
**sp** tumblers[1]

**tumbling** *adj*
'tɤmblɪn, -ɪŋ
**sp** tumbling[2]

**tumult** *n*
'tju:məlt
**sp** tumult[4], tumult's [tumult is][2]

**tumultuous** *adj*
tjʊ'mɤltɪəs
**sp** tumultuous[4]

**tun / ~s** *n*
tɤn / -z
**sp** tun[1], tunne[1] / tunnes[1], tuns[1]

**tun-dish** *n*
'tɤn-ˌdɪʃ
**sp** tunne-dish[1]

**tune / ~s** *n*
tju:n / -z
**sp** tune[50] / tunes[6]

**tun·e / ~ing / ~ed** *v*
tju:n / 'tju:nɪn, -ɪŋ / tju:nd
**sp** tune[8] / tuning[1] / tun'd[4]
> untune

**tuneable** *adj*
'tju:nəbəl
**sp** tuneable[2]
> untuneable

**tuned** *adj*
*m* 'tju:nɪd
**sp** tuned[1]
> care-, ill-, new-, un-, well-tuned

**tuner / ~s** *n*
'tju:nəɹ / -z
**sp** tuners[1]

**Tunis** *n*
'tju:nɪs
**sp** Tunis[9]

**tup / ~ping** *v*
'tɤpɪn, -ɪŋ
**sp** tupping[1]

**turban / ~s** *n*
'tɐ:ɹbənz
**sp** turbonds[1]

**turbanned** *adj*
'tɐ:ɹbənd
**sp** turbond-[Turke][1]

**turbulence** *n*
*m* 'tɐ:ɹbəˌlens
**sp** turbulence[1]

**turbulent** *adj*
*m* 'tɐ:ɹbəˌlent, -ələnt, -blənt
**sp** turbulent[2]

**turd**
> third

**turf** *n*
tɐ:ɹf
**sp** turfe[3], turph[3]

**turfy** *adj*
'tɐːɹfəɪ
**sp** turphie-[mountaines][1]

**Turk / ~'s / ~s** *n*
tɐːɹk / -s
**sp** Turke[16], [turbond]-Turke[1] / Turkes[1] / Turkes[7]
**rh** work *Oth 2.1.113*

**turkey / ~s** *n*
'tɐːɹkəɪz
**sp** turkies[1]

**Turkey** [name] *n*
'tɐːɹkəɪ
**sp** Turky[1]

**Turkish** *adj*
'tɐːɹkɪʃ
**sp** Turkish[9]

**turky-cock / ~s** *n*
'tɐːɹkəɪ-ˌkɒk / -s
**sp** turky-cock[1], turky cocke[1] / turky-cocks[1]
> cock

**Turlygod** *n*
'tɐːɹləɪ-ˌgɒd
**sp** Turlygod[1]

**turmoil** *n*
'tɐːɹməɪl
**sp** turmoile[1]

**turmoil / ~ed** *v*
*m* təɹ'məɪlɪd
**sp** turmoyled[1]

**turn / ~s** *n*
tɐːɹn / -z
**sp** turn[1], turne[45] / turnes[6]
**rh** burn *MND 3.1.105, VA 92*

**turn / ~est / ~s / ~eth / ~ing / ~ed** *v*
tɐːɹn / -s, -st / -z / 'tɐːɹn·əθ / -ɪn, -ɪŋ / *m* -ɪd, tɐːɹnd
**sp** turn[5], turne[209] / turn'st[2] / turnes[41] / turneth[1] / turning[15] / turnd[1], turn'd[90], turned[8], tur-ned[1]
**rh** burn *Per Epil.13* / **rh** *1* adjourned *Cym 5.4.80*; burned *AY 4.3.41, S 104.5*; **rh** *2* performed *Cym 5.4.80*
> overturn, a-turning; triple-, up-turned

**Turnbull** *n*
'tɐːɹnbʊl
**sp** Turnball-[street][1]

**turncoat / ~s** *n*
'tɐːɹnkoːt / -s
**sp** turne-coate[1] / turne-coats[1]
> coat

**turning** *adj / n*
'tɐːɹnɪn, -ɪŋ
**sp** turning[1] / turning[7], tur-ning[1]
**rh** *n* burning *RJ 1.2.47, VA 140*

**turning-up** *n*
'tɐːɹnɪn-'ɤp, -ɪŋ-
**sp** turning vp[1]

**turnip / ~s** *n*
'tɐːɹnɪps
**sp** turnips[1]

**Turph** [name] *n*
tɐːɹf
**sp** Turph[1]

**turpitude** *n*
*m* 'tɐːɹpɪˌtjuːd
**sp** turpitude[2]
**rh** conclude *TC 5.2.114*

**turquoise** *n*
'tɐːɹkəɪz
**sp** turkies[1]

**turret / ~'s / ~s** *n*
'tɤrət / -s
**sp** turret[1] / turrets[2] / turrets[2]

**turtle / ~s** *n*
'tɐːɹtl / -z
**sp** turtle[4] / turtles[5]

**turtle-dove / ~s** *n*
'tɐːɹtl-'dɤvz
**sp** turtle-doues[1]

**Tuscan** *adj*
'tɤskən
**sp** Tuscan[2]

**tush** *interj*
tɤʃ
**sp** tush[21]

**tut** *interj*
tɤt, t [*click*]
**sp** tut[38]

**tutor / ~s** *n*
'tjuːtəɹ / -z
**sp** tutor[10] / tutors[4]

**tutor / ~s / ~ed** *v*
'tjuːtəɹ / -z / -d
**sp** tutor[3], ture[1] / tutors[1] / tutor'd[4], tutord[1]
**rh** suitor *TG 2.1.131* / suitors *KL 3.2.83*
> untutored

**tutt·o / ~i** *Ital adj*
'tʊttiː
**sp** [con]tutti[1]

**tu-whit tu-whoo** *interj*
tuː-'ʍɪt tuː-'huː
**sp** tu-whit to-who[2]

**twain** *n*
twɛːn
**sp** twaine[35]
**rh** again *LLL 5.2.459, MV 3.2.326, R2 5.3.133, TNK 3.5.143, VA 123, 210*; brain *Ham 3.2.238*; Dumaine *LLL 5.2.48*; gain *S 42.11*; maintain, slain *Cym 5.4.70*; remain *MND 5.1.149, PT 45, S 36.1, 39.13*; slain *PT 25*; sustain *KL 5.3.317*
> a-twain

**twang / ~ed** *v*
=
**sp** twang'd[1]

**twangling** *adj*
'twaŋglɪn, -ɪŋ
**sp** twangling[2]

**tweak** *v*
=
**sp** tweakes[1]

**tween**
> between

**twelfth** *adj*
twelf, -t
**sp** twelfe[1]

**twelve** *adj*
=
**sp** twelue[22], twelue-[pence][1], twelue-[score][2], [sworne]-twelue[1]

**twelve** *n*
=
**sp** twelue[20]

**twelvemonth** *adj*
'twelvmɤnθ
**sp** twelvemonth[1]

**twelvemonth / ~'s** *n*
'twelvmɤnθ / -s
**sp** tweluemonth[10], twelue-month[1] / tweluemonths[1]

**twentieth** *adj*
'twentəɪət
**sp** twentieth[2]

**twenty** *adj*
'twentəɪ
**sp** twentie[36], 'twentie[1], twen-tie[3], twenty[91]

**twenty** *n*
'twentəɪ
**sp** twentie[26]
**rh** plenty *TN 2.3.49, VA 22*

**twenty-nine** *adj*
*m* 'twentəɪ-ˌnəɪn
**sp** twentie nine[1]

**twenty-seven** *n*
*m* ˌtwentəɪ-'sɛ:n, -'sevn
**sp** twentie seuen[1]

**twenty-six** *n*
*m* ˌtwentəɪ-'sɪks
**sp** twentie six[2]

**twenty-three** *adj*
*m* 'twentəɪ-ˌθri:
**sp** twentie three[1]

**twice** *adv*
twəɪs
**sp** twice[67]

**twice-sod** *adj*
'twəɪs-ˌsɒd
**sp** twice sod[1]

**twice-told** *adj*
'twəɪs-ˌto:ld
**sp** twice-told[1]

**twig / ~s** *n*
=
**sp** twig[1] / twigges[3], twigs[2]
> lime-twig

**twiggen-bottle** *n*
=
**sp** twiggen-bottle[1]
> bottle

**twilled** *adj*
*m* 'twɪlɪd
**sp** twilled[1]

**twin** *adj*
=
**sp** twyn-[brother][1]

**twin / ~s** *n*
=
**sp** twin[3] / twinnes[2], twins[2]

**twin / ~ned** *v*
=
**sp** twinn'd[1]

**twin-born** *adj*
*m* ˌtwɪn-'bɔ:ɹn
**sp** twin-borne[1]
> born

**twine** *n / v*
twəɪn
**sp** twine[2] / twine[2]
> untwine

**twink** *n*
=
**sp** twincke[1], twinke[1]

**twinkl·e / ~ing / ~ed** *v*
= / 'twɪŋklɪn, -ɪŋ / =
**sp** twinckle[1] / twinkling / twinkled[1]

**twinkling** *adj / n*
'twɪŋklɪn, -ɪŋ
**sp** twinkling[1] / twinkling[1]

**twinned** *adj*
=
**sp** twin'd[1], twinn'd, twyn'd[1]

**twist** *n*
=
**sp** twist[1]

**twist / ~ed** *v*
=
**sp** twist[1] / twisted[1]
> entwist

**twisted** *adj*
=
**sp** twisted[1]

**twit / ~s / ~ting** *v*
= / = / 'twɪtɪn, -ɪŋ
**sp** twit[2] / twits[1] / twitting[1]

**twixt**
> betwixt

**two** *adj*
=
**sp** too[3], two[447], *abbr* ii.[2]

**two / ~s** *n*
=, *Macmorris H5 3.2.115*
twɛ: / =
**sp** too[1], two[206], *Macmorris* tway[1] / twoes[2]
**rh** woo *MV 2.9.76*; you *Per 1.1.71*

**twofold** *adj*
'tu:ˌfo:ld
**sp** two-fold[5]
> fold

**two-hand** *adj*
'tu:-ˌand, -ˌha-
**sp** two-hand[1]
> hand

**two-headed** *adj*
*m* ˌtu:-'edɪd, -ˌhe-
**sp** two-headed[1]
> head

**two-legged** *adj*
'tu:-ˌlegd
**sp** two-legg'd[1]

**twopence / ~s** *n*
'tɤpəns / -ɪz
**sp** two pence[3] / two-pences[1]

**Tybalt / ~'s / ~s** *n*
'tɪbɑlt / -s
**sp** Tibalt[9], Tibalts [Tybalt is][1], Tybalt[42] / Tibalts[2], Tybalts[7] / Tibalts[1]

**Tyburn** *n*
'təɪbɐ:ɹn
**sp** Tiburne[1]

**tyke** *n*
təɪk
**sp** tyke[1]

**type / ~s** *n*
təɪp / -s
**sp** type[2] / types[1]

**Typhon / ~'s** *n*
'təɪfən / -z
**sp** typhon[1] / typhons[1]

**tyrannical** *adj*
tɪ'ranɪkɑl
**sp** tyrannicall[2]

**tyrannically** *adv*
tɪ'ranɪkləɪ
**sp** tyrannically[1]

**tyrannize** *v*
*m* 'tɪrəˌnəɪz
**sp** tirranize[1], tyrannize[2]
**rh** *1* cries *Luc 676;* **rh** *2* enemies *Luc 676*

**tyrannous** *adj*
*m* 'tɪrənəs, -əˌnɤs
**sp** tirrannous[1], tyrannous[10]

**tyranny** *n*
*m* 'tɪrənəɪ, -əˌnəɪ
**sp** tiranny[2], tirranie[2], tirranny[1], tirrany[3], tyrannie[10], tyranny[14], [high-sighted]-tyranny[1], tyrrany[1]
**rh** incertainty *S 115.9*; misery *VA 737*; perpetuity *1H6 4.7.19*

**tyrant** *adj*
'təɪrənt
**sp** tirant[1], tyrant[3]

**tyrant / ~'s / ~s** *n*
'təɪrənt / -s
**sp** tirant[5], tyrant[38] / tirants[1], tyrants[9] / tyrants[8]

**Tyre** *Per* *n*
təɪɹ
**sp** Tyre[25]
**rh** desire *Per 1.3.39, 2.Chorus.22, 3. Chorus.39, 4.Chorus.1*; inquire *Per 3. Chorus.21*

**Tyrian** *adj*
'tɪrɪən
**sp** Tirian[1]

**Tyrrel** *n*
'tɪrəl
**sp** Tirrel[1], Tirrell[3], Tyrrel[6]

# U

**U** [letter] / **~s** *n*
=
**sp** V's[2]

**ubique** *Lat adv*
u:'bi:kwe, -ke
**sp** vbique[1]

**udders** *n*
'ɤdəɹz
**sp** vdders[1]

**uglier** *n*
'ɤgləɪəɹ
**sp** vglier[1]

**ugl·y / ~iest** *adj*
'ɤgləɪ / -əst
**sp** ougly[4], vglie[1], vgly[18] / vgliest[1]

**ugl·y / ~ier** *adv*
'ɤgləɪ / -əɹ
**sp** vgly[1] / ouglier[1]

**ulcer** *n*
'ɤlsəɹ
**sp** vlcer[1]

**ulcerous** *adj*
'ɤlsrəs, -sər-
**sp** vlcerous[3]

**Ulysses** *n*
ju:'lɪsi:z
**sp** Vlisses[13], Vlysses[18]

**umber** *n*
'ɤmbəɹ
**sp** vmber[1]

**umbered** *adj*
'ɤmbəɹd
**sp** vmber'd[1]

**umbra** *Lat n*
'ʊmbra
**sp** vm-bra[1]

**Umfrevile** *n*
'ɤmfrəvɪl
**sp** Vmfreuill[1]

**umpire / ~s** *n*
'ɤmpi:ɹ / -z
**sp** vmpeere[1], vmper[1], vmpire[2] / vmpires[1]

**un / ~e** *Fr det*
œ̃ / yn
**sp** en[1], un[1], vn[1], vn[boyteere][1], *Caius MW 5.5.200* oon[2] / une[1], vn[1], vne[2]

**unable** *adj*
ɤn'ɛ:bəl
**sp** vnable[5]
> all-, self-unable

**unaccommodated** *adj*
*m* ˌɤnə'kɒməˌdɛ:tɪd
**sp** vnaccommo-dated[1]
> accommodate

**unaccompanied** *adj*
*m* ˌɤnə'kɒmpəˌnəɪd
**sp** vnaccompanied[1]
> accompany

**unaccustomed** *adj*
ˌɤnə'kɤstəmd
**sp** vnaccustom'd[5]
> accustomed, customed

**unaching** *adj*
ɤn'ɛ:kɪn, -ɪŋ
**sp** vnaking[1]
> ache

**unacquainted** *adj*
ˌɤnə'kwɛ:ntɪd
**sp** vnacquainted[3]
> acquaint

**unacted** *adj*
ɤn'aktɪd
**sp** vnacted[1]
**rh** compacted, enacted *Luc 527*
> act

**unactive** *adj*
ɤn'aktɪv
**sp** vnactiue[1]
> active

**unadvised** *adj*
ˌɤnəd'vəɪzd
**sp** vnaduis'd[3], vnaduised[3]
> advised

**unadvisedly** *adv*
*m* ˌɤnəd'vəɪzɪdˌləɪ
**sp** vnaduisedly[1]
> advised

**unagreeable** *adj*
ˌɤnə'gri:əbəl
**sp** vnagreeable[1]
> agree

**unaneled** *adj*
ˌɤnə'neld
**sp** vnnaneld[1]

**unanswered** *adj*
ɤn'ansəɹd, -'ɔ:n-
**sp** vn-answer'd[1]
> answer

**unappease / ~d** *v*
ˌɤnəˈpiːzd
**sp** vnappeas'd[1]
> appease

**unapt** *adj*
ɤnˈapt
**sp** vnapt[4]
> apt

**unaptness** *n*
ɤnˈaptnəs
**sp** vnaptnesse[1]
> apt

**unarm / ~ed** *v*
ɤnˈɑːɹm / *m* -d, -ɪd
**sp** vnarme[7] / vnarm'd[7], vnarmed[1]
> arm

**unassailable** *adj*
*m* ˌɤnəˈsɛːləˌbɤl
**sp** vnassayleable[1]
> assail

**unassailed** *adj*
ˌɤnəˈsɛːld
**sp** vnassail'd[1]
> assail

**unattainted** *adj*
ˌɤnəˈtɛːntɪd
**sp** vnattainted[1]
> attaint

**unattempted** *adj*
ˌɤnəˈtemtɪd, -mpt-
**sp** vnattempted[1]
> attempt

**unattended** *adj*
ˌɤnəˈtendɪd
**sp** vnattended[1]
> attend

**unauspicious** *adj*
*m* ˈɤnɒˌspɪsɪəs
**sp** vnauspicious[1]
> auspicious, inauspicious

**unauthorized** *adj*
*m* ˌɤnɔːˈtɒrəɪzd
**sp** vnauthoriz'd[1]
> authorize

**unavoided** *adj*
ˌɤnəˈvəɪdɪd
**sp** vnauoided[1], vnauoyded[3]
> avoid

**unaware / ~s** *adv*
ˌɤnəˈwɛːɹ / -z
**sp** vnaware[2] / vnawares[5]
**rh** are *VA 823*

**unbacked** *adj*
*m* ˈɤnbakt
**sp** vnback't[1]
> back

**unbaked** *adj*
ɤnˈbɛːkd
**sp** vnbak'd[1]
> bake

**unbanded** *adj*
ɤnˈbandɪd
**sp** vnbanded[1]
> band

**unbar** *v*
ɤnˈbɑːɹ
**sp** vnbarre[1]
> bar

**unbarbed** *adj*
ˈɤnbɑːɹbd, *m emend* ɤnˈbɑːɹbɪd
**sp** vnbarb'd[1]
> barb

**unbashful** *adj*
ɤnˈbaʃfʊl
**sp** vnbashfull[1]
> bashful

**unbated** *adj*
ɤnˈbɛːtɪd
**sp** vnbaited[1], vnbated[2]

**unbattered** *adj*
ɤnˈbatəɹd
**sp** vnbattered[1]
> battered

**unbecoming** *adj*
ˌɤnbɪˈkɤmɪn, -ɪŋ
**sp** vnbecomming[1]
> becoming

**unbefitting** *adj*
ˌɤnbɪˈfɪtɪn, -ɪŋ
**sp** vnbefitting[1]
> befit

**unbegot / ~ten** *adj*
ˌɤnbɪˈgɒt / -tən
**sp** vnbegot[1] / vnbegotten[1]
> beget

**unbelieved** *adj*
*m* ˌɤnbɪˈliːvɪd
**sp** vnbeleeued[1]
> believe

**unben·d / ~t** *v*
ɤnˈben·d / -t
**sp** vnbend[1] / vn-bent[1]
> bend

**unbewailed** *adj*
ˌɤnbɪˈwɛːld
**sp** vnbewayl'd[1]
> bewail

**unbid / ~den** *adj*
*m* ˈɤnbɪd / ɤnˈbɪdən
**sp** vnbid[1] / vnbidden[1]
> bid

**unbind** *v*
ɤnˈbəɪnd
**sp** vnbinde[2]
> bind

**unbitted** *adj*
ɤnˈbɪtɪd
**sp** vnbitted[1]
> bite

**unblessed** *adj*
ɤnˈblest
**sp** vnbless'd[1], vnblest[1]
> bless

**unbloodied** *adj*
ɤnˈblɤdəɪd
**sp** vnbloudied[1]
> bloody

**unblowed** *adj*
'ɤnblo:d
**sp** vnblowed[1]
> blow

**unbodied** *adj*
ɤn'bɒdəɪd
**sp** vnbodied[1]
> body

**unbolt** *v*
ɤn'bo:lt
**sp** vnbolt[1], vnboult[1]
> bolt

**unbolted** *adj*
ɤn'bo:ltɪd
**sp** vn-boulted[1]
> bolt

**unbonnetted** *adv*
ɤn'bɒnɪtɪd
**sp** vnbonnetted[1]
> bonnet

**unbookish** *adj*
ɤn'bʊkɪʃ
**sp** vnbookish[1]
> bookish

**unborn** *adj*
ɤn'bɔ:ɹn
**sp** vnborne[8]
**rh** thorn *R2 4.1.321*
> born

**unbosom** *v*
ɤn'bʊzəm
**sp** vnbosome[1]
> bosom

**unbound** *adj / v*
*m* 'ɤnbəʊnd
**sp** vnbound[1] / vnbound[2]
> bound

**unbounded** *adj*
ɤn'bəʊndɪd
**sp** vnbounded[1]
> bound

**unbowed** *adj*
*m* ɤn'bəʊɪd, -'bəʊd
**sp** vnbowed[1], vnbow'd[1]
> bow [head]

**unbraced** *adj*
*m* ɤn'brɛ:st, -sɪd
vnbrac'd[1], vnbraced[2]

**unbraided** *adj*
ɤn'brɛ:dɪd
**sp** vnbraided[1]

**unbreathed** *adj*
*m* 'ɤnbreθt, -ri:ðd
**sp** vnbreathed[1]
> breath

**unbred** *adj*
ɤn'bred
**sp** vnbred[1]
**rh** dead *S 104.13*

**unbreeched** *adj*
ɤn'bri:ʧt
**sp** vn-breech'd[1]
> breech

**unbridled** *adj*
ɤn'brəɪdld
**sp** vnbrideled[1], vnbridled[1]
> bridle

**unbroke** *adj*
ɤn'bro:k
vnbroke[1]
> break

**unbruised** *adj*
*m* ɤn'bru:zd, -zɪd
**sp** vnbruis'd[2], vn-bruis'd[1], vnbruised[1], vnbrused[1]
> bruise

**unbuckl·e / ~es / ~ing** *v*
ɤn'bɤk·əl / -əlz / -lɪn, -lɪŋ
**sp** vnbuckle[2] / vnbuckles[1] / vnbuckling[1]
> buckle

**unbuild** *v*
ɤn'bɪld
**sp** vnbuild[1]
> build

**unburied** *adj*
ɤn'berəɪd
**sp** vnburied[2]
> bury

**unburnt** *adj*
ɤn'bɐ:ɹnt
**sp** vnburnt[1]
> burn

**unburthen / ~s / ~ed** *v*
ɤn'bɐ:ɹðən, -dən / -z / -d
**sp** vnburthen[1] / vnburthens[1] / vnburthen'd[1]
> burden

**unbutton / ~ing** *v*
ɤn'bɤtən / -ɪn, -ɪŋ, -tn-
**sp** vn-button[1] / vnbuttoning[1]
> button

**unbuttoned** *adj*
ɤn'bɤtənd
**sp** vnbutton'd[1]
> button

**uncapable** *adj*
*m* ɤn'kɛ:pə,bɤl
**sp** vncapable[2]
> capable

**uncas·e / ~ing** *v*
ɤn'kɛ:s / -ɪn, -ɪŋ
**sp** vncase[1] / vncasing[1]
> case

**uncaught** *adj*
ɤn'kɔ:t
**sp** vncaught[2]
> catch

**uncertain** *adj*
ɤn'sɐ:ɹtən
**sp** vncertaine[10]
> certain, incertain

**uncertainly** *Luc* *adv*
*m* ɤn'sɐ:ɹtən,ləɪ
**sp** vncertainely[1]
**rh** quality, discovery *Luc 1311*

**uncertainty** *n*
*m* ɤn'sɐːɹtənˌtəɪ
**sp** vncertaintie[2], vncertainty[1]
**rh** fallacy *CE 2.2.194*
> certainty, incertainty

**unchain** *v*
ɤn'ʧɛːn
**sp** vnchaine[1]
> chain

**unchanging** *adj*
ɤn'ʧɛːnʤɪn, -ɪŋ
**sp** vnchanging[1]
> change

**uncharge** *v*
ɤn'ʧɑːɹʤ
**sp** vncharge[1]
> charge

**uncharged** *adj*
*m* ɤn'ʧɑːɹʤɪd
**sp** vncharged[1]
> charge

**uncharitable**
> incharitable

**uncharitably** *adv*
*m* ɤn'ʧarɪˌtabləɪ
**sp** vncharitably[1]
> charitably

**uncharmed** *adj*
ɤn'ʧɑːɹmd
**sp** vncharm'd[1]
**rh** armed *RJ 1.1.211*
> charm

**unchary** *adv*
ɤn'ʧarəɪ
**sp** vnchary[1]
> chary

**unchaste** *adj*
*m* ɤn'ʧast, 'ɤnʧast
**sp** vnchaste[4]
> chaste

**unchecked** *adj*
ɤn'ʧekt
**sp** vncheck'd[1], vncheckt[1]
> check

**unchild / ~ed** *v*
ɤn'ʧəɪldɪd
**sp** vnchilded[1]
> child

**uncivil** *adj*
ɤn'sɪvɪl
**sp** vnciuill[8]
> civil

**unclaim / ~ed** *v*
ɤn'klɛːmd
**sp** vnclaim'd[1]
> claim

**unclasp / ~ed** *v*
ɤn'klasp / -t
**sp** vnclaspe[3] / vnclasp'd[2]
> clasp

**uncle / ~'s / ~s** *n*
'ɤŋkəl / -z
**sp** vnckle[103], vncle[56], vnkle[26] / vnckles[5], vnkles[7] / vncles[1], vnckles[7], vnkles[7]
> great-uncle, nuncle

**uncle** *v*
'ɤŋkəl
**sp** vnckle[1]

**unclean** *adj*
ɤn'kliːn
**sp** vncleane[4]
**rh** scene *RJ Prol.4*
> clean

**uncleanliness** *n*
ɤn'klenlɪnəs
**sp** vncleanlinesse[1]
> cleanly

**uncleanly** *adj*
ɤn'klenləɪ
**sp** vncleanlie[1], vncleanly[4]
> cleanly

**uncleanness** *n*
ɤn'klenəs
**sp** vncleannesse[1]
> clean

**unclew** *v*
ɤn'kluː
**sp** vnclew[1]

**unclog** *v*
ɤn'klɒg
**sp** vnclogge[1]
> clog

**uncoined** *adj*
*m* 'ɤnkəɪnd, ɤn'kəɪnd
**sp** vncoyned[1]
> coin

**uncolted** *adj*
*m* 'ɤnkoːltɪd
**sp** vncolted[1]
> colt

**uncomeliness** *n*
ɤn'kɤmlɪnəs
**sp** vncomelinesse[1]
> comeliness

**uncomfortable** *adj*
*m* ɤn'kɤmfəɹˌtabəl
**sp** vncomfortable[1]
> comfortable

**uncompassionate** *adj*
ˌɤnkəm'pasɪənət
**sp** vncompassionate[1]
> compassionate

**uncomprehensive** *adj*
ɤnˌkɒmprɪ'ensɪv, -'he-
**sp** vncomprehensiue[1]
> comprehend

**unconfinable** *adj*
ˌɤnkən'fəɪnəbəl
**sp** vnconfinable[1]
> confine

**unconfirmed** *adj*
ˌɤnkən'fɐːɹmd
**sp** vnconfirm'd[1], vnconfirmed[1]
> confirm

**unconquered** *adj*
ɤn'kɒŋkəɹd, *m Luc* ɤn'kɒŋkəˌred
**sp** vnconquer'd[1], vnconquered[1]

**rh** bred, honoured *Luc 408*
> conquered

**unconsidered** *adj*
ˌɤnkən'sɪdəɹd
**sp** vnconsidered[2]
> considered

**unconstant** *adj*
ɤn'kɒnstənt
**sp** vnconstant[4]
> constant, inconstant

**unconstrained** *adj*
*m* ˌɤnkən'strɛ:nd, -nɪd
**sp** vnconstrained[1], vnconstrayn'd[1]
> constrain

**uncontemned** *adv*
ˌɤnkən'temd
**sp** vncontemn'd[1]
> contemn

**uncontrolled** *adj*
ˌɤnkən'tro:ld
**sp** vncontroul'd[1]
> control

**uncorrected** *adj*
ˌɤnkə'rektɪd
**sp** vncorrected[1]
> correct

**uncounted** *adj*
ɤn'kəʊntɪd
**sp** vncounted[1]
> count

**uncouple** *v*
ɤn'kɤpəl
**sp** vncouple[2]
> couple

**uncourteous** *adj*
ɤn'kɐ:ɹtəs, -ɪəs, -'kɔ:ɹ-
**sp** vncourteous[1]
> courteous

**uncouth** *adj*
ɤn'ku:θ
**sp** vncouth[2]

**uncover / ~ed** *v*
ɤn'kɤvəɹ / -d
**sp** vncouer[1] / vncouer'd[1]
> cover

**uncovered** *adj*
ɤn'kɤvəɹd
**sp** vncouer'd[2], vncouered[1]
> cover

**uncropped** *adj*
*m* ɤn'krɒpɪd
**sp** vncropped[1]
> crop

**uncrossed** *adj*
ɤn'krɒst
**sp** vncros'd[1]
> cross

**uncrown** *v*
ɤn'krəʊn
**sp** vncrowne[1]
> crown

**unction** *n*
'ɤŋksɪən
**sp** vnction[2]

**unctious** *adj*
'ɤŋksɪəs
**sp** vnctious[1]

**uncuckolded** *adj*
ɤn'kɤkəldɪd
**sp** vncuckolded[1]
> cuckold

**uncurable** *adj*
ɤn'kju:ɹəbəl
**sp** vncurable[1], vncureable[1]
> cure

**uncurbable** *adj*
ɤn'kɐ:ɹbəbəl
**sp** vncurbable[1]
> curb

**uncurbed** *adj*
*m* ɤn'kɐ:ɹbɪd
**sp** vncurbed[1]
> curb

**uncurl / ~s** *v*
ɤn'kɐ:ɹlz
**sp** vncurles[1]
> curl

**uncurrant** *adj*
ɤn'kɤɹənt
**sp** vncurrant[3]
> currant

**uncurse** *v*
ɤn'kɐ:ɹs
**sp** vncurse[1]
> curse

**undaunted** *adj*
ɤn'dɔ:ntɪd
**sp** vndaunted[4]
> daunt

**undeaf** *v*
ɤn'def
**sp** vndeafe[1]
> deaf

**undeck** *v*
ɤn'dek
**sp** vndeck[1]
> deck

**undeeded** *adj*
ɤn'di:dɪd
**sp** vndeeded[1]
> deed

**under** *adv*
'ɤndəɹ
**sp** vnder[7], [stand]-vnder[1], vn-der[1]
**rh** sunder *Luc 386*; wonder *VA 746*

**under** *prep*
'ɤndəɹ
**sp** vnder[252], vnder[saile][1], vn-der[8], vnder't[1], vn-der't [under it][1]

**under-bear / ~-borne** *v*
'ɤndəɹ-'bɛ:ɹ / -'bɔ:ɹn
**sp** vnder-beare[1] / vn-derborn[1]
> bear

**under-bearing** *n*
'ɤndəɹ-'bɛ:rɪn, -ɪŋ
**sp** vnder-bearing[1]
> bear

**under-crest** *v*
'ɤndəɹ-'krest
**sp** vnder-crest[1]
> crest

**under-fiend / ~s** *n*
'ɤndəɹ-'fi:ndz, -'fen-
**sp** vnder fiends[1]
> fiend

**underfoot** *adv*
'ɤndəɹ-'fʊt
**sp** vnderfoote[1]
> foot

**underglobe** *n*
'ɤndəɹ-'glo:b
**sp** vnder globe[1]
> globe

**under·go / ~goes / ~went / ~gone** *v*
*m* 'ɤndəɹ'go:, -ɹgo: / -z / 'ɤndəɹ-'went / -'gɒn
**sp** vndergo[6], vnder-go[1], vn-der-go[1], vndergoe[6], vnder-goe[2] / vndergoes[2] / vnderwent[1] / vndergon[1]
> go

**undergoing** *adj*
'ɤndəɹ-'go:ɪn, -ɪŋ
**sp** vndergoing[1]
> go

**underhand** *adj*
*m* 'ɤndəɹˌand, -ˌha-, -ɹa-
**sp** vnder-hand[2]
> hand

**under-hangman** *n*
'ɤndəɹ-'aŋmən, -'ha-
**sp** vnder hangman[1]
> hangman

**under-honest** *n*
'ɤndəɹ-'ɒnɪst
**sp** vnder honest[1]
> honest

**underling / ~s** *n*
'ɤndəɹlɪŋz
**sp** vnderlings[1]

**undermine** *v*
*m* 'ɤndəɹ'məɪn, -ɹm-
**sp** vndermine[2], vnder-mine[1]
> mine

**underminer / ~s** *n*
'ɤndəɹ'məɪnəɹz
**sp** vnderminers[1]
> mine

**underneath** *adv / prep*
*m* ˌɤndəɹ'ni:θ / 'ɤndəɹˌni:θ
**sp** vnder-neath[1] / vnderneath[13]

**under-peep** *v*
'ɤndəɹ-'pi:p
**sp** vnder-peepe[1]
> peep

**underpriz·e / ~ing** *v*
'ɤndəɹ-'prɛ:zɪn, -ɪŋ
**sp** vnderprising[1]
> prize

**under-prop** *v*
'ɤndəɹ-'prɒp
**sp** vnder-prop[2]
> prop

**underskinker** *n*
'ɤndəɹˌskɪŋkəɹ
**sp** vnder skinker[1]

**understand / ~eth / ~s / ~eth / ~ing / understood** *v*
ˌɤndəɹ'stand / -nst, -ndst / -dz / -əθ / -ɪn, -ɪŋ / ˌɤndəɹ'stʊd
**sp** vnderstand[89], vn-derstand[3], vnder-stand[5] / vnderstand'st[1] / vnderstands[4], vnder-stands[1] / vnderstandeth[1] / vnderstanding[1] / vnderstood[9], vnder-stood[1], vnderstoode[1]
**rh** a-land *Per 3.2.66*; hand *AY 2.7.204*; land *R2 5.3.123*; scanned *CE 2.2.160* / **rh** *1* good *R2 2.1.213*; **rh** *2* blood *LC 200*; their bud *LLL 5.2.294*; **rh** *3* mood *LC 200*
**pun** *TG 2.5.29, TN 3.1.77*
'ɤndəɹ-'stand

**understanding** *adj*
ˌɤndəɹ'standɪn, -ɪŋ
**sp** vnderstanding[3]

**understanding / ~s** *n*
ˌɤndəɹ'standɪn, -ɪŋ / -z
**sp** understanding[1], vnderstanding[12], vn-derstanding[1] / vn-derstandings[1]

**undertak·e / ~s / ~ing / under·took / ~ta'n** *v*
ˌɤndəɹ'tɛ:k / -s / -ɪn, -ɪŋ / ˌɤndəɹ·'tʊk / -tɛ:n
**sp** vndertake[42], vnder-take[1], vndertak't [undertake it][1] / vndertakes[3] / vndertaking[2] / vndertooke[5] / vnderta'ne[1]
> take

**undertaker** *n*
'ɤndəɹˌtɛ:kəɹ
**sp** vndertaker[2]
> take

**undertaking / ~s** *n*
ˌɤndəɹ'tɛ:kɪn, -ɪŋ / -z
**sp** vndertaking[3] / vndertakings[2], vnder-takings[1]
> take

**undervalued** *adj*
'ɤndəɹ'valjəd, -ju:d
**sp** vndervallewd[1], vndervalued[1]
> value

**under·work, ~-wrought** *v*
'ɤndə'rɔ:t
**sp** vnder-wrought[1]
> work

**under·write / ~-writ** *v*
'ɤndə'rɪt
**sp** vnder-writ[1]
> write

**undescried** *adj*
'ɤndɪ'skrəɪd
**sp** vndescry'd[1]
> descry

**undeserved** *adj*
*m* 'ɤndɪ'zɐ:ɹvɪd, -vd
**sp** vndeserued[4]
> deserve

**undeserver / ~s** *n*
'ɤndɪ'zɐɹvəɹ / -z
**sp** vndeseruer[2] / vndeseruers[1]
> deserver

**undeserving** *adj*
'ʏndɪ'zɐːɹvɪn, -ɪŋ
**sp** vndeseruing[2]
> deserving

**undetermined** *adj*
'ʏndɪ'tɐːɹmɪnd
**sp** vndetermin'd[1]
> determine

**undid**
> undo

**undinted** *adj*
ʏn'dɪntɪd
**sp** vndinted[1]
> dint

**undiscernable** *adj*
'ʏndɪ'sɐːɹnəbəl
**sp** vndiscerneable[1]
> discern

**undiscovered** *adj*
'ʏndɪs'kʏvəɹd
**sp** vndiscouer'd[2], vndiscouered[1]
> discover

**undishonoured** *adj*
*m* 'ʏndɪs'ɒnə,red
**sp** vndishonoured[1]
**rh** bed *CE 2.2.155*
> dishonoured

**undisposed** *adj*
'ʏndɪ'spoːzd
**sp** vndispos'd[1]
> dispose

**undistinguishable** *adj*
*m* 'ʏndɪ'stɪŋgwɪ,ʃabəl
**sp** vndistinguishable[2]
> distinguish

**undividable** *adj*
*m* 'ʏndɪ'vəɪdə,bʏl
**sp** vndiuidable[1]
> dividable

**undivulged** *adj*
*m* 'ʏndɪ'vʏlʤd, -ʤɪd
**sp** vndivulg'd[1], vndivulged[1]
> divulged

**un·do / ~does /~doing / ~did / ~done** *v*
ʏn·'duː / -'dʏz / -'duːɪn, -ɪŋ / -'dɪd / -'dʏn
**sp** vndo[9], vndoe[14], vndoo[4], vndoo't [undo it][1] / vndoes[1], vndo's[1] / vndoing[1] / vndid[2] / vndon[2], vndone[50], vn-done[2]
**rh** undo us to us *LLL 5.2.425*
> do

**undoing** *n*
ʏn'duːɪn, -ɪŋ
**sp** vndoing[3], vndooing[1]
> do

**undone** *adj*
ʏn'dʏn
**sp** vndone[1]
**rh** run *VA 783*; son *Per 1.1.118*; sun *Mac 5.5.50*
> do

**undoubted** *adj*
ʏn'dəʊtɪd
**sp** vndoubted[4]
> doubt

**undoubtedly** *adv*
*m* ʏn'dəʊtɪd,ləɪ
**sp** vndoubtedly[1]
> doubt

**undoubtful** *adj*
ʏn'dəʊtfʊl
**sp** vndoubtfull[1]
> doubtful

**undreamed** *adj*
'ʏndriːmd
**sp** vndream'd[1]
> dream

**undress** *v*
ʏn'dres
**sp** vndresse[1]
> dress

**undressed** *adj*
ʏn'drest
**sp** vndressed[1]
> dress

**undrowned** *adj*
ʏn'drəʊnd
**sp** vndrown'd[2]
> drown

**unduteous** *adj*
ʏn'djuːtɪəs
**sp** vnduteous[1]
> duteous

**undutiful** *adj*
ʏn'djuːtɪfʊl
**sp** vndutifull[1]
> dutiful

**une**
> un

**unearned** *adj*
*m* ʏn'ɐːɹnɪd
**sp** vnearned[1]
> earn

**unearthly** *adj*
ʏn'ɐːɹθləɪ
**sp** vn-earthly[1]
> earthly

**uneasiness** *n*
*m* ʏn'iːzɪ,nes
**sp** vneasinesse[1]
> easiness

**uneasy** *adj*
ʏn'iːzəɪ
**sp** vneasie[4]
> easy

**uneducated** *adj*
ʏn'edjə,kɛːtɪd
**sp** vneduca-ted[1]
> educate

**uneffectual** *adj*
'ʏnɪ'fektɪʊl
**sp** vneffectuall[1]
> effectual

**unelected** *adj*
'ʏnɪ'lektɪd
**sp** vnelected[1]
> elect

**unequal** *adj*
ɤn'iːkwɑl
**sp** vnequall[5]
> equal

**uneven** *adj*
ɤn'iːvən, -'ev-
**sp** vneeuen[1], vneuen[6]
**rh** seven *R2 2.2.120*
> even

**unexamined** *adj*
*m* 'ɤnɪg'zamɪnd
**sp** vnexamin'd[1]
> examine

**unexecuted** *adj*
*m* ɤn'eksɪˌkjuːtɪd
**sp** vnexecuted[1]
> execute

**unexpected** *adj*
'ɤnɪks'pektɪd
**sp** vnexpected[2]
> expected

**unexperienced** *adj*
'ɤnɪks'piːrɪənst
**sp** vnexperienc'd[1]
> experienced

**unexpressive** *adj*
'ɤnɪks'presɪv
**sp** vnexpressiue[1]
> expressive

**unfained** *adj*
*m* ɤn'fɛːnɪd
**sp** vnfained[2]
> fain

**unfainedly** *adv*
*m* ɤn'fɛːnɪdˌləɪ
**sp** vnfainedly[2]
> fain

**unfaithful** *n*
ɤn'fɛːθfʊl
**sp** vnfaith-full[1]
> faithful

**unfallible** *adj*
ɤn'falɪbəl
**sp** vnfallible[1]
> fallible, infallible

**unfamed** *adj*
ɤn'fɛːmd
**sp** vnfam'd[1]
> famed

**unfashionable** *adj*
*m* ɤn'faʃɪənˌabəl
**sp** vnfashionable[1]
> fashionable

**unfasten** *v*
ɤn'fasən
**sp** vnfasten[1]
> fasten

**unfathered** *adj*
ɤn'faðəɹd
**sp** vnfather'd[1]
**rh** gathered *S 124.2*
> father

**unfed** *adj*
'ɤnfed
**sp** vnfed[1]
> feed

**unfeed** *adj*
'ɤnfiːd
**sp** vnfeed[1]
> fee

**unfeeling** *adj*
ɤn'fiːlɪn, -ɪŋ
**sp** vnfeeling[4]
> feel

**unfeigned** *adj*
*m* ɤn'fɛːnɪd
**sp** vnfained[2], vnfayned[1]
> feigned

**unfeignedly** *adv*
*m* ɤn'fɛːnɪdˌləɪ
**sp** vnfainedly[2], vnfeignedly[1]
> feign

**unfelt** *adj*
*m* ɤn'felt, 'ɤnfelt
**sp** vnfelt[3]
> unfeel

**unfenced** *adj*
*m* ɤn'fensɪd
**sp** vnfenced[1]
> fence

**unfilled** *adj*
*m* ɤn'fɪld, 'ɤnfɪld
**sp** vnfill'd[2]
> fill

**unfilial** *adj*
ɤn'fɪlɪɑl
**sp** vnfilliall[1]
> filial

**unfinished** *adj*
ɤn'fɪnɪʃt
**sp** vnfinish'd[2], vn-finish'd[1]
**rh** diminished *VA 415*
> finish

**unfirm** *adj*
*m* ɤn'fɐːɹm, 'ɤnfɐːɹm
**sp** vnfirme[4]
> firm

**unfit** *adj*
ɤn'fɪt
**sp** vnfit[10]
> fit

**unfitness** *adj*
ɤn'fɪtnəs
**sp** vnfitnesse[1]
> fit

**unfix** *v*
ɤn'fɪks
**sp** vnfixe[3]
> fix

**unfledged** *adj*
ɤn'fledʒd
**sp** vnfledg'd[3]
> fledge

**unfold / ~s /~eth / ~ed** *v*
ɤn'foːld / -z / -əθ / -ɪd
**sp** vnfold[29], vn-fold[1] / vnfolds[3] / vnfoldeth[1] / vnfolded[4]
**rh** behold *MND 1.1.208*; behold, cold *Luc 1146*; behold, untold *Luc 754*; hold *MW 1.3.88*
> fold

**unfolding** *adj / n*
ɤn'fo:ldɪn, -ɪŋ
**sp** vnfolding[1] / vnfolding[1]
> fold

**unfool** *v*
ɤn'fʊl, -'fu:l
**sp** vnfoole[1]
> fool

**unforced** *adj*
ɤn'fɔ:ɹst
**sp** vnforc'd[1], vn-forc'd[1]
> forced

**unforfeited** *adj*
*m* ɤn'fɔ:ɹfɪˌtɪd
**sp** vnforfaited[1]
> forfeit

**unfortified** *adj*
*m* ɤn'fɔ:ɹtɪˌfəɪd
**sp** vnfortified[1]
> fortify

**unfortunate** *adj*
*m* ɤn'fɔ:ɹtnət, -tənˌɛ:t
**sp** vnfortunate[10]
> fortune, infortunate

**unfought** *adj*
ɤn'fɔ:t
**sp** vnfought[1]
> fight

**unfrequented** *adj*
'ɤnfrɪ'kwentɪd
**sp** vnfrequented[2]
> frequent

**unfriended** *adj*
ɤn'frendɪd
**sp** vnfriended[2]
> friend

**unfurnish / ~ed** *v*
ɤn'fɐ:ɹnɪʃ / -t
**sp** vnfurnish[1] / vnfurnisht[2]
> furnish

**unfurnished** *adj*
ɤn'fɐ:ɹnɪʃt
**sp** vnfurnish'd[1], vnfurnisht[2]
> furnish

**ungained** *adj*
ɤn'gɛ:nd
**sp** vngain'd[2]
> gain

**ungalled** *adj / adv*
*m* ɤn'gɑ:lɪd
**sp** vngalled[1] / vngalled[1]
> gall

**ungartered** *adj / adv*
ɤn'gɑ:ɹtəɹd
**sp** vngarter'd[1], vngartred[1] / vn-garter'd[1]
> garter

**ungenitured** *adj*
ɤn'ʤenɪtəɹd
**sp** vngenitur'd[1]

**ungentle** *adj*
ɤn'ʤentl
**sp** vngentle[11]
> gentle

**ungentleness** *n*
*m* ɤn'ʤentlˌnes
**sp** vngentlenesse[1]
> gentleness

**ungently** *adv*
ɤn'ʤentləɪ
**sp** vngently[3]
> ungently

**ungird** *v*
ɤn'gɐ:ɹd
**sp** vngird[1]
> gird

**ungodly** *adj*
ɤn'gɒdləɪ
**sp** vngodly[1]
> godly

**ungorged** *adj*
ɤn'gɔ:ɹʤd
**sp** vngorg'd[1]
> gorge

**ungot / ~ten** *adj*
ɤn'gɒt / -ən
**sp** vngot[1] / vngotten[1]
> get

**ungoverned** *adj*
ɤn'gɤvəɹnd
**sp** vngouern'd[5]
> govern

**ungracious** *adj*
ɤn'grɛ:sɪəs
**sp** vngracious[8]
> gracious

**ungrateful** *adj*
ɤn'grɛ:tfʊl
**sp** vngratefull[6]
> grateful, ingrateful

**ungravely** *adv*
ɤn'grɛ:vləɪ
**sp** vngrauely[1]
> gravely

**ungrown** *adj*
*m* 'ɤngro:n
**sp** vngrowne[1]
> grow

**unguarded** *adj*
ɤn'gɑ:ɹdɪd
**sp** vnguarded[3]
> guard

**unguem** *Lat n*
'ʊŋgwem
**sp** vnguem[1], *Costard LLL 5.1.72*
*error* dungil, *Holofernes 5.1.74* dunghel
> dunghill

**unguided** *adj*
ɤn'gəɪdɪd
**sp** vnguided[2]
> guided

**unhacked** *adj*
'ɤnˌakt, -ˌha-
**sp** vnhack'd[1], vnhackt[1]
> hack

**unhair** *v*
ɤn'ɛ:ɹ, -'hɛ:ɹ
**sp** vnhaire[1]
> hair

**unhallowed** *adj*
*m* ɤn'ɑləd, -ləwɪd, -lo:d, -lo:ɪd, -'hɑ-
**sp** vnhallow'd[2], vnhallowed[6]
> hallow

**unhand** *v*
ɤn'and, -'ha-
**sp** vnhand[1]
> hand

**unhandled** *adj*
ɤn'andld, -'ha-
**sp** vnhandled[2]
> handle

**unhandsome** *adj*
ɤn'ansəm-, -'ha-
**sp** vnhandsome[4]
> handsome

**unhanged** *adj*
ɤn'aŋd, -'ha-
**sp** vnhang'd[1]
> hang

**unhappily** *adv*
*m* ɤn'apləɪ, -pɪl-, -ɪˌləɪ, -'ha-
**sp** vnhappely[1], vnhappily[3]
> happily

**unhappiness** *n*
*m* ɤn'apɪˌnes, -ɪnəs, -'ha-
**sp** vnhappinesse[2]
> happiness

**unhappy** *adj*
ɤn'apəɪ, -'ha-
**sp** vnhappie[17], vnhappy[22]
> happy

**unhapp·y / ~ied** *v*
ɤn'apəɪd, -'ha-
**sp** vnhappied[1]
> happy

**unhardened** *adj*
ɤn'ɑ:ɹdənd, 'hɑ:-
**sp** vnhardned[1]
> harden

**unhatched** *adj*
*m* ɤn'aʧt, 'ɤnaʧt, -'ha-
**sp** vnhatch'd[2], vnhatch't[1]
> hatch

**unheard** *adj*
*m* ɤn'ɛ:ɹd, 'ɤnɛ:ɹd, -'hɛ:-, -ɑ:ɹd, -'hɑ:-
**sp** vnheard[2], vn-heard[2]
> hear

**unheart / ~s** *v*
ɤn'ɑ:ɹts, -'hɑ:-
**sp** vnhearts[1]
> heart

**unheedful** *adj*
ɤn'i:dfʊl, -'hi:-
**sp** vnheedfull[1], vn-heedfull[1]
> heedful

**unheedfully** *adv*
ɤn'i:dfləɪ, -fʊl-, -'hi:-
**sp** vnheedfully[1]
> heedfully

**unheedy** *adj*
ɤn'i:dəɪ, -'hi:-
**sp** vnheedy[1]
> heed

**unhelpful** *adj*
ɤn'elpfʊl, -'he-
**sp** vnhelpefull[1]
> help

**unhidden** *adj*
ɤn'ɪdən, -'hɪ-
**sp** vnhidden[1]
> hide

**unholy** *adj*
ɤn'o:ləɪ, 'ho:-
**sp** vnholy[3]
> holy

**unhoped** *adj*
'ɤno:pd, -ho:-
**sp** vnhop'd[1]
> hope

**unhopeful / ~est** *adj*
ɤn'o:pfləst, -fʊl-, -'ho:-
**sp** vnhopefullest[1]
> hopeful

**unhorse** *v*
ɤn'ɔ:ɹs, -'hɔ:-
**sp** vnhorse[1]
> horse

**unhospitable** *adj*
*m* ɤn'ɒspɪˌtabəl, -'hɒ-
**sp** vnhospitable[1]
> hospitable

**unhoused** *adj*
*m* ɤn'əʊzɪd, -'həʊ-
**sp** vnhoused[2]
> house *v*

**unhousled** *adj*
ɤn'əʊzəld, -'həʊ-
**sp** vnhouzzled[1]

**unhurtful** *adj*
ɤn'ɐ:ɹtfʊl, -'hɐ:-
vnhurtfull[1]
> hurt

**unicorn / ~s** *n*
'ju:nɪkɔ:ɹn / -z
**sp** vnicorne[1] / vnicornes[2]

**unimproved** *adj*
*m* 'ɤnɪm'prɤvɪd, -ru:v-
**sp** vnimproued[1]
> improve

**uninhabitable** *adj*
'ɤnɪn'abɪtəbəl, -'ha-
**sp** vninhabitable[1]
> inhabit

**unintelligent** *adj*
'ɤnɪn'telɪʤənt
**sp** vn-intelligent[1]
> intelligent

**union** *n*
'ju:nɪən
**sp** vnion[5]

**unite** *v*
jʊ'nəɪt
**sp** vnite[6]

**united** *adj*
jʊ'nəɪtɪd
**sp** vnited[5]

**unity** *n*
*m* 'ju:nɪtəɪ, -ˌtəɪ
**sp** vnitie[2], vnity[5]

**universal** *adj*
ˌju:nɪ'vɐ:ɹsal
**sp** vniuersal[1], vniuersall[12], vniuer-sall[1]

**universe** *n*
'ju:nɪˌvɐ:ɹs
**sp** vniuerse[1]

**universit·y / ~ies** *n*
ˌju:nɪ'vɐ:ɹsɪtəɪ / *m* -sɪˌtəɪz
vni-uersitie[1], vniuersity[1] / vniuersities[1]

**unjointed** *adj*
ɤn'ʤəɪntɪd
**sp** vnioynted[1]
> joint

**unjust** *adj*
*m* ɤn'ʤɤst, 'ɤnʤɤst
**sp** vniust[20]
**rh** dust *AW 5.3.63*; lust *Luc 189*; lust, mistrust *Luc 285*; trust *PP 18.21, S 138.9*
> just

**unjustly** *adv*
ɤn'ʤɤstləɪ
**sp** vniustly[7]
> justly

**unkennel** *v*
ɤn'kenəl
**sp** vnkennell[2]
> kennel

**unkept** *adv*
ɤn'kept
**sp** vnkept[1]
> keep

**unkind / ~est** *adj*
*m* ɤn'kəɪnd, 'ɤnkəɪnd / ɤn'kəɪndəst
**sp** vnkind[5], vnkinde[17] / vnkindest[4]
**rh** *1* blind *Tit 5.3.47*; find *KL 1.1.260*; mind *CE 4.2.21*; *Ham 3.1.101, VA 204, 310*; **rh** *2* wind *AY 2.7.176, VA 187*
> kind

**unkind** *n*
ɤn'kəɪnd
**sp** vnkinde[1]
**rh** mind *TN 3.4.359*
> kind

**unkindly** *adv*
ɤn'kəɪndləɪ
**sp** vnkindely[2], vnkindly[4]
> kindly

**unkindness** *n*
ɤn'kəɪndnəs
**sp** vnkindenesse[1], vnkindnes[1], vnkindnesse[18]
> kindness

**unking / ~ed** *v*
ɤn'kɪŋd
**sp** vn-king'd[1]
> king

**unkinged** *adj*
*m* 'ɤnkɪŋd
**sp** vn-king'd[1]
> king

**unkinglike** *adv*
ɤn'kɪŋləɪk
**sp** vn-kinglike[1]
> king

**unkiss** *v*
ɤn'kɪs
**sp** vn-kisse[1]
> kiss

**unkissed** *adj*
ɤn'kɪst
**sp** vnkist[1]
> kiss

**unknit** *v*
ɤn'nɪt, -'kn-
**sp** vnknit[4]
> knit

**unknowing** *n*
ɤn'no:ɪn, -ɪŋ, 'kn-
**sp** vnknowing[1]
> know

**unknown** *adj*
*m* ɤn'no:n, 'ɤn-no:n, -kn-
**sp** vnknown[4], vnknowne[37]
**rh** own *Luc 34*
> know

**unlace / ~d** *v*
ɤn'lɛ:s / -t
**sp** vnlace[1] / vnlac'd[1]
**rh** unlaced me embraced me *PP 11.7*
> lace

**unlaid** *adj*
ɤn'lɛ:d
**sp** vnlaid[1]
> lay

**unlawful** *adj*
ɤn'lɔ:fʊl
**sp** vnlawfull[10], vnlaw-full[1]
> lawful

**unlawfully** *adv*
*m* ɤn'lɔ:fʊˌləɪ, -fʊləɪ, -fləɪ
**sp** vn-lawfullie[1], vnlawfully[2]
> lawfully

**unlearned** *adj*
*m* ɤn'lɐ:ɹnd, -nɪd
**sp** vnlearn'd[2], vnlearned[2]
> learn

**unless** *conj*
ɤn'les
**sp** vnles[3], vnless[1], vnlesse[143]

**unlessoned** *adj*
ɤn'lesənd
**sp** vnlessoned[1]
> lesson

**unlettered** *adj*
ɤn'letəɹd
**sp** vnletered[1], vnletter'd[1], vnlettered[1]
> letter

**unlicked** *adj*
'ɤnlɪkt
**sp** vn-lick'd[1]
> lick

**unlike** *adj / prep*
ɤn'ləɪk
**sp** vnlike[4] / vnlike[10]
> like

**unlikely** *adj*
ɤn'ləɪkləɪ
**sp** vnlikely[3]
**rh** quickly *VA 989*
> likely

**unlimited** *adj*
ɤn'lɪmɪtɪd
**sp** vnlimited[1]
> limit

**unlineal** *adj*
ɤn'lɪnɪɑl
**sp** vnlineall[1]
> lineal

**unlink / ~ed** *v*
ɤn'lɪŋkt
**sp** vnlink'd[1]
> link

**unlived** *adj*
ɤn'ləɪvd
**sp** vnliued[1]
**rh** deprived, derived *Luc 1754*

**unload / ~s / ~ing / ~ed** *v*
ɤn'lo:d / -z / -ɪn, -ɪŋ / -ɪd
**sp** vnload[1], vnloade[1] / vnloads[1] / vnloading[1] / vnloaded[1]
> load

**unlock** *v*
ɤn'lɒk
**sp** vnlocke[4]
> lock

**unlocked** *adj*
ɤn'lɒkt
**sp** vnlock'd[1]
> lock

**unlooked** *adj*
ɤn'lʊkt
**sp** vnlook'd[1]
> look

**unlooked-for** *adj*
ɤn'lʊkt-ˌfɔ:ɹ
**sp** vnlook'd-for[1], vnlook'd for[5], vnlookt for[1]
> look

**unloose / ~d** *v*
ɤn'lu:s / -t
**sp** vnloose[5] / vnloos'd[1]
> loose

**unloved** *adj*
ɤn'lɤvd
**sp** vnlou'd[2]
> love

**unloving** *adj*
ɤn'lɤvɪn, -ɪŋ
**sp** vnlouing[1]
> love

**unluckily** *adv*
*m* ɤn'lɤkɪˌləɪ, -ɪl-
**sp** vnluckily[7]
> luckily

**unlucky** *adj*
ɤn'lɤkəɪ
**sp** vnluckie[4], vnlucky[1]
> lucky

**unmade** *adj*
'ɤnmɛ:d
**sp** vnmade[1]
> make

**unmake** *v*
'ɤnmɛ:k
**sp** vnmake[2]
> make

**unmanly** *adj*
ɤn'manləɪ
**sp** vnmanly[4]
> manly

**unmanned** *adj*
ɤn'mand
**sp** vnman'd[1], vnmann'd[1]
> man

**unmannered** *adj*
ɤn'manəɹd
**sp** vnmanner'd[2]
> manner

**unmannerly** *adj / adv*
*m* ɤn'manəɹˌləɪ, -ɹl-
**sp** vnmannerly[8], vn-mannerly[1] / vnmannerly[4]
**rh** by *1H4 1.3.42*
> manner

**unmarried** *adj*
ɤn'marəɪd
**sp** vnmarried[1]
> marry

**unmask** *v*
ɤn'mask
**sp** vnmaske[2]
> mask

**unmastered** *adj*
ɤn'mastəɹd
**sp** vnmastred[1]
> master

**unmatchable** *adj*
*m* ɤn'maʧəbəl, -ˌbɤl
**sp** vnmatchable[3], vnmatcheable[1]
> match

**unmatched** *adj*
*m* ɤn'maʧt, -ʧɪd
**sp** vnmatch'd[2], vnmatched[2]
> match

**unmeasurable** *adj*
*m* ɤn'mezəɹəbəl, -ˌbɤl
**sp** vnmeasurable[1], vnmeasureable[1]
> measure

**unmeet** *adj*
ɤn'mi:t
**sp** vnmeet[3], vnmeete[2]
**rh** sweet *LLL 4.3.111, PP 16.13*
> meet

**unmellowed** *adj*
ɤn'meləd, -lo:d
**sp** vn-mellowed[1]
> mellow

**unmerciful** *adj*
ɤn'mɐːɹsɪfəl
**sp** vnmercifull[1]
> merciful

**unmeritable** *adj*
*m* ɤn'merɪˌtabəl
**sp** vnmeritable[2]
> merit

**unmeriting** *adj*
ɤn'merɪtɪn, -ɪŋ
**sp** vn-meriting[1]
> merit

**unminded** *adj*
ɤn'məɪndɪd
**sp** vnminded[1]
> mind

**unmindful** *adj*
ɤn'məɪndfʊl
**sp** vnmindfull[1]
> mind

**unmingled** *adj*
ɤn'mɪŋgəld
**sp** vnmingled[2]
> mingle

**unmitigable** *adj*
*m* ɤn'mɪtɪˌgabəl
**sp** vnmittigable[1]
> mitigate

**unmitigated** *adj*
ɤn'mɪtɪˌgɛːtɪd
**sp** vnmittigated[1]
> mitigate

**unmix / ~ed** *v*
ɤn'mɪkst
**sp** vnmixt[1]
> mix

**unmoaned** *adj*
ɤn'moːnd
**sp** vnmoan'd[1]
> moan

**unmoved** *adj*
ɤn'mɤvd, -'muːvd
**sp** vnmou'd[1]
> move

**unmusical** *adj*
*m* ɤn'mjuːzɪˌkɑl
**sp** vnmusicall[1]
> musical

**unmuzzle** *v*
ɤn'mɤzəl
**sp** vnmuzzle[1]
> muzzle

**unmuzzled** *adj*
ɤn'mɤzəld
**sp** vnmuzled[1]
> muzzle

**unnatural** *adj*
*m* ɤn'natrəl, -tər-, -təˌrɑl
**sp** vnnaturall[37]
> natural

**unnaturally** *adv*
*m* ɤn'natrəˌləɪ
**sp** vnnaturally[1]
> naturally

**unneath** *adv*
ɤn'iːθ
**sp** vnneath[1]

**unnecessarily** *adv*
*m* ɤnˌnesɪ'sarɪˌləɪ
**sp** vnnecessarily[1]
> necessarily

**unnecessary** *adj*
*m* ɤn'nesɪˌsarəɪ, -ɪsrəɪ
**sp** vnnecessarie[1], vnnecessary[2]
> necessary

**unneighbourly** *adv*
*m* ɤn'nɛːbəɹˌləɪ
**sp** vn-neighbourly[1]
> neighbourly

**unnerved** *adj*
*m* ɤn'nɐːɹvɪd
**sp** vnnerued[1]
> nerve

**unnoble** *adj*
ɤn'noːbəl
**sp** vnnoble[1]
> noble

**unnoted** *adj*
ɤn'noːtɪd
**sp** vnnoted[2]
> note

**unnumbred** *adj*
ɤn'nɤmbəɹd
**sp** vnnumbred[2]
> number

**unowed** *adj*
*m* 'ɤnoːd
**sp** vn-owed[1]
> owe

**unpack** *v*
ɤn'pak
**sp** vnpacke[1]
> pack

**unpaid / ~-for** *adj*
ɤn'pɛːd / -ˌfɔːɹ
**sp** vnpaid[1], vnpaide[1] / vnpayd-for[1]
> unpay

**unparagoned** *adj*
*m* ɤn'parəˌgɒnd, -əgənd
**sp** vnparagon'd[2]
> paragon

**unparalelled** *adj*
*m* ɤn'parəˌleld
**sp** vnparalell'd[2], vnparallell'd[1]
> parallel

**unpardonable** *adj*
*m* ɤn'pɑːɹdəˌnabəl
**sp** vnpardonable[1]
> pardon

**unpartial** *adj*
ɤn'pɑːɹsɪɑl
**sp** vnpartiall[1]
> partial

**unpathed** *adj*
*m* 'ɤnpaθt
**sp** vnpath'd[1]
> path

**unpaved** *adj*
*m* 'ɤnpɛ:vd
**sp** vnpaued[1]
> pave

**unpay / unpaid** *v*
ɤn'pɛ: / -d
**sp** vnpay[1] / vnpayd[1]
> unpaid

**unpeaceable** *adj*
ɤn'pi:səbəl, -'pɛ:s-
**sp** vnpeaceable[1]
> peaceable

**unpeg** *v*
ɤn'peg
**sp** vnpegge[1]
> peg

**unpeople** *v*
ɤn'pi:pəl
**sp** vnpeople[2], vn-people[1], vnpeo-ple[1]
> people

**unpeopled** *adj*
ɤn'pi:pəld
**sp** vn-peopel'd[1], vnpeopled[2]
> people

**unperfectness** *n*
ɤn'pɐ:ɹfɪtnəs
**sp** vnperfectnesse[1]
> perfect

**unpicked** *adj*
ɤn'pɪkt
**sp** vnpickt[1]
> pick

**unpin** *v*
ɤn'pɪn
**sp** vn-pin[2]
> pin

**unpinked** *adj*
ɤn'pɪŋkt
**sp** vnpinkt[1]
> pink

**unpitied** *adj*
ɤn'pɪtəɪd
**sp** vnpittied[4]
> pity

**unpitifully** *adv*
ɤn'pɪtɪfləɪ, -fʊl-
**sp** vnpittifully[1]
> pitiful

**unplagued** *adj*
ɤn'plɛ:gd
**sp** vnplagu'd[1]
> plague

**unplausive** *adj*
ɤn'plɔ:zɪv
**sp** vnplausiue[1]
> plausive

**unpleasant / ~est** *adj*
ɤn'plezənst, -ntst
**sp** vnpleasant'st[1]
> pleasant

**unpleased** *adj*
ɤn'pli:zd
**sp** vnpleas'd[1]
> please

**unpleasing** *adj*
ɤn'pli:zɪn, -ɪŋ
**sp** vnpleasing[6]
> please

**unpolicied** *adj*
ɤn'pɒlɪsəɪd
**sp** vnpolicied[1]
> policy

**unpolished** *adj*
ɤn'pɒlɪʃt
**sp** vnpolished[1], vnpolisht[1], vnpollisht[1]
> polished

**unpolluted** *adj*
'ɤnpə'lu:tɪd
**sp** vnpolluted[1]
> pollute

**unpossessing** *adj*
'ɤnpə'zesɪn, -ɪŋ
**sp** vnpossessing[1]
> possessing

**unpossesed** *adj*
'ɤnpə'zest
**sp** vnpossest[1]
> possess

**unpractised** *adj*
ɤn'praktɪst
**sp** vnpractis'd[1], vnpractiz'd[1]
> practice

**unpregnant** *adj*
ɤn'pregnənt
**sp** vnpregnant[2]
> pregnant

**unpremeditated** *adj*
*m* 'ɤnprɪ'medɪˌtɛ:tɪd
**sp** vnpremeditated[1]
> premeditate

**unprepared** *adj*
'ɤnprɪ'pɛ:ɹd, -'pɑ:ɹd
**sp** vnprepar'd[2], vnpre-par'd[1], vnprepared[2]
> prepare

**unpressed** *adj*
ɤn'prest
**sp** vnprest[1]
> press

**unprevailing** *adj*
'ɤnprɪ'vɛ:lɪn, -ɪŋ
**sp** vnpreuayling[1]
> prevail

**unprevented** *adj*
'ɤnprɪ'ventɪd
**sp** vnpreuented[1]
> prevent

**unprizable** *adj*
*m* ɤn'prəɪzəbəl, -ˌbɤl
**sp** vnprizable[1], vnprizea-ble[1]
> prize

**unprized** *adj*
'ɤnprəɪzd
**sp** vnpriz'd[1]
> prize

**unprofitable** *adj*
*m* ɤn'prɒfɪtˌabəl

**sp** vnprofitable[4]
> profitable

**unprofited** *adj*
ɤn'prɒfɪtɪd
**sp** vnprofited[1]
> profit

**unproper** *adj*
ɤn'prɒpəɹ
**sp** vnproper[1]
> proper

**unproperly** *adv*
*m* ɤn'prɒpəɹ,ləɪ
**sp** vnproperly[1]
> properly

**unproportioned** *adj*
'ɤnprə'pɔ:ɹsɪənd
**sp** vnproportion'd[1]
> proportion

**unprovide** *v*
'ɤnprə'vəɪd
**sp** vnpro-uide[1]
> provide

**unprovided** *adj / adv*
'ɤnprə'vəɪdɪd
**sp** vnprouided[3] / vnprouided[3]
> provide

**unprovident** *S* *adj*
*m* ɤn'prɒvɪ,dent
**sp** vnprouident[1]
**rh** evident *S 10.2*
> provident

**unprovoke / ~s** *v*
'ɤnprə'vo:ks
**sp** vnprouokes[1]
> provoke

**unpruned** *adj*
*m* ɤn'pru:nɪd, -nd
**sp** vnpruin'd[1], vnpruned[2]
> prune

**unpublished** *adj*
ɤn'pɤblɪʃt
**sp** vnpublish'd[1]
> publish

**unpurged** *adj*
*m* ɤn'pɐ:ɹʤɪd
**sp** vnpurged[1]
> purge

**unpurposed** *adj*
ɤn'pɐ:ɹpəst
**sp** vnpurpos'd[1]
> purpose

**unqualitied** *adj*
ɤn'kwɑlɪtəɪd
**sp** vnqualitied[1]
> quality

**unqueened** *adj*
ɤn'kwi:nd
**sp** vnqueen'd[1]
> queen

**unquestionable** *adj*
ɤn'kwestɪənəbəl
**sp** vnquestionable[1]
> questionable

**unquestioned** *adj*
ɤn'kwestɪənd
**sp** vnquestion'd[2]
> question

**unquiet** *adj*
ɤn'kwəɪət
**sp** vnquiet[7]
> quiet

**unquietly** *adv*
ɤn'kwəɪətləɪ
**sp** vnquietly[1]
> quietly

**unquietness** *n*
*m* ɤn'kwəɪətnəs, -,nes
**sp** vnquietnesse[2]
> quietness

**unraised** *adj*
*m* ɤn'rɛ:zɪd
**sp** vnraysed[1]
> raise

**unraked** *adj*
ɤn'rɛ:kt
**sp** vnrak'd[1]
> rake

**unread** *n*
ɤn'red
**sp** vn-read[1]
> read

**unready** *adj*
ɤn'redəɪ
**sp** vnreadie[1], vnready[2]
> ready

**unreal** *adj*
ɤn'ri:ɑl
**sp** vnreall[2]
> real

**unreasonable** *adj*
*m* ɤn'rɛ:zə,nabəl, -znəbəl
**sp** vnreasonable[4]
> reasonable

**unreasonably** *adv*
*m* ɤn'rɛ:zə,nabləɪ
**sp** vnreasonably[1]
> reasonably

**unreclaimed** *adj*
*m* 'ɤnrɪ'klɛ:mɪd
**sp** vnreclaim'd[1]
> reclaim

**unreconciled** *adj*
ɤn'rekənsəɪld
**sp** vnreconcil'd[1]
> reconcile

**unreconciliable** *adj*
ɤn,rekən'səɪləbəl
**sp** vnreconciliable[1]
> reconcile

**unrecounted** *adj*
'ɤnrɪ'kəʊntɪd
**sp** vnrecounted[1]
> recount

**unrecuring** *adj*
'ɤnrɪ'kju:ɹɪn, -ɪŋ
**sp** vnrecuring[1]
> recure

**unregarded** *adj*
'ɤnrɪ'gɑ:ɹdɪd
**sp** vnregarded[1]
> regard

**unregister / ~ed** *v*
*m* ɤn'redʒɪˌstɐ:ɹd
**sp** vnregistred[1]
> register

**unrelenting** *adj*
'ɤnrɪ'lentɪn, -ɪŋ
**sp** vnrelenting[2], vn-relenting[1]
> relent

**unremovable** *adj*
'ɤnrɪ'mɤvəbəl, -mu:v-
**sp** vnremoueable[1]
> remove

**unremovably** *adj*
'ɤnrɪ'mɤvəbləɪ, -mu:v-
**sp** vnremoueably[1]
> remove

**unreprievable** *adj*
*m* 'ɤnrɪ'pri:vəˌbɤl
**sp** vnrepreeuable[1]
> reprieve

**unresolved** *adj*
'ɤnrɪ'sɒlvd, -'z-
**sp** vnresolu'd[1]
> resolve

**unrespected** *S* *adj*
'ɤnrɪ'spektɪd
**sp** unrespected[2]
**rh** directed *S 43.2*

**unrespective** *adj*
'ɤnrɪ'spektɪv
**sp** vnrespectiue[2]
> respect

**unrest** *n*
ɤn'rest
**sp** vnrest[6]
**rh** best *RJ 1.5.120*; breast *Luc 1725*; chest *Tit 2.3.8*; expressed *S 147.10*; west *R2 2.4.22*
> rest

**unrestored** *adj*
'ɤnrɪ'stɔ:ɹd
**sp** vnrestor'd[1]
> restore

**unrestrained** *adj*
*m* 'ɤnrɪ'strɛ:nɪd
**sp** vnrestrained[1]
> restrain

**unrevenged** *adj*
'ɤnrɪ'vendʒd
**sp** vnreueng'd[2]
> revenge

**unreverend** *adj*
ɤn'revrənd, -vər-
**sp** vnreuerend[3]
> reverence

**unreverent** *adj*
ɤn'revrənt, -vər-
**sp** vnreuerent[3]
> reverent

**unreversed** *adj*
'ɤnrɪ'vɐ:ɹst
**sp** vn-reuerst[1]
> reverse

**unrewarded** *adj*
'ɤnrɪ'wɑ:ɹdɪd
**sp** vn-rewarded[1]
> reward

**unrighteous** *adj*
ɤn'rəɪtɪəs
**sp** vnrighteous[1]
> righteous

**unrightful** *adj*
ɤn'rəɪtfʊl
**sp** vnrightfull[1]
> rightful

**unrip / ~est** *v*
ɤn'rɪps, -st
**sp** vnrip'st[1]
> ripe

**unripe** *adj*
ɤn'rəɪp
**sp** vnripe[1]
> ripe

**unrivalled** *adj*
ɤn'rəɪvəld
**sp** vn-riual'd[1]
> rival

**unroll / ~ed** *v*
ɤn'ro:l / -d
**sp** vnrowle[1] / vnrold[1]
> roll

**unroof / ~ed** *v*
ɤn'ru:ft, -'rʊ-
**sp** *Cor 1.1.216 emend of* unroo'st
> roof

**unroost / ~ed** *v*
ɤn'ru:stɪd
**sp** vnroosted[1]

**unroot** *v*
ɤn'ru:t
**sp** vnroote[1]
> root

**unrough** *adj*
*m* 'ɤnrɤf
**sp** vnruffe[1]
> rough

**unruly** *adj*
ɤn'ru:ləɪ
**sp** vnruly[12], vn-ruly[1]

**unsafe** *adj*
ɤn'sɛ:f
**sp** vnsafe[4]
> safe

**unsaluted** *adj*
'ɤnsə'lu:tɪd
**sp** vnsaluted[1]
> salute

**unsanctified** *adj*
*m* ɤn'saŋktɪˌfəɪd
**sp** vnsanctified[3]
> sanctify

**unsatiate** *adj*
ɤn'sasɪət
**sp** vnsatiate[1]
> satiate

**unsatisfied** *adj / n*
*m* ɤn'satɪsˌfəɪd
**sp** vnsatisfi'd[1], vnsatisfied[4] / vnsatisfied[1]
> satisfy

**unsavoury** *adj*
ɤn'sɛ:vrəɪ, -vər-
**sp** vnsauorie[1], vnsauory[1], vnsauoury[1]
> savoury

**unsay** *v*
ɤn'sɛ:
**sp** vnsay[3], vnsay't [unsay it][1]
**rh** away *MND 1.1.181*
> say

**unscalable** *adj*
*m* ɤn'skɛ:ləˌbɤl
**sp** vnskaleable[1]
> scale

**unscanned** *adj*
*m* 'ɤnskand
**sp** vnskan'd[1]
> scan

**unscarred** *adj*
*m* ɤn'skɑ:ɹd, 'ɤnskɑ:ɹd
**sp** vnscarr'd[2]
> scar

**unschooled** *adj*
ɤn'sku:ld
**sp** vnschool'd[2]
> school

**unscorched** *adj*
ɤn'skɔ:ɹʧt
**sp** vnscorch'd[1]
> scorch

**unscoured** *adj*
'ɤnsko:ɹd
**sp** vn-scowr'd[1]
> scour

**unscratched** *adj*
ɤn'skraʧt
**sp** vnscratch'd[1]
> scratch

**unseal / ~ed** *v*
ɤn'si:l / -d
**sp** vnseale[4] / vnseal'd[1]
> seal

**unseam / ~ed** *v*
ɤn'si:md
**sp** vnseam'd[1]
> seam

**unsearched** *adj*
ɤn'sɐ:ɹʧt
**sp** vnsearcht[1]
> search

**unseasonable** *adj*
*m* ɤn'sɛ:zəˌnabəl, -znəbəl
**sp** vnseasonable[3]
> season

**unseasonably** *adv*
ɤn'sɛ:znəbləɪ, -zən-
**sp** vnseasonably[1]
> season

**unseasoned** *adj*
ɤn'sɛ:zənd
**sp** vnseason'd[3]
> season

**unseconded** *adj*
ɤn'sekəndɪd
**sp** vn-seconded[1]
> second

**unsecret** *adj*
ɤn'si:krət
**sp** vnsecret[1]
> secret

**unseduced** *adj*
'ɤnsɪ'dju:st
**sp** vnse-duc'd[1]
> seduce

**unseeing** *adj*
ɤn'si:ɪn, -ɪŋ
**sp** vnseeing[1]
> see

**unseem / ~ing** *v*
ɤn'si:mɪn, -ɪŋ
**sp** vnseeming[1]
> seeming

**unseemly** *adj*
ɤn'si:mləɪ
**sp** vnseemely[1]
> seemly

**unseen** *adj*
ɤn'si:n
**sp** vnseene[15], vn-seene[1]
**rh** keen *S 118.3*
> see

**unseminared** *adj*
*m* ɤn'semɪˌnɑ:ɹd
**sp** vnseminar'd[1]

**unseparable** *adj*
*m* ɤn'sepəˌrabəl
**sp** vnseparable[1]
> separate

**unserviceable** *adj*
ɤn'sɐ:ɹvɪsəbəl
**sp** vn-seruiceable[1]
> service

**unset** *v*
ɤn'set
**sp** vnset[1]
**rh** counterfeit *S 16.6*
> set

**unsettle** *v*
ɤn'setl
**sp** vnsettle[1]
> settle

**unsettled** *adj*
ɤn'setld
**sp** vnsetled[6]
> settle

**unsevered** *adj*
ɤn'sɛ:vəɹd
**sp** vnseuer'd[1]
> sever

**unsex** *v*
ɤn'seks
**sp** vnsex[1]
> sex

**unshake·d / ~n** *adj*
ɤn'ʃɛ:k·t / -ən
**sp** vnshak'd[2] / vnshaken[2]
> shake

**unshape / ~s** *v*
ɤn'ʃɛ:ps
**sp** vnshapes[1]
> shape

**unshaped** *adj*
*m* ɤn'ʃɛ:pɪd
**sp** vnshaped[1]
> shape

**unsheath** *v*
ɤn'ʃi:ð
**sp** vnsheath[3]
> sheath

**unsheathed** *adj*
ɤn'ʃi:ðd
**sp** vnsheath'd[1]
**rh** breathed, bequeathed *Luc 1724*
> sheath

**unshout** *v*
ɤn'ʃəʊt
**sp** vnshoot[1]
> shoot

**unshown** *adj*
ɤn'ʃo:n
**sp** vnshewne[1]
> show

**unshrinking** *adj*
ɤn'ʃrɪŋkɪn, -ɪŋ
**sp** vnshrinking[1]
> shrink

**unshrubbed** *adj*
'ɤnʃrɤbd
**sp** vnshrubd[1]
> shrub

**unshunnable** *adj*
*m* ɤn'ʃɤnə,bɤl
**sp** vnshunnable[1]
> shun

**unshunned** *adj*
*m* 'ɤnʃɤnd
**sp** vnshun'd[1]
> shun

**unsifted** *adj*
ɤn'sɪftɪd
**sp** vnsifted[1]
> sift

**unsightly** *adj*
ɤn'səɪtləɪ
**sp** vnsightly[1]
> sight

**unsinewed** *adj*
ɤn'sɪnju:d
**sp** vnsinnowed[1]
> sinew

**unsisting** *adj*
ɤn'sɪstɪn, -ɪŋ
**sp** vnsisting[1]

**unskilful** *adj / n*
ɤn'skɪlfʊl
**sp** vnskilfull[2], vnskillfull[1] / vnskil-full[1]
> skilful

**unskilfully** *adv*
ɤn'skɪlfləɪ, -fʊl-
**sp** vnskilfully[1]
> skilfully

**unslipping** *adj*
ɤn'slɪpɪn, -ɪŋ
**sp** vn-slipping[1]
> slip

**unsmirched** *adj*
*m* ɤn'smɐ:ɹʧɪd
**sp** vnsmirched[1]
> smirch

**unsoiled** *adj*
*m* 'ɤnsəɪld
**sp** vnsoild[1]
> soil

**unsolicited** *adj*
*m* 'ɤnsə'lɪsɪ,tɪd, -stɪd
**sp** vnsolicited[1], vnsollicited[1]
> solicit

**unsorted** *adj*
ɤn'sɔ:ɹtɪd
**sp** vnsorted[1]
> sort

**unsought** *adj*
ɤn'sɔ:t
**sp** vnsought[3]
> seek

**unsound** *adj*
ɤn'səʊnd
**sp** vnsound[1]
> sound

**unsounded** *adj*
ɤn'səʊndɪd
**sp** vnsounded[2]
> sound

**unspeak** *adj*
ɤn'spi:k, -pɛ:k, -pek
**sp** vnspeake[1]
> speak

**unspeakable** *adj*
*m* ɤn'spi:kəbəl, -ə,bɤl, -pɛ:k-, -pek-
**sp** vnspeakable[3], vnspeakeable[2]
> speak

**unspeaking** *adj*
ɤn'spi:kɪn, -ɪŋ, -pɛ:k-, -pek-
**sp** vnspeaking[1]
> speak

**unsphere** *v*
ɤn'sfi:ɹ
**sp** vnsphere[1]
> sphere

**unspoke / ~n** *adj*
ɤn'spo:k / -ən
**sp** vnspoke[1] / vnspoken[1]
> speak

**unspotted** *adj*
ɤn'spɒtɪd
**sp** vnspotted[4]
**rh** allotted, rotted *Luc 821*
> spotted

**unsquared** *adj*
ɤn'skwɛ:ɹd
**sp** vnsquar'd[1]
> square

**unstable** *adj*
ɤn'stɛːbəl
**sp** vnstable[1]
> stable

**unstaid** *adj*
*m* ɤn'stɛːd, 'ɤnstɛːd
**sp** vnstaid[3]
> staid

**unstained** *adj*
*m* ɤn'stɛːnd, 'ɤnstɛːnɪd
**sp** vnstain'd[1], vnstained[3]
> stain

**unstanched** *adj*
*m* 'ɤnstanʧt, ɤn'stanʧɪd
**sp** vnstanched[2]
> stanch

**unstate** *v*
ɤn'stɛːt
**sp** vnstate[2]
> state

**unsteadfast** *adj*
ɤn'stedfast
**sp** vnstedfast[1]
> steadfast

**unstooping** *adj*
ɤn'stuːpɪn, -ɪŋ
**sp** vn-stooping[1]
> stooping

**unstringed** *adj*
*m* ɤn'strɪŋɪd
**sp** vnstringed[1]
> string

**unstuffed** *adj*
*m* 'ɤnstɤft
**sp** vnstuft[1]
> stuffed

**unsubstantial** *adj*
'ɤnsəb'stansɪɑl
**sp** vnsubstantiall[2]
> substantial

**unsuitable** *adj*
ɤn'ʃuːtəbəl, -'sjuː-
**sp** vnsuteable[2]
> suitable

**unsullied** *adj*
ɤn'sɤləɪd
**sp** vnsallied[1]
> sully

**unsunned** *adj*
'ɤnsɤnd
**sp** vn-sunn'd[1]
> sun

**unsure** *adj*
*m* ɤn'ʃuːɹ, 'ɤnʃuːɹ
**sp** vnsure[5]
**rh** endure *TN 2.3.47*
> sure

**unsured** *adj*
ɤn'ʃuːɹd
**sp** vnsur'd[1]
> sure

**unsuspected** *adj*
'ɤnsə'spektɪd
**sp** vnsuspected[2]
> suspect

**unswayable** *adj*
*m* ɤn'swɛːəˌbɤl
**sp** vnswayable[1]
> sway

**unswayed** *adj*
ɤn'swɛːd
**sp** vnsway'd[1]
> sway

**unswear** *v*
ɤn'swɛːɹ
**sp** vn-sweare[2]
> swear

**unswept** *adj*
ɤn'swept
**sp** vnswept[2]
**rh** *1* heaped *Cor 2.3.118*; **rh** *2* leap *MW 5.5.44*
> sweep

**unsworn** *adj*
ɤn'swɔːɹn
**sp** vnsworne[1]
> swear

**untainted** *adj*
ɤn'tɛːntɪd
**sp** vntainted[4]
> tainted

**untalked-of** *adj*
ɤn'tɔːkt-ˌɒv
**sp** vntalkt of[1]
> talk

**untangle / ~d** *v*
ɤn'taŋgəl / -d
**sp** vntangle[1] / vntangled[1]
> tangle

**untasted** *adj*
ɤn'tastɪd
**sp** vntasted[1]
> taste

**untaught** *adj / n*
*m* ɤn'tɔːt, 'ɤntɔːt / ɤn'tɔːt
**sp** vntaught[3], vn-taught[1] / vntaught[1]
> teach

**untempering** *adj*
ɤn'temprɪn, -ɪŋ, -pər-
**sp** vntempering[1]
> temper

**untender / ~ed** *adj*
ɤn'tendəɹ / -d
**sp** vntender[2] / vntender'd[1]
> tender

**untent** *v*
ɤn'tent
**sp** vntent[1]
> tent

**untented** *adj*
ɤn'tentɪd
**sp** vntented[1]
> tented

**unthankful** *adj*
ɤn'θaŋkfʊl
**sp** vnthankfull[1]
> thankful

**unthankfulness** *n*
*m* ɤn'θaŋkfʊl,nes, -lnəs
**sp** vnthankefulnesse[1], vnthankfulnes[1], vnthankfulnesse[1]
> thankfulness

**unthink** *v*
ɤn'θɪŋk
**sp** vnthinke[1]
> think

**unthought-of** *adj*
ɤn'θɔ:t-,ɒv
**sp** vnthought-of[1], vnthought of[1]
> think

**unthought-on** *adj*
ɤn'θɔ:t-,ɒn
**sp** vnthought-on[1]
> think

**unthread** *v*
ɤn'θred
**sp** vnthred[1]
> thread

**unthrift** *adj*
*m* 'ɤnθrɪft, ɤn'θrɪft
**sp** vnthrift[2]
> thrift

**unthrift / ~s** *n*
'ɤnθrɪfts
**sp** vnthrifts[1]
> thrift

**unthrifty** *adj*
ɤn'θrɪftəɪ
**sp** vnthriftie[3]
> thrifty

**untie** *v*
ɤn'təɪ
**sp** vntie[2], vnty[1], vntye[4]
**rh** I *TN 2.2.41*
> tie

**untied** *adj*
ɤn'təɪd
**sp** vnti'de[1]
> tie

**until** *prep*
=
**sp** vntil[2], vntill[72]
**rh** hill *Mac 4.1.91*
> till

**untimbered** *adj*
ɤn'tɪmbəɹd
**sp** vntimber'd[1]
> timbered

**untimely** *adj / adv*
ɤn'təɪmləɪ
**sp** vntimely[10] / vntimely[9]
> timely

**untirable** *adj*
ɤn'təɪrəbəl
**sp** vntyreable[1]
> tire

**untired** *adj*
*m* ɤn'təɪɹd, 'ɤntəɪɹd
**sp** vntyr'd[2]
> tired

**untitled** *adj*
ɤn'təɪtld
**sp** vntitled[1]
> titled

**unto** *prep*
*m* ɤn'tu:, 'ɤntu:
**sp** vnto[422], vn-to[1], vntoo't [unto it][3]
**rh** woo *emend of LC 181* vow; unto her woo her *VA 307*; unto him to woo him *VA 5*

**untold** *Luc, S* *adj*
ɤn'to:ld
**sp** vntold[2]
**rh** behold, unfold *Luc 753*; hold *S 136.9*
> tell

**untouched** *adj*
ɤn'tɤʧt
**sp** vntouch'd[1], vntoucht[1]
> touch

**untoward** *adj*
ɤn'to:ɹd
**sp** vntoward[2]
**rh** froward *TS 4.5.79*
> toward

**untowardly** *adv*
ɤn'to:ɹdləɪ
**sp** vntowardly[1]
> toward

**untraded** *adj*
ɤn'trɛ:dɪd
**sp** vntraded[1]
> trade

**untrained** *adj*
ɤn'trɛ:nd
**sp** vntrained[1], vntrayn'd[1]
> train

**untread** *v*
ɤn'tred
**sp** vntread[2]
> tread

**untreasured** *adj*
ɤn'trezəɹd
**sp** vntreasur'd[1]
> treasured

**untried** *adj*
ɤn'trəɪd
**sp** vntride[1]
**rh** slide *WT 4.1.6*
> try

**untrimmed** *adj*
*m* ɤn'trɪmɪd, *S* ɤn'trɪmd
**sp** vntrimmed[1], *S* vntrim'd[1]
**rh** dimmed *S 18.8*
> trim

**untrod / ~den** *adj*
*m* 'ɤntrɒd / ɤn'trɒdən
**sp** vntrod[1] / vntroden[1]
> untread

**untroubled** *adj*
ɤn'trɤbəld
**sp** vntroubled[1]
> troubled

**untrue** *adj*
ɤn'tru:
**sp** vntrue[4]
**rh** grew *LC 169*; you *AW 5.3.315, Cym 1.6.86, LLL 5.2.473, S 72.10, 113.14*
> true

**untrussing** *n*
ɤn'trɤsɪn, -ɪŋ
**sp** vntrussing[1]
> truss

**untruth / ~s** *n*
ɤn'tru:θ / -s
**sp** vntruth[1] / vntruths[3]
> truth

**untune** *v*
ɤn'tju:n
**sp** vn-tune[1]
> tune

**untuneable** *adj*
*m* ɤn'tju:nəbəl, -əˌbɤl
**sp** vntunable[1], vn-tuneable[1]
> tuneable

**untuned** *adj*
'ɤntju:nd
**sp** vntun'd[3]
> tune

**untutored** *adj*
ɤn'tju:təɹd
**sp** vntutor'd[1], vntutur'd[1]
> tutor

**untwine / ~d** *v*
ɤn'twəɪn / -d
**sp** vntwine[1] / vntwin'd[1]
**rh** vine *Cym 4.2.59*
> twine

**unurged** *adj*
*m* ɤn'ɐ:ɹʤd, 'ɤnɐ:ɹʤd
**sp** vn-urg'd[1], vn-vrg'd[1]
> urge

**unused** *adj*
*m* ɤn'ju:zɪd
**sp** vn-vsed[1]
> use

**unusual** *adj*
ɤn'ju:zwɑl, -zɑl
**sp** vnusall[1], vnusuall[3], vnvsuall[2]
> usual

**unvalued** *adj*
ɤn'valjəd, -ju:d
**sp** vnuallued[1], vnvalewed[1],
> value

**unvanquished** *adj*
ɤn'vaŋkwɪʃt
**sp** vn-vanquisht[1]
> vanquish

**unvarnished** *adj*
ɤn'vɑ:ɹnɪʃt
**sp** vn-varnish'd[1]
> varnish

**unveil** *v*
ɤn'vɛ:l
**sp** vnuaile[1]
> veil

**unvenerable** *adj*
ɤn'venrəbəl, -nər-
**sp** vnvenerable[1]
> venerable

**unvexed** *adj*
ɤn'vekst
**sp** vn-vext[1]
> vex

**unviolated** *adj*
*m* ɤn'vəɪəˌlɛ:tɪd
**sp** vnuiolated[1]
> violate

**unvirtuous** *adj*
ɤn'vɐ:ɹtjəs
**sp** vnuertuous[1]
> virtue

**unvisited** *adj*
ɤn'vɪzɪtɪd
**sp** vnuisited[1]
> violate

**unvulnerable** *adj*
*m* ɤn'vɤlnrəˌbɤl
**sp** vnvulnerable[1]
> invulnerable, vulnerable

**unwares** *adj*
ɤn'wɑ:ɹz
**sp** vnwares[1]
> ware

**unwarily** *adv*
ɤn'wɛ:rɪləɪ
**sp** vnwarily[1]
> wary

**unwashed** *adj*
ɤn'wɑʃt
**sp** vnwash'd[2], vnwasht[1]
> wash

**unwatched** *adj*
ɤn'wɑʧt
**sp** vnwatch'd[1]
> watch

**unwearied** *adj*
ɤn'wi:rəɪd, -'we-
**sp** vnwearied[1]
> weary

**unwed** *adj*
ɤn'wed
**sp** vnwed[1]
**rh** bed *CE 2.1.26*; head *PP 18.6*
> wed

**unwedgable** *adj*
*m* ɤn'weʤəˌbɤl
**sp** vn-wedgable[1]
> wedge

**unweeded** *adj*
ɤn'wi:dɪd
**sp** vnweeded[1]
> weed

**unweighed** *adj*
ɤn'wɛ:d
**sp** vnwaied[1]
> weigh

**unweighing** *adj*
ɤn'wɛ:ɪn, -ɪŋ
**sp** vnweighing[1]
> weigh

**unwelcome** *adj*
ɤn'welkəm
**sp** vnwelcom[1], vnwelcome[3], vn-welcome[1]
> welcome

**unwept** *adj*
ɤn'wept
**sp** vnwept[1]
> weep

**unwhip / ~ped** *v*
ɤn'ʍɪpt
**sp** vnwhipt[1]
> whip

**unwholesome** *adj*
ɤn'o:lsəm, -'ho:-
**sp** vnholdsome[1], vnwholesome[3], vnwholsome[3]
> wholesome

**unwieldy** *adj*
ɤn'wi:ldəɪ
**sp** vnwieldie[3]
> wield

**unwilling** *adj*
ɤn'wɪlɪn, -ɪŋ
**sp** vnwilling[8]
**rh** a-billing *VA 365*
> willing

**unwillingly** *adv*
*m* ɤn'wɪlɪn,ləɪ, -ɪŋ-
**sp** vnwillingly[7]
> willingly

**unwillingness** *n*
*m* ɤn'wɪlɪŋ,nes, -nəs
**sp** vnwillingnesse[3]
> willingness

**unwind** *v*
ɤn'wəɪnd
**sp** vnwind[1], vnwinde[1]
> wind

**unwiped** *adj*
ɤn'wəɪpt
**sp** vnwip'd[1]
> wipe

**unwise** *adj*
ɤn'wəɪz
**sp** vnwise[3]
> wise

**unwisely** *adv*
ɤn'wəɪzləɪ
**sp** vnwisely[1]
> wise

**unwish / ~ed** *v*
ɤn'wɪʃt
**sp** vnwisht[1]
> wish

**unwished** *adj*
*m* ɤn'wɪʃɪd
**sp** vnwished[1]
> wished

**unwit / ~ted** *v*
ɤn'wɪtɪd
**sp** vnwitted[1]
> wit

**unwittingly** *adv*
*m* ɤn'wɪtɪŋ,ləɪ
**sp** vnwittingly[1]
> wittingly

**unwonted** *adj*
ɤn'wo:ntɪd
**sp** vnwonted[2]
> wont

**unworthiest** *n*
ɤn'wɔ:ɹðɪəst
**sp** vnworthiest[1]
> worthiest

**unworthily** *adv*
*m* ɤn'wɔ:ɹðɪ,ləɪ
**sp** vnworthily[2]
> worthily

**unworthiness** *n*
*m* ɤn'wɔ:ɹðɪ,nes
**sp** vnworthinesse[4]
> worthiness

**unworth·y / ~ier / ~iest** *adj*
ɤn'wɔ:ɹðəɪ / -əɹ / -əst
**sp** vnworthie[2], [farre]-vnworthie[1], vnworthy[33] / vnworthier[1] / vnworthiest[1]
> worthy

**unwrung** *adj*
ɤn'rɤŋ
**sp** vnrung[1]
> wring

**unyoke** *v*
ɤn'jo:k
**sp** vnyoake[1], vnyoke[1]
> yoke

**unyoked** *adj*
*m* ɤn'jo:kt, 'ɤnjo:kt
**sp** vnyoak'd[2]
> yoke

**up** *adv, prep*
ɤp
**sp** vp[1021]
**rh** cup *S 114.10*
> up to

**upbraid / ~s / ~ed** *v*
ɤp'brɛ:d / -z / -ɪd
**sp** vpbraid[5], vpbraide[1], vpbraid's [upbraid us][1], vpbrayd[1], vpbray'd[1] / vpbraides[3] / vpbraided[3], vpbrayded[2]

**upbraiding / ~s** *n*
ɤp'brɛ:dɪnz, -ɪŋz
**sp** vpbraidings[2]

**upcast** *n*
'ɤpkast
**sp** vp-cast[1]
> cast

**upfill** *v*
ɤp'fɪl
**sp** vpfill[1]
> fill

**upheave / ~th** *VA* *v*
ɤp'i:vəθ / -'hi:
**sp** vpheaueth[1]
**rh** relieveth *VA 482*
> heave

**uphoard / ~ed** *v*
ɤp'o:ɹdɪd, -'ho:-
**sp** vp-hoorded[1]
> hoard

**uphold / ~s / ~eth / ~ing** *v*
ɤp'o:ld, -'ho:- / -z / -əθ / -ɪn, -ɪŋ
**sp** vphold[4] / vpholds[4] / vpholdeth[1] / vpholding[1]
**rh** cold *S 13.10*

**uplift / ~ed** *v*
ɤp'lɪft / -ɪd
**sp** vplift[2] / vplifted[2]
**rh** gift *Cym 5.4.103*

**uplifted** *adj*
ɤp'lɪftɪd
**sp** vp-lifted[2]

**upmost** *adj*
'ɤpmo:st
**sp** vpmost[1]

**upon** *prep*
=
**sp** vpon[1632], vpo[n][1], vp-on[9], vpon's[11], vpon't[27], vppon[24], vp-pon[1]
**rh** *1* gone *AW 3.4.6, MND 3.2.385*; upon you on you *Tem 4.1.108*; **rh** *2* moan *S 149.6*

**upper** *adj*
'ɤpəɹ
**sp** vpper[7]

**uprear** *S* *v*
*m* ɤp'ri:ɹ
**sp** vpreare[1]
**rh** here *S 49.11*
> rear

**upreared** *adj*
*m* ɤp'ri:ɹd, -i:rɪd
**sp** vprear'd[2], vp-reared[1]
> rear

**upright** *adj / adv*
*m* 'ɤprəɪt, ɤp'rəɪt
**sp** vpright[14] / vpright[8]
> right

**uprighteously** *adv*
ɤp'rəɪtɪəsləɪ
**sp** vprighteously[1]
> righteously

**uprightness** *n*
*m* ɤp'rəɪtnəs
**sp** vprightnesse[1]
> right

**uprise** *n*
*m* 'ɤprəɪz, ɤp'rəɪz
**sp** vprise[2]
> rise

**uprising** *n*
*m* ɤp'rəɪzɪn, -ɪŋ
**sp** vprising[1]
> rise

**uproar / ~s** *n*
ɤp'rɔ:ɹ / -z
**sp** vprore[2] / vprores[2]
> roar

**uproar** *v*
ɤp'rɔ:ɹ
**sp** vprore[1]
> roar

**uprouse / ~d** *v*
ɤp'rəʊzd
**sp** vprous'd[1]
> rouse

**upshoot** *n*
'ɤpʃu:t
**sp** vpshoot[1]
> shoot

**upshot** *n*
'ɤpʃɒt
**sp** vppe-shot[1], vpshot[1]

**upside down** *adv*
'ɤpsəɪd 'dəʊn
**sp** vpside downe[1]
> down

**upspring** *adj*
'ɤpsprɪŋ
**sp** vpspring[1]

**upstairs** *adv*
'ɤpstɛ:ɹz
**sp** vp-staires[1]
> stair

**up-staring** *adj*
ɤp'stɛ:rɪn, -ɪŋ
**sp** vp-staring[1]
> stare

**upstart** *adj / n*
'ɤpstɑ:ɹt
**sp** vpstart[1] / vpstart[1]

**upswarm / ~ed** *v*
ɤp'swɑ:ɹmd
**sp** vp-swarmed[1]
> swarm

**up to** *prep*
'ɤptə, -tʊ
**sp** vp to[18], vp to['th][1]
> up

**upturned** *adj*
*m* ɤp'tɑ:ɹnɪd
**sp** vpturned[1]
> turn

**upward** *adj / n*
'ɤpəɹd
**sp** vpward[2] / vpward[1]

**upward / ~s** *adv*
'ɤpəɹd / -z
**sp** vp-peer'd[1], vpward[9] /vpwards[1]

**urchin / ~s** *n*
'ɐ:ɹʧɪnz
**sp** vrchins[3]

**Urchinfield** *n*
'ɐ:ɹʧɪnfi:ld
**sp** Vrchinfield[1]

**urchin-show / ~s** *n*
'ɐ:ɹʧɪn-ˌʃo:z
**sp** vrchyn-shewes[1]
> show

**urg·e / ~est / ~es / ~ing / ~ed** *v*
ɐ:ɹʤ / 'ɐ:ɹʤ·əst / -ɪz / -ɪn, -ɪŋ / *m* -ɪd, ɐ:ɹʤd
**sp** vrge[32] / vrgest[2] / vrges[1] / vrging[7] / vrg'd[28], vrged[1]
**rh** purge *S 118.2* / purged *RJ 1.5.109*
> ill-urged, unurged

**urgent** *adj*
'ɐ:ɹʤənt
**sp** vrgent[2]

**urging** *n*
'ɐ:ɹʤɪn, -ɪŋ
**sp** vrging[2]

**urinal / ~s** *n*
'ju:rɪnɑl / -z
**sp** vrinal[1], vrinall[1], [castalion-king]-vrinall[1] / vrinalls[1]

**urine** *n*
'ju:rɪn
**sp** vrine[3]

**urn** *n*
ɐ:ɹn
**sp** vrne[3]

**Ursa Major** *n*
'ʊɹsə 'mɛ:dʒəɹ
**sp** Vrsa Maior[1]

**Ursula** *n*
'ɐ:ɹsjələ
**sp** Vrsula[15]

**us,** *abbr* **s** *pro*
=
**sp** us[1], *vs*[1670], *abbr* 's[245], s *with no apostrophe*[14]
**rh** *1* dangerous *Tim 3.5.74*; Demetrius *MND 1.1.220*; thus *LLL 5.2.119*; in us Proteus *TG 1.2.15*; **rh** *2* guess *LLL 5.2.119*
> we

**usage** *n*
=
**sp** vsage[10]

**usance / ~s** *n*
'ju:zəns, -ɔ:ns / -ɪz
**sp** vsance[2] / vsances[1]

**use / ~s** *n*
= [ju:s]
**sp** vse[103] / vses[8]
**rh** abuse *RJ 2.3.15, S 134.10, VA 164*; excuse *S 2.9*; Muse *S 78.3*; self-abuse *Mac 3.4.142*

**us·e / ~est / ~es / ~eth / ~ing / ~d** *v*
= [ju:z] / 'ju:z·əs, -st / -ɪz / -əθ / -ɪn, -ɪŋ / *m* -ɪd, ju:zd
**sp** vse[192] / vsest[4] / vses[9] / vseth[4] / vsing[7], v-sing[1] / vsd[1], vs'd[53], vsed[7]
**rh** abuse *S 4.7*; Muse *S 21.3, 82.3*; use it abuse it *Luc 862* / refusest *S 40.6* / abused *KL 1.3.20* [*Q*], *LLL 2.1.212, S 82.13*; confused *Oth 2.1.303*
> ill-, madly-, mis-, un-used

**used to** *aux v*
'ju:stə, -tʊ
**sp** vsd to[1], vs'd to[7], vse to[11]

**useful** *adj*
=
**sp** vsefull[2]

**useless** *adj*
=
**sp** vselesse[1]

**user** *Fr v*
y'ze
**sp** vser[1]

**usher / ~s** *n*
'ɤʃəɹ / -z
**sp** vsher[4] / vshers[1]

**usher / ~ed** *v*
'ɤʃəɹ / -d
**sp** vsher[1] / vsher'd[2]

**ushering** *n*
'ɤʃrɪn, -ɪŋ, -ʃər-
**sp** vshering[1]
**rh** sing *LLL 5.2.328*

**usual** *adj*
'ju:zwɑl, -zɑl
**sp** vsuall[6]
> unusual

**usually** *adv*
'ju:zwɑləɪ, -zɑl-
**sp** vsually[2]

**usurer / ~'s / ~s / ~s'** *n*
'ju:zjərəɹ, -zərəɹ, -zrəɹ / -z
**sp** vsurer[7] / vsurers[1], vsu-rers[1] / vsurers[2], vsu-rers[1] / vsurers[2]

**usuring** *adj*
'ju:zjərɪn, -ɪŋ, -zr-
**sp** vsuring[2]

**usurp / ~est / ~s / ~ing / ~ed** *v*
jʊ'zɐ:ɹp / -s, -st / -s / -ɪn, -ɪŋ / *m* -t, -ɪd
**sp** vsurp[1], vsurpe[19] / vsurp'st[3] / vsurpes[4] / vsur-ping[1] / vsurp'd[6], vsurped[1], vsurpt[6]
> long-usurped

**usurpation** *n*
*m* ˌju:zəɹ'pɛ:sɪən, -sɪˌɒn
**sp** vsurpation[3]

**usurper / ~'s / ~s** *n*
jʊ'zɐ:ɹpəɹ / -z
**sp** vsurper[6], vsurpers[2] / vsurpers[2]

**usurping** *adj / n*
jʊ'zɐ:ɹpɪn, -ɪŋ
**sp** vsurping[13] / vsurping[1]

**usurpingly** *adv*
jʊ'zɐ:ɹpɪnˌləɪ, -ɪŋ-
**sp** vsurpingly[1]

**usur·y / ~ies** *n*
*m* 'ju:zjərəɪ, -ˌrəɪ / -z
**sp** vsurie[2] / vsuries[2]
**rh** me *Tim 3.5.99*; thee *S 6.5*

**ut** *n*
ʊt
**sp** Cfavt [C fa ut][1]

**utensil / ~s** *n*
*m* 'ju:tənˌsɪl / -z
**sp** vtensile[1] / vtensils[1]

**utility** *n*
*m* ju:'tɪlɪˌtəɪ
**sp** vtilitie[1]

**utis** *n*
'ju:tɪs
**sp** vtis[1]

**utmost** *adj / n*
'ɤtmo:st
**sp** vtmost[13] / vtmost[4], vt-most[1]

**Utruvio** *n*
jʊ'tru:vɪo:
**sp** Vtru-uio[1]

**utter / ~s / ~eth / ~ing / ~ed** *v*
'ɤtəɹ / -z / -əθ, 'ɤtr- / -ɪn, -ɪŋ, 'ɤtr- / *m* -d, -ed
**sp** vtter[38] / vtters[5] / vttereth[1] / vttering[1] / vtter'd[4], vttered[7], vttred[3], vtt'red[2]
**rh** dead *MA 5.3.20*
> ill-uttering

**utterance** *n*
*m* 'ɤtrəns, -tər-, 'ɤtə,rans
**sp** vtterance[8], vttrance[1], vtt'rance[1]

**uttering** *n*
'ɤtrɪn, -ɪŋ, -tər-
**sp** vttering[1]

**utterly** *adv*
*m* 'ɤtəɹləɪ, ,ləɪ
**sp** vtterly[8]

**uttermost** *adj / n*
*m* 'ɤtəɹmo:st, ,mo:st
**sp** vttermost[1] / vttermost[7]

# V

**va** *Fr*
> aller

**vacancy** *n*
ˈvɛːkənˌsəɪ
**sp** vacancie[4]

**vacant** *adj*
ˈvɛːkənt
**sp** vacant[5]

**vacation** *n*
vəˈkɛːsɪən
**sp** vacation[1]

**vaded** *adj*
ˈvɛːdɪd
**sp** vaded[1]
**rh** shaded *PP 10.1*

**vagabond** *adj*
=
**sp** vagabond[2]

**vagabond / ~s** *n*
=
**sp** vagabond[2] / vagabonds[1]

**vagram** *adj*
ˈvɛːgrəm
**sp** vagram[1], vagrom[1]

**vail** *n / v*
vɛːl
**sp** vaile[1] / vaile[3], vale[3]

**vailed** *adj*
ˈvɛːlɪd
**sp** veyled[1]

**vailing** *adj*
ˈvɛːlɪn, -ɪŋ
**sp** vailing[3]

**vaillant** *Fr adj*
vaˈjɑ̃
**sp** valiant

**vain / ~er** *adj*
vɛːn / ˈvɛːnəɹ
**sp** vain[1], vaine[77] / vainer[1]
**rh** again *CE 3.2.27, 2H6 4.1.77, Luc 1665, MM 4.1.6, R2 2.2.141, 3.2.214, Tem 4.1.97, VA 771*; Aquitaine *LLL 1.1.137*; chain *CE 3.2.188*; pain *LLL 1.1.72, PP 20.19, R2 2.1.7*; slain *Luc 1044*

**vainglor·y / ~ies** *n*
*m* ˈvɛːnˌglɔːrəɪ, ˌvɛːnˈglɔːrəɪ / -z
**sp** vaine-glory[1], vainglorie[1], vainglory[1] / vaine-glories[1]
> glory

**vainly** *adv*
ˈvɛːnləɪ
**sp** vainly[6]

**vainness** *n*
ˈvɛːnəs
**sp** vainnesse[1], vain-nesse[1]

**vais** *Fr*
> aller

**valance** *n*
ˈvaləns
**sp** vallens[1]

**valanced** *adj*
ˈvalənst
*sp emend of Ham 2.2.422* valiant[1]

**vale / ~s** *n*
vɛːl / -z
**sp** vaile[1], vale[7] / vales[1]
**rh** pale, tale *LC 2*

**Valence** [name] *n*
ˈvaləns
**sp** Valence[1]

**Valentine / ~'s** *n*
ˈvaləntəɪn / -z
**sp** Valentine[67] / Valentines[4]
**rh** *1* mine *TG 5.4.125*; **rh** *2* betime *Ham 4.5.51*

**Valentinus** *n*
ˈvaləntəɪnəs
**sp** Valentinus[1]

**Valentio** *n*
vaˈlensɪoː
**sp** Valentio[1]

**Valentius** *n*
vaˈlensɪəs
**sp** Valencius[1]

**Valeria** *n*
vaˈliːrɪə
**sp** Valeria[6]

**Valerius** *n*
vaˈliːrɪəs
**sp** Valerius[1]

**valiant** *adj / n*
=
**sp** valiant[148], vali-ant[2], valliant[1] / valiant[4]
> active-, ever-, thrice-, tire-valiant

**valiantly** *adv*
ˈvalɪəntləɪ
**sp** valiantly[5]

**valiantness** *n*
=
**sp** valiantnesse[1]

**valiant-young** *adj*
'valɪənt-'jɒŋ
**sp** valiant young[1]

**validity** *n*
və'lɪdɪtəɪ
**sp** validitie[4], validity[1]
**rh** memory *Ham 3.2.199*

**valley / ~s** *n*
'valəɪ / -z
**sp** valley[3] / valleyes[3]

**valorous** *adj*
=, *Fluellen H5 3.2.74* 'falərəs
**sp** valorous[4], *Fluellen* falorous[1]

**valorously** *adv*
'valrəsləɪ, -lər-
**sp** valo-rously[1]

**valour / ~'s** *n*
'valər / -z
**sp** valor[10], valors [valour is][1], valour[92] / valors[2], valours[4]

**valuation** *n*
ˌvaljʊ'ɛ:sɪən
**sp** valewation[1], valuation[1]

**value / ~s** *n*
=
value[3] / valewes[1]

**valu·e / ~es / ~ing / ~ed** *v*
= / = / 'valʊɪn, -ɪŋ / =
**sp** valew[9], value[14] / valewes[2], values[3] / valewing[1] / valew'd[3], valewed[2], valu'd[1], valued[5]
> dis-, over-value; under-, un-valued

**valued** *adj*
'valju:d
**sp** valued[2]
> dearest-valued

**valueless** *adj*
*m* 'valju:ˌles
**sp** valuelesse[1]

**vane** *n*
vɛ:n
**sp** vaine[1], vane[1], veine[1]

**vanish / ~est / ~es / *VA* ~eth / ~ed** *v*
= / 'vanɪʃəst / = / = / *m* 'vanɪʃt, -ʃɪd
**sp** vanish[11] / vanishest[2] / vanishes[2] / vanisheth[1] / vanish'd[6], vanished[2], vanisht[3]
**rh** death, breath *Luc 1041*
> long-vanished

**vanit·y / ~ies** *n*
*m* 'vanɪˌtəɪ, -təɪ / -z
**sp** vanitie[8], vanity[13] / vanities[6]
**rh** thee *1H4 5.4.105*

**vanquish / ~est / ~eth / ~ed** *v*
= / 'vaŋkwɪʃəst / = / *m* 'vaŋkwɪʃt, -ʃɪd
**sp** vanquish[2] / vanquishest[1] / vanquisheth[1] / vanquish'd[5], vanquished[5], vanquisht[6]
> unvanquished

**vanquisher** *n*
'vaŋkwɪʃəɹ
**sp** vanquisher[2]

**vant** *n*
=
**sp** vant[1]

**vantage / ~s** *n*
=
**sp** vantage[39] / vantages[5]

**vantbrace** *n*
'vantbrɛ:s
**sp** vantbrace[1]

**Vapians** *n*
'vɛ:pɪənz
**sp** Vapians[1]

**vaporous** *adj*
'vɛ:prəs, -pər-
**sp** vaporous[1], vap'rous[1]

**vapour / ~s** *n*
'vɛ:pəɹ / -z
**sp** vapour[7] / vapours[6], va-pours[1]
**rh** vapour is thee it is *PP 3.9*

**vapour-vow** *n*
'vɛ:pəɹ-ˌvəʊ
**sp** vapor-vow[1]
> vow

**variable** *adj*
*m* 'varɪˌabəl
**sp** variable[6]

**variance** *n*
'varɪɔ:ns
**sp** variance[1]

**variation / ~s** *n*
ˌvarɪ'ɛ:sɪən / -z
**sp** variation[2] / va-riations[1]

**varied** *adj*
'varəɪd
**sp** varied[3], varried[1]

**variety** *n*
və'rəɪətəɪ
**sp** variety[1], *VA* varietie[1]
**rh** satiety *VA 21*

**varlet / ~s** *n*
'vɑ:ɹlət / -s
**sp** varlet[19], var-let[1], varlot[2], verlot[1] / varlets[3], varlots[1]

**varletry** *n*
'vɑ:ɹlətrəɪ
**sp** varlotarie[1]

**varletto** *n*
vɑ:ɹ'leto:
**sp** var-letto[1]

**varnish** *n / v*
'vɑ:ɹnɪʃ
**sp** varnish[2] / varnish[1]

**varnished** *adj*
'vɑ:ɹnɪʃt
**sp** varnisht[3]
> unvarnished

**Varrius** *n*
'varɪəs
**sp** Varrius[6]

**Varro / ~'s** *n*
'varo: / -z
**sp** Varro[7] / Varroes[1], Varro's[1]

**Varrus** *n*
'varəs
**sp** Varrus[3]

**vary** *n*
'varəɪ
**sp** varry[1]

**var·y / ~iest / ~ying** *v*
'varəɪ / -əst / -ɪn, -ɪŋ
**sp** varie[1], varry[1] / variest[1] / varying[1]

**varying** *adj*
'varəɪɪn, -ɪŋ
**sp** varrying[2], varying[1]

**vassal** *adj*
'vasɑl
**sp** vassall[4]

**vassal / ~s** *n*
'vasɑl / -z
**sp** vassaile[5], vassall[7] / vassailes[2], vassalls[1], vassals[3]

**vassalage** *n*
'vasəlɪʤ
**sp** vassalage[1]
**rh** embassage *S 26.1*

**vast** *adj / n*
vast
**sp** vast[7], vast-[shore-washet][1], vaste[3] / vast[2]

**vastidity** *n*
*m* vas'tɪdɪˌtəɪ
**sp** vastiditie[1]

**vasty** *adj*
'vastəɪ
**sp** vastie[4]

**Vaudemont** *n*
*m* ˌvo:də'mɒnt, 'vo:dəmɒnt, *Fr* -mɔ̃
**sp** Vandemont[2]

**Vaughan** *n*
'vɔ:ən
**sp** Vaughan[8]

**vault / ~s** *n*
vɔ:t, vɒlt / -s
**sp** vault[15], vaulte[1] / vaults[2]

**vault / ~ing / ~ed** *v*
'vɔ:t·ɪn, -ɪŋ, 'vɒlt- / -ɪd
**sp** vaulting[1], vawting[1] / vaulted[1]

**vaultage / ~s** *n*
'vɔ:tɪʤɪz, 'vɒlt-
**sp** vaultages[1]

**vaulted** *adj*
'vɔ:tɪd, 'vɒlt-
**sp** vaulted[1]

**vaulting** *adj*
'vɔ:t·ɪn, -ɪŋ, 'vɒlt-
**sp** vaulting[2]

**vaulty** *adj*
'vɔ:təɪ, 'vɒlt-
**sp** vaultie[2], vaulty[1]

**Vaumond** *n*
'vo:mɒnd
**sp** Vau-mond[1]

**vaunt / ~s** *n*
vɔ:nt / -s
**sp** vaunt[1] / vaunts[1]

**vaunt** *Luc* **/ ~s / ~ed** *v*
vɔ:nt / -s / 'vɔ:ntɪd
**sp** vant / vaunts[1] / vaunted[1]
**rh** want *Luc 41*

**vaunt-currier / ~s** *n*
ˌvɔ:nt-'kɤrɪəɹz
**sp** vaunt-curriors[1]
> currier

**vaunter** *n*
'vɔ:ntəɹ
**sp** vaunter[1]

**vaunting** *adj / n*
'vɔ:ntɪn, -ɪŋ
vaunting[2] / vaunting[1]

**vauntingly** *adv*
*m* 'vɔ:ntɪnˌləɪ, -ɪŋ-
**sp** vauntingly[1]

**vauvado** *nonsense word*
'vəʊvado:
**sp** vauvado[1]

**Vaux** *n*
vo:
**sp** Vaux[4]

**vaward** *n*
'vawəɹd
**sp** vauward[1], vaward[4]

**veal** *n*
=
**sp** veale[2]

**vedere / vede** *Ital*
've:de:
**sp** *emend of LLL 4.2.97* vnde[1]

**vehemence** *n*
'vi:məns, 'vi:ɪ-
**sp** ve-hemence[1]

**vehemency** *n*
*m* 'vi:mənsəɪ, -ˌsəɪ, 'vi:ɪ-
**sp** vehemencie[1], vehemency[2]

**vehement** *adj*
*m* 'vi:mənt, 'vi:ɪ-, 'vi:ɪˌment
**sp** vehement[5]

**vehemently** *adv*
*Evans MW 3.1.8* 'fi:ɪməntləɪ
**sp** fehemently[1]

**veho / ~r** *Lat v*
'vehɔ:ɹ
**sp** vehor[1]

**veil** *n*
vɛ:l
**sp** vaile[3], vale[1], veyle[2]

**veil / ~ed** *v*
vɛ:l / -d
**sp** vaile[1] / veyl'd[1]
> unveil

**veiled** *adj*
*m* vɛ:ld, 'vɛ:lɪd
**sp** vailed[1], vayl'd[1], veyl'd[1]

**vein / ~s** *n*
vɛ:n / -z
**sp** vaine[11], veine[4] / veines[22], vaines[3]
**rh** amain, again *LLL 5.2.541*; reign, remain *Luc 1454*; remain *MND 3.2.82*; slain *1H6 4.7.95* / gains *S 67.10*; restrains *Luc 427*

**velure** *n*
vɪ'lu:ɹ
**sp** velure[1]

**Velutus** *n*
ve'lu:təs
**sp** Velutus[2]

**velvet** *adj / n*
=
**sp** veluet[6], vel-uet[1] / veluet[9]

**velvet-guard / ~s** *n*
'velvɪt-'gɑ:ɹdz
**sp** veluet-guards[1]
> guard

**vendible** *adj*
=
**sp** vendible[2]
**rh** commendable *MV 1.1.112*

**venemous** *adj*
*m* 'venəˌmʏs, -nəm-, -nməs
**sp** venemous[3]

**venerable** *adj*
*m* 'venəˌrʏbəl, -nrəbəl
**sp** venerable[4]
> unvenerable

**venerial** *adj*
və'ni:rɪɑl
**sp** veneriall[1]

**Venetia** *Ital n*
və'netsɪa, -'ni:sɪa
**sp** *LLL 4.2.96 emend of* vem-chie[1], vencha[1]
**rh** pretia

**Venetian** *adj*
və'ni:sɪən
**sp** Venetian[4]

**Venetian / ~s** *n*
və'ni:sɪən / -z
**sp** Venecian[1], Venetian[4] / Venetians[1]

**veney / ~s** *n*
'venəɪz
**sp** veneys[1]

**venge** *v*
venʤ
**sp** venge[7]

**vengeance / ~s** *n*
'venʤəns / -ɪz
**sp** vengance[1], veng'ance[1], vengeance[49], 'vengeance[1] / vengeances[1]

**vengeful** *adj*
'venʤfʊl
**sp** vengefull[2]

**veni** *Lat*
> venio

**venial** *adj*
'venɪɑl
**sp** veniall[1]

**Venice** *n*
=
**sp** Venice[43], Ve-nice[1]

**venison** *adj / n*
=
**sp** venison[1] / venison[5]

**ven·io / ~it / veni** *Lat v*
'venɪt / 'vɛ:ni
**sp** venit[1] / ve-ni[1]

**venom** *adj / n*
=
**sp** venom[2], venome[2] / venom[6], venome[7]
> en-, out-venom

**venomed** *adj*
=
**sp** venom'd[5]

**venom-mouthed** *adj*
'venəm-ˌməʊðd
**sp** venom'd-mouth'd[1]
> mouth

**venomous** *adj*
'venməs, -nəm-
**sp** venomous[2]

**vent / ~s** *n*
=
**sp** vent[4] / vents[1]

**vent / ~s / ~ed** *v*
=
**sp** vent[14] / vents[1] / vented[2]

**ventage / ~s** *n*
=
**sp** ventiges[1]

**Ventidius** *n*
ven'tɪdɪəs, -ɪʤɪ-
**sp** Ventiddius[2], Ventidgius[2], Ventidius[6], Ventigius[5]

**ventricle** *n*
=
**sp** ventricle[1]

**venture / ~s** *n*
'ventəɹ / -z
**sp** venture[6] / ventures[6]

**venture / ~d** *v*
'ventəɹ / -d
**sp** venter[3], venture[17], ven-ture[1] / ventur'd[5], ventured[1]
**rh** enter *VA 628*

**venturing** *VA n*
'ventrɪn, -ɪŋ, -tər-
**sp** venturing[1]
**rh** tempring *VA 567*

**venturous** *adj*
'ventrəs, -tər-
**sp** venturous[5]
**rh** furious *R3 4.4.171*

**venue** *n*
'venju:
**sp** venewe[1]

**Venus / ~s'** *n*
= / 'vi:nəs
**sp** Venus[16] / Venus[5]

**venuto** *Ital n*
ve'nu:to:
**sp** venuto[3]
**rh** Petruchio *TS 1.2.25*; so *TS 1.2.279*

**Ver** *n*
vɛ:ɹ
**sp** Ver[2]
**rh** harbinger *TNK 1.1.7*

**verb** *n*
vɐ:ɹb
**sp** verbe[1]

**verba** *Lat*
> verbum

**verbal** *adj*
'vɐ:ɹbɑl
**sp** verball[2]

**verbatim** *adv*
vəɹ'bɑ:tɪm
**sp** verbatim[1]

**verbosity** *n*
vəɹ'bɒsɪtəɪ
**sp** verbositie[1]

**verb·um / ~a** *Lat n*
'veɹbɑ
**sp** verba[2]

**verdict** *n*
'vɐ:ɹdɪkt
**sp** verdict[5]
> party-verdict

**Verdon** *n*
'vɐ:ɹdən
**sp** Verdon[1]

**verdure** *n*
'vɐ:ɹdəɹ
**sp** verdure[2]

**Vere** *n*
vi:ɹ
**sp** Vere[1]

**verge** *n*
vɐ:ɹʤ
**sp** verge[8]

**verger / ~s** *n*
'vɐ:ɹʤəɹz
**sp** vergers[1]

**Verges** *n*
'vɐ:ɹʤɪz
**sp** Verges[3]

**verif·y / ~ied** *v*
*m* 'verɪfəɪ, -ˌfəɪ / -d
**sp** verifie[2] / verified[5], verify'd[1]

**verily** *adv*
'verɪləɪ
**sp** verely[6], verily[7]

**veritable** *adj*
*m* 'verɪˌtabəl
**sp** veritable[1]

**vérité** *Fr n*
veri'te
**sp** verite[1]

**verit·y / ~ies** *n*
*m* 'verɪtəɪ, -ˌtəɪ / -ˌtəɪz
**sp** veritie[4], verity[5] / verities[1]

**vermin** *n*
'vɐ:ɹmɪn
**sp** vermine[1]

**Vernon / ~'s** *n*
'vɐ:ɹnən / -z
**sp** Vernon[13] / Vernons[1]

**Verona / ~'s** *n*
və'ro:nə / -z
**sp** Verona[18] / Verona's[1], Veronas[1]

**Veronesa** *n*
ˌverə'nesə
**sp** Verennessa[1]

**versal** *adj*
'vɐ:ɹsɑl
**sp** versall[1]

**verse / ~s** *n*
vɐ:ɹs / 'vɐ:ɹsɪz
**sp** verse[17] / verses[19]
**rh** disperse *S 78.2*; inhearse *S 86.1*; rehearse *S 21.2, 38.2, 71.9, 81.9*

**vers·e / ~es / ~ing** *v*
'vɐ:ɹs·ɪz / -ɪn, -ɪŋ
**sp** verses[1] / versing[1]

**vert** *Fr adj*
vɛ:ɹ
**sp** verd[1]

**ver·y / ~ier / ~iest** *adv*
'verəɪ,
*Costard LLL 5.2.487* 'varə, *Evans MW 1.1.46ff* 'ferəɪ, *Macmorris H5 3.2.99*
'varəɪ / 'verəɪ·əɹ / -əst
**sp** verie[124], ve-rie[3], very[663], ve-ry[6], *Costard* vara[1], *Evans* ferry[3], fery[2], fery-[well][1], *Macmorris* vary[1] / verier[1], veryer[1] / veriest[4]

**vesper / ~'s** *n*
'vespəɹz
**sp** vespers[1]

**vessel / ~'s / ~s** *n*
=
**sp** vessel[1], vessell[30] / vessels[1] / vessells[1], vessels[3]

**vestal** *adj / n*
'vestɑl
**sp** vestal[1], vestall[1] / vestall[3]

**vestment / ~s** *n*
=
**sp** vestments[2]

**vesture** *n*
'vestəɹ
**sp** vesture[5]

**veux**
> vouloir

**vex / ~est / ~es / ~eth / ~ing / ~ed** *v*
= / = / = / = / 'veksɪn, -ɪŋ / =
**sp** vex[11], vexe[6] / vexest[1] / vexes[1] / vexeth[1] / vexing[1] / vex'd[2], vext[6]
> earth-vexing; soul-, un-vexed

**vexation / ~s** *n*
*m* vek'sɛ:sɪən, -sɪˌɒn / -sɪənz
**sp** vexation[9], vexati-on[1] / vexations[2]

**vexed** *adj*
=
**sp** vexed[2], vext[4]
> still-vexed

**via** *Eng / Fr interj*
'vəɪə / 'via
**sp** fia[1], via[5] / via[1]

**via** *Lat n*
'vi:a
**sp** via

**vial / ~s** *n*
'vəɪɑl / -z
**sp** viall[1], violl[3] / violles[2], viols[1]

**viand / ~s** *n*
'vəɪənd / -z
**sp** viand[1] / viands[6]

**vicar** *n*
'vɪkəɹ
**sp** vicar[4]

**vice / ~'s / ~s** *n*
vəɪs / 'vəɪsɪz
**sp** vice[47] / vices[1] / vices[13]
**rh** entice *PP 20.41*; trice *TN 4.2.124*
> high-viced

**vice** *v*
vəɪs
**sp** vice[1]

**vicegerent** *n*
ˌvəɪs'ʤerənt
**sp** vicegerent[1]

**viceroy / ~s** *n*
'vəɪsrəɪ / -z
**sp** viceroy[2] / vice-royes[1]

**vici** *Lat*
> vincere

**vicious** *adj*
'vɪsɪəs
**sp** vicious[7], vitious[1]

**viciousness** *n*
'vɪsɪəsnəs
**sp** viciousnesse[1]

**victor** *adj*
'vɪktəɹ
**sp** victor-[sword][1]

**victor / ~'s / ~s** *n*
'vɪktəɹ / -z
**sp** victor[4] / victors[1] / victors[5]

**victoress** *n*
'vɪktrəs
**sp** victoresse[1]

**victorious** *adj*
'vɪktɔ:rɪəs
**sp** victorious[15]

**victor·y / ~ies** *n*
*m* 'vɪktrəɪ, -təˌrəɪ / -z
**sp** victorie[22], victory[24] / victories[4]
**rh** *1* cheerfully *R3 5.3.271*; chivalry, Italy *Luc 110*; manly *2H6 4.8.51*; royally *1H6 1.6.31*; thee *R3 5.3.166*;
**rh** *2* way *3H6 5.1.113*

**victual / ~s** *n*
'vɪtl / -z
**sp** victuall[1] / victualles[1], victuals[2]

**victual / ~led** *v*
'vɪtl / -d
**sp** victuall[1] / victuall'd[1]

**victualler / ~s** *n*
'vɪtləɹz
**sp** victuallers[1]

**videlicet** *Lat adv*
vɪ'delɪset, *Evans MW 1.1.130f* fɪ-
**sp** videlicet[2], videlicit[1], videliset[1], *Evans* fidelicet[2]

**vid·eo / ~es / vidi** *Lat v*
'vɪd·eo: / -ez / 'vi:di
**sp** video[1]

**vie / ~d** *v*
vəɪ / -d
**sp** vie[1] / vi'd[1]
> outvied

**vie** *Fr n*
vi
**sp** vie[3]

**Vienna** *n*
=
**sp** Vienna[10]

**view / ~s** *n*
=
**sp** veiw[1], view[44] / viewes[2]
**rh** ensue *Luc 1261*; new *S 27.10, 56.12, 110.2*; true *MV 3.2.131, S 148.11*; withdrew *VA 1031*

**view / ~est / *Luc* ~s / ~eth / ~ing / ~ed** *v*
= / vju:st / = / = / 'vju:ɪn, -ɪŋ / =
**sp** view[22] / viewest[1] / vewes[1] / vieweth[1] / viewing[2] / view'd[3]
**rh** due *S 69.1*; hue *VA 343*; true *Luc 454* / renewest *S 3.1* / ensues, renews *Luc 1101* / ensuing *VA 1076*
> overview

**viewless** *adj*
=
**sp** viewlesse[1]

**vigil** *n*
=
**sp** vigil[1]

**vigilance** *n*
*m* ˈvɪʤɪˌlans
**sp** vigilance[3]

**vigilant** *adj*
*m* ˈvɪʤɪlənt, -ˌlant, *Dogberry MA 3.3.92* ˈvɪʤɪtənt
**sp** vigilant[3], *Dogberry* vigitant[1]

**vigour** *n*
ˈvɪgəɹ
**sp** vigor[4], vigour[6]
**rh** rigour *VA 953*

**vild / ~er / ~est** *adj*
vəɪld / ˈvəɪld·əɹ / -əst
**sp** vild[6], vil'd[3], vilde[34], vil'de[1] / vilder[1] / vildest[3]

**vild** *n*
vəɪld
**sp** vild[1], vilde[1]

**vildly** *adv*
ˈvəɪldləɪ
**sp** vildely[8], vildlie[1], vildly[4]

**vile / ~st** *adj*
vəɪl / ˈvəɪləst
**sp** vile[62] / vilest[1]
**rh** defile *MW 1.3.89*

**vile-concluded** *adj*
ˈvəɪl-kənˈklu:dɪd
**sp** vile-concluded[1]

**vilely** *adv*
ˈvəɪləɪ
**sp** vilely[2]

**vileness** *n*
ˈvəɪlnəs
**sp** vilenesse[1]

**village** *adj*
=
**sp** village[2]

**village / ~s** *n*
=
**sp** village[4] / villages[3], vil-lages[1]

**villager** *n*
ˈvɪlɪʤəɹ
**sp** villager[1]
**rh** here *TNK 3.5.103*

**villagery** *n*
ˈvɪlɪʤrəɪ
**sp** villagree[1]
**rh** he *MND 2.1.35*

**villain** *adj*
=
**sp** villaine[3], villaine-[mountainers][1], villaine-[slaue][1]

**villain / ~'s / ~s / ~s'** *n*
=
**sp** villain[12], villaine[223], [made-vp]-villaine[1], villaine's [villain is][1], vil-laine[3] / villaines[7] / villaines[41], villains[3], *Tit 4.2.9 emend of* villanie's[1] / villaines[1], villains[1]
> arch-villain, outvillained

**villain-like** *adj*
ˈvɪlən-ˌləɪk
**sp** villain-like[2]

**villainous** *adj / adv*
*m* ˈvɪlənəs, -ˌnɤs / ˈvɪlənəs
**sp** villanous[22], vil-lanous[2], villa-nous[2] / villanous[1]

**villainously** *adv*
*m* ˈvɪlənəsləɪ, -ˌləɪ
**sp** villanously[2]

**villain·y / ~ies** *n*
*m* ˈvɪlənəɪ, -ˌnəɪ / -z
**sp** vilany[1], villainie[1], villainy[2], villanie[20], vil-lanie[1], villa-nie[2], villany[22] / villanies[5]
**rh** flattery *Per 4.4.44*; Italy, jealousy *Cym 5.4.68*; mutually *MW 5.5.100*

**villiago** *n*
vɪlɪˈago:
**sp** villiago[1]

**villianda** *nonsense word*
vɪlɪˈanda
**sp** villianda[1]

**Vincentio / ~'s** *n*
vɪnˈsensɪo: / -z
**sp** Vincentio[19], Vin-centio[1], *TS 1.1.13 emend of* Vincentio's[1] / Vincentio's[2]

**vincere / vici** *Lat v*
ˈvɪnkere / ˈvi:si:
**sp** vincere[1] / vici[1]

**vindicative** *adj*
vɪnˈdɪkətɪv
**sp** vindecatiue[1]

**vine / ~s** *n*
vəɪn / -z
**sp** vine[7] / vines[4]
**rh** eyne *AC 2.7.111*; thine *CE 2.2.183*; untwine *Cym 4.2.60*

**vinegar** *adj / n*
ˈvɪnɪgəɹ, *Parolles AW 2.3.43* ˈvɪnaˌgɛ:ɹ
**sp** vineger[1] / vinegar[2], *Parolles* vinager[1]

**vinewed / ~est** *adj*
ˈvɪnju:dst
**sp** *emend of TC 2.1.14* whinid'st[1]

**vineyard / ~s** *n*
ˈvɪnjɑ:ɹd / -z
**sp** vineyard[5] / vineyards[2]
**rh** rocky-hard *Tem 4.1.68*

**vintner** *n*
ˈvɪntnəɹ
**sp** vintner[1]

**viol** *n*
ˈvəɪəl
**sp** vyall[1]

**Viola** *n*
ˈvəɪələ
**sp** Viola[11]

**violate / ~s** *v*
*m* ˈvəɪəˌlɛ:t,- əl- / -ˌlɛ:ts
**sp** violate[5] / violates[1]

**violated** *adj*
*m* ˈvəɪəˌlɛ:tɪd

**sp** violated[1]
> unviolated

**violation** *n*
*m* ˌvəɪəˈlɛːsɪən, -sɪˌɒn
**sp** violation[4]

**violator** *n*
*m* ˌvəɪəˈlɛːtəɹ
**sp** violator[1]

**viol-de-gamboys** *n*
ˌvəɪəl-də-ˈgambəɪz
**sp** viol-de-gam-boys[1]

**violence** *n*
*m* ˈvəɪəˌlens, ˈvəɪləns
**sp** violence[17], vio-lence[1]

**violent / ~est** *adj*
*m* ˈvəɪəˌlent, ˈvəɪlənt / ˈvəɪlənst
**sp** violent[39], vio-lent[1] / violent'st[1]

**Violenta** *n*
ˌvəɪəˈlentə
**sp** Violenta[2]

**violently** *adv*
ˈvəɪləntˌləɪ, -tləɪ, ˈvəɪə-
**sp** violently[5]

**violet / ~s** *n*
*m* ˈvəɪəˌlet, ˈvəɪlət / -s
**sp** violet[6] / violets[7]
**rh** set *VA 936*

**viper / ~s** *n*
ˈvəɪpəɹ / -z
**sp** viper[3] / vipers[3]

**viperous** *adj*
ˈvəɪprəs, -pər-
**sp** viperous[2], viporous[1]

**vir** *Lat n*
vɪɹ
**sp** vir[1]

**virago** *n*
vɪˈrɑːgoː
**sp** firago[1]

**Virgilia** *n*
vəɹˈʤɪlɪə
**sp** Virgilia[6]

**virgin** *adj*
ˈvɐːɹʤɪn
virgin[10], virgin-[branches][1], virgin-[knot][1], virgine[1]

**virgin / ~'s / ~s** *n*
ˈvɐːɹʤɪn / -z
**sp** virgin[20] / virgins[2] / virgins[7], vir-gins[2]

**virgin / ~ed** *v*
ˈvɐːɹʤɪnd
**sp** virgin'd[1]

**virginal** *adj*
ˈvɐːɹʤɪnɑl
**sp** virginall[2]

**virginal / ~ling** *v*
ˈvɐːɹʤɪnɑlɪn, -ɪŋ
**sp** virginalling[1]

**virginity** *n*
*m* vəɹˈʤɪnɪtəɪ, -ˌtəɪ
**sp** virginitie[12], virgini-tie[2], virginity[10], virgi-nity[1]

**Virginius** *n*
vəɹˈʤɪnɪəs
**sp** Virginius[2]

**virgin-like** *adj*
ˈvɐːɹʤɪn-ˌləɪk
**sp** virgin-like[1]

**Virgo / ~'s** *n*
ˈvɐːɹgoːz
**sp** Virgoes[1]

**virtue / ~'s / ~s** *n*
ˈvɐːɹtjə / -z
**sp** vertu[1], vertue[176], ver-tue[1] / vertues[10] / vertues[44], [bastard]-vertues[1], ver-tues[2]
> unvirtuous

**virtuous** *adj / n*
ˈvɐːɹtjəs, *Mistress Quickly MW 2.2.94* ˈfɐːɹ-
**sp** vertuous[88], ver-tuous[1], vertu-ous[3], *Mistress* fartuous[1] / vertuous[1]

**virtuously** *adv*
*m* ˈvɐːɹtjəsləɪ, -ˌləɪ
**sp** vertuously[5]

**visage / ~s** *n*
=
**sp** visage[31] / visages[4]
> grim-, humble-, pale-, tripe-visaged

**viscount** *n*
ˈvəɪkəʊnt
**sp** viscount[1]

**visible** *adj*
=
**sp** visible[4]
> invisible

**visibly** *adv*
*m* ˈvɪzɪˌbləɪ
**sp** visibly[1]

**vision / ~s** *n*
ˈvɪzɪən / -z
**sp** vision[15] / visions[3]
**rh** derision *MND 3.2.371*

**visit / ~s / ~ing / ~ed** *v*
= / = / ˈvɪzɪtɪn, -ɪŋ / =
**sp** visit[48], visite[7] / visits[2] / visiting[4] / visited[9]
**rh** bed *MND 3.2.430*
> unvisited

**visitation / ~s** *n*
*m* ˌvɪzɪˈtɛːsɪən, -sɪˌɒn / -sɪənz
**sp** visitation[16], visita-tion[1] / visitations[1]

**visited** *adj*
=
**sp** visited[1]

**visiting** *adj*
ˈvɪzɪtɪn, -ɪŋ
**sp** visiting[5]

**visiting / ~s** *n*
ˈvɪzɪtɪnz, -ɪŋz
**sp** visitings[1]

**visitor** *n*
'vɪzɪtəɹ / -z
**sp** visitor[1] / visitors[2]

**visor / Visor** [name] *n*
'vəɪzəɹ
**sp** visor[7], visore[1], vizor[1] / Visor[3]

**vit·a / ~ae** *Lat n*
'vi:te
**sp** vitae[1]
> aqua-vitae

**vital** *adj*
'vəɪtal
**sp** vitall[4]

**vitement** *Fr adv*
vit'mɑ̃
**sp** vistement[1]

**vivant** *Fr adj*
vi'vɑ̃
**sp** viuant[1]

**viva voce** *Lat n*
'vi:və 'vo:si:
**sp** viua voce[1]

**vivre / vive** *Fr v*
vi:v
**sp** viue[1]

**vixen** *n*
=
**sp** vixen[1]

**viz** *adv*
=
**sp** viz[1]

**vizaments** [*malap* advisements] *n*
'vəɪzəmənts
**sp** viza-ments[1]

**vizard / ~s** *n*
'vɪzəɹd / -z
**sp** vizard[5] / vizards[8]

**vizard / ~ed** *v*
'vɪzəɹdɪd
**sp** vizarded[2]

**vizard-like** *adj*
'vɪzəɹd-ˌləɪk
**sp** vizard-like[1]

**vlowting-stock**
> flouting-stock

**vocation** *n*
və'kɛ:sɪən
**sp** vocation[3], vocati-on[1]

**vocative** *n*
*Evans MW 4.1.46f* 'fɒkətɪv
**sp** focatiue[1], foca-tiue[1]

**vocativ·us / ~o** *Lat n*
vɒkə'ti:vo:
**sp** vocatiuo

**vocatur** *Lat v*
vɒ'kɑ:tʊɹ
**sp** vocatur[1]

**voice / ~s** *n*
vəɪs / 'vəɪsɪz
**sp** voice[61], voyce[94] / voices[9], voi-ces[1], voyces[43]
**rh** *1* choice *RJ 1.2.19*; rejoice *VA 978*; **rh** *2* juice *VA 134*; **rh** *3* noise *VA 921*
> low-, shrill-voiced

**voice / ~d** *v*
vəɪs / -t
**sp** voyce[1] / voic'd[1]
> outvoice

**void** *adj / v*
vəɪd
**sp** void[4], voide[1], voyd[2], voyde[2] / void[1], voide[1]
> avoid

**voiding** *adj*
'vəɪdɪn, -ɪŋ
**sp** voyding[1]

**volant / ~e** *Fr adj*
vɔ'lɑ̃t
**sp** volante[1]

**voliuorco** *nonsense word*
ˌvɒlɪu:'ɔ:ɹko:
**sp** voliuorco[1]

**volley** *n / v*
'vɒləɪ
**sp** volley[1], volly[2] / volly[1]

**Volquessen** *n*
vɒl'kesən
**sp** Volquessen[1]

**Volsce / ~s** *n*
'vɒlsi: / -z
**sp** Volce[3] / Volces[17], Volcies[2]

**Volsces** *adj*
'vɒlsi:z
**sp** Volces[1]

**Volscian** *adj*
'vɒlsɪən
**sp** Volcean[2], Volcian[2]

**Volscian / ~s / ~s'** *n*
'vɒlsɪən / -z
**sp** Volscian[1], Volcean[1] / Volceans[1], Volcians[3] / Volcians[1]

**Voltemand** *n*
'vɒltɪmand
**sp** Voltemand[3], Voltumand[2]

**volubility** *n*
*m* ˌvɒljə'bɪlɪtəɪ, -ˌtəɪ
**sp** volubilitie[1], volubility[1]

**voluble** *adj*
*m* 'vɒljəbəl, -ˌbɤl
**sp** voluble[4]

**volume / ~s** *n*
=
**sp** volume[10] / volumes[4]

**Volumnia** *n*
və'lɤmnɪə
**sp** Volumnia[8]

**Volumnius** *n*
və'lɤmnɪəs
**sp** Volumnius[8]

**voluntary** *adj*
*m* 'vɒlənˌtarəɪ, -trəɪ
**sp** voluntarie[2], voluntary[9], vo-luntary[1]

**voluntar·y / ~ies** *n*
*m* 'vɒlən,tarəɪ, -trəɪ / -,trəɪz
**sp** voluntary[1] / voluntaries[1]

**voluptuously** *adv*
və'lɤptjəsləɪ
**sp** voluptuously[1]

**voluptuousness** *n*
*m* və'lɤptjəs,nes
**sp** voluptuousnesse[2]

**vomissement** *Fr n*
vɔmis'mɑ̃
**sp** vemissement[1]

**vomit** *n*
=
**sp** vomit[2]

**vomit / ~s** *v*
=
**sp** vomit[2] / vomits[1]

**votaress** *n*
'vo:trəs
**sp** votresse[2]
**rh** Ephesus *Per 4.Chorus.4*

**votarist / ~s** *n*
*m* 'vo:trɪst, -tər-, -tə,r- / -trɪsts
**sp** votarist[2] / votarists[1]

**votar·y / ~ies** *n*
'vo:tə,rəɪ, -tər- / -tərəɪz
**sp** votarie[1], votary[2] / votaries[2]

**votre** *Fr*
> vous

**vouch / ~es** *n*
vəʊʧ / 'vəʊʧɪz
**sp** vouch[3], vouches[1]

**vouch / ~es / ~ing / ~ed** *v*
vəʊʧ / 'vəʊʧ·ɪz / -ɪn, -ɪŋ / vəʊʧt
**sp** vouch[8] / vouches[1] / vouching[1] / vouch'd[4]
> fore-vouched

**vouched** *adj*
vəʊʧt
**sp** voucht[1]

**voucher / ~s** *n*
'vəʊʧəɹ / -z
**sp** voucher[1] / vouchers[2]

**vouchsaf·e / ~es / ~ing / ~ed** *v*
'vəʊʧsɛ:f / -s / -ɪn, -ɪŋ / -t
**sp** vouchsafe[49], vouch-safe[2], voutsafe[1] / vouch-safes[1] / vouchsafing[1] / vouchsaf'd[1]

**vouchsafed** *adj*
'vəʊʧsɛ:ft
**sp** vouchsafed[2]

**vouloir / veux / voudrais** *Fr v*
vø / vu'drɛ
**sp** veus[1] / voudray[1]

**vous** *Fr pro*
vu, *followed by vowel* vuz
**sp** vos[1], vou[1], vous[24], vouz[1]

***votre*** *det*
'vɔtrə
**sp** vostre[9]

**vow / ~s** *n*
vəʊ / -z
**sp** vow[50], vowe[2] / vowes[57]
**rh** *1* allow, bow *Luc 1843*; brow, how *Luc 809, RJ 2.3.58*; now *LLL 5.2.345, RJ 1.1.223*; **rh** *2* unto LC 182 [*Q*] / boughs *AY 3.2.129*
> break-, marriage-, vapour-vow

**vow / ~s / ~ing / ~ed / ~edest** *v*
vəʊ / -z / 'vəʊ·ɪn, -ɪŋ / *m* -ɪd, vəʊd / vəʊds, -dst
**sp** vow[20], vowe[3] / vowes[6] / vowing[2] / vowd[2], vow'd[11], vowed[2] / vow'dst[1]
**rh** bowed *LLL 4.2.106, PP 5.2*

**vowed** *adj*
*m* 'vəʊɪd, vəʊd
**sp** vowed[2]

**vowel / ~s** *n*
'vəʊl / -z
**sp** vowell[1] / vowels[1]

**vow-fellow / ~s** *n*
'vəʊ-,feləz, -lo:z
**sp** vow-fellowes[1]
> fellow

**vox** *Lat n*
vɒks
**sp** vox[1]

**voyage / ~s** *n*
'vəɪɪʤ / -ɪz
**sp** voyage[20], voy-age[1] / voyages[2]

**vraiment** *Fr adv*
vrɛ'mɑ̃
**sp** verayment[2]

**Vulcan / ~'s** *n*
'vɤlkən / -z
**sp** Vulcan[3] / Vulcans[3]

**vulgar** *adj*
'vɤlgəɹ
**sp** vulgar[16]

**vulgar / ~s** *n*
'vɤlgəɹ / -z
**sp** vulgar[5] / vulgars[1]

**vulgarly** *adv*
*m* 'vɤlgəɹ,ləɪ
**sp** vulgarly[1]

**vulgo** *adv*
'vɤlgo:
**sp** vulgo[1]

**vulnerable** *adj*
*m* 'vɤlnə,rabəl
**sp** vulnerable[1]
> in-, un-vulnerable

**vulture / ~s** *n*
'vɤltəɹ / -z
**sp** vulture[3] / vultures[2]

**vulture** *v*
'vɤltəɹ
**sp** vulture[1]

# W

**wade / ~d** *v*
wɛːd / ˈwɛːdɪd
**sp** wade[3] / waded[2]

**waddle / ~d** *v*
ˈwɑdld
**sp** wadled[1]

**wafer-cake / ~s** *n*
ˈwɛːfəɹ-ˌkɛːks
**sp** wafer-cakes[1]

**waft / ~s / ~ing** *v*
wɑft / -s / ˈwɑftɪn, -ɪŋ
**sp** waft[6] / wafts[4] / wafting[1]

**waftage** *n*
ˈwɑftɪʤ
**sp** waftage[2]

**wafter** *n*
ˈwɑftəɹ
**sp** wafter[1]

**wag / ~s** *n*
=
**sp** wag[5], wagge[3] / wagges[1]

**wag / ~s / ~ging** *v*
= / = / ˈwagɪn, -ɪŋ
**sp** wag[6], wagg[1], wagge[4] / wagges[1], wags[1] / wagging[4]

**wage** *v*
ˈwɛːʤ / -d
**sp** wage[7] / wag'd[3]

**wager / ~s** *n*
ˈwɛːʤəɹ / -z
**sp** wager[18] / wagers[2]

**wager / ~ed** *v*
ˈwɛːʤəɹ / -d
wager[2] / wager'd[2]

**wages** *n*
ˈwɛːʤɪz
**sp** wages[11]
**rh** rages *Cym 4.2.261*

**waggish** *adj*
=
**sp** waggish[2]

**waggling** *n*
ˈwaglɪn, -ɪŋ
**sp** wagling[1]

**waggon** *adj / n*
=
**sp** waggon[2], waggon[2] / wagon[1]

**waggoner** *n*
*m* ˈwagəˌnɐːɹ
**sp** waggoner[2], wagoner[1]

**wagtail** *n*
ˈwagtɛːl
**sp** wagtaile[1]

**wail / ~s / ~ing / ~ed** *v*
wɛːl / -z / ˈwɛːlɪn, -ɪŋ / wɛːld
**sp** waile[15], wayle[6] / wailes[2] / wailing[1], wayling[3] / wail'd[2]
**rh** trundle-tail *KL 3.6.70*

**wailing** *adj*
ˈwɛːlɪn, -ɪŋ
**sp** wayling[1]

**wain** *n / v*
wɛːn
**sp** waine[1] / waine[1]

**wained** *adj*
ˈwɛːnɪd
**sp** wained[1]

**waining** *adj / n*
ˈwɛːnɪn, -ɪŋ
**sp** waining[1] / waining[1]
> beauty-waining

**wainrope / ~s** *n*
ˈwɛːnroːps
**sp** waine-ropes[1]

**wainscot** *n*
ˈwɛːnskət
**sp** wainscot[1]

**waist** *n*
wast
**sp** wast[1], waste[13]
**rh** 1 chaste *Luc 6*; **rh** 2 fast *LLL 4.3.183*
**pun** *2H4 1.2.144*, *MW 1.3.38* waste

**wait / ~s / ~eth / ~ing / ~ed** *v*
wɛːt / -s / ˈwɛːt·əθ / -ɪn, -ɪŋ / -ɪd
**sp** waight[1], wait[33], waite[25], wayt[1] / waites[5], waits[4], waytes[1] / waiteth[1] / waighting[1], waiting[1], wayting[1] / waighted[1], waited[3], wayted[4]
**rh** 1 conceit *LLL 5.2.401*; **rh** 2 gate *Per 1.1.80*

**waiting** *adj / n*
ˈwɛːtɪn, -ɪŋ
**sp** wayting[1] / waiting[1]

**waiting-gentlewoman** *n*
ˈwɛːtɪn-ˌʤentlwʊmən, -ɪŋ-

**sp** waiting-gentlewoman[2], waiting gentlewoman[2], waiting gentle-woman[1], wayting gentlewoman[1]
> gentlewoman

**waiting-woman** *n*
'wɛːt·ɪn-ˌwʊmən, -ɪŋ-
**sp** waiting woman[1], waiting women[1]
> woman

**wake** [awake] *n*
wɛːk
**sp** wake[3]
**rh** make *KL 3.2.34*

**wake** [fair] **/ ~s** *n*
wɛːks
**sp** wakes[3]

**wak·e / ~est / ~s / ~ing / ~ed** *v*
wɛːk / -s, -st / -s / 'wɛːkɪn, -ɪŋ / wɛːkt
**sp** wake[48] / wak'st[5] / wakes[13] / waking[2] / wak'd[13], waked[1], wakt[1], wak't[3]
**rh** betake *Luc 126* [*Q*] / sake, take *MND 2.2.33* / tak'st *MND 3.2.453* / a-shaking, taking *Luc 450*

**waked** *adj*
wɛːkt
**sp** wak'd[1]

**Wakefield** *n*
'wɛːkfiːld
**sp** Wakefield[1]

**waken** *v*
'wɛːkən / -d
**sp** waken[4] / waken'd[2], wakened[1]

**waking** *adj / n*
'wɛːkɪn, -ɪŋ
**sp** waking[15] / waking[3]
> still-waking

**waleful** *adj*
'wɛːlfʊl
**sp** walefull[1]

**Wales** *n*
'wɛːlz
**sp** Wales[38]

**walk** *n*
=
**sp** walke[2], walkes[7]

**walk / ~est / ~s / ~ing / ~ed** *v*
= / wɔːks, -st / = / 'wɔːkɪn, -ɪŋ / =
**sp** walk[2], walke[115] / walk'st[1] / walkes[23], walks[1] / walking[16] / walk'd[17], walked[2], walkt[5]
**rh** talk *TC 4.4.137* / stalks *Luc 367*
> overwalk

**walking** *adj / n*
'wɔːkɪn, -ɪŋ
**sp** walking[3] / walking[5]
> late-, night-walking

**wall / ~'s / ~s** *n*
wɑːl, = / -z
**sp** wal[2], wall[61], [brick]-wall[1] / wals[1], walls[1] / walles[31], walls[32], wals[7]
**rh** *1* all *MND 5.1.197, Tim 4.1.38*; befall *MND 5.1.154*; fall, withal *Luc 464*; hall *LLL 5.2.901*; parle *3H6 5.1.17*; thrall *Luc 723*; **rh** *2* perpetual *Luc 723*

**wall / ~s / ~ed** *v*
wɑːl, = / -z / -d
**sp** wall[2] / walls[1] / wal'd[1]
> outwall, sea-walled

**walled** *adj*
wɑːld, =
**sp** wall'd[3], walled[1]

**wall-eyed** *adj*
'wɑːl-ˌəɪd, 'wɔːl-
**sp** wall-ey'd[2]
> eye

**wallet / ~s** *n*
'wɑlət / -s
**sp** wallet[1] / wallets[1]

**wall-newt** *n*
'wɑːl-ˌnjuːt, 'wɔːl-
**sp** wall-neut[1]

**Wallon** *n*
wɑ'loːn
**sp** Wallon[2]

**wallow** *v*
'wɒlə, -loː
**sp** wallow[2]

**walnut** *n*
'wɑːlnət
**sp** wall-nut[1]

**walnut-shell** *n*
'wɑːlnət-ˌʃel
**sp** walnut-shell[1]
> shell

**Walter / ~'s** *n*
'wɑːtəɹ / -z
**sp** Walter[20] / Walters[1]
**pun** *2H6 4.1.31* water

**wan** *adj*
wɒn
**sp** wan[3]

**wan / ~ned** *v*
wɒnd
wan'd[1]

**wand** *adj*
wɑnd
**sp** wand[1]

**wand / ~s** *n*
wɑnd / -z
**sp** wand[3] / wands[2]

**wander / ~s / ~ing / ~ed** *v*
'wɑndəɹ / -z / 'wɑndrɪn, -ɪŋ / 'wɑndəɹd
**sp** wander[19] / wanders[1] / wandring[3], wand'ring[1] / wander'd[2], wandred[5]

**wanderer / ~s** *n*
'wɑndrəɹ / -z
**sp** wanderer[2] / wanderers[1]
night-wanderer

**wandering** *adj*
'wɑndrɪn, -ɪŋ, -dər-
**sp** wandering[4], wandring[6], wand'ring[2]

**wane** *n*
wɛːn
**sp** wane[1]

**wane / ~s** *v*
wɛːnz
**sp** wanes[1]

**waning** *adj / n*
'wɛːnɪn, -ɪŋ
**sp** wayning[1], *2H6 4.10.19 emend of* warning[1]

**want / ~s** *n*
wɑnt / -s
**sp** want[49] / wants[9]
**rh** scant *PP 20.36*

**want / ~est / ~s / ~eth / ~ing / ~ed** *v*
wɑnt / wɑnst, wɑnts, -tst / wɑnts / 'wɑnt·əθ / -ɪn, -ɪŋ / -ɪd
**sp** want[129] / want'st[7] / wants[32] / wanteth[3] / wanting[14] / wanted[8]
**rh** *1* enchant *Tem.Epil.13*; **rh** *2* vaunt *Luc 42* / granteth, panteth *Luc 557* / granting *S 87.7* / scanted *KL 1.1.279*

**wanting** *adj / n*
'wɑntɪn, -ɪŋ
**sp** wanting[3] / wanting[2]

**wanton** *adj / adv / v*
'wɑntən
**sp** wanton[44], wonton[1] / wanton[1] / wanton[3]

**wanton / ~'s / ~s** *n*
'wɑntən / -z
**sp** wanton[10] / wantons[1] / wantons[4]

**wantonly** *S* *adv*
*m* 'wɑntən,ləɪ
**sp** wantonly[1]
**rh** dye *S 54.7*

**wantonness** *n*
*m* 'wɑntən,nes, ənəs
**sp** wantonnes[1], wantonnesse[5]
**rh** excess *LLL 5.2.74*; less *S 96.1*

**want-wit** *n*
'wɑnt-,wɪt
**sp** want-wit[1]

**wappened** *adj*
'wɑpənd
**sp** wappen'd[1]

**war / ~'s / ~s** *n*
wɑːɹ / -z
**sp** war[12], warre[235], warres [war is][2] / warres[6] / warres[129], warrs[4], wars[9]
**rh** *1* afar, scar *Luc 831*; are *TC Prol.31*; bar *S 46.1*; far *AW 3.4.8*; jar *VA 98*; **rh** *2* stir *R2 2.3.52* / scars *H5 5.1.85*; stars *MND 3.2.408, Per 1.1.39*
> closet-war

**war / ~rest / ~red** *v*
wɑːɹ / -st / -d
**sp** warre[6] / war'st[1], warr'st[1] / war'd[1]

**warbl·e / ~ing** *v*
'wɑːɹb·əl / -lɪn, -lɪŋ
**sp** warble[2] / warbling[1]

**warbling** *adj*
'wɑːɹblɪn, -ɪŋ
**sp** warbling[1]

**ward / ~s** *n*
wɑːɹd / -z
**sp** ward[12] / wardes[2], wards[3]
**rh** *1* guard *S 133.9*; regard *Luc 303*; **rh** *2* heard *Luc 303*

**ward / ~ed** *v*
wɑːɹd / 'wɑːɹdɪd
**sp** ward[1] / warded[1]

**warden** *adj*
'wɑːɹdən
**sp** warden[1]

**warder / ~s / ~s'** *n*
'wɑːɹdəɹ / -z
**sp** warder[3] / warders[1] / warders[1]

**wardrobe** *n*
'wɑːɹdroːb
**sp** wardrobe[5]

**ware** *adj*
wɛːɹ
**sp** ware[5]
> unwares

**ware** *interj*
wɛːɹ
**sp** ware[2], ware-a[1]
**rh** *1* dear-a, **rh** *2* wear-a *WT 4.4.321* [*song*]
> beware

**Ware** [name] *n*
wɛːɹ
**sp** Ware[1]

**wares** *n*
wɛːɹz
**sp** wares[3]
**rh** fairs *LLL 5.2.317*

**warily** *adv*
'wɛːɹɪləɪ
**sp** warely[1], warily[1]
**rh** by *LLL 5.2.93*
> wary

**warlike** *adj*
'wɑːɹləɪk
**sp** warlicke[1], warlike[55], war-like[2], warrelike[2], warre-like[1]
> like

**warm / ~er** *adj*
wɑːɹm / 'wɑːɹməɹ
**sp** warme[33] / warmer[2]

**warm** *adv*
wɑːɹm
**sp** warme[2]
**rh** harm *VA 193*

**warm / ~s / ~ed** *v*
wɑːɹm / -z / -d
**sp** warm[3], warme[4] / warmes[3] / warm'd[7], warmed[1]
**rh** charmed, harmed *LC 191*; disarmed *S 154.6*

**war-man** *n*
'wɑːɹ-ˌman
**sp** war-man[1]

**war-marked** *adj*
'wɑːɹ-ˌmɑːɹkt
**sp** warre-markt-[footmen][1]
mark

**warming** *n*
'wɑːɹmɪn, -ɪŋ
**sp** warming[1]

**warming-pan** *n*
'wɑːɹmɪn-ˌpan, -ɪŋ-
**sp** warming-pan[1]

**warmth** *n*
wɑːɹmθ
**sp** warmth[5]

**warn / ~s / ~ed** *v*
wɑːɹn, *Edgar's assumed dialect KL 4.6.240* vɔːɹ / -z / -d
**sp** warne[5], *Edgar* vor'[1] / warnes[1] / warn'd[5]
> forewarn

**warning** *adj*
'wɑːɹnɪn, -ɪŋ
**sp** warning[1]

**warning / ~s** *n*
'wɑːɹnɪn, -ɪŋ / -z
**sp** warning[14] / warnings[2]

**warp / ~ed** *v*
wɑːɹp / -t
**sp** warpe[5] / warpt[1]
**rh** sharp *AY 2.7.188*

**warped** *adj*
*m* 'wɑːɹpɪd
**sp** warped[1]

**war-proof** *n*
*m* ˌwɑːɹ-'prɤf, 'pruːf
**sp** warre-proofe[1]

**warrant / ~s** *n*
'wɑrənt / -s
**sp** warrant[36], war-rant[3], warrant's [warrant is][1] / warrants[2]

**warrant / ~s / ~eth / ~ed** *v*
'wɑrənt / -s / -əθ / -ɪd
**sp** warrant[133], war-rant[1], *emend of AW 3.5.65* write / warrants[2] / warranteth[1] / warranted[1]
> well-warranted

**warranted** *adj*
'wɑrəntɪd
**sp** warranted[3]

**warrantize** *n*
*m* 'wɑrənˌtəɪz
**sp** warrantize[1]

**warranty** *n*
*m* 'wɑrənˌtəɪ
**sp** warrantie[3]

**warren** *n*
'wɑrən
**sp** warren[1]

**warrener** *n*
'wɑrənəɹ
**sp** warrener[1]

**warrior** *adj*
'wɑrɪəɹ
**sp** warrior[1]

**warrior / ~s** *n*
'wɑrɪəɹ / -z
**sp** warrior[3], warriour[8], war-riour[1] / warriers[1], warriors[12], warriours[3]

**wart** *n*
wɑɹt
**sp** wart[6]

**Wart / ~'s [name]** *n*
wɑɹt / -s
**sp** Wart[8] / Warts[1]

**war-thought / ~s** *n*
*m* ˌwɑːɹ-'θɔːts
**sp** warre-thoughts[1]

**war-wearied** *adj*
*m* ˌwɑːɹ-'wiːrəɪd, -'we-
**sp** warre-wearied[1]
> weary

**Warwick / ~'s** *n*
'wɒrɪk / -s
**sp** Warwick[42], Warwicke[172], War-wicke[1], *abbr in s.d.* War[1], Warw[icke][1] / Warwickes[12], Warwicks[1]

**Warwickshire** *n*
*m* 'wɒrɪkˌʃəɪɹ, -kʃəɹ
**sp** Warwickshire[3]

**war-worn** *adj*
'wɑːɹ-ˌwɔːɹn
**sp** warre-worne[1]
wear

**wary** *adj*
'wɛːrəɪ
**sp** warie[1], wary[9]
**rh** chary *S 22.9*
> unwarily, warily

**was** *v*
*unstr* wəs, *str* wɑs
**sp** was[2186]
**rh** glass *Luc 1764, S 5.12*; grass *Luc 393*; pass *Ham 2.2.417, S 49.7, WT 4.1.10*
> be, were

***it was*** *abbr*
twəz
**sp** twas[7], 'twas[144], t'was[1]

***was it*** *abbr*
wɑst
**sp** wast[39], was't[60]

**wash / ~es** *n*
wɑʃ / 'wɑʃɪz
**sp** wash[2] / washes[1], [Lincolne]-Washes[1]

**wash / ~es / ~ing / ~ed** *v*
wɑʃ / 'wɑʃ·ɪz / -ɪn, -ɪŋ / wɑʃt
**sp** wash[49] / washes[4] / washing[3] / washd[1], wash'd[8], washed[1], [vast-shore]-washet[1], washt[13]

**washed** *adj*
wɑʃt
**sp** wash'd[1]
> ale-washed

**washer** *n*
'wɑʃəɹ
**sp** washer[1]

**Washford** *n*
'wɑʃfəɹd
**sp** Washford[1]

**washing** *adj / n*
'wɑʃɪn, -ɪŋ
**sp** washing[1] / washing[2]
> buck-washing

**wasp / ~'s / ~s** *n*
wɑsp / -s
**sp** waspe[3] / waspes[1] / waspes[3]

**waspish** *adj*
'wɑspɪʃ
**sp** waspish[4]

**waspish-headed** *adj*
'wɑspɪʃ-ˌedɪd, -ˌhe-
**sp** waspish headed
> head

**wasp-tongued** *adj*
'wɑsp-ˌtɒŋd, -ˌtʊ-
**sp** waspe-tongu'd[1]
> tongue

**wassail / ~s** *n*
'wɑsəl / -z
**sp** wassell[1] / wassels[2]

**wassail-candle** *n*
'wasəl-ˌkandl
**sp** wassell-candle[1]

**waste** *adj / n*
wast
waste[1] / wast[7], waste[9]
**rh** *1* chaste *RJ 1.1.218*; taste *RJ 2.3.67*; **rh** *2* past *S 30.4*

**waste / ~s / ~d** *v*
wast / -s / 'wastɪd
**sp** wast[2], waste[18] / wastes[1], wasts[1] / wasted[13]
**rh** taste *S 77.2* / tasted *VA 130*
**pun** *MW 1.3.38, 2H4 1.2.143* waist

**wasted** *adj*
'wastɪd
**sp** wasted[2]
> time-bewasted

**wasteful** *adj*
'wastfʊl
**sp** wasteful[1], wastefull[4], wastfull[2]

**wasting** *adj*
'wastɪn, -ɪŋ
**sp** wasting[3]

**watch / ~es** *n*
wɑʧ / 'wɑʧ·ɪz
**sp** watch[69] / watches[3]
> night-watch

**watch / ~es / ~ing / ~ed** *v*
wɑʧ / 'wɑʧ·ɪz / -ɪn, -ɪŋ / wɑʧt
**sp** watch[49] / watches[2] / watching[2] / watch'd[4], watcht[16]
**rh** match *VA 584*
> unwatched

**watch-case** *n*
'wɑʧ-ˌkɛ:s
**sp** watch-case[1]
> case

**watchdog / ~s** *n*
'wɑʧdɒgz
**sp** watch-dogges[1]
> dog

**watcher** *n*
'wɑʧəɹz
**sp** watchers[2]

**watchful** *adj*
'wɑʧfʊl
**sp** watchfull[11]

**watching / ~s** *n*
'wɑʧɪn, -ɪŋ / -z
**sp** watching[6], wat-ching[1] / watchings[1]

**watch·man / ~men** *n*
'wɑʧmən
**sp** watchman /, watchmen[3], watch-men[1]

**watchword / ~s** *n*
'wɑʧˌwɔ:ɹd / *Evans MV 5.4.3* 'wɑʧˌɔ:ɹdz
**sp** watch-word[1] / watch-'ords[1]

**water / ~s** *n*
'wɑtəɹ, 'wɑ:- / -z
**sp** water[110], [holy]-water[3], [salt]-water[1], wa-ter[3] / waters[27]
**rh** flatter *Luc 1561*; matter *KL 3.2.82, LC 304, LLL 5.2.208*
**pun** *2H6 4.1.35* Walter
> sea-water

**water / ~ed** *v*
'wɑtəɹ, 'wɑ:- / -d
**sp** water[8] / watered[1]

**water-colour / ~s** *n*
'wɑtəɹ-ˌkɤləɹz, 'wɑ:-
**sp** water-colours[1]
> colour

**water-drop** *n*
'wɑtəɹ-ˌdrɒps, 'wɑ:-
**sp** water-drops[1]
**rh** crops *Luc 959*
> drop

**water-flowing** *adj*
'wɑtəɹ-ˌflo:ɪn, -ɪŋ, 'wɑ:-
**sp** water-flowing[1]
> flowing

**waterfl·y / ~ies** *n*
'wɑtəɹ-ˌfləɪ, 'wɑ:- / -z
**sp** waterflie[1] / water-flies[2]
> fly

**Waterford** *n*
'wɑtəɹˌfɔ:ɹd, 'wɑ:-
**sp** Waterford[1]

**watering** *n*
'wɑtrɪn, -ɪŋ, -tər-, 'wɑ:-
**sp** watering[1]

**waterish** *adj*
'wɑtrɪʃ, -tər-, 'wɑ:-
**sp** waterish[1], watrish[1]

**water-nymph** *n*
'wɑtəɹ-ˌnɪmf, 'wɑ:-
**sp** water-nymph[1]

**water-pot / ~s** *n*
'wɑtəɹ-ˌpɒts, 'wɑ:-
**sp** water-pots[1]
> pot

**water-rug / ~s** *n*
'wɑtəɹ-ˌrɤgz, 'wɑ:-
**sp** water-rugs[1]

**waterside** *n*
'wɑtəɹˌsəɪd, 'wɑ:-
**sp** water side[1]
> side

**water-spaniel** *n*
'wɑtəɹ-ˌspanɪəl, 'wɑ:-
**sp** water-spaniell[1]
> spaniel

**water-standing** *adj*
'wɑtəɹ-ˌstandɪn, -ɪŋ, 'wɑ:-
**sp** water-standing-[eye][1]
> stand

**Waterton** *n*
'wɑtəɹtən, 'wɑ:-
**sp** Waterton[1]

**water-walled** *adj*
*m* 'wɑtəɹ-ˌwɑ:lɪd, 'wɑ:-
**sp** water-walled[1]

**waterwork** *n*
'wɑtəɹˌwɔ:ɹk, 'wɑ:-
**sp** waterworke[1]
> work

**watery** *adj*
'wɑtrəɪ, -tər-, 'wɑ:-
**sp** waterie[4], watery[2], watrie[2], watry[7], watry-[starre][1], [grosse]-watry[1]

**wave / ~s** *n*
wɛ:v / -z
waue[5] / waues[13]
**rh** crave *VA 86*

**wav·e / ~es / ~ing / ~ed** *v*
wɛ:v / -z / 'wɛ:vɪn, -ɪŋ / wɛ:vd
**sp** waue[6] / waues[1] / wauing[6] / wau'd[1], waued[2]
**rh** grave *3H6 2.2.173*

**waver** *v*
'wɛ:vəɹ
**sp** wauer[1]

**waverer** *n*
*m* 'wɛ:vəˌrɐ:ɹ
**sp** wauerer[1]

**wavering** *adj*
'wɛ:vrɪn, -ɪŋ
**sp** wauering[4]

**wave-worn** *adj*
'wɛ:v-ˌwɔ:ɹn
**sp** waue-worne[1]
> worn

**waving** *adj*
'wɛ:vɪn, -ɪŋ
**sp** wauing[2]

**waw**
> pow-waw

**wawl** *v*
wɔ:l
**sp** wawle[1]

**wax** *n*
=
**sp** wax[10], waxe[10]
> ear-wax

**wax / ~es / ~ed / ~en** *v*
= / = / *m* wakst, 'waksɪd / =
**sp** wax[5], waxe[3] / waxes[3] / waxed[2], waxt[2] / waxen[2]

**waxen** *adj*
=
**sp** waxen[6]

**waxing** *adj*
'waksɪn, -ɪŋ
**sp** waxing[1]

**way / ~s** *n*
wɛ: / -z
**sp** waie[4], way[547], [towne]-way[1], wayes [way is][1] / waies[28], wayes[37], [crook'd]-wayes[1]
**rh** *1* assay, stay *LC 158*; astray *MND 3.2.359*; bay *VA 879*; convey *Per 4. Chorus.50*; day *CE 4.2.60, 1H4 5.5.41, Luc 1144, MND 2.2.42, 3.2.417, S 7.12, 34.3, WT 4.3.121*; day, grey *MA 5.3.29*; decay *S 16.1*; decay, slay *Luc 513*; delay *MND 5.1.199, Oth 2.3.376*; grey *TS 4.1.132*; lay *VA 828*; nay *MV 3.2.228*; pay *VA 90*; play *LLL 5.2.862*; play, stay *LLL 4.3.74*; pray *TG 1.2.39*; say *Cym 3.2.83, Luc 630, S 50.1*; slay *AW 2.1.178, VA 623*; stay *Luc 309, 1365, Per 5.3.84, R2 1.3.304, S 44.2, 48.1, VA 704, 871*; stray *R2 1.3.207*; **rh** *2* victory *3H6 5.1.112* / delays *VA 907*; praise *PP 18.13*
> church-, cross-, half-, high-, mid-, path-, road-way

**waylay / ~ed** *v*
ˌwɛ:'lɛ: / -d
**sp** way-lay[1] / way-layde[1]

**wayward / ~er** *adj*
'wɛ:wəɹd, 'wɛ:əɹd / -əɹ
**sp** waiward[2], wayward[6], way-ward[2] / waywarder[1]

**waywardness** *n*
'wɛ:wəɹdnəs, 'wɛ:əɹd-
**sp** way-wardnesse[1]

**we** *pro*
=
**sp** we[3023], wee[267], wea[4]
**rh** be *MND 5.1.393, Tim 3.5.47, TN 2.2.31*; me *2H6 3.2.411*; see *KL 1.1.262*; she *LLL 5.2.468*
> our, us

***we are*** *abbr*
wi:ɹ
**sp** w'are[1]

***we have*** *abbr*
wi:v
**sp** w'haue[1]

***we will*** *abbr*
wi:l
**sp** weel[3], wee'l[163], weele[39], wee'le[55], wee'll[28], we'l[7], well[1], we'll[18]

***we would*** *abbr*
wi:d, wi:ld
**sp** weed[1], wee'ld[2]

**weak / ~er / ~est** *adj*
= / 'wi:kəɹ / =
**sp** weak[2], weake[98] / weaker[11] / weakest[4]

**weak** *n*
=
**sp** weake[1]
**rh** speak *AW 2.1.176, 3.4.41, CE 3.2.35, Luc 1646, VA 1145*

**weaken / ~s / ~ed** *v*
=
**sp** weaken[1] / weakens[2] / weaken'd[1], weak'ned[1]

**weakest** *n*
=
**sp** wea-kest[1]

**weak-hearted** *adj*
*m* ˌwi:k-'ɑ:ɹtɪd, -'hɑ:-
**sp** weake-hearted[1]

**weak-hinged** *adj*
'wi:k-ˌɪnʤd, -ˌhɪ-
**sp** weake-hindg'd[1]

**weakling** *n*
=
**sp** weakeling[1]

**weakly** *adv*
'wi:kləɪ
sp weakely[1], weakly[2]

**weakness** *n*
'wi:knəs
**sp** weakenesse[8], weake-nesse[1], weaknesse[16]

**weal** *n*
=
**sp** weale[14]
**rh** steal *1H6 1.1.177*
> commonweal

**weals·man / ~men** *n*
'wi:lsmən
**sp** weales men

**wealth / ~'s** *n*
=
**sp** wealth[63], welth[1] / wealths-[sake][1]
**rh** stealth *CE 3.2.5, Tim 3.4.28*

**wealthily** *adv*
*m* 'welθɪˌləɪ
**sp** wealthily[2]

**wealth·y / ~iest** *adj*
'welθəɪ / -əst
**sp** wealthie[3], wealthy[8] / wealthiest[1]

**wean / ~ed** *v*
=
**sp** weane[2] / wean'd[1]

**weapon / ~'s / ~s** *n*
=
**sp** weapon[27], wea-pon[1] / weapons[1] / weapons[38], wea-pons[2]

**weaponed** *adj*
=
**sp** weapon'd[1]

**wear / ~-a** [*song*] *n*
wɛ:ɹ / wɛ:ɹ-ə
**sp** wear[1], weare[2] / weare-a[1]
**rh** dear-a, ware-a *WT 4.4.318*

**wear / ~est / ~s / ~ing / wor·e / ~st / ~n** *v*
wɛ:ɹ, wi:ɹ / -st / -z / 'wɛ:ɹɪn, -ɪŋ, 'wi:ɹ- / wɔ:ɹ / -st / -n
**sp** wear[5], weare[185] / wear'st[4] / weares[38], wears[1] / wearing[10] / wore[27] / wor'st[1] / worne[38]
**rh** *1* bear *AY 4.2.11, S 77.1, VA 163*; pear *RJ 2.1.37* [*emend of* were]; **rh** *2* appear, dear *Cor 2.1.171, LC 95, LLL 5.2.130, 456*; deer *AY 4.2.11*; deer, year *KL 3.4.131*; fear *VA 1081*; here *MND 2.2.77*; here, tear [cry] *LC 291*; year *KL 1.4.165, VA 506* / appears *Per Epil.10*; tears [cry] *Luc 680* / boar *VA 1107*; wore it bore it *AY 4.2.16* / new-born *LLL 4.3.240*
> outwear, wearing *adj*, well-worn, worn *adj*

**wearer / ~s** *n*
'wɛ:rəɹ, 'wi:- / -z
**sp** wearer[2] / wearers[1]

**wearied** *adj*
'wi:rəɪd, 'we-
**sp** wearied[3]
> day-, fore-, lust-, un-, war-, woe-, world-wearied

**wearily** *adv*
'wi:rɪləɪ, 'we-
**sp** wearily[1]

**weariness** *n*
*m* 'wi:rɪnəs, -ˌnes, 'we-
**sp** wearines[1], wearinesse[2]

**wearing** *adj / n*
'wɛ:rɪn, -ɪŋ, 'wi:-
**sp** wearing[1] / wearing[7]
> wear *v*

**wearisome** *adj*
*m* 'wi:rɪˌsɤm, 'we-
**sp** wearisome[3]

**wear·y / ~iest** *adj*
'wi:rəɪ, 'we- / -əst
**sp** wearie[29], weary[40] / weariest[1]
**rh** merry *Tem 4.1.134*
> a-, dog-, life-weary

**wear·y / ~ies / ~ied** *v*
'wi:rəɪ, 'we- / -z / -d
**sp** wearie[2], wea-rie[1], weary[2] / wearies[2] / wearied[2]

**weasel** *n*
'wi:zəl
**sp** weazel[1], weazell[5]

**weather / ~s** *n*
'weðəɹ / -z
**sp** weather[28], [leauen]-weather[1], wea-ther[2] / weathers[1]
**rh** *1* together *AY 5.4.133, PP 12.3, VA 972*; **rh** *2* hither *AY 2.5.8, 2.5.42*; thither *Luc 115*
> bell-weather

**weather-beaten** *adj*
'weðəɹ-ˌbi:tn
**sp** weather-beaten[1], weather-bitten[1]
> bitten

**weather-cock** *n*
'weðəɹ-ˌkɒk
**sp** weather-cocke[1], wethercocke[2]

**weather-fend / ~s** *v*
'weðəɹ-ˌfendz
**sp** weather-fends[1]

**weave / ~s / woven** *v*
= / = / 'wo:vən
**sp** weaue[1] / weaues[2] / wouen[3]
> ill-weaved

**weaved-up** *adj*
'wi:vd-ˌɤp
**sp** weau'd-vp[1]

**weaver / ~'s / ~s** *n*
'wi:vəɹ / -z
**sp** weauer[10] / weauers[1] / weauers[1]

**weaving** *adj*
'wi:vɪn, -ɪŋ
**sp** weauing[1]

**web** *n*
=
**sp** web[9], webbe[1]

**wed / ~dest / ~ding / ~ded** *v*
= / wedst / 'wedɪn, -ɪŋ / =
**sp** wed[30], wedde[2] / wed'st[1] / wedding[1] / wedded[14]
**rh** bed *AW 2.3.91, Ham 4.5.64, Per 2.5.94, PP 18.48*; dead *Ham 3.2.224*
> unwed

**wedded** *adj*
=
**sp** wedded[3], wedded-[lady][1]

**wedding** *adj / n*
'wedɪn, -ɪŋ
**sp** wedding[20] / wedding[12]

**wedge / ~s** *n*
=
**sp** wedges[2]

**wedge / -d** *v*
*m* weʤd, 'weʤɪd
**sp** wadg'd[1], wedg'd[1], wedged[1]
> unwedgable

**wedlock** *adj / n*
=
**sp** wedlocke[3] / wedlock[2], wedlocke[5]

**Wednesday** *n*
'wenzdɛ:
**sp** Wednesday[6], Wednes-day[1], Wendsday[2], Wensday[4], Wens-day[1]
> Ash Wednesday

**wee** *adj*
=
**sp** wee-[face][1]

**weed** [clothing] **/ ~s** *n*
=
**sp** weed[2] / weedes[12], weeds[7]
**rh** proceed *S 76.6* / speed's *MA 5.3.30*

**weed** [plant] **/ ~s** *n*
=
**sp** weed[3], weede[1] / weedes[7], weeds[13]
**rh** bleed *VA 1055*; deed *Luc 196* / deeds *S 69.12, 94.14*; needs *Mac 5.2.30*
> unweeded

**weed / ~s / ~ed** *v*
=
**sp** weed[4], weede[4] / weedes[1] / weeded[1]

**weeder-out** *n*
'wi:dəɹ-ˌəʊt
**sp** weeder out[1]

**weeding** *n*
'wi:dɪn, -ɪŋ
**sp** weeding[1]
**rh** reading *LLL 1.1.96*

**weedy** *adj*
'wi:dəɪ
**sp** weedy[1]

**week** *interj*
=
**sp** weeke[2]

**week / ~s** *n*
=
**sp** week[2], weeke[28] / weekes[5], [fiue]-weekes[1]
**rh** seek *AY 2.3.74, LLL 5.2.61, Luc 213* / cheeks *S 116.11*

**weekly** *adv*
'wi:kləɪ
**sp** weekly[1]

**ween / ~ing** *v*
= / 'wi:nɪn, -ɪŋ
**sp** weene[1] / weening[1]
> overween

**weep / ~est / ~s / ~ing / wept** *v*
= / wi:ps, -st / = / 'wi:pɪn, -ɪŋ / =
**sp** weep[7], weepe[150], weep't [weep it][1] / weep'st[7] / weepes[28], weeps[4] / weeping[22] / wept[28]
**rh** bo-peep *KL 1.4.171*; deep *LLL 4.3.31, Per 1.4.14*; deep, sleep *LC 124*; keep *LLL 4.3.37, RJ 5.3.17, S 9.5*; peep *VA 1090*; sleep *Ham 3.2.280, 1H6 4.3.28, PP 20.51* / sleeps *Luc 906* / peeping, sleeping *Luc 1087*
> a-weeping, unwept

**weeping** *adj*
'wi:pɪn, -ɪŋ
**sp** weeping[15]

**weeping / ~s** *n*
'wi:pɪn, -ɪŋ / -z
**sp** weeping[20] / weepings[1]
**rh** a-sleeping *Tim 1.2.65*; sleeping *Tim 4.3.489, VA 949*

**weet** *v*
=
**sp** weete[1]

**weigh** *v*
'wɛ: / -z / 'wɛ:ɪn, -ɪŋ / wɛ:d
**sp** waigh[8], weigh[31], weighe[1], *Ham 1.3.29 emend of* weight / waighes[1], weighes[4], weighs[2] / weighing[5] / waid[1], waigh'd[2], weigh'd[13], weighed[1]
**rh** fray *MND 3.2.131* / paying *MM 3.2.254* / maid *RJ 1.2.95*
> out-, over-weigh; un-, well-weighing; unweighed

**weight / ~s** *n*
'wɛ:t / -s
**sp** waight[22], weight[22] / waights[2]
**rh** straight *TNK 3.5.117*

**weightless** *adj*
'wɛ:tləs
**sp** weightlesse[1]

**weight·y / ~ier** *adj*
'wɛ:təɪ / -əɹ
**sp** waighty[4], weightie[5], weighty[5] / waightier[2], weightier[1]
**rh** why *TS 1.1.245*

**weird** *adj*
*m* 'wi:əɹd, 'wi:ɹd
**sp** weyard[3], weyward[3]

**welcome / ~st** *adj*
= / *m* 'welkəˌmest
**sp** welcom[5], welcome[105], wel-come[1] / welcommest[1]
> unwelcome

**welcome** *interj*
=
**sp** welcom[4], welcome[142], wel-come[1], well come[1]

**welcome / ~s** *n*
=
**sp** welcom[5], welcome[77], wel-come[1], wellcome[1] / welcomes[7]

**welcome / ~d** *v*
=
**sp** welcome[22] / welcom'd[3]

**welcomer** *n*
'welkəməɹ
**sp** welcommer[1]

**welfare** *n*
'welfɛ:ɹ
**sp** welfare[4]

**welked** *adj*
=
**sp** wealk'd[1]

**welkin / ~'s** *n*
=
**sp** welken[1], welkin[13] / welkins[3]

**well** *adj / interj*
=
**sp** wel[5], wel[178] / wel[20], well[508]

**well** *adv*
=, *Caius MW 1.4.76, 2.3.87* vel
**sp** wel[52], well[1371], [as]well[3], well-[belou'd][1], well-[fa-uourd][1], well-[sed][1], well-[winged][1], [farethee]-well[1], [farthee]well[2], [far-thee]-well[1], [farthe]well[1], [farye] well[2], [fareyou]wel[1], [faryou]well[1], [fareyou]well[4], [fery]-well[1], *Caius* vell[2]
**rh** *1* expel *VA 974*; farewell *R3 4.1.102*; fell *AW 3.1.21, LLL 5.2.113*; Florizel *WT 4.1.21*; hell *CE 2.2.221, 4.2.31, 39, KJ 1.1.271, LLL 4.3.254, MND 2.1.244, R2 5.5.115, R3 4.4.166, S 58.14, 129.13, TN 3.4.212*; parallel *TC 2.2.162*; passing-bell *VA 701*; sell *PP 18.11 [emend], S 21.13, TC 4.1.78*; sentinel *MND 2.2.31*; spell *RJ 2.3.83*; tell *CE 3.1.53, 3.2.186, 4.2.44, KL 1.4.343, 4.6.276, LC 255, MND 3.2.77, S 14.7, 103.10, WT 4.4.298*; **rh** *2* ill *KJ 3.4.4, RJ 4.5.76*; ill, Jill *MND 3.2.463*
> farewell

**well / ~s** *n*
=
**sp** well[17] / welles[1], wels[1]

**well-accomplished** *adj*
'welə'kɒmplɪʃt, -'kɤm-
**sp** well accomplish'd[1], well accomplisht[1]
> accomplished

**well-a-day** *interj*
'welə'dɛ:
**sp** weladay[3], well-a-day[1], welliday[1]
**rh** play *Per 4.4.49*

**well-advised** *adj*
*m* 'weləd'vəɪzɪd
**sp** well-aduised[1]
**rh** disguised *CE 2.2.223*
> advised

**well-a-near** *Per* *interj*
'welə'ni:ɹ, -nɛ:ɹ
**sp** wel-a-neare[1]
**rh** fear *Per 3.Chorus.51*

**well-appointed** *adj*
'welə'pəɪntɪd
**sp** well-appointed[2]
> appoint

**well-armed** *adj*
'wel-'ɑ:ɹmd
**sp** well armed[1]
> arm

**well-balanced** *adj*
'wel-'baləns t
**sp** weale-ballanc'd[1]
> balance

**well-behaved** *adj*
'welbɪ'ɛ:vd, -'hɛ:-
**sp** wel-behaued[1]
> behave

**well-beloved** *adj*
*m* 'welbɪ'lɤvd, -vɪd
**sp** welbeloued[1], wel-beloued[1], well belou'd[2]
> beloved

**well-beseeming** *adj*
'wel-bɪ'si:mɪn, -ɪŋ
**sp** well-beseeming[1], well beseeming[1]
> beseem

**well-born** *adj*
'wel-'bɔ:ɹn
**sp** well-borne[1], well borne[1]
> born

**well-bred** *adj*
'wel-'bred
**sp** well bred[1]
> breed

**well-chosen** *adj*
'wel-'ʧo:zən
**sp** well-chosen[1]
> choose

**well-dealing** *adj*
'wel-'dɛ:lɪn, -ɪŋ

**sp** well-dealing[1]
> deal

**well-derived** *adj*
*m* 'wel-dɪ'rəɪvɪd
**sp** well deriued[1]
> derive

**well-deserved** *adj*
*m* 'wel-dɪ'zɐ:ɹvɪd, -ɐ:ɹvd
**sp** well-deserued[1]
> deserved

**well-deserving** *adj*
'wel-dɪ'zɐ:ɹvɪn, -ɪŋ
**sp** well-deseruing[3]
> deserving

**well-disposed** *adj*
*m* 'wel-dɪs'po:zɪd
**sp** well-disposed[1]
> dispose

**well-divided** *adj*
'wel-dɪ'vəɪdɪd
**sp** well diuided[1]
> divide

**well-divulged** *adj*
'wel-dɪ'vɤlʤd
**sp** well divulg'd[1]
> divulged

**well-educated** *adj*
'wel-'edjəkɛ:tɪd
**sp** well educated[1]
> educate

**well-entered** *adj*
'wel-'entəɹd
**sp** well entred[1]
> enter

**well-famed** *adj*
'wel-'fɛ:md
**sp** well-fam'd[1]
> fame

**well-favoured** *adj*
'wel-'fɛ:vəɹd
**sp** wel fauor'd[1], wel-fauoured[1], well-fauourd[1], well fauour'd[1], well-fauour'd[1]
> favour

**well-foughten** *adj*
'wel-'fɔ:tən
**sp** well-foughten[1]
> fight

**well-found** *adj*
'wel-'fəʊnd
**sp** well-found[1]
> find

**well-graced** *adj*
'wel-'grɛ:st
**sp** well grac'd[1]
> grace

**well-hallowed** *adj*
'wel-'aləd, -'ha-
**sp** wel-hallow'd[1]
> hallow

**well-knit** *adj*
'wel-'nɪt, -'kn-
**sp** well-knit[1]
> knit

**well-known** *adj*
'wel-'no:n, -'kn-
**sp** well-knowne[1]
> know

**well-labouring** *adj*
'wel-'lɛ:brɪn, -ɪŋ, -bər-
**sp** well-labouring[1]
> labour

**well-learned** *adj*
'wel-'lɐ:ɹnɪd
**sp** well-learned[1]
> learn

**well-liking** *adj*
'wel-'ləɪkɪn, -ɪŋ
**sp** wel-liking[1]
> like

**well-lost** *adj*
'wel-'lɒst
**sp** well lost[1]
> lose

**well-meaning** *adj*
'wel-'mi:nɪn, -ɪŋ
**sp** well meaning[1]
> mean

**well-meant** *adj*
'wel-'ment
**sp** well-meant[1]
> mean

**well-minded** *adj*
'wel-'məɪndɪd
**sp** well-minded[1]
> mind

**well-nigh** *adv*
'wel-'nəɪ
**sp** wel-nye[1], well-nye[1]
> nigh

**well-noted** *adj*
'wel-'no:tɪd
**sp** well noted[1]
> note

**well-ordered** *adj*
'wel-'ɔ:ɹdəɹd
**sp** well-ordred[1]
> order

**well-paid** *adj*
'wel-'pɛ:d
**sp** well paid[1]
> pay

**well-painted** *adj*
'wel-'pɛ:ntɪd
**sp** well-painted[1]
> paint

**well-practised** *adj*
'wel-'praktɪst
**sp** well-practis'd[1]
> practice

**well-proportioned** *adj*
'wel-prə'pɔ:ɹsɪənd
**sp** well proportion'd[1]
> proportion

**well-remembered** *adj*
'wel-rɪ'membəɹd
**sp** well-remembred[1]
> remember

**well-reputed** *adj*
'wel-rɪ'pju:tɪd
**sp** well reputed[1]
> repute

**well-respected** *adj*
'wel-rɪ'spektɪd
**sp** well-respected[1]
> respect

**well-seeming** *adj*
'wel-'si:mɪn, -ɪŋ
**sp** well-seeming[1], welseeming[1]
> seem

**well-spoken** *adj*
'wel-'spo:kən
**sp** well-spoken[1], well spoken[1]
> speak

**well-took** *adj*
'wel-'tʊk
**sp** well-tooke[1]
> take

**well-tuned** *adj*
'wel-'tju:nd
**sp** well tun'd-[hornes][1]
> tune

**well-warranted** *adj*
'wel-'wɑɹntɪd, -ɹən-
**sp** well-warranted[1]
> warrant

**well-weighing** *adj*
'wel-'wɛ:ɪn, -ɪŋ
**sp** well-waighing[1]
> weigh

**well-willer / ~s** *n*
'wel-'wɪləɹ / -z
**sp** *TNK* well willer / well-willers[1]
**rh** pillar *TNK 3.5.115*
> will

**well-wished** *adj*
'wel-'wɪʃt
**sp** wel-wisht[1]
> wished

**well-worn** *adj*
'wel-'wɔ:ɹn
**sp** well-worne[1]
> wear

**Welsh** *adj / n*
=
**sp** Welch[5], Welch-[deuill][1], Welch-[hooke][1], Welsh[5] / Welch[2], Welsh[12]

**Welsh·man / ~men** *n*
=
**sp** Welchman[4], Welshman[1], Welsh-man[1] / Welchmen[3], Welshmen[2]

**Welsh·woman / ~women** *n*
*m* ˌwelʃ-'wɪmɪn
**sp** Welshwomen[1]
> woman

**wen** *n*
=
**sp** wen[1]

**wench / ~'s / ~s / ~s'** *n*
=
**sp** wench[57] / wenches[1] / wenches[20], wen-ches[1] / wenches[1]
**rh** French *1H6 4.7.41*
> flax-wench

**wenching** *adj*
'wenʃɪn, -ɪŋ
**sp** wenching[1]

**wench-like** *adj*
'wenʃ-ləɪk
**sp** wench-like[1]

**wend** *v*
=
**sp** wend[3]
**rh** end *CE 1.1.158, MND 3.2.372*

**went**
> go

**wept**
> weep

**were / wert** *v*
*str* wɛ:ɹ, *unstr* wəɹ / -t
**sp** wer[4], were[1529], were't [were it][2], wer't [were it][8] / wert[66], wer't[29]
**rh** *1* appear *Luc 631*; beer *Oth 2.1.155*; here *CE 4.2.10*; near *S 140.5*; **rh** *2* bear *S 13.6*; swear *LLL 4.3.116, PP 16.16;* **were it** bear it *Luc 1156*
> be, was

***it were*** *abbr*
twəɹ
**sp** 'twer[8], 'twere[108], t'were[2]

**west** *adj / n*
=
**sp** west[3] / west[26]
**rh** *1* best *TC 2.3.260*; nest *VA 530*; rest *S 73.6*; unrest *R2 2.4.21*; **rh** *2* east *S 132.8*
> north-north-west

**western** *adv*
'westəɹn
**sp** westerne[10]

**Westminster** *n*
'westmɪnstəɹ
**sp** Westminster[7]

**Westmoreland** *n*
*m* 'westməɹˌland, -lənd
**sp** Westmerland[47], West-merland[1]

**westward** *adv*
'westwəɹd
**sp** westward[4], west-ward[1]

**wet** *adj / n / v*
=
**sp** wet[8] / wet[1] / wet[7]
**rh** debt *VA 83*; jet, set *LC 40*; set *Luc 1228*

**wetting** *n*
'wetɪn, -ɪŋ
**sp** wetting[1]

**wezand** *n*
'wezənd
**sp** wezand[1]

**whale / ~'s** *n*
ʍɛ:l / -z
**sp** whale[6] / whales[1]

**wharf / ~s** *n*
ʍɑ:ɹf / -s
**sp** wharfe[1] / wharfes[1]

**what** *det, pro*
ʍɑt, *Caius MW 1.4.43* vɑt, *Katherine, Lady H5 5.2.108ff* wɑt
**sp** what[4395], whats [what is][7], what's [what is][323], *Caius* vat[9], *Katherine, Lady* wat[3]
**rh** wot *R2 2.2.39*

**whatever,** *abbr* **whate'er** *det / pro*
ʍɑt'ɛ:ɹ
**sp** what e're[1] / what ere[21], what e're[1]
> ever

**what ho** *interj*
ˌʍɑt 'ho:
**sp** what ho[7], what hoa[30], what hoe[2]

**whatsoever,** *abbr* **whatsoe'er** *det / pro*
*m* 'ʍɑtso:'evəɹ, *abbr* -'ɛ:ɹ
**sp** whatsoeuer[13], *abbr* whatsoere[1] / whatso-euer[1], *abbr* whatsoe're[1], whatsoere[2], what so ere[1]
> ever

**whatsomever,** *abbr* **whatsome'er** *pro*
'ʍɑtsəm'ɛ:ɹ
**sp** whatsomere[1], what somere[1]

**wheat** *n*
ʍi:t
**sp** wheate[8]

**wheaten** *adj*
'ʍi:tən
**sp** wheaten[1]

**wheel / ~s** *n*
ʍi:l / -z
**sp** wheele[19] / wheeles[8], [chariot]-wheeles, wheels[1]
**rh** steel *CE 3.2.154, Luc 952* / reels *RJ 2.2.191*
> millwheel

**wheel** *v*
ʍi:l
**sp** wheele[2]
> enwheel

**wheeled** *adj*
ʍi:ld
**sp** wheel'd[1]

**wheeling** *adj*
'ʍi:lɪn, -ɪŋ
**sp** wheeling[1]

**whelk / ~s** *n*
ʍelks
**sp** whelkes[1]

**whelm** *v*
ʍelm
**sp** whelme[1]
> overwhelm

**whelp / ~s** *n*
ʍelp
**sp** whelpe[8] / whelpes[2]
> bear-whelp

**whelp / ~ed** *v*
*m* 'ʍelpɪd, ʍelpt
**sp** whelped[1], whelpt[1]

**when** *adv / conj*
ʍen
**sp** when[85] / when[1842], whe[n][3], when's [when his][1], when't [when it][1]
**rh** again *R2 1.1.162*; men *AW 2.1.151, H8 1.1.5, MM 4.2.83*; pen *Per 4.Chorus.27*

**when as** *conj*
ʍen'az
**sp** when as[8]

**whence** *adv / conj*
ʍens
**sp** whence[23] / whence[52]
**rh** expense *Per 5.Chorus.17*

**whenever,** *abbr* **whene'er** *conj*
ʍen'ɛ:ɹ
**sp** when ere[2], when euer[3]
> ever

**whensoever** *conj*
'ʍenso:'evəɹ
**sp** whensoeuer[1]

**where** *adv*
ʍɛ:ɹ, *Caius MW 1.4.56 ff* vɛ:ɹ
**sp** wher[2], where[367], wheres [where is][1], where's [where is][90], wher's [where is][16], *Caius* ver[3], ver'[1], vere[1]
**rh** *1* swear *R2 5.3.142*; there *R2 1.2.72, S 5.8, S 100.12, TN 2.4.63*; **rh** appear *S 102.4*; clear *S 84.12*; here *RJ 1.1.198*; sphere *MND 2.1.6*; year *S 97.4*
> any-, every-, no-, some-where

**where** *conj / n*
ʍɛ:ɹ
**sp** wher[3], where[793], wher'e[1], where't [where it][2] / where[1]

**whereabout** *adv / n*
'ʍɛ:ɹəˌbəʊt
**sp** whereabout[1] / where-about[1]

**whereas** *conj*
ʍɛ:ɹ'az
**sp** whereas[4], where-as[1], where as[2]

**whereat** *adv*
ʍɛ:ɹ'at
**sp** whereat[7]

**whereby** *adv*
ʍɛ:ɹ'bəɪ
**sp** whereby[12]

**wherefore** *adv*
*m* ʍɛ:ɹ'fɔ:ɹ, 'ʍɛ:ɹ'fɔ:ɹ *Caius MW 3.1.73* vɛ:ɹ-
**sp** wherefore[130], wherefore's [wherefore is][1], wherfore[5], *Caius* vherefore[1]
**rh** door *CE 3.1.39*

**wherein** *adv*
*m* ʍɛ:ɹ'ɪn, 'ʍɛ:ɹ'ɪn
**sp** wherein[117], where-in[3], wherin[2]
**rh** din *Cym 5.4.109*

**whereinto** *adv*
'ʍɛ:ɹɪn'tu:
**sp** whereinto[1]

**whereof** *adv*
ʍɛ:ɹ'ɒv
**sp** whereof[75], where-of[3], wherof[3]

**whereon** *adv*
ʍɛːɹˈɒn
**sp** whereon[26]

**whereout** *adv*
ʍɛːɹˈəʊt
**sp** where-out[1]

**wheresoever**, *abbr*
**wheresoe'er** *adv / conj*
ˈʍɛːɹsoːˈevəɹ, *abbr* -ˈɛːɹ
wheresoeuer[1] / wheresoeuer[1], *abbr* wheresoere[7], wheresoe're[1], where so ere[1]
> ever

**wheresomever**, *abbr*
**wheresome'er** *conj*
ˈʍɛːɹsəmˈevəɹ, *abbr* -ˈɛːɹ
**sp** wheresomere[1]

**whereto** *adv*
ʍɛːɹˈtuː
**sp** whereto[20], where to[1]

**where-until** *conj*
ˈʍɛːɹənˈtɪl
**sp** where-vntill[2]

**whereunto** *adv*
ˈʍɛːɹənˈtuː
**sp** whereunto[2]

**whereupon** *adv*
ˈʍɛːɹəˈpɒn
**sp** whereupon[11], where-vpon[1]

**wherever**, *abbr*
**where'er** *conj*
ʍɛːɹˈevəɹ, *abbr* ʍɛːɹˈɛːɹ
**sp** where euer[5], where-euer[1], *abbr* where ere[7]
> ever

**wherewith** *adv*
ʍɛːɹˈwɪθ, -ɪð
**sp** wherewith[9]

**wherewithal** *adv / n*
ˈʍɛːɹwɪˈθɑːl, -ɪˈð-
**sp** wherewithall[1] / wherewithall[1]

**whet / ~test / ~ted** *v*
ʍet / -s, -st / ˈʍetɪd
**sp** whet[9] / whet'st[1] / whetted[2]

**whether** *conj*
ˈʍeðəɹ, *abbr* ʍɛːɹ
**sp** whether[83], whe-ther[2], *abbr* whe'r[1], where[3]
**rh** *1* feather *VA 304*; **rh** *2* neither *PP 7.17*; *rh 3* thither *PP 14.8*

**whetstone** *n*
ˈʍetstoːn
**sp** whetstone[4]
> stone

**whew** *interj*
ʍjuː
**sp** whew[1]

**whey** *n*
ʍɛː
**sp** whay[1]

**whey-face** *n*
ˈʍɛː-ˌfɛːs
**sp** whay-face[1]
> face

**which** *pro*
ʍɪʧ
**sp** which[2173]

**whiff** *n*
ʍɪf
**sp** whiffe[1]

**whiffler** *n*
ˈʍɪfləɹ
**sp** whiffler[1]

**while** *conj / n*
ʍəɪl
**sp** while[212] / while[16], [a-]while[2]
**rh** beguile *LLL 1.1.75, VA 1142*; guile *Luc 1536*; isle *KJ 4.2.100*; smile *H8 Epil.12*
> awhile

**whilere** *adv*
ʍəɪlˈɛːɹ
**sp** whileare[1]

**whiles** *conj / n*
ʍəɪlz
**sp** whiles[75] / whiles[1]
> otherwhiles

**whilst** *conj / n*
ʍəɪlst
**sp** whilest[14], whilst[22], whil'st[59] / whilst[4], whil'st[3]

**whine / ~d** *v*
ʍəɪn / -d
**sp** whine[2] / whin'd[2]

**whining** *adj*
ˈʍəɪnɪn, -ɪŋ
**sp** whining[3], whyning[1]

**whip / ~s** *n*
ʍɪp / -s
**sp** whip[10] / whips[2]

**whip / ~pest / ~s / ~ping / ~ped** *v*
ʍɪp / -st / -s / ˈʍɪpɪn, -ɪŋ / ʍɪpt
**sp** whip[25], whippe[1] / whip'st[1] / whips[3], whippes[3] / whipping[1] / whip'd[2], whipt[39]
> unwhipped

**whipper / ~s** *n*
ˈʍɪpəɹz
**sp** whippers[1]

**whipping** *n*
ˈʍɪpɪn, -ɪŋ
**sp** whipping[7] whip-ping[1]

**whipster** *n*
ˈʍɪpstəɹ
**sp** whipster[1]

**whipstock** *n*
ˈʍɪpstɒk
**sp** whip-stocke[1]
> stock

**whirl / ~s / ~ing / ~ed** *v*
ʍɐːɹl / -z / ˈʍɐːɹlɪn, -ɪŋ / ʍɐːɹld
**sp** whirle[2], whurle[1] / whirles[2] / whirling[1] / whirl'd[1] , whirled[1]

**whirlpool** *n*
'ʍɐːɹlpuːl
**sp** whirle-poole[1]

**whirlwind / ~s** *n*
'ʍɐːɹlwəɪnd / -z
**sp** whirlewind[1], whirle-winde[2] / whirle-windes[1], whirlewinds[1]

**whirlygig** *n*
'ʍɐːɹləɪgɪg
**sp** whirlegigge[1]

**whisper / ~s** *n*
'ʍɪspəɹ / -z
**sp** whisper[2] / whispers[2]

**whisper / ~s / ~ing / ~ed** *v*
'ʍɪspəɹ / -z / -ɪn, -ɪŋ, -pr- / -d
**sp** whisper[29], whis-per[1] / whispers[9] / whispering[1], whispring[1], whisp'ring[1] / whisper'd[2]
**rh** sinister *MND 5.1.162*

**whispering** *adj*
'ʍɪsprɪn, -ɪŋ, -pər-
**sp** whispering[1], whispring[1]

**whispering / ~s** *n*
'ʍɪsprɪnz, -ɪŋz, -pər-
**sp** whispering[2] / whisperings[1], whisp'rings[1]

**whist** *adj*
ʍɪst
**sp** whist[1]
**rh** kissed *Tem 1.2.378*

**whistle** *n*
'ʍɪsəl
**sp** whistle[3]

**whistl·e / ~es / ~ing** *v*
'ʍɪs·əl / -əlz / -lɪn, -lɪŋ
**sp** whistle[7] / whistles[1] / whisling[1]

**whistling** *adj / n*
'ʍɪslɪn, -ɪŋ
**sp** whistling[1] / whistling[1]

**whit** *n*
ʍɪt
**sp** whit[22]

**white / ~e / ~st** *adj*
ʍəɪt / 'ʍəɪt·əɹ / *m* -əst, -st
**sp** white[85], White-[heart][1] / whiter[4] / whitest[1], whit'st[1]
**rh** bite *KL 3.6.65*; delight *S 98.9, 130.5, VA 77, 398*; despite *Luc 56*; downright *VA 643*; night *1H6 2.4.126, MW 5.5.37*; right *PT 13*; write *MW 5.5.70*
> lily-, milk-, snow-white

**white** *adv*
ʍəɪt
**sp** white[1]

**white / ~s** *n*
ʍəɪt / -s
**sp** white[28] / whites[1]
**rh** appetite, delight *Luc 11*; fight *Luc 63*; fight, right *Luc 65*; fight, sight *Luc 1405*; light, night *Luc 394*; light *LLL 2.1.183*; night *S 12.4, TS 5.2.185*; sight *VA 1168*

**white-bearded** *adj*
'ʍəɪt-ˌbɛːɹdɪd, ˌbɐː
**sp** white-bearded[2]
> bearded

**white-faced** *adj*
'ʍəɪt-ˌfɛːst
**sp** white-fac'd[1]
> face

**Whitefriars** *n*
*m* ˌʍəɪt-'frəɪəɹz
**sp** White Friars[1]
> friar

**Whitehall** *n*
*m* ˌʍəɪt-'ɑːl, -'hɑːl
**sp** White-hall[1]
> hall

**white-handed** *adj*
*m* ˌʍəɪt-'andɪd, -'ha-
**sp** white handed[1]

**white-limbed** *adj*
'ʍəɪt-ˌlɪmd
**sp** white-limb'd[1]
> limb

**white-livered** *adj*
*m* ˌʍəɪt-'lɪvəɹd
**sp** white-liuer'd[2]
> liver *adj*

**whiteness** *n*
'ʍəɪtnəs
**sp** whitenes[1], whitenesse[4]

**whither** *adv*
'ʍɪðəɹ
**sp** whether[55], whe-ther[1], whither[33]
**rh** *1* neither *WT 4.4.306*; **rh** *2* thither *WT 4.4.297*; **rh** *3* together *VA 904*
> somewhither

**whiting** *adj*
'ʍəɪtɪn, -ɪŋ
**sp** whiting[1]

**whitly** *adj*
'ʍɪtləɪ
**sp** whitly[1]

**Whitmore** *n*
'ʍɪtmɔːɹ
**sp** Whitmore[3]

**whitster / ~s** *n*
'ʍɪtstəɹz
**sp** whit-sters[1]

**Whitsun** *adj*
'ʍɪtsən
**sp** Whitson[2], Whitson-[pastorals][1]

**whittle** *n*
'ʍɪtl
**sp** whittle[1]

**whiz / ~zing** *v*
'ʍɪzɪn, -ɪŋ
**sp** whizzing[1]

**who / ~m** *pro*
*str* uː, =, *unstr* ʊ / *str* uːm, =, *unstr* ʊm
**sp** who[1162] / whom[412], who[m][1], whome[2]
**rh** know *TN 2.5.96*

*who is* *abbr*
*str* u:z, hu:z, *unstr* ʊz, hʊz
**sp** who's[75]

*who will* *abbr*
*str* u:l, hu:l, *unstr* ʊl, hʊl
**sp** who'll[1]

**whoa** *interj*
'ho:ə
**sp** whoa[1], whoa-[ho-hoa][1]

**whoever,** *abbr* **whoe'er** *pro*
u:'evəɹ, *abbr* u:'ɛ:ɹ, hu:-
who-euer[1], *abbr* whoere[1], who ere[7], who e're[1]
> ever

**whole** *adj / adv / n*
o:l, ho:l
**sp** whol[1], whole[109] / whole[8] / whole[3]
**pun** *RJ 2.4.96* hole

**wholesome / ~st** *adj*
'o:lsəm, -'ho:- / -st
**sp** holesome[1], wholsom[1], wholesome[10], whole-some[1], wholsome[16], whol-some[1] / wholsomst[1]
> unwholesome

**wholly** *adv*
'o:ləɪ, 'ho:-, 'ʍo:-
**sp** wholly[6]

**whom**
> who

**whoop** *interj*
ʍu:p
**sp** whoop[3]

**whore / ~'s / ~s** *n*
ɔ:ɹ, hɔ:ɹ, o:ɹ, ho:ɹ / -z
**sp** whore[45] / whores[1] / whores[7]
**rh** *1* door, more, score *KL 1.4.123*; more *TC 4.1.67, 5.2.116*; **rh** *2* poor *KL 2.4.50*
**pun** *AY 2.7.24ff* hour

**whore / ~d** *v*
ɔ:ɹd, hɔ:-, o:ɹd, ho:-
**sp** whor'd[1]
> bewhored

**whoremaster** *adj / n*
'ɔ:ɹmastəɹ, 'hɔ:-, o:ɹ-, ho:-
**sp** whore-master-[man][1] / whoremaster[1], whore-master[1], whore-ma-ster[2]
> master

**whoremonger** *n*
'ɔ:ɹmɤŋgəɹ, 'hɔ:-, o:ɹ-, ho:-
**sp** whore-monger[1]

**whoring** *n*
'ɔ:ɹɪn, -ɪŋ , 'hɔ:-, o:ɹ-, ho:-
**sp** whoring[1]

**whorish** *adj*
'ɔ:ɹɪʃ, 'hɔ:-, o:ɹ-, ho:-
**sp** whorish[1]

**whorson** *adj*
'ɔ:ɹsən, 'hɔ:-, o:ɹ-, ho:-
**sp** horson[15], whoreson[7], whorson[15], whor-son[2]

**whorson / ~s** *n*
'ɔ:ɹsən, 'hɔ:- / -z, o:ɹ-, ho:-
**sp** horson[1] / whorsons[1]

**whose** *pro*
*str* u:z, =, *unstr* ʊz, hʊz
**sp** whose[590]

**whosoever,** *abbr* **whosoe'er** *pro*
'u:so:'evəɹ, *abbr* 'u:so:'ɛ:ɹ, 'hu:-
**sp** whosoeuer[2] / *abbr* whosoe're[2], who so ere[1]
> ever

**whosomever** *pro*
'u:səm'evəɹ, 'hu:-
**sp** who some euer[1]
> ever

**why** *adv / n*
ʍəɪ
**sp** why[1443] / why[2]
**rh** *1* I *Cym 5.4.132*; lie *S 115.3*; **rh** *2* amazedly *Mac 4.1.124*; weighty *TS 1.1.244*

**wicked / ~est** *adj*
= / 'wɪkɪdst
**sp** wicked[53], wick-ed[2] / wickedst[1]

**wicked** *n*
=
**sp** wicked[8]

**wickedness** *n*
*m* 'wɪkɪdˌnes, -dnəs
**sp** wickednes[2], wickednesse[7], wicked-nesse[1]

**wide / ~r** *adj*
wəɪd / 'wəɪdəɹ
**sp** wide[32], wide-[worlds][1] / wider[1]

**wide / ~r** *adv*
wəɪd / 'wəɪdəɹ
**sp** wide[16] / wider[3]
**rh** abide *S 27.7*; aside, espied *Luc 359*; belied *S 140.14*; glide *MND 5.1.370*; hide *VA 296*; ride *TNK 3.4.23*

**wide-chopped** *adj*
'wəɪd-ˌʧɒpt
**sp** wide-chopt-[rascall][1]
> chop

**wide-enlarged** *adj*
'wəɪd-ɪn'lɑ:ɹʤd
**sp** wide enlarg'd[1]
**rh** charged *AY 3.2.139*
> enlarge

**widen / ~s** *v*
'wəɪdənz
**sp** widens[1]

**wide-skirted** *adj*
*m* ˌwəɪd-'skɐ:ɹtɪd
**sp** wide-skirted[1]
> skirt

**widest** *n*
'wəɪdst
**sp** widst[1]

**wide-stretched** *adj*
*m* ˌwəɪd-'streʧɪd
**sp** wide-stretched[1]
> stretch

**widow** *adj*
'wɪdə, -do:
**sp** widow[7]

**widow / ~'s / ~s / ~s'** *n*
'wɪdə, -do: / -z
**sp** widdow[37], wid-dow[1], widdowe[1], widow[16], wi-dow[1], / widdowes[5], widdows[1], widowes[1] / widdowes[5], widowes[1], widows[1] / widdowes[1]

**widow / ~ed** *v*
'wɪdə, -do: / -d
**sp** widdow[1], widow[1] / widdowed[1]

**widow-comfort** *n*
'wɪdə-'kɤmfəɹt, -do:-
**sp** widow-comfort[1]
> comfort

**widow-dolour** *n*
'wɪdə-'dɒləɹ, -do:-
**sp** widdow-dolour[1]

**widowed** *adj*
*m* 'wɪdo:,ed
**sp** widowed[1]
**rh** bed *RJ 3.2.135*

**widower** *adj*
'wɪdəwəɹ, -do:-
**sp** widdower[1]

**widower / ~'s** *n*
'wɪdəwəɹ, -do:- / -z
**sp** widdower[2], widower[2] / widdowers[1]

**widowhood** *n*
'wɪdə,ʊd, -do:-, -,hʊd
**sp** widdow-hood[1]

**widow-maker** *n*
'wɪdə,mɛ:kəɹ, -do:-
**sp** widdow-maker[1]
> make

**wield** *v*
=
**sp** weild[1], wield[3]
**rh** field, yield *Luc 1432*
> unwieldy

**wife / ~'s / wive·s / ~s'** *n*
wəɪf / -s / wəɪv / -z
**sp** wife[454], [good]-wife[1], wife's [wife is][4] / wifes[1], wiues[23] / wiues[61] / wives'[2]
**rh** knife *Luc 1048, 1841*; life *AW 5.3.291, CE 3.2.68, 163, Luc 1802, 1806, Per Prol.37, 1.4.45, 5.1.243, R2 1.2.54, S 9.4, TN 5.1.134*; life, strife *Luc 235, 1376*; strife *AW 2.3.290, CE 3.2.26, Ham 3.2.233, Luc 1792, MV 2.3.21, TN 1.4.42*
> ale-, house-, mid-wife; wive

**wife-like** *adj*
'wəɪfləɪk
**sp** wife-like[2]

**wight / ~s** *n*
wəɪt / -s
**sp** wight[6] / wightes[1], wights[1]
**rh** knight *LLL 1.1.175* / knights *S 106.2*

**wild / ~er / ~est** *adj*
wəɪld / 'wəɪld·əɹ / -əst
**sp** wild[13], wild-[goose][2], wilde[66], wilde-[boares][1], wilde-[cat][2], wilde-[cats][1], wilde-[ducke][1], wilde-[fowle][1], wilde-[geese][3], wilde-[mare][1] / wilder[2] / wildest[3]
**rh** beguiled, child *Luc 956*; child *MND 2.1.25*; child, mild *Luc 1097*

**wild** *adv*
wəɪld
**sp** wilde[2]

**wild / ~s** *n*
wəɪld / -z
**sp** wilde[2] / wildes[1]

**wild-boar / ~s** *n*
'wəɪld-,bo:ɹz
**sp** wilde-boares[1]

**wilderness** *n*
*m* 'wɪldəɹnəs, -,nes
**sp** wildernes[1], wildernesse[7]

**wildest** *n*
'wəɪldəst
**sp** wildest[1]

**wildfire** *n*
'wəɪldfəɪɹ
**sp** wild-fire[1]

**wildly** *adv*
'wəɪldləɪ
**sp** wildely[8], wildly[3]
**rh** mildly *CE 5.1.88*

**wildness** *n*
'wəɪldnəs
**sp** wildenesse[5], wildnesse[4]
**rh** mildness *Luc 980*

**wiles** *n*
wəɪlz
**sp** wiles[2]

**wilful** *adj*
=
**sp** wilful[1], wilfull[11], wil-full[1], willfull[1]

**wilful-blame** *adj*
'wɪlfʊl-'blɛ:m
**sp** wilful blame[1]
> blame

**wilfull-negligent** *adj*
=
**sp** wilfull-negligent[1]
> negligence

**wilfull-opposite** *adj*
=
**sp** wilfull opposite[1]

**wilfully** *adv*
*m* 'wɪlfʊ,ləɪ
**sp** wilfully[4]

**wilfulness** *n*
*m* 'wɪlfʊl,nes
**sp** wilfulnesse[1]

**will / ~s** *n*
=
**sp** wil[5], [plessed]-wil[1], will[316], [free]-will[1], [Got's]-will[1] / willes[7], wills[11], wils[2], wil's[1]
**rh** fulfil *CE 4.1.113*; fulfil, kill *Luc 625, 1633*; hill *PP 9.7*; ill *CE 2.1.13, Luc 302, 1205, 1299, Per 1.1.104, 2.1.135, 166, RJ 1.1.202, 4.5.95, S 57.13, 89.7*; ill, quill *Luc 1299*; kill *Per 2.2.34, RJ 3.1.196*; kill, still *Luc 247*; skill *Cym 2.4.185, LC 126, MND 2.2.126, 5.1.108, TG 2.4.211*; still *CE 3.2.70, 4.2.18, 2H6 5.2.30, JC 5.5.51, Luc 728, PP 10.8, RJ 1.1.172, 2.3.24, S 134.2, 143.13, Tim 4.2.50, VA 479, 639*

**will / wilt / will·s / ~eth / ~ing / ~ed** *v*
= / = / = / = / 'wɪlɪn, -ɪŋ / =
**sp** wil[3], will[104] / wilt[26] / wills[5], wils[1] / willeth[1] / willing[4] / wil'd[2], will'd[3], willed[1]
**rh** kill *TNK Epil.7* / filleth *VA 550* / filling, spilling *Luc 1237* / filled *Per 5.2.16 [Chorus]*
> self-willed, well-willer

**will / wilt** *aux v*
=, *Caius MW 1.4.61ff* vɪl / =
**sp** wil[195], wil[be][2], will[4239], will's [will his][1], will't [will it][1], wil't [will it][4], *Caius* vill[9] / wilt[269], wil't[1], wilte[1]
**rh** ill *KJ 4.1.54, S 22.10*; ill, skill *Luc 1241*; kill *3H6 2.5.121*; skill *1H4 1.2.215*; still *CE 2.1.111*

***I will*** *abbr*
*str* əɪl, *unstr* əl, *Jamy H5 3.2.111* aɪl
**sp** Ile[1701], I'le[27], I'll[3], *Jamy* ayle[1]

***thou wilt*** *abbr*
*str* ðəʊlt, *unstr* ðəlt, ðəʊt
**sp** thou'lt[17], thou't[5]

***he will*** *abbr*
*str* i:l, hi:l, *unstr* ɪl
**sp** hee'l[57], heele[13], hee'le[19], hee'll[4], he'l[4], he'le[5], he'll[6]

***she will*** *abbr*
*str* ʃi:l, *unstr* ʃɪl
**sp** sheel[1], shee'l[13], sheele[4], shee'le[6], she'l[5], she'ld[1], she'l'd[1], she'le[3], she'll[4], shee'll[5]

***it will*** *abbr*
twɪl
**sp** 'twil[2], twill[3], 'twill[56], 'twill[be][1]

***we will*** *abbr*
*str* wi:l, *unstr* wɪl
**sp** weel[3], wee'l[163], weele[39], wee'le[55], wee'll[28], we'l[7], well[1], we'll[18]

***you will*** *abbr*
*str* ju:l, *unstr* jəl, jʊl
**sp** you'l[85], youle[16], you'le[31], you'll[25]

***they will*** *abbr*
*str* ðɛ:l, *unstr* ðəl
**sp** thei'le[1], they'l[21], theyle[2], they'le[14], they'll[10]

***who will*** *abbr*
*str* u:l, hu:l
**sp** who'll[1]

**Will** [name] *n*
=
**sp** Will[2]
**rh** fulfil *S 136.2*; kill *S 135.14, 135.1, 135.11, 136.14*

**William / ~'s** *n*
=
**sp** William[44] / Williams[1]

**Williams** *n*
=
**sp** Williams[3]

**willing** *adv*
'wɪlɪn, -ɪŋ
**sp** willing[5]

**willing / ~est** *adj*
'wɪlɪn, -ɪŋ / -st
**sp** willing[28] / willing'st[1]
**rh** shilling *H8 Prol.11*
> unwilling

**willingly** *adv*
*m* 'wɪlɪn,ləɪ, -nl-, -ɪŋ-
**sp** willinglie[1], willingly[34]
**rh** *1* majesty *2H6 1.3.210*; **rh** *2* die *TN 5.1.130*
> unwillingly

**willingness** *n*
*m* 'wɪlɪŋ,nes
**sp** willingnesse[2]
> unwillingness

**Willoughby** *n*
*m* 'wɪləbəɪ, -,bəɪ
**sp** Willoughby[7]

**willow** *adj / n*
'wɪlə, -lo:
**sp** willow[3] / willough[14], willow[3]

**willow-tree** *n*
'wɪlə-,tri:, -lo:
**sp** willow tree[1]
> tree

**Wilson** *n*
=
**sp** Wilson[1]

**Wiltshire / ~'s** *n*
'wɪltʃəɹ / -z
**sp** Wiltshire[6] / Wiltshires[1]

**wimpled** *adj*
=
**sp** wimpled[1]

**win / ~s / won** *v*
= / = / wɤn
**sp** win[70], winne[42] / winnes[5], wins[5] / won[28], wonne[63], woon[2]
**rh** *1* begin *H5 1.2.167*; sin *AW 4.2.76*; skin *2H6 3.1.301*; within *S 119.4*; win her dinner *TS 1.2.214*; **rh** *2* him *TC 3.3.212* / sins *TNK 4.2.155* / done *AW 4.2.64, 5.3.312, 333, 1H4 5.5.44, 1H6 4.5.26, Mac 1.2.70, R2 4.1.196*; done, sun *Mac 1.1.4*; run *TS 4.5.23*; son *1H6 4.6.50, S 41.5*; sun *LLL 1.1.86*

**wince** *v*
=
**sp** winch[22]

**Winchester** *adj*
'wɪntʃestəɹ
**sp** Winchester[1]

**Winchester / ~'s** *n*
'wɪnʧestəɹ / -z
**sp** Winchester[34] / Winchesters[1]

**Wincot** *n*
'wɪnkət
**sp** Wincot[1]

**wind / ~s** *n*
wəɪnd / -z
**sp** wind[19], [south]-wind[1], winde[133] / windes[42], winds[5]
**rh** behind, hind *CE 3.1.75*; find *LLL 4.3.103, MND 3.2.94, PP 16.5, 20.31, S 14.6, 51.7*; find, mind *LC 86*; mind *LLL 4.2.33, VA 338*; Rosalind *AY 3.2.86*; unkind *AY 2.7.175, VA 189* / minds *S 117.7*
> whirlwind; long-, short-winded

**wind / ~s / ~ing / ~ed / wound** *v*
wəɪnd / -z / 'wəɪnd·ɪn, -ɪŋ / -ɪd / wəʊnd
**sp** winde[16] / winds[1] / winding[2] / winded[1] / woon'd[1], wound[1]
> unwind

**wind-changing** *adj*
*m* ˌwəɪnd-'ʧɛ:nʤɪn, -ɪŋ
**sp** wind-changing[1]
> changing

**windgall / ~s** *n*
sp 'wəɪnˌgɑ:lz, -nd-
**sp** windegalls[1]

**winding** *adj*
'wəɪndɪn, -ɪŋ
**sp** winding[1]

**winding-sheet** *n*
'wəɪndɪn-ˌʃi:t, -ɪŋ
**sp** winding-sheet, winding sheet[1]
> sheet

**windlass / ~es** *n*
'wɪnləsɪz, -nd-
**sp** windlesses[1]

**windmill** *n*
'wɪnmɪl, -nd-
**sp** winde-mill[1], windmill[1]

**wind-obeying** *adj*
'wəɪnd-əˌbɛ:ɪn, -ɪŋ
**sp** winde-obeying[1]
> obey

**window / ~s / ~s'** *n*
'wɪndə:, -do: / -z
**sp** window[35], [chamber]-window[3], windowe[1] / windowes[16] / windowes[1]
> bay window

**window / ~ed** *v*
'wɪndəd, -do:d
**sp** window'd[1]

**windowed** *adj*
'wɪndəd, -do:d
**sp** window'd[1]

**windpipe / ~'s** *n*
'wɪnˌpəɪp, -nd- / -s
**sp** wind-pipe[1] / wind-pipes[1]
> pipe

**windring** *adj*
'wəɪndrɪn, -ɪŋ
**sp** windring[1]

**wind-shaked** *adj*
'wəɪnd-ˌʃɛ:kt
**sp** winde-shak'd-[surge][1]

**wind-shaken** *adj*
'wəɪnd-ˌʃɛ:kən
**sp** winde-shaken[1]

**Windsor** *adj / n*
'wɪnzəɹ
**sp** Windsor[23], Windsor-[bell][1], Windsor-[chimnies][1], Wind-sor[2]

**wind-swift** *adj*
'wəɪnd-ˌswɪft
**sp** wind-swift[1]
> swift

**windy** *adj*
'wɪndəɪ
**sp** windie[3], windy[3]

**wine** *n*
wəɪn
**sp** wine[80], [Reinish]-wine[1]
**rh** fine, mine *2H4 5.3.45*
> pipe-wine

**wing / ~s** *n*
=
**sp** wing[25], [sea]-wing[1] / wings[54], [battie]-wings[1]
**rh** king *PT 10, R3 4.3.54*; sing *S 78.7*; sting *Mac 4.1.17* / kings *R3 5.2.23*; sings *VA 306*; springs, things *Luc 949*; things *LLL 5.2.260*
> clip-, full-, light-, slow-, swift-, strong-winged

**wing / ~ed** *v*
= / *m* 'wɪŋɪd, wɪŋd
**sp** wing[2] / wing'd[2], winged[3]

**winged** *adj*
*m* 'wɪŋɪd, wɪŋd
**sp** wing'd[2], winged[8], [well]-winged[1]

**Wingfield** *n*
=
**sp** Wingefield[1]

**Wingham** *n*
'wɪŋəm
**sp** Wingham[1]

**wing-led** *adj*
=
**sp** wing-led[1]
> lead *v*

**wink / ~s** *n*
=
**sp** winke[5] / winkes[1]
> eye-wink

**wink / ~est / ~s / ~ing / ~ed** *v*
= / wɪŋkst / = / 'wɪŋkɪn, -ɪŋ / =
**sp** winck[1], wincke[1], wink[1], winke[18] / wink'st[1] / winks[1] / winking[3] / wink'd[2]

**winking** *adj / n*
'wɪŋkɪn, -ɪŋ
**sp** winking[3] / winking[4]

**winner / ~s** *n*
'wɪnəɹ / -z
**sp** winner[5] / winners[2]

**winning** *adj / n*
'wɪnɪn, -ɪŋ
**sp** winning[1] / winning[3]

**winnow / ~s / ~ed** *v*
'wɪnə, -no: / -z / -d
**sp** winnow[1] / winnowes[1] / winnowed[2]

**winnowed** *adj*
'wɪnəd, -no:
**sp** winnowed[2]

**winter / ~'s / ~s** *n*
'wɪntəɹ / -z
**sp** winter[42], winters [winter is][1] / winters[18] / winters[8]

**wintered** *adj*
'wɪntəɹd
**sp** wintred[1]

**winter-ground** *v*
'wɪntəɹ-ˌgrəʊnd
**sp** winter-ground[1]
> ground

**winterly** *adv*
*m* 'wɪntəɹˌləɪ
**sp** winterly[1]

**wip·e / ~es / ~ing / ~ed** *v*
wəɪp / -s / -ɪn, -ɪŋ / *m* -t, -ɪd
**sp** wipe[25] / wipes[1] / wiping[1] / wip'd[8], wiped[1], wipt[1]
> unwiped

**wire** *n*
wəɪɹ
**sp** wyer[1]

**wiry** *adj*
'wəɪrəɪ
**sp** wiery[1]

**wisdom / ~'s / ~s** *n*
=
**sp** wisdome[11], wis-dome[1], wisedom[4], wisedome[74] / wisedomes[3] wisedoms[1] / wisdomes[2], wisdoms[1], wisedomes[2], wise-domes[1]

**wise** *adj*
wəɪz / 'wəɪz·əɹ / -əst
**sp** wise[127], wise[man][4], wise-[mans][2], wise[men][6], wise-[men][2], wise[mens][1], wise-[ones][1], wise-[woman][1] / wiser[7] / wisest[9]
**rh** *1* eyes *Luc 1550;* **rh** *2* paradise *LLL 4.3.70, PP 3.13, Tem 4.1.123*
> unwise

**wise** *n*
wəɪz
**sp** wise[11]
**rh** sacrifice *Per 5.2.11* [*Chorus*]

**wise·ly / ~ier** *adv*
'wəɪzləɪ / -əɹ
**sp** wisely[31], wise-ly[1] / wiselier[1]
> unwisely

**wiseness** *n*
'wəɪznəs
**sp** wisenesse[1]

**wiser** *adv / n*
'wəɪzəɹ
**sp** wiser[2] / wiser[6]

**wisest** *n*
'wəɪzəst
**sp** wisest[4]

**wish / ~es / ~es'** *n*
=
**sp** wish[43] / wishes[25] / wishes'[1]
**rh** dish *LLL 4.3.79*

**wish / ~est / ~es / ~eth / ~ing / ~ed** *v*
= / 'wɪʃəst / = / = / 'wɪʃɪn, -ɪŋ / =
**sp** wish[164] / wishest[2] / wishes[7] / wisheth[1] / wishing[5] / wish'd[22], wisht[17]
> unwish

**wished** *adj*
*m* 'wɪʃɪd, wɪʃt
**sp** wish'd[1], wished[4]
> un-, well-wished

**wished-for** *adj*
'wɪʃt-ˌfɔ:ɹ
**sp** wisht-for[1]

**wisher / ~s** *n*
'wɪʃəɹz
**sp** wishers[2]

**wishful** *adj*
=
**sp** wishfull[1]

**wishing** *n*
'wɪʃɪn, -ɪŋ
**sp** wishing[3]

**wisp** *n*
=
**sp** wispe[1]

**wistly** *adv*
'wɪstləɪ
**sp** wistly[1]

**wit / ~'s / ~s** *n*
=
**sp** wit[238], wits [wit is][1], wit's [wit is][1], witte[12] / wits[3] / wits[69], wittes[8], witts[1]
**rh** *1* commit *TN 1.2.62*; fit *KL 1.2.179, 3.2.74, LLL 4.1.50, 143, Oth 2.1.131, TN 3.1.66*; hit *RJ 1.1.209*; it *CE 2.1.91, H5 1.2.296, LLL 4.3.145, Luc 153, Oth 2.1.128, TC 4.4.106*; knit *S 26.4*; nit *LLL 4.1.148*; sit *S 37.5*; writ *LLL 4.3.98, Per 4.4.31, S 23.14, 84.11*; **rh** *2* yet *LLL 4.2.34, VA 1008* / **rh** *1* bits *LLL 1.1.27*; fits *CE 5.1.86*; fits, sits *Luc 859*; pits *VA 249*; sits *Luc 290, RJ 1.4.47* / **rh** *2* Muscovites *LLL 5.2.264*; parasites *VA 850*
> mother-wit; beef-, blunt-, fat-, hasty-, high-, iron-, lean-, sodden-, subtle-, un-witted

**wit / ~ting** *v*
'wɪtɪn, -ɪŋ
**sp** witting[1]

**witch / ~'s / ~es** *n*
=
**sp** witch[39], 'witch[1] / witches[1] / witches[12]

**witch** *v*
=
**sp** witch[2]
> bewitch

**witchcraft** *n*
'wɪʧkraft
**sp** witchcraft[12], witch-craft[4], witchcraft's [witchcraft is][1]
> craft

**witched** *adj*
=
**sp** witcht[1]

**witching** *n*
'wɪʧɪn, -ɪŋ
**sp** witching[1]

**wit-cracker / ~s** *n*
'wɪt-ˌkrakəɹz
**sp** witte-crackers[1]

**with** *adv, prep*
wɪθ, wɪð
**sp** with[7360], with' [with the][2], with [all][4], with-[child][1], [big]-with[1], with's [with his][1], with's [with us][1], with't [with it][10]
**rh** teeth *VA 270*; with me guide thee, possess thee, tend thee *R3 4.1.94*; with thee behind thee *AY 3.3.95*

***be with ye/you*** *abbr*
'bɪjə
**sp** b'uy[1], bu'y[1], buy'[1], buy'ye[1]

**withal** *adv / prep*
wɪð'ɑ:l, -ɪθ-
**sp** withal[1], withall[63] / withal[8], withall[71], with-all[1]
**rh** *1* fall, wall *Luc 467*; **rh** *2* shall *LLL 5.2.142* / call *VA 847*; sprawl *Tit 5.1.52*
**pun** *JC 1.1.21* all, awl

**with·draw / ~drew / ~drawn** *v*
wɪð'drɔ:, -ɪθ- / =
**sp** withdraw[30], with-draw[5] / withdrew[2], with-drew[1] / withdrawn[1], withdrawne[1]
**rh** view *VA 1032*
> draw

**withdrawing** *n*
wɪð'drɔ:ɪn, -ɪŋ, -ɪθ-
**sp** with-drawing[1]

**wither / ~ing / ~ed** *v*
'wɪðəɹ / -ɪn, -ɪŋ, -ðr- / -d
**sp** wither[12] / withering[2] / wither'd[2]
> never-withering, overwithered

**withered** *adj*
'wɪðəɹd
**sp** wither'd[20], withered[10], [old]-wither'd[1]

**withers** *n*
'wɪðəɹz
**sp** withers[1], wi-thers[1]

**withhold / ~s / withheld** *v*
wɪð'old, -ɪθ-, -'ho:- / -z / wɪð'eld, -ɪθ-, -'he-
**sp** with-hold[7], with-holde[1] / with-holds[3] / with-held[4]
> hold

**within** *adv / prep*
wɪð'ɪn
**sp** within[112], with-in[1] / within[154], with-in[3], within's [within these][1]
**rh** begin *Cym 5.1.33*; shin *LLL 3.1.114*; win *S 119.2*

**without** *adv / conj / prep*
'wɪðəʊt
**sp** without[17] / without[2], with-out[2] / without[316], without-[dore-forme][1], with-out[7]
**rh** doubt *LC 98* / without her about her *TS 4.4.104*

**with·stand / ~stood** *v*
=
**sp** withstand[2] / withstood[1]
**rh** heart-blood *R2 1.1.173*

**witless** *adj*
=
**sp** witlesse[3]

**witness / ~es** *n*
=
**sp** witnes[4], witness[1], witnesse[61] / witnesses[10]

**witness / ~eth / ~ing / ~ed** *v*
= / = / 'wɪtnəsɪn, -ɪŋ / =
**sp** witnes[2], witnesse[53] / witnesseth[2] / witnessing[2] / witnest[2]

**witnessed** *adj*
=
**sp** witnest[1]

**wit-old** *adj*
'wɪt-ˌo:ld
**sp** wit-old[1]
> old

**wit-snapper** *n*
'wɪt-ˌsnapəɹ
**sp** witte-snapper[1]

**Wittenberg** *n*
'wɪtənˌbɐ:ɹg
**sp** Wittemberge[1], Wittenberg[3]

**wittily** *adv*
'wɪtɪləɪ
**sp** wittily[1]

**wittingly** *adv*
*m* 'wɪtɪnˌləɪ, -ɪŋ-
**sp** wittingly[3]
> unwittingly

**wittoll** *n*
'wɪtəl
**sp** wittoll[1]

**wittolly** *adj*
'wɪtələɪ
**sp** wittolly-[knaue][1]

**witt·y / ~iest** *adj*
'wɪtəɪ / -əst
**sp** wittie[5], witty[10] / wittiest[1]
**rh** city *H8 Epil.6*; ditty *VA 838*

**wive / ~d** *v*
wəɪv / -d
**sp** wiue[4] / wiu'd[3]
**rh** thrive *TN 5.1.394* / arrived *Oth 2.1.60*; thrived *Per 5.2.10* [*Chorus*]
> loose-wived

**wiving** *n*
'wəɪvɪn, -ɪŋ
**sp** wiuing[2]

**wizard / ~s** *n*
'wɪzəɹd / -z
**sp** wizard[3] / wizards[1]

**woe / ~'s / ~s** *n*
wo: / -z
**sp** woe[121] / woes[2] / woes[39]
**rh** *1* blow *Luc 1821*; blow, so *Luc 1661*; bow [weapon] *Per 5.1.246*; flow *H8 Prol.3, S 30.7*; foe, know *Luc 1605*; glow *MND 5.1.367*; go *MA 5.3.14, 33, MND 3.2.442, Per 3. Chorus.42, R2 3.4.97, 5.1.86, TC 2.2.112, 5.10.31*; go, moe, so *MA 2.3.66*; grow *R2 3.4.100, 5.6.45*; know *LC 63, Luc 1310, S 50.5*; low *LC 20, VA 1140*; moe, so *Luc 1482*; no *RJ 2.3.42, 3.2.51*; no, so *LLL 4.1.15*; overthrow *S 90.6*; Romeo *RJ 5.3.309*; show *Ham 1.2.86, LLL 4.3.33, Per 4.4.24, R2 3.3.70*; show, so *Luc 1509, 1808*; slow *S 44.14*; so *CE 2.1.15, 3H6 2.3.46, 2.5.20, Luc 1225, MM 2.1.271, 4.1.13, R2 2.1.152, 3.4.28, 4.1.149, S 71.8, 90.13, 127.13, 129.11, Tit 5.3.147, VA 714, 833, 839, 967*; toe *KL 3.2.33*;
**rh** *2* shrew *TS 5.2.29* / foes *KL 3.6.100* [*Q*]; foes, repose *Luc 935*; foes, shows *TNK 1.5.9*; foes, those *Luc 1458*; goes *Luc 1492, 1505*; goes, shows *Luc 1747*; grows *RJ 3.5.36*; shows *LC 307*

**woebegone** *adj*
'wo:bɪˌgɒn
**sp** woe-be-gone[1]

**woeful / ~lest** *adj*
'wo:fʊl / *m* -st, -ˌest
**sp** woefull[1], woful[1], wofull[31] / wofullest[1], wofulst[1], woful'st[1]

**woer / ~'s** *n*
'wu:əɹ / -z
**sp** woer[2] / woers[1]

**woe-wearied** *adj*
*m* ˌwo:-'wi:rəɪd, -'we-
**sp** woe-wearied[1]
> weary

**wold** *n*
wo:ld
**sp** old[1]

**wolf / wolves** *n*
=
**sp** wolfe[29] / wolues[18]
**rh** gulf *Mac 4.1.22*
> bitch-, demi-, she-wolf

**Wolsey** *n*
'wʊlzəɪ
**sp** Wolsey[12], Woolsey[1]

**wolvish** *adj*
=
**sp** woluish[2], wooluish[1]

**wolvish-rauening** *adj*
'wʊlvɪʃ-ˌravənɪn, -ɪŋ
**sp** woluish-rauening[1]
> raven

**woman / ~'s / women / ~'s** *n*
=, *Evans MW 1.1.211ff* 'ʊmən, -nz / =
**sp** woman[303], woma[n][1], [fat]-woman[1], [old-fat]-woman, [poore-old]-woman[1], [wise]-woman[1], [would]-woman[1], wo-man[11], womans [woman is][2], woman's [woman is][2], *Evans* 'oman[1], 'o-man[1], o'man[10], o'mans[1] / womans[70], wo-mans[3] / women[152], wo-men[1], [distaffe]-women[1] / womens[18]
**rh** no man *TG 3.1.105* / in *H8 Epil.10*
> beggar-, butter-, country-, day-, English-, French-, gentle-, kins-, mad-, tithe-, waiting-, Welsh-woman

**woman** *adj / v*
=
**sp** woman[1] / woman[2]

**womaned** *adj*
=
**sp** woman'd[1]

**womanhood** *n*
'wʊmənˌʊd, -ˌhʊd
**sp** womanhood[3], woman-hood[3], wooman-hood[1]

**womanish** *adj*
=
**sp** womanish[7]
**rh** devilish *R3 1.4.265*

**womankind** *n*
'wʊmənˌkəɪnd
**sp** womankind[1]

**womanly** *adj*
*m* 'wʊmənˌləɪ
**sp** womanlie[1], womanly[2]

**woman-queller** *n*
'wʊmən-ˌkweləɹ
**sp** woman-queller[1]
> quell

**woman-tired** *adj*
'wʊmənˌtəɪɹd
**sp** woman-tyr'd[1]

**womb / 's / ~s** *n*
wu:m, wʊm / -z
**sp** womb[3], wombe[47] / wombes[1] / wombes[1]
**rh** tomb *1H6 4.5.35, RJ 2.3.6, S 3.5*
> round-wombed

**womb / ~s** *v*
wu:mz, wʊ-
**sp** wombes[1]
> enwombed

**womby** *adj*
'wu:məɪ, 'wʊ-
**sp** wombie[1]

**women**
> woman

**won**
> win

**Woncot** *n*
'wɒnkət
**sp** Woncot[1]

**wonder / ~s** *n*
'wɤndəɹ / -z
**sp** wonder[64], won-der[1] / wonders[14]
**rh** asunder *1H6 4.7.48, PT 32*; thunder *LLL 4.2.113, PP 5.9*

**wonder / ~s / ~ing / ~ed** *v*
'wɤndəɹ / -z / -ɪn, -ɪŋ, -dr- / -d
**sp** wonder[49] / wonders[3] / wondering[1], wondring[1] / wonder'd[2], wondred[3]

**rh** sunder *MND 5.1.133*; under *VA 748*

**wondered** *adj*
'wɤndəɹd
**sp** wondred[1]

**wonderful** *adj*
'wɤndəɹfʊl
**sp** wonderful[3], wonderfull[19], wonder-full[2]

**wonderfully** *adv*
'wɤndəɹfləɪ
**sp** wonderfully[1]

**wondering** *adj / adv / n*
'wɤndrɪn, -ɪŋ
**sp** wondring[1] / wond'ring[1] / wondring[1], wond'ring[1]

**wonder-wounded** *adj*
'wɤndəɹ-ˌwəʊndɪd
**sp** wonder-wounded[1]
> wound

**wondrous** *adj / adv*
'wɤndrəs
**sp** wonderous[1], wondrous[13], won-drous[1] / wondrous[15], wond'rous[1], won-drous[1]

**wondrously** *adv*
'wɤndrəsləɪ
**sp** wondrously[1]

**wont** *adj / n / v*
wo:nt
**sp** wont[43] / wont[2] / woont[1]

**wonted** *adj*
'wo:ntɪd
**sp** wonted[10]

**woo / ~s / ~ing / ~ed** *v*
= / = / 'wu:ɪn, -ɪŋ / =
**sp** woe[20], woo[24], wooe[25] / woes[3], wooes[5] / woing[7], wooing[8] / woed[2], woo'd[21], wooed[9]
**rh** *1* do *LLL 5.2.299, MND 2.1.242, 2.2.136, Tim 4.3.470*; two *MV 2.9.75;* unto *LC 182* [*emend of* vow]; **woo her** unto her *VA 309*; **woo him** to him *PP 11.2*; **woo me** to me *AY 4.3.48*; **rh** *2* know *MND 5.1.137* / doing *TC 1.2.286*
> a-wooing

**wood** *adj*
=
**sp** wood[2]
**rh** blood *1H6 4.7.35, VA 740*

**wood / ~s** *n*
=
**sp** wood[50] / woods[13]
**rh** *1* good *Mac 4.1.96, MND 2.2.41*;
**rh** *2* flood *VA 826* / bloods *Tim 4.3.534*
> greenwood

**woodbine** *n*
'wʊdbəɪn
**sp** woodbine[2], wood-bine[1]
**rh** eglantine *MND 2.1.251*

**woodbird / ~s** *n*
'wʊdbɐ:ɹdz
**sp** wood birds[1]

**woodcock / ~s** *n*
=
**sp** woodcocke[6], wood-cocke[1] / woodcocks[2]

**wooden** *adj*
=
**sp** wodden[2], wodden-[prickes][1], woodden[5]

**woodland** *adj*
=
**sp** woodland[1]

**woodleaf / -leaves** *n*
=
**sp** wood-leaues[1]
> leaf

**woodman** *n*
=
**sp** woodman[3]

**woodmonger** *n*
'wʊdmɤŋgəɹ
**sp** woodmonger[1]

**Woodstock** *n*
=
**sp** Woodstock[1]

**Woodville** *n*
=
**sp** Woodeuile[1], Wooduile[2], Wooduill[2]

**wooer / ~s** *n*
'wu:əɹ / -z
**sp** wooer[7] / wooers[7]

**woof** *n*
wu:f, wʊf
**sp** woofe[1]

**wooing** *adj / n*
'wu:ɪn, -ɪŋ
**sp** woing[2], wooing[1] / woing[4], wooing[7]
**rh** *1* doing *TS 2.1.75*; suing *VA 358*;
**rh** *2* cunning *TS 2.1.403*

**wooingly** *adv*
'wu:ɪnləɪ, -ɪŋ-
**sp** wooingly[1]

**wool** *n*
=
**sp** wooll[3]

**woollen** *adj / n*
=
**sp** wollen[1], woollen[1] / woollen[1]

**woolly** *adj*
'wʊləɪ
**sp** woolly[2]

**woolsack** *n*
=
**sp** woolsacke[1]

**woolward** *adj*
'wʊlwəɹd
**sp** woolward[1]

**Worcester / ~'s** *n*
'wʊstəɹ / -z
**sp** Worcester[22], Worster[3] / Worcesters[1]

**word / ~'s / ~s / ~s'** *n*
wɔːɹd, *Evans MW 1.1.236* ɔːɹt / wɔːɹdz, *Evans MW 1.1.114* wɔːɹts
**sp** word[487], [all-changing]-word[1], worde[1], words [word is][1], *Evans* 'ord[1], ort[1] / words[3] / wordes[9], words[401], *Evans* worts[2] / words[2]
**rh** afford *S 79.9*; board *CE 3.2.20, LLL 2.1.203*; Ford *MW 5.5.236*; lord *2H4 5.5.74, 1H6 4.3.31, LLL 2.1.202, 4.1.101, 4.3.92, 5.2.238, 313, 370, 449, MND 2.2.158, Per 2.Chorus.4, R2 5.3.121, R3 3.7.3*; record, sword *Luc 1642*; sword *1H6 4.6.2, LLL 5.2.274, MND 2.2.112, 5.1.334* / affords *CE 3.1.25, Luc 1105, S 85.5, 105.10*; fords *Luc 1330*; lords *Luc 1610*; swords *Luc 1420, R2 3.3.131*
**pun** *MW 1.1.114* worts
> by-, court-, nay-, re-word

**word / ~s** *v*
wɔːɹd / -z
**sp** word[2], words[3]

**wore**
> wear

**work / ~s** *n*
wɔːɹk, *Evans MW 3.1.15* ɔːɹk / -s
**sp** work[3], worke[102], [a]-worke[2], work's [work has][1], *Evans* orke[1] / workes[8]

**work / ~s / ~ing / wrought** *v*
wɔːɹk, *Evans MW 1.1.135* ɔːɹk / -s / 'wɔːɹkɪn, -ɪŋ / =
**sp** work[4], worke[70], *Evans MW 1.1.135* orke[1] / workes[11], works[1] / working[4] / wrought[40]
**rh** lurk *PP 18.37*; Turk *Oth 2.1.114* / brought *R2 5.6.34*; fought *KL 4.7.96*; naught *VA 991*; sought, thought *Luc 341*; thought *S 44.11*
> a-, bed-, fire-, handi-, needle-, Night-, out-, sale-, water-, under-work; half-worker, high-wrought

**working** *adj*
'wɔːɹkɪn, -ɪŋ
**sp** working[1]

**working / ~s** *n*
'wɔːɹkɪn, -ɪŋ / -z
**sp** working[15] / workings[2]

**working-day** *adj*
'wɔːɹkɪn-ˌdɛː, -ɪŋ-
**sp** working day

**working-day / ~s** *n*
'wɔːɹkɪn-ˌdɛː, -ɪŋ- / -z
**sp** working day / working-daies[1], working dayes

**working-house** *n*
'wɔːɹkɪn-ˌəʊs, -ɪŋ-, -ˌhəʊs-
**sp** working-house[1]
> house

**work·man / ~men** *n*
'wɔːɹkmən
**sp** workeman[2], worke-man[1], workman[2] / workemen[3]

**workmanly** *adv*
*m* 'wɔːɹkmənˌləɪ
**sp** workmanlie[1]

**workmanship** *n*
*m* 'wɔːɹkmənˌʃɪp
**sp** workemanship[1]

**workyday** *adj*
'wɔːɹkəˌdɛː
**sp** worky day[1]
> day

**world / ~'s / ~s** *n*
wɔːɹld, *Caius MW 1.4.62, 2.3.28* vɔːɹld, *Evans MW 1.1.46, Fluellen H5 4.7.23ff* ɔːɹld / -z
**sp** world[591], [giant]-world[1], worlds [world is][1], world's [world is][5], *Caius* varld[1], vorld[1], *Evans, Fluellen* orld[3] / worldes[2], worlds[34], [wide]-worlds[1], *KJ 3.4.110 emend of* words / worlds[4]
> half-world

**worldling / ~s** *n*
'wɔːɹldlɪnz, -ɪŋz
**sp** worldlings[2]

**worldly** *adv*
'wɔːɹldləɪ
**sp** worldly[14], *emend of Oth 1.3.296* wordly[1]

**world-sharer / ~s** *n*
*m* ˌwɔːɹld-'ʃɛːrəɹz
**sp** world-sharers

**world-wearied** *adj*
*m* ˌwɔːɹld-'wiːrəɪd
**sp** world-wearied[1]
> weary

**world-without-end** *adj*
'wɔːɹld-wɪð'əʊt-ˌend
**sp** world-without-end[1]

**worm / ~'s / ~s / ~s'** *n*
wɔːɹm / -z
**sp** worm[2], worme[25], worme's [worm is][1], / wormes[1] / wormes[18], [blinde]-wormes[1] / wormes[meat][1]
> glow-, malt-worm

**worm-eaten** *adj*
*m* ˌwɔːɹm-'iːtən
**sp** worm-eaten[1], worme-eaten[1], worme-eaten-[hole][1]
> eat

**worm-hole / ~s** *n*
'wɔːɹm-ˌoːlz, -ˌhoː-
**sp** worme-holes[1]

**wormwood** *n*
'wɔːɹmwʊd
**sp** wormewood[1], worme-wood[2], wormwood[2]

**wormy** *adj*
'wɔːɹməɪ
**sp** wormie[1]

**worn** *adj*
wɔːɹn
**sp** worne[1]
> over-, war-, wave-worn; wear *v*

**worried** *adj*
'wʊrəɪd
**sp** worried[1]

**worr·y / ~ies / ~ing** *v*
'wʊrəɪ / -z / -ɪn, -ɪŋ
**sp** worry[1] / worryes[1] / worrying[1]

**wors·e / ~er / ~t** *adj*
wɔ:ɹs, wɑ:- / 'wɔ:ɹsəɹ,'wɑ:- / wɔ:ɹst, wɑ:-
**sp** worse[92], worsse[2] / worser[11], worsser[1] / worst[23]
**rh** curse *CE 4.2.26, R2 3.4.102, R3 4.4.122, S 84.14*
> bad

**wors·e / ~er / ~t** *adv*
wɔ:ɹs, wɑ:- / 'wɔ:ɹsəɹ,'wɑ:- / wɔ:ɹst, wɑ:-
**sp** worse[30], worsse[1] / worser[1] / worst[2]
**rh** curse *MND 3.2.45*; nurse *VA 774* / accursed *2H4 1.3.108*
> bad

**wors·e / ~er / ~t** *n*
wɔ:ɹs, wɑ:- / 'wɔ:ɹsəɹ,'wɑ:- / wɔ:ɹst, wɑ:-
**sp** worse[30] / worser[3] / worst[70]
**rh** accursed *TG 5.4.72*; curst *TS 1.2.128*; first *KL 5.3.4, TS 1.2.14, 35*
> bad

**worse-bodied** *adj*
'wɔ:ɹs-'bɒdəɪd, wɑ:-
**sp** worse bodied[1]
> body

**worship / ~'s / ~s** *n*
'wɔ:ɹʃɪp / -s
**sp** worship[11], wor-ship[2], worshippe[3], worship's [worship is][1] / worships[3] / worshippes[1], worships[5]

**worship / ~pest / ~s / ~ped** *v*
'wɔ:ɹʃɪp / -s, -st / -s / -t
**sp** worship[76] / worshipst[1] / worships[3] / worship'd[2], worshipt[6], wor-shipt[1]

**worshipful** *adj*
'wɔ:ɹʃɪpfʊl
**sp** worshipful[1], worshipfull[5]

**worshipfully** *adv*
'wɔ:ɹʃɪpfləɪ
**sp** worshipfully[1]

**worshipped** *adj*
'wɔ:ɹʃɪpt
**sp** worshipt[1]

**worshipper / ~s** *n*
'wɔ:ɹʃɪpəɹ / -z
**sp** worshipper[1] / worshippers[1]
**rh** cheer, fear *Luc 86*
> idiot-worshipper

**worsted-stocking** *adj*
'wʊstɪd-ˌstɒkɪn, -ɪŋ, 'wɔ:ɹs-
**sp** woosted-stocking[1]

**wort** *n*
wɔ:ɹt
**sp** wort[1]
**pun** *MW 1.1.115* words

**worth** *adj*
wɔ:ɹθ / 'wɔ:ɹðɪəɹ
**sp** woorth[2], worth[96]
**rh** *Ham 4.4.66* [*Q2*], *LC 267, S 72.14, VA 418*
> crown's-, out-, penny-worth

**worth / ~s** *n*
wɔ:ɹθ / -s
**sp** worth[81], wroth[1] / worths[1]
**rh** forth *AW 3.4.15, S 25.9, 38.9, 103.3, TC 1.3.241*
> halfpennyworth

**worthier** *n*
'wɔ:ɹðəɪəɹ
**sp** worthier[2], worthyer[1]

**worthiest** *n*
'wɔ:ɹðəɪəst
**sp** worthiest[5]
> unworthiest

**worthily** *adv*
*m* 'wɔ:ɹðɪˌləɪ, -ɪl-
**sp** worthily[13]
> unworthily

**worthiness** *n*
*m* 'wɔ:ɹðɪˌnes, -ɪnəs
worthinesse[13], worthi-nesse[1], worthynesse[1]
> unworthiness

**worthless** *adj*
'wɔ:ɹθləs
**sp** worthles[2], worthlesse[12], worth-lesse[1]

**worth·y / -ier** *adj*
'wɔ:ɹðəɪ / -əɹ / -əst
**sp** woorthie[1], woor-thy[1], worthie[20], worthy[191], wor-thy[2] / worthier[11] / worthiest[7], worthyest[1]
> all-, note-, thrice-, un-worthy

**worthy / ~'s / ~ies** *n*
'wɔ:ɹðəɪ / -z
**sp** worthie[2], wor-thie[1] / worthies[1] / worthies[13], wor-thies[2]

**worth·y / ~ied** *v*
'wɔ:ɹðəɪd
**sp** worthied[1]

**wot / ~test / ~s / ~ting** *v*
= / wɒts, -st / = / 'wɒtɪn, -ɪŋ
**sp** wot[24], wote[2] / wot'st[1] / wots[2] / wotting[1]
**rh** *1* forgot *PP 17.6, R2 5.6.18*; lot *Ham 2.2.415*; not *MND 3.2.422*; what *R2 2.2.40*; **rh** *2* boat *1H6 4.6.32*

**would / ~est** *v*
=, wʊld, *Macmorris H5 3.2.114* wad / wʊdst, wʊds, wʊt
**sp** wold[29], would[2212], wou'd[1], would't [would it][2], *Macmorris* wad[1] / wold'st[2], woo't[6], wouldest[5], wouldst[31], would'st[92]
**rh** should *LLL 1.1.141*
> will

***he would*** *abbr*
*str* i:d, =, i:ld, hi:ld, *unstr*
**sp** hee'd[1], hee'ld[4], heel'd[4]

***I would*** *abbr*
*str* əɪd, əɪld, *unstr* əd
**sp** Ide[1], I'de[24], I'ld[23], Il'd[11]

***it would*** *abbr*
*str* twʊd, twʊld, *unstr* twəd
**sp** 'twold[1], twoo'd[1], 'twould[21], t'would[2]

**wound / ~s / ~s'** *n*
wəʊnd / wəʊndz, -nz, [*in swearing*] wu:nz
**sp** wound[42] / woones[1], wounds[66], [honour-owing]-wounds[1] / wounds[1]
**rh** confound *Luc 1201*; found *RJ 2.2.1* [*rh with RJ 2.1.42*]; ground *MND 2.2.107, R3 3.2.139*; hound *VA 915*; round *VA 370*; sound *Luc 1466* / confounds, swounds *Luc 1488*

**wound / ~ing / ~ed** *v*
wəʊnd / 'wəʊnd·ɪn, -ɪŋ / -ɪd
**sp** wound[20] / wounding[7] / wounded[27]
**rh** confound *MND 5.1.288*; sound *Per 4.Chorus.23, RJ 4.5.125* / bounds *VA 267*; confounds *TC 3.1.116*

**wounded** *adj*
'wəʊndɪd
**sp** wounded[10]
> love-, wonder-wounded

**wounding** *adj*
'wəʊndɪn, -ɪŋ
**sp** wounding[2]
> back-wounding

**wounding / ~s** *n*
'wəʊndɪn, -ɪŋ / -z
**sp** *VA* wou[n]ding[1] / woundings[1]
**rh** harsh sounding *VA 432*

**woven** *adj*
'wo:vən
**sp** wouen[1]

**wrack / ~s** *n*
=
**sp** wrack[10], wracke[21] / wrackes[1]
**rh** alack *Per 4.Chorus.12*; back *Luc 841, 966, Mac 5.5.51, S 126.5, VA 558*
> shipwreck

**wrack / ~ed** *v*
=
**sp** wracke[1] / wrack'd[3], wrackt[9], wrack't[1]

**wrangle** *v*
=
**sp** wrangle[7]

**wrangler / ~s** *n*
'ranglər / -z
**sp** wrangler[1] / wranglers[1]

**wrangling** *adj / n*
'ranglɪn, -ɪŋ
**sp** wrangling[7] / wrangling[1]

**wrap / ~s / ~ped** *v*
=, rɒp / -s / -t
**sp** wrap[2] / wraps[1] / wrap'd[3], wrapt[5]

**wrastle**
> wrestle

**wrath / ~s** *n*
raθ, rɒθ, *MV 2.9.78* ro:θ / -s
**sp** wrath[54], wrath's [wrath is][1], wroth[1], *MV* wroath[1] / wraths[2]
**rh** *1* hath *LC 293, MND 2.1.20, Per 4.Chorus.44*; lath *TN 4.2.126*; **rh** *2* moth, oath *MV 2.9.78*; **rh** *3* death *TG 5.4.128*

**wrathful** *adj*
'raθfʊl, 'rɒθ-
**sp** wrathfull[12], wrath-full[1]

**wrathfully** *adv*
*m* 'raθfʊˌlər, 'rɒθ-
**sp** wrathfully[1]

**wrath-kindled** *adj*
*m* ˌraθ-'kɪndld, ˌrɒθ-
**sp** wrath-kindled[1]
> kindle

**wreak / ~s / ~ing** *v*
= / = / 'ri:kɪn, -ɪŋ
**sp** wreake[5] / wreakes[2] / wreaking[1]

**wreakful** *adj*
=
**sp** wreakefull[1], wrekefull[1]

**wreakless** *adj*
=
**sp** wreaklesse[3]

**wreath / ~s** *n*
ri:θ, ri:ð / -z
**sp** wreath[2] / wreathes[1], wreaths[1]

**wreathe / ~ed** *v*
=
**sp** wreath[1] / wreath'd[1]

**wreathed** *adj*
'ri:ðɪd
**sp** wreathed[1]

**wren / ~'s / ~s** *n*
=
**sp** wren[6] / wrens[1] / wrens[1]

**wrench** *n*
=
**sp** wrench[1]

**wrench / ~ing / ~ed** *v*
= / 'renʃɪn, -ɪŋ / =
**sp** wrench[3] / wrenching[1] / wrencht[2]

**wrenching** *adj / n*
'renʃɪn, -ɪŋ
**sp** wrenching[3]

**wrest** *n*
=
**sp** wrest[1]

**wrest / ~ed** *v*
=
**sp** wrest[5] / wrested[2]

**wrested** *adj*
=
**sp** wrested[1]

**wrestl·e / ~ing / ~ed** *v*
'ras·əl / -lɪn, -lɪŋ / -əld
**sp** wrastle[7] / wrastling[9], wrestling[1] / wrastled[3]

**wrestler / ~s** *n*
'raslər / -z
**sp** wrastler[6] / wrastlers[1]

**wretch / ~'s / ~es** *n*
=
**sp** wretch[54], [sharpe-looking]-wretch[1] / wretches[1] / wretches[12]
**rh** scratch *VA 703*

**wretched / ~est** *adj*
= / 'retʃɪdst
**sp** wretched[65] / wretched'st[1]

**wretched** *n*
=
**sp** wretched[2]

**wretchedness** *n*
=
**sp** wretchednesse[9]

**wring / ~s / ~ing / wrung** *v*
= / = / ˈrɪŋgɪn, -ɪŋ / rɤŋ
**sp** wring[11] / rings[1], wrings[3] / wringing[4] / wrung[4]

**wringer** *n*
ˈrɪŋgəɹ
**sp** ringer[1]

**wringing** *n*
ˈrɪŋgɪn, -ɪŋ
**sp** wringing[1]

**wrinkle / ~s** *n*
=
**sp** wrinckle[1], wrinkle[3] / wrinckles[3], wrinkles[5]

**wrinkle / ~s** *v*
=
**sp** wrinkles[1]

**wrinkled** *adj*
=
**sp** wrinckled[3], wrinkled[8], wrin-kled[1]

**wrist / ~s** *n*
=
**sp** wrist[2] / wrists[1]

**writ / ~s** *n*
=
**sp** writ[12] / writs[1]
**rh** it *Luc 1295, 1331*; wit *LLL 4.3.97, Per 4.4.32, S 23.13, S 84.9*

**writ·e / ~es / ~ing / wrote / writ / ~ten** *v*
rəɪt / -s / ˈrəɪtɪn, -ɪŋ / ro:t / =
**sp** write[114] / writes[23] / writing[5] / wrote[9] / writ[84], writt[1] / written[27], writ-ten[2]
**rh** bright *S 21.9*; fight *Luc 1296*; might *S 80.1*; night *S 86.5*; quite *S 103.5*; sprite *AY 3.2.133*; white *MW 5.5.69*
> underwrite

**writer / ~s** *n*
ˈrəɪtəɹ / -z
**sp** writer[2] / writers[5], wri-ters[1]
**rh** lighter *TNK Prol.19*

**writhled** *adj*
ˈrɪðəld
**sp** writhled[1]

**writing** *adj*
ˈrəɪtɪn, -ɪŋ
**sp** writing[1]

**writing / ~s** *n*
ˈrəɪtɪn, -ɪŋ / -z
**sp** writing[16] / writings[2]

**written** *adj*
=
**sp** written[4]

**wrong** *adj / adv*
=
**sp** wrong[13] / wrong[5]

**wrong / ~s** *n*
=
**sp** wrong[157] / wrongs[65], [true]-wrongs[1]
**rh** *1* along *RJ 1.1.196*; belong *S 88.14*; belong, strong *Luc 1264*; long *3H6 3.3.231, 4.1.110, Luc 1467, R2 2.1.164, TN 5.1.138*; strong *MND 3.2.28, Tim 5.4.10*; **rh** *2* tongue *LLL 1.1.166, 4.2.117, Luc 80, 1462, 1467, MND 2.2.11, 3.2.361, PP 5.13, R2 1.1.191, 1.3.246, 3.2.215, S 89.11, 112.8, 139.1, Tit 5.3.57, VA 219, 329, 429, 1005*; young *S 19.13* / **rh** *1* belongs *S 92.5*; **rh** *2* tongues *2H4 Induction.40, MA 5.3.5*

**wrong / ~est / ~s / ~ing / ~ed** *v*
= / rɒŋst / = / ˈrɒŋg·ɪn, -ɪŋ / *m* -ɪd, rɒŋd
**sp** wrong[46] / wrong'st[6] / wrongs[6] / wronging[1] / wrong'd[38], wronged[6]
> self-wrong

**wronged** *adj*
*m* rɒŋd, ˈrɒŋgɪd
**sp** wrong'd[2], wronged[8]

**wronger** *n*
ˈrɒŋgəɹ
**sp** wronger[3]

**wrongful** *adj*
=
**sp** wrongfull[2]

**wrongfully** *adv*
*m* ˈrɒŋfʊˌləɪ, -fləɪ
**sp** wrongfully[6], wrong-fully[1]

**wrong-incensed** *adj*
*m* ˈrɒŋ-ɪnˌsensɪd
**sp** wrong incensed[1]
> incense

**wrongly** *adv*
ˈrɒŋləɪ
**sp** wrongly[1]

**wrote**
> write

**wrought**
> wreak

**wrung**
> wring

**wry / ~ing** *v*
ˈrəɪɪn, -ɪŋ
**sp** wrying[1]

**wry-necked** *adj*
ˈrəɪ-ˌnekt
**sp** wry-neckt[1]
> neck

**Wye** *n*
wəɪ
**sp** Wye[3]

**Xanthippe** *n*
zan'tɪpi:
**sp** Zentippe[1]

# Y

**y** *Fr adv*
i
**sp** [mal]-y-[pence][1]

**yard / ~s** *n*
jɑːɹd / -z
**sp** yard[8] / yards[5]
> church-, meat-, tilt-yard

**yare** *adj*
jɑːɹ
**sp** yare[9]

**yarely** *adv*
'jɑːɹləɪ
**sp** yarely[2]

**yarn** *n*
jɑːɹn
**sp** yarne[1], yearne[1]

**Yaughan** *n*
'jɔːn
**sp** Yaughan[1]

**yawn / ~ed** *v*
=
**sp** yawne[5] / yawn'd[1]

**yawning** *adj*
'jɔːnɪn, -ɪŋ
**sp** yawning[3]

**yclad** *adj*
ɪ'klad
**sp** yclad[1]

**ycliped** *adj*
ɪ'klɪpt
**sp** ycliped[2]

**ye**
> you

**yea** *adv*
jɛː
**sp** yea[172], [rascally]-yea-[forsooth-knaue][1]

**yea / ~s** *n*
jɛːz
**sp** yeas[1]

**year / ~'s / ~s** *n*
'jiːɹ, jɛːɹ / -z
**sp** year[1], yeare[41], yeere[37], yere[4] / yeares[2], yeeres[1] / yeares[100], years[3], yeeres[83], yeers[1], yeres[5]
**rh** *1* appear *S 53.9*; cheer *2H4 5.3.18*; dear *2H4 5.3.18, KJ 1.1.152*; deer *KL 3.4.133*; fear *1H4 4.1.136*; here *Per 4.4.35*; peer *WT 4.3.3*; **rh** *2* bear *1H6 1.3.91*; everywhere *S 97.2*; there *2H4 5.3.18*; wear *KL 1.4.163, 3.4.133, VA 508* / **rh** *1* fears *Per 1.2.85*; peers *R2 1.3.94*; tears [cry] *Per 1.4.18, VA 1091*; **rh** *2* forbears *VA 524*
> goodyear, new-year's

**yearly** *adj / adv*
'jiːɹləɪ, 'jɛː-
**sp** yearely[1], yeerely[1] / yeerely[3]

**yearn / ~s / ~ed** *v*
jɐːɹn / -z / -d
**sp** yern[1] / yernes[1] / yern'd[1]

**yeast** *n*
jest
**sp** yest[1]

**yeasty** *adj*
'jestəɪ
**sp** yesty[2]

**Yedward,** *abbr* **Yed** *n*
'jedwəɹd, *abbr* jed
**sp** Yedward[1], *abbr* Yead[1]

**yell / ~s** *n*
=
**sp** yell[1] / yels[1]
**rh** smell *VA 688*

**yell / ~ed** *v*
=
**sp** yell[1] / yell'd[1]

**yellow** *adj*
'jelə, -oː
**sp** yellow[22], yel-low[1]

**yellow / ~s** *n*
'jelə, -loː / -z
**sp** yellow[3] / yel-lowes[1]
**rh** fellow *H8 Prol.16*

**yellowness** *n*
'jelənəs
**sp** yallow-nesse[1]

**yelping** *adj*
'jelpɪn, -ɪŋ
**sp** yelping[2]

**yeoman / ~'s / ~men / ~men's** *n*
'joː·mən / -z / -mən / -z
**sp** yeoman[9] / yeomans[1] / yeomen[3] / yeomens[1]

**yerewhile**
> erewhile

**yerk / ~ed** *v*
jɐːɹk / -t
**sp** yerke[1] / yerk'd[1]

**yes** *adv*
jɪs, jes
**sp** yes[215]

**yesterday / ~s** *adv*
*m* ˈjɪstəɹdɛː, ˈjes-, -ˌdɛː / -ˌdɛːz
**sp** yesterday[25] / yesterdayes[1]

**yesternight** *adv*
*m* ˈjɪstəɹnəɪt, -ˌnəɪt, ˈjes-
**sp** yesternight[11], yester-night[1]
> night

**yet** *adv*
jɪt, jet
**sp** yet[1501], yut[1]
**rh** sit *RJ 2.3.72*; wit *LLL 4.2.35, VA 1007*
> never-yet

**yew** *n*
=
**sp** eugh[1], yew[2]
**rh** Jew *Mac 4.1.27*; true *TN 2.4.54*

**yield / ~s / ~ing / ~ed** *v*
= / = / ˈjiːldɪn, -ɪŋ / =
**sp** yeeld[121], yeelde[13], yeild[4], yield[1] / yeeldes[1], yeelds[14] / yeelding[5] / yeelded[23]
**rh** *1* field *CE 3.2.40, H5 4.2.35, Luc 75, VA 452, 893*; field, wield *Luc 1433*; **rh** *2* killed *Luc 75* / fields *PP 19.4* / **rh** *1* shielded *LC 149*; **rh** *2* builded *LC 149*
> God

**yielder / ~s** *n*
ˈjiːldəɹz
**sp** yeelders[1]

**yielder-up** *n*
ˈjiːldəɹ-ˈɤp
**sp** yeelder vp[1]

**yielding** *adj / n*
ˈjiːldɪn, -ɪŋ
yeelding[2] / yeelding[8], yeilding[1]
> easy-yielding

**yoke / ~s** *n*
ˈjoːk / -s
**sp** yoake[18], yoke[5] / yoakes[2]
> unyoke

**yoke / ~th / ~d** *v*
joːk / ˈjoːk·əθ / *m* -ɪd, joːkd
**sp** yoake[5], yoke[2] / yoaketh[1] / yoak'd[3], yoaked[1], yoked[1]

**yoke-devil / ~s** *n*
ˈjoːk-ˌdɪvəlz
**sp** yoake diuels[1]
> devil

**yoke-fellow / ~s** *n*
*m* ˌjoːk-ˈfelə, -loː / -z
**sp** yoake-fellow[1] / yoke-fellowes[1]
> fellow

**yon** *det*
=
**sp** yon[9]

**yond** *adv / det*
=
**sp** yond[5], yonds [yond is][1] / yond[40], yon'd[5]

**yonder** *adv*
ˈjɒndəɹ
**sp** yonder[66], yon-der[1], yonders [yonder is][4], yon-ders [yonder is][1]

**yore** *S* *adv*
jɔːɹ
**sp** yore[1]
**rh** store *S 68.14*

**Yorick / ~'s** *n*
=
**sp** Yorick[1] / Yoricks[1]

**York / ~'s / ~s** *n*
jɔːɹk / -s
**sp** York[6], Yorke[245], Yorke-[Place, place][2] / Yorkes[6] / Yorkes[1]

**Yorkshire** *n*
ˈjɔːɹkʃəɹ
**sp** Yorkeshire[2]

**you** *pro*
*str* =, *unstr* jə, jʊ
**sp** yoe[1], you[13392], [dig]-you-[den][1], [far]you[well][1], [fare]you[wel][1], [la]-you[1], [lo]-you[1]
**rh** adieu *AC 5.2.188, 1H6 4.4.46, LLL 1.1.111, 2.1.200, 5.2.227, 235, 240, MND 1.1.225, RJ 3.5.58, S 57.6, TNK 1.4.13, VA 535*; do *Mac 3.5.13, Per 1.1.51, 2.5.25*; due *CE 4.1.2, TC 4.5.52*; ensue *Oth 2.3.10*; grew *S 84.2, 86.2*; new *CE 3.2.37, MV 3.2.133, S 15.13, 53.6, 76.9*; overview *LLL 4.3.174*; sue *LLL 5.2.428*; thereto *TG 1.3.88*; threw *S 145.14*; too *1H4 2.3.119*; true *LLL 5.2.428, 768, MM 2.4.169, MND 3.2.126, 5.1.196, MV 3.2.148, RJ 1.4.53, S 85.11, 114.1, 118.14, TC 4.5.44, Tem Epil.4, TN 3.4.367, 4.3.32*; two *Per 1.1.72*; untrue *AW 5.3.316, Cym 1.6.87, LLL 5.2.472, S 72.12, 113.13*; in you of you *TG 3.1.97*
**pun** *LLL 5.1.54* ewe

***ye***
*str* jiː, *unstr* jə
**sp** ye[268], 'ye[1], ye-[good-ev'n][1], ye'[haue][1], [far]ye[well][2], yee[22]
**rh** be *JC 4.3.130*; me *S 42.5, 111.13*; loves ye moved me *TG 1.2.28*

***you / ye are*** *abbr*
*str* jɑːɹ, *unstr* jəɹ
**sp** y'are[48], you'r[6], you're[15]

***you / ye have*** *abbr*
*str* jav, *unstr* jəv
**sp** y'haue[7]

***you must*** *abbr*
juːst, jʊst
**sp** you'st[1]

***your / ~s***
*str* juːɹ, *unstr* jəɹ, jʊɹ / juːɹz
**sp** your[6879], your'[1], [o']your[4], [peace-a]-your[1], [take-a]-your[1] / yours[250]

***yourself***
jəɹˈself, jʊɹ-
**sp** your self[6], your selfe[259]
**rh** myself *R3 4.4.421*

***you will*** *abbr*
*str* =, *unstr* jəl, jʊl
**sp** you'l[85], youle[16], you'le[31], you'll[25]

***you would*** *abbr*
*str* =, ju:ld, *unstr* jəd, jʊd, jʊld
**sp** you'd[1], you'ld[10], youl'd[7]

***be with ye / you***
'bɪjə
**sp** b'uy[1], bu'y[1], buy'[1], buy'ye[1]

**young** *adj*
jɒŋ / 'jɒŋ·gəɹ / *m* -st, -gəst
**sp** yong[256], yong-[man][3], yong [men][1], yong-[ones][1], young[171], young-[ones][1] / yonger[22], yon-ger[1], younger[2], youn-ger[1] / yongest[15], yong'st[1], youngest[4]
**rh** *1* belong *AW 1.3.123*; long *KL 5.3.323, LLL 5.2.825, PP 12.10, RJ 1.1.160, 4.5.78*; strong *VA 419*; wrong *S 19.14*; **rh** *2* tongue *PP 1.5, 1.9, 19.17, S 138.5*

**young / ~'s** *n*
'jɒŋ / -z
**sp** yong[4], young[2] / yongs[1]
**rh** long *KL 1.4.212*; long, strong *Luc 863*

**younger** *n*
'jɒŋgəɹ
**sp** yonger[4], younger[3]

**youngest** *n*
'jɒŋgəst
**sp** yongest[2], youngest[2]

**youngest-born** *n*
'jɒŋgəst-ˌbɔ:ɹn
**sp** yongest borne[1]
> born

**young-eyed** *adj*
'jɒŋ-ˌəɪd
**sp** young eyed[1]
> eye

**youngling** *n*
'jɒŋlɪŋ / -z
**sp** yongling[1], youngling[1] / young-lings[1]

**youngly** *adv*
'jɒŋləɪ
**sp** youngly[1]

**younker** *n*
'jɒŋkəɹ
**sp** yonker[1], younker[1]

**your**
> you

**youth / ~'s / ~s** *n*
=
**sp** youth[252], youths [youth is][2], youth's [youth is][2] / youths[1] / youths[4]
**rh** ruth *PP 9.9*; truth *AW 1.3.128, LC 104, PP 1.3, S 37.2, 41.10, 54.13, 60.9, 110.7, 138.3, TN 3.1.154*

**youthful** *adj*
=
**sp** youthful[1], youthfull[27]

# Z

**zan·y / ~ies** *n*
ˈzenəɪ / -z
**sp** zanie[1] / zanies[1]
**rh** comedy *LLL 5.2.463*

**zeal / ~s** *n*
=
**sp** zeale[32] / zeales[1]

**zealous** *adj*
=
**sp** zealous[3], zelous[2]

**zed** *n*
=
**sp** zed[1]

**Zenelophon** *n*
zəˈneləfɒn
**sp** Zenelophon[1]

**zenith** *n*
=
**sp** zenith[1]

**zephyr / ~s** *n*
ˈzefəɹz
**sp** zephires[1]

**zodiac / ~s** *n*
ˈzoːdɪak / -s
**sp** zodiacke[1] / zodiacks[1]

**zone** *n*
zoːn
**sp** zone[1]

**zounds** *interj*
zuːnz, -ndz
**sp** zounds[1]